Comhairle Contae Chorcaí
Cork County Council
LIBRARY SERVICE RULES

1. Readers must return this book on or before the last date shown below.
2. Books are loaned for 21 days and if kept beyond this time a fine will be charged.

www.corkcoco.ie/library

ARCHITECTURETODAY
LANDSCAPE

ARCHITECTURETODAY
LANDSCAPE

Editorial coordinator:
Claudia Martínez Alonso

Art director:
Mireia Casanovas Soley

Editor:
David Andreu Bach

Layout:
Cristina Simó Perales

Translation:
Macarena Abascal Valdenebro
Cayetano Cardelus

Editorial project:
2017 © **booq** Publishing, S.L.
c/ Domènech, 7-9, 2º 1ª
08012 Barcelona, Spain
T: +34 93 268 80 88
www.booqpublishing.com

ISBN 978-84-9936-961-7 (English edition)
ISBN 978-84-947172-0-8 (Edición española)

10	INTRODUCTION	158	LANDSKAP DESIGN
		164	LIQUIDAMBAR LANDSCAPE ARCHITECTS
12	3LHD	170	LUDWIG.SCHOENLE
16	70°N ARKITEKTUR	178	MADE ASSOCIATI ARCHITETTURA E PAESAGGIO
22	AGNES FEDL LANDSCAPE ARCHITECTURE	182	MARIANNE LEVINSEN LANDSKAB APS
30	ALDAYJOVER ARQUITECTURA Y PAISAJE	190	MCGREGOR COXALL
38	ANDREA COCHRAN	202	MICHAEL SINGER
44	ASPECT STUDIOS	210	MOSBACH PAYSAGISTES
54	BIRK NIELSEN	218	MVRDV
58	BROISSIN	222	NIEBERG ARCHITECT
66	DD\M – DI DATO & MENINNO ASSOCIATED ARCHITECTS	230	OKRA LANDSCAPE ARCHITECTS
74	DELTA VORM GROEP	238	OSLUND AND ASSOCIATES
82	DIETMAR FEICHTINGER ARCHITECTES	248	ØSTENGEN & BERGO LANDSCAPE ARCHITECTS
90	DISSING+WEITLING ARCHITECTURE	254	RAMSEYER WAISMAN ESTUDIO DE ARQUITECTURA
94	DURBACH BLOCK ARCHITECTS	266	REHWALDT LANDSCHAFTSARCHITEKTEN
98	EDAW	274	RIJNBOUTT
108	GERMÁN DEL SOL	282	ROMERA Y RUIZ ARQUITECTOS
112	GLASSER UND DAGENBACH	288	SASAKI
118	HAGER LANDSCHAFTSARCHITEKTUR	298	STUDIO KAPPO
124	JAMES CARPENTER DESIGN ASSOCIATES	306	TATJANA VON GRIESHEIM
138	JENSEN & SKODVIN ARKITEKTKONTOR	314	UTOPIA LANDSCAPES
134	JML ARQUITECTURA DEL AGUA	322	VALENTIEN + VALENTIEN LANDSCAPE ARCHITECTS
144	KARRES EN BRANDS LANDSCHAPSARCHITECTEN		
150	KWK PROMES	332	DIRECTORY

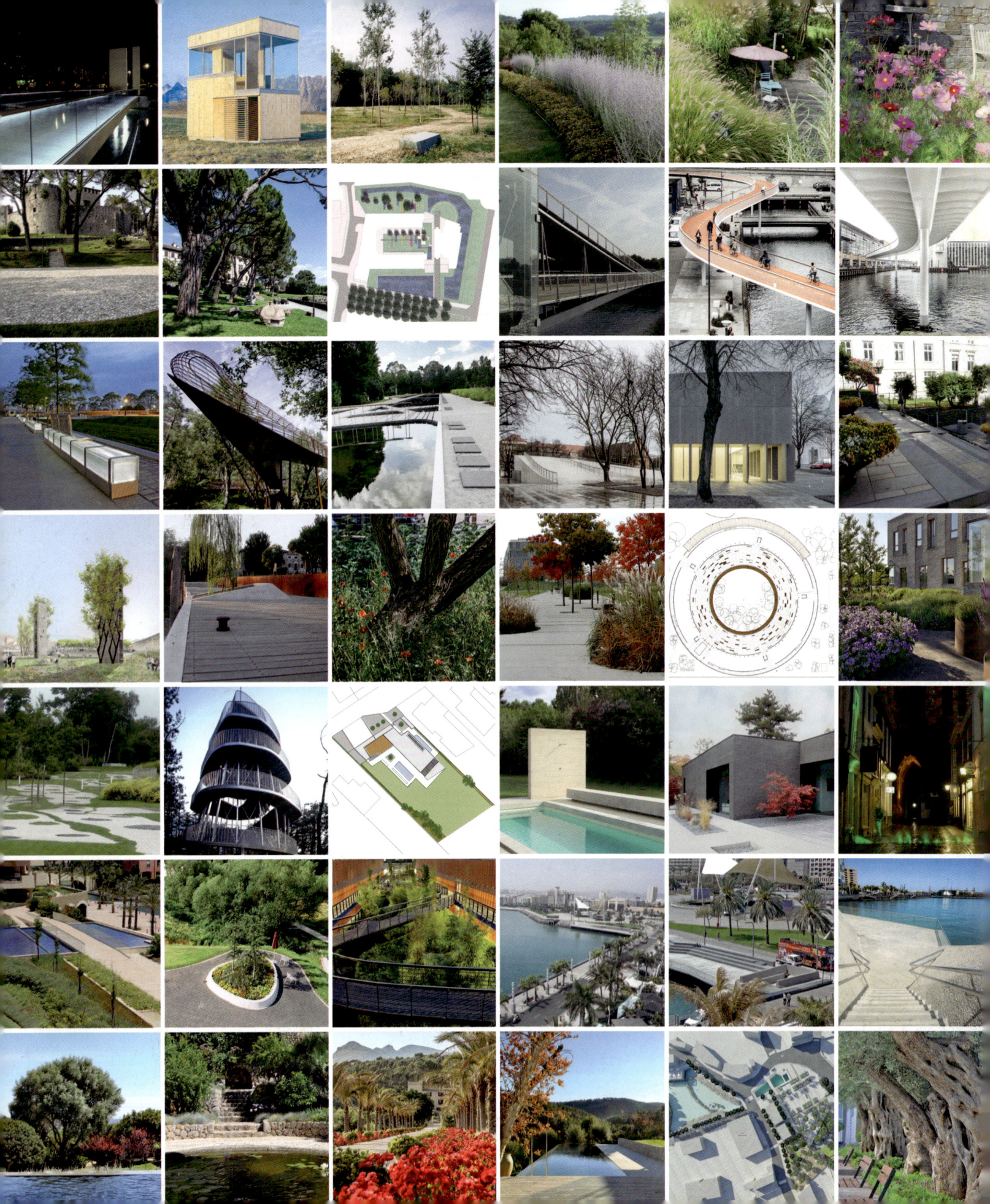

This book explores the relationships between landscape, architecture and art as means to integrate the life of man with the spaces he occupies.

In an urban context, this integration generates new organizational forms that transform the land into places suitable to the different activities that variously take place in it. The projects included in the book feature strategies that may be used in the reorganization of urban fabrics, the restoration of sensitive natural environments, the reclamation of derelict industrial zones, and the creation of parks, gardens and recreational areas. More specifically, some of these projects focus on renewable energy, urban ecology and green technologies, environmental education and art.

A common aspect that all the projects express is that landscape is to be understood as both material and process. The projects that affect the landscape are not inert entities but rather they are built of elements intended to transform through time. The principle instruments that define

these works are site and time. When working with outdoor spaces, both architects and artists engage into creations that establish relations of size and scale intrinsic to a particular site, which at the same time is bound to a surrounding context. Also, the projects that incorporate natural elements are inevitably tied to the notion of time. The authors of these projects, far from accepting the effects of time as a negative factor, have long learnt to use it to better integrate their artífice into the natural cycle incorporating the seasons, light at different times of the day, rain, snow and wind as dynamic element.

Transformed by man, the landscape is aimed to contribute to economic prosperity and environmental quality. At a conceptual level, architects and artists strive to bring a sense of place to the site and provide it with a special significance by releasing and enhancing the essence of the place.

This volume is a compilation of landscape architects and their projects that stand out for their sensitive and creative design, planning, and management of the land.

Este libro explora las relaciones entre el paisaje, la arquitectura y el arte como medio para integrar la vida del hombre con los espacios que ocupa.

En un contexto urbano, esta integración genera nuevas formas de organización que transforman la tierra en lugares adaptados a las diferentes actividades que se desarrollan en ella. Los proyectos incluidos en el libro presentan estrategias que pueden ser utilizadas en la reorganización de tejidos urbanos, la restauración de entornos naturales sensibles, la recuperación de zonas industriales abandonadas y la creación de parques, jardines y zonas recreativas. Más concretamente, algunos de estos proyectos se centran en las energías renovables, la ecología urbana y las tecnologías verdes, la educación medioambiental y el arte.

Un aspecto común que expresan todos los proyectos es que el paisaje debe ser entendido como material y como proceso. Los proyectos que afectan al paisaje no son entidades inertes, sino que están construidos de elementos destinados a transformarse a través del tiempo. Los principales instrumentos que definen estas obras son el lugar y el tiempo. Cuando se trabaja con espacios al aire libre, tanto los arquitectos como los artistas participan en creaciones que establecen relaciones de tamaño y escala intrínsecas a un lugar en particular, que al mismo tiempo está vinculado a un contexto circundante. Además, los proyectos que incorporan elementos naturales están inevitablemente ligados a la noción de tiempo. Los autores de estos proyectos, lejos de aceptar los efectos del tiempo como un factor negativo, han aprendido a utilizarlo para integrar mejor sus obras en el ciclo natural incorporando las estaciones, la luz en diferentes momentos del día, la lluvia, la nieve y el viento como elemento dinámico.

Transformado por el hombre, el paisaje tiene como objetivo contribuir a la prosperidad económica y la calidad ambiental. A nivel conceptual, los arquitectos y artistas se esfuerzan por darle un sentido de arraigo al lugar y le dan un significado especial al liberar y realzar su esencia.

Este volumen es una compilación de arquitectos paisajistas y sus proyectos que se destacan por su diseño sensible y creativo, planificación y gestión de la tierra.

3LHD

www.3lhd.com

N. Božidarevića 13/4
10000 Zagreb
Croatia

3LHD is a multi-discipline office that focuses on architecture, urban planning, design and art. Constantly exploring new possibilities, the studio participates in collaborations with other designers and has worked on projects as important as the Croatian Pavilion for the 2005 Expo in Japan or the Hotel Lone in Rovini. This young office has won awards both in Croatia and beyond its borders. Amongst these awards are the best sports building in the 2008 edition of the World Architecture Festival or the British *Architectural Review* Emerging Architects Award.

3LHD es un despacho multidisciplinar que engloba proyectos de arquitectura, urbanismo, diseño y arte. En constante exploración de nuevas posibilidades, el estudio participa en colaboraciones con otros creadores y ha trabajado en proyectos de la importancia del pabellón croata para la Expo 2005 en Japón, o el Hotel Lone de Rovini (Croacia). Pese a la juventud de sus integrantes, el estudio ha ganado diversos galardones tanto en Croacia como fuera de sus fronteras, entre ellos, el premio al mejor edificio deportivo en el World Architecture Festival de 2008 o el premio a los arquitectos emergentes otorgado por la revista británica Architectural Review.

RIVA SPLIT WATERFRONT
Riva Split Waterfront Split, Croatia — 2007 — Area: 24.000 m² / 258,000 sq ft
© Mario Jelavić, Domagoj Blažević

With an area of about 258,000 sq ft, the waterfront is the most active and busy zone of the city of Split. Facing the sea, this 820-foot-long by 180-foot-wide open space is also the main square of the city. The project integrates modular concrete elements in the pavement, which have colors ranging from white to light grey.

Con un área de más de 24.000 m², este paseo marítimo es la zona más viva y transitada de la ciudad de Split. Son 250 m de largo y 55 m de ancho los que, además de asomarse al mar, hacen las veces de plaza mayor. Entre otras facetas, el proyecto contempló la instalación de elementos modulares de hormigón, cuyo color varía del blanco al gris claro.

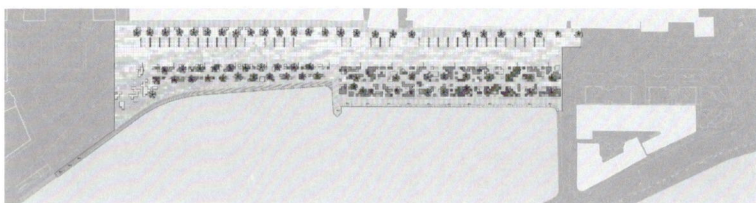

General plan

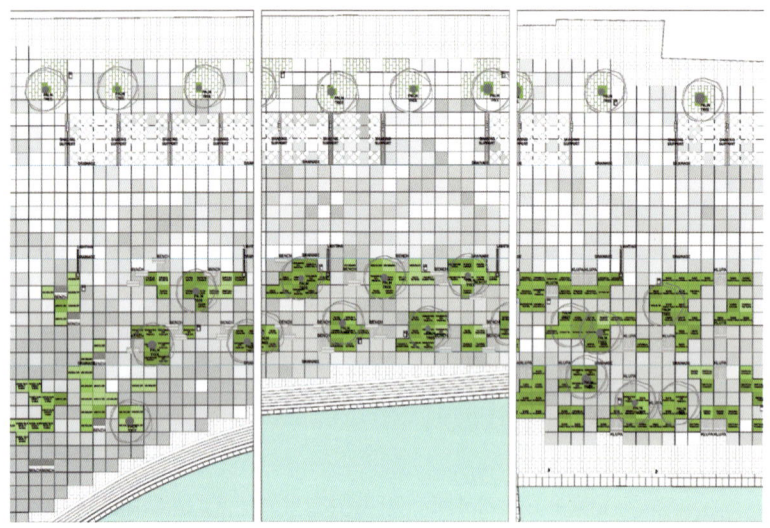

Urban restructuring plan

COMMEMORATIVE BRIDGE

Rijeka, Croatia — 2001 — Area: 310 m² / 3,337 sq ft
© Aljoša Brajdić

The main objective of this project was to confer a highly functional element with a monumental character. This was achieved by creating a symbolic object with tactile properties. The verticality of the monolithic columns, visually very heavy acts as a counterpoint to the horizontality of the bridge.

El objetivo primero de este proyecto era dotar de cierto carácter monumental a un elemento muy funcional. Se ha conseguido con creces crear un objeto simbólico, de cualidades táctiles, que contesta al plano horizontal de la pasarela con la verticalidad de los pilares monolíticos, de gran peso visual.

The 150-ton bridge element was assembled in a ship-yard and was transported to the site in one piece.

La pieza del puente, de 150 toneladas, se ensambló en un astillero y fue transportada entera hasta su ubicación.

70°N ARKITEKTUR

www.70n.no

Strandvegen 144, P.B. 1247
9262 Tromsø
Norway

Bjørn Otto Bratten, Gisle Løkken and Kjeld Nash founded 70°N arkitektur in 1995. Of the founding partners only Gisle Løkken remains, but the studio was joined by Joar Lillerust, Magdalena Haggärde and Petra Schnutenhaus. The multidisciplinary studio produces work in fields such as ephemeral architecture and set design, residential projects and landscape design. Experimenting and dialog are essential in their methodology, which results in an eclectic and modern style. Amongst the well-deserved prizes are the ArchitecturalReviewAward to the emerging studio in 2008, which put their name on the international scene.

Bjørn Otto Bratten, Gisle Løkken y Kjeld Nash fundaron 70°N arkitektur en 1995. De los socios fundadores hoy solo queda Gisle Løkken, y se han sumado a la directiva Joar Lillerust, Magdalena Haggärde y Petra Schnutenhaus. El suyo es un estudio multidisciplinar que trabaja en ámbitos tan dispares como la arquitectura efímera y de escenarios, los proyectos residenciales y el paisajismo. En su metodología son fundamentales la experimentación y el diálogo, lo cual redunda en un estilo ecléctico y moderno. Entre los premios recibidos por el equipo está el de la Architectural Review al estudio emergente de 2008, que los dio a conocer fuera de Noruega.

BIRD WATCHING TOWER
Lofoten, Norway — 2005 — Area: 35 m² / 377 sq ft
© Vegar Moen, Steinar Skaar, 70°N arkitektur

The design of these two 21.3-foot-tall towers in the Skjerpenvatnet and Gårdsvatnet nature reserve stands out for its simplicity. Both volumes are conceived so as to never cast shadows that would disturb the birds during the mating seasons.
The towers are sturdy steel constructions, clad in wood that need to withstand the strong winds common in the region.

El diseño de estas dos torres de 6,5 m de altura en las reservas de Skjerpenvatnet y Gårdsvatnet destaca por la sencillez de la estructura. Ambos volúmenes están pensados para que los observadores nunca proyecten sombras hacia el exterior, para no molestar a las aves durante las épocas de apareamiento.
Las torres son unas robustas construcciones de acero forradas de madera, pues debían soportar las fuertes rachas de viento típicas de la región.

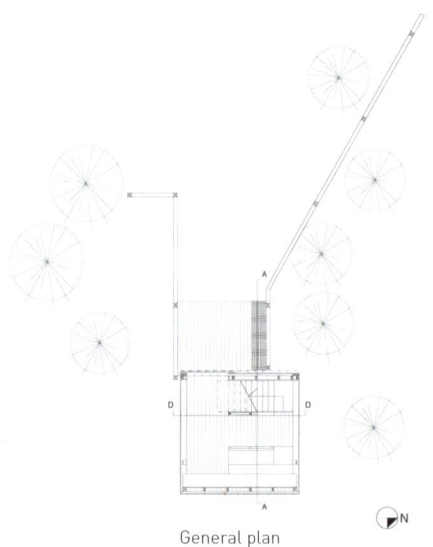

General plan

N

East elevation

West elevation

South elevation

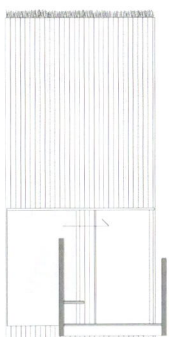

North elevation

SHELTER FOR BICYCLES AND LOOKOUT

Lofoten, Norway — 2005 — Area: 40 m² / 430.5 sq ft
© Vegar Moen, Steinar Skaar, 70°N arkitektur

This small shelter offers hikers some protection from the harsh weather the area is often subject to. The bicycles are parked on the access level, while the upper level offers a resting area with panoramic views.
The structure is designed to provide a 360° view of the surrounding landscape.

Este pequeño refugio da abrigo al excursionista en una zona con un clima riguroso. Las bicicletas se aparcan en el nivel de la entrada, mientras que la planta superior ofrece una zona de descanso con vistas panorámicas.
La estructura está diseñada para brindar una perspectiva de 360° del paisaje circundante.

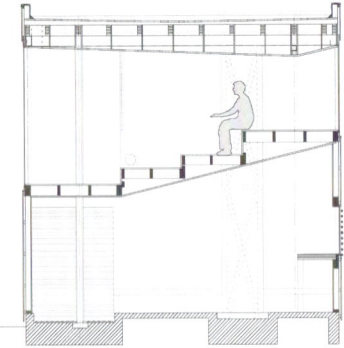
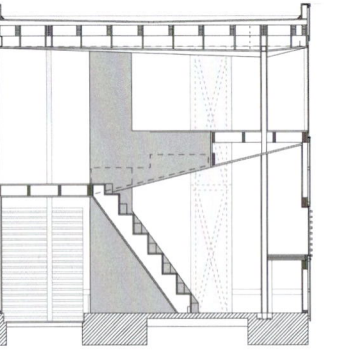

Longitudinal sections

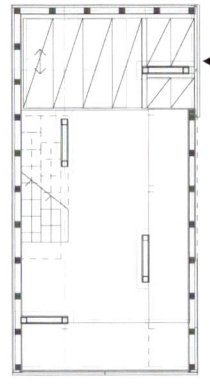

Floor plan

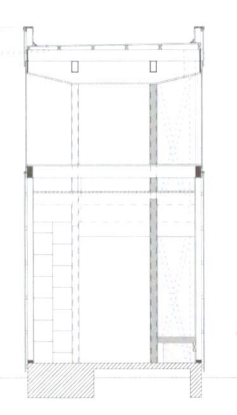

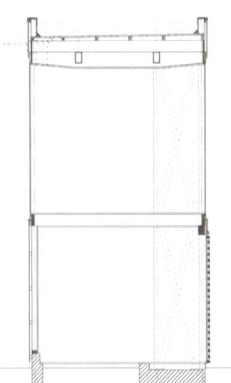

Cross sections

RESTING AREA IN TORVDALSHALSEN
Lofoten, Norway — 2005 — Area: 290 m² / 3,121.5 sq ft
© Vegar Moen, Steinar Skaar, 70°N arkitektur

Situated on the highway shoulder at the foot of the Eggum Mountains is a resting area with a horizontal disposition that favors the site as a lookout for visitors, a place to gaze at the landscape. A 197-foot-long wall separates the parking lot from the rest area and offers protection from the wind for those who decide to make a stop along the way. Although the wall is clad in wood, it is formed by a steel structure for stability.

A los pies de las montañas de Eggum se encuentra esta sencilla área de descanso para excursionistas que es, además, un lugar donde contemplar el paisaje gracias a su disposición horizontal. El muro vertical de 60 m separa la zona de descanso del aparcamiento y ayuda a proteger del viento a quienes decidan hacer un alto en el camino en este paraje. El muro, aunque forrado de madera, consta de una estructura de acero que le da estabilidad.

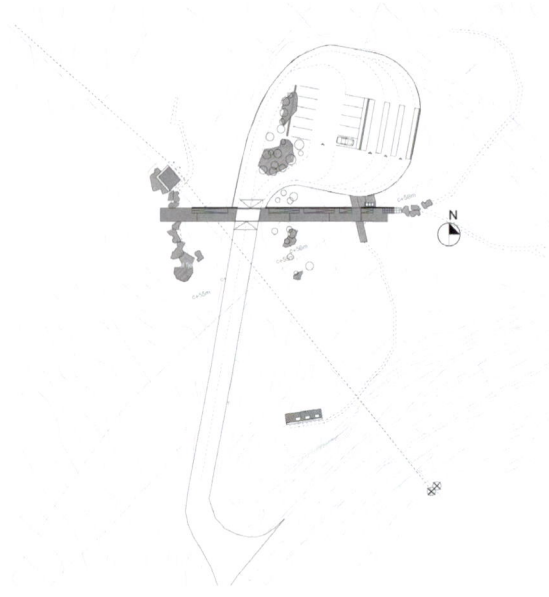

General plan

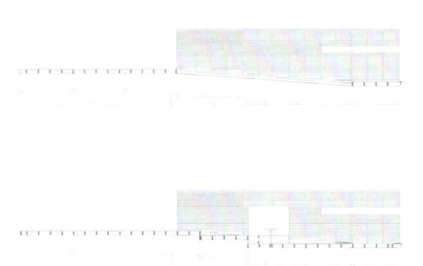

Sections

AGNES FEDL
LANDSCAPE ARCHITECTURE
Agnes Fedl
Nikolaus Fedl

www.fedl.eu
www.freiraumarchitektur.at

Fichtenweg 3
8072 Fernitz
Austria

The gardens and parks of Agnes Fedl are organic part of the landscape. She connects the beauty of the landscape with the functionality of the living area and create a harmonious unit for contemplation and experiences. The swinging forms, the plant structures, the play with colours, shades and light generate a joyful vividness. These spaces are breathing, are full of live and are in all of their structures harmonized with the needs of the owner and user.
The studio Agnes Fedl designs gardens, parks, landscape and public spaces since 1997 in and out of Austria.

Los jardines y parques de Agnes Fedl son parte orgánica del paisaje. Ella conecta la belleza del paisaje con la funcionalidad de la zona habitada y crea una unidad armoniosa para la contemplación y las experiencias. Las enérgicas formas, las composiciones de plantas y el juego de colores, sombras y luz generan una alegre vivacidad. Estos espacios respiran, están llenos de vida y están en armonía a todos los niveles con las necesidades del propietario y usuario.
El estudio Agnes Fedl diseña jardines, parques, paisajes y espacios públicos desde 1997 dentro y fuera de Austria.

MANOR HOUSE K
Southeast Styria, Austria — 2007 — 1.800 m² / 19,375 sq ft.
© Nikolaus Fedl, Klara Hutter

The property is gently embedded in the volcano mountains of east Styria. It was a special challenge for us to develop a modern garden around the old style manor house. As a calm middle we created a free lawn circle with panorama places in it, surrounded with spacious planted Terraces in harmonious colours, shades and structures, also as worthy frame for the landscape contemplation.

La propiedad está suavemente incrustada entre las montañas volcánicas del este de Styria. Para nosotros fue un desafío desarrollar un jardín moderno alrededor de la casa señorial. Como un apacible centro, creamos un círculo sin césped dotado de vistas panorámicas, rodeado de amplias terrazas plantadas con armoniosos colores, tonos y composiciones, que actúan también como marco para la contemplación del paisaje.

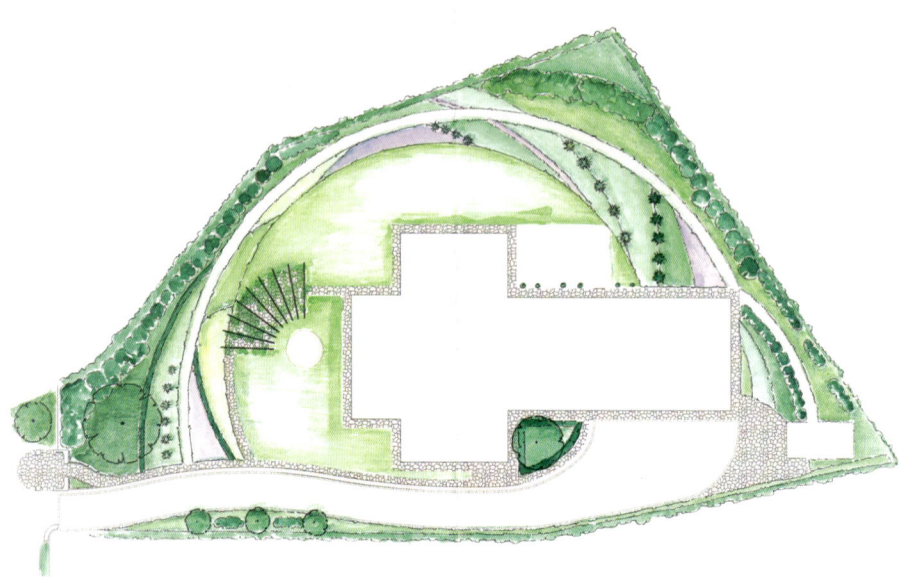

Site plan

RIVERSIDE GARDEN

Eibiswald, West Styria, Austria — 2015 — 2.200 m² / 23,681 sq ft.
© Nikolaus Fedl, Klara Hutter

The garden is a hidden refuge above the brook Saggau in west Styria. It extends, like a natural arena, to the bank over several terraces bordered with breathtaking plant arrangements. The colours and structures emphasize the picturesque panorama of the old trees overshadowed river landscape. Places invite the viewer enjoying this magical atmosphere and listening to the music of the rivulet.

El jardín es un refugio oculto sobre el arroyo Saggau en el oeste de Styria. Se extiende de forma natural hacia la orilla mediante terrazas bordeadas de impresionantes composiciones de plantas. Los colores y las formas enfatizan el pintoresco panorama del paisaje fluvial de viejos árboles en sombra. Sus rincones invitan a disfrutar de esta atmósfera mágica y a escuchar la música del riachuelo.

Site plan

VOLCANO VIEW GARDEN

Volcano Region in Styria, Austria — 2016 — 4.000 m² / 43,056 sq ft.
© Nikolaus Fedl, Klara Hutter

The uniqueness of this garden is hidden in its gentle elevated situation, through which it units with the ambient landscape and seems to be a part of it. Swinging paths expand supplementary the space. Birch grove and fruit trees built a natural frame. Delicate perennial and grass plantings next to the sitting places accompanies the panoramic view over the volcano landscape.

La singularidad de este jardín se oculta en su ligeramente elevada posición, a través de la cual se une con el paisaje y parece formar parte de él. Sinuosos senderos expanden de forma complementaria el espacio. Abedules y árboles frutales construyen un marco natural. Delicadas plantaciones perennes y de césped próximas a los asientos acompañan la vista panorámica sobre el paisaje del volcán.

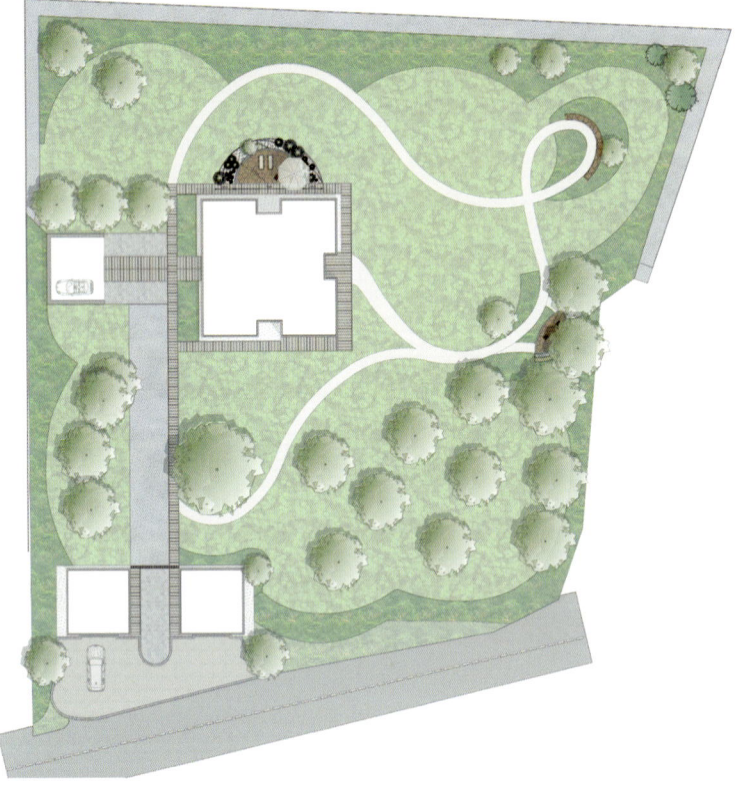

Site plan

MINIMUNDUS, LAKE CONSTANCE

Liebenau, Bad Württemberg, Germany — 2005 — 40.000 m² / 430,556 sq ft.
© Nikolaus Fedl, Klara Hutter

The model exhibition "the small world at the Lake Constance", initiated of Minimundus Klagenfurt, presented 90 models of architectural and technical monuments. The theme park was arranged as a harmonious unit. The visitors are guided through ever changing landscape with concentrated areas of model scenes, which are connected by gentle, following surface figurations, elevations and flanks that interact witch each other.

La exposición de maquetas "el pequeño mundo en el lago Constanza", promovida por Minimundus Klagenfurt, presentó 90 maquetas de monumentos arquitectónicos y técnicos. El parque temático fue organizado como una armoniosa unidad. Los visitantes son guiados a través de un paisaje siempre cambiante con áreas que concentran las escenas con maquetas, conectadas por suaves elevaciones y contornos que interactúan entre sí.

Site plan

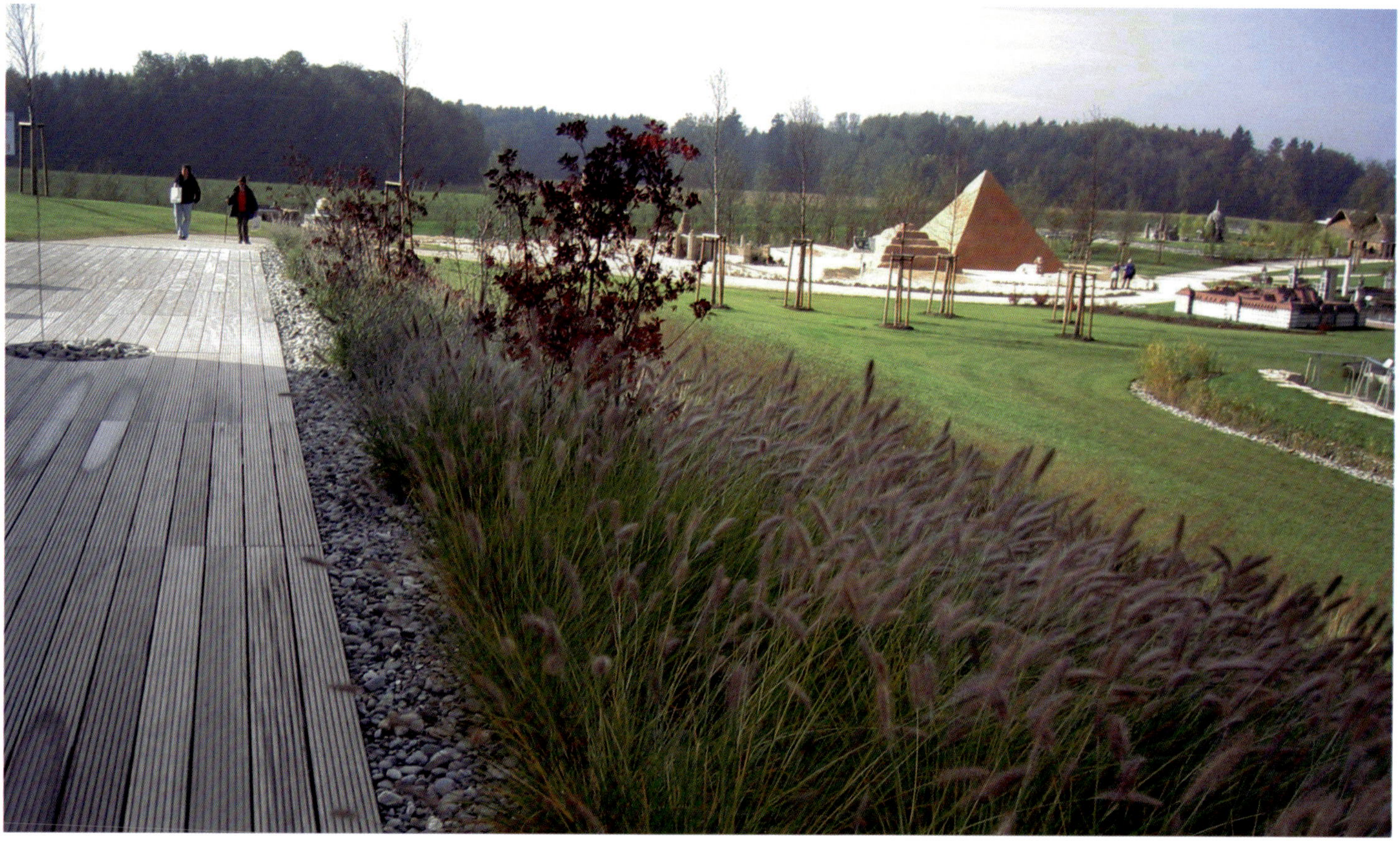

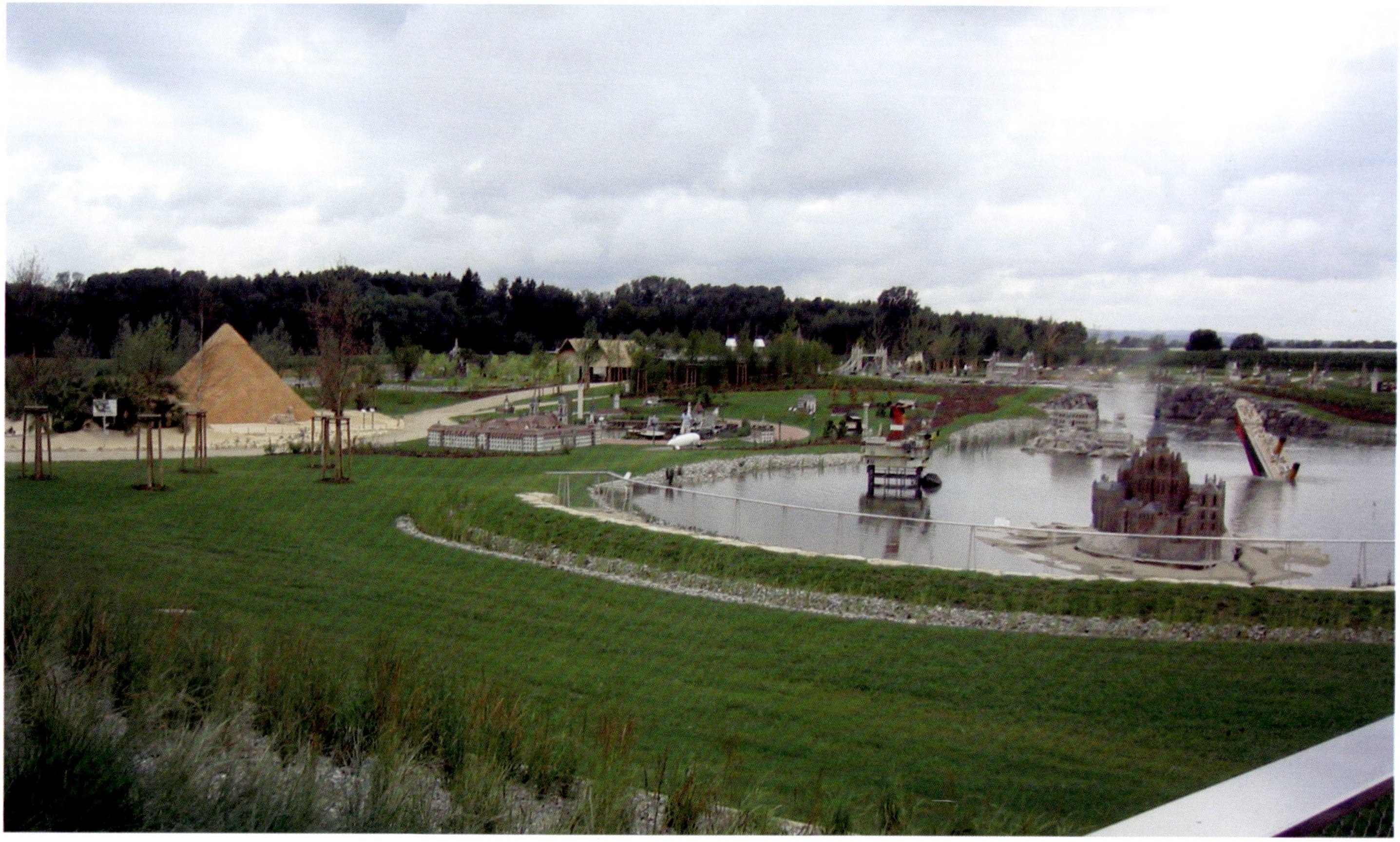

ALDAYJOVER
ARQUITECTURA Y PAISAJE

www.aldayjover.com

Av. Portal del Ángel, 3, 1º 2ª
08002 Barcelona
Spain

The works of aldayjover arquitectura y paisaje focus mainly on public facilities and spaces as well as landscape projects such as a Water Park for the Zaragoza International Exhibition in 2008. They also include single family and social housing (Gran Via Residence for mentally disabled in Barcelona), and restorations of highly valued historical buildings and city centers.
Recently, the Water Park has been nominated for the European Union Architecture Prize Mies van der Rohe.

Entre las obras de aldayjover arquitectura y paisaje se encuentran desde los principales espacios e instalaciones públicos hasta proyectos paisajísticos como el Parque del Agua de la Exposición Internacional de Zaragoza 2008. También realizan viviendas unifamiliares y equipamientos sociales (la Residencia Gran Vía para disminuidos psíquicos en Barcelona) y restauraciones de edificios de gran valor histórico y de centros urbanos.
Recientemente, el Parque del Agua ha sido nominado al Premio Mies van der Rohe de Arquitectura Contemporánea de la Unión Europea.

WATER PARK ZARAGOZA

Spain — 2008 — Area: 1.250.000 m² / 13,454,888 sq ft
© aldayjover, Jordi Bernadó

The idea for the design started with the original forest; expanding it, creating clearings and meadows, organizing the path of the water. Rather than introduce a radical design, the work emphasizes the qualities of the site: the landscape expresses the history of the territory and its relationship with its habitants.

La idea del diseño surgió del bosque original, expandiéndolo, creando claros y praderas, organizando el cauce del agua. En lugar de introducir un diseño radical, el trabajo enfatiza las cualidades del emplazamiento: el paisaje muestra la historia del territorio y el vínculo con sus habitantes.

Legend of uses and systems
A. Accesses
B. Circulation
C. Water system
D. Grand Canal Boulevard
E. Square and promenade on the aqueduct
F. Inhabited Forest
H. Gardens of the river Ebro
J. Gardens of the food
K. Exotic gardens
L. South plaza or botanical plaza
M. Grove

General plan

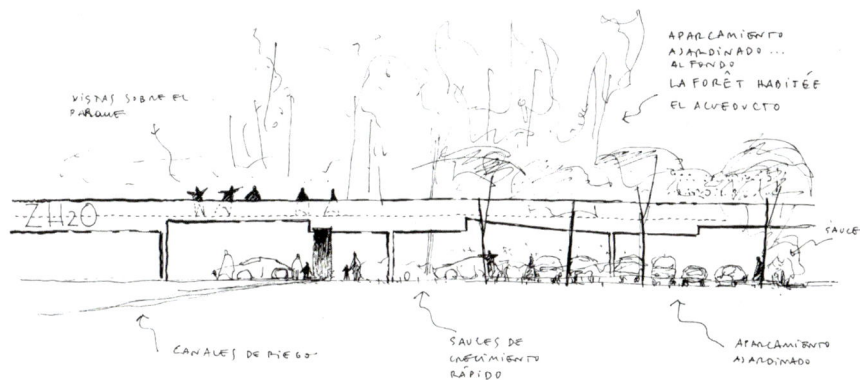

Sketch

The park is mainly a space for the river to overflow and filter through the ground naturally avoiding the areas where the service buildings are located.

El parque es principalmente un espacio para que el río se desborde y se filtre a través del suelo, evitando de forma natural las zonas donde se encuentran los edificios de servicio.

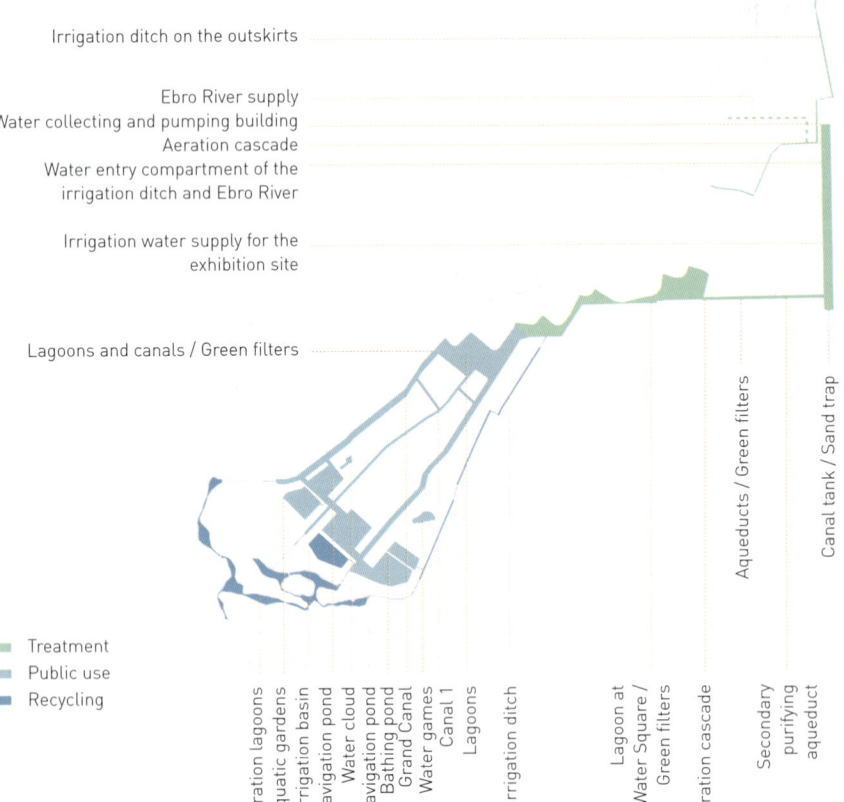

Irrigation ditch on the outskirts

Ebro River supply
Water collecting and pumping building
Aeration cascade
Water entry compartment of the
irrigation ditch and Ebro River

Irrigation water supply for the
exhibition site

Lagoons and canals / Green filters

Treatment
Public use
Recycling

Infiltration lagoons
Aquatic gardens
Irrigation basin
Navigation pond
Water cloud
Navigation pond
Bathing pond
Grand Canal
Water games
Canal 1
Lagoons
Irrigation ditch

Lagoon at
Water Square /
Green filters

Aeration cascade

Secondary
purifying
aqueduct

Aqueducts / Green filters

Canal tank / Sand trap

PHASES OF THE TREATMENT

EXTRACTION AND PUMPING

WATER CASCADE
Mechanical oxygenation

PRIMARY TREATMENT

Sedimentation and decantation
of solids in suspension

Filtration

SECONDARY TREATMENT

GRAVEL FILTERS

Retention of solids

HYGIENICS

Water under solar radiation

SUPERFICIAL FLUX (SF) AND
SUBSUPERFICIAL (SSF)

BED OF MACROPHITES

Decarbonisation
Elimination of phosphorus
De-nitrification

Reeds and yellow irises

CASCADES BY GRAVITY
Aeration
Mechanical oxygenation

TERCIARY TREATMENT

SUPERFICIAL FLUX (SF)

BED OF MACROPHITES

Decarbonisation
Elimination of phosphorus
De-nitrification

Elimination of germs Pathogens

Reeds (80%)
Yellow irises and others

Carps and gambusia species
(elimination of the risk of
mosquitoes)

MAINTENANCE OF WATER
QUALITY

USE FOR IRRIGATION

COMPLEMENTARY TREATMENT

MATURING LAGGON

INFILTRATION TO THE PHREATIC
SYSTEM OF THE PURIFIED WATER

Bulrushes and irises
Fauna of the river banks

Water treatment scheme

RECREATIONAL AND CONTEMPLATIVE USES
(ROOF TOP OF THE I.I.D.M.N.)

General view of the water system and the park

GRAND CANAL TANK

Promenade and access to the park

Distribution of water flow for irrigation purposes,
lagoons and water jets

PUTIFYING AQUEDUCT

ELEVATED PROMENADE
OVER THE PARK

EDUCATIONAL VISIT OF THE WATER PURIFIER

Environmental education: Visit of compartments that
recreatenatural ecosystems based on wetlands

Controlled experimental research of the application and
management of innovative systems of water purifying by means
of algae and plants inmonocultures and polycultures

CASCADE AT THE END OF THE AQUEDUCT

LAGOON AT THE WATER SQUARE

EDUCATIONAL PURPOSE
The recreational use is combined with
the environmental education

CASCADE

NAVIGABLE LAGOONS

Wharf

Draining for the renovation of canals and ponds

WHITE WATER RAFTING

NAVIGABLE CANALS

DISTRIBUTION OF THE WATER

Recreational use and transportation

WATER GAMES

RECREATIONAL PONDS OF PURIFIED WATER

Recreational and sportive use (bathingand rowing)

IRRIGATION DITCH

Reuse of the leftover treated water forirrigation

NATURAL LAGOONS

RESTORATION OF NATURALECOSYSTEMS

Fauna and flora richness

Promenades amongst lagoons

ARANZADI PARK

Pamplona, Spain — 2008 — Area: 20.000 m² / 215,278 sq ft
© aldayjover

The site located between Pamplona's city center and two adjacent neighborhoods presents a landscape of lush vegetation. The project recuperates the dynamism of a natural meander. It proposes a balance between the need for an open space of public use, riparian dynamics and the park's environmental role along the Arga River.

Este lugar, situado entre el centro de la ciudad de Pamplona y dos barrios adyacentes, presenta un paisaje de frondosa vegetación. El proyecto recupera el dinamismo de un meandro natural. Propone un equilibrio entre la necesidad de un espacio abierto de uso público, una dinámica ribereña y el papel medioambiental del parque a lo largo del río Arga.

Aerial view of Aranzadi Park

A. River banks
B. Orchard
C. Woodland in flood area
D. Playground garden
E. Celebrations garden
F. Aranzadi garden
G. English style garden
H. Garden parking

The design of the park is based on the flooding analysis of the Arga river. The landscape is therefore tied to the seasonal dynamics of the flood waters.

El diseño del parque se basa en el análisis de las inundaciones del río Arga, por lo tanto, el paisaje está sujeto a las dinámicas estacionales del agua de las crecidas.

Existing vegetation 55 ft

Riparian trees 39 ft

Riparian trees 26 ft

Forested flood plain (45.00)   Preserved agricultural fields

Existing tree (Ulmus minor)
Salix alba
Existing tree (Aesculus hippocastanum)
Populus alba
Salix alba
Populus alba
Populus alba
Populus tremula
Betula alba
Populus tremula

Gardens of the Aranzadi Park

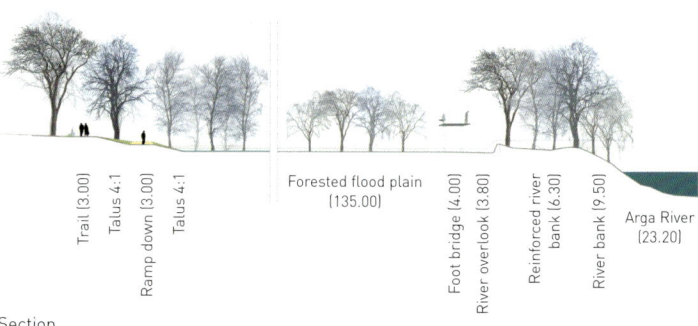

Trail (3.00)
Talus 4:1
Ramp down (3.00)
Talus 4:1
Forested flood plain (135.00)
Foot bridge (4.00)
River overlook (3.80)
Reinforced river bank (6.30)
River bank (9.50)
Arga River (23.20)

Section

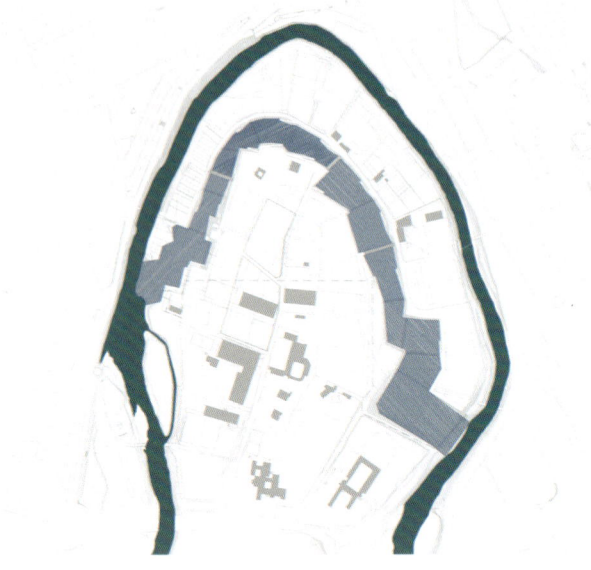

■ Natural bed of the Arga River in Aranzadi
▨ Woodland in flood area

Water system plan

▨ Playground garden   ▨ English style garden
▨ Celebrations garden   ▨ Garden's parking
▨ Aranzadi garden   ▨ Woodland in flood area

Vegetation plan

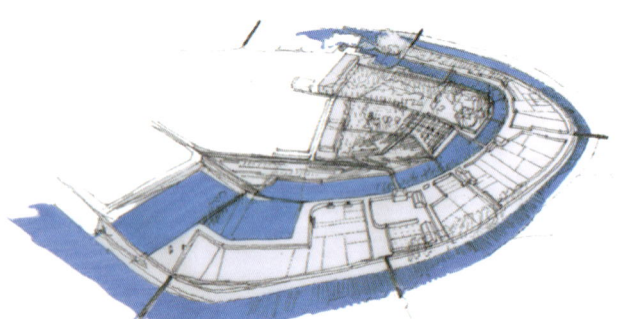

Sketch of the relationship between the water and its surroundings

Sketch of the relationship between the vegetation and its surroundings

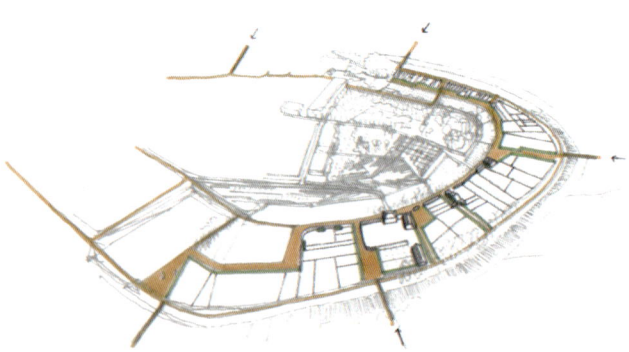

Sketch of the relationship between the orchard area and its surroundings

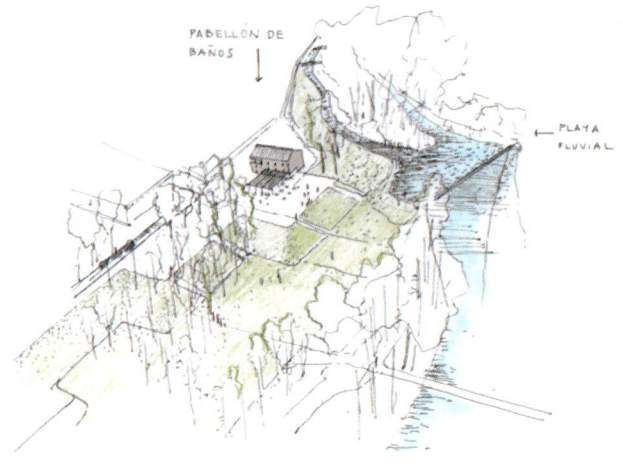

PABELLÓN DE BAÑOS

PLAYA FLUVIAL

Sketch of new constructions

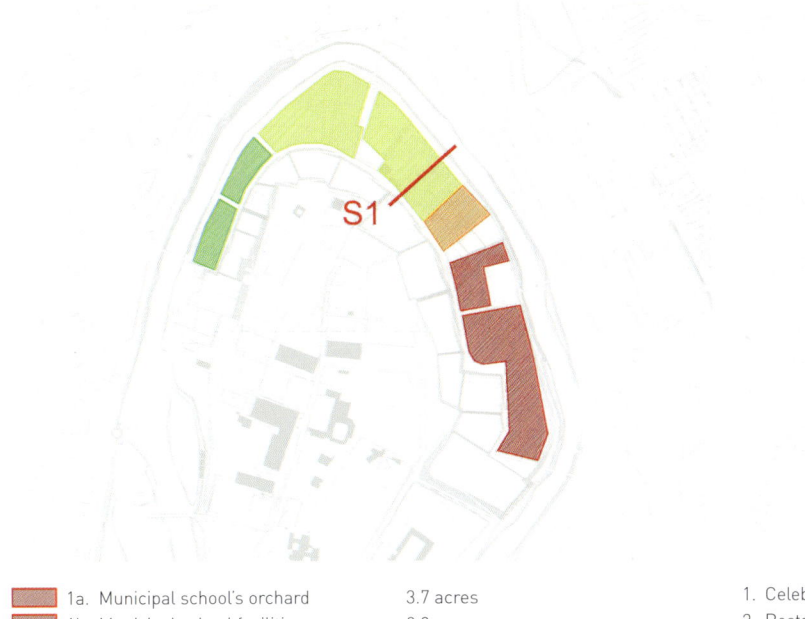

▨	1a. Municipal school's orchard	3.7 acres
▨	1b. Municipal school facilities	0.9 acres
▨	2. Experimental orchard	1.01 acres
▨	3. Production orchard	6.31 acres
▨	4. Social orchard	1.65 acres

Orchard system plan

1. Celebration pavilion and annexed residence
2. Restaurant
3. I+D center for horticultural varieties
4. Horticulture school
5. Public restrooms
6. Granary

▬ Municipal equipment
   a. Center for young creation
   b. Center for innovation
     (nurseries)
▭ New pedestrian bridges
▭ Viaduct in the flood area woodland

Sketch of new constructions

ANDREA COCHRAN

www.acochran.com

2325 Third Street #210
San Francisco
California 94107
United States

The work of Andrea Cochran is about sculpting and navigating space to achieve an integration of three elements: landscape, art and architecture. Her task consists of drawing the limits using a thought-out palette of materials to emphasize texture, the dynamism and the luminosity of the forms. Her studio has been awarded prizes such as the ASLA Merit Award in Design and the AIA Top Ten Green Project Award, and was a finalist in the National Design Awards in 2006.

Según sus propias palabras, el trabajo de Andrea Cochran esculpe y navega por el espacio a tratar para conseguir una integración orgánica de tres elementos: el paisaje, el arte y la arquitectura. Su labor consiste en trazar los límites haciendo uso de una paleta muy meditada de materiales para realzar la textura, el dinamismo y la luminosidad de las formas. El estudio ha cosechado premios como el Merit Award Design de la Sociedad Americana de Arquitectura del Paisaje, un Top Ten Green Award de la AIA y una mención como finalista en los National Design Awards de 2006.

WALDEN STUDIOS

Alexander Valley, California, United States — 2006 — Area: 24.000 m² / 258,333 sq ft
© Marion Brenner

This project consisted of the conversion of a fruit packing facility in the Russian River Valley. The new building is amix used center dedicated to the arts and its exterior maintains a spirit of modernity and calm. The gardenintegrates a series of piers that extend out into the vineyards.

Este proyecto consistió en la reconversión de un almacén de fruta en el valle del río Ruso. El nuevo edificio es un centro de uso mixto dedicado a las artes, y sus exteriores mantienen el espíritu moderno y tranquilo que transmite el interior. El jardín se extiende como un pantalán hacia un mar de viñedos. La exuberancia natural del entorno se ve realzada gracias a una intervención mínima, discreta.

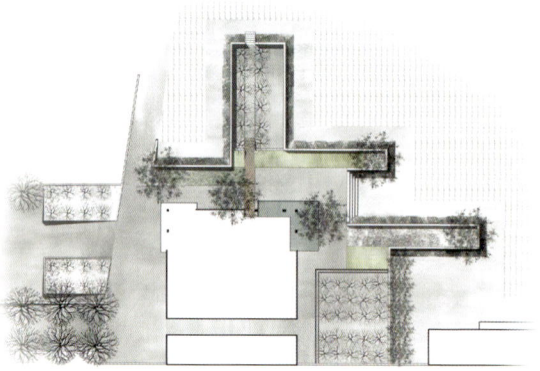

General plan

NUEVA SCHOOL

Hillsborough, California, United States — 2006 — Area: 2.400 m² / 25,833 sq ft
© Marion Brenner

When the architects received the commission to expand this suburban school, they agreed with the client that the program should include an amphitheater, a plaza, a classroom building, a dining space, and a library. The landscape helps weaving the different functions and ensures a secure and favorable space for games and for interaction amongst children.

Al recibir el encargo de expansión de este campus escolar suburbano, los arquitectos acordaron con el cliente la inclusión de un anfiteatro, una plaza, un edificio con aulas, un comedor y una biblioteca. La intervención paisajística ayuda a entretejer las distintas dependencias y asegura un espacio seguro y propicio para la interacción entre los alumnos.

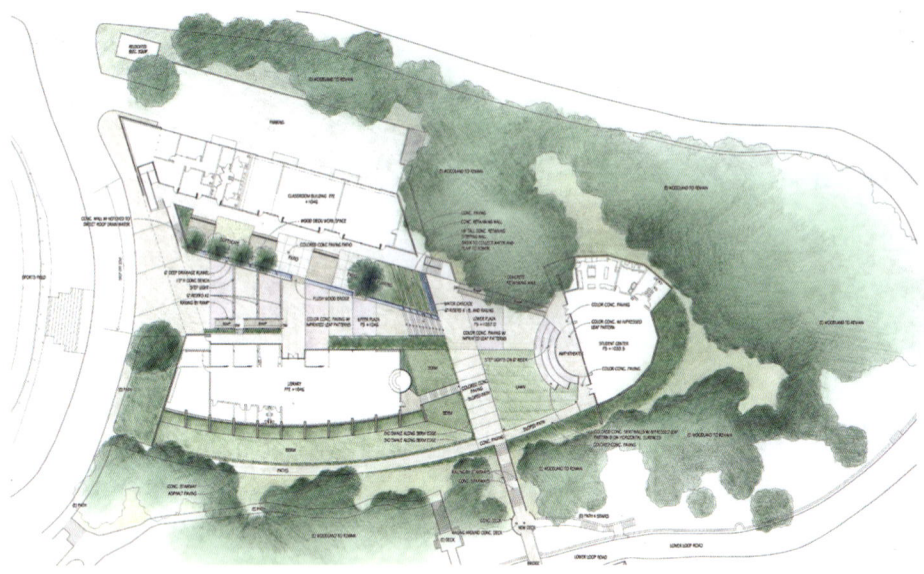

General plan

The project incorporates a green roof as an extension of the lawn, and a rainwatercanalization system.

El proyecto incorpora un tejado ecológico en el que se prolonga la superficie con césped y un sistema de canalización del agua de lluvia.

STONE EDGE FARM

Sonoma, California, United States — 2001 — Area: 11.000 m² / 118,403 sq ft
© Marion Brenner, Emily Rylander

Conceived as a retreat for the owner, this site achieves a tight relationship between building and nature. The project formed by a spa, an observatory and a native stone pyramid is interconnected by means of elements such as a reflecting pool and rows of olive trees.

The Corten steel stair, with its ochre tone, fits to perfection in this rustic landscape of drought-tolerant grasses.

Concebido como un lugar de retiro para el propietario, este proyecto consigue crear una estrecha relación entre el edificio y la naturaleza circundante. El conjunto que forman el spa, el observatorio y la pirámide de piedra está interconectado gracias a la inclusión de elementos como el estanque y las hileras de olivos. La escalera de acero corten, con su tono ocre, encaja a la perfección en este paisaje rústico de secano.

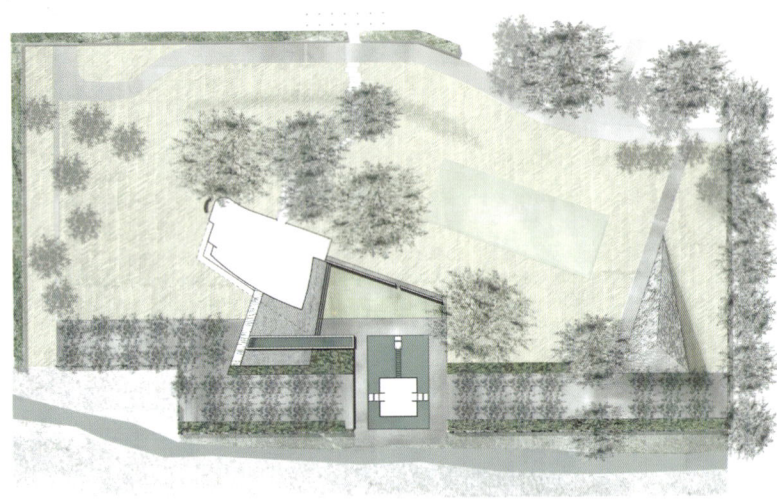

General plan

0   100ft

ASPECT STUDIOS

www.aspect.net.au

Marlborough Street, Studio 61, L6
2010 Surry Hills
New South Wales
Australia

Aspect Studios has four offices distributed in the main cities of the eastern Australian coast: Sydney, Melbourne and Brisbane. Aspect Studios delivers projects in landscape architecture, urban design and urban planning since 1993 when the office in Melbourne opened. The office has produced projects in Australia and abroad, and has received prestigious awards such as the AILA Victorian Awards and the City Pride Award. Many of the projects have appeared in publications by TeNeues, Harper Collins, and in the Daily Telegraph.

Aspect Studios tiene cuatro oficinas en las ciudades principales de la costa este australiana: Sídney, Melbourne y Brisbane. Especializados en paisajismo y planificación urbana, desde 1993 —fecha en que inauguraron su sede en Melbourne— han realizado proyectos tanto en Australia como en otros países. Han cosechado premios tan prestigiosos como los AILA Victorian Awards y el City Pride Award. Su obra ha sido reseñada en publicaciones de TeNeues y Harper Collins y en medios como el Daily Telegraph.

JACARANDA SQUARE
Sydney, Australia — 2008 — Area: 4.000 m² / 43,066 sq ft
© Kyla Sheehan, Simon Wood, Terence Chin

This park is one of the first constructions planned under the Sydney 2030 program, an effort to convert areas that belonged to the complex built for the 2000 Olympics, which remained partially unused since then. The site, known asthe Everyday Stadium, is aimed to increase the use of the area and to create an active and sustainable town center. The space is delimited by the orthogonal shape of the block, 164 x 260 feet.

Este parque es una de las primeras construcciones realizadas dentro del programa Sídney 2030, que busca reconvertir zonas del complejo construido para los Juegos Olímpicos 2000 y que han quedado parcialmente en desuso. Con esta idea, este parque fue bautizado como «el estadio de todos los días». El espacio viene determinado por la forma ortogonal de la manzana y mide 50 x 80 m.

General plan

Elevation

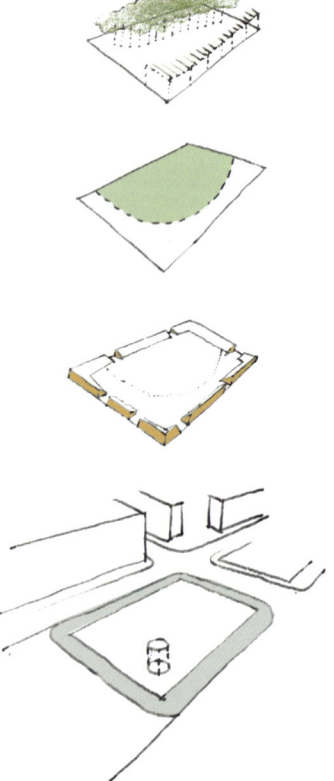

Axonometric view

The project was developed in collaboration with Mc-
Gregor Westlake Architecture and Deuce Design.

El proyecto se realizó en colaboración con McGregor
Westlake Architecture y Deuce Design.

WATER POLICE

Sydney, Australia — 2009 — Area:10.500 m² / 113,021 sq ft
© Florian Groehn

This project provides a clear example of how simple concepts can be used to convert an exterior space by providing it with a better use through the addition of a few elements to the original configuration. The facility for the Water Police now accommodates a park that helps the neighborhood to interact with the harbor.
The selection of urban furniture is key to creating a welcoming environment.

Este proyecto es un claro ejemplo de la sencillez con la que se puede reconvertir un espacio exterior y darle un uso mucho más favorable añadiendo muy pocos elementos a la configuración original. Las dependencias de la policía marina han pasado a albergar un parque que permite conectar el barrio con el puerto.
La elección del mobiliario urbano ha sido clave para crear un ambiente acogedor.

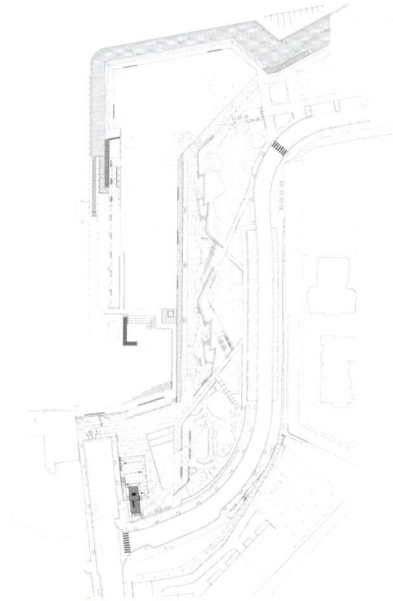

General plan

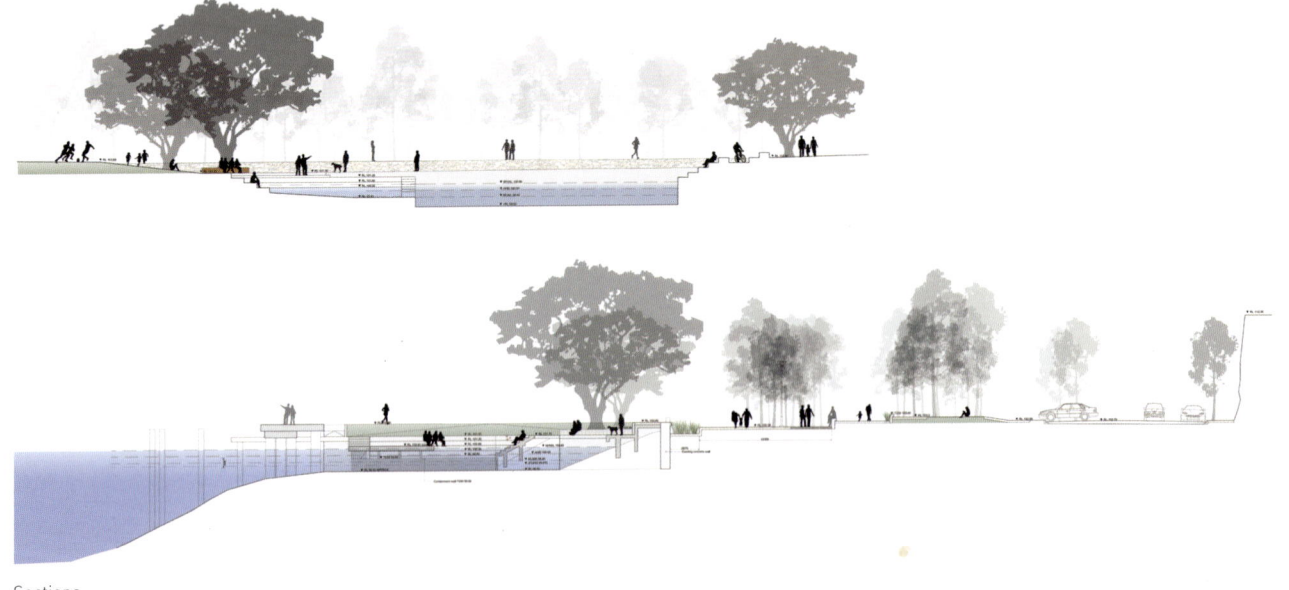

Sections

WETLAND 5

Sydney, Australia — 2007 — Area: 80.000 m² / 861,113 sq ft
© Simon Wood

The commission consisted in fitting out a reservoir, including the design of the retaining walls, the pedestrian ways, the urban furniture, and the landscape and lighting design. The result is a welcoming park worthy of a visit.

El proyecto consistía en acondicionar un pantano: diseñar los muros de contención y las vías peatonales, el mobiliario urbano, la disposición de la vegetación y el alumbrado. El resultado es una ordenación que convierte el entorno en un parque acogedor y que merece la pena visitar.

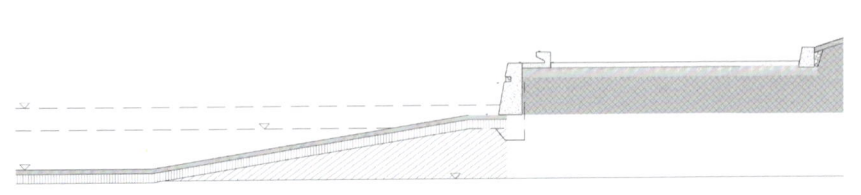

Construction detail

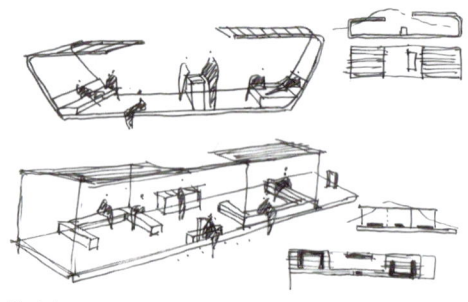

Sketch

General plan

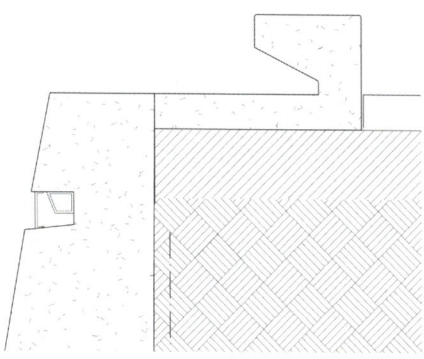

Construction detail

The continuous lighting system that delimits the body of water is a clever, functional solution that enhances the main element of the design.

El sistema de iluminación continuo que perfila la balsa de agua es un ejemplo de cómo se debe destacar visualmente el elemento protagonista de un proyecto.

BONDI TO BRONTE COAST WALK

Sydney, Australia — 2009 — Area: 1.800 m² / 19,375 sq ft
© Florian Groehn

This project consists of a spectacular 1,690-foot-long panoramic bridge that covers the shore near Waverley cemetery. The simplicity of the project is driven by materials which have been selected for their durability. Nonetheless, the final plan and the height of the structure were carefully developed. The main element of the intervention is the landscape, which generates the open character of the projects integrated in the orography.

Este proyecto consiste en una espectacular pasarela panorámica, de 515 m de longitud, que recorre la línea de la costa en los alrededores del cementerio de Waverley. Con unos materiales escogidos por su particular resistencia, la propuesta llama la atención por su aparente sencillez, aunque el trazado exacto fue cuidadosamente estudiado.
El verdadero protagonista de la intervención es el paisaje, de ahí el carácter abierto e integrado en la orografía de la estructura propuesta.

Section

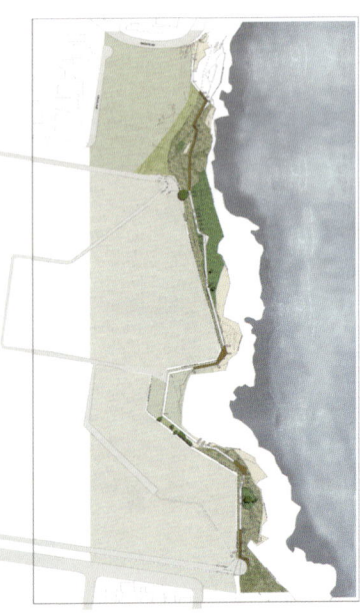

Site plan

BIRK NIELSEN
Urban Planners–
Landscape Architects

www.birknielsen.dk

Søndergade 1A
8000 Århus C
Denmark

Frode Birk founded his own architecture studio in 1988. Prior to that, he worked with the landscape architecture firm of Leth & Skaarup and under the direction of Professor Sven Hansen. He has been the coauthor of the book Wind Turbines and the Landscape: architecture and aesthetics, as well as of a film documentary with the same title. He has been recognized with, amongst other awards, a mention as a finalist to the European Land-scape Rosa Barba Prize in 2000 and the DAL Town Planning Prize in 2007.

Frode Birk fundó su propio estudio de arquitectura en 1988. Hasta entonces había trabajado en el estudio de paisajismo de Leth & Skaarup y, antes, bajo las órdenes del profesor Sven Hansen. Ha sido coautor del libro Wind Turbines and the Landscape: architecture and aesthetics, así como de un documental en vídeo con el mismo título. Entre las distinciones recibidas destacan una mención como finalista en el Premio Europeo de Paisaje Rosa Barba en 2000 y el DAL Town Planning Prize de 2007.

SQUARE IN AALBORG
Aalborg, Denmark — 2008 — 18.000 m² / 193,750 ft sq
© Birk Nielsen

The commission consisted in designing a plaza in the busiest pedestrian area of Aalborg. With virtually no verticalelements, the design identity is established with the various patterns applied to the different surfaces, and with theformation of geometric patterns using stone as the main element. A reflecting pool is the epicenter and the soul of the project. It offers a secluded corner for tranquility in the midst of a commercial zone.

En este proyecto, el encargo consistía en diseñar la plaza de la zona más concurrida de todo Aalborg. Sin apenas elementos verticales, la identidad del lugar se establece con el diseño cambiante de las distintas superficies y con la formación de patrones geométricos de variada naturaleza, formados con materiales pétreos de primera calidad.
Una serie de estanques constituyen el epicentro y el alma del proyecto, y ofrecen un rincón para la tranquilidad en mitad de una zona comercial.

Location map

General plan

SQUARE IN FREDERICIA

Fredericia, Denmark — 2008 — Area: 16.000 m² / 172,223 sq ft
© Birk Nielsen

This project constitutes the main square of Fredericia and links the historic district with the new city development areas located near the harbor. A striking paving design standsout with jigsaw elements that protrude from the granite mantle that delimits the square.

The fountains and the different water canalizations constitute the main ornamental elements of the project.

Este proyecto para la plaza central de la localidad de Fredericia tenía como objetivo prioritario unir el casco histórico con los nuevos barrios ubicados junto al puerto. Destaca un llamativo diseño de la pavimentación, con elementos dentados que sobresalen del manto de granito que delimita la plaza.

Las fuentes y las distintas canalizaciones de agua son los principales elementos ornamentales del proyecto.

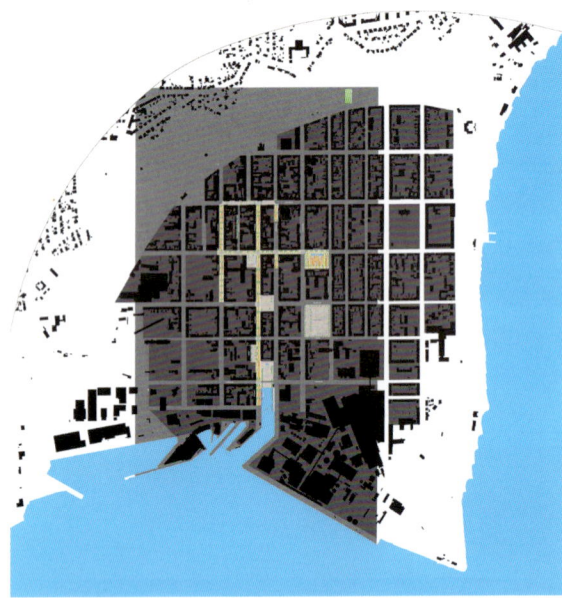

General plan

BROISSIN

www.broissin.com

**Mexico City
San Luis Potosí
Tijuana**

Broissin Architects is an office dedicated a 100% to architecture, design and interior and exterior design planning. They have gathered experience and ability to understand better the client's need, as well as an attractive design, a better use of the space, a good economic result and finishing time. They look forward on innovating with specialized design process for each project in different disciplines. They perceive architecture as one of the most efficient tools that any human being can use as a benefit to others. They have offices in Mexico City, San Luis Potosi and recently in Tijuana.

Broissin Architects es una oficina dedicada 100% a la arquitectura, el diseño y el diseño de interiores y exteriores. Acumulan experiencia y capacidad para entender mejor la necesidad del cliente, traducida en un diseño atractivo, un mejor uso del espacio y unos buenos resultados económicos. Esperan innovar con procesos de diseño especializados para cada proyecto en diferentes disciplinas. Perciben la arquitectura como una de las herramientas más eficientes que cualquier ser humano puede utilizar en beneficio de los demás. Tienen oficinas en la Ciudad de México, San Luis Potosí y recientemente en Tijuana.

GREEN HILLS KINDERGARTEN
Estado de México — 2012 — 1.800 m² / 19,375 sq ft
© Alexandre d'La Roche

The campus of Green Hills College to the north of the metropolitan area of the City of Mexico was planned in three stages, the first being a nursery dominated by the idea of letting buildings lie on the ground as if they were toys in a garden. This concept was behind the idea of locating all the prisms as if they were playing hide-and-seek with each other, leaving framed views of the nearby forest.

El plantel del colegio Green Hills en el norte del área metropolitana de la Ciudad de México es un campus planeado en tres etapas, la primera es la guardería en la que prevalece la idea de tumbar los edificios en el terreno a modo de juguetes en el jardín. Este concepto dió origen a la ubicación de todos los prismas que juegan a esconderse uno tras del otro dejando vistas enmarcadas del bosque inmediato.

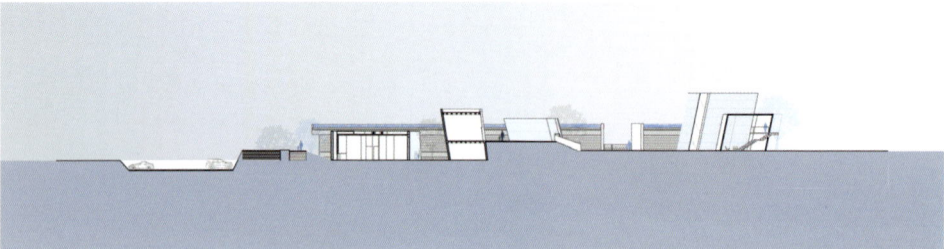

Cross section

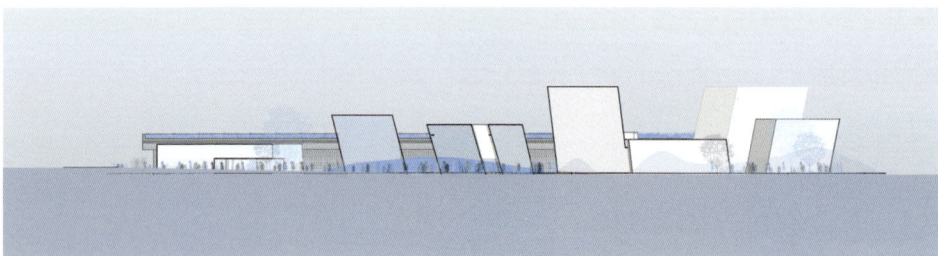

South elevation

Longitudinal section

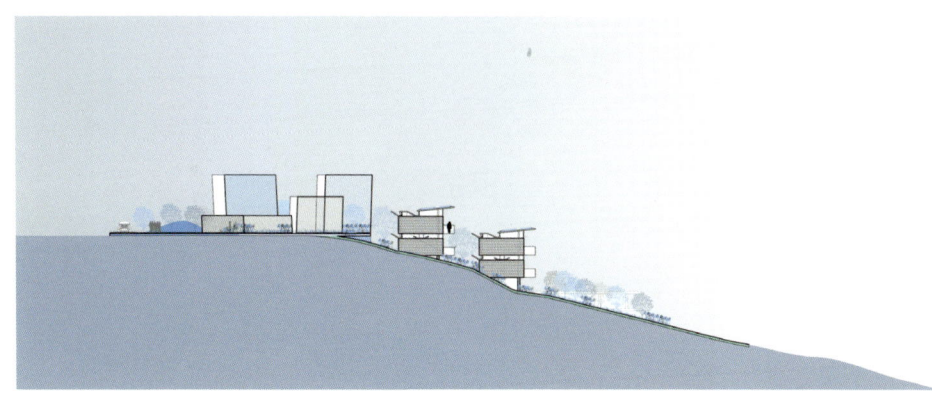

East elevation

It is a construction consisting of bays supported by stilts, encouraging the passage of rain water below the building as well as forming an ecological corridor for the species making up the region's cold forest ecosystem.

Es una construcción formada por crujías soportadas sobre pilotes, favoreciendo el paso del agua de lluvia por debajo del edificio así como la formación de un corredor ecológico para las especies que integran el ecosistema de bosque frio de la región.

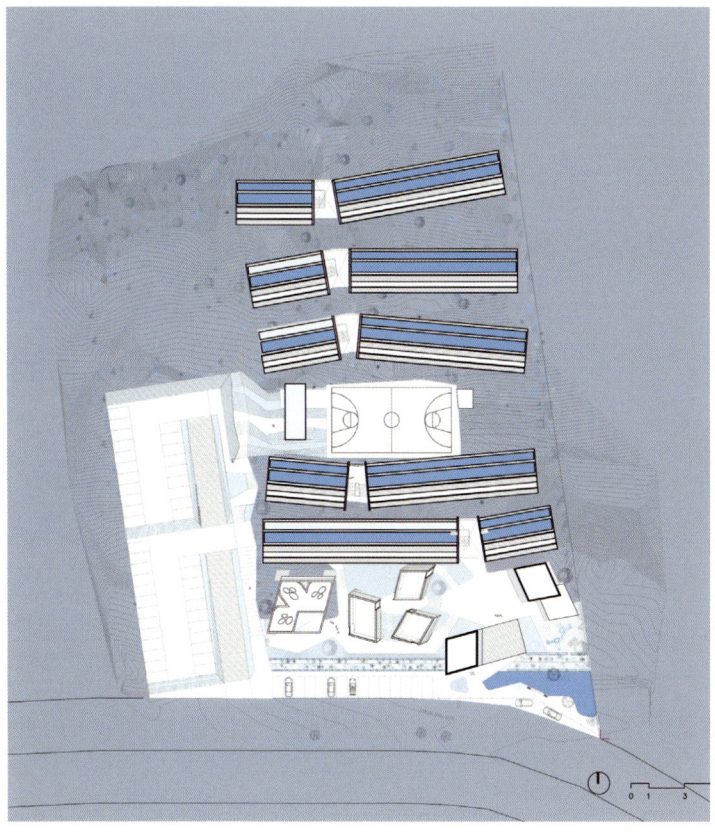

General plant

Kindergarden plan

A. **Building 1.**
   Primary classrooms
1. Cellar
2. Nurse station
3. Wash fountain
   8 children
4. W.C.
5. Computer room
6. K 1
7. K 2

B. **Maternity rooms**
8. Sandpit
9. Maternity playground

C. **Playground.**
   Classroom activities
10. Psychomotor skills
11. Mini-library
12. Art workshop

D. **Training courtyard**
13. Reception
14. Reception and
    student waiting area
15. Playground
16. Accounting
17. Address
18. Access

IREKUA ANATANI HOUSE

Avándaro, Estado de México — 2016 — 700 m² / 7,535 sq ft
© Alexandre d´La Roche

The name "Avandaro" comes from a Purépecha (a native language) word that means "place in the clouds", a territory originally inhabited by the tarasco indigenous people; who gave it this name, Irekua Anatani = Family house under the trees. Inspired by the land, which lies covered by oyamel trees, pine trees and encino trees, the house enjoys the splendor of living under this density and be intrinsically a part of it by safeguarding most of the existing forest.

El nombre de Avándaro proviene de la palabra purépecha que significa "lugar en las nubes", un territorio habitado originalmente por indígenas tarascos de cuya lengua este proyecto toma su alias, "Irekua Anatani" = Casa familiar bajo los árboles. Inspirada por un terreno cubierto por arboledas de oyameles, pinos y encinas, la casa goza del esplendor de vivir bajo esta espesura y es parte intrínseca de ella resguardando el bosque existente.

Cross section

The south west facade is mostly glass to capture the sunset in the evening and warm up the bedrooms to prepare them for the temperature decrease at night. The north facade tops towards Valle de Bravo's lake. The fifth facade is 100% green which maintains a uniform temperature throughout the whole year.

La fachada sur poniente en su mayoría es de vidrio para capturar los últimos rayos del sol de la tarde y calentar las habitaciones y baños. La fachada norte remata hacia el Valle de Bravo, pesenta la terraza principal y la alberca. La quinta fachada es 100% ecológica lo que mantiene una temperatura pareja durante todo el año.

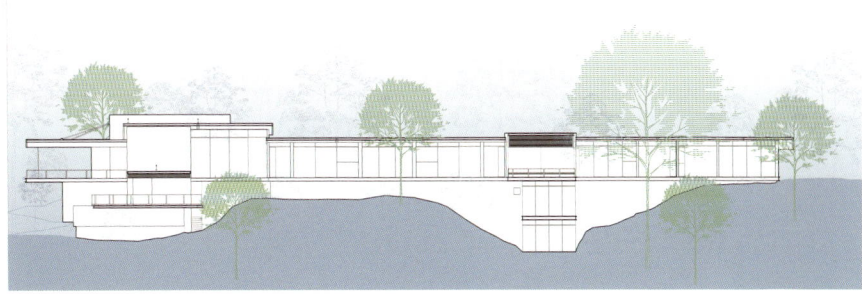

Rear elevation

The south east facade shows itself linear and dominated by a wood curtain that helps to let the sun's rays through in the morning in a diminished way, giving the necessary warmth.

La fachada sur se muestra lineal y dominada por una cortina de madera que ayuda a filtrar los rayos del sol de manera menguada dando la calidez necesaria.

Front elevation

Floor plan

1. Outdoor living
2. Terrace
3. Fire pit
4. Swimming pool
5. Jacuzzi
6. Sundeck
7. Dining room
8. Cupboard
9. Kitchen
10. Public area access
11. Hall
12. Family room
13. Boys room
14. Kids playroom
15. Girls room
16. Read / relax outside living
17. Foyer
18. Garden
19. Viewpoint / mountain terrace
20. Master bedroom
21. Closet
22. Garage
23. Bathroom

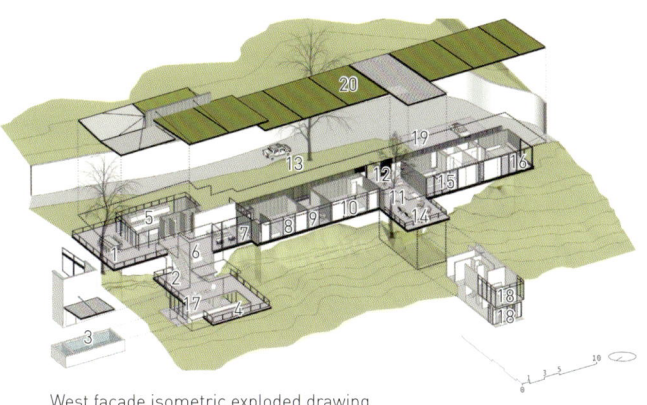

West façade isometric exploded drawing

1. Outdoor living	9. Kids playroom	15. Master bedroom w
2. Fire pit	10. Girls room	16. Master bedroom z
3. Swimming pool	11. Read / relax	17. Gym and steam
4. Sundeck	outside living	room
5. Kitchen	12. Foyer	18. Guest rooms
6. Hall	13. Garden	19. Garage
7. Family room	14. Viewpoint /	20. Green roof
8. Boys room	mountain terrace	

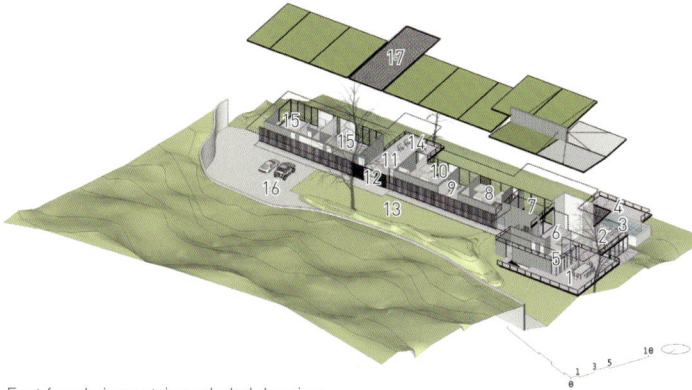

East façade isometric exploded drawing

1. Outdoor living	8. Boys room	14. Viewpoint /
2. Fire pit	9. Kids playroom	mountain terrace
3. Swimming pool	10. Girls room	15. Master bedroom
4. Sundeck	11. Read / relax	16. Garage
5. Kitchen	outside living	17. Green roof
6. Hall	12. Foyer	
7. Family room	13. Garden	

DD\M – DI DATO & MENINNO ASSOCIATED ARCHITECTS

---

www.didato-meninno.com

Corso Italia, 78
34170 Gorizia
Italy

Via Giacosa, 58
20127 Milan
Italy

DD\M Architects is a creative firm specialized in a multidisciplinary approach applied to many areas of design, from architecture to interior design, from urban and strategic design to landscape, from product design to graphic design and packaging.
The studio has considerable experience gained since 2004 and is characterized by the attention to quality, to design research and the ability to manage all the creative processes related to different disciplines.

DD\M arquitectos es una creativa firma especializada en un enfoque multidisciplinar aplicado a diferentes áreas del diseño, desde la arquitectura al diseño interior, desde el diseño urbano al paisajismo, desde el diseño de producto al diseño gráfico y al envasado. El estudio tiene una gran experiencia adquirida desde 2004 y se caracteriza por la atención a la calidad, la investigación y la capacidad de gestionar todos los procesos creativos de las diferentes disciplinas.

REDEVELOPMENT OF SEGHIZZI SQUARE AND THE BURG OF THE CASTLE OF GORIZIA

Gorizia, Italy — 2014 — 19.000 m² / 204,514 sq ft
© Massimo Crivellari

The renewal project for the "Borgo Castello", the historic village surrounding Gorizia's castle, has represented an opportunity to reconsider the symbol *par excellence* of the city. The new proposal have given birth to a new configuration, thus regenerating an area that recently had remained isolated from the rest of the city.

El proyecto de renovación del "Borgo Castello", la villa histórica que rodea el castillo de Gorizia, ha supuesto una oportunidad para reconsiderar el símbolo por excelencia de la ciudad. La nueva propuesta ha dado lugar a una nueva configuración, regenerando de esta manera un área que había quedado aislada del resto de la ciudad.

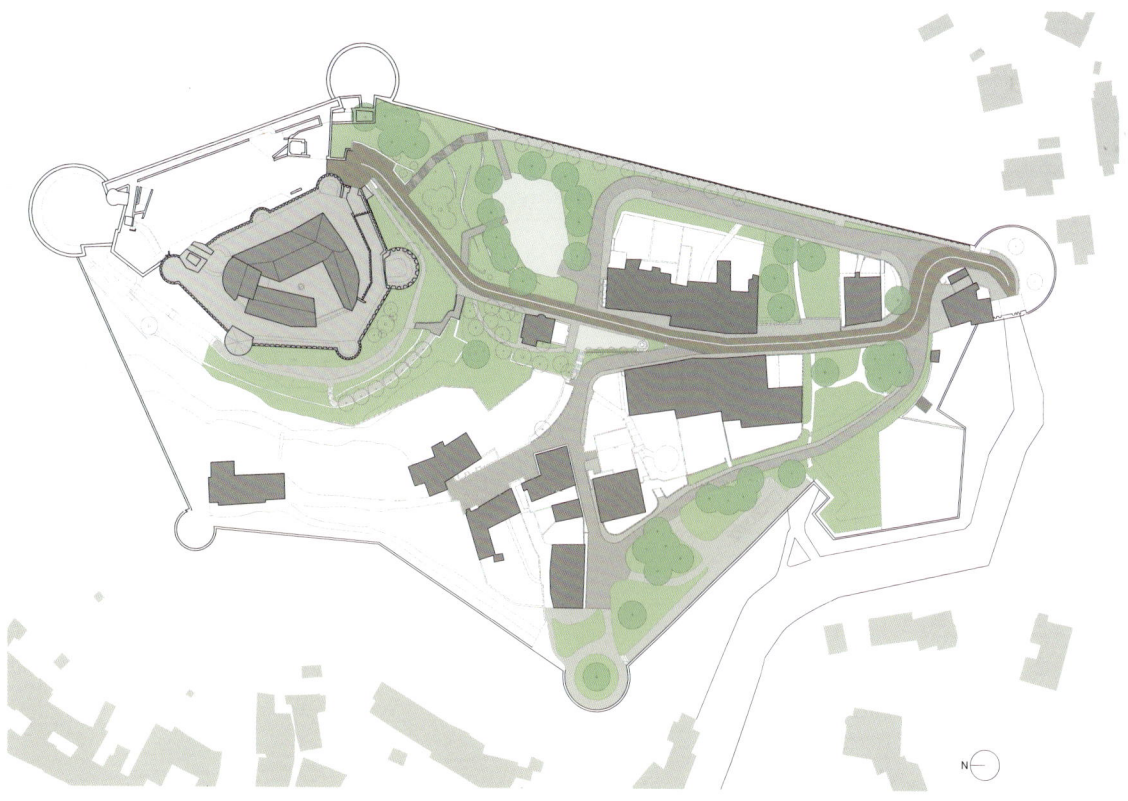

Site plan

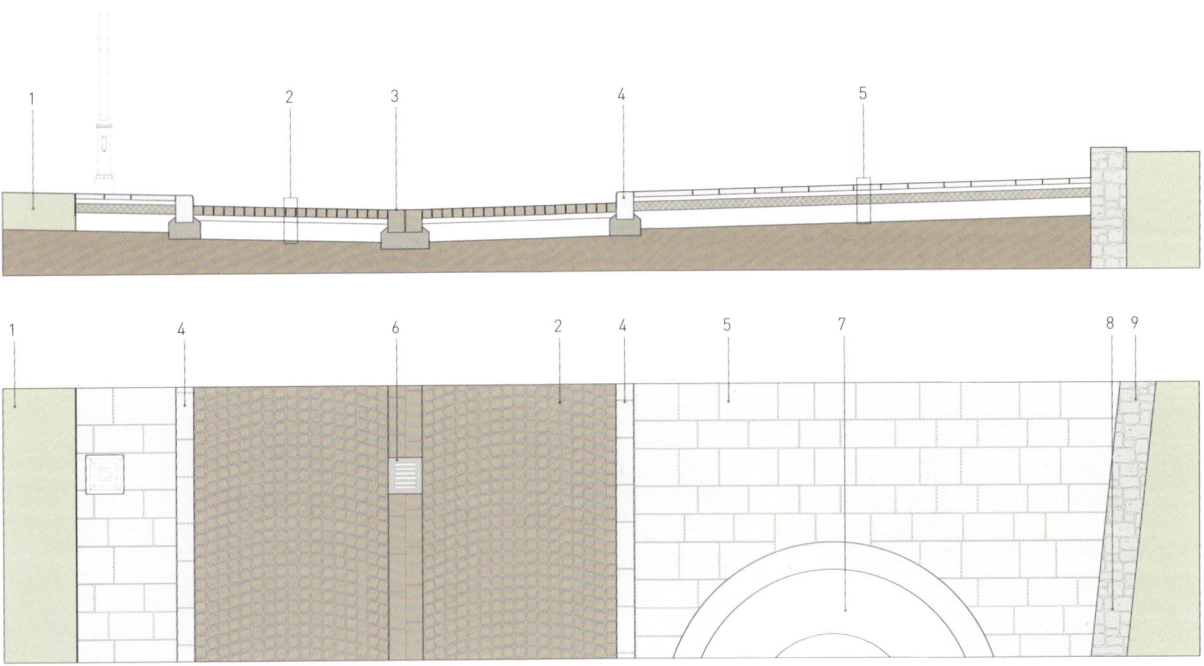

Central route paving detail

1. Flowerbed
2. Roadway
3. Roadway axis
4. Kerb
5. Sidewalk
6. Drainage grid
7. Existing well
8. Stone wall
9. Seat

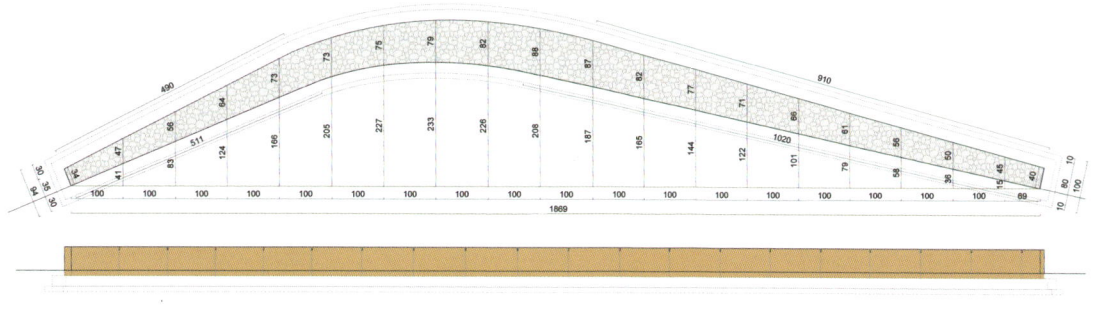

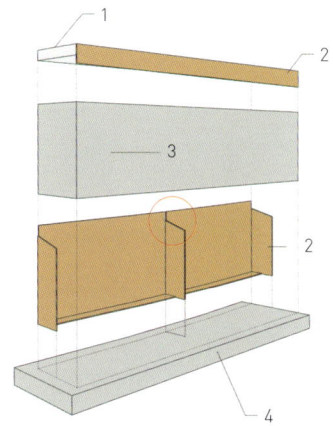

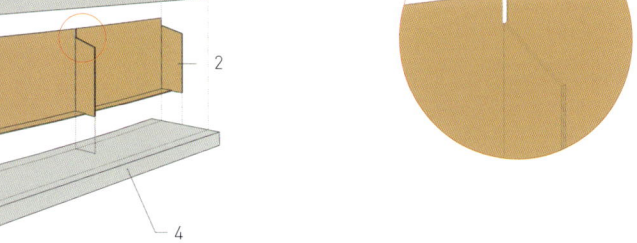

1. Split pebbles
2. Corten steel
3. Concrete retaining wall
4. Concrete basement
5. Corten joints detail

Seats details

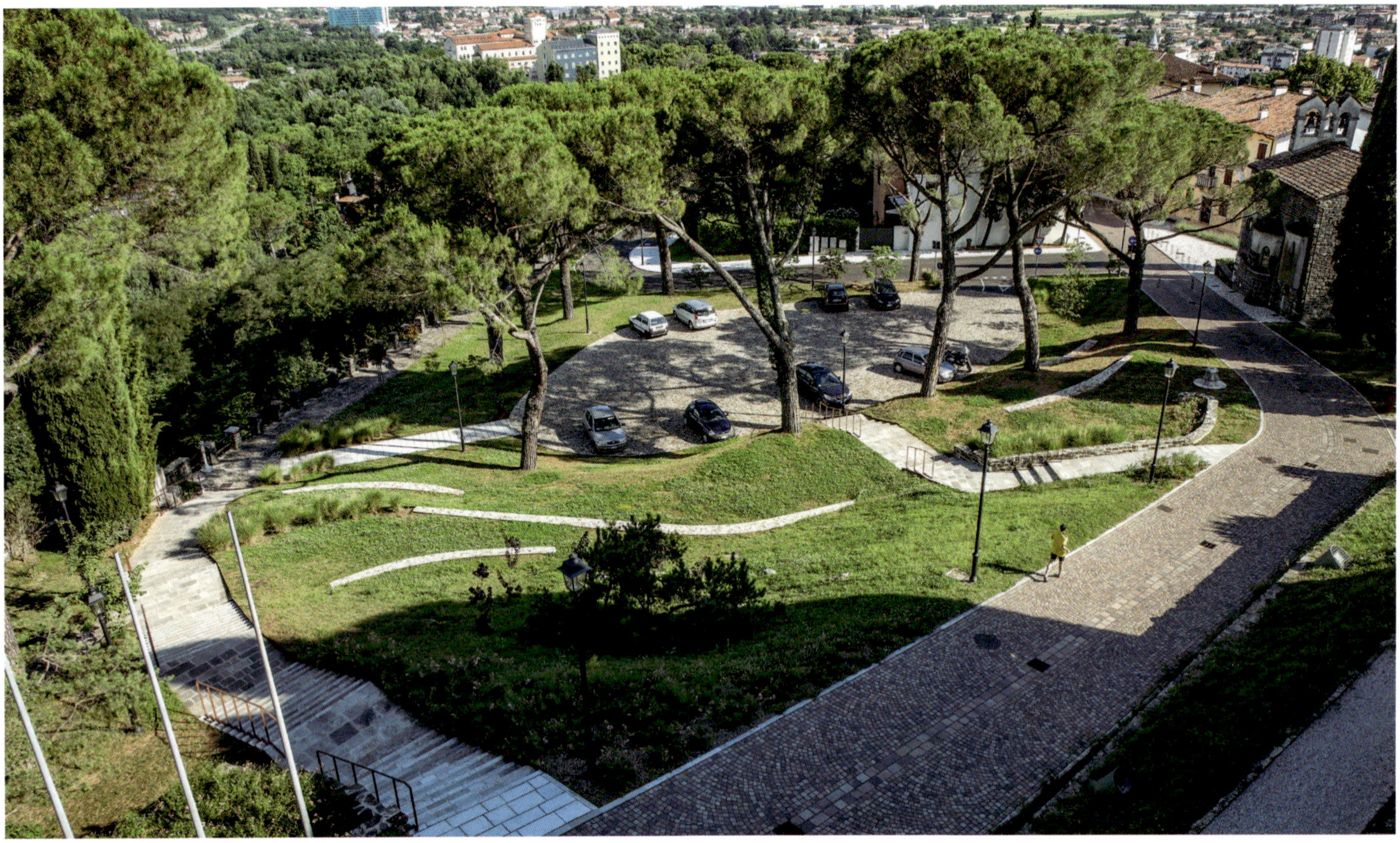

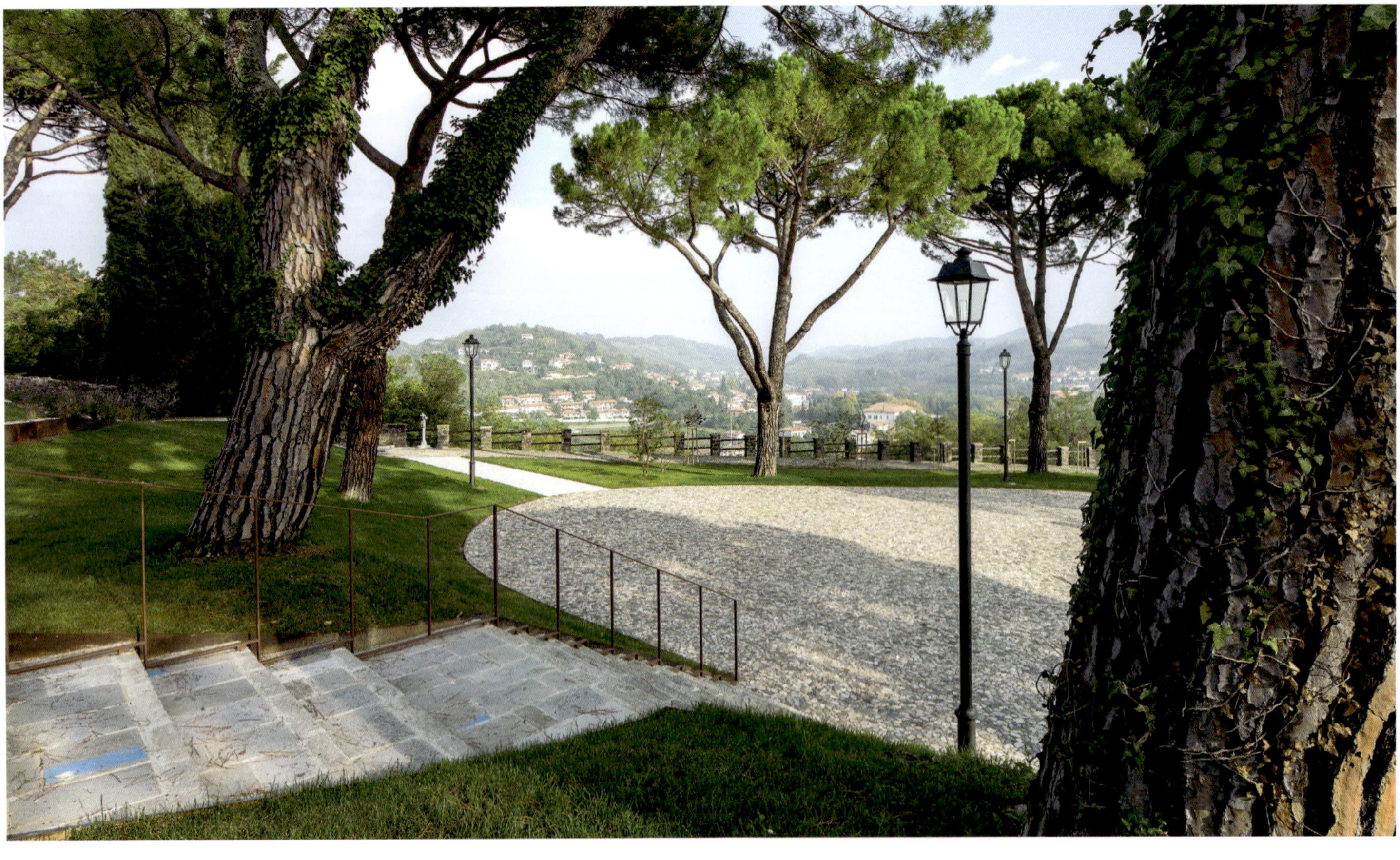

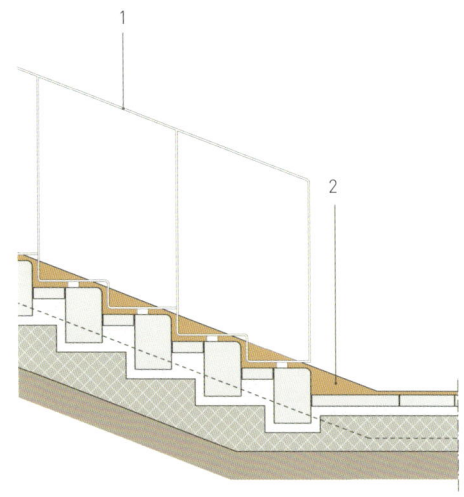

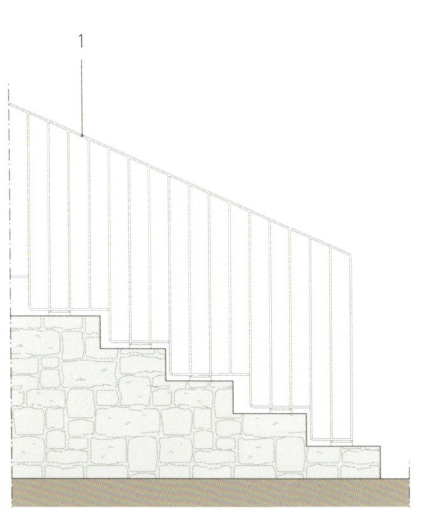

Railing tipologies details

1. Steel railing
2. Corten steel element

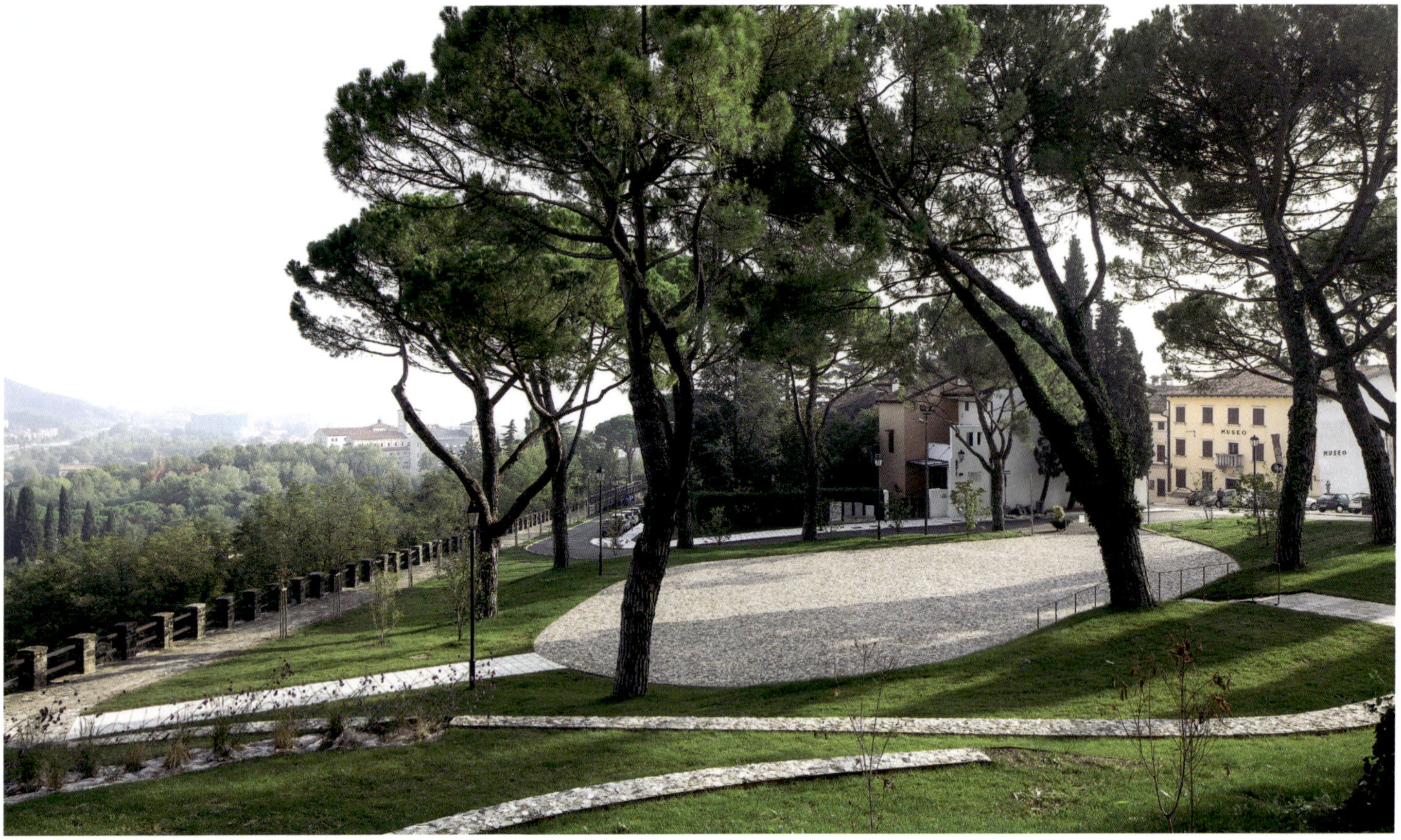
MUSEO
MUSEO

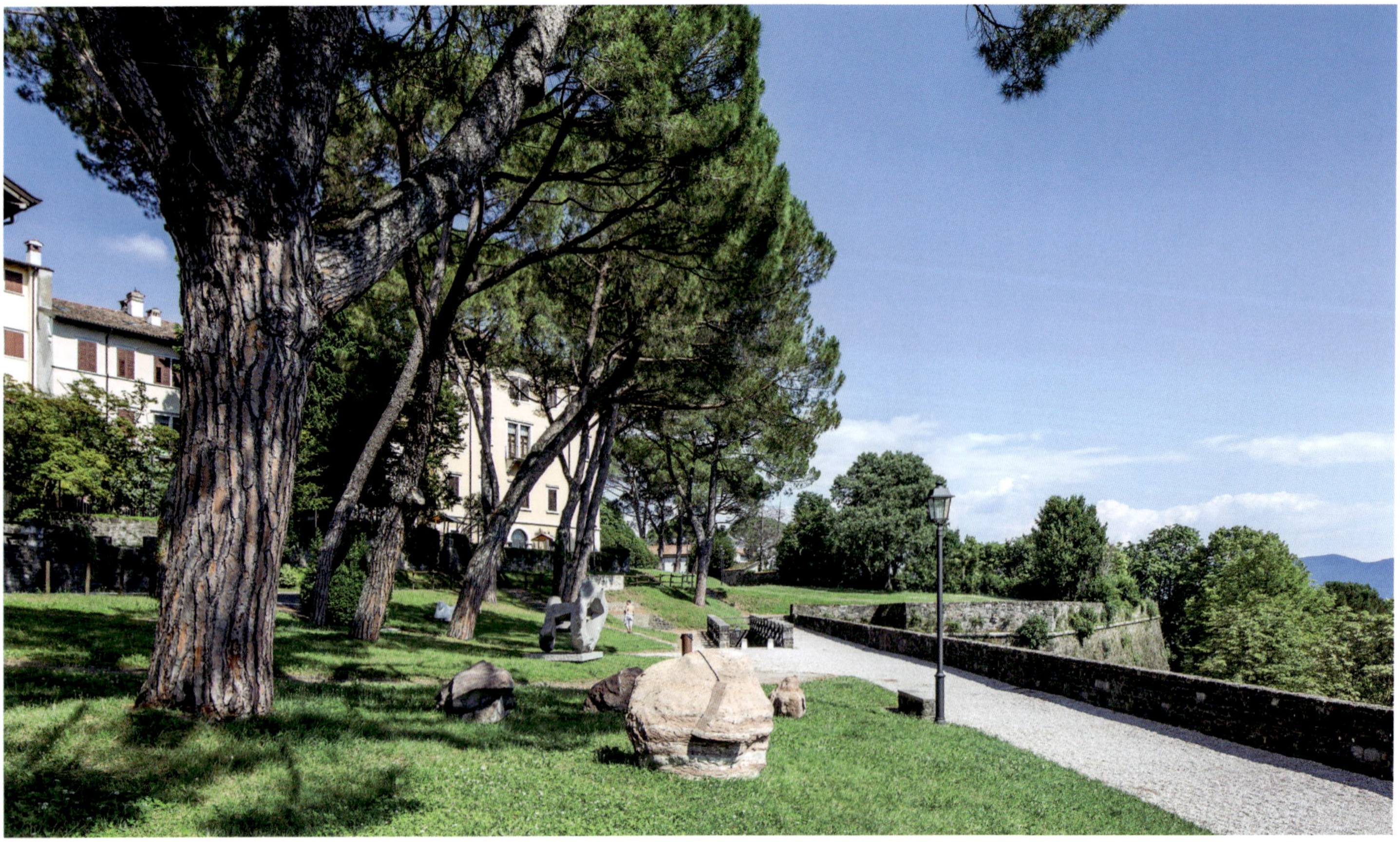

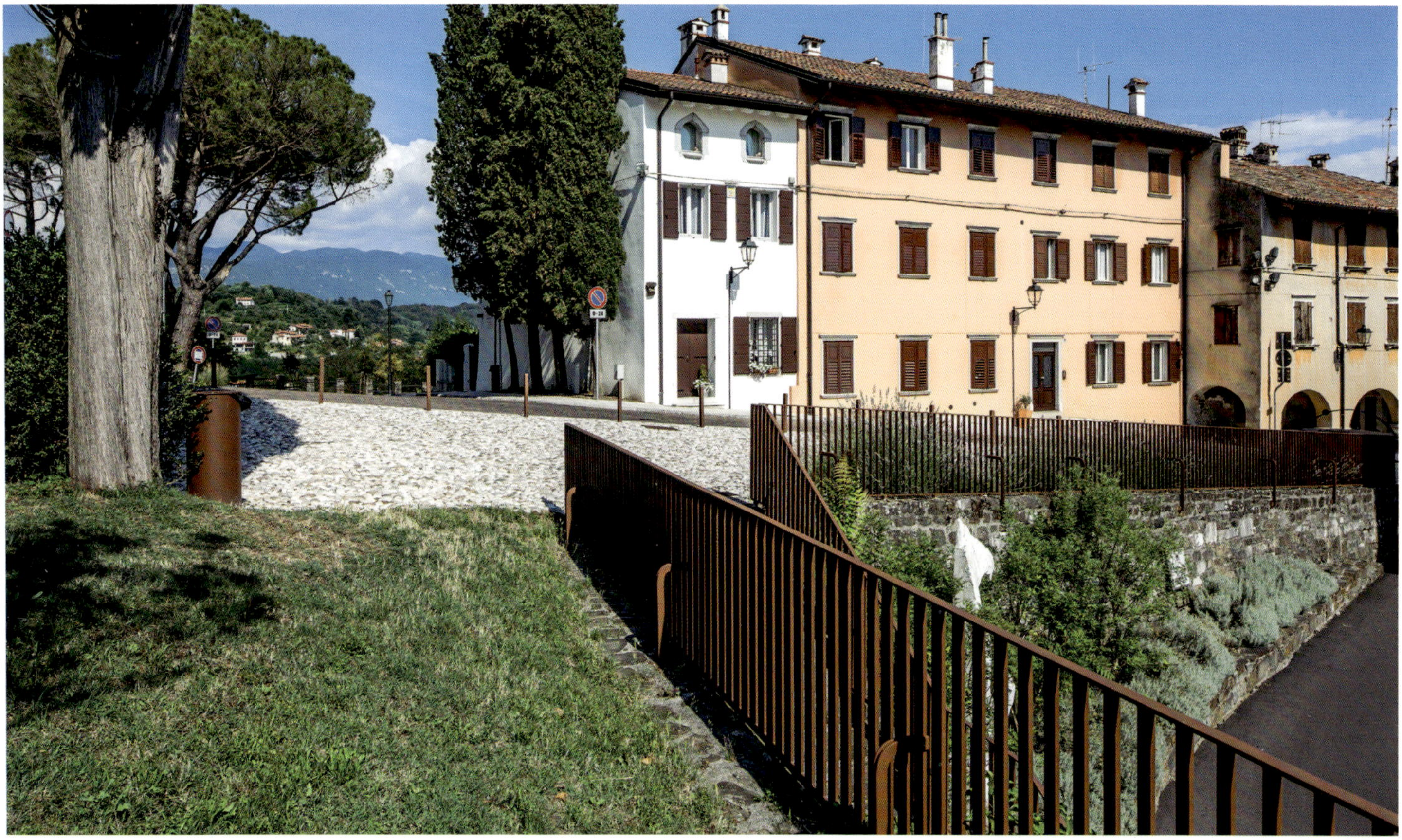

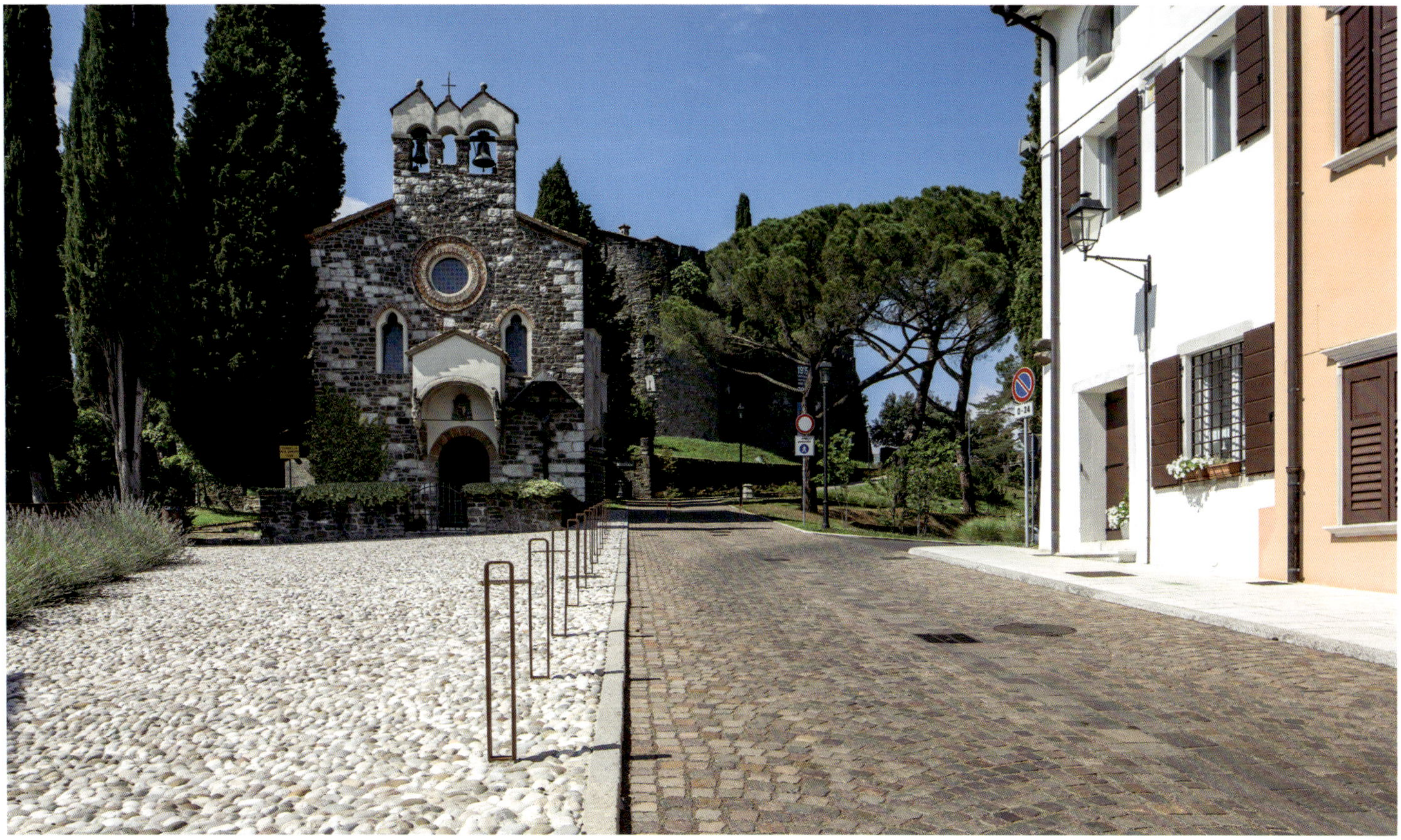

DELTA VORM GROEP

www.deltavormgroep.nl

Californiedreef 49
3565 bk Utrecht
The Netherlands

The Delta Vorm Groep Studio offers multidisciplinary design of exterior spaces focused in the fields of landscape and urban design. Architects and engineers converge in an atmosphere where interaction between the affiliated and parallel disciplines is fostered. Focusing their attention in the context of each particular project, the office aspires to use this information in a creative way to find solutions that are as logical as they are fascinating.

El estudio Delta Vorm Groep ofrece un servicio de diseño multidisciplinar para espacios exteriores, centrado en los ámbitos del paisajismo y el diseño urbano. Tanto arquitectos como ingenieros confluyen en su práctica, en la que se potencian las relaciones con disciplinas vecinas o tangenciales. Prestando una atención muy especial al contexto de cada proyecto, la firma aspira a usar esta información de manera creativa y a llegar a soluciones que siempre resultan tan lógicas como sorprendentes.

IBM RIEKERPOLDER
Amsterdam, The Netherlands — 2005 — Area: 25.000 m² / 172,223 sq ft
© Frank Colder, Picture7

An expanse of lawn serves as a background to the new headquarters for IBM, located on Riekerpolder Square, in the south part of the city of Amsterdam. The central element and visual focus of the project is the pond, which allowed planting the immediate surroundings with plants that need substantial amounts of water.

Una extensión inclinada de césped sirve de fondo a esta nueva sede de IBM que se encuentra en la plaza de Riekerpolder, en la zona sur de la ciudad de Ámsterdam. El elemento central del proyecto es el embalse de agua, lo cual ha posibilitado que los alrededores se vistieran de elementos vegetales que requieren de bastante hidratación.

General plan

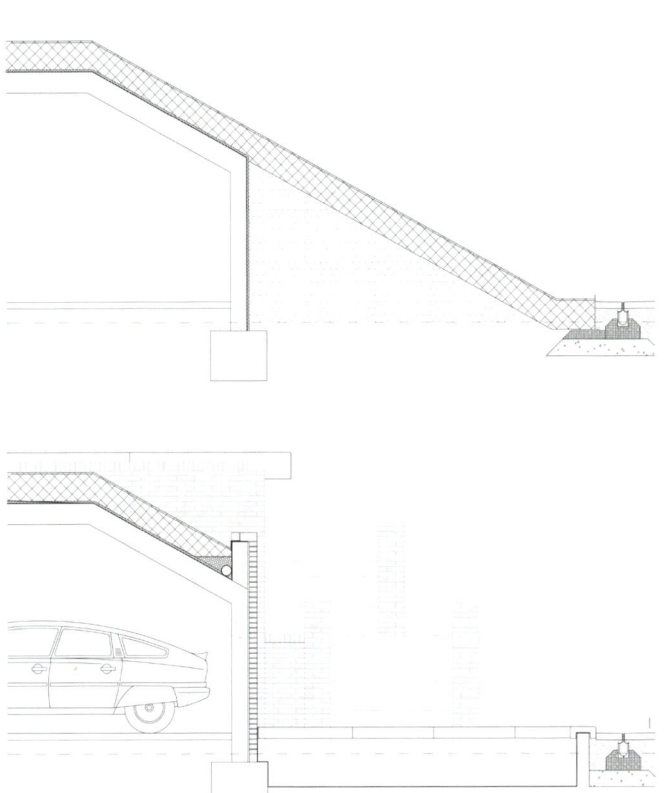

Sections

The central garden is a much more secluded space that keeps water still as the main element.

En el jardín central se crea un ambiente más recogido, aunque el agua sigue siendo el elemento protagonista.

GRAADT VAN ROGGENWEG

Utrecht, The Netherlands — 2001 — Area: 34.000 m² / 365,973 sq ft
© Frank Colder, Picture7

The recent construction of two buildings in the same area left an unused space between them, for which Delta Vorm Groep designed a hedge garden. The design of this garden is formed by a pattern of parallel lines that are perpendicular to the building's towers.

The hedges are uniformly 11.8 inches high, allowing the perception of the continuity of the design.

La reciente construcción de dos edificios en la misma zona dejó entre ambos un área sin utilizar, en la que Delta Vorm Groep ha diseñado un jardín cuyo principal protagonista son los setos de boj. Un patrón continuo de líneas estructurales paralelas marca el dibujo general de la planta, perpendiculares a las fachadas de los edificios.

Los setos de boj tienen una altura uniforme de 30 cm, de manera que se subraya el carácter continuo y unificador de las líneas transversales.

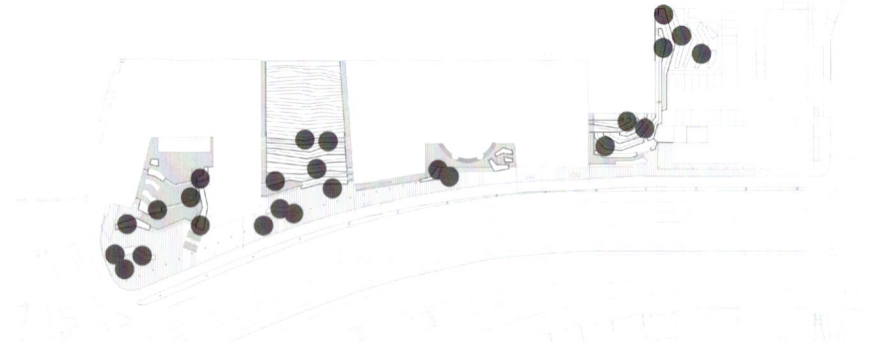

General plan

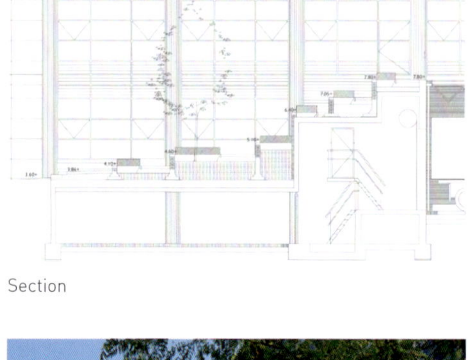

Section

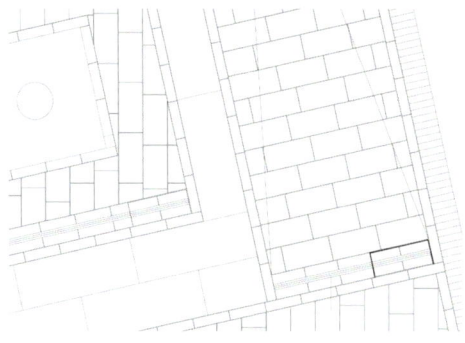

Pavement detail

MAANPLEIN

The Hague, The Netherlands — 2001 — Area: 6.500 m² / 69,965 sq ft
© Frank Colder, Picture7

The landscaping of this resting area among office buildings emphasizes the presence of the park as a continuous body that flows amongst the different volumes, imitating incidental forms of nature with sinuous paths, amorphous rocks and randomly planted vegetation.

El diseño del paisajismo de esta zona de descanso entre varios edificios de oficinas subraya la presencia del parque como un cuerpo continuo que fluye alrededor de los distintos volúmenes, imitando las formas arbitrarias de la naturaleza con senderos serpenteantes, rocas informes y plantas colocadas en forma de cuña.

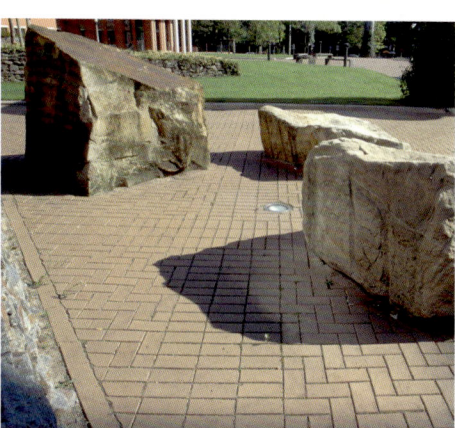

The design also includes a series of elements laid out in a pattern of lines and right angles, establishing contrasts between what is built and what is natural.

El diseño también cuenta con una serie de elementos dibujados a base de líneas y ángulos rectos, estableciendo un juego de contrastes entre lo construido y lo natural.

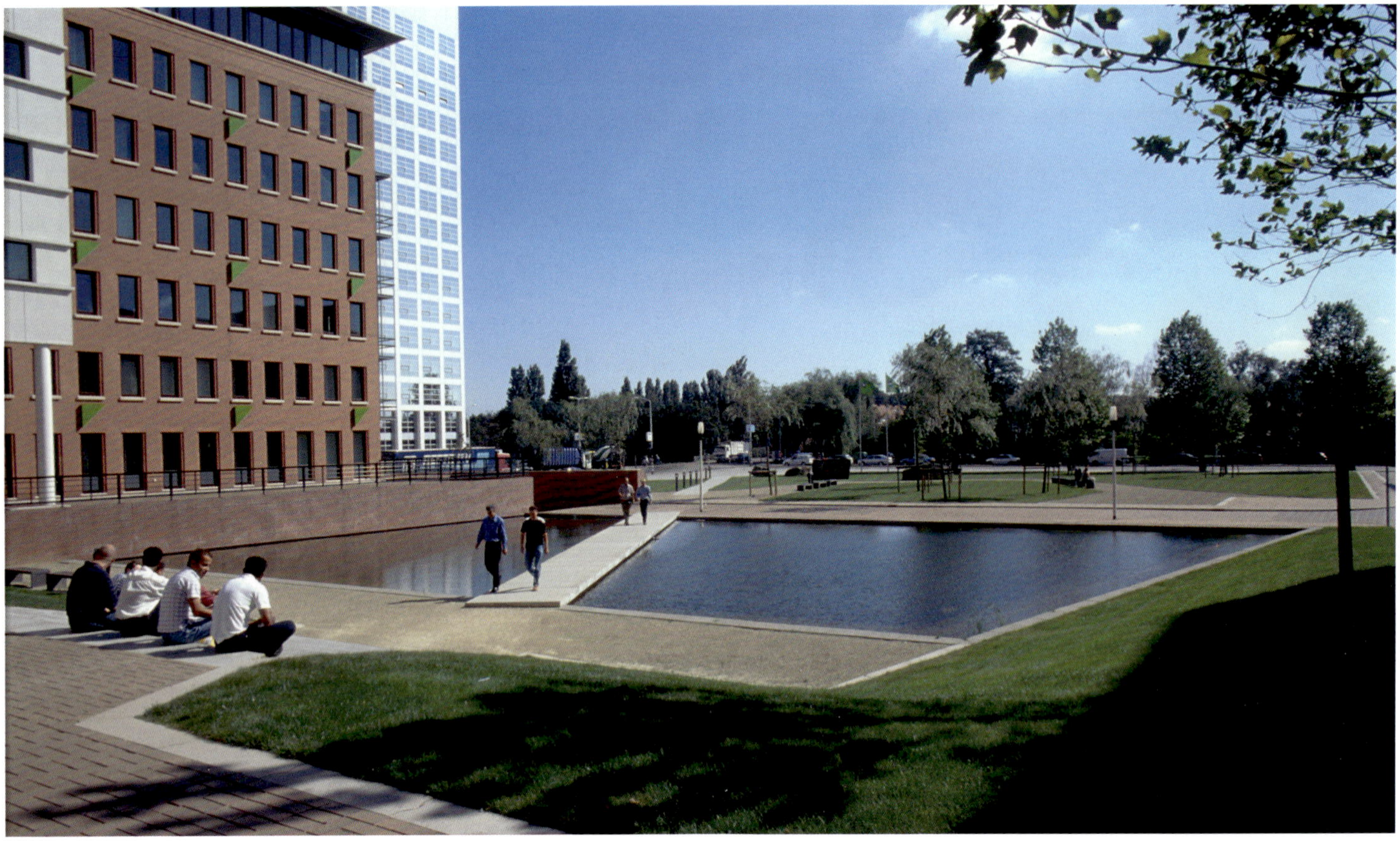

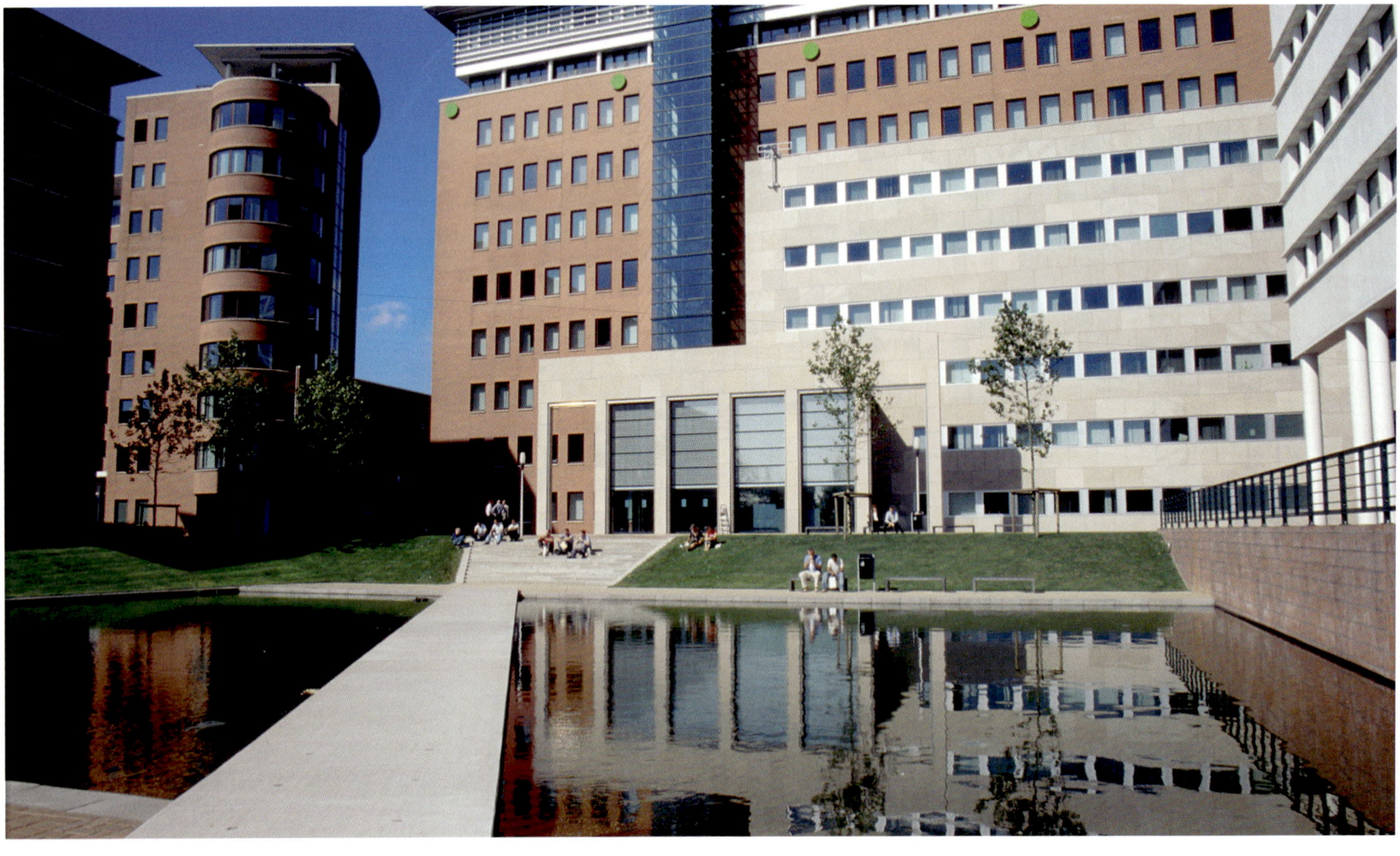

DIETMAR FEICHTINGER ARCHITECTES

www.feichtingerarchitectes.com

11, rue des Vignoles
75020 Paris
France

Dietmar Feichtinger studied architecture at the University of Graz, Austria, and from 1984 to 1988 worked at the same institution with his professors Giencke and Kada. He spent the following four years working with Philippe Chaix and Jean-Paul Morel and in 1994 opened his own architecture firm. He has taught at the University of Innsbruck and he still teaches at the University La Villette in Paris. In 2002 Feichtinger Architectes opened a second office in Vienna.

Dietmar Feichtinger estudió arquitectura en la Universidad de Graz (Austria), y de 1984 a 1988 trabajó en el mismo centro junto a los profesores Giencke y Kada. Los siguientes cuatro años los pasó en el estudio de Philippe Chaix y Jean-Paul Morel y en 1994 fundó su propia firma de arquitectura. Ha sido profesor de la Universidad de Innsbruck y todavía lo es de la Universidad La Villette de París. En 2002 Feichtinger Architectes estableció una delegación en Viena.

FOOTBRIDGE SIMONE DE BEAUVOIR
Paris, France — 2006 — 3.700 m² / 39,826 sq ft
© Jo Pesendorfer

With a total length of 997 ft and a free span of 623 ft, this impressive bridge connects Bercy Park with the François Mitterrand National Library, a route that could only be done by boat across the Seine River.
The intersection of the arcs with the suspended catenaries creates a symmetrical "lens". The resulting structure generates a 39-foot-wide and 164-foot-long space.

Con una longitud total de 304 m –de los cuales 190 discurren sin apoyos–, esta pasarela de impresionante aspecto conecta el parque de Bercy con la Biblioteca Nacional François Mitterrand, un camino que antes sólo podía hacerse a bordo de un barco que cruzara el Sena.
La intersección del arco con las curvas de la catenaria crea una lámina simétrica. Del entretejido resultante surge un espacio de 12 m de ancho y 50 m de largo.

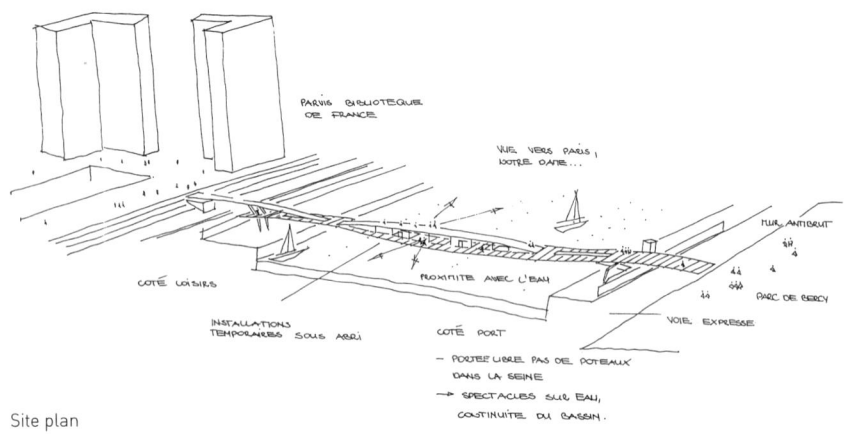

Site plan

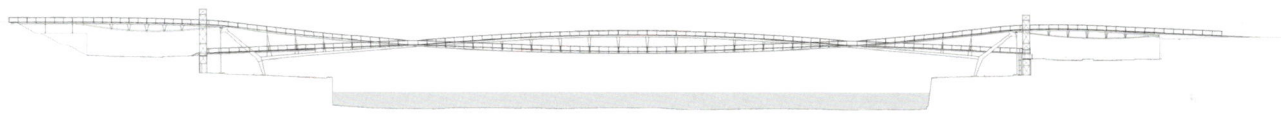

Elevation

FOOTBRIDGE OF THE MUSEUM

Hamburg, Germany — 2007 — Area: 160 m² / 1,722 sq ft
© Feichtinger Architectes

This bridge that connects the museum with the rest of the city is notable for it s simple structure. The two opposing arcs that form the structure of the bridge generate thenecessary tension to span the river without any support columns.
The unique oblique slopes of the bridge generate a highly sculptural geometrical environment.

Esta sencilla pasarela, que conecta el edificio del museo con el resto de la ciudad, llama la atención por su ligereza estructural, además de por los dos tramos de inclinación enfrentada que lo forman, enfrentados para propiciar la tensión necesaria para que se sujete sin necesidad de pilares.
La original trayectoria oblicua de la pasarela aporta un detalle escultórico a un entorno de rigurosa geometría de ángulos rectos.

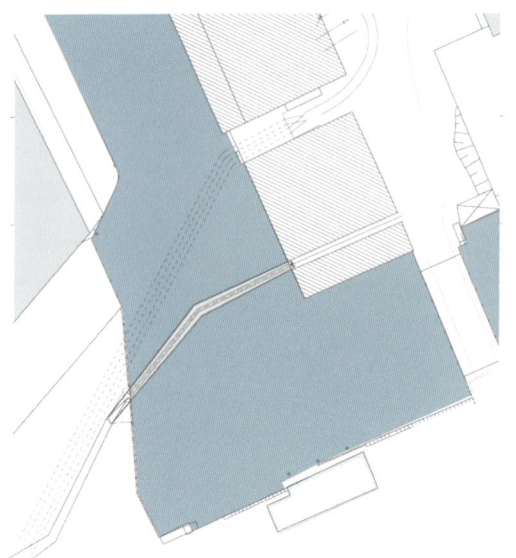

Location map

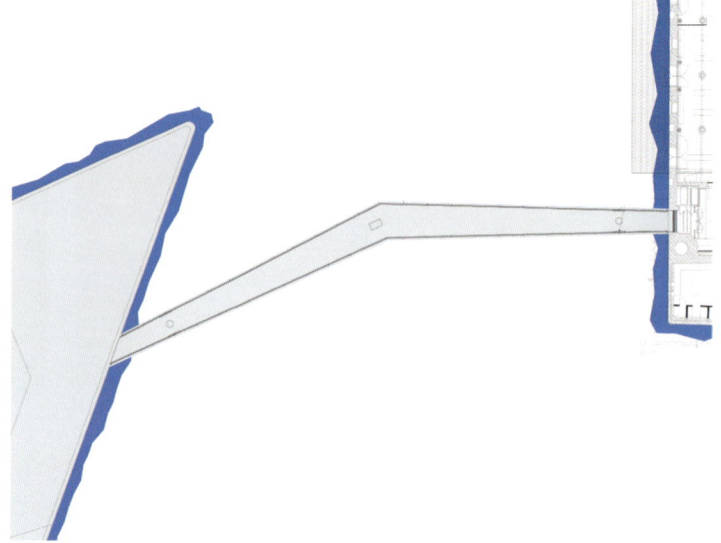

Site plan

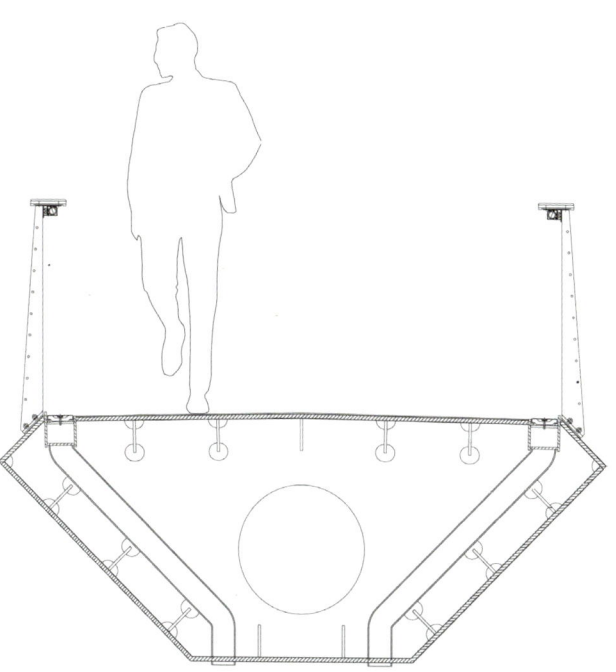

Cross section

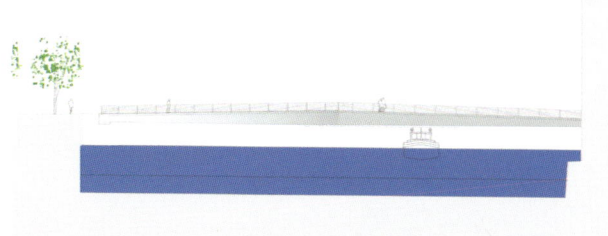

Longitudinal section

VALMY FOOTBRIDGE

Nanterre, France — 2008 — Area: 360 m² / 3,875 sq ft
© Feichtinger Architectes

This 295-foot-long bridge arcs through a dense urban fabric in the Paris financial district of La Défense. Especially resistant against possible torsion, the structure maintains itsrigidity thanks to a series of "vertebra" and "tendons".

Esta pasarela de 90 m de longitud se extiende a través de un denso tejido urbano en el distrito financiero parisino de La Défense. Especialmente resistente a posibles torsiones, la estructura mantiene su rigidez gracias a una serie de «vértebras» y «tendones».

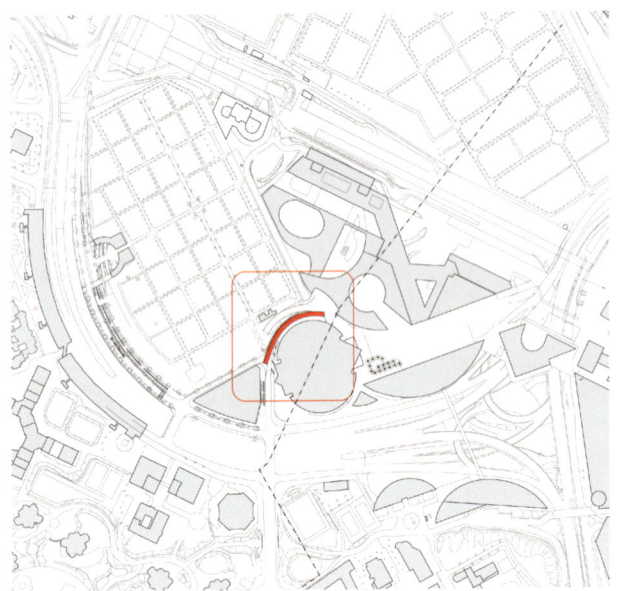

Location map

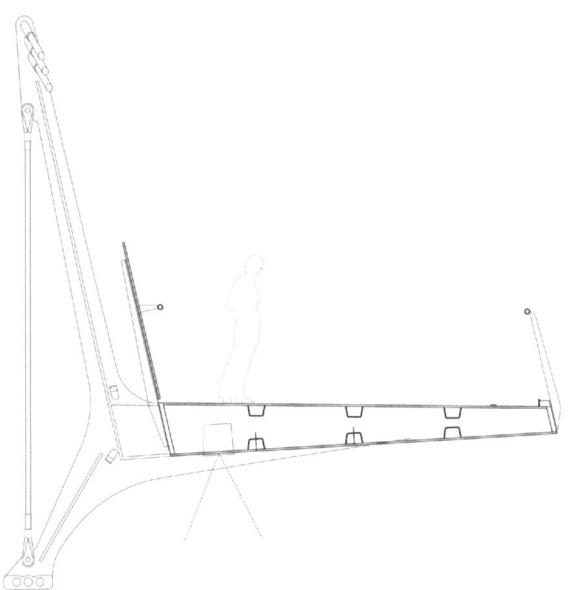

Cross section

FOOTBRIDGE IN STRASBOURG

Strasbourg, France — 2008 — Area: 190 m² / 2,045 sq ft
© Jo Persendorfer

The fundamental characteristics of this project derive from the immediate urban environment. The canal that these footbridges cross is also the site of a library. The hardindustrial character existing neighborhood is counterbalanced by the tranquility of the bridge design which invites walking through the site.

The light new structures contrast with the chaotic industrial environment.

Las características fundamentales de este proyecto vienen en gran parte definidas por su entorno urbano. El canal que permite atravesar la nueva pasarela es hoy en día el emplazamiento de una biblioteca. El aspecto industrial de los usos anteriores se combate con la intervención, que invita a la tranquilidad y al paseo.

La ligereza de la nueva construcción combate con el desordenado pasado industrial del entorno.

DISSING+WEITLING ARCHITECTURE

www.dw.dk

Artillerivej 86, 3 tv.
2300 Copenhagen S
Denmark

At DISSING+WEITLING the goal is to create optimal spaces for human activity – at work, in the home and in the public sphere with a clear and accommodating approach, characterized by user-centric solutions that pay attention to the physical, cultural and environmental context of each project.
DISSING+WEITLING was formed in 1971 to continue the work started by Arne Jacobsen. Since then, the company has refined and developed this Scandinavian design tradition with works that have set new standards in design and architecture.

En DISSING+WEITLING el objetivo es crear espacios óptimos para la actividad humana en el trabajo, el hogar y el ámbito público con un enfoque claro y útil, caracterizado por soluciones centradas en el usuario que prestan atención al contexto físico, cultural y medioambiental de cada proyecto.
DISSING+WEITLING fue creado en 1971 para continuar el trabajo iniciado por Arne Jacobsen. Desde entonces, la empresa ha refinado y desarrollado esta tradición de diseño escandinavo con obras que han establecido nuevos estándares en diseño y arquitectura.

CYKELSLANGEN (THE BICYCLE SNAKE)

Kalvebod Brygge, Copenhagen, Denmark — 2014 — 230 m long, 4,6 m wide / 756 ft long, 15 ft wide
© Ole Malling, Rasmus Hjortshøj

As a clever solution to a site-specific problem, The Bicycle Snake is an elevated 230 meter two-way bike lane at the first-floor level, wriggling its way over the harbour, connecting The Quay Bridge bridge crossing the inner harbour with a roadway some 5.5m above the level of the quay. Previously, bicyclists passing across the harbour had to bike through a narrow space haphazardly shared with pedestrians and push their bikes up a steep flight of stairs in order to continue their journey.

Como una solución inteligente a un problema específico del lugar, The Bicycle Snake es un carril bici elevado de dos vías y 230 metros de longitud, cuyo trazado serpentea sobre el puerto, conecta el puente del muelle y cruza el puerto interior a unos 5,5m sobre el suelo. Anteriormente, los ciclistas que cruzaban el puerto tenían que pedalear a través de un espacio estrecho compartido con los peatones y empujar sus bicicletas por un empinado tramo de escaleras para poder continuar su camino.

Even on our best behaviour, bad or insufficient city planning creates tension. However, clever urban planning and good design can relieve this, as is the case with The Bicycle Snake, which is a tremendous public success and has become an icon for Copenhagen's status as one of the most liveable cities in the world.

Incluso con nuestra mejor conducta, un deficiente planeamiento urbano crea tensión. Sin embargo, un planeamiento inteligente y un buen diseño pueden aliviar este hecho, como es el caso de The Bicycle Snake, un tremendo éxito de público convertido en un icono para el estatus de Copenhague como una de mejores las ciudades para vivir del mundo.

Site plan

With the added benefits of giving bike riders the joyful experience of meandering through the air at the first-floor level and thus leaving room for an attractive, vibrant urban space for pedestrians on the ground, The Bicycle Snake provides Copenhagen's numerous bicyclists with an easier access across the city's inner harbour and creates a less stressful atmosphere for both bicyclists and pedestrians.

Con el beneficio añadido de dar a los ciclistas la alegre experiencia de serpentear por el aire al nivel de una primera planta y dejar así espacio para una atractiva zona peatonal en el suelo, The Bicycle Snake ofrece a los numerosos ciclistas de Copenhague un recorrido más cómodo a través del puerto interior de la ciudad y crea una atmósfera menos estresante tanto para ciclistas como para peatones.

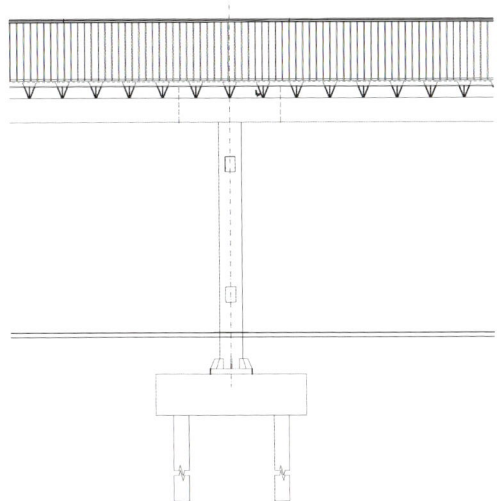

Elevation

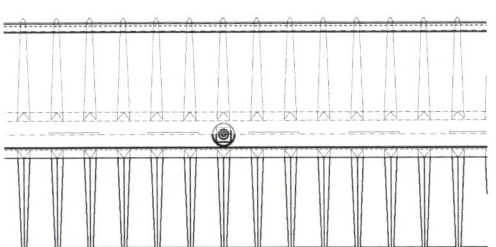

Plan and soffit plan

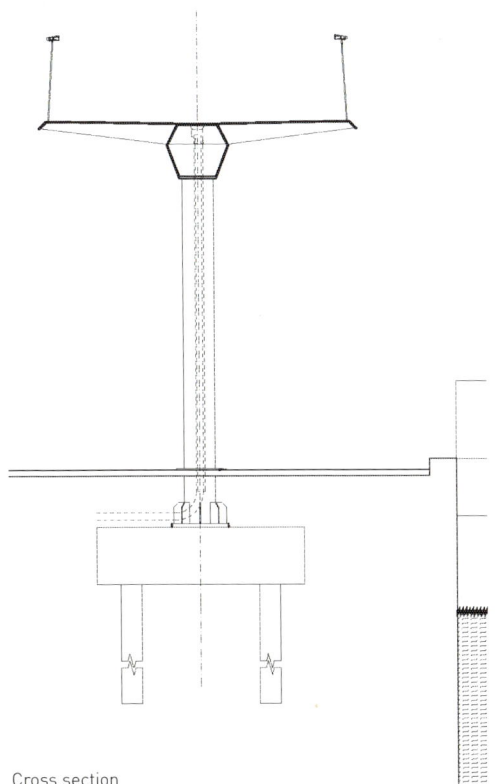

Cross section

DURBACH BLOCK ARCHITECTS

www.durbachblock.com

71 York Street, 5th Floor
2000 Sydney
New South Wales
Australia

Neil Durbach and Camila Block are two South African architects with their practice based in Sydney, Australia. The studio is formed of a team of eight professionals able to conceive creative projects in various fields from residential architecture to landscape architecture and public spaces. The firm has received the Wilkinson and Robin Boyd Residential House Award in two occasions.

Neil Durbach y Camilla Block son dos arquitectos sudafricanos radicados en Sídney. El estudio que fundaron, con una plantilla de ocho personas, cuenta con un equipo creativo capaz de concebir proyectos de gran calidad en campos muy variados, desde la arquitectura residencial al paisaje y los espacios públicos. Uno de los galardones más importantes que han recibido es el Wilkinson and Robin Boyd Residental House Award, que han ganado dos veces.

BRICKPIT RING
Sydney, Australia — 2005 — Area: 250 m² / 2,691 sq ft
© Craig Carlstrom

This former quarry is the last trace of an industrial exploitation that existed in the Homebush Bay. The elevated circular path designed by the architects acts as an outlook and a floating square made for the enjoyment of the immediate environment, somewhere between the natural and the artificial. The slender structure contrasts with the harshness of the landscape formed by the former quarry.

Esta antigua cantera es el último vestigio de una explotación industrial que hubo hace tiempo en la bahía de Homebush. El paseo circular aéreo diseñado por los arquitectos se convierte en un mirador y en una especie de plaza flotante que permite disfrutar de este entorno que oscila entre lo natural y lo artificial. La esbeltez de la estructura contrasta a la perfección con la dureza del paisaje que forma la cantera.

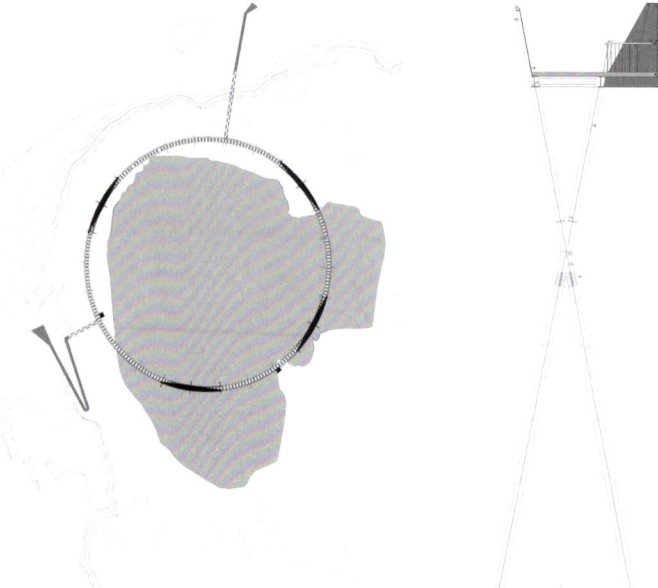

General plan

Section through elevated path

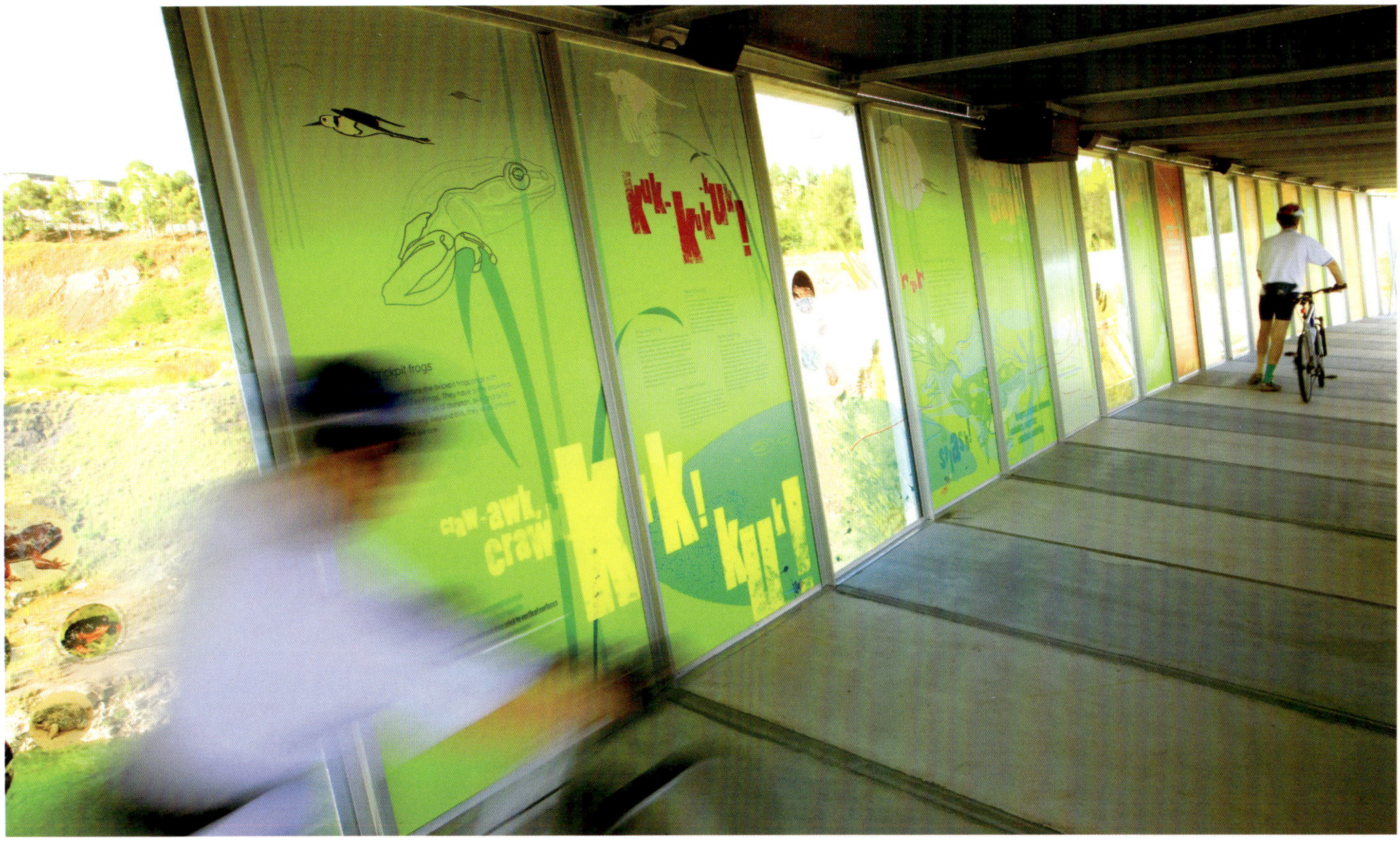
craw-awk,
craw

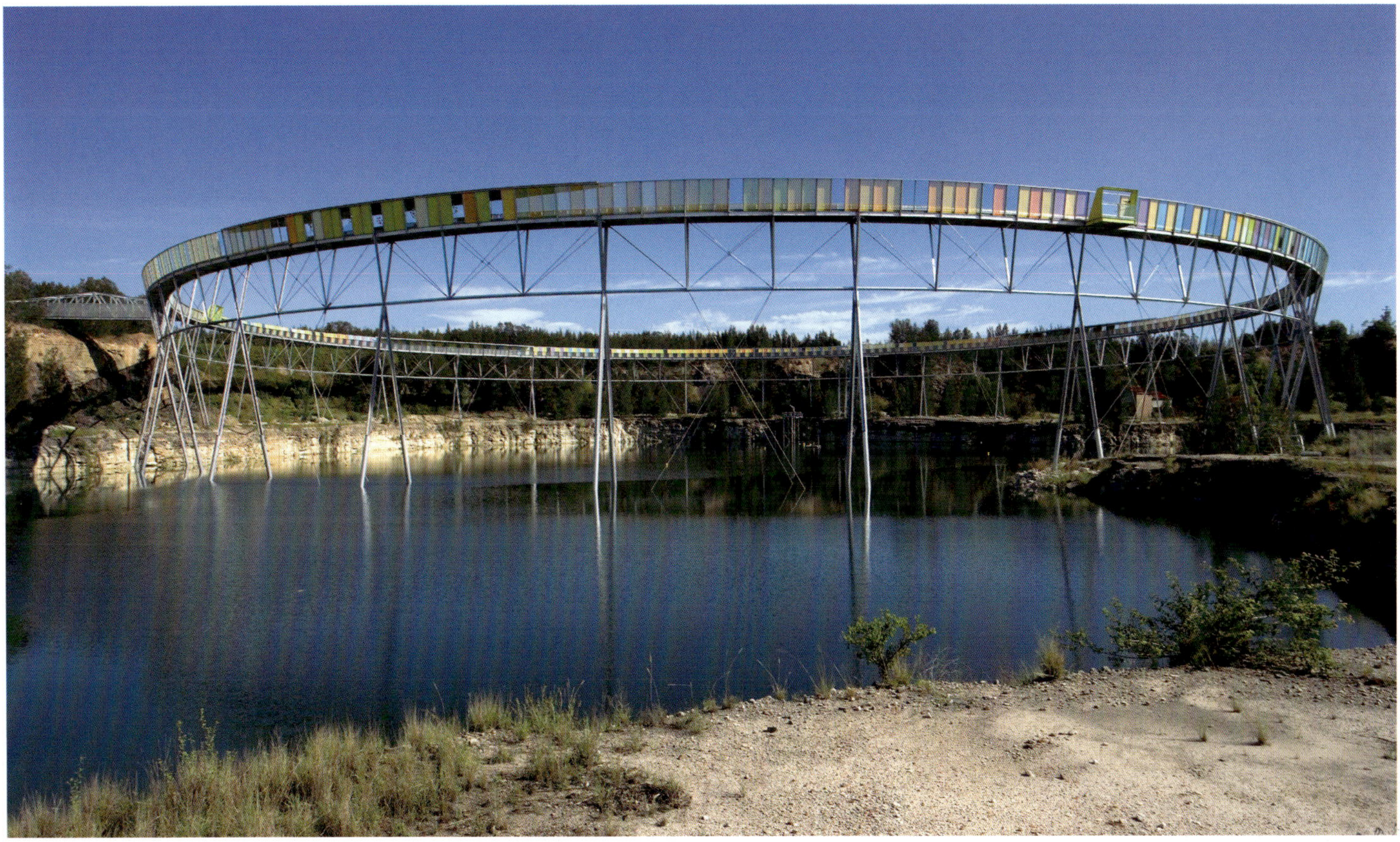

COMMONWEALTH PLACE
Canberra, Australia — 2002 — Area: 2.500 m² / 26,910 sq ft
© Anthony Browell

This meeting zone generates an effect of surprise due to the drama of the undulating landscape. The artificial hills of grass are the form of a roof of a large interior space with restaurants and cafeterias while on the exterior, the appearance is that of a conventional park.

Esta zona de reunión impacta por la interpretación grandiosa que hace de las ondulaciones del paisaje. El prado artificial discurre por unas colinas que ocultan, en un nivel inferior, una galería con restaurantes y cafeterías, mientras que desde el exterior el aspecto es el de un parque convencional.

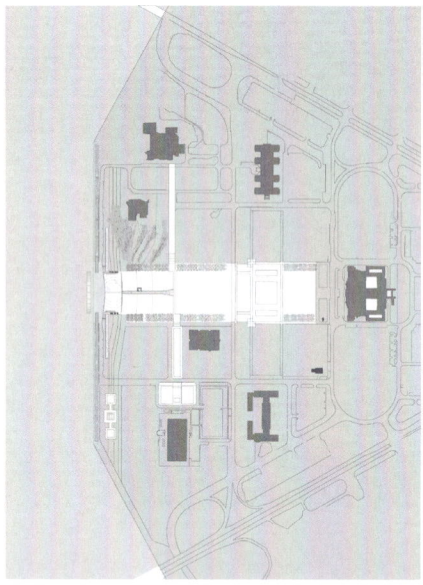

Location map

General plan

A privileged location makes the park a viewpoint that overlooks the river.

La privilegiada ubicación convierte al parque en un gran mirador que se asoma al río.

EDAW

www.edaw.com

150 Chestnut Street
San Francisco
California 94111
United States

The origin of AECOM, the firm from which-
derived from EDAW goes back to 1939.
Well-known for its "Californian style" architecture, the firm, founded by Garrett Eckbo
soonmarked a trend with its landscape architecture and urban planning designs. The
name of the firm was changed to EDAW
when Francis Dean and Don Austin became
directors. Nowadays, the firm has 1600 em-
ployees andover 30 offices. EDAW was selected as bestoffice by the American Society
of Landscape Architects.

El origen de AECOM, la firma de la que deriva
EDAW, se remonta hasta 1939. Famosa por
su arquitectura de «estilo californiano», la
empresa fundada por Garrett Eckbo pronto
marcó tendencia con sus proyectos de paisajismo y diseño y planificación urbana. Con
la llegada a la dirección de Francis Dean
y Don Austin, el estudio pasó a llamarse
EDAW. Actualmente cuenta con una plantilla
de 1.600 personas y más de 30 delegaciones.
EDAW mereció el premio al mejor estudio de
la Sociedad Americana de Paisajismo.

BLOOMINGTON CENTRAL STATION

Minneapolis, Minnesota, United States — 2009 — Area: 18.000 m² / 193,750 sq ft
© AECOM Design + Planning

The project is located a few minutes away from the
Minneapolis International Airport. The complex is
formed by residential towers, office buildings and
its center is constituted by a park and pedestrian
ways that cover the entire site.
Divisory canals with sculptural light posts along
them are elements that stand out from the design
of the park.

Esta estación de transportes se encuentra a unos
pocos minutos del aeropuerto internacional de
Minneapolis. El complejo consta de espacios residenciales y de oficinas, pero su centro neurálgico
lo constituyen el parque y las vías peatonales que
se distribuyen a lo largo de su planta.
Del diseño del parque destacan el uso de canales
divisorios y las escultóricas farolas que lo decoran.

SHEAF SQUARE

Sheffield, United Kingdom — 2008 — Area: 3.800 m² / 40,903 sq ft
© AECOM Design + Planning

This project is part of a regeneration plan in Sheffield's city center. Water is the main design element used in fountains and small waterfalls. The demolition of a building allows for a wide open space that welcomes visitors who arrive by train to the city.

The insertion of the square in this area has facilitated the proliferation of businesses and recreational areas.

Este proyecto es parte de un gran plan de regeneración del centro de la ciudad de Sheffield. El principal protagonista del diseño es el agua, que se emplea en fuentes y pequeñas cascadas. La demolición de un edificio ha permitido habilitar un espacio público amplio y acogedor que da la bienvenida a quien llegue en tren a la localidad.

La inclusión de la plaza en esta zona de la ciudad ha impulsado la proliferación de comercios y zonas de ocio.

JINJI LAKE

Suzhou, China — 2007 — Area: 5.500.000 m² / 59,201,507 sq ft
© AECOM Design + Planning

This park is part of a 1,359-acre regeneration area in the Jiangsu province, close to Shanghai. The project makes the most of the site on the lake's shore and subtly enhances its characteristics by means of pathways, benches and marshlands that visitors can enjoy.

Este parque forma parte de un área de regeneración de 550 ha situada en la provincia de Jiangsu, cerca de Shanghái. Las intervenciones en el parque, aunque discretas, logran sacar partido al entorno de la orilla del lago, permitiendo el disfrute por parte del visitante gracias a la instalación de paseos, bancos y pantalanes.

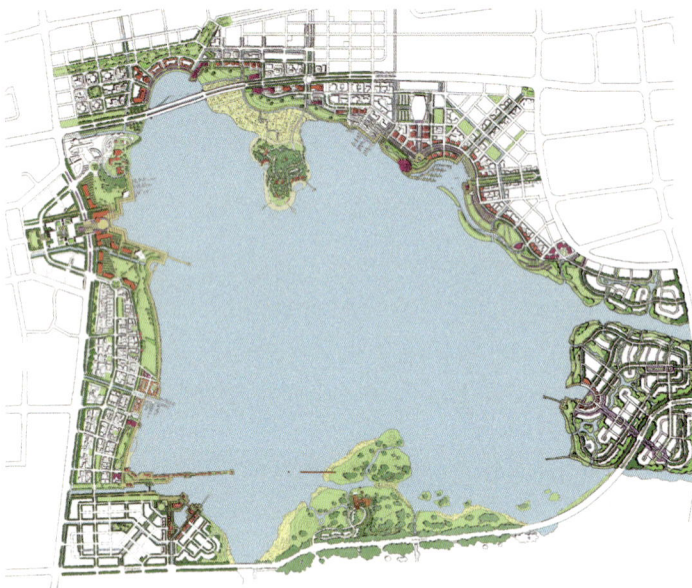

02

Site plan

Various bridges help overcoming the topographic irregularities of the shore without having to do long detours.

Una serie de pasarelas permite salvar, sin eternizar los recorridos, las irregularidades de la línea de la orilla.

BANKS OF THE RIVER HAI

Tianjin, China — 2004 — Area: 400.000 m² / 4,305,564 sq ft
© David Lloyd, Dix Carrillo, Frank Chow/EDAW

This project that deals with the renovation of the River Hai's 12.43-mile bank through Tianjin, was designed in four phases that correspond to the four districts, respecting the historic and cultural characteristics of each of them. The first phase affects the Cultural Heritage area which best preserves the national traditional identity.

Este proyecto, que aborda la rehabilitación de los 20 km de orilla del río Hai a su paso por Tianjin, fue diseñado en cuatro fases que se corresponden con los cuatro distritos por los que pasa el caudal, respetando las peculiaridades históricas y culturales de cada uno de ellos. La primera fase recorre la zona llamada del Patrimonio Cultural.

■ Historic building
■ District open space
■ Plaza
■ Sunken road
  1. Chinese temple
  2. Cathedral
  3. Fisherman's temple
  4. General's resident
  5. Renovated historic bridge

Site plan

The architects made the most of the height difference between the road and the river to create a space opened to pedestrians and closed to traffic.

Los arquitectos supieron sacar partido del desnivel existente entre la calzada y el cauce fluvial para crear un espacio abierto a los viandantes y cerrado al tráfico.

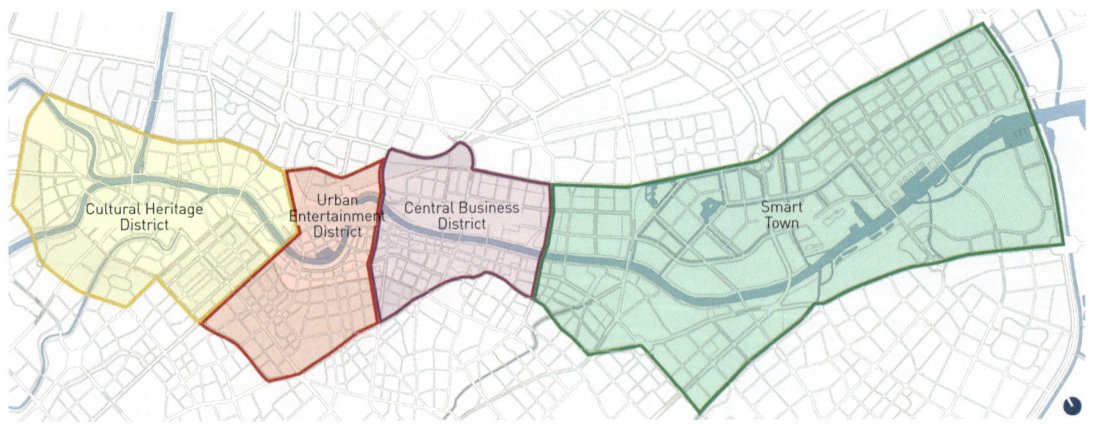

Location map

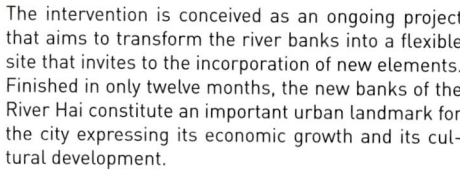

The intervention is conceived as an ongoing project that aims to transform the river banks into a flexible site that invites to the incorporation of new elements. Finished in only twelve months, the new banks of the River Hai constitute an important urban landmark for the city expressing its economic growth and its cultural development.

La intervención no está concebida como una obra terminada, sino que apuesta por hacer de los márgenes fluviales un escenario flexible que invite a la incorporación de nuevos elementos. Terminada en tan solo un año, la nueva ribera del Hai constituye un importante icono urbanístico, que refleja su crecimiento económico y su desarrollo cultural.

The site specific design combines stones collected from the river bed with a traditional paving using another type of local stone.

El diseño combina piedras procedentes del lecho del río con un tradicional losado en piedra grisácea, también de extracción local, diseñado específicamente para el proyecto.

GERMÁN DEL SOL

www.germandelsol.cl

Camino las Flores 11441
Las Condes, Santiago
Chile

Germán del Sol is a Chilean architect who isinspired by the spirit of the indigenous traditions. It is not rare to find in his work contemporary reinterpretations of elements in the vernacular architecture of his country. It iseasy to perceive the attempt to establish arelationship between the city and its constructions, and the culture and the nature of remote sites. He was the designer of the Chilean Pavilion for the 1992 Universal exhibition in Seville. He has been awarded the first prize of the Architecture Biennale in Santiago de Chile in many occasions, and he received the Gold Medal of Landscape Architecture Bienal Miami in 2001.

Germán del Sol es uno de los arquitectos chilenos que más se ha inspirado en el espíritu de las tradiciones indígenas. En su obra es muy frecuente encontrar elementos actualizados de la arquitectura local de su país, y también se percibe a menudo el intento por relacionar la ciudad y sus construcciones con la cultura y la naturaleza de lugares remotos. Fue el diseñador del pabellón de Chile para la Exposición Universal de Sevilla de 1992, y entre los premios que ha recibido están el I Premio de la Bienal de Arquitectura de Santiago de Chile, en varias ocasiones, y la Medalla de Oro de la Bienal de Arquitectura del Paisaje de Miami en 2001.

HOT SPRINGS COMPLEX
Villarrica National Park, Chile — 2008 — Area: 1.500 m² / 16,146 sq ft
© Guy Wenborne

The design of the circulation areas of this natural hot springs complex are an excellent example of intervention based on the respect of the environment, minimizing the impacton an area of great landscape and natural value.
A noble material such as wood is the only physical intrusion into the landscape and blends with it in the most organic way.

El diseño de las zonas de paso de este conjunto de termas naturales son un perfecto ejemplo de intervención que respeta en la mayor medida posible las condiciones del entorno, minimizando el impacto ambiental en una zona de gran valor paisajístico y ecológico.
Un elemento noble como la madera es la única interrupción física del paisaje y se ensambla en él de manera orgánica.

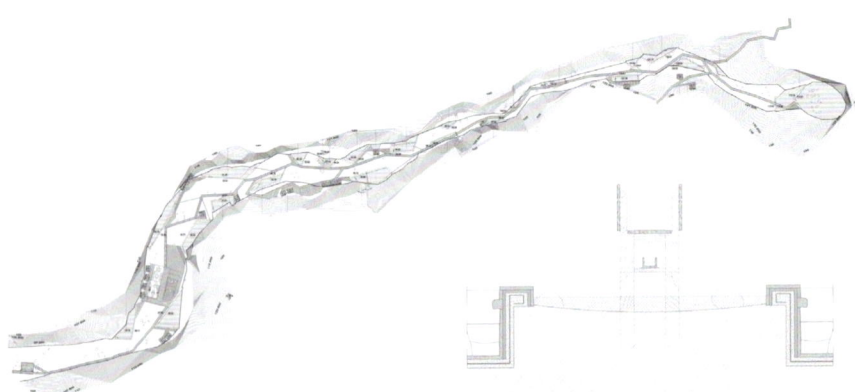

General plan   Boardwalk detail

REMOTA HOTEL

Patagonia, Chile — 2006 — Area: 3.200 m² / 34,444 sq ft
© Guy Wenborne

This rural hotel located in an unspoilt area of Patagonia shows in its design a deep respect for the natural elements surrounding it. So much so that it is arranged around an extension consisting of a wheat field with a series of scattered rocks, sculptural in nature.

The landscape is completely integrated with the construction since it rises up to the level of the structure's rooftop continuously and uninterruptedly.

Este hotel rural ubicado en una zona casi virgen de la Patagonia muestra en su diseño un profundo respeto por el elemento natural que lo envuelve. Tanto es así que está dispuesto en torno a una extensión formada por un trigal con una serie de rocas diseminadas de carácter escultórico.

El paisaje se integra totalmente en el conjunto al elevarse hasta los tejados de la estructura de forma continua, sin interrupciones.

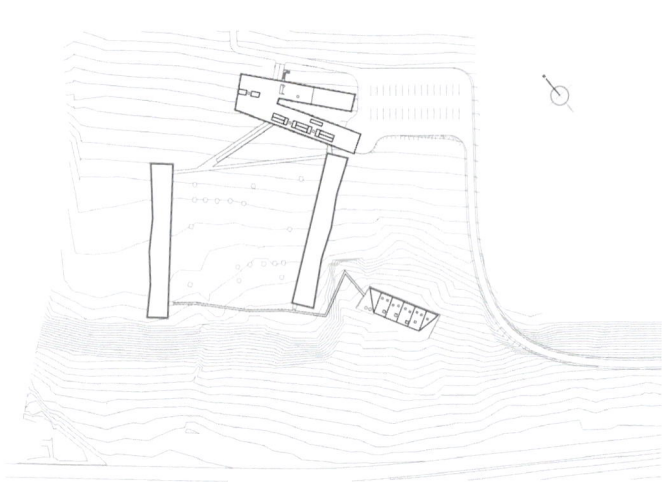

General plan

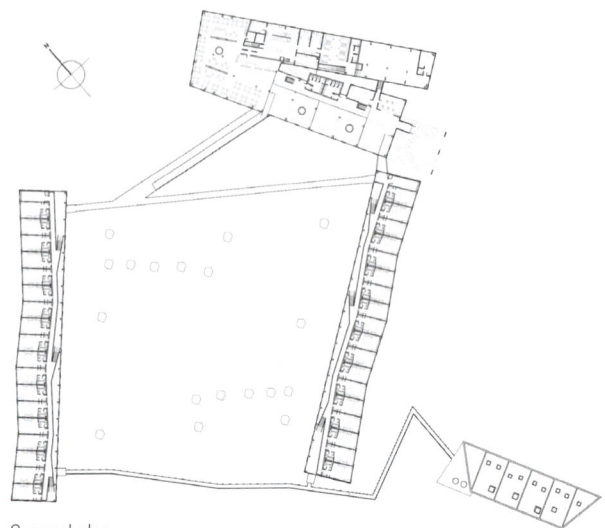

General plan

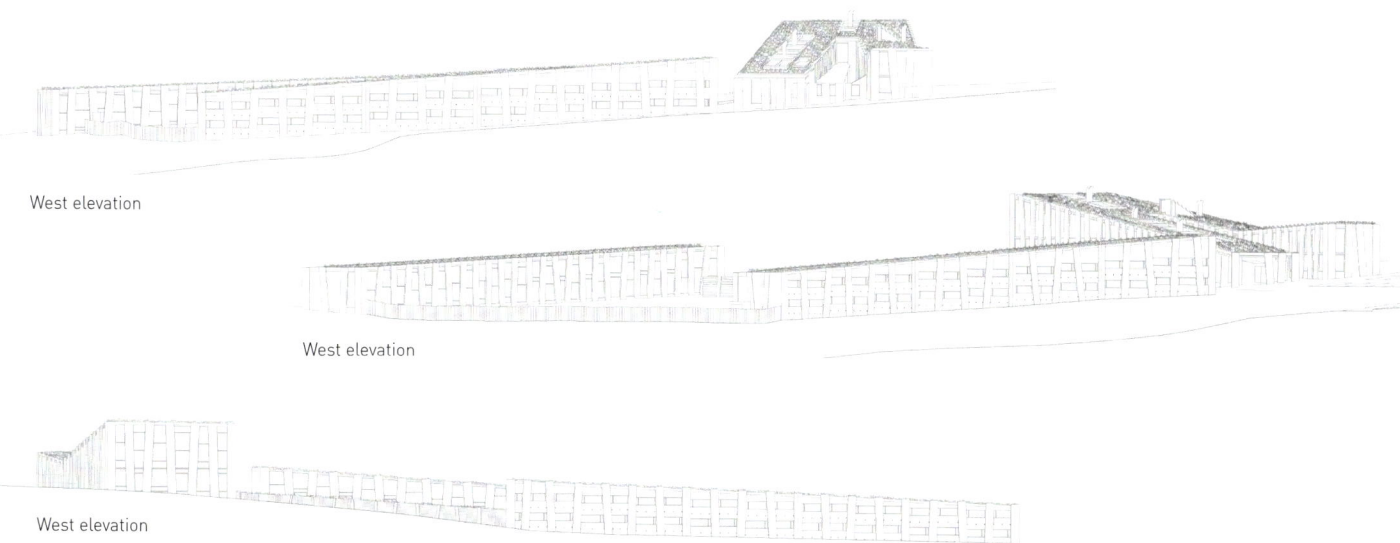

West elevation

West elevation

West elevation

GLASSER UND DAGENBACH

www.glada-berlin.de

Breitenbachplatz 17
14195 Berlin
Germany

Silvia Glaßer and Udo Dagenbach have been working as landscape designers on the design of parks and gardens since 1988. Silvia graduated in 1985 from the Nuertingen University and Udo graduated a year later from the Technical University of Berlin. The studio is formed by three landscape architects and five other professionals whose work is focused in the creation of open public spaces and the reconstruction of existing parks and gardens, as well as the design of natural environments in the private domain.

Silvia Glaßer y Udo Dagenbach llevan dedicándose al paisajismo y al diseño de parques y jardines desde 1988. Silvia se graduó en la Universidad de Nuertingen en 1985 y Udo lo hizo en la Técnica de Berlín un año más tarde. Su estudio cuenta con tres arquitectos paisajistas y cinco ayudantes, y su campo de actuación es la creación de espacios públicos al aire libre, así como los entornos naturales privados y la reconstrucción de parques y jardines ya existentes.

GARDENCENTER
Hamburg, Germany — 2007 — Area: 19.000 m² / 204,514 sq ft
© Udo Dagenbach

On this occasion the architects received a commission to renovate a nursery from a client they had beencollaborating with for fifteen years. The project consisted in combining old and new elements to capture thedifferent designs of gardens: from the French garden style to most minimalist of approaches.

En esta ocasión, los arquitectos aceptaron el encargo de un vivero con el que llevaban colaborando más de 15 años. El proyecto consistió en combinar elementos antiguos y modernos para plasmar las distintas corrientes del diseño de jardines, desde el clásico jardín de setos francés a formas más minimalistas.

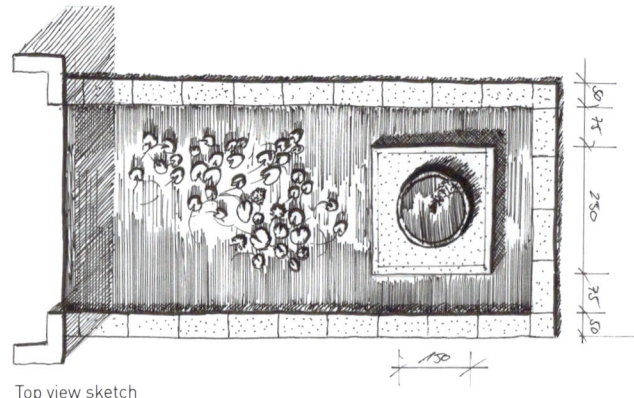

Top view sketch

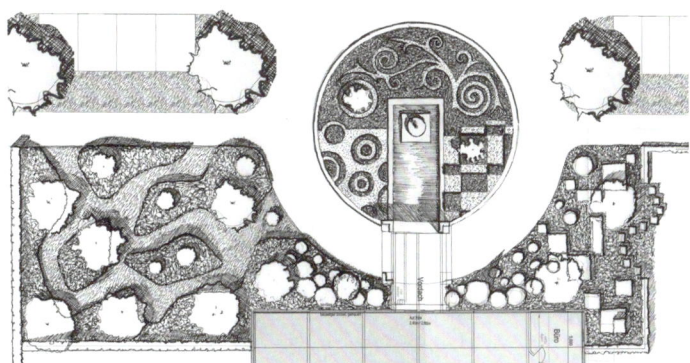

Partial plan of the entry

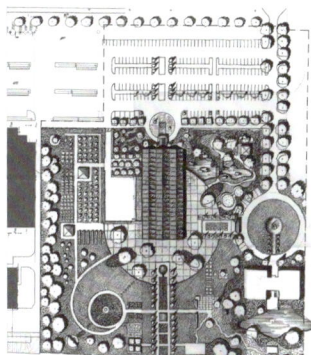

Partial plan of the entry

Most decisions were made on the site following the politics that the creators call taille directe.

Gran parte de las decisiones se tomaron *in situ*, mediante una técnica que los creadores llaman *taille directe*.

MOABIT PRISON HISTORICAL PARK

Berlin, Germany — 2006 — Area: 26.000 m² / 279,862 sq ft
© Udo Dagenbach

The design for the remodelling of this park responds to a large degree to the thorough study of the location's history, starting with the Moabit prison that occupied it for over acentury. The walls of the prison still enclose the star-shaped site.
The ubiquity of the walls encouraged to conceive open spaces with little interruptions caused by voluminous vegetation.

El diseño de la remodelación de este parque obedece en gran medida a un cuidado estudio de la historia del lugar, empezando por la prisión de Moabit, que ocupó este lugar hace 150 años. Los muros de esta cárcel siguen cercando la parcela y sirven de marco del recinto en forma de estrella. La ubicuidad de los muros animaba a concebir espacios muy abiertos, poco interrumpidos por vegetación voluminosa.

General plan

Sketches

VILNIUS VILLA

Vilnius, Lithuania — 2008 — Area: 14.000 m² / 150,694 sq ft
© Udo Dagenbach

The spacious garden of the modernist villa is composed of several of the most characteristic elements of this landscape architecture studio. One example of this are the spectacular geometric sculptures half made of granite, half made of hedges meticulously trimmed.

El amplio jardín de esta villa modernista cuenta con varios de los elementos más característicos de este estudio de paisajistas. Entre ellos, las espectaculares formas escultóricas realizadas con una mitad en granito y la otra a base de setos podados al milímetro para esculpir figuras geométricas.

General plan

Side view of the hedge

Plan and elevation at hedge

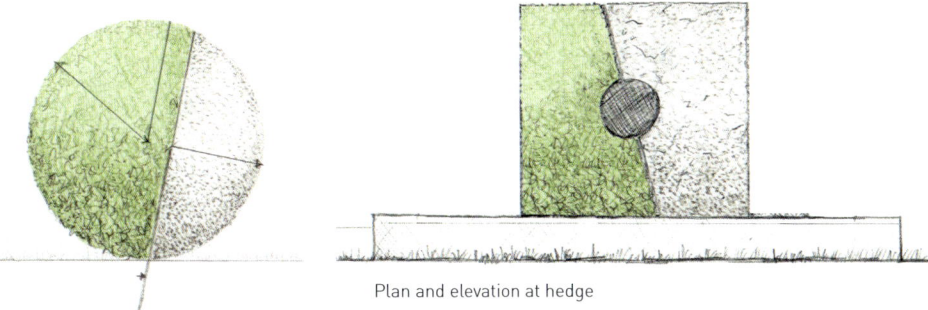

Detail of the spherical hedge

Plan and elevation at hedge

With Zen inspiration, this vegetable environment is conceived to take advantage of certain plant forms which are used to divide different zones.

Con algo de inspiración zen, este entorno vegetal saca el mayor partido posible a las estructuras vegetales como elementos divisorios.

HAGER
LANDSCHAFTSARCHITEKTUR

www.hager-ag.ch

Bergstrasse 50
8032 Zurich
Switzerland

Guido Hager was born in 1958 and studied atthe Rapperswill Technical University. In 1984 he established his own landscape office in Zurich specializing in the fields of conservation of monumental gardens and the design of urban furniture. In 2000, Patrick Altermatt joined the office. Currently, more than thirty professionals work in the office, which gives an indication of the number and variety of projects that the firm works on.

Guido Hager nació en 1958 y estudió en la Universidad Técnica de Rapperswill. En 1984 estableció su propio estudio de paisajismo en Zúrich, centrado en los campos de la conservación de jardines monumentales y el diseño de conceptos urbanos. Más adelante se unió al estudio el socio Patrick Altermatt, que dirige la empresa junto a Hager desde 2000. Actualmente trabajan en el estudio más de treinta personas, lo cual da una clara idea de la cantidad y la heterogeneidad de los proyectos en los que se embarca la firma hoy en día.

RUDOLF BECHAR PARK
Vienna, Austria — 2008 — 30.000 m² / 322,917 sq ft
© Rupert Steiner, Patrick Altermatt, Hager Landschaftsarchitektur

The park is located on a site previously occupied by a train station in the gentrified neighborhood of Leopoldstadt. The "veil of trees", orientated to the nearby Danube River, de limits the space, which is divided in different zones including several playgrounds.

Este parque se encuentra en el enclave anteriormente ocupado por una estación de tren, en el barrio recién regenerado de Leopoldstadt. Un «velo de árboles» con la misma orientación que el curso del Danubio delimita el espacio, que está dividido en parcelas con distintos tipos de plantas y cuenta con varias zonas de juegos para niños.

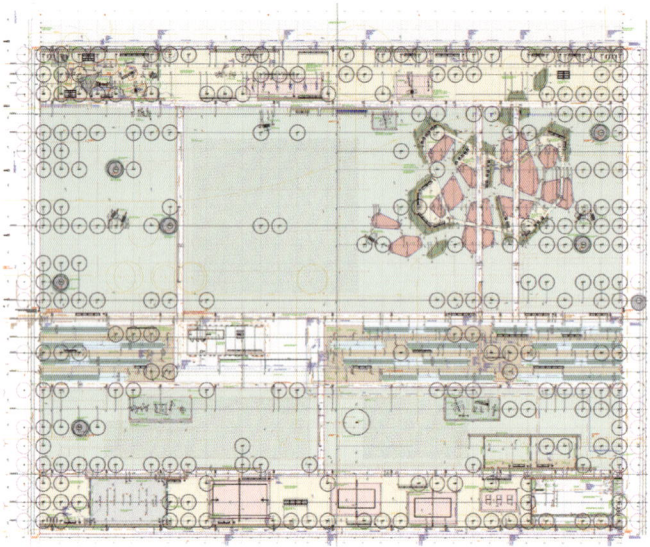

General plan

NEW URBAN AREA THU THIEM

Ho Chi Minh City, Vietnam — 2008 — Area: 350.000 m² / 3,767,369 sq ft
Renderings © Hager Landschaftsarchitektur

The design proposal for this park in Vietnam's Ho Chi Minh City takes advantage of its unique location amidst various bodies of water. Connected to the city by several bridges, the park would offer the citizens one of the largest green zones in town along with cultural and recreational facilities, all protected from the hustle and bustle of nearby neighborhoods.

La propuesta para este parque en Ho Chi Minh saca el mayor partido a una privilegiada ubicación entre distintos cuerpos de agua. Comunicado con el resto de la ciudad por una serie de puentes, el parque ofrece una de las mayores zonas verdes de la localidad, con espacios culturales y de recreo convenientemente separados del bullicio de otros barrios.

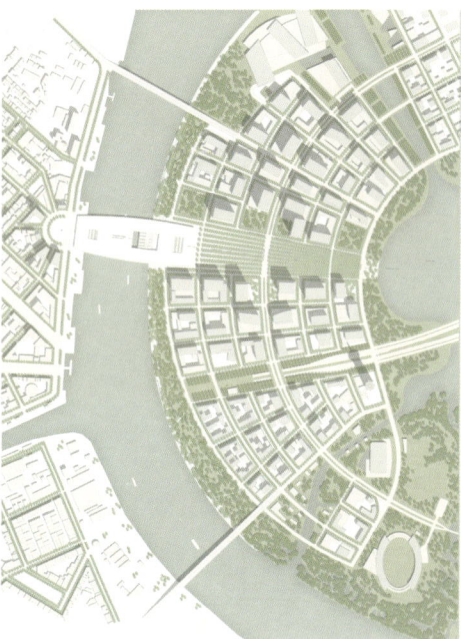

General plan

The proximity of the water emphasizes the open character of this area, isolated from the urban activity, which is very advisable in a city so densely populated.

La proximidad del agua hace del entorno un espacio diáfano, alejado de lo urbano, muy recomendable para una ciudad tan densamente poblada.

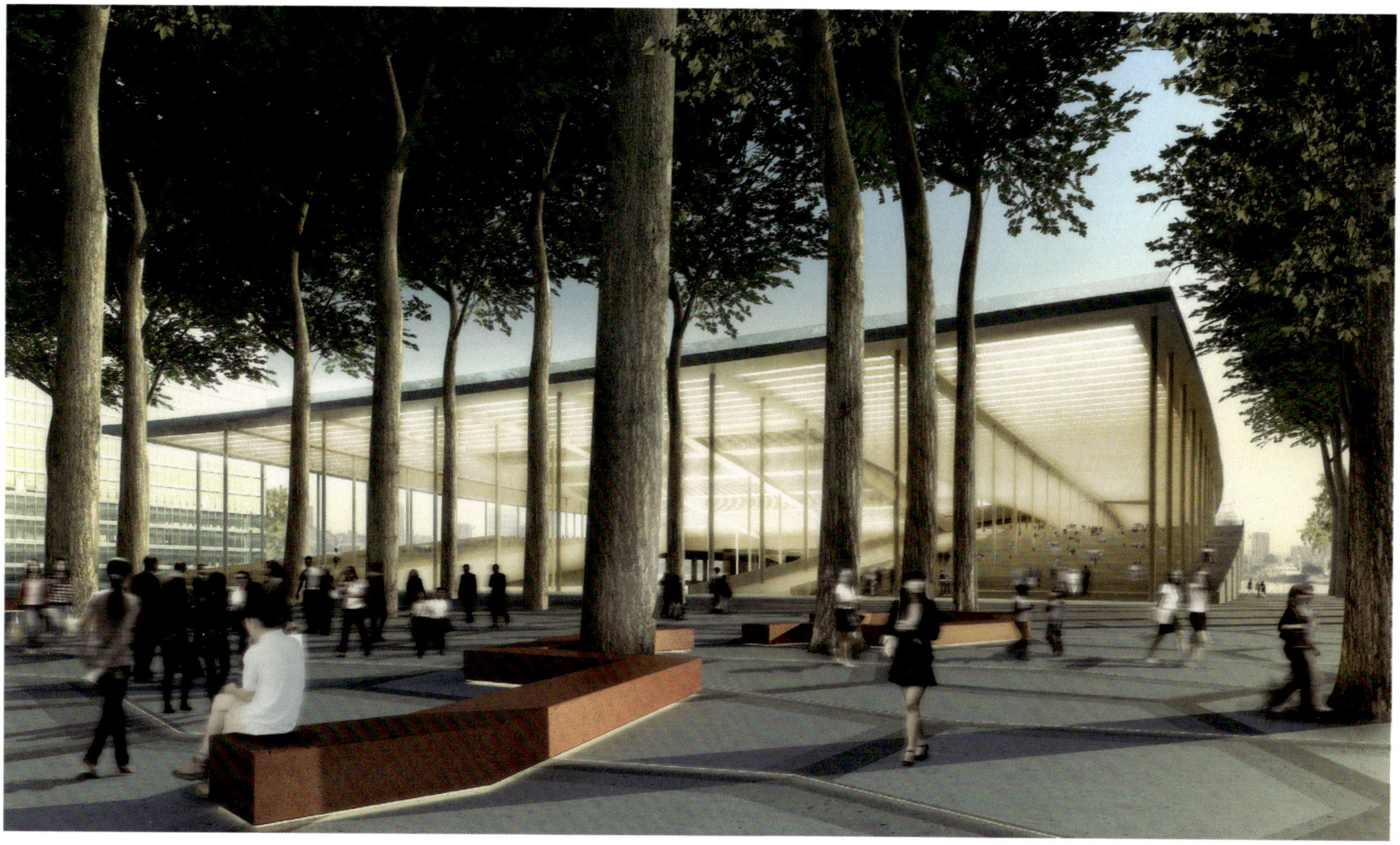

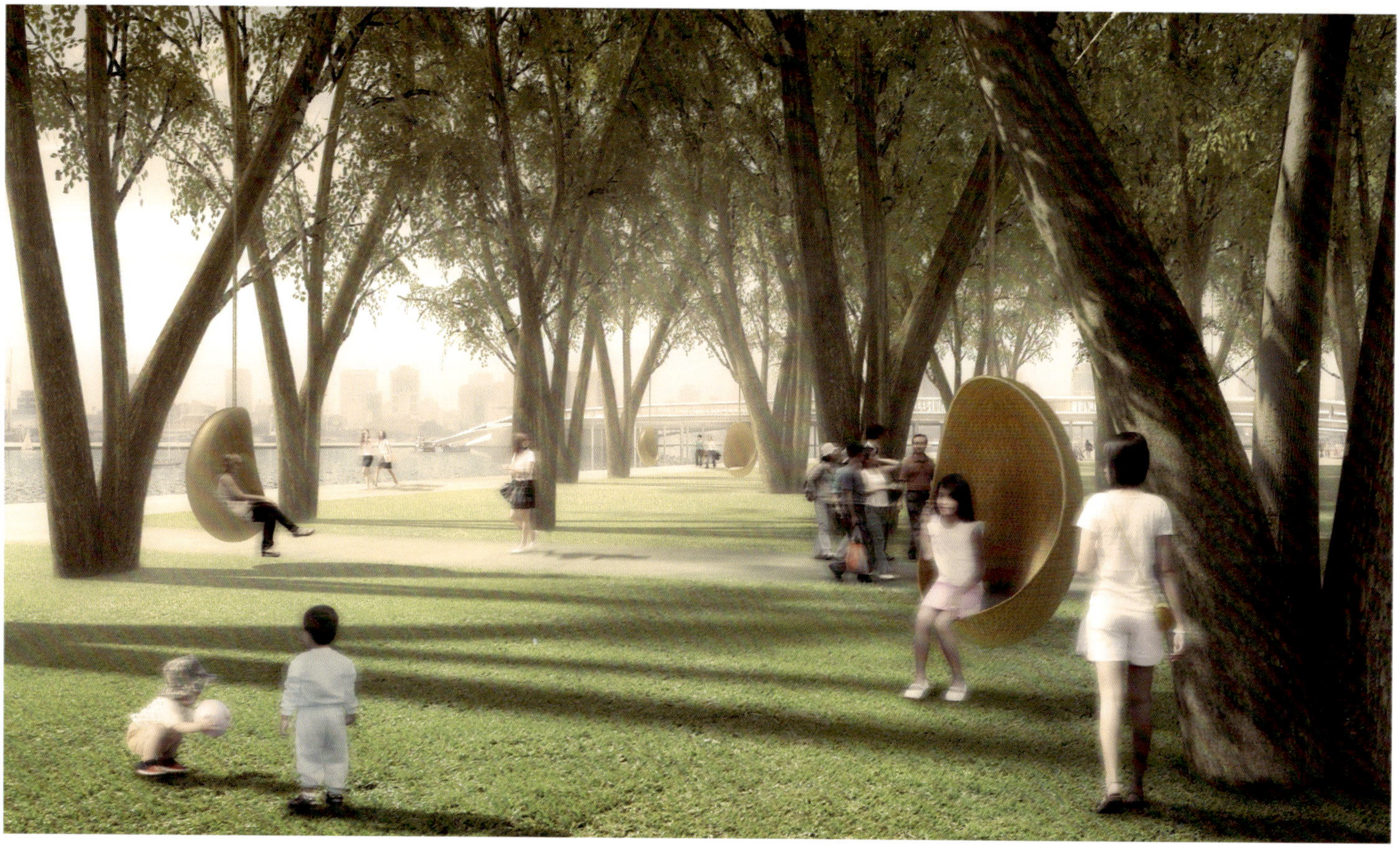

LIMMATWEST
Zurich, Switzerland — 2002 — 1.900 m² / 20,451,43 sq ft
© Hager Landschaftsarchitektur

This exterior space extends into three elongated areas. A row of plane trees separates the garden from the wide Hardturmstrasse while a less busy residential street is delimitedby means of different pavements on terraces and balconies. Also, a series of pools surround the parking area closer to the Limmat River.

Este espacio exterior se presenta en tres zonas longitudinales. Una hilera de plátanos separa este jardín de la calle Hardturmstrasse, mientras que la calle interior de la zona residencial está delimitada por el uso de distintos pavimentos. Por último, una serie de embalses de agua rodean la zona de aparcamiento más cercana al río Limmat.

The architects designed a heterogeneous plan to cover these exterior areas used by the community of residential buildings.

Los arquitectos apostaron por una tipología heterogénea para vestir estas zonas exteriores comunes entre varios edificios residenciales.

JAMES CARPENTER
Design Associates

www.jcdainc.com

145 Hudson Street, 4th floor
New York
New York 10013
United States

James Carpenter studied architecture and sculpture at the Rhode Island School of Design from which he graduated in 1972. Since 1978 he has worked on projects that combine both art and architecture to form structures with a strong visual impact. Amongst his most important works are the Pennsylvania Station in New York (2005), the exterior areas and the vestibule for the project Seven World Trade Center (2001-2006), which focuses on the transformation of the urban fabric of the area.

James Carpenter estudió arquitectura y escultura en la Escuela de Diseño de Rhode Island, donde se graduó en 1972. Desde 1978, trabaja en proyectos en los que el arte se combina con la arquitectura para formar estructuras de gran impacto visual, y entre sus trabajos más importantes están la nueva estación de Pensilvania, en Nueva York (2005), y las zonas exteriores y el vestíbulo del proyecto Seven World Trade Center (2001- 2006), centrado en la transformación del tejido urbano de la zona.

BATTERY PARK CITY STREETSCAPE
New York, New York, United States — 2006 — Area: 15.000 m² / 161,459 sq ft
© Andreas Keller

Located along Battery Park in the southwest of Manhattan, a promenade is developed perpendicular to Vesey Street and to the median strips of North End Avenue. The urban furniture stands out as an important part of the project (luminous benches) and the large metallic louvered pergola. One of the main objectives of the project was to insure an appropriate treatment of light both in day time and at night.

Situado a lo largo de Battery Park, en la zona sudoeste de Manhattan, este paseo discurre perpendicular a la travesía Versey y a las medianas de la avenida North End. Del proyecto destaca sobre todo el diseño del mobiliario urbano (los bancos luminiscentes) y la gran pérgola metálica, también a base de láminas transversales.
Uno de los principales objetivos del proyecto era asegurar un correcto tratamiento de la luz, tanto de día como de noche.

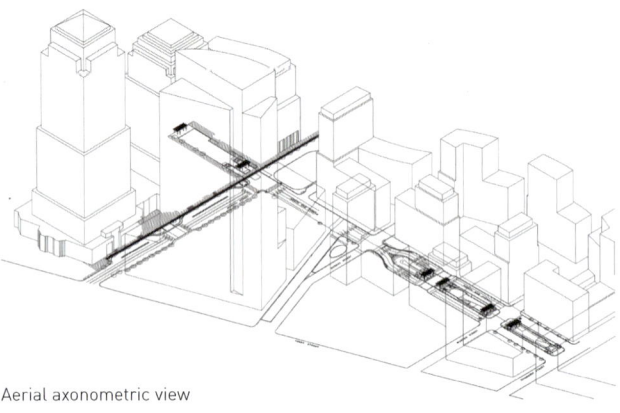

Aerial axonometric view

Detail at pergola

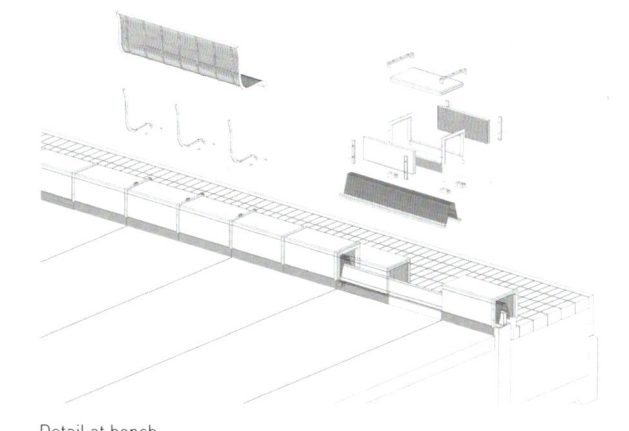

Detail at bench

LUMINOUS POSTS

Chattanooga, Tennessee, United States — 2005
© Andreas Keller

A park developed along the Tennessee River is part of the rejuvenation project for the river banks. The seven masts of light set in the park were designed to filter and direct the sunlight evoking the way the river interacts with the light.

Este parque que discurre junto al río Tennessee es parte del proyecto de renovación de la ribera. Los siete mástiles de luz que lo adornan filtran y redirigen la luz solar, evocando la manera en que lo hace el propio río. De noche, los triángulos de acero inoxidable y los prismas de cristal reparten la luz artificial de un modo parecido al de los faros marinos.

JENSEN & SKODVIN ARKITEKTKONTOR

www.jsa.no

Fredersborgveien 11
0177 Oslo
Norway

Jan Olav Jensen and Børre Skodvin founded JSA in 1995. The first teaches at the School of Architecture of the University of Oslo and the second teaches at the School of Design of the Norwegian capital. Their studio has won several nominations for the Mies van der Rohe Award, a Gluelam Award in 1999, a Grosch Medal, a Norwegian State Architectural Award and a Rosa Barba Landscape Award. Their works have been included in exhibits such as the Venice Biennale and the '20 under 40' in 1998.

Jan Olav Jensen y Børre Skodvin fundaron JSA en 1995. El primero es profesor en la Facultad de Arquitectura de la Universidad de Oslo, mientras que el segundo da clases en la Escuela de Diseño de la capital noruega. Su estudio ha conseguido varias candidaturas al Premio Mies van der Rohe, un premio Gluelam en 1999, una medalla Grosch, un Premio de Arquitectura del Estado de Noruega y un Premio Rosa Barba de paisajismo. Sus trabajos han sido incluidos en muestras como la Bienal de Venecia y la «20 under 40» de 1998.

VIEWING PLATFORM
Gudbransjuvet, Norway — 2008 — 60 m² / 646 sq ft
© Jensen & Skodvin Arkitektkontor

The main platform of the viewing point, located in an incomparable natural environment, is built of laser-cut 1-inch-thick steel sheets that are cantilevering over a cliff. The geometry of the design allows for a continuous route without jeopardizing security or obstructing views.
The integration of the architectural elements in the landscape is absolute, organic and natural.

La plataforma principal de este mirador, situada en un entorno natural incomparable, está construida con hojas de acero de 25 mm de grosor cortadas con láser e instaladas en voladizo sobre un acantilado. La geometría del recorrido permite un recorrido continuo sin que disminuya la seguridad ni se limiten las vistas.
La integración de los elementos arquitectónicos en el paisaje es total, orgánica, natural.

JUVET LANDSCAPE HOTEL

Gudbransjuvet, Norway — 2008 — 13.000 m² / 139,931 sq ft
© Jensen & Skodvin Arkitektkontor

In this peculiar hotel, each guest room is a detached independent small cabin elevated from the ground and occasionally having two glassed-in walls facing the woods.

The layout of the cabins is made so that no room looks at another. This enhances the impression of the occupants that they are isolated in the surrounding nature.

En este curioso hotel rural, cada habitación es una cabaña independiente, elevada sobre el terreno y con una de sus paredes asomada al bosque que la rodea por medio de una gran cristalera.

Ninguna cabaña está orientada hacia otra, de manera que se alimenta la ilusión de que los ocupantes están aislados en la naturaleza.

Site plan

General plan of space A

GURDBRANDSJUVET BRIDGE

Gudbrandsjuvet, Norway — 2008 — Area: 600 m² / 6,458 sq ft
© Jensen & Skodvin Arkitektkontor

This bridge composed of four parts act as a circulation platform cantilevered over the cliff, but also as a viewpoint to the incomparable landscape. The route in zigzag allows for a better exploration the vegetation that borders it. The main platform is constructed by 1-in laser-cut steel sheets.
The curvilinear path marked by the guardrails link the ensemble of bridges with the organic shapes of nature.

Este puente de cuatro tramos sirve como plataforma para salvar la altura de la ubicación, pero también como mirador de un paisaje realmente único. El recorrido que establece, en zigzag, permite adentrarse en el elemento vegetal que lo rodea. Su estructura se sostiene gracias a la tensión de cables de acero oxidado artificialmente.
Los trazados curvos de las barandillas vinculan el conjunto de puentes con las formas orgánicas de la naturaleza.

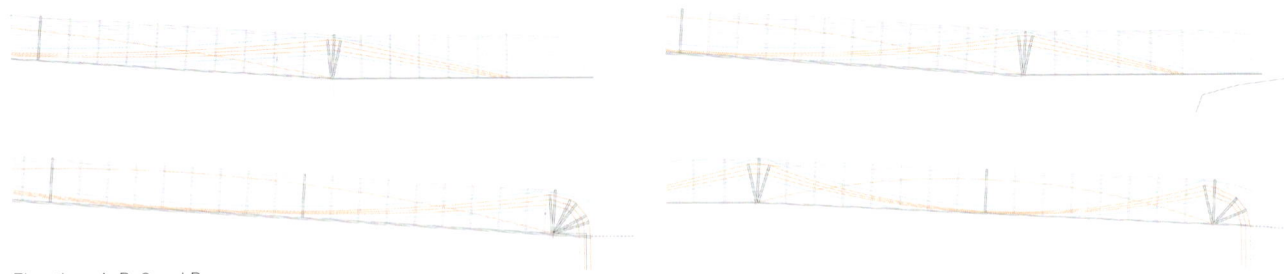

Elevations A, B, C and D

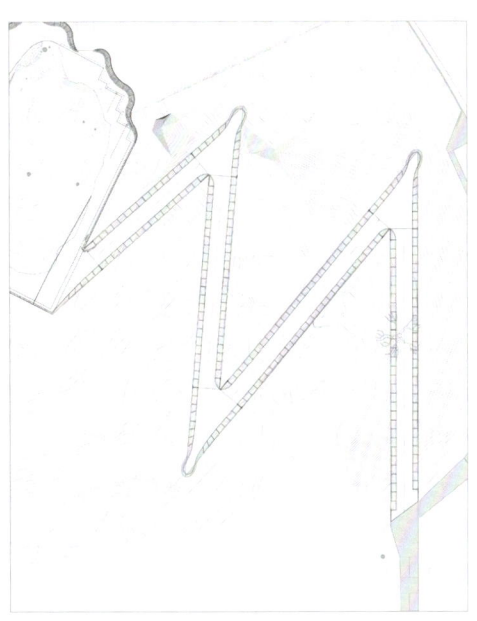

General plan

JML ARQUITECTURA DEL AGUA

www.jeanmaxllorca.com

Plaça Eusebi Güell, 12-13
08034 Barcelona
Spain

Jean Max Llorca was born in Albi, France, in 1947. In 1970 he joined the studio of Roger Anger and Mario Heymann. Eleven years later he opened JML, an office specializing in designs that feature water as the main element. During the eighties and the nineties he received important commissions from Paris. In 1996 he started collaborating with his son Stéphane, who in 2001 opened a branch in Barcelona. Since then, the quantity of the projects and their relevance have been continuously increasing.

Jean Max Llorca nació en Albi (Francia) en 1947. En 1970 se unió al estudio de Roger Anger y Mario Heymann y once años después fundó JML, estudio especializado en diseños en los que el elemento protagonista es el agua. A lo largo de las décadas de los ochenta y los noventa empieza a recibir encargos más importantes de París. En 1996 empieza a colaborar con él su hijo Stéphane, que en 2001 se pone al frente de una delegación en Barcelona. Desde entonces, el número de proyectos y la relevancia de los mismos no han dejado de ir en aumento.

MONTJUÏC TRADE FAIR
Barcelona, Spain — 2005 — Area: 60 m² / 646 sq ft
© Stéphane Llorca

This project is the result of the collaboration with the office of Toyo Ito & Architects. At the exterior spaces of this exhibition complex, JML connects the access spaces with the different pavilions configured as large atria. The studio was responsible for the development of the different concepts that deal with water treatment.

Este proyecto es fruto de una colaboración con el estudio de Toyo Ito & Architects Associates. En el exterior de este recinto ferial, JML se propuso interconectar los espacios de acceso a los diferentes pabellones, configurados como grandes atrios. El estudio se encargó de desarrollar los diferentes conceptos para el tratamiento del agua.

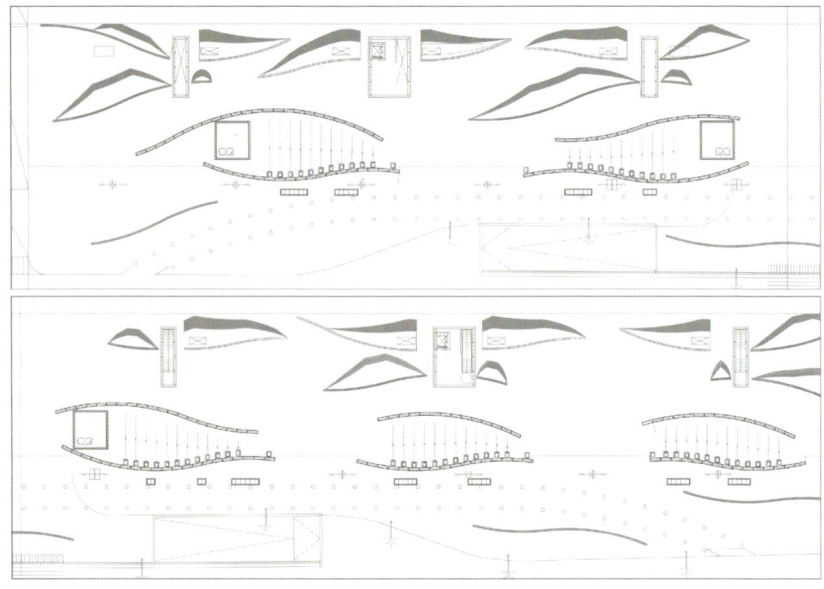

Site plan

The water jets are conceived so that they reflect the geometry of the architectural ensemble. The low arches that the jets create, emphasize the idea of an urban gate.

Los chorros de agua están concebidos de manera que reflejen la geometría del conjunto arquitectónico. Los suaves arcos que describen enfatizan el carácter de puerta urbana.

FRANÇOIS MITTERRAND SQUARE

Le Creuzot, France — 2005 — Area: 1.600 m² / 17,222 sq ft
© François Tribel, Services Techniques Ville du Creusot, Jean Max Llorca

This project is the result of the collaboration with architect François Tribel from the office of Atelier Grunig Tribel. Coeur de Ville (Heart of the City) is the name given to this projectundertaken in 2004 to recuperate the urban center. The area of the intervention covers 17,222 sq ft from the city hall to the wide esplanade formed by François Mitterrand Square.

Este proyecto es fruto de una colaboración con el arquitecto François Tribel, del Atelier Grunig Tribel. Coeur de Ville (Corazón de la Ciudad) es el nombre con el que se designó el proyecto emprendido en 2004 para recuperar el centro urbano. La zona de la intervención se prolonga desde el edificio del Ayuntamiento hasta la plaza François Mitterrand.

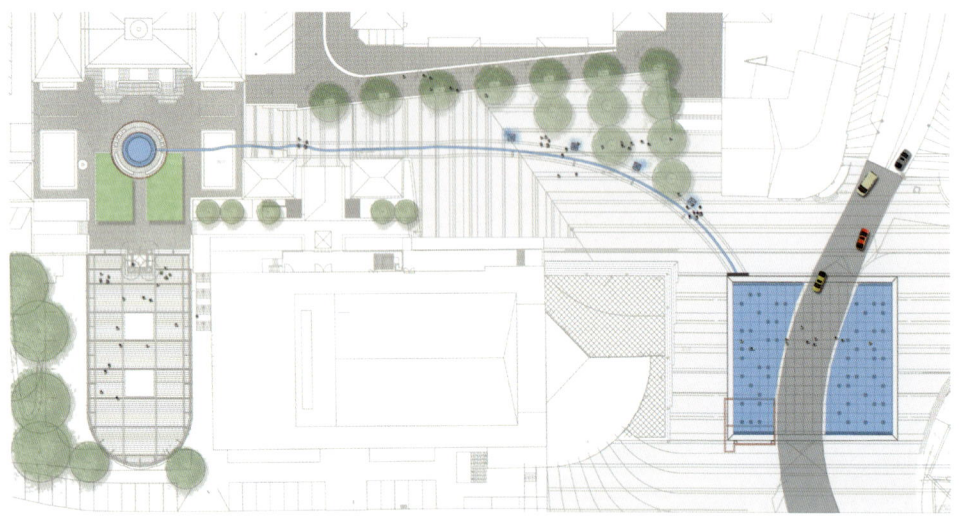

General plan

Several types of granite pavement are used to differentiate the uses of the different areas of the square, making a clear distinction between pedestrian areas and circulation ways.

Los distintos tipos de suelo de granito se han dispuesto de manera que demarcan el uso de cada zona de la plaza, distinguiendo las áreas peatonales de las vías de circulación.

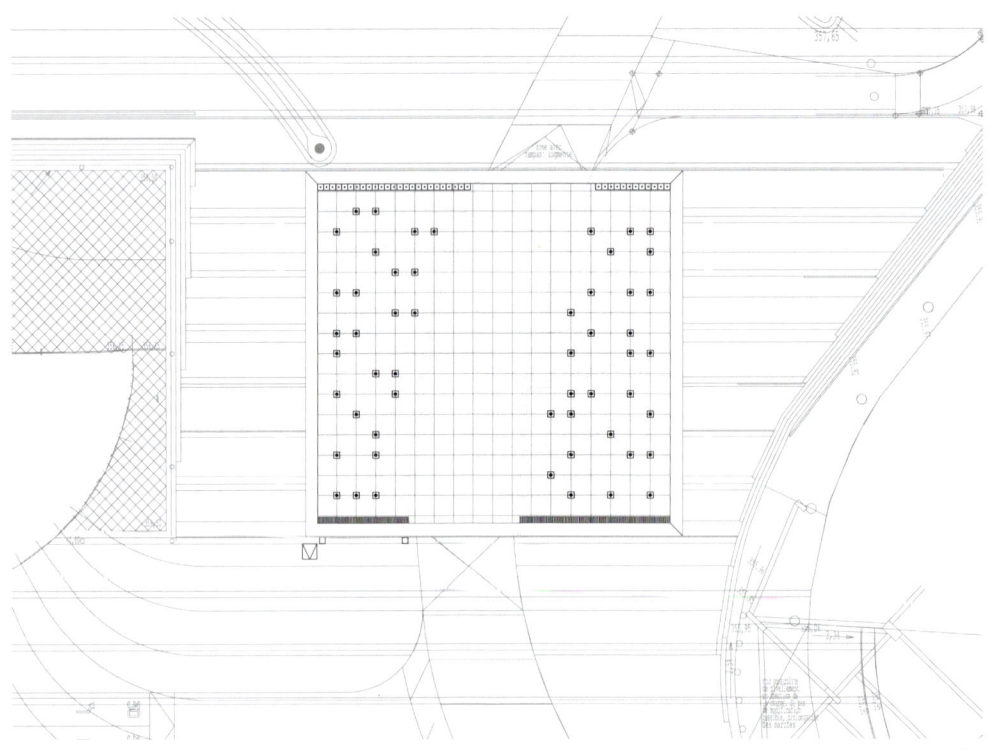

Site plan

At a larger scale and from a distance, these granite surfaces of subtly differentiated rich grey textures become compact and monolithic.

A una escala superior y con perspectiva, esta alfombra granítica y de texturas grises, sutilmente diferenciadas, se torna compacta y monolítica.

FLOODED SQUARE

Bordeaux, France — 2006 — Area: 2.700 m² / 29,062 sq ft
© Stéphane Llorca, CUB, Michel Corajoud

Located near the source of a river, the city of Bordeaux has centered large part of its economic activity on its quays. For many years the office of Corajoud has been responsiblefor the urban reorganization of these quays. Corajoud joined forces with JML for the design of the square.
The 29,062-sqft paved area is the site where different activities can take place, but it is also a place where one can freshen up during the summer.

Ubicada junto al cauce de un río, la ciudad de Burdeos siempre ha basado gran parte de su actividad económica en sus muelles. Durante años la agencia Corajoud se ha encargado de la reordenación urbana de estos muelles, proyecto general para el que contó con la colaboración de JML para esta plaza.
Estos 2.700 m² de pavimentación pueden ser el lugar para organizar distintas actividades, pero también un punto donde refrescarse en verano.

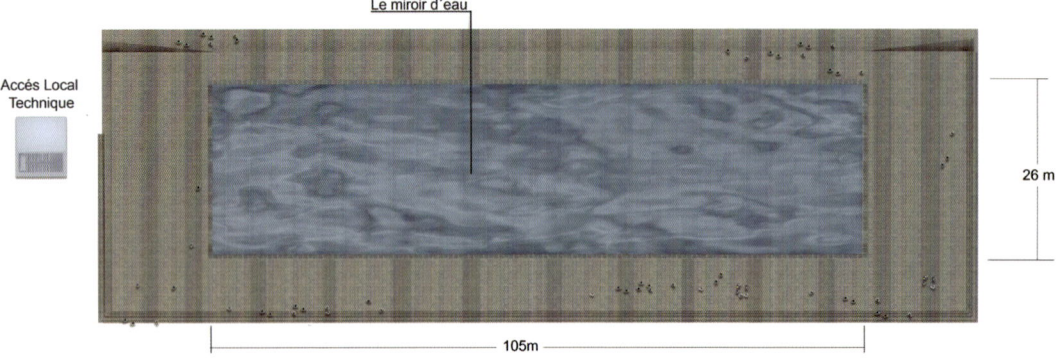

Reflecting pool plan

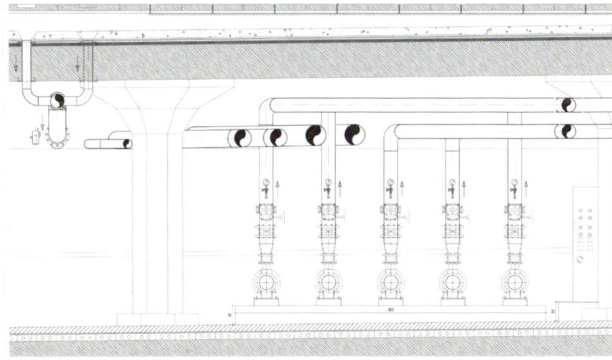

Partial elevation at water pump floor

When the weather and the activities program allow it, the water emerges from the surface and covers the rectangular square. The water is contained in a series of underground tanks from which water can be pumped up to create water jets or a mist effect.

Cuando la climatología y la programación de actividades lo permiten, el agua sale a la superficie y cubre el rectángulo de la plaza. El agua se almacena en una serie de depósitos subterráneos desde los que también se puede bombear para lograr el efecto de vapor y de fuentes de chorro.

The water jets create an artistic touch, almost sculptural that can prevent pedestrians to walk across the square if needed.

La función de los surtidores aporta al agua un toque artístico, casi escultural, que, según las necesidades, puede prevenir a los peatones de atravesar la zona.

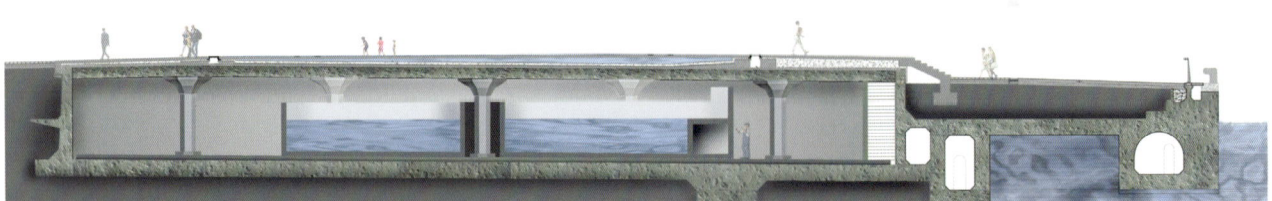

Section

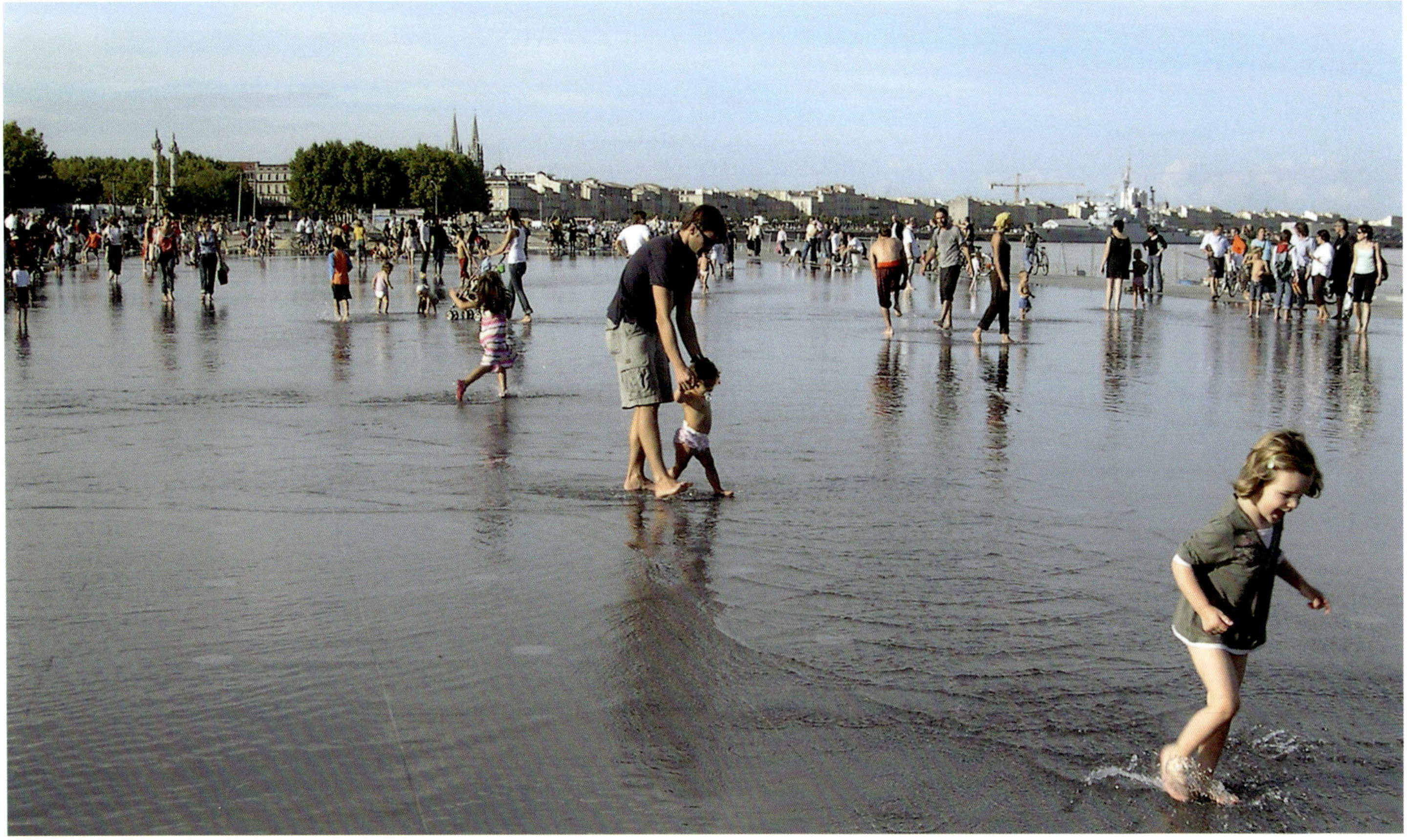

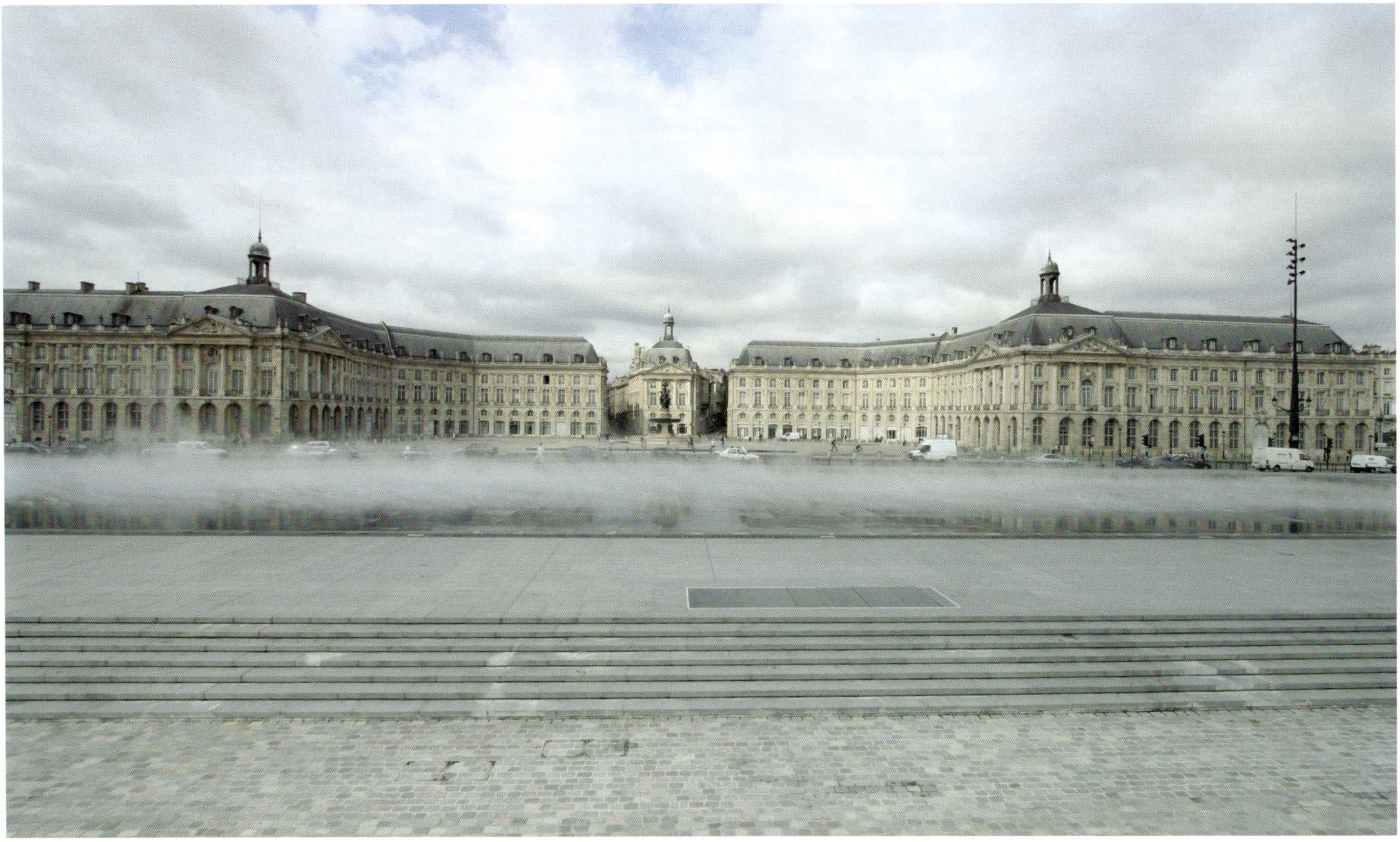

KARRES EN BRANDS
LANDSCHAPSARCHITECTEN

www.karresenbrands.nl

Oude Amersfoortseweg 123
1212 AA Hilversum
The Netherlands

Karres en Brands Landschapsarchitecten is a design office for landscape, architecture and urban planning founded in 1997 by Sylvia Karres and Bart Brands. The office projects include a wide range of commissions, competitions and studies in the Netherlands andabroad. The firm has produced many prize-winning projects such as De Nieuwe Ooster Cemetery in Amsterdam or Federation Square in Melbourne. In 2004 Karres en Brands received the Topos European LandscapeDesign Award.

Karres en Brands Landschapsarchitecten es un estudio de diseño paisajista, arquitectura y planificación urbana fundado por Sylvia Karres y Bart Brands en 1997. Entre los proyectos de la firma se incluyen una amplia gama de encargos, concursos y estudios, tanto en los Países Bajos como en el extranjero. Muchos de los proyectos que producen, como De Nieuwe Ooster Cemetery en Ámsterdam o la Federation Square en Melbourne, han sido galardonados en diferentes concursos y, por ejemplo, en 2004, Karres en Brands obtuvo el Topos European Landscape Design Award.

DE NIEUWE OOSTER CEMETERY
Amsterdam, The Netherlands — 2006 — Area: 6.600 m² / 71,042 sq ft
© Karres en Brands, Jeroen Musch

De Nieuwe Ooster cemetery in Amsterdam is the largest in the Netherlands. Built in three phases, the cemetery has undergone a recent renovation and extension that enhances the individual character of three different zones rather than unifying the site.

El cementerio De Nieuwe Ooster de Ámsterdam es el más grande de los Países Bajos. Construido en tres fases, el cementerio ha experimentado recientemente una renovación y una ampliación que, en lugar de unificar el emplazamiento, realzan el carácter individual de sus tres zonas.

Site plan

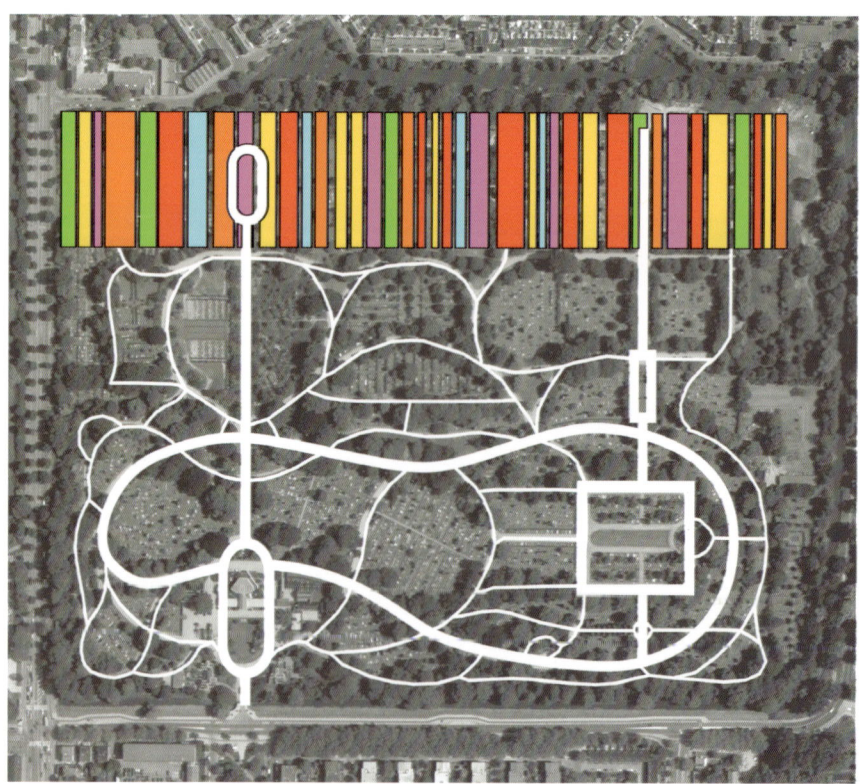

Conceptual plan

As an expression of equality, the burial chambers are long lines of stone slabs that, without any prime locations, mark the position of the grave.

En una expresión de igualdad, los sepulcros son losas de piedra que forman líneas alargadas y que, sin ubicaciones principales, marcan la posición de la tumba.

Linearity is also the spatial structure that defines the area where the cinerarium wall is set amongst green edges and silver birches spread loosely. The cinerarium is composed of a series of constructions with a sculptural character that generates intimate spaces that are open to the sky.

La linealidad también es la estructura espacial que define la zona ocupada por el muro del cinerario, entre bordes verdes y abedules blancos esparcidos libremente. El cinerario está formado por una serie de construcciones de carácter escultural que generan espacios íntimos abiertos al cielo.

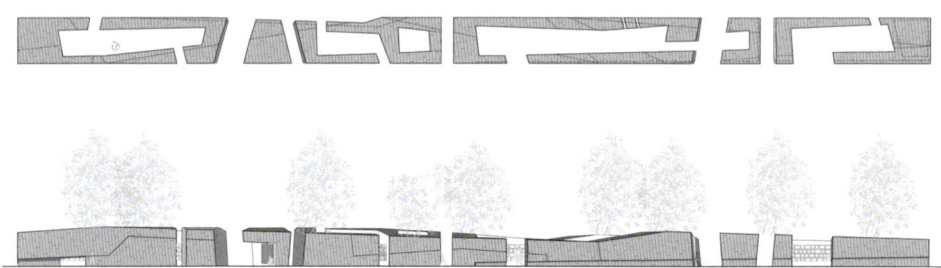

Plans and elevations

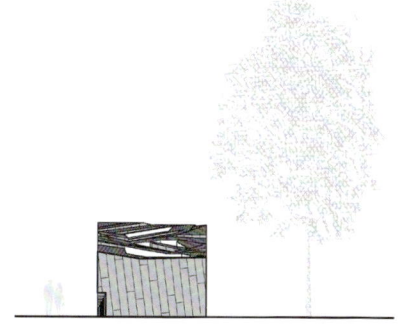
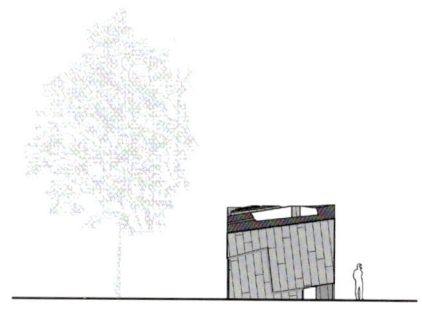

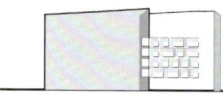

Elevations

The design team explores special forms of burial such as a long strip of water that holds cinerary urns.

El equipo de diseño estudia formas especiales de entierro, como una franja alargada de agua que alberga las urnas del cinerario.

DE OOSTERVAART CEMETERY

Langedijk, The Netherlands — 2008 — Area: 32.000 m² / 344,445 sq ft
© Karres en Brands, Jeroen Musch

The new De Oostervaart Cemetery was commissioned by the Municipality of Langedijk to be part of a green recreational area that also incorporates a leisure area, a park, sportsfields and allotment gardens in the direct neighborhood.

El nuevo cementerio De Oostervaart fue un encargo del municipio de Langedijk, como parte de un área recreativa verde, que también incorpora una zona de ocio, un parque, campos deportivos y huertos comunitarios en el barrio colindante.

Site plan

A large pond and several linear water elements organize the area. The cemetery is divided into small enclosed grave fields connected by a long path.

La zona está organizada por un gran estanque y diversos elementos acuáticos lineales. El cementerio se divide en dos pequeños camposantos cerrados y conectados por un sendero.

KWK PROMES
Robert Konieczny

www.kwkpromes.pl

ul. Rymera 3/5
40-048 Katowice
Poland

A leader and a founder of KWK Promes Architecture studio in 1999, he is a holder of the award for the House of the Year 2006, (Aatrial House) as the best housing project by World Architecture News. In 2007 the KWK Promes office was listed among 44 best young architects of the world. Year 2008 brought him another prize for The European Center for Architecture Art Design and Urban Studies and The Chicago Athenaeum for Europe's Emerging Young Architects 'Europe 40 under 40'. In 2016 National Museum – Dialogue Centre Przeomy was announced to be the Best Public Space in Europe by Centre de Cultura Contemporània de Barcelona.

Líder y fundador del estudio KWK Promes Architecture en 1999, Robert Konieczny es titular del premio de la Casa del Año 2006 (Aatrial House) como el mejor proyecto de vivienda de World Architecture News. En 2007, la oficina de KWK Promes figuraba entre los 44 mejores jóvenes arquitectos del mundo. El año 2008 le trajo otro premio del Centro Europeo de Arquitectura Diseño de Arte y Estudios Urbanos y El Ateneo de Chicago para los jóvenes arquitectos emergentes de Europa 'Europa 40 under 40'. En 2016 el Museo Nacional – Centro de Diálogo Przeomy en Szczecin fue anunciado como el Mejor Espacio Público en Europa por el Centro de Cultura Contemporánea de Barcelona.

NATIONAL MUSEUM IN SZCZECIN – DIALOGUE CENTRE PRZEŁOMY
Szczecin, Poland — 2016 — Area: 9.577 m² / 103,086 sq ft
© Juliusz Sokołowski

Szczecin is one of the largest victims of historical violence in Poland. For years, the Solidarności Square had been a square by name only —with vague borders, open frontages, burdensome busy street neighborhood and the absence of a defined function, despite the dominating one— to commemorate the events of December 1970, where the place was provided a monument in 2005. In 2014, the former Konzerthaus was replaced by a new philharmonic venue designed by Estudio Barozzi Veiga. The building became the new city icon, winning the main Mies van der Rohe award in 2015.

Szczecin es una de las mayores víctimas de la violencia histórica en Polonia. Durante años, la plaza de Solidarności fue una plaza sólo de nombre —con fronteras vagas, fachadas abiertas, un vecindario de agobiantes calles concurridas y la ausencia de una función definida— para conmemorar los hechos de diciembre de 1970, sobre los que se erigió un monumento en 2005. En 2014, el antiguo Konzerthaus fue reemplazado por un nuevo espacio filarmónico diseñado por el estudio Barozzi Vega. El edificio se ha convertido en el nuevo icono de la ciudad, ganando en 2015 el premio Mies Van der Rohe.

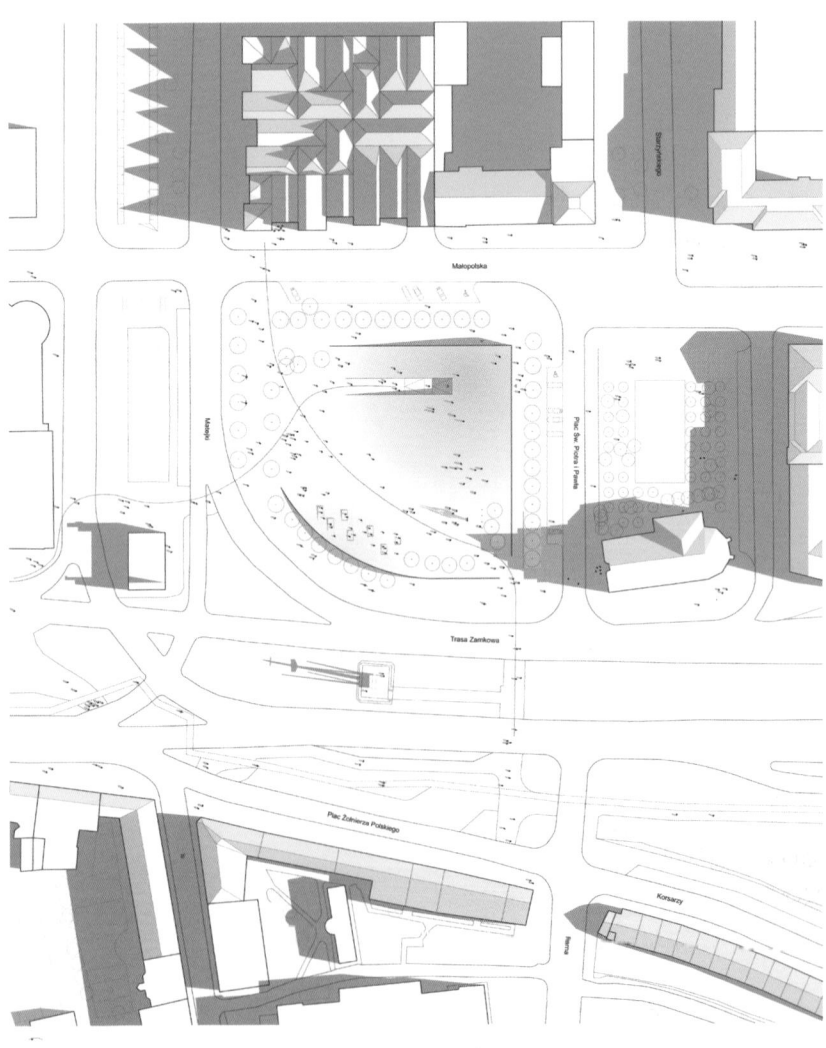

Site plan

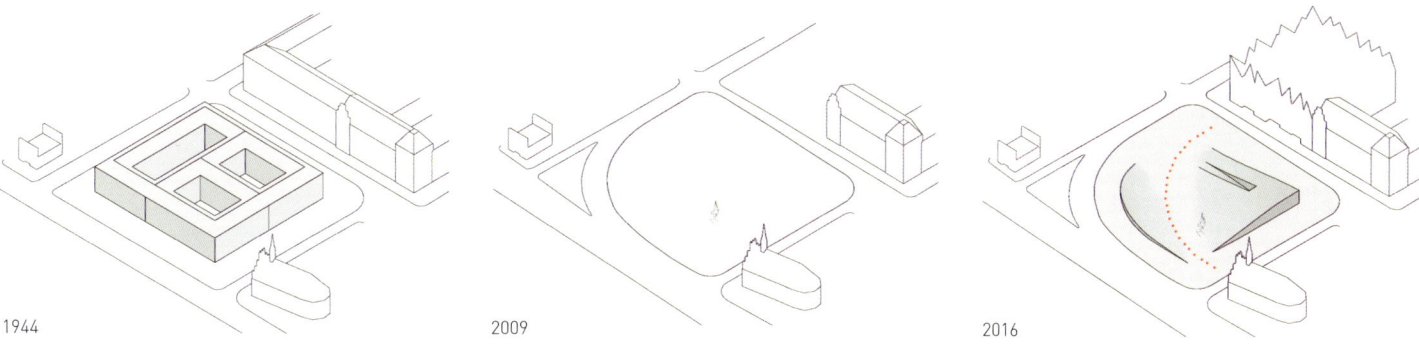

1944   2009   2016

Idea diagram

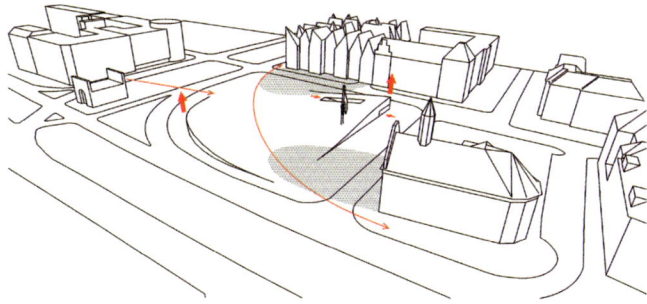

Diagram

Two contradictory traditions: an hybrid urban design which encloses the space as a quarter, while retaining the values of an open public space. The elevation houses the museum facillity, the other one is an artificial hill, closing up the urban interior and shielding it from the noise of the busy street.

Dos tradiciones contradictorias: un diseño urbano híbrido que encierra el espacio como un barrio, a la vez que conserva los valores de un espacio público abierto. La zona elevada alberga las instalaciones del museo, la otra es una colina artificial que delimita el interior de la plaza y la protege del ruido de la concurrida calle.

The museum's form is a continuation of the concrete floor of the square which is covered with rectangular tiles. In the elevated corner these tiles gain a 3rd dimension, becoming cuboidal blocks. The whole makes a monolith that transforms when the museum opens.

La forma del museo es una prolongación del suelo de hormigón de la plaza, cubierto con losas rectangulares. En la esquina elevada estas losas adquieren una tercera dimensión, convirtiéndose en cuboides. El conjunto deviene un monolito que se transforma cuando abre el museo.

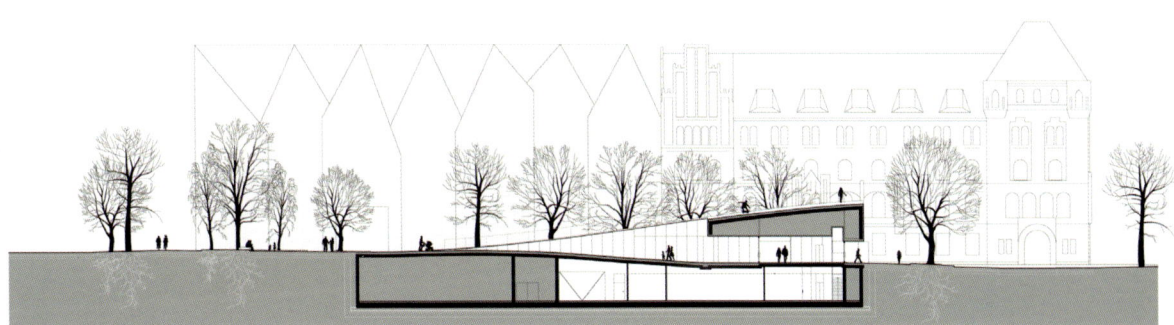

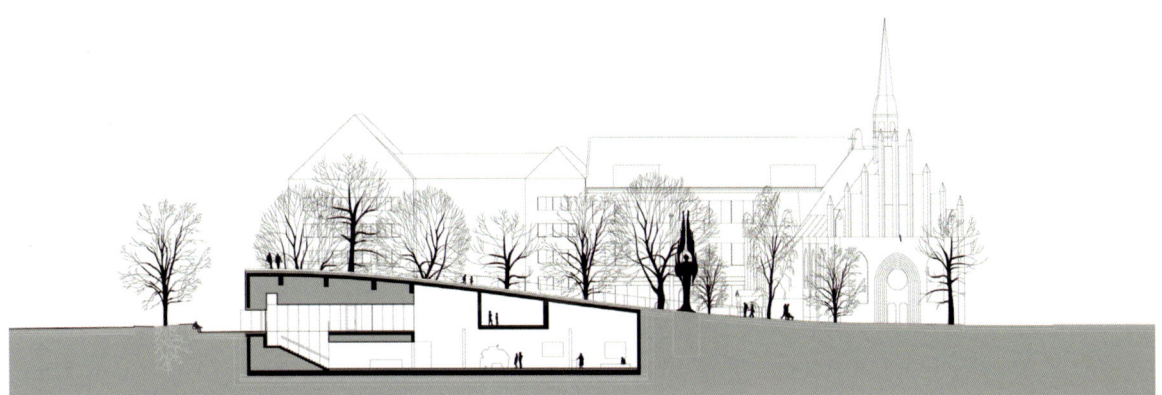

Sections

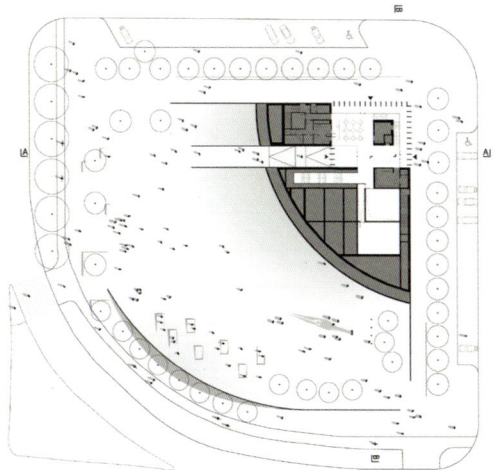

Ground floor plan

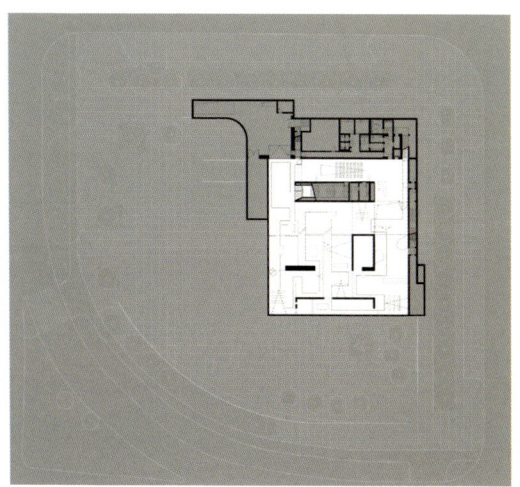

Basement plan

The exhibition space is hidden underground. The architects added a narration spinned by artists' masterpieces, historical works and the ones intentionally created for this venue. The blackness allows to focus on presented objects while giving the impression of an infinite space. This brand new formula for the exhibition makes a historical museum an art museum as well.

El espacio de exposición se esconde bajo tierra. Los arquitectos incorporaron una narración ilustrada con obras maestras de artistas, algunas existentes y otras creadas especialmente para el lugar. La oscuridad permite concentrar la atención en los objetos presentados y crea una impresión de espacio infinito. Esta nueva fórmula de exposición convierte un museo histórico también en museo de arte.

LANDSKAP DESIGN

www.landskapdesign.no

Formannsvei 50B
N-5035 Bergen
Norway

Landskap DESIGN AS was founded by professor, landscapearchitect Arne Sælen in 2001. After working two decades in a major architect company, he is now working alone, composing different groups of professionals and conduct workshops closely connected to the task in question. This has resulted in several internationally renown projects.
The works span from product design to strategic analysis for whole cities, as well as urban space design.

Landskap DESIGN AS fue fundada por el profesor y arquitecto paisájista Arne Sælen en 2001. Después de trabajar dos décadas en una importante empresa de arquitectura, ahora trabaja solo, formando diferentes grupos de profesionales y dirigiendo talleres vinculados a la tarea en cuestión. Esto se ha traducido en diversos proyectos reconocidos internacionalmente.
Las obras abarcan desde el diseño de producto hasta el análisis estratégico para ciudades, así como el diseño de espacio urbano.

STAIRCASE TO THE CHURCH OF S T. JOHN
Bergen, Norway — 2015 — 1.250 m² / 13,455 sq ft
© Arne Sælen, Bent René Synnevåg

Situated on top of a hill, the church dominates the cityscape.The red brick illuminated walls glow at night.The connecting street leads from the city center to the Church, divided by a crossing street. The upper part stairs are built as a granite construction in the late 1880s. The lower part had narrow stairs in both sides, with a broad gravel road in the middle. Asphalt was added in the 1930s. In 2015 the upper part was rebuilt to create an attractive recreation area focused on the use of water.

Situada en lo alto de una colina, la iglesia domina el paisaje urbano. Los muros de ladrillo rojo resplandecen por la noche. La calle que conecta la iglesia con el centro de la ciudad está dividida por una calle transversal. Las escaleras de granito superiores se construyeron a finales de 1880. La parte inferior tenía estrechas escaleras en ambos lados y una calzada central de grava. El asfalto se agregó en los años treinta. En 2015 se creó en la parte superior una atractiva zona lúdica basada en el uso del agua.

Ca. 1890

2016

Before

Construction

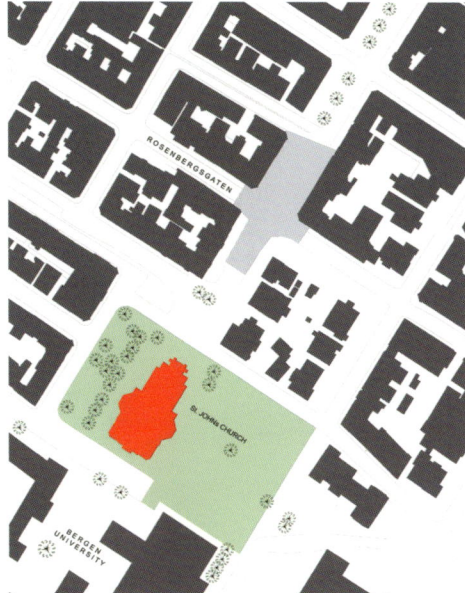

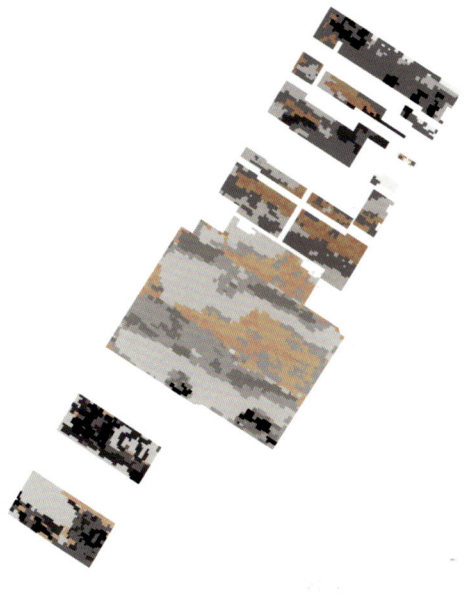

City plan

Site plan

Paving pattern

The new steps in the remodelling were made from a darker stone, with a pineapple surface on the insteps, and polished on the risings to create more contrast. Rusty wrought iron handrails were substituted by thick stainless steel rails. One high pylon with greenish light was the only light source in the upper part.

Los nuevos escalones de la remodelación se hicieron con una piedra más oscura, de textura rugosa en las huellas y pulida en las contrahuellas para crear más contraste. Los pasamanos oxidados de hierro fueron sustituidos por tubos de acero inoxidable. Un poste alto con luz verdosa fue la única fuente de luz en la parte superior.

Legend

	Red granite G354A
	Yellow granite G682
	Lys grå - Light grey granite
	Medium gray granite G654
	Dark grey granite G399
	Black granite G308
	Stairs single width
	Kurbstone with 2-stone drain
	New step duoble width
	Open drain
	Granite top
	Granite wall
	Pool edging
	Granite planter with grass and flowers
	Glass wall with rail
	Stainless steel rail
	Cobbled stones
	Asphalt
	Lowered drain
	Granite planter with tree
	Granite ramp
	Water disc
	Water jet
	Water fall

ROHRS GATE

ROSENBERGGATEN

Trappenummer

Construction plan

The driving range in the middle of the street was narrowed by large, granite planters used to rest. The whole square is levelled at pavement level and is really functioning as a shared space. The square is extended towards the city centre and a glass wall enable children and wheelchair users to view the city from above.

La zona de tráfico del centro de la calle se redujo con grandes jardineras de granito. Toda la plaza está nivelada a la altura del pavimento y funciona como un ámbito compartido. La plaza se extiende hacia el centro de la ciudad y un muro de vidrio permite a niños y usuarios de sillas de ruedas contemplar la ciudad desde lo alto.

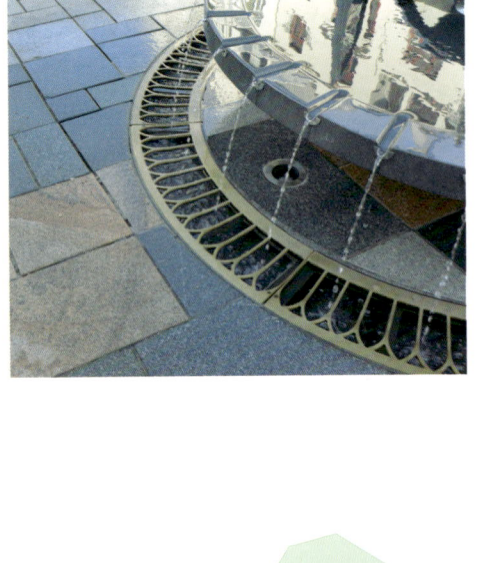

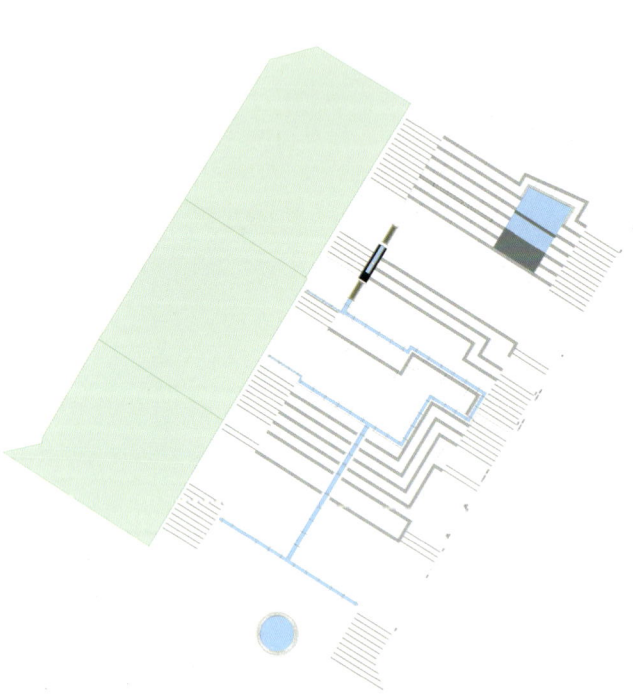

Water system diagram

The lower part is the major part of the construction. The water drain starts at the top and meander down various plateaus and stairs until it finally stops at another water installation: a huge polished black granite block with a single water jet falling in two steps until it rests in a deep, polished pond where the water disappears. The water reappears in a mighty waterfall at the base of the stairs.

La parte inferior es la parte principal de la construcción. El recorrido del agua comienza en la parte superior y serpentea por varias mesetas y escaleras hasta que finalmente se detiene en otra instalación: un gran bloque de granito negro pulido con un único chorro que cae en dos fases hasta un estanque profundo donde el agua desaparece. Esta reaparece en una gran cascada situada en la base de las escaleras.

LIQUIDAMBAR LANDSCAPE ARCHITECTS

---

www.liquidambar.es

**Vallehermoso, 110
28003 Madrid
Spain**

LIQUIDAMAR is a multidisciplinary studio dedicated to Landscape Architecture since 1999. Our vocation focuses on the optimization of exterior spaces from conception to accurate detail. Our philosophy is to conceive spaces where beauty prevails, the search for harmony in forms, the poetics of the garden, and the intense interior-exterior transition. But we also look for the spaces' suitability and adaptation to its users, and to climate. Our designs for exterior spaces are aimed at distilling the nature to have it close to our vital space. In form, content and essence, our garden seeks timelessness.

LIQUIDAMBAR es un estudio multidisciplinar, dedicado a la Arquitectura del Paisaje, desde 1999. Nuestra vocación es optimizar los espacios exteriores desde la primera idea hasta el último detalle.
Nuestra filosofía es concebir espacios exteriores donde prime la belleza, la búsqueda de la armonía en las formas, la poética del jardín y la intensa transición interior-exterior. Pero también buscamos su idoneidad, su adecuación a sus moradores, y a su clima. Nuestros diseños de exterior intentan destilar la naturaleza para tenerla próxima a nuestro espacio vital. En la forma, contenido y esencia, nuestro jardín busca la intemporalidad.

CAMPUS BBVA LA MORALEJA
Alcobendas, Madrid — 2012 — 37.000 m² / 398,265 sq ft
© Liquidambar

BBVA Campus has achieved LEED® Gold certification, awarded by the United States Green Building Council (USGBC) in order to recognise the degree of sustainability and health of the most representative buildings in the world. The great plains are replaced by plantings of native shrubs, with water requirements which are compatible with the Spanish climate and soil. A Mediterranean garden designed with great aesthetic effectiveness.

Campus BBVA ha conseguido la certificación LEED® Oro, por el United States Green Building Council (USGBC) para el reconocimiento de los niveles de sostenibilidad y de salud de los edificios más representativos del mundo. Las grandes praderas son sustituidas por plantaciones de especies arbustivas de carácter autóctono, con una necesidad hídrica y de suelo compatible con el clima español y su edafología. Un jardín mediterráneo con un diseño de gran efectividad estética.

CENTRO DE INNOVACIÓN BBVA SANTA BÁRBARA

Santa Bárbara, Madrid — 2016 — 3.000 m² / 32,292 sq ft
© Liquidambar

This garden covers two courtyards of a townhouse in the city centre, destined for the construction of innovation offices. The access courtyard has two geometric and symmetrical designed parterres, Mediterranean plants, olive trees and boxwood. A layer of black gravel minimises maintenance and a line through great contrast of colour and texture. The second courtyard is made up of a planter border with hydrangeas and virgin vines, an extension paved with limestone, various flower parterres and a land art installation.

Este jardín está incluido en dos patios de un palacete en el centro de la ciudad, destinado a oficinas de innovación. El patio de acceso posee dos parterres de diseño geométrico y simétrico, de plantas mediterráneas, olivos y boj. Una capa de grava negra alivia el mantenimiento y permite un gran contraste de color y de texturas. El segundo patio lo componen una jardinera perimetral con hortensias y parra virgen, una extensión pavimentada de piedra caliza, varios parterres de jardinería y una instalación de *land art*.

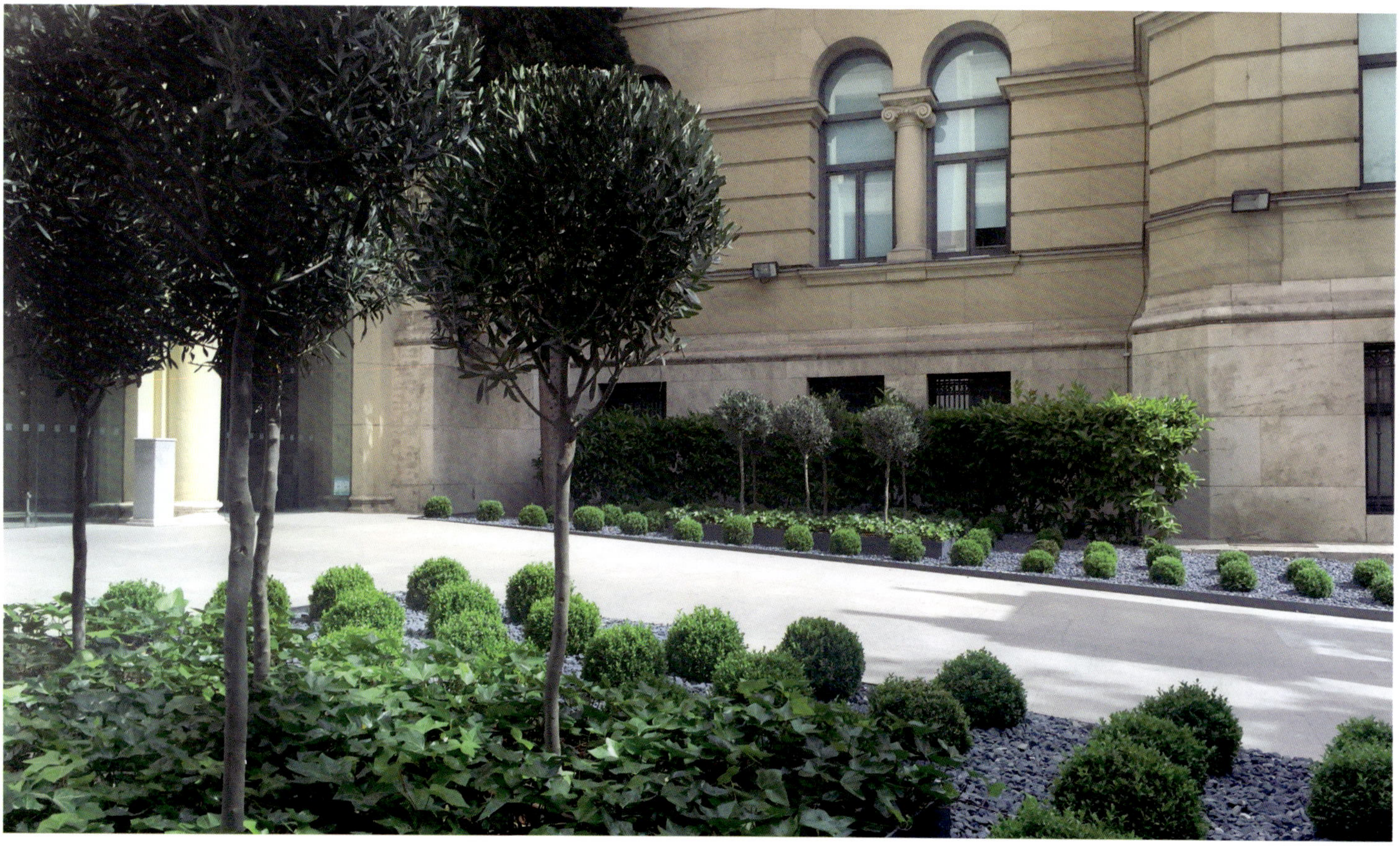

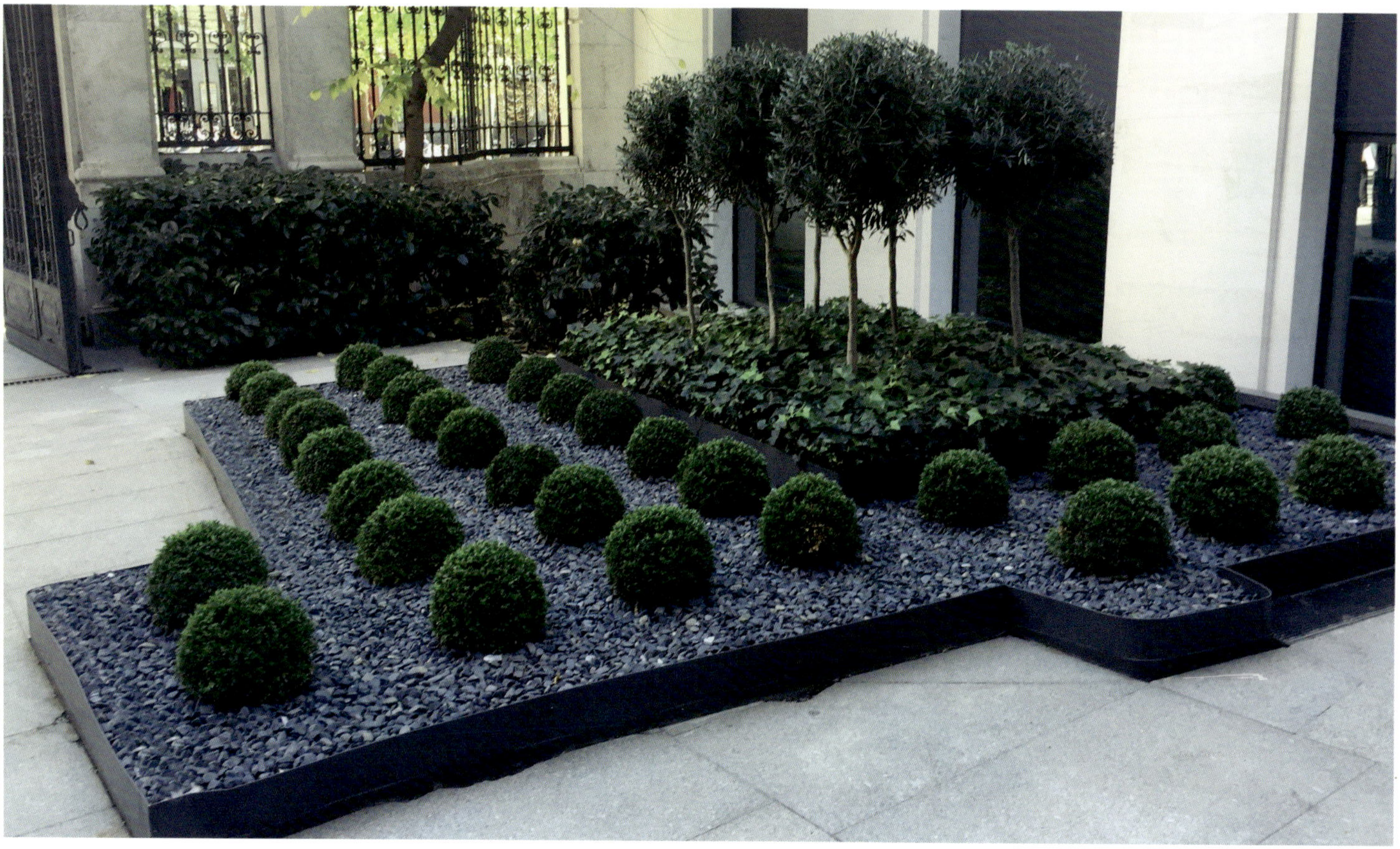

JARDIN CON PALMERAS

Pozuelo de Alarcón, Madrid — 2016 — 2.280 m² / 24,542 sq ft
© Liquidambar

We transformed an old garden with a tennis court into a different garden with a padel tennis court, taking advantage of the spare ground for parties and activities. We were able to unify the spaces and create an exterior designed for leisure, relaxation, practising sport and dinner. The idea was to arrange an orderly alignment of palm trees, decrease the amount of grass limiting it to the areas near the pool, thus arranging paved-over areas to improve spatial integration.

Transformamos un jardín antiguo con pista de tenis en un jardín diferente con una pista de padel, aprovechando la zona resultante para fiestas y actividades. Logramos unificar los espacios y crear un exterior pensado para disfrutar, descansar, hacer deporte y cenar. La idea fue trazar una alineación ordenada de palmeras, se redujo la cantidad de césped acotándolo a las zonas próximas a la piscina, estableciendo así mismo pisas de pavimento para mejorar la integración de los espacios.

Site plan

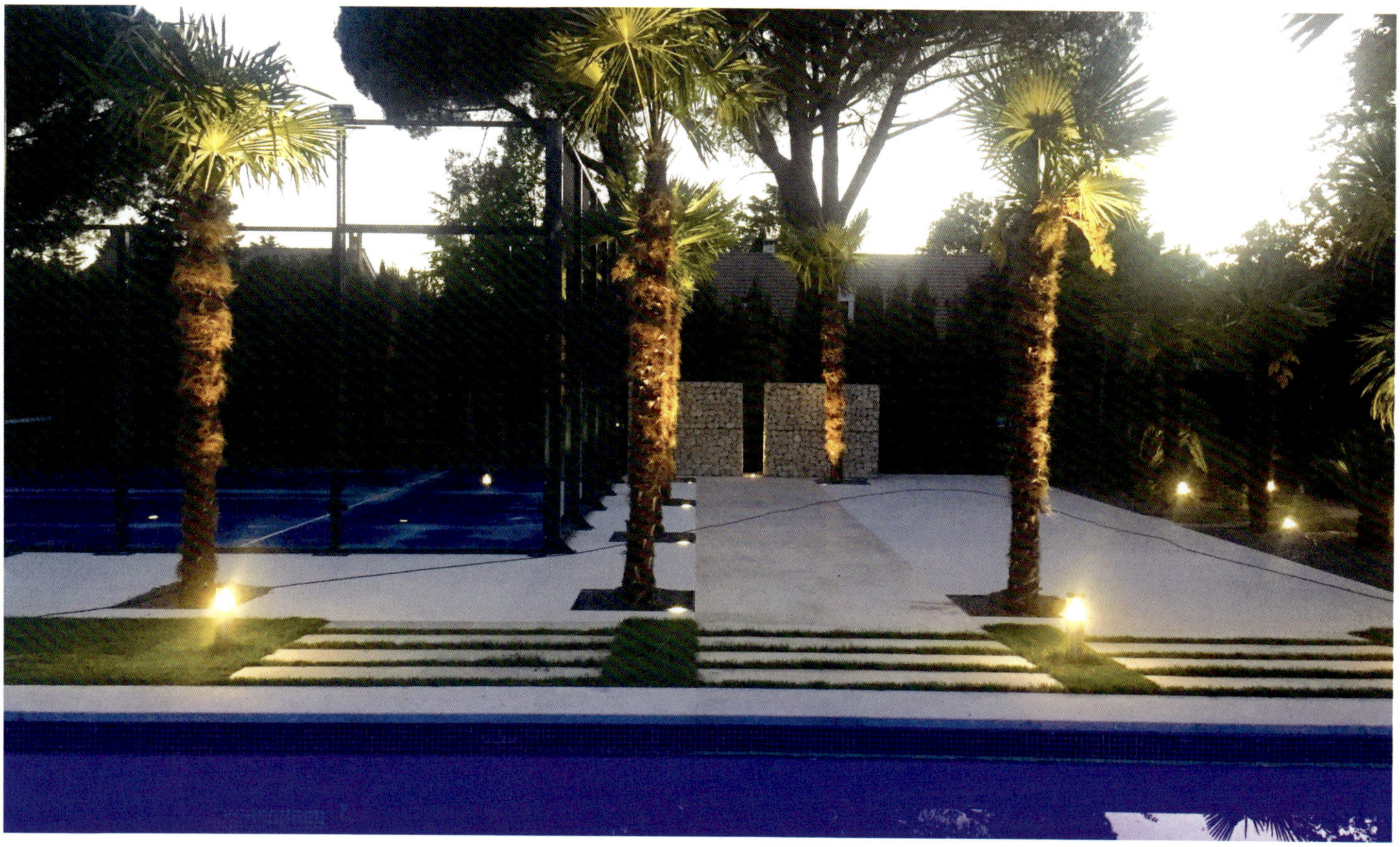

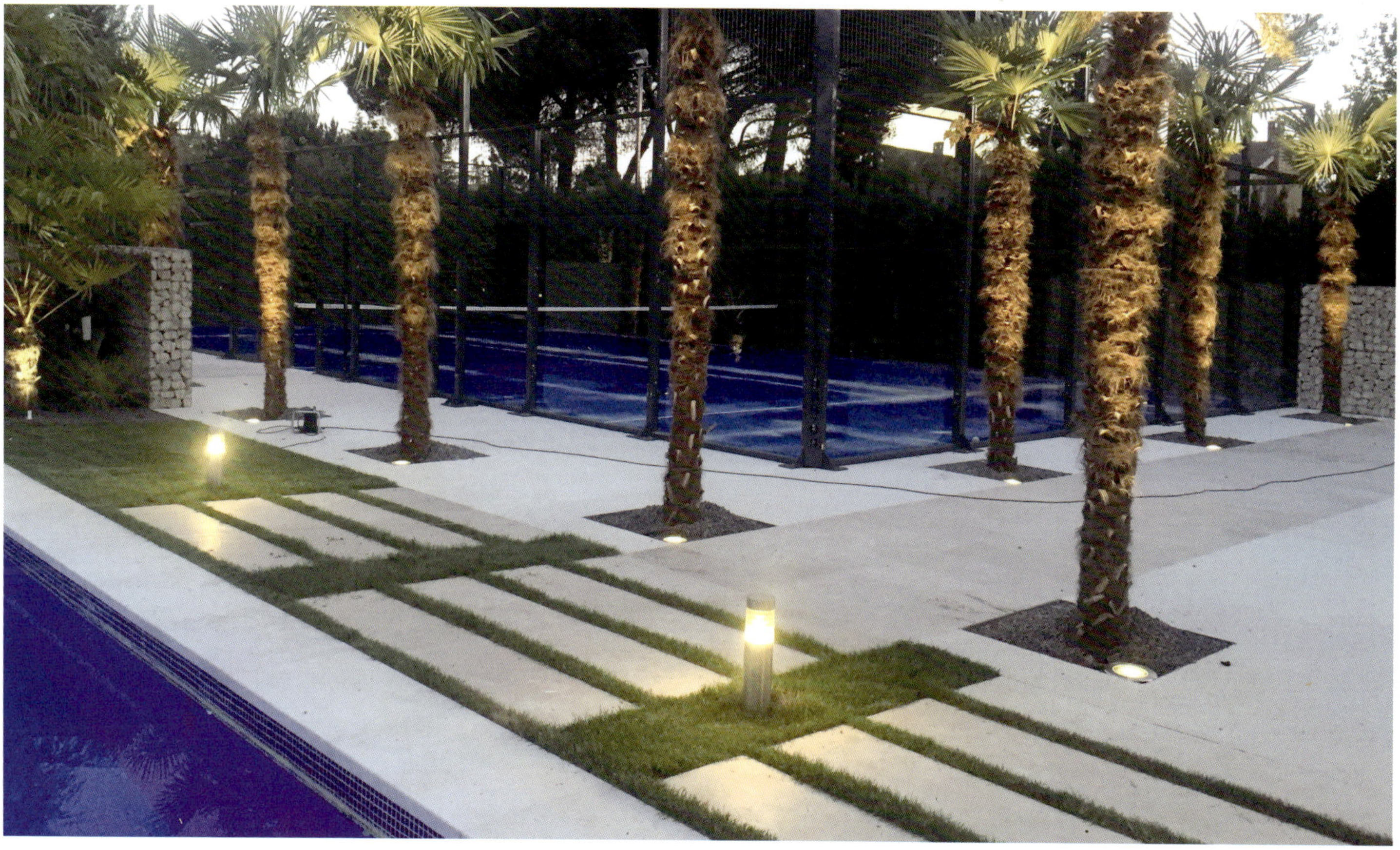

© Ferdinando Iannone

LUDWIG.SCHOENLE
(Ferdinand Ludwig
and Daniel Schönle)

www.ludwig-schoenle.de

**Charlottenstraße 29
70182 Stuttgart
Germany**

The focus of ludwig.schoenle is on "Baubotanik", an innovative field of research and practice dealing with the topic of living architecture in various scales. In their interdisciplinary work, the partners Ferdinand Ludwig and Daniel Schönle aim to apply the spatial, aesthetical, ecological, constructive and processual potentials of trees in new ways. By doing so, the office tries to implement the visionary idea of growing structures in the practice of architecture, urban planning and landscape design.

El foco de ludwig.schoenle está puesto en "Baubotanik", un innovador campo de investigación relacionado con la Arquitectura Residencial a varios niveles.
En su trabajo interdisciplinar, los socios Ferdinand Ludwig y Daniel Schönle investigan las nuevas aplicaciones de los árboles y de sus propiedades espaciales, estéticas, ecológicas y constructivas. De esta forma, su estudio implementa la idea visionaria de estructuras orgánicas en crecimiento, en relación a la arquitectura, el urbanismo y el diseño paisajístico.

PLANE TREE CUBE NAGOLD
South Germany — 2012 — 120 m² / 1,292 sq ft
© ludwig.schoenle

Plane-Tree-Cube Nagold is a long-term Baubotanik experiment within an urban context. Initially it is made of 1200 young plane trees that are arranged in containers on six levels. Over the years the trees fuse into one organism and become the main load bearing structure. Then the project will serve as a multifunctional vertical pocket park.

Plane-Tree-Cube Nagold es un experimento baubotanik a largo plazo en un contexto urbano. Inicialmente está hecho de 1200 plátanos jóvenes dispuestos en containers distribuidos en seis niveles. Con los años, los árboles se funden en un solo organismo y devienen la estructura portante principal. Entonces el proyecto actuará de pequeño parque vertical multifuncional.

Top view

After completion

Elevation - phase 01

Elevation - phase 02

Elevation - phase 03

Construction site

Possible situation in about 20 years

Section after completion and after approx. 15 years

Impressions from the first years

Concept of plant addition

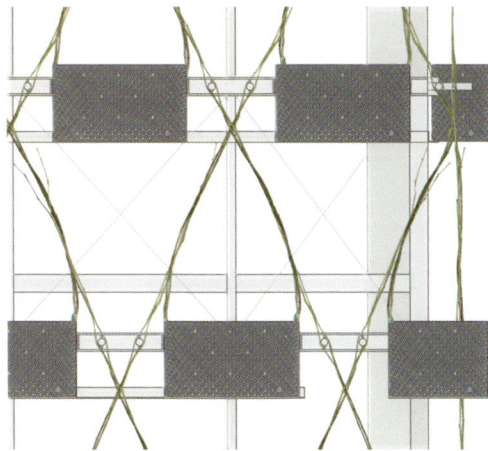

Construction detail after completion

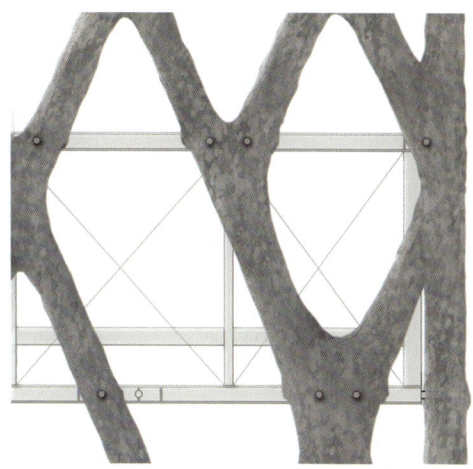

Construction detail after approx. 15 years

Left, detail ingrowth point after 1 year (reference project)
Right, detail ingrowth point after 5 years (reference project)

Izquierda, detalle de punto de crecimiento después de 1año (proyecto de referencia)
Derecha, detalle de punto de crecimiento después de 5 años (proyecto de referencia)

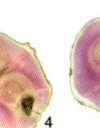

Section through inosculation (research sample)

PRATUM IN CAELO
North Italy — 2016 (date of competition) — 31.000 m² / 333,681 sq ft
© ludwig.schoenle

The proposal for a new park in the historic centre of Prato is based on a processual approach, interlinking natural growth and urban development. The process of change is curated as a unique event for the users of the park from begin on. Remnants of a hospital are transformed into iconic tree towers, representing change and history at the same time.

El propósito del nuevo parque en el centro histórico de Prato se basa en un enfoque funcional, interconectando crecimiento natural con desarrollo urbano. Desde el principio, el proceso de cambio fue asumido por los usuarios del parque como un evento singular. Los restos de un hospital se transforman en icónicas torres, representando a la vez el cambio y la historia.

Site plan

View into the park from the western entrance area. The access cores (elevator towers) as remnants of the former hospital are transformed into tree towers.

Vista hacia el parque desde la zona de la entrada oeste. Los núcleos de acceso (torres de ascensores) como restos del antiguo hospital, son transformados en tres torres.

View from the entrance with the Baubotanik Towers

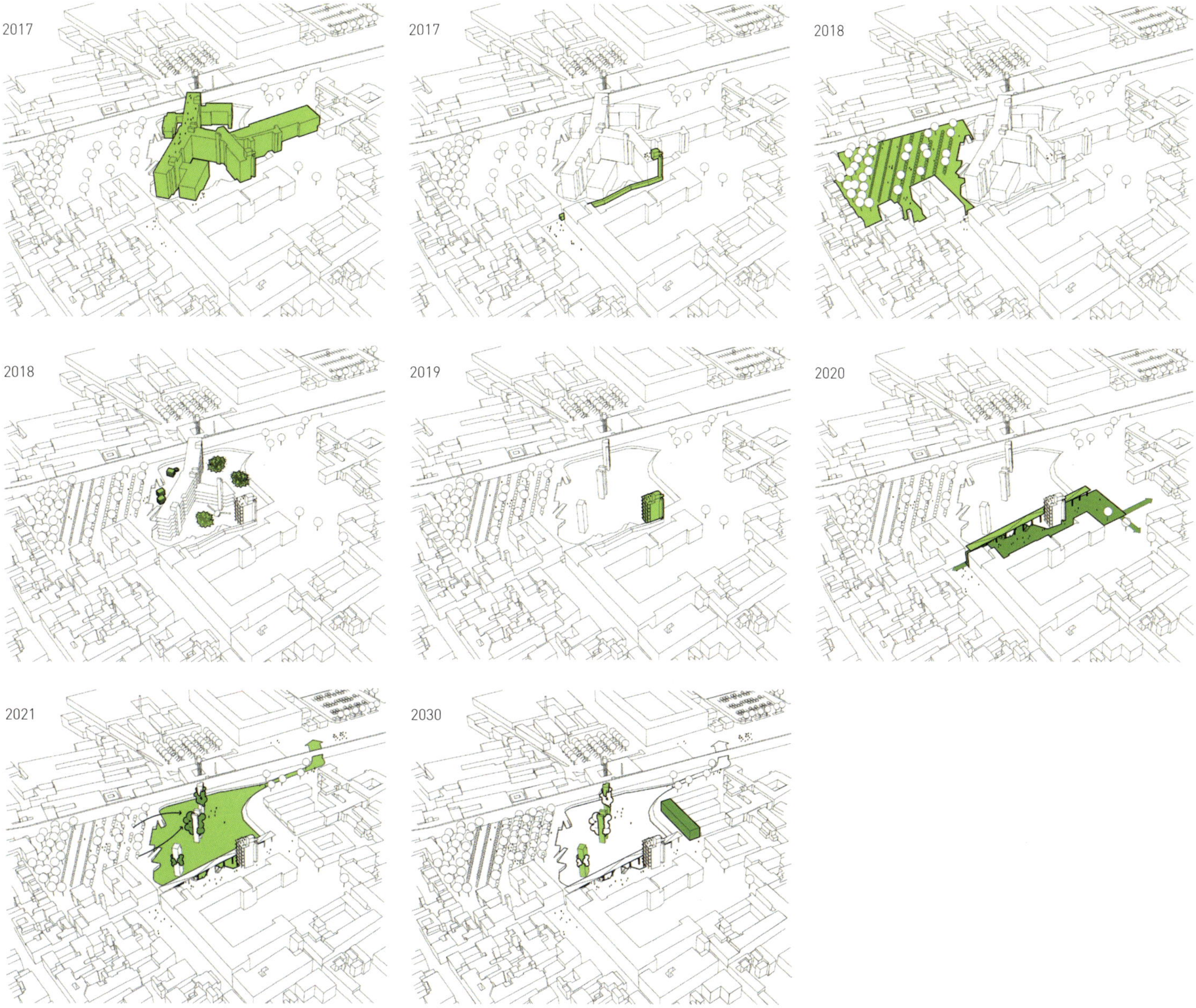

2017

2017

2018

2018

2019

2020

2021

2030

Developmental process of the wohle park.

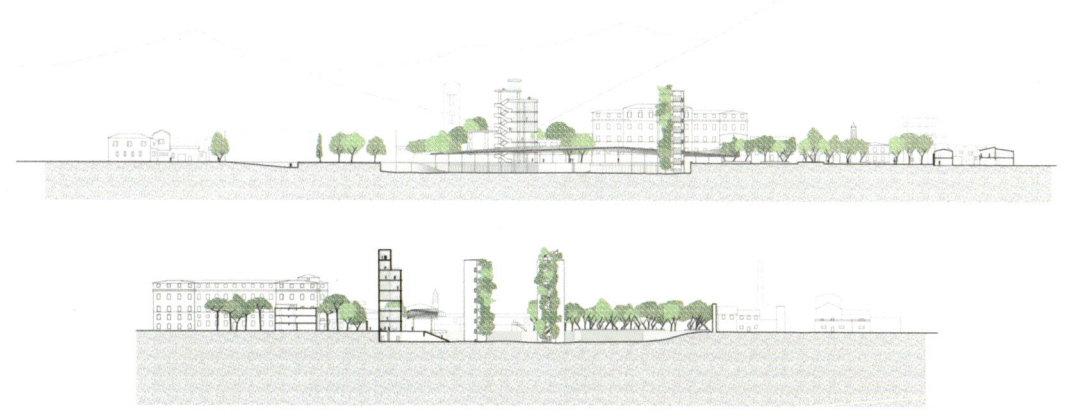

Sections

General concept towers in the city

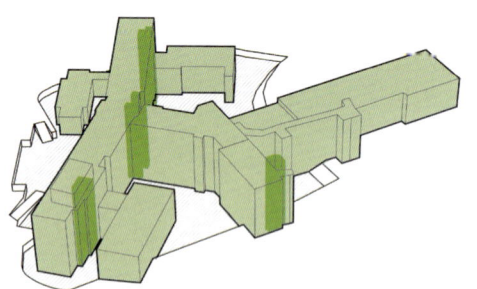
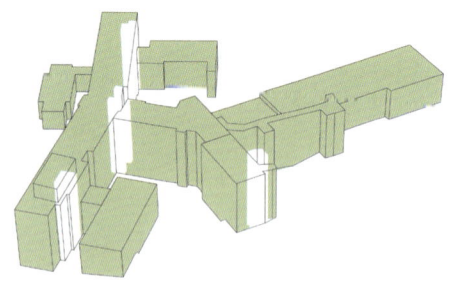
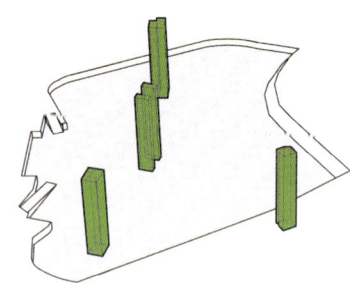

Concept of demolition and preservation

Inside the Baubotanik elevator tower

Meadow, pergola and art tower

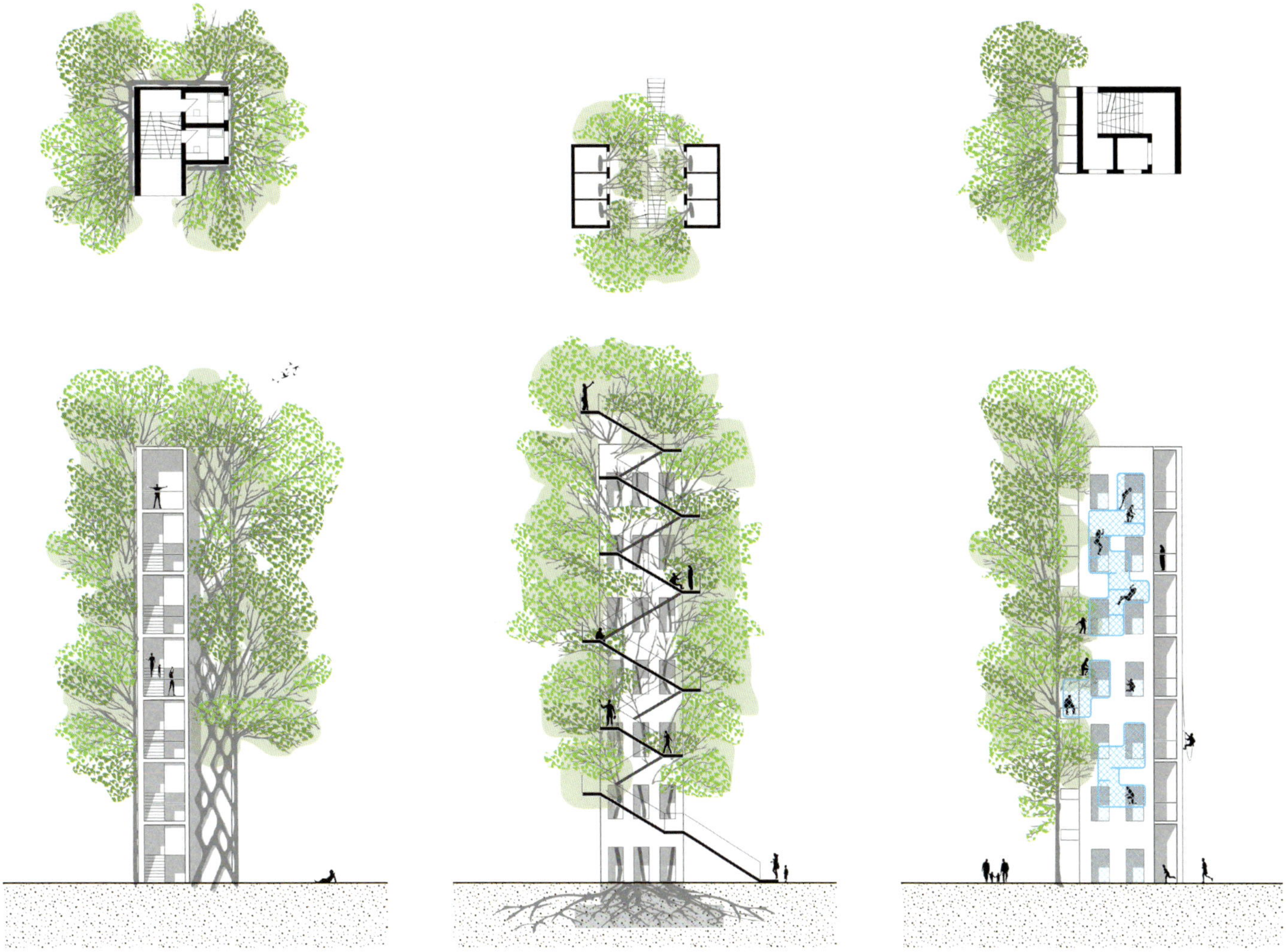

Baubotanik Towers

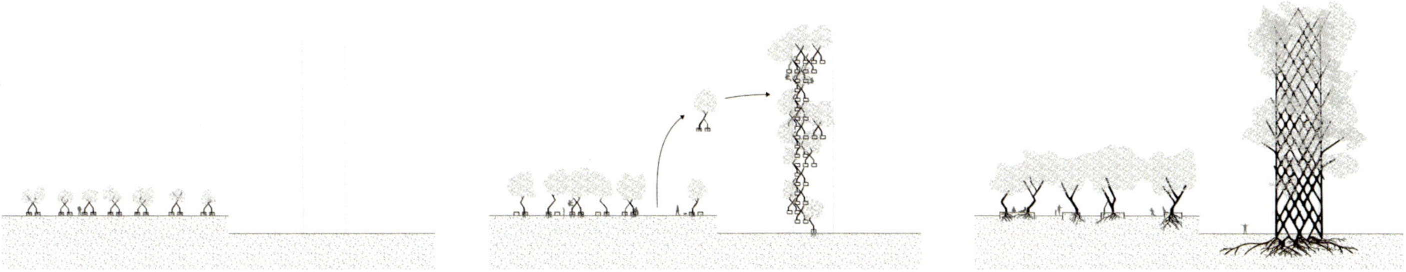

Concept of plant production on site and development of Baubotanik Towers

| February | April | July | August | October |

Detail vegetation meadow

MADE ASSOCIATI
Architettura e Paesaggio

www.madeassociati.it

Vicolo Pescatori 2
31100 Treviso
Italy

Michela De Poli and Adriano Marangon founded the Made Associati office in Treviso, Italy in 2001. The architectural office focuses on architectural planning, urban planning, and landscape architecture through the analysis of sites with particular landscape or environmental importance. The team participates innational and international competitions and has obtained various awards. Their projects are published in the main international architectural reviews. "Our way of working is one in which we are constantly stimulated by doubt, its most positive aspect."

Michela De Poli y Adriano Marangon fundaron Made Associati en Treviso (Italia) en 2001. Este estudio de arquitectura se centra en la planificación arquitectónica, urbanística y paisajística a través del análisis de los emplazamientos con especial importancia panorámica o medioambiental. El equipo participa en concursos nacionales e internacionales y ha obtenido diversos galardones. Sus proyectos se han publicado en las principales revistas internacionales de arquitectura. «Nuestro método de trabajo es aquel en el que la duda nos estimula constantemente, su aspecto más positivo».

CENDON DI SILEA
Cendon di Silea, Italy — 2005 — Area: 8.000 m² / 86,111 sq ft
© Adriano Marangon, Corrado Piccoli

The project presents a new reading and a reorganization of the space to recuperate traditional elements, related to both the landscape and history of the site, that wereinsufficiently explored until now. It also provides the inhabitants of the town with a new public space: an area that opens up to the river and connects it with the urban center.

La intervención propone una relectura y una reorganización del espacio para recuperar los elementos tradicionales —tanto paisajísticos como históricos— del lugar, poco aprovechados hasta entonces, al tiempo que proporciona un nuevo espacio público para los habitantes de la ciudad, una zona que se abre al río y lo conecta con el centro urbano.

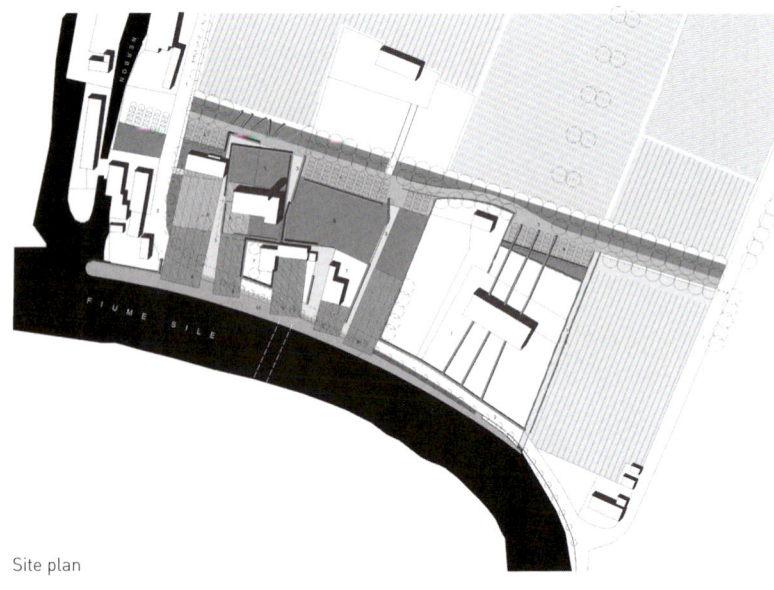

Site plan

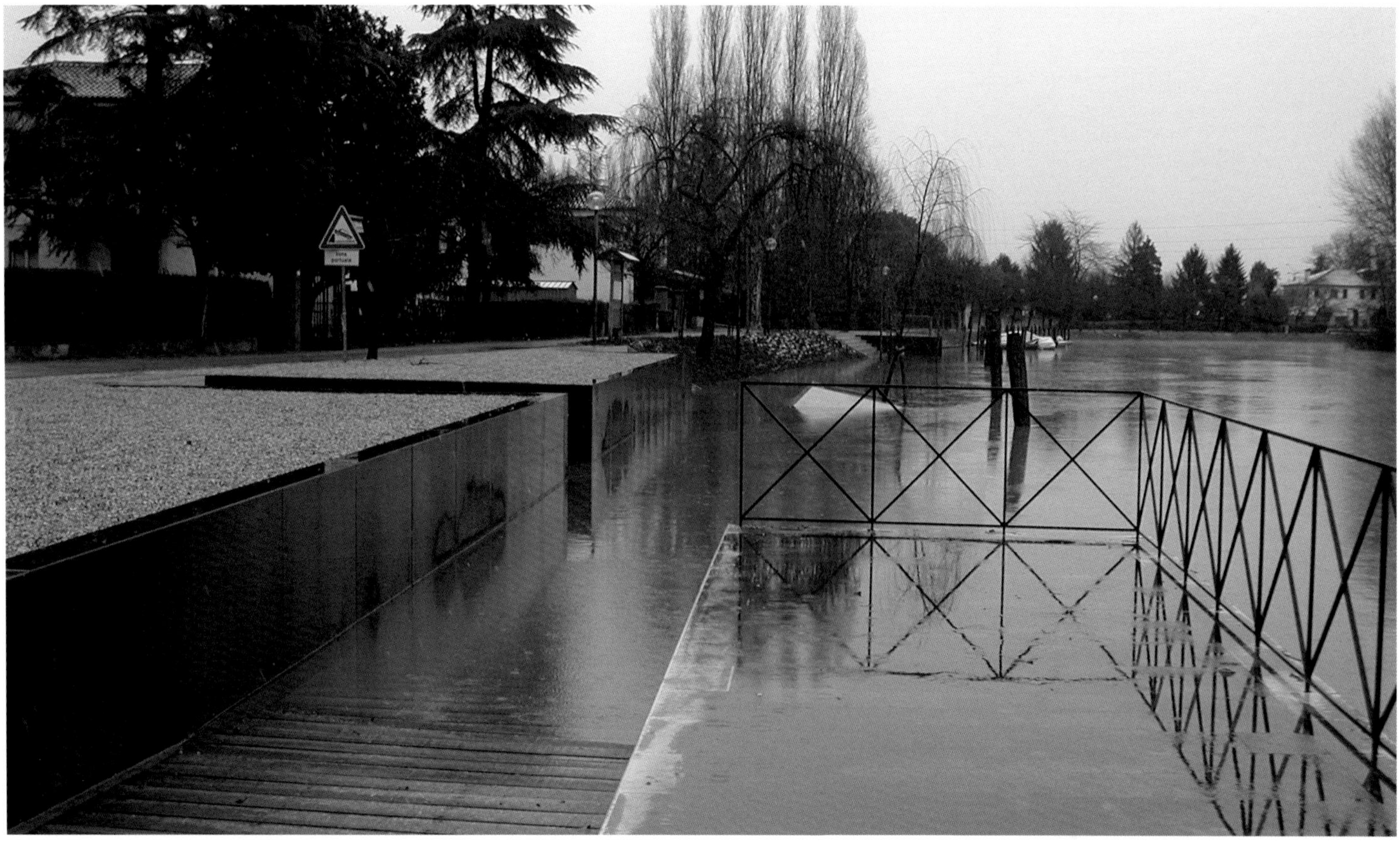

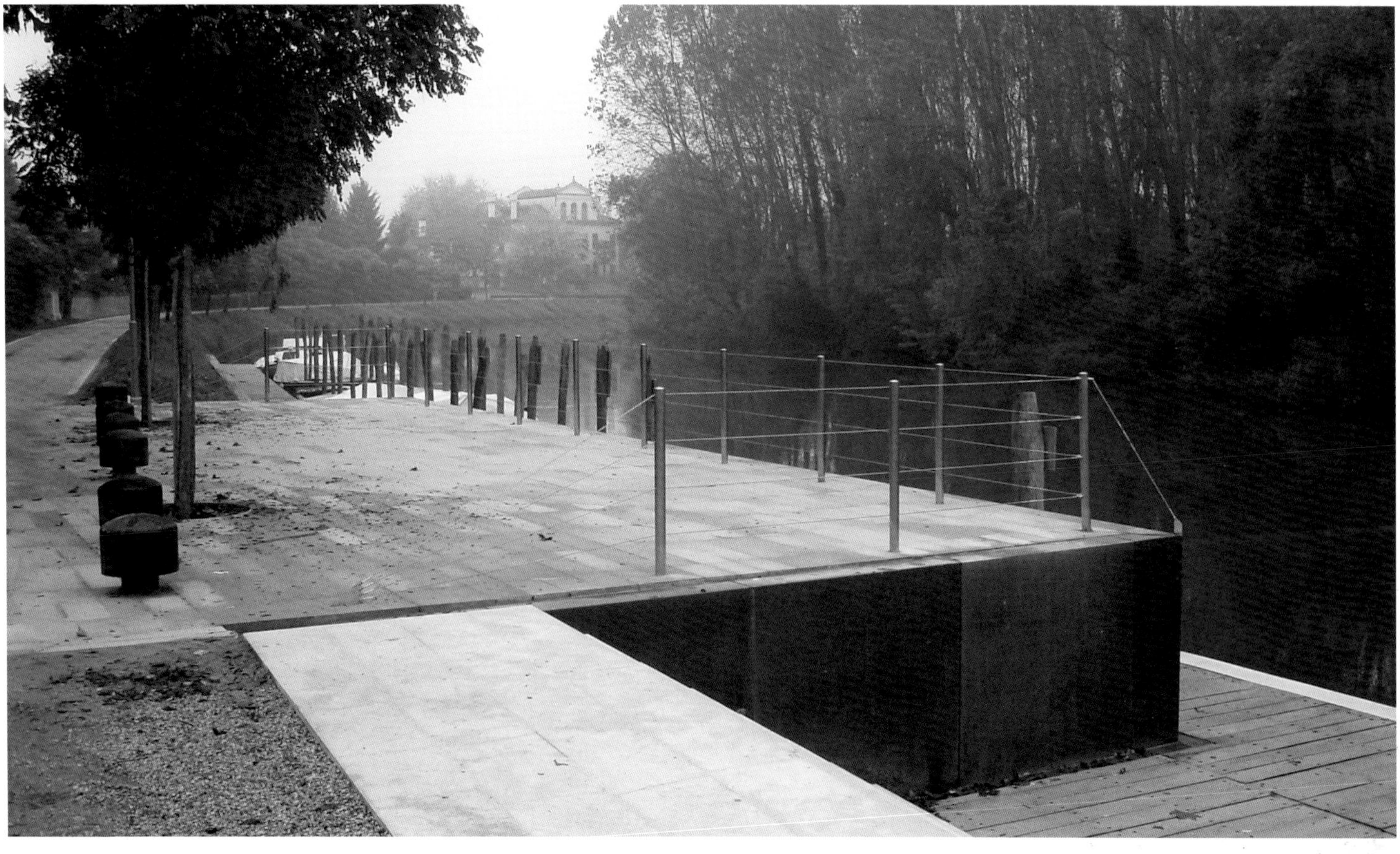

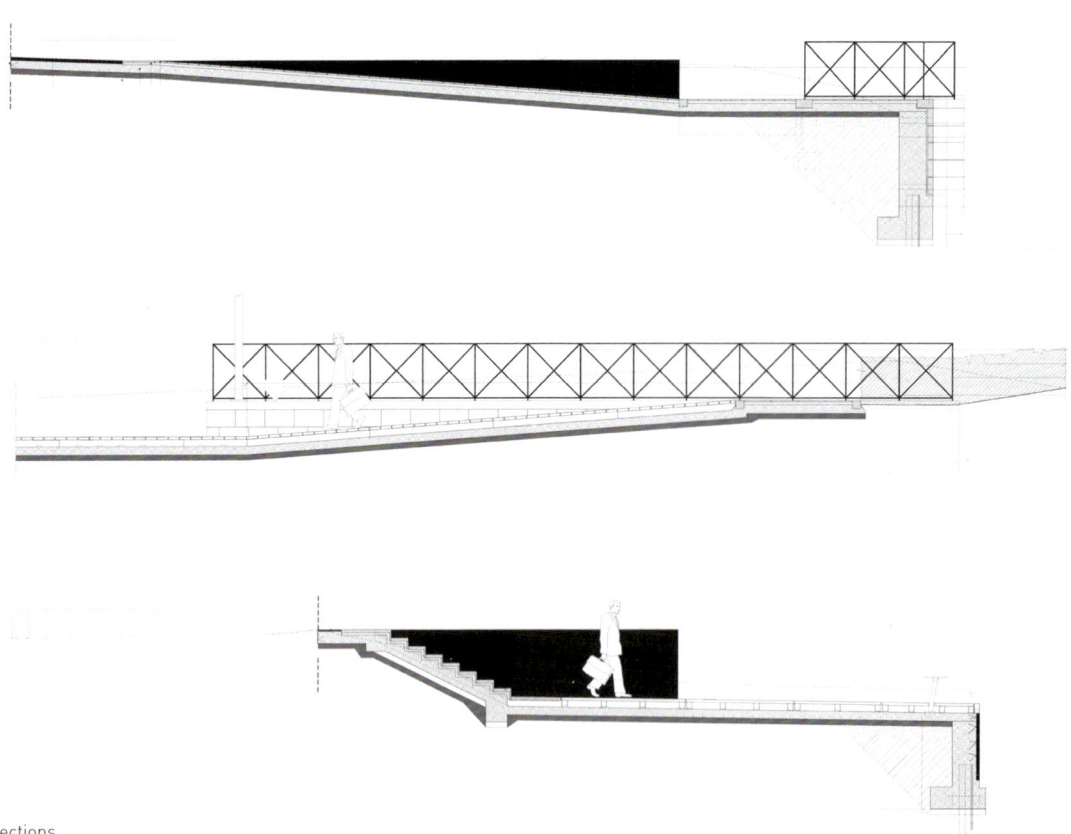

Sections

The design maintains the continuity between the different spaces that extend towards the Sile river.

Se han empleado hileras de setos y vegetación autóctona para deconstruir los elementos y espacios de la ribera y crear escenarios superpuestos.

MARIANNE LEVINSEN LANDSKAB APS

www.mariannelevinsen.dk

Blegdamsvej 28G
2200 Copenhagen N
Denmark

The architectural practice of Marianne Levinsen embodies a contemporary awareness of the environmental and social challenges in our urban spaces. Since starting her own office in Copenhagen in 2002, Marianne Levinsen has realized a large number of public and private projects, and gained wide recognition for her unique sense of place, space and materiality. Her projects range in scale, yet always maintaining a focus on the intimate relationship between the human scale and the built environment.

La práctica arquitectónica de Marianne Levinsen contiene una contemporánea concienciación sobre los desafíos medioambientales y sociales en nuestros espacios urbanos. Desde que inauguró su propia oficina en Copenhague en 2002, Marianne Levinsen ha realizado un gran número de espacios públicos y privados y obtenido amplio reconocimiento por su singular sentido del lugar, espacio y materialidad. Sus proyectos varían en escala, pero siempre se centran en la íntima relación entre la escala humana y el entorno construido.

LINDEVANGS PARK
Frederiksberg, Denmark — 2015 — 21.000 m² / 226,042 sq ft
© Torben Petersen

Cloudbursts and increased flooding is the outlook for many urban areas. The mission of Lindevangs Park is to respond to the challenges of a wetter future by looking at ways to adapt the urban landscape. This solution solves the water inundation problem and also doubles as the public space "Sløjfen". Residents and school classes are invited to come experiment with the water playground or visit the shared city garden.

Aguaceros y un incremento de las inundaciones representan el futuro para muchas áreas urbanas. La misión de Lindevangs Park es responder a los desafíos de un futuro más húmedo buscando maneras de adaptar el paisaje urbano. Esta solución resuelve el problema de las inundaciones y a la vez configura el espacio público "Sløjfen". Residentes y escuelas son invitados a experimentar con los juegos de agua o a visitar el jardín urbano.

COPENHAGEN BUSINESS SCHOOL "KILEN"

Frederiksberg, Denmark — 2006 — 34.020 m² / 366,186 sq ft
© Torben Petersen

The idea of the promenade is to keep a joint space and identity in the large scale and to connect the University building volumes situated near the promenade. The promenade is made of concrete poured on site with circular holes which give space respectively to different trees and grasses —a stylised picture of closed or worn out urban areas where wild grasses and pioneer plants break through from below as soon as there is a hole, a crack in the trail.

La idea del paseo es mantener un espacio y una identidad comunes dentro de la gran escala y conectar los volúmenes de los edificios de la universidad situados cerca del paseo. El paseo está hecho de hormigón in situ con agujeros circulares que alojan diferentes árboles y arbustos —una imagen estilizada de áreas urbanas deterioradas donde las hierbas silvestres y las plantas colonizadoras se abren paso desde abajo tan pronto encuentran un agujero, una grieta en el camino.

NAVITAS HARBOUR FRONT
Ørestad, Denmark — 2014 — 13.000 m² / 139,930 sq ft
© Torben Petersen

This project was to create an outdoor space around the building Navitas, Engineering and Technical Engineering School. This space creates outdoor life for the students and citizens by inviting city life to the new harbour. The main landscape elements are the large wooden steps/seating space, as well as the inner courtyards, which create green oases in the middle of the large building.

Este proyecto consistió en crear un espacio exterior alrededor del edificio Navitas, Ingeniería y Escuela de Ingeniería Técnica. Este espacio genera vida al aire libre para estudiantes y ciudadanos invitando a la vida ciudadana al nuevo puerto. Los principales elementos del paisaje son los grandes escalones/asientos de madera, así como los patios interiores, que crean oasis verdes en el centro del gran edificio.

COURTYARD AND SURROUNDING AREA OF TIETGEN DORMITORY

Ørestad, Denmark — 2002 — 13. 390 m² / 144,128 sq ft
© Jens Lindhe

The overall concept is to connect the green common, surrounding grass, and wetland area with the existing urban canal. The dormitory courtyard consists of a recessed grass area surrounded by a 2 metre wide circular wooden bench as the only piece of furniture in the courtyard. Tall, pruned silver willow trees connect the open courtyard to the sky.

El concepto general consiste en conectar la zona verde contigua y la zona del humedal con el canal urbano existente. El patio de la residencia se compone de un área cerrada de césped rodeada por un banco circular de madera de 2 metros de ancho como única pieza de mobiliario. Altos y podados sauces blancos conectan el patio abierto con el cielo.

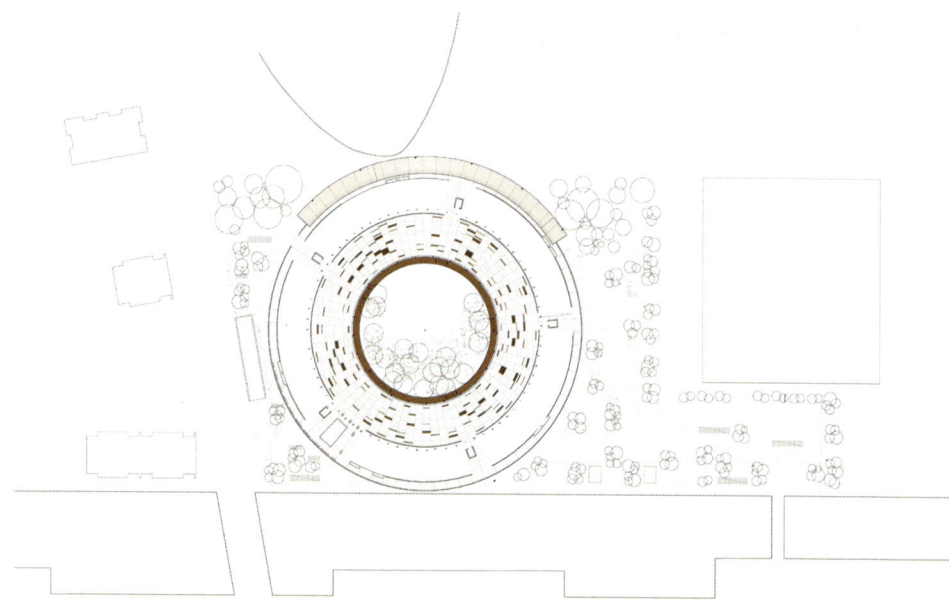

Site plan

KOKKEDAL WEST CARE CENTRE

Kokkedal, Denmark — 2010 — 50.000 m² / 538,193 sq ft
© Torben Petersen

The buildings of the care centre are placed around a communal garden space that gathers and connects the buildings. The area serves as shared space with pedestrians vehicular traffic. The surface's slope is adjusted according to regulations, to avoid ramps and railings and the access to all buildings is adapted in soft terrain elevations for walking-impaired and wheelchair users.

Los edificios del centro de asistencia se sitúan alrededor de un jardín comunitario que los reúne y los conecta. El área constituye un espacio compartido por peatones y vehículos. La pendiente de su superficie se ajusta a la normativa para evitar rampas y barandillas, y el acceso a todos los edificios se adapta para minusválidos y usuarios de sillas de ruedas mediante suaves elevaciones del terreno.

Site plan

MCGREGOR COXALL

www.mcgregorcoxall.com

1C Whistler Street
Manly
New South Wales
Australia

McGregor Coxall are a multi-disciplinary design firm located in Australia, China and the UK dedicated to assisting cities achieve sustainable prosperity. The international team provides services through Landscape Architecture, Urbanism and Environment disciplines. Embracing leading digital technologies, they deliver design solutions for complex urban and environmental challenges. CEO Adrian McGregor founded the firm in 1998 and was joined by Philip Coxall in 2000. Biocity Research was established in 2006 to enable partnerships with universities and scientific agencies. Primacy is given to design excellence throughout the entire organisation and is managed by the design group.

McGregor Coxall es una multidisciplinar firma de diseño ubicada en Australia, China y el Reino Unido que promueve la prosperidad sostenible de las ciudades. El equipo internacional ofrece servicios que abarcan la arquitectura del paisaje, el urbanismo y el medio ambiente. Utilizando tecnologías digitales punteras, ofrecen soluciones de diseño para complejos desafíos urbanos y medioambientales. Adrian McGregor fundó la firma en 1998 y en 2000 se le unió Philip Coxall. Biocity Research se creó en 2006 para fomentar la asociación con agencias universitarias y científicas. La excelencia en el diseño es prioritaria en toda la organización y está dirigida por el grupo de diseño.

BALLAST POINT PARK
Sydney Harbour, Australia — 2002 — 2.500 m² / 269,098 sq ft

This 2.5 ha post industrial waterfront park is located on a contaminated former lubricant production site in Sidney. The site's richly layered history included occupation by indigenous people, construction of the 'Menevia' marine villa in the 1860's, quarry use for ship ballast and finally petroleum distillation from the 1920's until 2002. McGregor Coxall undertook project management, design development, and construction driven by a strong environmental agenda where recycled materials are used site wide.

Este parque postindustrial de 2.5 ha frente al mar se sitúa sobre una contaminada antigua zona de producción de lubricante. La rica historia del lugar incluye la ocupación por indígenas, la construcción de la villa "Menevia" sobre 1860, el uso como cantera para lastre de barcos y, hasta 2002, la destilación de petróleo. McGregor Coxall asumieron la gestión del proyecto, el desarrollo del diseño y la construcción guiados por un programa medioambiental que impone el uso de materiales reciclados en todo el ámbito.

1. Wharf road amenities building
2. Upper lawn terrace picnic area.
3. Refelction on Tank 101 (former oil storage) with wind turbines
4. Tank impressions in rock shelf
5. The ridge spine pedestrian path
6. Upper viewing terrace
7. Southern Promenade
8. Terraced Promontory viewing decks
9. Eastern Viewing platform to the Sydney Harbour Bridge
10. Timber Jetty fishing platform
11. Footprints of past storage tanks as grass rings and wetland
12. Menevia Interpretation & display
13. Bund wall Stair and Path
14. Ballast Garden and bridge
15. Ampetheatre

Site plan

© Droneheadz

90

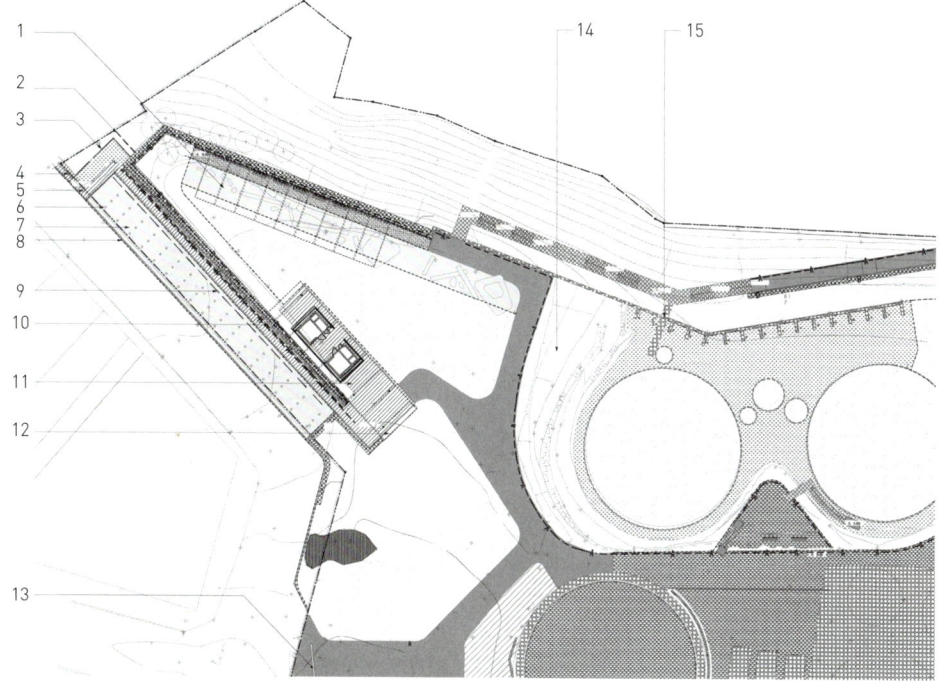

© McGregor Coxall

Site plan

1. Playground to Australian standards
2. 1000 mm high metal balustrade between existing boundary fence and gabion wall
3. Extent of sandstone edge wall to biotope, biotope to filter and clean storm water run off from car park prior to entering the storm water system
4. Ramp up from existing footpath
5. Timber bridge over biotope
6. Driveover LED maker lights indicating parking bays
7. New Bitumen Car park
8. Sandstone disch drain
9. 150 mm high 50 x 50 mm GMS finished SHS wheel stops bolt fixed to a concrete footing
10. 200mm wide recycled gravel strip between gabion + timber deck entry path
11. Location for coffee wagon
12. Timber bench top to gabion wall
13. Entry gates 2.50 m high with 150 x 150 mm SHS frame and 10 x 100 mm MS flat bars central gate to be operable opening on a recessed metal rail embeded in the concrete pavement
14. Existing rock slope retained
15. Cut out to heritage wall layed flat as path on GMS support piers

© McGregor Coxall

© Mark Skye

Wind turbine generators reflect a movement away from fossil fuels and an integrated stormwater management and recycle system ensures that all stormwater entering Sydney Harbour from the site has been cleaned and polished prior to its discharge.

Los generadores eólicos reflejan un movimiento alejado de los combustibles fósiles, y un sistema integrado de gestión y reciclado garantiza que todas las aguas pluviales del parque que se vierten en el puerto de Sydney han sido previamente tratadas.

© McGregor Coxall

© McGregor Coxall

© Mark Skye

© Mark Skye

© McGregor Coxall

© McGregor Coxall

© McGregor Coxall

LINGANG BIRD AIRPORT

Tianjin, China — Construction completion expected 2018 — 1.020.000 m² / 10,979,189 sq ft
© McGregor Coxall

Each year more than 50 Million birds make the return journey from the Antarctic reaches to the northern tip of the earth seeking food and shelter. The East Asian-Australian corridor is now the world's most threatened due to loss of bird foraging habitat by coastal urbanisation. In a bid to increase critical bird habitat, the Asian Development Bank encouraged the Port of Tianjin to embark upon an international design competition for a wetland bird sanctuary on a degraded land fill site in the Lingang area.

Cada año más de 50 millones pájaros hacen el viaje de regreso desde la Antártida hacia el norte de la tierra buscando comida y refugio. El corredor Este de Asia-Australia es ahora el más amenazado del mundo debido a la urbanización de la costa. En un intento de aumentar los hábitats para aves, el Banco de Desarrollo de Asia animó al puerto de Tianjin a embarcarse en un concurso de diseño internacional para un humedal santuario de aves en una zona degradada del área de Lingang.

Actual state

Spanning 61 ha the landscape has been specifically designed to support the needs of more than fifty species of birds in three different water habitats including an island lake with shallow rapids, reed zone and mud flats.

El paisaje, que abarca 61 ha, ha sido modificado específicamente para satisfacer las necesidades de más de cincuenta especie de pájaros en tres hábitats diferentes que incluyen un lago con rápidos poco profundos, zona de juncos y marismas.

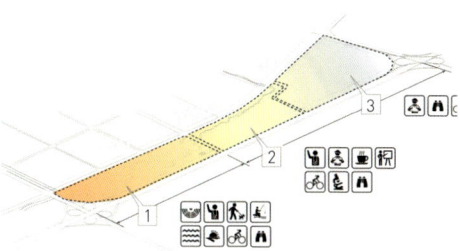

Visitor activity Control in areas of high bird activity

1. Unrestricted visitor access
2. Visitor volume and activity controlled
3. Low volume visitor activity Controlled

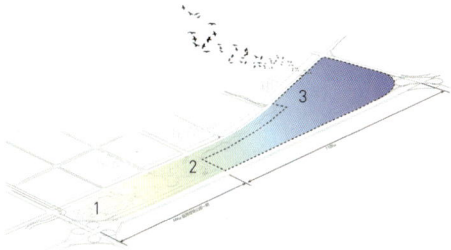

Bird activity and distribution

1. Low bird activity
2. Moderate bird activity
3. High bird activity

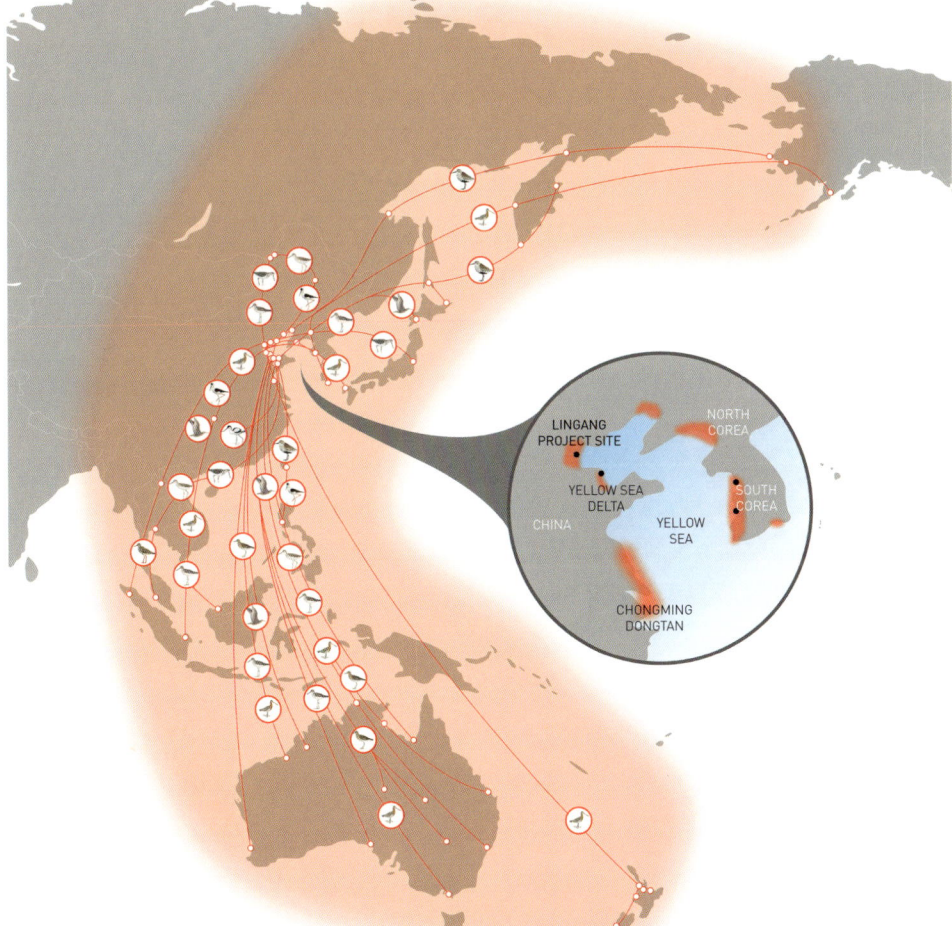

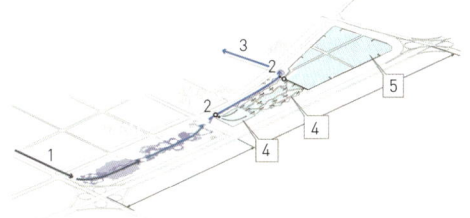

Flow and water level controlled and optimised

1.	Grey water	4.	Southern Zone Mudflat
2.	Pump	5.	Northern Zone Reedbed
3.	Treated water		and Mudflat

East asian australasian flyway (EAAF selected species)

 Marsh Sandpiper

 Black-tailed Godwit

Spotted Redshank

Sharp-tailed
Sandpiper

Black winged Stilt

 Pled Avocet

 Common Greenshank

 White-winged Tern

Little Egret

Relict Gull

Great Knot

Red Knot

 Curlew Sandpiper

Eurasian Curlew

Dunlin

Broadbilled Sandpiper

Spoonbilled Sandpiper

Red-necked Stint

Asian Dowitcher

Black-headed Gull

McGregor Coxall were awarded first prize in the competition with a design that proposes the world's first migratory 'Bird Airport'. The masterplan recognises the importance of the site both to China, Australia and the earth's ecosystems by proposing a 60 ha wetland park and bird sanctuary.

McGregor Coxall ganaron el primer premio en el concurso con un diseño que propone el primer "aeropuerto de pájaros" migratorio del mundo. El plan reconoce la importancia del lugar para China, Australia y los ecosistemas de la tierra con la propuesta de un parque de humedales y santuario de aves de 60 ha.

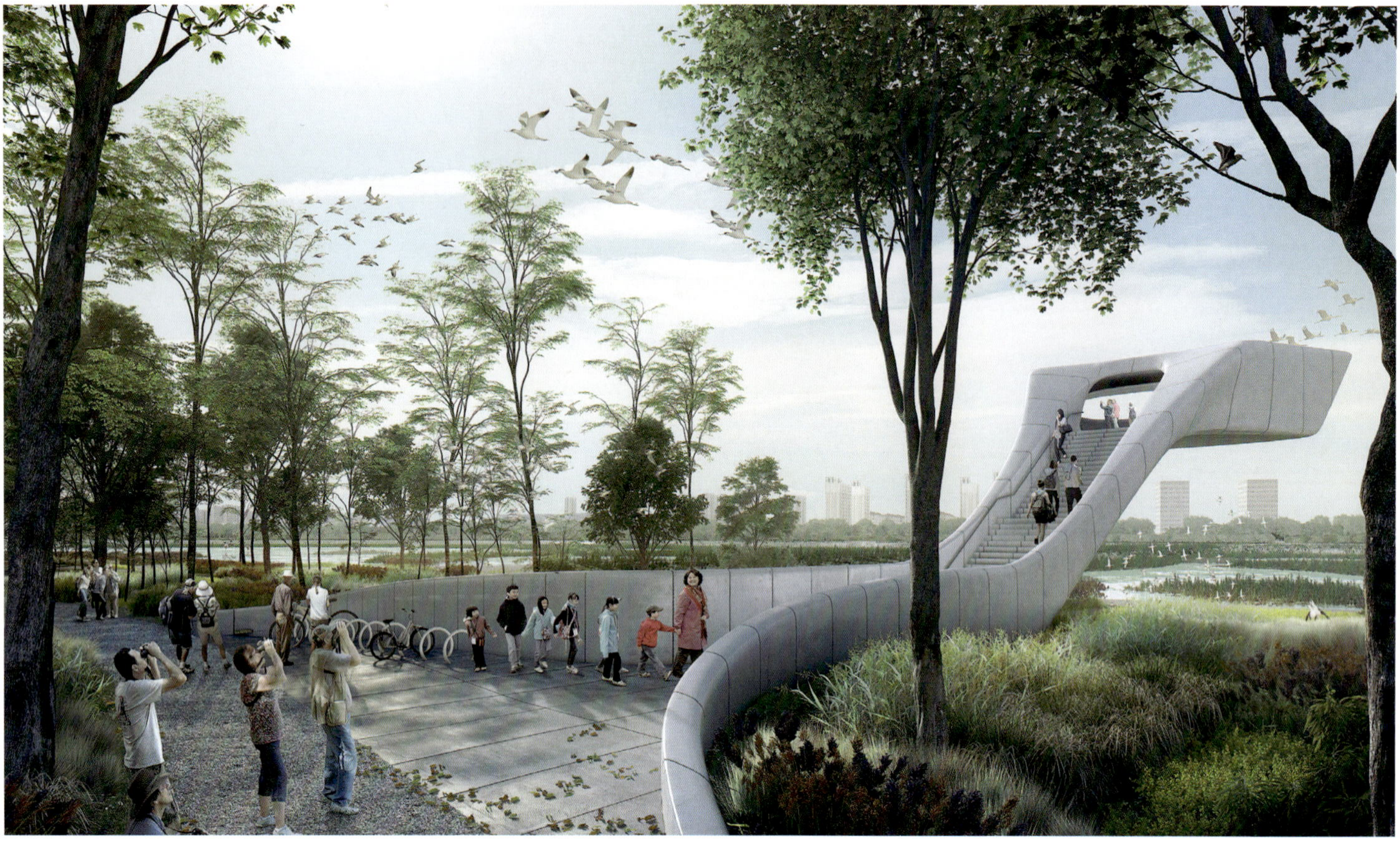

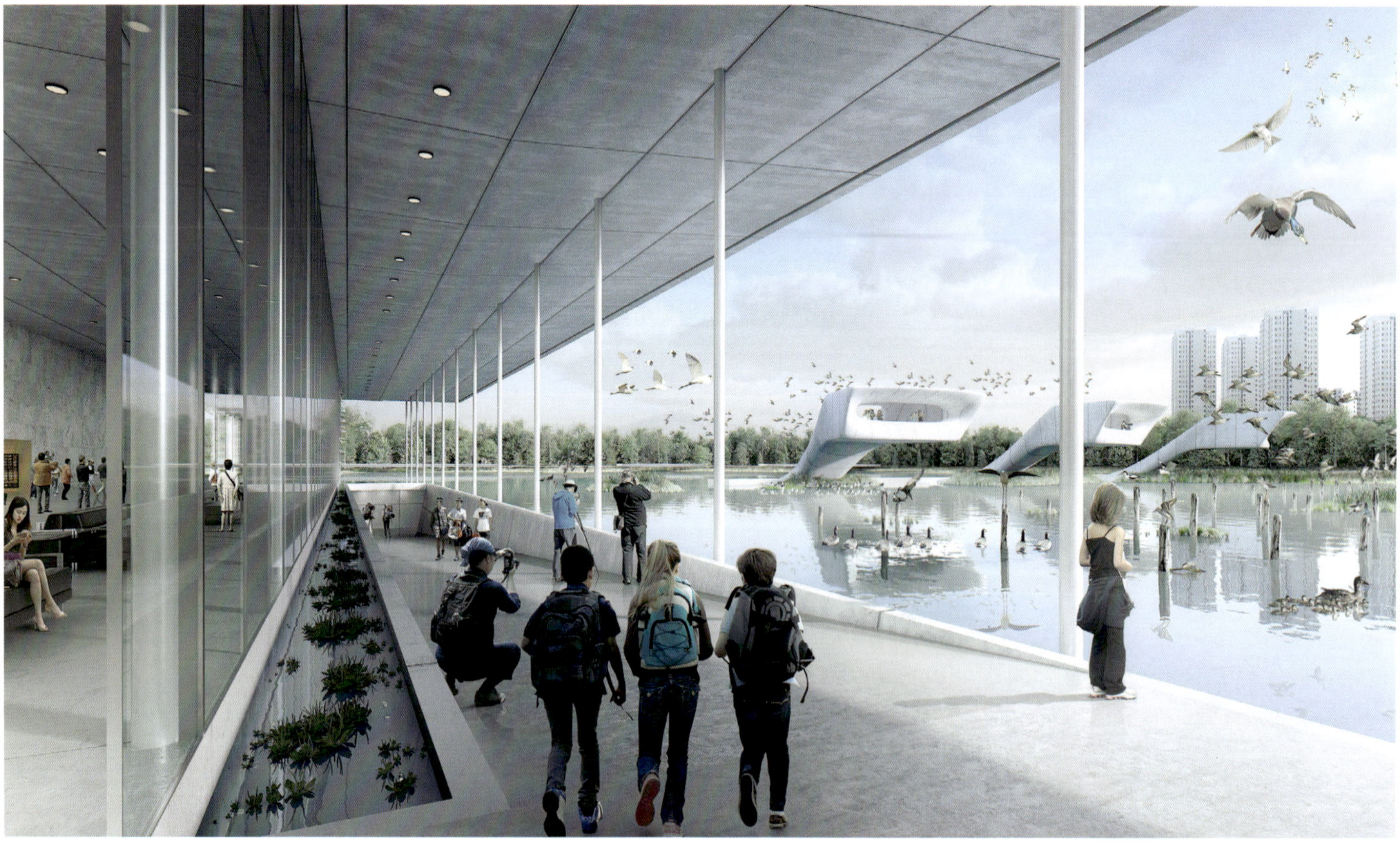

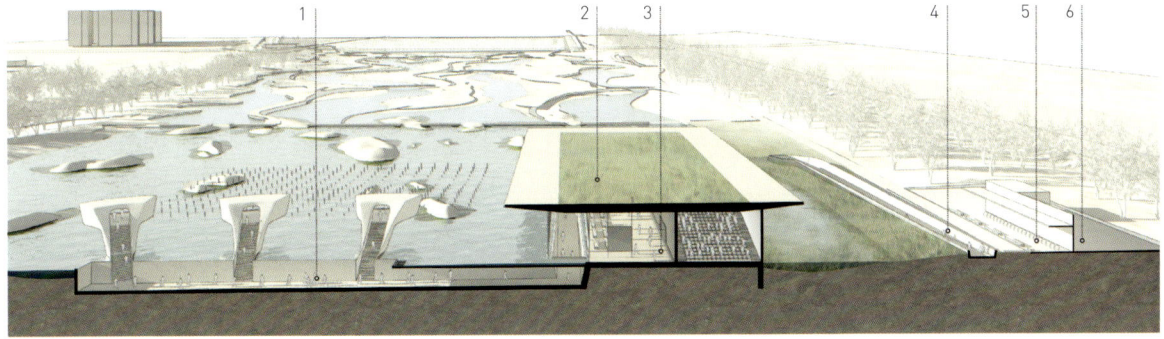

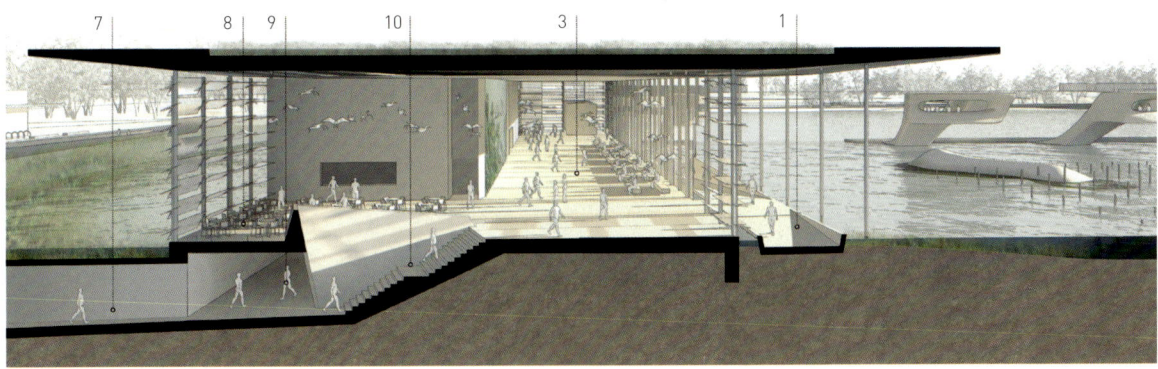

1. Slot to bird hides
2. Green roof
3. Exhibition space
4. Main entry ramp
5. Seating & shelter
6. Goods delivery & services
7. Underground entry corridor
8. Cafe seating
9. B1 lobby below
10. Entry stair

Renders

THE LEVEE. HIGH STREET MAITLAND

Maitland, Australia — 2015 — 8.000 m² / 86,111 sq ft
Renders © McGregor Coxall / Photos © Simon Wood

Central Maitland has been repositioned as a retail activity centre. The design juxtaposes a minimalist, high tech public domain with the grand heritage fabric of this historical city. The project has successfully enabled economic regeneration with retail vacancy having dropped from 50% to zero. The McGregor Coxall masterplan utilised targeted urbanism strategies to revive the local economy. Underpinning the design was a change of use from pedestrian mall to shared zone as a means of activating the street.

El centro de Maitland ha sido reconvertido a zona de actividad de retail. El diseño yuxtapone un ámbito público minimalista y de alta tecnología con el patrimonio histórico de la ciudad. El proyecto ha permitido una regeneración económica que ha reducido del 50% al 0% el número de locales de retail disponibles. El plan de McGregor Coxall utilizó estrategias urbanísticas dirigidas a revitalizar la economía local. El diseño cambió el uso de zona comercial peatonal a zona compartida como medio de activación de la calle.

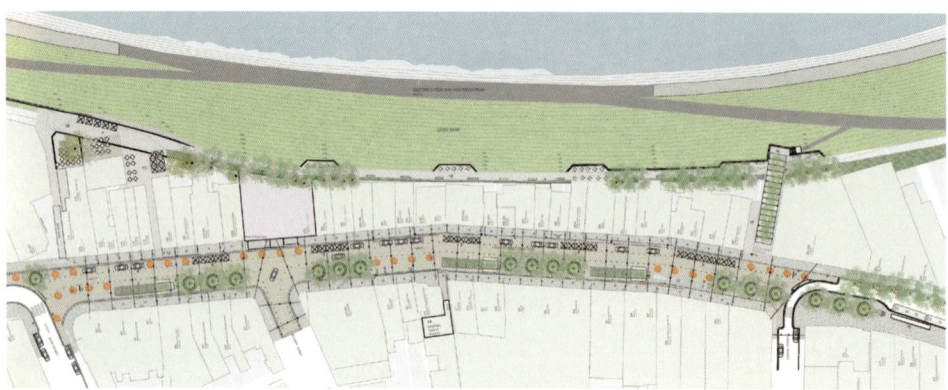

Site plan

Render

The long term strategy set out in the masterplan is to reposition central Maitland as a leisure based retail centre. The street construction is the first step in securing a share for the city. Stage two will begin construction shortly commencing with refurbishment of the riverwalk and a new River Link public building and community space designed to reconnect High Street to the adjacent Hunter River.

La estrategia a largo plazo fijada en el plan general transforma el centro de Maitland en un área de retail basada en el ocio. La construcción de la calle es el primer paso para garantizar un beneficio ciudadano. La segunda fase comenzará pronto con la remodelación del paseo junto al río y un nuevo edificio público con espacios comunitarios diseñado para volver a conectar High Street con el vecino río Hunter.

The $7 million street renovation has been heralded a success with vacancy rates now at zero. Local business and the community have adopted the design as their own. The behaviour of the community has changed as drivers and pedestrians mix safely at low speed in the space. The outdoor tables are filled with people and the space is filled with public life and activity.

La reforma de las calles por valor de 7 millones supuso un éxito con la reducción a cero del número de locales disponibles. Los negocios y la comunidad adoptaron el diseño como propio. El comportamiento de la comunidad cambió a medida que conductores y peatones se mezclaron de forma segura. Las mesas al aire libre se llenan de gente y el espacio se llena de vida pública y actividad.

PARRAMATTA CITY RIVER STRATEGY

Sydney, Australia — 2015 — 310.000 m² / 3,336,812 sq ft
© McGregor Coxall

The banks of Parramatta River have been inhabited for thousands of years, providing fresh water, food and transport for the Aboriginal clans that lived along its course. The Parramatta City River Strategy is a multi million dollar regeneration scheme for the 31 ha Parramatta River urban waterfront in Sydney's second largest metro centre. The strategy uses design to bridge the gap between environment and development, and takes a multi-disciplinary approach to innovation and research-based project solutions.

Los bordes del rio Parramatta han estado deshabitados durante miles de años, proveyendo de agua fresca, comida y transporte a los aborígenes que vivieron en la zona. Este proyecto paisajístico es una regeneración multimillonaria de 31 ha del frente marítimo de Sídney, Australia. La estrategia consiste en la conexión del espacio existente entre paisaje y construcción a través de un concepto multidisciplinar de I+D.

Site plan

The project proposes a world-class public domain and a high quality collection of mixed-use buildings that seamlessly respond to a dense network of accessible and active spaces. The plan aims to catalyse growth along the river corridor through an innovative urban realm and four dynamic, mixed-use quarters that link place and the environment together.

El proyecto propone una colección de una mezcla de edificios de gran calidad de acabados como respuesta a una zona de enorme densidad. El plan trata de catalizar el crecimiento junto al curso del río a través de una reconstrucción urbana de carácter innovador que se concentra en una serie de barrios de uso mixto que conectan el lugar con las características del paisaje.

MICHAEL SINGER

---

www.michaelsinger.com

**321 NW 1st Avenue
Delray Beach
Florida 33444
United States**

The work of Michael Singer has been key to the transformation of land art, architecture and landscape architecture into a discipline that offers models for urban renovation within an ecological framework. In 1993, the *New York Times* chose his project for a recycling plant of residues as one of the eight best designs of the year. As an artist, he has been part of exhibits in prestigious centers such as the Museum of Modern Art and the Guggenheim Museum, both in New York.

El trabajo de Michael Singer ha sido clave en la transformación del land art, la arquitectura y el paisajismo en una disciplina que ofrece modelos para la renovación urbana de ámbito ecológico. En 1993, el New York Times escogió su proyecto para una planta de reciclaje de residuos como uno de los ocho mejores diseños del año. Como artista, ha expuesto en centros tan prestigiosos como el Museo de Arte Moderno y el Museo Guggenheim, ambos de Nueva York.

WEST PALM BEACH WHARFS
West Palm Beach, Florida, United States — 2009 — Area: 50.500 m² / 543,577 sq ft
© Tom Hurst

The project for the new waterfront promenade and recreational areas of West Palm Beach includes three new wharfs that generate zones for sailboats and ferries. The largecentral wharf integrates a row of pergolas that shade the urban furniture and form a pleasant promenade.

El proyecto del nuevo paseo marítimo y de zonas de ocio de West Palm Beach incluye tres nuevos muelles que dan lugar a una serie de pantalanes para embarcaciones de recreo y atracaderos de taxis acuáticos. El gran muelle central incorpora una hilera de pérgolas que da sombra al mobiliario urbano y conforma una atractiva zona de paseo.

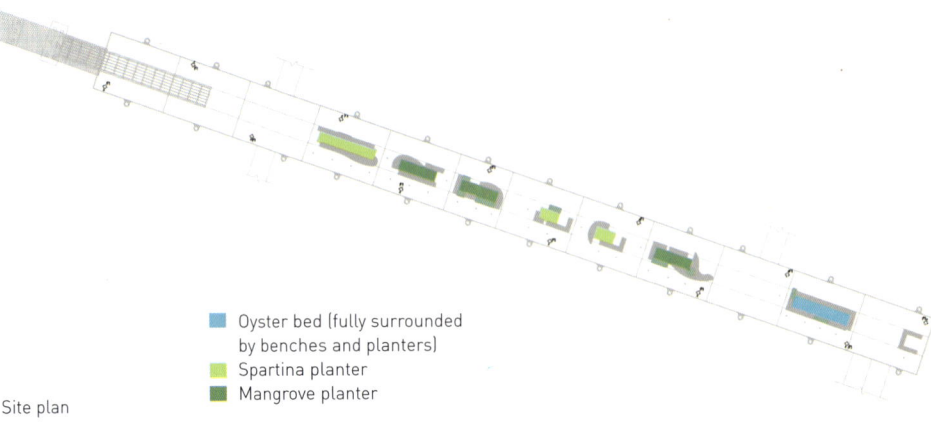

■ Oyster bed (fully surrounded by benches and planters)
■ Spartina planter
■ Mangrove planter

Site plan

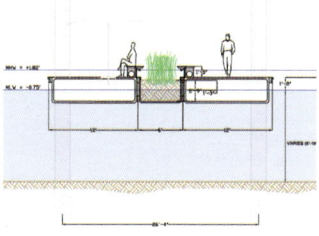

Cross section A

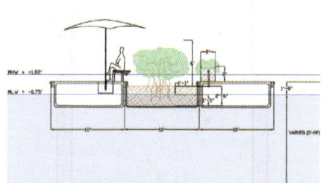

Cross section B

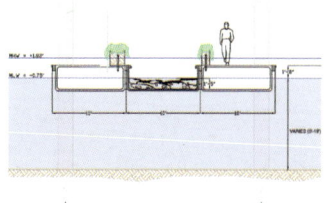

Cross section C

GARDEN SCULPTURE
Athens, Greece — 2007 — Area: 780 m² / 8,396 sq ft
© David Stansbury

In 2005, Michael Singer was selected to design the gardens of the US Embassy in Athens. The new building, work of Kallman, McKinnell & Wood, as well as the old one, by Walter Gropius, required a new landscape design that would integrate them. The central element of the project is a 65.6-foot-tall sculpture on a marble pedestal.

En 2005, Michael Singer fue seleccionado para diseñar los jardines de la Embajada de los Estados Unidos en Atenas. El edificio nuevo, obra de Kallman, McKinnell & Wood, y el antiguo, de Walter Gropius, requerían de un nuevo diseño paisajístico que ayudara a integrarlos. El elemento central del proyecto es una gran escultura de mármol de más de 20 m.

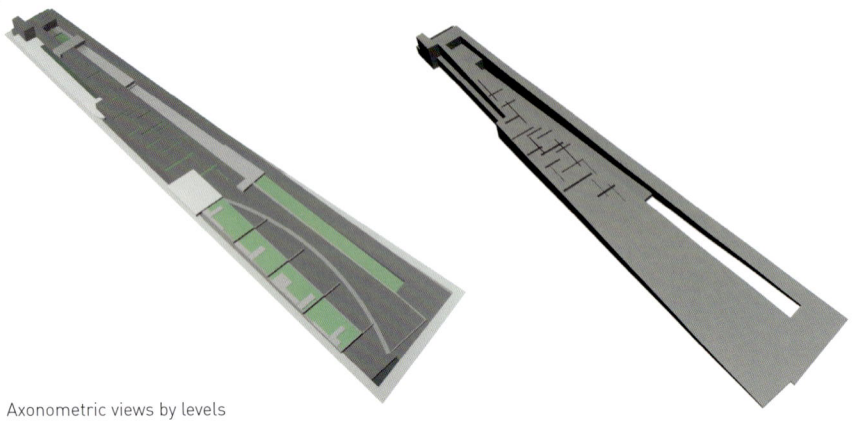

Axonometric views by levels

The design makes reference to the importance of archaeological findings in Greek history by integrating an "artificial arqueological site".

El diseño pretende hacer referencia a la importancia de los descubrimientos arqueológicos en la historia griega, integrando un «yacimiento artificial».

GARDEN OF THE SEASONS

Middlebury, Vermont, United States — 2005 — Area: 900 m² / 9,687 sq ft
© David Stansbury

The Garden of the Seasons, situated on the main pedestrian way that leads to the new library of the Middlebury College campus, offers the students a sensorial experience as well as a very peculiar quiet atmosphere. Access to it is through a small semi-circular portico where a granite bench with views to the mountains has been placed.

El Jardín de las Estaciones, situado en la principal vía peatonal que lleva a la nueva biblioteca del campus de Middlebury College, ofrece a los estudiantes una experiencia sensorial y un ambiente de quietud particular. Se accede a él por una pequeña ágora semicircular, donde se ha instalado un banco de granito con vistas a las montañas.

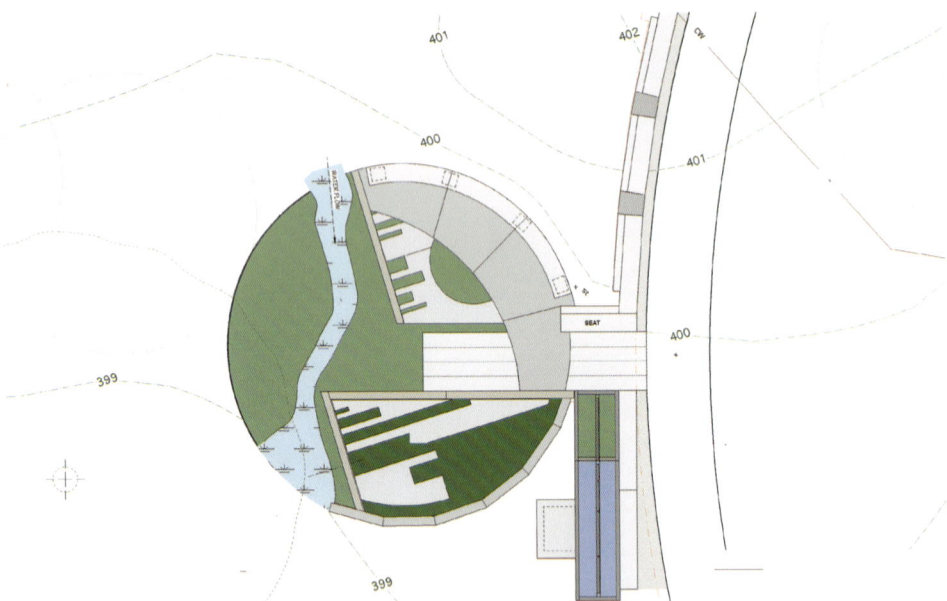

Site plan

The benches act as gigantic flower pots with a selection of native plants and integrate the vegetable element within the project.

Con una selección de plantas autóctonas, los bancos actúan de maceteros gigantes y ayudan à integrar el elemento vegetal en el conjunto.

COMMEMORATIVE GARDEN

Stuttgart, Germany — 1992 — Area: 450 m² / 4,843 sq ft
© K. D. Bus

Michael Singer was commissioned by the city of Stuttgart for the design of a cloistered garden in one of the most extensive parks of in the city, exactly where two streams converge. Singer has conceived a system of wells and canalizations that distribute the flow of water by means of sculptural pieces reminiscent of lost civilizations such as the Maya's or the Inca's.

La ciudad de Stuttgart encargó a Michael Singer el diseño de este jardín enclaustrado en uno de los parques, justo donde convergían dos arroyos. Singer ha concebido un sistema de pozos y canalizaciones que redistribuye el cauce de estos arroyos a base de piezas escultóricas con reminiscencias de civilizaciones perdidas como la maya o la inca.

The cuts on the granite planes give the environment
a sense of harshness that reinforces the paradisiacal
atmosphere that the garden aspires to.

Los cortes en las láminas de granito dan al entorno el
aspecto de crudeza inacabada que refuerza la atmósfera de paraíso perdido que inspira el jardín.

MOSBACH PAYSAGISTES

www.mosbach.fr

81 Rue des Poissónniers
75018 Paris
France

Mosbach is graduated from the landscape architecture school of Versailles. She founded with Claramunt, Jacotot and Tricaud Pages Paysage and opened her studio in Paris, 1987. Among her projects, the archaeological park of Solutre, the walk Canal of Saint-Denis, the Botanical Garden of Bordeaux, "the other side" in Quebec City, Shan Shui garden in Xian, the museum park Louvre Lens and Phases Shifts Parks, Taichung Taiwan. The equerre d'argent award goes to the Louvre Lens museum park, Paris, 2013. Phase Shifts Park got the Iconic Concept award category German Design Council, Munich 2014. Mosbach is chevalier dans l'ordre national de la Légion d'honneur promotion 14th July 2016.

Mosbach se graduó en la escuela de arquitectura del paisaje de Versalles. Fundó con Claramunt, Jacotot y Tricaud Pages Paysage y abrió su estudio en París en 1987. Entre sus proyectos, el parque arqueológico de Solutre, el paseo canal de Saint-Denis, el jardín botánico de Burdeos, "the oher side" en Quebec, el jardín Shan Shui en Xian, el parque del museo Louvre en Lens y el parque Phase Shifts en Taichung. El premio Équerre d'argent se concedió al parque del museo Louvre en Lens, París, 2013. El parque Phase Shifts obtuvo el premio del Consejo Alemán de Diseño en la categoría de "concepción icónica", Múnich 2014. Mosbach es caballero en el orden de la Legión de Honor, promoción 14 de Julio de 2016.

LOUVRE LENS MUSEUM PARK
North Pas de Calais, France — 2009-2014 — 200.000 m² / 2,152,782 sq ft

This project addresses the question of compartmentalizing and de-compartmentalizing what pertains to the realm of art, architecture, landscape, economics and history. It restores the disturbed link between skin (recording surface) and depth (resource of yesterday and tomorrow).The project outline the challenges of a programmatic content (triggers of active memory), the space strategy of a cultural facility (park-museum) and potential landscape events (Louvre park).

Este proyecto aborda la cuestión de separar y reunir lo que pertenece al ámbito del arte, la arquitectura, el paisaje, la economía y la historia. Restablece el vínculo alterado entre piel (superficie de grabación) y profundidad (recurso del ayer y del mañana). El proyecto subraya los desafíos de un contenido programático (disparadores de la memoria activa), la estrategia del espacio de un centro cultural (museo-parque) y potenciales eventos paisajísticos (parque del Louvre).

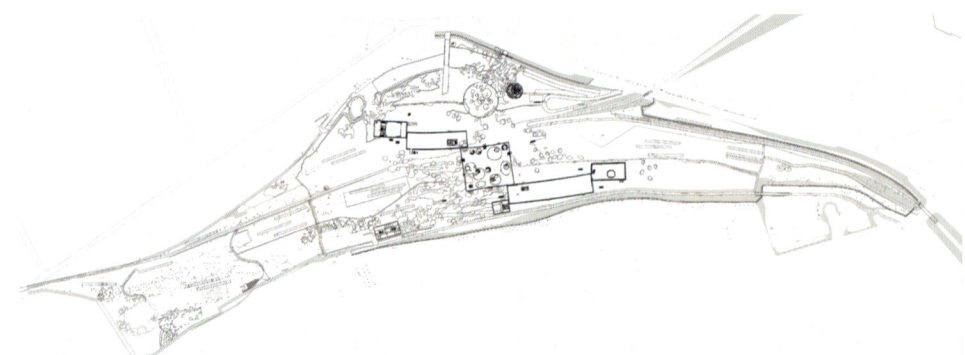

Site plan

© Francis Bocquet

© Francis Bocquet

The Louvre Lens develops the concept of museum-park that combines art, architecture, landscape, nature and urban history. The installation of the museum on one of the pitheads means having the capacity to change over from economic production to an economy regenerated by a way of inhabiting and revisiting the memories of an area in contact with the memories of art and culture in the broad sense.

El Louvre de Lens desarrolla el concepto de museo-parque que combina arte, arquitectura, paisaje, naturaleza e historia urbana. La instalación del museo sobre una de los accesos a la mina simboliza la capacidad de cambiar de la producción económica a una economía regenerada por una forma de habitar y de revivir los recuerdos de una zona al contactar con los recuerdos del arte y la cultura en el sentido amplio.

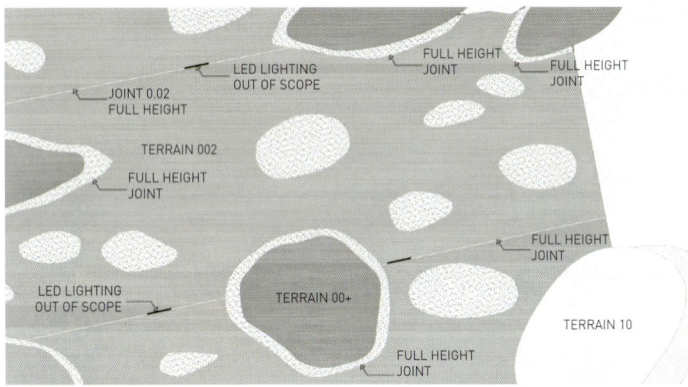

© Philippe Frutier (Altimage)

Detail parvis west

LAWN

TERRAIN 003

LAWN

Detail parvis west

MVRDV

www.mvrdv.nl

**Dunantstraat 10
3024 BC Rotterdam
The Netherlands**

Founded in Rotterdam in 1993 by Winy Maas, Jacob van Rijs and Nathalie de Vries, this studio of architecture, urbanism and landscape design has won international acclaim. Its team of 60 professionals develops projects that stand out for their visual appeal and for a clever use of the resources resulting in functional yet creative creations. Finalist of the Mies van der Rohe on many occasions, the office has won prizes such as the Dutch Institute of Architecture award in 2002, and the Marcus Corporation Foundation award in 2005.

Fundado en Róterdam en 1993 por Winy Maas, Jacob van Rijs y Nathalie de Vries, este estudio de urbanismo, arquitectura y paisajismo es una de las firmas europeas de mayor proyección internacional. Actualmente cuenta con una plantilla de más de 60 personas. De estilo práctico y desenfadado, sus proyectos destacan por un atractivo visual más que notable y por el inteligente aprovechamiento de los recursos. Finalistas de los premios Mies van de Rohe en numerosas ocasiones, han ganado, entre otros, galardones como el de la Marcus Corporation Foundation en 2005 y el del Instituto holandés de Arquitectura en 2002.

ANYANG PEAK
Anyang, South Korea — 2006 — Area: 160 m² / 1,722 sq ft
© MVRDV

This look-out tower was built to give the Anyang Resort the appeal that attracted visitors during the seventies and eighties. Taking advantage of the spectacular setting on the Anyang Peak, the tower stands out with its curvy forms, which seem to extend the trail into a spiral that reaches this site.
A 479-foot-long ramp spirals up to form the 49-foot-high tower over an area of 1,722 sq ft.

Esta torre mirador se construyó para devolver al parque recreativo de Anyang el encanto que tuvo para el visitante entre los años setenta y ochenta. Sacándole todo el partido al envidiable emplazamiento en el pico de Anyang, la torre destaca por sus formas sinuosas, que parecen prolongar el sendero en espiral por el que se accede a ella.
Un recorrido de 146 m y cuatro vueltas permite la subida hasta los 15 m de altura que tiene la torre, sobre un área de 160 m².

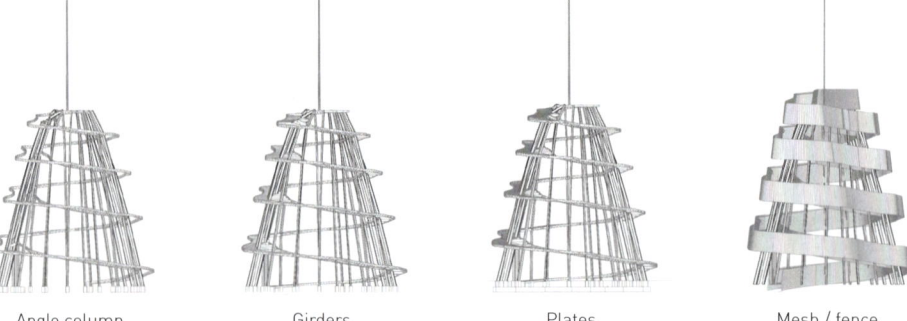

Angle column | Girders | Plates | Mesh / fence
Construction process

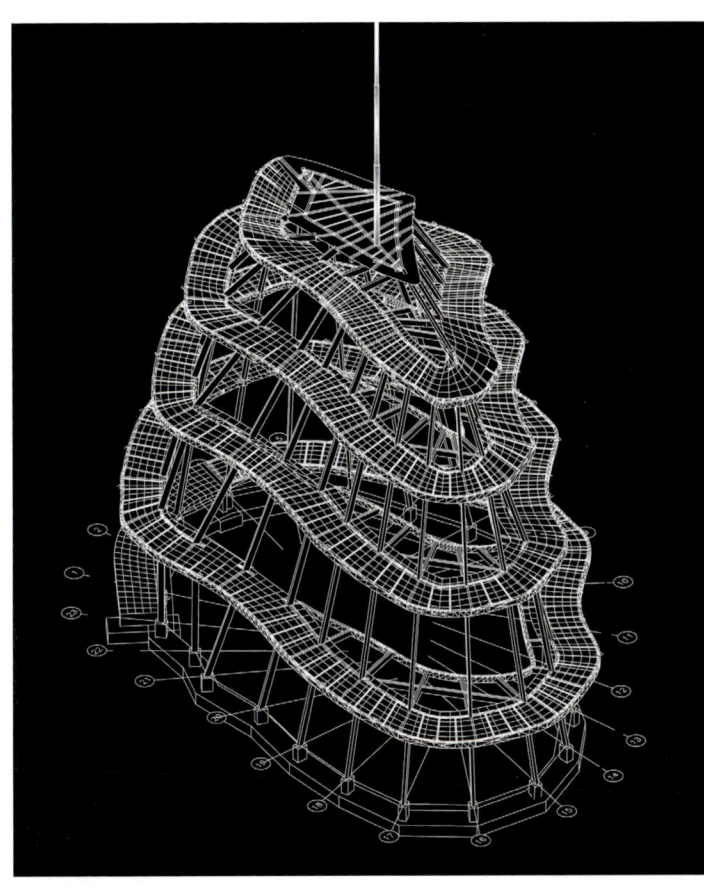

LEIRIA PEDESTRIAN BRIDGES

Leiria, Portugal — Project — Area: 725 m² / 7,804 sq ft
Renderings © MVRDV

The starting point of this project was the necessity of building various bridges to solve the difficult connections over the river in an area of the city that accommodates sports facilities. These bridges are not only overhead land connections but also a solution to avoid constructions that interrupts pedestrian access across the river.

El proyecto partía de la necesidad de construir varios puentes para resolver las complicadas comunicaciones de esta parte del río, en una zona llena de instalaciones deportivas. Estos puentes no sólo conectan terrenos de distintas alturas, sino que también actúan como pasarelas que salvan zonas muy escarpadas.

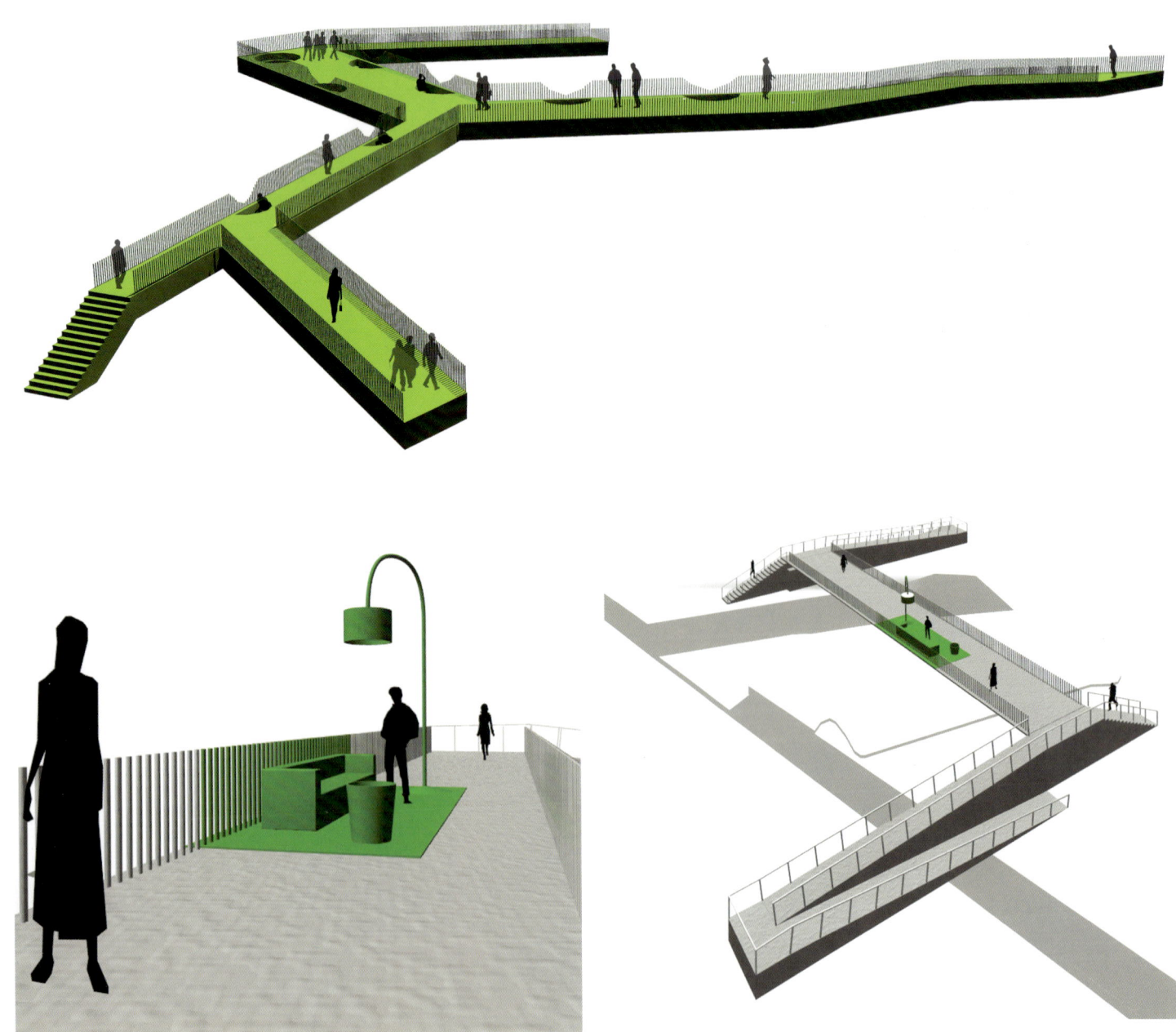

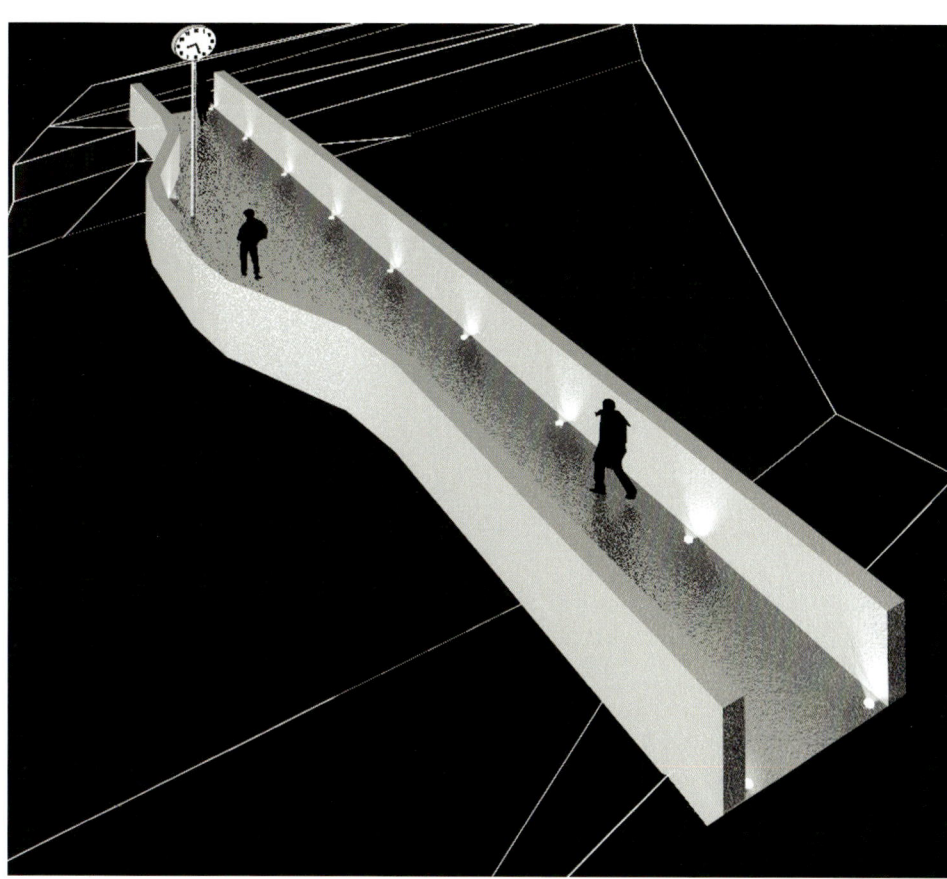

The different configurations of the bridges adapt to the various sites, which the designers analyze to their full advantage.

De inclinación y longitud muy diferentes, el vínculo visual entre los distintos puentes son sus robustas barandillas.

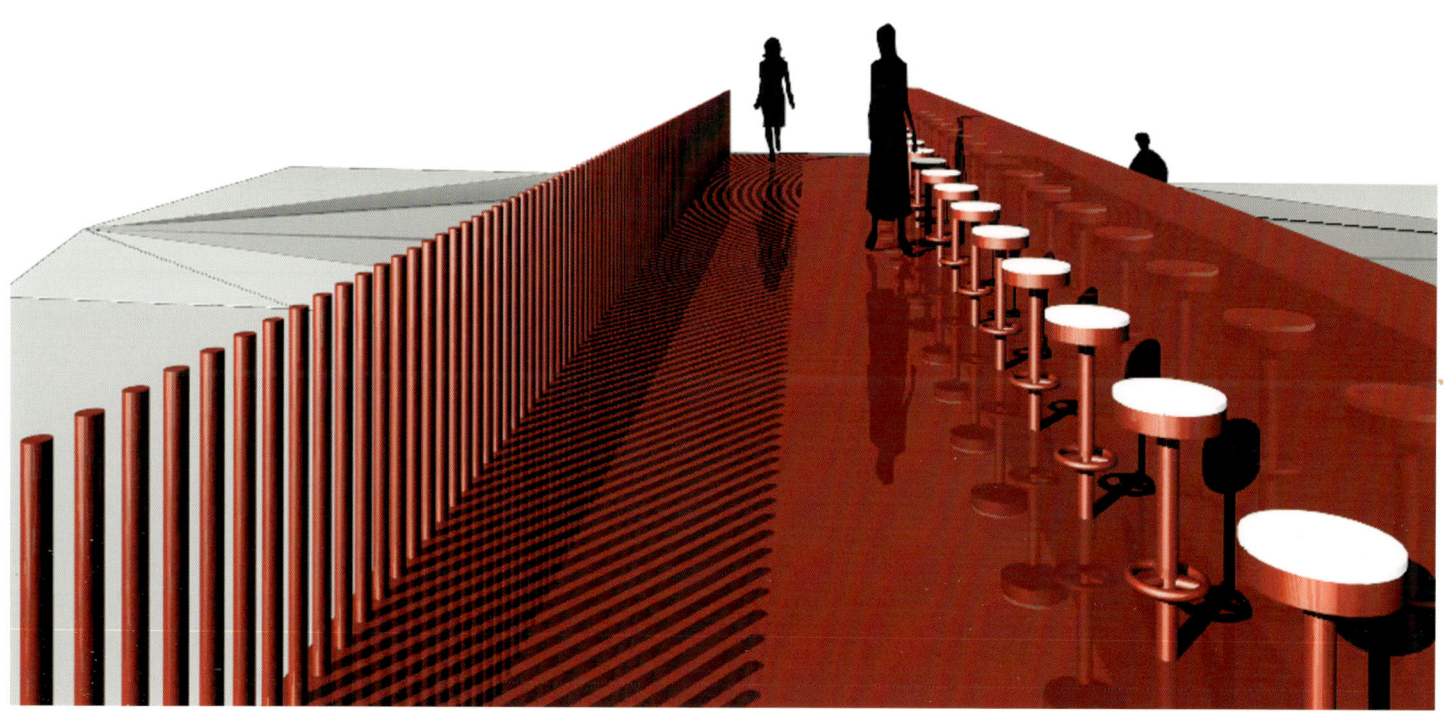

NIEBERG ARCHITECT
atelieraxelnieberg

www.nieberg-architect.de

Waterloo strasse 1
30169 Hannover
Germany

The studio of Axel Nieberg has been working on various tasks in the fields of architecture, interior design, landscaping, lighting design and product design for over 15 years. Axel Nieberg is well known for the minimalistic use of forms and the extraordinary way of directing light in combination with natural materials. In terms of the Japanese Wabi-sabi doctrine, great value is set upon simplicity and a natural aging process of the materials, which are increased by the development of a patina. His landscape architecture corresponded with the minimalist character of the buildings. Numerous international publications and awards indicate the quality of his work.

El estudio de Axel Nieberg ha estado trabajando en diferentes tareas en los campos de arquitectura, diseño interior, paisajismo, diseño de iluminación y diseño de producto durante más de 15 años. Axel Nieberg es conocido por el uso minimalista de las formas y la extraordinaria manera de dirigir la luz en combinación con materiales naturales. En términos de la doctrina japonesa *Wabi-sabi*, concede un gran valor a la sencillez y al proceso de envejecimiento natural de los materiales, aumentado con el desarrollo de una pátina. Su arquitectura del paisaje se corresponde con el carácter minimalista de los edificios. Numerosas publicaciones internacionales y premios avalan la calidad de su trabajo.

LANDSCAPE ARCHITECTURE FOR A RESIDENTIAL BUILDING IN BRUNSWICK
Brunswick, Lower Saxony, Germany — 2013 — 2.000 m² / 21,528 sq ft
© Axel Nieberg

The 2.000 m² property lies in a district of Brunswick, Germany and borders directly on a nature preserve. The design of the outside areas assisted the expression of the L-shaped building cube. The space in front of the exposed concrete house is simple and designed with restraint. A line of Japanese cherries forms an interesting eyecatcher. The charcoal grey basalt grit serves as contrast to the bright concrete of the building.

La finca de 2.000 m² se encuentra en un distrito de Brunswick, Alemania y limita directamente con una reserva natural. El diseño de las zonas exteriores realza la expresividad del edificio en forma de L. El espacio frente de la casa de hormigón visto es simple y diseñado con contención. Una línea de cerezos japoneses constituye un interesante centro de atención. La grava gris basalto sirve de contraste al brillante hormigón del edificio.

Site plan

In the atrium at the entrance an expressive marple tree forms a special accent. On the eastside a water bassin is directly positioned at a large window and has an effect thus as reflecting surface. The terraces are made of wood as well as of concrete.

A longstretched swimming pool forms the centre of the terraces. A roofed terrace area allows the stay outside also in the transitional seasons.

En el atrio de entrada un expresivo arce enfatiza la composición. En el lado este un estanque se sitúa directamente bajo una gran ventana, creando así un efecto de superficie reflectante. Las terrazas están construidas de madera así como de hormigón. Una larga y estrecha piscina constituye el centro de las terrazas. Una zona de terraza cubierta permite la estancia en el exterior también en las temporadas de transición.

LANDSCAPE ARCHITECTURE FOR A RESIDENTIAL BUILDING IN CELLE

Celle, Lower Saxony, Germany — 2016 — 2.000 m² / 21,528 sq ft
© Axel Nieberg

The 2.000 m² property is situated in a developed residential area along the Aller River near the city of Celle in Germany. The property is set back from the road with a 30-meter-long driveway and the eastern edge of the property is bordered by forest. The western side of the property features a stand of old trees with an overall topography that slopes from the northeast to the southwest.

La finca de 2.000 m² se sitúa en una zona residencial situada a lo largo del río Aller, cerca de la ciudad de Celle, en Alemania. La finca se separa de la calle por un camino de 30 metros de longitud y el lado oriental de la propiedad limita con un bosque. El lado oeste de la finca muestra un conjunto de viejos árboles y una topografía que se inclina desde el noreste hacia el sudoeste.

Site plan

The outdoor space corresponded with the minimalism of the architecture. The new maple trees set in the visual indoor axis. For the minimal character and the expression increase the trees planted in basalt grit areas.

El espacio exterior se corresponde con el minimalismo de la arquitectura. Los nuevos arces se colocan en el eje visual interior. El carácter minimalista y expresivo se incrementa con los árboles plantados en las zonas de grava de basalto.

OKRA
Landscape Architects

www.okra.nl

Oudegracht 23
3511 AB Utrecht
The Netherlands

OKRA was founded in 1993 by Hans Oerlemans, Martin Knuijt, Christ-Jan van Rooij and Boudewijn Almekinders and has grown into a well-established agency, executing both national and international projects that have won the team many awards. The office is a mix of landscape architects, urban and regional planners, architects, artists, graphic and industrial designers, and civil technical advisors.
The team is driven by the idea of society submitted to perpetual change and constant shifts in the spatial reflections of society.

Hans Oerlemans, Martin Knuijt, Christ-Jan van Rooij y Boudewijn Almekinders fundaron OKRA en 1993. En la actualidad, la agencia está bastante consolidada y ejecuta proyectos nacionales e internacionales que han reportado numerosos premios al equipo. El estudio es una mezcla de arquitectos paisajistas, planificadores urbanos y regionales, arquitectos, artistas, diseñadores gráficos e industriales y asesores técnicos. Lo que motiva al equipo es la idea de una sociedad sujeta al cambio perpetuo y la constante alteración de sus reflexiones espaciales.

AFRIKAANDERPLEIN
Rotterdam, The Netherlands — 2005 — Area: 50.600 m² / 544,654 sq ft
© Ben ter Mull

As part of a national program initiated to improve public spaces in heavily populated urban areas, a particular effort was directed towards revitalizing the Afrikaanderplein, a large but seriously neglected area in Rotterdam, whose residents are multicultural.
The Afrikaanderplein is characterized on the one hand by greenery (the park) and on the other hand, by the diversity of cultures in the neighborhood which meet here.

Dentro de un programa nacional destinado a mejorar los espacios públicos en las áreas urbanas densamente pobladas, se incluyó una campaña especial para la revitalización de Afrikaanderplein, una amplia aunque descuidada zona de Róterdam habitada por personas de diferentes culturas.
Por un lado, Afrikaanderplein se caracteriza por su vegetación (el parque) y, por el otro, por la diversidad cultural que alberga el barrio.

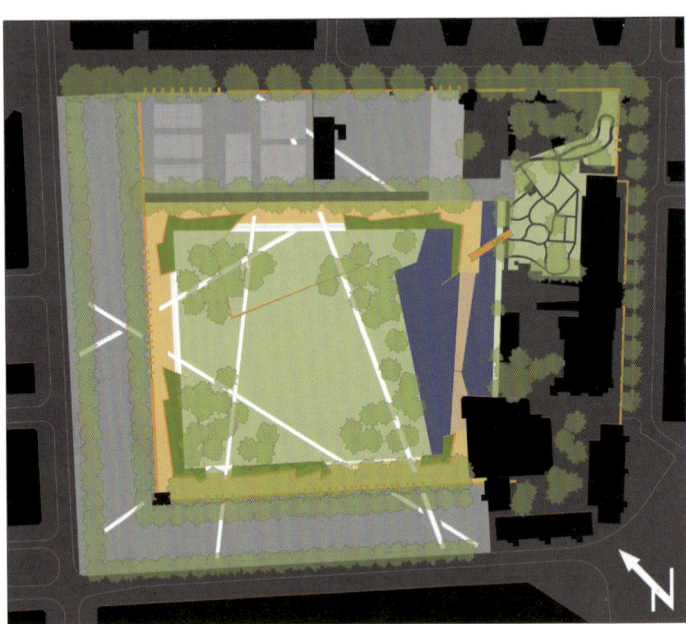

Site plan

MELAAN

Mechelen, Belgium — 2006 — Area: 25.000 m² / 269,098 sq ft
© Ben ter Mull

The Melaan canal was restored and reintegrated in the old city center of Mechelen. The canal's logical identity is restored by bringing water back into the dry bed, which acts as a catalysis for urban development by bestowing the city with a charm that was lost.

Between the street and the canal, a promenade establishes a connection between the city and the Melaan.

El canal de Melaan fue restaurado y reintegrado en el casco histórico de la ciudad belga de Malinas. Al devolver el agua al cauce seco, el canal recupera su identidad lógica y actúa como catalizador del desarrollo urbanístico, dotando a la zona de un encanto que había perdido.

Entre la calle y el canal, un paseo conecta la ciudad con el Melaan.

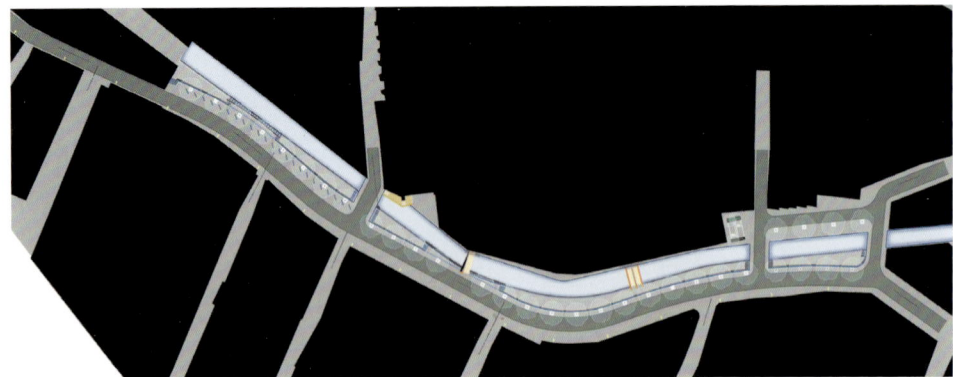

Site plan

QUAY AND BRIDGES ON THE RIVER IJSSEL

Doesburg, The Netherlands — 2001 — Area: 35.000 m² / 376,737 sq ft
© Ben ter Mull

OKRA has designed a new Ijssel waterfront inspired in the medieval character of the city center and the atmosphere of former industrial areas along the river. The waterfront, lined with houses and work places, allows for future construction opportunities and for the development of new public spaces.

OKRA ha diseñado una nueva ribera para el Ijssel inspirada en el carácter medieval del centro de la ciudad y la atmósfera de las antiguas zonas industriales que bordeaban el río. El muelle, donde se alinean casas y oficinas, ofrece la oportunidad de construir en el futuro y permite el desarrollo de nuevos espacios públicos.

Site plan

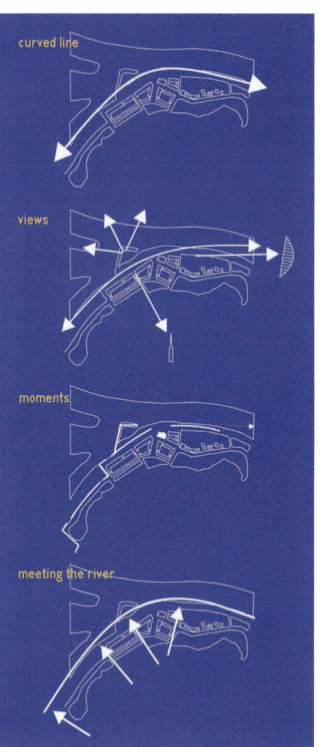

Site diagrams

The highlights of the waterfront are formed by two prominent places: a grandstand stair and an observation tower on a pontoon yet to be developed.

Los reflejos del muelle vienen dados por dos lugares destacados: una magnífica escalinata y una torre de observación sobre un pontón aún por desarrollar.

DOMPLEIN
Utrecht, The Netherlands — 2010 — Area: 160 m² / 1,722 sq ft
© Ben ter Mull

The heart of the city of Utrecht is built on top of a castellum. The Domplein (cathedral square) is redesigned to revive the history of the city. The castellum wall, 13 feet below ground level, is metaphorically revealed at street level and in the square.

El corazón de la ciudad de Utrecht está edificado sobre las ruinas de un castellum. La Domplein (plaza de la catedral) se ha rediseñado para revivir la historia de la urbe. El muro del castellum, a 4 metros por debajo del nivel del suelo, se revela en forma de metáfora tanto en la calle como en la plaza.

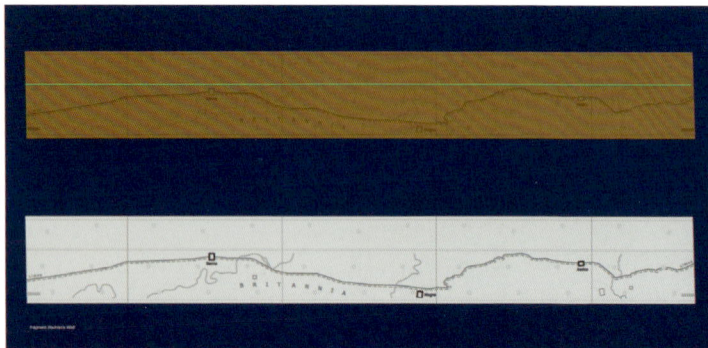
Drawing of a fragment of Hadrian's Wall

3D model of metal plate set in the pavement

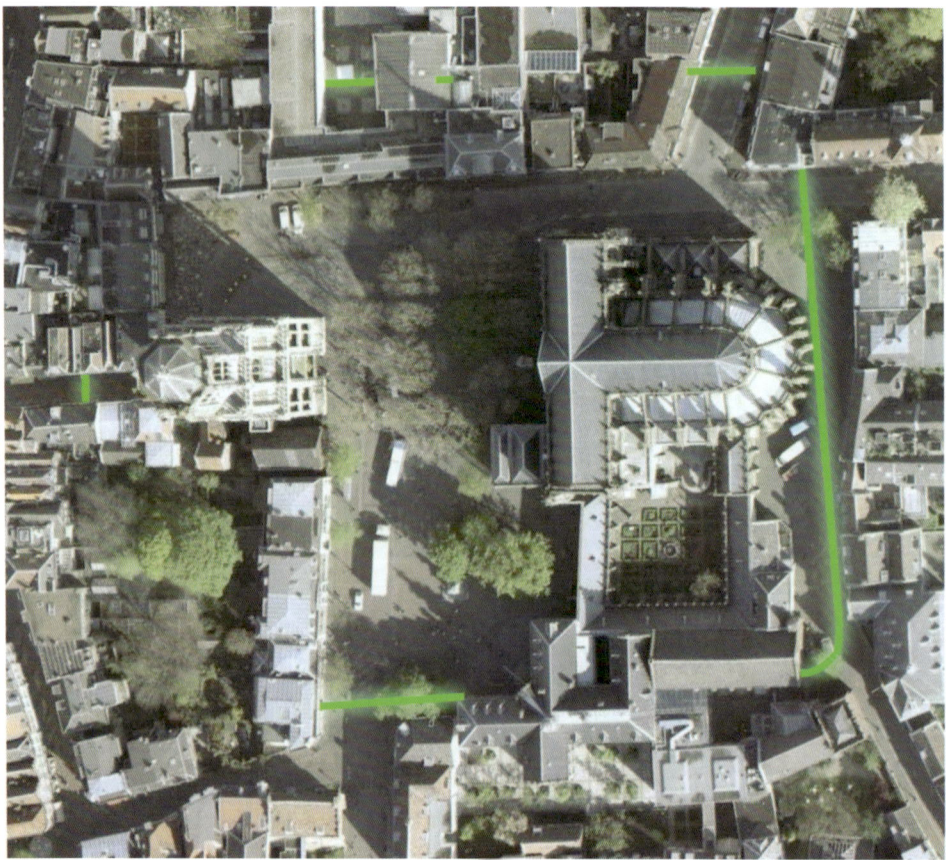

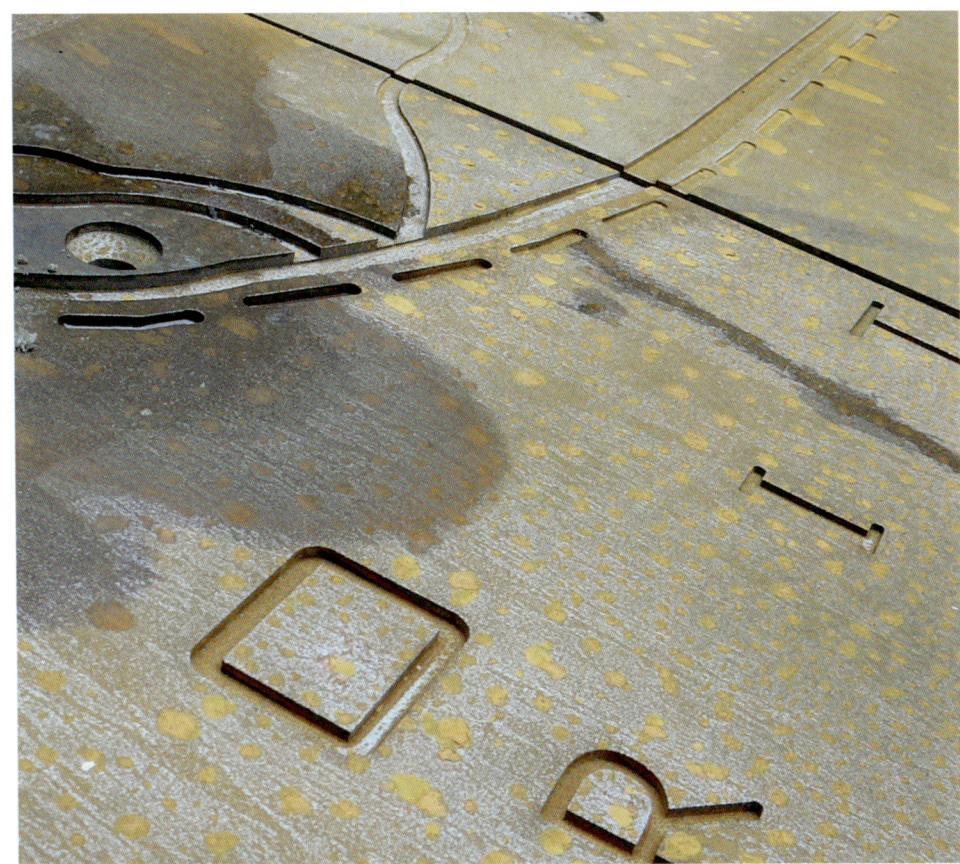

The dramatic presence of the Domplein is intensified with a mysterious bright light emerging from the ground.

Una misteriosa luz brillante que emerge desde el suelo realza la espectacular presencia de la Domplein.

OSLUND AND ASSOCIATES

www.oaala.com

115 N Washington Avenue
Suite 200
Minneapolis
Minnesota 55401
United States

Tom Oslund is one of the most acclaimed landscape architects in the United States. His work has been recognized with many awards from the American Society of Landscape Architects and the AIA, among others. For more than twenty years, he has created projects of different typologies, from universities and public buildings to private residences and religious temples. He also has a long career as a lecturer at institutions such as the Corcoran School of Art in Washington, the Walker Art Center in Minneapolis and at the Botanical Garden of Chicago.

Tom Oslund is one of the most acclaimed landscape architects in the United States. His work has been recognized with many awards from the American Society of Landscape Architects and the AIA, among others.
For more than twenty years, he has created projects of different typologies, from universities and public buildings to private residences and religious temples. He also has a long career as a lecturer at institutions such as the Corcoran School of Art in Washington, the Walker Art Center in Minneapolis and at the Botanical Garden of Chicago.

GOLD MEDAL PARK

Minneapolis, Minnesota, United States — 2007 — Area: 13.000 m² / 139,940 sq ft
© Michael Migo, Tom Oslund

Centrally located in the Mill District of Minneapolis, the design of this park involved various paths, an artificial mound with panoramic views, and the planting of close to 300 mature trees.

Ubicado en pleno centro del Mill District de Minneapolis, el diseño de este parque implicaba el trazado de varios caminos flanqueados por árboles, así como una colina con vistas panorámicas esculpida artificialmente y la colocación de 300 árboles adultos.

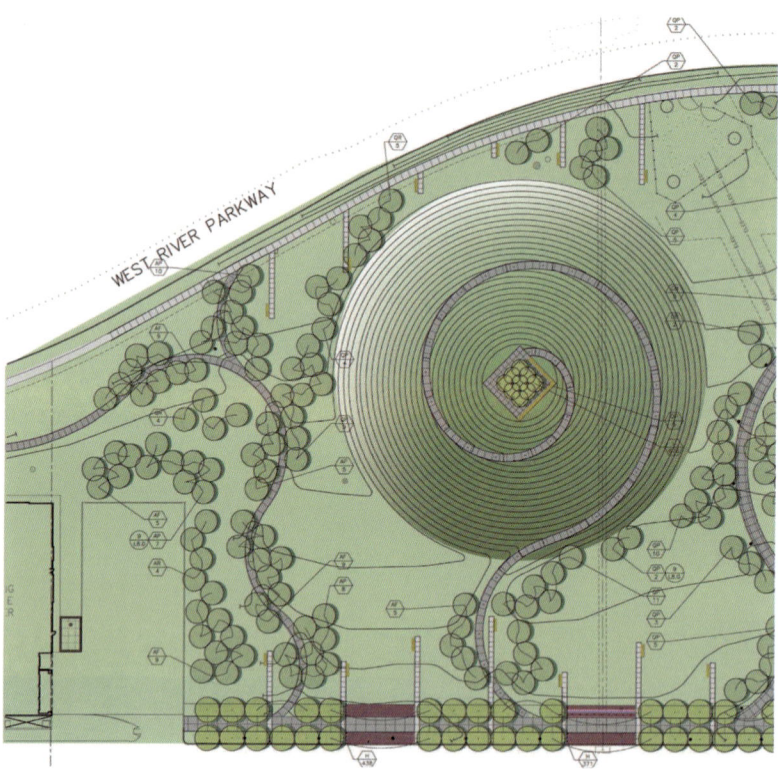

General plan

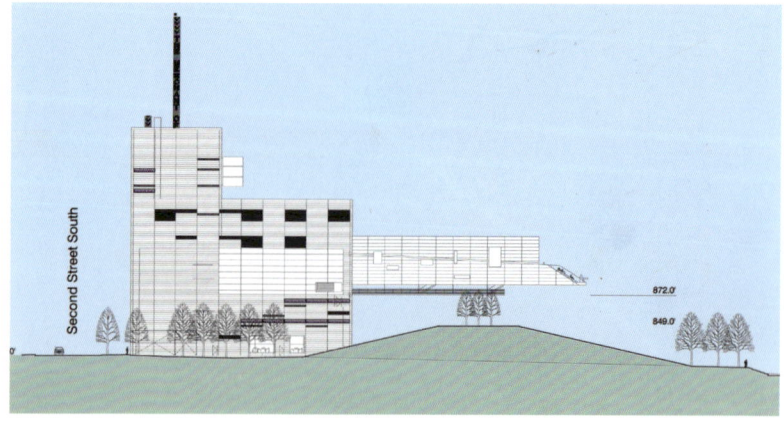

Elevation

The benches lit from within with LED lights are a source of illumination after dark.

The benches lit from within with LED lights are a source of illumination after dark.

HARLEY DAVIDSON MUSEUM

Milwaukee, Wisconsin, United States — 2008 — Area: 32.000 m² / 344,445 sq ft
© Michael Mingo

The exterior spaces of the Harley Davidson Museum achieve the objective of providing visitors with meeting areas, using details that clearly identify the brand. At the same time, the elements that link the site with its industrial past are a historic witness to the development of the company.

Los espacios exteriores del Harley Davidson Museum cumplen con su objetivo de ofrecer espacios de reunión y de ocio para los visitantes, sin dejar de contar con elementos que se identifiquen con la marca. Al mismo tiempo, se siguen conservando los elementos que vinculan el lugar con su pasado industrial, testigo histórico del desarrollo de la empresa.

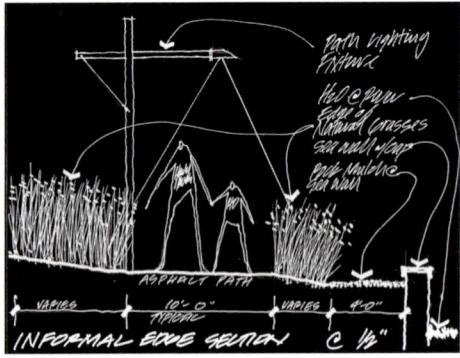 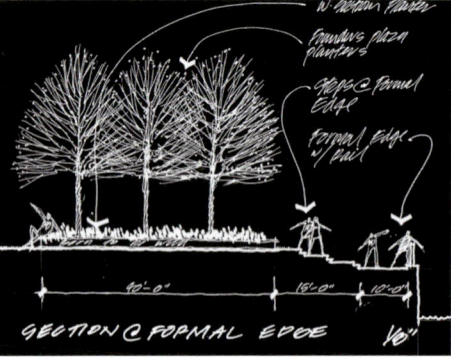

Sketches

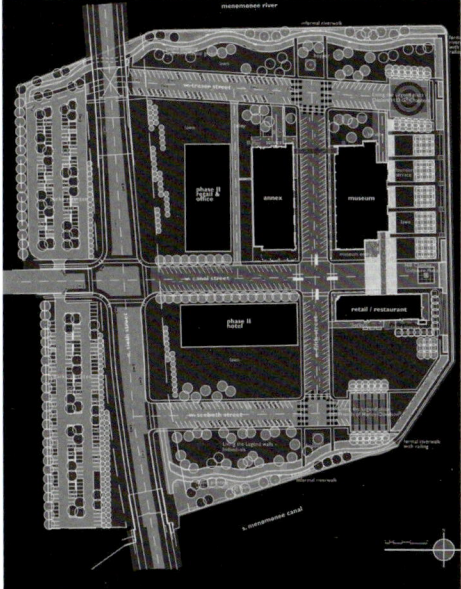

Site plan

The vegetation and the Corten steel walls emphasize the contrast between the former and current uses of the site.

La vegetación y los muros de acero corten bastan para dejar claro el contraste entre el uso pasado y futuro del emplazamiento.

GENERAL MILLS CORPORATION

Golden Valley, Minnesota, United States — 2004 — Area: 28.000 m² / 301,389 sq ft
© George Heinrich, Tadd Kreun

The challenge tied to this project lies on the design of exterior spaces that are welcoming and complimentary to the modernist style of the pre-existing buildings. Both the ponds and the green zones form a striking horizontality that accentuates the geometric relations of the landscape and create a tranquil atmosphere. The vegetation in the form of trees is scarce so there is no visual obstruction that would compromise the feeling of openness provided by the large expanse of lawn.

El reto de este proyecto estribaba en diseñar unos exteriores que fueran acogedores y a la vez ayudaran a realzar el estilo modernista del resto de edificios del campus. Tanto las balsas de agua como las zonas verdes forman un eje horizontal marcado, muy plano, que acentúa las relaciones geométricas del paisaje y ayuda a crear un ambiente tranquilo. La vegetación arbórea es escasa, con la idea de no interrumpir la sensación de amplitud que aporta la extensión llana de césped.

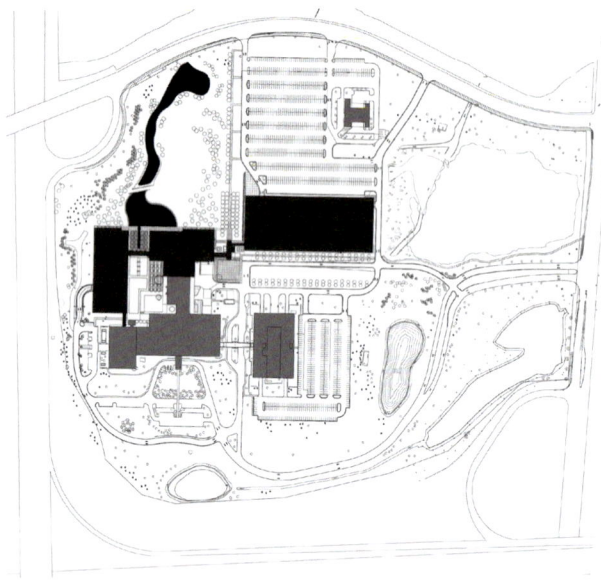

Site plan

I-35W STREET ANTHONY FALLS BRIDGE

Minneapolis, Minnesota, United States — 2008 — Area: 12.000 m² / 129,167 sq ft
© Oslund and Associates, T. Kreun, J. Hom, A. Krautbauer

The design of this bridge's surroundings is based on simplicity. Vegetation is replaced with a natural element of much easier maintenance like stone, with a seemingly random placement that confers a dramatic effect.

The zigzag design of the pedestrian way brings a geometric order into what seems to be "controlled chaos."

El diseño de los aledaños de este puente se basa en una máxima de simplicidad. La vegetación se sustituye por un elemento natural pero de mantenimiento más sencillo, la piedra, cuya distribución en pilas aparentemente aleatorias consigue un efecto espectacular.

El zigzag de la vía peatonal procura líneas rectas a un diseño en el que reina una especie de «caos controlado».

Improvement plan at North

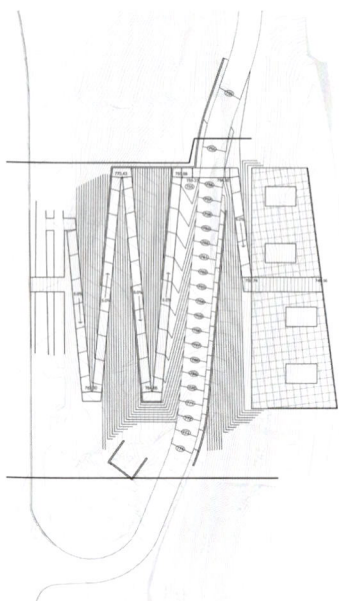

General plan

Artist's impressions

LABORATORY SCIENCE BUILDING AT THE UNIVERSITY OF MINNESOTA

Minnesota, United States — 2007 — Area: 6.000 m² / 64,583 sq ft
© T. Oslund, G. Heinrich, J. Hom

Inspiration for the design of this exterior space derives from the concept of Science on Display, a leitmotif that bestows the environment with a high level of visibility. The lightness of the stair and the sculptural character of the pond are the central elements of the design.

La inspiración para el diseño de este espacio exterior deriva del concepto de *Science on display* («ciencia en exposición»), un leitmotiv que inspira el alto grado de visibilidad que se ha conferido al entorno, con la ligereza de la escalera y el carácter escultórico del estanque como principales rasgos estructurales.

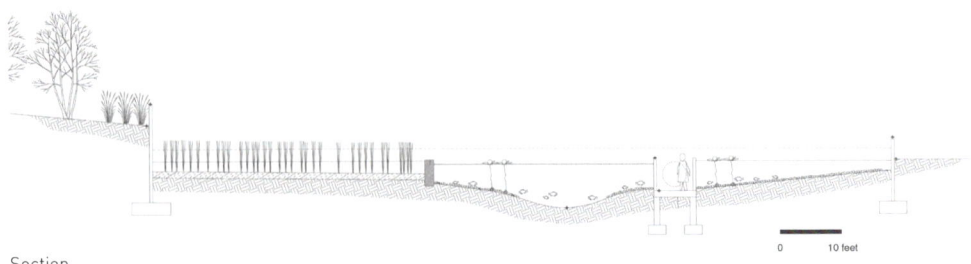

Section

0   10 feet

Artist's impression

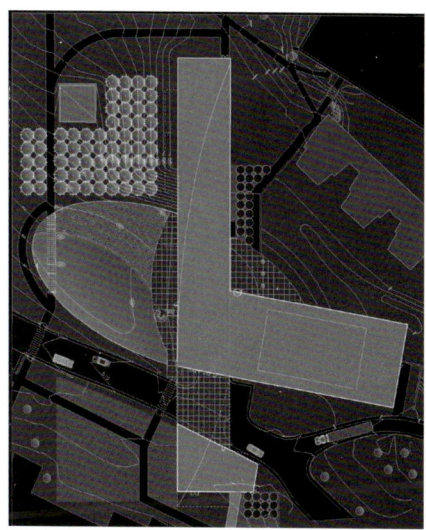

General plan

The warp of the ellipsoidal shapes that form the stair and the pond confers the site with a singularity.

La urdimbre de formas elipsoidales que forman la escalera y el estanque dota de gran personalidad al conjunto.

ØSTENGEN & BERGO
LANDSCAPE ARCHITECTS

www.ostengen-bergo.no

Fred Olsens gate 3b
0152 Oslo
Norway

Østengen & Bergo is a renowned landscape architect office founded in 1996 by the partners Kari Bergo and Johan Østengen. We are based in Oslo, Norway. Østengen & Bergo is involved in a wide range of tasks in landscape architecture, from landscape analysis and urban planning, to building details. Østengen & Bergo is seeking to emphasize the uniqueness of a place. Our aim is to create sustainable and functional solutions that inspire and invites us all to use our common grounds. We create spaces for biodiversity and natural experiences, recreation and activity, special occasions and everyday life.

Østengen & Bergo es una reconocida oficina de arquitectos paisajistas ubicada en Oslo, Noruega, y fundada en 1996 por Kari Bergo y Johan Østengen. Østengen & Bergo está implicada en una amplia gama de tareas en arquitectura del paisaje, desde análisis paisajístico y planeamiento urbano, hasta los detalles constructivos. Østengen & Bergo busca enfatizar la singularidad de un lugar. Nuestro objetivo es crear soluciones sostenibles y funcionales que inspiren y nos inviten a utilizar nuestros argumentos comunes. Creamos espacios para experiencias naturales y de biodiversidad, recreación y actividad, ocasiones especiales y vida cotidiana.

DALSNIBBA SKYWALK
Stranda municipality, Møre og Romsdal, Norway — 2016 — 78.200 m² / 841,738 sq ft
© Arild Solberg, Østengen & Bergo, Geiranger Skysslag

Dalsnibba is a mountain in Møre og Romsdal county, Norway, approximately 1.500 m. above sea level. The increase of visitors has arisen and it was a need for expanded parking facilities, to restore the old path to the top, and to create a more spectacular viewing platform. The terrain is steep, and the project had great emphasis on finding a balance between the existing qualities of the landscape, the traces of abandoned pathways and acting within the area's conservation requirements.

Dalsnibba es una montaña del condado de Møre og Romsdal, Noruega, a unos 1.500 m. sobre el nivel del mar. Del incremento de visitantes surgió la necesidad de ampliar las instalaciones del parking, recuperar el antiguo camino hasta la cima y crear una plataforma panorámica más espectacular. El terreno es escarpado, y el proyecto buscó un equilibrio entre las cualidades inherentes al paisaje, los rastros de senderos abandonados y el respeto de la normativa de conservación de la zona.

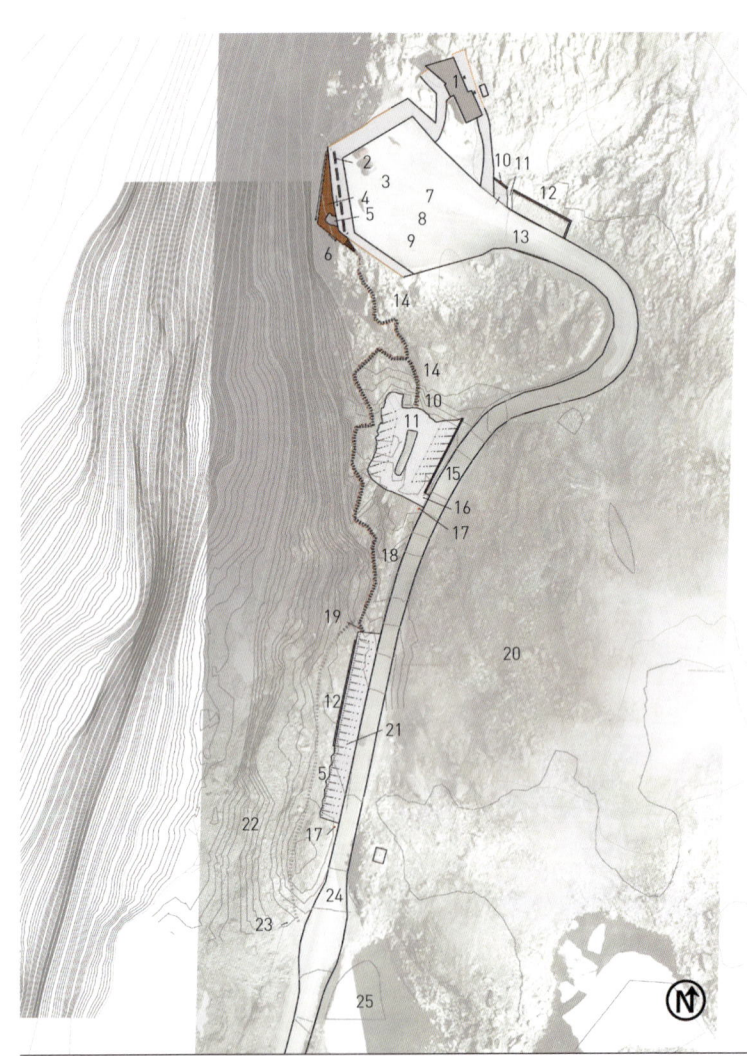

Site plan

1. Service building
2. Bench
3. Universal access to platform
4. Platform
5. Visible mountain
6. Stair meets stone filling
7. Dalsnibba
8. Parking area
9. Plateau
10. Sign
11. Ridge preserved
12. Wall with stone markers
13. 8 parking stalls incl
14. Path w/handrail
15. Slope w/rock edge
16. Parking north 16 stalls
17. P-sign
18. Terrain preserved
19. New path
20. Limit to landscape protection area
21. Parking south 19 stalls
22. Existing path (no restoration)
23. Existing info-sign
24. Nibbevegen
25. Towards Geirainger

It has been important to preserve the nature surfaces and the vulnerable artic vegetation and interact the constructions to the mountain formations. The color scheme is carefully adapted to the environment.

Fue importante preservar las superficies de la naturaleza y la vulnerable vegetación ártica, y hacer interactuar las construcciones con las formaciones montañosas. La combinación de colores se adapta cuidadosamente al entorno.

The new parking spaces are carefully fit in between the rocks, and built up on local stone walls, with direct access to the restored pathway.
The trail is based on the traces of the old path and smoothly winds up to the top. The railing is designed so that the trail is evident and arouse interest.

Los nuevos espacios de aparcamiento se asientan cuidadosamente entre las rocas, sobre muros de piedra del lugar y con acceso directo al sendero restaurado. El camino se apoya en los rastros de la antigua ruta y serpentea suavemente hasta la cima. La barandilla está diseñada para que el camino se haga visible.

The new platform, the "Skywalk", is cantilevered outside the old platform. A staircase leads down to the trail to the ancient pathway.
Glass railing and a fiberglass reinforced plastic grate on platform provides spectacular views of both the surrounding landscape and the rocks below.

La nueva plataforma, "Skywalk", está en vuelo respecto de la antigua plataforma. Una escalera conduce al inicio del antiguo camino.
Una barandilla de vidrio y una rejilla de plástico reforzado con fibra de vidrio en el suelo ofrecen espectaculares vistas del paisaje y de las rocas inferiores.

SKJERVET

Granvin, Norway — 2015 — 40.000 m² / 430,556 sq ft
© Paal Hoff, Østengen & Bergo

The landscape surrounding the waterfall is a narrow valley formed like a deep bowl. The waterfall drop 135 m. over two sections divided by a terrace and a road bridge. The terrain is steep and a trail made of natural stone became a central nerve of a project that invites visitors to teem into and enjoy the landscape. At the bottom of the valley, a universally designed pathway leads into the foot of the fall.

El paisaje que rodea la cascada es un estrecho valle con forma de profundo cuenco. La cascada cae 135 m. sobre dos secciones divididas por una terraza y un puente. El terreno es escarpado y un camino de piedra natural constituye el nervio central de un proyecto que invita a los visitantes a entrar en él y a disfrutar del paisaje. En el fondo del valle, un camino de diseño accesible conduce a los pies de la cascada.

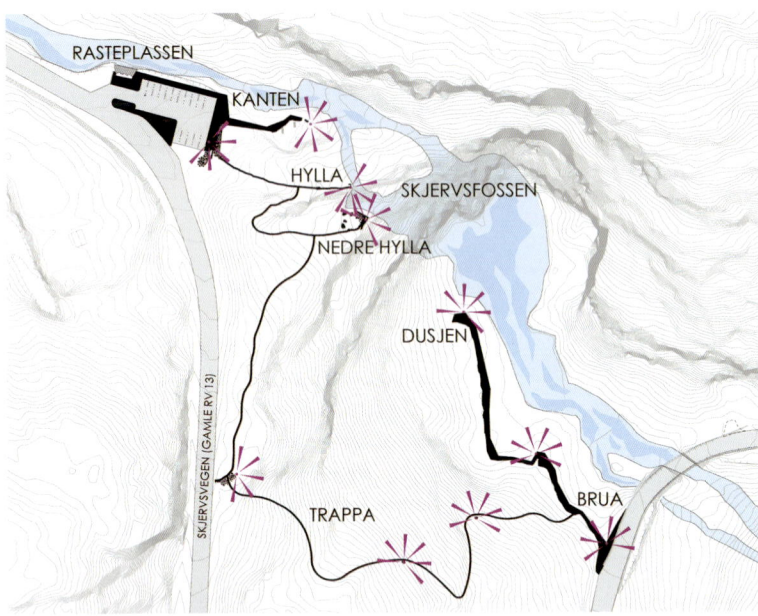

Site plan

Local natural stone is the main material in the project, used in the restroom building, service area and nature trails. The color scheme is carefully adapted to the environment, with robust designed fences in rebar and benches in concrete. The abrupt rising figure of the restroom building creates a landmark seen from the road, but it does not interfere with the landscape.

La piedra natural es el principal material del proyecto, utilizado en el edificio de aseos, área de servicio y caminos naturales. La combinación de colores se adapta cuidadosamente al entorno, con bancos de hormigón y robustas vallas diseñadas con armaduras de acero. La abrupta figura del edificio de aseos supone un hito perceptible desde la carretera que no interfiere con el paisaje.

Norwegian landscape contractors made the straight lines and precise walls of natural stone. Nepalese Sherpas shaped the natural stairs of stone in terrain. The intention is that the combination of contemporary form, ancient craft and local material, create a timeless dimension.

Contratistas noruegos trazaron las líneas rectas y los precisos muros de piedra natural. Sherpas nepalís dieron forma a las escaleras de piedra natural sobre el terreno. La intención es que la combinación de forma contemporánea, arte antiguo y material local cree una dimensión intemporal.

RAMSEYER WAISMAN ARQUITECTOS – RWA

www.rwa.es

Paseo de la Castellana, 151
28046 Madrid
Spain

RWA has a solid reputation thanks to the end results of its interventions and to its capacity for undertaking projects of different magnitudes with maximum guarantees of quality and efficiency.

The team at RWA understands that architecture happens in relation to a place and a time, so attention is paid to social responsibility, to controlling the use of resources, and to contributing other intangible values.

In Landscaping, coherence with the climatic and geographic position is the starting point for any project. Selecting trees and plants suited to the climate means rainfall will maintain them, keeping the need for irrigation to a minimum.

RWA tiene una sólida reputación por los resultados de sus intervenciones y por su capacidad de acometer proyectos de diferentes magnitudes con plenas garantías de calidad y eficiencia.

El equipo de RWA entiende que la arquitectura se produce en relación a un tiempo y a un lugar, prestando atención a la responsabilidad social, al uso controlado de los recursos y debe aportar otros valores intangibles.

En Paisajismo, el punto de partida de todos los proyectos es la coherencia con el lugar climático y geográfico. La selección de árboles y plantas adecuadas al clima, permiten un mantenimiento con el régimen de lluvias, minimizando la necesidad de riego.

GRAN RESERVA DE SOTOGRANDE

Sotogrande, Cádiz, Spain — 2010 — Area: 500.000 m² / 5,381,955 sq ft
© Google

The location of *La Gran Reserva de Sotogrande* boasts a number of optimum conditions for the development of a residential estate. This enclave with varied sea and mountain views is situated on the crest of a hill. Its most striking features are:
- Its natural surroundings.
- A very close location to facilities for the pursuit of all types of recreational activities.
- Its international transport links thats facilitate accessibility.

La Gran Reserva de Sotogrande está situada en un lugar que reúne diversas condiciones óptimas para el desarrollo de una propuesta residencial: su entorno natural invita al disfrute de los sentidos, su situación está muy próxima a centros para la práctica de todo tipo de actividades recreativas y sus conexiones con infraestructuras de transporte internacionales facilitan su acceso. En el conjunto, solo están permitidas construcciones para uso residencial unifamiliar privado.

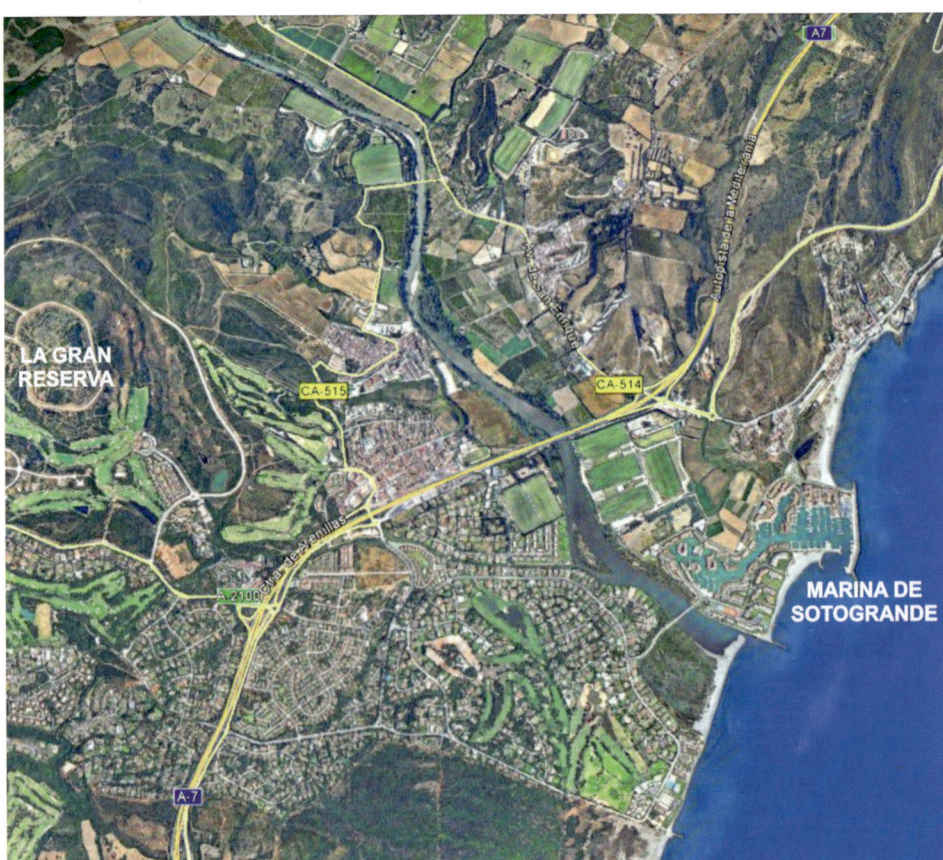

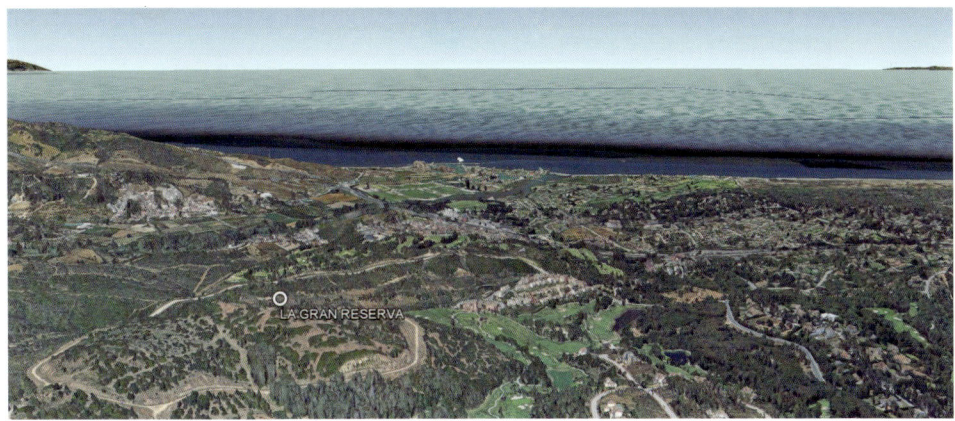

ORGANISATION OF THE ESTATE

La Gran Reserva de Sotogrande is situated at the top of a hill and its organisation is a function of this principal characteristic.

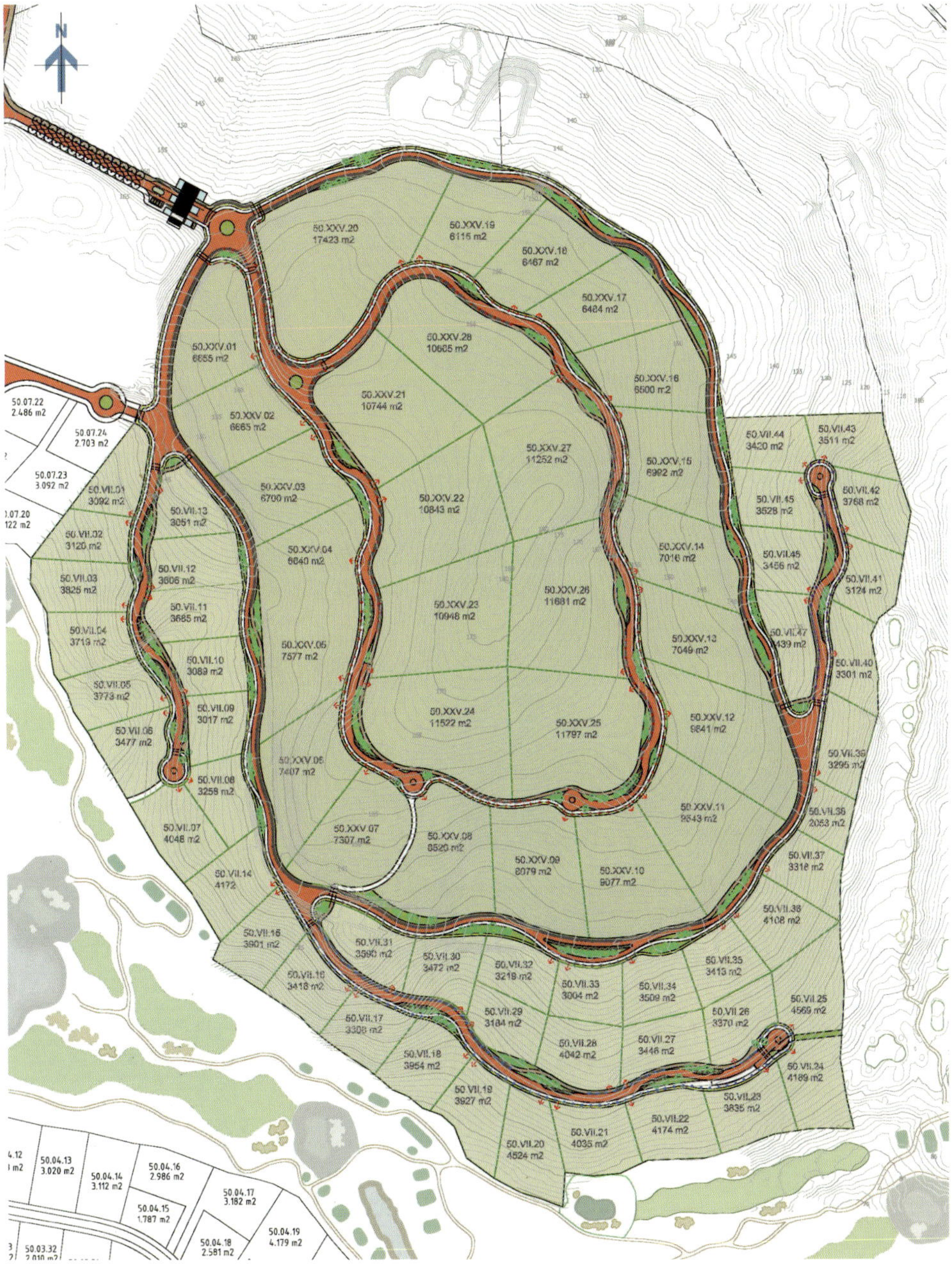

The arrangement of the plots and both internal and access pathways is the result of a desire to optimise the unique potential afforded by the location.

The estate is organised in three zones differentiated by their location on the hill:
- The upper part of the crest, with plots of surface area greater than 10.000 m²
- The intermediate part, with plots of surface area of between 6.000 and 10.000 m²
- The lower part, most of which abuts the Campo de,Golf La Reserva, with plots of surface areas between 3.000 and 5.000 m²

Only buildings for private single-family residential use are permitted on the estate, whith some mandatory considerations:
- Integrate the building with existing vegetation. For this reason, the building design must be accompanied by a landscaping proposal that analyses impact on several levels; respect setback constraints so that the building profile does not protrude above the foreseen envelope for the terrain profile and the vegetation profile.
- Do not modify the vegetation established for the highest area of the hillside.
- Minimise the impact of buildings by integrating vegetation with the architectural design.

ORGANIZACIÓN DEL CONJUNTO

La Gran Reserva de Sotogrande está situada en lo alto de una colina y su organización corresponde a esta característica principal. La disposición de las parcelas y de los recorridos panorámicos y de acceso obedecen a la voluntad de singularizar el potencial que brinda el lugar.

El conjunto está organizado en tres zonas diferenciadas por su situación en la colina:
- La parte alta de la cima, con parcelas de superficies mayores de 10.000 m².
- La parte intermedia, con parcelas de superficies entre 6.000 y 10.000 m².
- La parte baja, lindando en su mayor parte con el Campo de Golf La Reserva, con parcelas de superficies entre 3.000 y 5.000 m².

En el conjunto, sólo están permitidas construcciones para uso residencial unifamiliar con una serie de consideraciones obligatorias:
- Integrar la arquitectura con la vegetación existente, a través de una propuesta de paisajismo adecuada.
- Respetar los retranqueos de las edificaciones para que su perfil no se recorte por encima de la vegetación establecida.
- No alterar la vegetación establecida para la zona más alta de la colina.
- Minimizar el impacto de lo construido integrando la vegetación con el proyecto arquitectónico.

Site plan

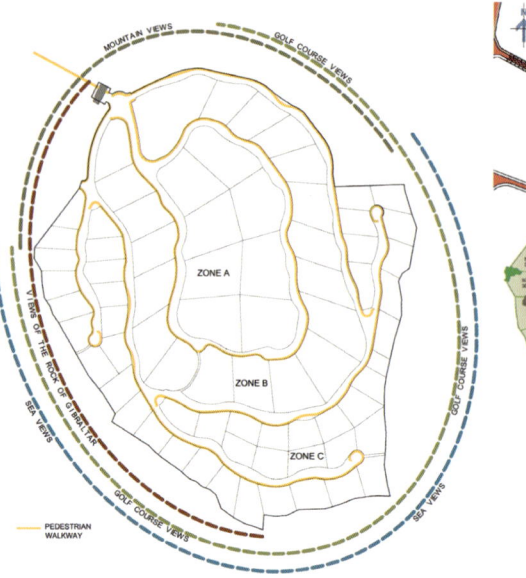

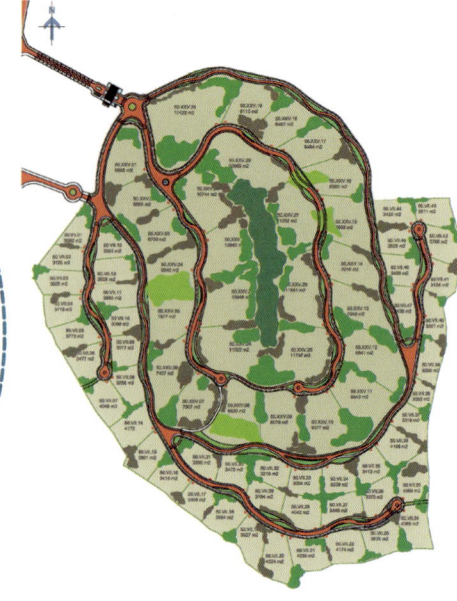

ORGANISATION OF THE SYSTEM
This system is conceived as a homogenous whole with a balanced distribution, in such a manner as to enable all users enjoy the same services.

A priority design consideration for this system is the objective of respecting the exclusive and peaceful nature of the location.

ORGANIZACIÓN DEL SISTEMA
El sistema de circulaciones y de espacios comunes se ha concebido como un todo homogéneo y equilibrado en su distribución, de forma que todos los usuarios puedan disfrutar de los mismos servicios.

En su diseño se ha considerado prioritario el objetivo de respetar el carácter exclusivo y tranquilo del lugar.

PEDESTRIAN WALKWAYS
The network of pedestrian walkways is for the exclusive enjoyment of users of the La Gran Reserva residential estate and affords a number of diverse routes that enhance the enjoyment of the landscape for those walking or jogging.

In order to guarantee the safety, the walkways are situated at the edge of the pathway system. The walkway is separated from the golf buggy / bicycle lane and, to enhance the sense of amplitude of the route, the curb is laid flush with the paving. Trees to provide shade are placed every eight (8) metres along the dividing line between the pedestrian walkway and the golf buggy / bicycle lane.

PASEOS PEATONALES
La red de paseos peatonales, exclusiva para los usuarios de la urbanización, proporciona diversos recorridos para disfrutar del paisaje caminando o corriendo. Para garantizar la seguridad de los usuarios, los paseos están situados en el borde exterior de los viales, separados del carril buggies-bicicletas y para aumentar la sensación de amplitud del recorrido, el bordillo está enrasado con el pavimento. Cada ocho metros, se disponen árboles para dar sombra, en alcorques a nivel y en la separación con el carril buggy-bicicleta.

PROTECTION AGAINST WIND
The direction of the prevailing wind is indicated for each plot in order to protect buildings from the problems and inconveniences occasioned by the wind and to help predict the means that may be required by each plot in this respect. Based on this study, vegetative barriers of a general nature are recommended and these should not interfere with views or sun exposure.

PROTECCIÓN CONTRA VIENTOS
Para preservar las construcciones de los problemas que ocasiona el viento y preveer los medios necesarios, se ha señalado la dirección de los vientos dominantes en cada parcela. Basándose en este estudio, se han previsto barreras vegetales de carácter general, evitando su interferencia con las vistas o el soleamiento.

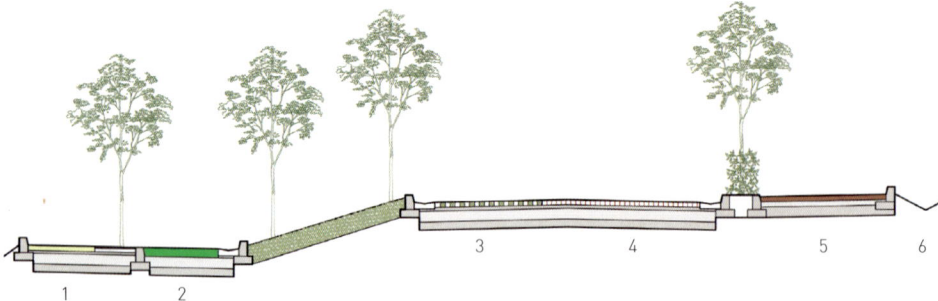

Section of two-way pathway. Parking area

1. Pedestrians
2. Golf buggies /bikes
3. Parking area
4. Automobile roadway
5. Pipeclay path
6. Dicht

COMMON OPEN SPACES
The common open areas enrich the routes of the pathways, offering spaces that are cared for meticulously. Criteria appropriate to Mediterranean gardens are employed. Special attention has been paid to the selection of species in accordance with the climate and the arrangement of an efficient irrigation system coherent with the location of the estate, whilst facilitating savings in energy and natural resources.

ESPACIOS ABIERTOS COMUNES
Las zonas abiertas comunes enriquecen el trazado de los viales con espacios cuidados, entendidos como continuidad con el entorno natural que rodea el conjunto. Se han seguido criterios propios de jardines mediterráneos, atendiendo especialmente a la selección de especies según el clima, a la disposición de un sistema de riego eficiente y coherente con la ubicación del conjunto y al ahorro de energía y recursos naturales.

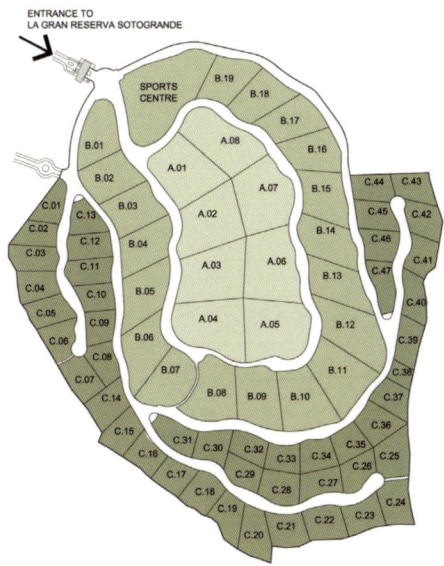

ENTRANCE TO
LA GRAN RESERVA SOTOGRANDE

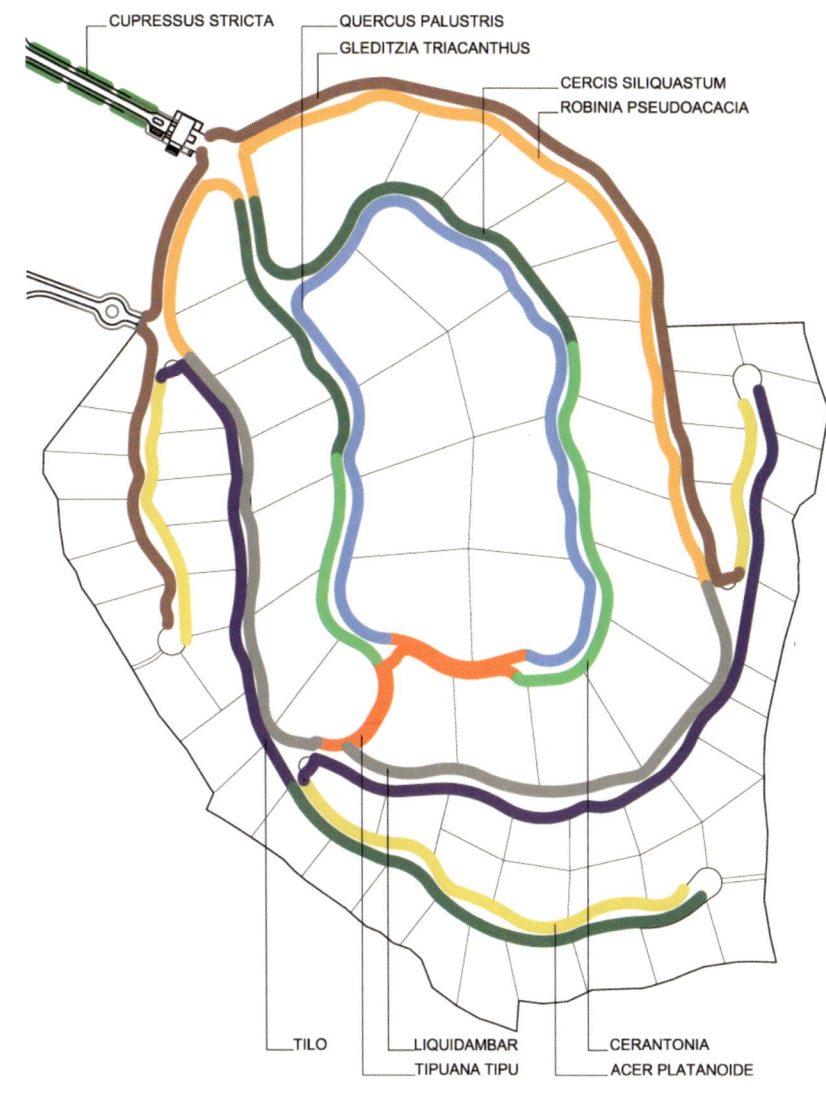

CUPRESSUS STRICTA

QUERCUS PALUSTRIS

GLEDITZIA TRIACANTHUS

CERCIS SILIQUASTUM

ROBINIA PSEUDOACACIA

TILO

LIQUIDAMBAR

TIPUANA TIPU

CERANTONIA

ACER PLATANOIDE

LANDSCAPING

The landscaping design at *La Gran Reserva de Sotogrande* is conceived as a coherent whole in harmony with the natural surroundings.

The existing vegetation is the basis for the landscaping design Criteria appropriate to Mediterranean gardens are employed. Special attention has been paid to the selection of species in accordance with the climate and the arrangement of an efficient irrigation system coherent with the location of the estate, whilst facilitating savings in energy and natural resources.

The landscaping design was completed with the application of the corresponding advanced techniques for the implementation of these criteria. All species selected are suited to the climate of the location.

In the design different strategies are coordinated for vegetation associated with pathways, for the arrangement of singular vegetation in relation to common open spaces and for the distribution of mass vegetation. The mass vegetation for the common spaces has been correlated with that of the private spaces.

PAISAJISMO

El proyecto de paisajismo de La Gran Reserva de Sotogrande se ha pensado como un conjunto coherente y armónico con la naturaleza que lo rodea.

La vegetación existente se ha considerado como base del diseño paisajista de La Gran Reserva. Se han seguido criterios propios de jardines mediterráneos, atendiendo especialmente a la selección de especies según el clima, a la disposición de un sistema de riego eficiente y coherente con la ubicación del conjunto y al ahorro de energía y recursos naturales.

El paisajismo se completó con la aplicación de técnicas avanzadas para la implementación de dichos criterios. Todas las especies seleccionadas se caracterizan por su adecuación al clima del lugar.

En el diseño se han coordinado diferentes estrategias para la vegetación asociada a los viales, para la disposición de la vegetación singular en relación a los espacios abiertos comunes y para la distribución de la vegetación en masa, que en los espacios comunes se ha interrelacionado con la de los espacios privados.

Tilo   *Cerantonia siliqua*   *Tipuana tipu*   *Acer platanoide*   *Robinia pseudoacacia*

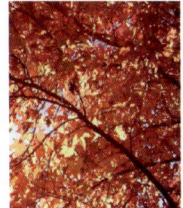

Liquidambar   *Cupressus stricta*   *Cercis siliquastum*   *Gledizia triacanthus*   *Quercus palustris*

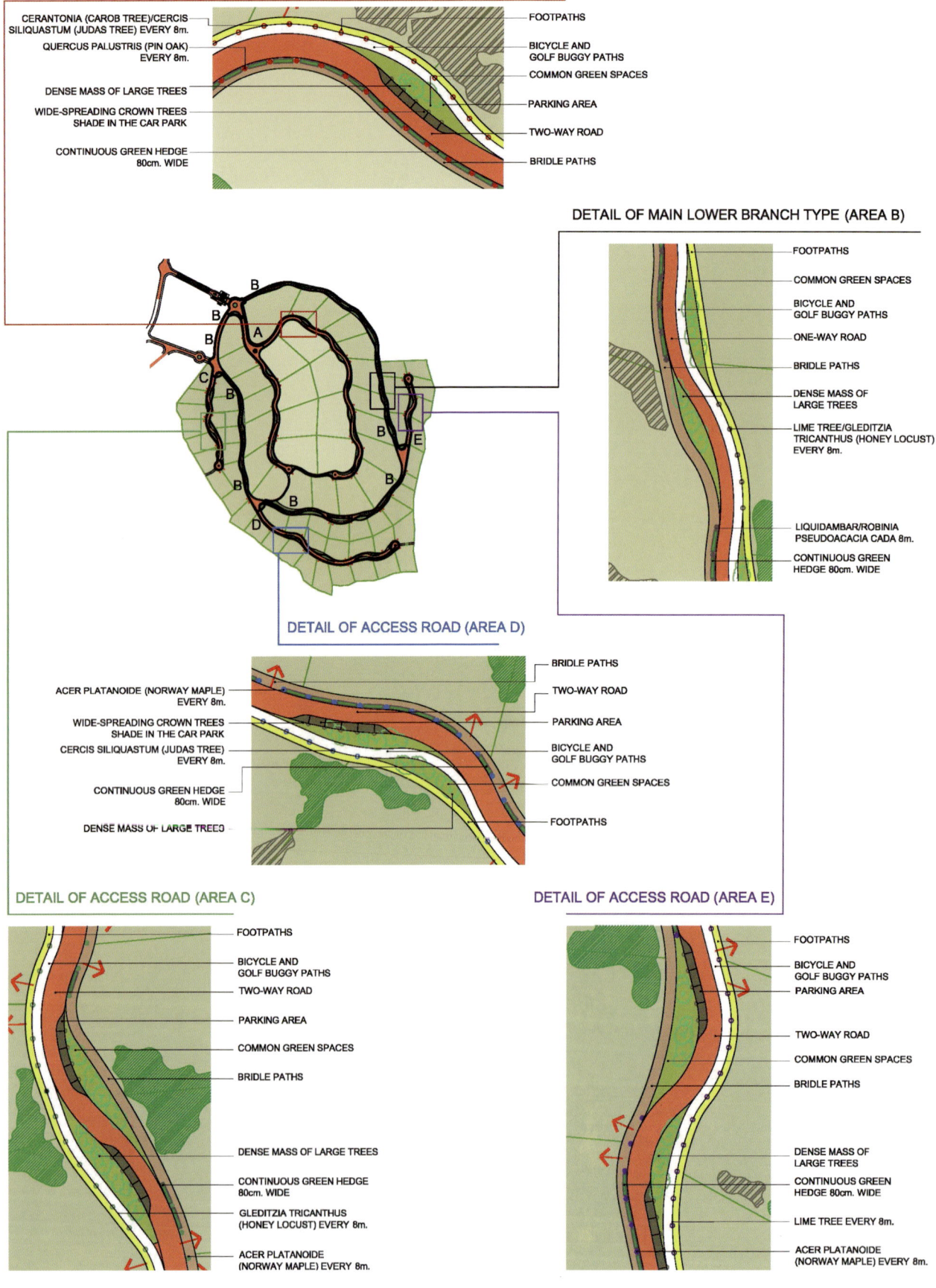

DETAIL OF MAIN UPPER BRANCH TYPE (AREA A)

CERANTONIA (CAROB TREE)/CERCIS SILIQUASTUM (JUDAS TREE) EVERY 8m.

QUERCUS PALUSTRIS (PIN OAK) EVERY 8m.

DENSE MASS OF LARGE TREES

WIDE-SPREADING CROWN TREES SHADE IN THE CAR PARK

CONTINUOUS GREEN HEDGE 80cm. WIDE

FOOTPATHS

BICYCLE AND GOLF BUGGY PATHS

COMMON GREEN SPACES

PARKING AREA

TWO-WAY ROAD

BRIDLE PATHS

DETAIL OF MAIN LOWER BRANCH TYPE (AREA B)

FOOTPATHS

COMMON GREEN SPACES

BICYCLE AND GOLF BUGGY PATHS

ONE-WAY ROAD

BRIDLE PATHS

DENSE MASS OF LARGE TREES

LIME TREE/GLEDITZIA TRICANTHUS (HONEY LOCUST) EVERY 8m.

LIQUIDAMBAR/ROBINIA PSEUDOACACIA CADA 8m.

CONTINUOUS GREEN HEDGE 80cm. WIDE

DETAIL OF ACCESS ROAD (AREA D)

ACER PLATANOIDE (NORWAY MAPLE) EVERY 8m.

WIDE-SPREADING CROWN TREES SHADE IN THE CAR PARK

CERCIS SILIQUASTUM (JUDAS TREE) EVERY 8m.

CONTINUOUS GREEN HEDGE 80cm. WIDE

DENSE MASS OF LARGE TREES

BRIDLE PATHS

TWO-WAY ROAD

PARKING AREA

BICYCLE AND GOLF BUGGY PATHS

COMMON GREEN SPACES

FOOTPATHS

DETAIL OF ACCESS ROAD (AREA C)

FOOTPATHS

BICYCLE AND GOLF BUGGY PATHS

TWO-WAY ROAD

PARKING AREA

COMMON GREEN SPACES

BRIDLE PATHS

DENSE MASS OF LARGE TREES

CONTINUOUS GREEN HEDGE 80cm. WIDE

GLEDITZIA TRICANTHUS (HONEY LOCUST) EVERY 8m.

ACER PLATANOIDE (NORWAY MAPLE) EVERY 8m.

DETAIL OF ACCESS ROAD (AREA E)

FOOTPATHS

BICYCLE AND GOLF BUGGY PATHS

PARKING AREA

TWO-WAY ROAD

COMMON GREEN SPACES

BRIDLE PATHS

DENSE MASS OF LARGE TREES

CONTINUOUS GREEN HEDGE 80cm. WIDE

LIME TREE EVERY 8m.

ACER PLATANOIDE (NORWAY MAPLE) EVERY 8m.

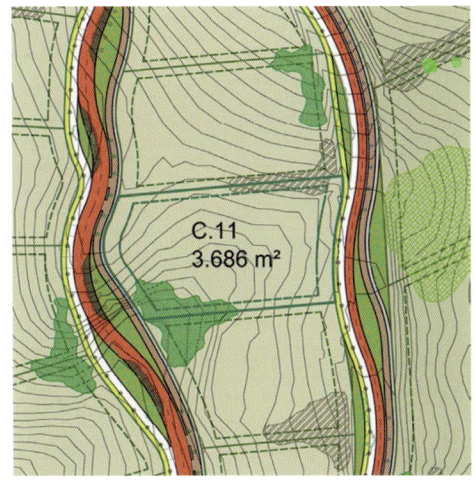

C.11
3.686 m²

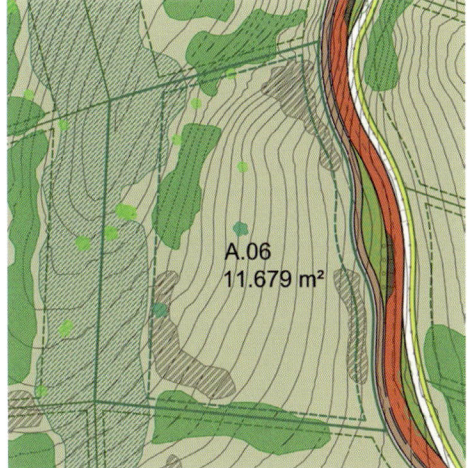

A.06
11.679 m²

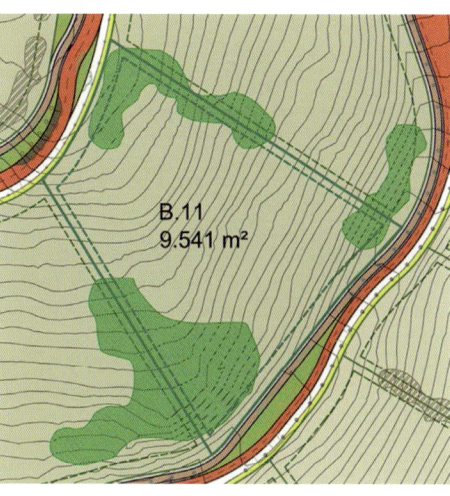

B.11
9.541 m²

PLOT CHARACTERISTICS

In determining the plots on La Gran Reserva de Sotogrande, it was considered that a southern orientation was optimal for residential use, bearing in mind the excellence of the estate's views of the sea, the golf courses, the Rock of Gibraltar and the mountains.

These were priority considerations in determining the regular shape and proportional dimensions of the plots and the aim is to ensure that the viable location of buildings is coherent with the characteristics of each plot.

Each plot has its own distinctive features that differentiate it from others. These include views, orientation, solar radiation, existing vegetation, access to pathways, gradient of the terrain and surface area.

CARACTERÍSTICAS DE LAS PARCELAS

Las parcelas de *La Gran Reserva de Sotogrande* se handeterminado considerando la orientación sur como la mejor para el uso residencial y atendiendo al potencial de sus vistas panorámicas sobre el mar, los campos de golf, el Peñón de Gibraltar y las montañas. Estas consideraciones han sido prioritarias para determinar una forma regular y unas dimensiones proporcionadas en las parcelas, procurando que la viabilidad de la ubicación de las construcciones sea coherente con las características de cada una de ellas. Cada parcela tiene valores propios y diferentes a los del resto, como las vistas, la orientación, el soleamiento, la vegetación existente, el acceso a las circulaciones, las pendientes del terreno y la superficie.

RESIDENCIAL RIBERA DEL MARLÍN

Sotogrande, Cádiz, Spain — Completition phase 1: 2010 /phase 2: 2014 — 75.000 m² / 807,293 sq ft
© RWA y Sotogrande SA

Ribera del Marlin Complex configures and completes one of the margins of the Sotogrande Marina. The aim requested by the client was to harmonize a triple programme formulating the commercial, residential and leisure uses as complementary. The sea is the main reference of the setting, so it is towards the sea - parallel to the coast - that both the residential buildings and the gardens surrounding them are laid out, as well as the facades of the commercial premises and the promenade where they are situated.

El conjunto configura y completa uno de los márgenes de la Marina de Sotogrande y consigue el objetivo, solicitado por el cliente, de hacerlo armonizando un triple programa commercial, residencial y de ocio, planteando estos usos como complementarios.
El mar es la principal referencia del lugar y hacia él se orientan, configurándose en paralelo a la costa, tanto los edificios de viviendas y los jardines que los rodean como el frente de locales comerciales y el paseo peatonal en el que éstos de encuentran.

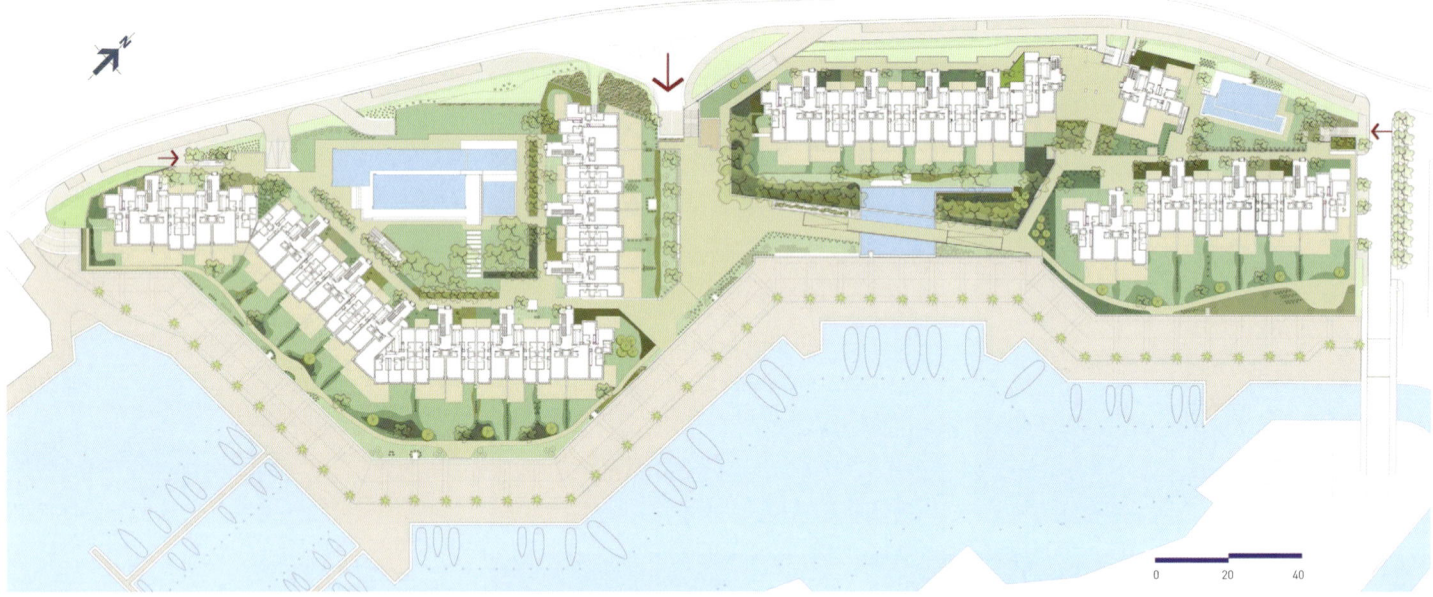

General plan

The *Ribera del Marlín* Complex is situated near the Rock of Gibraltar, on the coast of the straits that separate the Mediterranean Sea from the Atlantic Ocean. This unique setting and its corresponding weather patterns were fundamental when considering the design of the complex.

In its setting, the complex makes up a large part of the waterfront, with the layout of the buildings arranged to look out to the sea, though without forgetting their relationship with nature and the countryside and which spreads out on the side opposite the waterfront.

Ribera del Marlin Complex está situado próximo al Peñón de Gibraltar, en la costa que forma el estrecho que separa el Mar Mediterráneo del Océano Atlántico. Esta singular localización y las condiciones climáticas que le corresponden se consideraron primordiales en el diseño del conjunto.

En su emplazamiento, el conjunto construye una extensa parte del *waterfront* orientando la disposición de las construcciones hacia el mar, pero, sin olvidar su relación con el campo y la naturaleza que se extienden en el lado opuesto al *waterfront*.

The housing blocks are arranged so that they benefits from the best of sunlight and views.
All the dwellings are oriented onto two sides, to encourages natural cross-ventilation, minimizing the need for energy consumption in air- conditioning.
The volumes are highlighted by tricks of light and shade produced by the overhanging balconies, which prolong seawards the indoor space of the dwellings.
The residential units participate in the promenade´s comercial life, but with privacy lent by setting back the buildings behind protecting gardens.

Los bloques de viviendas se disponen hacia las mejores orientaciones solares y visuales.
Todas las viviendas tienen doble orientación para permitir la ventilación cruzada natural, minimizando el consumo energético en refrigeración.
En sus volúmenes destaca el juego de luces y sombras producido por los grandes voladizos de sus terrazas, que prolongan hacia el mar el espacio interior de las viviendas.
Las viviendas participan de la vida comercial del paseo, pero con la intimidad y el confort que consiguen el retranqueo y el jardín que las protege.

Section

1. Easterly wind
2. Westerly wind
3. Protection devices for windows in facades with high exposure to winds
4. Direct access to berths, storages and dwellings
5. Noise sources
6. Commercial premises
7. Commercial storage area
8. Dwelling
9. Residencial parking
10. Commercial parking

The difference generated in height level allows a clear functional separation of the vehicle access, parking areas and storage zones of each programme, which optimises their interrelation. The construction of service areas underground, which allowed exterior traffic space to be liberated, was a technical and construction challenge due to the situation below sea level.

La diferencia de cota que se genera permite una clara separación funcional de circulaciones, aparcamientos y almacenes de cada programa, que optimiza sus relaciones. La construcción de las plantas de servicio bajo rasante, que permitieron liberar los espacios de circulación exteriores, supuso un reto técnico y constructivo por su situación por debajo del nivel del mar.

The comercial premises make up the frontline of a promenade, which also includes nautical activity at the mooring points and enjoys a sense of spaciousness provided by residential buildings'gardens, situated on the roofs of saids premises. The direct connection to the nautical activity determines the functional and formal organisation of the commercial areas.

Los Locales comerciales constituyen el frente de un paseo peatonal que también integra la actividad náutica de los puntos de atraque y disfruta de la amplitud espacial que proporciona el jardín de las viviendas, situado sobre la cubierta de dichos locales. La conexión directa a la actividad náutica determina la organización funcional y formal de los espacios comerciales.

1. Delivery access
2. Public parking access
3. Residential parking access
4. Green facade
5. Residential parking
6. Commercial premises
7. Commercial waterfront
8. Pedestrian marina
9. Berths

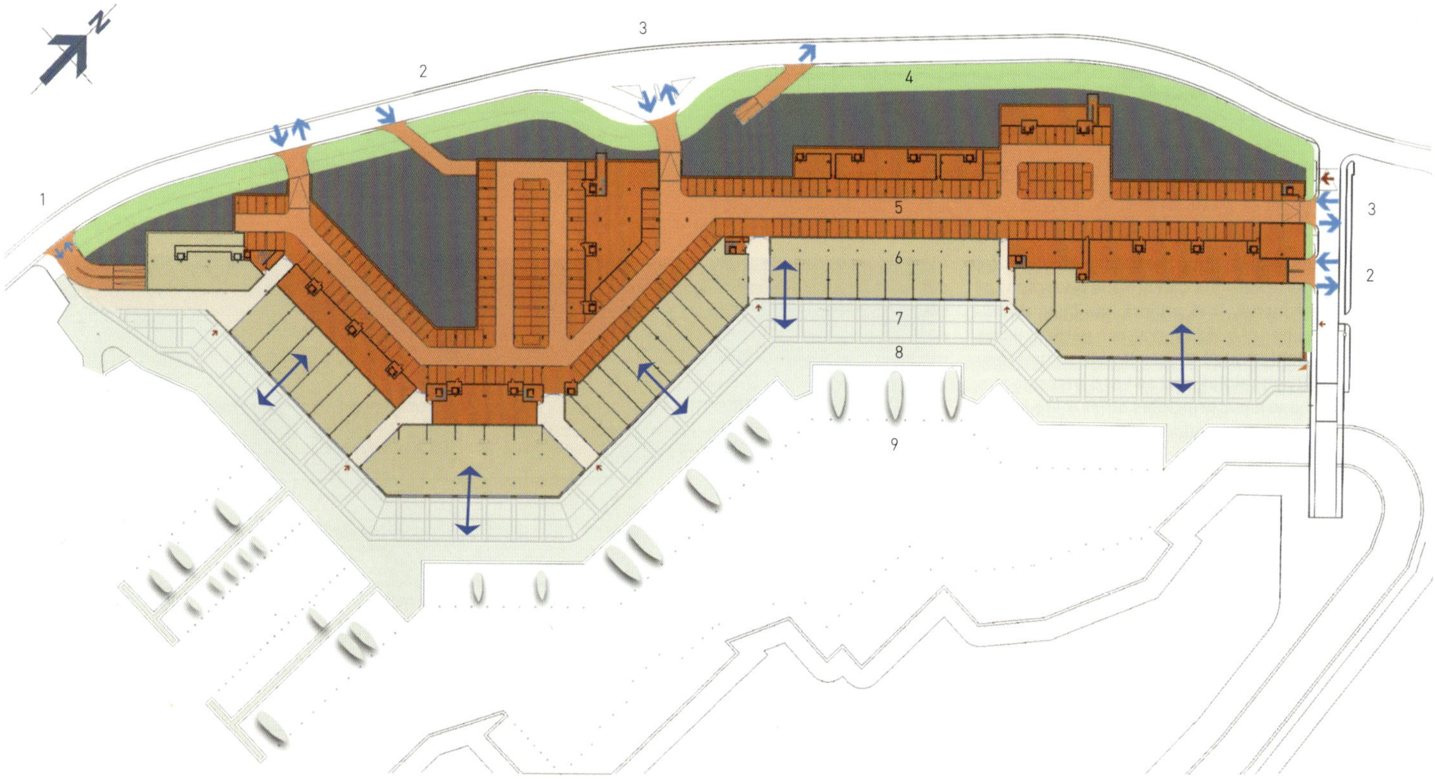

Development Layout

REHWALDT
Landschaftsarchitekten

www.rehwaldt.de

Bautzner Strasse 133
01099 Dresden
Germany

Since founding his practice in 1993 in Dresden, landscape architect Till Rehwaldt has been producing works of urban design, plans for recreation and entertainment, and town planning. Participation in design competitions has been a recurring challenge and many projects have been acquired this way. His design process is aimed at bestowing sites with a new identity arising from the spatial, chronological, and programmatic context while progressively defining the formal language of surfaces, plant selections, functional elements and details.

Desde que fundó su estudio en Dresde, en 1993, el arquitecto paisajista Till Rehwaldt ha producido trabajos de diseño urbano, planos de recreación y entretenimiento y planificación urbana. Para él, los concursos de diseño han sido un desafío recurrente y muchos proyectos los ha conseguido de este modo.
El objetivo de su proceso de diseño es dotar a los lugares de una nueva identidad a partir del contexto espacial, cronológico y programático, al tiempo que, progresivamente, define el lenguaje formal de las superficies, las selecciones de plantas, los elementos funcionales y los detalles.

ZOOLOGICAL GARDEN DRESDEN – GIRAFFE ENCLOSURE
Dresden, Germany — 2008 — Area: 18.000 m² / 193,750 sq ft
© Rehwaldt Landschaftsarchitekten

The imposing scenery around the park is used as a visual extension of the zoo. The paths designed to guide visitors extend beyond the limits of the site towards the headlands. The enclosure does not impede the visitors feeling of being amongst the animals.

El imponente escenario que rodea el parque se utiliza como extensión visual del zoo. Los caminos diseñados para guiar a los visitantes se extienden hacia los cabos, más allá de los límites del emplazamiento. Las vallas no impiden que los visitantes tengan la sensación de estar entre animales.

1.   Window (at the old zoo entrance)
2.   Access
3.   Zebras enclosure
4.   Waders enclosure
5.   Zebras' and waders' habitat
6.   Tree planting
7.   Ditch
8.   Giraffes enclosure
9.   Depot
10. Access
11. Moat
12. Waders' island
13. Gate
14. Riverbed
15. Giraffes' savanna
16. Fruit tree
17. Giraffes' habitat
18. Terrarium
19. Sand dune
20. Bushes
21. Water hole
22. Benches
23. Low plants
24. Observation tree
25. Info
26. African route
27. Safari – Playground
28. Rhododendrons
29. Lions habitat
30. Rose garden

Site plan

To showcase the giraffes, the enclosure was divided in different zones representing the various natural habitats such as the savanna, a water hole and scrubland.

Para las jirafas, el recinto se dividió en distintas zonas que representan diversos hábitats naturales como la sabana, con un abrevadero y monte bajo.

BAVARIAN GARDEN EXHIBITION NATURE IN WALDKIRCHEN

Waldkirchen, Germany — 2007 — Area: 32.000 m² / 344,445 sq ft
© Rehwaldt Landschaftsarchitekten

This project, designed for a garden exhibition, adopted the form of a promenade to allow visitors to experience the city in various ways. The promenade integrates different zones: the market place, the cemetery, the city park, a sports field, and Bellevue, representing the city's character.

Este proyecto, diseñado como jardín para exposiciones, adquirió la forma de un paseo para permitir que los visitantes experimenten la ciudad de distintos modos. El paseo integra distintas zonas: el mercado, el cementerio, el parque de la ciudad, varios campos deportivos y el Bellevue, que representan el carácter de la ciudad.

General plan

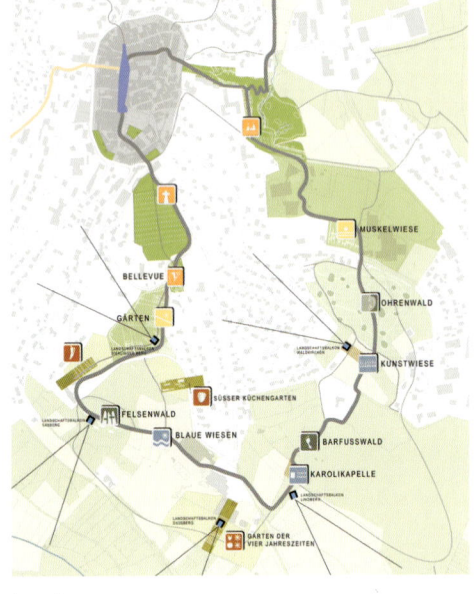

Location map

1. Garden
2. Underground garage
3. Wall
4. Alley City Wall
5. City wall symbol
6. Option stair tower
7. Activity square
8. Lighting pole
9. Kindergarten
10. Kindergarten's playground
11. Gardens
12. Benches
13. Cherry garden
14. Game terrace
15. Schoolyard
16. School garden
17. School
18. Outlook
19. Plantation
20. Promenade
21. Hedges
22. Footpath
23. Bridge
24. Water jungle
25. Wäshlbach Creek
26. Lake source
27. Water ramp
28. Lookout
29. Passage
30. Bus parking space
31. 14 parking places
32. Driving training area
33. Meadow
34. Island
35. Artificial lake
36. Marshland
37. Pond
38. 68 parking places
39. Passage
40. Stone ridge

The promenades in the woods are planned to enhance the sensual experience. Scenic balconies equipped with information panels offer views of the surrounding landscape.

Los paseos en el bosque están diseñados para mejorar la experiencia sensorial. Los balcones panorámicos, equipados con paneles informativos, ofrecen vistas del paisaje que los rodea.

ULAP PARK

Berlin, Germany — 2008 — Area: 4.800 m² / 51,667 sq ft
© Rehwaldt Landschaftsarchitekten

A small area with trees in the predominantly geometrical urban fabric of Berlin city center was strengthened by developing a spatially cohesive green zone. This allows for events to happen, most of them responding to the activities taking place in the buildings that delimit the square.

Mediante la creación de una zona verde que aporta cohesión espacial, se reforzó una pequeña zona de árboles en el tejido urbano fundamentalmente geométrico del centro de Berlín. Esto permite la celebración de eventos, la mayoría de ellos relacionados con las actividades que tienen lugar en los edificios que delimitan la plaza.

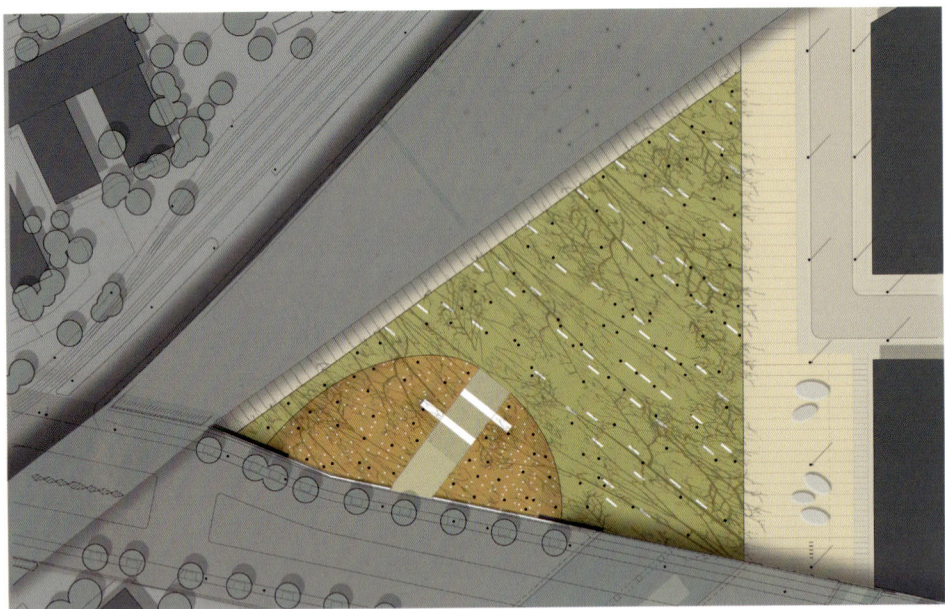

General plan

The ULAP area is a space for all age groups. Generous open spaces and the tree canopy create a clearly defined urban open space.

La zona del ULAP es un espacio para personas de todas las edades. Los generosos espacios abiertos y la bóveda de árboles generan un espacio urbano despejado y bien definido.

WUPPERTAL ZOOLOGICAL GARDEN

Wuppertal, Germany — 2007 — Area: 18.000 m² / 193,750 sq ft
© Rehwaldt Landschaftsarchitekten

The Wuppertal Zoo underwent improvements in landscaping and circulation. In particular, a depression that used to be cut off by a railroad embankment was generously extended beneath the new Sambabrücke (Samba Bridge). The Sambastrasse (Samba Route) became an integral part of the new landscape.

El zoo de Wuppertal experimentó una serie de mejoras en cuanto a paisajismo y vialidad. En concreto, una depresión en el terreno, que quedaba aislada por el terraplén de una vía, se amplió generosamente bajo el nuevo Sambabrücke (puente de la samba). La Sambastrasse (ruta de la samba) pasó a ser una parte integrante del nuevo paisaje.

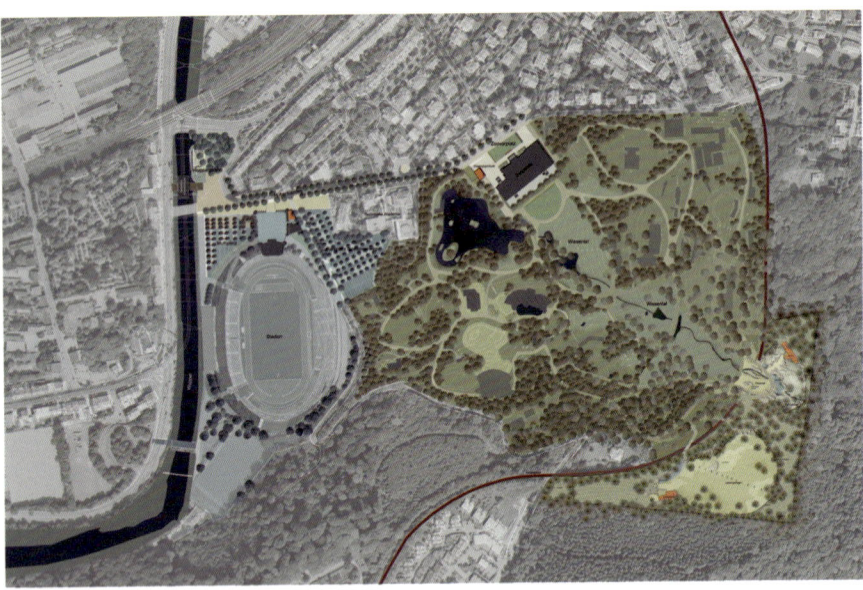

Site plan

The tiger vivarium was designed as a rock forest while the lions' enclosure was given the look of the wide open savanna.

El recinto de los tigres se diseñó como un bosque de rocas, mientras que a la zona de los leones se le confirió el aspecto de la sabana más auténtica.

RIJNBOUTT

www.rijnboutt.nl

Postbus 59316
1040 KH Amsterdam
The Netherlands

Richard Koek studied architecture and urban design at the Delft University of Technology between 1981 and 1988. After graduating, he enrolled in the Centrum Herengracht studio, which in 1993, when he became a partner, was renamed as CH & Partners. This studio has been one of the most prolific in the field of landscape architecture during the past two decades. In 2009 CH & Partners merged with Rijnboutt Van der Vossen Rijnboutt where Koek continues developing high quality landscape projects.

Richard Koek estudió arquitectura y desarrollo urbano en la Universidad Tecnológica de Delft entre 1981 y 1988. Nada más graduarse, ingresó en el estudio Centrum Herengracht, que en 1993, al pasar a ser él uno de los socios, fue rebautizado como CH & Partners. Este estudio ha sido en las últimas dos décadas uno de los más importantes de Holanda en el ámbito del paisajismo. En 2009 CH & Partners se fusionó con la firma Rijnboutt Van der Vossen Rijnboutt, bajo la cual Koek sigue desarrollando proyectos paisajísticos de calidad.

SHELL TERRAIN

Rijswik, The Netherlands — 2007 — Area: 86.000 m² / 925,696 sq ft
© Kees Hummel

This investigation center built in the fifties needed some improvement work for some time, especially on its exterior. The remodeling project not only included the adaptation of the green zones but also had to add a parking garage for 800 cars. The most striking element of the project is the "green roof" at the top floor.

Este centro de investigación, construido en la década de los cincuenta, hacía tiempo que necesitaba una reforma, sobre todo en sus zonas exteriores. El proyecto de remodelación incluyó la adaptación de zonas verdes y un aparcamiento de 800 plazas. El elemento más llamativo es el «tejado verde» acondicionado en el nivel superior.

Site plan

An 8,611 sq ft bamboo garden enlivens one of the exterior spaces of the complex, which acquires the dynamism of a modern campus thanks to this intervention.

Un jardín de bambú de 800 m² anima uno de los espacios exteriores del complejo, el cual, gracias a la intervención, adquiere el dinamismo de un campus moderno.

NAARDEN WALLS

Naarden, The Netherlands — 2005 — Area: 92.000 m² / 990,280 sq ft
© Harry Verkuylen

This restoration project for the Naarden city walls had to face a triple challenge: preserve the historic and cultural character of the site, insure an appropriate use of the space and respect nature.
Pruning the trees and improving the dikes and ponds generated an open space, which was much safer and more pleasant.

Este proyecto de restauración de las murallas de la localidad de Naarden tuvo que afrontar el triple reto de preservar el carácter histórico y cultural del emplazamiento, garantizar una utilización del espacio y respetar la naturaleza.
La poda de muchos árboles y la mejora de diques y estanques generó un espacio más abierto, seguro y agradable.

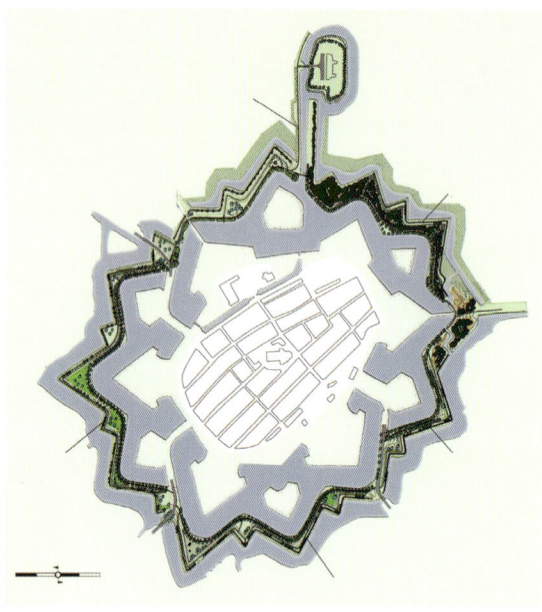

Site plan

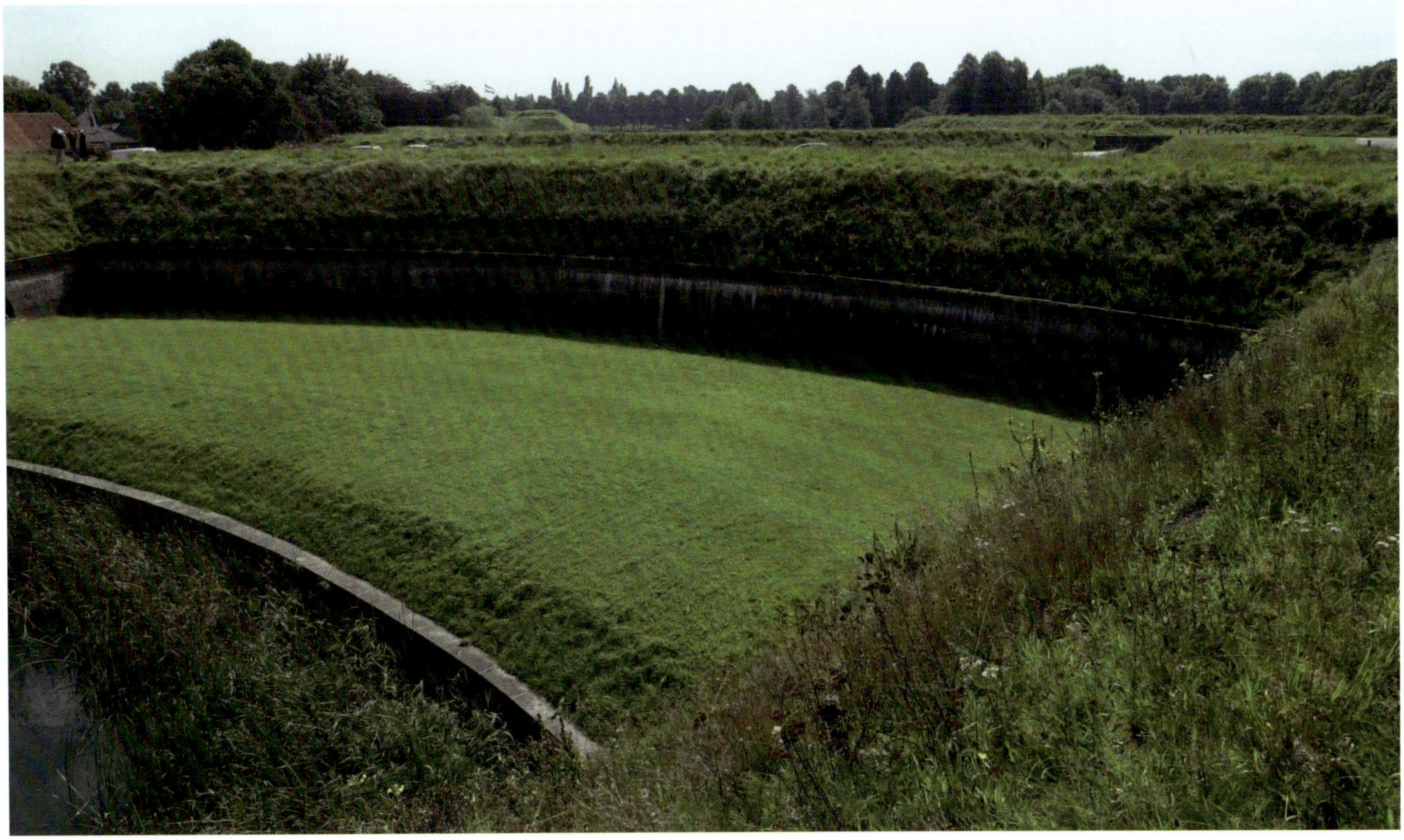

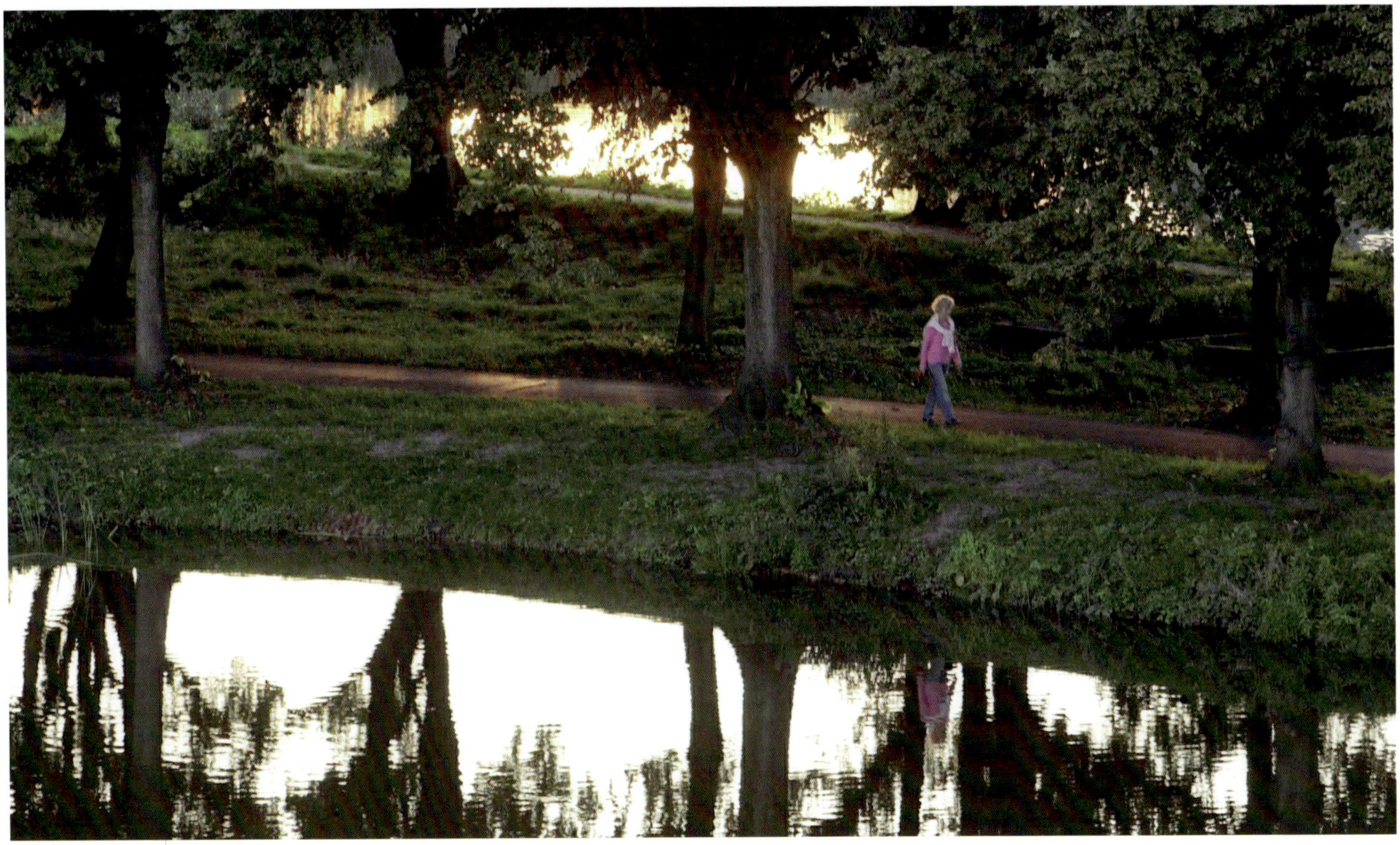

DIE WIELDEN

Eindhoven, The Netherlands — 2004 — Area: 24.000 m² / 258,334 sq ft
© Kees Hummel

When the architects received the commission to design the gardens of the Delft University of Technology, they decided to plant six rows of pine trees on a gravel podium surrounded by a 9.8-foot-wide canal into which the rainwater collected on the entire property flows.

A series of pedestrian bridges across the canal establish paths between the different buildings on the campus.

Al recibir el encargo de diseñar los jardines de la entrada de la Universidad Técnica de Delft, los arquitectos optaron por plantar seis hileras de pinos, situados en un podio de grava bordeado por un canal de 3 m de ancho en el que desembocan las aguas pluviales de toda la extensión.

Una serie de puentes para peatones salvan el curso del canal y establecen los recorridos entre los distintos edificios del campus.

Site plan

MAHLER 4

Amsterdam, The Netherlands — 2004 — Area: 21.000 m² / 226,042 sq ft
© Rijnboutt Architects

This neighborhood south of Amsterdam has been submitted to a radical transformation. The Zuidplein Square was first to be remodeled within this transformation program. The design consists of the longitudinal disposition of three islands with vegetation, which at the same time help to align the urban furniture.
The selection of plants included native species that comply with criteria for hardiness and longevity.

Este barrio del sur de Ámsterdam ha sufrido una transformación radical. Insertada en este proceso, la plaza de Zuidplein ha sido la primera del entorno en ser reformada. El diseño se basa en la disposición longitudinal de tres islas con vegetación, que a su vez ayudan a alinear el mobiliario urbano.
La selección de flora se ha llevado a cabo entre especies autóctonas, obedeciendo a criterios de resistencia y longevidad.

Elevation

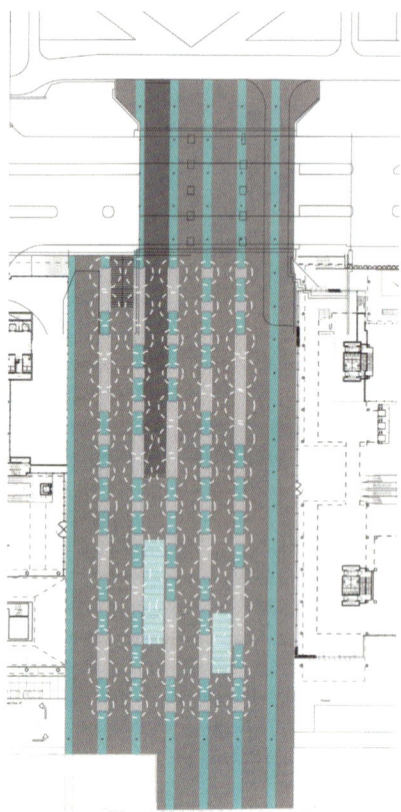

General plan

ROMERA Y RUIZ
ARQUITECTOS

---

www.romerayruiz.com

Angel Guerra, 14, Local bajo
35003 Las Palmas de Gran Canaria
Spain

ÁNGELA RUIZ MARTÍNEZ, Doctor in architecture. Associate Professor of the University of Las Palmas de Gran Canaria. Department of graphical expression & architectural design.
PEDRO ROMERA GARCIA, Doctor in architecture and Professor of architectural design at the School of Architecture of Las Palmas from 1999.
ROMERA Y RUIZ ARQUITECTOSSLP (1999, Las Palmas de Gran Canaria). They have undertaken several projects, builds, and works and taken part in numerous cultural activities. Their work has been awarded, exhibited and published in various international media.

ÁNGELA RUIZ MARTÍNEZ, Doctora arquitecta. Profesora asociada de la Universidad de Las Palmas de Gran Canaria. Departamento de Expresión Gráfica y Proyectos Arquitectónicos.
PEDRO ROMERA GARCÍA, Doctor Arquitecto y Profesor de Proyectos Arquitectónicos en la Escuela de Arquitectura de Las Palmas desde 1999.
ROMERA Y RUIZ ARQUITECTOS SLP (1999, Las Palmas de Gran Canaria). Ha desarrollado diferentes proyectos, planes, obras y ha participado en numerosas actividades culturales. Su obra ha sido premiada, expuesta y publicada en diversos medios internacionales.

MARITIME PARK
Las Palmas de Gran Canaria — 2015 — 6.560,42 m² / 70,616 sq ft
© Juan E. Correa, Miquel Oliva

The project has been shaped over three layers, set at three different heights. The first is flush with the existing promenade and shares the same material giving rise to a continuity integrating the intervention with the existing promenade. The remaining two layers are concrete and below the promenade.

La formalización del proyecto se resuelve en tres estratos, a tres cotas distintas. La primera está enrasada con el paseo existente y comparte el mismo material para provocar una continuidad que integre la intervención con el paseo existente. Los otros dos estratos son de hormigón y están por debajo del paseo.

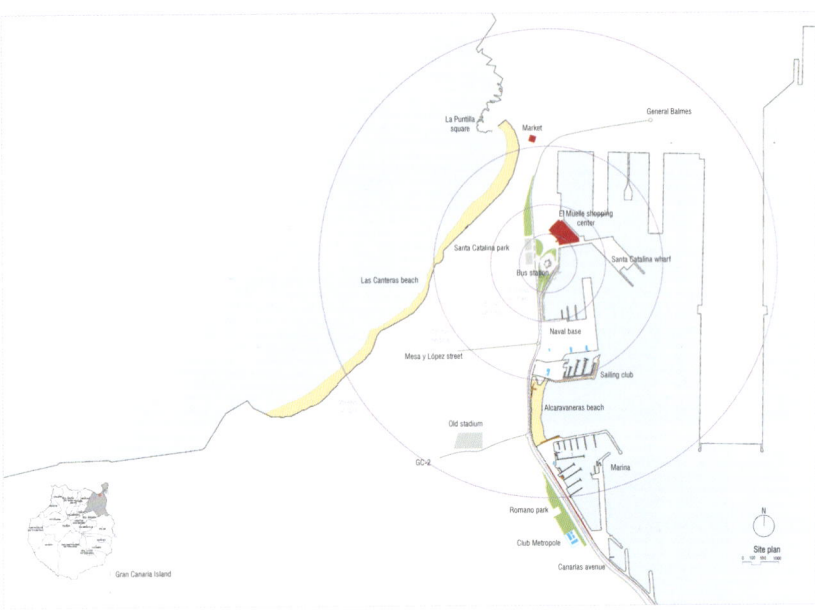

Site plan

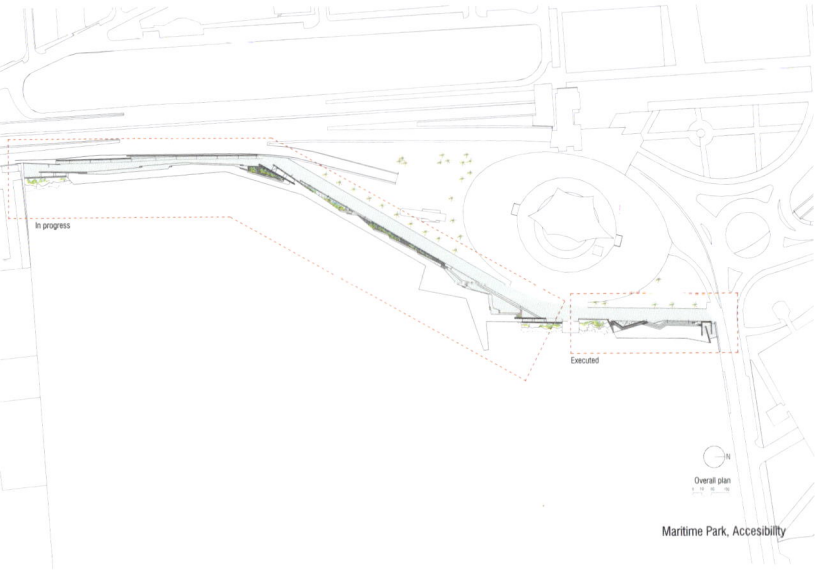

Accesibility

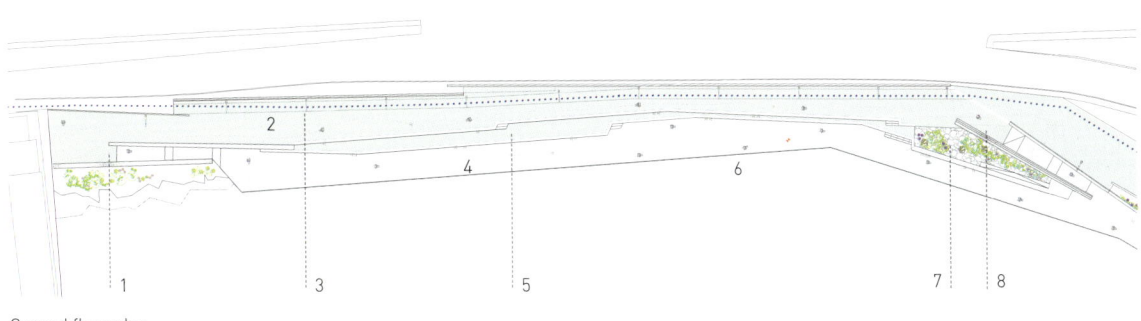

Ground floor plan

1. Adapted access
2. Bicicle lane
3. Light
4. Plataform
5. Grandstand
6. Glass rail
7. Natural stone and vegetation
8. Seafront existing

···· Bicycle lane
--- Itinerary

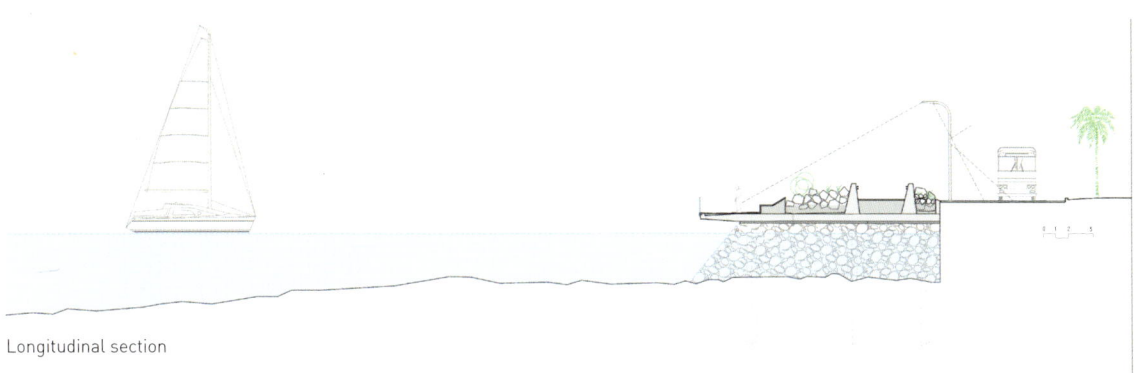

Longitudinal section

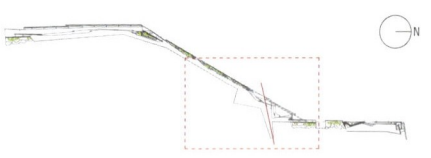

1. Adapted access
2. Bicicle lane
3. Light
4. Plataform
5. Grandstand
6. Glass rail
7. Natural stone and vegetation
8. Seafront existing
9. Pergola
10. Canary Island Square

.... Bicycle lane
--- Itinerary

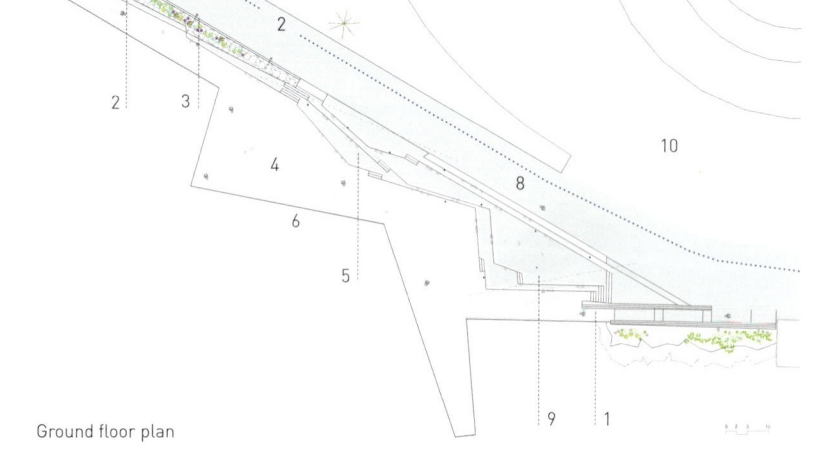

Ground floor plan

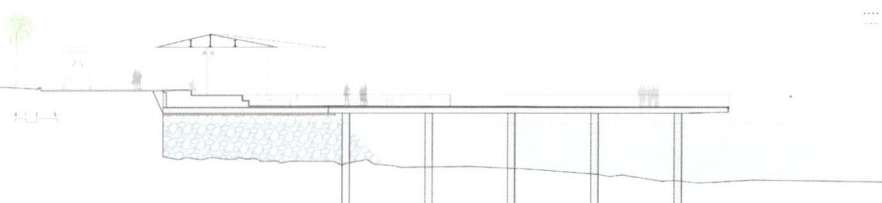

Longitudinal section

Las Palmas de Gran Canaria owes its urban maritime development to the existence of the port. The project area has a privileged location regarding the city's development since it lies on the edge of the urban experience and port activity.

Las Palmas de Gran Canaria debe su desarrollo urbano-marítimo a la existencia del puerto. El área del proyecto tiene una situación privilegiada respecto al desarrollo de la ciudad ya que está en el límite de la experiencia urbana y la actividad portuaria.

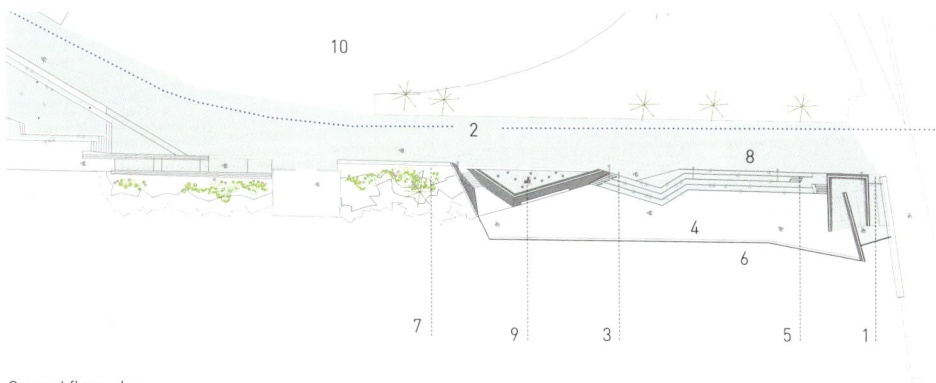

Ground floor plan

1. Adapted access
2. Bicicle lane
3. Light
4. Plataform
5. Grandstand
6. Glass rail
7. Natural stone and vegetation
8. Seafront existing
9. Accesible Nebulized water area
10. Canary Island Square

···· Bicycle lane
--- Itinerary

Longitudinal section

The space where the platforms meet each other is designed using bleachers that were set up as a viewing site, stage or as a tourist attraction, and many more applications have been discovered while developing the project. The entire intervention is accessible to travel.

El encuentro entre las plataformas está diseñado mediante graderíos que se plantearon como estancia contemplatoria, escenario o como atractor turístico, y muchos más usos que se han ido descubriendo con el desarrollo del proyecto. El recorrido a lo largo de toda la intervención es accesible.

SASAKI

www.sasaki.com

64 Pleasant Street
Watertown
Massachusetts 02472
United States

For over sixty years, Sasaki has brought together the best of landscape architecture, planning, urban design, architecture, interior design, civil engineering, graphic design, place branding, and data science to shape the places in which we live. Out of their Boston and Shanghai offices they define the contours of place and redefine what's possible along the way. Today, they are a diverse practice of 270 professionals who share a singular passion for creating spaces and places around the world that prove human potential.

Durante más de sesenta años, Sasaki ha reunido lo mejor de la arquitectura paisajista, de la planificación, del diseño urbano, de la arquitectura, del diseño de interiores, de la ingeniería civil, del diseño gráfico, de la identidad de lugar y la ciencia de datos para dar forma a los lugares en los que vivimos. Más allá de sus oficinas en Boston y Shanghai definen los contornos del lugar y redefinen lo que es posible por el camino. Hoy en día, son un equipo multidisciplinar de 270 profesionales que comparten una singular pasión por crear espacios y lugares con potencial humano por todo el mundo.

CHICAGO RIVERWALK, PHASES 2 AND 3
Chicago, United States — 2016 — 14.164 m² / 152,460 sq ft
© Christian Phillips, Kate Joyce Studios

Keeping with a trend happening in cities across America, the design team, Sasaki and Ross Barney Architects, transformed underutilized infrastructure on the waterfront into a downtown amenity that maximizes underleveraged real estate.
For decades, the Chicago River's edge was not a place people had any reason to visit, but is now a connected, inviting, and comfortable public destination.

Siguiendo una tendencia en boga en las ciudades americanas, el equipo Sasaki y Ross Barney Arquitectos convirtió una infraestructura poco utilizada en el margen del río en un atractivo para el centro de la ciudad, que revaloriza la zona.
Durante décadas, la gente no tuvo razón alguna para visitar la orilla del río Chicago, pero ahora es un destino público sugerente, confortable y bien comunicado.

The Chicago Riverwalk project plays a central role in enhancing the downtown Chicago experience by giving visitors and residents of Chicago a place to engage in recreation and leisure in the heart of the city.

El proyecto Chicago Riverwalk juega un papel central en la mejora del centro de Chicago, ofreciendo a los visitantes y residentes un lugar que invita a participar en la recreación y el ocio en el corazón de la ciudad.

The new connective spaces also act as critical linkages to existing open space systems in the city. Lowering the Riverwalk to river's edge and connecting each section into one continuous path means that for the first time, pedestrians can move seamlessly from the city's core to the lakefront along the river.

Los nuevos espacios actúan también como vínculos vitales con los sistemas de espacios abiertos de la ciudad. Guiar el paseo hasta la orilla y conectar cada tramo en un recorrido continuo significa que por primera vez los peatones pueden moverse sin problemas a lo largo del río desde el corazón de la ciudad hasta el lago.

THE LAWN ON D
Boston, United States — 2014 — 10.927 m² / 117,612 sq ft
© Christian Philips

The Massachusetts Convention Center Authority in partnership with its design team, conceived of the 2.7 acre Lawn on D — a flexible, vibrant, and temporary urban space — setting the tone for civic impact and expressing the ambitions of a new interactive district, flexible, technologically advanced, inspired by art and events, and inclusive of many constituents.

La autoridad del centro de convenciones de Massachusetts en asociación con su equipo de diseño concibieron el Lawn on D, un flexible, vibrante y temporal espacio urbano de 2,7 acres, que marca la pauta del impacto ciudadano y expresa las ambiciones de un nuevo distrito interactivo, flexible, inclusivo, tecnológicamente avanzado e inspirado por el arte y los eventos.

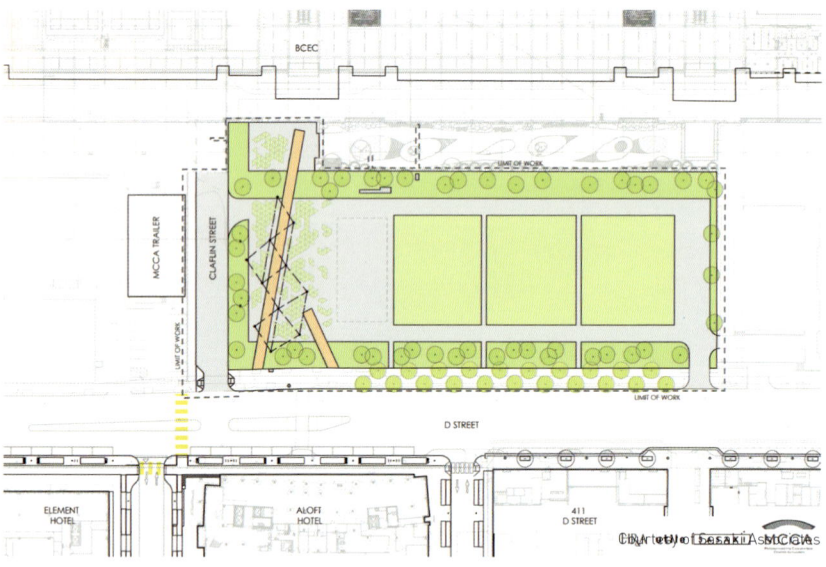

Site plan

SACRED HEART UNIVERSITY CAMPUS LANDSCAPES

Fairfield, Connecticut, United States — 2009-2015 — 230.671 m² / 152,460 sq ft
© Robert Benson, Jane Messinger, Anton Grassl/ESTO

Sasaki's 15-year relationship with Sacred Heart University began with a comprehensive master plan for the University's 57-acre campus in Fairfield, Connecticut. Following the master plan, Sasaki completed three significant and transformative projects a new Chapel (2009), a new Student Commons (2012) and the recently completed Martire Center for Business and Communications (2015). The projects are knitted together through a series of distinct yet harmonious landscapes.

La relación de 15 años de Sasaki con la Sacred Heart University comenzó con el plan integral del campus de 57 acres de la universidad en Fairfield, Connecticut. Siguiendo el plan, Sasaki completó tres importantes proyectos: una nueva capilla (2009), una nueva residencia de estudiantes (2012) y el recientemente terminado Martire Center for Business and Communications (2015). Los proyectos se enlazan entre sí a través de una sucesión de diferentes pero armoniosos paisajes.

STUDIO KAPPO

www.studio-kappo.com

Centener 40
52210 Rovinj
Croatia

Studio KAPPO was founded in 2001 and since then we provide a wide range of services from landscape architecture, planning, urban design, consultancy, GIS and environmental assessment.
Awareness of how important the landscape quality is leads us to a responsible attitude toward natural and constructed landscape with innovative approach, sustainable solutions and unique design at every task we undertake, regardless of the scale, from large multifunctional sites to small, intimate spaces.

Studio KAPPO fue fundado en 2001 y desde entonces ofrecemos una amplia gama de servicios relacionados con la arquitectura del paisaje, planeamiento, diseño urbano, consultoría, SIG y evaluación medioambiental. La percepción de la importancia de la calidad del paisaje nos empuja a una actitud responsable hacia el paisaje natural y el construido, con un enfoque innovador, soluciones sostenibles y un diseño singular para cada tarea, sin importar su escala, desde grandes áreas multifuncionales a pequeños espacios íntimos.

HIDROBAZA BATHING COMPLEX
Štinjan, Croatia — Completition phase 1: 2016 — 52.500 m² / 565,105 sq ft
© Studio KAPPO, Damir Bošnjak

Hidrobaza bathing complex is an adaptive reuse project of the former Military seaplane station Puntižela. Main goal was to preserve historical character of the area and integration of historical elements and matrix. The complex has several distinct components: beach, recreational and natural areas.

El complejo de baño Hidrobaza es un proyecto de reutilización de la antigua estación de hidroaviones militar de Puntizela. El objetivo fue preservar el carácter histórico de la zona y la integración de los elementos históricos con la matriz del proyecto. El complejo consta de varios componentes: playa y áreas recreativas y naturales.

Site plan

HOTEL LONE LANDSCAPE DESIGN
Rovinj, Croatia — 2011 — 16.975 m² / 182,717 sq ft
© Studio KAPPO

The landscape design relies on a balanced relationship between natural and built elements and their transitions, the use of native species to enforce the sustainability and the concept that forms links between existing and new in creation of an unique Mediterranean landscape.

El diseño del paisaje se basa en una equilibrada relación entre elementos naturales y construidos y en sus transiciones, el uso de especies autóctonas para subrayar la sostenibilidad y el concepto de construir vínculos entre lo existente y lo nuevo para crear un paisaje mediterráneo singular.

Site plan

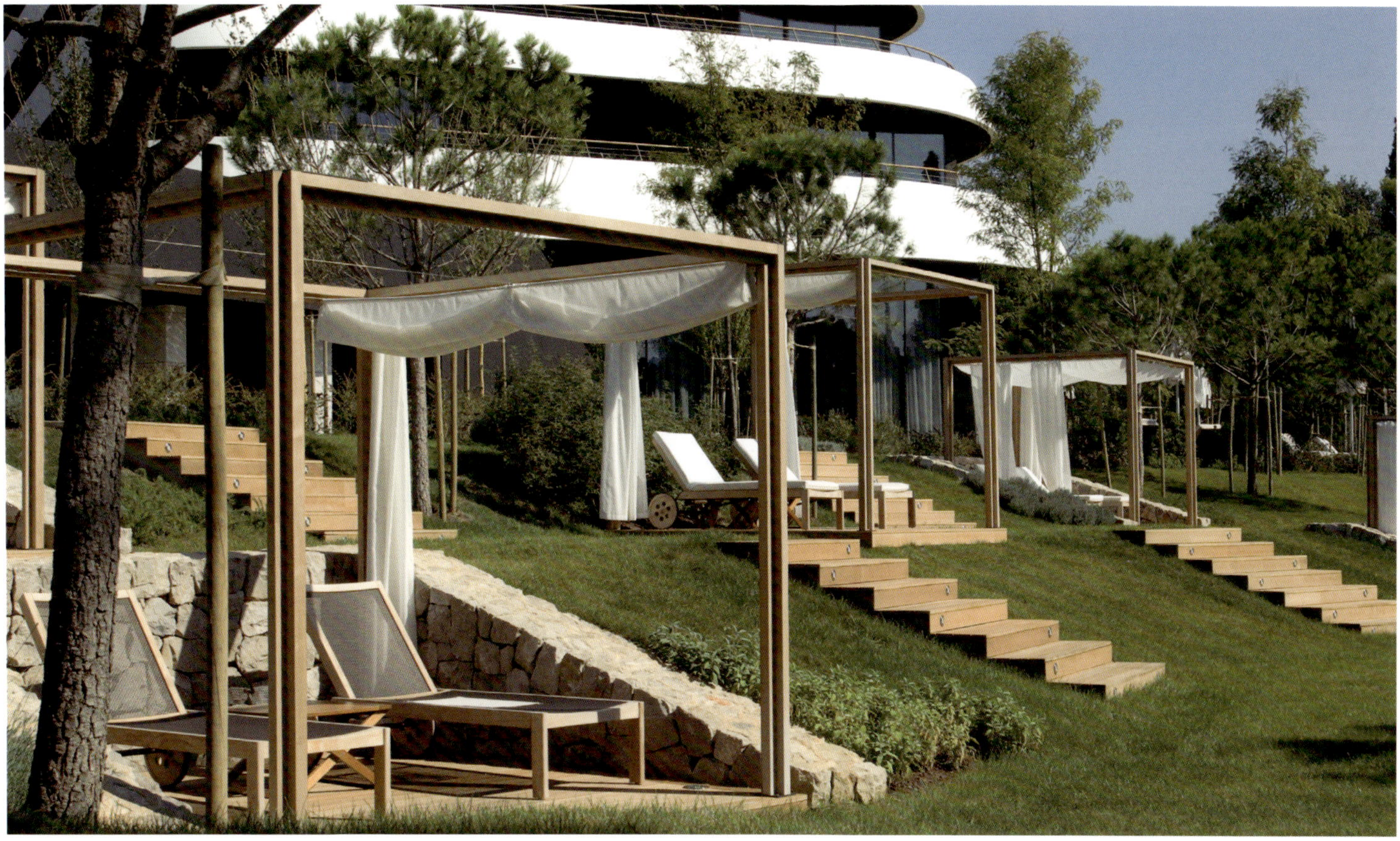

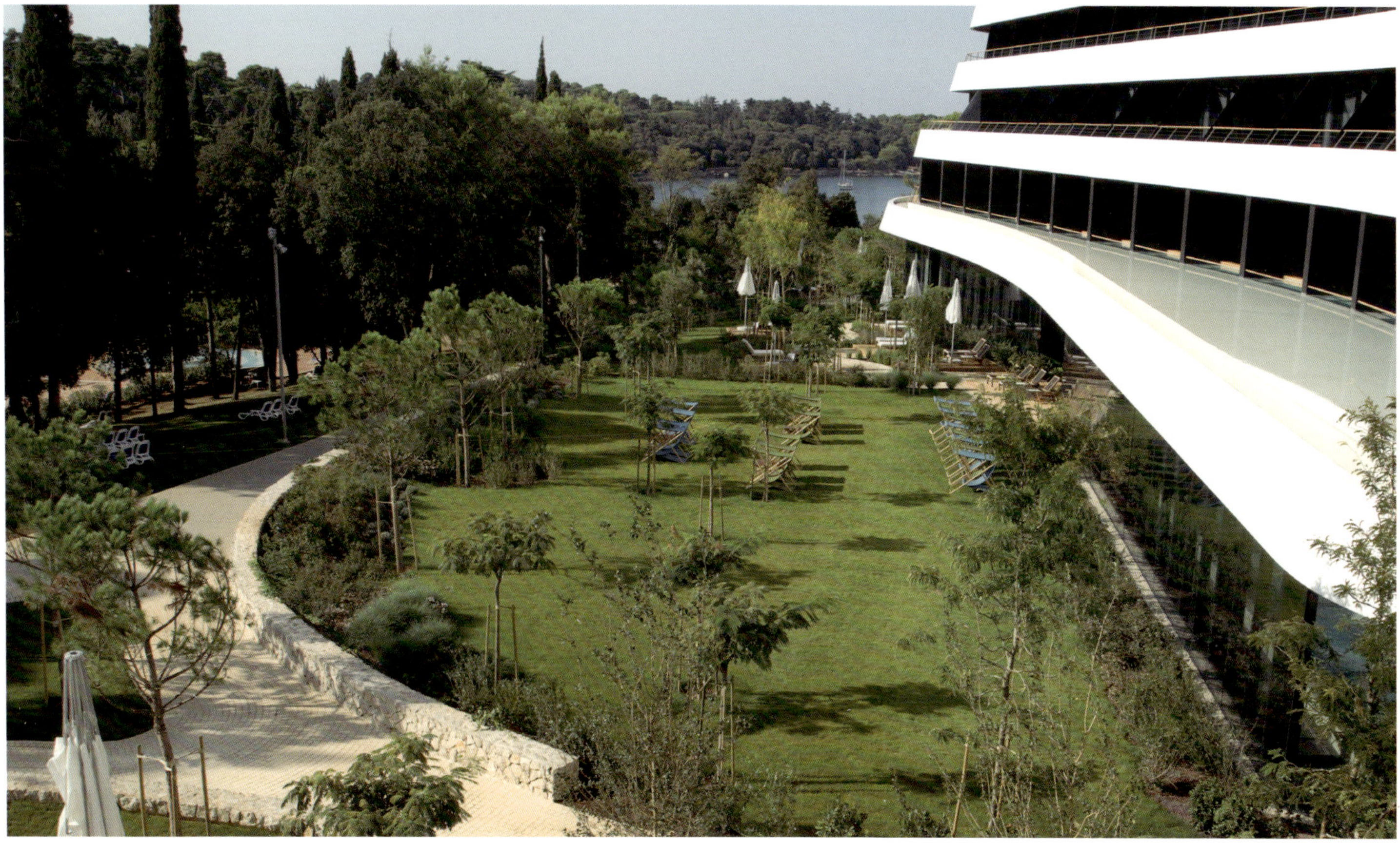

TITO'S MEMORIAL PARK

Pula, Croatia — 2013 — 7.200 m² / 77,500 sq ft
© Studio KAPPO, Damir Bošnjak

The main goals of the redesign was to maintain and emphasize the memorial character of the park positioning the remaining busts together in a stable and respectful setting. The redesign provides a range of spaces and supports commemoration while facilitating people's everyday activities.

Los principales objetivos del rediseño fueron mantener y enfatizar el carácter conmemorativo del parque colocando los bustos existentes juntos en un escenario permanente y respetuoso. El rediseño genera espacios variados y permite la conmemoración a la vez facilita las actividades cotidianas de la gente.

Site plan

HOTEL MONTE MULINI ENTRANCE FOUNTAIN

Rovinj, Croatia — 2008 — 160 m² / 1,722 sq ft
© Studio KAPPO, Virgilio Giuricin

The fountain represents a dynamic feature at the hotel entrance where visitors can sit and listen to the tumbling sound and enjoy the coolness of water. The cascades, water pool and slope lined with pebbles provide variable water texture impressions that become complete in collision with light.

La fuente representa un elemento dinámico de la entrada del hotel, donde los visitantes se sientan y escuchan el sonido del agua cayendo y disfrutan de su frescor. Las cascadas, el estanque y la pendiente revestida de guijarros producen impresiones variables en la textura del agua que se completan al colisionar con la luz.

© Anna Tarragona

TATJANA VON GRIESHEIM, LANDSCAPE ARCHITECT

---

www.tatjanavongriesheim.com

**Mortitx, 53
07013 Palma de Mallorca
Spain**

During her architectural landscaping studies in Belgrade, Tatjana contributed to an in-depth analysis of the environmental situation in Beirut (1996) and in 1998 completed her thesis 'National Parks of North and South Rhodesia'. Fascinated by its rich flora and fauna, she returned to Africa to work on urban and residential projects. In Spain, where she's been working since 2001, she graduated as "Master de Análisis de Paisaje". While most of her projects have been residential, Tatjana has realized several commercial and urban landscaping works.

Durante sus estudios de arquitectura del paisaje en Belgrado, Tatjana contribuyó a un análisis en profundidad de la situación medioambiental en Beirut (1996) y en 1998 completó su tesis 'Parques Nacionales de Rhodesia del Norte y del Sur'. Fascinada por su rica flora y fauna, regresó a África para trabajar en proyectos urbanos y residenciales. En España, donde trabaja desde 2001, se graduó como "Máster de Análisis del Paisaje". Aunque la mayoría de sus proyectos han sido residenciales, Tatjana ha realizado varios proyectos comerciales y de paisaje urbano.

HOTEL «CASTELL SON CLARET»
Capdella, Mallorca — 2014 — Area: 23.000 m² / 247,570 sq ft
© Marco Moog

When designing the landscape for this massive Majorcan heritage property, the landscaper thought of giving the visitor a moment to return to those days when the castle was built and enchant the hotel client with a mix of feelings hence the vegetation and water elements respecting a Majorcan ambient. The organic forms give a romantic sensation whilst the strong architecture of the ancient building and the water elements represent the strong character of the landscape.

Al diseñar el paisaje para esta inmensa propiedad del patrimonio mallorquín, la paisajista quiso ofrecer al visitante un retorno a los días en que el castillo fue construdo y encantar al cliente con una mezcla de sentimientos, de ahí la vegetación y los elementos de agua que reflejan una atmósfera mallorquina. Las formas orgánicas generan una sensación romántica mientras que la potente arquitectura del viejo edificio y los elementos de agua representan el carácter fuerte del paisaje.

Site plan

Sketch

Sketch

The large garden invites you to take long walks through alternating vegetation and offers secluded areas to rest, read and relax or jogging ways for the sportive ones.

El gran jardín invita a dar largos paseos a través de la variada vegetación y ofrece zonas aisladas para descansar, leer y relajarse o rutas de *jogging* para los deportistas.

HOUSE «MONTENEGRO»

Son Vida, Palma, Mallorca — 2015 — 1.200 m² / 12,917 sq ft
© Xisco Taberne, TvG

This contemporary garden follows the main lines of the house's architecture. The mixture of water elements, the swimming pool reflecting local nature, the pond with its natural stone at the entrance, and the grenade trees form a cohesive combination.
"Less is more" is the motto of this garden.

Este jardin contemporáneo sigue la lineas principales de la arquitectura de la casa. La mezcla de los elementos de agua con la piscina que refleja la naturaleza autóctona, el estanque con sus piedras naturales en la entrada y los granados forman un conjunto coherente.
"Lo menos es mas" es el lema de este jardin.

FINCA «SON BERNADI»

S´Alqueria, Mallorca — 2009 — Area: 4.900 m² / 52,743 sq ft
© TvG

This project, both the garden as well as the house, show the taste and romanticism of their owners. The impeccable liaison between client and landscaping architect created this romantic Mediterranean garden. Very colourful yet undemonstrative, with covered pergolas illuminated by antique lamps, a contemporary design swimming pool and a water cascade, terraces, old stone steps, four season trees, etc. All of this give the finca, located in one of Mallorca's most sought after areas, a very special feel.

Este proyecto, tanto el jardín como la casa, demuestran el gusto y romanticismo de sus propietarios. La colaboración entre el cliente y la paisajista en todo momento fue fluida creándose un bellísimo jardín romántico. Muy colorido, con elementos como pérgolas iluminadas por lámparas antiguas, una piscina de forma contemporánea y una cascada de agua, bancales, árboles de cuatro estaciones... dando toque especial a esta finca situada en una de las zonas mas cotizadas de Mallorca.

FINCA DEIA
Tramuntana, Mallorca — 2013 — Area: 5.300 m² / 57,049 sq ft
© Tatjana Von Griesheim

This Finca has long maintained its natural vegetation being tucked away in the highly protected mountainous part of Mallorca. Centenary olive trees were planted in their respective *bancales* and surrounded in new plantations of aromatic shrubs. Keeping the old stonewalls and terraces a new garden was created that invokes what Mallorca originally was... 'the island of tranquility'.

Esta finca está situada en una zona montañosa de la parte oeste de la isla y relativamente protegida, por lo cual ha mantenido su encanto salvaje. La plantación de olivos centenarios en sus correspondientes bancales y el resto de la vegetación autóctona, han guiado el diseño de este proyecto. Introduciendo plantas aromáticas y manteniendo los detalles constructivos a la antigua se ha conseguido un jardín que en todo momento transmite la Mallorca como era hace tiempo... "la isla de la calma".

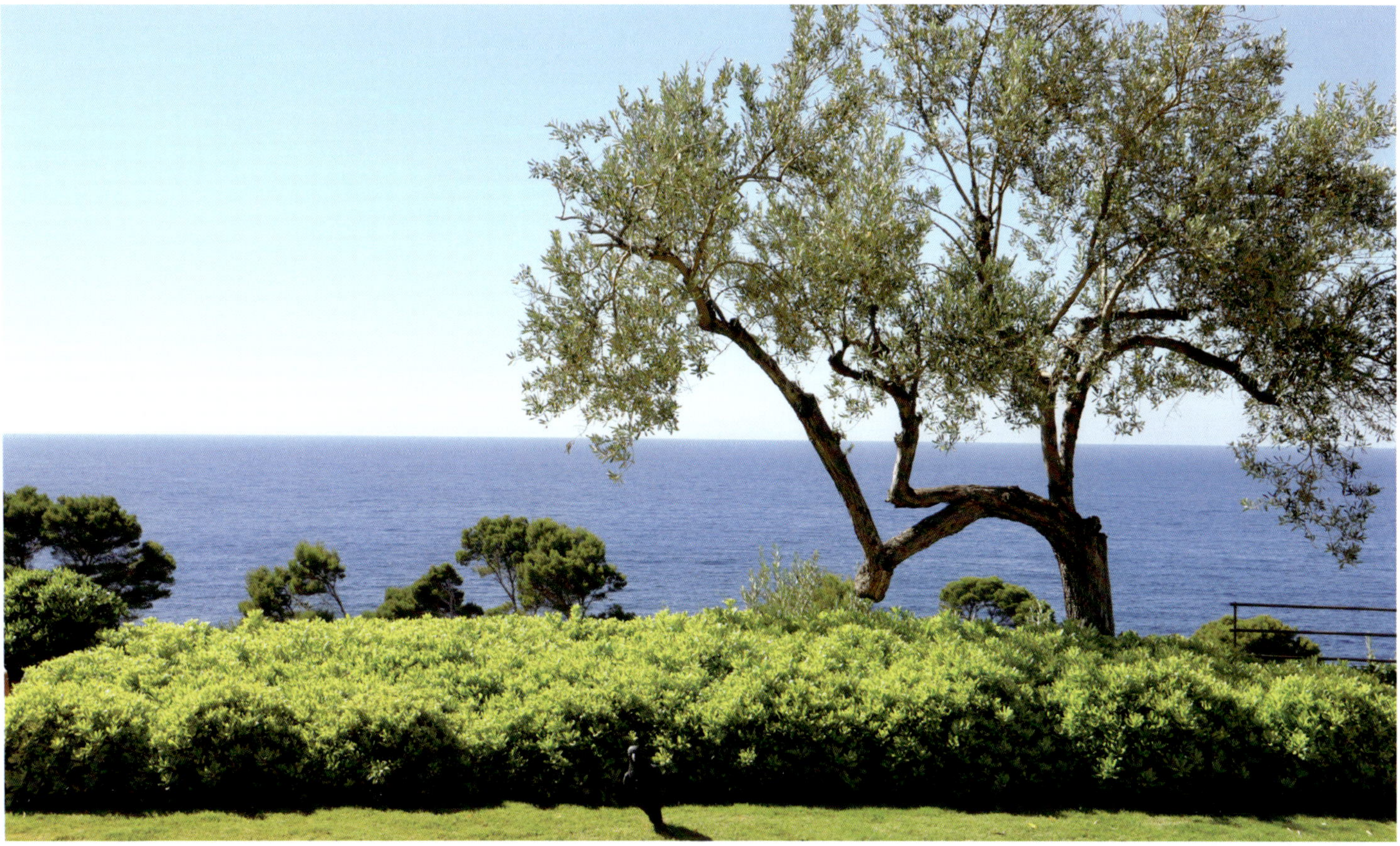

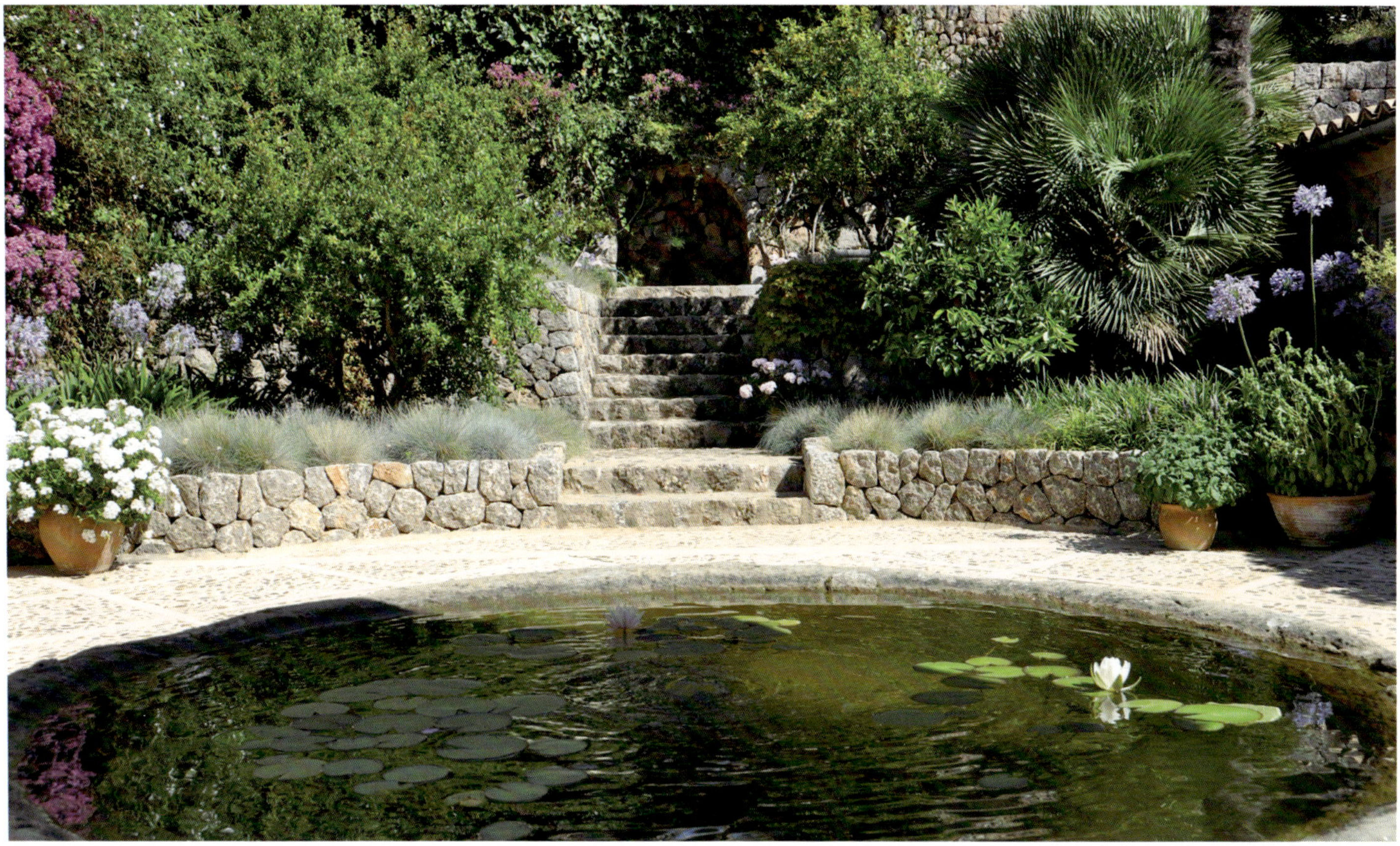

UTOPIA LANDSCAPES

www.utopia-landscapes.gr

sami Karatasou st. 44
Filopappos hill
1742 Athens
Greece

Utopia landscapes is a creative architectural office which specializes in landscape design, urban planning and hotel design. Founded in 2005 by the landscape architect Anastasios Tserpelis, it has accumulated substantial experience in the design and implementation of landscape plans in both the public and the private sphere. Each project space is studied independently and transformed after a process of careful observation, inspiration and creative design. The focus is on underlining the qualitative contribution of the 'green design' and ensuring a harmonious relationship between the proposal for regeneration and the broader architectural and natural surroundings of the area under study.

Utopia landscapes es una creativa oficina de arquitectura especializada en diseño del paisaje, planeamiento urbano y diseño de hoteles. Fundada en 2005 por el arquitecto paisajista Anastasios Tserpelis, ha acumulado sustancial experiencia en el diseño e implantación de planes paisajísticos tanto en la esfera privada como en la pública. Cada espacio proyectual es estudiado de forma independiente y transformado después de un proceso de cuidadosa observación, inspiración y diseño creativo. El objetivo es subrayar la contribución cualitativa del diseño ecológico y asegurar una relación armoniosa entre la propuesta de regeneración y el entorno natural y arquitectónico del área de estudio.

PIGON SQUARE REGENERATION
City of Skala, Lakonia, Greece — 2015 — 5.600 m² / 60,278 sq ft
© Utopia Landscapes

In Greek, the name 'Pigon' means springs and indeed the site is located on natural water springs. The primary aim of the design was to protect this delicate freshwater ecosystem, while transforming it into a destination capable of catering for the needs of the local community and also attracting visitors. A green design approach was followed so as to protect and restore the natural water systems and integrate pedestrian spaces into a coherent whole.

En griego, el nombre "Pigon" significa manantial y de hecho el emplazamiento se sitúa sobre manantiales de agua. El objetivo del diseño fue proteger este delicado ecosistema de agua dulce y a la vez transformarlo en un destino capaz de atender las necesidades de la comunidad local y también de atraer visitantes. Se siguió un enfoque de diseño ecológico para proteger y restaurar los sistemas naturales de agua e integrar los espacios peatonales en un conjunto coherente.

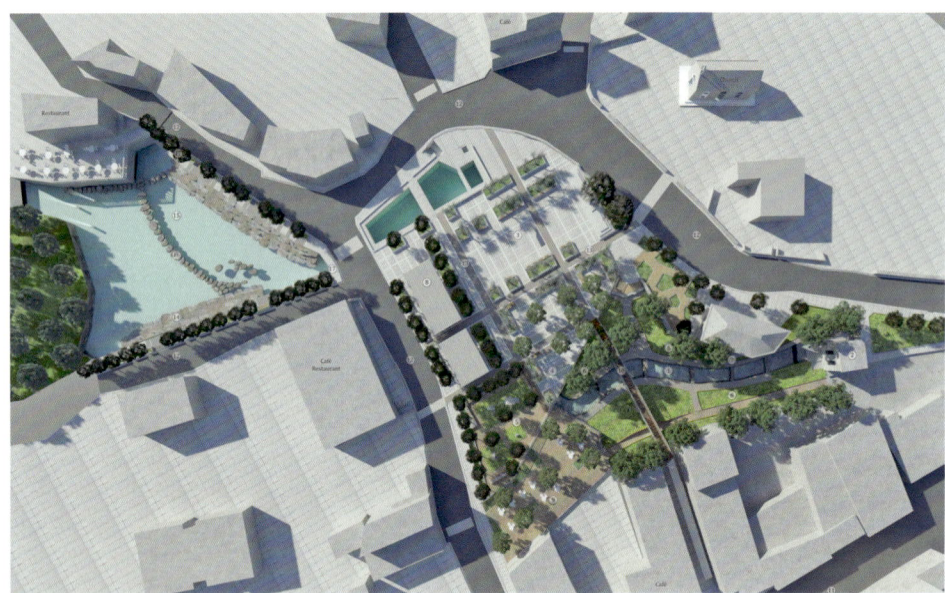

Site plan

Renderings

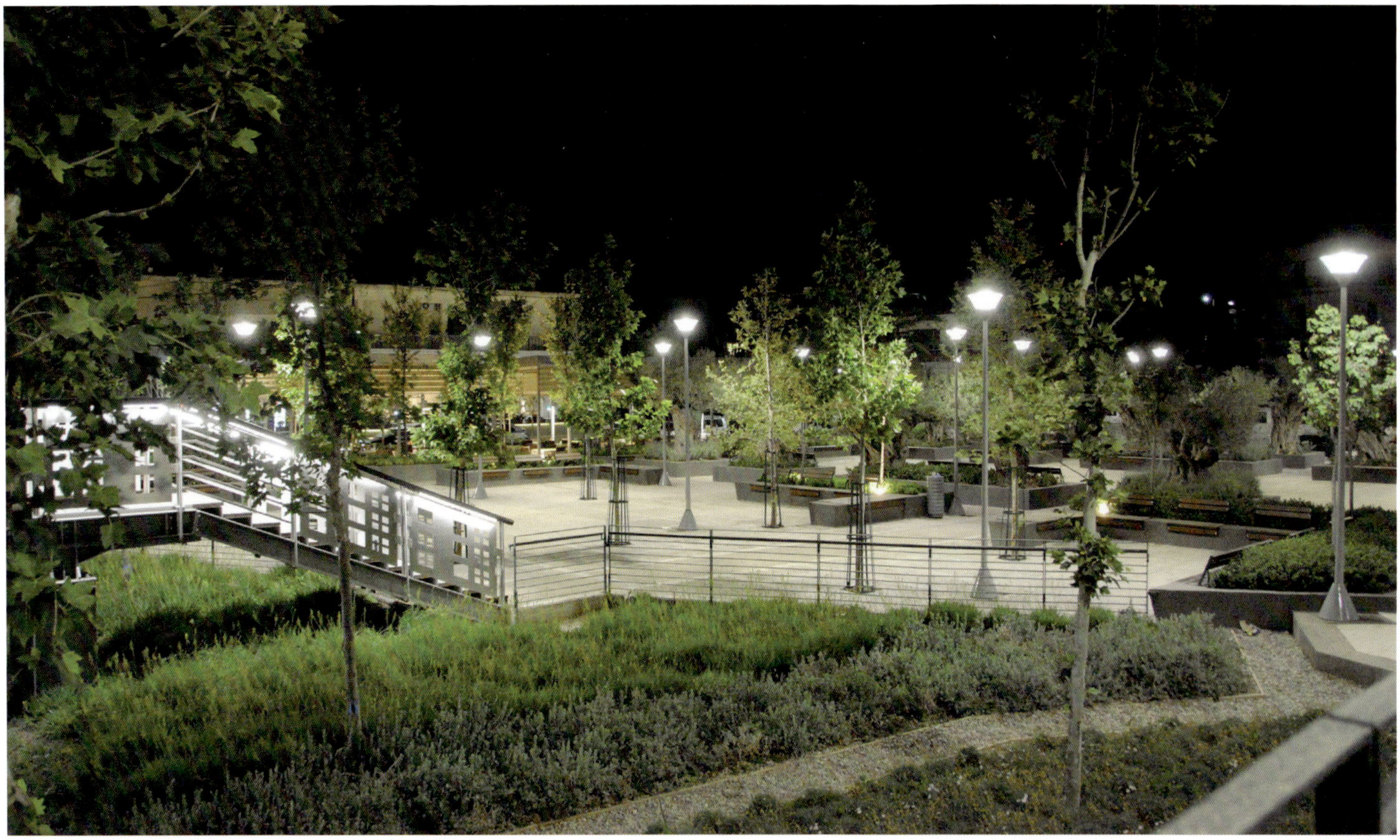

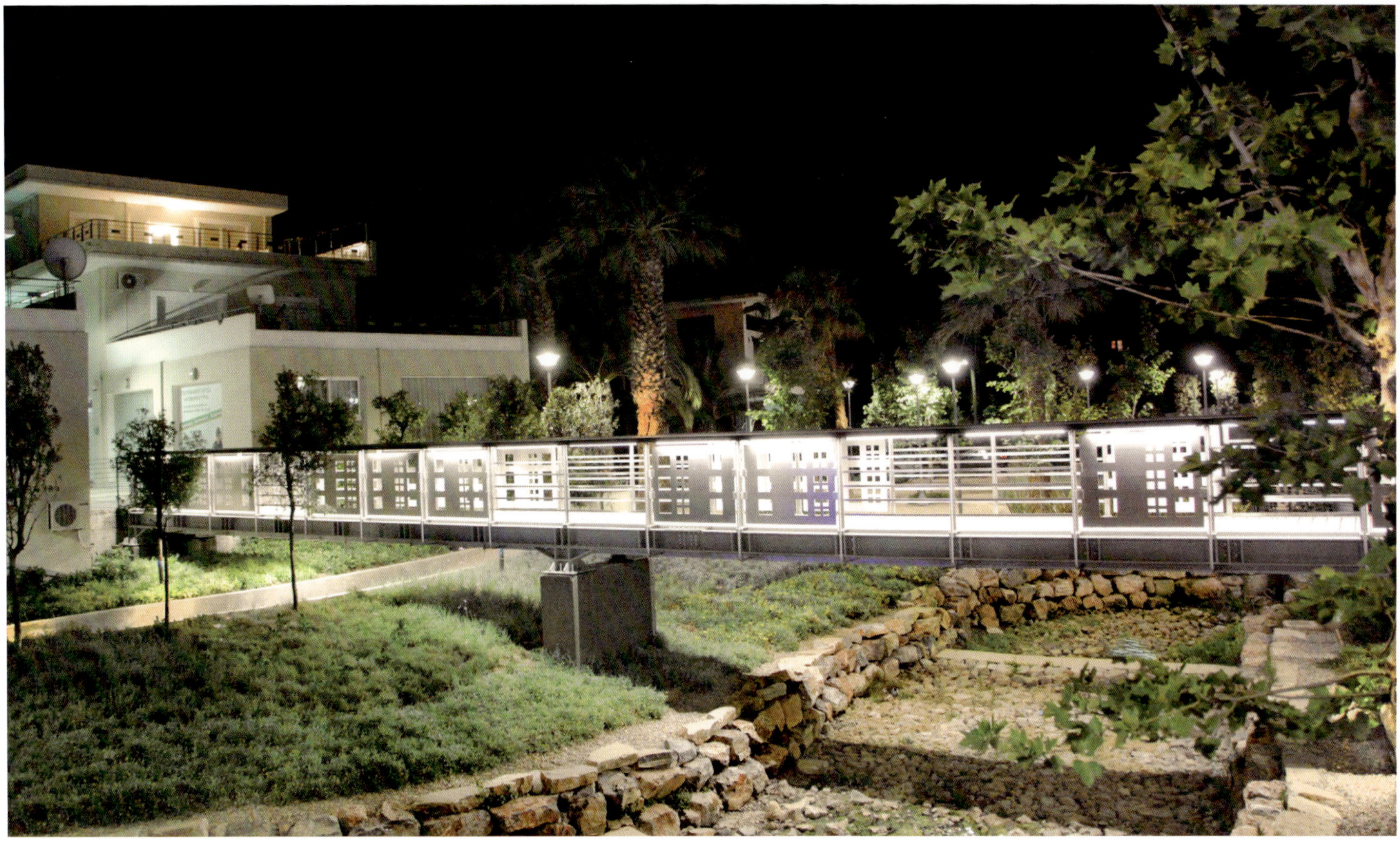

THE BOTANICAL GARDEN IN PARK FLOISVOS
City of Paleo Faliro, Athens, Greece — 2014 — 3.710 m² / 39,934 sq ft
© Utopia Landscapes

The Botanical Garden in Park Floisvos. The objective of this project was to create a neoteristic botanical garden, with symbolisms drawn from the floral kingdom, which would inspire the visitors and especially the children. An interplay of the senses is provoked by the landscape design of this botanical garden, where colours, scents and the variety of forms are merged into a hymn for the nature of the Mediterranean.

El jardín botánico en el parque Floisvos. El objetivo de este proyecto fue crear un jardín botánico neotérico, con simbolismos extraídos del reino floral que inspiraran a los visitantes, en especial a los niños. Una interacción con los sentidos es provocada por el diseño del paisaje de este jardín botánico, donde los colores, los olores y las formas variadas se combinan en un himno por la naturaleza del Mediterráneo.

Site plan

A. The room of colours
B. The room of scents
C. The room of textures
D. The Mediterranean parterres
E. The labyrinth

Built elements
1. Primary path
2. Secondary path
3. Green parterre
4. Main green parterre
5. Space
6. Main entrance
7. Entrance room

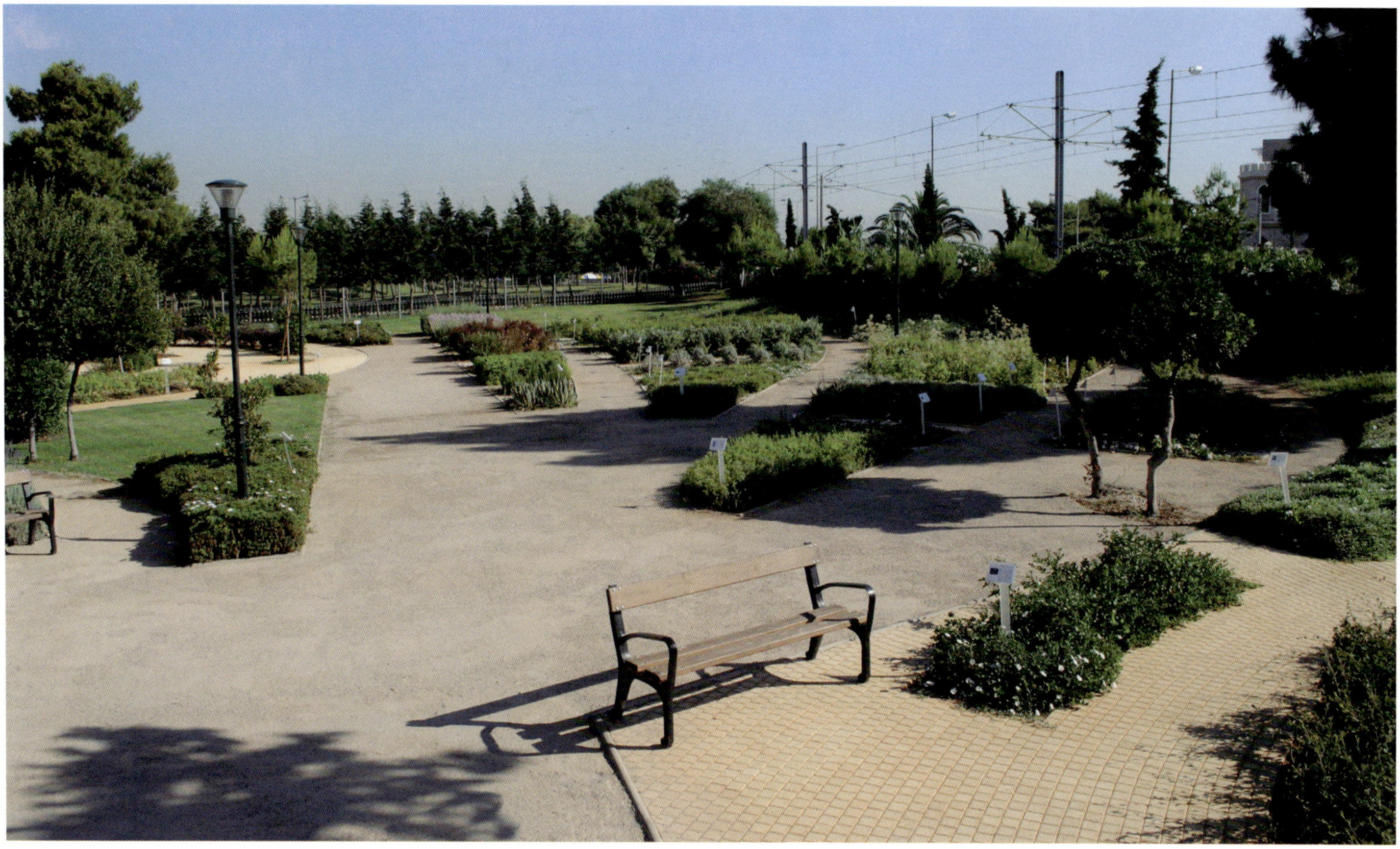

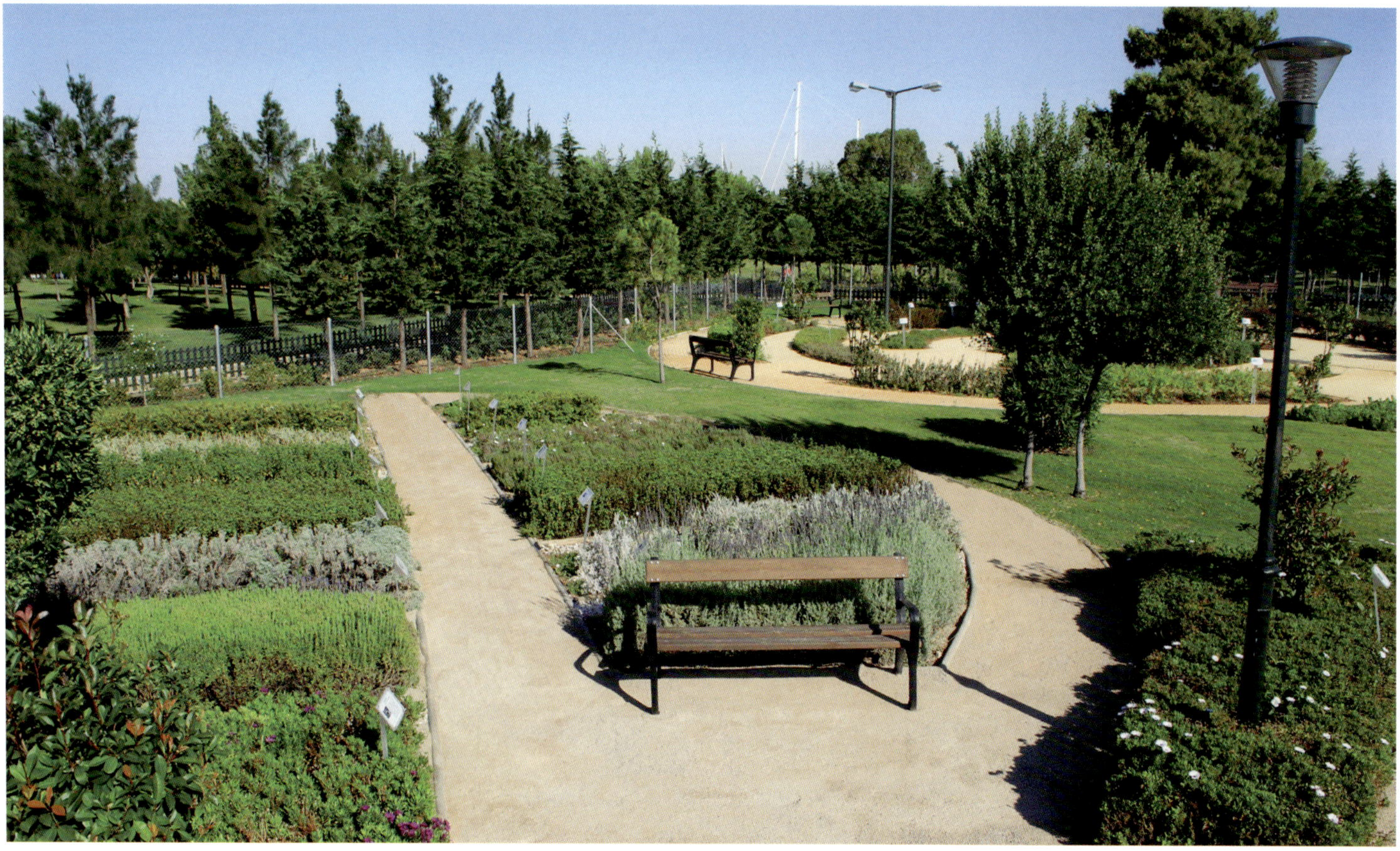

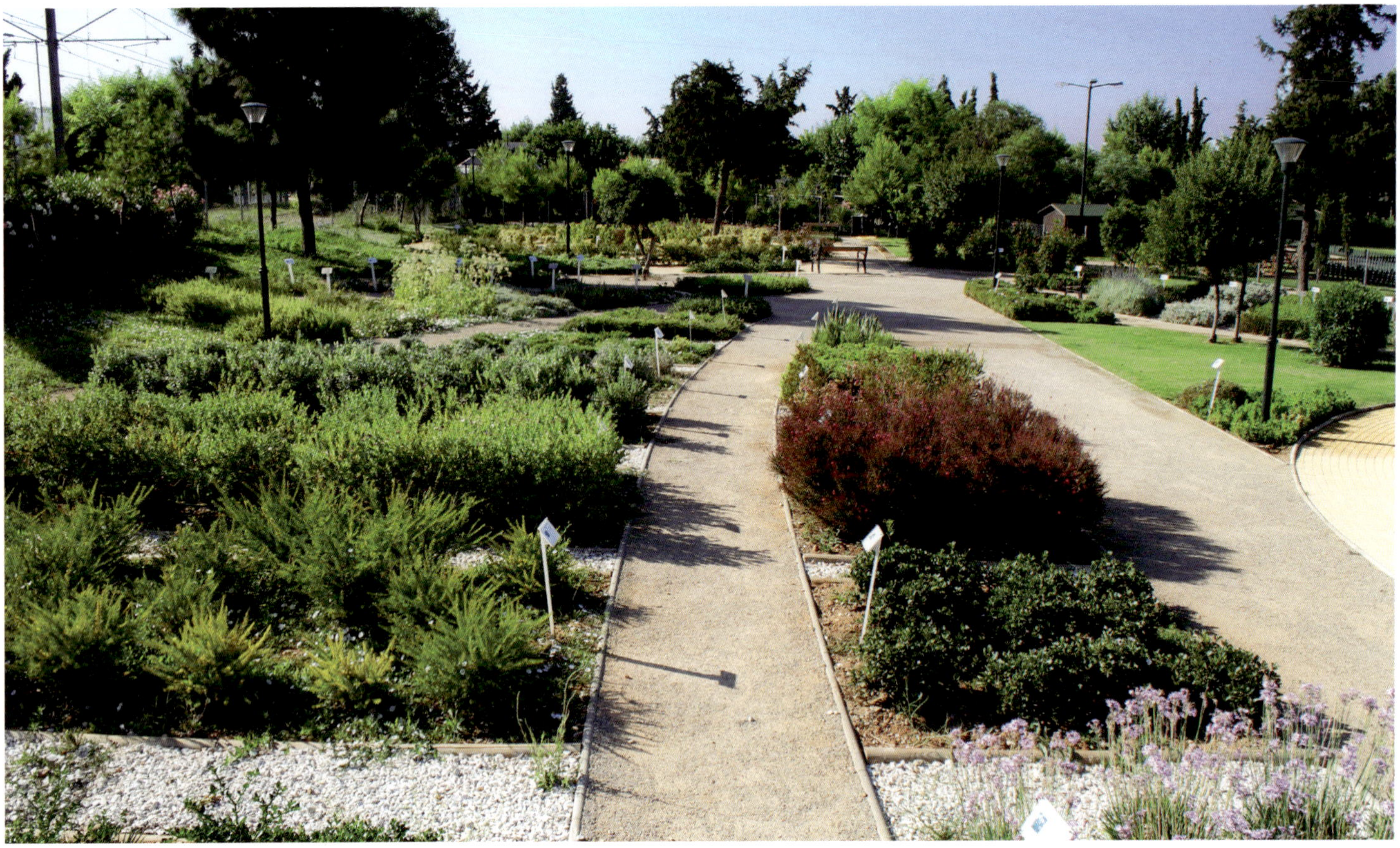

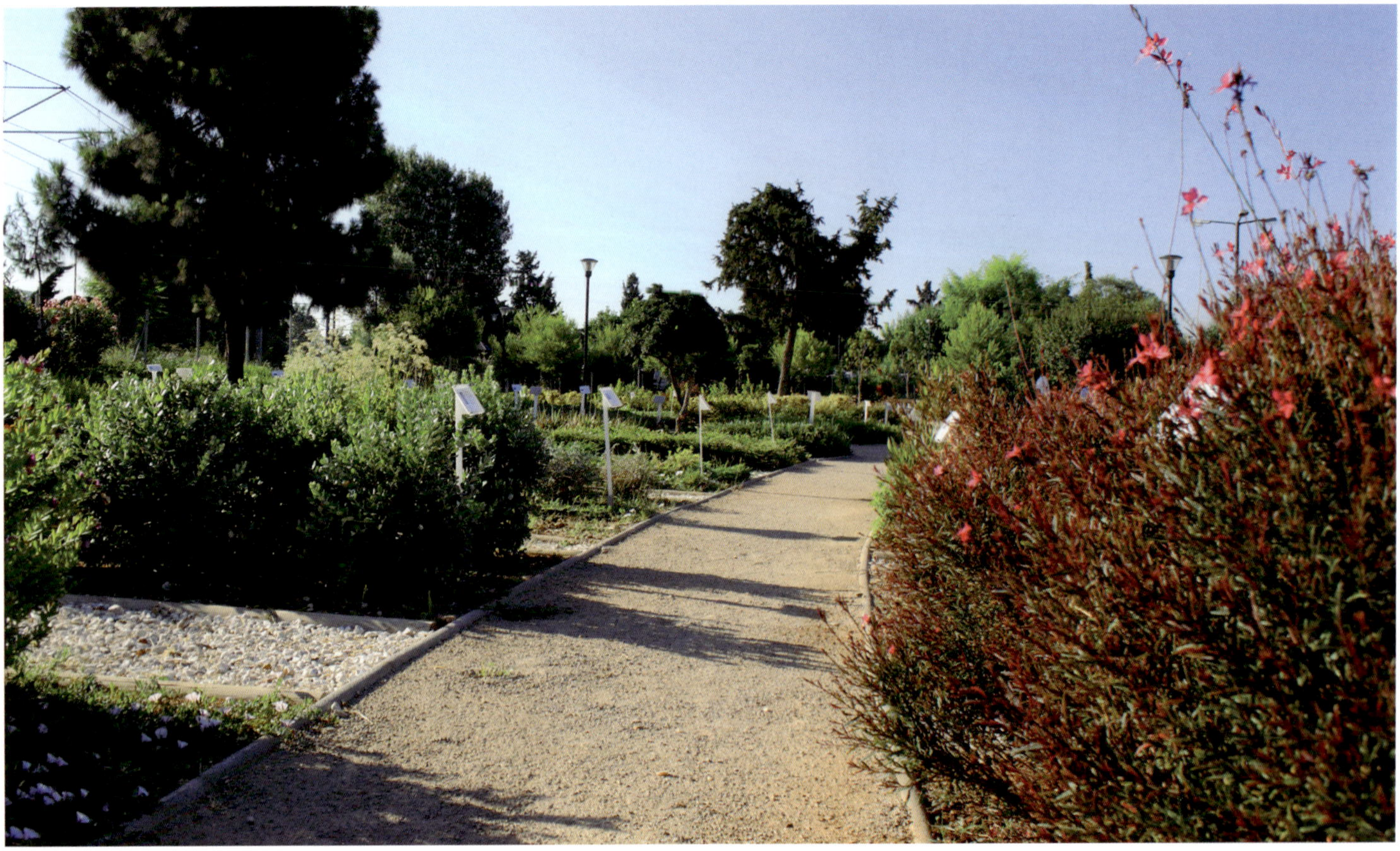

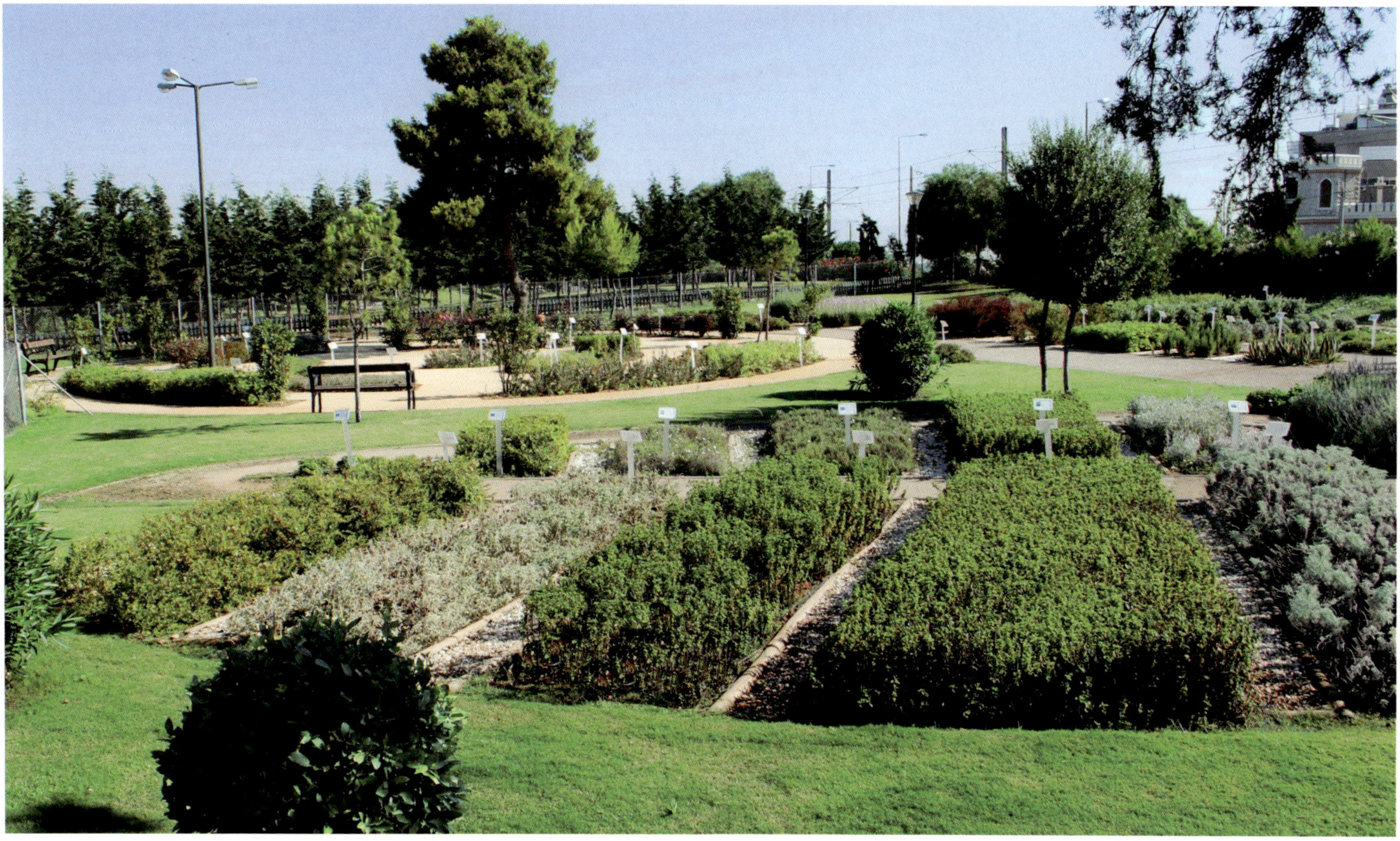

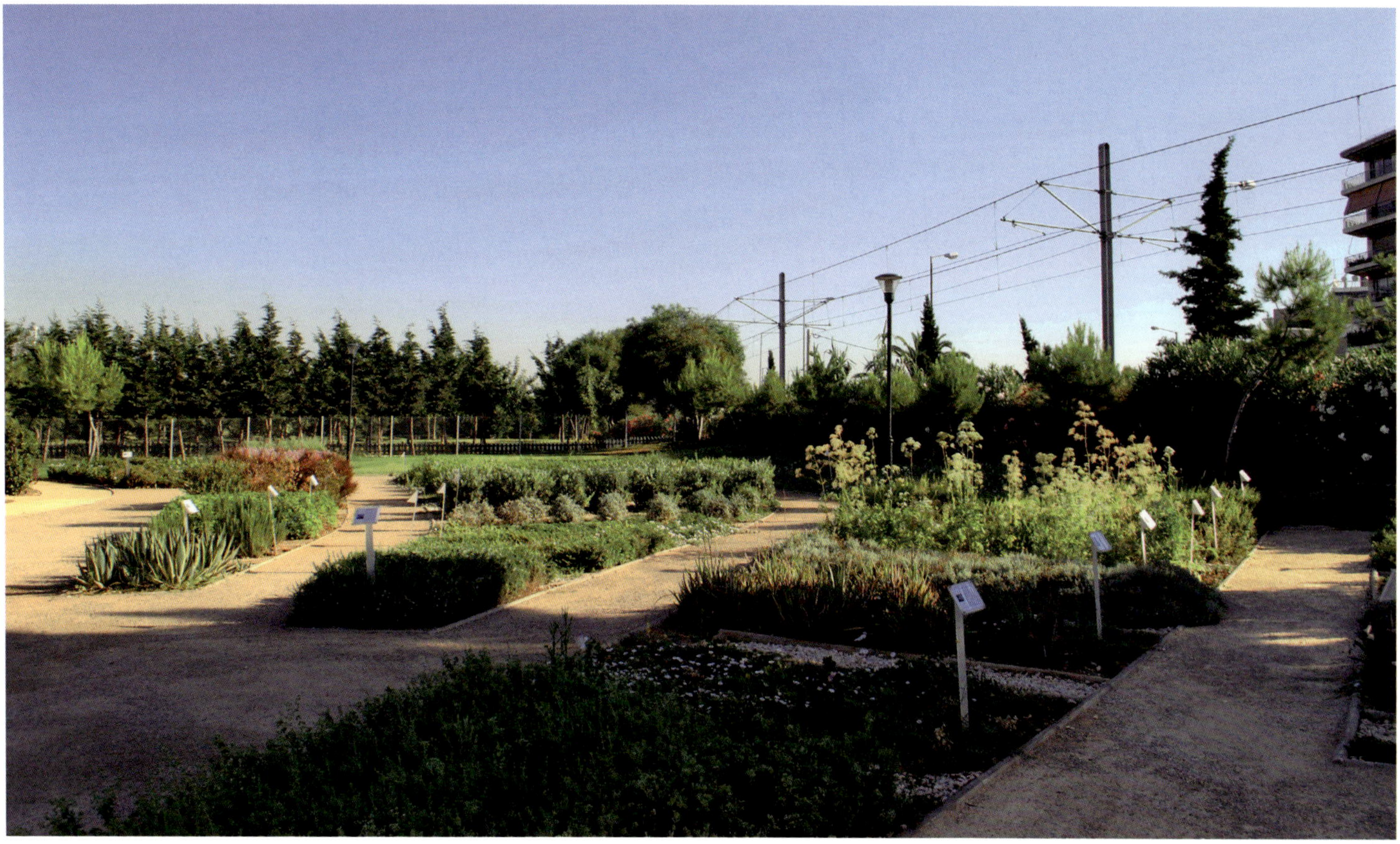

VALENTIEN + VALENTIEN LANDSCAPE ARCHITECTS and Town Planner SRL Molenaar. Architects and Town Planner

www.valentien.de

Tulbeckstraße 39
D-80339 Munich
Germany

The office Valentien+Valentien Landscape Architects was founded in Stuttgart by Christoph and Donata Valentien in 1971. Due to the appointment of Christoph Valentien as professor at the University Munich to the chair of Landscape Architecture and Design in 1980, the office has been moved to Weßling/ Bavaria two years after. Key activities have been consulting and planning for landscape architecture, urban development, and ecological and urban surveys, as well as design and construction planning.

El despacho Valentien + Valentien Landscape Architects fue fundado en Stuttgart por Christoph y Donata Valentien en 1971. Debido al nombramiento de Christoph Valentien como profesor de la Universidad de Munich en la cátedra de Arquitectura y Diseño de Paisajes en 1980, el despacho se trasladó a Weßling / Baviera dos años después. Las principales actividades han sido la consultoría y planificación en arquitectura del paisaje y desarrollo urbano.

NEW TOWN CENTRE FOR THE CITY OF SCIENCE AND TECHNOLOGY „TAIHU TPARK" IN WUXI

The City of Wuxi, China — 2013 — 187.000 m² / 2,012,851 sq ft
© Jan Siefke, Klaus Molenaar

In the city of Wuxi, located about 200 km north west of Shanghai, a national High-Tech development, of an area of 100 km², was established in 1995. Part of this zone forms the new City of Science and Technology, with 100,000 residents and creating 250,000 jobs in the area. The challenge was to create an attractive public city space out of the 6ha, centrally located open area. Critical was the integration of the spaces surrounding the two skyscrapers and the surrounds of the convention and culture centre.

En la ciudad de Wuxi, situada a unos 200 km al noroeste de Shanghai, se estableció en 1995 un área de desarrollo nacional de alta tecnología, de 100 km2. Parte de esta zona conforma la nueva Ciudad de las Ciencias y la Tecnología, de 100.000 habitantes y que crea 250.000 empleos en la zona. El desafío fue crear un atractivo espacio público de 6ha, una zona céntrica y abierta. Crítica fue la integración de los espacios que rodean los dos rascacielos y de los alrededores del centro de cultura y convenciones.

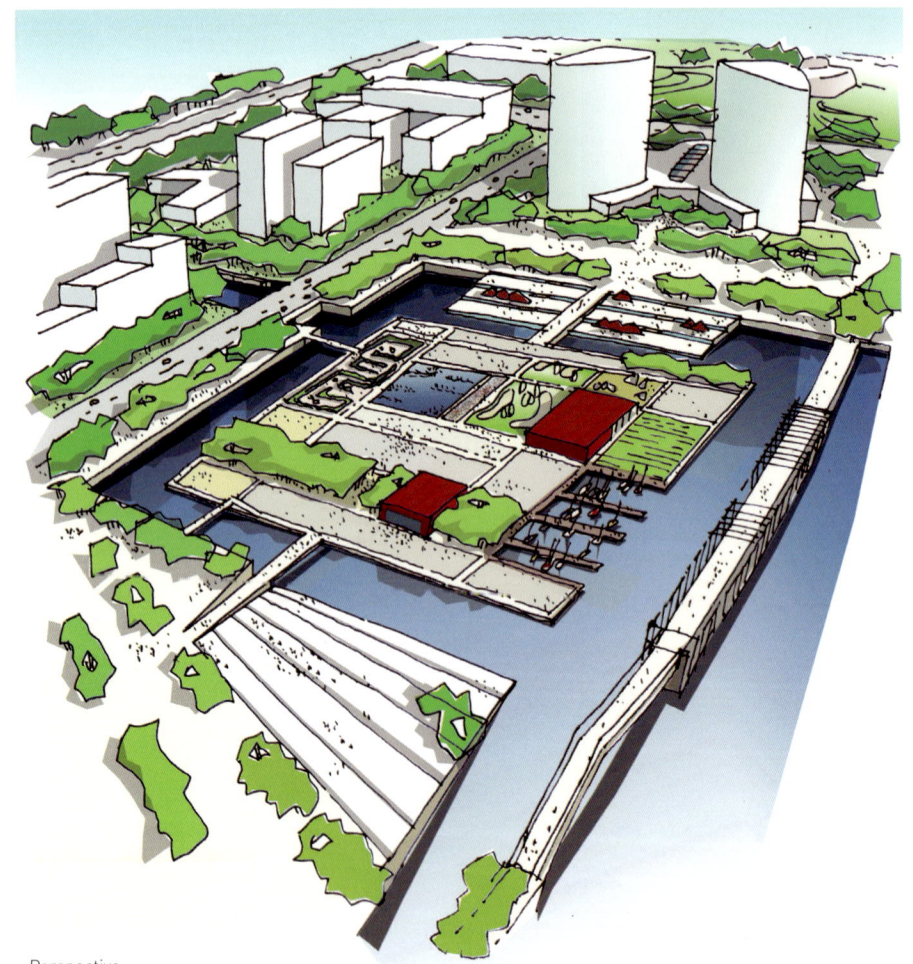

Perspective

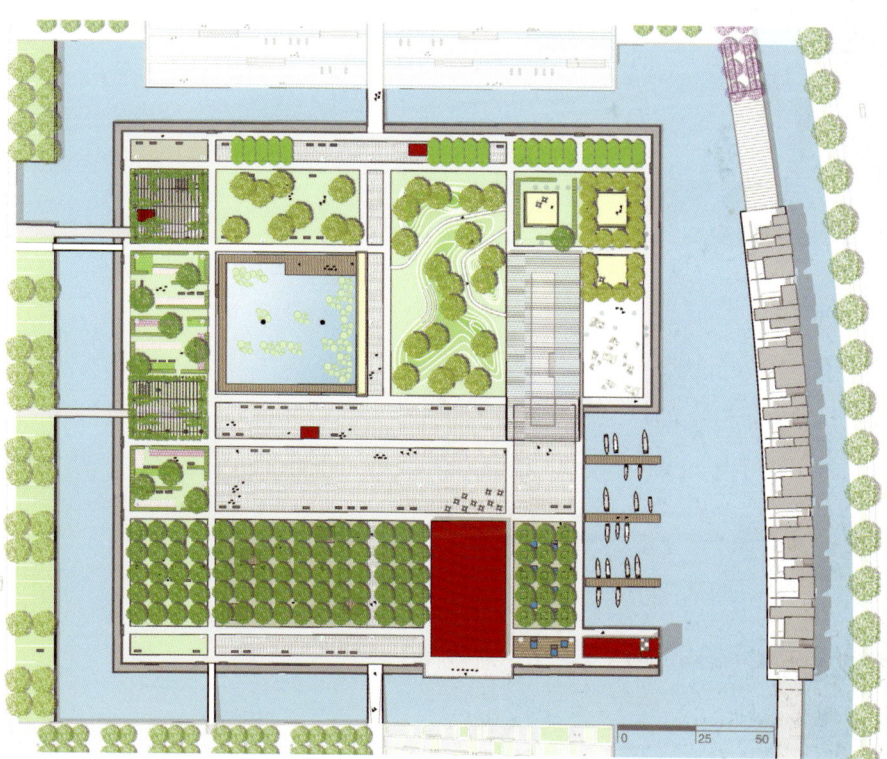

Plan Overview

Plan Wasseplatz

The concept was to encompass numerous streams and channels and in doing so, to create an urban landscape characterized by water, offering both diverse, small scale spaces to rest as well as possibilities for large scale events.

El concepto fue aglutinar numerosos arroyos y canales y así crear un paisaje urbano caracterizado por el agua, ofreciendo a la vez diversos espacios de pequeña escala para el descanso y posibilidades para eventos a gran escala.

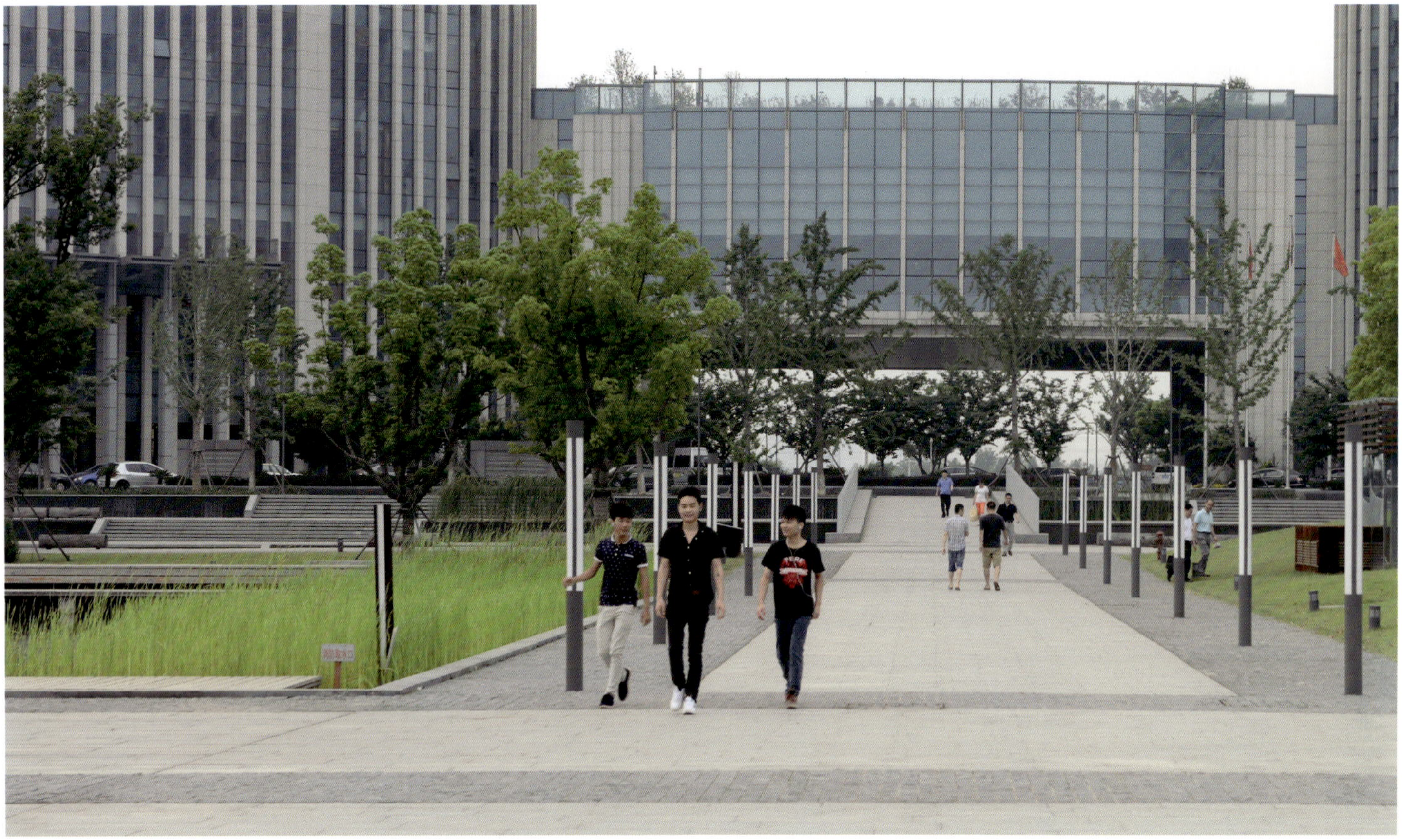

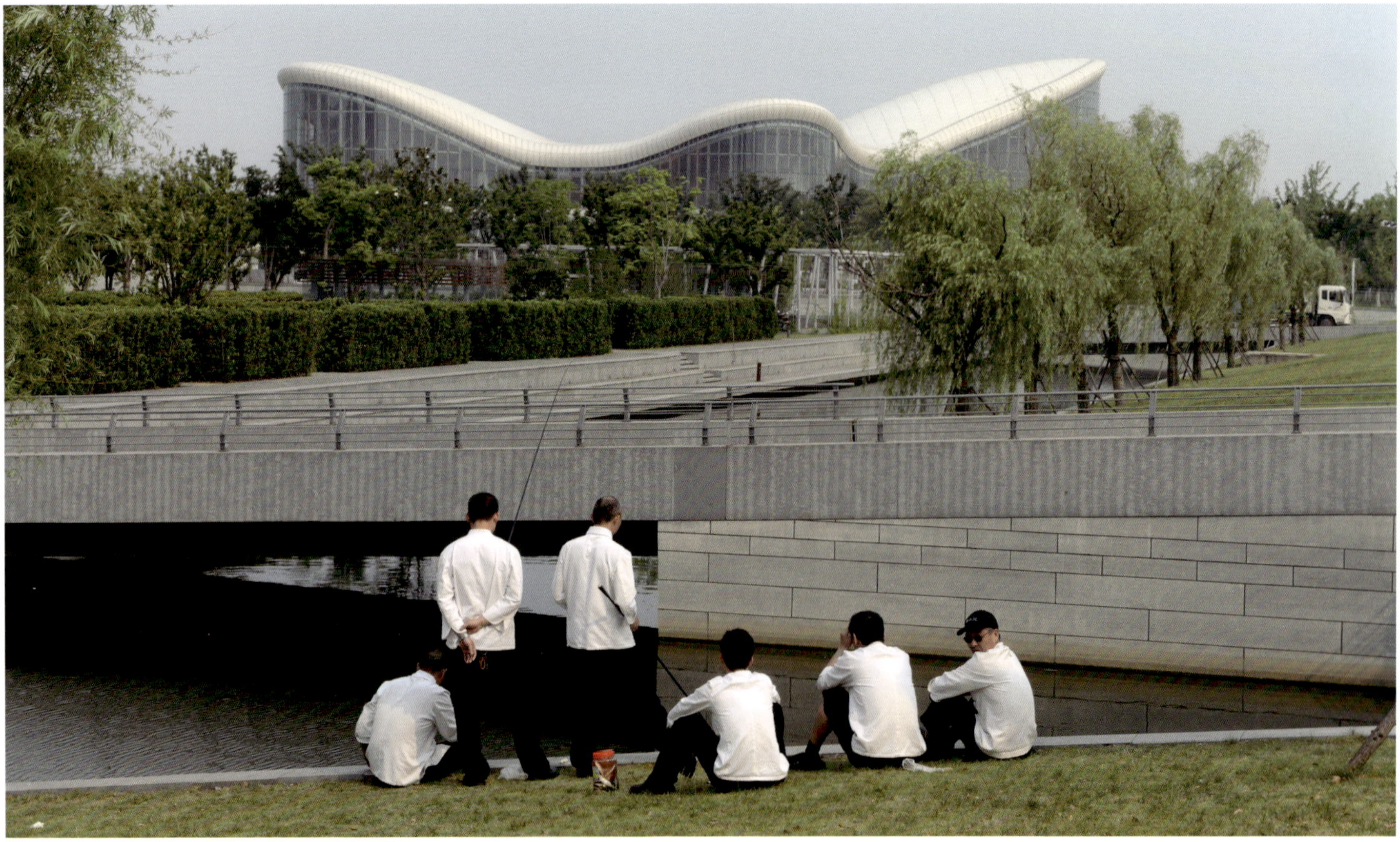

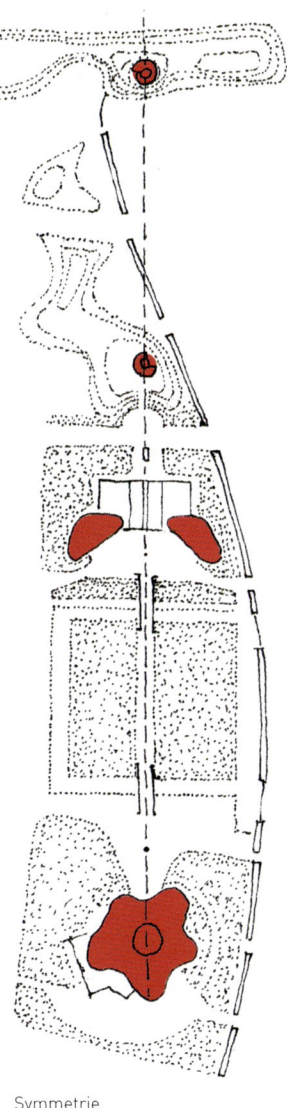

Symmetrie

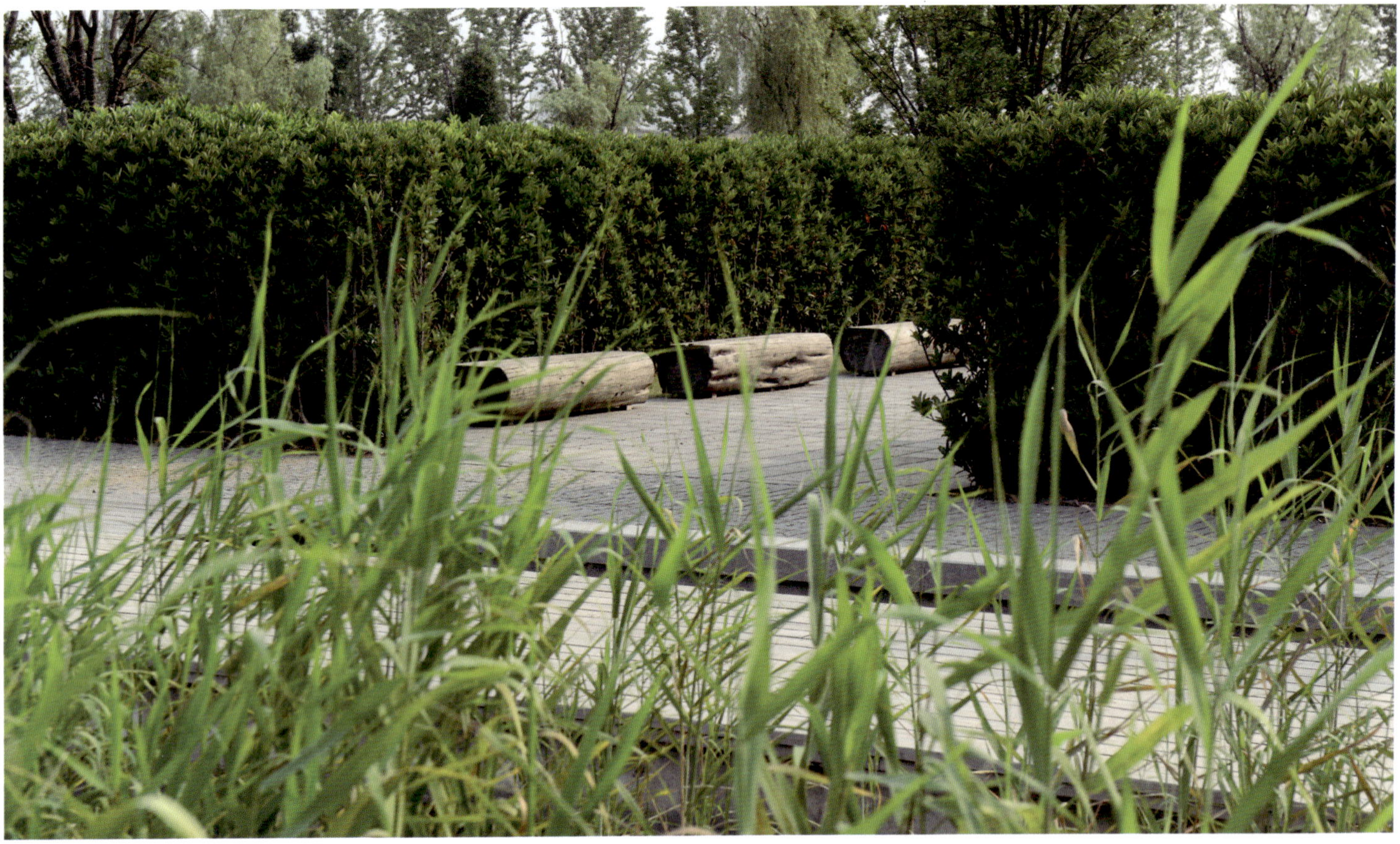

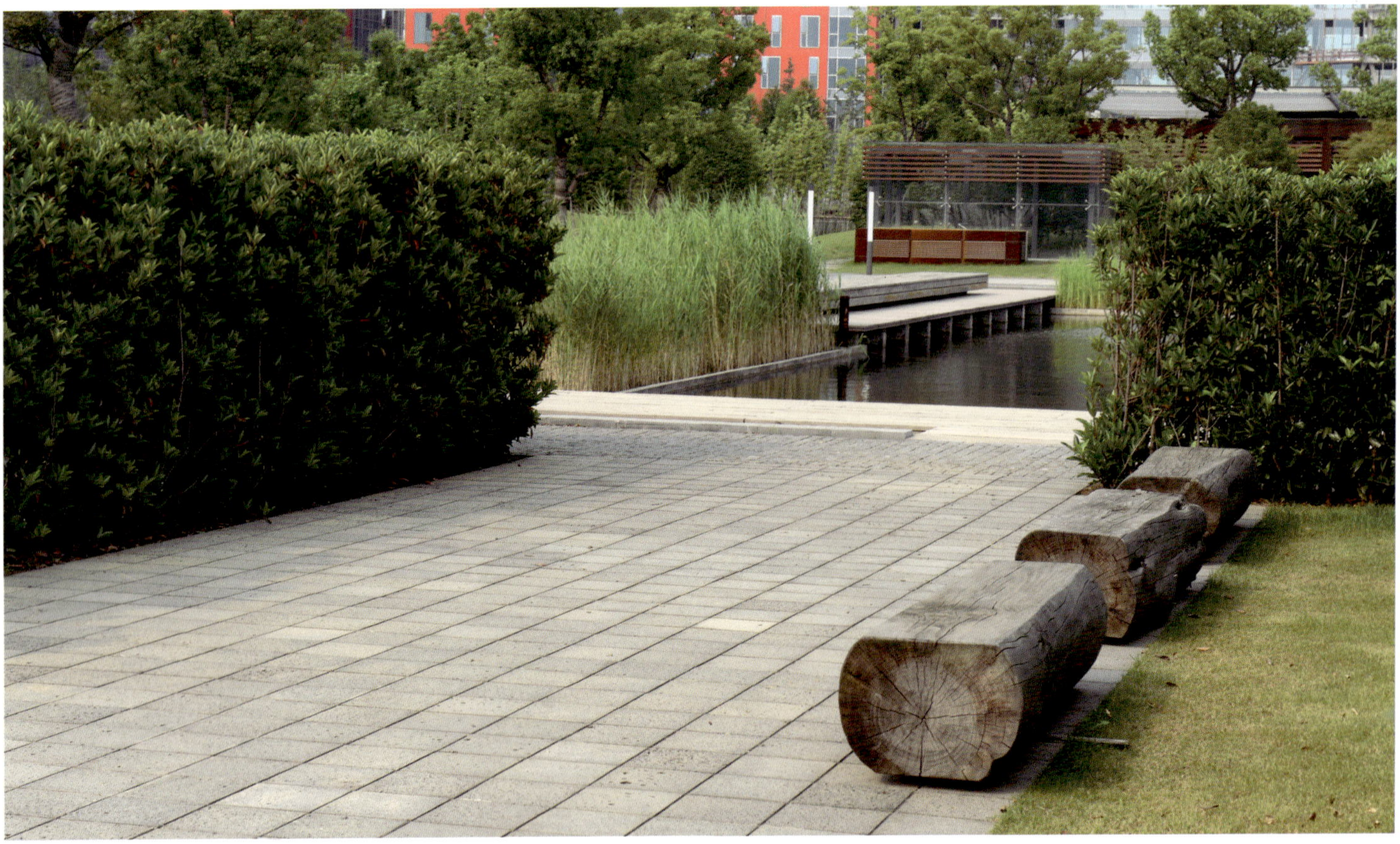

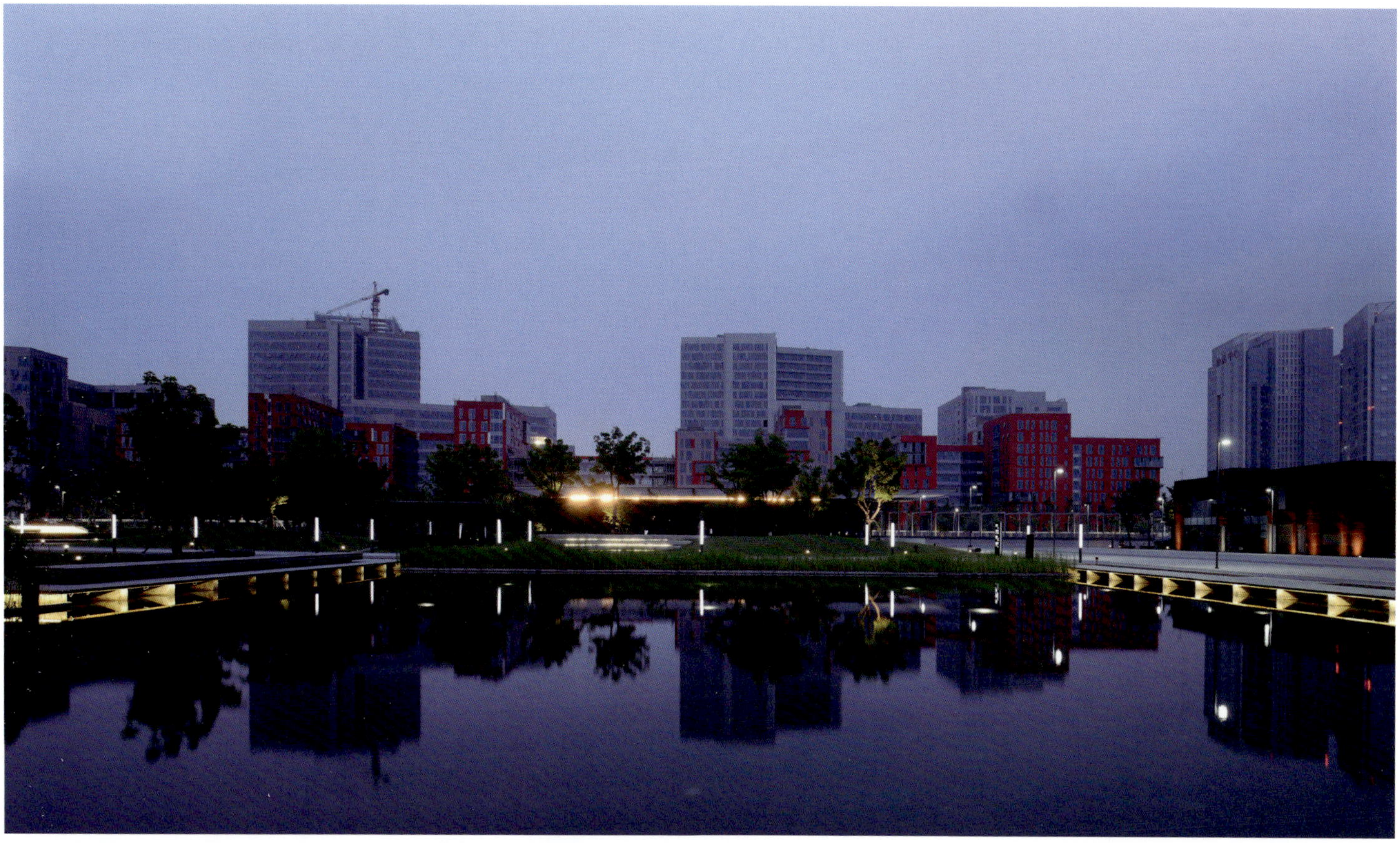

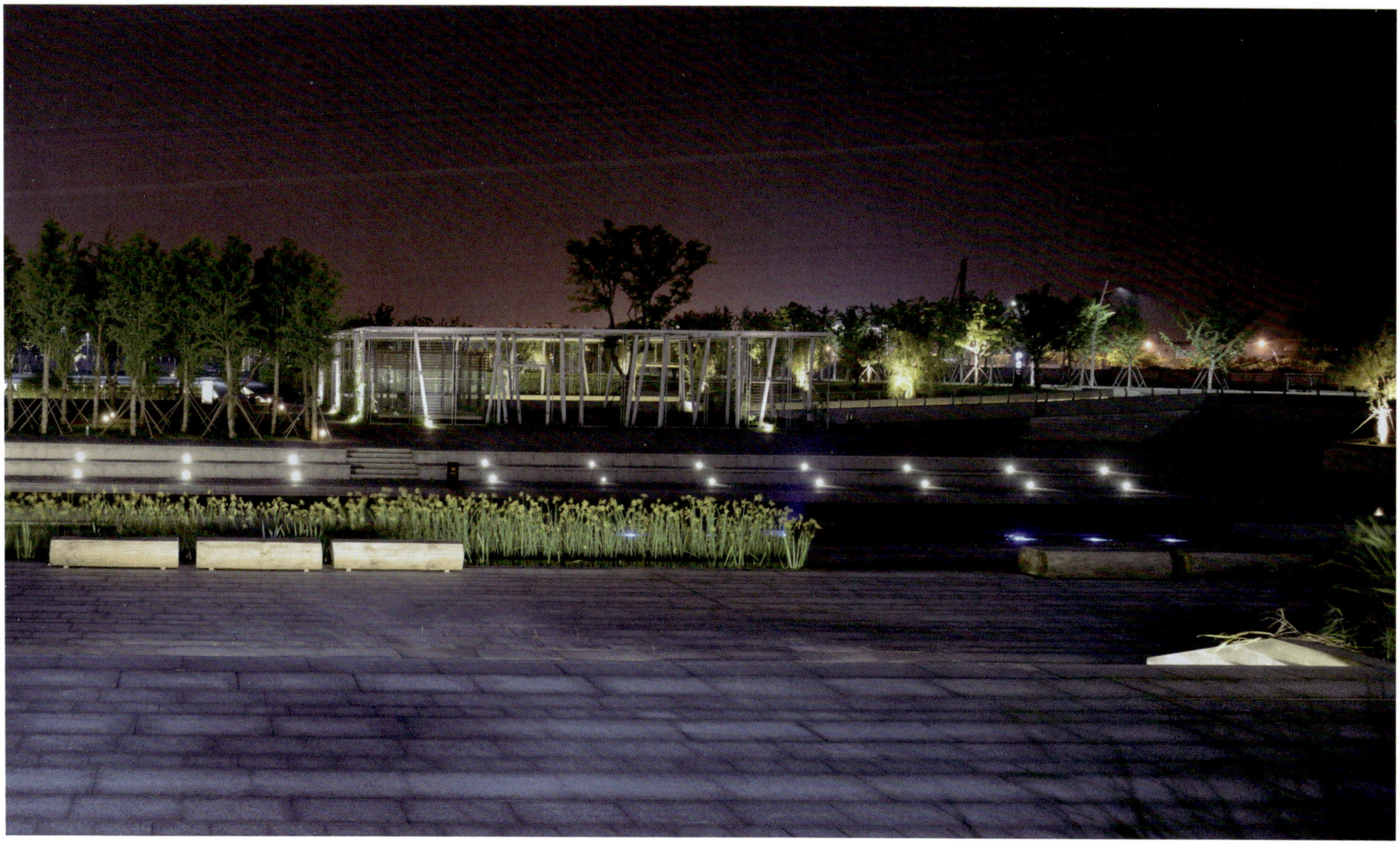

DIRECTORY

3LHD

Riva Split Waterfront
Commemorative Bridge

70°N ARKITEKTUR

Bird Watching Tower
Shelter for Bicycles and Lookout
Resting Area in Torvdalshalsen

AGNES FEDL LANDSCAPE ARCHITECTURE

Manor House K
Riverside Garden
Volcano View Garden
Minimundus, Lake Constance

Landscape Architects: Agnes Fedl, Nikolaus Fedl

ALDAYJOVER ARQUITECTURA Y PAISAJE

Water Park Zaragoza
Aranzadi Park

ANDREA COCHRAN

Walden Studios
Nueva School
Stone Edge Farm

ASPECT STUDIOS

Jacaranda Square
Water Police
Wetland 5
Bondi to Bronte Coast Walk

BIRK NIELSEN

Square in Aalborg
Square in Fredericia

BROISSIN

Green Hills Kindergarten
Partner in Charge: Gerardo Broissin
Project Leader: José Luis García
Design Team: Enrique Guillén, Mauricio Cristóbal, Alfonso Vargas,
Rodrigo Jiménez, David Suárez, Alejandro Rocha, Noé Morales,
Gabriela Maldonado, Adrián Téllez, Pablo Moncada

Irekua Anatani House
Partner in Charge: Gerardo Broissin
Project Leader: Adrián Téllez
Design Team: Mauricio Cristóbal, Alejandro Rocha, Adrián Téllez,
Thelma Blake
Collaborators: Monserrat Jiménez, Oscar Aguilar, Damariz González,
Alejandra Carranza, Alejandro Dávalos, Pablo Morales

DD\M – DI DATO & MENINNO ASSOCIATED ARCHITECTS

Redevelopment of Seghizzi Square and the Burg of the Castle of Gorizia
Architectural Project: DD\M (project leader),
Asstecaa (www.asstecaa.it),
mP Settanta (www.mpsettanta.it), arch. Ravera
Electric Plant Project: p.i. Mariagrazia Wilfinger
Landscape Project: Studio Lai Valenti (www.studiolaivalenti.it)
Collaborators: Valentina Cantarutti, Andrea Bisiach, Michele Marangon

DELTA VORM GROEP

IBM Riekerpolder
Graadt van Roggenweg
Maanplein

DIETMAR FEICHTINGER ARCHITECTES

Footbridge Simone de Beauvoir
Footbridge of the Museum
Valmy Footbridge
Footbridge in Strasbourg

DISSING+WEITLING ARCHITECTURE

Cykelslangen (The Bicycle Snake)
Client: The City of Copenhagen
Engineer: Rambøll
Landscape Architect: Marianne Levinsen Landskab
Light Design: Lightconstructor Cph

DURBACH BLOCK ARCHITECTS

Brickpit Ring
Commonwealth Place

EDAW

Bloomington Central Station
Sheaf Square
Jinji Lake
Banks of the River Hai

GERMÁN DEL SOL

Hot Springs Complex
Remota Hotel

GLASSER UND DAGENBACH

Gardencenter
Moabit Prison Historical Park
Vilnius Villa

HAGER LANDSCHAFTSARCHITEKTUR

Rudolf Bechar Park
New Urban Area Thu Thiem
Limmatwest

JAMES CARPENTER DESIGN ASSOCIATES

Battery Park City Streetscape
Luminous Posts

JENSEN & SKODVIN ARKITEKTKONTOR

Viewing Platform
Juvet Landscape Hotel
Gurdbrandsj Uvet Bridge

JML ARQUITECTURA DEL AGUA

Montjuïc Trade Fair
François Mitterrand Square
Flooded Square

KARRES EN BRANDS LANDSCHAPSARCHITECTEN

De Nieuwe Ooster Cemetery
De Oostervaart Cemetery

KWK PROMES Robert Konieczny

National Museum In Szczecin – Dialogue Centre Przełomy

Authors of the Square and Building: Robert Konieczny, Michał Lisiński
Authors of the Competition Entrance: Robert Konieczny, Dorota Żurek,
Katarzyna Furgalińska
Collaboration: architects Aleksandra Stolecka, Piotr Tokarski,
Adam Radzimski, Joanna Biedna, Magdalena Adamczak
General Contractor: Skanska
Investor: National Museum in Szczecin (Muzeum Narodowe w Szczecinie)

LANDSKAP DESIGN

Staircase to the Church of St. John
Lighting Designer: landskap DESIGN AS
Landscape architect: professor Arne Sælen
In cooperation with In´By AS: Landscape architects Ola Bettum,
Peer Lehn-Pedersen
Client: Bergen municipality
Constructor: Bergen Bydrift AS
Engineer and Construction Manager: Prosjekt Konsult Kvinnherad AS

LIQUIDAMBAR LANDSCAPE ARCHITECTS

Campus BBVA La Moraleja
Collaborators: Liquidambar, IsabelGarcía Puente, Helia García Puente,
Carlos García Puente, Kiko Almazán

Centro de Innovación BBVA Santa Bárbara
Jardín con Palmeras
Isabel García Puente, Carlos García Puente

LUDWIG.SCHOENLE
Ferdinand Ludwig and Daniel Schönle

Plane Tree Cube Nagold
Brocke Engineers (Stuttgart)
Helix Plant Systems (Kornwestheim)
SecOp (Sulzbach-Laufen)

Pratum in Caelo
Studio Umschichten (Stuttgart)
Sergio Sanna (Palermo/Barcelona)
Allmann Sattler Wappner (München)
Carlo Scoccianti (Prato)
Green4Cities (Vienna)

MADE ASSOCIATI ARCHITETTURA E PAESAGGIO

Cendon di Silea

MARIANNE LEVINSEN LANDSKAB APS

Lindevangs Park
Client: Frederiksberg Council, Frederiksberg Water Supplier
Engineer: Niras A/S

Copenhagen Business School "Kilen"
Client: Copenhagen Business School
Lead Consultant: Lundgaard/Tranberg A/S

Navitas Harbour Front
Client: INCUBA, Engineering and Technical Engineering School
Lead Consultant: Kjær & Richter, CCO

Courtyard and surrounding area of Tietgen Dormitory
Client: Tietgen Fonden
Lead Consultant: Lundgaard/Tranberg A/S

Kokkedal West Care Centre
Client: Hørsholm Council, DAB
Lead Consultant: Lundgaard/Tranberg A/S

MCGREGOR COXALL

Ballast Point Park
Director in Charge: Philip Coxall
Team: Larissa Blanch, Christian Borchert, Adrian McGregor, Jack Qian

Lingang Bird Airport
Director in Charge: Adrian McGregor
Project Manager: Jack Qian
WSUD Leader: David Knights
Project Production: Ya You
Team: Hong Lee, Yang Li, Don Do, Ann Deng, Kemi Amede, Sibilla Macens

The Levee. High Street Maitland
Director in Charge: Adrian McGregor
Team: Maria Sabria, Michael Cowdy, Dave Knights, Ann Deng,
Christian Borchert, Matthew Ritson, Jack Qian

Parramatta City River Strategy
Director in Charge: Adrian McGregor
Project Manager: Michael Cowdy
Team: Dave Knights, Nicola Balch, Jack Qian

MICHAEL SINGER

West Palm Beach Wharfs
Garden Sculpture
Garden of the Seasons
Commemorative Garden

MOSBACH PAYSAGISTES

Louvre Lens Museum Park
Client: Region Nord Pas de Calais
Landscaper Mosbach Paysagistes: Catherine Mosbach, Atelier 122,
Delphine Elie, Jessica Gramcko, Marion Dervout, Etienne Haller,
Jennifer Mui, Solène Leray, Pauline Rabin Le Gall, Marie Ross,
Jean François Seage, Eiko Tomura
Team Head: Architect Sanaa, Sejima Kazuyo + Ryue Nishizawa.
Yumiko Yamada, Yoshitaka Tanase, Louis-Antoine Grégo,
Rikiya Yamamoto, Kohji Yoshida, Lucy Styles, Erika Hidaka,
Nobuhiro Kitazawa, Bob Van den Brande, Arrate Arizaga Villalba,
Guillaume Choplain, Osamu Kato, Naoto Noguchi, Shohei Yoshida,
Takashige Yamashita, Takashi Suo, Ichio Matsuzawa, Andreas Krawczyk

MVRDV

Anyang Peak
Leiria Pedestrian Bridges

NIEBERG ARCHITECT
atelieraxelnieberg

Landscape Architecture for a Residential Building in Brunswick
Collaborators: Friedrich, Gardening firm, Brunswick

Landscape Architecture for a Residential Building in Celle
Collaborators: Gehlhaar, Nursery Garden, Hanover

OKRA LANDSCAPE ARCHITECTS

Afrikaanderplein
Melaan
Quay and Bridges on the River Ijssel
Domplein

OSLUND AND ASSOCIATES

Gold Medal Park
Harley Davidson Museum
General Mills Corporation
I-35W Street Anthony Falls Bridge
Laboratory Science Building at the University of Minnesota

ØSTENGEN & BERGO LANDSCAPE ARCHITECTS

Dalsnibba Skywalk
Landscape Architect: Østengen & Bergo Landscape Architects
Client: Geiranger skysslag
Engineer and Construction Manager: ART arkitekter og ingeniører
Contractor: Eide og Frilund AS, Christie & Opsahl AS, Sherpas from Nepal

Skjervet
Client: Statens Vegvesen, Norwegian Public Roads Administration/
National Tourist Routes
Architect (Restroom Building): Fortunen Architects http://fortunen.no/
Contractor: Aakerholt, Steen & Lund

RAMSEYER WAISMAN ARQUITECTOS – RWA

Gran Reserva de Sotogrande
Residencial Ribera del Marlín
Design Team: Sixto Fernández, Susana Milla, Inés Ramseyer,
Angela Rodríguez, Cristina Rodríguez, Inma Ruiz, Cris Sarráchaga,
Catalina Cortiguera
Work Team: J. A. Andrade, Fco. Lamparero, Inma Ruiz, Adolfo Waisman
Structure: Soluciones Técnicas Arq. Ingeniería
Installations: JG Ingenieros
Quality Control: SGS - Intemac

REHWALDT LANDSCHAFTSARCHITEKTEN

Zoological Garden Dresden – Giraffe Enclosure
Bavarian Garden Exhibition Nature in Waldkirchen
ULAP Park
Wuppertal Zoological Garden

RIJNBOUTT

Shell Terrain
Naarden Walls
Die Wielden
Mahler 4

ROMERA Y RUIZ ARQUITECTOS

Maritime Park
Architects: Pedro Romera García and Ángela Ruiz Martínez
Client: Council of Las Palmas de Gran Canaria
Collaborators: Rocío Acosta Martínez, Carlota Ardanaz Petit,
Yudit Barreto Martín, Paula Cabrera Fry, José M. López Cabrera,
Carlos Marrero Macías, Rocío Narbona Flores, Tamara Narbona Flores,
Paula de La Rosa Rodríguez and Rosalba Santana González
Technical Architect: Edward Lynch
Structure: Ventura and Machado Arquitectos
Engineer: Constantino J. Gonzalvo Ortiz
Building Company: Hermanos García Álamo S.L.

SASAKI

Chicago Riverwalk, Phases 2 and 3
Sasaki, Ross Barney Architects, CDOT, 2FM,
Alfred Benesch & Company, Jacobs – Ryan

The Lawn on D
Sasaki, Massachusetts Convention Center Authority (MCCA), Utile, Inc.,
I.W. Harding Construction Co., Inc., Tetra Tech, Cosentini Associates,
Zaragunda, Howeler + Yoon Architecture

Sacred Heart University Campus Landscapes
Sasaki, Sacred Heart University, Simpson Gumpertz & Heger,
Lam Partners Inc., Tillotson Design Associates,
Horton Lees Brogden Lighting Design, R.J. Van Seters Co. Ltd.,
Rist-Frost-Shumway Engineering, LeMessurier, Cosentini Associates,
Schirmer Engineering Corporation, Acoustic Dimensions, Acentech,
Colburn and Guyette

STUDIO KAPPO

Hidrobaza Bathing Complex
Design Team: Katja Sosic, Andrea Puorro, Marko Sosic, Sanja Bibulic,
Dunja Dukic, Andreja Bencic, Ivana Smoljan - Antolović
Civil Engineering: I.F. Projekt
Lightning: San Polo

Hotel Lone Landscape Design
Design Team: Katja Sosic, Andrea Puorro, Marko Sosic, Lido Sosic
Hotel Lone Architects: 3LHD

Tito's Memorial Park
Design Team: Katja Sosic, Andrea Puorro, Marko Sosic, Sanja Bibulic

Hotel Monte Mulini Entrance Fountain
Design Team: Katja Sosic, Andrea Puorro, Marko Sosic, Lido Sosic
Mechanical Engineering: Macro 5

TATJANA VON GRIESHEIM, LANDSCAPE ARCHITECT

Hotel «Castell Son Claret»
House «Montenegro»
Finca «Son Bernadi»
Finca Deia

UTOPIA LANDSCAPES

Pigon Square Regeneration
Landscape Architect: 'Utopia Landscapes' A. Tserpelis & Co E.E.
Topographical Engineering: Christos Patalas, Nikolaos Legakis
Electrological Engineering: Vasileios Minakakis
Structural and Civil Engineering: George Skouras
Bioclimatic Consultant: Michalis Kavousanakis
Lighting Design: Ioanna Dimantoni
General Contractor: Technogea Co.
Pergola Fabricator: Cospico S.A.
Lighting Supplier: Gravani Bros S.A.
Plants Supplier: Alexiou Plants Ltd

The Botanical Garden in Park Floisvos
Landscape Architect: 'Utopia Landscapes' A. Tserpelis & Co E.E.
Topographical Engineering: Christos Galatsiatos
Structural Engineering: Odos Ate.
Landscape Contractor: Antonis Eliopoulos
Lighting Supplier: E. Gavalas & Co E.E
Plants Supplier: Alexiou Plants Ltd

VALENTIEN + VALENTIEN LANDSCAPE ARCHITECTS

**New Town Centre for the City of Science and Technology
„Taihu TPark" in Wuxi**
Designer: Valentien + Valentien Landscape Architects and
Town Planner SRL, Molenaar. Architects and Town Planner
Technical Implementation: Shanghai Huabang Corporation for Town
Planning and Design Coordination China / Germany: Yiju Ding

E–F

History: America

Library of Congress Classification
2011

LIBRARY OF CONGRESS

Prepared by the Policy and Standards Division

LIBRARY OF CONGRESS
Cataloging Distribution Service
Washington, D.C.

This edition cumulates all additions and changes to Classes E-F through Weekly List
2010/45, dated November 10, 2010. Additions and changes made subsequent to that date
are published in weekly lists posted on the World Wide Web at

<http://www.loc.gov/aba/cataloging/classification/weeklylists/>

and are also available in Classification Web, the online Web-based edition of the Library of
Congress Classification.

Library of Congress Cataloging-in-Publication Data

Library of Congress.
 Library of Congress classification. E-F. History, American (Western Hemisphere) / prepared
by the Policy and Standards Division. -- 2011 edition.
      pages cm
  "This edition cumulates all additions and changes to Classes E-F through Weekly list
2010/45, dated November 10, 2010. Additions and changes made subsequent to that date
are published in weekly lists posted on the World Wide Web ... and are also available in *Clas-
sification Web*, the online Web-based edition of the Library of Congress classification"--T.p.
verso.
 Includes index.
 ISBN 978-0-8444-9522-4
 1. Classification, Library of Congress. 2. Classification--Books--History. 3. Classification-
-Books--America. I. Library of Congress. Policy and Standards Division. II. Title. III. Title:
History, American (Western Hemisphere).
   Z696.U5E3 2011   025.4'697--dc22   2010052342

For sale by the Library of Congress Cataloging Distribution Service,
101 Independence Avenue, S.E., Washington, DC 20541-4912.
Product catalog available on the Web at **www.loc.gov/cds.**

PREFACE

The schedule for classes E-F, *History: America*, was the first Library of Congress Classification schedule to be published. The first edition was published in 1901, the second in 1913, and the third in 1958. The latter edition was reprinted in 1965 with supplementary pages of additions and changes to January 1965. Editions published in 1995, 2000, and 2007 cumulated additions and changes made during the periods 1965-1995, 1995-2000, and 2000-2007 respectively. This 2011 edition cumulates changes made since the publication of the 2007 edition.

Classification numbers or spans of numbers that appear in parentheses are formerly valid numbers that are now obsolete. Numbers or spans that appear in angle brackets are optional numbers that have never been used at the Library of Congress but are provided for other libraries that wish to use them. In most cases, a parenthesized or angle-bracketed number is accompanied by a "see" reference directing the user to the actual number that the Library of Congress currently uses, or a note explaining Library of Congress practice.

Access to the online version of the full Library of Congress Classification is available on the World Wide Web by subscription to *Classification Web*. Details about ordering and pricing may be obtained from the Cataloging Distribution Service at

<http://www.loc.gov/cds/>

New or revised numbers and captions are added to the L.C. Classification schedules as a result of development proposals made by the cataloging staff of the Library of Congress and cooperating institutions. Upon approval of these proposals by the weekly editorial meeting of the Policy and Standards Division, new classification records are created or existing records are revised in the master classification database. Weekly lists of newly approved or revised classification numbers and captions are posted on the World Wide Web at

<http://www.loc.gov/aba/cataloging/classification/weeklylists/>

Janis Young, senior subject cataloging policy specialist in the Policy and Standards Division, is responsible for coordinating the overall intellectual and editorial content of classes E and F. Kent Griffiths, assistant editor of classification schedules, is responsible for creating new classification records, maintaining the master database, and creating index terms for the captions.

Barbara B. Tillett, Chief
Policy and Standards Division

January 2011

OUTLINE

America **E11-143**

United States **E151-909**

United States Local History **F1-975**

British America **F1001-1145.2**

French America **F1170**

Latin America. Spanish America **F1201-3799**

TABLES

INDEX

E11-143	America
E11-29	General
E29	Elements in the population
E31-49.2	North America
E51-73	Pre-Columbian America. The Indians
E75-99	Indians of North America
E81-83	Indian wars
E99	Indian tribes and cultures
E101-135	Discovery of America and early explorations
E103-110	Pre-Columbian period
E111-120	Columbus
E121-135	Post-Columbian period. El Dorado
E141-143	Descriptive accounts of America. Earliest to 1810
E151-889	United States
E151-169.12	General
E171-183.9	History
E171-180	General
E173	Sources and documents
E175-175.7	Historiography
E176-176.8	Biography
E179.5	Historical geography
E181	Military history
E182	Naval history
E183-183.3	Political history
E183.7-183.9	Diplomatic history. Foreign and general relations.
E183.8	Relations with individual countries
E184-185.98	Elements in the population
E184.5-185.98	Afro-Americans
E185.2-185.89	Status and development since emancipation
E185.96-185.98	Biography. Genealogy
E186-199	Colonial history (1607-1775)
E186-189	General
E191-199	By period
E191	1607-1689
E195-199	1689-1775
E196	King William's War, 1689-1697
E197	Queen Anne's War, 1702-1713
E198	King George's War, 1744-1748
E199	French and Indian War, 1755-1763
E201-298	The Revolution, 1775-1783
E300-453	Revolution to the Civil War, 1775/1783-1861
E300-302.6	General
E302	Collected works of American statesmen

OUTLINE

United States
 Revolution to the Civil War, 1775/1783-1861
  General - Continued

E302.1	Political history
E302.5-302.6	Biography (Late eighteenth century)
E303-440.5	By period
E303-309	1775-1789. The Confederation, 1783-1789
E310-337	1789-1809. Constitutional period
E310.7	Diplomatic history. Foreign and general relations
E311-320	Washington's administrations, 1789-1797
E321-330	John Adams' administration, 1797-1801
E323	Troubles with France, 1796-1800
E331-337	Jefferson's administrations, 1801-1809
E333	Purchase of Louisiana, 1803
E335	War with Tripoli, 1801-1805
E336-336.5	Neutral trade and its restrictions, 1800-1810
E337.5	Nineteenth century (General)
E337.8-400	Early nineteenth century, 1801/1809-1845
E337.8-340	General
E337.8	Collected works of American statesmen
E339-340	Biography
E341-370	Madison's administrations, 1809-1817
E351.5-364.9	War of 1812
E365	War with Algeria, 1815
E371-375	Monroe's administrations, 1817-1825
E373	Missouri Compromise, 1820
E374	Diplomatic history. Foreign relations
E376-380	John Quincy Adams' administration, 1825-1829
E381-385	Jackson's administrations, 1829-1837
E384.3	Nullification
E386-390	Van Buren's administration, 1837-1841
E391-392	William H. Harrison's administration, March 4-April 4, 1841
E396-400	Tyler's administration, April 4, 1841-1845
E398	Northeastern boundary disputes, 1783-1845
E401-415.2	Mexican War, 1846-1848
E408	Mexican cessions of 1848
E415.6-440.5	Middle nineteenth century, 1845/1848-1861
E415.6-415.9	General
E415.6	Collected works of American statesmen
E415.8-415.9	Biography
E416-420	Polk's administration, 1845-1849

United States
  Revolution to the Civil War, 1775/1783-1861
    By period
      Middle nineteenth century, 1845/1848-1861 - Continued
E421-423   Taylor's administration, 1849-July 9, 1850
E423   Slavery question, 1849-1853
E426-430   Fillmore's administration, July 9, 1850-1853
E431-435   Pierce's administration, 1853-1857
E433   Slavery question, 1853-1857
E436-440.5   Buchanan's administration, 1857-1861
E438   Slavery question, 1857-1861
E440.5   State of the country, November 1860-
                    March 4, 1861
E441-453   Slavery in the United States.   Antislavery
                  movements
E456-655   Civil War period, 1861-1865
E456-459   Lincoln's administrations, 1861-April 15, 1865
E461-655   The Civil War, 1861-1865
E482-489   Confederate States of America
E491-586   Armies.   Troops
E591-600   Naval history
E660-738   Late nineteenth century, 1865-1900
E660-664   General
E660   Collected works of American statesmen
E661.7   Diplomatic history.   Foreign and general
                  relations
E663-664   Biography
E666-670   Johnson's administration, April 15, 1865-1869
E668   Reconstruction, 1865-1877
E669   Purchase of Alaska, 1867
E671-680   Grant's administrations, 1869-1877
E681-685   Hayes' administration, 1877-1881
E686-687.9   Garfield's administration, March 4-September
                  19, 1881
E691-695   Arthur's administration, September 19, 1881-1885
E696-700   Cleveland's first administration, 1885-1889
E701-705   Benjamin Harrison's administration, 1889-1893
E706-710   Cleveland's second administration, 1893-1897
E711-738   McKinley's first administration, 1897-1901
E713   Annexation in 1898 of Hawaii, the Philippines,
                  and Puerto Rico
E714-735   War of 1898 (Spanish-American War)

OUTLINE

United States - Continued

E740-837.7	Twentieth century
E740-749	General
E740.5	Sources and documents
E742.5	Collected works of American statesmen
E743-743.5	Political history
E743.5	Un-American activities
E744-744.5	Diplomatic history. Foreign and general relations
E745	Military history
E746	Naval history
E747-748	Biography
E751	McKinley's second administration, March 4-September 14, 1901
E756-760	Theodore Roosevelt's administrations, September 14, 1901-1909
E761-765	Taft's administration, 1909-1913
E766-783	Wilson's administrations, 1913-1921
E768	Purchase of Danish West Indies (Virgin Islands), 1917
E780	Internal history during World War I
E784-805	1919-1933. Harding-Coolidge-Hoover era. "The twenties"
E785-786	Harding's administration, 1921-August 2, 1923
E791-796	Coolidge's administration, August 2, 1923-1929
E801-805	Hoover's administration, 1919-1933
E806-812	Franklin Delano Roosevelt's administrations, 1933-April 12, 1945
E813-816	Truman's administrations, April 12, 1945-1953
E835-837.7	Eisenhower's administrations, 1953-1961
E838-889	Later twentieth century, 1961-2000
E838-840.8	General
E838.3	Sources and documents
E839.5-839.8	Political history
E839.8	Un-American activities
E840-840.2	Diplomatic history. Foreign and general relations
E840.6-840.8	Biography (General)
E841-843	Kennedy's administration, 1961-November 22, 1963
E842.9	Assassination, funeral, memorial services, etc.
E846-851	Johnson's administrations, November 22, 1963-1969
E855-861	Nixon's administrations, 1969-August 9, 1974
E860-861	Watergate Affair. Resignation

United States
   Later twentieth century, 1961-2000 - Continued
E865-868   Ford's administration, August 9, 1974-1977
E872-875   Carter's administration, 1977-1981
E876-880   Reagan's administrations, 1981-1989
E877.3   Assassination attempt
E881-884   George H.W. Bush's administration, 1989-1993
E885-889   Clinton's administrations, 1993-2001
E895-904   Twenty-first century
E902-906   George W. Bush's administrations, 2001-2009
E907-909   Barack Obama's administration, 2009-

F1-975   United States local history
F1-15   New England
F16-30   Maine
F31-45   New Hampshire
F46-60   Vermont
F61-75   Massachusetts
F76-90   Rhode Island
F91-105   Connecticut
F106   Atlantic coast.   Middle Atlantic States
F116-130   New York
F131-145   New Jersey
F146-160   Pennsylvania
F161-175   Delaware
F176-190   Maryland
F191-205   District of Columbia.   Washington
F206-220   The South.   South Atlantic States
F221-235   Virginia
F236-250   West Virginia
F251-265   North Carolina
F266-280   South Carolina
F281-295   Georgia
F296-301   Gulf States.   West Florida
F306-320   Florida
F321-335   Alabama
F336-350   Mississippi
F350.5-355   Mississippi River and Valley.   Middle West
F366-380   Louisiana
F381-395   Texas
F396   Old Southwest.   Lower Mississippi Valley
F406-420   Arkansas
F431-445   Tennessee

OUTLINE

United States local history
Old Southwest.   Lower Mississippi Valley - Continued

F446-460	Kentucky
F461-475	Missouri
F476-485	Old Northwest. Northwest Territory
F486-500	Ohio
F516-520	Ohio River and Valley
F521-535	Indiana
F536-550	Illinois
F550.5-553.2	The Lake region. Great Lakes
F561-575	Michigan
F576-590	Wisconsin
F590.3-596.3	The West. Trans-Mississippi Region. Great Plains
F597	The Northwest
F598	Missouri River and Valley
F601-615	Minnesota
F616-630	Iowa
F631-645	North Dakota
F646-660	South Dakota
F661-675	Nebraska
F676-690	Kansas
F691-705	Oklahoma
F721-722	Rocky Mountains. Yellowstone National Park
F726-740	Montana
F741-755	Idaho
F756-770	Wyoming
F771-785	Colorado
F786-790	New Southwest. Colorado River, Canyon, and Valley
F791-805	New Mexico
F806-820	Arizona
F821-835	Utah
F836-850	Nevada
F850.5-851.5	Pacific States
F851.7	Cascade Range
F852-854	Pacific Northwest. Columbia River and Valley. Northwest boundary since 1846
F856-870	California
F871-885	Oregon
F886-900	Washington
F901-951	Alaska
F951	Bering Sea and Aleutian Islands
	Hawaii, see DU620+
F965	The territories of the United States (General)

United States local history - Continued

F970	Insular possessions of the United States (General)
F975	Central American, West Indian, and other countries protected by and having close political affiliations with the United States (General)
F1001-1145.2	British America
F1001-1145.2	Canada
F1001-1035	General
F1035.8	Maritime provinces. Atlantic coast of Canada
F1036-1040	Nova Scotia. Acadia
F1041-1045	New Brunswick
F1046-1049.7	Prince Edward Island
F1050	St. Lawrence Gulf, River and Valley (General)
F1051-1055	Quebec
F1056-1059.7	Ontario
F1060-1060.97	Canadian Northwest. Northwest Territories
F1061-1065	Manitoba
F1067	Assiniboia
F1070-1074.7	Saskatchewan
F1075-1080	Alberta
F1086-1089.7	British Columbia
F1090	Rocky Mountains of Canada
F1090.5	Arctic regions
F1091-1095.5	Yukon
F1096-1100.5	Mackenzie
F1101-1105.7	Franklin
F1106-1110.5	Keewatin
F1121-1139	Newfoundland
F1135-1139	Labrador
F1140	The Labrador Peninsula
F1141-1145.2	Nunavut
	Other than Canada
	Bahamas, see F1650+
	Bermudas, see F1630+
	British East and West Florida, 1763-1783, see F301, F314
	British Guiana, see F2361+
	British Honduras (Belize), see F1441+
	British West Indies, see F2131+
	Falkland Islands, see F3031+
	Thirteen North American Colonies before 1776, see E186+

OUTLINE

Dutch America
  Colony in Brazil, 1625-1661, see F2532
  Dutch Guinea, see F2401+
  Dutch West Indies, see F2141
  New Netherlands to 1664, see F122.1
  New Sweden (Dutch possession, 1655-1664), see F167
French America

F1170	Saint Pierre and Miquelon
	Other French America
	Colony in Brazil, 1555-1567, see F2529
	Colony in Florida, 1562-1565, see F314
	French Guiana, see F2441+
	French West Indies, see F2151
	Louisiana, 1698-1803, see F372
	New France and Acadia, 1600-1763, see F1030, F1038
F1201-3799	Latin America. Spanish America
F1201-1392	Mexico
F1218.5-1221	Antiquities. Indians
F1401-1419	Latin America (General)
F1421-1440	Central America
F1435-1435.3	Mayas
F1441-1457	Belize
F1461-1477	Guatemala
F1481-1497	Salvador (El Salvador)
F1501-1517	Honduras
F1521-1537	Nicaragua
F1541-1557	Costa Rica
F1561-1577	Panama
F1569.C2	Canal Zone. Panama Canal
F1601-1629	West Indies
F1630-1640	Bermudas
F1650-1660	Bahamas
F1741-1991	Greater Antilles
F1751-1854.9	Cuba
F1788-1788.22	Communist regime
F1861-1896	Jamaica
F1900-1941	Haiti (Island). Hispaniola
F1912-1930	Haiti (Republic)
F1931-1941	Dominican Republic
F1951-1983	Puerto Rico
F1991	Navassa

Latin America.   Spanish America
West Indies - Continued

F2001-2151   Lesser Antilles
                     Groups of islands, by geographical distribution
F2006   Leeward islands
F2011   Windward Islands
F2016   Islands along Venezuela coast
F2033-2129   Individual islands
                     Groups of islands, by political allegiance
F2131-2133   British West Indies
F2136   Virgin Islands of the United States
F2141   Netherlands West Indies.   Dutch West Indies
F2151   French West Indies
F2155-2191   Caribbean area.   Caribbean Sea
F2201-3799   South America
F2201-2239   General
F2251-2299   Colombia
F2301-2349   Venezuela
F2351   Guiana
F2361-2391   Guyana.   British Guiana
F2401-2431   Surinam
F2441-2471   French Guiana
F2501-2659   Brazil
F2661-2699   Paraguay
F2701-2799   Uruguay
F2801-3021   Argentina
F3031-3031.5   Falkland Islands
F3051-3285   Chile
F3301-3359   Bolivia
F3401-3619   Peru
F3701-3799   Ecuador

E11-143

America

General

E11-E29 are reserved for works that are actually comprehensive in scope. A book on travel would only occasionally be classified here; the numbers for the United States, Spanish America, etc., would usually accommodate all works, the choice being determined by the main country or region covered

11	Periodicals. Societies. Collections (serial)
	For international American Conferences see F1404+
	Collections (nonserial). Collected works
12	Several authors
13	Individual authors
14	Dictionaries. Gazetteers. Geographic names
	General works see E18
	History
16	Historiography
16.5	Study and teaching
	Biography
17	Collective
	Individual, see country, period, etc.
18	General works
	Including comprehensive works on America
18.5	Chronology, chronological tables, etc.
18.7	Juvenile works
18.75	General special
	By period
	Pre-Columbian period see E51+; E103+
18.82	1492-1810
	Cf. E101+ Discovery and exploration of America
	Cf. E141+ Earliest accounts of America to 1810
18.83	1810-1900
18.85	1901-
19	Pamphlets, addresses, essays, etc.
	Including radio programs, pageants, etc.
20	Social life and customs. Civilization. Intellectual life
21	Historic monuments (General)
21.5	Antiquities (Non-Indian)
21.7	Historical geography
	Description and travel. Views
	Cf. F851 Pacific coast
	Cf. G419+ Travels around the world and in several parts of the world including America and other countries
	Cf. G575+ Polar discoveries
	Earliest to 1606 see E141+
	1607-1810 see E143
27	1811-1950

1

General
    Description and travel. Views -- Continued

27.2	1951-1980
27.5	1981-

    Elements in the population

29.A1	General works
29.A2-Z	Individual elements, A-Z
29.A43	Akan
29.A73	Arabs
29.A75	Asians
29.B35	Basques
	Blacks see E29.N3
29.B75	British
29.C35	Canary Islanders
29.C37	Catalans
29.C5	Chinese
29.C73	Creoles
29.C75	Croats
29.C94	Czechs
29.D25	Danube Swabians
29.E37	East Indians
29.E87	Europeans
29.F8	French
29.G26	Galicians (Spain)
29.G3	Germans
29.H9	Huguenots
29.I74	Irish
29.I8	Italians
29.J3	Japanese
29.J5	Jews
29.N3	Negroes. Blacks
(29.O6)	Orientals
29.P6	Poles
29.R83	Russian Germans
29.R84	Russians
29.S65	Spaniards
29.S83	Swedes
29.Y67	Yoruba

North America
    The numbers "E31-46" like "E11-29" are to be assigned to works actually comprehensive in scope; for example, a book dealing principally with British America with a few pages at the end on the United States would be classed in F1001-F1035, regardless of title. Most works having United States in the title relate so largely to this country that they are classed in E151-E839

31	Periodicals. Societies. Collections

E11-143

North America -- Continued

35	Dictionaries. Gazetteers. Geographic names
	Guidebooks see E41
	Biography
36	Collective
	Individual, see country, period, etc.
38	General works
38.5	Juvenile works
39	Pamphlets, addresses, essays, etc.
39.5	Pictorial works
40	Social life and customs. Civilization. Intellectual life
40.5	Geography
41	Description and travel. Guidebooks
43	Antiquities (non-Indian)
43.5	National and state parks and reservations (Collective descriptive works)
	History
	Cf. E101+ Discovery and exploration of America
	Cf. F1411+ History of Latin America
45	General works
46	General special
46.5	Military history
	Elements in the population
49	General works
49.2.A-Z	Individual elements, A-Z
	For a list of of racial, ethnic, and religious elements (with Cutter numbers) see E184.A+
	South America see F2201+
	Pre-Columbian America. The Indians
	For language, see PM
51	Periodicals. Societies. Collections (serial)
	Including anthropological records, Archaeological Institute of America
	For American Antiquarian Society see E172
51.5	Congresses
	Collections (nonserial). Collected works
53	Several authors
54	Individual authors
54.5	Dictionaries. Directories. Guides to tribes
	Study and teaching. Research
55.5	General works
	Audiovisual aids
55.6.A1-.Z8	General works
55.6.Z9	Catalogs of audiovisual materials
56	Museums. Exhibitions
	Subarrange by author
	Including collections of antiquities

Pre-Columbian America. The Indians -- Continued

57	Theory. Methods of investigation
	Including biography (arranged by biographee), e.g., William Jones
58	General works
58.4	Juvenile works
59.A-Z	Topics, A-Z
59.A32	Aesthetics
59.A35	Agriculture
59.A5	Anthropometry
	Antiquities see E61
59.A67	Architecture
59.A68	Arms and armor. Weapons
59.A7	Art
59.A73	Arts
59.A8	Astronomy
59.B3	Baskets
59.B43	Beadwork
	Boats see E59.C2
59.C18	Cannibalism
59.C2	Canoes. Boats
59.C22	Captivities
59.C25	Cartography
59.C46	Children
59.C5	Chronology
59.C55	City planning
59.C58	Colonization
59.C59	Commerce
59.C6	Costume. Adornment
59.C73	Craniology
59.C9	Cremation
	Culture see E58
59.D35	Dance
59.D45	Dentistry
59.D58	Diseases
59.D66	Dolls
59.D69	Domestic animals
59.D9	Dwellings
59.E3	Economic conditions
	Including employment
59.E4	Education
59.E75	Ethnic identity
59.F53	First contact with Europeans
59.F6	Folklore. Legends
59.F63	Food
59.G3	Games. Recreation. Sports
59.G55	Goldwork

Pre-Columbian America. The Indians
Topics, A-Z

	Government, Tribal see E59.T75
	Government and politics see E59.P73
59.G6	Government relations
59.H54	Hindu influences
59.I4	Implements
59.I5	Industries
59.I53	Influence on other civilizations
59.I58	Intellectual life
59.L3	Land tenure
59.L4	Leatherwork. Tanning
	Legends see E59.F6
	Literature see PM151+
59.M3	Masks
59.M33	Material culture
59.M34	Mathematics
59.M4	Medicine
59.M47	Metalwork
59.M58	Migrations
59.M65	Missions
59.M66	Mixed descent
59.M7	Money
59.M8	Mortuary customs
59.N5	Narcotics
59.N8	Numeration
59.P42	Petroglyphs. Rock paintings
59.P45	Philosophy
	Picture writing see E59.W9
	Popular attitudes toward Indians see E59.P89
59.P73	Politics and government
59.P75	Population
59.P8	Pottery
59.P87	Psychology
59.P89	Public opinion. Popular attitudes toward Indians
59.P92	Public welfare
	Recreation see E59.G3
59.R38	Religion. Mythology
59.R56	Rites and ceremonies
59.R6	Roads. Trails
	Rock paintings see E59.P42
59.S35	Science
59.S37	Sculpture
59.S45	Sexual behavior
59.S54	Shell engraving
59.S63	Slavery
59.S64	Social conditions

	Pre-Columbian America. The Indians
	Topics -- Continued
	Sports see E59.G3
59.S65	Social life and customs
59.S7	Statistics
59.T35	Textile fabrics
59.T6	Tobacco pipes
	Trails see E59.R6
59.T73	Transpacific influences
59.T75	Tribal government
59.W3	Warfare
	Weapons see E59.A68
59.W8	Women
59.W9	Writing. Picture writing
61	Archaeology of the Americans. Origin of the Indians in general
65	Latin America (General)
	For special, class in local history, usually under the country; in certain cases with state or province; e.g., F1219, Mexico; F1529.M9, Mosquito Reservation
	For Spanish treatment of the Indians see F1411
	North America (north of Mexico)
71	General works
	For works on Indians only see E77+
73	Mound builders. Mounds
	Class here general works only
	For mounds in a particular state, province, or region see E78.A+
(74.A-Z)	By state, province, or region, A-Z
	Indians of North America
75	Periodicals. Societies. Collections
76	Congresses
76.2	Dictionaries. Directories. Guides to tribes
	Biography of Indianists
76.4	Collective
76.45.A-Z	Individual, A-Z
	Subarrange each by Table E1
76.6	Study and teaching
76.7	Research
76.8	Historiography
	Museums. Exhibitions
76.85	General works
76.86.A-Z	Special institutions. By place, A-Z
	General works
77	Comprehensive works
77.2	Addresses, essays, lectures
77.4	Juvenile works

Indians of North America

General works -- Continued

77.5	Pictorial works
77.6	Minor works
	Archaeology
77.8	Periodicals. Societies. Collections. Congresses
77.9	General treatises
77.92	Juvenile works
77.94	Minor works
78.A-Z	By state, province, or region, A-Z

Including Indian antiquities. Class all mounds and
archaeological sites within a county or other division of a
state, subarranging by author, e.g., mounds
in Franklin County, Ohio, are classed in E78.O3

Class Indian reservations here under state unless held by a
single tribe, when they are classed in E99

For Canada (General) see E78.C2

For works limited to specific tribes see E99.A+

Acadia see E78.N9

78.A28	Alabama
78.A3	Alaska
78.A34	Alberta
78.A66	Appalachian Region

Including Blue Ridge Mountains

78.A7	Arizona
78.A8	Arkansas
78.A88	Atlantic States
	Blue Ridge Mountains see E78.A66
78.B9	British Columbia
78.C15	California
78.C2	Canada (General)

Including the Canadian Northwest

Cf. E78.B9 British Columbia; E78.N9 Nova Scotia; etc.

Cf. E92 Government relations

78.C45	Chattahoochee River Valley
78.C5	Churchill River Watershed (Sask. and Man.)
78.C6	Colorado
78.C617	Colorado Plateau
78.C62	Colorado River Valley
78.C63	Columbia Plateau
78.C64	Columbia River Valley
78.C7	Connecticut
78.D2	Dakota Territory

For North Dakota see E78.N75

For South Dakota see E78.S63

78.D3	Delaware
78.D5	Delaware Valley

Indians of North America

By state, province, or region, A-Z -- Continued

78.D54	Delmarva Peninsula
78.D6	District of Columbia
78.E2	Eastern North America. Woodlands
78.F6	Florida
78.F73	Franklin (District)
78.G3	Georgia
78.G67	Great Basin
78.G7	Great Lakes
78.G73	Great Plains
78.H83	Hudson Valley
78.I18	Idaho
78.I3	Illinois
78.I5	Indian Territory

Including the five civilized tribes before 1907

For the five civilized tribes after 1907 see E78.O45

78.I53	Indiana
78.I6	Iowa
78.K15	Kankakee Valley
78.K16	Kansas
78.K25	Keewatin (District)
78.K3	Kentucky
78.L3	Labrador
78.L58	Little Colorado River Valley (New Mexico and Arizona)
78.L8	Louisiana
78.M16	Mackenzie
78.M2	Maine
78.M25	Manitoba
78.M28	Maritime Provinces
78.M3	Maryland
78.M4	Massachusetts
78.M6	Michigan
78.M65	Middle Atlantic States
78.M67	Middle West
78.M7	Minnesota
78.M73	Mississippi
78.M75	Mississippi Valley
78.M8	Missouri
78.M82	Missouri Valley
78.M9	Montana
78.N3	Nebraska
78.N4	Nevada
78.N46	New Brunswick
78.N5	New England
78.N54	New Hampshire
78.N6	New Jersey

Indians of North America
By state, province, or region, A-Z -- Continued

78.N65	New Mexico
78.N7	New York
78.N72	Newfoundland
78.N74	North Carolina
78.N75	North Dakota
	Northeastern States see E78.E2
78.N76	Northwest (Old)
78.N77	Northwest (Pacific)
78.N78	Northwest coast of North America
78.N79	Northwest Territories
78.N8	Northwestern States
78.N9	Nova Scotia. Acadia
78.O3	Ohio
78.O4	Ohio Valley
78.O45	Oklahoma

Including the five civilized tribes after 1907
For the five civilized tribes before 1907 see E78.I5

78.O5	Ontario
78.O6	Oregon
78.O9	Ozark Mountains
78.P2	Pacific Coast
78.P24	Pacific Crest Trail
78.P4	Pennsylvania
	Plains Indians see E78.G73
	Plateau Indians see E78.G67
78.P7	Prairie Provinces
78.P8	Puget Sound
78.Q3	Québec
78.R37	Republican River Valley (Nebraska and Kansas)
78.R4	Rhode Island
78.R56	Rio Grande Valley
78.R63	Rocky Mountains
78.S2	Saskatchewan
78.S6	South Carolina
78.S63	South Dakota
78.S65	Southern States
78.S7	Southwest, New

Including Four Corners Region
Cf. F802.B25 Cliff dwellings in Frijoles Canyon
Cf. F817.C3 Cliff dwellings in Canyon de Chelly
National Monument

78.S8	Southwest, Old
78.S87	Superior, Lake
78.S9	Susquehanna Valley
78.T3	Tennessee

Indians of North America
By state, province, or region, A-Z -- Continued

78.T33	Tennessee River Region
78.T4	Texas
	Ungava see E78.Q3
78.U55	Utah
78.V5	Vermont
78.V7	Virginia
78.W3	Washington (State)
78.W5	The West
78.W6	West Virginia
78.W8	Wisconsin
	Woodlands see E78.E2
78.W95	Wyoming
78.Y44	Yellowstone National Park. Yellowstone River Valley
78.Y8	Yukon Territory

Indian wars

81	General works
82	Wars of the colonial period (General)

Individual wars
Arranged chronologically
For biographies, assign first cutter for biographee
For wars and uprisings in Virginia, 1609-1676
(Massacres of 1622 and 1641, etc.) see F229

83.63	Pequot War, 1636-1638
83.65	Dutch-Indian War, 1643-1645. Kieft's War
83.655	New York Uprising, 1655
83.663	Esopus wars, 1659-1676
83.67	King Philip's War, 1675-1676
83.69	Frontenac's Expedition, 1696
	King William's War, 1689-1697 see E196
	Queen Anne's War, 1702-1713 see E197
83.71	Tuscarora War, 1711-1713
83.713	Yamassee War, 1715-1716
83.72	Eastern Indian Wars (New England), 1722-1726
	Including Pigwacket Fight, 1725; Sébastien Rasles (Râle, Rasle); etc.
83.73	Natchez Massacre, 1729
83.739	Chickasaw War, 1739-1740
	King George's War, 1744-1748 see E198
	French and Indian War, 1755-1763 see E199
83.759	Cherokee War, 1759-1761
83.7595	Wyoming Massacre, 1763
83.76	Pontiac's Conspiracy, 1763-1765
	Biography: Henry Bouquet, etc.
83.77	Dunmore's War, 1774. Battle of Point Pleasant
83.775	Indian Wars, 1775-1783

	Indians of North America
	Indian wars
	Individual wars
	Indian wars, 1775-1783 -- Continued
	Campaigns of the Revolution see E230+
	Wyoming Massacre, 1778 see E241.W9
	Cherry Valley Massacre, 1778 see E241.C5
	Sullivan's Campaign, 1779 see E235
	Crawford's Campaign, 1782 see E238
83.79	Northwestern Indian wars (Ohio Valley), 1790-1795
	Including Harmar's Expedition, 1790; Scott's Expedition, May 1791; Wilkinson's Expedition, August 1791; St. Clair's Campaign, Novmber 1791
83.794	Wayne's Campaign, 1793-1795
83.81	Battle of Tippecanoe, 1811
83.812	Indian wars, 1812-1815
	Campaigns of the War of 1812 see E355.2
83.813	First Creek War, 1813-1814
	Including Jackson's execution of the Tennessee militiamen
83.817	First Seminole War, 1817-1818
	Including the execution of Ambrister and Arbuthnot
83.818	Arikara War, 1823
83.83	Black Hawk War, 1832
	Biography: Black Hawk, the Sauk chief, etc.
83.835	Second Seminole War, 1835-1842
83.836	Second Creek War, 1836
	Thomas Sidney Jesup, etc.
83.837	Comanche War, 1840
83.838	Temecula Massacre, 1847
83.84	Pacific Northwest Indian wars, 1847-1865
	Including Cayuse War, 1847-1850; Rogue River War, 1850; Yakima War, 1855-1858; Spokane Expedition, 1858
83.854	Dakota Indian or Sioux war, 1855-1856
	Including Harney's Expedition
83.855	Third Seminole War, 1855-1858
83.8565	Battle of Maricopa Wells, 1857
	Mountain Meadow Massacre, 1857 see F826
83.857	Spirit Lake Massacre, 1857
83.8575	Battle of Solomon's Fork, 1857
83.8577	Battle of Crooked Creek, 1859
83.858	Mill Creek War, 1857-1865
83.859	Navaho (Navajo) War, 1858-1868
83.8596	Battle of Pease River, 1860

Indians of North America
Indian wars
Individual wars -- Continued
83.86 Dakota Indian or Sioux War, 1862-1865
Including uprising in Minnesota (Battles of Birch Coulee,
Fort Ridgely, New Ulm, Wood Lake), 1862; Battle of
Whitestone Hill, 1863; Battle of Killdeer Mountain, July
1864; Platt Bridge Fight, July 1865; Powder River
Campaign, July-October 1865
83.863 Indian wars, 1862-1865
Including Shoshoni War, 1863-1865; Cheyenne War, 1864;
Sand Creek Massacre, 1864; Battle of Adobe Walls,
1864
Cf. E83.858 Mill Creek War
Cf. E83.859 Navaho War
Cf. E83.86 Sioux War
83.864 Snake War, 1864-1868
83.866 Indian wars, 1866-1898
Including Fort Phil Kearney Massacre, 1866; Warren
Wagon Train Massacre, 1871; Red Cloud War, 1866-
1867
Biography: George Crook, Nelson Appleton Miles, etc.
83.867 Black Hawk War (Utah), 1865-1872
83.8675 Battle of Camp Cady, 1866
83.868 Battle of Beecher Island, 1868
83.869 Washita Campaign, 1868-1869
83.8695 Battle of Summit Springs, 1869
83.8697 Battle of Belly River, 1870
83.87 Modoc War, 1872-1873
83.875 Red River War, 1874-1875
Including Cheyenne Outbreak
83.876 Dakota Indian or Sioux War, 1876
Including Battle of the Little Big Horn
83.8765 Battle of the Butte, 1877
83.877 Nez Percé War, 1877
Including Battle of the Big Hole
83.879 Ute War, 1879
Including White River Massacre
Riel Rebellion see F1060.9
83.88 Apache War, 1882-1886
83.89 Dakota Indian or Sioux War, 1890-1891. Messiah War
Including Death of Chief Sitting Bull; Wounded Knee
Massacre, 1890
83.895 Chippewa War, 1898
Captivities
Including adventures and experiences of those taken captive by
the Indians

Indians of North America
    Captivities -- Continued
85   General works. Collected narratives
87.A-Z   Individual captivities, A-Z
               Prefer classification in E83.63+ or E99.A+ if captivity relates to a particular war or tribe
88   Individual memoirs of early explorers, traders, trappers, etc., giving accounts of their experiences among the Indians
               For memoirs relating to a specific tribe see E99.A+
        Biography
89   Collective
               Including portraits
89.5   Individual and collective biography as a literary form
90.A-Z   Individual, A-Z
               Subarrange each by Table E1
               Class individuals identified with specific tribes in E99 unless better known in connection with specific wars in which case class with the war in E83.63-.895
               e.g.
               Black Hawk, Sauk chief see E83.83
               Pocahontas see E99.P85
               Sitting Bull, Dakota chief see E99.D1
90.T2   Tegakouita, Catharine
        Government relations
               Including government agencies dealing with Indians, Indian rights associations, biography, treatment of Indians, reservations (General), and government services for Indians (General)
               For works limited to specific regions or states see E78.A+
               For works limited to specific tribes see E99.A+
91   General works
92   Canada
               Cf. E78.C2 Indians in Canada
93   United States
(94)   Law
               see class K
(95)   Treaties
               see class K
        Social life and customs see E98.S7
        Education
               For works limited to specific tribes see E99.A+
96   General works
           Canada
96.2   General works
            Indian schools
96.5   General works

Indians of North America
Education
Canada
Indian schools -- Continued

96.6.A-Z	Individual schools. By name, A-Z
	e.g.
96.6.S17	St. Paul's Indian Residential School, Cardston, Alta.
96.65.A-Z	By region or province, A-Z

United States

97	General works
97.3	Finance
	Indian schools
97.5	General works
97.55	Tribal colleges. Indian community colleges
97.6.A-Z	Individual schools. By name, A-Z
	e.g.
97.6.B87	Bureau of Indian Affairs School, Bethel, Alaska
97.6.C35	Cherokee National Female Seminary, Tahlequah, Okla.
97.6.F66	Fort Shaw Indian School (Great Falls, Mont.)
97.6.H3	Hampton Institute, Hampton, Va.
	Cf. LC2851.H27+ African American education at Hampton Institute
97.6.J69	Johnson's Indian School, White Sulphur, Ky.
97.6.M5	Moor's Indian Charity School, Lebanon, Conn.
	Cf. LD1420+ Dartmouth College, Hanover, N.H.
97.6.R35	Rapid City Indian School
97.6.S2	Santee Normal Training School, Santee, Nebr.
97.6.T4	Thomas Indian School, Iroquois, N.Y.
97.6.U54	University of California. Tecumseh Center
97.65.A-Z	By region or state, A-Z
97.8	Indian libraries. Library service to Indians
	Cf. E98.B65 Books and reading for Indians
97.9	Indian archives
98.A-Z	Other topics, A-Z
	For works limited to specific geographic areas, if specific tribes are not indicated see E78.A+
	For works limited to specific tribes see E99.A+
98.A15	Adoption
98.A2	Aesthetics
	African Americans relations see E98.R28
98.A27	Aged. Older Indians
98.A3	Agriculture
	Alcohol use see E98.L7
98.A55	Anthropometry
	Antiquities see E77.8+; E78.A+
	Appropriations see E91+

Indians of North America
Other topics, A-Z -- Continued

98.A63	Architecture
98.A65	Arms and armor. Weapons
98.A7	Art
	For modern art by Indian artists, see class N
98.A73	Arts
98.A84	Asian influences
98.A88	Astronomy
98.B3	Baskets
98.B46	Beadwork
98.B54	Biology. Ethnobiology
98.B6	Boats. Canoes
98.B65	Books and reading
	Cf. E97.8 Indian libraries
98.B7	Botany (Economic). Ethnobotany
98.B8	Buffalo
	Burial customs see E98.M8
98.B87	Business enterprises
98.C14	Calendar
	Captivities see E85+
98.C17	Cartography
	Including works about maps of Indian lands
98.C3	Census
98.C47	Charitable contributions. Philanthropy
98.C5	Children
	Citizenship see E91+
98.C55	Chronology
	Claims
98.C6	By Indians
98.C62	Against Indians
98.C7	Commerce
98.C73	Communication
98.C76	Copperwork
98.C79	Cosmology
98.C8	Costume. Adornment
	Crafts see E98.I5
98.C85	Craniology
98.C87	Crime. Police
	Including Indian reservation police
	Criminal justice system
	see class K
98.C89	Cultural assimilation
	Cf. E91+ Government relations and treatment of
	Indians
	Culture see E77
98.D2	Dance

	Indians of North America
	Other topics, A-Z -- Continued
98.D6	Diseases
98.D65	Dolls
98.D67	Domestic animals
98.D8	Drama
98.D9	Dwellings. Furniture
98.E2	Economic conditions
	Education see E97+
98.E5	Embroidery
98.E6	Employment
98.E83	Ethics
98.E85	Ethnic identity
	Ethnobiology see E98.B54
	Ethnobotany see E98.B7
98.F3	Financial affairs

        Including trust estates, revolving credit fund, relief
        Cf. E98.P3 Pensions

98.F38	Fire use
98.F39	First contact with Europeans
98.F4	Fishing
98.F58	Folk literature

        For legends and tales see E98.F6

| 98.F6 | Folklore. Legends |

        For individual tribes see E99.A+

98.F7	Food
98.F73	Footwear
98.G18	Gambling

        Including gambling on Indian reservations

98.G2	Games. Recreation. Sports
98.G44	Genealogy
	Government relations see E91+
	Handicraft see E98.I5
98.H35	Handicapped Indians. Indians with disabilities
	History see E77+
	Homosexuality see E98.S48
98.H55	Horses
	Hospitals see RA981.A35
98.H58	Housing
98.H77	Humor
98.H8	Hunting
98.I4	Implements. Utensils
98.I5	Industries

        Including handicraft, mining, etc.
        For basketry see E98.B3
        For silversmithing see E98.S55
        For textile industry see E98.T35

Indians of North America
Other topics, A-Z -- Continued

98.I54	Interviews
98.I75	Irrigation
98.J48	Jewelry
98.K48	Kinship
98.K54	Knives
98.L3	Land tenure
	Land transfers see E91+
	Language see PM1+
98.L4	Leatherwork. Tanning
	Legends see E98.F6
98.L7	Liquor use. Alcohol use
98.M2	Magic
98.M27	Marriage customs and rites
98.M3	Masks
	Mass media see P94.5.I53+
98.M34	Material culture
98.M35	Medals
98.M4	Medicine. Medicine men
	Cf. E98.D6 Diseases
	Mental health see RC451.5.I5
98.M45	Metalwork
98.M5	Military capacity and organization. Indians as soldiers
98.M6	Missions (General)
	Including biography of missionaries.
	Prefer tribe or local
	For Jesuit missions in New France see F1030.7+
98.M63	Mixed descent
98.M7	Money. Wampum
98.M8	Mortuary customs
	Music (Music scores) see M1669
	Music (History and criticism of Indian music) see ML3557
98.N2	Names
98.N5	Narcotics. Drugs
	Newspapers see PN4883
	Older Indians see E98.A27
	Origin see E61
98.O7	Oratory. Speeches, addresses, etc.
	Ornaments see E98.C8
98.O76	Orphanages
	Cf. HV959+ Indian orphanages
98.P23	Painting
98.P3	Pensions
98.P34	Petroglyphs. Rock paintings
	Philanthropy see E98.C47
98.P5	Philosophy

Indians of North America
Other topics, A-Z -- Continued

98.P53	Physical anthropology
	Including physical characteristics, beauty, etc.
	Cf. E98.A55 Anthropometry
(98.P6)	Picture writing. Rock writing
	see E98.P34
(98.P74)	Poetry
	For poetry by Indians in non-Indian languages, see PR, PS, etc.
	For poetry in Indian languages see PM151+
	Police see E98.C87
	Politics and government see E98.T77
98.P76	Population
	Portraits (Collected) see E89+
98.P8	Pottery
98.P86	Powwows
98.P9	Property
	Including appraisal, removal of restrictions, timber contracts, wills, etc.
98.P95	Psychology
	Cf. BF432.I5 Intelligence of Indians
98.P99	Public opinion about Indians. Popular attitudes toward Indians
	Recreation see E98.G2
98.R28	Relations with African Americans
98.R3	Religion. Mythology
	Including creation, future life, katcinas, occultism, revivalism, rites and ceremonies, shamanism, etc.
98.R4	Removal
	Reservations see E78.A+; E91+; E99.A+
98.R5	Riding gear
98.R53	Rites and ceremonies
	Rock paintings see E98.P34
98.S26	Salt
98.S3	Sandpaintings
	Scalping see E98.W2
98.S43	Science
98.S46	Services for
98.S48	Sexual behavior
	Including homosexuality
98.S5	Sign language
98.S55	Silversmithing
98.S6	Slavery
	Smoking see E98.T6
98.S67	Social conditions
98.S7	Social life and customs

	Indians of North America
	Other topics, A-Z -- Continued
98.S75	Societies
	Speeches, addresses, etc see E98.O7
	Sports see E98.G2
	Suffrage see E91+
98.S9	Suicide
98.S94	Sweatbaths
98.T2	Tattooing
98.T24	Taxation
98.T35	Textile fabrics. Weaving
	Including blankets, rugs, etc.
98.T6	Tobacco pipes. Smoking
98.T65	Totems
	Including totem poles
98.T7	Trails
98.T73	Transatlantic influences
98.T75	Trapping
	Treaties
	see class K
98.T77	Tribal government. Politics and government
98.U72	Urban residence
	Utensils see E98.I4
98.W2	Warfare. Scalping
	Wars see E81+
	Weapons see E98.A65
	Weaving see E98.T35
98.W49	Wife abuse
	Wills see E98.P9
98.W8	Women
98.W86	Writing
98.Y68	Youth
99.A-Z	Tribes and cultures, A-Z
	For biographies, assign second Cutter number for the biographee
	Including those Mexican tribes that are also found in the United States
99.A12	Abitibi
99.A13	Abnaki. Abenaki
99.A15	Achomawi
99.A16	Acoma
99.A18	Adena culture
99.A28	Ahtena
99.A34	Aleuts
99.A349	Algonkin
99.A35	Algonquian
99.A4	Alibamu

Indians of North America
Tribes and cultures, A-Z -- Continued

99.A45	Alsea
	Anasazi culture see E99.P9
99.A6	Apache
	For biography of Cochise see E99.C68C63
99.A62	Apalachee
99.A63	Apalachicola
99.A7	Arapaho
99.A8	Arikara
99.A82	Arosaguntacook
99.A83	Assateague
99.A84	Assiniboin
99.A86	Athapascan
	Atikamekw see E99.T33
99.A87	Atsina. Gros Ventre (Montana)
99.A875	Atsugewi
99.A88	Attacapa
99.B33	Bannock
99.B37	Basket-Maker
99.B376	Bearlake
(99.B38)	Bellabella
	see E99.H45
99.B39	Bellacoola
99.B4	Beothuk
99.B5	Biloxi
99.B6	Bocootawwonauke
99.B7	Brotherton
99.B8	Brulé
99.C12	Caddo
99.C13	Caddoan
99.C15	Cahokia
99.C155	Cahuilla
99.C18	Calusa
99.C19	Campo
99.C2	Capote
	Carrier see E99.T17
99.C23	Casas Grandes culture
99.C24	Catawba
99.C26	Cathlamet
(99.C27)	Caughnawaga
	see E99.M8
99.C3	Cayuga
99.C32	Cayuse
99.C37	Chaco culture
99.C4	Chakchiuma
99.C48	Chasta

Indians of North America
Tribes and cultures, A-Z -- Continued

99.C483	Chastacosta
99.C49	Chehalis
99.C4925	Chelan
99.C493	Chemehuevi
99.C495	Cheraw
	Cheroenhaka see E99.N93
99.C5	Cherokee
99.C526	Chetco
99.C53	Cheyenne
99.C55	Chickasaw
	Chilcotin see E99.T78
99.C552	Chilkat
99.C5523	Chilliwack
99.C553	Chilula
99.C56	Chimariko
99.C565	Chimmesyan
99.C57	Chinook
99.C58	Chinookan
99.C59	Chipewyan
99.C6	Chippewa
99.C68	Chiricahua
99.C68C63	Biography of Cochise
99.C7	Chitimacha
99.C8	Choctaw
99.C815	Chumash. Chumashan
99.C82	Clallam
99.C83	Clayoquot
99.C832	Clovis culture
99.C834	Coahuiltecan
99.C835	Cochimi
99.C84	Cochiti
99.C842	Cocopa
	Coeur d'Alene see E99.S63
99.C844	Colville
99.C85	Comanche
99.C86	Comox
99.C87	Conestoga
99.C873	Conoy
	Including Piscataway
99.C874	Coos
99.C87414	Coosa
99.C8742	Coquille
99.C8743	Coree
(99.C8744)	Costanoan
	see E99.O32

Indians of North America
Tribes and cultures, A-Z -- Continued

99.C875	Cowichan
99.C877	Cowlitz
99.C88	Cree
99.C9	Creek
99.C91	Croatan. Lumbee
99.C92	Crow
99.C94	Cupeño
99.D1	Dakota. Sioux
	Including Chief Sitting Bull
	For death of Chief Sitting Bull see E83.89
99.D18	Deg Hit'an. Ingalik
99.D2	Delaware
	Dena'ina see E99.T185
99.D25	Dene Thá
99.D4	Dhegiha
99.D5	Diegueño
99.D8	Dudley
99.D9	Duwamish
99.E42	Entiat
99.E5	Erie
99.E7	Eskimos
	Including Inuit
99.E8	Esopus
99.E85	Esselen
99.E9	Eyak
	Five civilized tribes see E78.I5; E99.C5; E99.C55; E99.C8; E99.C9; E99.S28
99.F65	Folsom culture
99.F67	Fort Ancient culture
99.F7	Fox
99.F75	Fremont culture
99.G15	Gabrieleño
	Gitksan see E99.K55
99.G67	Gosiute
	Gros Ventre (Montana) see E99.A87
99.G82	Guale
99.H15	Hackensack
99.H2	Haida
99.H23	Haisla
99.H26	Han
99.H28	Hasinai
99.H3	Havasupai
99.H45	Heiltsuk
99.H6	Hidatsa
99.H65	Hitchiti

Indians of North America
Tribes and cultures, A-Z -- Continued

99.H68	Hohokam culture
99.H69	Hopewell culture
99.H7	Hopi
99.H72	Houma
99.H75	Hualapai
99.H77	Hul'qumi'num
99.H795	Hunkpapa
99.H8	Hupa
99.H9	Huron
	Including Wyandot Indians
99.I2	Illinois
(99.I5)	Ingalik
	see E99.D18
	Inuit see E99.E7
99.I6	Iowa
99.I69	Iroquoian
99.I7	Iroquois
99.I8	Isleta
99.J4	Jemez
99.J5	Jicarilla
99.J8	Juaneño
99.J9	Jumano
99.K15	Kainah
99.K16	Kalapuyan
99.K17	Kalispel
99.K18	Kamia
99.K2	Kansa
99.K23	Karankawa
99.K25	Karok
99.K258	Kashaya
99.K26	Kaska
99.K264	Kaskaskia
99.K267	Kato
99.K269	Kawaiisu
99.K28	Kawchottine
99.K3	Keeche
99.K39	Keresan
99.K396	Kichai
99.K4	Kickapoo
99.K5	Kiowa
99.K52	Kiowa Apache
99.K55	Kitksan. Gitksan
99.K59	Kiyuksa
99.K7	Klamath
99.K76	Klikitat

Indians of North America
   Tribes and cultures, A-Z -- Continued

99.K77	Koasati
	Kootenai see E99.K85
99.K79	Koyukon
99.K82	Kuitsh
99.K83	Kusso
99.K84	Kutchin
99.K85	Kutenai
99.K9	Kwakiutl
99.L2	Laguna
	Lakes Indians see E99.S546
	Lakota Indians see E99.T34
99.L25	Lamar culture
99.L3	Lassik
99.L35	Lekwungen. Songhees
99.L4	Lillooet
99.L5	Lipan
99.L9	Luiseño
	Lumbee see E99.C91
99.L95	Lummi
99.L98	Lutuamian
99.M115	Madehsi
99.M12	Mahican
99.M18	Maidu
99.M19	Makah
99.M195	Malecite
99.M198	Manahoac
99.M2	Mandan
99.M22	Manhattan
99.M23	Manso
99.M25	Maricopa
99.M27	Martis culture
99.M3	Mascouten
99.M4	Mashpee
99.M42	Massachuset
99.M424	Massawomeck
99.M43	Mattole
99.M433	Mayas
	Cf. F1435+ Central America
	Cf. F1445+ British Honduras
	Cf. F1465+ Guatemala
99.M435	Mdewakanton
99.M44	Menominee
99.M45	Mescalero
99.M46	Methow
99.M47	Métis

Indians of North America
Tribes and cultures, A-Z -- Continued

99.M48	Miami
99.M6	Micmac
99.M615	Mikasuki
99.M62	Mikinakwadshiwininiwak
99.M625	Mill Creek
99.M63	Mimbreño
	Mimbres culture see E99.M76
99.M64	Mingo
99.M642	Miniconjou
99.M65	Minisink
99.M68	Missisauga
99.M6815	Mississippian culture
99.M682	Missouri
99.M683	Mistassin
99.M69	Miwok
99.M693	Mixed descent
	For Métis see E99.M47
99.M697	Moache
99.M698	Mobile
99.M7	Modoc
99.M75	Mogollon Apache
99.M76	Mogollon culture
	Including Mimbres culture
99.M77	Mohave
99.M8	Mohawk
99.M83	Mohegan
99.M84	Molala
99.M85	Monacan
99.M86	Mono
99.M87	Montagnais
99.M88	Montauk
99.M89	Moquelumnan
99.M9	Moravian
99.M917	Muckleshoot
99.M92	Multnomah
99.M93	Munsee
99.M95	Muskhogean
99.N125	Nahane
99.N14	Nanticoke
99.N16	Narranganset
99.N18	Naskapi
99.N19	Natchesan
99.N2	Natchez
99.N22	Natsitkutchin
99.N23	Naugatuck

Indians of North America
Tribes and cultures, A-Z -- Continued

99.N25	Nauset
99.N3	Navajo
99.N45	Nehalem
99.N46	Nespelim
99.N48	Neutral Nation
99.N5	Nez Percé
99.N6	Niantic
99.N65	Nipissing
99.N7	Nipmuc
99.N73	Nisenan
99.N734	Niska
99.N74	Nisqually
99.N815	Nomlaki
99.N84	Nooksack
99.N85	Nootka
99.N9	Norridgewock
99.N93	Nottoway
99.N96	Ntlakyapamuk
99.N97	Numic
99.O22	Occaneechi
99.O3	Oglala
99.O32	Ohlone
	Ojibwa see E99.C6
(99.O33)	Oka
	see E99.M8
99.O35	Okinagan
99.O4	Omaha
99.O45	Oneida
99.O5	Oneota (Great Plains)
99.O58	Onondaga
99.O63	Oohenonpa
99.O68	Oowekeeno
99.O8	Osage
99.O87	Oto
99.O9	Ottawa
99.P2	Paiute
99.P215	Palaihnihan
99.P22	Paloos
99.P225	Pamlico
99.P23	Pamunkey
99.P24	Panamint
99.P244	Panhandle culture
99.P25	Papago. Tohono O'Odham
99.P26	Pascagoula
99.P27	Passamaquoddy

Indians of North America
Tribes and cultures, A-Z -- Continued

99.P29	Patwin
99.P292	Paugusset
99.P3	Pawnee
99.P32	Payaya
99.P34	Pecos
99.P35	Pee Dee
99.P4	Pennacook
99.P5	Penobscot
99.P515	Peoria
99.P52	Pequawket
99.P53	Pequot
99.P57	Piankashaw
99.P575	Picuris
99.P58	Piegan
99.P6	Pima
99.P62	Piman
99.P63	Piro Pueblo
	Piscataway see E99.C873
	Plains Indians see E78.G73
99.P635	Plaquemine
99.P64	Pocasset
99.P65	Pomo
99.P7	Ponca
99.P8	Potawatomi
99.P83	Potomac
99.P84	Poverty Point culture
99.P85	Powhatan
	Including Pocahontas
99.P9	Pueblo
	Including Anasazi culture and cliff dwellings
99.P98	Puyallup
99.Q2	Quapaw
99.Q5	Quileute
99.Q6	Quinaielt
99.Q7	Quinnipiac
99.R18	Rappahannock
99.S14	Saclan
(99.S15)	Saint Regis
	see E99.M8
99.S16	Sakonnet
	Salado culture see E99.S547
99.S17	Salinan
99.S2	Salish
99.S21	Salishan
	Including Coast Salish and Puget Sound Salish

Indians of North America
Tribes and cultures, A-Z -- Continued

99.S2115	Samish
99.S212	San Felipe
99.S213	San Ildefonso
99.S214	Sandia
99.S215	Sanpoil
99.S217	Sans Arc
99.S22	Santee
99.S223	Santo Domingo
99.S225	Saone
99.S226	Saponi
99.S227	Sarsi
99.S23	Sauk
(99.S25)	Scaticook (Connecticut)
	see E99.S252
99.S252	Scaticook
99.S258	Sechelt
99.S26	Sekani
99.S28	Seminole
99.S3	Seneca
	Senijextee see E99.S546
99.S31	Serrano
99.S32	Sewee
99.S325	Shahaptian
99.S33	Shasta
99.S332	Shastan
99.S35	Shawnee
99.S38	Shinnecock
99.S39	Shoshonean
99.S4	Shoshoni
99.S45	Shuswap
(99.S5)	Sia
	see E99.Z52
99.S53	Sihasapa
99.S54	Siksika
99.S544	Siletz
99.S546	Sin Aikst. Senijextee. Lakes Indians
99.S547	Sinagua culture
	Including Salado culture
99.S55	Sinkiuse-Columbia
99.S56	Sinkyone
99.S6	Siouan
	Sioux see E99.D1
99.S62	Sisseton
99.S622	Siuslaw
99.S623	Siwanoy

Indians of North America
Tribes and cultures, A-Z -- Continued

99.S627	Skagit
99.S63	Skitswish. Coeur d'Alene
99.S64	Skokomish
99.S65	Slavey
99.S66	Snoqualmie
99.S665	Sokoki
	Songhees see E99.L35
99.S68	Spokan
99.S7	Squawmish
99.S72	Stalo
99.S75	Stillaquamish
99.S8	Stockbridge
99.S85	Suquamish
99.S95	Susquehanna
99.T114	Tabeguache
99.T115	Taensa
99.T12	Tahltan
99.T15	Takelma
99.T17	Takulli
99.T18	Tamaroa
99.T185	Tanai. Dena'ina
99.T187	Tanana
99.T189	Tanoan
99.T2	Taos
99.T315	Tawakoni
99.T32	Tenino
99.T325	Tequesta
99.T33	Têtes de Boule. Atikamekw
99.T34	Teton
99.T35	Tewa
99.T4	Thlingchadinne
99.T52	Tigua. Tiwa
99.T53	Tillamook
99.T54	Timiskaming
99.T55	Timucua
99.T56	Tinne
99.T57	Tionontati
	Tiwa see E99.T52
99.T58	Tlakluit
99.T6	Tlingit
	Tohono O'Odham see E99.P25
99.T7	Tolowa
99.T73	Tonikan
99.T75	Tonkawa
99.T77	Tsattine

Indians of North America
   Tribes and cultures, A-Z -- Continued

99.T772	Tsetsaut
99.T78	Tsilkotin
99.T8	Tsimshian
99.T83	Tubatulabal
99.T845	Tukkuthkutchin
99.T85	Tukuarika
99.T87	Tulalip
99.T875	Tunica
99.T88	Tunxis
99.T9	Tuscarora
99.T92	Tutchone
99.T96	Tutelo
99.T97	Tututni
99.T98	Twana
99.T986	Tzotzil
	Cf. F1221.T9 Mexico
99.U35	Uinta
99.U4	Umatilla
99.U45	Umpqua
99.U8	Ute
99.U85	Uto-Aztecan
99.V8	Vuntakutchin
99.W114	Waccamaw
99.W12	Wachuset
99.W125	Waco
99.W13	Wahpekute
99.W135	Wahpeton
99.W15	Wailaki
99.W16	Wakashan
99.W18	Walla Walla
99.W185	Walpapi
99.W19	Wamesit
99.W2	Wampanoag
99.W3	Wanapum
99.W34	Wappinger
99.W35	Wappo
99.W36	Warm Spring Apache
99.W37	Wasco
99.W38	Washoe. Washo
99.W4	Wawenock
99.W45	Wea
99.W48	Weeden Island culture
99.W5	Welsh
	Including the tradition and theories about this mythic tribe
99.W53	Wenatchi

Indians of North America
　　Tribes and cultures, A-Z -- Continued

99.W54	Wenrohronon
99.W56	Wet'suwet'en
99.W6	Wichita
99.W63	Wiechquaeskeck
99.W65	Wiminuche
99.W7	Winnebago
99.W78	Wintu
99.W79	Wintun
99.W8	Wiyat
99.W84	Woodland culture
99.W9	Wyam
99.Y18	Yahuskin
99.Y2	Yakama. Yakima
99.Y212	Yakonan
99.Y22	Yamassee
99.Y225	Yampa
99.Y23	Yana
99.Y25	Yankton
99.Y26	Yanktonai
	Yaqui see F1221.Y3
99.Y5	Yavapai
99.Y54	Yazoo
99.Y7	Yokayo
99.Y75	Yokuts
99.Y77	Yoncalla
99.Y9	Yuchi
99.Y92	Yukian
99.Y94	Yuma
99.Y95	Yuman
99.Y97	Yurok
99.Z52	Zia. Sia
99.Z9	Zuñi

Discovery of America and early explorations
　　Including early to about 1607

101	General works
	Pre-Columbian period
103	General works
	Special
105	Norse. Vinland

　　　　　　　Including biography of Leiv Eiriksson, Kensington rune
　　　　　　　　stone
　　　　　　　For Greenland see G725+

109.A-Z	Other, A-Z
109.A35	African
109.B3	Basque

Discovery of America and early explorations
   Pre-Columbian period
      Special
         Other, A-Z -- Continued

109.C37	Catalan
109.C44	Celtic
109.C5	Chinese
109.D2	Danish
109.D9	Dutch
109.E2	East Indian
109.E3	Egyptian
109.G7	Greek
109.I57	Indonesian
109.I6	Irish
109.I8	Italian

            Including voyages of the brothers Niccolò and Antonio Zeno

109.M34	Malian
109.P5	Phoenician
109.P65	Polynesian
109.P8	Portuguese
109.S7	Spanish
109.T74	Trojan
109.W4	Welsh

            For the tradition of the Welsh Indians see E99.W5

110   Background factors of the discovery, and resulting conditions
        Including the influence of Paolo del Pozzo Toscanelli, Martin Behaim
    Columbus (Cristoforo Colombo)

111   General works
        Including biography

112   Special
        Including autographs, birthplace, canonization, celebrations, coat of arms, education, friends, iconography, landfall, language, marriage, monuments, name, relics, ships, tomb
        For bibliography of Columbus see Z8187

113   Family
        Including the Colombo, Colón, Moniz, and Perestrello families
      Writings of Columbus

114   Collected works
          Arranged alphabetically by editor
          Including collected letters and collections of documents concerning him
        Individual works
          First letter (Santangel)

Discovery of America and early explorations
  Columbus (Cristoforo Colombo)
    Writings of Columbus
      Individual works
        First letter (Santangel) -- Continued

115	Spanish text. By date
	Including facsimiles and reprints without translation
115.2	Translations. By language, A-Z, and date of imprint
	With or without facsimiles or reprints of Spanish text
115.3	Paraphrases and works about the letter. By author
	Second letter (Sánchez)
116	Spanish text. By date
	Including facsimiles and reprints without translation
	Translations
116.1	Latin. By date
	Including the earliest translation as well as others made from it; facsimiles and texts
116.2	Other. By initial letter of language and date
	With or without facsimiles or reprints of Spanish text
116.3	Paraphrases and works about the letter. By author
117	Other writings
	For his journal see E118
118	Voyages. Journal of Columbus
119	Columbus celebrations, 1892-1893
	Arranged alphabetically by place
	Cf. T400+ National and international exhibitions
119.2	Columbus quincentennial, 1992-1993
120	Pamphlets, addresses, essays, etc.
	Including poetry, drama, Columbus Day celebrations and programs
	Cf. PN-PZ, Literature
	Post-Columbian period. El Dorado
	Including successors of Columbus to about 1607
121	General works
	Cf. G199.2+ History of geographical discoveries, explorations, and travels
	Cf. G575+ Polar discoveries
	Cf. G640+ Search for the Northwest Passage
	Spanish and Portuguese

Discovery of America and early explorations
Post-Columbian period. El Dorado
Spanish and Portuguese -- Continued

123   General works
Including Line of Demarcation drawn by Pope Alexander VI
in 1493 and modified by Treaty of Tordesillas, 1494
Cf. E141+ Descriptive accounts of America before
1607
Cf. F314 Spanish settlement in Florida before 1821
Cf. F1230 Spanish settlement in Mexico before 1810
Cf. F1411 History of Spanish America before 1600
Cf. F3442 Spanish settlement in Peru before 1820
Cf. G278+ History of geographical discoveries by the
Spanish and the Portuguese

125.A-Z   Individual explorers, A-Z
e.g.
125.A3   Aguilar, Jerónimo de (Table E1)
125.A35   Aguirre, Lope de (Table E1)
125.B2   Balboa, Vasco Núñez de (Table E1)
125.B7   Boyl, Bernardo (Table E1)
125.C11   Cabral, Pedro Alvares (Table E1)
125.C12   Cabrillo, Juan Rodríquez (Table E1)
125.C2   Caminha, Pedro Vaz de (Table E1)
125.C4   Casas, Bartolomé de las (Table E1)
For the tracts of Las Casas see F1411
Coronado, Francisco see E125.V3
125.C8   Cosa, Juan de la (Table E1)
125.F3   Federmann, Nikolaus (Table E1)
125.F35   Fernández, Juan (Table E1)
125.F9   Fuca, Juan de (Table E1)
125.G2   García, Diego de Moguer (Table E1)
125.G6   Gómez, Esteban (Table E1)
125.G8   Grijalva, Juan de (Table E1)
125.M3   Marco da Nizza, Father (Table E1)
125.N3   Narváez, Pánfilo de (Table E1)
125.N9   Núñez Cabeza de Vaca, Alvar (Table E1)
125.O58   Ordás, Diego de (Table E1)
125.O6   Orellano, Francisco de (Table E1)
125.P2   Pancaldo, León (Table E1)
125.P5   Pinzón, Martín Alonso (Table E1)
125.P52   Pinzón, Vincente Yáñez (Table E1)
125.P7   Ponce de León, Juan (Table E1)
125.S23   Sarmiento de Gamboa, Pedro (Table E1)
125.S3   Schmidel, Ulrich (Table E1)
125.S7   Soto, Hernando de (Table E1)
125.U8   Ursúa, Pedro de (Table E1)
125.V3   Vázquez de Coronado, Francisco (Table E1)

Discovery of America and early explorations
Post-Columbian period. El Dorado
Spanish and Portuguese
Individual explorers, A-Z -- Continued
125.V5   Vespucci, Amerigo (Table E1)
125.V6   The name "America"
English
127   General works
129.A-Z   Individual explorers, A-Z
129.C1   Cabot, John and Sebastian (Table E1)
129.D7   Drake, Sir Francis (Table E1)
                   Cf. G420.D7 Voyage of circumnavigation
129.G4   Gilbert, Sir Humphrey (Table E1)
129.H4   Hawkins, Sir Richard (Table E1)
129.H8   Hudson, Henry (Table E1)
                   Cf. F127.H8 Hudson: Fulton celebration, 1909
129.R2   Raleigh, Sir Walter (Table E1)
                   Cf. DA86.22.R2 Biography
                   Cf. F229 Raleigh's Roanoke colonies, 1584-1590
French
                   Cf. F314 French colony in Florida
                   Cf. F1030 New France
131   General works
133.A-Z   Individual explorers, A-Z
133.C3   Cartier, Jacques (Table E1)
133.P3   Paulmier de Gonneville, Binot (Table E1)
133.T47   Thevet, André (Table E1)
133.V5   Verrazzano, Giovanni da (Table E1)
135.A-Z   Other, A-Z
                   e.g.
135.D9   Dutch
135.G3   German. Welsers
135.I8   Italian
(139)   Allusions
                   Including works on subjects other than America, containing
                      allusions to the discovery and to the New World
                   For the books being classified with the subjects of which they
                      treat or the literature to which they belong, e.g., the polyglot
                      Psalter edited by Agostino Giustiniani, see BS1419 and the
                      Sentencias catholocias del divi, poeta Dant, compiled by
                      Jaume Ferrer de Blanes, see PS3937.F4
Descriptive accounts of America. Earliest to 1810
141   Earliest to 1606
                   Including 16th century travels
                   Cf. E101+ Discoveries
                   Cf. F1411 History of Latin America to 1600

143

Descriptive accounts of America. Earliest to 1810 -- Continued
    1607-1810. Latin America
        For other local, see corresponding country and period divisions
            in F
        For English colonies see E162
        For New France, 1603-1763 see F1030
        For Latin America since 1810 see F1409

	United States
	General
151	Periodicals. Societies. Collections
	Including general societies for the preservation of historic or other national interest, e.g., American Scenic and Historic Preservation Society
	For historical periodicals and societies, see E171+ E186 etc.
	For patriotic societies, see E172.7 E181 E182 E186 E202 etc.
	For geographic societies see G3
154	Gazetteers
	Directories
154.5	General
154.7	Social directories. Social registers
(154.9)	Business and trade directories
	see HF5035+
	Recreational directories see E158
155	Geographic names
	Cf. E98.N2 Indian names
	Cf. G104+ Geographic names and terms (General)
156	General works
	Electronic information resource catalogs see E175.88
158	Guidebooks. Handbooks
	Including directories of summer and winter resorts, excursions
159	Historic monuments (General)
	Including mansions, mission buildings, public buildings
	For individual mansions, mission buildings, public buildings, etc., see local divisions
	For historical and descriptive works on regions traversed by a road, see class F
	For general questions of the location and removal of the national capital see F195
	For roads see HE356.A+
	Cf. E179.5 Boundaries
	Cf. G109+ Distances
159.5	Antiquities (non-Indian)
160	National and state parks and reservations (Collective descriptive works)
	For works on individual parks, including theory, management and description, see the subject or local division, e.g., E475.81 Chickamauga and Chattanooga National Military Park; F868.Y6, Yosemite National Park
	Including national forests as parks
	For works on theory, management and history, etc. of U.S. parks and public reservations in general see SB482.A1+
	Cf. SD426+ Forest reserves

E151-909

General -- Continued

161	Social life and customs (General)

Including antiquities, museums, etc., illustrative of American life,
e.g., Henry Ford Museum and Greenfield Village,
Dearborn, Mich.

Cf. E169.1+ Civilization, intellectual life

By period see E162+

161.3	Geography

Description and travel

For regions, see class F, Local history, e. g. F106 Atlantic
coast; F206+ Southern States; F351+ Mississippi Valley;
F476+ Old Northwest; F591+ The West

For travel before era of settlement see E141+

161.5	History of travels. Travel anthologies

By period

Including works on civilization, social life

Class a general work of travel through the country in 1785 in
E164, not in F106, Atlantic States

162	1607-1764

Including general descriptive works on the British colonies
in America including Thanksgiving Day and customs

Cf. F7 Thanksgiving Day in New England

Cf. GT4975 Festivals

163	1765-1783
164	1784-1811
165	1812-1844
166	1845-1860
167	1861-1865

For travels in the Confederate States see F214

168	1866-1913
169.A-.Z7	1914-1944
169.Z8	1945-1980
169.Z82	1981-2000
169.Z83	2001-
(169.02)	1945-1980

see E169.Z8

(169.04)	1981-2000

see E169.Z82; E169.Z83

Civilization. Intellectual life

Including national characteristics, ideals, Americanization

Cf. E161 Social life and customs (General)

Cf. JK1758 Manuals for foreign-born citizens

169.1	General works

By period

Early to 1865 see E162+

1866-1945 see E169.1

169.12	1945-

	General
	Civilization. Intellectual life -- Continued
	Biography (Americanization literature) see E184+
	History
171	Periodicals. Yearbooks
172	Societies

E151-909

171   Periodicals. Yearbooks
172   Societies
                Including historical departments of other organizations, e.g., museums, libraries
                Cf. E175.4 Historiography
              Geographic societies see G3
              Patriotic hereditary societies
172.7   General works
              Individual societies
                see E181+ E186 E202 etc.
              Political and patriotic societies primarily interested in social objectives see HS2321+
172.9   Congresses, seminars, etc.
173   Sources and documents. Collections. Collected works
              Including exhibitions of source materials
174   Dictionaries and encyclopedias
174.5   Chronology. Chronological tables, etc.
            Historiography
              For general works on state and local historiography see E180+
175   General works. History
175.1   Pamphlets, etc.
175.4   Institutions
              Including programs, reports, methods of organization and work
              Including the work of government commissions, historical societies, etc.
175.4.C3   Carnegie Institution of Washington. Division of Historical Research
            Biography of historians
              Including general criticism of their works
              For criticism of a particular work, see the work
175.45   Collective
175.5.A-Z   Individual, A-Z
              Subarrange each by Table E1
              e.g.
175.5.B38   Beard, Charles Austin
175.7   Methodology
              Including theory, comparison and criticism, etc. Research

	History -- Continued
175.8	Study and teaching
	Class here study and teaching in colleges, universities, and secondary schools
	For primary schools see LB1530
	For elementary schools see LB1581+
175.85	Criticism of textbooks (General)
	Cf. E468.5 Criticism of textbooks on the Civil War
175.87	Film catalogs
175.88	Electronic information resource catalogs
175.9	Philosophy of American history
	Biography (Collective)
176	General
	For biography of individual periods, see the period, e.g., E302.5, 1775-1829
	For general United States biography not limited to political life see CT210+
176.1	Presidents
	For the biography of each president, see his administration, e. g. E312 Washington; E322 Jefferson
	Presidential inaugurations are classed in local history, e.g, F128.44, New York City, for Washington's first inauguration in 1789; but F158.44, Philadelphia, for his second in 1793; F197-200, Washington, D.C., for the inauguration of Jefferson and succeeding presidents
	For White House see F204.W5
176.2	Wives of Presidents
176.25	Fathers of Presidents
176.3	Mothers of Presidents
176.4	Relations with women
176.45	Children and grandchildren of Presidents
176.47	Staff
176.472.A-Z	Relations with specific ethnic groups, A-Z
176.472.A34	African Americans
176.472.J47	Jews
176.48	Pets
176.49	Vice-Presidents
176.5	Portraits
	Class here works emphasizing historical aspects
	For works emphasizing the artistic aspect or the artist see N7593+
176.6	Hall of Fame, New York University
176.8	Juvenile works

History -- Continued
  Biography (Individual)
        see under periods in national or state history, e.g., E195, United
            States, 1689-1775; E207, Revolution; F122, New York
            State before 1775; also under topics, e. g. E181-E182,
            Military and naval leaders; E185.97, African-Americans. For
            the life of a representative in Congress and governor of a
            state, see state history unless his national career has been
            decidedly more prominent
  General works

178	Comprehensive works
178.1	Textbooks
178.2	Outlines, syllabi, etc.
	For chronology see E174.5
178.25	Examinations, questions, etc.
178.3	Juvenile works
	Including collections of stories from American history for children
	Cf. PE1127.H5+ English readers on United States history
178.4	Comic and satirical works
	Including humor of American history
178.5	Pictorial works
178.6	Addresses, essays, lectures, etc.
178.9	Poetical works. Rhyming histories
	Collections or single poems on a particular event are classed with the subject, e.g., E233, Ballads and poems relating to the Burgoyne campaign
	For general collections of American historical poems see PS595.H5
179	General special
	Including topics such as disasters, floods, pageants, vigilance committees, etc., in general not otherwise provided for
	For local, see class F
179.5	Historical geography
	Including Boundaries (General), the frontier, history of territorial expansion, public domain, regionalism
	For anthropogeography see GF503+
	Cf. E713 Expansion controversy, imperialism, etc.
	Cf. JK2556 Territorial government and administration

History
Historical geography -- Continued
Boundaries (Special)
For Northeast (1783-1845) see E398
For Northeast (Maine) see F27.B7
For Northeast (New Hampshire) see F42.B7
For Northeast (Vermont) see F57.B7
For Northeast (New York) see F127.B7
For Southeast (Florida) see F317.B7
For Southwest (Texas) see F392.B7
For North (Great Lakes) see F550.5+
For Northwest see F597
For Southwest see F786
For Pacific Northwest see F854
For Oregon see F880
For Alaska see F912.B7
History of states and counties, collectively
Class counties limited to one state with that state
180   General works
180.5   State and local historiography
181   Military history
Including battles of more than two wars
Including military societies, veterans' organizations, etc.,
covering more than one war: Medal of Honor Legion of the
United States, Military Order of Foreign Wars of the United
States; Military Order of the Purple Heart; Society of
American Wars of the United States, etc.
Including military biography not limited to one war: William
Selby Harney, John Joseph Pershing, Hugh Lenox Scott,
Leonard Wood, etc.
For military history of individual wars, see the war, e.g., E230-
239, Revolution; E470-478, Civil War
For Grand Army of the Republic (Civil War) see E462.1
For battles of more than two wars in the twentieth century
see E745
Cf. U52+ Biography (Military science)

History -- Continued

182   Naval history (United States Navy and Marine Corps)
Including naval battles of more than two wars
Including naval societies, veterans' organizations, etc., covering
more than one war: Naval Order of the United States,
United States Navy Veteran Association, etc.
Naval biography not limited to one war: Smedley Darlington
Butler; Stephen Decatur, 1752-1808; Robley Dunglison
Evans; Ernest Joseph King; Edward Yorke Macauley;
Alfred Thayer Mahan; Richard Worsam Meade; Hiram
Paulding; Matthew Calbraith Perry; John Woodward Philip;
George Henry Preble; Francis Asbury Roe; Stephen Clegg
Rowan; Benjamin Franklin Sands; Charles Steedman;
Thomas Truxtun, etc.
For naval history of individual wars, see the war, e.g., E271,
Revolution; E591-600, Civil War
For National Association of Naval Veterans (Civil War)
see E462.5
For naval history of the twentieth century see E746
Cf. V62+ Biography (Naval science)
Political history
Political history of a period or administration is classed with the
period or administration, e.g., E188, Colonial history; E801,
Hoover's administration
183   General works
183.3   Political collectibles. Political Americana
Diplomatic history. Foreign and general relations
General works on the diplomatic history of a period or
administration are classed with the period or administration,
e.g., E313, Washington's administration; E661.7, Period
since the Civil War; E744, Twentieth century. All works on
relations with a specific country are classed in E183.8,
regardless of administration or period
Cf. JZ1482 Monroe Doctrine
183.7   General works

E151-909

	History
	Diplomatic history. Foreign and general relations -- Continued
(183.75)	Relations with special groups of countries
	For Europe (1945-) see D1065.U5
	For Islamic countries see DS35.74.U6
	For Near East see DS63.2.U5
	For East Asia see DS518.8
	For Africa see DT38+
	For Oceania see DU30
	For Barbary States (1801-1809) see E335
	For Central American, West Indian, and other countries protected by and having close political affiliations with the United States see F975
	For International American Conference see F1404.5+
	For Latin America see F1418
	For West Indies see F1622
183.8.A-Z	Relations with individual countries, A-Z
183.9	Other (not A-Z)
	Elements in the population
184.A-Z	Elements, A-Z
	Including racial, ethnic, and religious groups that have significance in the history of the United States, and including collective and individual biography of members of these groups
	Elements in individual regions, states, cities, etc., are classed with the region, state, city, etc., e.g., F128.9.G3, Germans in New York (City)
	The Cutter numbers are intended to be used as a guide for the best distribution of numbers and not to be used as a fixed standard or to affect numbers already assigned
	Cf. BX, Special churches and sects
	For voyages of discovery of various nationalities see E101+
	For voyages of discovery by various nationalities see G220+
184.A1	General works
	Including foreign elements (General), minorities, race conflicts, and problems
184.A2	Acadians. Cajuns
184.A23	Afghans

Elements in the population
Elements, A-Z -- Continued

184.A24	Africans

For African Americans, see E184.4+ E441+ or class F
For works on African Americans in the United States in
general or in individual regions or states, see E185.5+ or
E441+ For works on African Americans in individual
counties, cities or towns, see class F. If the pertinent
number in F provides for an A-Z arrangement for
elements in the population, assign ".N4".

184.A26	Afrikaners
184.A3	Albanians
184.A4	Alsatians
	Amish see E184.M45
184.A65	Arabs
184.A67	Argentines
184.A7	Armenians
184.A75	Asians
184.A8	Assyrians
184.A9	Austrians
184.A94	Azerbaijanis
184.A95	Azoreans
184.B13	Bangladeshis
184.B15	Basques
184.B2	Belgians
184.B26	Bengali
184.B67	Bohemians. Czechs
184.B674	Bolivians
184.B675	Bosnians
184.B676	Brass Ankles
184.B68	Brazilians
184.B69	Bretons
184.B7	British

Including the English
For other nationalities, see the nationality, e.g., E184.S3,
Scotch

184.B8	Bulgarians
184.B89	Burundians
	Byelorussians see E184.W6
	Cajuns see E184.A2
	Cambodians see E184.K45
184.C2	Canadians
184.C22	Canary Islanders
184.C24	Cape Verdeans
184.C27	Caribbeans
184.C29	Catalans

E151-909

	Elements in the population
	Elements, A-Z -- Continued
184.C3	Catholics
	For the Catholic Church see BX1404+
	For Catholic religious orders see BX2505+
	Cf. E184.C36 Chaldean Catholics
184.C34	Central Americans
184.C36	Chaldean Catholics
184.C4	Chileans
184.C5	Chinese
184.C58	Colombians
184.C6	Cornish
184.C8	Covenanters
184.C87	Creoles
184.C9	Cretans
184.C93	Croats. Croatians
184.C97	Cubans
184.C98	Cypriots
	Czechs see E184.B67
	Danes see E184.S19
184.D6	Dominicans (Dominican Republic)
184.D78	Druzes
184.D9	Dutch
184.E17	East Europeans
184.E2	East Indians
	Cf. E184.G84 Gujaratis
	Cf. E184.K35 Kanarese
	Cf. E184.M37 Marathas
	Cf. E184.P28 Pakistanis
	Cf. E184.P36 Panjabis
184.E28	Ecuadorians
184.E38	Egyptians
(184.E5)	English
	see E184.B7
184.E7	Estonians
184.E74	Ethiopians
184.E95	Europeans
	Cf. E184.E17 East Europeans
184.F4	Filipinos
184.F5	Finns
184.F57	Flemings
184.F8	French
	Cf. E184.A2 Acadians
	Cf. E184.F85 French Canadians
	Cf. E184.H9 Huguenots
184.F85	French Canadians
	Cf. E184.A2 Acadians

E151-909

Elements in the population

Elements, A-Z -- Continued

184.F89	Friends. Society of Friends. Quakers
	For American yearly meetings see BX7607.A+
	For Friends as religious body see BX7635+
	For individual meeting houses see BX7780
184.F894	Frisians
184.G24	Gambians
184.G27	Georgians (South Caucasians)
184.G3	Germans
	For Palatines see E184.P3
	Cf. E184.M7 Moravians
	Cf. E184.R85 Russian Germans
	Cf. E184.S78 Swabians
184.G44	Ghanaians
184.G7	Greeks
184.G75	Grenadians
184.G82	Guatemalans
184.G84	Gujaratis
184.G86	Guyanese
184.H27	Haitians
184.H3	Hawaiians
	Hispanic Americans see E184.S75
184.H55	Hmong (Asian people)
184.H66	Hondurans
184.H9	Huguenots
184.H95	Hungarians
184.H97	Hutterite Brethren
184.I3	Icelanders
	Indians see E75+
184.I43	Indochinese
184.I45	Indonesians
184.I5	Iranians
184.I55	Iraqis
184.I6	Irish
	Cf. E184.S4 Scots-Irish
184.I7	Israelis
184.I8	Italians
184.I96	Ivoirians
	Jackson Whites see E184.R3
184.J27	Jamaicans
184.J3	Japanese
	For Japanese-American war relocation see D769.8.A6

Elements in the population
Elements, A-Z -- Continued

(184.J5)	Jews

This number is not valid for works about Jews in the United States as a whole. The Cutter number .J5 may be used under those numbers in the United States local history that are subarranged by this list of Cutter numbers, e.g. F73.9.J5, Jews in Massachusetts
see E184.3+

Jugoslavs see E184.Y7

184.K3	Kalmyks
184.K35	Kanarese
184.K37	Kashubes
184.K43	Kenyans
184.K45	Khmers. Cambodians
184.K6	Koreans
184.K87	Kurds
184.L27	Laos
184.L34	Lebanese
184.L4	Letts. Latvians
184.L53	Liberians
184.L55	Liechtensteiners
184.L7	Lithuanians
184.L88	Luxemburgers
184.M3	Macedonians
184.M33	Malians
184.M34	Maltese
184.M37	Marathas
184.M44	Melungeons
184.M45	Mennonites. Amish

For the Mennonite Church see BX8116+

184.M47	Mestizos
184.M5	Mexicans
184.M52	Middle Easterners
184.M53	Minorcans
184.M66	Montenegrins
184.M7	Moravians

For Moravian Church see BX8566+; BX8581

184.M8	Mormons
184.M83	Mountain people

Cf. F210 Southern States

184.M88	Muslims
(184.N4)	Negroes

see E184.5+, E441+, or class F
Assign the Cutter .N4 only for numbers in class F that provide for an A-Z arrangement for elements in the population

184.N53	Nicaraguans

Elements in the population
Elements, A-Z -- Continued

184.N55	Nigerians
	Norwegians see E184.S2
(184.O6)	Orientals
	see E184.A75
184.P25	Pacific Islanders
184.P28	Pakistanis
184.P3	Palatines
184.P33	Palestinians
184.P35	Panamanians
184.P36	Panjabis
	Persians see E184.I5
184.P47	Peruvians
184.P7	Poles
184.P8	Portuguese
184.P85	Puerto Ricans
184.R3	Ramapo Mountain people
184.R8	Romanians
	Romanies see DX201
184.R85	Russian Germans
184.R9	Russians
	Ruthenians see E184.U5
184.R93	Rwandans
184.R97	Ryukyuans
184.S15	Salvadorans
184.S16	Sami Americans
184.S17	Samoans
184.S18	Scandinavians
184.S19	Danes
184.S2	Norwegians
184.S23	Swedes
184.S3	Scotch. Scots
184.S4	Scots-Irish
184.S48	Senegalese
184.S5	Serbs
184.S53	Shakers
184.S54	Sierra Leoneans
184.S55	Sikhs

E151-909

Elements in the population

Elements, A-Z -- Continued

184.S6	Slavs
	Cf. E184.B67 Bohemians. Czechs
	Cf. E184.B8 Bulgarians
	Cf. E184.C93 Croats
	Cf. E184.P7 Poles
	Cf. E184.R9 Russians
	Cf. E184.S5 Serbs
	Cf. E184.S64 Slovaks
	Cf. E184.S65 Slovenes
	Cf. E184.U5 Ukrainians
	Cf. E184.Y7 Yugoslavs
184.S64	Slovaks
184.S65	Slovenes
184.S67	Somalis
184.S68	Sorbs
184.S69	South Asians
184.S695	Southeast Asians
184.S7	Spaniards
184.S75	Spanish Americans
	Cf. E184.C34 Central Americans
	Cf. E184.M5 Mexicans
184.S77	Sudanese
184.S78	Swabians
	Swedes see E184.S23
184.S9	Swiss
184.S98	Syrians
184.T35	Taiwanese
184.T4	Thais
184.T53	Tibetans
184.T88	Turks
184.U5	Ukrainians
	Including Ruthenians
184.V53	Vietnamese
184.W35	Walloons
184.W4	Welsh
184.W5	Wesorts
184.W54	West Indians
184.W6	White Russians
184.Y36	Yao (Southeast Asian people)
184.Y44	Yemenites
184.Y66	Yoruba
184.Y7	Yugoslavs
184.2	Americans in foreign countries
	Americans in a particular country are classified with that country

	Elements in the population -- Continued
	Jews
	Including Italian Jews, Russian Jews, etc.
184.3	Periodicals
184.312	Congresses
184.32	Collections. Sources
184.33	Historiography
184.34	Study and teaching
184.35	History (General). General works
	For history of Judaism in the United States, including individual synagogues and congregations see BM205+
	By period
184.3512	Colonial period to 1776
184.352	1776-1880
184.353	1880-1925
184.354	1925-1945
184.355	1945-
184.36.A-Z	Special topics, A-Z
184.36.A34	African American-Jewish relations
	Antisemitism see DS146.U6
184.36.E25	Economic conditions
	For special aspects of economic conditions, see class H
184.36.E84	Ethnic identity
	For relations between American Jews and Israel see DS132
184.36.E86	Ethnic relations
184.36.I58	Intellectual life
184.36.P64	Politics and government
184.36.S65	Social conditions. Social life and customs
	Including family, youth, children, etc.
	For special aspects of social conditions, including specific activities, services, etc., see class H
	For religious life see BM723+
184.36.W64	Women
	Including collective biography
	By region, state, etc.
	see class F
	Biography and memoirs
184.37.A1-.A19	Collective
	For collective biography of women see E184.36.W64
184.37.A2-Z	Individual, A-Z
	African Americans
	Including works on free African Americans in the United States before 1863
	Periodicals, societies, etc. see E185.5
184.5	Congresses

E151-909

Elements in the population
African Americans -- Continued
184.6   Collections. Sources
184.65   Historiography
               Study and teaching. African American studies
184.7.A1-.Z8   General works
184.7.Z9   Catalogs of audiovisual materials
185   General works. History (General)
                  Cf. E441+ Slavery in the United States
                  Cf. E448 Colonization
                  Cf. E453 Emancipation
                  Cf. GN645 Black race (Anthropology)
                  Cf. HT973.2+ Slave trade (General)
                  Cf. HV3181+ Protection, assistance, and relief for
                     African Americans
                  Cf. LC2701+ Education of African Americans
               History (By period)
185.18   To 1863
                     Including free African Americans
                     For free African Americans in an individual state see
                        E185.93.A+
185.2   1863-1877
                     Including from emancipation to the end of the
                        reconstruction period, the African American as a ward
                        of the nation, ex-slaves, slave pensions, Freedmen's
                        Bureau (Bureau of Refugees, Freedmen, and
                        Abandoned Lands).
                     For Reconstruction in individual southern states, see the
                        state, eg., F231, Virginia; F259, North Carolina
                     For Freedmen, by state see E185.93.A+
                     For Reconstruction (General), 1865-1877 see E668
                  1877-1964. Reconstruction to Civil Rights Act of 1964
185.5   Periodicals. Societies. Collections
                     Including periodicals and societies before emancipation,
                        and post 1964
                     Cf. HS2259+ Fraternal and social societies
                  Museums. Exhibitions, etc.
185.53.A1   General works
185.53.A3-Z   By city and museum, A-Z
185.6   General works

E151-909

Elements in the population
 African Americans
  History (By period)
   1877-1964. Reconstruction to Civil Rights Act of 1964 --
    Continued
185.61   Race relations
      Including attitudes, discriminations, loyalties, prejudices;
        civil rights; interracial cooperation, movements, and
        practices; segregation
      For relations with Indians see E98.R28
      For relations with Jewish Americans see
        E184.36.A34
      Cf. BP221+ Black Muslims
      Cf. JK1924+ African American suffrage
      Cf. LC212.5+ Racial segregation in schools
185.615   1964-
      Including race relations
      For periodicals, societies, etc. see E185.5
    Special topics
185.62   Intermarriage of races. Miscegenation. Mulattoes
185.625   Psychosocial factors. Race identity
185.63   African Americans in the Armed Forces
      Cf. D639.N4 World War I, 1914-1918
      Cf. E269.N3 Revolution, 1775-1783
      Cf. E540.N3 Civil War, 1861-1865 (Union Army)
      Cf. E585.A35 Civil War, 1861-1865 (Confederate
        Army)
      Cf. E725.5.N3 Spanish-American War, 1898
    Crime. Delinquency see HV6197.A+
(185.7)   Religion. African American churches
      For African American religions not limited to
        Christianity see BL1+
      For Black Muslims see BP221+
      For African American churches (General), African
        American clergy, etc. see BR563.N4
      For missions to African Americans (Individual
        denominations) see BV2766.A+
      For missions to African Americans (General) see
        BV2783
      For individual Christian sects, denominations, local
        churches see BX1+
185.8   Economic conditions
      For special aspects of economic conditions, see class H
    The professions
      see the individual profession
185.86   Social conditions. Social life and customs
      Including family, women, youth, children, etc.

	Elements in the population
	African Americans
	Special topics -- Continued
	Health. Physical condition
	see class R
185.89.A-Z	Other topics, A-Z
185.89.E8	Ethnobotany
	Gay African Americans see HQ76.27.A37
	Housing see HD7293+
	Iconography
	see class N
185.89.I56	Intellectual life
185.89.N3	Names
	Relations with Jewish Americans see E184.36.A34
185.89.R45	Reparations
	Transportation see HE1+
	By region, state, etc.
185.9	African Americans in the North
185.912	African Americans in the Appalachian Region
185.915	African Americans in the Middle West and Old Northwest
185.917	African Americans in New England
185.92	African Americans in the South
	For pre-1964 material see E185; E185.6
185.925	African Americans in the West
185.93.A-.W	By state, A-W
	For African Americans in an individual county, city, or town, see F, e.g., F128.9.N3, African Americans in New York
	For slavery in an individual state see E445.A+
185.93.A3	Alabama
185.93.A4	Alaska
185.93.A7	Arizona
185.93.A8	Arkansas
185.93.C2	California
185.93.C6	Colorado
185.93.C7	Connecticut
185.93.D4	Delaware
185.93.D6	District of Columbia
185.93.F5	Florida
185.93.G4	Georgia
185.93.H3	Hawaii
185.93.I15	Idaho
185.93.I2	Illinois
185.93.I4	Indiana
185.93.I64	Iowa
185.93.K16	Kansas
185.93.K3	Kentucky
185.93.L6	Louisiana

Elements in the population
  African Americans
    By region, state, etc.
      By state, A-W -- Continued

185.93.M15	Maine
185.93.M2	Maryland
185.93.M3	Massachusetts
185.93.M5	Michigan
185.93.M55	Minnesota
185.93.M6	Mississippi
185.93.M7	Missouri
185.93.M8	Montana
185.93.N5	Nebraska
185.93.N52	Nevada
185.93.N53	New Hampshire
185.93.N54	New Jersey
185.93.N55	New Mexico
185.93.N56	New York
185.93.N6	North Carolina
185.93.N7	North Dakota
185.93.O2	Ohio
185.93.O4	Oklahoma
185.93.O7	Oregon
185.93.P41	Pennsylvania
185.93.R4	Rhode Island
185.93.S7	South Carolina
	Including the Sea Islands
185.93.S8	South Dakota
185.93.T3	Tennessee
185.93.T4	Texas
185.93.U8	Utah
185.93.V4	Vermont
185.93.V8	Virginia
185.93.W3	Washington
185.93.W5	West Virginia
185.93.W58	Wisconsin
185.93.W9	Wyoming
185.94	African Americans living in foreign countries (Collectively)
	For African Americans in a particular country, see the country
	Biography. Genealogy

Elements in the population
  African Americans
    Biography. Genealogy -- Continued
      Collective
185.96
        Including biographical dictionaries and directories
        Class here general collected biography, including collected
          biography of African Americans in public life covering
          several or all periods of United States history
        For biography of African Americans in public life covering a
          single period of United States history, see the period
        For African Americans associated with a special field, see
          the field
        For African Americans of an individual county, city or town,
          see F
        For African Americans of special regions or states
          see E185.9+
      Individual, A-Z
185.97.A-Z
        Cutter numbers listed below are provided as examples
        For African Americans associated with a special field
          (including politics), see the field or period of activity
        For African Americans in an individual county, city or town,
          see F, e.g., F128.9.N3, New York (City)
        For African Americans of special regions or states
          see E185.9+
        For biography of slaves (1775-1861) see E444
        For biography of slaves (1830-1863) see E449+
        Carver, George Washington see S417.A+
185.97.R63   Robeson, Paul (Table E1)
185.97.T8   Truth, Sojourner (Table E1)
185.97.W4   Washington, Booker Taliaferro (Table E1)
185.97.Z9   Anonymous
      Biography of persons other than African Americans
        identified primarily with African Americans
185.98.A1   Collective
185.98.A3-Z   Individual, A-Z
          Subarrange each by Table E1
    Colonial history, 1607-1775
      From earliest permanent English settlements on the Atlantic
        Coast to the American Revolution
      Including the thirteen colonies
186   Periodicals. Societies
        e.g., The Prince Society and its publications
      Patriotic societies
186.3   Society of Colonial Wars (Table E4)
186.4   National Society of the Colonial Dames of America (Table
          E4)
186.5   Colonial Dames of America (Table E4)

56

Colonial history, 1607-1775

Patriotic societies -- Continued

186.6	Order of the Founders and Patriots of America (Table E4)
186.7	Colonial Daughters of the Seventeenth Century (Table E4)
186.8	Daughters of Founders and Patriots of America (Table E4)
186.99.A-Z	Other, A-Z
186.99.C55	Colonial Dames of the XVII Century (Table E5)
186.99.D3	Daughters of the American Colonists (Table E5)
186.99.H55	Hereditary Order of Descendants of Colonial Governors (Table E5)
186.99.N33	National Society of the Colonial Daughters of America (Table E5)
186.99.O6	Order of Colonial Lords of Manors in America (Table E5)
	Order of Washington see E202.7
186.99.P6	The Pilgrims (Table E5)
186.99.S5	Sons and Daughters of the Pilgrims (Table E5)
187	Collections. Collected works
	Including monographs, essays, documents, sources
187.A5	American colonial tracts monthly
187.A53	American political tracts
187.C72	Colonial pamphlets
187.F69	Force, Peter. Tracts and other papers
187.H42	Hazard, Ebenezer. Historical collections
187.O7	Original narratives of early American history
187.2	Historiography
	Biography
187.5	Collective. Genealogy
	Including comprehensive lists of English immigrants
	For biography of later colonial period, beginning with French and Indian War, is classed in E302.5; genealogy of New England in F3; etc.
	For lists of immigrants of other nationalities see E184.A+
	Individual
	see E191+ E302.6 and individual wars

E151-909

Colonial history, 1607-1775 -- Continued
188   General works
       Cf. E82 Indian wars (General)
       Cf. E83.63+ individual Indian wars
       Cf. E101+ Discovery and exploration of America to 1607
       Cf. E141+ General accounts of America to 1810
       Cf. E162 Travel and description
       Cf. F7 New England to 1775
       Cf. F229 Raleigh's Roanoke colonies, 1584-1590
       Cf. F314 French Huguenot colonies
       Cf. F1030 British North America
       Cf. F2131 British West Indies
       Cf. F2361+ British Guiana
       Cf. JV1000+ Administration of British colonies
188.5   Addresses, essays, lectures, sermons, etc.
189   Minor works
       Including pamphlets, pageants, etc., and otherwise unprovided-
         for topics
       Discussions on European origin of American institutions are
         classed in D unless largely American history
   By period
191   1607-1689
       Cf. E83.63 Pequot War, 1636-1638
       Cf. E83.663 War with Esopus Indians, 1658-1664
       Cf. E83.67 King Philip's War, 1675-1676
       Cf. F7 Council for New England, 1620; Plymouth
         Company, 1606; United Colonies of New England,
         1643-1684; etc.
       Cf. F7.5 Governor Andros and his government, 1688
       Cf. F22 Popham Colony, Maine
       Cf. F229 Virginia Company of London
     1689-1775
       Including attempts at union; Albany Congress of 1754; last
         years of colonial government, 1763-1775
       Biography: Sir William Johnson, William Shirley, etc.
       Cf. E83.71 Tuscarora War, 1711-1713
       Cf. E83.72 Wars with the eastern Indians (New
         England)
       Cf. E83.739 Wars with Chickasaw Indians, 1739-1740
       Cf. E83.76 Pontiac's Conspiracy, 1763-1765
       Cf. E210+ Political history, disputes with Great Britain
       Cf. E215.2 Stamp Act Congress, 1765
       Cf. F517 Ohio Company
       Cf. F1032 Quebec Act, 1774
       Cf. F2272.5 Cartagena Expedition, 1741
195   General works

E151-909

Colonial history, 1607-1775
By period
1689-1775 -- Continued
196   King William's War, 1689-1697
Including the destruction of Schenectady, 1690; capture of
Port Royal (Nova Scotia), 1690; Quebec Expedition,
1690; Massacre at Haverhill, 1697
197   Queen Anne's War, 1702-1713
Including Massacres at Deerfield (1704), Haverhill (1708),
etc.; Church's expedition to the eastward; capture of
Port Royal (Nova Scotia), 1710; Walker's expedition to
Quebec, 1711
Cf. D281+ War of Spanish Succession, 1710-1714
Cf. E83.71 Tuscarora War, 1711-1713
198   King George's War, 1744-1748
Including siege and capture of Louisburg (Cape Breton
Island), 1745
Biography: Sir William Pepperell, etc.
Cf. D291+ War of the Austrian Succession, 1740-
1748
Cf. F1036+ Nova Scotia, Acadia, Cape Breton Island
199   French and Indian War, 1755-1763
Including Washington at Fort Necessity, 1754; Braddock's
defeat, 1755; Battle of Lake George, 1755; siege of
Fort Beauséjour, 1755; siege of Fort William Henry,
1757; expeditions against Ticonderoga and Crown
Point, 1755-1759; second siege and capture of
Louisburg, 1758; capture of Fort Frontenac, 1758;
Niagara and Quebec campaigns, 1759
Biography: John Bradstreet; Francois Gaston, duc de
Levis; Louis Joseph de Montcalm-Gozon, marquis de
Saint-Veran; Robert Rogers, etc.
Cf. DD409+ Seven Years' War, 1756-1763
Cf. E83.759 Cherokee War, 1759-1761
Cf. E195+ Albany Congress, 1754
Cf. F1038 Winslow's expedition for expulsion of the
Acadians, 1755
Cf. F1781 Siege of Havana, 1762-1763
Elements in the population see E184.A+
The Revolution, 1775-1783
201   Periodicals. Societies
202   Societies (Patriotic and hereditary)
Including reports, registers
For publications of the Seventy-Six Society, see E203.S49
For collections of documents, memoirs, etc. see E203
202.1   Society of the Cincinnati (Table E4)
202.2   Daughters of the Cincinnati (Table E4)

The Revolution, 1775-1783
　　Societies (Patriotic and hereditary) -- Continued
202.3　　　　　　　Sons of the American Revolution (Table E4)
202.4　　　　　　　Sons of the Revolution (Table E4)
　　　　　　　　　　Including proposals for the union of Sons of the Revolution
　　　　　　　　　　　　and Sons of the American Revolution
202.5　　　　　　　Daughters of the American Revolution (Table E4)
202.6　　　　　　　Daughters of the Revolution (Table E4)
202.7　　　　　　　Order of Washington (Table E4)
202.8　　　　　　　Washington Society of Maryland (Table E4)
202.9　　　　　　　Children of the American Revolution (Table E4)
202.99.A-Z　　　　Other, A-Z
　　　　　　　　　　Subarrange each by Table E5
　　　　　　　　　　e.g.
202.99.M64　　　　Military Order of Pulaski (Table E5)
202.99.O63　　　　Order of LaFayette (Table E5)
202.99.O65　　　　Order of the Descendants of the Signers of the Secret
　　　　　　　　　　　　Pact or Prior Declaration of Independence (Table E5)
　　　　　　　　Museums, exhibitions see E289
203　　　　　　　Collections. Collected works
　　　　　　　　　　Including documents, essays, letters, journals, memoirs
　　　　　　　　　　For Collections of anecdotes see E296
204　　　　　　　Congresses, seminars, etc.
　　　　　　　　Biography
　　　　　　　　　　Including portraits
206　　　　　　　　Collective
　　　　　　　　　　Especially military and naval leaders
　　　　　　　　　　For signers of the Declaration of Independence see
　　　　　　　　　　　　E221
　　　　　　　　　　For statesmen of the Revolutionary period see E302.5
207.A-Z　　　　　　Individual, A-Z
　　　　　　　　　　Including lives of military and naval commanders and staff
　　　　　　　　　　　　officers
　　　　　　　　　　e.g.
　　　　　　　　　　For regimental officers and privates see E263.A+;
　　　　　　　　　　　　E275.A2+
　　　　　　　　　　For scouts and spies see E279+
　　　　　　　　　　Cf. E302.6.A+ Lives of individual statesmen
207.A3　　　　　　　Alexander, William (Table E1)
　　　　　　　　　　　Called Lord Sterling
207.A4　　　　　　　Allen, Ethan (Table E1)
207.B2　　　　　　　Barry, John (Table E1)
207.B48　　　　　　Biddle, Nicholas (Table E1)
207.B5　　　　　　　Biddle, Owen (Table E1)
207.B58　　　　　　Bigelow, Timothy (Table E1)
207.B8　　　　　　　Brown, John, 1744-1780 (Table E1)
207.C5　　　　　　　Clark, George Rogers (Table E1)

The Revolution, 1775-1783
  Biography
    Individual, A-Z -- Continued

207.C62	Clinton, James (Table E1)
207.D3	Davidson, William Lee (Table E1)
207.D9	Duportail, Louis Lebegue de Presle (Table E1)
207.E3	Elbert, Samuel (Table E1)
207.G2	Gadsden, Christopher (Table E1)
207.G3	Gates, Horatio (Table E1)
207.G56	Glover, John (Table E1)
207.G9	Greene, Nathanael (Table E1)
207.H7	Hopkins, Ezek (Table E1)
207.H85	Howe, Robert (Table E1)
207.J7	Jones, John Paul (Table E1)
207.K14	Kalb, Jean, baron de (Table E1)
207.K74	Knox, Henry (Table E1)
207.K8	Kośsciusko, Tadeusz Andrzej (Table E1)
	Cf. DK4348.K67 Polish patriot
207.L2	Lafayette, Marquis de (Table E1)
	Including Lafayette in America
	Cf. DC146.L2 Lafayette in France
207.L22	Lamb, John (Table E1)
207.L47	Lee, Charles (Table E1)
207.L5	Lee, Henry (Table E1)
207.M3	Marion, Francis (Table E1)
207.M5	Mercer, Hugh (Table E1)
207.M6	Mifflin, Thomas (Table E1)
207.M7	Montgomery, Richard (Table E1)
207.M8	Morgan, Daniel (Table E1)
207.M85	Moultrie, William (Table E1)
207.M9	Moylan, Stephen (Table E1)
207.M95	Muhlenberg, John Peter Gabriel (Table E1)
207.N2	Nash, Francis (Table E1)
207.O13	O'Brien, Jeremiah (Table E1)
207.P2	Parsons, Samuel Holden (Table E1)
207.P3	Paterson, John (Table E1)
207.P63	Pickens, Andrew (Table E1)
207.P68	Pitcairn, John (Table E1)
207.P7	Pomeroy, Seth (Table E1)
207.P75	Prescott, William (Table E1)
207.P8	Pułaski, Kazimierz (Table E1)
	Cf. DK4348.P8 Polish patriot
207.P9	Putnam, Israel (Table E1)
207.R32	Reed, James (Table E1)
207.S3	Schuyler, Philip John (Table E1)
207.S79	Stark, John (Table E1)
207.S8	Steuben, Friederich Wilhelm, Baron von (Table E1)

E151-909

The Revolution, 1775-1783
  Biography
    Individual, A-Z -- Continued

207.S9	Sullivan, John (Table E1)
207.S95	Sumter, Thomas (Table E1)
207.T13	Talbot, Silas (Table E1)
207.T45	Thomas, John (Table E1)
207.T57	Tilghman, Tench (Table E1)
207.T8	Tucker, Samuel (Table E1)
207.W2	Ward, Artemas (Table E1)
207.W26	Ward, Samuel (Table E1)
207.W27	Warner, Seth (Table E1)
207.W35	Wayne, Anthony (Table E1)
207.W63	Wickes, Lambert (Table E1)
207.W65	Willett, Marinus (Table E1)
207.W7	Williams, Otho Holland (Table E1)
207.W78	Wood, James (Table E1)
207.W8	Woodhull, Nathaniel (Table E1)
207.W9	Wooster, David (Table E1)
208	General works. History (General)
	For travel, manners, and customs of the period see E163
209	General special
	Including pamphlets, pictorial works, chronological tables, etc., and otherwise unprovided-for topics, such as historiography, the Revolution as a social movement, religious aspects, legends
	Political history
	Including the causes and origins of the Revolution and the controversies that preceded it, 1763-1775; the influence of the American clergy, legal aspects, trade, western lands
	For controversies in individual colonies before 1763 see E263.A+
210	General works (Other than contemporary)
211	Contemporary works
	For sermons and addresses of a general character see E297
215	Special questions and events
215.1	Commercial restrictions (General). Enforcement of trade and navigation laws. Writs of assistance
215.2	Stamp Act, 1765. Stamp Act Congress, New York, 1765
215.3	Townshend Acts, 1767. Nonimportation agreements of 1768-1769
	Including Townshend Acts repealed in April 1770, except for a tax on tea
215.4	Mutiny Act, 1765. Boston Massacre, March 5, 1770
	Including the quartering of troops in Boston
215.5	Taxation and representation

The Revolution, 1775-1783
Political history
Special questions and events -- Continued

215.6	Gaspee affair, June 1772
215.7	Resistance to the tea tax. Boston Tea Party, December 1773
215.8	Boston Port Bill, 1774
215.9	Mecklenburg Resolves, 1775
	Including the so-called Mecklenburg Declaration of Independence
215.95	The "Olive branch" petition to George III, 1775
216	Other special topics (not A-Z)

       Including Committees of correspondence and safety; efforts to enlist aid of other British possessions, as Canada and Ireland; Paul Revere's ride; Sons of Liberty; the Duché letters

       For Loyalists in the colonies see E277+

       For The parsons' cause, Va. see F229

       For War of the Regulators, N.C. see F257

221	Declaration of Independence
	Including collective biography of the signers

Military operations
    Cf. E271+ Naval history

230	General works

       Including campaigns and battles (General) and lists of battles

       For Indian wars, 1775-1783 see E83.775

       For orderly books which are classed with campaigns see E231+

       For individual battles see E241.A+

       For orderly books which are classed with the military organization to which they belong see E251+

230.5.A-Z	By region, A-Z

       Regions within a state are classed under the name of the state
       e.g.

230.5.M6	Middle States
230.5.N4	New York (State). Hudson Valley
230.5.O3	Ohio Valley
230.5.V3	Vermont. Mount Independence

Campaigns. By year

231	1775
	Including beginnings, Canadian invasion, siege of Boston (1775-1776), Patriots' Day (April 19)
232	1776
	Including British occupation of New York, Washington's retreat up the Hudson and through New Jersey

E151-909

The Revolution, 1775-1783
Military operations
Campaigns. By year -- Continued

233	1777
	Including Burgoyne's invasion, St. Leger's invasion, Howe's occupation of Philadelphia, Jane McCrea
	For Saratoga Campaign see E241.S2
234	1778
	Including Clark's Expedition, Butler's Indian Campaign, Valley Forge
235	1779
	Including Penobscot Expedition, Sullivan's Indian Campaign
236	1780
	Including Benedict Arnold's treason, campaigns in the South
	Cf. E278.A7 Arnold as a loyalist
237	1781
	Including campaigns in the Carolinas and Virginia, Clark's Expedition against Detroit
	For Mutiny of the Pennsylvania line see E255
238	1782
	Including Crawford's Indian Campaign
239	1783
	Including British evacuation of New York, Evacuation Day
	For Newburgh addresses see E255
241.A-Z	Individual battles, A-Z
	Including attacks, capture and burning of cities, massacres, sieges
	Battles, sieges, etc., may be classed in E231+ if preferred
241.B33	Bedford, N.Y. (Westchester County), 1779
241.B4	Bennington, Vt., 1777
241.B65	Blue Licks, Ky., 1782
	Boston siege, 1775-1776 see E231
241.B76	Bound Brook, N.J., 1777
241.B8	Brandywine, Pa., 1777
	Brooklyn N.Y., 1776 see E241.L8
241.B87	Bull's Ferry, N. J., 1780
241.B9	Bunker Hill, Mass, 1775
241.C17	Camden, S.C., 1780
241.C2	Carleton's Raid, 1778
241.C4	Charleston, S.C., 1780
241.C48	Chelsea, Mass, 1775
241.C5	Cherry Valley, N.Y., 1778
241.C515	Chesapeake Bay, Va., 1781
241.C52	Chestnut Hill, Pa., 1777
241.C56	Clapps Mill, N.C., 1781

E151-909

The Revolution, 1775-1783
Military operations
Individual battles, A-Z -- Continued

241.C7	Concord, Mass., 1775
241.C73	Cooch's Bridge, Del., 1777
241.C8	Cowan's Ford, Tenn., 1781
241.C9	Cowpens, S. C., 1781
241.C94	Crooked Billet, Pa., 1778
241.C96	Cumberland, Fort, N.B., 1776
241.D2	Danbury, Conn., 1777
241.E39	Elizabeth, N.J., 1780
241.E4	Elizabethtown, N.C., 1781
241.E86	Eutaw Springs, S.C., 1781
241.F16	Fairfield, Conn., 1779
	Falmouth, Me. see E241.P8
241.F55	Flamborough Head, England, 1779
241.F74	Freeland, Fort, Warrior Run, Pa. 1779
241.G3	Germantown, Pa., 1777
241.G6	Great Bridge, Va., 1775
241.G8	Groton Heights, Conn., 1781
241.G9	Guilford Court House, N.C., 1781
241.H2	Harlem Heights, N.Y., 1776
241.H8	Hubbardton, Vt., 1777
241.K48	Kettle Creek, Ga., 1779
241.K5	King's Mountain, S.C., 1780
241.K6	Kingston, N.Y., 1777
241.L6	Lexington, Mass., 1775
241.L65	Lindley's Mill, N.C., 1781
241.L7	Little Egg Harbor, N.J., 1778
241.L8	Long Island, N.Y., 1776
241.M5	Mercer, Fort, N.J., 1777
241.M6	Minisink, N.Y., 1779
241.M7	Monmouth, N.J., 1778
241.M8	Moore's Creek Bridge, N.C., 1776
241.M9	Moultrie, Fort, S.C., 1776
241.N5	New Haven, Conn., 1779
241.N59	Newtown, N.Y., 1779
241.O6	Oriskany, N.Y., 1777
241.P2	Paoli, Pa., 1777
241.P24	Paulus Hook, N.J., 1779
241.P3	Pell's Point, N.Y., 1776
241.P46	Pensacola, Fla., 1781
241.P55	Piqua, Ohio, 1780
241.P8	Portland, Me., 1775
241.P9	Princeton, N.J., 1777
241.Q3	Québec (City), 1775-1776
241.R3	Red Bank, N.J., 1777

The Revolution, 1775-1783
Military operations
Individual battles, A-Z -- Continued
241.R4   Rhode Island, 1778
241.R53   Ridgefield, Conn., 1777
241.S2   Saratoga, N.Y., 1777
241.S26   Savannah, Ga., 1779
241.S53   Short Hills, N.J., 1777
241.S6   Springfield, N.J., 1780
241.S7   Stanwix, Fort, N.Y., 1777
241.S8   Stony Point, N.Y., 1779
241.T5   Ticonderoga, N.Y., 1775
241.T7   Trenton, N.J., 1776
241.V14   Valcour Island, Lake Champlain, 1776
241.W3   Washington, Fort, N.Y., 1776
241.W5   White Plains, N.Y., 1776
241.W9   Wyoming, Pa., 1778
241.Y6   Yorktown, Va., 1781
249   Diplomatic history. Treaty of Paris, 1783
                    Including alliances, claims of foreigners against the United
                        States, diplomatic relations with individual countries,
                        missions to foreign powers, propaganda, Treaty of 1778
                    Cf. E265 French participation in the war, French
                        auxiliaries
                    Cf. E313+ Final withdrawal of British troops from western
                        posts
249.3   Foreign public opinion
                Armies. Troops
251   General works
255   The American Army
                    Including bounties; the Conway Cabal; Mutiny of the
                        Pennsylvania Line, 1781; Newburgh addresses;
                        pensioners; registers and lists not confined to single
                        states; war claims
                    For orderly books see E231+
                    Cf. E281 Lists of prisoners
                    Cf. UB373+ Military pensions (General)
                  Continental army
259   General works
260   Military organizations raised by Congress directly
                    Including Commander in Chief's Guard, Lee's Legion,
                        etc.

The Revolution, 1775-1783
Armies. Troops
The American Army -- Continued

263.A-.W   By state, A-W

Including the British American colonies; each state's part in the war and previous controversy

Including collections; histories (General and regional); rolls and orderly books; registers; addresses honoring patriots; diaries, journals, letters, and memoirs of officers, etc.; state continental line; state troops and militia, including minutemen

Histories of counties and towns in the war are classed in local history, e.g., F74.W9, Worcester, Mass.

E151-909

Cf. E230+ Military operations in a state

Cf. E277+ American loyalists in individual states

263.C2   Canada (Province of Quebec)

Biography: Antoine Paulint, etc.

Cf. E216 Efforts to enlist aid of Canada

Cf. E263.N9 Nova Scotia and dependencies

Cf. E269.C27 Canadians in the American army

263.C5   Connecticut

Biography: Jonathan Trumbell, etc.

263.D3   Delaware. Delmarva Peninsula

Biography: Thomas Rodney, etc.

263.F6   Florida (East and West)

263.G3   Georgia

Biography: Lyman Hall, etc.

263.I5   Indiana

263.K4   Kentucky

263.L68   Louisiana

Maine see E263.M4

263.M3   Maryland

Including biography: John Gunby, John Eager Howard, etc.

Cf. E263.D3 Delmarva Peninsula

263.M4   Massachusetts (and Maine)

Biography: Joseph Hawley, Josiah Quincy (1744-1775), Joseph Warren, etc.

263.N4   New Hampshire

Biography: Joseph Cilley, etc.

263.N5   New Jersey

Including biography: Moore Furnam, Margaret (Hill) Morris, etc.

263.N6   New York

Including biography: Simon Boerum, Henry Ludington, etc.

The Revolution, 1775-1783
Armies. Troops
The American Army
By state, A-W -- Continued

263.N8	North Carolina (and Tennessee)
	Biography: Joseph Graham, etc.
	For Tennessee alone see E263.T4
	Cf. E215.9 Mecklenburg Resolutions
	Cf. F257 War of the Regulators, 1766-1771
263.N84	Old Northwest
263.N9	Nova Scotia (and dependencies)
	Cf. E263.C2 Canada (Province of Quebec)
263.O3	Ohio
263.P4	Pennsylvania and Delaware Valley (General)
	Biography: John Bayard, John Rosbrugh, etc.
	Quebec see E263.C2
263.R4	Rhode Island
	Biography: Israel Angell, etc.
	Cf. E215.6 Gaspee Affair, June 1772
263.S7	South Carolina
	Biography: John Drayton, Eliza (Yonge) Wilkinson, etc.
263.T4	Tennessee
	For Tennessee with North Carolina see E263.N8
263.T45	Texas
263.V5	Vermont
263.V8	Virginia
	Biography: Theodorick Bland, John Champe, Filippo Mazzei, Leven Powell, etc.
	Cf. E83.77 Dunmore's War, 1774
	Cf. E263.D3 Delmarva Peninsula
263.W5	West Indies. Bermudas
265	Auxiliaries
	Including French participation; histories; lists; personal letters, journals and narratives of soldiers and sailors
	Biography: Comte de Rochambeau, etc.
	For Marquis de Lafayette see E207.L2
	The British Army
	Including histories; lists; personal diaries; journals, letters, and narratives
	For Tory regiments see E277.6.A+
267	General works
268	German mercenaries. Hessians
	For Germans in the American Army see E269.G3
269.A-Z	Participation by race, ethnic group, religious group, etc., A-Z
	African Americans see E269.N3
269.B2	Baptists
269.C27	Canadians

	The Revolution, 1775-1783
	Participation by race, ethnic group, religious group, etc., A-Z
	-- Continued
269.C3	Catholics
269.C5	Church of England (Anglicans)
269.D88	Dutch
269.F67	Foreigners (General)
	French auxiliaries see E265
269.F8	Friends. Quakers
	German mercenaries see E268
269.G3	Germans
269.H3	Haitians
269.I5	Indians
269.I6	Irish
269.J5	Jews
	Loyalists see E277+
269.M6	Moravians
269.N3	Negroes. African Americans
269.P6	Poles
269.P9	Presbyterians
269.S36	Scots-Irish
269.S63	Spaniards
269.S8	Swedes
269.W4	Welsh
	Colleges and their participation
270.A1	General works
270.A2-Z	Individual colleges, A-Z
	e.g.
270.P9	Princeton University
270.Y2	Yale University
	Naval history. Naval operations
	Including British and French fleets in the West Indies; narratives of sailors, privateers
	For lives of naval leaders see E206+
	For naval operations forming part of military movements see E231+
271	General works
273.A-Z	Individual ships, A-Z
273.P75	Providence

E151-909

The Revolution, 1775-1783 -- Continued
    Personal narratives and other accounts (General)
        Including diaries, journals, letters, memoirs, reminiscences, etc.
        For narratives relating to special campaigns, etc., by year
            see E231+
        For narratives relating to special campaigns, etc., by
            state see E263.A+
        For narratives of French auxiliaries see E265
        For narratives of British soldiers see E267+
        For narratives of German mercenaries see E268
        For narratives of naval service see E271+
        For narratives of loyalists see E278.A+
        For narratives of prisoners see E281
        Cf. E203 Collections of source material
        Cf. E296 Anecdotes

275.A2	Collections
275.A3-Z	Individual narratives
276	Women and the war

    Loyalists. Traitors
        Including biography and narratives of loyalists; loyalists in exile
            (General) and in England; treatment of Tories, e.g.,
            sequestration, confiscation, and sale of estates
        For loyalists in Nova Scotia, Acadia see F1036+
        For loyalists in New Brunswick see F1041+
        For loyalists in Ontario see F1056+

277	General works
277.6.A-Z	Loyalist regiments, etc.
	e.g.
277.6.B9	Butler's Rangers
277.6.D3	De Lancey's Brigade (Loyalist)
277.6.M2	Maryland Loyalists Regiment
277.6.N5	New Jersey Volunteers
277.6.Q6	Queen's Rangers
278.A-Z	Individual loyalists, A-Z
	e.g.
278.A3	Alexander, Robert (Table E1)
278.A4	Allen, Jolley (Table E1)
278.A7	Arnold, Benedict (Table E1)
	Cf. E236 Arnold's treason
278.A72	Arnold, Margaret (Shippen) (Table E1)
278.B9	Butler, Walter (Table E1)
278.C4	Chandler, John (Table E1)
278.C5	Christie, James (Table E1)
278.C7	Connolly, John (Table E1)
278.C8	Cornell, Samuel (Table E1)
278.C9	Curwen, Samuel (Table E1)
278.D94	Dulany, Daniel (Table E1)

	The Revolution, 1775-1783
	Loyalists. Traitors
	Individual loyalists, A-Z -- Continued
278.F2	Fanning, David (Table E1)
278.G14	Galloway, Joseph (Table E1)
278.G4	Gilbert, Thomas (Table E1)
278.L5	Leonard, Daniel (Table E1)
278.M13	McAlpine, John (Table E1)
278.M8	Moody, James (Table E1)
278.M98	Murray, James (Table E1)
278.S6	Smyth, John Ferdinand Dalziel (Table E1)
278.T9	Tuttle, Stephen (Table E1)
278.V27	Van Schaack, Henry Cruger (Table E1)
278.V54	Vernon, Thomas (Table E1)
278.W6	Wilkins, Isaac (Table E1)
	Secret service. Spies
279	General works
280.A-Z	Individual spies, A-Z
	e.g.
280.A5	André, John (Table E1)
	Including his captors: John Paulding, Isaac Van Wart, David Williams
280.C95	Crosby, Enoch (Table E1)
280.H2	Hale, Nathan (Table E1)
280.H8	Howe, John (Table E1)
280.T7	Townsend, Robert (Table E1)
281	Prisoners and prisons
	Including exchanges, prison life, prison ships, prisoners' narratives
283	Medical and hospital services. Hospitals, etc.
	Biography: Jonathan Potts, etc.
	Celebrations. Anniversaries
	Monuments and memorials are classed by place in F
	For special celebrations in the form of expositions see T400+
285	General works
	Special centennials
	1876
	For works limited to the 1876 exposition see T825
285.2	General works
285.25.A-.W	By state, A-W

Under each:

.x	General works
.x2A-.x2Z	By city, A-Z

	1926 exposition see T826.3
	1976
	Cf. BV4254.75 Bicentennial sermons

	The Revolution, 1775-1783
	Celebrations. Anniversaries
	Special centennials
	1976 -- Continued
285.3	General works
285.4.A-.W	By state, A-W

Under each:

.x	*General works*
.x2A-.x2Z	*By city, A-Z*

	Special days
	Evacuation Day, November 25 see E239
	Fourth of July
	Class here general works on the observance of the day, including specific celebrations and addresses
	For works of distinct local interest, see F
286.A1-.A19	General works
286.A2-Z	Individual celebrations and addresses. By place and date
	e. g.
286.B74 1774	Boston, 1774
286.B74 1933	Boston, 1933
	Patriots Day, April 19 see E231
289	Museums. Exhibitions
	Including bells, flags, relics, trophies, etc.
(295)	Poetry, ballads, songs. Drama, pageants
	see class P
296	Anecdotes
	Cf. E203 Collections of source materials
	Cf. E275.A2+ Personal narratives
297	Sermons. Prayers
	For sermons on a specific subject, see the subject
298	Comic and satirical histories. Humor, caricatures, etc.
	Revolution to the Civil War, 1775/1783-1861
	For history of the Revolutionary War see E201+
	For history of the Civil War see E461+
300	Historiography
301	General works
	Including works covering the preliminaries of the Revolution to the close of the Civil War, 1765-1865
	For political history of slavery, E338+
	Cf. E183.7+ Diplomatic history, 1783-1865
	Cf. E398 Northeast boundary question
	Cf. E441+ Slavery and the antislavery movement
	Cf. F550.5+ Northern boundary (Great Lakes)
	Cf. F597 Northern boundary
	Cf. F854 Pacific Northwest boundary
	Cf. F880 Northwest boundary

	Revolution to the Civil War, 1775/1783-1861 -- Continued
302.A-Z	Collected works of American statesmen (Revolutionary group), A-Z
	e.g.
	For works of statesmen of the early nineteenth century see E337.8.A+
	For works of statesmen of the middle nineteenth century see E415.6.A+
302.A26-.A269	Adams, John (Table E3)
302.F82	Franklin, Benjamin (Collected and selected works). By date
	For his literary works and biography see PS745+
302.H2-.H29	Hamilton, Alexander (Table E3)
302.J44-.J449	Jefferson, Thomas (Table E3)
302.M19-.M199	Madison, James (Table E3)
302.M74-.M749	Monroe, James (Table E3)
	Washington, George see E312.7
302.1	Political history
	Including the supremacy of the fathers of the republic
	Cf. E210+ Political history of the Revolution
	Cf. E357+ Political history of the War of 1812
	Cf. E407 Political history of the War with Mexico
	Biography (Late eighteenth century)
	For Revolutionary leaders, especially military commanders see E206+
302.5	Collective
	For signers of the Declaration of Independence, collectively see E221
302.6.A-Z	Individual, A-Z
	e.g.
302.6.A2	Adams, Samuel (Table E2A)
302.6.A5	Ames, Fisher (Table E2A)
302.6.A7	Armstrong, John (Table E2A)
302.6.B14	Bache, Benjamin Franklin (Table E2A)
302.6.B17	Baldwin, Abraham (Table E2A)
302.6.B19	Baldwin, Simeon (Table E2A)
302.6.B2	Bartlett, Josiah (Table E2A)
302.6.B3	Bayard, James Asheton (Table E2A)
302.6.B6	Blount, William (Table E2A)
302.6.B7	Boudinot, Elias (Table E2A)
302.6.B8	Bradley, Stephen Row (Table E2A)
302.6.B84	Breckinridge, John (Table E2A)
302.6.B9	Burr, Aaron (Table E2A)
	For Burr's conspiracy see E334
302.6.B91	Jumel, Eliza (Bowen) (Table E2A)
302.6.B93	Burr, Esther (Edwards) (Table E2A)
302.6.B954	Alston, Theodosia Burr (Table E2A)
302.6.C11	Cabot, George (Table E2A)

E151-909

Revolution to the Civil War, 1775/1783-1861
Biography (Late eighteenth century)
Individual, A-Z -- Continued

302.6.C2	Campbell, George Washington (Table E2A)
302.6.C3	Carroll, Charles (Table E2A)
	Charles Carroll of Carrollton
302.6.C33	Carroll, Daniel (Table E2A)
302.6.C4	Chase, Samuel (Table E2A)
302.6.C55	Clark, Abraham (Table E2A)
302.6.C6	Clinton, George (Table E2A)
302.6.C7	Cooper, Thomas (Table E2A)
302.6.D14	Dallas, Alexander James (Table E2A)
302.6.D16	Dana, Francis (Table E2A)
302.6.D2	Davie, William Richardson (Table E2A)
302.6.D25	Deane, Silas (Table E2A)
302.6.D3	Dearborn, Henry (Table E2A)
302.6.D45	Dexter, Samuel (Table E2A)
302.6.D5	Dickinson, John (Table E2A)
302.6.D8	Duane, James (Table E2A)
302.6.D82	Duane, William (Table E2A)
302.6.E16	Eaton, William (Table E2A)
302.6.E3	Ellery, William (Table E2A)
302.6.E4	Ellsworth, Oliver (Table E2A)
302.6.F24	Farragut, George (Table E2A)
302.6.F56	FitzSimons, Thomas (Table E2A)
302.6.F6	Fowler, John (Table E2A)
	Franklin, Benjamin
	For his collected works see E302.F82
	Autobiography
302.6.F7A2	English. By date
302.6.F7A3-.F7Z3	Translations. By language and date
302.6.F7Z4-.F7Z99	Commentaries
	Letters
302.6.F75A1-.F75A6	Collections. By title
302.6.F75A7	Single letters. By date
302.6.F8	Biography
302.6.G16	Gallatin, Albert (Table E2A)
302.6.G37	Gerry, Elbridge (Table E2A)
302.6.G47	Giles, William Branch (Table E2A)
302.6.G66	Gorham, Nathaniel (Table E2A)
302.6.G95	Gwinnett, Button (Table E2A)
302.6.H2	Hamilton, Alexander (Table E2A)
	For his collected works see E302.H2+
302.6.H22	Hamilton, Elizabeth (Schuyler) (Table E2A)
	Hancock, John
302.6.H23	General works (Table E2A)
302.6.H24	Hancock, Dorothy (Quincy) (Table E2A)

Revolution to the Civil War, 1775/1783-1861
Biography (Late eighteenth century)
Individual, A-Z -- Continued

302.6.H27	Hanson, John (Table E2A)
302.6.H29	Harper, Robert Goodloe (Table E2A)
302.6.H4	Henry, John (Table E2A)
302.6.H5	Henry, Patrick (Table E2A)
302.6.H6	Hillegas, Michael (Table E2A)
302.6.H63	Hillhouse, James (Table E2A)
302.6.H65	Hindham, William (Table E2A)
302.6.H7	Hooper, William (Table E2A)
302.6.H78	Hopkins, Stephen (Table E2A)
302.6.H8	Hosmer, Titus (Table E2A)
302.6.H89	Humphreys, David (Table E2A)
302.6.H9	Huntingdon, Benjamin (Table E2A)
302.6.H93	Husbands, Herman (Table E2A)
302.6.I6	Ingersoll, Jared (Table E2A)
302.6.I7	Iredell, James (Table E2A)
302.6.J4	Jay, John (Table E2A)
	For Jay's Treaty see E314
302.6.J65	Johnson, Thomas (Table E2A)
302.6.J7	Johnson, William Samuel (Table E2A)
302.6.K3	Kavanagh, Edward (Table E2A)
302.6.K5	King, Rufus (Table E2A)
302.6.L26	Langdon, John (Table E2A)
302.6.L3	Laurens, Henry (Table E2A)
302.6.L4	Lee, Richard Henry (Table E2A)
302.6.L6	Lewis, Francis (Table E2A)
302.6.L66	Livermore, Edward St. Loe (Table E2A)
302.6.L67	Livingston, Anne Home (Shippen) (Table E2A)
302.6.L68	Livingston, Edward (Table E2A)
302.6.L684	Livingston, Louise (Davezac) Moreau (Table E2A)
302.6.L7	Livingston, Philip (Table E2A)
302.6.L72	Livingston, Robert R. (Table E2A)
302.6.L75	Livingston, William (Table E2A)
302.6.L8	Logan, George (Table E2A)
302.6.L9	Lyon, Matthew (Table E2A)
302.6.M12	McHenry, James (Table E2A)
302.6.M13	McKean, Thomas (Table E2A)
302.6.M14	Maclay, William (Table E2A)
302.6.M17	Macon, Nathaniel (Table E2A)
302.6.M35	Marshall, Humphrey (Table E2A)
302.6.M4	Marshall, John (Table E2A)
	Including John Marshall Day
302.6.M432	Mason, Armistead Thomson (Table E2A)
302.6.M45	Mason, George (Table E2A)
302.6.M6	Morgan, George (Table E2A)

E151-909

Revolution to the Civil War, 1775/1783-1861
Biography (Late eighteenth century)
Individual, A-Z -- Continued

302.6.M7	Morris, Gouverneur (Table E2A)
302.6.M8	Morris, Robert (Table E2A)
302.6.M81	Morris, Mary (White) (Table E2A)
302.6.M88	Mulligan, Hercules (Table E2A)
302.6.O8	Otis, James (Table E2A)
302.6.P14	Paine, Robert Treat (Table E2A)
302.6.P3	Paterson, William (Table E2A)
302.6.P5	Pickering, Timothy (Table E2A)
302.6.P54	Pinckney, Charles (Table E2A)
302.6.P55	Pinckney, Charles Cotesworth (Table E2A)
302.6.P57	Pinckney, Thomas (Table E2A)
302.6.P6	Pinkney, William (Table E2A)
302.6.P73	Plumer, William (Table E2A)
302.6.P84	Pollock, Oliver (Table E2A)
302.6.P86	Pope, John (Table E2A)
302.6.P93	Preston, Francis (Table E2A)
302.6.Q7	Quincy, Josiah, 1772-1864 (Table E2A)
302.6.R18	Randolph, Edmund (Table E2A)
302.6.R2	Randolph, John (Table E2A)
302.6.R27	Read, George (Table E2A)
302.6.R3	Reed, Joseph (Table E2A)
302.6.R6	Rodney, Caesar (Table E2A)
302.6.R61	Rodney, Caesar Augustus (Table E2A)
302.6.R77	Ross, Betsy (Griscom) (Table E2A)
302.6.R79	Ross, George, 1730-1779 (Table E2A)
302.6.R8	Ross, James (Table E2A)
302.6.R85	Rush, Benjamin (Table E2A)
302.6.R89	Rutledge, John, 1739-1800 (Table E2A)
302.6.R9	Rutledge, John, 1766-1819 (Table E2A)
302.6.S13	Sailly, Peter (Table E2A)
302.6.S17	Salomon, Haym (Table E2A)
302.6.S3	Sawyer, Lemuel (Table E2A)
302.6.S45	Sevier, John (Table E2A)
302.6.S5	Sherman, Roger (Table E2A)
302.6.S57	Smith, Jeremiah (Table E2A)
302.6.S59	Smith, William Stephens (Table E2A)
302.6.S7	Spaight, Richard Dobbs (Table E2A)
302.6.S85	Stockton, Richard (Table E2A)
302.6.S98	Symmes, John Cleves (Table E2A)
302.6.T18	Tait, Charles (Table E2A)
302.6.T2	Tallmadge, Benjamin (Table E2A)
302.6.T23	Taylor, John (Table E2A)
302.6.T4	Thomas, Ebenezer Smith (Table E2A)
302.6.T48	Thomson, Charles (Table E2A)

Revolution to the Civil War, 1775/1783-1861
Biography (Late eighteenth century)
Individual, A-Z -- Continued

302.6.T8	Tompkins, Daniel D. (Table E2A)
302.6.T93	Tyler, Mary Hunt (Palmer) (Table E2A)
302.6.V33	Varnum, James Mitchell (Table E2A)
302.6.V4	Varnum, Joseph Bradley (Table E2A)
302.6.W15	Washington, Bushrod (Table E2A)
302.6.W2	Webster, Pelatiah (Table E2A)
302.6.W4	Weems, Mason Locke (Table E2A)
302.6.W5	Whipple, William (Table E2A)
302.6.W55	Williams, William (Table E2A)
302.6.W6	Williamson, Hugh (Table E2A)
302.6.W62	Willing, Thomas (Table E2A)
302.6.W64	Wilson, James (Table E2A)
302.6.W67	Wingate, Paine (Table E2A)
302.6.W68	Wisner, Henry (Table E2A)
302.6.W7	Witherspoon, John (Table E2A)
302.6.W85	Wolcott, Oliver (Table E2A)

E151-909

By period
1775-1789. The Confederation, 1783-1789

303   General works
                Including Continental Congress, 1774-1788. Articles of
                    Confederation. The Constitution. Foreign relations,
                    1783-1789
                For Revolution see E201+
                For Shay's Rebellion see F69
                For Constitutional history see JK116+

303.2   Bicentennial celebrations for the Constitution
309   Territorial questions
                Including cession of western land claims to the general
                    government by Connecticut, Massachusetts, New York,
                    North Carolina and Virginia, 1781-1786. Northwest
                    Ordinance, 1787
                For Georgia land cessions of 1802 see F290
                For South Carolina cession of 1787 see F292.B7
                For Old Northwest see F476+

1789-1809. Constitutional period
310   General works
310.7   Diplomatic history. Foreign and general relations
                For diplomatic history of special periods, see E313-314,
                  E323, E333-336, E357, etc.
         Washington's administrations, 1789-1797
                For wars with the northwestern Indians, 1790-1795
                  see E83.79
                Cf. HG2525+ United States banks (First and second)
311   General works

Revolution to the Civil War, 1775/1783-1861
    By period
        1789-1809. Constitutional period
            Washington's administrations, 1789-1797 -- Continued
            Biography of George Washington, 1732-1799
                For bibliography see Z8950

312	General works. Washington as president
312.1	Societies
312.15	Reminiscences of contemporaries, anecdotes, calendars, etc.
312.17	Special

                        Including personality, character, religion, etc.; relations
                            with special classes or individuals; etc.

312.19	Ancestry. Family. Servants

        Including biography, e.g., Martha Washington
        For genealogy of the Washingtons and
            genealogical tables see CS71.A+

312.195	Sulgrave Manor

        Including home of the Washington family in England
        Including publications of the Sulgrave Institution

        By period

312.2	Early life to 1775
312.23	Expeditions to the Ohio, 1753-1754. Participation in French and Indian War

        For general accounts of Braddock's Campaign
            see E199

312.25	Military career as commander-in-chief, 1775-1783

        Cf. E201+ The American Revolution

312.27	Itineraries, etc.

        Class individual headquarters with locality in F

312.29	Period after the Revolution, 1783-1799

        For period of the Presidency, 1789-1797 see
            E311+

312.3	Death. Funeral. Memorial services

        Including memorial publications
        For tomb see E312.5
        For funeral addresses and sermons see
            E312.62+

      Iconography

312.4	General works
312.43	Portraits, etc.

        For medals see CJ5801+

      Monuments, statues, etc.

312.45	General works

      Local monuments, statues, etc.
        see class F, e. g. F203.4.W3 Washington
            monument in Washington, D. C.

Revolution to the Civil War, 1775/1783-1861
By period
1789-1809. Constitutional period
Washington's administrations, 1789-1797
Biography of George Washington, 1732-1799 --
Continued

312.5	Homes and haunts
	Including birthplace, Wakefield, Va.; Mount Vernon; Washington estate; Washington's tomb and relics
312.6	Anniversaries. Celebrations. Memorials (since 1800 only)
	Including Washington's birthday, centennial celebrations, etc.
	For funeral and memorial services, 1799-1800 see E312.3
	Addresses, essays, lectures. Sermons
312.62	Collections
312.63	Individual
(312.65)	Poetry. Drama. Fiction
	see subclasses P - PZ
312.66	Juvenile works
	Music
	see class M
312.67	Other works
	Including questions and answers on his life
	Writings of Washington
312.7	Collected works. By date
312.72	Partial collections. Selected works. By date
	Letters
	Collections
312.74	General. By date
312.75.A-Z	By subject, A-Z
	e.g.
312.75.A2-.A3	Agriculture
312.75.M4-.M5	Freemasons
312.75.R3-.R4	Religion
	Revolution see E203
312.75.S6-.S7	Society of the Cincinnati
312.76	Individual letters. By date
312.77	Spurious letters. Editions, by date
312.78	Rules of civility. By date
312.79	Selections. Extracts
	Including maxims, prayers, sayings, etc.
312.8	Diaries. Journals. By date
	For selected Revolutionary orders see E230
312.81	Accounts. Editions. By date
	Addresses and messages

E151-909

Revolution to the Civil War, 1775/1783-1861
By period
1789-1809. Constitutional period
Washington's administrations, 1789-1797
Writings of Washington
Addresses and messages -- Continued

312.83	Addresses to officers of the army, March 15, 1783
312.85	Circular letter, June 18, 1783
	Another edition has title "Last official address ... to the legislatures of the United States"
	Addressed to the governors of the several states
	Editions arranged by place of publication
312.87	Farewell address to the army, November 2, 1783
312.9	Speeches and messages as President. By date
312.95	Farewell address, 1796. By date
	Subarranged by place of publication
312.952	History and criticism
312.99	Will. Editions, by date
	Diplomatic history. Foreign relations
	Including Neutrality proclamation of 1793; withdrawal of British garrisons from western posts; embargo of 1794; Treaty with Spain, 1795
	Including activities of foreign ministers Adet, Genet, and Casa Yrujo
313	General works
314	Jay's Treaty
	Signed November 1794, ratified August, 1795
	For British right of search see E357.2
315	Whiskey insurrection of Pennsylvania, 1794
320	Presidential campaign of 1796
	John Adams' administration, 1797-1801
	For Washington, D.C. selected as capital see F195
321	General works
	Biography of John Adams, 1735-1826
	For his collected works see E302.A26+
	For speeches and messages as President see J82.A2+
322	General works (Table E2)
322.1	Adams family (not genealogy)
323	Troubles with France, 1796-1800
	Including "XYZ" letters, naval conflicts
326	Fries Rebellion, 1798-1799
327	Alien and sedition laws, 1798
328	Kentucky and Virginia Resolutions
330	Presidential campaign of 1800

Revolution to the Civil War, 1775/1783-1861
By period
1789-1809. Constitutional period -- Continued
Jefferson's administrations, 1801-1809
For impressment of American sailors see E357.2
For Chesapeake Affair see E357.3
For Lewis and Clark Expedition, 1804-1806 see
F592.3+

331	General works
	Biography of Thomas Jefferson, 1743-1826
	For bibliography see Z8452
332	General works. Jefferson as president and statesman
	For autobiography see E332.9.A8
332.15	Reminiscences of contemporaries. Anecdotes
332.2	Special

Including Jefferson's personality, character, religion,
catholicity, etc.; attitude toward civil and religious
liberty, state rights, freedom of the press, etc.;
knowledge of government, language, science, the
fine and useful arts
Including Jefferson as scholar, humanist, author,
architect, musician, educator, social reformer,
farmer, inventor
Including Jefferson's relations with special classes,
e.g., Jews, slaves; relations with contemporaries,
e.g., Alexander Hamilton, James Madison
For Jefferson as a philosopher see B885
For Jefferson as president and statesman see
E332
For Jefferson as legislator see E332.3+
For Jefferson as diplomat see E332.45
For Jefferson as traveler see E332.745

332.25	Ancestry. Family. Family life

Including biography, e.g., Martha (Jefferson) Randolph,
his daughter

	By period
332.27	Early life

Including frontier life in western Virginia; education;
admission to the bar, 1764; professional career,
1767-1774; marriage

	Public life
332.3	General works
332.4	State politics

Including service in Virginia House of Burgesses,
1770; Virginia legislature, 1776-1778;
governor, 1779-1781

Revolution to the Civil War, 1775/1783-1861
  By period
    1789-1809. Constitutional period
      Jefferson's administrations, 1801-1809
        Biography of Thomas Jefferson, 1743-1826
          By period
            Public life -- Continued

332.45   International diplomacy
                Including treaty negotiator with European powers,
                   1784; Minister to France, 1785-1789

332.5   National politics
                Including delegate to the Continental Congress,
                   1775-1776, 1781, 1783-1784; Secretary of
                   State, 1790-1793; Vice-president, 1796-1800
                For Presidency, 1801-1809 see E331+
                Cf. E221 Declaration of Independence
                Cf. E320 Presidential campaign, 1796
                Cf. E330 Presidential campaign, 1800
                Cf. E337 Presidential campaign, 1808
                Cf. HG521 History of United States money,
                   1783-1860
                Cf. JK2311+ Democractic (Democratic-
                   Republican) Party

332.6   Later life
                Including financial difficulties; sale of library to
                   Congress, 1815; death and burial; funeral and
                   memorial services, 1826-1827; memorial
                   publications
                For tomb see E332.74
                For funeral addresses and sermons see
                   E332.76+
                For the founding of the University of Virginia,
                   1819 see LD5660+

             Iconography
332.7   General works
332.72   Portraits, etc.
                Cf. subclass NE, Engraved portraits
                For medals see CJ5801+
332.73   Monuments, statues, etc.
                Includes foreign monuments and statues, e.g., the
                   Jefferson statue at Angers, France
                For local monuments and statues, see F, e.g., the
                   Thomas Jefferson Memorial in Washington,
                   F203.4.J4.

Revolution to the Civil War, 1775/1783-1861
  By period
    1789-1809. Constitutional period
      Jefferson's administrations, 1801-1809
        Biography of Thomas Jefferson, 1743-1826 --
          Continued

332.74	Homes and haunts
	Including his birthplace, Shadwell, Va.; Monticello with tomb and relics; Graff House, Philadelphia; Hotel de Langear, Paris; etc.
332.745	Journeys
	Including those in America and Europe
332.75	Anniversaries. Celebrations. Memorials
	Including memorials since 1827; Jefferson's birthday; centennial celebrations
	For funeral and memorial services, 1826-1827 see E332.6
	Addresses, essays, lectures. Sermons
332.76	Collections
332.77	Individual
(332.78)	Poetry. Drama. Fiction
	see subclasses P - PZ
	Music
	see class M
332.79	Juvenile works
332.795	Other works
	Including The Thomas Jefferson quiz book
332.799	Uncataloged pamphlets, clippings, etc.
	Writings of Jefferson
	For speeches and messages as President see J82.A3+
(332.8)	Collected works
	see E302.J44
(332.82)	Selected works
	see E302.J44
	Correspondence
332.84	Calendar of correspondence
332.85	Collections of letters (General). By date
332.86	Selected letters (General). By date
	Special
(332.87.A-Z)	Letters, by subject, A-Z
	see the subject, e.g., PA70.U6, Letters concerning philology and the classics
332.88.A-Z	Letters. By correspondent, A-Z
	e.g.
332.88.D8	Dupont de Nemours, Pierre Samuel
332.88.J4	Jefferson, Randolph

E151-909

Revolution to the Civil War, 1775/1783-1861
  By period
    1789-1809. Constitutional period
      Jefferson's administrations, 1801-1809
        Writings of Jefferson -- Continued

332.9.A-Z	Individual works, A-Z
	e.g.
	In general, prefer classification by subject in classes, A-Z
332.9.A8	Autobiography (1743-1790)
332.9.C6	Commonplace books. Literary Bible
	Declaration of Independence see E221
	Jefferson Bible see BT304.95.J44
	Literary Bible see E332.9.C6
	Notes on the state of Virginia see F230
	Summary view of the rights of British America see E211
(332.95)	Addresses, essays, lectures
	see E302.J44
(332.98)	Doubtful or spurious works
	see classification by subject
(332.99)	Criticism and evaluation of Jefferson's writings
	see E332.2
333	Purchase of Louisiana, 1803
	Including Treaty of Paris, 1803; diplomatic and political aspects; etc.
	For the region purchased see F351; F352+; F366+
333.7	Presidential campaign of 1804
334	Burr's conspiracy, 1805-1807. Wilkinson's participation
	For Burr, Aaron (Biography) see E302.6.B9
	For Wilkinson, James (Biography) see E353.1.W6
	For Mississippi Valley see F353
335	War with Tripoli, 1801-1805
	Called also Tripolitan or Tripoline War
	Including general relations with Barbary States; Treaty of Peace and Amity; the capture and destruction of the frigate Philadelphia; etc.
	Biography: James Barron, Richard Valentine Morris, Mordecai Manuel Noah, Edward Preble, Richard Somers, etc.
	For War with Algeria see E365
	Neutral trade and its restriction, 1800-1810
	Including French spoliations after 1800
	For controversies with England see E357+
	Cf. HF3505.8 Early 19th century British commerce
336	General works

Revolution to the Civil War, 1775/1783-1861
By period
1789-1809. Constitutional period
Jefferson's administrations, 1801-1809
Neutral trade and its restriction, 1800-1810 --
Continued

336.5	Embargo, December 1807-March 1809
	For Embargo effects on commerce see HF3025
337	Presidential campaign of 1808
337.5	Nineteenth century (General)

Early nineteenth century, 1801/1809-1845
Including slavery controversy in politics, general works on
"manifest destiny," territorial expansion
For Antimasonic controversy, 1827-1845 see HS525+
Cf. E441+ Moral and economic aspects of slavery in
the United States

E151-909

337.8.A-Z	Collected works of American statesmen, A-Z
	e.g.
	For works of statesmen of the middle nineteenth
	century see E415.6.A+
337.8.A2	Adams, John Quincy
337.8.C13	Calhoun, John Caldwell
337.8.C55	Clay, Henry
337.8.E9	Everett, Edward
337.8.J3	Jackson, Andrew
337.8.W24	Webster, Daniel
338	General works
	Biography
	For middle nineteenth century see E415.8+
339	Collective
340.A-Z	Individual, A-Z
	e.g.
340.A4	Allen, Charles (Table E2A)
340.B2	Bancroft, George (Table E2A)
340.B4	Benton, Thomas Hart (Table E2A)
340.B57	Binney, Horace, 1780-1875 (Table E2A)
340.B6	Birney, James Gillespie (Table E2A)
340.B67	Branch, John (Table E2A)
340.B8	Brockenbrough, William Henry (Table E2A)
340.B88	Brown, James (Table E2A)
340.B9	Burges, Tristam (Table E2A)
340.B98	Butler, Benjamin Franklin, 1795-1858 (Table E2A)
340.C15	Calhoun, John Caldwell (Table E2A)
340.C3	Cass, Lewis (Table E2A)
340.C4	Choate, Rufus (Table E2A)
340.C5	Cilley, Jonathan (Table E2A)
	Including the Graves-Cilley duel

Revolution to the Civil War, 1775/1783-1861
By period
Early nineteenth century, 1801/1809-1845
Biography
Individual, A-Z -- Continued

340.C6	Clay, Henry (Table E2A)
340.C62	Clayton, Augustin Smith (Table E2A)
340.C65	Clinton, De Witt (Table E2A)
340.C7	Cook, Daniel Pope (Table E2A)
340.C76	Corwin, Thomas (Table E2A)
340.C89	Crawford, William Harris (Table E2A)
340.C9	Crittenden, John Jordan (Table E2A)
340.D14	Dallas, George Mifflin (Table E2A)
340.D4	DeForest, David Curtis (Table E2A)
340.D7	Dodge, Henry (Table E2A)
340.E8	Everett, Edward (Table E2A)
340.E9	Ewing, Thomas (Table E2A)
340.F16	Fairfield, John (Table E2A)
340.F86	Frelinghuysen, Theodore (Table E2A)
340.G2	Gaston, William (Table E2A)
340.G48	Gilpin, Henry Dilworth (Table E2A)
340.G8	Grundy, Felix (Table E2A)
340.H2	Hammond, Charles (Table E2A)
340.H26	Hardin, Benjamin (Table E2A)
340.H4	Hayne, Robert Young (Table E2A)
340.H9	Huntington, Jabez Williams (Table E2A)
340.I5	Ingersoll, Charles Jared (Table E2A)
340.I53	Ingersoll, Joseph Reed (Table E2A)
340.J3	Jarvis, Leonard (Table E2A)
340.J69	Johnson, Richard Mentor (Table E2A)
340.K2	Kaufman, David Spangler (Table E2A)
340.K33	Kendall, Amos (Table E2A)
340.K54	King, William Rufus (Table E2A)
340.L4	Lawrence, Abbott (Table E2A)
340.L5	Legaré, Hugh Swinton (Table E2A)
340.L7	Linn, Lewis Fields (Table E2A)
340.M17	McDuffie, George (Table E2A)
340.M2	McLean, John (Table E2A)
340.M3	Mangum, Willie Person (Table E2A)
340.M34	Mason, Jeremiah (Table E2A)
340.M4	Menefee, Richard Hickman (Table E2A)
340.M5	Mercer, Charles Fenton (Table E2A)
340.M7	Monroe, James, 1799-1870 (Table E2A)
340.M8	Morris, Thomas (Table E2A)
340.M83	Morrow, Jeremiah (Table E2A)
340.O8	Otis, Harrison Gray (Table E2A)
340.P3	Pearce, James Alfred (Table E2A)

Revolution to the Civil War, 1775/1783-1861

By period

Early nineteenth century, 1801/1809-1845

Biography

Individual, A-Z -- Continued

340.P54	Phelps, Samuel Shethar (Table E2A)
340.P75	Poindexter, George (Table E2A)
340.P77	Poinsett, Joel Roberts (Table E2A)
340.P88	Prentiss, Samuel (Table E2A)
340.P9	Prentiss, Seargent Smith (Table E2A)
	Including the Prentiss-Tucker duel

E151-909

340.R6	Ritchie, Thomas (Table E2A)
340.R7	Robertson, George (Table E2A)
340.R88	Royall, Anne (Newport) (Table E2A)
340.R9	Rush, Richard (Table E2A)
340.S18	Saltonstall, Leverett (Table E2A)
340.S75	Stevenson, Andrew (Table E2A)
	Story, Joseph see KF8745.A+
	Taney, Roger Booke see KF8745.A+
340.T47	Thompson, Richard Wiggington (Table E2A)
340.V7	Vinton, Samuel Finley (Table E2A)
340.W3	Wayne, James Moore (Table E2A)
340.W4	Webster, Daniel (Table E2A)
340.W53	White, Hugh Lawson (Table E2A)
340.W65	Wilmot, David (Table E2A)
340.W73	Winthrop, Robert Charles (Table E2A)
340.W79	Wirt, William (Table E2A)
340.W8	Woodbury, Levi (Table E2A)
340.W95	Wright, Silas (Table E2A)
	Jefferson's administrations, 1801-1809 see E331+
	Madison's administrations, 1809-1817
	For War with Algeria, 1815 see E365
	For Presidential campaign of 1816 see E370
	Cf. E83.81 Battle of Tippecanoe, 1811
	Cf. E83.813 First Creek War, 1813-1814
	Cf. E357+ Troubles with England since 1797
	Cf. F314 Seizure of West Florida west of the Perdido
341	General works
342	Biography of James Madison, 1751-1836 (Table E2)
	For his collected works see E302.M19+
	For speeches and messages as President see J82.A4+
342.1	Madison's family (not genealogy)
	Including biography, e.g., Dorothy (Payne) Todd Madison (Dolley Madison)
349	Presidential campaign of 1812
	War of 1812

Revolution to the Civil War, 1775/1783-1861
By period
Early nineteenth century, 1801/1809-1845
Madison's administrations, 1809-1817
War of 1812 -- Continued

351	Periodicals. Societies. Collections
	Societies of veterans
351.2	National Convention of the Soldiers of the War of 1812
351.23	Pennsylvania Association of the Defenders of the Country in the War of 1812
351.27	New England Association of Soldiers of the War of 1812
351.28	New York State Convention of the Soldiers of the War of 1812
	Patriotic societies of descendants
351.3	Society of the War of 1812 (Table E6)
351.32	Society of the Second War with Great Britain in the State of New York (Table E6)
351.5	Military Society of the War of 1812 (Table E6)
351.6	National Society of United States Daughters of 1812 (Table E6)
	Biography
353	Collective
	Chiefly military and naval leaders
	For statesmen and politicians see E302.5+; E339+
353.1.A-Z	Individual
	e.g.
353.1.A19	Adair, John (Table E1)
353.1.B2	Bainbridge, William (Table E1)
353.1.B26	Barney, Joshua (Table E1)
353.1.B5	Biddle, James (Table E1)
353.1.B8	Brock, Sir Isaac (Table E1)
353.1.B9	Brown, Jacob (Table E1)
353.1.C75	Covington, Leonard (Table E1)
353.1.C8	Croghan, George (Table E1)
353.1.D29	Decatur, Stephen, 1779-1820 (Table E1)
353.1.E4	Elliot, Jesse Duncan (Table E1)
353.1.G14	Gaines, Edmund Pendleton (Table E1)
353.1.H2	Hampton, Wade, 1754-1835 (Table E1)
353.1.H8	Hull, Isaac (Table E1)
353.1.H9	Hull, William (Table E1)
353.1.J7	Jones, Jacob (Table E1)
353.1.L4	Lawrence, James (Table E1)
353.1.M15	McArthur, Duncan (Table E1)
353.1.M2	Macdonough, Thomas (Table E1)

Revolution to the Civil War, 1775/1783-1861

By period

Early nineteenth century, 1801/1809-1845

Madison's administrations, 1809-1817

War of 1812

Biography

Individual -- Continued

353.1.M3	Macomb, Alexander (Table E1)
353.1.M8	Morris, Charles (Table E1)
353.1.P4	Perry, Oliver Hazard (Table E1)
353.1.P7	Porter, David (Table E1)
353.1.R5	Ripley, Eleanor Wheelock (Table E1)
353.1.R7	Rodgers, John (Table E1)
353.1.S8	Stewart, Charles (Table E1)
353.1.W6	Wilkinson, James (Table E1)
354	General works

E151-909

Cf. E165 Manners and customs, and general
travel, 1812-1845

Military operations, 1812-1815

Cf. E83.812 Indian wars, 1812-1815

355   General works

Including campaigns and battles (General) and lists
of battles

For individual battles see E356.A+

355.1.A-Z   By region, A-Z

Campaigns of the northwestern army, the war in the
north, in the south, etc., in general

355.1.N5   Campaigns on the Niagara frontier

Campaigns. By year

355.2   1812

Including campaigns in the north and northwest
covering Detroit, Lake Champlain, Niagara

355.4   1813

Including campaigns in the east, north, and
northwest covering Chesapeake Bay, Lake
Champlain, Lake Erie, Lake Ontario, St.
Lawrence River

Cf. E83.813 First Creek War, 1813-1814

355.6   1814-1815

Including campaigns in the east, north, and
northwest covering Chesapeake Bay, Lake
Champlain, New Orleans, Niagara

For the capture and burning of Washington
see E356.W3

Revolution to the Civil War, 1775/1783-1861
By period
Early nineteenth century, 1801/1809-1845
Madison's administrations, 1809-1817
War of 1812
Military operations, 1812-1815 -- Continued

356.A-Z	Individual battles, A-Z
	Including attacks; capture and burning of cities; sieges
	Battles, sieges, etc., may be classed in E355.2+
356.B2	Baltimore, 1814
	Including the battle of North Point and the bombardment of Fort McHenry
	Class here also the Fort McHenry National Monument and Historic Shrine
356.B3	Beaver Dams, Ont., 1813
356.B5	Bladensburg, Md. 1814
356.B6	Boquet River, N.Y., 1814
	Bridgewater, Ont. see E356.L9
356.B8	Brownstown, Mich., 1812
356.C2	Campbell's Island, 1814
	In Mississippi River east of Moline, Ill.
356.C3	Caulk's Field, Md., 1814
	Champlain, Lake see E356.P7
356.C4	Chateauguay, N.Y., 1813
356.C53	Chicago, 1812
	Including the Fort Dearborn Massacre
356.C55	Chippewa, Ont., 1814
356.C74	Cook's Mills, Ont., 1814
356.C8	Craney Island, Va., 1813
	Dearborn, Fort see E356.C53
356.D4	Detroit, 1812
356.D8	Dudley's defeat
356.E5	Erie, Fort, Ont., 1814
356.E6	Erie, Lake, 1813
	Including Perry Memorial, Put-in-Bay, Ohio
	Frenchtown, Mich. see E356.R2
356.G4	George, Fort, Ont., 1812
356.H3	Harrison, Fort, Ind., 1812
356.L9	Lundy's Lane, Ont., 1814
356.M15	Mackinac, Mich., 1812
	On Mackinac Island, Lake Huron
	McHenry, Fort see E356.B2
356.M5	Meigs, Fort, Ohio, 1813
356.N5	New Orleans, 1815
	Including Chalmette National Historical Park
	Niagara, Ont. see E356.L9

Revolution to the Civil War, 1775/1783-1861
By period
Early nineteenth century, 1801/1809-1845
Madison's administrations, 1809-1817
War of 1812
Military operations, 1812-1815
Individual battles, A-Z -- Continued
North Point see E356.B2

	North Point see E356.B2
356.P6	Pigeon Roost, Ind., 1812
356.P7	Plattsburg, N.Y., 1814
356.Q3	Queenston (Queenston Heights), Ont., 1812
356.R2	Raisin River, Mich., 1813
356.S34	Sackets Harbor, N.Y., Battle of, 1813
356.S7	Stephenson, Fort, Ohio, 1813
356.S8	Stonington, Conn., 1814
356.T3	Thames, Ont., 1813
356.T68	Toronto, 1813
356.W3	Washington, D.C., 1814
	York, Ont. see E356.T68

E151-909

Political history
Including controversy with England, 1797-1812
Cf. E314 Jay's Treaty
Cf. E336+ Neutral trade and its restrictions, 1800-1810
Cf. E336.5 Embargo, December 1807-March 1809

357	General works
357.2	Right of search and impressment
357.3	The Chesapeake-Leopard Affair, 1807
	Opposition to the war by the New England Federalists
357.6	General works
357.7	Hartford Convention, 1814
357.9	Effects of the war
358	Diplomatic history. Foreign relations
	Including Treaty of Ghent, 1814; treatment of alien enemies; fisheries; boundaries
	Armies. Troops
359	General works
	The American Army
359.2	Regulars
359.24	Infantry
359.25	Cavalry
359.26	Artillery
359.3	Militia
359.4	Pensioners. Bounties. Claims
359.5.A-.W	The states and their participation, A-W

Revolution to the Civil War, 1775/1783-1861
  By period
    Early nineteenth century, 1801/1809-1845
      Madison's administrations, 1809-1817
        War of 1812
          Armies. Troops
            The American Army
              The states and their participation, A-W --
                Continued

359.5.C7	Connecticut
359.5.F6	Florida
359.5.G4	Georgia
359.5.I53	Indiana
359.5.K5	Kentucky
359.5.L8	Louisiana
359.5.M2	Maryland
359.5.M3	Massachusetts
359.5.N3	New Hampshire
359.5.N4	New Jersey
359.5.N6	New York
359.5.N7	North Carolina
359.5.O2	Ohio
359.5.P3	Pennsylvania
359.5.T47	Texas
359.5.V3	Vermont
359.5.V8	Virginia
359.8	The British Army
359.85	Canadian participation
359.9.A-Z	Participation by race, ethnic group, etc., A-Z
359.9.A35	African Americans
359.9.J5	Jews
	Negroes see E359.9.A35
360	Naval history

            Including naval battles on the ocean; naval blockades;
              narratives of sailors, privateers
            For biography of naval leaders see E353+
            For naval battles in connection with military
              operations see E355+
            For Chesapeake-Leopard Affair see E357.3
          Secret service. Spies

360.5	General works
360.6.A-Z	Individual spies, A-Z
360.6.H5	Henry, John (British) (Table E1)
361.A-Z	Personal narratives, A-Z

            For sailor's narratives see E360
            For prisoners' narratives see E362

Revolution to the Civil War, 1775/1783-1861
  By period
    Early nineteenth century, 1801/1809-1845
      Madison's administrations, 1809-1817
        War of 1812 -- Continued

362	Prisoners and prisons
	Including lists of prisoners, prison life, prisoners' narratives, etc., as well as accounts of the Dartmoor Massacre, 1815 (Dartmoor Military Prison, England).
362.5	Medical and hospital services. Hospitals
362.7	Women
363	Celebrations. Anniversaries. Museums
	Including exhibitions
	Illustrative material
(364)	Poetry, ballads, songs. Drama, pageants
	see class P
364.3	Anecdotes
	Cf. PN-PT, Literature
	Cf. E360 Personal narratives of sailors and soldiers
	Cf. E361.A+ Personal narratives of soldiers
364.5	Addresses, essays, lectures. Sermons. Prayers
364.9	Other (not A-Z)
365	War with Algeria, 1815
	Cf. E335 Relations with the Barbary States in general
370	Presidential campaign of 1816

      Monroe's administrations, 1817-1825
        For First Seminole War, 1817-1818 see E83.817

371	General works
372	Biography of James Monroe, 1758-1831 (Table E2)
	For his collected works see E302.M74+
	For speeches and messages as President see J82.A5+
373	Missouri Compromise, 1820
	Cf. E433 Repeal of the Missouri Compromise, 1854
	Cf. E446 Early American slavery and political agitation growing out of it
	Cf. F466 Missouri history
374	Diplomatic history. Foreign relations
	For execution of Arbuthnot and Ambrister, 1818 see E83.817
	For cession of Florida see F314
	For Monroe Doctrine see JZ1482

E151-909

Revolution to the Civil War, 1775/1783-1861

By period

Early nineteenth century, 1801/1809-1845

Monroe's administrations, 1817-1825 -- Continued

375   Presidential campaign of 1824

Including charge of a corrupt bargain between Adams and Clay

John Quincy Adams' administration, 1825-1829

For Northeastern boundary dispute see E398

For Panama Congress, 1826 see F1404

For Tariff of 1828 see HF1754

376   General works

Biography of John Quincy Adams, 1767-1845

For his collected works see E337.8.A2

For speeches and messages as President see J82.A6+

377   General works (Table E2)

377.2   Adams' family (not genealogy)

Including biography of individual families

Diplomatic history see E376+

380   Presidential campaign of 1828

Jackson's administrations, 1829-1837

For Black Hawk War see E83.83

For Second Seminole War see E83.835

For Second Creek War see E83.836

For Northeastern boundary troubles see E398

For Tariff of 1833 see HF1754

For Bank of the United States, 1816-1836 see HG2525+

381   General works

382   Biography of Andrew Jackson, 1767-1845 (Table E2)

For his collected works see E337.8.J3

For speeches and messages as President see J82.A7+

Cf. E83.813 Execution of Tennessee militiamen, First Creek War

Jackson's family

382.1.A1   General works

382.1.D6   Donelson, Emily Tennessee (Donelson)

382.1.J2   Jackson, Rachel (Donelson)

383   Presidential campaign of 1832

384.3   Nullification

For Tariff controversy see HF1754

Cf. F273 South Carolina politics, 1775-1865

               Revolution to the Civil War, 1775/1783-1861
                 By period
                 Early nineteenth century, 1801/1809-1845
                   Jackson's administrations, 1829-1837 -- Continued

384.7   Removal of deposits from the Bank of the United
                     States. Vote of censure, 1834. Expunging
                     resolutions, 1834-1837
                      Cf. HG2525+ Bank of the United States, 1816-1836
384.8   Diplomatic history. Foreign relations
                     For Mexican protest against advance of United
                     States troops see F390
385   Presidential campaign of 1836
                 Van Buren's administration, 1837-1841
                   For Second Seminole War, 1835-1842 see E83.835
                   For removal of the Creek Indians to the West see
                     E99.C9
                   For Aroostook War, and Northeast boundary troubles
                     see E398
                   For "Armistad" case see E447
                   For movement for annexation of Texas see F390
                   For Alton riot, 1837 see F549.A4
                   For Canadian Rebellion 1837, and destruction of the
                     "Caroline" see F1032
                   For Panic of 1837 see HB3717
                   For independent treasury see HG2535+
386   General works
387   Biography of Martin Van Buren, 1782-1862 (Table E2)
                   For his collected works see E337.8.A2
                   For speeches and messages as President see
                     J82.A8+
390   Presidential campaign of 1840
                 W. H. Harrison's administration, March 4-April 4, 1841
391   General works
392   Biography of William H. Harrison, 1773-1841 (Table
                     E2)
                   For his collected works see E337.8.A+
                   For speeches and messages as President see
                     J82.B1+
                 Tyler's administration, April 4, 1841-1845
                   For Dorr's Rebellion, 1842 see F83.4
                   For question of the annexation of Texas see F390
                   For tariff see HF1754
                   For attempt to reestablish Bank of the United States
                     see HG2525+
396   General works
                   Including explosion of the frigate "Princeton," 1844

E151-909

Revolution to the Civil War, 1775/1783-1861
By period
Early nineteenth century, 1801/1809-1845
Tyler's administration, April 4, 1841-1845 -- Continued
397 Biography of John Tyler, 1790-1862 (Table E2)
For his collected works see E337.8.A+
For speeches and messages as President see
J82.B2+
398 Northeastern boundary dispute, 1783-1845
Including the Aroostook War, 1839; Webster-Ashburton
Treaty (known also as Treaty of Washington,
Ashburton Treaty), 1842
After 1845 reports on boundary disputes are classed with
locality, e.g. F27.B7, Maine; F42.B7, New
Hampshire; F127.B7, New York
400 Presidential campaign of 1844
Mexican War, 1846-1848
401 Periodicals
Societies
401.1 Aztec Club of 1847
401.2 Guadalupe Club of 1848, Washington, D.C.
401.3 National Association of Veterans of the Mexican War
401.34 Michigan Association of Veterans of the War with
Mexico
401.36 Ohio State Association of Mexican War Veterans
401.7 Dames of 1846
Biography
Chiefly military and naval leaders
For statesmen and politicians see E339+; E415.8+
403 Collective
403.1.A-Z Individual, A-Z
e.g.
403.1.B9 Butler, William Orlando (Table E1)
403.1.C7 Connor, David (Table E1)
Cf. E410 Naval history
403.1.D6 Doniphan, Alexander William (Table E1)
403.1.H2 Hamer, Thomas Lyon (Table E1)
403.1.H87 Hungerford, Daniel Elihu (Table E1)
403.1.K2 Kearny, Stephen Watts (Table E1)
403.1.P6 Pillow, Gideon Johnson (Table E1)
For Pillow's court martial see E405.6
403.1.Q8 Quitman, John Anthony (Table E1)
403.1.R2 Ransom, Truman Bishop (Table E1)
403.1.S4 Scott, Winfield (Table E1)
403.1.S5 Shields, James (Table E1)
403.1.S6 Sloat, John Drake (Table E1)
403.1.S8 Stockton, Robert Field (Table E1)

Revolution to the Civil War, 1775/1783-1861

By period

Mexican War, 1846-1848

Biography

Individual, A-Z -- Continued

403.1.W8	Wool, John Ellis (Table E1)
	Cf. E405.4 Wool's campaign in Mexico
	Cf. E601+ Civil War reminiscences
403.1.W9	Worth, William Jenkins (Table E1)
404	General works
	Military operations
	For individual battles see E406.A+
	Cf. E410 Naval history
405	General works
	Campaigns
	For general campaigns see E405
405.1	Taylor's Campaign, 1846-1847
	Including campaign along the Rio Grande and in northern Mexico
405.2	Campaigns in and the occupation of New Mexico and California
	Including expeditions made by Doniphan, Kearny, Stockton
405.4	Chihuahua Campaign, 1846-1848
	Including Wool's march from San Antonio to Saltillo
405.6	Scott's Campaign, 1847
	From Veracruz to Mexico City
406.A-Z	Individual battles, A-Z
406.A48	Alvarado, Veracruz, Mexico, 1846
406.B9	Buena Vista, Mexico, 1847
406.C4	Cerro Gordo, Mexico, 1847
406.C47	Chapultepec, Mexico, 1847
406.C5	Churubusco, Mexico, 1847
406.C6	Contreras, Mexico, 1847
406.M3	Matamoros, Mexico, 1846
406.M6	Mexico City, 1847
406.M65	Molino del Rey, Mexico, 1847
406.M7	Monterrey, Mexico, 1846
406.P3	Palo Alto, Mexico, 1846
406.R4	Resaca de la Palma, Mexico, 1846
406.S2	San Pasqual, Calif., 1846
406.S25	Santa Clara, Calif., 1847
406.V4	Veracruz, Mexico, 1847
407	Political history
	Including causes of the war
	Cf. F390 Revolt and annexation of Texas

E151-909

Revolution to the Civil War, 1775/1783-1861
By period
Mexican War, 1846-1848 -- Continued

408   Diplomatic history. Treaty of Guadalupe Hidalgo, 1848
Including Mexican cessions of 1848
Cf. F786 Mexican boundary after 1848, and the
Gadsden Purchase, 1853

Armies. Troops
409   General works
The American Army
409.2   Regulars
409.4   Pensioners. Bounties. Claims
For United States military pensions (General) see
UB373+
409.5.A-.W   The states and their participation, A-W
409.5.A8   Arkansas
409.5.C6   Connecticut
409.5.D6   District of Columbia
409.5.F5   Florida
409.5.I4   Illinois
409.5.I7   Indiana
409.5.I72   Iowa
409.5.K4   Kentucky
409.5.M2   Maryland
409.5.M56   Mississippi
409.5.N6   New York
409.5.O3   Ohio
409.5.P3   Pennsylvania
409.5.S7   South Carolina
409.5.T4   Tennessee
409.5.T45   Texas
409.7   Registers, lists of the dead and wounded, etc.
409.8   The Mexican Army
410   Naval history
Including narratives of sailors
For biography of naval leaders see E403+
For operations in connection with military campaigns
see E405+
411   Personal narratives
For sailors' narratives see E410
For prisoners' narratives see E412
412   Prisoners and prisons
Including lists of prisoners, prison life, prisoners' narratives
412.5   Medical and hospital services. Hospitals
413   Celebrations. Anniversaries
Cf. E401.1+ Societies of veterans

Revolution to the Civil War, 1775/1783-1861
  By period
    Mexican War, 1846-1848 -- Continued
      War poetry, drama, etc.
        see class P

415	Addresses, essays, lectures. Sermons
415.2.A-Z	Special topics, A-Z
415.2.A78	Art and the war
	Censorship see E415.2.P74
415.2.D48	Desertions
415.2.P74	Press. Censorship
415.2.P82	Public opinion
415.2.S43	Secret service

    Middle nineteenth century, 1845/1848-1861

415.6.A-Z	Collected works of American statesmen, A-Z

        e.g.
          For works of statesmen of the early nineteenth
            century see E337.8.A+

415.6.D16-.D169	Dana, Richard Henry (Table E3)
415.6.J65-.J659	Johnson, Andrew (Table E3)
415.6.J94-.J949	Julian, George Washington (Table E3)
	Lincoln, Abraham see E457.91+
415.6.P55-.P559	Phillips, Wendell (Table E3)
415.6.S51-.S519	Seward, William Henry (Table E3)
415.6.S93-.S939	Sumner, Charles (Table E3)
415.6.T57-.T579	Tilden, Samuel Jones (Table E3)
415.7	General works

        From the outbreak of the Mexican War through the period
          of reconstruction after the Civil War, 1845-1877
        Including political aspects of the slavery question,
          extension of slavery to the territories, squatter
          sovereignty
        For the wars with the Pacific coast Indians, 1847-
          1865 see E83.84
        Cf. F1783 Cuban question, 1810-1899
        Cf. JK2341 American Party (Know-Nothing Pary)
      Biography
        For military leaders of the Mexican War see E403+
        For military leaders of the Civil War see E467+

415.8	Collective
415.9.A-Z	Individual, A-Z

        e.g.

415.9.B4	Bell, John (Table E2A)
415.9.B45	Belmont, August (Table E2A)
415.9.B6	Black, Jeremiah Sullivan (Table E2A)
415.9.B79	Breckinridge, John Cabell (Table E2A)
415.9.B84	Broderick, David Colbreth (Table E2A)

Revolution to the Civil War, 1775/1783-1861
By period
Middle nineteenth century, 1845/1848-1861
Biography
Individual, A-Z -- Continued

415.9.B88	Browning, Orville Hickman (Table E2A)
415.9.B9	Brownlow, William Gannaway (Table E2A)
415.9.C18	Cameron, Simon (Table E2A)
415.9.C19	Campbell, John Archibald (Table E2A)
415.9.C4	Chase, Salmon Portland (Table E2A)
415.9.C55	Clay, Cassius Marcellus (Table E2A)
415.9.C6	Clayton, John Middleton (Table E2A)
415.9.C63	Clingman, Thomas Lanier (Table E2A)
415.9.C68	Colfax, Schuyler (Table E2A)
415.9.C96	Curtis, Benjamin Robbins (Table E2A)
415.9.C98	Cushing, Caleb (Table E2A)
415.9.D15	Dana, Richard Henry (Table E2A)
	For his collected works see E415.6.D16+
415.9.D26	Davis, Henry Winter (Table E2A)
	For his collected works see E415.6.A+
415.9.D27	Dayton, William Lewis (Table E2A)
415.9.D48	Dickinson, Anna Elizabeth (Table E2A)
415.9.D5	Dickinson, Daniel Stevens (Table E2A)
415.9.D6	Dix, John Adams (Table E2A)
415.9.D73	Douglas, Stephen Arnold (Table E2A)
	For Lincoln-Douglas debates see E457.4
415.9.D9	Dunn, William McKee (Table E2A)
415.9.F4	Fessenden, William Pitt (Table E2A)
415.9.F5	Field, David Dudley (Table E2A)
415.9.F55	Field, Maunsell Bradhurst (Table E2A)
415.9.F64	Floyd, John Buchanan (Table E2A)
415.9.F7	Foote, Henry Stuart (Table E2A)
415.9.F8	Frémont, John Charles (Table E2A)
415.9.G4	Giddings, Joshua Reed (Table E2A)
415.9.G7	Graham, William Alexander (Table E2A)
415.9.G8	Greeley, Horace Alexander (Table E2A)
	For presidential campaign of 1872 see E675
415.9.G85	Grimes, James Wilson (Table E2A)
415.9.G86	Grinnell, Josiah Bushnell (Table E2A)
415.9.G89	Grow, Galusha Aaron (Table E2A)
415.9.H15	Hale, John Parker (Table E2A)
415.9.H2	Hamlin, Hannibal (Table E2A)
415.9.H28	Harris, Benjamin Gwinn (Table E2A)
	For Harris court-martial, 1865 see E458.8
415.9.H35	Haskin, John Bussing (Table E2A)
415.9.H6	Hicks, Thomas Holliday (Table E2A)
415.9.H65	Hilliard, Henry Washington (Table E2A)

Revolution to the Civil War, 1775/1783-1861
  By period
    Middle nineteenth century, 1845/1848-1861
      Biography
        Individual, A-Z -- Continued

E151-909

415.9.H9	Hunter, Robert Mercer Taliaferro (Table E2A)
415.9.J5	Jenckes, Thomas Allen (Table E2A)
415.9.J6	Jones, George Wallace (Table E2A)
415.9.J7	Jones, J. Glancy (Table E2A)
415.9.J95	Julian, George Washington (Table E2A)
	For his collected works see E415.6.J94+
415.9.K35	Kennedy, John Pendleton (Table E2A)
415.9.K52	King, Horatio (Table E2A)
415.9.K7	Körner, Gustav Philip (Table E2A)
415.9.L2	Lane, Joseph (Table E2A)
415.9.L38	Lawrence, Amos Adams (Table E2A)
415.9.L4	Lawrence, William Beach (Table E2A)
415.9.L7	Lieber, Francis (Table E2A)
415.9.L89	Lovejoy, Owen (Table E2A)
415.9.M16	Maclay, William Brown (Table E2A)
415.9.M18	Marcy, William Learned (Table E2A)
415.9.M19	Mason, Charles (Table E2A)
415.9.M2	Mason, James Murray (Table E2A)
415.9.M3	Maury, Dabney Herndon (Table E2A)
415.9.M4	Memminger, Christopher Gustavus (Table E2A)
415.9.M5	Meredith, William Morris (Table E2A)
415.9.P4	Pendleton, George Hunt (Table E2A)
415.9.P78	Pomeroy, Samuel Clarke (Table E2A)
415.9.R75	Rollins, Edward Henry (Table E2A)
415.9.R76	Rollins, James Sidney (Table E2A)
415.9.S4	Seward, William Henry (Table E2A)
	For his collected works see E415.6.S51+
415.9.S5	Seymour, Horatio (Table E2A)
415.9.S53	Sickles, Daniel Edgar (Table E2A)
415.9.S58	Slidell, John (Table E2A)
415.9.S64	Smith, Gerrit (Table E2A)
415.9.S72	Soulé, Pierre (Table E2A)
415.9.S74	Speed, James (Table E2A)
415.9.S84	Stevens, Thaddeus (Table E2A)
415.9.S88	Stuart, Alexander Hugh Holmes (Table E2A)
415.9.S9	Sumner, Charles (Table E2A)
	For his collected works see E415.6.S93+
	For works on Brooks' assault see E434.8
415.9.T12	Taft, Alphonso (Table E2A)
415.9.T45	Thompson, Jacob (Table E2A)
415.9.T5	Tilden, Samuel Jones (Table E2A)
	For his collected works see E415.6.T57+

Revolution to the Civil War, 1775/1783-1861
  By period
    Middle nineteenth century, 1845/1848-1861
      Biography
        Individual, A-Z -- Continued

415.9.T6	Toombs, Robert Augustus (Table E2A)
415.9.T86	Trumbell, Lyman (Table E2A)
415.9.T88	Tuck, Amos (Table E2A)
415.9.T93	Tyler, Robert (Table E2A)
415.9.V2	Vallandigham, Clement Laird (Table E2A)
415.9.W16	Wade, Benjamin Franklin (Table E2A)
415.9.W2	Walker, Robert James (Table E2A)
415.9.W39	Weed, Thurlow (Table E2A)
415.9.W6	Wilson, Henry (Table E2A)
415.9.W8	Wise, Henry Alexander (Table E2A)
415.9.Y2	Yancey, William Lowndes (Table E2A)
415.9.Y9	Yulee, David Levy (Table E2A)

Polk's administration, 1845-1849
    Including government of the newly acquired Spanish
        possessions in the Southwest; slavery in the territories;
        slavery question in politics; Wilmot Proviso, 1846
    For Annexation of Texas, 1845 see F390
    For Oregon question and Northwestern boundary to
        1846 see F880

416	General works

Biography of James K. Polk, 1795-1849
    For his collected works see E415.6.A+
    For speeches and messages as President see
        J82.B3+

417	General works (Table E2)
417.1	Polk, Sarah (Childress)
420	Presidential campaign of 1848

Taylor's administration, 1849-July 9, 1850
    For organization of New Mexico see F801
    For organization of Utah territory see F826
    For admission of California see F864

421	General works
422	Biography of Zachary Taylor, 1784-1850 (Table E2)

    For his campaign, 1846-1847 see E405.1
    For his collected works see E415.6.A+
    For speeches and messages as President see
        J82.B4+

423	Slavery question, 1849-1853

    Including Clay's Omnibus Bill (Compromise of 1850);
        Southern Convention, Nashville, 1850
    For fugitive slaves and the new law of 1850 see
        E450

E151-909

Revolution to the Civil War, 1775/1783-1861
    By period
        Middle nineteenth century, 1845/1848-1861 -- Continued
        Fillmore's administration, July 9, 1850-1853
426   General works
427   Biography of Millard Fillmore, 1800-1874 (Table E2)
                    For his collected works see E415.6.A+
                    For speeches and messages as President see
                        J82.B5+
429   Diplomatic history, 1849-1853. Foreign relations
                    Including intervention; political refugees from abroad
                    For Clayton-Bulwer Treaty, 1850 see F1438
                    For the Cuban question see F1783
430   Presidential campaign of 1852
                Pierce's administration, 1853-1857
                    For the wars with Pacific coast Indians see E83.84
                    For the Third Seminole War, 1855-1858 see E83.855
                    For the Gadsden Purchase see F786
                    For the Filibuster War in Nicaragua, 1855-1857 see
                        F1526
                    For the Bombardment of Greytown, Nicaragua, 1854
                        see F1536.S2
                    For the Cuban question see F1783
                    For the American Party (Know-Nothing Party) see
                        JK2341
431   General works
                    Including diplomatic history; the Ostend Manifesto,
                        October 1854
                Biography of Franklin Pierce, 1804-1869
                    For his collected works see E415.6.A+
                    For speeches and messages as President see
                        J82.B6+
432   General works (Table E2)
432.2   Pierce family (not genealogy)
                    Including biography of individual members
433   Slavery question, 1853-1857
                    Including repeal of the Missouri Compromise, 1854;
                        Kansas-Nebraska Bill, May 1854
                    For squatter sovereignty see E415.7
                    For moral and economic aspects of the slavery
                        question see E449+
                    For Kansas troubles see F685
434.5   Election of speaker of the House
434.8   Brooks' assault on Senator Sumner, 1856
435   Presidential campaign of 1856

Revolution to the Civil War, 1775/1783-1861
   By period
     Middle nineteenth century, 1845/1848-1861 -- Continued
      Buchanan's administration, 1857-1861
         For Spirit Lake Massacre, 1857 see E83.857
         For Mill Creek War, 1857-1865 see E83.858
         For Mormon Rebellion, 1857-1859 see F826
         For Walker's Filibuster wars, 1855-1860 see F1526
         For Cuban question see F1783
         For Paraguay Expedition see F2686

436	General works
	Biography of James Buchanan, 1791-1868
	For his collected works see E337.8.A+
	For speeches and messages as President see J82.B7+
437	General works (Table E2)
437.1	Buchanan family (not genealogy)
	Including biography, e.g., Harriet Lane, 1830-1903
438	Slavery question, 1857-1861
	Including attempt to revive slave trade, 1858, Lincoln's Cooper Institute address
	For Squatter sovereignty see E415.7
	For Dred Scott decision, 1857 see E450
	For Harpers Ferry raid, 1859 see E451
	For Lincoln-Douglas debates, 1858 see E457.4
	For Kansas and the Lecompton Constitution see F685
440	Presidential campaign of 1860
440.5	State of the country, November 1860-March 4, 1861
	Including attempts at compromise (Crittenden Compromise, December 18, 1860; Crittenden Resolution, July 22, 1861; etc.); Peace Conference at Washington (Border Slave State Convention), 1861; secession of certain states
	Cf. E458.1 Political history, March 4-December 31, 1861
	Cf. E471.1 Opening events of the Civil War

   Slavery in the United States. Antislavery movements
     Including general works on slavery in the South
     For various political aspects of the slavery question of the Revolution to the Civil War period, see E301, including especially E373, E407, E415.7, E416, E423, E433, E438, E440.5
     For general works on African Americans, including the period since the Civil War see E185
     Cf. HT851+ Slavery and the slave trade (General)

Revolution to the Civil War, 1775/1783-1861
    Slavery in the United States. Antislavery movements --
    Continued

441	General works
	Including history of slavery in general
	For history to 1830 see E446+
	For history, 1830-1863 see E449+
	Periodicals (To 1830) see E446
	Periodicals (1830-1863) see E449
442	The internal slave trade. Slave markets and auctions
443	Slave life
	Including duties of slaves and masters, overseers
444	Biography. Personal narratives of slaves
	For biography of fugitive slaves see E450
	Cf. E449 Life and writings of Frederick Douglass
445.A-.W	By state, A-W
	Including history of antislavery movements
	Slavery in an individual county is to be classed here under
	the state
	Cf. E185.93.A+ African Americans in the individual
	states
445.A3	Alabama
445.C7	Connecticut
445.D3	Delaware
445.D6	District of Columbia
445.F6	Florida
445.G3	Georgia
445.I2	Illinois
445.I3	Indiana
445.K16	Kansas
	Cf. F685 Struggle between proslavery and antislavery
	parties
445.K5	Kentucky
445.L8	Louisiana
445.M3	Maryland
445.M4	Massachusetts
445.M6	Mississippi
445.M67	Missouri
445.N2	Nebraska
445.N5	New England
445.N54	New Jersey
445.N55	New Mexico
445.N56	New York
	Cf. F128.4 Negro plot in New York City, 1741
445.N8	North Carolina
445.P3	Pennsylvania
445.R4	Rhode Island

Revolution to the Civil War, 1775/1783-1861
Slavery in the United States. Antislavery movements
By state, A-W -- Continued

445.S7   South Carolina
                Cf. F273 Trouble with Massachusetts over its African
                    American citizens in South Carolina
                Cf. F279.C4+ Charleston Insurrection (Denmark
                    Vesey's Rebellion), 1822
445.T3   Tennessee
445.T47   Texas
445.V8   Virginia
                Cf. F232.S7 Southampton Insurrection (Nat Turner's
                    Rebellion), 1831
                Cf. F234.R5+ Richmond Insurrection (Gabriel's
                    Insurrection), 1800
445.W8   Wisconsin
            History of slavery to 1830
                Including controversial literature
446   General works
                Including attempts to revive slave trade, early anti-slavery
                    movements
                Cf. E309 Northwest Ordinance of 1787
                Cf. E373 Missouri Compromise, 1820
447   Slave insurrections (General)
                Including mutiny on slave ships, e.g., Amistad (Schooner);
                    Creole (Brig)
                For individual insurrections, see local history, e.g.,
                    Charleston Insurrection (Denmark Vesey's Rebellion),
                    1822 in F279.C4; New York Negro plot, 1741 in
                    F128.4; Richmond Insurrection (Gabriel's Insurrection),
                    1800 in F234.R5; Southampton Insurrection (Nat
                    Turner's Rebellion), 1831, in F232.S7
448   Colonization
                Including the American Colonization Society and affiliated
                    organizations: their origin, plans, history, etc.; also
                    modern colonization societies
                Cf. DT621+ Liberia

Revolution to the Civil War, 1775/1783-1861
Slavery in the United States. Antislavery movements --
Continued
History of slavery, 1830-1863. Period of abolition agitation
Including controversial literature
Cf. E337.8+ Political aspects of slavery question
Cf. E416+ Wilmot Proviso, 1846
Cf. E423 Compromise of 1850
Cf. E434.8 Brooks' assault on Senator Sumner, 1856
Cf. F273 Dispute between Massachusetts and South
Carolina over African American citizens of
Massachusetts, 1845
Cf. F549.A4 Alton Riot, 1837
Cf. F685 Struggle between proslavery and antislavery
parties in Kansas

449   General works
Biography: Frederick Douglass, William Lloyd Garrison,
William Jay, Lucretia (Coffin) Mott, Wendell Phillips

450   Fugitive slaves
Including biographies and narratives of fugitive slaves, e.g.,
John Anderson, Eliza Harris, James Williams; Fugitive
Slave Law; personal liberty laws; slaves in free states;
Underground Railroad; biographies and narratives of
protectors of slaves, e.g., Levi Coffin, Jonathan Walker,
Laura S. Haviland
Including such events and cases as the Garrison mob,
Boston, 1835; case of the slave child, Med Slater,
1836; Isaac Brown case, 1847; Dred Scott case, 1848-
1857; South Bend slave case, 1849; Randolph epistles,
1850; Christiana Riot, 1851, and trial of Castner
Hanway and others for assault on Edward Gorsuch;
Sherman M. Booth case, 1854; Anthony Burns case in
Boston, 1854; Addison White rescue, 1857; Oberlin-
Wellington rescue, 1858; Jonathan Lemmon slave
case, 1860
For court records of individual trials see KF223.A+
Cf. KF4545.S5 Fugitive slave act

451   John Brown's Raid at Harpers Ferry, W. Va., 1859
Including the capture, trial, execution and biography of
John Brown
Cf. F685 John Brown in Kansas

Revolution to the Civil War, 1775/1783-1861
Slavery in the United States. Antislavery movements
History of slavery, 1830-1863. Period of abolition agitation -
- Continued

453   Slaves and the slavery question in the Civil War
Including "Contrabands"; slavery in the Confederate States
of America; emancipation of the slaves in general;
Emancipation Proclamation (manifesto by Abraham
Lincoln on September, 22, 1862, that on January 1,
1863, he would declare free all slaves held in parts of
the United States not in the possession of the Union
armies)
For local material see E185.93.A+; E445.A+
Cf. E185.2 Freedmen, Freedmen's Bureau
Cf. E185.93.S7 Port Royal Mission, S.C.
Cf. E540.N3 African American soldiers in the Union
Army
Cf. E585.A35 African American soldiers in the
Confederate Army
Civil War period, 1861-1865
Lincoln's administrations, 1861-April 15, 1865
For wars with Dakota Indians, 1862-1863 see E83.86
For other Indian wars, 1862-1863 see E83.863
For election and events preceding inauguration see
E440; E440.5
For presidential campaign of 1864 see E458.4

456   General works
Biography of Abraham Lincoln, 1809-1865
For his collected works see E457.91+
For his speeches and messages as President see
E457.94

457   General works. Lincoln as president and statesman
(Table E2)
Including campaign biographies of 1860 and 1864
Cf. E456 Political history of the country, 1861-1865
Cf. E458+ Political history of the country, 1861 -1865

457.1   Societies
457.15   Anecdotes relating to Lincoln
Including personal reminiscences of contemporaries, but
not formal biographies

Civil War period, 1861-1865

Lincoln's administrations, 1861-April 15, 1865

Biography of Abraham Lincoln, 1809-1865 -- Continued

457.2 Special

Including Lincoln's personality (character, kindness, loyalty, etc.), religion, education, books and reading, etc.

Attitude toward slavery, temperance and prohibition

Lincoln as lawyer, freemason, writer, speaker

Lincoln's relations with special classes, e.g., Jews, private soldiers

For Lincoln as president and statesman see E457

E151-909

457.25 Family life

Including biography, e.g., Mary (Todd) Lincoln, Thomas (Tad) Lincoln

By period

457.3 Early life to 1861

For campaign biographies see E457

Cf. F532.S6 Lincoln Boyhood National Memorial

Cf. F549.S7 Lincoln's home in Springfield, Ill.

457.32 To 1830

Including lineage, family, and parents (Thomas Lincoln, Nancy (Hanks) Lincoln, Sarah (Bush) Johnston Lincoln)

Including birthplace (Hodgenville, Ky.), boyhood and youth in Kentucky and Indiana

Cf. F532.S6 Nancy Hanks Lincoln Memorial

457.35 1830-1846

Including first years in Illinois; Black Hawk War, 1832; Illinois legislature, professional career

Including Ann Rutledge, marriage

Cf. E457.25 Family life

457.4 1846-1861

Including national politics; congressional service; Lincoln-Douglas debates, 1858; journey to Washington

Cf. E415.7 Slavery question

Cf. E440 Presidential campaign of 1860

Cf. E440.5 State of the country, November 1860-March 1861

Cf. E449 The slavery question

1861-1865

Cf. E458.4 Presidential campaign of 1864

Cf. E461+ The Civil War

Cf. E475.55 Gettysburg address

457.45 General works

Civil War period, 1861-1865
Lincoln's administrations, 1861-April 15, 1865
Biography of Abraham Lincoln, 1809-1865
By period
1861-1865 -- Continued

457.5 Assassination
Including the conspirators (Booth, Surratt, etc.)
For the trials of Booth, Surratt, etc. see KF223.A+

457.52 Death
Including funeral journey to Springfield, burial,
memorial services throughout the country and
abroad, guard of honor, tomb
Cf. E457.8 Funeral sermons

457.6 Monuments. Statues. Portraits
Including life and death masks, etc. Class here also
monuments, statues, etc. located in foreign countries
For local monuments, statues, etc., in the United States,
see F, e.g., in Washington, D.C., F203.4.L72, Lincoln
Statue (Lincoln Park); F203.4.L73, Lincoln Memorial
For medals see CJ5801+
Cf. E457.32 Birthplace, Hodgenville, Kentucky
Cf. E457.52 Lincoln Tomb, Springfield, Ill.

457.63 Caricatures and cartoons
Including satirical and comic works

457.64 Homes and haunts of Lincoln (General)
For early years to 1830 see E457.32
For early years, 1830-1846 see E457.35
For Springfield home see F549.S7

457.65 Museums. Exhibitions. Lincoln relics
Including Lincoln Museum (Ford Theatre), Washington,
D.C.; Oldroyd collection of Lincoln relics
For medals see CJ5801+

457.7 Anniversaries. Celebrations. Memorials since 1865
Including centennials, Lincoln Day
For funeral and memorial services see E457.52

457.8 Addresses, essays, lectures. Sermons (Funeral, etc.)
Class here the addresses that have been delivered since
the assassination
For addresses delivered before April, 1865, see E440,
E457, or E458.1-5
Cf. E457.15 Personal reminiscences
Cf. E457.52 Funeral services

(457.9) Poetry. Drama. Fiction
see class P
Music
see class M

457.905 Juvenile works

Civil War period, 1861-1865
<blockquote>
Lincoln's administrations, 1861-April 15, 1865
<blockquote>
Biography of Abraham Lincoln, 1809-1865 -- Continued
</blockquote>
</blockquote>

457.909	Lincolniana

> > > > Including miscellaneous printed matter, minor pamphlets
> > > > Reserved for material not separately cataloged

> > > Writings of Lincoln
> > > > Classification by subject is preferred

E151-909

457.91	Collected works. By date
457.92	Partial collections. Selected works. Selections. By date

> > > > Including collections of speeches (three or more)

457.94	State papers, messages, inaugural addresses. By date

> > > > *Under each:*
> > > > | | |
> > > > |---|---|
> > > > | .A2-.A29 | Text |
> > > > | .A3-.Z | History and criticism |
> > > > e.g.

457.94 1861	First inaugural address
457.94 1865	Second inaugural address
457.95	Addresses, essays, lectures. By date

> > > > For Lincoln-Douglas debates, 1858 see E457.4
> > > > For collections of speeches see E457.92

> > > Letters

457.96	Individual. By date
457.962	Collections. By date
457.98	Minor works

> > > > Including history of the Fisher murder mystery; a facsimile
> > > > of an indenture drawn up, October 25, 1841, by Lincoln
> > > > and signed by his father

457.99	Stories, anecdotes, poems, axioms, brief extracts, etc., attributed to Lincoln

> > > > Arranged alphabetically by editor or title

> > Political history (Contemporary works)
> > > Including questions at issue between North and South, the
> > > internal policies of the United States, etc.
> > > For treaties published after the close of the war see
> > > E459
> > > For foreign public opinion see E469.8
> > > For sermons and addresses see E649+

458	General works

> > > Including collections and works covering more than a single
> > > year

458.1	March 4-December 31, 1861

> > > Cf. E440.5 State of the nation, November 1860-
> > > March 4, 1861

458.2	1862
458.3	1863

> > > Cf. E453 Emancipation of the slaves

       Civil War period, 1861-1865

        Lincoln's administrations, 1861-April 15, 1865

         Political history (Contemporary works) -- Continued

458.4   1864

           Including presidential campaign of 1864; campaign
            literature; etc.

458.5   January-May 1865

458.7   Union men in the South. Refugees

458.8   Confederate sympathizers in the North. "Copperheads,"
          "Butternuts," etc.

          Including conspiracies, e.g., Northwestern Conspiracy, 1864;
           disloyal organizations: Knights of the Golden Circle,
           Order of American Knights or Sons of Liberty, Order of
           the Lone Star, etc.; suspension of the writ of habeas
           corpus; prisoners of state; Harris court-martial, 1865; etc.
          Cf. E615+ Union prisons

459   Political history (Non-contemporary works)

          Including publications since May 1865; treatises only
          For contemporary publications see E458+
          For addresses, sermons, etc. see E649+

        The Civil War, 1861-1865

461   Periodicals

          For Confederate periodicals see E482

         Societies of veterans, etc.

          For Confederate societies see E483
          For regimental associations of veterans see E492

462   General works

462.Z7   Minor publications not separately cataloged

         Individual societies, etc.

462.1   Grand Army of the Republic (Table E4)

462.15   Women's Relief Corps (Table E4)

462.17   Ladies of the Grand Army of the Republic (Table E4)

462.18   Legion of Loyal Women, Washington, D.C. (Table E4)

462.2   Military Order of the Loyal Legion of the United States
          (Table E4)

462.25   Dames of the Loyal Legion (Table E4)

462.3   Military Order of the Medal of Honor (Table E4)

462.4   Union Veteran Legion of the United States (Table E4)

462.5   National Association of Naval Veterans (Table E4)

462.6   Veteran Brotherhood of the State of Kansas (Table E4)

462.7   Union League of America (Table E4)

462.84   Union clubs (Table E4)
           For local Union clubs see HS2721+

462.9   Sons of Union Veterans of the Civil War (Table E4)

462.92   Soldiers' and Sailors' National Union League of
          Washington, D.C. (Table E4)

462.93   Washington, D.C. Old Guard (Table E4)

The Civil War, 1861-1865
    Societies of veterans, etc.
      Individual societies, etc. -- Continued

462.94	Order of American Freemen (Table E4)
462.96	Union White Boys in Blue (Table E4)
462.97	Philadelphia. War Veterans' Club (Table E4)
462.98	National Soldiers Historical Association (Table E4)
462.99.A-Z	Other societies, etc.

          Subarrange each by Table E5
          e.g.

462.99.D2	Daughters of Union Veterans of the Civil War (Table E5)

E151-909

          First Defenders see E493.9
          National Association of Civil War Army Nurses see E621

462.99.N27	National Veteran Club of the United States (Table E5)
462.99.O65	Order of Stars and Stripes (Table E5)
462.99.S6	Society for Correct Civil War Information (Table E5)
462.99.S62	Society of the Army and Navy of the Gulf (Table E5)
462.99.U53	Union Society of the Civil War (Table E5)
462.99.U57	Union Soldiers' Alliance, Washington, D.C. (Table E5)
462.99.U63	Union Veterans' Union (Table E5)

          United States Veteran Signal Corps Association see E608

463	Patriotic societies during the war

          Including Loyal League of Union Citizens, Loyal National League of the State of New York, Loyal Publication Society
          For Loyal Union League clubs see HS2721+

464	Collections. Collected works

          Including papers read before Loyal Legion, Grand Army of the Republic
          Cf. E458+ Collections of political pamphlets
          Cf. E484 Confederate collections
          Cf. E655 Anecdotes of the Civil War

    Biography

467	Collective (Union and Confederate)

          For rolls of college men in the war see E541.A+; E586.A+
          For prisoners of war see E611+
          For nurses see E621+

The Civil War, 1861-1865

Biography -- Continued

467.1.A-Z	Individual, A-Z

Including chiefly lives of commanders and other officers
e.g.

Cf. E415.9.A+ Biography of political leaders except a
few like Davis, Stanton, and Benjamin whose
careers culminated in the war

Cf. E495+ Regimental officers and privates

Cf. E545+ Regimental officers and privates

Cf. E601+ Personal narratives of war service

467.1.A2	Adams, Charles Francis, 1807-1886 (Table E1)
467.1.A3	Alexander, Andrew Jonathan (Table E1)
467.1.A4	Allen, Henry Watkins (Table E1)
467.1.A54	Anderson, Richard Heron (Table E1)
467.1.A78	Arrowsmith, George (Table E1)
467.1.A8	Ashby, Turner (Table E1)
467.1.B14	Bailey, Theodorus (Table E1)
467.1.B16	Baker, Edward Dickenson (Table E1)
467.1.B23	Banks, Nathaniel Prentice (Table E1)
467.1.B25	Barlow, Francis Channing (Table E1)
467.1.B26	Barnes, James (Table E1)
467.1.B29	Bartlett, William Francis (Table E1)
467.1.B3	Bayard, George Dashiell (Table E1)
467.1.B38	Beauregard, Pierre Gustave Toutant (Table E1)
467.1.B39	Beaver, James Addams (Table E1)
467.1.B397	Benedict, Lewis (Table E1)
467.1.B4	Benjamin, Judah Philip (Table E1)
467.1.B5	Berry, Hiram Gregory (Table E1)
467.1.B6	Birney, David Bell (Table E1)
467.1.B7	Boomer, George Boardman (Table E1)
467.1.B73	Bowen, John Steven (Table E1)
467.1.B75	Bragg, Braxton (Table E1)
467.1.B77	Brown, Joseph Newton (Table E1)
467.1.B8	Burnside, Ambrose Everett (Table E1)
467.1.B87	Butler, Benjamin Franklin (Table E1)
467.1.B9	Butterfield, Daniel (Table E1)
467.1.C52	Chetlain, Augustus Louis (Table E1)
467.1.C97	Curtis, Samuel Ryan (Table E1)
467.1.C98	Cushing, William Barker (Table E1)
467.1.C99	Custer, George Armstrong (Table E1)
467.1.D13	Dahlgren, John Adolphus Bernard (Table E1)
467.1.D24	Davis, Charles Henry (Table E1)
467.1.D26	Davis, Jefferson (Table E1)
467.1.D27	Davis, Varina (Howell). "Mrs. Jefferson Davis" (Table E1)
467.1.D28	Davis, Varina Anne Jefferson (Table E1)
467.1.D6	Dodge, Grenville Mellen (Table E1)

The Civil War, 1861-1865
Biography
Individual, A-Z -- Continued

467.1.D9	Du Pont, Samuel Francis (Table E1)
467.1.E13	Early, Jubal Anderson (Table E1)
467.1.E4	Elliott, Stephen (Table E1)
467.1.E47	Ellsworth, Ephraim Elmer (Table E1)
467.1.E86	Ewell, Richard Stoddert (Table E1)
467.1.E9	Ewing, Charles (Table E1)
467.1.F23	Farragut, David Glasgow (Table E1)
467.1.F64	Flusser, Charles Williamson (Table E1)
467.1.F68	Foote, Andrew Hull (Table E1)
467.1.F72	Forrest, Nathan Bedford (Table E1)
467.1.F83	Franklin, William Buel (Table E1)
467.1.F87	French, Samuel Gibbs (Table E1)
467.1.F9	Fritchie, Barbara (Hauer) (Table E1)
467.1.G29	Geary, John White (Table E1)
467.1.G6	Gooding, Oliver Paul (Table E1)
467.1.G66	Gordon, John Brown (Table E1)
467.1.G68	Gorgas, Josiah (Table E1)
467.1.G79	Greene, George Sears (Table E1)
467.1.G88	Grout, William Wallace (Table E1)
467.1.H18	Halleck, Henry Wager (Table E1)
467.1.H19	Hampton, Wade, 1818-1902 (Table E1)
467.1.H2	Hancock, Winfield Scott (Table E1)
467.1.H4	Hartranft, John Frederick (Table E1)
467.1.H44	Hatton, Robert (Table E1)
467.1.H58	Hood, John Bell (Table E1)
467.1.H6	Hooker, Joseph (Table E1)
467.1.H7	Hovey, Alvin Peterson (Table E1)
467.1.H8	Howard, Oliver Otis (Table E1)
467.1.H885	Humphreys, Andrew Atkinson (Table E1)
467.1.H89	Hunt, Henry Jackson (Table E1)
467.1.H9	Hunter, David (Table E1)
467.1.J15	Jackson, Thomas Jonathan (Table E1)
467.1.J73	Johnston, Albert Sidney (Table E1)
467.1.J74	Johnston, Joseph Eggleston (Table E1)
467.1.K24	Kearny, Philip (Table E1)
467.1.L4	Lee, Robert Edward (Table E1)
467.1.L5	Logan, Thomas Muldrup (Table E1)
467.1.L55	Longstreet, James (Table E1)
467.1.L6	Lowell, Charles Russell (Table E1)
467.1.L9	Lyon, Nathaniel (Table E1)
467.1.M2	McClellan, George Brinton (Table E1)
	Cf. E458.4 Presidential campaign of 1864
467.1.M24	McCulloch, Ben (Table E1)
467.1.M35	Maffitt, John Newland (Table E1)

E151-909

The Civil War, 1861-1865
Biography
Individual, A-Z -- Continued

467.1.M38	Meade, George Gordon (Table E1)
467.1.M4	Meagher, Thomas Francis (Table E1)
467.1.M6	Mitchel, Ormsby Macknight (Table E1)
467.1.M86	Morgan, John Hunt (Table E1)
467.1.M87	Mosby, John Singleton (Table E1)
467.1.O7	Ord, Edward Otho Cresap (Table E1)
467.1.P26	Parsons, Lewis Baldwin (Table E1)
467.1.P365	Pemberton, John Clifford (Table E1)
467.1.P37	Pendleton, William Nelson (Table E1)
467.1.P4	Perkins, George Hamilton (Table E1)
467.1.P51	Pettigrew, James Johnston (Table E1)
467.1.P57	Pickett, George Edward (Table E1)
467.1.P7	Polk, Leonidas (Table E1)
467.1.P78	Porter, David Dixon (Table E1)
467.1.P8	Porter, Fitz-John (Table E1)

For conduct at 2d battle of Bull Run and court-martial see E473.772

467.1.P82	Porter, Horace (Table E1)
467.1.R2	Ramseur, Stephen Dodson (Table E1)
467.1.R25	Rawlins, John Aaron (Table E1)
467.1.R4	Reynolds, John Fulton (Table E1)
467.1.R7	Rosecrans, William Starke (Table E1)
467.1.S32	Schenck, Robert Cumming (Table E1)
467.1.S35	Schofield, John McAllister (Table E1)
467.1.S4	Sedgwick, John (Table E1)
467.1.S47	Semmes, Raphael (Table E1)
467.1.S54	Sheridan, Philip Henry (Table E1)
467.1.S55	Sherman, William Tecumseh (Table E1)
467.1.S552	Sherman, Ellen (Ewing) (Table E1)
467.1.S58	Sigel, Franz (Table E1)
467.1.S63	Slocum, Henry Warner (Table E1)
467.1.S75	Smith, William Farrar (Table E1)
467.1.S8	Stanton, Edwin McMasters (Table E1)
467.1.S84	Steedman, James Barrett (Table E1)
467.1.S85	Stephens, Alexander Hamilton (Table E1)
467.1.S87	Stone, Charles Pomeroy (Table E1)
467.1.S9	Stuart, James Ewell Brown (Table E1)
467.1.T4	Thomas, George Henry (Table E1)
467.1.T8	Tucker, John Randolph (Table E1)
467.1.T9	Tyler, Daniel (Table E1)
467.1.T98	Tyndale, Hector (Table E1)
467.1.W13	Wadsworth, James Samuel (Table E1)

The Civil War, 1861-1865
  Biography
    Individual, A-Z -- Continued

467.1.W2	Wallace, Lewis (Table E1)
	Cf. PS3130+ Wallace as an author, his works, and
	criticism of those works
467.1.W3	Wallace, William Henry Lamme (Table E1)
467.1.W4	Warren, Gouverneur Kemble (Table E1)
	Cf. E477.675 Warren court-martial
467.1.W46	Welles, Gideon (Table E1)
467.1.W5	Wheeler, Joseph (Table E1)
467.1.W61	Whiting, William Henry Chase (Table E1)
467.1.W69	Wilder, John Thomas (Table E1)
467.1.W72	Williams, Alpheus Starkey (Table E1)
467.1.W74	Wilson, James Harrison (Table E1)
467.1.W77	Winslow, John Ancrum (Table E1)
467.1.W81	Wistar, Isaac Jones (Table E1)
467.1.W94	Wright, Marcus Joseph (Table E1)

  Comprehensive works. General histories
    Cf. E167 Description and travel, 1861-1865
    Cf. E458+ Causes, aims, etc., of the war
    Cf. E470+ Military operations
    Cf. E482+ The Confederate States of America
    Cf. F214 The Confederate States of America

468	General works
468.3	Chronology
	Cf. E470.1 Chronological lists of battles
468.5	Historiography
	Including criticism of histories and textbooks, accuracy and
	bias of writers
	Cf. E175.85 Criticism of textbooks (General)
468.7	Pictorial works
	Including works important solely or chiefly for the illustrations
468.8	Soldiers' almanacs
468.9	General special
	Including otherwise unprovided for topics such as
	propaganda, name of the war, influence, etc.
	Cf. E488.5 Confederate propaganda in foreign
	countries

E151-909

The Civil War, 1861-1865 -- Continued
Diplomatic history
Including Trent Affair, 1861; Gilmore and Jacquess' conference
with Jefferson Davis, 1864; Hampton Roads Conference,
1865; construction of Confederate war vessels in England;
etc.
Cf. E440.5 Washington Peace Conference, 1860
Cf. E470.95 Confederates in Canada, and St. Albans
Raid
Cf. E488 Confederate diplomatic history
Cf. E596+ Confederate navy
Cf. F1233 French intervention in Mexico

469   General works
469.8   Foreign public opinion
Cf. E458+ Contemporary addresses on the war
Military operations
470   General works
Including campaigns and battles (General); military histories
of the war; narratives of commanders
For works restricted to a special region, campaign, or
battle see E470+
For lists of battles see E470.1
Cf. E468+ General history of the war
Cf. E601+ Personal narratives of minor officers and
privates
470.1   Battles (Alphabetical or chronological lists)
For individual battles see E471+
By region
Including military operations of individual armies
Eastern border states
Including Virginia, Maryland, District of Columbia, and
Pennsylvania. Army of the James, Army of the
Potomac, Army of Virginia, Army of Northern Virginia
(C.S.A.)
For personal narratives of service in the Army of the
Potomac, if not classed under campaign or regiment,
see E601, rather than E470.2
470.2   General works

E151-909

The Civil War, 1861-1865
Military operations
By region
Eastern border states -- Continued
470.3   Shenandoah Valley
Including the Romney Campaign
Cf. E472.16 Operations in the Shenandoah Valley,
July 2-25, 1861
Cf. E473.74 Operations in the Shenandoah Valley,
May 15-June 17, 1862
Cf. E476.66 Operations in the Shenandoah Valley,
June 23-August 3, 1864
Cf. E477.33 Operations in the Shenandoah Valley,
August 7-November 28, 1864
Cf. E477.65 Operations in the Shenandoah Valley,
1865
Western border states
Including Ohio Valley and central Mississippi Valley (West
Virginia, Kentucky, Tennessee, Ohio, Indiana, Illinois,
Missouri, Arkansas). Army of West Virginia
470.4   General works
470.45   Border warfare. Guerrillas
470.5   Cumberland and Tennessee Valleys. Chattanooga region
Including armies of the Cumberland and the Tennessee,
Army of Tennessee (C.S.A.)
470.6   Lower South
Including North Carolina, South Carolina, Georgia, and
regions west
For Sherman's march see E476.69
470.65   South Atlantic coast line
Including siege of Charleston, 1863-1865; supplies for
Savannah
For Naval operations and blockade running see
E591+
Cf. E473.96 Engagement in Charleston Harbor, April
7, 1863
Cf. E475.6+ Engagements in Charleston Harbor,
1863
Cf. E476.4+ Engagements in Charleston Harbor,
1864
470.7   Gulf States
Including Florida, Alabama, Mississippi, Louisiana, Texas
For Society of the Army and Navy of the Gulf see
E462.99.S62
For naval operations and blockade running see
E591+
470.8   Mississippi Valley

The Civil War, 1861-1865
Military operations
By region -- Continued

470.9   Trans-Mississippi region
Including Texas, Indian Territory, Kansas, New Mexico, Missouri, Arkansas, etc. Army of the Pacific

470.95   Northern frontier of the United States
Including Confederates in Canada; St. Albans (Vt.) Raid, 1864

By campaign and battle

A history of a regiment in a particular campaign or battle is classed in E471-478, rather than E495-582

The literature of the national military parks at Chickamauga and Chattanooga, Gettysburg, Vicksburg, etc. is classed with the battle as are descriptive works dealing with the battlefield

Naval operations in connection with military movements are classed here, rather than in E591

For local guidebooks, see class F, e.g., F44.C4, Chattanooga

Cf. E467.1.A+ Biography of leaders

Cf. E468+ Comprehensive histories of the war

Cf. E470 General military histories, and memoirs of commanders

Cf. E470.2+ Military operations by region, and history of armies

Cf. E493.1 History of corps and divisions

Cf. E493.5 History of brigades

Cf. E495+ History of regiments

Cf. E547 History of corps, divisions, and brigades

Cf. E551+ History of regiments

Opening events

471   General works

471.1   South Carolina, December 20, 1860-April 14, 1861
Including Charleston Harbor (Fort Sumter)

471.5   Other southern states
Cf. E440.5 General political history
Cf. E458.1 General political history
Cf. E551+ General political history

471.51   Georgia, January 3-26, 1861

471.52   Alabama and Mississippi, January 4-20, 1861

471.53   Florida, January 6-August 31, 1861
Including Fort Jefferson, Dry Tortugas

471.54   North Carolina, January 9-May 20, 1861

471.55   Louisiana, January 10-February 19, 1861

471.56   Texas and New Mexico, February 1-June 11, 1861

471.57   Arkansas, Indian Territory, and Missouri, February 7-May 9, 1861

The Civil War, 1861-1865
   Military operations
      By campaign and battle -- Continued

472.1	Maryland, Pennsylvania and Virginia, and West Virginia, April 16-July 31, 1861
472.13	Conflict between United States troops and mob in Baltimore, April 19
472.14	Engagement at Big Bethel, June 10
472.16	Operations in Shenandoah Valley, July 2-25
472.17	Campaign in West Virginia, July 6-17
	Including Battle of Rich Mountain, July 11; Battle of Scary Creek, July 17
472.18	Bull Run Campaign, July 16-22
	Including First battle of Bull Run (Manassas), July 21
472.182	Manassas Battlefield Confederate Park
472.183	Manassas National Battlefield Park
472.2	Missouri, Arkansas, Kansas and Indian Territory, May 10-November 19, 1861
	Including battles of Carthage, Mo., July 5; Athens, Mo., August 5; Fredericktown, Mo., October 17-21
472.23	Battle of Wilson's Creek, August 10
472.25	Siege of Lexington, Mo., September 13-20
472.28	Engagement at Belmont, Mo., and demonstration from Paducah upon Columbus, Ky., November 7
472.3	Texas, New Mexico, and Arizona, June 11-February 1, 1862
472.32	Skirmish at Mesilla, evacuation of Fort Fillmore, and surrender of Union forces at San Augustine, July 25-27
472.4	Kentucky and Tennessee, July 1-November 19, 1861
472.5	North Carolina and southeastern Virginia, August 1, 1861-January 11, 1862
472.6	Maryland, northern Virginia, and West Virginia, August 1, 1861-March 17, 1862
	Including battles of Kessler's Cross Lanes, W.V., August 26; Carnifex Ferry, W.V., September 10; Cheat Mountain, W.V., September 12-15; Greenbrier River, W.V., October 3
472.63	Operations on the Potomac near Leesburg, Va.
	Including engagement at Ball's Bluff and action near Edward's Ferry, October 21-24
472.7	Coasts of South Carolina, Georgia, and middle and east Florida, August 21, 1861-April 11, 1862
	Including Port Royal Expedition, November, 1861
472.79	Bombardment and capture of Fort Pulaski, Ga., April 10-11

E151-909

The Civil War, 1861-1865

Military operations

By campaign and battle -- Continued

472.8	West Florida, southern Alabama, southern Mississippi, and Louisiana, September 1, 1861-May 12, 1862
472.88	Bombardment and capture of Forts Jackson and Saint Philip and occupation of New Orleans, by Union Forces, April 18-May 1
	Cf. E510+ General Butler's government of Louisiana
472.9	Kentucky, Tennessee, north Alabama, and southwest Virginia, November 19, 1861-March 4, 1862
	Including Anna E. Carroll's claim; battles of Rowlett's Station, Ky., December 17, 1861; Middle Creek, Ky., January 10, 1862; Mill Springs, Ky., January 19, 1862
472.96	Capture of Fort Henry, Tenn., February 6
472.97	Siege and capture of Fort Donelson, Tenn., February 12-16
473.1	Missouri, Arkansas, Kansas, and Indian Territory, November 19, 1861-April 10, 1862
473.15	Operations at New Madrid, Mo., and Island No. 10, and descent upon Union City, Tenn., February 28-April 8
473.17	Battle of Pea Ridge, March 6-8
473.2	Southeastern Virginia, January 11-March 17, 1862
	Including naval engagement in Hampton Roads, Merrimac and Monitor
473.3	North Carolina, January 11-August 20, 1862
	Including Burnside's Expedition; seige of Fort Macon, N.C., March 23-26; Battle of South Mills, April 19; and capture of Elizabeth City, N.C., September 10
473.31	Battle of Roanoke Island, February 8
473.34	Battle of New Bern, March 14
473.4	Texas, New Mexico, and Arizona, February 1-September 20, 1862
	Including battles of Valverde, N.M., February 20-21, Glorieta Pass, N.M., March 26-28; Nueces River, August 10
473.46	Expedition from southern California through Arizona to northwestern Texas and New Mexico, April 13-September 20
	Including California column
473.5	Kentucky, Tennessee, northern Mississippi, northern Alabama, and southwest Virginia, March 4-June 10, 1862
	Including Battle of Memphis, Tenn., June 6
473.52	Cumberland Gap campaign, March 28-June 18

The Civil War, 1861-1865
  Military operations
    By campaign and battle
      Kentucky, Tennessee, northern Mississippi, northern
        Alabama, and southwest Virginia, March 4-June 10,
        1862 -- Continued

473.54	Battle of Shiloh, April 6-7
	Including Shiloh National Military Park
473.55	Raid on Confederate line of communication between Chattanooga, Tenn., and Marietta, Ga., April 7-12
	Including Andrews' railroad raid
473.56	Advance upon and siege of Corinth, Miss., and pursuit of the Confederate forces, April 29-June 10
473.59	Attack on Chattanooga, Tenn., June 7-8
473.6	Peninsular campaign, Va., March 17-September 2, 1862
	Including Battle of Hanover Court House, Va., May 27
473.61	Siege of Yorktown, April 5-May 4
473.63	Battle of Williamsburg, May 5
473.64	Occupation of Norfolk and Portsmouth, May 10
473.65	Battle of Fair Oaks, May 31-June 1
473.66	Stuart's raid, June 13-15
473.68	Seven days' battles, June 25-July 1
	Including Battles of Mechanicsville (Beaver Dam Creek), June 26; Gaines' Mill, June 27; White Oak Swamp, June 28-30; Savage Station, June 29; Glendale (Frayser's Farm), June 30; Malvern Hill, July 1
473.7	Northern Virginia, West Virginia, and Maryland, March 17-September 2, 1862
	Including General Pope's Virginia campaign; battles of McDowell, Va., May 8; Port Republic, June 9
473.72	Battle of Kernstown, Va., March 23
473.74	Operations in the Shenandoah Valley, May 15-June 17
	Including 1st Battle of Winchester, May 25; and Battle of Cross Keys, Va., June 8
473.76	Battle of Cedar Mountain, August 9
473.77	Campaign in northern Virginia, August 16-September 2
	Including Battles of Groveton, August 28-29; Bull Run (Second battle), August 30; Chantilly, September 1
473.772	Fitz-John Porter case
473.8	Missouri, Arkansas, Kansas, Indian Territory, and the Department of the Northwest, April 10-November 20, 1862
	Including battles of Searcy Landing, Ark., May 19; Locust Grove, Okla., July 3; and Clark's Mill, Mo., November 7
	Cf. E83.86 Sioux Indian War, 1862-1865

E151-909

The Civil War, 1861-1865
Military operations
By campaign and battle -- Continued
473.9   Coasts of South Carolina, Georgia, and middle and east Florida, April 12, 1862-June 11, 1863
Including Battle of Pocotaligo, S.C., October 22, 1862
473.92   Engagement at Secessionville (James Island), S.C., June 16, 1862
473.96   Engagement in Charleston Harbor, April 7, 1863
474.1   West Florida, southern Alabama, southern Mississippi, and Louisiana, May 12, 1862-May 14, 1863. Texas, New Mexico and Arizona, September 20, 1862-May 14, 1863
Including Battle of Galveston, January 1, 1863
For Grierson's raid, April 17-May 2, 1863 see E475.23
474.11   Operations against Vicksburg, Miss., and Baton Rouge, La., May 18-August 6, 1862
Including the Essex (U.S. ironclad) and Arkansas (Confederate ironclad)
474.17   Operations against and about Port Hudson, La., March 7-27, 1863
For seige of Port Hudson see E475.42
474.18   Operations in west Louisiana, April 9-May 14, 1863
474.3   Kentucky, middle and east Tennessee, north Alabama, and southwest Virginia, June 10-October 31, 1862
Including Battle of Snow's Pond, Ky., September 25
474.32   Morgan's first Kentucky raid, July 4-28
474.34   Action at and surrender of Murfreesboro, Tenn., July 13
474.37   Battle of Richmond, Ky., August 30
474.38   Evacuation of Cumberland Gap, Tenn., September 17-October 3
474.39   Battle of Perryville, Ky., October 8
474.4   West Tennessee and northern Mississippi, June 10, 1862-January 20, 1863
474.42   Engagement at Iuka, Miss., September 19
474.44   Battle of Corinth, Miss., and pursuit of the Confederate forces, October 3-12
474.46   Forrest's expedition into west Tennessee, December 15-January 2
474.47   Operations against Vicksburg, December 20-January 3
474.48   Expedition against Arkansas Post or Fort Hindman, Ark., and operations in that vicinity, January 4-17

The Civil War, 1861-1865
Military operations
By campaign and battle -- Continued

474.5   North Carolina and southeastern Virginia, August 20,
                 1862-June 3, 1863
                     Including battles of New River, N.C., November 23-25,
                         1862 and Whitehall, N.C., December 16; and siege of
                         Suffolk, Va.
474.52   Expedition from New Bern, to Goldsboro, N.C.,
                 December 11-20, 1862
474.55   Siege of Washington, N.C., and pursuit of the
                 Confederate forces, March 30-April 20, 1863
474.6   Northern Virginia, West Virginia, Maryland and
                 Pennsylvania, September 3-November 14, 1862
474.61   The Maryland campaign, September 3-20
                     Including siege of Harper's Ferry, September 14-15; and
                         battles of Crampton's Gap, Md., September 14; and
                         South Mountain, Md., September 14
474.65   Battle of Antietam, September 17
                     Including Antietam National Cemetery
474.67   Stuart's expedition into Maryland and Pennsylvania,
                 October 9-12
474.7   Kentucky, middle and east Tennessee, north Alabama,
                 and southwest Virginia, November 1, 1862-January
                 20, 1863
474.75   Morgan's second Kentucky raid, December 22-January
                 2
474.77   The Stone's River or Murfreesboro, Tenn. campaign,
                 December 26-January 5
                     Including Stones River National Military Park
474.8   Northern Virginia, West Virginia, Maryland, and
                 Pennsylvania, November 15, 1862-January 25, 1863
474.85   Battle of Fredericksburg, Va., December 11-15
                     Including Fredericksburg and Spotsylvania County
                         National Military Park
474.9   Missouri, Arkansas, Kansas, Indian Territory, and the
                 Department of the Northwest, November 20, 1862-
                 December 31, 1863
                     Including battles of Cane Hill., Ark., November 28, 1862;
                         Chalk Bluff, May 1-2, 1863; Helena, Ark., July 4, 1863;
                         Honey Springs, Okla., July 17, 1863; and Baxter
                         Springs, Kan., October 6, 1863
                     Cf. E83.86 Sioux Indian War, 1862-1865
474.92   Battle of Prairie Grove, Ark., December 7, 1862
474.94   Battle of Fayetteville, Ark., April 18, 1863
474.96   Advance of Union forces upon Little Rock, Ark., August
                 1-September 14, 1863

E151-909

The Civil War, 1861-1865
  Military operations
    By campaign and battle
      Missouri, Arkansas, Kansas, Indian Territory, and the
        Department of the Northwest, November 20, 1862-
        December 31, 1863 -- Continued

474.97   Quantrill's raid into Kansas and pursuit by Union forces,
              August 20-28
                Including the Lawrence massacre and burning, August 21
474.98   Shelby's raid in Arkansas and Missouri, September 22-
              October 26
475.1   Kentucky, middle and east Tennessee, north Alabama,
              and southwest Virginia, January 21-August 10, 1863
                Including Streight's raid toward Rome, Ga., April-May 1863;
                and Battle of Thompson's Station, Tenn., March 5
475.16   The middle Tennessee or Tullahoma campaign, June
              23-July 7
475.18   Morgan's raid in Kentucky, Indiana, and Ohio, July 2-26
                Including Battle of Corydon, Ind., July 9
475.2   Mississippi and west Tennessee
                Including operations in Arkansas and Louisiana connected
                with the siege of Vicksburg, January 20-August 10,
                1863
475.22   Yazoo Pass expedition, February 24-April 8
475.23   Grierson's raid from La Grange, Tenn., to Baton
              Rouge, La., April 17-May 2
475.24   Battle of Port Gibson, Miss., May 1
475.26   Battle of Champion's Hill, May 16
475.27   Siege of Vicksburg, Miss., May 19-July 4
                Including Vicksburg National Military Park
475.29   The Jackson, Miss., campaign and siege, July 5-25,
              1863. Battle of Jackson, May 13, 1863
475.3   Northern Virginia, West Virginia, Maryland and
              Pennsylvania, January 26-June 3, 1863
                Including Battle of Kelly's Ford, March 17
475.35   The Chancellorsville campaign, April 27-May 6
                Including the Battle of Salem Church, May 3-4
475.38   The Stoneman raid, April 29-May 7
475.4   West Florida, southern Alabama, southern Mississippi,
              Louisiana, Texas, and New Mexico, May 14-
              December 31, 1863
                Including engagements at Milliken's Bend, June 7, and
                Sabine Pass, September 8
              For Siege of Vicksburg see E475.27
475.42   Siege of Port Hudson, La., May 22-July 8

The Civil War, 1861-1865
Military operations
By campaign and battle -- Continued

475.5	North Carolina, Virginia, West Virginia, Maryland, Pennsylvania, and Department of the East, June 3-August 3, 1863

Including 2nd Battle of Winchester, Va., June 12-15; and
Battle of Middleburg, Va., June 17-18
Cf. F128.44 Draft riots in New York City, June 13-16

475.51	The Gettysburg campaign, June 3-August 1

Including battles of Brandy Station, Va., June 9; and
Hanover, Pa., June 30

475.53	Battle of Gettysburg
475.55	Gettysburg National Cemetery

Including dedication, national monument, and Lincoln's
Gettysburg address

475.56	Gettysburg National Military Park

Including state, regimental, and other monuments
For accounts of the battle see E475.53

475.57	Fiftieth anniversary celebration, 1913
475.58	Seventy-fifth anniversary celebration, 1938
475.582	One-hundredth anniversary celebration, 1963
	Coasts of South Carolina and Georgia. Middle and east Florida, June 12-December 31, 1863
475.6	General works
475.62	Charleston Harbor, April-December, 1863

Cf. E473.96 Engagement in Charleston Harbor,
April 7, 1863

475.63	Operations on Morris Island, S.C., July 10-September 7

Including attack and fall of Battery Wagner

475.65	Bombardment of Fort Sumter, August 17-December 31
475.68	Engagement in Charleston Harbor, September 7-8
475.7	North Carolina, Virginia, West Virginia, Maryland and Pennsylvania, August 4-December 31, 1863

Including Battle of Bulltown, W.V., October 13; and 2nd
Battle of Rappahannock Station, November 7; Salem
Raid, December 8-25

475.75	The Bristoe, Va., campaign, October 9-22

Including Battle of Bristoe Station, Va., October 14

475.76	Expeditions from Beverly and Charleston against Lewisburg, W. Va., November 1-7

Including Battle of Droop Mountain, W. Va., November 6

475.78	Mine Run, Va., campaign, November 26-December 2
475.8	Kentucky, southwest Virginia, Tennessee, Mississippi, north Alabama, and north Georgia, August 11-October 19, 1863

Including Battle of Blue Springs, Tenn., October 10

The Civil War, 1861-1865
  Military operations
    By campaign and battle
      Kentucky, southwest Virginia, Tennessee, Mississippi,
        north Alabama, and north Georgia, August 11-
        October 19, 1863 -- Continued

475.81   Chickamauga, Ga., campaign, August 16-September
        22
          Including Chickamauga and Chattanooga National Park
475.85   East Tennessee campaign, August 16-October 19
475.87   Wheeler and Roddey's raid, September 30-October 17
475.88   Chalmer's raid in west Tennessee and northern
        Mississippi, October 4-17
475.9   Kentucky, southwest Virginia, Tennessee, Mississippi,
        north Alabama, and north Georgia, October 20-
        December 31, 1863
          Including Battle of Mossy Creek, Tenn., December 29
475.92   Reopening of the Tennessee River, October 26-29
          Including skirmish at Brown's Ferry and engagement at
          Wauhatchie, Tenn., October 29
475.94   Knoxville, Tenn., campaign, November 4-December 23
          Including attack upon Fort Sanders, November 29; and
          seige of Knoxville
475.97   Chattanooga-Ringgold campaign, November 23-27
          Including battles of Lookout Mountain and Missionary
          Ridge
476.1   Kentucky, southwest Virginia, Tennessee, Mississippi,
        Alabama, and north Georgia, January 1-April 30,
        1864
          Including Battle of Cloyds Mountain, Va., May 9
476.14   The Meridian, Miss., expedition, February 3-March 6
          Including cooperating expeditions from Memphis and up
          the Yazoo River; Battle of Okolona, Feb. 22
476.17   Forrest's expedition into west Tennessee and
        Kentucky, March 16-April 14
          Including Massacre at Fort Pillow, April 12
476.2   North Carolina, Virginia, West Virginia, Maryland, and
        Pennsylvania, January 1-April 30, 1864
          Including Battle of Plymouth, Va., April 17-20
476.23   Expedition against New Bern, N.C., January 28-
        February 10
476.27   Kilpatrick's expedition against Richmond, February 28-
        March 4
          Including Dahlgren's raid
476.3   Louisiana and the trans-Mississippi states and territories,
        January 1-June 30, 1864
          Including Battle of Calcasieu Pass, La., May 6

The Civil War, 1861-1865
  Military operations
    By campaign and battle
      Louisiana and the trans-Mississippi states and territories, January 1-June 30, 1864 -- Continued
476.33   Red River, La., campaign, March 10-May 22
                Including battles of Mansfield, La., April 8; and Pleasant Hill, La., April 9
476.35   Camden, Ark., expedition, March 23-May 3
                Including battles of Fitzhugh's Woods, April 1; Poison Spring, April 18; Marks' Mill, April 25; and Jenkins' Ferry, April 30
              South Carolina, Florida, and coast of Georgia, January 1-November 13, 1864
                Including Battle of Chapman's Fort, May 26
476.4   General works
476.41   Operations in Charleston Harbor and vicinity, January 1-November 13
476.43   Florida expedition, February 5-22
                Including Battle of Olustee, February 20
476.5   Southeastern Virginia and North Carolina, May 1-June 12, 1864
476.52   Campaign from the Rapidan to the James, May 4-June 12
                Including Overland Campaign: battles of the Wilderness, May 5-7; Spotsylvania, May 8-21; North Anna River, May 23-26; Wilson's Wharf, Va., May 24; Totopotomoy Creek, Va., May 26-30; Hawes Shops, Va., May 28; Cold Harbor, June 3
476.57   Operations on the south side of the James, May 4-June 2
                Including Battle of Drewrys Bluff, Va., May 12-16 and Bermuda Hundred, Va., May 16-30
476.59   Engagement at Petersburg, Va., June 9
476.6   Northern Virginia, West Virginia, Maryland, and Pennsylvania, May 1-August 3, 1864
                Including Battle of Piedmont, June 5; Battle of Trevilian Station, Va., June 11-12
476.62   Expedition against the Virginia and Tennessee Railroad, May 2-19
476.64   Engagement at New Market, Va., May 15
476.65   Lynchburg campaign, May 26-June 29

E151-909

The Civil War, 1861-1865
  Military operations
    By campaign and battle
      Northern Virginia, West Virginia, Maryland, and
        Pennsylvania, May 1-August 3, 1864 -- Continued

476.66	Operations in the Shenandoah Valley, Maryland, and Pennsylvania, June 23-August 3

          Including Battle of Cool Spring, Va., July 17-18; Battle of Rutherford's Farm, July 20; 2nd Battle of Kernstown, Va., July 24, 1864; and Maryland campaign: Battle of Monocacy River, July 9; attack on Fort Stevens, Washington, D.C., July 11-12

          For burning of Chambersburg, Pa., July 30 see F159.C4

476.69	Sherman's march, May 1864-April 1865

          Cf. E476.7 Atlanta, Ga., campaign, May 1-September 8, 1864

          Cf. E476.87 Operations in north Georgia and north Alabama, September 29-November 13, 1864

          Cf. E477.41 Savannah campaign, November 15-December 21

          Cf. E477.7 North Carolina (from February 1), South Carolina, southern Georgia, and east Florida, January 1-June 30, 1865

476.7	Atlanta, Ga., campaign, May 1-September 8, 1864

          Including battles of Resaca, May 13-15; New Hope Church, May 24-82; Kennesaw Mountain, June 27; Peachtree Creek, July 20; Jonesboro (Jonesborough), August 31-September 1; capture of Atlanta, September 1

          Including Kennesaw Mountain National Battlefield Park

476.8	Kentucky, southwest Virginia, Tennessee, Mississippi, Alabama, and north Georgia, May 1-November 13, 1864

          Including Battle of Blue Springs, Tenn., August 23; and Battle of Johnsonville, November 4-5

          For Atlanta campaign see E476.7

476.82	Morgan's raid into Kentucky, May 31-June 20
476.83	Expedition from Memphis, Tenn., into Mississippi, June 1-13

          Inlcuding Battle of Brice's Crossroads, June 10

476.84	Expedition from La Grange, Tenn., to Tupelo, Miss., July 5-21

          Including Battle of Tupelo, Miss., July 14-15

476.85	Operations in Mobile Bay, August 2-23
476.87	Operations in north Georgia and north Alabama, September 29-November 13

          Including Battle of Allatoona, October 5

The Civil War, 1861-1865
Military operations
By campaign and battle -- Continued

476.9	Southeastern Virginia and North Carolina, June 13-July 31, 1864
476.91	Richmond campaign, June 13-July 31
	Including Wilson-Kautz Raid, Va., June 22-29
476.93	Siege of Petersburg. Battle of Petersburg Crater
	Including Petersburg National Military Park and battles of Ream's Station, August 22-25; and Boydton Plank Road, October 27-28
477.1	Louisiana and the trans-Mississippi states and territories, July 1-December 31, 1864
	Including 2nd Battle of Cabin Creek, Okla., September 19
	Cf. E83.863 Indian campaigns in Dakota
477.16	Price's Missouri expedition, August 29-December 2
	Including Battles of Pilot Knob, September 27; Westport, October 21-23; Big Blue, October 22; Mine Creek, Kan., October 25
477.2	Southeastern Virginia and North Carolina, August 1-December 31, 1864
477.21	Richmond campaign, August 1-December 31
	Including Weldon Railroad; Hicksford Raid, Emporia, Va., December 7; battle and capture of Fort Harrison, September 29-30
477.28	Expedition to and operations against Fort Fisher, N.C., December 7-27
477.3	Northern Virginia, West Virginia, Maryland, and Pennsylvania, August 4-December 31, 1864
477.33	Shenandoah Valley campaign, August 7-November 28
	Including Battles of Winchester, September 19; Fisher's Hill, September 22; Cedar Creek, October 19
477.4	South Carolina, Georgia, and Florida, November 14-December 31, 1864
477.41	Savannah campaign, November 15-December 21
	Including Battle of Griswoldville, Ga., November 22
477.44	Engagement at Honey Hill, S.C., November 30
477.5	Kentucky, southwest Virginia, Tennessee, Mississippi, Alabama, and north Georgia, November 14, 1864-January 23, 1865
477.52	Campaign in north Alabama and middle Tennessee, November 14, 1864-January 23, 1865
	Including Battles of Spring Hill, Tenn., November 29; Franklin, Tenn., November 30; Nashville, December 15-16

E151-909

The Civil War, 1861-1865
 Military operations
  By campaign and battle -- Continued

477.6	Northern and southeastern Virginia, North Carolina (January 1-31), West Virginia, Maryland, and Pennsylvania, January 1-June 30, 1865
477.61	Richmond campaign, January 1-April 3
	Including attack on Fort Stedman, March 25; evacuation of Petersburg, April 2
477.63	Expedition to and capture of Fort Fisher, N.C., January 3-17
477.65	Expedition from Winchester to the front of Petersburg, February 27-March 28
	Including operations in the Shenandoah Valley
477.67	Appomattox campaign, March 29-April 9
	Including Battles of Gravelly Run, Dinwiddie Courthouse, Five Forks, Sailor's Creek
477.675	Warren court-martial
477.7	North Carolina (from February 1), South Carolina, southern Georgia, and east Florida, January 1-June 30, 1865
	Including Sherman's March through the Carolinas and battles of Aiken, S.C., February 11; Monroe's Crossroads, N.C., March 10; Bentonville, N.C., March 19-21; and Asheville, N.C., April 6; and Potter's Raid, N.C., April 9
477.75	Capture and burning of Columbia, S.C., February 17-18
477.8	Louisiana and the trans-Mississippi states and territories, January 1 -June 30, 1865
	Including Battle of Palmito Ranch, Tex., May 12-13
	Cf. E83.863 Indian campaigns
477.9	Kentucky, southwestern Virginia, Tennessee, northern and central Georgia, Mississippi, Alabama and West Florida, January 1-June 30, 1865
	Including Stoneman's raid, March 24-April 15; Gillem's raid, April 15-25
477.94	Mobile campaign, March 17-May 4
477.96	Wilson's raid from Chickasaw to Selma, Ala., and Macon, Ga., March 22-April 24
	Including capture of Columbus, Ga., April 16; Battle of West Point, Ga., April 16
477.98	Pursuit and capture of Jefferson Davis, May 1-10

The Civil War, 1861-1865
　　Military operations
　　　By campaign and battle -- Continued
478.1　　　　　Pacific coast, January 1, 1861-June 30, 1865
　　　　　　　　For Expedition from southern California through
　　　　　　　　　　Arizona to northwestern Texas and New Mexico,
　　　　　　　　　　April 13-September 20, 1862 see E473.46
　　　　　　　　Cf. E83.86 Indian campaigns
　　　　　　　　Cf. E83.863 Indian wars
480　　　　　Finance. Commerce. Confiscations, etc.
　　　　　　　Including abandoned and confiscable property, blockade,
　　　　　　　　　government contracts, purchase of products from
　　　　　　　　　insurgents, war claims
　　　　　　　Cf. HF3027.6 History of United States commerce during
　　　　　　　　　Civil War
　　　　　　　Cf. HJ251+ Public finance of the Civil War
　　　　　　　Cf. HJ2371+ Revenue and taxation during Civil War
480.5　　　　Confederate States of America
　　　　　　Confederate States of America
482　　　　　Periodicals
483　　　　　Societies
483.1　　　　　United Confederate Veterans
483.2　　　　　Confederate Veteran Association of Kentucky
483.25　　　　Society of the Army and Navy of the Confederate States,
　　　　　　　　　Maryland
483.28　　　　Grand Camp Confederate Veterans, Department of
　　　　　　　　　Virginia
483.4　　　　　Sons of Confederate Veterans
　　　　　　　　Formerly United Sons of Confederate Veterans
483.5　　　　　United Daughters of the Confederacy
483.55　　　　Children of the Confederacy
483.7　　　　　Southern Historical Society
483.72　　　　Confederate Southern Memorial Association
483.75　　　　Confederate Memorial Literary Society
483.99.A-Z　　Other societies, A-Z
　　　　　　　　e.g.
483.99.C78　　　Confederate Veterans' Association of Fulton County,
　　　　　　　　　Georgia
484　　　　　Collections. Collected works
　　　　　Biography (Collective and individual) see E467+
　　　　　Description and travel, social conditions, etc. see F214

E151-909

The Civil War, 1861-1865

Confederate States of America -- Continued

487   History (General). Political history

Including administration of Jefferson Davis and memoirs and reminiscences of civil officials and noncombatants

Cf. E458+ Political history and causes of the war

Cf. E468+ General histories of the war

Cf. E470+ Military operations

Cf. JK9663+ C.S.A. documents

488   Diplomatic history

Cf. E469+ Diplomatic history of the United States

Cf. E596+ Confederate navy

Military history see E470.2+; E545+

Naval history see E591+

Economic history see HC105.65

Addresses, sermons, etc. see E650

Commemorations, Memorial Day see E645

Battle Abbey, Richmond see F234.R5+

Flags see E646

Hospitals see E625

Military prisons see E611

488.5   Propaganda in foreign countries

Secret Service, Signal Corps see E608

Union men in the South see E458.7

489   Other (not A-Z)

Armies. Troops

The Union Army

491   General works

Including administration, organization, volunteering, conscription, Southern federals, statistics, numbers and losses, Civil War medals of honor, transportation, supplies

492   Arms of the service

492.3   United States regular troops

For general histories of regular army organizations see UA24+

492.4   Infantry

Subarranged by number or name of regiment, A-Z, and by author, A-Z

492.5   Cavalry

Subarranged by number or name of regiment, A-Z, and by author, A-Z

492.6   Artillery

Subarranged by number or name of regiment, A-Z, and by author, A-Z

The Civil War, 1861-1865
  Armies. Troops
    The Union Army
      Arms of the service
        United States regular troops -- Continued
492.7   Other (not A-Z)
                Including Balloon Service, Corps of Engineers,
                  Sharpshooters
                For Secret Service, Signal Corps see E608
492.9   African American regiments
                For various state regiments of African Americans
                  see E495+
                For general subject of African Americans in the war
                  see E540.N3
492.94   Infantry
                   Subarranged by number or name of regiment, A-Z, and
                     by author, A-Z
492.95   Cavalry
                   Subarranged by number or name of regiment, A-Z, and
                     by author, A-Z
493.1   Corps. Divisions
                Subarranged by number or name of corps, A-Z, and by
                  author, A-Z
                Including associations, societies, unions, etc., of
                  individual corps
493.5   Brigades
                Subarranged by number or name of brigade, A-Z, and by
                  author, A-Z
                Including associations, reunions, etc., of individual
                  brigades
                A brigade consisting entirely of troops from a single state
                  whether infantry or cavalry, may be classed in E496-
                  537, subdivision ".4" under state number, e.g.,
                  E507.4.C9, Crocker's Iowa Brigade
493.9   First defenders or Minute Men of 1861
                Including works on troops who responded to President
                  Lincoln's first call of April 15, 1861
494   Registers, lists of the dead and wounded, etc.
                Including lists of soldiers and officers from more than one
                  state and veterans residing in particular states
                Veterans residing in a county or town are classed with
                  local biography in F
                For lists of prisoners see E611

E151-909

The Civil War, 1861-1865
   Armies. Troops
      The Union Army -- Continued
         By state
            Including state political history, 1861-1865; quotas in the
               war; war governors
            For military operations in a state see E470.2+
            For relief associations see E629
            For a comprehensive history of a state militia
               regiment see UA50+
         Alabama
            For Lower South military operations see E470.6
            For Gulf States military operations see E470.7
            For campaigns and battles see E471+
            For Confederate history see E471.52; E551+

495	General works
495.1	Official publications on the raising, equipment, and service of the troops in the war
495.2	Adjutant General's reports for 1861-1865
495.3	Lists of soldiers. Lists of the state's dead
	Class here Union troops
495.4	Histories of the states' troops
	Including collected biographies or lists of officers, general associations of survivors, the draft, state brigades, state memorials and monuments, the state's battle flags, lists of citizens serving kin organizations of other states
	Class here Union troops
	Military organizations
	Class here Union troops
495.5	Infantry
	Subarranged by number or name of regiment, A-Z, and by author, A-Z, e.g., E527.5.L6, Logan Guards
	Class here Union troops
495.6	Cavalry
	Subarranged by number or name of regiment, A-Z, and by author, A-Z
	Class here Union troops
495.7	Artillery, Heavy
	Subarranged by number or name of regiment, A-Z, and by author, A-Z
	Class here Union troops
495.8	Artillery, Light
	Subarranged by number or name of regiment, A-Z, and by author, A-Z
	Class here Union troops

The Civil War, 1861-1865
Armies. Troops
The Union Army
By state
Alabama
Military organizations -- Continued

495.9   Other (not A-Z)
Class here Union troops
History of a town or county's participation in the Civil War, and local lists of soldiers, are classed in local history (F1-900). If, however, the town was the seat of military operations, as Chambersburg, Pa., the literature is found in E471-478, or where several sieges or battles are covered, in E470.2-9 (e.g., a history of all military operations around Richmond)

495.95   Arizona
Arizona is not to be further subdivided
Arkansas
For general military operations see E470.4+
For campaigns and battles see E470.8; E470.9; E471+
For Confederate history see E471.57; E553+

496   General works
496.1   Official publications on the raising, equipment, and service of the troops in the war
496.2   Adjutant General's reports for 1861-1865
496.3   Lists of soldiers. Lists of the state's dead
Class here Union troops
496.4   Histories of the states' troops
Including collected biographies or lists of officers, general associations of survivors, the draft, state brigades, state memorials and monuments, the state's battle flags, lists of citizens serving kin organizations of other states
Class here Union troops
Military organizations
Class here Union troops
496.5   Infantry
Subarranged by number or name of regiment, A-Z, and by author, A-Z, e.g., E527.5.L6, Logan Guards
Class here Union troops
496.6   Cavalry
Subarranged by number or name of regiment, A-Z, and by author, A-Z
Class here Union troops

The Civil War, 1861-1865
 Armies. Troops
  The Union Army
   By state
    Arkansas
     Military organizations -- Continued

496.7   Artillery, Heavy
       Subarranged by number or name of regiment, A-Z,
        and by author, A-Z
       Class here Union troops

496.8   Artillery, Light
       Subarranged by number or name of regiment, A-Z,
        and by author, A-Z
       Class here Union troops

496.9   Other (not A-Z)
       Class here Union troops
       History of a town or county's participation in the Civil
        War, and local lists of soldiers, are classed in
        local history (F1-900). If, however, the town was
        the seat of military operations, as
        Chambersburg, Pa., the literature is found in
        E471-478, or where several sieges or battles are
        covered, in E470.2-9 (e.g., a history of all military
        operations around Richmond)
    California
     Cf. E473.46 The California column, 1862

497   General works
497.1   Official publications on the raising, equipment, and
      service of the troops in the war
497.2   Adjutant General's reports for 1861-1865
497.3   Lists of soldiers. Lists of the state's dead
497.4   Histories of the states' troops
      Including collected biographies or lists of officers,
       general associations of survivors, the draft, state
       brigades, state memorials and monuments, the
       state's battle flags, lists of citizens serving kin
       organizations of other states
     Military organizations

497.5   Infantry
       Subarranged by number or name of regiment, A-Z,
        and by author, A-Z

497.6   Cavalry
       Subarranged by number or name of regiment, A-Z,
        and by author, A-Z

497.7   Artillery, Heavy
       Subarranged by number or name of regiment, A-Z,
        and by author, A-Z

The Civil War, 1861-1865
Armies. Troops
The Union Army
By state
California
Military organizations -- Continued

497.8   Artillery, Light
                    Subarranged by number or name of regiment, A-Z,
                       and by author, A-Z
497.9   Other (not A-Z)
                    History of a town or county's participation in the Civil
                       War, and local lists of soldiers, are classed in
                       local history (F1-900). If, however, the town was
                       the seat of military operations, as
                       Chambersburg, Pa., the literature is found in
                       E471-478, or where several sieges or battles are
                       covered, in E470.2-9 (e.g., a history of all military
                       operations around Richmond)

E151-909

                 Colorado
498   General works
498.1   Official publications on the raising, equipment, and
                    service of the troops in the war
498.2   Adjutant General's reports for 1861-1865
498.3   Lists of soldiers. Lists of the state's dead
498.4   Histories of the states' troops
                    Including collected biographies or lists of officers,
                       general associations of survivors, the draft, state
                       brigades, state memorials and monuments, the
                       state's battle flags, lists of citizens serving kin
                       organizations of other states
                 Military organizations
498.5   Infantry
                    Subarranged by number or name of regiment, A-Z,
                       and by author, A-Z
498.6   Cavalry
                    Subarranged by number or name of regiment, A-Z,
                       and by author, A-Z
498.7   Artillery, Heavy
                    Subarranged by number or name of regiment, A-Z,
                       and by author, A-Z
498.8   Artillery, Light
                    Subarranged by number or name of regiment, A-Z,
                       and by author, A-Z

The Civil War, 1861-1865
Armies. Troops
The Union Army
By state
Colorado
Military organizations -- Continued
498.9   Other (not A-Z)
History of a town or county's participation in the Civil
War, and local lists of soldiers, are classed in
local history (F1-F900). If, however, the town
was the seat of military operations, as
Chambersburg, Pa., the literature is found in
E471-E478, or where several sieges or battles
are covered, in E470.2-E470.9 (e.g., a history of
all military operations around Richmond)
Connecticut
Including biography: William Alfred Buckingham
For Dakota Territory see E530+
499   General works
499.1   Official publications on the raising, equipment, and
service of the troops in the war
499.2   Adjutant General's reports for 1861-1865
499.3   Lists of soldiers. Lists of the state's dead
499.4   Histories of the states' troops
Including collected biographies or lists of officers,
general associations of survivors, the draft, state
brigades, state memorials and monuments, the
state's battle flags, lists of citizens serving kin
organizations of other states
Military organizations
499.5   Infantry
Subarranged by number or name of regiment, A-Z,
and by author, A-Z
499.6   Cavalry
Subarranged by number or name of regiment, A-Z,
and by author, A-Z
499.7   Artillery, Heavy
Subarranged by number or name of regiment, A-Z,
and by author, A-Z
499.8   Artillery, Light
Subarranged by number or name of regiment, A-Z,
and by author, A-Z

The Civil War, 1861-1865
  Armies. Troops
    The Union Army
      By state
        Connecticut
          Military organizations -- Continued

499.9	Other (not A-Z)

E151-909

History of a town or county's participation in the Civil War, and local lists of soldiers, are classed in local history (F1-F900). If, however, the town was the seat of military operations, as Chambersburg, Pa., the literature is found in E471-E478, or where several sieges or battles are covered, in E470.2-E470.9 (e.g., a history of all military operations around Richmond)

        Dakota Territory see E530+
        Delaware

500	General works
500.1	Official publications on the raising, equipment, and service of the troops in the war
500.2	Adjutant General's reports for 1861-1865
500.3	Lists of soldiers. Lists of the state's dead
500.4	Histories of the states' troops

Including collected biographies or lists of officers, general associations of survivors, the draft, state brigades, state memorials and monuments, the state's battle flags, lists of citizens serving kin organizations of other states

          Military organizations

500.5	Infantry

Subarranged by number or name of regiment, A-Z, and by author, A-Z

500.6	Cavalry

Subarranged by number or name of regiment, A-Z, and by author, A-Z

500.7	Artillery, Heavy

Subarranged by number or name of regiment, A-Z, and by author, A-Z

500.8	Artillery, Light

Subarranged by number or name of regiment, A-Z, and by author, A-Z

The Civil War, 1861-1865
 Armies. Troops
  The Union Army
   By state
    Delaware
     Military organizations -- Continued
500.9   Other (not A-Z)
       History of a town or county's participation in the Civil War, and local lists of soldiers, are classed in local history (F1-F900). If, however, the town was the seat of military operations, as Chambersburg, Pa., the literature is found in E471-E478, or where several sieges or battles are covered, in E470.2-E470.9 (e.g., a history of all military operations around Richmond)
    District of Columbia
     For campaigns and battles see E470.2+; E471+
501   General works
501.1   Official publications on the raising, equipment, and service of the troops in the war
501.2   Adjutant General's reports for 1861-1865
501.3   Lists of soldiers. Lists of the state's dead
501.4   Histories of the states' troops
      Including collected biographies or lists of officers, general associations of survivors, the draft, state brigades, state memorials and monuments, the state's battle flags, lists of citizens serving kin organizations of other states
     Military organizations
501.5   Infantry
       Subarranged by number or name of regiment, A-Z, and by author, A-Z
501.6   Cavalry
       Subarranged by number or name of regiment, A-Z, and by author, A-Z
501.7   Artillery, Heavy
       Subarranged by number or name of regiment, A-Z, and by author, A-Z
501.8   Artillery, Light
       Subarranged by number or name of regiment, A-Z, and by author, A-Z

The Civil War, 1861-1865
Armies. Troops
The Union Army
By state
District of Columbia
Military organizations -- Continued
501.9   Other (not A-Z)

History of a town or county's participation in the Civil War, and local lists of soldiers, are classed in local history (F1-F900). If, however, the town was the seat of military operations, as Chambersburg, Pa., the literature is found in E471-E478, or where several sieges or battles are covered, in E470.2-E470.9 (e.g., a history of all military operations around Richmond)

E151-909

Florida
For Lower South military operations see E470.6
For Gulf States military operations see E470.7
For campaigns and battles see E471+
For Confederate history see E471.53; E558+

502   General works
502.1   Official publications on the raising, equipment, and service of the troops in the war
502.2   Adjutant General's reports for 1861-1865
502.3   Lists of soldiers. Lists of the state's dead
           Class here Union troops
502.4   Histories of the states' troops
           Including collected biographies or lists of officers, general associations of survivors, the draft, state brigades, state memorials and monuments, the state's battle flags, lists of citizens serving kin organizations of other states
           Class here Union troops

Military organizations
           Class here Union troops
502.5   Infantry
           Subarranged by number or name of regiment, A-Z, and by author, A-Z, e.g., E527.5.L6, Logan Guards
           Class here Union troops
502.6   Cavalry
           Subarranged by number or name of regiment, A-Z, and by author, A-Z
           Class here Union troops

The Civil War, 1861-1865
Armies. Troops
The Union Army
By state
Florida
Military organizations -- Continued

502.7   Artillery, Heavy
            Subarranged by number or name of regiment, A-Z, and by author, A-Z
            Class here Union troops

502.8   Artillery, Light
            Subarranged by number or name of regiment, A-Z, and by author, A-Z
            Class here Union troops

502.9   Other (not A-Z)
            Class here Union troops
            History of a town or county's participation in the Civil War, and local lists of soldiers, are classed in local history (F1-F900). If, however, the town was the seat of military operations, as Chambersburg, Pa., the literature is found in E471-E478, or where several sieges or battles are covered, in E470.2-E470.9 (e.g., a history of all military operations around Richmond)

      Georgia
        For Lower South military operations see E470.6
        For campaigns and battles see E471+
        For Confederate history see E471.51; E559+

503   General works
503.1   Official publications on the raising, equipment, and service of the troops in the war
503.2   Adjutant General's reports for 1861-1865
503.3   Lists of soldiers. Lists of the state's dead
        Class here Union troops
503.4   Histories of the states' troops
        Including collected biographies or lists of officers, general associations of survivors, the draft, state brigades, state memorials and monuments, the state's battle flags, lists of citizens serving kin organizations of other states
        Class here Union troops
      Military organizations
        Class here Union troops

The Civil War, 1861-1865
Armies. Troops
The Union Army
By state
Georgia
Military organizations -- Continued

503.5 Infantry
Subarranged by number or name of regiment, A-Z,
and by author, A-Z, e.g., E527.5.L6, Logan
Guards
Class here Union troops

503.6 Cavalry
Subarranged by number or name of regiment, A-Z,
and by author, A-Z
Class here Union troops

503.7 Artillery, Heavy
Subarranged by number or name of regiment, A-Z,
and by author, A-Z
Class here Union troops

503.8 Artillery, Light
Subarranged by number or name of regiment, A-Z,
and by author, A-Z
Class here Union troops

503.9 Other (not A-Z)
Class here Union troops
History of a town or county's participation in the Civil
War, and local lists of soldiers, are classed in
local history (F1-F900). If, however, the town
was the seat of military operations, as
Chambersburg, Pa., the literature is found in
E471-E478, or where several sieges or battles
are covered, in E470.2-E470.9 (e.g., a history of
all military operations around Richmond)

Illinois
For general military operations see E470.4+
For campaigns and battles see E471+

505   General works
505.1 Official publications on the raising, equipment, and
service of the troops in the war
505.2 Adjutant General's reports for 1861-1865
505.3 Lists of soldiers. Lists of the state's dead
505.4 Histories of the states' troops
Including collected biographies or lists of officers,
general associations of survivors, the draft, state
brigades, state memorials and monuments, the
state's battle flags, lists of citizens serving kin
organizations of other states

E151-909

The Civil War, 1861-1865
  Armies. Troops
   The Union Army
    By state
     Illinois -- Continued
      Military organizations

505.5	Infantry
	Subarranged by number or name of regiment, A-Z, and by author, A-Z
505.6	Cavalry
	Subarranged by number or name of regiment, A-Z, and by author, A-Z
505.7	Artillery, Heavy
	Subarranged by number or name of regiment, A-Z, and by author, A-Z
505.8	Artillery, Light
	Subarranged by number or name of regiment, A-Z, and by author, A-Z
505.9	Other (not A-Z)
	History of a town or county's participation in the Civil War, and local lists of soldiers, are classed in local history (F1-F900). If, however, the town was the seat of military operations, as Chambersburg, Pa., the literature is found in E471-E478, or where several sieges or battles are covered, in E470.2-E470.9 (e.g., a history of all military operations around Richmond)
505.95	Indian Territory
	Not to be further subdivided
	For Indian tribes see E99.A+
	For campaigns and battles see E470.9; E471+
	For Confederate history see E471.57; E561
	Indiana
	Including biography: Oliver Perry Morton
	For general military operations see E470.4+
	For campaigns and battles see E471+
506	General works
506.1	Official publications on the raising, equipment, and service of the troops in the war
506.2	Adjutant General's reports for 1861-1865
506.3	Lists of soldiers. Lists of the state's dead
506.4	Histories of the states' troops
	Including collected biographies or lists of officers, general associations of survivors, the draft, state brigades, state memorials and monuments, the state's battle flags, lists of citizens serving kin organizations of other states

The Civil War, 1861-1865
Armies. Troops
The Union Army
By state
Indiana -- Continued
Military organizations

506.5	Infantry
	Subarranged by number or name of regiment, A-Z, and by author, A-Z
506.6	Cavalry
	Subarranged by number or name of regiment, A-Z, and by author, A-Z
506.7	Artillery, Heavy
	Subarranged by number or name of regiment, A-Z, and by author, A-Z
506.8	Artillery, Light
	Subarranged by number or name of regiment, A-Z, and by author, A-Z
506.9	Other (not A-Z)

E151-909

506.9 Other (not A-Z)

History of a town or county's participation in the Civil War, and local lists of soldiers, are classed in local history (F1-F900). If, however, the town was the seat of military operations, as Chambersburg, Pa., the literature is found in E471-E478, or where several sieges or battles are covered, in E470.2-E470.9 (e.g., a history of all military operations around Richmond)

Iowa
Including biography: Samuel Jordan Kirkwood

507	General works
507.1	Official publications on the raising, equipment, and service of the troops in the war
507.2	Adjutant General's reports for 1861-1865
507.3	Lists of soldiers. Lists of the state's dead
507.4	Histories of the states' troops
	Including collected biographies or lists of officers, general associations of survivors, the draft, state brigades, state memorials and monuments, the state's battle flags, lists of citizens serving kin organizations of other states

Military organizations

507.5	Infantry
	Subarranged by number or name of regiment, A-Z, and by author, A-Z
507.6	Cavalry
	Subarranged by number or name of regiment, A-Z, and by author, A-Z

The Civil War, 1861-1865
Armies. Troops
The Union Army
By state
Iowa
Military organizations -- Continued
507.7   Artillery, Heavy
Subarranged by number or name of regiment, A-Z,
and by author, A-Z
507.8   Artillery, Light
Subarranged by number or name of regiment, A-Z,
and by author, A-Z
507.9   Other (not A-Z)
History of a town or county's participation in the Civil
War, and local lists of soldiers, are classed in
local history (F1-F900). If, however, the town
was the seat of military operations, as
Chambersburg, Pa., the literature is found in
E471-E478, or where several sieges or battles
are covered, in E470.2-E470.9 (e.g., a history of
all military operations around Richmond)
Kansas
For campaigns and battles see E470.9; E471+
508   General works
508.1   Official publications on the raising, equipment, and
service of the troops in the war
508.2   Adjutant General's reports for 1861-1865
508.3   Lists of soldiers. Lists of the state's dead
508.4   Histories of the states' troops
Including collected biographies or lists of officers,
general associations of survivors, the draft, state
brigades, state memorials and monuments, the
state's battle flags, lists of citizens serving kin
organizations of other states
Military organizations
508.5   Infantry
Subarranged by number or name of regiment, A-Z,
and by author, A-Z
508.6   Cavalry
Subarranged by number or name of regiment, A-Z,
and by author, A-Z
508.7   Artillery, Heavy
Subarranged by number or name of regiment, A-Z,
and by author, A-Z
508.8   Artillery, Light
Subarranged by number or name of regiment, A-Z,
and by author, A-Z

The Civil War, 1861-1865
    Armies. Troops
      The Union Army
        By state
          Kansas
            Military organizations -- Continued

508.9	Other (not A-Z)
	For the seceded states, this subdivision is used for Union troops
	History of a town or county's participation in the Civil War, and local lists of soldiers, are classed in local history (F1-F900). If, however, the town was the seat of military operations, as Chambersburg, Pa., the literature is found in E471-E478, or where several sieges or battles are covered, in E470.2-E470.9 (e.g., a history of all military operations around Richmond)

E151-909

          Kentucky
            For general military operations see E470.4+
            For campaigns and battles see E470.5; E470.8; E471+
            For Confederate history see E564+

509	General works
509.1	Official publications on the raising, equipment, and service of the troops in the war
509.2	Adjutant General's reports for 1861-1865
509.3	Lists of soldiers. Lists of the state's dead
509.4	Histories of the states' troops
	Including collected biographies or lists of officers, general associations of survivors, the draft, state brigades, state memorials and monuments, the state's battle flags, lists of citizens serving kin organizations of other states

            Military organizations

509.5	Infantry
	Subarranged by number or name of regiment, A-Z, and by author, A-Z
509.6	Cavalry
	Subarranged by number or name of regiment, A-Z, and by author, A-Z
509.7	Artillery, Heavy
	Subarranged by number or name of regiment, A-Z, and by author, A-Z
509.8	Artillery, Light
	Subarranged by number or name of regiment, A-Z, and by author, A-Z

The Civil War, 1861-1865
Armies. Troops
The Union Army
By state
Kentucky
Military organizations -- Continued

509.9   Other (not A-Z)

History of a town or county's participation in the Civil War, and local lists of soldiers, are classed in local history (F1-F900). If, however, the town was the seat of military operations, as Chambersburg, Pa., the literature is found in E471-E478, or where several sieges or battles are covered, in E470.2-E470.9 (e.g., a history of all military operations around Richmond)

Louisiana

Including the administration of the Department of the Gulf by General Benjamin Franklin Butler in 1862
For Gulf States military operations see E470.7
For campaigns and battles see E470.8; E471+
For Confederate history see E471.55; E565+

510   General works

510.1   Official publications on the raising, equipment, and service of the troops in the war

510.2   Adjutant General's reports for 1861-1865

510.3   Lists of soldiers. Lists of the state's dead
Class here Union troops

510.4   Histories of the states' troops

Including collected biographies or lists of officers, general associations of survivors, the draft, state brigades, state memorials and monuments, the state's battle flags, lists of citizens serving kin organizations of other states
Class here Union troops

Military organizations
Class here Union troops

510.5   Infantry

Subarranged by number or name of regiment, A-Z, and by author, A-Z, e.g., E527.5.L6, Logan Guards
Class here Union troops

510.6   Cavalry

Subarranged by number or name of regiment, A-Z, and by author, A-Z
Class here Union troops

The Civil War, 1861-1865
Armies. Troops
The Union Army
By state
Louisiana
Military organizations -- Continued

510.7   Artillery, Heavy
Subarranged by number or name of regiment, A-Z,
and by author, A-Z
Class here Union troops

510.8   Artillery, Light
Subarranged by number or name of regiment, A-Z,
and by author, A-Z
Class here Union troops

510.9   Other (not A-Z)
Class here Union troops
History of a town or county's participation in the Civil
War, and local lists of soldiers, are classed in
local history (F1-F900). If, however, the town
was the seat of military operations, as
Chambersburg, Pa., the literature is found in
E471-E478, or where several sieges or battles
are covered, in E470.2-E470.9 (e.g., a history of
all military operations around Richmond)

Maine
Including biography: Abner Coburn, Israel Washburn

511   General works

511.1   Official publications on the raising, equipment, and
service of the troops in the war

511.2   Adjutant General's reports for 1861-1865

511.3   Lists of soldiers. Lists of the state's dead

511.4   Histories of the states' troops
Including collected biographies or lists of officers,
general associations of survivors, the draft, state
brigades, state memorials and monuments, the
state's battle flags, lists of citizens serving kin
organizations of other states
Military organizations

511.5   Infantry
Subarranged by number or name of regiment, A-Z,
and by author, A-Z

511.6   Cavalry
Subarranged by number or name of regiment, A-Z,
and by author, A-Z

511.7   Artillery, Heavy
Subarranged by number or name of regiment, A-Z,
and by author, A-Z

E151-909

The Civil War, 1861-1865
Armies. Troops
The Union Army
By state
Maine
Military organizations -- Continued
511.8 Artillery, Light
Subarranged by number or name of regiment, A-Z,
and by author, A-Z
511.9 Other (not A-Z)
History of a town or county's participation in the Civil
War, and local lists of soldiers, are classed in
local history (F1-F900). If, however, the town
was the seat of military operations, as
Chambersburg, Pa., the literature is found in
E471-E478, or where several sieges or battles
are covered, in E470.2-E470.9 (e.g., a history of
all military operations around Richmond)
Maryland
For prisoners of state see E458.8
For campaigns and battles see E470.2+; E471+
For Confederate history see E566+
512 General works
512.1 Official publications on the raising, equipment, and
service of the troops in the war
512.2 Adjutant General's reports for 1861-1865
512.3 Lists of soldiers. Lists of the state's dead
512.4 Histories of the states' troops
Including collected biographies or lists of officers,
general associations of survivors, the draft, state
brigades, state memorials and monuments, the
state's battle flags, lists of citizens serving kin
organizations of other states
Military organizations
512.5 Infantry
Subarranged by number or name of regiment, A-Z,
and by author, A-Z
512.6 Cavalry
Subarranged by number or name of regiment, A-Z,
and by author, A-Z
512.7 Artillery, Heavy
Subarranged by number or name of regiment, A-Z,
and by author, A-Z
512.8 Artillery, Light
Subarranged by number or name of regiment, A-Z,
and by author, A-Z

The Civil War, 1861-1865
Armies. Troops
The Union Army
By state
Maryland
Military organizations -- Continued

512.9	Other (not A-Z)

      History of a town or county's participation in the Civil War, and local lists of soldiers, are classed in local history (F1-F900). If, however, the town was the seat of military operations, as Chambersburg, Pa., the literature is found in E471-E478, or where several sieges or battles are covered, in E470.2-E470.9 (e.g., a history of all military operations around Richmond)

E151-909

Massachusetts
    Including biography: John Albion Andrew

513	General works
513.1	Official publications on the raising, equipment, and service of the troops in the war
513.2	Adjutant General's reports for 1861-1865
513.3	Lists of soldiers. Lists of the state's dead
513.4	Histories of the states' troops

      Including collected biographies or lists of officers, general associations of survivors, the draft, state brigades, state memorials and monuments, the state's battle flags, lists of citizens serving kin organizations of other states

Military organizations

513.5	Infantry

      Subarranged by number or name of regiment, A-Z, and by author, A-Z, e.g., E527.5.L6, Logan Guards

513.6	Cavalry

      Subarranged by number or name of regiment, A-Z, and by author, A-Z

513.7	Artillery, Heavy

      Subarranged by number or name of regiment, A-Z, and by author, A-Z

513.8	Artillery, Light

      Subarranged by number or name of regiment, A-Z, and by author, A-Z

The Civil War, 1861-1865
Armies. Troops
The Union Army
By state
Massachusetts
Military organizations -- Continued
513.9   Other (not A-Z)
History of a town or county's participation in the Civil War, and local lists of soldiers, are classed in local history (F1-F900). If, however, the town was the seat of military operations, as Chambersburg, Pa., the literature is found in E471-E478, or where several sieges or battles are covered, in E470.2-E470.9 (e.g., a history of all military operations around Richmond)

Michigan
514   General works
514.1   Official publications on the raising, equipment, and service of the troops in the war
514.2   Adjutant General's reports for 1861-1865
514.3   Lists of soldiers. Lists of the state's dead
514.4   Histories of the states' troops
Including collected biographies or lists of officers, general associations of survivors, the draft, state brigades, state memorials and monuments, the state's battle flags, lists of citizens serving kin organizations of other states

Military organizations
514.5   Infantry
Subarranged by number or name of regiment, A-Z, and by author, A-Z, e.g., E527.5.L6, Logan Guards
514.6   Cavalry
Subarranged by number or name of regiment, A-Z, and by author, A-Z
514.7   Artillery, Heavy
Subarranged by number or name of regiment, A-Z, and by author, A-Z
514.8   Artillery, Light
Subarranged by number or name of regiment, A-Z, and by author, A-Z

The Civil War, 1861-1865
  Armies. Troops
    The Union Army
      By state
        Michigan
          Military organizations -- Continued
514.9   Other (not A-Z)
                       History of a town or county's participation in the Civil
                         War, and local lists of soldiers, are classed in
                         local history (F1-F900). If, however, the town
                         was the seat of military operations, as
                         Chambersburg, Pa., the literature is found in
                         E471-E478, or where several sieges or battles
                         are covered, in E470.2-E470.9 (e.g., a history of
                         all military operations around Richmond)
          Minnesota
            For Indian wars see E83.86; E83.863
515   General works
515.1   Official publications on the raising, equipment, and
                 service of the troops in the war
515.2   Adjutant General's reports for 1861-1865
515.3   Lists of soldiers. Lists of the state's dead
515.4   Histories of the states' troops
                   Including collected biographies or lists of officers,
                     general associations of survivors, the draft, state
                     brigades, state memorials and monuments, the
                     state's battle flags, lists of citizens serving kin
                     organizations of other states
          Military organizations
515.5   Infantry
                 Subarranged by number or name of regiment, A-Z,
                   and by author, A-Z
515.6   Cavalry
                 Subarranged by number or name of regiment, A-Z,
                   and by author, A-Z
515.7   Artillery, Heavy
                 Subarranged by number or name of regiment, A-Z,
                   and by author, A-Z
515.8   Artillery, Light
                 Subarranged by number or name of regiment, A-Z,
                   and by author, A-Z

E151-909

The Civil War, 1861-1865
  Armies. Troops
    The Union Army
      By state
        Minnesota
          Military organizations -- Continued

515.9   Other (not A-Z)

History of a town or county's participation in the Civil War, and local lists of soldiers, are classed in local history (F1-F900). If, however, the town was the seat of military operations, as Chambersburg, Pa., the literature is found in E471-E478, or where several sieges or battles are covered, in E470.2-E470.9 (e.g., a history of all military operations around Richmond)

        Mississippi

For Lower South military operations see E470.6
For Gulf States military operations see E470.7
For campaigns and battles see E471+
For Confederate history see E471.52; E568+; E568

516   General works
516.1   Official publications on the raising, equipment, and service of the troops in the war
516.2   Adjutant General's reports for 1861-1865
516.3   Lists of soldiers. Lists of the state's dead

Class here Union troops

516.4   Histories of the states' troops

Including collected biographies or lists of officers, general associations of survivors, the draft, state brigades, state memorials and monuments, the state's battle flags, lists of citizens serving kin organizations of other states
Class here Union troops

        Military organizations

Class here Union troops

516.5   Infantry

Subarranged by number or name of regiment, A-Z, and by author, A-Z, e.g., E527.5.L6, Logan Guards
Class here Union troops

516.6   Cavalry

Subarranged by number or name of regiment, A-Z, and by author, A-Z
Class here Union troops

The Civil War, 1861-1865
Armies. Troops
The Union Army
By state
Mississippi
Military organizations -- Continued

516.7   Artillery, Heavy
Subarranged by number or name of regiment, A-Z,
and by author, A-Z
Class here Union troops

516.8   Artillery, Light
Subarranged by number or name of regiment, A-Z,
and by author, A-Z
Class here Union troops

516.9   Other (not A-Z)
Class here Union troops
History of a town or county's participation in the Civil
War, and local lists of soldiers, are classed in
local history (F1-F900). If, however, the town
was the seat of military operations, as
Chambersburg, Pa., the literature is found in
E471-E478, or where several sieges or battles
are covered, in E470.2-E470.9 (e.g., a history of
all military operations around Richmond)

Missouri
For general military operations see E470.4+
For campaigns and battles see E470.8; E470.9;
E471+
For Confederate history see E471.57; E569+

517   General works
517.1   Official publications on the raising, equipment, and
service of the troops in the war
517.2   Adjutant General's reports for 1861-1865
517.3   Lists of soldiers. Lists of the state's dead
517.4   Histories of the states' troops
Including collected biographies or lists of officers,
general associations of survivors, the draft, state
brigades, state memorials and monuments, the
state's battle flags, lists of citizens serving kin
organizations of other states
Military organizations
517.5   Infantry
Subarranged by number or name of regiment, A-Z,
and by author, A-Z
517.6   Cavalry
Subarranged by number or name of regiment, A-Z,
and by author, A-Z

E151-909

The Civil War, 1861-1865
Armies. Troops
The Union Army
By state
Missouri
Military organizations -- Continued

517.7   Artillery, Heavy

Subarranged by number or name of regiment, A-Z,
and by author, A-Z

517.8   Artillery, Light

Subarranged by number or name of regiment, A-Z,
and by author, A-Z

517.9   Other (not A-Z)

History of a town or county's participation in the Civil
War, and local lists of soldiers, are classed in
local history (F1-F900). If, however, the town
was the seat of military operations, as
Chambersburg, Pa., the literature is found in
E471-E478, or where several sieges or battles
are covered, in E470.2-E470.9 (e.g., a history of
all military operations around Richmond)

Nebraska

518   General works

518.1   Official publications on the raising, equipment, and
service of the troops in the war

518.2   Adjutant General's reports for 1861-1865

518.3   Lists of soldiers. Lists of the state's dead

518.4   Histories of the states' troops

Including collected biographies or lists of officers,
general associations of survivors, the draft, state
brigades, state memorials and monuments, the
state's battle flags, lists of citizens serving kin
organizations of other states

Military organizations

518.5   Infantry

Subarranged by number or name of regiment, A-Z,
and by author, A-Z

518.6   Cavalry

Subarranged by number or name of regiment, A-Z,
and by author, A-Z

518.7   Artillery, Heavy

Subarranged by number or name of regiment, A-Z,
and by author, A-Z

518.8   Artillery, Light

Subarranged by number or name of regiment, A-Z,
and by author, A-Z

The Civil War, 1861-1865
Armies. Troops
The Union Army
By state
Nebraska
Military organizations -- Continued

518.9   Other (not A-Z)

       History of a town or county's participation in the Civil War, and local lists of soldiers, are classed in local history (F1-F900). If, however, the town was the seat of military operations, as Chambersburg, Pa., the literature is found in E471-E478, or where several sieges or battles are covered, in E470.2-E470.9 (e.g., a history of all military operations around Richmond)

E151-909

Nevada

519   General works

519.1   Official publications on the raising, equipment, and service of the troops in the war

519.2   Adjutant General's reports for 1861-1865

519.3   Lists of soldiers. Lists of the state's dead

519.4   Histories of the states' troops

       Including collected biographies or lists of officers, general associations of survivors, the draft, state brigades, state memorials and monuments, the state's battle flags, lists of citizens serving kin organizations of other states

Military organizations

519.5   Infantry

       Subarranged by number or name of regiment, A-Z, and by author, A-Z

519.6   Cavalry

       Subarranged by number or name of regiment, A-Z, and by author, A-Z

519.7   Artillery, Heavy

       Subarranged by number or name of regiment, A-Z, and by author, A-Z

519.8   Artillery, Light

       Subarranged by number or name of regiment, A-Z, and by author, A-Z

The Civil War, 1861-1865
  Armies. Troops
    The Union Army
      By state
        Nevada
          Military organizations -- Continued

519.9   Other (not A-Z)

                History of a town or county's participation in the Civil War, and local lists of soldiers, are classed in local history (F1-F900). If, however, the town was the seat of military operations, as Chambersburg, Pa., the literature is found in E471-E478, or where several sieges or battles are covered, in E470.2-E470.9 (e.g., a history of all military operations around Richmond)

         New Hampshire

520   General works

520.1   Official publications on the raising, equipment, and service of the troops in the war

520.2   Adjutant General's reports for 1861-1865

520.3   Lists of soldiers. Lists of the state's dead

520.4   Histories of the states' troops

            Including collected biographies or lists of officers, general associations of survivors, the draft, state brigades, state memorials and monuments, the state's battle flags, lists of citizens serving kin organizations of other states

         Military organizations

520.5   Infantry

            Subarranged by number or name of regiment, A-Z, and by author, A-Z

520.6   Cavalry

            Subarranged by number or name of regiment, A-Z, and by author, A-Z

520.7   Artillery, Heavy

            Subarranged by number or name of regiment, A-Z, and by author, A-Z

520.8   Artillery, Light

            Subarranged by number or name of regiment, A-Z, and by author, A-Z

The Civil War, 1861-1865
Armies. Troops
The Union Army
By state
New Hampshire
Military organizations -- Continued

520.9   Other (not A-Z)
History of a town or county's participation in the Civil
War, and local lists of soldiers, are classed in
local history (F1-F900). If, however, the town
was the seat of military operations, as
Chambersburg, Pa., the literature is found in
E471-E478, or where several sieges or battles
are covered, in E470.2-E470.9 (e.g., a history of
all military operations around Richmond)

E151-909

New Jersey
Including biography: Joel Parker, etc.

521   General works
521.1   Official publications on the raising, equipment, and
service of the troops in the war
521.2   Adjutant General's reports for 1861-1865
521.3   Lists of soldiers. Lists of the state's dead
521.4   Histories of the states' troops
Including collected biographies or lists of officers,
general associations of survivors, the draft, state
brigades, state memorials and monuments, the
state's battle flags, lists of citizens serving kin
organizations of other states
Military organizations
521.5   Infantry
Subarranged by number or name of regiment, A-Z,
and by author, A-Z
521.6   Cavalry
Subarranged by number or name of regiment, A-Z,
and by author, A-Z
521.7   Artillery, Heavy
Subarranged by number or name of regiment, A-Z,
and by author, A-Z
521.8   Artillery, Light
Subarranged by number or name of regiment, A-Z,
and by author, A-Z

The Civil War, 1861-1865
Armies. Troops
The Union Army
By state
New Jersey
Military organizations -- Continued
521.9   Other (not A-Z)
History of a town or county's participation in the Civil
War, and local lists of soldiers, are classed in
local history (F1-F900). If, however, the town
was the seat of military operations, as
Chambersburg, Pa., the literature is found in
E471-E478, or where several sieges or battles
are covered, in E470.2-E470.9 (e.g., a history of
all military operations around Richmond)
New Mexico
For campaigns and battles see E470.9; E471+
For Confederate history see E471.56; E571+
522   General works
522.1   Official publications on the raising, equipment, and
service of the troops in the war
522.2   Adjutant General's reports for 1861-1865
522.3   Lists of soldiers. Lists of the state's dead
522.4   Histories of the states' troops
Including collected biographies or lists of officers,
general associations of survivors, the draft, state
brigades, state memorials and monuments, the
state's battle flags, lists of citizens serving kin
organizations of other states
Military organizations
522.5   Infantry
Subarranged by number or name of regiment, A-Z,
and by author, A-Z
522.6   Cavalry
Subarranged by number or name of regiment, A-Z,
and by author, A-Z
522.7   Artillery, Heavy
Subarranged by number or name of regiment, A-Z,
and by author, A-Z
522.8   Artillery, Light
Subarranged by number or name of regiment, A-Z,
and by author, A-Z

The Civil War, 1861-1865
Armies. Troops
The Union Army
By state
New Mexico
Military organizations -- Continued
522.9   Other (not A-Z)
History of a town or county's participation in the Civil
War, and local lists of soldiers, are classed in
local history (F1-F900). If, however, the town
was the seat of military operations, as
Chambersburg, Pa., the literature is found in
E471-E478, or where several sieges or battles
are covered, in E470.2-E470.9 (e.g., a history of
all military operations around Richmond)

E151-909

New York
Cf. F128.44 Draft riots, New York City
523   General works
523.1   Official publications on the raising, equipment, and
service of the troops in the war
523.2   Adjutant General's reports for 1861-1865
523.3   Lists of soldiers. Lists of the state's dead
523.4   Histories of the states' troops
Including collected biographies or lists of officers,
general associations of survivors, the draft, state
brigades, state memorials and monuments, the
state's battle flags, lists of citizens serving kin
organizations of other states
Military organizations
523.5   Infantry
Subarranged by number or name of regiment, A-Z,
and by author, A-Z
523.6   Cavalry
Subarranged by number or name of regiment, A-Z,
and by author, A-Z
523.7   Artillery, Heavy
Subarranged by number or name of regiment, A-Z,
and by author, A-Z
523.8   Artillery, Light
Subarranged by number or name of regiment, A-Z,
and by author, A-Z

The Civil War, 1861-1865
Armies. Troops
The Union Army
By state
New York
Military organizations -- Continued

523.9   Other (not A-Z)

        History of a town or county's participation in the Civil War, and local lists of soldiers, are classed in local history (F1-F900). If, however, the town was the seat of military operations, as Chambersburg, Pa., the literature is found in E471-E478, or where several sieges or battles are covered, in E470.2-E470.9 (e.g., a history of all military operations around Richmond)

North Carolina

        For Lower South military operations see E470.6
        For campaigns and battles see E471+
        For Confederate history see E471.54; E573+

524   General works

524.1   Official publications on the raising, equipment, and service of the troops in the war

524.2   Adjutant General's reports for 1861-1865

524.3   Lists of soldiers. Lists of the state's dead
        Class here Union troops

524.4   Histories of the states' troops

        Including collected biographies or lists of officers, general associations of survivors, the draft, state brigades, state memorials and monuments, the state's battle flags, lists of citizens serving kin organizations of other states
        Class here Union troops

Military organizations
        Class here Union troops

524.5   Infantry

        Subarranged by number or name of regiment, A-Z, and by author, A-Z, e.g., E527.5.L6, Logan Guards
        Class here Union troops

524.6   Cavalry

        Subarranged by number or name of regiment, A-Z, and by author, A-Z
        Class here Union troops

524.7   Artillery, Heavy

        Subarranged by number or name of regiment, A-Z, and by author, A-Z
        Class here Union troops

The Civil War, 1861-1865
Armies. Troops
The Union Army
By state
North Carolina
Military organizations -- Continued

524.8	Artillery, Light
	Subarranged by number or name of regiment, A-Z, and by author, A-Z
	Class here Union troops
524.9	Other (not A-Z)
	Class here Union troops
	History of a town or county's participation in the Civil War, and local lists of soldiers, are classed in local history (F1-F900). If, however, the town was the seat of military operations, as Chambersburg, Pa., the literature is found in E471-E478, or where several sieges or battles are covered, in E470.2-E470.9 (e.g., a history of all military operations around Richmond)

E151-909

North Dakota see E530+
Ohio
For general military operations see E470.4+
For campaigns and battles see E471+

525	General works
525.1	Official publications on the raising, equipment, and service of the troops in the war
525.2	Adjutant General's reports for 1861-1865
525.3	Lists of soldiers. Lists of the state's dead
525.4	Histories of the states' troops
	Including collected biographies or lists of officers, general associations of survivors, the draft, state brigades, state memorials and monuments, the state's battle flags, lists of citizens serving kin organizations of other states
	Military organizations
525.5	Infantry
	Subarranged by number or name of regiment, A-Z, and by author, A-Z
525.6	Cavalry
	Subarranged by number or name of regiment, A-Z, and by author, A-Z
525.7	Artillery, Heavy
	Subarranged by number or name of regiment, A-Z, and by author, A-Z

The Civil War, 1861-1865
Armies. Troops
The Union Army
By state
Ohio
Military organizations -- Continued
525.8   Artillery, Light
Subarranged by number or name of regiment, A-Z,
and by author, A-Z
525.9   Other (not A-Z)
History of a town or county's participation in the Civil
War, and local lists of soldiers, are classed in
local history (F1-F900). If, however, the town
was the seat of military operations, as
Chambersburg, Pa., the literature is found in
E471-E478, or where several sieges or battles
are covered, in E470.2-E470.9 (e.g., a history of
all military operations around Richmond)
Oklahoma see E505.95
Oregon
526   General works
526.1   Official publications on the raising, equipment, and
service of the troops in the war
526.2   Adjutant General's reports for 1861-1865
526.3   Lists of soldiers. Lists of the state's dead
526.4   Histories of the states' troops
Including collected biographies or lists of officers,
general associations of survivors, the draft, state
brigades, state memorials and monuments, the
state's battle flags, lists of citizens serving kin
organizations of other states
Military organizations
526.5   Infantry
Subarranged by number or name of regiment, A-Z,
and by author, A-Z
526.6   Cavalry
Subarranged by number or name of regiment, A-Z,
and by author, A-Z
526.7   Artillery, Heavy
Subarranged by number or name of regiment, A-Z,
and by author, A-Z
526.8   Artillery, Light
Subarranged by number or name of regiment, A-Z,
and by author, A-Z

The Civil War, 1861-1865
Armies. Troops
The Union Army
By state
Oregon
Military organizations -- Continued
526.9   Other (not A-Z)
History of a town or county's participation in the Civil
War, and local lists of soldiers, are classed in
local history (F1-F900). If, however, the town
was the seat of military operations, as
Chambersburg, Pa., the literature is found in
E471-E478, or where several sieges or battles
are covered, in E470.2-E470.9 (e.g., a history of
all military operations around Richmond)

E151-909

Pennsylvania
For campaigns and battles see E470.2+; E471+
527   General works
527.1   Official publications on the raising, equipment, and
service of the troops in the war
527.2   Adjutant General's reports for 1861-1865
527.3   Lists of soldiers. Lists of the state's dead
527.4   Histories of the states' troops
Including collected biographies or lists of officers,
general associations of survivors, the draft, state
brigades, state memorials and monuments, the
state's battle flags, lists of citizens serving kin
organizations of other states
Military organizations
527.5   Infantry
Subarranged by number or name of regiment, A-Z,
and by author, A-Z, e.g., E527.5.L6, Logan
Guards
527.6   Cavalry
Subarranged by number or name of regiment, A-Z,
and by author, A-Z
527.7   Artillery, Heavy
Subarranged by number or name of regiment, A-Z,
and by author, A-Z
527.8   Artillery, Light
Subarranged by number or name of regiment, A-Z,
and by author, A-Z

The Civil War, 1861-1865
Armies. Troops
The Union Army
By state
Pennsylvania
Military organizations -- Continued
527.9 Other (not A-Z)
History of a town or county's participation in the Civil
War, and local lists of soldiers, are classed in
local history (F1-F900). If, however, the town
was the seat of military operations, as
Chambersburg, Pa., the literature is found in
E471-E478, or where several sieges or battles
are covered, in E470.2-E470.9 (e.g., a history of
all military operations around Richmond)
528 General works
Rhode Island
528.1 Official publications on the raising, equipment, and
service of the troops in the war
528.2 Adjutant General's reports for 1861-1865
528.3 Lists of soldiers. Lists of the state's dead
528.4 Histories of the states' troops
Including collected biographies or lists of officers,
general associations of survivors, the draft, state
brigades, state memorials and monuments, the
state's battle flags, lists of citizens serving kin
organizations of other states
Military organizations
528.5 Infantry
Subarranged by number or name of regiment, A-Z,
and by author, A-Z
528.6 Cavalry
Subarranged by number or name of regiment, A-Z,
and by author, A-Z
528.7 Artillery, Heavy
Subarranged by number or name of regiment, A-Z,
and by author, A-Z
528.8 Artillery, Light
Subarranged by number or name of regiment, A-Z,
and by author, A-Z

The Civil War, 1861-1865
  Armies. Troops
    The Union Army
      By state
        Rhode Island
          Military organizations -- Continued
528.9   Other (not A-Z)
                 History of a town or county's participation in the Civil
                   War, and local lists of soldiers, are classed in
                   local history (F1-F900). If, however, the town
                   was the seat of military operations, as
                   Chambersburg, Pa., the literature is found in
                   E471-E478, or where several sieges or battles
                   are covered, in E470.2-E470.9 (e.g., a history of
                   all military operations around Richmond)
        South Carolina
          For Lower South military operations see E470.6
          For campaigns and battles see E471+
          For Confederate history see E471.1; E577+
          Cf. E185.93.S7 African Americans in the Sea Island
            District
529   General works
529.1   Official publications on the raising, equipment, and
             service of the troops in the war
529.2   Adjutant General's reports for 1861-1865
529.3   Lists of soldiers. Lists of the state's dead
             Class here Union troops
529.4   Histories of the states' troops
             Including collected biographies or lists of officers,
               general associations of survivors, the draft, state
               brigades, state memorials and monuments, the
               state's battle flags, lists of citizens serving kin
               organizations of other states
             Class here Union troops
          Military organizations
            Class here Union troops
529.5   Infantry
               Subarranged by number or name of regiment, A-Z,
                 and by author, A-Z, e.g., E527.5.L6, Logan
                 Guards
               Class here Union troops
529.6   Cavalry
               Subarranged by number or name of regiment, A-Z,
                 and by author, A-Z
               Class here Union troops

E151-909

The Civil War, 1861-1865
Armies. Troops
The Union Army
By state
South Carolina
Military organizations -- Continued
529.7 Artillery, Heavy
Subarranged by number or name of regiment, A-Z,
and by author, A-Z
Class here Union troops
529.8 Artillery, Light
Subarranged by number or name of regiment, A-Z,
and by author, A-Z
Class here Union troops
529.9 Other (not A-Z)
Class here Union troops
History of a town or county's participation in the Civil
War, and local lists of soldiers, are classed in
local history (F1-F900). If, however, the town
was the seat of military operations, as
Chambersburg, Pa., the literature is found in
E471-E478, or where several sieges or battles
are covered, in E470.2-E470.9 (e.g., a history of
all military operations around Richmond)
South Dakota
For Indian wars see E83.86; E83.863
530 General works
530.1 Official publications on the raising, equipment, and
service of the troops in the war
530.2 Adjutant General's reports for 1861-1865
530.3 Lists of soldiers. Lists of the state's dead
530.4 Histories of the states' troops
Including collected biographies or lists of officers,
general associations of survivors, the draft, state
brigades, state memorials and monuments, the
state's battle flags, lists of citizens serving kin
organizations of other states
Military organizations
530.5 Infantry
Subarranged by number or name of regiment, A-Z,
and by author, A-Z
530.6 Cavalry
Subarranged by number or name of regiment, A-Z,
and by author, A-Z
530.7 Artillery, Heavy
Subarranged by number or name of regiment, A-Z,
and by author, A-Z

The Civil War, 1861-1865
 Armies. Troops
  The Union Army
   By state
    South Dakota
     Military organizations -- Continued
530.8   Artillery, Light
                 Subarranged by number or name of regiment, A-Z,
                     and by author, A-Z
530.9   Other (not A-Z)
                 History of a town or county's participation in the Civil
                     War, and local lists of soldiers, are classed in
                     local history (F1-F900). If, however, the town
                     was the seat of military operations, as
                     Chambersburg, Pa., the literature is found in
                     E471-E478, or where several sieges or battles
                     are covered, in E470.2-E470.9 (e.g., a history of
                     all military operations around Richmond)
    Tennessee
         For general military operations see E470.4+
         For campaigns and battles see E470.8; E471+
         For Confederate history see E579+
531   General works
531.1   Official publications on the raising, equipment, and
             service of the troops in the war
531.2   Adjutant General's reports for 1861-1865
531.3   Lists of soldiers. Lists of the state's dead
             Class here Union troops
531.4   Histories of the states' troops
             Including collected biographies or lists of officers,
                 general associations of survivors, the draft, state
                 brigades, state memorials and monuments, the
                 state's battle flags, lists of citizens serving kin
                 organizations of other states
             Class here Union troops
         Military organizations
             Class here Union troops
531.5   Infantry
                 Subarranged by number or name of regiment, A-Z,
                     and by author, A-Z, e.g., E527.5.L6, Logan
                     Guards
                 Class here Union troops
531.6   Cavalry
                 Subarranged by number or name of regiment, A-Z,
                     and by author, A-Z
                 Class here Union troops

E151-909

The Civil War, 1861-1865
　　Armies. Troops
　　　The Union Army
　　　　By state
　　　　　Tennessee
　　　　　　Military organizations -- Continued
531.7　　　　　　　Artillery, Heavy
　　　　　　　　　Subarranged by number or name of regiment, A-Z,
　　　　　　　　　　and by author, A-Z
　　　　　　　　　Class here Union troops
531.8　　　　　　　Artillery, Light
　　　　　　　　　Subarranged by number or name of regiment, A-Z,
　　　　　　　　　　and by author, A-Z
　　　　　　　　　Class here Union troops
531.9　　　　　　　Other (not A-Z)
　　　　　　　　　Class here Union troops
　　　　　　　　　History of a town or county's participation in the Civil
　　　　　　　　　　War, and local lists of soldiers, are classed in
　　　　　　　　　　local history (F1-F900). If, however, the town
　　　　　　　　　　was the seat of military operations, as
　　　　　　　　　　Chambersburg, Pa., the literature is found in
　　　　　　　　　　E471-E478, or where several sieges or battles
　　　　　　　　　　are covered, in E470.2-E470.9 (e.g., a history of
　　　　　　　　　　all military operations around Richmond)
　　　　　Texas
　　　　　　For campaigns and battles see E470.7; E470.9;
　　　　　　　E471+
　　　　　　For Confederate history see E471.56; E580+
532　　　　　　General works
532.1　　　　　Official publications on the raising, equipment, and
　　　　　　　service of the troops in the war
532.2　　　　　Adjutant General's reports for 1861-1865
532.3　　　　　Lists of soldiers. Lists of the state's dead
　　　　　　　Class here Union troops
532.4　　　　　Histories of the states' troops
　　　　　　　Including collected biographies or lists of officers,
　　　　　　　　general associations of survivors, the draft, state
　　　　　　　　brigades, state memorials and monuments, the
　　　　　　　　state's battle flags, lists of citizens serving kin
　　　　　　　　organizations of other states
　　　　　　　Class here Union troops
　　　　　Military organizations
　　　　　　Class here Union troops

The Civil War, 1861-1865
  Armies. Troops
    The Union Army
      By state
        Texas
          Military organizations -- Continued

532.5   Infantry
                     Subarranged by number or name of regiment, A-Z,
                        and by author, A-Z, e.g., E527.5.L6, Logan
                        Guards
                     Class here Union troops

532.6   Cavalry
                     Subarranged by number or name of regiment, A-Z,
                        and by author, A-Z
                     Class here Union troops

532.7   Artillery, Heavy
                     Subarranged by number or name of regiment, A-Z,
                        and by author, A-Z
                     Class here Union troops

532.8   Artillery, Light
                     Subarranged by number or name of regiment, A-Z,
                        and by author, A-Z
                     Class here Union troops

532.9   Other (not A-Z)
                     Class here Union troops
                     History of a town or county's participation in the Civil
                        War, and local lists of soldiers, are classed in
                        local history (F1-F900). If, however, the town
                        was the seat of military operations, as
                        Chambersburg, Pa., the literature is found in
                        E471-E478, or where several sieges or battles
                        are covered, in E470.2-E470.9 (e.g., a history of
                        all military operations around Richmond)

532.95   Utah
                   Not to be further subdivided
                 Vermont
                   Cf. E470.95 St. Albans Raid, 1864
533   General works
533.1   Official publications on the raising, equipment, and
                   service of the troops in the war
533.2   Adjutant General's reports for 1861-1865
533.3   Lists of soldiers. Lists of the state's dead

The Civil War, 1861-1865
  Armies. Troops
    The Union Army
      By state
        Vermont -- Continued

533.4	Histories of the states' troops
	Including collected biographies or lists of officers, general associations of survivors, the draft, state brigades, state memorials and monuments, the state's battle flags, lists of citizens serving kin organizations of other states
	Military organizations
533.5	Infantry
	Subarranged by number or name of regiment, A-Z, and by author, A-Z
533.6	Cavalry
	Subarranged by number or name of regiment, A-Z, and by author, A-Z
533.7	Artillery, Heavy
	Subarranged by number or name of regiment, A-Z, and by author, A-Z
533.8	Artillery, Light
	Subarranged by number or name of regiment, A-Z, and by author, A-Z
533.9	Other (not A-Z)
	History of a town or county's participation in the Civil War, and local lists of soldiers, are classed in local history (F1-F900). If, however, the town was the seat of military operations, as Chambersburg, Pa., the literature is found in E471-E478, or where several sieges or battles are covered, in E470.2-E470.9 (e.g., a history of all military operations around Richmond)
	Virginia
	Including biography of Governor Francis Harrison Pierpont
	For campaigns and battles see E470.2+; E471+
	For Confederate history see E581.1+
534	General works
534.1	Official publications on the raising, equipment, and service of the troops in the war
534.2	Adjutant General's reports for 1861-1865
534.3	Lists of soldiers. Lists of the state's dead
	Class here Union troops

The Civil War, 1861-1865
   Armies. Troops
     The Union Army
       By state
         Virginia -- Continued

534.4
          Histories of the states' troops
           Including collected biographies or lists of officers, general associations of survivors, the draft, state brigades, state memorials and monuments, the state's battle flags, lists of citizens serving kin organizations of other states
           Class here Union troops

E151-909

          Military organizations
           Class here Union troops

534.5
           Infantry
            Subarranged by number or name of regiment, A-Z, and by author, A-Z, e.g., E527.5.L6, Logan Guards
            Class here Union troops

534.6
           Cavalry
            Subarranged by number or name of regiment, A-Z, and by author, A-Z
            Class here Union troops

534.7
           Artillery, Heavy
            Subarranged by number or name of regiment, A-Z, and by author, A-Z
            Class here Union troops

534.8
           Artillery, Light
            Subarranged by number or name of regiment, A-Z, and by author, A-Z
            Class here Union troops

534.9
           Other (not A-Z)
            Class here Union troops
            History of a town or county's participation in the Civil War, and local lists of soldiers, are classed in local history (F1-F900). If, however, the town was the seat of military operations, as Chambersburg, Pa., the literature is found in E471-E478, or where several sieges or battles are covered, in E470.2-E470.9 (e.g., a history of all military operations around Richmond)

         Washington (State)
535
          General works
535.1
          Official publications on the raising, equipment, and service of the troops in the war
535.2
          Adjutant General's reports for 1861-1865
535.3
          Lists of soldiers. Lists of the state's dead

The Civil War, 1861-1865
Armies. Troops
The Union Army
By state
Washington (State) -- Continued

535.4   Histories of the states' troops
                 Including collected biographies or lists of officers,
                    general associations of survivors, the draft, state
                    brigades, state memorials and monuments, the
                    state's battle flags, lists of citizens serving kin
                    organizations of other states
             Military organizations
535.5   Infantry
                     Subarranged by number or name of regiment, A-Z,
                        and by author, A-Z
535.6   Cavalry
                     Subarranged by number or name of regiment, A-Z,
                        and by author, A-Z
535.7   Artillery, Heavy
                     Subarranged by number or name of regiment, A-Z,
                        and by author, A-Z
535.8   Artillery, Light
                     Subarranged by number or name of regiment, A-Z,
                        and by author, A-Z
535.9   Other (not A-Z)
                     History of a town or county's participation in the Civil
                        War, and local lists of soldiers, are classed in
                        local history (F1-F900). If, however, the town
                        was the seat of military operations, as
                        Chambersburg, Pa., the literature is found in
                        E471-E478, or where several sieges or battles
                        are covered, in E470.2-E470.9 (e.g., a history of
                        all military operations around Richmond)
             West Virginia
                 For general military operations see E470.4+
                 For campaigns and battles see E471+
                 For Confederate history see E582+
536   General works
536.1   Official publications on the raising, equipment, and
                 service of the troops in the war
536.2   Adjutant General's reports for 1861-1865
536.3   Lists of soldiers. Lists of the state's dead

The Civil War, 1861-1865
  Armies. Troops
    The Union Army
      By state
        West Virginia -- Continued
536.4   Histories of the states' troops
                 Including collected biographies or lists of officers,
                     general associations of survivors, the draft, state
                     brigades, state memorials and monuments, the
                     state's battle flags, lists of citizens serving kin
                     organizations of other states
               Military organizations

E151-909

536.5   Infantry
                 Subarranged by number or name of regiment, A-Z,
                     and by author, A-Z
536.6   Cavalry
                 Subarranged by number or name of regiment, A-Z,
                     and by author, A-Z
536.7   Artillery, Heavy
                 Subarranged by number or name of regiment, A-Z,
                     and by author, A-Z
536.8   Artillery, Light
                 Subarranged by number or name of regiment, A-Z,
                     and by author, A-Z
536.9   Other (not A-Z)
                 History of a town or county's participation in the Civil
                     War, and local lists of soldiers, are classed in
                     local history (F1-F900). If, however, the town
                     was the seat of military operations, as
                     Chambersburg, Pa., the literature is found in
                     E471-E478, or where several sieges or battles
                     are covered, in E470.2-E470.9 (e.g., a history of
                     all military operations around Richmond)
             Wisconsin
537   General works
537.1   Official publications on the raising, equipment, and
                 service of the troops in the war
537.2   Adjutant General's reports for 1861-1865
537.3   Lists of soldiers. Lists of the state's dead
537.4   Histories of the states' troops
                 Including collected biographies or lists of officers,
                     general associations of survivors, the draft, state
                     brigades, state memorials and monuments, the
                     state's battle flags, lists of citizens serving kin
                     organizations of other states
             Military organizations

The Civil War, 1861-1865
Armies. Troops
The Union Army
By state
Wisconsin
Military organizations -- Continued

537.5   Infantry
                                       Subarranged by number or name of regiment, A-Z,
                                           and by author, A-Z
537.6   Cavalry
                                       Subarranged by number or name of regiment, A-Z,
                                           and by author, A-Z
537.7   Artillery, Heavy
                                       Subarranged by number or name of regiment, A-Z,
                                           and by author, A-Z
537.8   Artillery, Light
                                       Subarranged by number or name of regiment, A-Z,
                                           and by author, A-Z
537.9   Other (not A-Z)
                                       History of a town or county's participation in the Civil
                                           War, and local lists of soldiers, are classed in
                                           local history (F1-F900). If, however, the town
                                           was the seat of military operations, as
                                           Chambersburg, Pa., the literature is found in
                                           E471-E478, or where several sieges or battles
                                           are covered, in E470.2-E470.9 (e.g., a history of
                                           all military operations around Richmond)
540.A-Z   Participation by race, ethnic group, religious group, etc.,
                                   A-Z
                               African Americans see E540.N3
540.B4   Belgians
540.C25   Canadians
540.C3   Catholics
540.C47   Children
540.C5   Christians. Clergy. Churches (General)
540.C94   Czechs
540.F6   Foreigners (General). Immigrants
                                   Cf. E540.G3 Germans
                                   Cf. E540.H6 Hungarians
                                   Cf. E540.I6 Irish
540.F8   Friends
540.G3   Germans
540.H6   Hungarians
                               Immigrants see E540.F6
540.I3   Indians
                                   For Indian wars, 1861-1865 see E83.86
                                   For Indian wars, 1861-1863 see E83.863

	The Civil War, 1861-1865
	Armies. Troops
	The Union Army
	Participation by race, ethnic group, religious group, etc., A-Z -- Continued
540.I6	Irish
540.I8	Italians
540.J5	Jews
540.M5	Methodists
540.M54	Mexicans
540.N3	Negroes. African Americans
	For United States African American regiments see E492.9
	For State African American regiments see E495+
	Cf. E453 Slavery as affected by the war
540.P64	Poles
540.P9	Presbyterians
540.S8	Swedes
541.A-Z	Colleges, schools, etc., and their participation, A-Z
	e.g.
	Cf. E586.A+ Confederate colleges, schools, etc.
541.A5	Amherst College
541.B7	Bowdoin College
541.B8	Brown College
541.D22	Dartmouth College
541.E13	East Maine Conference Seminary, Bucksport
541.H2	Harvard University
541.I6	Iowa. University
541.M3	Marietta College
541.N2	Nazareth Hall, Nazareth, Pa.
541.N5	New York. City College
541.O2	Oberlin College
541.P4	Pennsylvania. University
541.P9	Princeton University
541.U5	Union University, Schenectady, N.Y.
541.W7	Williams College
541.Y2	Yale University
	The Confederate States Army
545	General works
	Including administration, organization, volunteering, conscription, statistics, transportation, supplies
	For Separate armies see E470.2+
	For Flags see E646
	For Amnesty see E668
	Arms of service

The Civil War, 1861-1865
  Armies. Troops
    The Confederate States Army
      Arms of service -- Continued
546   General works
                  Individual corps, divisions, etc., that are confined to a
                      single state are classed in E551-582 with subdivision
                      ".4" under each
546.4   Infantry
546.5   Cavalry
546.6   Artillery
546.7   Other (not A-Z)
                  For Secret Service, Signal Corps see E608
547   Corps. Divisions. Brigades
                  Including associations
                  e.g.
547.C6   Cleburne's Division
547.F6   Forrest's Cavalry Corps
547.H2   Hampton's Cavalry Division
547.M8   Morgan's Cavalry Division
547.P5   Pickett's Division
547.W5   Wheeler's Cavalry Corps
548   Registers, lists of the dead and wounded, etc.
                  In general, lists of soldiers and officers from more than
                      one state and veterans residing in particular states
                      are classed here
                  For veterans residing in county or town, see F
                  For lists of prisoners see E615+
            By state
                  Subdivided like E495-537. Under the border states
                      (Kentucky, Maryland, Missouri, and West Virginia, and
                      territory of New Mexico), the subdivisions ".3-.9" are
                      used for Confederate troops, all general and political
                      history of the state being classed in E509, 512, 517,
                      522, and 536
                  Including individual Confederate States and border states
                      with troops in the Confederate States Army
                  For military operations in a state see E470.2+
                  For Southern relief agencies see E634
            Alabama
                  For Lower South military operations see E470.6
                  For Civil War, campaigns and battles see E471+
                  For preliminaries of the war see E471.52
                  For Union history see E495+
551   General works
551.1   Official publications on the raising, equipment, and
                  service of the troops in the war

The Civil War, 1861-1865
  Armies. Troops
    The Confederate States Army
      By state
        Alabama -- Continued

551.2	Adjutant General's reports for 1861-1865
551.3	Lists of soldiers. Lists of the state's dead
551.4	Histories of the states' troops

            Including collected biographies or lists of officers, general associations of survivors, the draft, state brigades, state memorials and monuments, the state's battle flags, lists of citizens serving in organizations of other states, etc.

E151-909

          Military organizations

            For regimental associations of veterans, see the regiment

            A comprehensive history of a state militia regiment is classed in UA50-549 even if Civil War service is given

551.5	Infantry

            Subarranged by number or name of regiment, A-Z, and by author, A-Z, e.g., E527.5.L6, Logan Guards

551.6	Cavalry

            Subarranged by number or name of regiment, A-Z, and by author, A-Z

551.7	Artillery, Heavy

            Subarranged by number or name of regiment, A-Z, and by author, A-Z

551.8	Artillery, Light

            Subarranged by number or name of regiment, A-Z, and by author, A-Z

551.9	Other (not A-Z)

        Arizona

552	General works
552.1	Official publications on the raising, equipment, and service of the troops in the war
552.2	Adjutant General's reports for 1861-1865
552.3	Lists of soldiers. Lists of the state's dead
552.4	Histories of the states' troops

            Including collected biographies or lists of officers, general associations of survivors, the draft, state brigades, state memorials and monuments, the state's battle flags, lists of citizens serving in organizations of other states

          Military organizations

The Civil War, 1861-1865
Armies. Troops
The Confederate States Army
By state
Arizona
Military organizations -- Continued

552.5	Infantry
	Subarranged by number or name of regiment, A-Z, and by author, A-Z, e.g., E527.5.L6, Logan Guards
552.6	Cavalry
	Subarranged by number or name of regiment, A-Z, and by author, A-Z
552.7	Artillery, Heavy
	Subarranged by number or name of regiment, A-Z, and by author, A-Z
552.8	Artillery, Light
	Subarranged by number or name of regiment, A-Z, and by author, A-Z
552.9	Other (not A-Z)
	Arkansas
	For general military operations see E470.4+
	For campaigns and battles see E470.8
	For Civil War, campaigns and battles see E471+
	For preliminaries of the war see E471.57
	For Union history see E496+
553	General works
553.1	Official publications on the raising, equipment, and service of the troops in the war
553.2	Adjutant General's reports for 1861-1865
553.3	Lists of soldiers. Lists of the state's dead
553.4	Histories of the states' troops
	Including collected biographies or lists of officers, general associations of survivors, the draft, state brigades, state memorials and monuments, the state's battle flags, lists of citizens serving in organizations of other states
	Military organizations
553.5	Infantry
	Subarranged by number or name of regiment, A-Z, and by author, A-Z, e.g., E527.5.L6, Logan Guards
553.6	Cavalry
	Subarranged by number or name of regiment, A-Z, and by author, A-Z

The Civil War, 1861-1865
　　Armies. Troops
　　　The Confederate States Army
　　　　By state
　　　　　Arkansas
　　　　　　Military organizations -- Continued
553.7　　　　　　　Artillery, Heavy
　　　　　　　　　Subarranged by number or name of regiment, A-Z,
　　　　　　　　　　and by author, A-Z
553.8　　　　　　　Artillery, Light
　　　　　　　　　Subarranged by number or name of regiment, A-Z,
　　　　　　　　　　and by author, A-Z
553.9　　　　　　　Other (not A-Z)
　　　　　Florida
　　　　　　For Civil War, campaigns and battles see E471+
　　　　　　For preliminaries of the war see E471.53
　　　　　　For Union history see E502+
558　　　　　General works
558.1　　　　　Official publications on the raising, equipment, and
　　　　　　　service of the troops in the war
558.2　　　　　Adjutant General's reports for 1861-1865
558.3　　　　　Lists of soldiers. Lists of the state's dead
558.4　　　　　Histories of the states' troops
　　　　　　　Including collected biographies or lists of officers,
　　　　　　　　general associations of survivors, the draft, state
　　　　　　　　brigades, state memorials and monuments, the
　　　　　　　　state's battle flags, lists of citizens serving in
　　　　　　　　organizations of other states
　　　　　　Military organizations
558.5　　　　　　Infantry
　　　　　　　　Subarranged by number or name of regiment, A-Z,
　　　　　　　　　and by author, A-Z, e.g., E527.5.L6, Logan
　　　　　　　　　Guards
558.6　　　　　　Cavalry
　　　　　　　　Subarranged by number or name of regiment, A-Z,
　　　　　　　　　and by author, A-Z
558.7　　　　　　Artillery, Heavy
　　　　　　　　Subarranged by number or name of regiment, A-Z,
　　　　　　　　　and by author, A-Z
558.8　　　　　　Artillery, Light
　　　　　　　　Subarranged by number or name of regiment, A-Z,
　　　　　　　　　and by author, A-Z
558.9　　　　　　Other (not A-Z)

E151-909

The Civil War, 1861-1865
Armies. Troops
The Confederate States army
By state
Georgia
For Lower South military operations see E470.6
For Civil War, campaigns and battles see E471+
For preliminaries of the war see E471.51
For Union history see E503+

559	General works
559.1	Official publications on the raising, equipment, and service of the troops in the war
559.2	Adjutant General's reports for 1861-1865
559.3	Lists of soldiers. Lists of the state's dead
559.4	Histories of the states' troops

Including collected biographies or lists of officers, general associations of survivors, the draft, state brigades, state memorials and monuments, the state's battle flags, lists of citizens serving in organizations of other states

Military organizations

559.5	Infantry

Subarranged by number or name of regiment, A-Z, and by author, A-Z, e.g., E527.5.L6, Logan Guards

559.6	Cavalry

Subarranged by number or name of regiment, A-Z, and by author, A-Z

559.7	Artillery, Heavy

Subarranged by number or name of regiment, A-Z, and by author, A-Z

559.8	Artillery, Light

Subarranged by number or name of regiment, A-Z, and by author, A-Z

559.9	Other (not A-Z)
561	Indian Territory

Not to be further subdivided
For individual Indian tribes see E99.A+
For campaigns and battles see E470.9
For Civil War, campaigns and battles see E471+
For preliminaries of the war see E471.57

Kentucky
For general military operations see E470.4+
For campaigns and battles see E470.5; E470.8
For Civil War, campaigns and battles see E471+
For Union history see E509+

564	General works

The Civil War, 1861-1865
 Armies. Troops
  The Confederate States Army
   By state
    Kentucky

564.1	Official publications on the raising, equipment, and service of the troops in the war
564.2	Adjutant General's reports for 1861-1865
564.3	Lists of soldiers. Lists of the state's dead
564.4	Histories of the states' troops

      Including collected biographies or lists of officers, general associations of survivors, the draft, state brigades, state memorials and monuments, the state's battle flags, lists of citizens serving in organizations of other states

      This subdivision is used for Confederate troops

E151-909

     Military organizations

564.5	Infantry

      Subarranged by number or name of regiment, A-Z, and by author, A-Z, e.g., E527.5.L6, Logan Guards

      This subdivision is used for Confederate troops

564.6	Cavalry

      Subarranged by number or name of regiment, A-Z, and by author, A-Z

      This subdivision is used for Confederate troops

564.8	Artillery, Light

      Subarranged by number or name of regiment, A-Z, and by author, A-Z

      This subdivision is used for Confederate troops

564.9	Other (not A-Z)

      This subdivision is used for Confederate troops

    Louisiana

     For campaigns and battles see E470.8
     For Civil War, campaigns and battles see E471+
     For preliminaries of the war see E471.55
     For Union history see E510+

565	General works
565.1	Official publications on the raising, equipment, and service of the troops in the war
565.2	Adjutant General's reports for 1861-1865
565.3	Lists of soldiers. Lists of the state's dead

The Civil War, 1861-1865
  Armies. Troops
    The Confederate States Army
      By state
        Louisiana -- Continued
565.4   Histories of the states' troops
              Including collected biographies or lists of officers,
                general associations of survivors, the draft, state
                brigades, state memorials and monuments, the
                state's battle flags, lists of citizens serving in
                organizations of other states
            Military organizations
565.5   Infantry
                Subarranged by number or name of regiment, A-Z,
                  and by author, A-Z, e.g., E527.5.L6, Logan
                  Guards
565.6   Cavalry
                Subarranged by number or name of regiment, A-Z,
                  and by author, A-Z
565.7   Artillery, Heavy
                Subarranged by number or name of regiment, A-Z,
                  and by author, A-Z
565.8   Artillery, Light
                Subarranged by number or name of regiment, A-Z,
                  and by author, A-Z
565.9   Other (not A-Z)
                This subdivision is used for Confederate troops
        Maryland
            For campaigns and battles see E470.2+
            For Civil War, campaigns and battles see E471+
            For Union history see E512+
566   General works
566.1   Official publications on the raising, equipment, and
              service of the troops in the war
566.2   Adjutant General's reports for 1861-1865
566.3   Lists of soldiers. Lists of the state's dead
566.4   Histories of the states' troops
              Including collected biographies or lists of officers,
                general associations of survivors, the draft, state
                brigades, state memorials and monuments, the
                state's battle flags, lists of citizens serving kin
                organizations of other states
              This subdivision is used for Confederate troops
            Military organizations

The Civil War, 1861-1865
  Armies. Troops
    The Confederate States Army
      By state
        Maryland
          Military organizations -- Continued

566.5   Infantry
  Subarranged by number or name of regiment, A-Z, and by author, A-Z, e.g., E527.5.L6, Logan Guards
  This subdivision is used for Confederate troops

566.6   Cavalry
  Subarranged by number or name of regiment, A-Z, and by author, A-Z
  This subdivision is used for Confederate troops

566.7   Artillery, Heavy
  Subarranged by number or name of regiment, A-Z, and by author, A-Z
  This subdivision is used for Confederate troops

566.8   Artillery, Light
  Subarranged by number or name of regiment, A-Z, and by author, A-Z
  This subdivision is used for Confederate troops

566.9   Other (not A-Z)
  This subdivision is used for Confederate troops

     Mississippi
  For Lower South military operations see E470.6
  For Civil War, campaigns and battles see E471+
  For preliminaries of the war see E471.52
  For Union history see E516+

568   General works
568.1   Official publications on the raising, equipment, and service of the troops in the war
568.2   Adjutant General's reports for 1861-1865
568.3   Lists of soldiers. Lists of the state's dead
     Military organizations

568.5   Infantry
  Subarranged by number or name of regiment, A-Z, and by author, A-Z, e.g., E527.5.L6, Logan Guards

568.6   Cavalry
  Subarranged by number or name of regiment, A-Z, and by author, A-Z

568.7   Artillery, Heavy
  Subarranged by number or name of regiment, A-Z, and by author, A-Z

E151-909

The Civil War, 1861-1865
 Armies. Troops
  The Confederate States Army
   By state
    Mississippi
     Military organizations -- Continued
568.8   Artillery, Light
       Subarranged by number or name of regiment, A-Z, and by author, A-Z
568.9   Other (not A-Z)
       This subdivision is used for Confederate troops
    Missouri
     For general military operations see E470.4+
     For campaigns and battles see E470.8
     For Civil War, campaigns and battles see E471+
     For preliminaries of the war see E471.57
     For Union history see E517+
569   General works
569.1   Official publications on the raising, equipment, and service of the troops in the war
569.2   Adjutant General's reports for 1861-1865
569.3   Lists of soldiers. Lists of the state's dead
569.4   Histories of the states' troops
      Including collected biographies or lists of officers, general associations of survivors, the draft, state brigades, state memorials and monuments, the state's battle flags, lists of citizens serving kin organizations of other states
      This subdivision is used for Confederate troops
     Military organizations
569.5   Infantry
       Subarranged by number or name of regiment, A-Z, and by author, A-Z, e.g., E527.5.L6, Logan Guards
       This subdivision is used for Confederate troops
569.6   Cavalry
       Subarranged by number or name of regiment, A-Z, and by author, A-Z
       This subdivision is used for Confederate troops
569.7   Artillery, Heavy
       Subarranged by number or name of regiment, A-Z, and by author, A-Z
       This subdivision is used for Confederate troops
569.8   Artillery, Light
       Subarranged by number or name of regiment, A-Z, and by author, A-Z
       This subdivision is used for Confederate troops

The Civil War, 1861-1865
  Armies. Troops
    The Confederate States Army
      By state
        Missouri
          Military organizations -- Continued

569.9	Other (not A-Z)
	This subdivision is used for Confederate troops

New Mexico
  For campaigns and battles see E470.9
  For Civil War, campaigns and battles see E471+
  For preliminaries of the war see E471.56

E151-909

571	General works
571.2	Adjutant General's reports for 1861-1865
571.3	Lists of soldiers. Lists of the state's dead
571.4	Histories of the states' troops

  Including collected biographies or lists of officers,
    general associations of survivors, the draft, state
    brigades, state memorials and monuments, the
    state's battle flags, lists of citizens serving in
    organizations of other states

Military organizations

571.5	Infantry
	Subarranged by number or name of regiment, A-Z, and by author, A-Z, e.g., E527.5.L6, Logan Guards
571.6	Cavalry
	Subarranged by number or name of regiment, A-Z, and by author, A-Z
571.7	Artillery, Heavy
	Subarranged by number or name of regiment, A-Z, and by author, A-Z
571.8	Artillery, Light
	Subarranged by number or name of regiment, A-Z, and by author, A-Z
571.9	Other (not A-Z)
	This subdivision is used for Confederate troops

North Carolina
  For campaigns and battles see E470.6
  For Civil War, campaigns and battles see E471+
  For preliminaries of the war see E471.54
  For Union history see E524+

573	General works
573.1	Official publications on the raising, equipment, and service of the troops in the war
573.2	Adjutant General's reports for 1861-1865
573.3	Lists of soldiers. Lists of the state's dead

The Civil War, 1861-1865
Armies. Troops
The Confederate States Army
By state
North Carolina -- Continued
573.4 Histories of the states' troops
Including collected biographies or lists of officers,
general associations of survivors, the draft, state
brigades, state memorials and monuments, the
state's battle flags, lists of citizens serving in
organizations of other states
Military organizations
573.5 Infantry
Subarranged by number or name of regiment, A-Z,
and by author, A-Z, e.g., E527.5.L6, Logan
Guards
573.6 Cavalry
Subarranged by number or name of regiment, A-Z,
and by author, A-Z
573.7 Artillery, Heavy
Subarranged by number or name of regiment, A-Z,
and by author, A-Z
573.8 Artillery, Light
Subarranged by number or name of regiment, A-Z,
and by author, A-Z
573.9 Other (not A-Z)
This subdivision is used for Confederate troops
Oklahoma see E561
South Carolina
For campaigns and battles see E470.6
For Civil War, campaigns and battles see E471+
For preliminaries of the war see E471.1
For Union history see E529+
577 General works
577.1 Official publications on the raising, equipment, and
service of the troops in the war
577.2 Adjutant General's reports for 1861-1865
577.3 Lists of soldiers. Lists of the state's dead
577.4 Histories of the states' troops
Including collected biographies or lists of officers,
general associations of survivors, the draft, state
brigades, state memorials and monuments, the
state's battle flags, lists of citizens serving in
organizations of other states
Military organizations

The Civil War, 1861-1865
  Armies. Troops
    The Confederate States Army
      By state
        South Carolina
          Military organizations -- Continued

577.5	Infantry
	Subarranged by number or name of regiment, A-Z, and by author, A-Z, e.g., E527.5.L6, Logan Guards
577.6	Cavalry
	Subarranged by number or name of regiment, A-Z, and by author, A-Z
577.7	Artillery, Heavy
	Subarranged by number or name of regiment, A-Z, and by author, A-Z
577.8	Artillery, Light
	Subarranged by number or name of regiment, A-Z, and by author, A-Z
577.9	Other (not A-Z)
	This subdivision is used for Confederate troops

E151-909

          Tennessee
            For general military operations see E470.4+
            For campaigns and battles see E470.5
            For Civil War, campaigns and battles see E471+
            For Union history see E531+

579	General works
579.1	Official publications on the raising, equipment, and service of the troops in the war
579.2	Adjutant General's reports for 1861-1865
579.3	Lists of soldiers. Lists of the state's dead
579.4	Histories of the states' troops
	Including collected biographies or lists of officers, general associations of survivors, the draft, state brigades, state memorials and monuments, the state's battle flags, lists of citizens serving in organizations of other states

          Military organizations

579.5	Infantry
	Subarranged by number or name of regiment, A-Z, and by author, A-Z, e.g., E527.5.L6, Logan Guards
579.6	Cavalry
	Subarranged by number or name of regiment, A-Z, and by author, A-Z

The Civil War, 1861-1865
　Armies. Troops
　　The Confederate States Army
　　　By state
　　　　Tennessee
　　　　　Military organizations -- Continued
579.7　　　　　　Artillery, Heavy
　　　　　　　　Subarranged by number or name of regiment, A-Z,
　　　　　　　　　and by author, A-Z
579.8　　　　　　Artillery, Light
　　　　　　　　Subarranged by number or name of regiment, A-Z,
　　　　　　　　　and by author, A-Z
579.9　　　　　　Other (not A-Z)
　　　　　　　　This subdivision is used for Confederate troops
　　　　　Texas
　　　　　　For campaigns and battles see E470.9
　　　　　　For preliminaries of the war see E471.56
　　　　　　For Union army see E532+
580　　　　　General works
580.1　　　　　Official publications on the raising, equipment, and
　　　　　　service of the troops in the war
580.2　　　　　Adjutant General's reports for 1861-1865
580.3　　　　　Lists of soldiers. Lists of the state's dead
580.4　　　　　Histories of the states' troops
　　　　　　Including collected biographies or lists of officers,
　　　　　　　general associations of survivors, the draft, state
　　　　　　　brigades, state memorials and monuments, the
　　　　　　　state's battle flags, lists of citizens serving in
　　　　　　　organizations of other states
　　　　　Military organizations
580.5　　　　　Infantry
　　　　　　Subarranged by number or name of regiment, A-Z,
　　　　　　　and by author, A-Z, e.g., E527.5.L6, Logan
　　　　　　　Guards
580.6　　　　　Cavalry
　　　　　　Subarranged by number or name of regiment, A-Z,
　　　　　　　and by author, A-Z
580.7　　　　　Artillery, Heavy
　　　　　　Subarranged by number or name of regiment, A-Z,
　　　　　　　and by author, A-Z
580.8　　　　　Artillery, Light
　　　　　　Subarranged by number or name of regiment, A-Z,
　　　　　　　and by author, A-Z
580.9　　　　　Other (not A-Z)
　　　　　　This subdivision is used for Confederate troops
　　　　　Virginia
　　　　　　For Union history see E534+

The Civil War, 1861-1865
Armies. Troops
The Confederate States Army
By state
Virginia

581.1	Official publications on the raising, equipment, and service of the troops in the war
581.2	Adjutant General's reports for 1861-1865
581.3	Lists of soldiers. Lists of the state's dead
581.4	Histories of the states' troops

Including collected biographies or lists of officers, general associations of survivors, the draft, state brigades, state memorials and monuments, the state's battle flags, lists of citizens serving in organizations of other states

Military organizations

581.5	Infantry

Subarranged by number or name of regiment, A-Z, and by author, A-Z, e.g., E527.5.L6, Logan Guards

581.6	Cavalry

Subarranged by number or name of regiment, A-Z, and by author, A-Z

581.7	Artillery, Heavy

Subarranged by number or name of regiment, A-Z, and by author, A-Z

581.8	Artillery, Light

Subarranged by number or name of regiment, A-Z, and by author, A-Z

581.9	Other (not A-Z)

West Virginia

For general military operations see E470.4+
For Union history see E536+

582	General works
582.1	Official publications on the raising, equipment, and service of the troops in the war
582.2	Adjutant General's reports for 1861-1865
582.3	Lists of soldiers. Lists of the state's dead
582.4	Histories of the states' troops

Including collected biographies or lists of officers, general associations of survivors, the draft, state brigades, state memorials and monuments, the state's battle flags, lists of citizens serving kin organizations of other states

This subdivision is used for Confederate troops

Military organizations

E151-909

The Civil War, 1861-1865
Armies. Troops
The Confederate States Army
By state
West Virginia
Military organizations -- Continued

582.5	Infantry
	Subarranged by number or name of regiment, A-Z, and by author, A-Z, e.g., E527.5.L6, Logan Guards
	This subdivision is used for Confederate troops
582.6	Cavalry
	Subarranged by number or name of regiment, A-Z, and by author, A-Z
	This subdivision is used for Confederate troops
582.7	Artillery, Heavy
	Subarranged by number or name of regiment, A-Z, and by author, A-Z
	This subdivision is used for Confederate troops
582.8	Artillery, Light
	Subarranged by number or name of regiment, A-Z, and by author, A-Z
	This subdivision is used for Confederate troops
582.9	Other (not A-Z)
	This subdivision is used for Confederate troops
	Participation by race, ethnic group, religious group, etc., A-Z
585.A35	African Americans
585.C54	Children
585.I53	Indian
585.I75	Irish
	Negroes see E585.A35
586.A-Z	Colleges, schools, etc., and their participation, A-Z
	e.g.
586.N8	North Carolina. University
586.S5	Shreveport, La. Centenary College of Louisiana
586.S7	South Carolina. University
586.U5	U.S. Military Academy, West Point
586.V5	Virginia Military Institute, Lexington, Va.
586.V6	Virginia. University
	Naval history

The Civil War, 1861-1865

Naval history -- Continued

591   General works. The Union Navy

Including naval operations, registers, naval reminiscences,
individual fleets or squadrons

Cf. E462.5 National Association of Naval Veterans

Cf. E467+ Lives of naval commanders

Cf. E470+ Naval operations in combination with military
campaigns (e.g., Monitor-Merrimac battle)

Cf. E480 Naval contracts

595.A-Z   Individual ships, A-Z

e.g.

595.C5   Cherokee (Steamer)

595.C9   Cumberland (Frigate)

595.H2   Hartford (Sloop)

595.K2   Kearsarge (Corvette)

595.L5   Lehigh (Monitor)

595.M7   Monitor (Ironclad)

595.R6   Roanoke (Steamer)

The Confederate States Navy

Including registers, naval reminiscences, privateers and
cruisers

Cf. E469+ Construction of cruisers abroad

596   General works

599.A-Z   Individual ships, A-Z

e.g.

599.A3   Alabama (Confederate cruiser)

599.A4   Albemarle (Ram)

599.A8   Atlanta (Ram)

599.F6   Florida (Privateer)

599.M5   Merrimac (Frigate)

599.S2   Savannah (Privateer)

599.S5   Shenandoah (Cruiser)

599.S8   Sumter (Cruiser)

600   Blockade and blockade running

E151-909

The Civil War, 1861-1865 -- Continued
Personal narratives and other accounts
The narratives of general or staff officers are usually classed in
E470 unless relating to special armies or campaigns, in
which case they are classed in E470.2-9 or E471-478
The narratives of regimental officers and privates are classed in
E495-537 or E551-552 if they contain rolls or are otherwise
valuable for regimental histories
The narratives of noncombatants are classed in E470-478, if
relating to military operations; otherwise in E456, E468,
E491, E545, F214, or under state in E495-582
For biography of commanding officers see E467+
For narratives of regimental officers and privates if they
are of value for military history of special campaigns
see E471+
Cf. E464 Collections of narratives
Cf. E484 Collections of narratives
Cf. E591+ Sailors' narratives
Cf. E611+ Prisoners' narratives
Cf. E621+ Nurses' narratives
Cf. E628 Women
Cf. E655 Collections of anecdotes

601	Union narratives
	Including journals, diaries, letters
	Cf. E458.7 Refugees from the South
605	Confederate narratives
	Cf. E487 Memoirs and reminiscences of Confederate
	civil officials and noncombatants
	Cf. F214 The South (Travel and description during the
	Civil War)
607	Army life. The private soldier
608	Secret Service. Signal Corps
	Including United States Veteran Signal Corps Association,
	telegraph service, United States Military Telegraph Corps,
	spies, scouts, etc. (North and South)
	Cf. E473.55 Andrews' Railroad Raid, 1862
609	Press. Censorship
	Prisoners and prisons
	Including prison life
611	Confederate prisons
	Including general lists of prisoners, exchanges
612.A-Z	Individual prisons, by name of prison or city, A-Z
	e.g.
612.A5	Andersonville, Ga. Military Prison
612.B3	Belle Isle Prison, Richmond
612.C2	Cahaba, Ala. Military Prison
612.D2	Danville, Va. Military Prison

The Civil War, 1861-1865
  Prisoners and prisons
    Confederate prisons
      Individual prisons, by name of prison or city, A-Z --
        Continued

612.L6	Libby Prison, Richmond
612.L7	Liggon's Tobacco Warehouse Prison, Richmond
612.M1	Macon, Ga. Military Prison
612.M2	Madison, Ga. Military Prison
612.R6	Richmond prisons (Collective)
612.S15	Salisbury, N.C. Military Prison
612.T9	Tyler, Tex. Camp Ford

      Union prisons
        Cf. E458.8 Treason and traitors in the North, prisoners
          of state, and suspension of habeas corpus

615	General works
616.A-Z	Individual prisons, by name of prison or city, A-Z
	e.g.
616.A4	Alton, Ill. Military Prison
616.C4	Camp Chase, Columbus, Ohio
616.D3	Fort Delaware, Del.
616.D4	Camp Dennison, Ohio
616.D7	Camp Douglas, Chicago, Ill.
616.E4	Elmira, N.Y. Military Prison
616.J7	Johnson's Island, Lake Erie
616.L2	Fort Lafayette, N.Y.
616.L8	Point Lookout, Md.
616.M8	Camp Morton, Ind.
616.O4	Old Capitol Prison, Washington, D.C.
616.R6	Rock Island, Ill. Military Prison
	Washington, D.C. Old Capitol see E616.O4

  Medical and hospital services. Sanitary services
    Including ambulance service; hospitals; mortality and health
      statistics; nurses, physicians, surgeons; transportation of
      the wounded

621	General, and the North
	Including National Association of Army Nurses of the Civil War
	Including biography: Mary Ann Bickerdyke, John Hill Brinton
625	The South
	Including biography
628	Women

  Relief. Charities

629	General, and the North
	Including southern relief agencies and associations
	United States Sanitary Commission
631.A1-.A7	Official publications

E151-909

The Civil War, 1861-1865
Relief. Charities
General, and the North
United States Sanitary Commission -- Continued

631.A8-.Z4	Branch societies. By name
	Including publications of and about these societies
631.Z5	General works
	Western Sanitary Commission
631.5.A1-.A7	Official publications
631.5.A8-Z	General works
631.7.A-Z	Local sanitary commissions. By state, city, etc., A-Z
631.7.A1	General works
632	Sanitary fairs
634	The South
	Including southern relief agencies
635	Religion in the armed forces (North and South)

Including religious life of the personnel; work of chaplains,
church denominations, United States Christian
Commission, Young Men's Christian Association, etc.
Including religious and other tracts

Celebrations. Memorials. Monuments

National cemeteries located on battlefields are classed in E471-
478. Those located elsewhere are classed in local history,
e.g., F234.A7, Arlington, Va.
For Registers of the dead (Union) see E494
For Registers of the dead (Confederate) see E548
For Registers of deceased prisoners of war see E611+
Cf. E495+ Civil War history of the states

641	General, and the North
642	Memorial Day services and addresses
	Cf. BV4279 Memorial Day sermons
645	The South. Confederate Memorial Day
	Including services and addresses
646	War museums. Exhibitions. Flags. Trophies
	Cf. E495+ subdivision ".4" Battle flags of individual
	states
646.5	Antiquities
	Illustrative material
647	Cartoons
	Addresses, essays, lectures. Sermons, prayers
649	The North

Including those delivered since the war
For Lincoln memorial address see E457.8
For those delivered during the war see E458+
For Memorial Day addresses see E642

The Civil War, 1861-1865

Illustrative material

Addresses, essays, lectures. Sermons, prayers --
Continued

650	The South
	Including southern addresses and sermons made during the war and after
	For Confederate Memorial Day addresses see E645
655	Anecdotes. Collections of short narratives
	For literature, see PN-PT
	Cf. E464 General collections
	Cf. E484 Confederate collections

E151-909

656	Motion pictures about the war
	Late nineteenth century, 1865-1900
660.A-Z	Collected works of American statesmen, A-Z
	Including works of statesmen of the twentieth century to 1921
	e.g.
660.B6-.B69	Blaine, James Gillespie (Table E3)
660.B87-.B879	Bryan, William Jennings (Table E3)
660.D3-.D39	Depew, Chauncey Mitchell (Table E3)
660.G2-.G29	Garfield, James Abram (Table E3)
660.G756-.G7569	Grant, Ulysses Simpson (Table E3)
660.H29-.H299	Harrison, Benjamin (Table E3)
660.L75-.L759	Lodge, Henry Cabot (Table E3)
660.M14-.M149	McKinley, William (Table E3)
660.R7-.R79	Roosevelt, Theodore (Table E3)
660.S3-.S39	Schurz, Carl (Table E3)
660.T11-.T119	Taft, William Howard (Table E3)
660.W71-.W719	Wilson, Woodrow (Table E3)
661	General works
	Cf. E83.866 Indian wars, 1866-1898
	Cf. E185 African Americans, the race question
	Cf. E668 Reconstruction
	Cf. E741 Twentieth century
661.7	Diplomatic history. Foreign and general relations
	For relations with individual countries see E183.8.A+
	For relations with Latin America see F1418
	Biography
	Including biography of statesmen of the early twentieth century
663	Collective
664.A-Z	Individual, A-Z
	e.g.
664.A19	Adams, Charles Francis, 1835-1915 (Table E2A)
664.A55	Angell, James Burrill (Table E2A)
664.A6	Anthony, Henry Bowen (Table E2A)
664.B123	Bacon, Robert (Table E2A)
664.B2	Bailey, Joseph Weldon (Table E2A)

Late nineteenth century, 1865-1900
Biography
Individual, A-Z -- Continued

664.B3	Bayard, Thomas Francis (Table E2A)
664.B5	Belmont, Perry (Table E2A)
664.B55	Bigelow, John (Table E2A)
664.B6	Blaine, James Gillespie (Table E2A)
	For his collected works see E660.B6+
664.B62	Blaine, Harriet Bailey (Table E2A)
	"Mrs. J.G. Blaine"
664.B64	Bland, Richard Parks (Table E2A)
664.B69	Bonaparte, Charles Joseph (Table E2A)
664.B819	Brandeis, Louis Dembitz (Table E2A)
664.B87	Bryan, William Jennings (Table E2A)
	For his collected works see E660.B87+
664.C22	Cannon, Joseph Gurney (Table E2A)
664.C29	Carpenter, Matthew Hale (Table E2A)
664.C4	Chandler, Zachariah (Table E2A)
664.C45	Choate, Joseph Hodges (Table E2A)
664.C49	Clark, Champ (Table E2A)
664.C543	Cockran, William Bourke (Table E2A)
664.C75	Conkling, Roscoe (Table E2A)
664.C78	Cox, Jacob Dolson (Table E2A)
664.C8	Cox, Samuel Sullivan (Table E2A)
664.D28	Davis, Jeff (Table E2A)
664.D4	Depew, Chauncey Mitchell (Table E2A)
	For his collected works see E660.D3+
664.D58	Dingley, Nelson Jr. (Table E2A)
664.E88	Evarts, William Maxwell (Table E2A)
664.F46	Field, Stephen Johnson (Table E2A)
664.F52	Fish, Hamilton (Table E2A)
664.F53	Fisk, Clinton Bowen (Table E2A)
664.F69	Foraker, Joseph Benson (Table E2A)
664.G2	Gardner, Augustus Peabody (Table E2A)
664.G34	George, James Zachariah (Table E2A)
664.G67	Gorman, Arthur Pue (Table E2A)
664.G73	Grady, Henry Woodfin (Table E2A)
664.H24	Hanna, Marcus Alonzo (Table E2A)
664.H27	Harlan, James (Table E2A)
664.H31	Harris, Isham Green (Table E2A)
664.H41	Hay, John (Table E2A)
664.H49	Hendricks, Thomas Andrews (Table E2A)
664.H53	Hill, Benjamin Harvey (Table E2A)
664.H65	Hoar, George Frisbie (Table E2A)
664.H73	Hobart, Garret Augustus (Table E2A)
664.H86	Hughes, Charles Evans (Table E2A)
664.I4	Ingalls, John James (Table E2A)

Late nineteenth century, 1865-1900
  Biography
    Individual, A-Z -- Continued

664.K4	Kerr, Michael Crawford (Table E2A)
664.L16	LaFollette, Robert Marion (Table E2A)
664.L2	Lamar, Lucius Quintus Cincinnatus (Table E2A)
664.L7	Lodge, Henry Cabot (Table E2A)
	For his collected works see E660.L75+
664.L83	Logan, John Alexander (Table E2A)
664.M8	Morrill, Justin Smith (Table E2A)
664.M82	Morton, Julius Sterling (Table E2A)
664.M85	Morton, Levi Parsons (Table E2A)
664.N4	Nelson, Knute (Table E2A)
664.P15	Page, Walter Hines (Table E2A)
664.P2	Palmer, John McAuley (Table E2A)
664.P41	Penrose, Boies (Table E2A)
664.P53	Phelps, William Walter (Table E2A)
664.P62	Pinchot, Gifford (Table E2A)
664.P7	Platt, Orville Hitchcock (Table E2A)
664.P72	Platt, Thomas Collier (Table E2A)
664.P73	Plumb, Preston B. (Table E2A)
664.Q2	Quay, Matthew Stanley (Table E2A)
664.R3	Reed, Thomas Brackett (Table E2A)
664.R35	Reid, Whitelaw (Table E2A)
664.R7	Root, Elihu (Table E2A)
664.R93	Rusk, Jeremiah McLain (Table E2A)
664.S39	Schurz, Carl (Table E2A)
	For his collected works see E660.S3+
664.S57	Sherman, John (Table E2A)
664.S68	Smoot, Reed (Table E2A)
664.S78	Stanford, Leland (Table E2A)
664.S896	Straus, Oscar Solomon (Table E2A)
664.T2	Teller, Henry Moore (Table E2A)
664.T57	Tillman, Benjamin Ryan (Table E2A)
664.V2	Vance, Zebulon Baird (Table E2A)
664.W24	Wanamaker, John (Table E2A)
664.W337	Watson, Thomas Edward (Table E2A)
664.W55	Wharton, Francis (Table E2A)
664.W675	Williams, John Sharp (Table E2A)
664.W76	Windom, William (Table E2A)
664.W8	Wolcott, Edward Oliver (Table E2A)

  Andrew Johnson's administration, April 15, 1865-1869

666	General works
	Including impeachment of the President
	Cf. E83.868 Beecher Island Fight
	Cf. F1032 Fenian invasion of Canada, 1866

E151-909

Late nineteenth century, 1865-1900
Andrew Johnson's administration, April 15, 1865-1869 --
Continued
Biography of Andrew Johnson, 1808-1875
For his collected works see E415.6.J65+
For speeches and messages as President see J82.B9+

667   General works (Table E2)
667.1   Johnson family (not genealogy) (Table E2)
Including biography of individual families
668   Reconstruction, 1865-1877
Including amnesty; Ku-Klux Klan; relations of seceded states
to the Union; removal of political disabilities
For reconstruction in individual states, see the state in class F
Cf. E185.2 African Americans during reconstruction
Cf. F216 Travel in the South during reconstruction
669   Diplomatic history. Foreign relations
Including proposed annexation of Danish West Indies, 1867-
1869; purchase of Alaska, 1867
Cf. F901+ Alaska, Klondike region, Bering Sea, and
Aleutian Islands
Cf. F1233 French in Mexico
670   Presidential campaign of 1868
Grant's administrations, 1869-1877
671   General works
Including Grant and Sumner controversy; Liberal Republicans
Cf. E83.87 Modoc War, 1872-1873
Cf. E83.876 Dakota Indian War, Custer Massacre,
1876
Cf. E668 Reconstruction
Cf. HB3717 Panic of 1873
Cf. HG527 Specie Resumption Act, January 1875
Cf. HJ5021 Whiskey Ring, 1875
Cf. JK681 Civil service reform
Cf. T825 Centennial Exposition, Philadelphia, 1876
Biography of Ulysses Simpson Grant, 1822-1885
For his collected works see E660.G756+
For speeches and messages as President see J82.C1+
672   General works (Table E2)
672.1   Grant family (not genealogy)
Including biography of individual members

Late nineteenth century, 1865-1900
Grant's administrations, 1869-1877 -- Continued
673   Diplomatic history. Foreign relations
     Including proposed annexation of Santo Domingo, 1869-
       1871; sale of arms to France
     Cf. F854 Northwest San Juan border
     Cf. F1033 Fenian invasions of Canada, 1870-1871
     Cf. F1785 Cuban question; Virginius affair, October-
       December, 1873
     Cf. F1938.2+ Dominican Republic foreign relations
675   Presidential campaign of 1872
680   Presidential campaign of 1876
     Including Hayes-Tilden contest, Electoral Commission
Hayes' administration, 1877-1881
681   General works
     Cf. E83.877 Nez Percé War, 1877
     Cf. E83.879 Ute War, 1879
     Cf. HG527 Resumption of gold payments, 1879
Biography of Rutherford Birchard Hayes, 1822-1893
     For his collected works see E660.A+
     For speeches and messages as President see J82.C2+
682   General works (Table E2)
682.1   Hayes family (not genealogy)
     Including biography of individual members
685   Presidential campaign of 1880
Garfield's administration, March 4-September 19, 1881
686   General works
     Including Blaine's foreign policy
     Cf. E691 Arthur's administration
     Cf. E701 Harrison's administration
Biography of James Abram Garfield, 1831-1881
     For his collected works see E660.A+
     For speeches and messages as President see J82.C3+
687   General works (Table E2)
687.2   Garfield's family (not genealogy)
     Including biography of individual members
687.9   Assassination. Guiteau
Arthur's administration, September 19, 1881-1885
691   General works
     Cf. E83.88 Apache War, 1883-1886
692   Biography of Chester Alan Arthur, 1830-1886 (Table E2)
     For his collected works see E660.A+
     For speeches and messages as President see J82.C4+
695   Presidential campaign of 1884
Cleveland's first administration, 1885-1889

E151-909

Late nineteenth century, 1865-1900
Cleveland's first administration, 1885-1889 -- Continued
696   General works
               For Cleveland's second administration see E706+
               Cf. E83.88 Apache War, 1883-1886
697   Biography of Grover Cleveland, 1837-1908 (Table E2)
               For his collected works see E660.A+
               For speeches and messages as President see J82.C5+
697.5   Cleveland family (not genealogy)
               Including biography of individual members
700   Presidential campaign of 1888
Benjamin Harrison's administration, 1889-1893
701   General works
               Cf. E83.89 Dakota Indian War, 1890-1891
               Cf. F1404.5+ International American Conference,
                  1889-1890
               Cf. HF1755 McKinley Tariff Act, 1890
           Biography of Benjamin Harrison, 1833-1901
               For his collected works see E660.H29+
               For speeches and messages as President see J82.C6+
702   General works (Table E2)
702.2   Harrison family (not genealogy)
               Including biography of individual members
705   Presidential campaign of 1892
Cleveland's second administration, 1893-1897
706   General works
               For Cleveland's first administration see E696+
               Cf. DU627.19+ Hawaiian Revolution, 1893-1898
               Cf. F2331.B7+ Venezuela-British Guiana boundary
                  controversy
               Cf. HF1755 Wilson-Gorman Tariff Act, 1894
               Cf. HG529+ Currency question, 1890-1900
710   Presidential campaign of 1896
McKinley's first administration, 1897-1901
711   General works
               For McKinley's second administration see E751+
               Cf. DS770+ Boxer Insurrection in China, 1900
               Cf. E713 Territorial expansion
           Biography of William McKinley, 1843-1901
               For his collected works see E660.M14+
               For speeches and messages as President see J82.C8+
711.6   General works (Table E2)
711.9   Assassination. Czolgosz
711.95   McKinley, Ida (Saxton)

Late nineteenth century, 1865-1900
McKinley's first administration, 1897-1901 -- Continued
713 Diplomatic history. Foreign relations
Including imperialism; territorial expansion, e.g., Hawaiian
Islands, Philippine Islands
Cf. DS679 Annexation of Philippine Islands, 1898
Cf. DU627.3+ Annexation of Hawaiian Islands, 1898
Cf. E179.5 Historical geography of United States
Cf. F970 Insular possessions of the United States as a
whole
Cf. F1786 Question of Cuban annexation
Cf. F1975 Annexation of Puerto Rico, 1898
War of 1898 (Spanish-American War)
714 Periodicals. Collections
714.3.A-Z Societies
e.g.
714.3.A12 Spanish War Veterans (1899-1904)
714.3.N2-.N8 Naval and Military Order of the Spanish-American War
714.3.S48-.S5 Service Men of the Spanish War (1899-1904)
714.3.S67-.S68 Society of the Army of Santiago de Cuba
714.3.U57-.U95 United Spanish War Veterans
Biography
For individual narratives see E729
714.5 Collective
714.6.A-Z Individual, A-Z
e.g.
714.6.D51 Dewey, George (Table E2A)
714.6.D55 Dickinson, Walter Mason (Table E2A)
714.6.R8 Rowan, Andrew Summers (Table E2A)
714.6.S3 Schley, Winfield Scott (Table E2A)
Cf. E727 Court-martial
715 Comprehensive works. General histories
Military operations. Campaigns and battles
717 General works
717.1 Cuban Campaign
Including Santiago Campaign; battles of El Caney, San
Juan Hill, Santiago
Cf. E727 Naval battle off Santiago
Cf. F1786 Cuban Revolution, 1895-1898
717.3 Puerto Rican Campaign
717.7 Philippine Campaign. Battle of Manila Bay
Cf. DS679 Philippine Insurrection
Battles see E717+
721 Political history
Including question of intervention after destruction of the
"Maine"; public opinion

	Late nineteenth century, 1865-1900
	McKinley's first administration, 1897-1901
	War of 1898 (Spanish-American War)
	Political history -- Continued
721.6	Destruction of the Maine (Battleship), February 15, 1898
723	Diplomatic history. Treaty of Paris, 1898
	For legal works, including texts of the treaty and related documents see KZ1389+
	Armies. Troops
725	General works
725.3	United States Army. Corps. Brigades
725.4	Infantry
	Subarranged by regiment, e.g., E725.4.9th for Ninth regiment (Volunteer)
	Including regulars and volunteers
725.45	Cavalry
	Subarranged by regiment, e.g., E725.45.1st for First regiment (Volunteer), "The Rough Riders"
	Including regulars and volunteers
725.46	Artillery
725.47	Other (not A-Z)
	Including engineers, Signal Corps
725.5.A-Z	Participation by race, ethnic group, etc., A-Z
	African Americans see E725.5.N3
725.5.C5	Churches
725.5.G3	Germans
725.5.J4	Jews
725.5.N3	Negroes. African Americans
725.6.A-Z	Colleges, schools, etc., and their participation, A-Z
	e.g.
725.6.H3	Harvard University
725.6.P7	Princeton University
725.8	Registers, lists of the dead and wounded, etc.
725.9	Spanish Army
726.A-.W	By state, A-W. Regimental histories
726.A3	Alabama
726.C1	California
726.C7	Connecticut
726.F6	Florida
726.I2	Illinois
726.I3	Indiana
726.I4	Iowa
726.K2	Kansas
726.K37	Kentucky
726.L8	Louisiana
726.M4	Massachusetts

Late nineteenth century, 1865-1900
McKinley's first administration, 1897-1901
War of 1898 (Spanish-American War)
By state, A-W. Regimental histories -- Continued

726.M6	Michigan
726.M7	Minnesota
726.M8	Missouri
726.N3	New Hampshire
726.N4	New Jersey
726.N5	New York
726.N8	North Carolina
726.O3	Ohio
726.P4	Pennsylvania
726.R4	Rhode Island
726.T4	Tennessee
726.V5	Vermont
726.W6	Wisconsin

E151-909

Naval history
727   General works. United States Navy
Including naval operations including battle of Santiago
and destruction of Cervera's fleet but not battle of
Manila Bay, which is classed in E717.7; court-martial
of Schley; individual squadrons and ships
Cf. E721.6 Destruction of the Maine (Battleship)
727.8   Spanish Navy
729   Personal narratives and other accounts
Including diaries, letters, reminiscences
Cf. E727 Sailors' narratives
Cf. E730 Prisoners' narratives
730   Prisoners and prisons
Including prison life
731   Medical and hospital services. War relief work
Including camps, Red Cross, sanitary services
733   Celebrations. Monuments
734   Museums. Exhibitions. Flags. Trophies
735   Addresses, essays, lectures
738   Presidential campaign of 1900
Twentieth century
740   Periodicals. Societies. Collections (serial)
740.5   Sources and documents
740.7   Dictionaries and encyclopedias
741   General works
742   Addresses, essays, lectures, etc. (Collected)
By several authors or an individual author

	Twentieth century -- Continued
742.5.A-Z	Collected works of American statesmen, A-Z
	For works of statesmen of the early 20th century see E660.A+
	For works of statesmen prominent after 1960 see E838.5.A+
742.5.E37-.E379	Eisenhower, Dwight David (Table E3)
742.5.H66-.H669	Hoover, Herbert Clark (Table E3)
742.5.R6-.R69	Roosevelt, Franklin Delano (Table E3)
742.5.T6-.T69	Truman, Harry S. (Table E3)
	Political history
743	General works
743.5	Un-American activities
	Including propaganda, spies and espionage, subversive activities, fifth column
	For Soviet propaganda in the United States see DK272.A+
	For Anti-Soviet propaganda in the United States see DK272.7.A+
	Diplomatic history. Foreign and general relations
	For relations with individual countries see E183.8.A+
	For relations with Latin America see F1418
744	General works
744.5	Cultural relations (General)
	Including the work and publications of the U.S. Department of State's Office of Information and Educational Exchange; the U.S. Information Agency; Voice of America
	Cultural relations with individual countries or groups of countries are classed with foreign countries, e.g, E183.8; F1418; etc.
	For works treating only of American information libraries see Z675.G7
745	Military history
	Including military biography of World War I-II and the Korean War, e.g., Claire Lee Chennault, Douglas MacArthur, George Catlett Marshall, George Smith Patton, Jonathan Mayhew Wainright
	For military history of individual wars, see the war, e.g. D509+ World War I, 1914-1918; D731+ World War II, 1939-1945; DS918+ Korean War, 1950-1953
	For military societies established before 1951 see E181
	For biographees whose careers extend into the Vietnam War see E840.5.A+

Twentieth century -- Continued

746   Naval history

           Including naval battles of more than two wars

           Including naval biography, not limited to one war (Collective and individual): William Frederick Halsey

           For naval history of individual wars, see the war, e.g., Korean War, DS920

      Biography

747   Collective

748.A-Z   Individual, A-Z

           e.g.

E151-909

748.B32   Baruch, Bernard Mannes (Table E2A)
748.B63   Bloom, Sol (Table E2A)
748.B7   Borah, William Edgar (Table E2A)
748.D22   Dawes, Charles Gates (Table E2A)
748.D48   Dewey, Thomas Edmund (Table E2A)
748.D868   Dulles, John Foster (Table E2A)
748.F24   Farley, James Aloysius (Table E2A)
748.G23   Garner, John Nance (Table E2A)
748.G53   Glass, Carter (Table E2A)
748.H93   Hull, Cordell (Table E2A)
748.I28   Ickes, Harold Le Claire (Table E2A)
748.L23   La Guardia, Fiorello Henry (Table E2A)
748.L7   Lilienthal, David Eli (Table E2A)
748.L86   Long, Huey Pierce (Table E2A)
748.L893   Lucas, Scott Wike (Table E2A)
748.M52   Mellon, Andrew William (Table E2A)
748.M75   Morrow, Dwight Whitney (Table E2A)
748.N65   Norris, George William (Table E2A)
748.S63   Smith, Alfred Emanuel (Table E2A)
748.S88   Stimson, Frederic Jesup (Table E2A)
748.T2   Taft, Robert Alphonso (Table E2A)
748.W225   Walker, Frank C. (Table E2A)
748.W23   Wallace, Henry Agard (Table E2A)
748.W7   Wilke, Wendell Lewis (Table E2A)
748.Y74   Young, Owen D. (Table E2A)
749   Pamphlets, addresses, etc.

      McKinley's second administration, March 4-September 14, 1901

        For McKinley's first administration see E711+

        For presidential campaign of 1900 see E738

751   General works

        Biography and assassination of McKinley see E711.6+

      Theodore Roosevelt's administrations, September 14, 1901-1909

Twentieth century

Theodore Roosevelt's administrations, September 14, 1901-
1909 -- Continued

756   General works

Including negotiations for purchase of Danish West Indies,
policy in Russo-Japanese War

Cf. F912.B7 Alaska boundary question, 1903

Cf. F1566.5 Panama foreign relations, 1903

Biography of Theodore Roosevelt, 1858-1919

For his collected works see E660.R7+

For speeches and messages as President see J82.C9+

757   General works (Table E2)

757.2   Roosevelt memorials

Including reports

Cf. F129.O98 Sagamore Hill, Oyster Bay, N.Y.

Cf. F203.4.T5 Theodore Roosevelt Island, D.C.

757.3   Roosevelt family (not genealogy)

758   Presidential campaign of 1904

760   Presidential campaign of 1908

Taft's administration, 1909-1913

761   General works

Cf. HD2771+ Regulation of corporations

Biography of William Howard Taft, 1857-1930

For his collected works see E660.T11+

For speeches and messages as President see J82.D1+

762   General works (Table E2)

762.1   Taft family (not genealogy)

Including biography, e.g., Helen (Herron) Taft

765   Presidential campaign of 1912

Wilson's administrations, 1913-1921

766   General works

For period of World War I see E780

Cf. HG2559+ Establishment of Federal Reserve
System

Cf. HV5089 18th amendment to the Constitution, 1919
(Prohibition)

Cf. JK1880+ 19th amendment to Constitution, 1920
(Woman suffrage)

Biography of Woodrow Wilson, 1856-1924

For his collected works see E660.W71+

For speeches and messages as President see J82.D2+

767   General works (Table E2)

767.1   Special (not A-Z)

767.3   Wilson family (not genealogy)

Including biography, e.g., Edith (Bolling) Galt Wilson

Twentieth century
Wilson's administrations, 1913-1921 -- Continued

768   Diplomatic history. Foreign relations
Including purchase of Danish West Indies (Virgin Islands)
For frontier trouble with Mexico, 1913 see F1234
Cf. D570+ Participation of the United States in World
War I
Cf. D619 Relation of United States to World War I prior
to its entry

769   Presidential campaign of 1916
772   Woodrow Wilson Foundation
780   Internal history during World War I
783   Presidential campaign of 1920
784   1919-1933. Harding-Coolidge-Hoover era. "The twenties"
Harding's administration, 1921-August 2, 1923
785   General works
Including history of Teapot Dome oil scandal
Cf. HD242.5 Oil leases
786   Biography of Warren Gamaliel Harding, 1865-1923
(Table E2)
For his collected works see E742.5.A+
For speeches and messages as President see
J82.D3+
786.2   Harding family (not genealogy)
Including biography, e. g. Florence Kling Harding
Coolidge's administrations, August 1923-1929
791   General works
Cf. D649.G3A4+ Dawes and Young plans
Biography of Calvin Coolidge, 1872-1933
For his collected works see E742.5.A+
For speeches and messages as President see
J82.D4+
792   General works (Table E2)
792.1   Coolidge family (not genealogy)
Including biography, e.g., Calvin Coolidge, Jr.
795   Presidential campaign of 1924
796   Presidential campaign of 1928
796.Z9   Campaign literature not separately cataloged
796.Z93   Democratic
796.Z95   Republican
Hoover's administration, 1929-1933
801   General works
Cf. HB3717 Stock market crash, 1929
Cf. HG3729.A+ Reconstruction Finance Corporation
(created 1932)

Twentieth century
1919-1933. Harding-Coolidge-Hoover era. "The twenties"
Hoover's administration, 1929-1933 -- Continued
Biography of Herbert Clark Hoover, 1874-1964
For his collected works see E742.5.A+
For speeches and messages as President see J82.D5+

802	General works (Table E2)
802.1	Hoover family (not genealogy)
	Including biography, e.g., Lou (Henry) Hoover
805	Presidential campaign of 1932

F.D. Roosevelt's administrations, 1933-April 12, 1945

806	General works

Period of the "New Deal." Including works covering the Roosevelt and Truman administrations, 1933-1953
Cf. D731+ World War II, 1939-1945
Cf. DS686+ Commonwealth of the Philippines, 1935-1946
Cf. HD7121+ Social security
Cf. TK1421+ Tennessee Valley Authority (created 1932)
Biography of Franklin Delano Roosevelt, 1882-1945
For his collected works see E742.5.R6+
For speeches and messages as President see J82.D6+
Cf. F129.H99 Hyde Park

807	General works (Table E2)
807.1	Roosevelt family (not genealogy)
	Including biography, e.g., Eleanor Roosevelt
807.3	Assassination attempt
	Including biography of Giuseppe Zangara
810	Presidential campaign of 1936
811	Presidential campaign of 1940
812	Presidential campaign of 1944

Truman's administrations, April 12, 1945-1953

813	General works

Including period of the "Fair Deal"
Cf. D845 North Atlantic Treaty, 1949
Cf. DS686.5+ Republic of the Philippines, 1946-
Cf. DS919 Participation in the Korean War, 1950-1953
Cf. HC60 Point four program, Technical assistance program
Cf. HC240+ Marshall Plan (European Recovery Program), Foreign Assistance Act, 1948
Cf. HD7795+ Taft-Hartley Labor Act, 1947
Cf. UA646.3+ North Atlantic Treaty Organization
Cf. UB343 Selective Service Act, 1948

Twentieth century
  Truman's administrations, April 12, 1945-1953 -- Continued
    Biography of Harry S. Truman, 1884-1972
      For his collected works see E742.5.T6+
      For speeches and messages as President see J82.D7+

814	General works (Table E2)
814.1	Truman family (not genealogy)
	Including biography, e.g., Margaret (Truman) Daniels
815	Presidential campaign of 1948
816	Presidential campaign of 1952

  Eisenhower's administrations, 1953-1961

835	General works
	Cf. DS921.7 Korean armistice, 1953
	Cf. E743.5 Internal security, subversive activities, etc.
	Cf. HD242.5 Tidelands oil controversy
	Cf. HD9698+ Atoms for peace program
	Cf. LC212.5+ Segregation in schools

    Biography of Dwight David Eisenhower, 1890-1969
      For his collected works see E742.5.E37+
      For speeches and messages as President see J82.D8+

836	General works (Table E2)
837	Eisenhower family (not genealogy)
	Including biography, e.g., Mamie (Doud) Eisenhower
837.5	Presidential campaign of 1956
837.7	Presidential campaign of 1960

  Later twentieth century, 1961-2000

838	Periodicals. Societies
	Collections
838.3	Sources and documents
838.5.A-Z	Collected works of American statesmen, A-Z
838.5.K4-.K49	Kennedy, John Fitzgerald (Table E3)
838.6	Dictionaries and encyclopedias
839	General works
839.3	Minor works. Pamphlets
839.4	Addresses, essays, lectures, etc. (Collected)
	By several authors or an individual author
	Political history
839.5	General works
839.8	Un-American activities
	Including propaganda, spies and espionage, subversive activities
	Diplomatic history. Foreign and general relations
	For relations with individual countries or groups of countries see E183.8.A+
840	General works

E151-909

	Later twentieth century, 1961-2000
	Diplomatic history. Foreign and general relations -- Continued
840.2	Cultural relations (General)
	e.g., The work and publications of the U.S. Department of State's Office of Information and Educational Exchange; the U.S. Information Agency; Voice of America; etc.
	Cultural relations with individual countries or groups of countries are classed with foreign relations, e.g., E183.8; F1418; etc.
	For works treating only of American information libraries see Z675.G7
840.4	Military, naval and air force history
840.5.A-Z	Biography, A-Z
	Subarrange each by Table E1
	Biography (General)
840.6	Collective
840.8.A-Z	Individual, A-Z
	e.g.
840.8.K4	Kennedy, Robert F. (Table E2A)
840.8.K58	Kissinger, Henry (Table E2A)
	Kennedy's administration, 1961-November 22, 1963
	Including Cuban missile crisis
841	General works
	Biography of John Fitzgerald Kennedy, 1917-1963
	General works. Kennedy as President and statesman
	For his collected works see E838.5.K4+
	For speeches and messages as President see J82.D9+
	For his speeches and messages issued as official documents see KF70.A47+
842.A3	Autobiography, diaries, etc. By date
842.A4	Letters. By date
842.A6-Z8	Biography and criticism
842.Z9	Juvenile works on all or portions of Kennedy's life
842.1	Special (not A-Z)
	By period
842.3	Naval career, 1941-1945
842.47	Visit to Ireland, 1963
842.5	Monuments, portraits, statues, etc.
	Class here also monuments, etc. located in foreign countries
	For medals see CJ5801+
842.9	Assassination, funeral, memorial services, etc.
843	Kennedy family (not genealogy)
	Including biography, e.g., Jacqueline (Bouvier) Kennedy. For Jacqueline (Kennedy) Onassis see CT275.A+

Later twentieth century, 1961-2000 -- Continued
Lyndon Johnson's administrations, November 22, 1963-1969

846   General works
Biography of Lyndon Baines Johnson, 1908-1973
For his collected works see E838.5.A+
For speeches and messages as President see J82.E1+
847   General works (Table E2)
847.2   Special (not A-Z)
848   Johnson family (not genealogy)
Including biography, e.g., Claudia Alta (Taylor) Johnson
850   Presidential campaign of 1964
851   Presidential campaign of 1968
Nixon's administrations, 1969-August 9, 1974
855   General works
Biography of Richard Milhous Nixon, 1913-
For his collected works see E838.5.A+
For speeches and messages as President see J82.E2+
856   General works (Table E2)
857   Nixon family (not genealogy)
Including biography, e.g., Thelma (Ryan) Nixon
859   Presidential campaign of 1972
860   Watergate Affair, 1972-1974
861   Impeachment question. Resignation
Ford's administration, August 9, 1974-1977
865   General works
Biography of Gerald R. Ford, 1913-
For his collected works see E838.5.A+
For speeches and messages as President see J82.E3+
866   General works (Table E2)
866.3   Assassination attempts
Including biography of Lynette Fromme
867   Ford family (not genealogy)
Including biography of individual members
868   Presidential campaign of 1976
Carter's administration, 1977-1981
872   General works
Biography of Jimmy Carter, 1924-
For his collected works see E838.5.A+
For speeches and messages as President see J82.E4+
873   General works (Table E2)
873.2   Special (not A-Z)
874   Carter family (not genealogy)
Including biography of individual members
Iran Hostage Crisis, 1979-1981 see E183.8.A+
875   Presidential campaign of 1980
Reagan's administrations, 1981-1989
876   General works

E151-909

<table>
<tr><td></td><td>Later twentieth century, 1961-2000</td></tr>
<tr><td></td><td>Reagan's administrations, 1981-1989 -- Continued</td></tr>
<tr><td></td><td>Biography of Ronald Reagan, 1911-</td></tr>
<tr><td></td><td>For his collected works see E838.5.A+</td></tr>
<tr><td></td><td>For speeches and messages as President see J82.E5+</td></tr>
<tr><td></td><td>For his acting career see PN2287.A+</td></tr>
<tr><td>877</td><td>General works (Table E2)</td></tr>
<tr><td>877.2</td><td>Special (not A-Z)</td></tr>
<tr><td>877.3</td><td>Assassination attempt</td></tr>
<tr><td></td><td>Including biography of John Hinckley</td></tr>
<tr><td>878</td><td>Reagan family (not genealogy)</td></tr>
<tr><td></td><td>Including biography of individual members</td></tr>
<tr><td>879</td><td>Presidential campaign of 1984</td></tr>
<tr><td>880</td><td>Presidential campaign of 1988</td></tr>
<tr><td></td><td>George H. W. Bush's administration, 1989-1993</td></tr>
<tr><td>881</td><td>General works</td></tr>
<tr><td>882</td><td>Biography of George H. W. Bush, 1924- (Table E2)</td></tr>
<tr><td></td><td>For his collected works see E838.5.A+</td></tr>
<tr><td></td><td>For speeches and messages as President see J82.E6+</td></tr>
<tr><td>882.2</td><td>Special (not A-Z)</td></tr>
<tr><td>883</td><td>Bush family (not genealogy)</td></tr>
<tr><td></td><td>Including biography of individual members</td></tr>
<tr><td>884</td><td>Presidential campaign of 1992</td></tr>
<tr><td></td><td>Clinton's administrations, 1993-2001</td></tr>
<tr><td>885</td><td>General works</td></tr>
<tr><td></td><td>Biography of Bill Clinton, 1946-</td></tr>
<tr><td></td><td>For his collected works see E838.5.A+</td></tr>
<tr><td></td><td>For his speeches as President see J82.E7+</td></tr>
<tr><td>886</td><td>General (Table E2)</td></tr>
<tr><td>886.2</td><td>Special (not A-Z)</td></tr>
<tr><td>887</td><td>Clinton family (not genealogy)</td></tr>
<tr><td></td><td>Including biography of individual members</td></tr>
<tr><td>888</td><td>Presidential campaign of 1996</td></tr>
<tr><td>889</td><td>Presidential campaign of 2000</td></tr>
<tr><td></td><td>Twenty-first century</td></tr>
<tr><td></td><td>Collections</td></tr>
<tr><td>891</td><td>Sources and documents</td></tr>
<tr><td>891.5</td><td>Collected works of American statesmen, A-Z</td></tr>
<tr><td>891.5.B87-.B879</td><td>Bush, George W. (George Walker), 1946- (Table E3)</td></tr>
<tr><td>891.5.O33-.O339</td><td>Obama, Barack (Table E3)</td></tr>
<tr><td>895</td><td>Diplomatic history. Foreign and general relations</td></tr>
<tr><td></td><td>For relations with individual countries see E183.8.A+</td></tr>
<tr><td></td><td>For relations with Latin America see F1418</td></tr>
<tr><td></td><td>Military history</td></tr>
<tr><td>897</td><td>General works</td></tr>
<tr><td></td><td>Biography</td></tr>
<tr><td>897.3</td><td>Collective</td></tr>
</table>

Twenty-first century
Military history
Biography -- Continued
897.4.A-Z   Individual, A-Z
        Subarrange each by Table E1
Biography (General)
901   Collective
901.1.A-Z   Individual, A-Z
George W. Bush's administrations, 2001-2009
902   General works
Biography of G.W. Bush, 1946-
    For his collected works see E891.5.B87+
      For speeches and messages as president see
        J82.E8+
903   General works (Table E2)
903.3   Special (not A-Z)
904   Bush family (not genealogy)
    Including biography of individual members
905   Presidential campaign of 2004
906   Presidential campaign of 2008
Barack Obama's administration, 2009-
    For his collected works see E891.5.O33+
    For speeches and messages as president see J82.E9+
907   General works
Biography of Barack Obama
908   General works (Table E2)
908.3   Special (not A-Z)
909   Obama family (not genealogy)
    Including biography of individual members

E151-909

United States local history
New England

1	Periodicals. Societies. Collections
1.5	Museums. Exhibitions, exhibits
2	Gazetteers. Dictionaries. Geographic names
2.3	Guidebooks
3	Biography (Collective). Genealogy (Collective)
3.2	Historiography
	Historians see E175.5.A+
3.5	Study and teaching
4	General works. Histories
4.3	Juvenile works
4.5	Pamphlets, addresses, essays, etc.
4.6	Anecdotes, legends, pageants, etc.
5	Historic monuments (General). Illustrative material
6	Antiquities (Non-Indian)
	By period
7	Early to 1775

Including the Plymouth Company, 1606; Council for New
England, 1620; United Colonies of New England, 1643-
1684; Puritans; Pilgrims; Thanksgiving Day in New
England
Including individual voyagers after 1607, e.g., Bartholomew
Gosnold, John Smith, George Waymouth
Cf. BF1575 Witchcraft in New England
Cf. E83.63 Pequot War, 1636-1638
Cf. E83.67 King Philip's War, 1675-1676
Cf. E83.72 War with eastern Indians, 1722-1726
Cf. E105 Norsemen, Vinland
Cf. E121+ Early voyages before 1607
Cf. E162 Thanksgiving Day in the United States
Cf. E196 King William's War, 1689-1697
Cf. E197 Queen Anne's War, 1702-1713
Cf. E198 King George's War, 1744-1748
Cf. E199 French and Indian War, 1755-1763
Cf. F22 Popham Colony
Cf. F67 Puritans in Massachusetts
Cf. F68 Pilgrims in New Plymouth Colony

7.5	Dominion of New England, 1686-1689

Including consolidation of New England colonies and
regions into one province; later (1688), enlarged by the
addition of New York and New Jersey
Including relations with Governor Edmund Andros;
Revolution of 1689

8	1775-1865

Cf. E357.6+ Opposition to War of 1812

	New England
	By period -- Continued
9	1865-1950
	Including New England hurricane, 1938
	For effects of hurricane on an individual state or city, see the local classification number
10	1951-
12.A-Z	Regions, A-Z
12.A74	Atlantic Coast
	Berkshire Hills see F72.B5
12.C7	Connecticut River and Valley
	Cf. F42.C65 New Hampshire
	Cf. F57.C7 Vermont
	Cf. F72.C7 Massachusetts
	Cf. F102.C7 Connecticut
	Isle of Shoals see F42.I8
	Merrimac River and Valley see F42.M4; F72.M6
	White Mountains see F41
	Elements in the population
15.A1	General works
15.A2-Z	Individual elements
	For list of racial, ethnic, and religious elements (with Cutter numbers) see E184.A+

F1-975

	Maine
	Historical note from the second edition (1913) of Class F:
	"Various grants, sometimes conflicting, were made in this region by the Plymouth company, and the Council for New England. The eastern portion was usually considered part of Acadia. The territory between the Kennebec and the St. Croix was granted by the Council in 1635-1638 to Sir William Alexander, sold to the Duke of York in 1663 and included in his province of New York 1664-1686 as Cornwall County. In the latter year it was set off to Massachusetts. Grants were made to Gorges and others covering the region west of the Kennebec, and settlement begun at several points. In the 17th century the whole of the English settlements were absorbed by Massachusetts, formally annexed by the province charter of 1691 and thenceforth known as the District of Maine. State 1820."
16	Periodicals. Societies. Collections
16.5	Museums. Exhibitions, exhibits
17	Gazetteers. Dictionaries. Geographic names
17.3	Guidebooks
18	Biography (Collective). Genealogy (Collective)
18.2	Historiography
	Historians see E175.5.A+
18.5	Study and teaching

Maine -- Continued

19	General works. Histories
19.3	Juvenile works
19.5	Pamphlets, addresses, essays, etc.
19.6	Anecdotes, legends, pageants, etc.
20	Historic monuments (General). Illustrative material
21	Antiquities (Non-Indian)
	By period
22	Early to 1620
	Including attempts at colonization: Pemaquid, Me.; Popham Colony
23	1620-1775
	Including Lygonia Colony (Plough Patent); Trelawney Plantation
	Biography: Edward Godfrey
	Cf. E83.72 War with Eastern Indians, 1722-1726
	Cf. F27.K3 Kennebec Patent
	Cf. F27.M95 Muscongus or Waldo Patent
	Cf. F29.B9 Pejepscot Purchase
	Cf. F1036+ Acadia
	Cf. F1039.B7 Boundary between French and English possessions in Acadia
24	1775-1865
	Including separation from Massachusetts and admission as a state, March 15, 1820
	Including biography: William King
	Cf. E230+ Military operations and battles
	Cf. E263.M4 Maine in the Revolution (General)
	Cf. E398 International boundary troubles and the Aroostook War, 1839
	Cf. E511+ Civil War, 1861-1865 (General)
25	1865-1950
	Including biography: Harris Merrill Plaisted, etc.
	Cf. D570.85.M2+ World War I, 1914-1918
	Cf. D769.85.M2+ World War II, 1939-1945
	1951-
26	General works
	Biography
26.3	Collective
26.32.A-Z	Individual, A-Z
	Subarrange each by Table F5
27.A-Z	Regions, counties, etc., A-Z
27.A15	Counties
27.A16	Mountains
27.A17	Rivers
27.A18	Lakes
27.A19	Islands

Maine
Regions, counties, etc., A-Z -- Continued
Acadia National Park see F27.M9

27.A4	Allagash River and Valley
27.A5	Androscoggin County
	Including Lake Androscoggin, Snow Falls
27.A53	Androscoggin River and Valley
27.A7	Aroostook County
	Including general works on the Aroostook River and Valley, as well as works limited to the part located in Maine
	For works limited to the portion of the Aroostook River And Valley located in New Brunswick see F1044.A7
27.A75	Atlantic Coast
	Bartlett Island see F27.M9
	Baxter State Park see F27.P5
27.B49	Blue Hill Bay
	Bluff Island see F27.Y6
27.B7	Boundaries
	Cf. E398 Northeastern boundary disputes, 1783-1845
	Cf. F42.B7 New Hampshire boundary
	Cf. F1039.B7 Ancient boundary of Acadia
27.C3	Casco Bay and islands (Collectively)
	For Individual islands see F27.C9
27.C9	Cumberland County
	Including Orr's Island, Peak Island, Sebago Lake
	For Saco River and Valley see F27.S15
	For Saco Bay see F27.Y6
27.D2	Dead River and Valley
	Dochet Island see F27.W3
27.F8	Franklin County
	Including Temple Stream
	Friendship Long Island see F27.K7
	Great Gott Island see F27.H3
27.H3	Hancock County
	Including Great Gott Island, Little Cranberry Island, Little Gott Island, Long Island, Placentia Island, Swans Island, Union River and Valley, Union River Bay
	For Mount Desert Island see F27.M9
	Isles of Shoals see F42.I8
	Islesboro Island see F27.W16
	Kennebago Lake see F27.R2
27.K2	Kennebec County
	Including Lake Cobbosseecontee
27.K3	Kennebec Patent. Plymouth Company (1749-1816)
27.K32	Kennebec River and Valley

F1-975

Maine

Regions, counties, etc., A-Z -- Continued

27.K7	Knox County
	Including Friendship Long Island
	For Matinicus Island see F27.M3
27.L7	Lincoln County
	For Monhegan Island see F27.M7
	Little Cranberry Island see F27.H3
	Little Gott Island see F27.H3
	Long Island see F27.H3
	Machias Bay see F27.W3
27.M18	Magalloway Island
27.M3	Matinicus Island
27.M7	Monhegan Island
27.M8	Moosehead Lake region
27.M9	Mount Desert Island
	Including Acadia National Park, Bartlett Island
	Cf. F1038 Jesuit station, 1609
	Moxie Pond see F27.S7
27.M95	Muscongus or Waldo Patent
	Including greater part of Waldo and Knox and a portion of Lincoln counties
27.O9	Oxford County
	Including Oxford Hills, Parmachenee Lake
	Oxford Hills see F27.O9
	Parmachenee Lake see F27.O9
27.P3	Passamaquoddy Bay, Maine
	Cf. F1044.P3 New Brunswick
	Pejepscot Patent (Brunswick) see F29.B9
27.P37	Penobscot Bay region
27.P38	Penobscot County
27.P4	Penobscot River and Valley
27.P48	Piscataqua River and Valley
	Class here works limited to the part of the Piscataqua River and Valley located in Maine
	For general works on the Piscataqua River and Valley, as well as works limited to the part located in New Hampshire see F42.P4
27.P5	Piscataquis County
	Including Baxter State Park, Debsconeag Lake region, Mount Kathadin, Chesuncook Lake, Sebec Lake
	Placentia Island see F27.H3
	Pond Island see F27.W3
27.R2	Rangeley Lakes. Kennebago Lake
	Roque Island see F27.W3
	Saco Bay see F27.Y6
27.S15	Saco River and Valley

	Maine
	Regions, counties, etc., A-Z -- Continued
27.S18	Sagadahoc County
	Saint Croix (Dochet) Island see F27.W3
27.S2	Saint Croix River and Valley
	Class here general works on the Saint Croix River and Valley, as well as works limited to the part located in Maine
	For works limited to the part of the Saint Croix River and Valley located in New Brunswick see F1044.S17
27.S25	Saint George (George's) River
27.S3	Saint John River and Valley
	Class here on the part of the Saint John River and Valley located in Maine
	For general works on the Saint John River and Valley, as well as works on the part located in New Brunswick see F1044.S2
27.S42	Sebasticook River and Valley
	Sebec Lake see F27.P5
	Sheepscot River and Valley see F27.W16
	Snow Falls see F27.A53
27.S7	Somerset County
	Including Moxie Pond, Great Moose Lake
	Stratton Island see F27.Y6
	Swans Island see F27.H3
	Temple Stream see F27.F8
27.T48	Thompson Lake and Region
	Union River and Valley. Union River Bay see F27.H3
27.W16	Waldo County
	Including Islesboro Island, Sheepscot River and Valley
	For Waldo Patent see F27.M95
27.W3	Washington County
	Including Narraguagus Valley, Pond Island, St. Croix (Dochet) Island, Roque Island, Machias Bay
27.Y6	York County
	Including Bluff Island, Boon Island, Saco Bay, Stratton Island
	For Saco River and Valley see F27.S15
29.A-Z	Cities, towns, etc., A-Z
	e.g.
29.A9	Augusta
29.B2	Bangor
29.B3	Bar Harbor
29.B9	Brunswick
	Including Pejepscot Purchase. Pejepscot Company (Brunswick Proprietors)
29.K3	Kennebunk
29.P9	Portland

F1-975

	Maine
	Cities, towns, etc., A-Z -- Continued
29.Y6	York
	Elements in the population
30.A1	General works
30.A2-Z	Individual elements
	For list of racial, ethnic, and religious elements (with Cutter numbers) see E184.A+
	New Hampshire
31	Periodicals. Societies. Collections
31.5	Museums. Exhibitions, exhibits
32	Gazetteers. Dictionaries. Geographic names
32.3	Guidebooks
33	Biography (Collective). Genealogy (Collective)
33.2	Historiography
	Historians see E175.5.A+
33.5	Study and teaching
34	General works. Histories
34.3	Juvenile works
34.5	Pamphlets, addresses, essays, etc.
34.6	Anecdotes, legends, pageants, etc.
35	Historic monuments (General). Illustrative material
36	Antiquities (Non-Indian)
	By period
37	Early to 1775. Mason's Grant
	Including biography: John Mason
	Cf. E83.72 Wars with eastern Indians, 1722-1726
	Cf. E199 French and Indian War, 1755-1763
	Cf. F52 New Hampshire Grants
38	1775-1865
	Including biography: William Henry Young Hackett, Isaac Hill, etc.
	Cf. E263.N4 New Hampshire in the Revolution
	Cf. E359.5.N3 War of 1812
	Cf. E520+ Civil War, 1861-1865 (General)
39	1865-1950
	Including biography: Harry Bingham, Charles Doe
	Cf. D570.85.N25+ World War I, 1914-1918
	Cf. D769.85.N25+ World War II, 1939-1945
	Cf. E726.N3 War of 1898 (Spanish-American War)
40	1951-
41	White Mountains
41.1	Periodicals. Societies. Collections
41.2	Gazetteers. Dictionaries. Geographic names
41.25	Guidebooks
41.3	General works
41.32	Pamphlets, addresses, essays, etc.

	New Hampshire
	White Mountains -- Continued
41.37	Historic monuments (General). Illustrative material
	By period
41.44	Early to 1865
41.5	1865-1950
41.52	1951-
41.6.A-Z	Regions, places, etc., A-Z
	e.g.
	For political subdivisions see F42.A+
	For political divisions see F44.A+
41.6.F8	Franconia Notch
	Old Man of the Mountain see F41.6.P9
41.6.P9	The Profile
41.6.W3	Washington, Mount
42.A-Z	Regions, counties, etc., A-Z
42.A15	Counties
42.A16	Mountains
42.A17	Rivers
42.A18	Lakes
42.A19	Islands
42.B4	Belknap County
42.B7	Boundaries
	For New York-New Hampshire dispute over New Hampshire Grants see F52
42.C3	Carroll County
	Including Mount Pequawkwet (Kearsarge), Ossipee Mountain Park
	For Mount Kearsarge, Merrimack Co. see F42.M5
42.C5	Cheshire County
	Including Mount Monadnock
42.C65	Connecticut River and Valley, N.H.
	Cf. F12.C7 New England
42.C7	Coos County
	Including Indian Stream
42.G7	Grafton County
	Including Newfound (Pasquaney) Lake, Mount Moosilaukee
42.H6	Hillsboro (Hillsborough) County
	Including Uncanoonuc Mountains
42.I8	Isles of Shoals
	Kearsarge, Mount, Carroll Co. see F42.C3
	Kearsarge, Mount, Merrimack Co. see F42.M5
	Magalloway Valley see F27.M18

F1-975

	New Hampshire
	Regions, counties, etc., A-Z -- Continued
42.M4	Merrimac River and Valley
	Class here works limited to the part of the Merrimac River and Valley located in New Hampshire
	For general works on the Merrimac River and Valley, as well as works limited to the part located in Massachusetts see F72.M6
42.M5	Merrimac County
	Including Mount Kearsarge
	Odiorne Point State Park see F42.R7
42.P4	Piscataqua River and Valley
	Class here general works on the Piscataqua River and Valley, as well as works limited to the part located in New Hampshire
	For works limited to the part of the Piscataqua River and Valley located in Maine see F27.P48
42.R7	Rockingham County
	Including Lake Massabesic, Odiorne Point State Park
	For Isles of Shoals see F42.I8
42.S8	Strafford County
42.S87	Sullivan County
42.S9	Sunapee Lake
	Waterville Valley see F44.W32
	Welch Island see F42.W7
	White Mountains see F41
42.W7	Winnipesaukee, Lake
	Including Welch Island
44.A-Z	Cities, towns, etc., A-Z
	e.g.
44.C7	Concord
44.D7	Dover
44.M2	Manchester
44.N2	Nashua
44.P8	Portsmouth
44.W32	Waterville
	Including Waterville Valley
	Elements in the population
45.A1	General works
45.A2-Z	Individual elements
	For list of racial, ethnic, and religious elements (with Cutter numbers) see E184.A+

Vermont

> Historical note from the second edition (1913) of Class F: "This region was practically unsettled down to the middle of the 18th century and the question of its ownership scarcely thought of. In 1749 the dispute began between the governments of New Hampshire and New York. During the next few years the former state disposed of a large part of the area by means of township grants (whence the name "New Hampshire Grants" by which it was commonly known). In 1765 the King of England adjudged the Connecticut River to be New York's eastern boundary, north of Massachusetts. At first the whole "New Hampshire Grants" were annexed to Albany County; later (1768) Cumberland County was erected in the southeast, Gloucester in the northeast (1770), and the northwestern half of the "Grants" in 1772 formed the eastern part of Charlotte County (the remainder lying west and south of Lake Champlain). New York insisted on annulling the land grants of New Hampshire; the settlers resisted and from 1777 to 1791 formed an independent state, but were denied representation in Congress. In 1791 the state was admitted to the union."

F1-975

46	Periodicals. Societies. Collections
46.5	Museums. Exhibitions, exhibits
47	Gazetteers. Dictionaries. Geographic names
47.3	Guidebooks
48	Biography (Collective). Genealogy (Collective)
48.2	Historiography
	Historians see E175.5.A+
48.5	Study and teaching
49	General works. Histories
49.3	Juvenile works
49.5	Pamphlets, addresses, essays, etc.
49.6	Anecdotes, legends, pageants, etc.
50	Historic monuments (General). Illustrative material
51	Antiquities. (Non-Indian)
	By period
52	Early to 1791

>   Including New Hampshire Grants; Green Mountain boys
>   Including biography: Ira Allen, Thomas Chittenden
>   Cf. E230+ Military operations and battles
>   Cf. E263.V5 Vermont in the Revolution (General)
>   Cf. F37 New Hampshire colonial history
>   Cf. F122 New York colonial history
>   Cf. F127.A3 Albany Co., N.Y.
>   Cf. F127.W3 Charlotte (now Washington) County, N.Y.

	Vermont
	By period -- Continued
53	1791-1865
	Including admission as a state, March 4, 1791
	Biography: Jacob Collamer, etc.
	Cf. E355 Military operations
	Cf. E359.5.V3 War of 1812
	Cf. E470.95 St. Alban's Raid
	Cf. E533+ Civil War, 1861-1865 (General)
54	1865-1950
	Cf. D570.85.V5+ World War I, 1914-1918
	Cf. D769.85.V5+ World War II, 1939-1945
	Cf. E726.V5 War of 1898 (Spanish-American War)
	1951-
55	General works
	Biography
55.2	Collective
55.22.A-Z	Individual, A-Z
	Subarrange each by Table F5
57.A-Z	Regions, counties, etc., A-Z
57.A15	Counties
57.A16	Mountains
57.A17	Rivers
57.A18	Lakes
57.A19	Islands
57.A2	Addison County
	Including Lake Dunmore
57.B4	Bennington County
	Including works on the part of the Hoosic River and Valley located in Vermont
	For the part of the Hoosic River and Valley located in Massachusetts see F72.B5
	For general works on the Hoosic River and Valley, as well as works limited to the part located in New York State see F127.H73
57.B7	Boundaries
	For New Hampshire-New York dispute over land in the present state of Vermont see F52
	Cf. F42.B7 New Hampshire boundary
	Cf. F72.B7 Massachusetts boundary
	Cf. F127.B7 New York boundary
57.C2	Caledonia County

Vermont

Regions, counties, etc., A-Z -- Continued

57.C4	Champlain, Lake, Region

Class here works limited to the part of the Lake Champlain
Region located in Vermont

For general works on the Lake Champlain Region, as
well as works limited to the part located in New
York State see F127.C6

Cf. F57.G7 Grand Isle Co.

57.C5	Chittenden County
57.C7	Connecticut River and Valley, Vt.

Cf. F12.C7 New England

57.E7	Essex County
57.F8	Franklin County

For Missisquoi River and Valley see F57.M7

57.G7	Grand isle County
57.G8	Green Mountains

Hoosic River and Valley, Vt. see F57.B4

57.L2	Lamoille County
57.L22	Lamoille River and Valley
57.M25	Mad River and Valley
57.M3	Mount Mansfield
57.M5	Memphremagog, Lake, region, Vt.

Cf. F1054.M5 Quebec

57.M7	Missisquoi River and Valley

Class here works limited to the part of the Missisquoi River
and Valley located in Vermont

For general works on the Missisquoi River and Valley,
as well as works limited to the part in and Quebec
see F1054.B8

57.O56	Ompompanoosuc Parish

Cf. F59.N9 Norwich
Cf. F59.T4 Thetford

57.O6	Orange County
57.O7	Orleans County

Including Willoughby Lake
For Missisquoi River and Valley see F57.M7

57.R9	Rutland County

Including Lake Bomoseen

57.W3	Washington County

Willoughby Lake see F57.O7

57.W6	Windham County
57.W7	Windsor County
57.W73	Winooski River
59.A-Z	Cities, towns, etc., A-Z

e.g.

59.B4	Bennington

Vermont
    Cities, towns, etc., A-Z -- Continued

59.B8	Brattleboro
59.B9	Burlington
59.M7	Montpelier
59.N9	Norwich
	Ompompanoosuc Parish see F57.O56
59.T4	Thetford

    Elements in the population

60.A1	General works
60.A2-Z	Individual elements

        For a list of racial, ethnic, and religious elements (with Cutter numbers) see E184.A+

Massachusetts

    Historical note from the second edition (1913) of Class F: "Part of the grant to the Plymouth Company 1606 and later to the Council for New England. Settlements were chiefly made under latter's grants. (Pilgrims at Plymouth 1620. Wessagusset or Weymouth 1622. Cape Ann 1624. Wollaston or Quincy 1625. Massachusetts Bay company 1628-1630.) The province charter 1691 united all the separate settlements within the present state limits, as well as the District of Maine. Western lands claimed under early charters were ceded to U.S., 1785 except those in western N.Y. which were surrendered to that state in 1786."

61	Periodicals. Societies. Collections
61.5	Museums. Exhibitions, exhibits
62	Gazetteers. Dictionaries. Geographic names
62.3	Guidebooks
63	Biography (Collective). Genealogy (Collective)
63.2	Historiography
	Historians see E175.5.A+
63.5	Study and teaching
64	General works. Histories
64.3	Juvenile works
64.5	Pamphlets, addresses, essays, etc.
64.6	Anecdotes, legends, pageants, etc.
65	Historic monuments (General). Illustrative material
66	Antiquities (Non-Indian)
	By period

Massachusetts

By period -- Continued

67 Early to 1775

Including Dorchester Company; Massachusetts Bay
Company; persecution of Quakers; Province of
Massachusetts; Puritans

Including biography: Roger Conant, Thomas Dudley, John
Endecott, Daniel Gookin, Anne (Marbury) Hutchinson,
Thomas Hutchinson, Cotton Mather, Increase Mather,
Peter Oliver, Thomas Pownall, John Read, Timothy
Ruggles, Samuel Sewall, John Winthrop (1588-1649),
etc.

Cf. BF1575 Witchcraft delusion

Cf. E83.67 King Philip's War, 1675-1676

Cf. E83.72 Wars with eastern Indians, 1722-1726

Cf. E196 King William's War, 1689-1697

Cf. E197 Queen Anne's War, 1702-1713

Cf. E198 King George's War, 1744-1748

Cf. E199 French and Indian War, 1755-1763

Cf. F7.5 Andros and his province of New England,
1688-1689

F1-975

68 New Plymouth Colony

Including Pilgrims; annexation to Massachusetts, 1691
(forming the counties of Barnstable, Bristol, and
Plymouth); etc., Pilgrim Society, Plymouth; Society of
Mayflower Descendants

Including biography: Isaac Allerton, William Bradford,
William Brewster, Miles Standish, etc.

For Old Colony Historical Society, Taunton see
F74.T2

Massachusetts
By period -- Continued
69 1775-1865
Including Shays' Rebellion, 1786-1787
Biography: James Bowdoin, Christopher Gore, David
Henshaw, Samuel Howe, Amos Lawrence, Theophilus
Parsons, Samuel Phillips, William Phillips, Paul Revere,
Caleb Strong
Cf. E210+ Preliminaries (Revolution)
Cf. E216 Paul Revere's ride
Cf. E230+ Military operations and battles
Cf. E263.M4 Massachusetts and the Revolution
Cf. E309 Cession of western lands
Cf. E359.5.M3 War of 1812
Cf. E513+ Civil War, 1861-1865 (General)
Cf. F127.G2 Lands in western New York
Cf. F127.H2 Lands in western New York
Cf. F127.T6 Lands in western New York
Cf. F273 Trouble with South Carolina over African
American citizens, 1845
Cf. F483 Cession of western lands
70 1865-1950
Including biography: James Michael Curley, Frederic Thomas
Greenhalge, Samuel Hoar, Roger Wolcott, etc.
Cf. D570.85.M4+ World War I, 1914-1918
Cf. D769.85.M4+ World War II, 1939-1945
Cf. E726.M4 War of 1898 (Spanish-American War)
1951-
71 General works
Biography
71.2 Collective
71.22.A-Z Individual, A-Z
Subarrange each by Table F5
72.A-Z Regions, counties, etc., A-Z
72.A15 Counties
72.A16 Mountains
72.A17 Rivers
72.A18 Lakes
72.A19 Islands
Barnstable Co. see F72.C3

Massachusetts

Regions, counties, etc., A-Z -- Continued

72.B5   Berkshire County

Including Berkshire Hills, Greylock Mountain, Mount Everest, and the part of the Hoosic River and Valley and the Mohawk Trail located in Massachusetts

For works limited to the part of the Hoosic River and Valley located in Vermont see F57.B4

For general works on the Hoosic River and Valley, as well as works limited to the part located in New York State see F127.H73

For works limited to the part of the Mohawk Trail located in New York State see F127.M55

72.B57   Blackstone River and Valley

Class here works limited to the part of the Blackstone River and Valley located in Massachusetts

For general works on the Blackstone River and Valley, as well as works limited to the part located in Rhode Island see F87.B55

F1-975

Boon Lake see F72.M7

"Boston Ten Townships," N.Y. see F127.T6

72.B7   Boundaries

For Massachusetts territorial claims to western New York see F127.G2

Cf. F42.B7 New Hampshire boundary

Cf. F1039.B7 Ancient boundary of Acadia

72.B8   Bristol County
72.B9   Buzzards Bay region
72.C3   Cape Cod. Barnstable County

Including Cape Cod Bay, Sparrow-hawk (Ship) wreck (1626), Nauset Beach

Chappaquiddick Island see F72.M5

72.C46   Charles River
72.C7   Connecticut River and Valley, Mass.

Cf. F12.C7 New England

Dukes Co. see F72.M5

72.E5   Elizabeth Islands

Including Cuttyhunk, Nashawena, Naushon, Nonamesset, Pasque, and Penikese Islands

72.E7   Essex County

Including Cape Ann, Ipswich (Agawam) River, North Shore, Saugus River

72.F8   Franklin County

Including Deerfield River, Pocumtuck Valley

72.H2   Hampden County
72.H3   Hampshire County

Including Mill River, Mount Holyoke, Mount Tom

Massachusetts
Regions, counties, etc., A-Z -- Continued

72.H7	Housatonic River and Valley
	Class here works limited to the part of the Housatonic River and Valley located in Massachusetts
	For general works on the Housatonic River and Valley, as well as works limited to the part located in Connecticut see F102.H7
72.M5	Martha's Vineyard. Dukes County
	Including Chappaquiddick Island
	"Massachusetts Ten Townships," N.Y. see F127.T6
72.M6	Merrimac River and Valley
	Class here general works on the Merrimac River and Valley, as well as works limited to the part located in Massachusetts
	For works limited to the part of the Merrimac River and Valley located in New Hampshire see F42.M4
72.M7	Middlesex County
	Including Lake Boon, Concord River, Middlesex Fells Reservation, Minute Man National Historical Park, Walden Pond
	Middlesex Fells Reservation see F72.M7
72.M73	Millers River and Valley
	Minute Man National Historical Park see F72.M7
72.N2	Nantucket County
	Including Nantucket, Muskeget, and Tuckernuck Islands
	Nauset Beach see F72.C3
72.N6	No Mans Land (Island)
72.N8	Norfolk County
	Peddocks Island see F72.P7
	Pioneer Valley see F72.C7
72.P6	Plum Island
72.P7	Plymouth County
	Including North River, South Shore, Peddocks Island
72.S86	Sudbury River and Valley
72.S9	Suffolk County
	Cf. F73 Boston
72.S94	Swift River Valley. Quabbin Reservoir. Ware River Valley
	Walden Pond see F72.M7
72.W9	Worcester County
	Including Wachusett Mountain, Lake Quinsigamond
73	Boston
73.1	Periodicals. Societies. Collections
73.15	Museums. Exhibitions, exhibits
	For Foreign Exhibition, 1883 see T460
73.18	Guidebooks

	Massachusetts
	Boston -- Continued
73.25	Biography (Collective). Genealogy (Collective)
	Including vital records, epitaphs
73.27	Historiography
73.29	Study and teaching
73.3	General works. Histories
73.33	Juvenile works
73.35	Pamphlets, addresses, essays, etc.
73.36	Anecdotes, legends, pageants, etc.
73.37	Historic monuments (General). Illustrative material
73.39	Antiquities (Non-Indian)
	By period
73.4	Early to 1775
	Including the fires of 1711, 1737, 1760, etc.
	Including biography: William Blackstone, etc.
	Cf. E215 Events just prior to the Revolution
73.44	1775-1865
	Cf. E450 Fugitive slave riots
73.5	1865-1950
	Including fire of 1872
	1951-
73.52	General works
	Biography
73.53	Collective
73.54.A-Z	Individual, A-Z
	Subarrange each by Table F5
	Sections. Localities. Districts, etc.
73.6	General works
73.61	Cemeteries
	Including Copp's Hill Burial Ground, Granary Burial Ground, King's Chapel Burial Ground, Mount Hope Cemetery
73.62	Churches
	For religious aspects see BX1+
73.625	Hotels, taverns, etc.
73.627	Places of amusement
73.63	Harbor
73.64	Monuments. Statues
	e.g.
73.64.A1	General works
73.64.B4	Beacon Hill Monument
73.64.W4	Wendell Phillips Statue
73.65	Parks. Squares. Circles
	Including Boston Common, Franklin Park
73.67	Streets. Bridges. Railroads, etc.
	e.g.
73.67.A1	General works

F1-975

	Massachusetts
	Boston
	Sections. Localities. Districts, etc.
	Streets. Bridges. Railroads, etc. -- Continued
73.67.P3	Park Street
73.67.S7	State Street
73.67.T7	Tremont Street
73.67.W3	Washington Street
73.68.A-Z	Suburbs. Sections of the city. Rivers
73.68.B32	Back Bay
73.68.B4	Beacon Hill
	Brighton see F74.B73
73.68.C3	Castle Island
	Charlestown see F74.C4
	Dorchester see F74.D5
73.68.E2	East Boston
73.68.L43	Leather District
73.68.N65	North End
73.68.R2	Rainsford Island
73.68.R67	Roslindale
	Roxbury see F74.R9
73.68.S7	South Boston
73.68.T5	Thompson Island
	West Roxbury see F74.W59
73.68.W47	West End
73.69	Wards
	Buildings
73.7	Collective
73.8.A-Z	Individual, A-Z
	e.g.
73.8.C9	Crown Coffee House
73.8.F2	Faneuil Hall Market
73.8.O4	Old State House
73.8.P3	Parker House
73.8.S8	State House
	Elements in the population
73.9.A1	Collective
73.9.A2-Z	Individual elements
	For list of racial, ethnic, and religious elements (with Cutter numbers) see E184.A+
74.A-Z	Other cities and towns, etc., A-Z
	e.g.
74.B73	Brighton
74.C1	Cambridge
74.C4	Charlestown
74.C8	Concord
74.D5	Dorchester

Massachusetts
  Other cities and towns, etc., A-Z -- Continued

74.G9	Groton
74.L98	Lynn
	Old Sturbridge Village see F74.S93
74.P8	Plymouth
74.P96	Provincetown
74.R9	Roxbury
74.S1	Salem
74.S8	Springfield
74.S84	Sterling
74.S88	Stoneham
74.S89	Stow
74.S93	Sturbridge
	Including Old Sturbridge Village
74.T2	Taunton
	Including Old Colony Historical Society
74.W59	West Roxbury
74.W9	Worcester

F1-975

  Elements in the population

75.A1	Collective
75.A2-Z	Individual elements
	For a list of racial, ethnic, and religious elements (with Cutter numbers) see E184.A+

Rhode Island

76	Periodicals. Societies. Collections
76.5	Museums. Exhibitions, exhibits
77	Gazetteers. Dictionaries. Geographic names
77.3	Guidebooks
78	Biography (Collective). Genealogy (Collective)
78.2	Historiography
	Historians see E175.5.A+
78.5	Study and teaching
79	General works. Histories
79.3	Juvenile works
79.5	Pamphlets, addresses, essays, etc.
79.6	Anecdotes, legends, pageants, etc.
80	Historic monuments (General). Illustrative material
81	Antiquities (Non-Indian)
	By period
82	Early to 1775
	Including First Rhode Island Charter, 1663; the Narragansett country; union of plantations at Newport, Portsmouth, Providence, and Warwick, 1636-1643
	Including biography: John Clarke, Samuel Gorton, Roger Williams, etc.
	Cf. E83.67 King Philip's War, 1675-1676

Rhode Island

By period -- Continued

83	1775-1865
	Cf. E215.6 Gaspee affair
	Cf. E230+ Military operations and battles
	Cf. E263.R4 Rhode Island in the Revolution (General)
	Cf. E528.1+ Civil War, 1861-1865 (General)
83.4	Dorr Rebellion, 1842
	Including biography: Thomas Wilson Dorr, etc.
84	1865-1950
	Cf. D570.85.R4+ World War I, 1914-1918
	Cf. D769.85.R4+ World War II, 1939-1945
	Cf. E726.R4 War of 1898 (Spanish-American War)
85	1951-
87.A-Z	Regions, counties, etc., A-Z
87.A15	Counties
87.A16	Mountains
87.A17	Rivers
87.A18	Lakes
87.A19	Islands
87.B55	Blackstone River and Valley
	Class here general works on the Blackstone River and Valley, as well as works limited to the part located in Rhode Island
	For works limited to the part of the Blackstone River and Valley located in Massachusetts see F72.B57
87.B6	Block Island (Manisees)
87.B7	Boundaries
	Cf. F72.B7 Massachusetts boundary
	Cf. F82 Massachusetts claims to Narragansett country
	Cf. F102.B7 Connecticut boundary
87.B86	Bristol County
87.K3	Kent County
87.N2	Narragansett Bay region
87.N5	Newport County
	For Block Island see F87.B6
	For Rhode Island (Island) see F87.R4
87.P3	Pawtuxet River and Valley
87.P5	Pettaquamscutt Purchase
87.P9	Providence County
87.R4	Rhode Island (Island) (Aquidneck)
87.S25	Sakonnet River and Region
87.W3	Washington County
89.A-Z	Cities, towns, etc., A-Z
	e.g.
89.N5	Newport
89.P9-.P99	Providence (Table F2)

Rhode Island -- Continued
Elements in the population

90.A1   General works
90.A2-Z   Individual elements
            For a list of racial ethnic, and religious elements (with
                Cutter numbers) see E184.A+

Connecticut
            Historical note from the second edition (1913) of Class F: "The
                whole region was claimed by the Council for New England
                and grants made under its authority. Connecticut River and
                region west was also claimed by the Dutch of New
                Netherland, and trading posts established. The English
                settlements at Windsor, Saybrook, Wethersfield and Hartford
                (1633-1636) organized a government as Connecticut in 1639.
                New Haven, settled 1638, maintained a separate existence till
                1662 when a royal charter united it to Connecticut.
                Connecticut had some pretensions to jurisdiction over eastern
                Long Island till the latter was confirmed to N.Y. 1674-5.
                Claims to western lands were surrendered to U.S. in 1786,
                the state retaining only the right to sell to settlers the tract
                known as the Western Reserve. Connecticut's claim to a strip
                of territory south of Pennsylvania's northern boundary was
                the cause of an extended controversy with the latter state."

F1-975

91   Periodicals. Societies. Collections
91.5   Museums. Exhibitions, exhibits
92   Gazetteers. Dictionaries. Geographic names
92.3   Guidebooks
93   Biography (Collective). Genealogy (Collective)
93.2   Historiography
              Historians see E175.5.A+
93.5   Study and teaching
94   General works. Histories
94.3   Juvenile works
94.5   Pamphlets, addresses, essays, etc.
94.6   Anecdotes, legends, pageants, etc.
94.8   Geography
95   Historic monuments (General). Illustrative material
96   Antiquities (Non-Indian)
            By period

	Connecticut
	By period -- Continued
97	Early to 1775
	Including early grants by the Council for New England; Dutch posts
	Including biography: John Winthrop, 1606-1676
	Cf. E83.63 Pequot War, 1636-1638
	Cf. E83.67 King Philip's War, 1675-1676
	Cf. E199 French and Indian War, 1755-1763
	Cf. F7.5 Government of Andros, 1688-1689
	Cf. F157.W9 Claims to Wyoming Valley, Susquehanna Company
98	New Haven Colony
	Cf. F102.N5 New Haven County
	Cf. F104.N6+ New Haven
99	1775-1865
	Cf. E230+ Military operations and battles in the Revolution
	Cf. E263.C5 Connecticut in the Revolution (General)
	Cf. E309 Cession of western lands
	Cf. E357.7 Hartford Convention, 1814
	Cf. E359.5.C7 War of 1812
	Cf. E409.5.C6 War with Mexico, 1845-1848
	Cf. E499+ Civil War, 1861-1865 (General)
	Cf. F157.W9 Susquehanna claims
	Cf. F483 Cession of western lands
	Cf. F497.W5 Cession of western lands
100	1865-1950
	Cf. D570.85.C8+ World War I, 1914-1918
	Cf. D769.85.C8+ World War II, 1939-1945
	Cf. E726.C7 War of 1898 (Spanish-American War)
	1951-
101	General works
	Biography
101.2	Collective
101.3.A-Z	Individual, A-Z
	Subarrange each by Table F5
102.A-Z	Regions, counties, etc., A-Z
102.A15	Counties
102.A16	Mountains
102.A17	Rivers
102.A18	Lakes
102.A19	Islands
102.A85	Atlantic Coast

	Connecticut
	Regions, counties, etc., A-Z -- Continued
102.B7	Boundaries
	Cf. F72.B7 Massachusetts boundary
	Cf. F127.B7 New York boundary
	Cf. F157.W9 Pennsylvania-Connecticut boundary
	dispute ("Connecticut Gore," Susquehanna
	Company)
102.C2	Candlewood, Lake
102.C7	Connecticut River and Valley, Conn.
	Cf. F12.C7 New England
102.F2	Fairfield County
	Including Norwalk Islands including Sheffield Island
	Firelands see F497.W5
	Fishers Island see F127.F5
102.H3	Hartford County
102.H7	Housatonic River and Valley
	Class here general works on the Housatonic River and
	Valley, as well as works limited to the part located in
	Connecticut
	For works limited to the part of the Housatonic River
	and Valley located in Massachusetts see F72.H7
102.L6	Litchfield County
	Including Highland Lake, Litchfield Hills
	For Berkshire Hills see F72.B5
	Long Island see F127.L8
102.M6	Middlesex County
102.N2	Naugatuck River and Valley
102.N5	New Haven County
	Including Leetes Island
	Cf. F98 New Haven Colony
102.N7	New London County
102.T4	The Thimbles
102.T6	Tolland County
	Western Reserve see F497.W5
	Westmoreland (township, 1774; county, 1775) see
	F157.W9
102.W7	Windham County
104.A-Z	Cities, towns, etc. A-Z
	e.g.
104.H3	Hartford
104.L7	Litchfield
104.N6-.N69	New Haven (Table F2)
104.N7	New London
104.N93	Norwich
104.S8	Stamford
	Elements in the population

F1-975

Connecticut
Elements in the population -- Continued
105.A1   General works
105.A2-Z   Individual elements
                       For a list of racial, ethnic, and religious elements (with
                           Cutter numbers) see E184.A+
106   Atlantic coast of North America. Middle Atlantic States
                   Including the eastern United States as a whole; Atlantic States
                       (Maine to Florida); Middle States; Appalachian Mountains
                       (General)
                   Class here descriptive and historic works after 1825
                   For earlier works, see E162-165; E186-375
                   Cf. F157.D4 Delaware River and Valley
                   Cf. F157.S8 Susquehanna River and Valley
                   Cf. F172.D3 Delaware Bay and Region
                   Cf. F187.C5 Chesapeake Bay and region
                   Cf. F187.P8 Potomac River and Valley
                   Cf. F217.A65 Appalachian Mountains, Southern
                   Cf. F1035.8 Atlantic coast of Canada
               New York
                   Historical note from the second edition (1913) of Class F: "Settled
                       by the Dutch. New Netherland in its broadest extent included
                       the Hudson Valley and eastward to the Connecticut, the lower
                       Mohawk, Long Island and the Dutch and Swedish settlements
                       on the Delaware River (Delaware, New Jersey, and
                       southeastern Pennsylvania). It was conquered by the English
                       in 1664 and reduced in limits, though the claim still extended
                       to the Connecticut River, while N.J. was for many years
                       attached to N.Y. under the same governor; also Martha's
                       Vineyard and Nantucket, and modern Maine east of the
                       Kennebec, for a time. Claims to the west bank of the
                       Connecticut River were surrendered to Connecticut and
                       Massachusetts in colonial times, and later to Vermont. During
                       the early colonial period, what is now the western part of the
                       state was Indian country with a few missionaries, and having
                       relations quite as much with New France as with New York.
                       After the revolution, Massachusetts enforced territorial claims
                       to western New York, under her charters, but never exercised
                       governmental rights."
116   Periodicals. Societies. Collections
               New York Historical Society
                   Collections
116.N62   First and second series, 1811-1859
116.N63   John Watts de Peyster Publication Fund series
                       Formerly Publication Fund series
116.N638   Quarterly bulletin, 1917-
116.N64   Proceedings, 1843-1849

New York
  Periodicals. Societies. Collections
   New York Historical Society -- Continued

116.N65	Annual report of the Executive Committee
116.N66	Charter, constitution, etc. Editions by date
116.N67	Lists of members. Editions by date
116.N68	Anniversary address. By date
116.N69	Inaugural address of President. By date
116.N7-.N76	Other official publications. By title
116.N77A-.N77Z	Publications about the society or its officer. By author or name of officer
116.5	Museums. Exhibitions, exhibits
117	Gazetteers. Dictionaries. Geographic names
117.3	Guidebooks
118	Biography (Collective). Genealogy (Collective)
118.2	Historiography
	Historians see E175.5.A+
118.5	Study and teaching
119	General works. Histories
119.3	Juvenile works
119.5	Pamphlets, addresses, essays, etc.
119.6	Anecdotes, legends, pageants, etc.
120	Historic monuments (General). Illustrative material
121	Antiquities (Non-Indian)
	By period
	Early to 1775
	Including English province, 1664-1774; Dutch reconquest, 1673-1674; Leisler's Rebellion, 1689; Agrarian conflicts, 1711-1715
	Including biography: Nicholas Bayard; William Burnet; Cadwallader Colden; Thomas Dongan, Earl of Limerick; Caleb Heathcote; Jacob Leisler; etc.
	Cf. E101+ Early voyages to America
	Cf. E196 King William's War, 1689-1697
	Cf. E199 French and Indian War, 1755-1763
	Cf. F7.5 Andros and his government, 1688-1689
	Cf. F52 New Hampshire Grants
	Cf. F1030 French explorations, invasions, and missionaries in western New York
122	General works

F1-975

	New York
	By period
	Early to 1775 -- Continued
122.1	New Netherlands. Dutch Colony, 1610-1664

Including biography: Arent van Curler, Adriaen van der Donck, Jonas Michaelius, Peter Minuit, Peter Stuyvesant, etc.

Cf. E83.655 Indian uprising of 1655

Cf. E83.663 Esopus Indian War, 1663-1664

Cf. F127.R32 Rensselaerswyck

Cf. F167 Subjugation of the Swedes on the Delaware, 1655

123	1775-1865

Including biography: John Watts DePeyster, James Kent, John Alsop King, Elias Warner Leavenworth, Henry Cruse Murphy, Daniel D. Tompkins, Stephen Van Rensselaer, etc.

Cf. E230+ Military operations and battles in the Revolution

Cf. E263.N6 New York in the Revolution (General)

Cf. E355+ Military operations and battles

Cf. E359.5.N6 War of 1812 (General)

Cf. E409.5.N6 War with Mexico, 1845-1848

Cf. E523+ Civil War, 1861-1865 (General)

Cf. F1032 Burning of the "Caroline"; the McLeod case

Cf. HD199 Antirent War, New York (State) 1839-1846

Cf. HS525+ Antimasonic controversy, 1827-1845

Cf. TC625.E6 Erie Canal

124	1865-1950

Including biography: John Alden Dix, Daniel Drew, Roswell Pettibone Flower, Herbert Henry Lehman, Patrick Henry McCarren, James Aloysius O'Gorman, John Boyd Thatcher, etc.

Cf. D570.85.N4+ World War I, 1914-1918

Cf. D769.85.N4+ World War II, 1939-1945

Cf. E726.N5 War of 1898 (Spanish-American War)

	1951-
125	General works
	Biography
125.2	Collective
125.3.A-Z	Individual, A-Z
	Subarrange each by Table F5
126.9	Western New York
127.A-Z	Regions, counties, etc., A-Z
127.A15	Counties
127.A16	Mountains
127.A17	Rivers

	New York
	Regions, counties, etc., A-Z -- Continued
127.A18	Lakes
127.A19	Islands
127.A2	Adirondack Mountains
	Including Esther Mountain, Mount Marcy, etc.
127.A3	Albany County
	Including Helderberg Mountains
	Cf. F52 New Hampshire
	Cf. F127.R32 Rensselaerswyck
127.A4	Allegany County
127.A43	Allegany State Park
127.A45	Allegheny River and Valley
	Class here works limited to the part of the Allegheny River and Valley located in New York State
	Allens Creek and Valley see F127.M6
	Altona Flat Rock see F127.C77
	Au Sable River and Valley see F127.E8
	Bear Mountain State Park see F127.R6
127.B4	Beaver Kill and Beaver Kill Valley
	Big Moose Lake see F127.H5
127.B48	Black River
	"Boston Ten Townships" see F127.T6
127.B7	Boundaries
	For New Hampshire-New York dispute over New Hampshire Grants see F52
	For Massachusetts territorial claims to western New York see F127.G2
	Cf. F72.B7 Massachusetts boundary
	Cf. F142.B7 New Jersey boundary
	Bronx Co. see F128.68.B8
127.B8	Broome County
	Cf. F127.G2 Genesee region
	Cf. F127.T6 "Massachusetts (or Boston) Ten Townships"
	Canandaigua Lake see F127.O7
127.C28	Castleton Island State Park
127.C3	Catskill Mountains
	Including Kaaterskill Park, Rip Van Winkle Trail
127.C4	Cattaraugus County
127.C5	Cayuga County
	Including Fair Haven Beach State Park
127.C52	Cayuga Lake
127.C56	Cedar River and Valley

F1-975

	New York
	Regions, counties, etc., A-Z -- Continued
127.C6	Champlain, Lake, Region
	Class here general works on the Lake Champlain Region, as well as works limited to the part located in New York State
	Including Champlain Valley; Lake Champlain Tercentenary, 1909
	For works limited to the part of the Lake Champlain Region located in Vermont see F57.C4
	Cf. F57.G7 Grand Isle Co., Vt.
	Charlotte Co. (1772) see F127.W3
127.C7	Chautauqua County
	Including Chautauqua Creek and Valley, Lake Chautauqua, Portage Trail
127.C72	Chemung County
127.C73	Chemung River and Valley
	Class here general works on the Chemung River and Valley, as well as works limited to the part located in New York State
	For works limited to the part of the Chemung River and Valley located in Pennsylvania see F157.C37
127.C76	Chenango County
127.C765	Chenango River and Valley. Chenango Canal
	Clermont State Park see F127.L73
127.C77	Clinton County
	Including Altona Flat Rock
127.C8	Columbia County
127.C83	Constitution Island
	Cornwall Co. see F23
127.C85	Cortland County
	Cumberland Co. (1768) see F52
127.D3	Delaware County
127.D4	Delaware River and Valley
	Class here works limited to the part of the Delaware River and Valley located in New York State
	For works limited to the part of the Delaware River and Valley located in New Jersey see F142.D4
	For general works on the Delaware River and Valley, as well as works limited to the part located in Pennsylvania see F157.D4
	For works limited to the part of the Delaware River and Valley located in Delaware see F172.D4
	Denning Point see F127.D8
127.D8	Dutchess County
	Including Little (or Upper) Nine Partners Patent, Denning Point

New York
Regions, counties, etc., A-Z -- Continued

(127.E5) Erie Canal
  see HE396.E6

127.E6 Erie County

127.E65 Erie, Lake, region, N.Y.
  Cf. F555 Lake Erie (General)

127.E8 Essex County
  Including Au Sable River and Valley, Au Sable Chasm
  Esther Mountain see F127.A2
  Fair Haven Beach State Park see F127.C5

127.F4 Finger Lakes region
  Cf. F127.C52 Cayuga Lake, etc.
  Fire Island see F127.S9

127.F5 Fishers Island
  Cf. F129.S74 Southold

127.F8 Franklin County
  Including Mount Seward, Saranac Lakes

127.F88 Fulton Chain Lakes and Region

127.F9 Fulton County
  Gardiner's Island see F129.E13

127.G15 Gateway National Recreation Area
  Class here general works on the Gateway National
   Recreation Area, as well as works limited to the part
   located in New York
  For works limited to the part of the Gateway National
   Recreation Area located in New Jersey see
   F142.G37

127.G19 Genesee County

127.G2 Genesee region. Genesee River and Valley
  Phelps-Gorham Purchase (1788), etc.
  Cf. F127.H7 Holland Purchase
  Cf. F127.T6 "Massachusetts (or Boston) Ten
   Townships"

127.G3 George, Lake
  Gloucester Co. (1770) see F52
  Grand Island see F129.G68

127.G67 Great Sacandaga Lake

127.G7 Greene County
  For Catskill Mountains see F127.C3
  Grindstone Island see F127.T5

127.H2 Hamilton County
  Including Blue Mountain Lake, Long Lake, Racquette Lake
  Hamptons see F127.S9
  Helderberg Mountains see F127.A3

127.H5 Herkimer County
  Including West Canada Creek, Big Moose Lake

F1-975

New York
   Regions, counties, etc., A-Z -- Continued
      Hiawatha Island see F127.S96

127.H7	Holland Purchase. Treaty of Big Tree, 1797
127.H73	Hoosic River and Valley

         Class here general works on the Hoosic River and Valley, as well as works limited to the part located in New York State
         For works limited to the part of the Hoosic River and Valley located in Vermont see F57.B4
         For works limited to the part of the Hoosic River and Valley located in Massachusetts see F72.B5

127.H8	Hudson River and Valley

         Class here general works on the Hudson River and Valley, as well as works limited to the part in New York State
         Including Highlands; Hudson-Fulton Celebration, 1909; Palisades
         For works limited to the part of the Hudson River and Valley located in New Jersey see F142.H83
         Cf. F142.B4 New Jersey Palisades
      Irondequoit Creek and Valley see F127.M6

127.J4	Jefferson County

      Jones Beach State Park see F127.N2

127.K4	Keuka Lake
127.K5	Kings County

         Cf. F129.B7 Borough of Brooklyn

127.L57	Letchworth State Park
127.L6	Lewis County
127.L7	Livingston County

         Including Hemlock Lake

127.L73	Livingston Manor. Clermont State Park
127.L8	Long Island

         For Fishers Island see F127.F5
         For Shelter Island see F127.S54
         Cf. F127.K5 Kings Co.
         Cf. F127.N2 Nassau Co.
         Cf. F127.Q3 Queens Co.
         Cf. F127.S9 Suffolk Co.

127.M2	Madison County

      Manhasset Neck see F127.N2
      Marcy, Mount see F127.A2
      "Massachusetts (or Boston) Ten Townships" see F127.T6

127.M4	Military tract (set off from Tryon County, 1782)
127.M5	Minisink region

         For Minisink Patent (1704) see F142.B7

	New York
	Regions, counties, etc., A-Z -- Continued
127.M55	Mohawk River and Valley
	Including the part of the Mohawk Trail located in New York State
	For the part of the Mohawk Trail located in Massachusetts see F72.B5
127.M6	Monroe County
	Including Allens Creek and Valley, Irondequoit Creek and Valley
127.M7	Montgomery County
	Including Tryon Co. (1772-1784)
127.N2	Nassau County
	Including Manhasset Neck, Jones Beach State Park
	New Hampshire Grants see F52
	New York Co. see F128+
127.N38	New York State Seaway Trail
127.N5	Niagara County
127.N6	Niagara River and Region
	Class here general works on the Niagara River and Region, as well as works limited to the part located in New York State
	Including Niagara Frontier, Niagara River and Valley
	Cf. F1059.N5 Niagara Peninsula, Ontario
127.N8	Niagara Falls
	Including State Reservation, Goat Island
	Cf. F1059.Q3 Queen Victoria Niagara Falls Park, Ontario
127.O5	Oneida County
	Including Sauquoit Valley
127.O52	Oneida Lake
127.O6	Onondaga County
	Including Onondaga Lake
127.O7	Ontario County
	Including Canandaigua Lake
	Cf. F127.G2 Genesee region
	Cf. F127.H7 Holland Purchase
127.O72	Ontario, Lake, region, N.Y.
	Cf. F556 Lake Ontario (General)
127.O8	Orange County
	Including Newburgh Bay, Orange Lake
	For Highlands see F127.H8
	For Minisink region see F127.M5
	For Wawayanda Patent (1703) see F142.B7
	Orange Lake see F127.O8
127.O9	Orleans County
127.O908	Oswegatchie River

F1-975

New York
  Regions, counties, etc., A-Z -- Continued

127.O91	Oswego County
127.O93	Otsego County
	Ozonia Lake see F127.S2
	Palisades of the Hudson see F127.H8
	Phelps-Gorham Purchase (1788) see F127.G2
	Poesten Kill see F127.R3
127.P9	Putnam County
127.Q3	Queens County
	Cf. F128.68.Q4 Borough of Queens
	Raquette Lake see F127.H2
127.R3	Rensselaer County
	Including Taconic Mountains, Poesten Kill
127.R32	Rensselaerswyck. The Van Rennsselaer Manor
	Cf. HD199 Antirent War, New York (State), 1839-1846
	Richmond Co. see F127.S7
	Robins Island see F127.S9
127.R6	Rockland County
	Including Bear Mountain State Park
127.S2	Saint Lawrence County
	Including Black Lake, Ozonia Lake, Sylvia Lake
127.S23	Saint Lawrence River and Valley, N.Y.
	Cf. F127.T5 Thousand Islands
	Cf. F1050 General, and Canada
127.S235	Sampson State Park
	Saranac Lakes see F127.F8
127.S26	Saratoga County
	Including Mount McGregor, etc.
	Sauquoit Valley see F127.O5
127.S27	Schenectady County
127.S3	Schoharie County
	Including Schoharie Creek and Valley
127.S33	Schroon River and Valley
127.S34	Schuyler County
	Including Watkins Glen
	Seaway Trail see F127.N38
127.S4	Seneca County
127.S43	Seneca Lake
	Shawangunk Mountains see F127.U4
127.S54	Shelter Island
127.S7	Staten Island. Richmond County Borough of Richmond
127.S8	Steuben County
	Including Canisteo River

New York
    Regions, counties, etc., A-Z -- Continued

127.S9	Suffolk County
	Including Fire Island, Fire Island State Park, Hamptons, Robins Island
	For Fishers Island see F127.F5
127.S91	Sullivan County
	For Minisink region see F127.M5
127.S96	Susquehanna River and Valley
	Class here works limited to the part of the Susquehanna River and Valley located in New York State
	Including Hiawatha Island
	For general works on the Susquehanna River and Valley, as well as works limited to the part located in Pennsylvania see F157.S8
	For works limited to the part of the Susquehanna River and Valley located in Maryland see F187.S8
	Sylvia Lake see F127.S2
127.T5	Thousand Islands
	Including Carleton Island, Grenell Island, Grindstone Island
127.T6	Tioga County "Massachusetts (or Boston) Ten Townships."
	Cf. F127.G2 Genesee region
127.T7	Tompkins County
	Tryon Co. (1772-1784) see F127.M7
127.T83	Tug Hill region
127.U4	Ulster County
	Including Lake Minnewaska, Mohonk Lake, Mount Meenahga, Shawangunk Mountains
	For Catskill Mountains see F127.C3
	For Minisink region see F127.M5
127.U54	Unadilla River and Valley
127.W2	Warren County
	Including Luzerne Lake
	Cf. F127.G3 Lake George
127.W3	Washington County
	Including Charlotte County (1772)
	Cf. F52 New Hampshire Grants
	Cf. F127.G3 Lake George
	Wawayanda Patent (1703) see F142.B7
127.W4	Wayne County
127.W5	Westchester County
	Including Fordham Manor, Philipsburg Manor, Van Cortlandt Manor
	Cf. F128.68.B8 Borough of the Bronx
127.W9	Wyoming County
127.Y3	Yates County

F1-975

	New York -- Continued
	New York City
	Class here general works on New York City, as well as works limited to Manhattan (New York County)
128	Periodicals. Societies. Collections
128.15	Museums. Exhibitions, exhibits
	For World's Fair, 1939-1940 see T785
128.18	Guidebooks
128.25	Biography (Collective). Genealogy (Collective)
128.27	Historiography
128.29	Study and teaching
128.3	General works. Histories
128.33	Juvenile works
128.35	Pamphlets, addresses, essays, etc.
128.36	Anecdotes, legends, pageants, etc.
128.37	Historic monuments. Illustrative material
128.39	Antiquities. (Non-Indian)
	By period
128.4	Early to 1775
	Including New Amsterdam; Negro plot, 1741
	Including biography: Annetje Jane Bogardus, etc.
	Cf. F122+ New York (State)
128.44	1775-1865
	Including Fire, 1835; Draft riot, 1863
	Including biography: Michael Floy, Philip Hone, Fernando Wood, etc.
	Cf. E230+ Military operations and battles
	Cf. E263.N6 New York in the Revolution
128.47	1865-1900
	Including Riot, 1871; Blizzard, 1888
	Including biography: Richard Croker, Andrew Haswell Green, John Kelly, Abram Stevens Hewitt, William Marcy Tweed, etc.
128.5	1901-1950. Greater New York
	Including "General Slocum" disaster, 1904
	Including biography: Edward Joseph Flynn, William Jay Gaynor, Seth Low, James John Walker, etc.
	Cf. F127.Q3 Queens Co.
	Cf. F127.S7 Staten Island, Richmond County
	Cf. F129.B7 Brooklyn
	1951-1980
128.52	General works
	Biography
128.53	Collective
128.54.A-Z	Individual, A-Z
	Subarrange each by Table F5
	1981-

	New York
	New York City
	By period
	1981- -- Continued
128.55	General works
	Biography
128.56	Collective
128.57.A-Z	Individual, A-Z
	Subarrange each by Table F5
	Sections. Localities. Districts, etc.
128.6	General works
128.61.A-Z	Cemeteries
	e.g.
128.61.A1	General works
128.61.W8	Woodlawn Cemetery
128.62	Churches
	For architecture, see NA; for religious aspects, see BX
128.625	Hotels, taverns, etc.
128.627	Places of amusement
128.63	Harbor
128.64.A-Z	Monuments. Statues
	e.g.
128.64.A1	General works
128.64.G7	Grant Monument (Grant's Tomb)
128.64.L6	Statue of Liberty
128.65.A-Z	Parks. Squares. Circles
	e.g.
128.65.A1	General works
128.65.B3	Battery
128.65.B8	Bronx Parkway
128.65.C3	Central Park
128.65.C5	City Hall Park
128.65.R5	Riverside Park
128.65.Z6	Zoological Park
128.67.A-Z	Streets. Bridges. Railroads
	e.g.
128.67.A1	General works
128.67.B6	Bowery
128.67.B7	Broadway
128.67.F4	Fifth Avenue
128.67.F7	Forty-second Street
128.67.P3	Park Avenue
128.67.R6	Riverside Drive
128.67.W2	Wall Street
128.68.A-Z	Suburbs. Sections of the city. Rivers
	e.g.
128.68.A1	General works

F1-975

	New York
	New York City
	Sections. Localities. Districts, etc.
	Suburbs. Sections of the city. Rivers -- Continued
128.68.B6	Bloomingdale
128.68.B8	Bronx (Borough)
	Including Morrisania Manor, Pelham Manor
	Cf. F127.W5 Westchester Co.
	Brooklyn (Borough) see F129.B7
128.68.C47	Chinatown
128.68.C5	City Island
	Coney Island see F129.C75
128.68.C76	Crown Heights
	Flatbush see F129.F5
128.68.G7	Governor's Island
128.68.G8	Greenwich Village
128.68.H3	Harlem
128.68.H4	Harlem River
128.68.L5	Little Italy
	Long Island City see F129.L78
	Manhattan see F128+
128.68.Q4	Queens (Borough)
	Cf. F127.Q3 Queens Co.
	Richmond (Borough) see F127.S7
	Rockaway Beach see F129.R8
	Staten Island see F127.S7
128.68.S9	Stuyvesant Village
128.68.W2	Washington Heights
128.69	Wards
	Buildings
128.7	General works. Collective
128.8.A-Z	Individual, A-Z
	e.g.
128.8.M8	Morris Mansion (Jumel Mansion)
128.8.P4	Pennsylvania Station
128.8.R7	Rockefeller Center
128.8.V2	Van Cortlandt Mansion
128.8.W82	Woolworth Building
	Elements in the population
128.9.A1	General works
128.9.A2-Z	Individual elements
	For a list of racial, ethnic, and religious elements (with Cutter numbers) see E184.A+
129.A-Z	Other cities, towns, etc., A-Z
	e.g.
129.A1	General works
129.A3-.A39	Albany (Table F2)

New York
  Other cities, towns, etc., A-Z -- Continued

129.B7	Brooklyn
	A borough of New York (City)
129.B8-.B89	Buffalo (Table F2)
129.C75	Coney Island
129.E13	East Hampton
	Including Gardiner's Island, Gardiner Manor
129.F5	Flatbush (New York, N.Y.)
129.F503	Flatbush (Ulster County)
129.G68	Grand Island
129.H99	Hyde Park
129.L78	Long Island City
129.O98	Oyster Bay
	Including Sagamore Hill
129.R7-.R79	Rochester (Table F2)
129.R8	Rockaway Beach
129.S3	Saratoga Springs
129.S74	Southold
	Cf. F127.F5 Fishers Island

Elements in the population

130.A1	General works
130.A2-Z	Individual elements
	For a list of racial, ethnic, and religious elements (with Cutter numbers) see E184.A+

New Jersey
  Historical note from the second edition (1913) of Class F: "This region was claimed by the Dutch of New Netherland as part of their dominion, and such Swedes as had obtained a footing in the southern part were subjugated in 1655. The English crown, however, never relinquished its claim to the whole Atlantic coast of North America, and the claim was made by the Plowden family and heirs that a royal grant was made in 1634 to Sir Edmund Plowden, of "New Albion" covering Long Island and the whole region between New York and Virginia. Explorations were made but no settlement. In 1664 the Duke of York conquered New Netherland, granting New Jersey to Berkeley and Carteret. The former in 1674 sold his undivided half to Fenwick and Byllinge of the Society of Friends, by whom in turn it was transferred to trustees. In 1676 was executed the "Quintipartite deed" whereby the eastern part was given to Carteret under name of East Jersey, and the western part to the Trustees, as West Jersey. Carteret's portion was sold in 1682 to a board of proprietors, also Friends. The two provinces maintained separate governments till 1702 when Queen Anne united them as the province of New Jersey."

F1-975

New Jersey -- Continued

131	Periodicals. Societies. Collections
131.5	Museums. Exhibitions, exhibits
132	Gazetteers. Dictionaries. Geographic names
132.3	Guidebooks
133	Biography (Collective). Genealogy (Collective)
133.2	Historiography
	Historians see E175.5.A+
133.5	Study and teaching
134	General works. Histories
134.3	Juvenile works
134.5	Pamphlets, addresses, essays, etc.
134.6	Anecdotes, legends, pageants, etc.
135	Historic monuments (General). Illustrative material
136	Antiquities (Non-Indian)
	By period
137	Early to 1775

Including Plowden's New Albion Grant; East and West Jersey, 1676-1702

Including biography: Sir George Carteret, John Fenwick, William Franklin, etc.

Cf. E198 King George's War, 1744-1748

Cf. F142.S2 Fenwick's Colony

Cf. F167 New Sweden

138	1775-1865

Including biography: Richard Stockton Field, William Churchill Houston, Andrew Kirkpatrick, etc.

Cf. E230+ Military operations and battles

Cf. E263.N5 New Jersey in the Revolution

Cf. E359.5.N4 War of 1812 (General)

Cf. E521+ Civil War, 1861-1865 (General)

139	1865-1950

Including biography: Harold Giles Hoffman, John Peter Jackson, Henry Cooper Pitney, etc.

Cf. D570.85.N3+ World War I, 1914-1918

Cf. D769.85.N3+ World War II, 1939-1945

Cf. E726.N4 War of 1898 (Spanish-American War)

	1951-
140	General works
	Biography
140.2	Collective
140.22.A-Z	Individual, A-Z
	Subarrange each by Table F5
142.A-Z	Regions, counties, etc., A-Z
142.A15	Counties
142.A16	Mountains
142.A17	Rivers

	New Jersey
	Regions, counties, etc., A-Z -- Continued
142.A18	Lakes
142.A19	Islands
142.A79	Atlantic Coast
142.A8	Atlantic County
	Barnegat Bay see F142.O2
142.B4	Bergen County

          Including Hackensack River and Valley; New Jersey
             Palisades
          Cf. F127.H8 New Jersey Palisades

| 142.B7 | Boundaries |

          Including Minisink and Wawayanda Patents
          Cf. F172.B7 Delaware boundary

| 142.B9 | Burlington County |

          Including Rancocas Valley

142.C16	Camden County
142.C2	Cape May County
142.C9	Cumberland County
	Deal Lake see F142.M7
142.D3	Delaware Bay and Region

          Class here works limited to the part of the Delaware Bay and
             Region located in New Jersey
          For general works on the Delaware Bay and Region, as
             well as works limited to the part located in Delaware
             see F172.D3

| 142.D4 | Delaware River and Valley |

          Class here works limited to the part of the Delaware River
             and Valley located in New Jersey
          For works limited to the part of the Delaware River and
             Valley located in New York State see F127.D4
          For general works on the Delaware River and Valley,
             as well as works limited to the part located in
             Pennsylvania see F157.D4
          For works limited to the part of the Delaware River and
             Valley located in Delaware see F172.D4

      Delaware Water Gap see F157.D5

| 142.E8 | Essex County |

          Including Nutley area

| 142.G37 | Gateway National Recreation Area |

          Class here works limited to the part of the Gateway National
             Recreation Area locate in New Jersey
          For general works on the Gateway National Recreation
             Area, as well as works limited to the part located in
             New York see F127.G15

| 142.G5 | Gloucester County |
| 142.H35 | Hackensack Meadowlands |

F1-975

New Jersey
 Regions, counties, etc., A-Z -- Continued
  Hacklebarney State Park see F142.M8
142.H7   Hopatcong, Lake
142.H8   Hudson County
142.H83   Hudson River and Valley
           Class here works limited to the part of the Hudson River and
            Valley located in New Jersey
           For general works on the Hudson River and Valley, as
            well as works limited to the part in New York State
            see F127.H8
           Cf. F142.B4 New Jersey Palisades
142.H9   Hunterdon County
142.J4   Jersey Shore
142.L65   Long Beach Island
142.M5   Mercer County
142.M6   Middlesex County
142.M64   Millstone River and Valley
142.M7   Monmouth County
           Including Deal Lake, Monmouth Patent, Navesink River and
            Valley, Shark River
142.M8   Morris County
           Including Hacklebarney State Park
142.M85   Morristown National Historical Park
142.M9   Mullica River
          Navesink River and Valley see F142.M7
          New Albion Grant see F137
142.N48   New Jersey Coastal Heritage Trail
142.O2   Ocean County
           Including Barnegat Bay, Long Beach, Sedge Islands
          Palisades of New Jersey see F142.B4
          Palisades of the Hudson (Interstate park) see F127.H8
142.P2   Passaic County
           Including Ringwood Manor
142.P3   Passaic River and Valley
142.P5   Pine Barrens. Pinelands National Reserve
          Pinelands National Reserve see F142.P5
142.R16   Ramapo River and Valley, N.J.
142.R2   Raritan River and Valley
142.S2   Salem County
           Including John Fenwick's colony
          Sedge Islands see F142.O2
142.S6   Somerset County
          Staten Island see F127.S7
142.S9   Sussex County
           For Minisink region see F127.M5
           For Minisink Patent see F142.B7

New Jersey
Regions, counties, etc., A-Z -- Continued
142.U5 Union County
142.W2 Warren County
For Delaware Water Gap see F157.D5
142.W47 Wharton State Forest
144.A-Z Cities, towns, etc., A-Z
e.g.
144.A1 General works
144.A8 Atlantic City
144.C2 Camden
East Orange see F144.O6
144.E4 Elizabeth
144.J5-.J59 Jersey City (Table F2)
144.N6-.N69 Newark (Table F2)
144.O6 Orange (East, South, West)
144.P4 Paterson
South Orange see F144.O6
144.T7-.T79 Trenton (Table F2)
West Orange see F144.O6
Elements in the population
145.A1 General works
145.A2-Z Individual elements
For a list of racial, ethnic, and religious elements (with
Cutter numbers) see E184.A+
Pennsylvania
Historical note from the second edition (1913) of Class F: "The
southeast part was colonized by Swedes and was a portion of
the colony of New Sweden; in 1655 it was conquered by the
Dutch of New Netherland and formed a part of that colony. In
1664 the Duke of York's conquest of New Netherland
transferred it to his control. 1680-82 William Penn received
his royal grant of Pennsylvania, extending west from the
Delaware River, the Duke of York releasing his claim there,
and selling at the same time the region covered by modern
Delaware (which was also claimed by Lord Baltimore as
forming part of Maryland). The southern boundary was in
dispute with Maryland for many years. Connecticut claimed a
strip along the northern border and Virginia considered the
Forks of the Ohio [Pittsburgh] and region south and east as
included in her territory, and organized county governments."
146 Periodicals. Societies. Collections
146.5 Museums. Exhibitions, exhibits
147 Gazetteers. Dictionaries. Geographic names
147.3 Guidebooks
148 Biography (Collective). Genealogy (Collective)
148.2 Historiography

F1-975

Pennsylvania

Historiography -- Continued

Historians see E175.5.A+

148.5	Study and teaching
149	General works. Histories
149.3	Juvenile works
149.5	Pamphlets, addresses, essays, etc.
149.6	Anecdotes, legends, pageants, etc.
149.8	Geography
150	Historic monuments (General). Illustrative material
151	Antiquities (Non-Indian)

By period

152	Early to 1775

Including Grant to Penn, 1681; the Paxton boys

Including biography: Andrew Hamilton, Sir William Keith, James Logan, Francis Daniel Pastorius, Richard Peters, Michael Schlatter, Conrad Weiser, etc.

Cf. E83.76 Pontiac's Conspiracy, 1763-1765

Cf. E198 King George's War, 1744-1748

Cf. E199 French and Indian War, 1755-1763

Cf. F157.W5 Virginia claims in southwestern Pennsylvania

Cf. F157.W9 Connecticut claims in northeastern Pennsylvania

152.2	The proprietors: William Penn and family
153	1775-1865

Including Harrisburg Convention, 1788; Buckshot War, 1838

Including biography: Charles Biddle, Benjamin Chew, James Cooper, William John Duane, Thomas Earle, John Bannister Gibson, Joseph Hiester, Ellis Lewis, Joseph Ritner, William Rodman, George Washington Woodward, etc.

Cf. E230+ Military operations and battles

Cf. E263.P4 Pennsylvania in the Revolution

Cf. E315 Whiskey Rebellion, 1794

Cf. E326 Fries' Rebellion, 1798-1799

Cf. E359.5.P3 War of 1812

Cf. E409.5.P3 War with Mexico, 1845-1848

Cf. E470.2+ Campaigns and battles

Cf. E471+ Civil War campaigns and battles

Cf. E527+ Civil War, 1861-1865 (General)

Cf. F157.W9 Connecticut settlers in Wyoming Valley, Susquehanna claim

	Pennsylvania
	By period -- Continued
154	1865-1950
	Including biography: John Wallace Crawford, John A. Lemon, Arthur George Olmsted, Samuel Whitaker Pennypacker, George Ross, 1841-1894, etc.
	Cf. D570.85.P4+ World War I, 1914-1918
	Cf. D769.85.P4+ World War II, 1939-1945
	Cf. E726.P4 War of 1898 (Spanish-American War)
	Cf. HV6452.A+ Molly Maguires
	1951-
155	General works
	Biography
155.2	Collective
155.3.A-Z	Individual, A-Z
	Subarrange each by Table F5
157.A-Z	Regions, counties, etc., A-Z
157.A15	Counties
157.A16	Mountains
157.A17	Rivers
157.A18	Lakes
157.A19	Islands
157.A2	Adams County
	For Conewago Creek and Valley see F157.C75
157.A4	Allegheny County
157.A45	Allegheny Mountains
	Class here works limited to the part of the Allegheny Mountains located in Pennsylvania
	For general works on the Allegheny Mountains see F217.A3
157.A5	Allegheny River and Valley
	Class here general works on the Allegheny River and Valley, as well as works limited to the part located in Pennsylvania
	For the part of the Allegheny River and Valley located in New York State see F127.A45
157.A7	Armstrong County
157.B16	Bald Eagle Mountain
157.B2	Beaver County
	Including Ohio River and Valley, Pa.
	Cf. F516+ General
157.B23	Beaver River and Valley
157.B25	Bedford County
157.B3	Berks County
	Including Oley Valley
157.B5	Blair County
157.B65	Blue Mountains

Pennsylvania

Regions, counties, etc., A-Z -- Continued

157.B7	Boundaries. Mason and Dixon's Line

For Virginia claim to land south and east of the Ohio
River see F157.W5

For Connecticut claims in northeastern Pennsylvania
see F157.W9

Cf. F127.B7 New York boundary

Cf. F497.B7 Ohio boundary

157.B76	Bradford County
157.B77	Brandywine Creek and Valley

Class here general works on the Brandywine Creek and
Valley, as well as works limited to the part located in
Pennsylvania

For works limited to the part of the Brandwyine Creek
and Valley located in Delaware see F172.B78

157.B8	Bucks County

For Perkiomen River and Valley see F157.M7

Buffalo Creek and Valley see F157.U5

157.B87	Butler County
157.C16	Cambria County
157.C18	Cameron County
157.C2	Carbon County
157.C3	Centre County

Including Penn's Cave

157.C37	Chemung River and Valley

Class here works limited to the part of the Chemung River
and Valley located in Pennsyslvania

For general works on the Chemung River and Valley,
as well as works limited to the part located in New
York State see F127.C73

157.C4	Chester County
157.C5	Clarion County
157.C52	Clarion River
157.C53	Clearfield County
157.C6	Clinton County
157.C67	Cocalico Creek and Valley
157.C7	Columbia County
157.C73	Conemaugh River and Valley

Conestoga Creek and Valley see F157.L2

157.C75	Conewago Creek and Valley
157.C76	Cook Forest Park

Coxton Lake see F157.W35

157.C77	Crawford County

Including Conneaut Lake

157.C8	Cumberland County

Including Old Cumberland Co. (Formed 1750)

Pennsylvania

Regions, counties, etc., A-Z -- Continued

157.C85	Cumberland Road. National Road
	Cf. HE356.C8 Traffic engineering
157.C9	Cumberland (Kittochtinny) Valley
	Including Cumberland and Franklin Counties
	For Franklin County only see F157.F8
157.D2	Dauphin County
157.D28	Delaware and Lehigh National Heritage Corridor
157.D3	Delaware County
157.D4	Delaware River and Valley
	Class here general works on the Delaware River and Valley, as well as works limited to the part located in Pennsylvania
	For works limited to the part of the Delaware River and Valley located in New York State see F127.D4
	For works limited to the part of the Delaware River and Valley located in New Jersey see F142.D4
	For works limited to the part of the Delaware River and Valley located in Delaware see F172.D4
157.D5	Delaware Water Gap
157.E4	Elk County
157.E45	Endless Mountains
157.E6	Erie County
	Including Lake Erie region, Pa.
	Cf. F555 Lake Erie (General)
157.F2	Fayette County (Formed 1783)
	Cf. F157.W5 Old Westmoreland Co.
157.F65	Forbes Road
157.F7	Forest County
157.F8	Franklin County
	Including Cumberland Valley (the part in Franklin Co.,), Conococheague Creek and Valley
	Cf. F157.C9 Cumberland Valley (General, and Cumberland Co.)
	Cf. F187.W3 Conococheague Creek, Md.
157.F9	Fulton County
157.G8	Greene County (Formed 1796)
	Cf. F157.W5 Old Westmoreland Co.
157.H9	Huntingdon County
	Independence National Historical Park see F158.65.I3
157.I3	Indiana County
157.J4	Jefferson County
157.J6	Juniata County
157.J7	Juniata River and Valley
157.L15	Lackawanna County
157.L17	Lackawanna River and Valley

F1-975

	Pennsylvania
	Regions, counties, etc., A-Z -- Continued
157.L2	Lancaster County
	Including Conestoga Creek, Mill Creek and Valley, Pequea Creek
157.L3	Lawrence County
	League Island see F158.68.L4
157.L4	Lebanon County
157.L5	Lehigh County
157.L6	Lehigh River and Valley
157.L8	Luzerne County
157.L9	Lycoming County
157.M2	McKean County
157.M3	Mahoning River and Valley
	Class here works limited to the part of the Mahoning River and Valley located in Pennsylvania
	For general works on the Mahoning River and Valley, as well as works limited to the part located in Ohio see F497.M2
	Mason and Dixon's Line see F157.B7
157.M5	Mercer County
157.M55	Mifflin County
	Mill Creek and Valley see F157.L2
157.M58	Monongahela River and Valley
	Class here general works on the Monongahela River and Valley, as well as works limited to the part located in Pennsylvania
	For works limited to the part of the Monongahela River and Valley located in West Virginia see F247.M6
157.M6	Monroe County
	Including Pocono Mountains
	For Delaware Water Gap see F157.D5
157.M7	Montgomery County
	Including Perkiomen River and Valley
157.M8	Montour County
157.N57	Nippenose Valley
157.N7	Northampton County
157.N8	Northumberland County
157.O26	Octoraro Creek and Valley
	Class here general works on the Octoraro Creek and Valley, as well as works limited to the part located in Pennsylvania
	For works limited to the part of the Octoraro Creek and Valley located in Maryland see F187.O27
	Ohio River and Valley see F157.B2
	Oley Valley see F157.B3

	Pennsylvania
	Regions, counties, etc., A-Z -- Continued
157.P44	Pennsylvania Dutch Country
	Cf. F157.L2 Pennsylvania Dutch in Lancaster County
157.P5	Perry County
157.P56	Philadelphia County
	Cf. F158.44 Consolidation Act merging the county into the city in 1854
157.P6	Pike County
	Including Promised Land State Park and Wallenpaupack Creek and Valley
157.P63	Pine Creek and Valley (Potter County-Lycoming County)
157.P64	Pine Creek Gorge Natural Area
157.P8	Potter County
	Promised Land State Park see F157.P6
157.S3	Schuylkill County
157.S33	Schuylkill River and Valley
157.S47	Shenango River and Valley
157.S49	Sinnamahoning Creek
157.S5	Snyder County
157.S6	Somerset County
157.S67	Sullivan County
	Including Eagle's Mere
157.S7	Susquehanna County
157.S8	Susquehanna River and Valley
	Class here general works on the Susquehanna River and Valley, as well as works limited to the part located in Pennsylvania
	For works limited to the part of the Susquehanna River and Valley located in New York State see F127.S96
	For works limited to the part of the Susquehanna River and Valley located in Maryland see F187.S8
157.S9	West Branch of the Susquehanna
157.T5	Tioga County
157.U5	Union County
	Including Buffalo Creek and Valley
157.V4	Venango County
	Wallenpaupack Creek and Valley see F157.P6
157.W2	Warren County
157.W3	Washington County (Formed 1781)
	Cf. F157.W5 Old Westmoreland Co.
157.W35	Wayne County
	Including Coxton Lake

F1-975

	Pennsylvania
	Regions, counties, etc., A-Z -- Continued
157.W5	Westmoreland County

        Including Old Westmoreland County, formed 1773 (present-day Westmoreland, Washington, Fayette, and Greene counties); boundary disputes with Virginia until 1784 over land south and east of the Ohio River (Virginia's so-called District of West Augusta: counties of Monongalia, Yohogania, and Ohio)

        Cf. F157.W9 Connecticut's old county of Westmoreland

        Cf. F247.M7 Monongalia Co., W. Va.

        Cf. F247.O3 Ohio Co., W. Va.

157.W62	Wissahickon Creek and Valley
157.W8	Wyoming County
157.W9	Wyoming Valley

        Including Connecticut claims, Susquehanna Company, "Connecticut Gore," Connecticut town and county of Westmoreland

| 157.Y6 | York County |

        For Conewago Creek and Valley see F157.C75

| 157.Y7 | York Road |
| 157.Y72 | Youghiogheny River and Valley |

        Class here general works on the Youghiogheny River and Valley, as well as works limited to the part located in Pennsylvania

        For works limited to the part of the Youghiogheny River and Valley located in Maryland see F187.Y68

        For works limited to the part of the Youghiogheny River and Valley located in West Virginia see F247.Y68

	Philadelphia
158.1	Periodicals. Societies. Collections
158.15	Museums. Exhibitions, exhibits

        For Centennial Exposition, 1876 see T825

        For Sesquicentennial International Exposition, 1926 see T826.3

158.18	Guidebooks
158.25	Biography (Collective). Genealogy (Collective)
158.27	Historiography
158.29	Study and teaching
158.3	General works. Histories
158.33	Juvenile works
158.35	Pamphlets, addresses, essays, etc.
158.36	Anecdotes, legends, pageants, etc.
158.37	Historic monuments. Illustrative material
158.39	Antiquities (Non-Indian)
	By period
158.4	Early to 1775

	Pennsylvania
	Philadelphia
	By period -- Continued
158.44	1775-1865
	Including merging of the county of Philadelphia into the city; burning of the Orphan Asylum, 1822; riots of 1831, 1838, 1844
	Cf. E233 Howe's occupation in 1777
158.5	1865-1950
	1951-
158.52	General works
	Biography
158.53	Collective
158.54.A-Z	Individual, A-Z
	Subarrange each by Table F5
	Sections. Localities. Districts, etc.
158.6	General works
158.61.A-Z	Cemeteries
158.61.A1	General works
158.61.M8	Monument Cemetery
158.62.A-Z	Churches
	For religious aspects see BX1+
158.62.A1	General works
158.62.C5	Christ Church
158.62.F5	First Presbyterian Church
158.625	Hotels, taverns, etc.
158.627	Places of amusement
158.63	Harbor
158.64.A-Z	Monuments. Statues
	e.g.
158.64.A1	General works
158.64.G3	Garfield Memorial
158.64.M2	McKinley Statue
158.64.P4	Pennypacker Memorial
158.64.W3	Washington monuments
158.65.A-Z	Parks. Squares. Circles
	e.g.
158.65.A1	General works
158.65.F2	Fairmount Park
158.65.I3	Independence National Historical Park
	For Independence Hall alone see F158.8.I3
158.67.A-Z	Streets. Bridges. Railroads
	e.g.
158.67.A1	General works
158.67.F17	Fairmount Parkway
158.67.I33	Independence Square
158.67.M34	Market Street

F1-975

Pennsylvania
Philadelphia
Sections. Localities. Districts, etc. -- Continued

158.68.A-Z	Suburbs. Sections of the city. Rivers, etc.
	e.g.
158.68.A1	General works
158.68.E4	Elmwood
158.68.F2	Falls of Schuylkill
	Germantown see F159.G3
158.68.L4	League Island
158.68.N8	North Penn Village
158.68.N9	Northern Liberties
158.68.O8	Oxford Township
158.68.P8	Port Royal Farm
158.68.S6	Southwark
158.68.W5	West Philadelphia
158.68.W7	Windmill Island
158.68.W8	Wissahickon Creek
158.69	Wards
	Buildings
158.7	General works. Collective
158.8.A-Z	Individual, A-Z
	e.g.
158.8.A7	Arsenal, Frankford
158.8.C2	Carpenters' Hall
158.8.C5	City Hall
158.8.C7	Congress Hall
158.8.I3	Independence Hall
	Including Liberty bell
158.8.P4	Pennsylvania Hall
158.8.S8	Strawberry Mansion
158.8.W3	Washington Mansion
	Elements in the population
158.9.A1	General works
158.9.A2-Z	Individual elements
	For a list of racial, ethnic, and religious elements (with Cutter numbers) see E184.A+
159.A-Z	Other cities, towns, etc., A-Z
	e.g.
159.C4	Chambersburg
159.E7	Erie
159.G3	Germantown
159.H3	Harrisburg
	Jim Thorpe see F159.M4
159.J7	Johnstown
159.M4	Mauch Chunk. Jim Thorpe
159.P6-.P69	Pittsburgh (Table F2)

	Pennsylvania
	Other cities, towns, etc., A-Z -- Continued
159.R2	Reading
159.S4	Scranton
159.W6	Wilkes-Barre
	Elements in the population
160.A1	General works
160.A2-Z	Individual elements

> For a list of racial, ethnic, and religious elements (with Cutter numbers) see E184.A+

Delaware

> Historical note from the second edition (1913) of Class F: "The first settlements in the region were made by the Dutch about 1629. 1638 the Swedes colonized the region about the lower Delaware River and Bay, in Del., southeastern Pa. and N. J., calling their colony New Sweden. In 1655 the Dutch of New Nether-land conquered and held it till 1664 when it was included in the English conquest. Claimed by both Lord Baltimore and William Perm, and adjudged to the latter. Knownasthe "Lower Counties on the Delaware." A separate province 1703."

F1-975

161	Periodicals. Societies. Collections
161.5	Museums. Exhibitions, exhibits
162	Gazetteers. Dictionaries. Geographic names
162.3	Guidebooks
163	Biography (Collective). Genealogy (Collective)
163.2	Historiography
	Historians see E175.5.A+
163.5	Study and teaching
164	General works. Histories
164.3	Juvenile works
164.5	Pamphlets, addresses, essays, etc.
164.6	Anecdotes, legends, pageants, etc.
165	Historic monuments (General). Illustrative material
166	Antiquities (Non-Indian)
	By period
167	Early to 1775

> Including Swedish settlements on the Delaware River; New Sweden; Dutch conquest, 1655; English conquest, 1664; part of Penn's grant, 1681; the "Lower Counties on the Delaware"
> Including biography: Johan Classon Rising, etc.

| 168 | 1775-1865 |

> Including biography: Jacob Broom, etc.
> Cf. E230+ Military operations and battles
> Cf. E263.D3 Delaware in the Revolution (General)
> Cf. E500+ Civil War, 1861-1865 (General)

	Delaware
	By period -- Continued
169	1865-1950
	Including biography: John Edward Addicks, Edward Woodward Gilpin, etc.
	Cf. D570.85.D4+ World War I, 1914-1918
	1951-
170	General works
	Biography
170.3	Collective
170.4.A-Z	Individual, A-Z
	Subarrange each by Table F5
172.A-Z	Regions, counties, etc., A-Z
172.A15	Counties
172.A16	Mountains
172.A17	Rivers
172.A18	Lakes
172.A19	Islands
172.B7	Boundaries
	Cf. F157.B7 Pennsylvania boundary, Mason and Dixon's line
	Cf. F187.B7 Maryland boundary
172.B78	Brandywine Creek and Valley
	Class here works limited to the part of the Brandywine Creek and Valley located in Delaware
	For general works on the Brandywine Creek and Valley, as well as works limited to the part located in Pennsylvania see F157.B77
172.D3	Delaware Bay and Region
	Class here general works on the Delaware Bay and Region, as well as works limited to the part located in Delaware
	For works limited to the part of the Delaware Bay and Region located in New Jersey see F142.D3
172.D4	Delaware River and Valley
	Class here works limited to the part of the Delaware River and Valley located in Delaware
	For works limited to the part of the Delaware River and Valley located in New York State see F127.D4
	For works limited to the part of the Delaware River and Valley located in New Jersey see F142.D4
	For general works on the Delaware River and Valley, as well as works limited to the part located in Pennsylvania see F157.D4
	Delmarva Peninsula see F187.E2
172.K3	Kent County

Delaware
Regions, counties, etc., A-Z -- Continued

172.N35	Nanticoke River and Valley
	Class here general works on the Nanticoke River and Valley, as well as works limited to the part located in Delaware
	For works limited to the part of the Nanticoke River and Valley located in Maryland see F187.N35
172.N5	New Castle County
	Including Christina River (Creek)
	For Bohemia Manor see F187.C3
172.S8	Sussex County
174.A-Z	Cities, towns, etc. A-Z
	e.g.
174.D74	Dover
174.W7-.W79	Wilmington (Table F2)
	Elements in the population
175.A1	General works
175.A2-Z	Individual elements
	For a list of racial, ethnic and religious elements (with Cutter numbers) see E184.A+

F1-975

Maryland

176	Periodicals. Societies. Collections
178	Museums. Exhibitions, exhibits
179	Gazetteers. Dictionaries. Geographic names
179.3	Guidebooks
180	Biography (Collective). Genealogy (Collective)
180.2	Historiography
	Historians see E175.5.A+
180.5	Study and teaching
181	General works. Histories
181.3	Juvenile works
181.5	Pamphlets, addresses, essays, etc.
181.6	Anecdotes, legends, pageants, etc.
181.8	Geography
182	Historic monuments (General). Illustrative material
183	Antiquities (Non-Indian)
	By period
184	Early to 1775
	Including the Calverts, proprietors of Maryland; Kent Island and Claiborne; toleration in Maryland
	Including biography: George Calvert, 1st Baron of Baltimore; Cecilius Calvert, 2d Baron of Baltimore; William Claiborne, etc.
	Cf. E199 French and Indian Wars, 1755-1763
	Cf. F157.B7 Mason and Dixon's line

	Maryland
	By period -- Continued
185	1775-1865
	Including biography: Enoch Louis Lowe, John Van Lear McMahon, etc.
	Cf. E230+ Military operations and battles in the Revolution
	Cf. E263.M3 Maryland in the Revolution (General)
	Cf. E355+ War of 1812, Military operations and battles
	Cf. E359.5.M2 War of 1812 (General)
	Cf. E409.5.M2 War with Mexico, 1845-1848
	Cf. E470.2+ Civil War general military operations
	Cf. E471+ Civil War campaigns and battles
	Cf. E512+ Civil War, 1861-1865 (General)
	Cf. E566+ As a Confederate state
	Cf. F189.B1+ Baltimore Riot, 1812
186	1865-1950
	Including Reconstruction, 1865-1877
	Biography: Aloysius Leo Knott, Charles Edward Phelps
	Cf. D570.85.M3+ World War I, 1914-1918
	Cf. D769.85.M3+ World War II, 1939-1945
	1951-
186.2	General works
	Biography
186.3	Collective
186.35.A-Z	Individual, A-Z
	Subarrange each by Table F5
186.9	Western Maryland
187.A-Z	Regions, counties, etc., A-Z
187.A15	Counties
187.A16	Mountains
187.A17	Rivers
187.A18	Lakes
187.A19	Islands
187.A4	Allegany County
187.A6	Anne Arundel County
	Including Severn River and Valley, Saint Anne's Parish, Saint James' Parish
	Assateague Island National Seashore see F187.W7
187.B2	Baltimore County
	Including Patapsco Neck and River, Hampton National Historic Site
	Blackwater River and Valley see F187.D6
187.B7	Boundaries
	Cf. F157.B7 Pennsylvania boundary; Mason and Dixon's line
	Cf. F202.B7 District of Columbia boundary

	Maryland
	Regions, counties, etc., A-Z -- Continued
187.C15	Calvert County
	Including Christ Church Parish, Solomons Island
187.C2	Caroline County
187.C25	Carroll County
	Catoctin Mountain see F187.F8
187.C3	Cecil County
	Including Saint Mary Anne's Parish, Bohemia Manor, Worwell Manor
187.C4	Charles County
187.C47	Chesapeake and Ohio Canal area
187.C5	Chesapeake Bay Region
	Class here general works on the Chesapeake Bay Region, as well as works limited to the part located in Maryland
	Including Kent Island, Magothy River and Valley, Smith Island
	For works limited to the part of the Chesapeake Bay Region located in Virginia see F232.C43
	Cf. F187.E2 Eastern Shore, Md.
	Cf. F232.E2 Eastern Shore, Va.
187.C6	Cobb Island
187.D6	Dorchester County
	Including Blackwater River and Valley, Elliott Island, Hooper Islands
187.E2	Eastern Shore of Maryland. Delmarva Peninsula
	Including Pocomoke River
	Elliott Island see F187.D6
187.F8	Frederick County
	Including Catoctin Mountain, Prince George's Parish, Sugar Loaf Mountain
187.G2	Garrett County
	Great Falls of the Potomac see F187.M7
187.G89	Gwynns Falls Watershed
	Hampton National Historic Site see F187.B2
187.H2	Harford County
	Including Deer Creek, Saint George's Parish
	Hooper Islands see F187.D6
187.H8	Howard County
187.K3	Kent County
	Including Chester Parish
	Kent Island see F187.C5
	Magothy River and Valley see F187.C5
	Maryland Heights see F187.W3
	Mason and Dixon's line see F157.B7
187.M7	Montgomery County
	Including Great Falls of the Potomac, Prince George's Parish

F1-975

	Maryland
	Regions, counties, etc., A-Z -- Continued
187.N35	Nanticoke River and Valley

Class here works limited to the part of the Nanticoke River
and Valley located in Maryland

For general works on the Nanticoke River and Valley,
as well as works limited to the part located in
Delaware see F172.N35

187.O27   Octoraro Creek and Valley

Class here works limited to the part of the Octoraro Creek
and Valley located in Maryland

For general works on the Octoraro Creek and Valley,
as well as works limited to the part located in
Pennsylvania see F157.O26

Patapsco Neck and River see F187.B2

187.P38   Patuxent River and Valley

187.P56   Piscataway Park

Pocomoke River see F187.E2

187.P8   Potomac River and Valley

Class here general works on the Potomac River and Valley,
as well as works limited to the part located in Maryland

For Great Falls see F187.M7

For works limited to the part of the Potomac River and
Valley located in Washington, D.C. see F202.P8

For works limited to the part of the Potomac River and
Valley located in Virginia see F232.P8

For works limited to the part of the Potomac River and
Valley located in West Virginia see F247.P8

187.P9   Prince Georges County

Including King George's Parish, Queen Anne's Parish

187.Q3   Queen Annes County

Saint Catherine Island (Saint Mary's County) see F187.S2

187.S2   Saint Marys County

Including Saint Catherine Island

Severn River and Valley see F187.A6

Smith Island see F187.C5

Solomons Island see F187.C15

187.S7   Somerset County

Sugar Loaf Mountain see F187.F8

187.S8   Susquehanna River and Valley

Class here works limited to the part of the Susquehanna
River and Valley located in Maryland

For works limited to the part of the Susquehanna River
and Valley located in New York State see F127.S96

For general works on the Susquehanna River and
Valley, as well as works limited to the part located
in Pennsylvania see F157.S8

Maryland

Regions, counties, etc., A-Z -- Continued

187.T2   Talbot County
187.W3   Washington County
                    Including Antietam Creek, Conococheague Creek and Valley,
                        Md., Maryland Heights
                    Cf. F157.F8 Conococheague Creek and Valley,
                        Pennsylvania
187.W5   Wicomico County
187.W7   Worcester County
                    Including Assateague Island National Seashore
187.Y68   Youghiogheny River and Valley
                    Class here works limited to the part of the Youghiogheny
                        River and Valley located in Maryland
                    For general works on the Youghiogheny River and
                        Valley, as well as works limited to the part located
                        in Pennsylvania see F157.Y72
                    For works limited to the part of the Youghiogheny River
                        and Valley located in West Virginia see F247.Y68

F1-975

189.A-Z   Cities, towns, etc., A-Z
                    e.g.
189.A6-.A69   Annapolis (Table F2)
189.B1-.B19   Baltimore (Table F2)
                Elements in the population
190.A1   General works
190.A2-Z   Individual elements
                    For a list of racial, ethnic, and religious elements (with
                        Cutter numbers) see E184.A+
                District of Columbia. Washington
                    Historical note from the second edition (1913) of Class F:
                        "Cessions authorized by Maryland and Virginia 1788-89.
                        District located under acts of Congress 1790-1791, and
                        established by proclamation in latter year. In 1801 it was
                        divided into two counties. Washington and Alexandria,
                        separated by the Potomac River, 1846 Alexandria County
                        was retroceded to Virginia. Before 1871 there was no general
                        government for the District. Georgetown was already a city
                        when ceded by Maryland, and Washington received a
                        municipal charter in 1802. The rural portions of the District
                        were under county governments at the head of which were
                        Levy courts. In 1871 the city charters were revoked and the
                        county government abolished, and the entire District
                        consolidated under a governor and Legislative assembly. In
                        1874 three temporary commissioners were substituted, and
                        1878 came the reorganization in present form, with two
                        civilian and one engineer commissioner."
191   Periodicals. Societies. Collections

District of Columbia. Washington -- Continued

191.5	Museums. Exhibitions, exhibits
192	Gazetteers. Dictionaries. Geographic names
192.3	Guidebooks
193	Biography (Collective). Genealogy (Collective)
193.2	Historiography
	Historians see E175.5.A+
193.5	Study and teaching
194	General works. Histories
194.3	Juvenile works
194.5	Pamphlets, addresses, essays, etc.
194.6	Anecdotes, legends, pageants, etc.
195	Historic monuments. Illustrative material
	Including location of national capital, L'Enfant and his plan, retrocession
195.5	Antiquities (Non-Indian)
196	Political and social life
	By period
	Including Inauguration ceremonies, 1801-
197	Early to 1815
	Cf. E356.W3 Capture by the British, 1814
198	1815-1878
	Including biography: William Albert Bradley, Joseph Gales, Walter Lenox, Alexander Robey Shepherd, etc.
	Cf. E396 Explosion of frigate Princeton, 1844
	Cf. E409.5.D6 War with Mexico, 1845-1848
	Cf. E470.2+ Civil War general military operations
	Cf. E471+ Civil War campaigns and battles
	Cf. E501+ Civil War, 1861-1865 (General)
	Cf. F195 Retrocession of Alexandria County to Virginia, 1846
199	1878-1950
	Including Bonus Expeditionary Force, 1932, 1933
	Cf. D570.85.D6 World War I, 1914-1918
	Cf. D769.85.D6 World War II, 1939-1945
	1951-1980
200	General works
	Biography and memoirs
200.2	Collective
200.3.A-Z	Individual, A-Z
	Subarrange each by Table F5
	1981-
201	General works
	Biography and memoirs
201.2	Collective
201.3.A-Z	Individual, A-Z
	Subarrange each by Table F5

District of Columbia. Washington -- Continued

202.A-Z	Regions, suburbs, etc., A-Z
202.A5	Anacostia River and Valley
202.B7	Boundaries
	Cf. F195 Retrocession of Alexandria County to Virginia
202.B8	Brightwood
202.B9	Brookland
	For West Brookland see F202.W5
202.C2	Capitol Hill
202.C46	Chinatown
202.C6	Columbia Heights
202.F64	Foggy Bottom
202.G3	Georgetown
202.L4	Le Droit Park
202.M9	Mount Pleasant
202.N5	Northeast Washington
202.N7	Northwest Washington
202.P8	Potomac River and Valley
	Class here works limited to the part of the Potomac River and Valley located in Washington, D.C.
	For general works on the Potomac River and Valley, as well as works limited to the part located in Maryland see F187.P8
	For works limited to the part of the Potomac River and Valley located in Virginia see F232.P8
	For works limited to the part of the Potomac River and Valley located in West Virginia see F247.P8
	Cf. F203.3 Washington Harbor
202.S6	Southeast Washington
202.S7	Southwest Washington
202.T4	Temple Heights
202.T43	Tenleytown
	Theodore Roosevelt (Analostan) Island see F203.4.T5
202.W5	West Brookland
203	Localities, etc.
203.1.A-Z	Cemeteries
	e.g.
	Cf. RA626+ Management, laying-out, etc., of cemeteries
203.1.A1	General works
	Arlington National Cemetery see F234.A7
203.1.C7	Congressional Cemetery
203.1.G5	Glenwood Cemetery
203.1.O12	Oak Hill Cemetery
203.2.A-Z	Churches
	e.g.
	For religious aspects see BX1+

F1-975

	District of Columbia. Washington
	Localities, etc.
	Churches -- Continued
203.2.A1	General works
203.2.N4	New York Avenue Presbyterian Church
203.2.S14	Saint John's Church, Georgetown
203.3	Harbor
203.35	Hotels, taverns, etc.
203.4.A-Z	Monuments. Statues. Memorials
	e.g.
203.4.A1	General works
	Cf. F204.C2 The Capitol, Statuary Hall
203.4.B7	Braddock's Rock
203.4.C7	Columbus Monument
203.4.E6	Ericsson Monument
203.4.G2	Garfield Statue
203.4.G7	Grant Memorial
203.4.J4	Jefferson Memorial
203.4.L73	Lincoln Memorial
203.4.M5	Meade Monument
203.4.T5	Theodore Roosevelt Island
203.4.W3	Washington Monument
203.5.A-Z	Parks. Squares. Circles
	e.g.
203.5.A1	General works
203.5.C2	Capitol Grounds
203.5.L2	Lafayette Park
203.5.M2	The Mall
203.5.P86	Potomac Park
203.5.R6	Rock Creek Park
203.7.A-Z	Streets. Bridges. Railroads
	e.g.
203.7.A1	General works
203.7.A6	Arlington Memorial Bridge
203.7.C7	Constitution Avenue
203.7.F7	Fourteenth Street
203.7.L8	Long Bridge
203.7.P4	Pennsylvania Avenue
203.7.S6	Sixteenth Street
203.9	Wards
204.A-Z	Buildings
	e.g.
204.A1	General works
204.B5	Blair House
204.C2	Capitol
204.C3	Cathedral of St. Peter and Paul
204.C5	City Hall

District of Columbia. Washington
  Buildings -- Continued

204.D43	Department of Commerce Building
204.F6	Ford Theatre
204.H8	House Office Building
204.M5	Memorial Continental Hall
204.N23	National Theatre
204.O2	Octagon House
204.P47	Petersen House
204.S9	Supreme Court Building
204.U5	Union Railroad Station
204.W5	White House

  Elements in the population

205.A1	General works
205.A2-Z	Individual elements

      For a list of racial, ethnic, and religious elements (with Cutter numbers) see E184.A+

The South. South Atlantic States

F1-975

  Including region south of Mason and Dixon's line and Ohio River
  Cf. E441+ Slavery in the United States

206	Periodicals. Societies. Collections
206.5	Museums. Exhibitions, exhibits
207	Gazetteers. Dictionaries. Geographic names
207.3	Guidebooks
207.7	Dictionaries and encyclopedias of history
208	Biography (Collective). Genealogy (Collective)
208.2	Historiography

    Historians see E175.5.A+

208.5	Study and teaching
209	General works. Histories
209.3	Juvenile works
209.5	Pamphlets, addresses, essays, etc.
209.6	Anecdotes, legends, pageants, etc.
209.8	Geography
210	Historic monuments (General). Illustrative material

    Including life and conditions of Appalachian people (General)

211	Antiquities (Non-Indian)
	By period
212	Early to 1775

    Cf. F229 Early grants of Virginia, Raleigh's colonies, etc.

213	1775-1865

    Including plantation life
    Cf. E230+ Campaigns of the Revolution
    Cf. E423 Southern Convention, Nashville, 1850
    Cf. E441+ Slavery

	The South. South Atlantic States
	By period
	1775-1865 -- Continued
214	Period of the Civil War
	Including description and travel
	Cf. E468+ Civil War, 1861-1865 (General)
	Cf. E482+ Confederate States of America
215	1865-1951
216	1865-1877. Reconstruction
	Including northern societies formed to ameliorate conditions in the South
	Cf. E668 Histories of reconstruction
216.2	1951-
217.A-Z	Regions, A-Z
217.A15	Counties
217.A16	Mountains
217.A17	Rivers
217.A18	Lakes
217.A19	Islands
217.A3	Allegheny (Alleghany) Mountains
	For works limited to the part of the Allegheny Mountains in Pennsylvania see F157.A45
217.A65	Appalachian Mountains, Southern
	Atlantic Coast see F106
217.B6	Blue Ridge Mountains
	For works limited to the part of the Blue Ridge Mountain located in North Carolina see F262.B6
	Cf. F232.S48 Shenandoah National Park (Va.)
217.B67	Border States
	Class here works on the border states of the Civil War era, Delaware, Kentucky, Maryland, Missouri, and West Virginia, treated collectively
	Chesapeake Bay region see F187.C5
217.C45	Chattooga River and Valley
	Gulf Coast see F296
217.N37	Natchez Trace
	Ohio River and Valley see F516+
	Old Southwest, Lower Mississippi Valley see F396
	Pickwick Landing Reservoir see F217.T3
217.P53	Piedmont Region
	Potomac River and Valley see F187.P8

The South. South Atlantic States
Regions, A-Z -- Continued

217.T3   Tennessee River and Valley
                   Including Pickwick Landing Reservoir
                   For works limited to the part of the Tennessee River
                      and Valley located in Alabama see F332.T2
                   For works limited to the part of the Tennessee River
                      and Valley located in Tennessee see F443.T3
                   For works limited to the part of the Tennessee River
                      and Valley located in Kentucky see F457.T3

217.W57   Wiregrass Country
                Elements in the population
220.A1   General works
220.A2-Z   Individual elements, A-Z
                   For a list of racial, ethnic, and religious elements (with
                      Cutter numbers) see E184.A+

                Virginia

F1-975

                   Historical note from the second edition (1913) of Class F: "Name
                      first applied in the reign of Queen Elizabeth to the region
                      extending indefinitely northward from Florida. First attempted
                      settlement was that of Raleigh under his patent of 1584.
                      Virginia was defined under King James' 1st, 2d and 3d
                      charters 1606-1612. The later Pa., Md., and Carolina charters
                      took off large sections of land already given to Virginia. The
                      Quebec act of 1774 cut off her western territory north of the
                      Ohio River until it was won back by G. R. Clark during the
                      revolution. At the close of that war Great Britain abandoned
                      her claim to that region. Others of the states had conflicting
                      charter rights, all of which were eventually given up to the IT.
                      S. Virginia surrendered the territory northwest of the Ohio
                      1784, and that south of the same river in 1789 (in addition to
                      relinquishing in 1789 claims to land in southwest Pa.). While
                      the civil war was in progress, a Union government with capital
                      at Alexandria was recognized by the IT. S. and that part of
                      the state held by United States troops. West Virginia was lost
                      to Va. during the war, that section of the state declaring
                      against secession."

221   Periodicals. Societies. Collections
223   Museums. Exhibitions, exhibits
224   Gazetteers. Dictionaries. Geographic names
224.3   Guidebooks
225   Biography (Collective). Genealogy (Collective)
225.2   Historiography
                   Historians see E175.5.A+
225.5   Study and teaching
226   General works. Histories
226.3   Juvenile works

Virginia -- Continued

226.5	Pamphlets, addresses, essays, etc.
226.6	Anecdotes, legends, pageants, etc.
227	Historic monuments (General). Illustrative material
228	Antiquities (Non-Indian)
	By period
229	Early to 1775

Including Raleigh's explorations and colonies, 1584-1590; Virginia Company of London; Jamestown settlement; Indian massacres; Bacon's Rebellion, 1676; the Parsons' Cause, 1763

Including biography: William Claiborne, Virginia Dare, Nicolas Martiau, John Smith, Alexander Spotswood, etc.

Cf. E83.759 Cherokee War, 1759-1761

Cf. E83.76 Pontiac's Conspiracy, 1763-1765

Cf. E83.77 Dunmore's War, 1774; Battle of Point Pleasant

Cf. E99.P85 Pocahontas

Cf. E199 French and Indian War, 1755-1763

Cf. F517 Explorations in the Ohio Valley

230	1775-1865

Including biography: Archibald Cary, John Floyd, Edmund Pendleton, John Howe Peyton, Edmund Ruffin, etc.

For Kentucky County and District see F454

Cf. E230+ The Revolution, Military operations and battles

Cf. E234 Clark's conquest of the Northwest

Cf. E263.V8 Virginia in the Revolution (General)

Cf. E309 Cession of territory north of Ohio River

Cf. E328 Virginia Resolutions, 1798

Cf. E355+ War of 1812, Military operations and battles

Cf. E359.5.V8 War of 1812 (General)

Cf. E451 John Brown at Harper's Ferry

Cf. E471+ Civil War campaigns and battles

Cf. E534+ Civil War, 1861-1865 (General)

Cf. E581.1+ Civil War, 1861-1865 (General)

Cf. F157.W5 Relinquishment of claims in southwestern Pennsylvania

Cf. F232.S7 Nat Turner's Insurrection, 1831

Cf. F241 Separation of West Virginia

For Kentucky County and District see F454

Cf. F483 Cession of territory north of the Ohio River

231	1865-1950. Reconstruction

Biography: William Mahone, John Edward Massey

Cf. D570.85.V8+ World War I, 1914-1918

Cf. D769.85.V8+ World War II, 1939-1945

Cf. F241 Controversies with West Virginia

	Virginia
	By period -- Continued
231.2	1951-
	Biography
231.3.A2	Collective
231.3.A3-Z	Individual, A-Z
	Subarrange each by Table F5
231.9	Southwest Virginia
232.A-Z	Regions, counties, etc., A-Z
232.A15	Counties
232.A16	Mountains
232.A17	Rivers
232.A18	Lakes
232.A19	Islands
232.A2	Accomac (Accomack) County
	Including Chincoteague Island
	Cf. F232.E2 Eastern Shore of Virginia
232.A3	Albemarle County
232.A35	Albemarle Parish
232.A4	Alexandria County (To June 6, 1920). Arlington County
	(Since June 6, 1920)
	For Retrocession from the District of Columbia see
	F195
	Cf. F202.B7 District of Columbia boundary
232.A5	Alleghany County
232.A54	Amelia County
232.A55	Amherst County
232.A6	Appomattox County
	Arlington Co. see F232.A4
	Arlington National Cemetery see F234.A7
	Assateague Island National Seashore see F187.W7
232.A9	Augusta County
	Including Weyer's (Wier's) Cave
	Cf. F157.W5 West Augusta District and boundary
	disputes with Pennsylvania
232.B24	Back Creek and Valley
	Class here general works on Back Creek and Valley, as well
	as works limited to the part located in Virginia
	For works limited to the part of Back Creek and Valley
	located in West Virginia see F247.B14
232.B3	Bath County
232.B4	Bedford County
	Blacks Run and Valley see F232.R7
232.B5	Bland County
232.B55	Blissland (Blisland) Parish
232.B6	Botetourt County

F1-975

	Virginia
	Regions, counties, etc., A-Z -- Continued
232.B7	Boundaries
	For Mason and Dixon's line see F157.B7
	For Virginia's claims in southwestern Pennsylvania see F157.W5
	Cf. F187.B7 Maryland boundary
	Cf. F202.B7 District of Columbia boundary
232.B8	Bristol Parish
	Brocks Gap see F232.R7
232.B9	Brunswick County
232.B94	Buchanan County
232.B96	Buckingham County
	Burkes Garden Basin see F232.T2
	Cabell Co. see F247.C2
232.C15	Campbell County
	Including Timber Lake
232.C2	Caroline County
232.C27	Carroll County
	Cedar Creek and Belle Grove National Historical Park see F232.S5
232.C3	Charles City County
232.C4	Charlotte County
232.C43	Chesapeake Bay Region
	Class here works limited to the part of the Chesapeake Bay Region located in Virginia
	Including Governor's Land Archaeological District
	For general works on the Chesapeake Bay Region, as well as works limited to the part located in Maryland see F187.C5
232.C52	Chesterfield County
232.C54	Chickahominy River and Valley
	Chincoteague Island see F232.A2
	Clark Mountain see F232.O6
232.C59	Clarke County
	Including Cunningham Chapel Parish, Frederick Parish
232.C65	Clinch River and Valley
	Class here general works on the Clinch River and Valley, as well as works limited to the part located in Virginia
	For works limited to the part of the Clinch River and Valley located in Tennessee see F443.C57
232.C7	Colonial National Historical Park
232.C8	Craig County
232.C9	Culpepper County
	Cf. F232.S2 Saint Mark's Parish
232.C93	Cumberland County
232.C94	Cumberland Parish

Virginia
Regions, counties, etc., A-Z -- Continued
Dean Mountain see F232.S48
Delmarva Peninsula see F187.E2

232.D2	Dickenson County
232.D6	Dinwiddie County
232.D7	Dismal Swamp. Lake Drummond

Class here general works on the Dismal Swamp, as well as
works limited to the part located in Virginia
For works limited to the part of the Dismal Swamp
located in North Carolina see F262.D7

232.E2	Eastern Shore of Virginia

Cf. F187.E2 Maryland

232.E5	Elizabeth City County
232.E6	Elizabeth City Parish
232.E62	Elizabeth River and Valley

Endless Caverns see F232.S47

232.E7	Essex County

Including Rappahannock Co. (1656-1692)

232.F2	Fairfax County

Including Great Falls Park, Fort Hunt Park

232.F3	Fauquier County
232.F38	Fincastle County
232.F4	Floyd County
232.F6	Fluvanna County

Fort Hunt Park see F232.F2

232.F7	Franklin County
232.F75	Frederick County

Frederick Parish see F232.C59

232.F76	Fredericksville Parrish
232.G38	George Washington Memorial Parkway. Mount Vernon Memorial Highway
232.G4	Giles County

Including Mountain Lake

232.G6	Gloucester County

Cf. F232.K54 Kingston Parish
Cf. F232.P45 Petsworth Parish

232.G65	Goochland County

Governor's Land Archaeological District see F232.C43

232.G7	Grayson County

Great Falls of the Potomac see F187.M7
Great Falls Park see F232.F2

232.G8	Greene County
232.G85	Greensville County

Gwynn Island see F232.M3

232.H17	Halifax County
232.H2	Hamilton Parish

F1-975

Virginia
   Regions, counties, etc., A-Z -- Continued

232.H23	Hampton Roads
	Cf. F232.J2 James River and Valley
232.H3	Hanover County
232.H4	Henrico County
232.H5	Henrico Parish
232.H6	Henry County
232.H8	Highland County
	Holmans Creek see F232.S47
	Hungry Mother Creek and Valley see F232.S6
232.I8	Isle of Wight County
232.J13	Jackson River and Valley
	Class here general works on the Jackson River and Valley, as well as works limited to the part located in Virginia
	For works limited to the part of the Jackson River and Valley located in West Virginia see F247.J22
232.J15	James City County
	Cf. F232.B55 Blissland Parish
232.J2	James River and Valley
	Including Mulberry Island
	Cf. F232.H23 Hampton Roads
	Jones Mountain see F232.S48
	Kentucky County and District see F454
232.K4	King and Queen County
232.K45	King George County
232.K5	King William County
232.K54	Kingston Parish
232.L2	Lancaster County
232.L4	Lee County
	Lewis Mountain see F232.S48
232.L8	Loudoun County
	Including Lowes area
232.L85	Louisa County
232.L9	Lunenburg County
	Luray Caverns see F232.P2
232.M2	Madison County
232.M3	Mathews County
	Including Gwynn Island
	Cf. F232.K54 Kingston Parish
232.M4	Mecklenburg County
232.M6	Middlesex County
	Monongalia Co. see F247.M7
232.M7	Montgomery County
	Mount Vernon Memorial Highway see F232.G38
	Mulberry Island see F232.J2
232.N2	Nansemond County

Virginia

Regions, counties, etc., A-Z -- Continued

Natural Bridge see F232.R68

Natural Tunnel, Natural Tunnel State Park see F232.S3

232.N25	Nelson County
	Including Tye River and Valley
232.N3	New Kent County
	Including Saint Peter's Parish
	Cf. F232.B55 Blissland Parish

New Market Endless Caverns see F232.S47

232.N5   New River and Valley

               Class here works limited to the part of the New River and
                   Valley located in Virginia

               For general works on the New River and Valley, as well
                   as works limited to the part located in West Virginia
                   see F247.N5

               For works limited to the part of the New River and
                   Valley located in North Carolina see F262.N6

F1-975

232.N8	Norfolk County
232.N85	Northampton County
	Cf. F232.E2 Eastern Shore of Virginia
232.N86	Northern Neck
232.N867	Northern Virginia
232.N87	Northumberland County
232.N9	Nottoway County
	Ohio Co. see F247.O3
232.O6	Orange County
	Including Clark Mountain
232.O85	Otter, Peaks of
232.O9	Overwharton Parish
232.P2	Page County
	Including Luray Caverns
232.P25	Pamunkey River and Valley
232.P3	Patrick County
232.P45	Petsworth Parish
232.P5	Piedmont
232.P7	Pittsylvania County

Virginia

Regions, counties, etc., A-Z -- Continued

232.P8	Potomac River and Valley
	Class here works limited to the part of the Potomac River and Valley located in Virginia
	For Great Falls see F187.M7
	For general works on the Potomac River and Valley, as well as works limited to the part located in Maryland see F187.P8
	For works limited to the part of the Potomac River and Valley located in Washington, D.C. see F202.P8
	For works limited to the part of the Potomac River and Valley located in West Virginia see F247.P8
232.P816	Powell River and Valley
	Class here general works on the Powell River and Valley, as well as works limited to the part located in Virginia
	For works limited to the part of the Powell River and Valley located in Tennessee see F443.P78
232.P82	Powhatan County
232.P83	Prince Edward County
232.P85	Prince George County
232.P86	Prince William County
	Including Prince William Forest Park
232.P87	Princess Anne County
	Including Lynnhaven Parish
232.P9	Pulaski County
232.R18	Rapidan River and Valley
232.R2	Rappahannock County
	Cf. F232.E7 Rappahannock Co. (1656-1692)
232.R4	Richmond County
232.R6	Roanoke County
232.R63	Roanoke River and Valley
	Class here works limited to the part of the Roanoke River and Valley located in Virginia
	For general works on the Roanoke River and Valley, as well as works limited to the part located in North Carolina see F262.R5
232.R68	Rockbridge County
	Including Natural Bridge
232.R7	Rockingham County
	Including Blacks Run and Valley, Brocks Gap
232.R9	Russell County
232.S15	Saint George's Parish
232.S2	Saint Mark's Parish
232.S3	Scott County
	Including Natural Tunnel, Natural Tunnel State Park

Virginia

Regions, counties, etc., A-Z -- Continued

232.S47	Shenandoah County
	Including Endless Caverns, Holmans Creek
232.S48	Shenandoah National Park
	Including Dean Mountain, Jones Mountain, Lewis Mountain
232.S5	Shenandoah River and Valley
	Class here general works on the Shenandoah River and Valley, as well as works limited to the part located in Virginia
	For individual caves, see the county
	For works limited to the part of the Shenandoah River and Valley located in West Virginia see F247.S5
232.S6	Smyth County
	Including Hungry Mother Creek and Valley
232.S7	Southampton County
	Including Southampton Insurrection, 1831 (Nat Turner's Insurrection, Turner's Negro Insurrection)
232.S8	Spotsylvania County
	Cf. F232.S15 Saint George's Parish
232.S86	Stafford County
	Cf. F232.O9 Overwharton Parish
232.S9	Surry County
	Cf. F232.A35 Albemarle Parish
232.S96	Sussex County
	Cf. F232.A35 Albemarle Parish
232.T15	Tangier Island
232.T2	Tazewell County
	Including Burkes Garden Basin
232.T54	Tidewater Region
	Timber Lake see F232.C15
232.T8	Truro Parish
	Tye River and Valley see F232.N25
	Valley of Virginia see F232.S5
232.W25	Warren County
232.W27	Warwick County
	Including Lake Maury
232.W3	Washington County
	West Augusta District see F157.W5
232.W4	Westmoreland County
232.W8	Wise County
	Wood Co. see F247.W8
232.W9	Wythe County
	Yohogania Co. see F157.W5
232.Y6	York County
234.A-Z	Cities, towns, etc., A-Z
	e.g.

F1-975

	Virginia
	Cities, towns, etc., A-Z -- Continued
234.A3	Alexandria
234.A7	Arlington
	Including Arlington National Cemetery, Lee Mansion
234.F8	Fredericksburg
234.J3	Jamestown
	Monticello see E332.74
	Mount Vernon see E312.5
234.N48	New Market
	For Endless Caverns see F232.S47
234.N8	Norfolk
234.R5-.R59	Richmond (Table F2)
234.S865	Stratford Hall
234.W7	Williamsburg
234.Y6	Yorktown
	Cf. F232.C7 Colonial National Historical Park
	Elements in the population
235.A1	General works
235 A2-7	Individual elements
	For a list of racial, ethnic, and religious elements (with Cutter numbers) see E184.A+
	West Virginia
	Historical note from the second edition (1913) of Class F: "Those counties of Virginia which refused to secede in 1861. Admitted as a state June 19,1863."
236	Periodicals. Societies. Collections
238	Museums. Exhibitions, exhibits
239	Gazetteers. Dictionaries. Geographic names
239.3	Guidebooks
240	Biography (Collective). Genealogy (Collective)
240.2	Historiography
	Historians see E175.5.A+
240.5	Study and teaching

West Virginia -- Continued

241	General works. Histories
	Including by period (early to 1950) as well as general
	Including controversies between Virginia and West Virginia growing out of separation; admission as a state, June 20, 1863
	Biography: Anne Bailey
	For 1951 and later see F245
	Cf. D570.85.W4+ World War I, 1914-1918
	Cf. D769.85.W4+ World War II, 1939-1945
	Cf. E470.3 Civil War campaigns and battles
	Cf. E471+ Civil War campaigns and battles
	Cf. E534+ Union government of Virginia
	Cf. E536+ West Virginia in the Civil War and organization of the state (General)
	Cf. E582+ Confederate history
	Cf. F229 Virginia (Early to 1865)
	Cf. F230 Virginia (Early to 1865)
241.3	Juvenile works
241.5	Pamphlets, addresses, essays, etc.
241.6	Anecdotes, legends, pageants, etc.
242	Historic monuments (General). Illustrative material
243	Antiquities (Non-Indian)
	By period
	Early to 1950 see F229; F230; F241
	1951-
245	General works
	Biography
245.4	Collective
245.42.A-Z	Individual, A-Z
	Subarrange each by Table F5
247.A-Z	Regions, counties, etc., A-Z
247.A15	Counties
247.A16	Mountains
247.A17	Rivers
247.A18	Lakes
247.A19	Islands
	Babcock State Park see F247.F2
247.B14	Back Creek and Valley
	Class here works limited to the part of Back Creek and Valley located in West Virginia
	For general works on Back Creek and Valley, as well as works limited to the part located in Virginia see F232.B24
247.B2	Barbour County
247.B5	Berkeley County
247.B54	Big Coal River and Valley

F1-975

West Virginia
>Regions, counties, etc., A-Z -- Continued

247.B55	Birch River and Valley
247.B56	Blennerhassett Island
247.B6	Boone County
	Including Turtle Creek and Valley
247.B7	Boundaries
	Cf. F187.B7 Maryland and old Maryland-Virginia
	boundary
	Cf. F497.B7 Ohio boundary
247.B8	Braxton County
247.B9	Brooke County
247.C2	Cabell County
247.C24	Cacapon River and Valley
247.C3	Calhoun County
	Campbell's Creek and Valley see F247.K2
	Canaan Valley see F247.T8
	Cheat Mountain see F247.R2
247.C5	Clay County
247.D6	Doddridge County
247.D79	Dry Fork River and region
247.E4	Elk River and Valley
247.F2	Fayette County
	Including Babcock State Park
247.G5	Gilmer County
247.G67	Grant County
	Great Kanawha River and Valley see F247.K3
247.G7	Greenbrier County
247.G73	Greenbrier River Trail
247.H17	Hacker's Creek and Valley
247.H2	Hampshire County
247.H24	Hancock County
	Including Tomlinson Run, Tomlinson Run State Park
247.H28	Hardy County
247.H3	Harrison County
	Indian Creek and Valley (Ritchie County) see F247.R6
247.J2	Jackson County
247.J22	Jackson River and Valley
	Class here works limited to the part of the Jackson River and
	Valley located in West Virginia
	For general works on the Jackson River and Valley, as
	well as works limited to the part located in Virginia
	see F232.J13
247.J4	Jefferson County
247.K2	Kanawha County
	Including Campbell's Creek and Valley
247.K3	Kanawha River and Valley

West Virginia
Regions, counties, etc., A-Z -- Continued

247.L6	Lewis County
247.L7	Lincoln County
247.L8	Logan County
247.M2	McDowell County
247.M26	Marion County
247.M3	Marshall County
247.M4	Mason County
247.M5	Mercer County
247.M55	Mineral County
247.M57	Mingo County
247.M59	Monongahela National Forest
247.M6	Monongahela River and Valley

Class here works limited to the part of the Monongahela River
and Valley located in West Virginia
For general works on the Monongahela River and
Valley, as well as works limited to the part located
in Pennsylvania see F157.M58

F1-975

247.M7	Monongalia County

Cf. F157.W5 West Augusta District and Virginia
boundary disputes with Pennsylvania

247.M75	Monroe County
247.M8	Morgan County
247.N5	New River and Valley

Class here general works on the New River and Valley, as
well as works limited to the part located in West Virginia
For works limited to the part of the New River and
Valley located in Virginia see F232.N5
For works limited to the part of the New River and
Valley located in North Carolina see F262.N6

247.N6	Nicholas County
247.O3	Ohio County

Cf. F157.W5 West Augusta District and Virginia
boundary disputes with Pennsylvania

247.O4	Ohio River and Valley, W. Va.

Cf. F516+ General

247.P3	Pendleton County
247.P5	Pleasants County
247.P7	Pocahontas County

West Virginia

Regions, counties, etc., A-Z -- Continued

247.P8	Potomac River and Valley
	Class here works limited to the part of the Potomac River and Valley located in West Virginia
	For general works on the Potomac River and Valley, as well as works limited to the part located in Maryland see F187.P8
	For works limited to the part of the Potomac River and Valley located in Washington, D.C. see F202.P8
	For works limited to the part of the Potomac River and Valley located in Virginia see F232.P8
247.P9	Preston County
247.P95	Putnam County
247.R15	Raleigh County
247.R2	Randolph County
	Including Cave of Dry Fork of Cheat River, Cheat Mountain
247.R6	Ritchie County
	Including Indian Creek and Valley
247.R8	Roane County
247.S5	Shenandoah River and Valley
	Class here works limited to the part of the Shenandoah River and Valley located in West Virginia
	For general works on the Shenandoah River and Valley, as well as works limited to the part located in Virginia see F232.S5
247.S9	Summers County
247.T3	Taylor County
247.T4	Tenmile Creek and Valley
	Tomlinson Run see F247.H24
	Tomlinson Run State Park see F247.H24
247.T8	Tucker County
	Including Canaan Valley
247.T86	Tygart River and Valley
	Turtle Creek and Valley see F247.B6
247.T9	Tyler County
247.U6	Upshur County
247.W3	Wayne County
247.W37	Webster County
247.W5	Wetzel County
247.W6	Wirt County
247.W8	Wood County
247.W9	Wyoming County

West Virginia

Regions, counties, etc., A-Z -- Continued

247.Y68   Youghiogheny River and Valley

Class here works limited to the part of the Youghiogheny River and Valley located in West Virginia

For general works on the Youghiogheny River and Valley, as well as works limited to the part located in Pennsylvania see F157.Y72

For works limited to the part of the Youghiogheny River and Valley located in Maryland see F187.Y68

249.A-Z   Cities, towns, etc., A-Z

e.g.

249.C4   Charleston
249.H2   Harpers Ferry
249.H95   Huntington
249.W5   Wheeling
249.W6   White Sulphur Springs

Elements in the population

250.A1   General works
250.A2-Z   Individual elements

For a list of racial, ethnic, and religious elements (with Cutter numbers) see E184.A+

F1-975

North Carolina

Historical note from the second edition (1913) of Class F: "Within the limits of the present N. C. was planted the first English colony in America, Raleigh's, in 1585 (F 229). The territory comprising the modern Carolinas was all known as Virginia, and formed part of the grant to the Virginia company of London 1606. Not being occupied by the Jamestown settlers, the region was granted in 1629 to Sir Robert Heath under the name of "Caro-lana." No colony was established and the tract between Virginia and the Spanish colony of Florida was re-granted in 1663 as Carolina to a company of proprietors. Settlement was made at once at Albemarle and Clarendon (the Cape Fear region) in N. C, and a few years later at Charleston in S. C. These settlements were so remote from each other that during most of the proprietary period, their governments were separate in fact, though the colony was not divided till about 1712. 1729 the proprietors released their claims to the crown. The western portion of the state was ceded to the U. S. in 1790 and became the state of Tennessee."

251   Periodicals. Societies. Collections
251.5   Museums. Exhibitions, exhibits
252   Gazetteers. Dictionaries. Geographic names
252.3   Guidebooks
253   Biography (Collective). Genealogy (Collective)

North Carolina -- Continued

253.2	Historiography
	Historians see E175.5.A+
253.5	Study and teaching
254	General works. Histories
254.3	Juvenile works
254.5	Pamphlets, addresses, essays, etc.
254.6	Anecdotes, legends, pageants, etc.
254.8	Geography
255	Historic monuments (General). Illustrative material
256	Antiquities (Non-Indian)
	By period
257	Early to 1775

        Including grant of Carolina to eight proprietors, 1663;
            Albemarle and Clarendon settlements; Royal province;
            Regulator Insurrection;, 1766-1771

        Including biography: George Burrington, Sir Richard Everard,
            William Tryon, etc.

        Cf. E83.71 Tuscarora War, 1711-1713

        Cf. E83.759 Cherokee War, 1759-1761

        Cf. E197 Queen Anne's War, 1702-1713

        Cf. F229 Raleigh's Roanoke colonies, 1584-1590

        Cf. F272 Original Carolina grant

        Cf. F314 War with Spaniards of Florida, 1740

258	1775-1865

        Biography: Charles Manley, John Motley Morehead, Thomas
            Ruffin, Benjamin Smith

        Cf. E215.9 Mecklenburg Resolves, 1775

        Cf. E230+ The Revolution, Military operations and
            battles

        Cf. E263.N8 North Carolina in the Revolution (General)

        Cf. E309 North Carolina cessions of 1784 and 1790

        Cf. E359.5.N7 War of 1812

        Cf. E470.6 Civil War general military operations

        Cf. E471+ Civil War campaigns and battles

        Cf. E524+ Civil War, 1861-1865 (General)

        Cf. E573+ Civil War, 1861-1865 (General)

259	1865-1950. Reconstruction

        Biography: Charles Brantley Aycock, William Woods Holden,
            Jonathan Worth

        Cf. D570.85.N8+ World War I, 1914-1918

        Cf. D769.85.N8+ World War II, 1939-1945

        Cf. E726.N8 War of 1898 (Spanish-American War)

	1951-
260	General works
	Biography
260.4	Collective

	North Carolina
	By period
	1951-
	Biography -- Continued
260.42.A-Z	Individual, A-Z
	Subarrange each by Table F5
261	Western North Carolina
262.A-Z	Regions, counties, etc., A-Z
262.A15	Counties
262.A16	Mountains
262.A17	Rivers
262.A18	Lakes
262.A19	Islands
262.A3	Alamance County
262.A33	Albemarle region (Northeast coast region)
262.A4	Alexander County
262.A45	Allegheny County
262.A5	Anson County
262.A7	Ashe County
	Including Pond Mountain
262.A84	Atlantic Coast
262.A9	Avery County
	Including North Toe River and Valley
	Bald Head Island see F262.B9
262.B3	Bald Mountains
	Class here works limited to the part of the Bald Mountains located in North Carolina
	For general works on the Bald Mountains, as well as works limited to the part located in Tennessee see F443.B3
262.B37	Beaufort County
262.B38	Bertie County
	Big Bald Mountain see F262.B3
	Big Pine Creek and Valley see F262.M25
262.B4	Black Mountains
	Including Mount Mitchell
262.B45	Bladen County
262.B6	Blue Ridge Mountains
	Class here works limited to the part of the Blue Ridge Mountains located in North Carolina
	Including Grandfather Mountain
	For general works on the Blue Ridge Mountains see F217.B6
	Bogue Banks see F262.C23
262.B7	Boundaries
	Cf. F232.B7 Virginia boundary
	Cf. F292.B7 Georgia boundary

F1-975

North Carolina

Regions, counties, etc., A-Z -- Continued

262.B89	Broad River and Valley
	Class here works limited to the part of the Broad River and Valley located in North Carolina
	For general works on the Broad River and Valley, as well as works limited to the part located in South Carolina see F277.B73
262.B9	Brunswick County
	Including Cape Fear, Smith Island, Bald Head Island
262.B94	Buncombe County
262.B96	Burke County
262.B97	Bute County
262.C12	Cabarrus County
262.C15	Caldwell County
262.C17	Camden County
	Cape Fear see F262.B9
262.C2	Cape Fear River and Valley
	Cape Hatteras National Seashore see F262.O96
	Cape Lookout National Seashore see F262.C23
262.C23	Carteret County
	Including Bogue Banks, Harkers Island, Portsmouth Island, Cape Lookout National Seashore
	Cashiers Valley see F262.J2
262.C26	Caswell County
262.C28	Catawba County
262.C3	Catawba River and Valley, N.C.
	Cf. F277.C3 South Carolina
	Charlotte and Mecklenburg County see F264.C4
262.C4	Chatham County
262.C43	Cherokee County
	Chimney Rock Park see F262.R9
262.C44	Chowan County
262.C47	Clay County
	Including Matheson Cove
262.C5	Cleveland County
262.C6	Columbus County
262.C8	Craven County
262.C9	Cumberland County
262.C95	Currituck County
262.D2	Dare County
	Cf. F262.R4 Roanoke Island
262.D3	Davidson County
262.D4	Davie County

North Carolina
Regions, counties, etc., A-Z -- Continued

262.D7	Dismal Swamp
	Class here works limited to the part of the Dismal Swamp located in North Carolina
	For general works on the Dismal Swamp, as well as works limited to the part located in Virginia see F232.D7
262.D77	Duplin County
262.D8	Durham County
262.E2	Edgecombe County
262.F7	Forsyth County Wachovia
	Including Tanglewood Park
262.F8	Franklin County
262.F85	French Broad River and Valley
	Class here works limited to the part of the French Broad River and Valley located in North Carolina
	For general works on the French Broad River and Valley, as well as works limited to the part located in Tennessee see F443.F8
262.G2	Gaston County
262.G3	Gates County
	Goose Creek Island see F262.P2
262.G8	Graham County
	Grandfather Mountain see F262.B6
262.G85	Granville County
	Great Smoky Mountains see F443.G7
262.G86	Greene County
262.G9	Guilford County
262.H2	Halifax County
	Harkers Island see F262.C23
262.H3	Harnett County
262.H35	Haywood County
	Including Maggie Valley
	Hazel Creek and Valley see F262.S95
262.H47	Henderson County
262.H5	Hertford County
262.H7	Hoke County
262.H74	Hominy Creek and Valley
262.H9	Hyde County
	Including Ocracoke Island
262.I7	Iredell County
262.J2	Jackson County
	Including Whiteside Cove, Cashiers Valley
262.J6	Johnston County
262.J7	Jones County
262.L4	Lee County

F1-975

North Carolina
Regions, counties, etc., A-Z -- Continued

262.L5	Lenoir County
262.L6	Lincoln County
	Linville Gorge Wilderness see F262.P57
262.L64	Little Laurel Creek and Valley
262.M15	McDowell County
262.M2	Macon County

Including Tellico Creek and Valley

262.M25	Madison County

Including Big Pine Creek and Valley, Shelton Laurel Creek
and Valley

Maggie Valley see F262.H35

262.M3	Martin County

Matheson Cove see F262.C47

262.M4	Mecklenburg County

Mitchell, Mount see F262.B4

262.M5	Mitchell County
262.M6	Montgomery County
262.M7	Moore County
262.N2	Nash County
262.N48	Neuse River and Valley
262.N5	New Hanover County

New River and Valley (Onslow Co.) see F262.O5

262.N6	New River and Valley

Class here works limited to the part of the New River and
Valley located in North Carolina
Including Ingles Ferry
For works limited to the part of the New River and
Valley located in Virginia see F232.N5
For general works on the New River and Valley, as well
as works limited to the part located in West Virginia
see F247.N5

262.N67	Norman, Lake

North Toe River and Valley see F262.A9

262.N7	Northampton County

Ocracoke Island see F262.H9

262.O5	Onslow County

Including New River and Valley, Topsail Island

262.O7	Orange County
262.O96	Outer Banks (General)

Including Cape Hatteras National Seashore

262.P2	Pamlico County

Including Goose Creek Island

262.P25	Pasquotank County

Pee Dee (Pedee) River and Valley see F262.Y2; F277.P3

262.P35	Peltier Creek and Valley

North Carolina
Regions, counties, etc., A-Z -- Continued

262.P37	Pender County
262.P4	Perquimans County
262.P5	Person County
262.P57	Pisgah National Forest
	Including Linville Gorge Wilderness
262.P6	Pitt County
262.P65	Polk County
	Pond Mountain (Ashe County) see F262.A7
	Portsmouth Island see F262.C23
	Raleigh's Roanoke Colonies, 1584-1590 see F229
262.R2	Randolph County
262.R25	Reed Gold Mine State Historic Site
262.R3	Richmond County
262.R39	Roan Mountain
	Class here general works on Roan Mountain, as well as works limited to the part located in North Carolina
	For works limited to the part of Roan Mountain located in Tennessee see F443.R49
262.R4	Roanoke Island
	Including Fort Raleigh National Historic Site
	For Raleigh's Roanoke Colonies, 1584-1590 see F229
262.R5	Roanoke River and Valley
	Class here general works on the Roanoke River and Valley, as well as works limited to the part located in North Carolina
	For works limited to the part of the Roanoke River and Valley located in Virginia see F232.R63
262.R6	Robeson County
262.R7	Rockingham County
262.R8	Rowan County
262.R9	Rutherford County
	Including Chimney Rock Park
262.S3	Sampson County
262.S34	Sandhills
	Class here general works on Sandhills, as well as works limited to the part located in North Carolina
	For works limited to the part of Sandhills located in South Carolina see F277.S27
	For works limited to the part of Sandhills located in Georgia see F292.S25
262.S4	Scotland County
	For Smoky Mountains (The Smokies) see F443.G7
	Shelton Laurel Creek and Valley see F262.M25
	Smith Island see F262.B9
262.S7	Stanly County

F1-975

	North Carolina
	Regions, counties, etc., A-Z -- Continued
262.S8	Stokes County
262.S9	Surry County
262.S95	Swain County
	Including Hazel Creek and Valley
	Tanglewood Park see F262.F7
	Tellico Creek and Valley see F262.M2
	Topsail Island see F262.O5
262.T7	Transylvania County
262.T73	Trent River and Valley
	Tryon Co. (to 1778) see F262.L6; F262.R9
262.T9	Tyrrell County
262.U5	Union County
262.V3	Vance County
262.W18	Waccamaw River and Valley
	Class here works limited to the part of the Waccamaw River and Valley located in North Carolina
	For general works on the Waccamaw River and Valley, as well as works limited to the part located in South Carolina see F277.W33
	Wachovia see F262.F7
262.W2	Wake County
262.W27	Warren County
262.W3	Washington County
262.W34	Watauga County
	For New River and Valley see F262.N6
262.W37	Waxhaws
	Cf. F277.W39 South Carolina
262.W4	Wayne County
	Western North Carolina see F261
	Whiteside Cove see F262.J2
262.W6	Wilkes County
262.W7	Wilson County
262.Y19	Yadkin County
262.Y2	Yadkin (Pee Dee) River and Valley
	Cf. F277.P3 Pee Dee River of South Carolina
262.Y3	Yancey County
264.A-Z	Cities, towns, etc., A-Z
	e.g.
264.A8	Asheville
264.C4	Charlotte
264.R1	Raleigh
264.W8	Winston-Salem
	Elements in the population
265.A1	General works

North Carolina
   Elements in the population -- Continued
265.A2-Z   Individual elements
                     For a list of racial, ethnic, and religious elements (with
                        Cutter numbers) see E184.A+
         South Carolina
                  Historical note from the second edition (1913) of Class F: "Like
                     North Carolina, South Carolina was included within the
                     original grants of Virginia. The whole province of Carolina
                     was granted in 1663 to 8 proprietors. The settlements were
                     so remote from each other that necessarily the governments
                     were separate during most of the proprietary period. About
                     1712 the province was divided, and 1729 the 8 proprietors
                     sold their claims to the crown. Georgia and the territory
                     extending west from it, were taken from South Carolina.
                     Western lands still claimed by the state, consisting of a
                     narrow strip south of Tenn., were granted to the U.S. 1787."

266   Periodicals. Societies. Collections
266.5   Museums. Exhibitions, exhibits

F1-975

267   Gazetteers. Dictionaries. Geographic names
267.3   Guidebooks
268   Biography (Collective). Genealogy (Collective)
268.2   Historiography
                     Historians see E175.5.A+
268.5   Study and teaching
269   General works. Histories
269.3   Juvenile works
269.5   Pamphlets, addresses, essays, etc.
269.6   Anecdotes, legends, pageants, etc.
269.8   Geography
270   Historic monuments (General). Illustrative material
271   Antiquities (Non-Indian)
                  By period
272   Early to 1775
                        Including the "Carolana" grant of 1629; province of Carolina
                           (1663-1712); Charleston settlement; Locke's
                           Fundamental constitutions; Spanish attack from Florida in
                           1680; separation of the two Carolinas
                        Including biography: Eliza (Lucas) Pinckney, etc.
                        Cf. E83.759 Cherokee War, 1759-1761
                        Cf. E197 Queen Anne's War, 1702-1713
                        Cf. F257 North Carolina settlement
                        Cf. F289 Georgia settlement, Montgomery's
                           Margravate of Azilia
                        Cf. F314 Huguenot colony at Port Royal, 1562; St.
                           Augustine Expedition, 1740

South Carolina

By period -- Continued

273 1775-1865

Including dispute with Massachusetts over the latter's African American citizens, 1845; secession

Biography: James Henry Hammond, Thomas Lee, James Louis Petigru, Robert Barnwell Rhett

Cf. E185.93.S7 African Americans in the Sea Islands, Port Royal mission

Cf. E230+ The Revolution, military operations and battles

Cf. E263.S7 South Carolina in the Revolution (General)

Cf. E384.3 Nullification

Cf. E409.5.S7 War with Mexico, 1845-1849

Cf. E470.6 Civil War general military operations

Cf. E471+ Civil War campaigns and battles

Cf. E529+ Civil War, 1861-1865, Union history

Cf. E577+ Civil War, 1861-1865 (General)

Cf. F292.B7 South Carolina's cession of 1787

Cf. HF1754 Tariff of 1828

274 1865-1950. Reconstruction

Including biography: David Henry Chamberlain, Benjamin Franklin Perry, Frederick Adolphus Sawyer, etc.

Cf. D570.85.S6+ World War I, 1914-1918

Cf. D769.85.S6+ World War II, 1939-1945

1951-

275 General works

Biography

275.4 Collective

275.42.A-Z Individual, A-Z

Subarrange each by Table F5

277.A-Z Regions, counties, etc., A-Z

277.A15 Counties

277.A16 Mountains

277.A17 Rivers

277.A18 Lakes

277.A19 Islands

277.A2 Abbeville County

277.A3 Aiken County

277.A4 Allendale County

277.A5 Anderson County

277.A84 Ashley River and Valley

277.A86 Atlantic Coast

277.B2 Bamberg County

277.B25 Barnwell County

	South Carolina
	Regions, counties, etc., A-Z -- Continued
277.B3	Beaufort County Sea Islands, S.C.
	Including Hilton Head Island, Hunting Island, Kiawah Island, Parris Island, Saint Helena Island, Edisto Island, Fripp Island
	Cf. E185.93.S7 African Americans in the Sea Islands District
277.B5	Berkeley County. Craven County
	Including Cooper River, Daniel Island
277.B63	Black River and Valley
277.B7	Boundaries
	For South Carolina cession south of Tennessee see F292.B7
	Cf. F262.B7 North Carolina boundary
277.B73	Broad River and Valley
	Class here general works on the Broad River and Valley, as well as works limited to the part located in South Carolina
	For works limited to the part of the Broad River and Valley located in North Carolina see F262.B89
	Bull Island see F277.C4
	Bullock Creek and Valley see F277.Y6
277.C2	Calhoun County
277.C22	Camden District
	Cape Romain see F277.C4
277.C3	Catawba River and Valley, S.C.
	Cf. F262.C3 North Carolina
277.C4	Charleston County
	Including Folly Island, Wadmalaw Island, Seabrook Island, Hampton Plantation State Park, Tea Farm Park, Jehossee Island, Bull Island, Johns Island, Dewees Island, James Island, Cape Romain
	For Sea Islands, S.C. see F277.B3
277.C5	Cherokee County
277.C55	Chester County
277.C57	Chesterfield County
277.C7	Clarendon County
277.C8	Colleton County
	Including Poco Sabo Plantation
277.C85	Congaree Swamp and Region
	Cooper River see F277.B5
	Craven County see F277.B5
	Daniel Island see F277.B5
277.D2	Darlington County
	Dewees Island see F277.C4
277.D5	Dillon County
277.D6	Dorchester County

F1-975

	South Carolina
	Regions, counties, etc., A-Z -- Continued
277.E2	Edgefield County
	Edisto Island see F277.B3
277.E25	Edisto River and Valley
277.F3	Fairfield County
277.F5	Florence County
	Folly Island see F277.C4
	Fripp Island see F277.B3
277.G35	Georgetown County
	Including Hobcaw Barony, Pawleys Island
277.G6	Greenville County
277.G7	Greenwood County
277.H3	Hampton County
	Hampton Plantation State Park see F277.C4
	Hilton Head Island see F277.B3
	Hobcaw Barony see F277.G35
277.H6	Horry County
	Hunting Island see F277.B3
	James Island see F277.C4
277.J3	Jasper County
	Jehossee Island see F277.C4
277.K3	Kershaw County
	Kiawah Island see F277.B3
277.K5	Kings Mountain National Military Park
277.L2	Lancaster County
277.L3	Laurens County
	Including Rosemont Plantation
277.L4	Lee County
277.L5	Lexington County
277.L94	Lynches Scenic River
277.M15	McCormick County
277.M2	Marion County
277.M3	Marlboro County
277.M87	Murray, Lake, and Region
277.N5	Newberry County Newberry District
277.N6	Ninety-Six (District)
277.O3	Oconee County
277.O5	Orangeburg County
277.O6	Orangeburgh District
	Parris Island see F277.B3
277.P3	Pee Dee region. Pee Dee River and Valley (Great Pedee and Little Pedee Rivers)
	Cf. F262.Y2 North Carolina
277.P35	Pendleton County Pendleton District
277.P5	Pickens County
	Poco Sabo Plantation see F277.C8

	South Carolina
	Regions, counties, etc., A-Z -- Continued
277.P95	Prince Frederick Parish
277.P97	Prince William's Parish
277.R49	Richard B. Russell Lake and Region

Class here works limited to the part of Richard B. Russell Lake and Region located in South Carolina

For general works on Richard B. Russell Lake and Region, as well as works limited to the part located in Georgia see F292.R49

277.R5	Richland County
	Saint Helena Island see F277.B3
277.S2	Saint Mark's Parish
277.S24	Saint Thomas and Saint Denis Parish
277.S26	Saluda County
277.S27	Sandhills

Class here works limited to the part of Sandhills located in South Carolina

For general works on Sandhills, as well as works limited to the part located in North Carolina see F262.S34

For works limited to the part of Sandhills located in Georgia see F292.S25

| 277.S28 | Santee River. Santee River system |
| 277.S3 | Savannah River and Valley |

Class here works limited to the part of the Savannah River and Valley located in South Carolina

Including Argyle Island

For general works on the Savannah River and Valley, as well as works limited to the part located in Georgia see F292.S3

Sea Islands, S.C. see F277.B3

Seabrook Island see F277.C4

277.S7	Spartanburg County
277.S77	Sullivans Island
277.S8	Sumter County
	Tea Farm Park see F277.C4
277.U5	Union County
277.W33	Waccamaw River and Valley

Class here general works on the Waccamaw River and Valley, as well as works limited to the part located in South Carolina

For works limited to the part of the Waccamaw River and Valley located in North Carolina see F262.W18

Wadmalaw Island see F277.C4

| 277.W39 | Waxhaws |

Cf. F262.W37 North Carolina

	South Carolina
	Regions, counties, etc., A-Z -- Continued
277.W7	Williamsburg County
277.Y6	York County
	Including Bullock Creek and Valley
277.Y62	York District
279.A-Z	Cities, towns, etc., A-Z
	e.g.
279.C4-.C49	Charleston (Table F2)
279.C7	Columbia
279.G79	Greenville
279.S7	Spartanburg
	Elements in the population
280.A1	General works
280.A2-Z	Individual elements
	For a list of racial, ethnic, and religious elements (with Cutter numbers) see E184.A+
	Georgia
	Historical note from the second edition (1913) of Class F: "A part of the Carolina grant (1663-1665), but not colonized. 1717 Sir Robert Montgomery obtained from the Proprietors of Carolina a grant between the Savannah and the Altamaha, which was forfeited 3 years later as no settlement was made. In 1732 the tract between the Savannah and Altamaha Rivers was granted by the Crown for 21 years to Trustees. At the expiration of the trust it became a royal province. In 1763 the land between the Altamaha and St. Mary's River and region west to the Mississippi was added to Georgia. In 1802 the state assumed its present form by ceding its western lands to the U. S. and receiving so much of the S. C. cession of 1787 as lay north of its reduced limits."
281	Periodicals. Societies. Collections
283	Museums. Exhibitions, exhibits
284	Gazetteers. Dictionaries. Geographic names
284.3	Guidebooks
285	Biography (Collective). Genealogy (Collective)
285.2	Historiography
	Historians see E175.5.A+
285.5	Study and teaching
286	General works. Histories
286.3	Juvenile works
286.5	Pamphlets, addresses, essays, etc.
286.6	Anecdotes, legends, pageants, etc.
287	Historic monuments (General). Illustrative material
288	Antiquities (Non-Indian)
	By period

	Georgia
	By period -- Continued
289	Early to 1775
	Including Indian affairs; Spanish claims and attacks; Montgomery's Margravate of Azilia; Trustees for establishing the colony of Georgia in America; Royal province
	Including biography: James Edward Oglethorpe, etc.
	Cf. E197 Queen Anne's War, 1701-1713
	Cf. F295.S1 Salzburger immigration
	Cf. F314 St. Augustine Expedition, 1740
290	1775-1865
	Including cession of western lands to United States, 1802
	Including biography: Elijah Clarke, Howell Cobb, Herschel Vespasian Johnson, Charles James McDonald, Thomas Spalding, Linton Stephens, etc.
	Cf. E83.813 First Creek War, 1813-1814
	Cf. E83.817 First Seminole War, 1817-1818
	Cf. E83.836 Second Creek War, 1836
	Cf. E99.C5 Cherokee troubles
	Cf. E230+ The Revolution, Military operations and battles
	Cf. E263.G3 Georgia in the Revolution
	Cf. E359.5.G4 War of 1812
	Cf. E470.6 Civil War general military operations
	Cf. E471+ Civil War campaigns and battles
	Cf. E503+ Civil War, 1861-1865, Union history
	Cf. E559+ Civil War, 1861-1865 (General)
	Cf. F296 Western lands ceded to the United States (General)
	Cf. F341 Yazoo land companies, Yazoo fraud
291	1865-1950. Reconstruction
	Including biography: Rufus Brown Bullock, William Harrell Felton, Charles Jones Jenkins, Eugene Talmadge, etc.
	Cf. D570.85.G4+ World War I, 1914-1918
	Cf. D769.85.G4+ World War II, 1939-1945
	1951-
291.2	General works
	Biography
291.3.A2	Collective
291.3.A3-Z	Individual, A-Z
	Subarrange each by Table F5
291.7	North Georgia
291.8	South Georgia
292.A-Z	Regions, counties, etc., A-Z
292.A15	Counties
292.A16	Mountains

F1-975

Georgia
    Regions, counties, etc., A-Z -- Continued

292.A17	Rivers
292.A18	Lakes
292.A19	Islands
292.A48	Altamaha River and Valley
292.A6	Appling County
	Argyle Island see F277.S3
292.A7	Atkinson County
292.A74	Atlantic coast
292.B13	Bacon County
292.B14	Baker County
292.B15	Baldwin County
292.B2	Banks County
292.B27	Barrow County
292.B3	Bartow County
292.B4	Ben Hill County
292.B45	Berrien County
292.B5	Bibb County
	Billys Island see F292.O5
292.B6	Bleckley County
292.B7	Boundaries. South Carolina cession south of Tennessee
	Cf. F277.B7 South Carolina boundary
	Cf. F317.B7 Florida boundary
	Cf. F443.B7 Tennessee boundary
292.B8	Brantley County
292.B83	Brooks County
292.B85	Bryan County
292.B9	Bulloch County
292.B95	Burke County
292.B97	Butts County
292.C15	Calhoun County
292.C17	Camden County
	Including Kings Bay
	Campbell Co. see F292.F9
292.C18	Candler County
292.C19	Carroll County
292.C2	Catoosa County
292.C3	Charlton County
292.C36	Chatham County
	Including Ossabaw Island, Tybee Island
292.C39	Chattahoochee County

Georgia
　　Regions, counties, etc., A-Z -- Continued
292.C4　　　　　Chattahoochee River and Valley
　　　　　　　Class here general works on the Chattahoochee River and
　　　　　　　　Valley, as well as works limited to the part located in
　　　　　　　　Georgia
　　　　　　　For works limited to the part of the Chattahoochee
　　　　　　　　River and Valley located in Florida see F317.J2
　　　　　　　For works limited to the part of the Chattahoochee
　　　　　　　　River and Valley located in Alabama see F332.C4
292.C43　　　　Chattooga County
292.C47　　　　Cherokee County
292.C5　　　　Clarke County
292.C53　　　　Clay County
292.C54　　　　Clayton County
292.C55　　　　Clinch County
292.C6　　　　Cobb County
292.C63　　　　Coffee County
　　　　　　　Colonel's Island see F292.G5
292.C7　　　　Colquitt County
292.C73　　　　Columbia County
292.C76　　　　Cook County
292.C8　　　　Coweta County
292.C85　　　　Crawford County
292.C93　　　　Crisp County
292.C94　　　　Cumberland Island. Cumberland Island National Seashore
292.D15　　　　Dade County
292.D2　　　　Dawson County
292.D27　　　　Decatur County
292.D3　　　　De Kalb County
292.D5　　　　Dodge County
292.D55　　　　Dooly County
292.D6　　　　Dougherty County
292.D65　　　　Douglas County
292.E2　　　　Early County
292.E25　　　　Echols County
292.E3　　　　Effingham County
292.E4　　　　Elbert County
292.E5　　　　Emanuel County
292.E9　　　　Evans County
292.F2　　　　Fannin County
292.F3　　　　Fayette County
292.F57　　　　Flint River and Valley
292.F6　　　　Floyd County
292.F67　　　　Forsyth County
292.F7　　　　Fort Frederica National Monument
292.F8　　　　Franklin County

F1-975

Georgia

Regions, counties, etc., A-Z -- Continued

292.F9	Fulton County
	Including Campbell County, Milton Co.
292.G3	Gilmer County
292.G4	Glascock County
292.G5	Glynn County
	Including Colonel's Island
	For Fort Frederica National Monument see F292.F7
292.G58	Golden Isles
	Including Jekyl Island, St. Simon's Island
292.G6	Gordon County
292.G66	Grady County
292.G7	Greene County
292.G9	Gwinnett County
292.H2	Habersham County
292.H25	Hall County
292.H3	Hancock County
292.H5	Haralson County
292.H55	Harris County
292.H6	Hart County
292.H7	Heard County
292.H73	Henry County
292.H8	Houston County
292.I67	Irwin County
292.J13	Jackson County
292.J2	Jasper County
292.J25	Jeff Davis County
292.J28	Jefferson County
	Jekyl Island see F292.G58
292.J4	Jenkins County
292.J6	Johnson County
292.J7	Jones County
	Kings Bay see F292.C17
292.L2	Lamar County
	Lanier, Lake see F292.S53
292.L25	Lanier County
292.L3	Laurens County
292.L4	Lee County
292.L6	Liberty County
292.L63	Lincoln County
	Little Tennessee River and Valley see F443.L64
292.L66	Long County
	Lookout Mountain see F443.L8
292.L7	Lowndes County
292.L8	Lumpkin County
292.M13	McDuffie County

Georgia
>Regions, counties, etc., A-Z -- Continued

292.M15	McIntosh County
	Including Sapelo Island
292.M17	Macon County
292.M2	Madison County
292.M25	Marion County
	McLemore Cove see F292.W16
292.M5	Meriwether County
292.M6	Miller County
	Milton Co. see F292.F9
292.M65	Mitchell County
292.M7	Monroe County
292.M73	Montgomery County
292.M76	Morgan County
292.M8	Murray County
292.M9	Muscogee County
292.N4	Newton County
292.O27	Ocmulgee River
292.O3	Oconee County
292.O33	Oconee River and Valley
292.O38	Ogeechee River and Valley
292.O4	Oglethorpe County
292.O5	Okefenokee Swamp
	Including Billys Island
	Ossabaw Island see F292.C36
292.P3	Paulding County
292.P4	Peach County
292.P57	Pickens County
292.P61	Pierce County
292.P65	Pike County
292.P7	Polk County
292.P85	Pulaski County
292.P9	Putnam County
292.Q5	Quitman County
292.R3	Rabun County
292.R35	Randolph County
292.R49	Richard B. Russell Lake and Region
	Class here general works on Richard B. Russell Lake and Region, as well as works limited to the part located in Georgia
	For works limited to the part of Richard B. Russell Lake and Region located in South Carolina see F277.R49
292.R5	Richmond County
	Rock City Gardens see F443.L8
292.R6	Rockdale County

F1-975

	Georgia
	Regions, counties, etc., A-Z -- Continued
292.S2	Saint Mary's River and Valley
	Class here works limited to the part of the Saint Mary's River and Valley located in Georgia
	For general works on the Saint Mary's River and Valley, as well as works limited to the part located in Florida see F317.S3
	Saint Simon's Island see F292.G58
292.S25	Sandhills
	Class here works limited to the part of Sandhills located in Georgia
	For general works on Sandhills, as well as works limited to the part located in North Carolina see F262.S34
	For works limited to the part of Sandhills located in South Carolina see F277.S27
	Sapelo Island see F292.M15
292.S3	Savannah River and Valley
	Class here general works on the Savannah River and Valley, as well as works limited to the part located in Georgia
	Including Argyle Island
	For works limitd to the part of the Savannah River and Valley located in South Carolina see F277.S3
292.S33	Schley County
292.S35	Screven County
292.S4	Seminole County
292.S53	Sidney Lanier, Lake
292.S6	Spalding County
292.S7	Stephens County
292.S8	Stewart County
292.S85	Stone Mountain Memorial
292.S9	Sumter County
292.T2	Talbot County
292.T23	Taliaferro County
292.T27	Tattnall County
292.T3	Taylor County
292.T35	Telfair County
292.T37	Terrell County
292.T4	Thomas County
292.T5	Tift County
292.T6	Toombs County
292.T65	Towns County
292.T7	Treutlen County
292.T75	Troup County
292.T8	Turner County
292.T9	Twiggs County

	Georgia
	Regions, counties, etc., A-Z -- Continued
	Tybee Island see F292.C36
292.U5	Union County
292.U6	Upson County
292.W16	Walker County
	Including McLemore Cove
292.W17	Walton County
292.W2	Ware County
292.W23	Warren County
292.W25	Washington County
292.W3	Wayne County
292.W35	Webster County
292.W45	Wheeler County
292.W48	White County
292.W5	Whitfield County
292.W65	Wilcox County
292.W7	Wilkes County
292.W75	Wilkinson County
292.W9	Worth County
294.A-Z	Cities, towns, etc., A-Z
	e.g.
294.A8-.A89	Atlanta (Table F2)
294.A9	Augusta
294.C7	Columbus
294.M2	Macon
294.S2	Savannah
	Elements in the population
295.A1	General works
295.A2-Z	Individual works
	For a list of racial, ethnic, and religious elements (with Cutter numbers) see E184.A+
295.S1	Salzburgers
296	Gulf States
	Including Gulf coast after 1803; Gulf of Mexico
	For South Atlantic States see F206+
	For West Florida see F301
	For Mississippi Territory (1798) see F336+
	For Gulf coast early to 1803 see F372
	For Lower Mississippi Valley see F396
	Cf. F332.G9 Gulf coast of Alabama
	Cf. F392.G9 Gulf coast of Texas

301 West Florida

Historical note from the second edition (1913) of Class F: "The portion of the Louisiana coast east of the Mississippi; settled by French about 1700. Ceded to Great Britain 1763, with the other French possessions east of the Mississippi. Great Britain also received Spanish Florida from Spain in 1763, and soon after divided her possessions on the Gulf coast into the two colonies of East and West Florida, the Chattahoochee-Apalachicola River forming the boundary between them. The northern limit of West Florida was at first 31°; after 1764, 32°, 30'. The 31° was agreed upon as boundary in the American-British treaty of 1783, but both Floridas were ceded to Spain by Great Britain the same year and the former country claimed the 32°, 30' line as the northern boundary. (The territory in dispute, sometimes known as the Natchez district of West Florida, was surrendered by Spain to the U.S. in 1798 and organized as the Territory of Mississippi; and enlarged 1804 by the addition of Georgia's western lands, and that part of the S.C. cession of 1787 north of it, thus including all modern Ala. and Miss. north of 31). West Florida, consisting of the Gulf coast south of 31° between the Chattahoochee and the Mississippi, continued a Spanish colony. The inhabitants revolted in 1810, and a presidential proclamation declared West Florida under the jurisdiction of the U.S. The part west of the Pearl River (Baton Rouge district) was added to Louisiana on the latter's admission as a state 1812; the remainder as far east as the Perdido River (Mobile district), annexed to Mississippi Territory the same year. The small remnant east of the Perdido (the Pensacola district, which continued to be known as West Florida) was conquered by Jackson in the 1st Seminole war 1818, returned to Spain nest year, and formed part of the Florida purchase of 1819."

Cf. F317.W5 Pensacola District after 1819
Cf. F334.M6 Mobile
Cf. F341 Natchez District
Cf. F377.B7 Louisiana boundary
Cf. F377.F6 Florida parishes of Louisiana, Baton Rouge District since 1812

Florida

Historical note from the second edition (1913) of Class F: "Early claims to this region were made by Spain, France and England. Colonized by the two former nations, hut soon recognized as a Spanish possession. Boundaries not defined, but limited by the English on the north and the French on the west. Ceded to Great Britain 1763, who reorganized it as East Florida, bounded west by the Chattahoochee-Apalachicola River and north by 31° and St. Mary's River. Returned to Spain 1783, and after a generation of border troubles with northern neighbors, sold to U.S. 1819 with the part of West Florida still in Spanish hands. A territory 1822. Admitted as a state 1845."

306	Periodicals. Societies. Collections
308	Museums. Exhibitions, exhibits
309	Gazetteers. Dictionaries. Geographic names
309.3	Guidebooks
310	Biography (Collective). Genealogy (Collective)
310.2	Historiography
	Historians see E175.5.A+
310.5	Study and teaching
311	General works. Histories
311.3	Juvenile works
311.5	Pamphlets, addresses, essays, etc.
311.6	Anecdotes, legends, pageants, etc.
311.8	Geography
312	Historic monuments (General). Illustrative material
313	Antiquities (Non-Indian)
	By period
314	Early to 1821

Including French Huguenot colonies, 1562-1565; Spanish Colony, 1565-1763, 1783-1821; St. Augustine expeditions, 1740, 1743; East Florida; English Colony, 1763-1783; "Republic of Florida," 1812-1816; MacGregor at Amelia Island, 1817; Treaty of Washington, 1819 (with Spain); Spanish Florida claims (General)

Including biography: Dominique de Gourgues, René Goulaine de Laudonnière, Pedro Menéndez de Avilés, Jean Ribaut (Ribault), etc.

For West Florida see F301

Cf. E83.813 First Creek War, 1813-1814

Cf. E83.817 First Seminole War, 1817-1818; execution of Arbuthnot and Ambrister

Cf. E359.5.F6 War of 1812

Cf. F319.S2 Saint Augustine

Cf. F372 Gulf coast before 1763

Cf. F1410 Spaniards in North America (General)

F1-975

	Florida
	By period -- Continued
315	1821-1865
	Including Andrew Jackson's administration as governor; admission as a state, 1845
	Cf. E83.835 Second Seminole War, 1835-1842
	Cf. E83.855 Third Seminole War, 1855-1858
	Cf. E470.7 Civil War general military operations
	Cf. E471+ Civil War campaigns and battles
	Cf. E502+ Civil War, Union history
	Cf. E558+ Civil War, 1861-1865 (General)
316	1865-1950
	Including Reconstruction; hurricane disasters, 1926, 1927
	Cf. D769.85.F5+ World War II, 1939-1945
	Cf. E726.F6 War of 1898 (Spanish-American War)
	1951-
316.2	General works
	Biography
316.22	Collective
316.23.A-Z	Individual, A-Z
	Subarrange each by Table F5
317.A-Z	Regions, counties, etc., A-Z
317.A15	Counties
317.A16	Mountains
317.A17	Rivers
317.A18	Lakes
317.A19	Islands
317.A4	Alachua County
	Including Paynes Prairie
	Amelia Island see F317.N3
317.A6	Apalachicola River and Valley
317.A74	Atlantic Coast
317.B2	Baker County
317.B3	Bay County
	Biscayne Bay see F317.D2
317.B54	Big Bend Region
317.B7	Boundaries
	Cf. F332.B7 Alabama boundary
317.B75	Bradford County
317.B8	Brevard County
	Including Cape Canaveral, Indian River, Merritt Island
317.B85	Broward County
	Caladesi Island see F317.P6
317.C3	Calhoun County
	Cape Canaveral see F317.B8
317.C4	Charlotte County
	Chattahoochee River and Valley, Fla. see F317.J2

Florida
   Regions, counties, etc., A-Z -- Continued

317.C5	Citrus County
317.C6	Clay County
317.C7	Collier County
	Including Marco Island
317.C75	Columbia County
317.D2	Dade County Miami-Dade County
	Including Biscayne Bay, Lake Worth
	For Everglades see F317.E9
317.D4	De Soto County
317.D5	Dixie County
317.D9	Duval County
	Emerald Coast see F317.G8
317.E7	Escambia County
	For Perdido River and Valley see F317.P4
317.E9	Everglades
	Including Everglades National Park
317.F6	Flagler County
	Florida Keys see F317.M7
317.F63	Florida National Scenic Trail
	Fort Jefferson National Monument see F317.M7
317.F7	Franklin County
317.G2	Gadsden County
317.G5	Gilchrist County
317.G6	Glades County
317.G8	Gulf coast of Florida
	Including Gulf Islands National Seashore (General, and
	Florida), Emerald Coast
	Cf. F347.G9 Gulf Islands National Seashore
	(Mississippi)
317.G9	Gulf County
	Gulf Islands National Seashore see F317.G8
317.H2	Hamilton County
317.H3	Hardee County
317.H4	Hendry County
317.H5	Hernando County
317.H54	Highlands County
317.H6	Hillsborough County
317.H7	Holmes County
317.H73	Holmes Creek and Valley
	Class here general works on Holmes Creek and Valley, as
	well as works limited to the part located in Florida
	For works limited to the part of Homles Creek and
	Valley located in Alabama see F332.H56
317.I24	Ichetucknee River
	Indian River see F317.B8

F1-975

Florida

Regions, counties, etc., A-Z -- Continued

317.I5	Indian River County
317.J2	Jackson County

Including works on the part of the Chattahoochee River and
Valley located in Florida

For general works on the Chattahoochee River and
Valley, as well as works limited to the part located
in Georgia see F292.C4

For works limited to the part of the Chattahoochee
River and Valley located in Alabama see F332.C4

Cf. F317.A6 Apalachicola River and Valley

317.J4	Jefferson County
	Jupiter Inlet see F317.P2
317.K57	Kissimmee River and Valley
317.L15	Lafayette County
317.L2	Lake County
	Lake Worth see F317.D2
317.L3	Lee County

Including Pine Island

For Everglades see F317.E9

317.L5	Leon County
317.L6	Levy County
317.L7	Liberty County
317.M15	Madison County
317.M18	Manasota Key
317.M2	Manatee County

Including Manatee River

Marco Island see F317.C7

317.M3	Marion County

Including Lake Weir

317.M35	Martin County
	Merritt Island see F317.B8
	Miami-Dade Co. see F317.D2
317.M7	Monroe County

Including Florida Keys, Fort Jefferson National Monument

For Everglades see F317.E9

317.M92	Myakka River State Park
317.N3	Nassau County

Including Amelia Island

Cf. F314 Amelia Island, History before 1819

317.O25	Ocala National Forest
317.O27	Okaloacoochee Slough
317.O3	Okaloosa County
317.O4	Okeechobee, Lake
317.O43	Okeechobee County
	Okefenokee Swamp see F292.O5

Florida

Regions, counties, etc., A-Z -- Continued

317.O46	Oklawaha River and Valley
317.O6	Orange County
317.O7	Osceola County
317.P2	Palm Beach County
	Including Jupiter Inlet
317.P3	Pasco County
	Paynes Prairie see F317.A4
317.P4	Perdido River and Valley
	Class here works limited to the part of the Perdido River and Valley located in Florida
	For general works on the Perdido River and Valley, as well as works limited to the part located in Alabama see F332.P4
	Pine Island see F317.L3
317.P6	Pinellas County
	Including Caladesi Island
317.P7	Polk County
317.P8	Putnam County
317.R43	Red Hills
317.S18	Saint Johns County
317.S2	Saint Johns River and Valley
	Including Timucan Ecological and Historic Preserve
317.S27	Saint Lucie County
317.S3	Saint Mary's River and Valley
	Class here general works on the Saint Mary's River and Valley, as well as works limited to the part located in Florida
	For works limited to the part of the Saint Mary's River and Valley located in Georgia see F292.S2
317.S37	Sanibel Island
317.S4	Santa Rosa County
317.S45	Sarasota County
317.S5	Seminole County
317.S75	Sumter County
317.S78	Suwannee County
317.S8	Suwannee River and Valley
317.T3	Taylor County
	Timucuan Ecological and Historic Preserve see F317.S2
	Tomoka River see F317.V7
317.U5	Union County
317.V7	Volusia County
	Including Tomoka River
317.W23	Wakulla County
317.W24	Walton County

F1-975

Florida

Regions, counties, etc., A-Z -- Continued

317.W3	Washington County
	Including St. Andrews Bay
317.W5	West Florida region
	The Pensacola District after 1819
	For the Pensacola District, early to 1819 see F301
317.W57	Withlacoochee River and Valley
319.A-Z	Cities, towns, etc., A-Z
	e.g.
319.J1	Jacksonville
319.K4	Key West
319.M6	Miami
319.P4	Pensacola
319.S2	Saint Augustine
319.S24	Saint Petersburg
319.T14	Tallahassee
319.T2	Tampa
	Elements in the population
320.A1	General works
320.A2-Z	Individual elements
	For a list of racial, ethnic, and religious elements (with Cutter numbers) see E184.A+

Alabama

Historical note from the second edition (1913) of Class F: "The territory included in the present state of Alabama was, all but the southern extremity, embraced in the Carolina grants 1663-1665; and again under the original Georgia charter of 1732 or the extension thereof, in 1763, (all except a narrow strip along the northern border which belonged to S.C. till ceded to the national government in 1787.) The portion between 31° and 32° 30' extending west to the Mississippi was detached to form part of the English province of West Florida 1764-1783, and in 1798 was organized as Mississippi Territory. 1804 the remainder, up to 35°, including that part surrendered by Ga. 1802, and S. C. cession, was added. 1812, the Gulf coast from the Perdido to the Pearl River (the Mobile district of West Florida) became part of the Territory. 1817, on the admission of Mississippi as a state, Alabama was organized as a territory with its present limits. State 1819."

321	Periodicals. Societies. Collections
323	Museums. Exhibitions, exhibits
324	Gazetteers. Dictionaries. Geographic names
324.3	Guidebooks
325	Biography (Collective). Genealogy (Collective)
325.2	Historiography

	Alabama
	Historiography -- Continued
	Historians see E175.5.A+
325.5	Study and teaching
326	General works. Histories
	Including admission as a state, December 14, 1819
	Including By period (Early to 1950)
	Including Secession; Reconstruction; Ku-Klux Klan
	Including biography: John Hollis Bankhead, William Parish
	Chilton, Thomas Erby Kilby, Thomas Hill Watts, etc.
	For West Florida see F301
	Cf. D570.85.A2+ World War I, 1914-1918
	Cf. D769.85.A2+ World War II, 1939-1945
	Cf. E83.813 First Creek War, 1813-1814
	Cf. E83.836 Second Creek War, 1836
	Cf. E99.C5 Cherokee Indians
	Cf. E470.7 Civil War general military operations
	Cf. E471+ Civil War campaigns and battles
	Cf. E495+ Civil War, 1861-1865, Union history
	Cf. E551+ Civil War, 1861-1865 (General)
	Cf. E726.A3 War of 1898 (Spanish-American War)
	Cf. F292.B7 South Carolina cession south of Tennessee
	Cf. F341 Mississippi Territory
	Cf. F372 Early French settlements on the coast
	(Louisiana)
326.3	Juvenile works
326.5	Pamphlets, addresses, essays
326.6	Anecdotes, legends, pageants, etc.
327	Historic monuments (General). Illustrative material
328	Antiquities (Non-Indian)
	By period
	Early to 1950 see F326
	1951-
330	General works
	Biography
330.2	Collective
330.3.A-Z	Individual, A-Z
	Subarrange each by Table F5
332.A-Z	Regions, counties, etc., A-Z
332.A15	Counties
332.A16	Mountains
332.A17	Rivers
332.A18	Lakes
332.A19	Islands
332.A8	Autauga County

F1-975

Alabama

Regions, counties, etc., A-Z -- Continued

332.B2	Baldwin County
	For Mobile Bay see F332.M58
	For Perdido River and Valley see F332.P4
332.B3	Barbour County
332.B5	Bibb County
332.B6	Blount County
	Including Garfield Colony, Rickwood Caverns State Park
332.B7	Boundaries
	Cf. F443.B7 Tennessee boundary
332.B8	Bullock County
332.B9	Butler County
332.C25	Calhoun County
332.C35	Chambers County
332.C4	Chattahoochee River and Valley
	Class here works limited to the part of the Chattahoochee River and Valley located in Alabama
	For general works on the Chattahoochee River and Valley, as well as works limited to the part located in Georgia see F292.C4
	For works limited to the part of the Chattahoochee River and Valley located in Florida see F317.J2
332.C44	Cherokee County
	Including Weiss Lake
332.C46	Chilton County
332.C48	Choctaw County
332.C6	Clarke County
332.C62	Clay County
332.C63	Cleburne County
332.C65	Coffee County
332.C68	Colbert County
332.C7	Conecuh County
332.C74	Coosa County
332.C75	Coosa River and Valley
332.C8	Covington County
332.C85	Crenshaw County
332.C9	Cullman County
332.D17	Dale County
332.D3	Dallas County
	Dauphin Island see F332.M6
332.D4	De Kalb County
332.E4	Elmore County
332.E7	Escambia County
332.E8	Etowah County
332.F4	Fayette County
332.F83	Franklin County

Alabama
Regions, counties, etc., A-Z -- Continued

332.G4	Geneva County
332.G7	Greene County
332.G9	Gulf coast of Alabama
	For Mobile Bay see F332.M58
	Cf. F296 Gulf coast (General)
332.H3	Hale County
332.H4	Henry County
332.H56	Holmes Creek and Valley
	Class here works limited to the part of Holmes Creek and Valley located in Alabama
	For general works on Holmes Creek and Valley, as well as works limited to the part located in Florida see F317.H73
332.H6	Houston (Huston) County
332.J2	Jackson County
332.J4	Jefferson County
	Including Rouges Creek and Valley
332.L2	Lamar County
332.L3	Lauderdale County
332.L4	Lawrence County
332.L5	Lee County
332.L6	Limestone County
332.L7	Lowndes County
332.M2	Macon County
332.M3	Madison County
332.M35	Marengo County
332.M37	Marion County
332.M4	Marshall County
332.M58	Mobile Bay
332.M6	Mobile County
	Including Dauphin Island
332.M7	Monroe County
332.M73	Montgomery County
332.M8	Morgan County
	Muscle Shoals see F332.T2
	Oliver Dam see F332.T9
332.P34	Paint Rock River
	Class here general works on the Paint Rock River, as well as works limited to the part located in Alabama
	For works limited to the part of the Paint Rock River located in Tennessee see F443.P34
332.P37	Pea River and Valley

F1-975

	Alabama
	Regions, counties, etc., A-Z -- Continued
332.P4	Perdido River and Valley
	Class here general works on the Perdido River and Valley, as well as works limited to the part located in Alabama
	For works limited to the part of the Perdido River and Valley located in Florida see F317.P4
332.P45	Perry County
332.P5	Pickens County
332.P55	Pike County
332.R3	Randolph County
	Rickwood Caverns State Park see F332.B6
	Rouges Creek and Valley see F332.J4
332.R87	Russell County
332.S2	Saint Clair County
332.S5	Shelby County
332.S8	Sumter County
332.T14	Talladega County
332.T15	Tallapoosa County
332.T17	Tannehill Historical State Park
332.T2	Tennessee River and Valley
	Class here works limited to the part of the Tennessee River and Valley located in Alabama
	Including Muscle Shoals (Topography)
	For general works on the Tennessee River and Valley see F217.T3
332.T6	Tombigbee River and Valley
	Class here general works on the Tombigbee River and Valley, as well as works limited to the part located in Alabama
	For works limited to the part of the Tombigbee River and Valley located in Mississippi see F347.T6
332.T9	Tuscaloosa County
	Including Oliver Dam
332.W3	Walker County
332.W4	Washington County
	Weiss Lake see F332.C44
332.W48	Wheeler Lake and region
332.W5	Wilcox County
332.W54	William B. Bankhead National Forest
332.W6	Winston County
334.A-Z	Cities, towns, etc., A-Z
	e.g.
334.B6-.B69	Birmingham (Table F2)
334.M6	Mobile
334.M7-.M79	Montgomery (Table F2)
334.T9	Tuscaloosa

Alabama -- Continued

Elements in the population

335.A1	General works
335.A2-Z	Individual elements

For a list of racial, ethnic, and religious elements (with Cutter numbers) see E184.A+

Mississippi

Historical note from the second edition (1913) of Class F: "Like Alabama, the state of Mississippi, with the exception of its southern extremity, was embraced in the Carolina grants of 1663-1665, and again under the original Georgia charter of 1732 and its extension in 1763; (a narrow strip along the northern border belonging to S.C. till ceded to the U.S. in 1787.) This region was first occupied by the French, and claimed by them as part of Louisiana till ceded to Great Britain in 1763. The territory south of 32° 3C and west of Georgia formed the English province of West Florida 1764-1783. The area bounded by 31°, 32° 30' and the Mississippi and Chattahoochee rivers was organized as Mississippi Territory 1798. In 1804 the Ga. cession of 1802, and the part of the S.C. cession of 1787 north of it, was added. In 1812, Spanish West Florida between the Pearl River and the Perdido was joined to it. Admitted as a state, 1817, with present limits, the eastern part being set off as Alabama Territory."

F1-975

336	Periodicals. Societies. Collections
338	Museums. Exhibitions, exhibits
339	Gazetteers. Dictionaries. Geographic names
339.3	Guidebooks
340	Biography (Collective). Genealogy (Collective)
340.2	Historiography
	Historians see E175.5.A+
340.5	Study and teaching

Mississippi -- Continued

341 General works. Histories

Including admission as a state, December 10, 1817

By period (Early to 1950), as well as general

Including secession; Reconstruction; Yazoo land companies, etc. Including Natchez District of West Florida

Including biography: Albert Gallatin Brown, Winthrop Sargent, etc.

For West Florida, Mobile District before 1812 see F301

For 1951 and later see F345+

Cf. D769.85.M7+ Mississippi

Cf. E83.813 First Creek War, 1813-1814

Cf. E99.N2 Natchez Indians

Cf. E470.7 Civil War general military operations

Cf. E471+ Civil War campaigns and battles

Cf. E516+ Civil War, 1861-1865, Union history

Cf. E568+ Civil War, 1861-1865 (General)

Cf. E568 Civil War, 1861-1865 (General)

Cf. F292.B7 South Carolina cession south of Tennessee

341.3 Juvenile works

341.5 Pamphlets, addresses, essays

341.6 Anecdotes, legends, pageants, etc.

342 Historic monuments (General). Illustrative material

By period

Early to 1950 see F341

1951-

345 General works

Biography

345.2 Collective

345.3.A-Z Individual, A-Z

Subarrange each by Table F5

347.A-Z Regions, counties, etc., A-Z

347.A15 Counties

347.A16 Mountains

347.A17 Rivers

347.A18 Lakes

347.A19 Islands

Ackia Battleground National Monument see F347.L45

347.A2 Adams County

347.A4 Alcorn County

347.A5 Amite County

347.A7 Attala County

347.B4 Benton County

347.B6 Bolivar County

Mississippi

Regions, counties, etc., A-Z -- Continued

347.B7	Boundaries
	Cf. F332.B7 Alabama boundary
	Cf. F377.B7 Louisiana boundary
	Cf. F443.B7 Tennessee boundary
347.C2	Calhoun County
347.C3	Carroll County
347.C4	Chickasaw County
347.C45	Choctaw County
347.C5	Claiborne County
	Including Grand Gulf State Military Park
347.C55	Clarke County
347.C6	Clay County
347.C7	Coahoma County
347.C75	Copiah County
347.C8	Covington County
347.D4	De Soto County
347.F6	Forrest County
347.F7	Franklin County
347.G4	George County
	Grand Gulf State Military Park see F347.C5
347.G65	Greene County
347.G7	Grenada County
347.G9	Gulf coast of Mississippi
	Including Gulf Islands National Seashore
	Cf. F296 Gulf coast (General)
	Cf. F317.G8 Gulf Islands National Seashore (General, and Florida)
347.H2	Hancock County
347.H3	Harrison County
	Including Ship Island
347.H5	Hinds County
347.H6	Holmes County
347.H8	Humphreys County
347.I7	Issaquena County
347.I8	Itawamba County
347.J3	Jackson County
347.J4	Jasper County
347.J48	Jefferson County
347.J5	Jefferson Davis County
347.J6	Jones County
347.K3	Kemper County
347.L2	Lafayette County
347.L25	Lamar County
347.L3	Lauderdale County
347.L35	Lawrence County

F1-975

Mississippi

Regions, counties, etc., A-Z -- Continued

347.L4	Leake County
347.L45	Lee County
	Including Ackia Battleground National Monument
347.L47	Leflore County
347.L6	Lincoln County
347.L8	Lowndes County
347.M15	Madison County
347.M25	Marion County
347.M3	Marshall County
347.M6	Mississippi River and Valley, Miss.,
	Cf. F350.3+ General
	Cf. F396 Lower Mississippi Valley
347.M7	Monroe County
347.M75	Montgomery County
347.N4	Neshoba County
347.N48	Newton County
347.N6	Noxubee County
347.O4	Oktibbeha County
347.P2	Panola County
347.P26	Pascagoula River and Valley
347.P3	Pearl River and Valley
	Class here general works on the Pearl River and Valley, as well as works limited to the part located in Mississippi
	For works limited to the part of the Pearl River and Valley located in Louisiana see F377.P3
347.P33	Pearl River County
347.P4	Perry County
347.P6	Pike County
347.P63	Piney Woods
347.P7	Pontotoc County
347.P8	Prentiss County
347.Q5	Quitman County
347.R3	Rankin County
347.S3	Scott County
347.S45	Sharkey County
347.S5	Simpson County
347.S6	Smith County
347.S8	Stone County
347.S9	Sunflower County
347.T3	Tallahatchie County
347.T35	Tate County
347.T45	Tippah County
347.T5	Tishomingo County

	Mississippi
	Regions, counties, etc., A-Z -- Continued
347.T6	Tombigbee River and Valley
	Class here works limited to the part of the Tombigbee River and Valley located in Mississippi
	For general works on the Tombigbee River and Valley, as well as works limited to the part located in Alabama see F332.T6
347.T8	Tunica County
347.U5	Union County
347.W24	Walthall County
347.W29	Warren County
347.W35	Washington County
347.W4	Wayne County
347.W45	Webster County
347.W65	Wilkinson County
347.W7	Winston County
347.Y15	Yalobusha County
347.Y2	Yazoo County
347.Y3	Yazoo River and Valley
349.A-Z	Cities, towns, etc., A-Z
	e.g.
349.B5	Biloxi
349.J13	Jackson
349.M5	Meridian
349.N2	Natchez
349.V6	Vicksburg
	Elements in the population
350.A1	General works
350.A2-Z	Individual elements
	For a list of racial, ethnic, and religious elements (with Cutter numbers) see E184.A+
	Mississippi River and Valley. Middle West
350.3	Guidebooks
350.5	Biography (Collective). Genealogy (Collective)
350.8	Antiquities (Non-Indian)

F1-975

Mississippi River and Valley. Middle West -- Continued

351 General works

Including the Mississippi Valley under Spain, France, Great Britain, and the United States. History; description, exploration, and travel; manners and customs

Including periodicals, societies, collections, collective biography

For Louisiana purchase (Diplomatic and political aspects) see E333

Cf. F347.B7 Mississippi-Arkansas boundary

Cf. F366+ Louisiana

Cf. F377.B7 Mississippi-Louisiana boundary

Cf. F396 Lower Mississippi River and Valley

Cf. F516+ Ohio River and Valley

Cf. F547.I2 Illinois River and Valley

Cf. F597 Upper Mississippi River and Valley

Cf. F598 Missouri River and Valley

By period

352 Early to 1803

Including early explorations and discoveries, by Hennepin, La Salle, Marquette

Cf. E125.S7 Soto's explorations (General)

Cf. E234 Clark's Expedition, 1778

Cf. E333 Purchase of Louisiana by the United States (Diplomatic and political aspects)

Cf. F372 Louisiana (To 1803)

Cf. F373 Louisiana (1764-1803)

Cf. F597 Carver's explorations (Upper Mississippi Valley)

Cf. F1030 New France

Cf. F1030.2 Marquette's explorations (General)

Cf. F1030.3 Joliet's exploration (General)

Cf. F1030.4 Hennepin's explorations (General)

Cf. F1030.5 La Salle's explorations (General)

Cf. HG6007 Law's Mississippi Scheme

353 1803-1865

Cf. E83.83 Black Hawk War, 1832

Cf. E334 Burr's Conspiracy, 1805-1807

Cf. E470.8 Civil War general military operations

Cf. E471+ Civil War campaigns and battles

Cf. F592 Lewis and Clark Expedition, 1804-1806; Pike's Expedition, 1805-1807

354 1865-1950

Including floods, cruises down the river

Cf. TC425.M65 Jetties of the Mississippi

355 1951-

Elements in the population

358 General works

Mississippi River and Valley. Middle West
Elements in the population -- Continued
358.2.A-Z   Individual elements
For a list of racial, ethnic, and religious elements (with
Cutter numbers) see E184.A+
Louisiana
Historical note from the second edition (1913) of Class F: "Region
lying between Florida and New Spain, claimed by both
France and Spain on right of discovery. Settled by Le Moyne
d'Iberville 1698; detached from New France as a separate
province in 1712, to include the region between the Allegheny
and Rocky Mountains, New France and New Spain. The
earliest capitals and centres of population were Biloxi and
Mobile. Portion east of the Mississippi ceded to Great Britain
1763 (becoming known as West Florida); that west of the
Mississippi to Spain, the previous year. The latter region was
secretly re-ceded to France in 1800 and by that power sold to
U.S. 1803. 1804 the province was divided on the line of 33
into the territory of Orleans and the district of Louisiana. The
territory of Orleans with the addition of the Baton Rouge
district of West Florida was admitted as the state of Louisiana
in 1812, the district of Louisiana becoming the territory of
Missouri the same year."

366	Periodicals. Societies. Collections
366.5	Museums. Exhibitions, exhibits
367	Gazetteers. Dictionaries. Geographic names
367.3	Guidebooks
367.5	Directories
368	Biography (Collective). Genealogy (Collective)
368.2	Historiography
	Historians see E175.5.A+
368.5	Study and teaching
369	General works. Histories
369.3	Juvenile works
369.5	Pamphlets, addresses, essays
369.6	Anecdotes, legends, pageants, etc.
370	Historic monuments (General). Illustrative material
371	Antiquities (Non-Indian)
	By period

F1-975

Louisiana

By period -- Continued

372   Early to 1803

Including French Louisiana; Settlement of 1698; Crozat's Grant, 1712-1717; Cession to Spain, 1763

Including biography: Jean Baptiste Le Moyne de Bienville, Pierre Le Moyne d'Iberville, etc.

Cf. E83.739 Chickasaw War, 1739-1740

Cf. F334.M6 Mobile, Ala.

Cf. F352 Mississippi Valley

Cf. HG6007 Law's Mississippi scheme, 1717, 1720

373   1764-1803

Including Spanish Louisiana; right of navigation of the Mississippi; retrocession to France, 1800-1801

Including biography: Esteban Miró, etc.

For Purchase of Louisiana by the United States see E333

For Spaniards in North America (General) see F1410

374   1803-1865

Including admission as a state, April 30, 1812.

Including Province of Louisiana, 1803-1804; Territory of Orleans, 1804-1812; boundary disputes with Spain

Including biography: William Charles Cole Claiborne, Thomas Jefferson Durant, Charles Étienne Arthur Gayarré, Jean Lafitte, Alexander Porter, etc.

Cf. E334 Burr's Conspiracy, 1805-1807

Cf. E355 War of 1812 (Military operations)

Cf. E470.7 Civil War general military operations

Cf. E471+ Civil War campaigns and battles

Cf. E510+ Union history

Cf. E565+ Civil War, 1861-1865 (General)

Cf. F301 West Florida

Cf. F314 Spanish Treaty of 1819

Cf. F592 Lewis and Clark Expedition

Cf. F697 "Indian country"

375   1865-1950. Reconstruction

Including carpet-bag misrule; Committee of Seventy; Ku-Klux Klan

Including biography: Edgar Howard Farrar, Samuel Douglas McEnery, etc.

Cf. D769.85.L6+ World War II, 1939-1945

Cf. E726.L8 War of 1898 (Spanish-American War)

     1951-

376   General works

     Biography and memoirs

376.2   Collective

F1-975

Louisiana
  By period
    1951-
      Biography and memoirs -- Continued

376.3.A-Z	Individual, A-Z
	Subarrange each by Table F5
377.A-Z	Regions, parishes, etc., A-Z
377.A15	Counties
377.A16	Mountains
377.A17	Rivers
377.A18	Lakes
377.A19	Islands
377.A2	Acadia Parish
377.A4	Allen Parish
377.A7	Ascension Parish
377.A75	Assumption Parish
377.A78	Atchafalaya River and Swamp
	Including Bayou Chene and other bayous in the region
377.A8	Attakapas District
	Avery Island see F377.F57
377.A9	Avoyelles Parish
	Bayou Lafourche see F377.L24
	Bayou Manchac see F377.M23
	Bayou Teche see F377.T4
377.B37	Bartholomew Bayou
	Class here works limited to the part of the Bartholomew Bayou located in Louisiana
	For general works on the Bartholomew Bayou, as well as works limited to the part located in Arkansas see F417.B27
377.B4	Beauregard Parish
377.B5	Bienville Parish
377.B6	Bossier Parish
377.B7	Boundaries
	Cf. F377.F6 Florida parishes
	Caddo Lake see F377.C15
377.C15	Caddo Parish
	Including works on the part of Caddo Lake located in Louisiana
	For general works on Caddo Lake, as well as works limited to the part located in Texas see F392.C17
377.C2	Calcasieu Parish
377.C23	Caldwell Parish
377.C25	Cameron Parish
	Cane River Lake see F377.N4
377.C3	Catahoula Parish
	Chalmette National Historical Park see E356.N5

	Louisiana
	Regions, parishes, etc., A-Z -- Continued
377.C5	Claiborne Parish
377.C7	Concordia Parish
	Cotile Lake see F377.R25
377.D4	Delta region
377.D45	De Soto Parish
377.E17	East Baton Rouge Parish
377.E2	East Carroll Parish
377.E3	East Feliciana Parish
377.E8	Evangeline Parish
377.F57	Five Islands
	Including Avery Island
377.F6	Florida parishes. Baton Rouge district of West Florida since 1812 (between Pearl and Mississippi rivers)
	For early to 1812 see F301
377.F7	Franklin Parish
	Grand Isle see F377.J4
377.G7	Grant Parish
377.G9	Gulf coast of Louisiana
	Cf. F296 Gulf coast (General)
377.I15	Iberia Parish
377.I2	Iberville Parish
	Isles Dernieres see F377.T5
377.J2	Jackson Parish
377.J4	Jefferson Parish
	Including Grand Isle
377.J43	Jefferson Davis Parish
377.L2	Lafayette Parish
377.L24	Lafourche Bayou
377.L25	Lafourche Parish
377.L3	La Salle Parish
377.L5	Lincoln Parish
377.L6	Livingston Parish
377.M2	Madison Parish
377.M23	Manchac, Bayou
377.M6	Mississippi River and Valley, La.
	Cf. F350.3+ General
	Cf. F396 Lower Mississippi Valley
377.M7	Morehouse Parish
	Murphys Lake see F377.N4
377.N4	Natchitoches Parish
	Including Murphys Lake and Cane River Lake
377.O7	Orleans Parish
377.O78	Ouachita Parish

Louisiana
Regions, parishes, etc., A-Z -- Continued

377.O8	Ouachita River and Valley

           Class here general works on the Ouachita River and Valley,
               as well as works limited to the part located in Louisiana
           For works limited to the part of the Ouachita River and
               Valley located in Arkansas see F417.O83

377.P27	Pass Manchac
377.P3	Pearl River and Valley

           Class here works limited to the part of the Pearl River and
               Valley located in Louisiana
            For general works on the Pearl River and Valley, as
               well as works limited to the part located in
               Mississippi see F347.P3

377.P45	Plaquemines Parish
377.P55	Pointe Coupee Parish
377.P6	Pontchartrain, Lake
377.R25	Rapides Parish

           Including Cotile Lake

377.R3	Red River and Valley

           Class here general works on the Red River and Valley, as
               well as works limited to the part located in Louisiana
            For works limited to the part of the Red River and
               Valley located in Texas see F392.R3
            For works limited to the part of the Red River and
               Valley located in Arkansas see F417.R3
            For works limited to the part of the Red River and
               Valley located in Oklahoma see F702.R3
            For works limited to the part of the Red River and
               Valley located in New Mexico see F802.R36

377.R32	Red River Parish
377.R5	Richland Parish
377.R58	River Road
377.S115	Sabine Parish
377.S116	Sabine River and Valley

           Class here general works on the Sabine River and Valley, as
               well as works limited to the part located in Louisiana
            For works limited to the part of the Sabine River and
               Valley located in Texas see F392.S12

377.S12	Saint Bernard Parish
377.S124	Saint Charles Parish
377.S13	Saint Helena Parish
377.S134	Saint James Parish
377.S135	Saint John the Baptist Parish
377.S14	Saint Landry Parish
377.S16	Saint Martin Parish
377.S2	Saint Mary Parish

	Louisiana
	Regions, parishes, etc., A-Z -- Continued
377.S3	Saint Tammany Parish
377.T3	Tangipahoa Parish
377.T4	Bayou Teche
377.T45	Tensas Parish
377.T5	Terrebonne Parish
	Including Isles Dernieres
377.T6	Toledo Bend Reservoir. Toledo Bend region
377.U5	Union Parish
377.V5	Vermilion Parish
377.V6	Vernon Parish
377.W3	Washington Parish
377.W4	Webster Parish
377.W45	West Baton Rouge Parish
377.W47	West Carroll Parish
377.W5	West Feliciana Parish
377.W6	Winn Parish
379.A-Z	Cities, towns, etc., A-Z
	e.g.
379.A15	Cities and towns (Collective and selective)
379.B33	Baton Rouge
379.N5-.N59	New Orleans (Table F2)
379.S4	Shreveport
	Elements in the population
380.A1	General works
380.A2-Z	Individual elements
	For a list of racial, ethnic, and religious elements (with Cutter numbers) see E184.A+

Texas

Historical note from the second edition (1913) of Class F:
"Considered by the Spaniards as part of New Spain, but not colonized. The site of La Salle's French colony 1685-1687. Under Spanish Louisiana but few colonists came in. The region was claimed by the U. S. as part of the Louisiana purchase 1803, but in the treaty of 1819 by which Florida was acquired, these claims were abandoned and the Sabine River recognized as the boundary. 1821-1834 the country was parcelled out by the Mexican government into colonies under proprietors called "impresarios"; the immigrants coming chiefly from the U.S. It was organized as the province of Texas 1821 and joined to Coalmila as the "Department of Coahuila and Texas" 1824. By the revolution of 1835-1836 Texas won her independence. At once the movement for annexation to the II. S. began. Admitted as a state 1845. In 1850 it sold to the national government nearly a third of its area, consisting of the northwestern part (now forming the eastern half of New Mexico and portions of Okl., Kan., Col. and Wy.)"

F1-975

381	Periodicals. Societies. Collections
383	Museums. Exhibitions, exhibits
384	Gazetteers. Dictionaries. Geographic names
384.3	Guidebooks
385	Biography (Collective). Genealogy (Collective)
385.2	Historiography
	Historians see E175.5.A+
385.5	Study and teaching
386	General works. Histories
386.3	Juvenile works
386.5	Pamphlets, addresses, essays
386.6	Anecdotes, legends, pageants, etc.
386.8	Geography
387	Historic monuments (General). Illustrative material
388	Antiquities (Non-Indian)
	By period
389	Early to 1835

Including Impresarios; Province of Mexico; Coahuila and Texas (Mexican state); Austin's Colony; De Witt's Colony; Las Casas and Sambrano Revolutions, 1811; Fredonian Insurrection, 1826-1827

Including biography: Stephen Fuller Austin, David Gouverneur Burnet, Anson Jones, Thomas Jefferson Rusk, etc.

Cf. E359.5.T47 War of 1812

Cf. F352 La Salle's Colony, 1685-1687

	Texas
	By period -- Continued
390	1835-1846
	Including admission as a state, December 29, 1845
	Including War of Independence, 1835-1836 (Siege of the Alamo, 1836; Battle of San Jacinto, 1836; etc.); Republic of Texas, 1836-1846; Santa Fe Expedition, 1841; Mier Expedition, 1842; annexation to the United States
	Including biography: Samuel Houston, Mirabeau Bonaparte Lamar, Henry Smith, William Alexander Anderson Wallace, etc.
	1846-
	Including frontier troubles with Mexico; Session and Reconstruction; frontier and ranch life; Texas Rangers
	Including biography: Roy Bean, Charles Goodnight, George Washington Littlefield, William Jesse McDonald, Wilbert Lee O'Daniel, etc.
	Cf. D570.85.T4+ World War I, 1914-1918
	Cf. D769.85.T4+ World War II, 1939-1945
	Cf. E401+ War with Mexico, 1845-1848
	Cf. E470.9 Civil War general military operations
	Cf. E471+ Civil War campaigns and battles
	Cf. E532+ Civil War, 1861-1865, Union history
	Cf. E580+ Civil War, 1861-1865 (General)
	Cf. F801 Sale of claims to northwest lands, 1850
	Cf. F1232 Mexican frontier troubles (General)
391	General works
	1951-
391.2	General works
	Biography
391.3	Collective
391.4.A-Z	Individual, A-Z
	Subarrange each by Table F5
392.A-Z	Regions, counties, etc., A-Z
392.A15	Counties
392.A16	Mountains
392.A17	Rivers
392.A18	Lakes
392.A19	Islands
392.A195	Amistad National Recreation Area
392.A2	Anderson County
392.A25	Andrews County
392.A3	Angelina County
392.A6	Aransas County
392.A65	Archer County
	Armand Bayou Park and Nature Center see F392.H38
392.A7	Armstrong County

Texas
    Regions, counties, etc., A-Z -- Continued

392.A8	Atascosa County
392.A9	Austin County
392.B15	Bailey County
392.B17	Balcones Canyonlands National Wildlife Refuge
392.B2	Bandera County
392.B23	Bastrop County
392.B25	Baylor County
392.B3	Bee County
392.B34	Bell County
	Including Tennessee Valley
392.B5	Bexar County
392.B53	Big Bend National Park
392.B54	Big Bend region
	Big Thicket see F392.H37
392.B546	Blacklands
392.B55	Blanco County
392.B57	Bolivar Peninsula
392.B58	Borden County
392.B6	Bosque County
392.B7	Boundaries
	For International boundary see F786
	Cf. F377.B7 Louisiana boundary
392.B74	Bowie County
392.B82	Brazoria County
392.B84	Brazos County
392.B842	Brazos River and Valley
	Including South Bend Reservoir
392.B85	Brewster County
	For Big Bend National Park see F392.B53
392.B86	Briscoe County
392.B88	Brooks County
392.B89	Brown County
392.B95	Burleson County
392.B97	Burnet County
392.C17	Caddo Lake
	Class here general works on Caddo Lake, as well as works
	limited to the part located in Texas
	For works limited to the part of Caddo Lake located in
	Louisiana see F377.C15
392.C2	Caldwell County
392.C22	Calhoun County
392.C23	Callahan County
392.C25	Cameron County
392.C26	Camp County

Texas

Regions, counties, etc., A-Z -- Continued

392.C27	Canadian River and Valley

Class here works limited to the part of the Canadian River and Valley located in Texas

For general works on the Canadian River and Valley, as well as works limited to the part located in Oklahoma see F702.C2

392.C28	Carson County
392.C287	Casa Blanca Land Grant
392.C29	Cass County
392.C3	Castro County
392.C4	Chambers County
392.C44	Cherokee County
392.C45	Childress County
	Choke Canyon Reservoir see F392.F92
392.C5	Clay County
392.C517	Coastal Bend
392.C52	Cochino Bayou and Valley
392.C53	Cochran County
392.C54	Coke County
392.C55	Coleman County
392.C56	Collin County
392.C57	Collingsworth County
392.C58	Colorado County
392.C6	Colorado River and Valley
392.C7	Comal County
392.C75	Comanche County
392.C77	Concho County
392.C773	Concho River and Valley
392.C78	Cooke County
392.C79	Cooper Lake
392.C8	Coryell County

Including Mother Neff State Park

392.C82	Cottle County
392.C83	Crane County
392.C84	Crockett County
392.C85	Crosby County
392.C9	Culberson County
392.D13	Dallam County
392.D14	Dallas County
392.D25	Dawson County
392.D3	Deaf Smith County
392.D35	Delta County
392.D4	Denton County

Including Green Valley

392.D47	Devils River and Valley

	Texas
	Regions, counties, etc., A-Z -- Continued
392.D5	De Witt County
392.D6	Dickens County
392.D65	Dimmit County
	Dinosaur Valley State Park see F392.S65
392.D7	Donley County
392.D9	Duval County
392.E16	Eastland County
	Ecleto Creek and Valley see F392.W7
392.E25	Ector County
392.E3	Edwards County
392.E33	Edwards Plateau
392.E36	El Camino Real de Tierra Adentro National Historic Trail

> Class here works limited to the part of the El Camino Real de
> Tierra Adentro National Historic Trail located in Texas
> For general works on the El Camino Real de Tierra
> Adentro National Historic Trail, as well as works
> limited to the part located in New Mexico see
> F802.E45

F1-975

392.E38	El Paso County
392.E4	Ellis County
392.E64	Enchanted Rock State Natural Area
392.E7	Erath County
392.F15	Falls County
392.F17	Fannin County
392.F2	Fayette County
392.F4	Fisher County
392.F6	Floyd County
392.F65	Foard County
392.F7	Fort Bend County
	Fort Leaton State Park see F392.P7
392.F8	Franklin County
392.F85	Freestone County
392.F9	Frio County
392.F92	Frio River and Valley
	Including Choke Canyon Reservoir
392.G2	Gaines County
392.G25	Galveston County
392.G3	Garza County
392.G5	Gillespie County
392.G55	Glasscock County
392.G6	Goliad County
	Including Goliad State Park
392.G65	Gonzales County
392.G68	Gray County
392.G7	Grayson County

Texas

Regions, counties, etc., A-Z -- Continued

392.G73	Gregg County
392.G75	Grimes County
392.G85	Guadalupe County
392.G86	Guadalupe Mountains. Guadalupe Mountains National Park

Class here works limited to the part of the Guadalupe Mountains located in Texas

For general works on the Guadalupe Mountains, as well as works limited to the part located in New Mexico see F802.G93

392.G9	Gulf coast of Texas

For Padre Island see F392.P14

Cf. F296 Gulf coast (General)

392.H3	Hale County
392.H33	Hall County
392.H34	Hamilton County
392.H35	Hansford County
392.H36	Hardeman County
392.H37	Hardin County

Including Big Thicket

392.H38	Harris County

Including Armand Bayou Park and Nature Center

392.H39	Harrison County
392.H4	Hartley County
392.H43	Haskell County
392.H46	Hays County
392.H5	Hemphill County
392.H54	Henderson County
392.H56	Hidalgo County
392.H57	Hill County
392.H6	Hockley County
392.H65	Hood County
392.H67	Hopkins County
392.H7	Houston County
392.H75	Howard County
392.H8	Hudspeth County
392.H82	Hueco Mountains

Class here general works on the Hueco Mountains, as well as works limited to the part located in Texas

For works limited to the part of the Hueco Mountains located in New Mexico see F802.H84

392.H9	Hunt County
392.H95	Hutchinson County

Including Lake Meredith National Recreation Area

392.I6	Irion County

Texas

Regions, counties, etc., A-Z -- Continued

392.J22	Jack County
392.J24	Jackson County
392.J27	Jasper County
392.J3	Jeff Davis County
392.J33	Jefferson County
	Including Sabine Pass Battlefield State Historical Park
392.J48	Jim Hogg County
392.J5	Jim Wells County
392.J6	Johnson County
392.J7	Jones County
392.K2	Karnes County
392.K25	Kaufman County
392.K3	Kendall County
392.K32	Kenedy County
392.K33	Kent County
392.K35	Kerr County
392.K4	Kimble County
392.K45	King County
392.K47	King Ranch
392.K5	Kinney County
392.K6	Kleberg County
392.K7	Knox County
392.L33	La Junta de los Rios
	Lake Meredith National Recreation Area see F392.H95
392.L36	Lamar County
392.L37	Lamb County
392.L38	Lampasas County
392.L4	La Salle County
392.L42	Lavaca County
392.L45	Lee County
392.L46	Leon County
392.L5	Liberty County
392.L54	Limestone County
392.L55	Lipscomb County
392.L58	Live Oak County
392.L6	Llano County
392.L62	Llano Estacado (Staked Plain)
392.L66	Long Cove
392.L7	Loving County
392.L8	Lubbock County
392.L87	Lyndon B. Johnson Historical Park
392.L9	Lynn County
392.M15	McCulloch County
392.M2	McLennan County
392.M23	McMullen County

F1-975

Texas
   Regions, counties, etc., A-Z -- Continued

392.M25	Madison County
392.M3	Marion County
392.M33	Martin County
392.M36	Mason County
392.M4	Matagorda County
	Including Matagorda Bay
392.M43	Maverick County
392.M44	Medina County
392.M45	Menard County
	Meredith, Lake, National Recreation Area see F392.H95
392.M5	Midland County
392.M54	Milam County
392.M56	Mills County
392.M6	Mitchell County
392.M67	Montague County
392.M7	Montgomery County
392.M74	Moore County
392.M8	Morris County
	Mother Neff State Park see F392.C8
392.M85	Motley County
	Mustang Island State Park see F392.N8
392.N2	Nacogdoches County
392.N24	Nacogdoches District
392.N3	Navarro County
392.N35	Neches River and Valley
392.N4	Newton County
392.N6	Nolan County
392.N8	Nueces County
392.N82	Nueces River and Valley
392.O2	Ochiltree County
392.O4	Oldham County
392.O7	Orange County
392.P14	Padre Island
392.P16	Palo Duro State Park. Palo Duro Canyon
392.P165	Palo Pinto County
392.P168	Panhandle
392.P17	Panola County
392.P2	Parker County
392.P24	Parmer County
392.P28	Pecos County
392.P3	Pecos River and Valley
	Class here general works on the Pecos River and Valley, as well as works limited to the part located in Texas
	For works limited to the part of the Pecos River and Valley located in New Mexico see F802.P3

Texas
Regions, counties, etc., A-Z -- Continued

392.P55	Polk County
392.P6	Potter County
392.P7	Presidio County
	Including Fort Leaton State Park
392.R15	Rains County
392.R2	Randall County
392.R22	Ray Roberts Lake
392.R25	Reagan County
392.R26	Real County
392.R3	Red River and Valley

Class here works limited to the part of the Red River and
Valley located in Texas
For general works on the Red River and Valley, as well
as works limited to the part located in Louisiana see
F377.R3

392.R33	Red River County
392.R4	Reeves County
392.R45	Refugio County
392.R48	Richland Creek and Valley
	Including Richland-Chambers Dam and Reservoir
392.R5	Rio Grande and Valley

Class here general works on the Rio Grande and Rio Grande
Valley, as well as works limited to the part located in
Texas
For Big Bend National Park see F392.B53
For works limited to the part of the Rio Grande and Rio
Grande Valley located in New Mexico see F802.R5
For works limited to the part of the Rio Grande and Rio
Grande Valley located in Mexico see F1334

392.R6	Roberts County
392.R63	Robertson County
392.R64	Rocking Chair Ranche
392.R65	Rockwall County
392.R75	Runnels County
392.R8	Rusk County
392.S11	Sabine County
	Sabine Pass Battlefield State Historical Park see F392.J33
392.S12	Sabine River and Valley

Class here works limited to the part of the Sabine River and
Valley located in Texas
For general works on the Sabine River and Valley, as
well as works limited to the part located in
Louisiana see F377.S116

392.S19	San Antonio River and Valley
392.S23	San Augustine County

Texas

    Regions, counties, etc., A-Z -- Continued

392.S234	San Gabriel River and Valley
392.S235	San Jacinto County
392.S236	San Marcos River and Valley
392.S237	San Patricio County
392.S24	San Saba County
392.S35	Schleicher County
392.S4	Scurry County
392.S46	Shackelford County
392.S5	Shelby County
392.S52	Sherman County
392.S55	Smith County
392.S65	Somervell County
	Including Dinosaur Valley State Park
	South Bend Reservoir see F392.B842
	Staked Plain see F392.L62
392.S75	Starr County
392.S78	Stephens County
392.S8	Sterling County
392.S85	Stonewall County
392.S9	Sutton County
392.S95	Swisher County
392.T25	Tarrant County
392.T3	Taylor County
	Tennessee Valley see F392.B34
392.T4	Terrell County
392.T45	Terry County
392.T47	Texas Hill Country
392.T5	Throckmorton County
392.T55	Titus County
	Toledo Bend Reservoir and Toledo Bend region see F377.T6
392.T6	Tom Green County
392.T7	Travis County
392.T8	Trinity County
392.T83	Trinity River and Valley
392.T9	Tyler County
392.U5	Upshur County
392.U6	Upton County
392.U9	Uvalde County
392.V17	Val Verde County
392.V2	Van Zandt County
392.V5	Victoria County
392.W24	Walker County
392.W25	Waller County
392.W27	Ward County

Texas

Regions, counties, etc., A-Z -- Continued

392.W3	Washington County
392.W33	Washita River and Valley

Class here general works on the Washita River and Valley, as well as works limited to the part located in Texas

For works limited to the part of the Washita River and Valley located in Oklahoma see F702.W36

392.W4	Webb County
392.W45	Wharton County
392.W47	Wheeler County
392.W55	Wichita County
392.W6	Wilbarger County
392.W64	Willacy County
392.W66	Williamson County
392.W7	Wilson County

Including Ecleto Creek

392.W75	Winkler County
392.W8	Wise County
392.W9	Wood County
392.X2	XIT Ranch
392.Y6	Yoakum County
392.Y7	Young County
392.Z3	Zapata County
392.Z4	Zavala County
394.A-Z	Cities, towns, etc., A-Z

e.g.

394.A4	Amarillo
394.A9-.A99	Austin (Table F2)
394.B3	Beaumont
394.C78	Corpus Christi
394.D21-.D219	Dallas (Table F2)
394.E4	El Paso
394.F7	Fort Worth
394.G2	Galveston
394.H8-.H89	Houston (Table F2)
394.S211-.S2119	San Antonio (Table F2)
394.W12	Waco

Elements in the population

395.A1	General works
395.A2-Z	Individual elements

For a list of racial, ethnic, and religious elements (with Cutter numbers) see E184.A+

F1-975

396	Old Southwest. Lower Mississippi Valley
	Biography: John A. Murrell
	Cf. E78.S8 Indians of the Old Southwest
	Cf. E334 Burr's Conspiracy
	Cf. F296 Gulf coast
	Cf. F350.3+ Mississippi River and Valley
	Cf. F366+ Louisiana
	Cf. F377.R3 Red River, La.
	Cf. F392.B7 Texas boundaries
	Cf. F417.O9 Ozark Mountain region
	Cf. F786 Mexican boundaries (United States)

Arkansas

Historical note from the second edition (1913) of Class F: "Part of the province of Louisiana under France and Spain. On the division of Louisiana in 1804 it belonged to the northern portion, or District of Louisiana which became the Territory of Missouri in 1812. In 1819 the Territory of Arkansas was set off from Missouri, containing all Louisiana between 33° and 36 °30', west to the Spanish possessions. 1824-1828 the territory gave up its western portion as Indian country, and in 1836 was admitted as a state with substantially its present limits."

406	Periodicals. Societies. Collections
408	Museums. Exhibitions, exhibits
409	Gazetteers. Dictionaries. Geographic names
409.3	Guidebooks
410	Biography (Collective). Genealogy (Collective)
410.2	Historiography
	Historians see E175.5.A+
410.5	Study and teaching
411	General works. Histories
	Including admission as a state, June 15, 1836
	Including by period (Early to 1950), as well as general
	Including Reconstruction
	Including biography: Thomas Chipman McRae, etc.
	For 1951 and later see F415+
	Cf. D769.85.A8+ World War II, 1939-1945
	Cf. E470.4+ Military operations
	Cf. E471+ Civil War campaigns and battles
	Cf. E532+ Civil War, 1861-1865, Union history
	Cf. E553+ Civil War, 1861-1865 (General)
411.3	Juvenile works
411.5	Pamphlets, addresses, essays
411.6	Anecdotes, legends, pageants, etc.
412	Historic monuments (General). Illustrative material
413	Antiquities (Non-Indian)
	By period
	Early to 1950 see F411

	Arkansas
	By period -- Continued
	1951-
415	General works
	Biography and memoirs
415.2	Collective
415.3.A-Z	Individual, A-Z
	Subarrange each by Table F5
417.A-Z	Regions, counties, etc., A-Z
417.A15	Counties
417.A16	Mountains
417.A17	Rivers
417.A18	Lakes
417.A19	Islands
417.A65	Arkansas County
417.A67	Arkansas Delta
417.A7	Arkansas River and Valley
	Class here general works on the Arkansas River and Valley, as well as works limited to the part located in Arkansas
	For works limited to the part of the Arkansas River and Valley located in Kansas see F687.A7
	For works limited to the part of the Arkansas River and Valley located in Oklahoma see F702.A7
	For works limited to the part of the Arkansas River and Valley located in Colorado see F782.A7
417.A8	Ashley County
417.B27	Bartholomew Bayou
	Class here general works on the Bartholomew Bayou, as well as works limited to the part located in Arkansas
	For works limited to the part of the Bartholomew Bayou located in Louisiana, see F377.B37
417.B3	Baxter County
417.B4	Benton County
	Blue Mountain Lake see F417.L75
417.B6	Boone County
417.B7	Boundaries
	Cf. F347.B7 Mississippi boundary
417.B8	Bradley County
417.B85	Buffalo River and Valley
417.B86	Bull Shoals Lake and Region
	Class here general works on Bull Shoals Lake and Region, as well as works limited to the part located in Arkansas
	For works limited to the part of Bull Shoals Lake and Region located in Missouri see F472.B94
417.C27	Cadron Creek and Valley
417.C3	Calhoun County
	Including Sparta Mine

F1-975

Arkansas

Regions, counties, etc., A-Z -- Continued

417.C4	Carroll County
417.C45	Chicot County
417.C5	Clamorgan land grant (Arkansas and Missouri)
417.C53	Clark County
417.C54	Clay County
417.C55	Cleburne County
417.C56	Cleveland County
417.C6	Columbia County
417.C7	Conway County
	Including Cypress Creek and Valley
417.C8	Craighead County
	Crater of Diamonds State Park see F417.P5
417.C87	Crawford County
417.C9	Crittenden County
417.C95	Cross County
	Cypress Creek and Valley see F417.C7
417.D3	Dallas County
417.D4	Desha County
417.D7	Drew County
417.F3	Faulkner County
417.F7	Franklin County
417.F8	Fulton County
417.G3	Garland County
417.G7	Grant County
417.G8	Greene County
417.H4	Hempstead County
417.H6	Hot Spring County
417.H7	Howard County
417.I5	Independence County
417.I9	Izard County
417.J3	Jackson County
417.J4	Jefferson County
417.J6	Johnson County
417.L2	Lafayette County
417.L4	Lawrence County
417.L45	Lee County
417.L6	Lincoln County
417.L64	Little River and Valley
	Class here works limited to the part of the Little River and Valley located in Arkansas
	For general works on the Little River and Valley, as well as works limited to the part located in Oklahoma see F702.L55
417.L65	Little River County

Arkansas

Regions, counties, etc., A-Z -- Continued

417.L75	Logan County
	Including Blue Mountain Lake
417.L8	Lonoke County
417.M3	Madison County
417.M35	Marion County
417.M5	Miller County
417.M58	Mississippi County
417.M6	Mississippi River and Valley, Ark.
	Cf. F350.3+ General
	Cf. F396 Lower Mississippi Valley
417.M7	Monroe County
417.M75	Montgomery County
417.N4	Nevada County
417.N5	Newton County
417.N56	Nimrod Lake and Region
417.O75	Ouachita County
417.O77	Ouachita Mountains
	Class here works limited to the part of the Ouachita Mountains located in Arkansas
	For general works on the Ouachita Mountains, as well as works limited to the part located in Oklahoma see F702.O9
417.O8	Ouachita National Forest (Arkansas National Forest)
417.O83	Ouachita River and Valley
	Class here works limited to the part of the Ouachita River and Valley located in Arkansas
	For general works on the Ouachita River and Valley, as well as works limited to the part located in Louisiana see F377.O8
417.O9	Ozark Mountains
	Class here general works on the Ozark Mountains, as well as works limited to the part located in Arkansas
	For works limited to the part of the Ozark Mountains located in Missouri see F472.O9
417.P4	Perry County
417.P43	Petit Jean Mountain
417.P45	Phillips County
417.P5	Pike County
	Including Crater of Diamonds State Park
417.P65	Poinsett County
417.P7	Polk County
417.P75	Pope County
417.P85	Prairie County
417.P98	Pulaski County
417.R2	Randolph County

Arkansas

Regions, counties, etc., A-Z -- Continued

417.R3	Red River and Valley
	Class here works limited to the part of the Red River and Valley located in Arkansas
	For general works on the Red River and Valley, as well as works limited to the part located in Louisiana see F377.R3
417.S15	Saint Francis County
417.S2	Saint Francis River and Valley
	Class here general works on the Saint Francis River and Valley, as well as works limited to the part located in Arkansas
	For works limited to the part of the Saint Francis River and Valley located in Missouri see F472.S25
417.S23	Saline County
417.S25	Scott County
417.S3	Searcy County
417.S33	Sebastian County
417.S4	Sevier County
417.S5	Sharp County
	Sparta Mine see F417.C3
417.S8	Stone County
417.U5	Union County
417.V3	Van Buren County
417.V55	Village Creek and Valley
417.W3	Washington County
417.W4	White County
417.W5	White River and Valley
	Class here general works on the White River and Valley, as well as works limited to the part located in Arkansas
	For works limited to the part of the White River and Valley located in Missouri see F472.W5
417.W6	Woodruff County
417.Y4	Yell County
	For Blue Mountain Lake see F417.L75
419.A-Z	Cities, towns, etc., A-Z
	e.g.
419.H8	Hot Springs
419.L7	Little Rock
	Elements in the population
420.A1	General works
420.A2-Z	Individual elements
	For a list of racial, ethnic, and religious elements (with Cutter numbers) see E184.A+

Tennessee

Historical note from the second edition (1913) of Class F: "Part of North Carolina under her early grants. Settled first, 1769-72, in the neighborhood of the Watauga River in eastern extremity. A local government called the Watauga association was organized in 1772, but soon absorbed by N.C. 1784 that state ceded her western territory to the U.S.; and the Watauga colony formed an independent State (Frankland or Franklin) and applied for admission to the union. N.C. thereupon withdrew her cession, and reestablished her jurisdiction west of the mountains. In 1790, it was again ceded to the U.S. and organized as the "Territory South of the Ohio." Admitted as a state 1796."

431	Periodicals. Societies. Collections
433	Museums. Exhibitions, exhibits
434	Gazetteers. Dictionaries. Geographic names
434.3	Guidebooks
435	Biography (Collective). Genealogy (Collective)
435.2	Historiography

F1-975

Historians see E175.5.A+

435.5	Study and teaching
436	General works. Histories

Including the state of Franklin, 1784-1788; admission as a state, June 1, 1796

By period (Early to 1950) as well as general

Including pioneer days; Secession and Reconstruction

Including biography: David Crockett, Jefferson Dillard Goodpasture, Austin Peay, Archibald Roane, James Robertson, William Tatham, Alfred Alexander Taylor, Robert Love Taylor, etc.

For 1951 and later see F440

Cf. D570.85.T2+ World War I, 1914-1918

Cf. D769.85.T2+ World War II, 1939-1945

Cf. E83.813 First Creek War, 1813-1814

Cf. E263.T4 Tennessee in the Revolution, 1775-1783

Cf. E309 North Carolina cessions of 1784 and 1790

Cf. E409.5.T4 War with Mexico, 1845-1848

Cf. E470.4+ Civil War general military operations

Cf. E470.5 Civil War military operations

Cf. E471+ Civil War campaigns and battles

Cf. E531+ Civil War, 1861-1865, Union history

Cf. E579+ Civil War, 1861-1865 (General)

Cf. E726.T4 War of 1898 (Spanish-American War)

436.3	Juvenile works
436.5	Pamphlets, addresses, essays
436.6	Anecdotes, legends, pageants, etc.
437	Historic monuments (General). Illustrative material

	Tennessee -- Continued
438	Antiquities (Non-Indian)
	By period
	Early to 1950 see F436
	1951-
440	General works
	Biography and memoirs
440.2	Collective
440.22.A-Z	Individual, A-Z
	Subarrange each by Table F5
442.1	East Tennessee
	Including Association of the Territorial Company of
	Philadelphia, Ocoee District
	Cf. F210 Mountain whites of the South
442.2	Middle Tennessee. Cumberland Valley
	Cf. F457.C9 Cumberland Valley, Ky.
442.3	West Tennessee
	Cf. F443.M6 Mississippi Valley, Tenn.
443.A-Z	Regions, counties, etc., A-Z
443.A15	Counties
443.A16	Mountains
443.A17	Rivers
443.A18	Lakes
443.A19	Islands
443.A5	Anderson County
443.B3	Bald Mountains
	Class here general works on the Bald Mountains, as well as
	works limited to the part located in Tennessee
	Including Big Bald Mountain
	For works limited to the part of the Bald Mountains
	located in North Carolina see F262.B3
443.B33	Bays Mountain
443.B35	Bedford County
	Including Liberty Gap
443.B4	Benton County
	Big Bald Mountain see F443.B3
443.B55	Bledsoe County
443.B6	Blount County
443.B7	Boundaries
	For South Carolina cession south of Tennessee see
	F292.B7
	Cf. F262.B7 North Carolina boundary
	Cf. F457.B7 Kentucky boundary
443.B74	Boyd's Creek and Valley
443.B8	Bradley County
	Including Chatata Creek and Valley
443.C3	Campbell County

Tennessee

Regions, counties, etc., A-Z -- Continued

443.C313	Cannon County
443.C316	Carroll County
443.C32	Carter County
	Including Lost Cove
	Chatata Creek and Valley see F443.B8
443.C4	Cheatham County
443.C45	Chester County
443.C47	Chickamauga Lake and region
443.C5	Claiborne County
443.C55	Clay County
443.C56	Clear Fork River and Valley
	Class here works limited to the part of the Clear Fork River and Valley located in Tennessee
	For general works on the Clear Fork River and Valley, as well as works limited to the part located in Kentucky see F457.C58
443.C57	Clinch River and Valley
	Class here works limited to the part of the Clinch River and Valley located in Tennessee
	For general works on the Clinch River and Valley, as well as works limited to the part located in Virginia see F232.C65
443.C6	Cocke County
443.C65	Coffee County
443.C7	Crockett County
	Cumberland Caverns see F443.W2
443.C78	Cumberland County
	Cumberland River and Valley see F442.2
443.D18	Dale Hollow Lake and Region
	Class here general works on Dale Hollow Lake and Region, as well as works limited to the part located in Tennessee
	For works limited to the part of Dale Hollow Lake and Region located in Kentucky see F457.D26
443.D2	Davidson County
443.D25	Decatur County
443.D3	De Kalb County
443.D5	Dickson County
443.D9	Dyer County
443.F3	Fayette County
443.F34	Fentress County
	Fort Loudoun Lake see F443.L9
	Fort Pillow State Park see F443.L35
443.F7	Franklin County

F1-975

	Tennessee
	Regions, counties, etc., A-Z -- Continued
443.F8	French Broad River and Valley
	Class here general works on the French Broad River and Valley, as well as works limited to the part located in Tennessee
	For works limited to the part of the French Broad River and Valley located in North Carolina see F262.F85
443.G35	Gibson County
443.G4	Giles County
443.G65	Grainger County
443.G7	Great Smoky Mountains
	Including Great Smoky Mountains National Park
443.G75	Greene County
443.G85	Grundy County
	Hales Bar Dam Region see F443.M32
443.H17	Hamblen County
443.H19	Hamilton County
443.H24	Hancock County
443.H28	Hardeman County
443.H3	Hardin County
443.H37	Hawkins County
443.H4	Haywood County
443.H45	Henderson County
443.H5	Henry County
443.H6	Hickman County
443.H7	Holston River and Valley
443.H75	Houston County
443.H8	Humphreys County
443.J3	Jackson County
443.J35	James County
443.J5	Jefferson County
443.J7	Johnson County
443.K6	Knox County
443.L25	Lake County
443.L35	Lauderdale County
	Including Fort Pillow State Park
443.L4	Lawrence County
	LeConte, Mount see F443.S45
443.L5	Lewis County
	Liberty Gap see F443.B35
443.L6	Lincoln County
443.L63	Little River and Valley
443.L64	Little Tennessee River and Valley
443.L8	Lookout Mountain
	Including Rock City Gardens, Ga.
	Lost Cove (Carter Cove) see F443.C32

Tennessee

Regions, counties, etc., A-Z -- Continued

443.L9	Loudon County
	Including Fort Loudoun Lake
443.M15	McMinn County
443.M2	McNairy County
443.M23	Macon County
443.M25	Madison County
443.M32	Marion County
	Including Hale's Bar Dam Region
443.M35	Marshall County
443.M4	Maury County
443.M5	Meigs County
443.M6	Mississippi River and Valley, Tenn.
	Cf. F350.3+ General
	Cf. F396 Lower Mississippi Valley
443.M7	Monroe County
	Including Fort Loudoun
443.M8	Montgomery County
443.M83	Moore County
443.M85	Morgan County
443.N67	Norris Lake
443.O2	Obion County
443.O9	Overton County
443.P34	Paint Rock River
	Class here works limited to the part of the Paint Rock River located in Tennessee
	For general works on the Paint Rock River, as well as works limited to the part located in Alabama see F332.P34
443.P4	Perry County
443.P5	Pickett County
443.P7	Polk County
443.P75	Possum Trot Hollow
443.P78	Powell River and Valley
	Class here works limited to the part of the Powell River and Valley located in Tennessee
	For general works on the Powell River and Valley, as well as works limited to the part located in Virginia see F232.P816
443.P9	Putnam County
443.R34	Reelfoot Lake and region
443.R4	Rhea County

F1-975

	Tennessee
	Regions, counties, etc., A-Z -- Continued
443.R49	Roan Mountain
	Class here works limited to the part of Roan Mountain located in Tennessee
	For general works on Roan Mountain, as well as works limited to the part located in North Carolina see F262.R39
443.R5	Roane County
443.R55	Robertson County
443.R8	Rutherford County
443.S2	Scott County
443.S35	Sequatchie County
443.S36	Sequatchie River and Valley
443.S45	Sevier County
	Including Mount LeConte, Sugarlands
443.S5	Shelby County
443.S6	Smith County
	Smoky Mountains (The Smokies) see F443.G7
443.S7	Stewart County
	Sugarlands see F443.S45
443.S8	Sullivan County
443.S9	Sumner County
443.S97	Sweetwater Valley
443.T3	Tennessee River and Valley
	Class here works limited to the part of the Tennessee River and Valley located in Tennessee
	For general works on the Tennessee River and Valley see F217.T3
443.T5	Tipton County
443.T7	Trousdale County
443.U5	Unicoi County
443.U6	Union County
443.V3	Van Buren County
443.W17	Walden Ridge
443.W2	Warren County
	Including Cumberland Caverns
443.W3	Washington County
443.W33	Watts Bar Reservoir and region
443.W4	Wayne County
443.W5	Weakley County
443.W6	White County
443.W7	Williamson County
443.W75	Wilson County
444.A-Z	Cities, towns, etc., A-Z
	e.g.
444.C4-.C49	Chattanooga (Table F2)

Tennessee
Cities, towns, etc., A-Z -- Continued
For Lookout Mountain see F443.L8

444.K7	Knoxville
444.M5-.M59	Memphis (Table F2)
444.N2-.N29	Nashville (Table F2)
444.O3	Oak Ridge
	Elements in the population
445.A1	General works
445.A2-Z	Individual elements

For a list of racial, ethnic, and religious elements (with Cutter numbers) see E184.A+

Kentucky

Historical note from the second edition (1913) of Class F: "Included in the original limits of Virginia. Small settlements were made by pioneers from N.C. and Va. 1766-1775. The Transylvania colony in 1775 tried to secure recognition from the Continental Congress. Va. organized the region as the county of Kentucky 1776 and later as the district of Kentucky including several counties. 1789 Virginia gave her consent for the formation of a new state, and 1792 Kentucky was admitted."

F1-975

446	Periodicals. Societies. Collections
448	Museums. Exhibitions, exhibits
449	Gazetteers. Dictionaries. Geographic names
449.3	Guidebooks
450	Biography (Collective). Genealogy (Collective)
450.2	Historiography
	Historians see E175.5.A+
450.5	Study and teaching
451	General works. Histories
451.3	Juvenile works
451.5	Pamphlets, addresses, essays
451.6	Anecdotes, legends, pageants, etc.
452	Historic monuments (General). Illustrative material
453	Antiquities (Non-Indian)
	By period
454	Early to 1792

Including Transylvania; County and District of Kentucky
Including biography: Daniel Boone, James Harrod, Richard Henderson, etc.
Cf. E83.79 Wars with northwestern Indians, 1790-1795
Cf. F517 Early explorations on Ohio River

	Kentucky
	By period -- Continued
455	1792-1865

Including admission as a state, June 1, 1792

Including biography: George Michael Bedinger, Joseph
Hamilton Daveiss, Harry Innes, Benjamin Sebastian,
Isaac Shelby, etc.

Cf. E328 Kentucky and Virginia Resolutions, 1798
Cf. E359.5.K5 War of 1812
Cf. E409.5.K4 War with Mexico, 1845-1848
Cf. E470.4+ Civil War general military operations
Cf. E471+ Civil War campaigns and battles
Cf. E509+ Civil War, 1861-1865 (General)
Cf. E564+ Civil War, Confederate history
Cf. F210 Mountain whites of the South

| 456 | 1865-1950 |

Including biography: William Goebel, etc.
Cf. D570.85.K4+ World War I, 1914-1918
Cf. D769.85.K4+ World War II, 1939-1945
Cf. E726.K37 War of 1898 (Spanish-American War)

	1951-
456.2	General works
	Biography and memoirs
456.25	Collective
456.26.A-Z	Individual, A-Z
	Subarrange each by Table F5
457.A-Z	Regions, counties, etc., A-Z
457.A15	Counties
457.A16	Mountains
457.A17	Rivers
457.A18	Lakes
457.A19	Islands
457.A3	Adair County
457.A5	Allen County
457.A6	Anderson County
457.B16	Ballard County
457.B2	Barren County
	Including Diamond Cave, Great Onyx Cave
457.B23	Bath County
457.B4	Bell County
	Big Bone Lick see F457.B65
457.B5	Big Sandy River and Valley
457.B6	Bluegrass region
457.B65	Boone County
	Including Big Bone Lick
457.B7	Boundaries
457.B8	Bourbon County

Kentucky
  Regions, counties, etc., A-Z -- Continued

457.B82	Boyd County
457.B83	Boyle County
457.B84	Bracken County
457.B85	Breathitt County
457.B9	Breckinridge County
457.B92	Bullitt County
457.B95	Butler County
457.C15	Caldwell County
457.C17	Calloway County
457.C2	Campbell County
457.C25	Carlisle County
457.C3	Carroll County
457.C35	Carter County
457.C37	Casey County
457.C55	Christian County
457.C56	Clark County
457.C57	Clay County
457.C58	Clear Fork River and Valley

Class here general works on the Clear Fork River and Valley,
    as well as works limited to the part located in Kentucky
For works limited to the part of the Clear Fork River and
    Valley located in Tennessee see F443.C56

457.C6	Clinton County
457.C66	Crittenden County
457.C7	Cumberland County
457.C77	Cumberland Gap National Historical Park
457.C8	Cumberland Mountains

    Cf. F210 Mountain whites of the South

457.C9	Cumberland River and Valley, Ky.

    Cf. F442.2 Tennessee

    Cypress Creek and Valley see F457.U5

457.D26	Dale Hollow Lake and Region

Class here works limited to the part of Dale Hollow Lake and
    Region located in Kentucky
For general works on the Dale Hollow Lake and
    Region, and those limited to the part located in
    Tennessee see F443.D18

457.D3	Daviess County

    Diamond Cave see F457.B2

457.E2	Edmonson County

    For Mammoth Cave see F457.M2

457.E4	Elliott County
457.E7	Estill County
457.F2	Fayette County
457.F4	Fleming County

F1-975

	Kentucky
	Regions, counties, etc., A-Z -- Continued
457.F6	Floyd County
457.F8	Franklin County
457.F9	Fulton County
457.G16	Gallatin County
457.G2	Garrard County
457.G6	Grant County
457.G77	Graves County
457.G78	Grayson County
	Great Onyx Cave see F457.B2
457.G82	Green County
457.G85	Green River and Valley
457.G86	Greenup County
457.H16	Hancock County
457.H2	Hardin County
457.H3	Harlan County
457.H4	Harrison County
457.H43	Hart County
457.H5	Henderson County
457.H6	Henry County
457.H7	Hickman County
457.H8	Hopkins County
457.J2	Jackson County
457.J23	Jackson Purchase region
457.J4	Jefferson County
457.J5	Jessamine County
457.J7	Johnson County
457.K28	Kenton County
457.K29	Kentucky Lake
457.K3	Kentucky River and Valley
457.K5	Knott County
457.K6	Knox County
457.L2	Larue County
457.L25	Laurel County
457.L27	Lawrence County
457.L45	Lee County
457.L47	Leslie County
457.L48	Letcher County
457.L5	Lewis County
457.L6	Lincoln County
457.L7	Livingston County
457.L8	Logan County
457.L9	Lyon County
457.M14	McCracken County
457.M15	McCreary County
457.M16	McLean County

Kentucky

Regions, counties, etc., A-Z -- Continued

457.M17	Madison County
457.M18	Magoffin County
457.M2	Mammoth Cave
	Including Mammoth Cave National Park
457.M3	Marion County
457.M34	Marshall County
457.M36	Martin County
457.M4	Mason County
457.M5	Meade County
457.M54	Menifee County
457.M56	Mercer County
457.M57	Metcalfe County
457.M6	Mississippi River and Valley, Ky.
	Cf. F350.3+ General
457.M7	Monroe County
457.M74	Montgomery County
457.M8	Morgan County
457.M9	Muhlenberg County
457.N2	Nelson County
457.N5	Nicholas County
457.O2	Ohio County
457.O3	Ohio River and Valley, Ky.
	Cf. F516+ General
457.O4	Oldham County
457.O97	Owen County
457.O98	Owsley County
	Payne Hollow see F457.T65
457.P3	Pendleton County
457.P4	Perry County
457.P6	Pike County
457.P7	Powell County
457.P8	Pulaski County
457.R4	Red River and Valley
	Including Red River Gorge
457.R6	Robertson County
457.R65	Rockcastle County
457.R7	Rowan County
457.R8	Russell County
457.S24	Salt Lick Creek and Valley
457.S3	Scott County
457.S4	Shelby County
457.S5	Simpson County
457.S7	Spencer County
457.T25	Taylor County

F1-975

	Kentucky
	Regions, counties, etc., A-Z -- Continued
457.T3	Tennessee River and Valley
	Class here works limited to the part of the Tennessee River and Valley located in Kentucky
	For general works on the Tennessee River and Valley see F217.T3
	For Kentucky Lake see F457.K29
457.T5	Todd County
457.T6	Trigg County
457.T65	Trimble County
	Including Payne Hollow
457.U5	Union County
	Including Cypress Creek and Valley
457.W2	Warren County
457.W3	Washington County
457.W4	Wayne County
457.W5	Webster County
457.W6	Whitley County
457.W7	Wolfe County
457.W8	Woodford County
459.A-Z	Cities, towns, etc., A-Z
	e.g.
459.C8	Covington
459.F8	Frankfort
459.L6	Lexington
459.L8-.L89	Louisville (Table F2)
	Elements in the population
460.A1	General works
460.A2-Z	Individual elements
	For a list of racial, ethnic, and religious elements (with Cutter numbers) see E184.A+
	Missouri

Historical note from the second edition (1913) of Class F: "Part of the province of Louisiana. In 1804 all that portion above 33 was separated from the lower Louisiana (then called the territory of Orleans) and styled the District of Louisiana, comprising all the possessions of the U.S. west of the Mississippi, above the present state of Louisiana. It became the territory of Louisiana 1805, and territory of Missouri, 1812. 1819 the southern part was detached as the territory of Arkansas, and 1821 Missouri was admitted as a state with nearly its present limits, the irregular northwest corner of the state being added in 1836. The portion of the old province of Louisiana to the north and west, remained unorganized; sometimes designated as 'Missouri Territory' but more often as 'The Indian country.'"

Missouri -- Continued

461	Periodicals. Societies. Collections
463	Museums. Exhibitions, exhibits
464	Gazetteers. Dictionaries. Geographic names
464.3	Guidebooks
465	Biography (Collective). Genealogy (Collective)
465.2	Historiography
	Historians see E175.5.A+
465.5	Study and teaching
466	General works. Histories
	Admission as a state, August 10, 1821
	Including by period (Early to 1950) as well as general
	Including the Platt Purchase
	Including biography: Frederick Bates, Joseph Wingate Folk, etc.
	For 1951 and later see F470
	Cf. D570.85.M8+ World War I, 1914-1918
	Cf. D769.85.M8+ World War II, 1939-1945
	Cf. E373 Missouri Compromise, 1820
	Cf. E470.4+ Civil War general military operations
	Cf. E470.8 Civil War general military operations
	Cf. E470.9 Civil War general military operations
	Cf. E471+ Civil War campaigns and battles
	Cf. E569+ Civil War, Confederate history
	Cf. E571+ Civil War, 1861-1865 (General)
	Cf. E726.M8 War of 1898 (Spanish-American War)
	Cf. F685 Kansas troubles, 1854-1859
466.3	Juvenile works
466.5	Pamphlets, addresses, essays
466.6	Anecdotes, legends, pageants, etc.
467	Historic monuments (General). Illustrative material
468	Antiquities (Non-Indian)
	By period
(469)	Early to 1950
	see F466
470	1951-
472.A-Z	Regions, counties, etc., A-Z
472.A15	Counties
472.A16	Mountains
472.A17	Rivers
472.A18	Lakes
472.A19	Islands
472.A2	Adair County
472.A5	Andrew County
472.A8	Atchison County
472.A9	Audrain County
472.B27	Barry County
472.B28	Barton County

F1-975

	Missouri
	Regions, counties, etc., A-Z -- Continued
472.B3	Bates County
472.B38	Bellevue Valley
472.B4	Benton County
	Including Harry S. Truman Dam and Reservoir
472.B57	Bollinger County
472.B6	Boone County
472.B7	Boundaries
472.B9	Buchanan County
472.B94	Bull Shoals Lake and Region
	Class here works limited to the part of Bull Shoals Lake and Region located in Missouri
	For general works on Bull Shoals Lake and Region, as well as works limited to the part located in Arkansas see F417.B86
472.B96	Butler County
472.C2	Caldwell County
472.C3	Calloway County
472.C32	Camden County
472.C33	Cape Girardeau County
472.C35	Carroll County
472.C36	Carter County
472.C37	Cass County
472.C4	Cedar County
472.C44	Chariton County
472.C45	Christian County
	Clamorgan land grant see F417.C5
472.C47	Clarence Cannon Reservoir
472.C48	Clark County
472.C5	Clay County
472.C53	Clinton County
472.C65	Cole County
472.C7	Cooper County
472.C8	Crawford County
472.C9	Current River and Valley
	Class here general works on the Current River and Valley, as well as works limited to the part located in Missouri
472.D15	Dade County
472.D2	Dallas County
472.D25	Daviess County
472.D3	De Kalb County
472.D35	Dent County

Missouri

Regions, counties, etc., A-Z -- Continued

472.D4	Des Moines River and Valley

Class here works limited to the part of the Des Moines River and Valley located in Missouri

For general works on the Des Moines River and Valley, as well as works limited to the part located in Iowa see F627.D43

472.D6	Douglas County
472.D9	Dunklin County
472.E4	Eleven Point Wild and Scenic River
472.F6	Franklin County
472.G3	Gasconade County
472.G4	Gentry County
472.G8	Greene County
472.G88	Grundy County
472.H3	Harrison County
	Harry S. Truman Dam and Reservoir see F472.B4
472.H6	Henry County Rives County
472.H65	Hickory County

For Harry S. Truman Dam and Reservoir see F472.B4

472.H7	Holt County
472.H8	Howard County
472.H9	Howell County
472.I7	Iron County
472.J2	Jackson County
472.J3	Jasper County

Including Prosperity Lake and region

472.J4	Jefferson County
472.J6	Johnson County
472.K6	Knox County
472.L15	Laclede County
472.L2	Lafayette County
472.L4	Lawrence County
472.L6	Lewis County
472.L7	Lincoln County
472.L8	Linn County
472.L85	Livingston County
472.L88	Loess Hills

Class here works limited to the part of the Loess Hills located in Missouri

For general works on the Loess Hills, as well as works limited to the part located in Iowa see F627.L76

Long Branch Lake and region see F472.M2

472.M13	McDonald County

Including Jacob's Cavern

F1-975

Missouri
    Regions, counties, etc., A-Z -- Continued

472.M2	Macon County
	Including Long Branch Lake and region
472.M23	Madison County
472.M29	Maries County
472.M3	Marion County
472.M4	Mercer County
472.M45	Miller County
	Including Bone Cave
472.M48	Mingo Swamp
472.M55	Mississippi County
472.M6	Mississippi River and Valley, Mo.
	Cf. F350.3+ General
472.M7	Missouri River and Valley, Mo.
	Cf. F598 General
472.M75	Moniteau County
472.M76	Monroe County
472.M77	Montgomery County
472.M8	Morgan County
472.N4	New Madrid County
472.N5	Newton County
472.N7	Nodaway County
472.O6	Oregon County
472.O7	Osage County
472.O74	Osage River and Valley
472.O85	Ozark County
472.O9	Ozark Mountains
	Class here works limited to the part of the Ozark Mountains located in Missouri
	For general works on the Ozark Mountains, as well as works limited to the part located in Arkansas see F417.O9
472.O93	Ozarks, Lake of the
472.P3	Pemiscot County
472.P4	Perry County
	Including Tower Rock
472.P5	Pettis County
472.P55	Phelps County
472.P6	Pike County
472.P64	Pine Ford Dam and Reservoir
472.P7	Platte County
472.P8	Polk County
	Prosperity Lake and region see F472.J3
472.P9	Pulaski County
472.P95	Putnam County
472.R14	Ralls County

	Missouri
	Regions, counties, etc., A-Z -- Continued
472.R15	Randolph County
472.R2	Ray County
472.R4	Reynolds County
472.R6	Ripley County
	Rives Co. see F472.H6
472.S2	Saint Charles County
472.S23	Saint Clair County
472.S25	Saint Francis River and Valley
	Class here works limited to the part of the Saint Francis River and Valley located in Missouri
	For general works on the Saint Francis River and Valley, as well as works limited to the part located in Arkansas see F417.S2
472.S28	Saint Francois County
472.S3	Saint Louis County
472.S33	Ste. Genevieve County
472.S35	Saline County
472.S4	Schuyler County
472.S42	Scotland County
472.S43	Scott County
472.S48	Shannon County
472.S5	Shelby County
472.S65	Stoddard County
472.S7	Stone County
472.S8	Sullivan County
472.T16	Taney County
472.T4	Texas County
472.V4	Vernon County
472.W17	Warren County
472.W2	Washington County
472.W3	Wayne County
472.W4	Webster County
472.W5	White River and Valley
	Class here works limited to the part of the White River and Valley located in Missouri
	For general works on the White River and Valley, as well as works limited to the part located in Arkansas see F417.W5
472.W6	Worth County
472.W7	Wright County
474.A-Z	Cities, towns, etc., A-Z
	e.g.
474.J4	Jefferson City
474.K2-.K29	Kansas City (Table F2)
474.S18	Saint Joseph

F1-975

Missouri
   Cities, towns, etc., A-Z -- Continued
474.S2-.S29   Saint Louis (Table F2)
474.S7   Springfield
   Elements in the population
475.A1   General works
475.A2-Z   Individual elements
        For a list of racial, ethnic, and religious elements (with
           Cutter numbers) see E184.A+
Old Northwest. Northwest Territory
   Historical note from the second edition (1913) of Class F: "First
      explored by the French from New France in the latter part of
      the 17th century, and various trading posts established. On
      the formation of the province of Louisiana, the entire
      Mississippi Valley with the Illinois country was incorporated in
      it, the northern and eastern portions of the Old Northwest (the
      Great Lake region and Ohio Valley above modern Louisville)
      continuing under New France. Certain of the English
      colonies, notably Virginia, had charter claims to this region,
      and the dispute over jurisdiction helped to bring on the
      French and Indian war, one result of which was to transfer all
      territory east of the Mississippi River to England. But the
      claims of the individual colonies were ignored by the mother
      country, and the region west of the Alleghanies as far south
      as the Ohio was annexed to the province of Quebec in 1774.
      Then came the Revolution, with Clark's conquest of the
      Northwest, which led to the abandonment of the British claim
      in the peace of 1783. New York, Virginia, Massachusetts and
      Connecticut all ceded their claims to the general government,
      1781-1786; and 1787 there was passed an ordinance
      organizing the "Territory of the United States Northwest of the
      Ohio". The British posts, however, were not surrendered till
      1796. In 1800 the Territory was divided by a line drawn north
      from the mouth of the Kentucky River, the eastern portion
      retaining the old name, and including all of Ohio, eastern
      Michigan and a strip along the eastern edge of Indiana; the
      western part received the name of Indiana Territory. 1803
      Ohio was admitted as a state with substantially its present
      limits, the remainder of the Northwest Territory being
      annexed to Indiana Territory."
   Including region between the Ohio and Mississippi Rivers and the
      Great Lakes
   Cf. F366+ Louisiana
   Cf. F516+ Ohio Valley
   Cf. F597 Upper Mississippi Valley
476   Periodicals. Societies. Collections
476.5   Museums. Exhibitions, exhibits

Old Northwest. Northwest Territory -- Continued
477	Gazetteers. Dictionaries, Geographic names
477.3	Guidebooks
478	Biography (Collective). Genealogy (Collective)
478.2	Historiography
	Historians see E175.5.A+
478.5	Study and teaching
479	General works. Histories
	Cf. E78.N76 Indians of the Old Northwest
479.3	Juvenile works
479.5	Pamphlets, addresses, essays
479.6	Anecdotes, legends, pageants, etc.
480	Historic monuments (General). Illustrative material
481	Antiquities (Non-Indian)
	By period
482	Early to 1763
	Cf. E199 French and Indian War, 1755-1763
	Cf. F517 Ohio Company, 1749
	Cf. F544 Illinois country
	Cf. F572.M16 Mackinac region
	Cf. F574.D4+ Detroit, 1701
	Cf. F1030 New France
483	1763-1803

Including cessions by Virginia and other states, 1781-1786; settlement; Virginia military lands (Chillicothe); the Seven Ranges; Ohio Company, 1786-1795 (Marietta); American and French Scioto companies (Gallipolis); the Miami or Symmes Purchase (Cincinnati)

Biography: Manasseh Cutler, Nathaniel Massie, Rufus Putnam, Arthur St. Clair

Cf. E83.76 Pontiac's Conspiracy, 1763-1765
Cf. E83.775 Indian wars, 1775-1783
Cf. E83.79 Indian wars, 1790-1795
Cf. E83.794 Wayne's Campaign, 1793-1795
Cf. E234 Clark's campaign, 1778
Cf. E237 Clark's campaign, 1781
Cf. E263.N84 Old Northwest in the Revolution
Cf. E309 Northwest Ordinance of 1787
Cf. F230 Virginia
Cf. F497.W5 Western Reserve of Connecticut
Cf. F534.V7 Vincennes
Cf. F1032 Province of Quebec (Canada); Quebec Act

484.3	1803-1865
	Cf. E83.81 Tippecanoe Campaign, 1811
	Cf. E355 War of 1812 (Military operations)
484.5	1865-1950
484.6	1951-

Old Northwest. Northwest Territory -- Continued
Elements in the population
485.A1   General works
485.A2-Z   Individual elements
      For Individual elements see E184.A+
Ohio
486   Periodicals. Societies. Collections
488   Museums. Exhibitions, exhibits
489   Gazetteers. Dictionaries. Geographic names
489.3   Guidebooks
490   Biography (Collective). Genealogy (Collective)
490.2   Historiography
      Historians see E175.5.A+
490.5   Study and teaching
491   General works. Histories
491.3   Juvenile works
491.5   Pamphlets, addresses, essays
491.6   Anecdotes, legends, pageants, etc.
491.8   Geography
492   Historic monuments (General). Illustrative material
493   Antiquities (Non-Indian)
By period
495   Early to 1865
      Including admission as a state, February 19, 1803
      Including biography: Jacob Burnet, Alfred Kelley, Edward
        Tiffin, Allen Trimble, Thomas Worthington, etc.
      Cf. E83.81 Tippecanoe Campaign, 1811
      Cf. E355+ War of 1812, Military operations
      Cf. E359.5.O2 War of 1812 (General)
      Cf. E409.5.O3 War with Mexico, 1845-1848
      Cf. E470.4+ Civil War general military operations
      Cf. E471+ Civil War campaigns and battles
      Cf. E525+ Civil War, 1861-1865 (General)
      Cf. F483 History before 1803 (Old Northwest)
      Cf. F497.B7 Toledo War, 1836
496   1865-1950
      Including biography: William Allen, Asa Smith Bushnell,
        George Barnsdale Cox, Donn Piatt, Tom Loftin Johnson,
        Charles Reemelin, etc.
      Cf. D570.85.O3+ World War I, 1914-1918
      Cf. D769.85.O3+ World War II, 1939-1945
      Cf. E726.O3 War of 1898 (Spanish-American War)
    1951-
496.2   General works
    Biography
496.3   Collective

Ohio
By period
1951-
Biography -- Continued

496.4.A-Z	Individual, A-Z
	Subarrange each by Table F5
497.A-Z	Regions, counties, etc., A-Z
497.A15	Counties
497.A16	Mountains
497.A17	Rivers
497.A18	Lakes
497.A19	Islands
497.A2	Adams County
497.A4	Allen County
497.A7	Ashland County
497.A73	Ashtabula County
497.A8	Athens County
497.A9	Auglaize County
	Bass Islands see F497.O8
497.B3	Bean Creek and Valley
	Class here general works on Bean Creek and Valley, as well as works limited to the part located in Ohio
	For works limited to the part of Bean Creek River and Valley located in Michigan see F572.B36
497.B4	Belmont County
	Including Raven Rocks
	Blennerhassett Island see F247.B56
497.B7	Boundaries
	Including Toledo War, 1836 (Ohio-Michigan boundary)
497.B8	Brown County
497.B86	Buckeye Lake
497.B9	Butler County
497.C2	Carroll County
497.C4	Champaign County
497.C5	Clark County
	Including George Rogers Clark Memorial Park
497.C53	Clermont County
497.C55	Clinton County
497.C6	Columbiana County
	Including Sandy Beaver Canal
	Connecticut Reserve see F497.W5
497.C7	Coshocton County
497.C8	Crawford County
497.C9	Cuyahoga County
	Including Euclid Creek
497.C95	Cuyahoga River and Valley
	Including Tinkers Creek and Valley

Ohio
     Regions, counties, etc., A-Z -- Continued

497.D2	Darke County
497.D25	Defiance County
497.D3	Delaware County
497.E5	Erie County
	Including Kelleys Island
	For Firelands see F497.W5
497.E6	Erie, Lake, region, Ohio
	For Kelleys Island see F497.E5
	For Bass Islands see F497.O8
	For Sandusky Bay see F497.S23
	Cf. F555 General
	Euclid Creek see F497.C9
497.F15	Fairfield County
497.F2	Fayette County
	Firelands see F497.W5
497.F8	Franklin County
497.F9	Fulton County
497.G15	Gallia County
497.G2	Geauga County
	George Rogers Clark Memorial Park see F497.C5
497.G7	Greene County
497.G93	Guernsey County
497.H2	Hamilton County
	Including Duck Creek, Mill Creek
497.H3	Hancock County
497.H35	Hanging Rock iron region
497.H4	Hardin County
497.H5	Harrison County
497.H55	Henry County
497.H6	Highland County
497.H68	Hocking County
497.H7	Hocking River and Valley
497.H74	Holmes County
497.H8	Huron County
	For Firelands see F497.W5
497.J2	Jackson County
497.J4	Jefferson County
	Including Yellow Creek
	Kelleys Island see F497.E5
497.K7	Knox County
497.L2	Lake County
497.L3	Lawrence County
497.L4	Leatherwood Creek and Valley
497.L6	Licking County

Ohio

Regions, counties, etc., A-Z -- Continued

497.L7	Little Miami River and Valley
	Cf. F497.M64 Miami (Great Miami) River and Valley
497.L8	Logan County
497.L86	Lorain County
497.L9	Lucas County
497.M14	Madison County
497.M18	Mahoning County
497.M2	Mahoning River and Valley
	Class here general works on the Mahoning River and Valley, as well as works limited to the part located in Ohio
	For works limited to the part of the Mahoning River and Valley located in Pennsylvania see F157.M3
497.M3	Marion County
497.M4	Maumee River and Valley
	Class here general works on the Maumee River and Valley as well as works limited to the part located in Ohio
	For works limited to the part of the Maumee River and Valley located in Indiana see F532.M62
497.M5	Medina County
497.M53	Meigs County
497.M56	Mercer County
497.M6	Miami County
497.M64	Miami (Great Miami) River and Valley
	Cf. F497.L7 Little Miami River and Valley
497.M67	Monroe County
497.M7	Montgomery County
	Including Twin Valley
497.M76	Morgan County
497.M8	Morrow County
497.M9	Muskingum County
497.M92	Muskingum River and Valley
497.N6	Noble County
497.O3	Ohio River and Valley, Ohio
	Cf. F516+ General
497.O8	Ottawa County
	Including Bass Islands, Put-in Bay
497.P2	Paulding County
497.P4	Perry County
497.P5	Pickaway County
497.P55	Pike County
497.P8	Portage County
497.P9	Preble County
	Put-in Bay see F497.O8
497.P96	Putnam County
	Raven Rocks see F497.B4

F1-975

	Ohio
	Regions, counties, etc., A-Z -- Continued
497.R5	Richland County
497.R7	Rocky River and Valley
497.R8	Ross County
497.S2	Sandusky County
497.S23	Sandusky River and Valley. Sandusky Bay
	Sandy Beaver Canal see F497.C6
497.S3	Scioto County
497.S32	Scioto River and Valley
497.S4	Seneca County
497.S54	Shelby County
497.S7	Stark County
497.S9	Summit County
	Including Portage Path
	Tiffin River and Valley see F497.B3
	Tinkers Creek and Valley see F497.C95
497.T8	Trumble County
497.T9	Tuscarawas County
497.T93	Tuscarawas River and Valley
497.U5	Union County
497.V2	Van Wert County
497.V5	Vinton County
497.W13	Wabash and Erie Canal
	Class here works limited to the part of the Wabash and Erie Canal located in Ohio
	For general works on the Wabash and Erie Canal, as well as works limited to the part located in Indiana see F532.W16
497.W2	Warren County
497.W3	Washington County
	For Blennerhassett Island see F247.B56
497.W4	Wayne County
497.W5	Western Reserve (Connecticut Reserve). Firelands
497.W7	Williams County
497.W8	Wood County
497.W9	Wyandot County
499.A-Z	Cities, towns, etc., A-Z
	e.g.
499.A3	Akron
499.C2	Canton
499.C4	Chillicothe
499.C5-.C59	Cincinnati (Table F2)
499.C6-.C69	Cleveland (Table F2)
499.C7-.C79	Columbus (Table F2)
499.D2-.D29	Dayton (Table F2)
499.M3	Marietta

	Ohio
	Cities, towns, etc., A-Z -- Continued
499.S7	Springfield
499.T6	Toledo
499.Y8	Youngstown
	Elements in the population
500.A1	General works
500.A2-Z	Individual elements
	For a list of racial, ethnic, and religious elements (with Cutter numbers) see E184.A+
	Ohio River and Valley
	Cf. E78.O4 Indians of the Ohio Valley
	Cf. F157.B2 Pennsylvania
	Cf. F350.3+ Mississippi River and Valley
	Cf. F457.O3 Kentucky
	Cf. F476+ Old Northwest
	Cf. F497.O3 Ohio
	Cf. F532.O4 Indiana
516	General works
	Including periodicals, societies, collections, biographies, etc.
	By period
517	Early to 1795
	Including Celoron's Expedition, 1749; Ohio Company, 1747-1779
	Biography: Michael Cresap, Simon Girty, Simon Kenton, Lewis Wetzel
	Cf. E83.79 Wars with northwestern Indians, 1790-1795
	Cf. E199 French and Indian War, 1755-1763
	Cf. E234 Clark's Campaign, 1778
	Cf. F372 Louisiana before 1803
	Cf. F534.V7 Vincennes
	Cf. F1030 New France
518	1795-1865
	Cf. E470.4+ Civil War general military operations
	Cf. E471+ Civil War campaigns and battles
519	1865-1950
	Including floods, 1884, 1913
520	1951-
	Elements in the population
520.5	General works
520.6.A-Z	Individual elements, A-Z
	For a list of racial, ethnic, and religious elements (with Cutter numbers) see E184.A+

F1-975

Indiana

> Historical note from the second edition (1913) of Class F: "First explored from New France; the southwest portion set off to Louisiana 1712 as part of the Illinois country. Ceded to Great Britain 1763 and annexed to the province of Quebec 1774. Conquered by Clark for Virginia 1779 and British title surrendered to U.S. by treaty of 1783. On relinquishment of claims of certain states under their colonial charters,1781-1786, the "Territory of the United States Northwest of the Ohio" was created 1787. In 1800 Indiana Territory was formed by setting off the part west of the meridian of the Kentucky River, including nearly all of the modern Indiana, the western part of Mich, and all of Ill. and Wis. and northeast Minn. 1803, on the admission of Ohio, Indiana received an accession of a strip along her eastern border, and the rest of Mich. 1805 the Territory of Michigan was set off from Indiana (including the lower peninsula only) 1809 the Territory of Indiana was reduced to substantially its present limits, and the region of the west and northwest established as the Territory of Illinois. Indiana was admitted as a state 1816."

521	Periodicals. Societies. Collections
523	Museums. Exhibitions, exhibits
524	Gazetteers. Dictionaries. Geographic names
524.3	Guidebooks
525	Biography (Collective). Genealogy (Collective)
525.2	Historiography
	Historians see E175.5.A+
525.5	Study and teaching
526	General works. Histories

> Including admission as a state, December 11, 1816
> Including biography: James Franklin Doughty Lanier, etc.
> For 1951 and later see F530
> Cf. D570.85.I6+ World War I, 1914-1918
> Cf. D769.85.I6+ World War II, 1939-1945
> Cf. E83.81 Tippecanoe Campaign, 1811
> Cf. E355 War of 1812 (Military operations)
> Cf. E409.5.I7 War with Mexico (1845-1848
> Cf. E470.4+ Civil War, Military operations
> Cf. E471+ Civil War campaigns and battles
> Cf. E506+ Civil War, 1861-1865 (General)
> Cf. E726.I3 War of 1898 (Spanish-American War)

526.3	Juvenile works
526.5	Pamphlets, addresses, essays
526.6	Anecdotes, legends, pageants, etc.
527	Historic monuments (General). Illustrative material
528	Antiquities (Non-Indian)
	By period

	Indiana
	By period -- Continued
	Early to 1950 see F526
	1951-
530	General works
	Biography and memoirs
530.2	Collective
530.22.A-Z	Individual, A-Z
	Subarrange each by Table F5
532.A-Z	Regions, counties, etc., A-Z
532.A15	Counties
532.A16	Mountains
532.A17	Rivers
532.A18	Lakes
532.A19	Islands
532.A2	Adams County
532.A4	Allen County
	For Maumee River see F532.M62
532.B2	Bartholomew County
532.B4	Benton County
532.B5	Blackford County
532.B6	Boone County
532.B7	Boundaries
532.B76	Brown County
	Calumet region see F532.L2
532.C3	Carroll County
532.C4	Cass County
532.C5	Clark County
532.C6	Clay County
	Clifty Falls State Park see F532.J5
532.C65	Clinton County
532.C8	Crawford County
	Including Wyandotte Cave
532.D17	Daviess County
532.D18	Dearborn County
532.D2	Decatur County
532.D25	De Kalb County
532.D3	Delaware County
532.D8	Dubois County
	Dune region see F532.M67
	Dunes State Park see F532.I5
532.E4	Elkhart County
532.F2	Fayette County
532.F6	Floyd County
532.F77	Fountain County
532.F8	Franklin County
532.F9	Fulton County

F1-975

Indiana
   Regions, counties, etc., A-Z -- Continued

532.G4	Gibson County
532.G7	Grant County
532.G75	Greene County
532.H2	Hamilton County
532.H3	Hancock County
532.H4	Harrison County
532.H5	Hendricks County
532.H6	Henry County
532.H75	Hoosier National Forest
532.H8	Howard County
532.H9	Huntington County
532.I5	Indiana Dunes State Park
532.J14	Jackson County
532.J3	Jasper County
532.J4	Jay County
532.J5	Jefferson County

        Including Clifty Falls State Park

532.J53	Jennings County
532.J6	Johnson County

     Kankakee-St. Joseph portage see F532.S2

532.K2   Kankakee River and Valley

        Class here general works on the Kankakee River and Valley,
           as well as works limited to the part located in Indiana
        For works limited to the part of the Kankakee River and
           Valley located in Illinois see F547.K27

532.K6	Knox County
532.K8	Kosciusko County
532.L17	Lagrange County
532.L2	Lake County

        Including Calumet region, Ind.
        Cf. F547.C7 Illinois

532.L3	La Porte County
532.L4	Lawrence County

        Including Spring Mill State Park
     Lost River and Valley see F532.O63

532.M2	Madison County
532.M4	Marion County
532.M6	Marshall County
532.M613	Martin County
532.M62	Maumee River and Valley

        Class here works limited to the part of the Maumee River and
           Valley located in Indiana
        For general works on the Maumee River and Valley, as
           well as works limited to the part located in Ohio see
           F497.M4

Indiana
    Regions, counties, etc., A-Z -- Continued

532.M65	Miami County
532.M67	Michigan, Lake, region, Ind.
	Including the dunes of Indiana
	For Indiana Dunes State Park see F532.I5
	Cf. F553 General
532.M7	Monroe County
532.M75	Montgomery County
532.M8	Morgan County
532.M87	Muscatatuck National Wildlife Refuge
532.N5	Newton County
	Including Beaver Lake
532.N6	Noble County
532.O3	Ohio County
532.O4	Ohio River and Valley, Ind.
	Cf. F516+ General
532.O63	Orange County
	Including Lost River and Valley
532.O9	Owen County
532.P2	Parke County
	Including Turkey Run State Park
532.P4	Perry County
532.P6	Pike County
	Pokagon State Park see F532.S8
532.P8	Porter County
532.P85	Posey County
532.P88	Pulaski County
532.P9	Putnam County
532.R3	Randolph County
532.R5	Ripley County
532.R95	Rush County
532.S2	Saint Joseph County
	Including Saint Joseph-Kankakee portage
	Cf. F572.S43 Saint Joseph River and Valley, Mich.
532.S3	Saint Joseph River and Valley
	Class here general works on the Saint Joseph River and Valley, as well as works limited to the part located in Indiana
	For works limited to the part of the Saint Joseph River and Valley located in Michigan see F572.S43
532.S35	Scott County
532.S47	Shakamak State Park
532.S5	Shelby County
532.S6	Spencer County
	Including Lincoln Boyhood National Memorial and Nancy Hanks Lincoln Memorial

F1-975

	Indiana
	Regions, counties, etc., A-Z -- Continued
	Spring Mill State Park see F532.L4
532.S7	Starke County
532.S8	Steuben County
	Including Pokagon State Park
532.S9	Sullivan County
532.S97	Switzerland County
532.T6	Tippecanoe County
532.T63	Tipton County
	Turkey Run State Park see F532.P2
532.U5	Union County
532.V2	Vanderburgh County
532.V5	Vermillion County
532.V7	Vigo County
532.W16	Wabash and Erie Canal
	Class here general works on the Wabash and Erie Canal, as well as works limited to the part located in Indiana
	For works limited to the part of the Wabash and Erie Canal located in Ohio see F497.W13
532.W18	Wabash County
532.W2	Wabash River and Valley
	Class here general works on the Wabash River and Valley, as well as works limited to the part located in Indiana
	For works limited to the part of the Wabash River and Valley located in Illinois see F547.W14
532.W3	Warren County
532.W4	Warrick County
532.W45	Washington County
532.W5	Wayne County
532.W55	Wells County
532.W58	White County
532.W59	Whitewater (White Water) River and Valley
532.W6	Whitley County
534.A-Z	Cities, towns, etc., A-Z
	e.g.
534.E9	Evansville
534.F7	Fort Wayne
534.I3-.I39	Indianapolis (Table F2)
534.N5	New Harmony
534.S7	South Bend
534.T3	Terre Haute
534.V7	Vincennes
	Elements in the population
535.A1	General works

	Indiana
	Elements in the population -- Continued
535.A2-Z	Individual elements
	For a list of racial, ethnic, and religious elements (with cutter numbers) see E184.A+

Illinois

Historical note from the second edition (1913) of Class F: "The Illinois country was explored and colonized by New France in the 17th century. A part of Louisiana 1712. Ceded to Great Britain 1763 and annexed to the province of Quebec 1774. Conquered by Clark for Virginia 1779 and confirmed to the U.S. by treaty 1783. The states with claims to the region under colonial charters having ceded them to the general government 1781-1786, the "Territory of the United States Northwest of the Ohio" was organized 1787. On the division of the Northwest Territory in 1800, Illinois became part of the Indiana Territory. 1809 the Territory of Illinois was organized, consisting of the present states of Illinois and Wisconsin, and the upper peninsula of Mich, and northeast Minn. 1818 Illinois was admitted as a state with boundaries substantially as at present, the remainder of the territory being annexed to Mich."

F1-975

536	Periodicals. Societies. Collections
538	Museums. Exhibitions, exhibits
539	Gazetteers. Dictionaries. Geographic names
539.3	Guidebooks
540	Biography (Collective). Genealogy (Collective)
540.2	Historiography
	Historians see E175.5.A+
540.5	Study and teaching
541	General works. Histories
541.3	Juvenile works
541.5	Pamphlets, addresses, essays
541.6	Anecdotes, legends, pageants, etc.
541.8	Geography
542	Historic monuments (General). Illustrative material
543	Antiquities (Non-Indian)
	By period
544	Early to 1775. The Illinois country
	Including Illinois under French rule
	Cf. F352 Mississippi River and Valley before 1803
	Cf. F1030 New France, 1603-1763

Illinois
By period -- Continued
545 1775-1865
Including admission as a state, December 3, 1818
Including biography: John Boyle, Peter Cartwright, Edward
Coles, Joseph Duncan, Ninian Edwards, Thomas Ford,
Adam Wilson Snyder, Richard Yates, etc.
Cf. E83.83 Black Hawk War, 1832
Cf. E234 Clark's Campaign, 1778
Cf. E355 War of 1812 (Military operations)
Cf. E409.5.I4 War with Mexico, 1845-1848
Cf. E470.4+ Civil War, Military operations
Cf. E471+ Civil War campaigns and battles
Cf. E505+ Civil War, 1861-1865 (General)
Cf. F547.E3 English settlement in Edwards County
546 1865-1950
Biography: John Peter Altgeld, Edward Fitzsimons Dunne,
Frank Orren Lowden, Adlai Ewing Stevenson, John Riley
Tanner
Cf. D570.85.I3+ World War I, 1914-1918
Cf. D769.85.I3+ World War II, 1939-1945
Cf. E726.I2 War of 1898 (Spanish-American War)
1951-
546.2 General works
Biography
546.3 Collective
546.4.A-Z Individual, A-Z
Subarrange each by Table F5
547.A-Z Regions, counties, etc., A-Z
547.A15 Counties
547.A16 Mountains
547.A17 Rivers
547.A18 Lakes
547.A19 Islands
547.A2 Adams County
547.A3 Alexander County
Including Horseshoe Lake
547.B6 Bond County
547.B65 Boone County
547.B7 Boundaries
547.B75 Brown County
547.B8 Bureau County
547.C13 Cache River and Valley
547.C15 Calhoun County
Calumet region see F547.C7
547.C2 Carroll County
547.C3 Cass County

Illinois
Regions, counties, etc., A-Z -- Continued

547.C37	Chain O' Lakes
547.C4	Champaign County
547.C45	Chicago River
547.C5	Christian County
547.C53	Clark County
547.C55	Clay County
547.C57	Clinton County
547.C6	Coles County
547.C7	Cook County
	Including Calumet region, Ill.
	Cf. F532.L2 Indiana
547.C8	Crawford County
547.C9	Cumberland County
547.D3	De Kalb County
547.D4	Des Plaines River and Valley, Ill.
547.D5	De Witt County
547.D7	Douglas County
547.D9	Du Page County
	Dunes of Illinois see F547.M56
547.E25	Edgar County
547.E3	Edwards County
	Including English settlement
547.E4	Effingham County
547.F35	Fayette County
547.F7	Ford County
547.F77	Fox River and Valley
	Class here works limited to the part of the Fox River and Valley located in Illinois
	For general works on the Fox River and Valley, as well as works limited to the part located in Kenosha, Racine, and Waukesha Counties, Wisconsin see F587.F7
547.F78	Franklin County
547.F8	Fulton County
547.G3	Gallatin County
	Giant City State Park see F547.J2
547.G7	Greene County
547.G8	Grundy County
547.H17	Hamilton County
547.H2	Hancock County
547.H3	Hardin County
547.H4	Henderson County
547.H52	Henry County
	Horseshoe Lake see F547.A3
547.I13	Illinois and Michigan Canal National Heritage Corridor

F1-975

	Illinois
	Regions, counties, etc., A-Z -- Continued
547.I2	Illinois River and Valley
547.I7	Iroquois County
547.J2	Jackson County
	Including Giant City State Park
547.J3	Jasper County
547.J5	Jersey County
547.J6	Jo Daviess County
547.J8	Johnson County
	Jubilee College State Park see F547.P4
547.K2	Kane County
547.K25	Kankakee County
547.K27	Kankakee River and Valley
	Class here works limited to the part of the Kankakee River and Valley located in Illinois
	Including Willow Creek and Valley
	For general works on the Kankakee River and Valley, as well as works limited to the part located in Indiana see F532.K2
547.K4	Kendall County
547.K7	Knox County
547.L2	Lake County
547.L3	La Salle County
	Including Starved Rock State Park
547.L4	Lawrence County
547.L5	Lee County
547.L78	Livingston County
547.L8	Logan County
547.M13	McDonough County
547.M14	McHenry County
547.M16	McLean County
547.M18	Macoupin County
547.M2	Madison County
547.M3	Marion County
547.M34	Marshall County
547.M37	Mason County
547.M4	Massac County
547.M5	Menard County
547.M55	Mercer County
547.M56	Michigan, Lake region, Ill.
	Including the dunes of Illinois
	Cf. F553 General
547.M6	Military lands between the Mississippi and Illinois Rivers
	Cf. E359.4 Military bounties (War of 1812)

Illinois
Regions, counties, etc., A-Z -- Continued

547.M65	Mississippi River and Valley, Ill.
	Cf. F350.3+ General
	Cf. F597 Upper Mississippi Valley
547.M68	Monroe County
547.M7	Montgomery County
547.M8	Morgan County
547.M9	Moultrie County
547.O3	Ogle County
547.O4	Ohio River and Valley, Ill.
	Cf. F516+ General
547.P4	Peoria County
	Including Jubilee College State Park
547.P45	Perry County
	Including White Walnut Creek and Valley
547.P5	Piatt County
547.P6	Pike County
547.P7	Pope County
547.P78	Pulaski County
547.P8	Putnam County
547.R2	Randolph County
547.R5	Richland County
547.R6	Rock Island County
547.R64	Rock Island Trail State Park
547.R7	Rock River and Valley
	Class here general works on the Rock River and Valley, as well as works limited to the part located in Illinois
	For works limited to the part of the Rock River and Valley located in Wisconsin see F587.R63
547.S2	Saint Clair County
547.S24	Saline County
547.S3	Sangamon County
547.S33	Sangamon River and Valley
547.S4	Schuyler County
547.S45	Scott County
547.S6	Shelby County
547.S65	Spoon River and Valley
547.S7	Stark County
	Starved Rock State Park see F547.L3
547.S8	Stephenson County
547.S94	Sugar Creek and Valley, Macoupin County and Sangamon County
547.T2	Tazewell County
547.U5	Union County
547.V2	Vermilion County
547.W12	Wabash County

	Illinois
	Regions, counties, etc., A-Z -- Continued
547.W14	Wabash River and Valley
	Class here works limited to the part of the Wabash River and Valley located in Illionis
	For general works on the Wabash River and Valley, as well as works limited to the part located in Indiana see F532.W2
547.W2	Warren County
547.W23	Washington County
547.W25	Wayne County
547.W3	White County
	White Walnut Creek and Valley see F547.P45
547.W4	Whiteside County
547.W5	Will County
547.W6	Williamson County
	Willow Creek and Valley see F547.K27
547.W7	Winnebago County
547.W8	Woodford County
	Chicago
548.1	Periodicals. Societies. Collections
548.15	Museums. Exhibitions, exhibits
	Cf. T500 World's Columbian Exposition, 1893
	Cf. T501 Century of Progress International Exposition, 1933-1934
548.18	Guidebooks
548.25	Biography (Collective). Genealogy (Collective)
548.27	Historiography
548.29	Study and teaching
548.3	General works. Histories
548.33	Juvenile works
548.35	Pamphlets, addresses, essays
548.36	Anecdotes, legends, pageants, etc.
548.37	Historic monuments. Illustrative material
548.39	Antiquities (Non-Indian)
	By period
548.4	Early to 1875
	Cf. E356.C53 Fort Dearborn Massacre, 1812
548.42	1865-1875
	Including great fire of 1871
548.45	1875-1892
	Cf. T500 World's Columbian Exposition, 1893
548.5	1892-1950
	1951-
548.52	General works
	Biography
548.53	Collective

	Illinois
	Chicago
	By period
	1951-
	Biography -- Continued
548.54.A-Z	Individual, A-Z
	Subarrange each by Table F5
	Sections. Localities. Districts, etc.
548.6	General works
	Cemeteries
548.61	General works
548.612.A-Z	Individual, A-Z
548.612.G72	Graceland Cemetery, Chicago
548.62	Churches
548.625	Hotels, taverns, etc.
548.627	Places of amusement
548.63	Harbor
548.64	Monuments. Statues
	e.g.
548.64.A1	General works
548.64.G4	George Washington-Robert Morris-Haym Salomon Monument
548.65	Parks. Squares. Circles
	e.g.
548.65.A1	General works
548.65.D2	Dearborn Park
548.65.L7	Lincoln Park
548.65.S7	South Park
548.67	Streets. Bridges. Railroads
	e.g.
548.67.A1	General works
548.67.M75	Monroe Street
548.68	Suburbs. Sections of the city. Rivers, etc.
	e.g.
548.68.A1	General works
548.68.I7	Irving Park
548.68.N7	North Shore
548.68.R8	Roseland
548.68.S7	South Shore
548.68.W8	Wolf's Point
548.68.W82	Woodlawn
548.69	Wards
	Buildings
548.7	General works. Collective
548.8.A-Z	Individual, A-Z
	e.g.
548.8.A9	Auditorium Building

	Illinois
	Chicago
	Buildings
	Individual, A-Z -- Continued
548.8.C9	Custom House
548.8.G7	Grand Central Passenger Station
548.8.P17	Palmer House
	Elements in the population
548.9.A1	General works
548.9.A2-Z	Individual elements

For a list of racial, ethnic, and religious elements (with Cutter numbers) see E184.A+

549.A-Z	Other cities, towns, etc., A-Z
	e.g.
549.A4	Alton
549.B6	Bishop Hill Colony
549.B65	Bloomington
549.C44	Champaign
549.C56	Cicero
549.D3	Decatur
549.E2	East St. Louis
549.E8	Evanston
549.J7	Joliet
549.O13	Oak Park
549.P4	Peoria
549.Q6	Quincy
549.R6	Rock Island
549.R7	Rockford
549.S7	Springfield
	Elements in the population
550.A1	General works
550.A2-Z	Individual elements

For a list of racial, ethnic, and religious elements (with Cutter numbers) see E184.A+

The Lake region. Great Lakes

Including the portion of the northern boundary of the United States between the St. Lawrence River and the Lake of the Woods; early French explorations; British posts

Cf. F476+ Old Northwest

Cf. F1030 New France

Cf. GB1627.G8+ Physical geography

550.5	Biography (Collective). Genealogy (Collective)
551	General works

The Lake region. Great Lakes -- Continued
552   Lake Superior
                          Cf. F572.S9 Lake Superior region, Mich.
                          Cf. F587.A8 Apostle Islands and Chequamegon Bay
                          Cf. F587.S9 Lake Superior region, Wis.
                          Cf. F612.S9 Lake Superior region, Minn.
                          Cf. F1059.S9 Lake Superior region, Ontario
                          Cf. F1059.T5 Thunder Bay region, Ontario
553   Lake Michigan
                          Cf. F532.M67 Lake Michigan region, Ind.
                          Cf. F547.M56 Lake Michigan region, Ill.
                          Cf. F572.M16 Mackinac Straits and region
                          Cf. F572.M57 Lake Michigan region, Mich.
                          Cf. F587.G6 Green Bay
                          Cf. F587.M57 Lake Michigan region, Wis.
554   Lake Huron
                          Cf. F572.H92 Lake Huron region, Mich.
                          Cf. F572.S15 Saginaw Bay
                          Cf. F572.S34 Lake St. Clair
                          Cf. F1059.G3 Georgian Bay
                          Cf. F1059.H95 Lake Huron region, Ontario

F1-975

555   Lake Erie
                          Cf. F127.E65 Lake Erie region, N.Y.
                          Cf. F127.N6 Niagara region
                          Cf. F157.E6 Lake Erie region, Pa. (Erie Co.)
                          Cf. F497.E6 Lake Erie region, Ohio
                          Cf. F497.W5 Western Reserve
                          Cf. F1059.E6 Lake Erie region, Ontario
556   Lake Ontario
                          Cf. F127.O72 Lake Ontario region, N.Y.
                          Cf. F1050 St. Lawrence River
                          Cf. F1059.O6 Lake Ontario region
                     Elements in the population
558   General works
558.2.A-Z   Individual elements
                          For a list of racial, ethnic, and religious elements (with
                              Cutter numbers) see E184.A+

Michigan

Historical note from the second edition (1913) of Class F: "For early political history of this region see note under F476+ The present Michigan formed part of the original Northwest Territory in 1787; was divided in 1800, with its western part in Indiana Territory. 1803 the eastern part also was annexed to Indiana Territory. In 1805 the territory of Michigan was set off from Indiana, consisting at that time of the lower peninsula only (the upper peninsula continuing a part of Indiana Territory till the organization of Illinois Territory in 1809). 1818, on the admission of Illinois as a state, the northern portion of the former Illinois Territory (including the northern peninsula, all of Wis. and northeast Minn.) was added to Mich. In 1834, all the region west, bounded by Missouri, the Missouri River and the Canadian line, was annexed, including the rest of Minn., Iowa and parts of the Dakotas. This was followed by agitation for the erection of a new state east of Lake Michigan and the organization of the region west of that lake as a new territory. The matter was complicated by a controversy between O. and Mich, over their boundary, (the Toledo war). Congress took action by organizing Wisconsin Territory under an act approved April, 1836, and offering statehood to Mich, in June, 1836, on her acceptance of the northern peninsula in compensation for the tract in dispute with Ohio. Michigan, which had already organized a state government in 1835, accepted statehood on these terms in December, 1836."

561	Periodicals. Societies. Collections
563	Museums. Exhibitions, exhibits
564	Gazetteers. Dictionaries. Geographic names
564.3	Guidebooks
565	Biography (Collective). Genealogy (Collective)
565.2	Historiography
	Historians see E175.5.A+
565.5	Study and teaching

Michigan -- Continued

566	General works. Histories
	Including admission as a state, January 26, 1837
	Including by period (early to 1950) as well as general
	Including biography: Aaron Thomas Bliss, Stevens Thomson
	Mason, Chase Salmon Osborn, William Woodbridge, etc.
	For 1951 and later see F570+
	Cf. D570.85.M5+ World War I, 1914-1918
	Cf. D769.85.M5+ World War II, 1939-1945
	Cf. E83.76 Pontiac's War, 1763-1765
	Cf. E83.81 Tippecanoe Campaign, 1881
	Cf. E237 Clark's campaign against Detroit, 1781
	Cf. E355 War of 1812 (Military operations)
	Cf. E471+ Civil War campaigns and battles
	Cf. E514+ Civil War, 1861-1865 (General)
	Cf. E726.M6 War of 1898 (Spanish-American War)
	Cf. F497.B7 Toledo War, 1836
566.3	Juvenile works
566.5	Pamphlets, addresses, essays
566.6	Anecdotes, legends, pageants, etc.
567	Historic monuments (General). Illustrative material
568	Antiquities (Non-Indian)
	By period
	Early to 1950 see F566
	1951-
570	General works
	Biography
570.2	Collective
570.25.A-Z	Individual, A-Z
	Subarrange each by Table F5
572.A-Z	Regions, counties, etc., A-Z
572.A15	Counties (Collective and selective)
	For Northern Michigan see F572.N7
	For Northern (Upper) Peninsula see F572.N8
572.A16	Mountains
572.A17	Rivers
572.A18	Lakes
572.A19	Islands
572.A2	Alcona County
572.A25	Alger County
572.A3	Allegan County
572.A4	Alpena County
	Including Thunder Bay
572.A5	Antrim County
	Including Torch Lake
572.A7	Arenac County
	Including Point Lookout

	Michigan
	Regions, counties, etc., A-Z -- Continued
572.B15	Baraga County
572.B2	Barry County
572.B3	Bay County
	Including Tobico Marsh
572.B36	Bean Creek and Valley
	Class here works limited to the part of Bean Creek and Valley located in Michigan
	For general works on Bean Creek and Valley, as well as works limited to the part located in Ohio see F497.B3
572.B38	Beaver Island
572.B4	Benzie County
	Including Crystal Lake, Herring Lake
572.B5	Berrien County
	Including Paw Paw Lake
572.B7	Boundaries
	For Toledo War, 1836 (Michigan-Ohio boundary) see F497.B7; F497.B7
	Cf. F532.B7 Indiana boundary
572.B8	Branch County
572.B86	Brule River and Valley
	Class here general works on the Brule River and Valley, as well as works limited to the part located in Michigan
	For works limited to the part of the Brule River and Valley located in Wisconsin see F587.B85
572.C2	Calhoun County
572.C3	Cass County
572.C4	Charlevoix County
	For Beaver Island see F572.B38
572.C5	Cheboygan County
	Including Douglas Lake
	Cheneaux Islands see F572.L57
572.C54	Chippewa County
	For Drummond Island see F572.D88
572.C65	Clare County
572.C7	Clinton County
572.C9	Crawford County
	Crystal Lake see F572.B4
572.D4	Delta County
572.D46	Detroit River and Valley
	Class here general works on the Detroit River and Valley, as well as works limited to the part located in Michigan
	For works limited to the part of the Detroit River and Valley located in Ontario see F1059.D46
	Devils Lake (Lenawee County) see F572.L5

Michigan
    Regions, counties, etc., A-Z -- Continued

572.D5	Dickinson County
	Douglas Lake see F572.C5
572.D88	Drummond Island
572.E2	Eaton County
572.E5	Emmet County
	Fox Islands see F572.L45
572.G3	Genesee County
572.G38	Gladwin County
572.G44	Gogebic County
572.G45	Grand Island
572.G46	Grand River and Valley
572.G5	Grand Traverse Bay region. The Traverse region

                Including Power Island
                Cf. F572.L7 Little Traverse Bay region

572.G6	Grand Traverse County
572.G8	Gratiot County
572.G87	Green Bay Region

                Class here works limited to the part of the Green Bay Region
                    located in Michigan
                For general works on the Green Bay Region, as well as
                    works limited to the part located in Wisconsin see
                    F587.G6

572.H6	Hillsdale County
572.H8	Houghton County
	Houghton Lake see F572.R6
572.H9	Huron County
	Huron Mountains see F572.M33
572.H92	Huron, Lake, region, Mich.

                Cf. F554 General

572.H93	Huron-Manistee National Forests
572.I5	Ingham County
572.I6	Ionia County

                Including Long Lake

572.I63	Iosco County
572.I66	Iron County
572.I7	Isabella County
572.I8	Isle Royale
572.J2	Jackson County
572.K2	Kalamazoo County
572.K22	Kalamazoo River and Valley
572.K23	Kalkaska County
572.K3	Kent County
572.K4	Keweenaw County

                For Isle Royale see F572.I8

572.K43	Keweenaw Peninsula

Michigan

Regions, counties, etc., A-Z -- Continued

572.L2	Lake County
572.L3	Lapeer County
572.L45	Leelanau County
	Including Fox Islands
572.L5	Lenawee County
	Including Devils Lake
572.L57	Les Cheneaux Islands (The Snows)
572.L7	Little Traverse Bay region
	Cf. F572.G5 Grand Traverse Bay region
572.L8	Livingston County
	Long Lake (Ionia County) see F572.I6
	Lookout, Point (Arenac Co.) see F572.A7
572.L9	Luce County
572.M14	Mackinac (Mackinaw) County Mackinac region. Straits of Mackinac, etc.
	For Les Cheneaux Islands see F572.L57
572.M16	Mackinac Island. Mackinac Island (City)
572.M2	Macomb County
572.M3	Manistee County
572.M33	Marquette County
	Including Huron Mountains
572.M36	Mason County
572.M4	Mecosta County
572.M5	Menominee County
572.M516	Menominee Range
	Class here general works on the Menominee Range, as well as works limited to the part located in Michigan
	For works limited to the part of the Menominee Range located in Wisconsin see F587.M49
572.M52	Menominee River and Valley
	Class here general works on the Menominee River and Valley, as well as works limited to the part located in Michigan
	For works limited to the part of the Menominee River and Valley located in Wisconsin see F587.M5
572.M57	Michigan, Lake, region, Mich.
	Cf. F553 General
	Michilimackinac see F572.M16
572.M6	Midland County
572.M65	Missaukee County
572.M7	Monroe County
572.M8	Montcalm County
572.M83	Montmorency County
572.M9	Muskegon County
572.M93	Muskegon River and Valley

Michigan
    Regions, counties, etc., A-Z -- Continued

572.N5	Newaygo County
572.N7	Northern Michigan (Northern part of Lower Peninsula)
572.N8	Northern (Upper) Peninsula
572.O2	Oakland County
572.O3	Oceana County
572.O4	Ogemaw County
572.O6	Ontonagon County
572.O62	Ontonagon River and Valley
572.O7	Osceola County
572.O73	Oscoda County
572.O78	Otsego County
572.O8	Ottawa County
	Paw Paw Lake see F572.B5
572.P38	Paw Paw River and Valley
572.P46	Pere Marquette River and Valley
572.P5	Pictured Rocks National Lakeshore
572.P53	Pigeon River and Valley. Pigeon River Country State Forest, etc.
	Point Lookout (Arenac Co.) see F572.A7
	Power Island see F572.G5
572.P7	Presque Isle County
572.R6	Roscommon County
	Including Houghton Lake
572.S15	Saginaw Bay region
	Including Fort Saginaw
572.S17	Saginaw County
572.S2	Saginaw River and Valley
572.S3	Saint Clair County
572.S34	Saint Clair, Lake, Mich.
	Cf. F1059.S3 Ontario
572.S4	Saint Joseph County
572.S43	Saint Joseph River and Valley
	Class here works limited to the part of the Saint Joseph River and Valley located in Michigan
	For general works on the Saint Joseph River and Valley, as well as works limited to the part located in Indiana see F532.S3
572.S5	Sanilac County
572.S6	Schoolcraft County
572.S7	Shiawassee County
572.S8	Sleeping Bear Dunes National Lakeshore
	The Snows (Islands) see F572.L57
572.S86	South Manitou Island
572.S9	Superior, Lake, region, Mich.
	Cf. F552 General

F1-975

Michigan

  Regions, counties, etc., A-Z -- Continued

572.T58	Thumb District. Thumb Area
	Thunder Bay see F572.A4
	Tiffin River and Valley see F572.B36
	Tobico Marsh see F572.B3
	Torch Lake see F572.A5
	Traverse region see F572.G5
572.T9	Tuscola County
	Upper Peninsula see F572.N8
572.V3	Van Buren County
572.W24	Walloon Lake
572.W3	Washtenaw County
572.W4	Wayne County
572.W5	Wexford County
574.A-Z	Cities, towns, etc., A-Z
	e.g.
574.A6	Ann Arbor
574.B3	Bay City
574.D2	Dearborn
	For Edison Institute (Henry Ford Museum and Greenfield Village), Dearborn, Mich. see E161
574.D4-.D49	Detroit (Table F2)
574.G7	Grand Rapids
574.K1	Kalamazoo
574.L2	Lansing
	Mackinac Island (City) see F572.M16
574.M17	Mackinaw
574.M9	Muskegon
574.S15	Saginaw
574.S3	Sault Ste. Marie
	Elements in the population
575.A1	General works
575.A2-Z	Individual elements
	For a list of racial, ethnic, and religious elements (with Cutter numbers) see E184.A+

Wisconsin
  Historical note from the second edition (1913) of Class F:
      "Explored by the French from New France. Ceded to Great
      Britain with other French territory east of the Mississippi,
      1763, and annexed to Quebec 1774. Transferred to the U.S.
      by the peace of 1783 and included in Northwest Territory
      1787, in Indiana Territory 1800, in Illinois Territory 1809, in
      Michigan Territory 1818. Wisconsin Territory was organized
      1836, to include the modern states of Wis., Iowa and Minn,
      and eastern North and South Dakota. In 1838 the Territory of
      Iowa was set off, taking the region between the Mississippi
      and Missouri rivers. Wisconsin was admitted as a state with
      substantially its present limits, 1848 (the northwestern part of
      the territory forming part of Minnesota Territory organized
      1849)."

F1-975

576	Periodicals. Societies. Collections
578	Museums. Exhibitions, exhibits
579	Gazetteers. Dictionaries. Geographic names
579.3	Guidebooks
580	Biography (Collective). Genealogy (Collective)
580.2	Historiography
	Historians see E175.5.A+
581	General works. Histories
581.3	Juvenile works
581.5	Pamphlets, addresses, essays
581.6	Anecdotes, legends, pageants, etc.
581.8	Geography
582	Historic monuments (General). Illustrative material
583	Antiquities (Non-Indian)
	By period
584	Early to 1848
	Including biography: Thomas Pendleton Burnett, etc.
585	1836-1848. Wisconsin Territory
586	1848-1950
	Including admission as a state, May 29, 1848
	Including biography: Benjamin Franklin Hopkins, Morgan Lewis Martin, Cadwallader Colden Washburn, etc.
	Cf. D570.85.W6+ World War I, 1914-1918
	Cf. D769.85.W6+ World War II, 1939-1945
	Cf. E470.4+ Civil War, Military operations
	Cf. E471+ Civil War campaigns and battles
	Cf. E537+ Civil War, 1861-1865 (General)
	Cf. E726.W6 War of 1898 (Spanish-American War)
	1951-
586.2	General works
	Biography
586.4	Collective

	Wisconsin
	By period
	1951-
	Biography -- Continued
586.42.A-Z	Individual, A-Z
	Subarrange each by Table F5
587.A-Z	Regions, counties, etc., A-Z
587.A15	Counties
587.A16	Mountains
587.A17	Rivers
587.A18	Lakes
587.A19	Islands
587.A2	Adams County
	Apostle Islands see F587.A8
587.A8	Ashland County
	Including Apostle Islands, Chequamegon Bay, Madeline Island, Copper Falls State Park
587.B25	Barron County
587.B3	Bayfield County
	For Chequamegon Bay see F587.A8
587.B55	Black River and Valley
	Blue Lake see F587.O5
587.B7	Boundaries
	Cf. F547.B7 Illinois boundary
	Cf. F612.B7 Minnesota boundary
587.B8	Brown County
587.B85	Brule River and Valley
	Class here works limited to the part of the Brule River and Valley located in Wisconsin
	For general works on the Brule River and Valley, as well as works limited to the part located in Michigan see F572.B86
587.B9	Buffalo County
587.B95	Burnett County
587.C2	Calumet County
	Chain O'Lakes see F587.W3
	Chequamegon Bay see F587.A8
587.C48	Chippewa County
587.C5	Chippewa River and Valley
587.C6	Clark County
587.C76	Columbia County
	Copper Falls State Park see F587.A8
587.C8	Crawford County
	Dalles of the Wisconsin see F587.W8
587.D3	Dane County
	Including Cave of the Mounds, Lake Mendota
	Dells of the Wisconsin see F587.W8

Wisconsin

Regions, counties, etc., A-Z -- Continued

587.D6	Dodge County
587.D7	Door County
	Including Peninsula State Park, Rock Island, Washington Island
587.D8	Douglas County
587.D9	Dunn County
587.E2	Eau Claire County
587.F5	Florence County
587.F6	Fond du Lac County
587.F65	Forest County
587.F7	Fox River and Valley (Kenosha County, Racine County, and Waukesha County)
	Class here general works on the Fox River and Valley, as well as works limited to the part located in Kenosha, Racine, and Waukesha Counties, Wisconsin
	For works limited to the part of the Fox River and Valley located in Illinois see F547.F77
587.F72	Fox River and Valley (Columbia County-Brown County)
	Lake Geneva see F587.W18
587.G5	Grant County
587.G6	Green Bay Region
	Class here general works on the Green Bay Region, as well as works limited to the part located in Wisconsin
	For works limited to the part of the Green Bay Region located in Michigan see F572.G87
587.G7	Green County
587.G74	Green Lake County
587.I6	Iowa County
587.I7	Iron County
587.J2	Jackson County
587.J4	Jefferson County
587.J9	Juneau County
587.K3	Kenosha County
587.K35	Kewaunee County
587.K4	Kickapoo River and Valley, Wisc.
587.L14	La Crosse County
587.L2	Lafayette County
587.L3	Langlade County
587.L5	Lincoln County
	Madeline Island see F587.A8
587.M2	Manitowoc County
587.M3	Marathon County
587.M35	Marinette County
587.M4	Marquette County

	Wisconsin
	Regions, counties, etc., A-Z -- Continued
587.M49	Menominee Range
	Class here works limited to the part of the Menominee Range located in Wisconsin
	For general works on the Menominee Range, as well as works limited to the part located in Michigan see F572.M516
587.M5	Menominee River and Valley
	Class here works limited to the part of the Menominee River and Valley located in Wisconsin
	For general works on the Menominee River and Valley, as well as works limited to the part located in Michigan see F572.M52
587.M57	Michigan, Lake, region, Wis.
	Cf. F553 General
587.M6	Milwaukee County
587.M63	Mississippi River and Valley, Wis.
	Cf. F350.3+ General
	Cf. F597 Upper Mississippi Valley
587.M7	Monroe County
587.O2	Oconto County
587.O5	Oneida County
	Including Blue Lake
587.O93	Outagamie County
587.O98	Ozaukee County
	Peninsula State Park see F587.D7
587.P4	Pepin County
587.P6	Pierce County
	Pike Lake Chain see F587.P9
587.P7	Polk County
587.P8	Portage County
587.P83	Porte des Morts Strait
587.P9	Price County
	Including Pike Lake Chain
587.R2	Racine County
587.R4	Richland County
587.R6	Rock County
	Rock Island see F587.D7
587.R63	Rock River and Valley (Sinissippi Valley)
	Class here works limited to the part of the Rock River and Valley located in Wisconsin
	For general works on the Rock River and Valley, as well as works limited to the part located in Illinois see F547.R7
587.R8	Rusk County
587.S13	Saint Croix County

Wisconsin
Regions, counties, etc., A-Z -- Continued

587.S14	Saint Croix River and Valley
	Class here general works on the Saint Croix River and Valley, as well as works limited to the part located in Wisconsin
	For works limited to the part of the Saint Croix River and Valley located in Minnesota see F612.S2
587.S2	Sauk County
	Including Devil's Island, Durward's Glen
587.S3	Sawyer County
587.S45	Shawano County
587.S5	Sheboygan County
587.S9	Superior, Lake, region, Wis.
	Cf. F552 General
587.T3	Taylor County
587.T79	Trempealeau County
587.V5	Vernon County
587.V6	Vilas County
587.W18	Walworth County
	Including Lake Geneva
587.W185	Washburn County
587.W19	Washington County
	Washington Island see F587.D7
587.W2	Waukesha County
587.W3	Waupaca County
	Including Chain O'Lakes
587.W35	Waushara County
587.W5	Winnebago County
587.W8	Wisconsin River and Valley
	Including Dells (Dalles) of the Wisconsin
587.W86	Wolf River. Wolf National Scenic Riverway
587.W9	Wood County
589.A-Z	Cities, towns, etc., A-Z
	e.g.
589.G7	Green Bay
589.K3	Kenosha
589.L1	La Crosse
589.M1-.M19	Madison (Table F2)
589.M6-.M69	Milwaukee (Table F2)
589.O8	Oshkosh
589.P8	Prairie du Chien
589.R2	Racine
589.S95	Superior
	Elements in the population
590.A1	General works

  Wisconsin

                                              Elements in the population -- Continued

590.A2-Z   Individual elements

                                    For a list of racial, ethnic, and religious elements (with Cutter numbers) see E184.A+

                        The West. Trans-Mississippi Region. Great Plains

                                For Middle West see F350.3+

                                For Louisiana (Province) see F374

                                For Northwest (Upper Mississippi Valley) see F597

                                For Missouri River and Valley see F598

                                For "Indian country," 1803-1854 see F697

                                For Rocky Mountains see F721

                                For The Southwest see F786

                                For Pacific coast see F851

                                For Pacific Northwest see F852

                                Cf. E81+ Indian wars (General)

590.2   Museums. Exhibitions, exhibits

590.3   Guidebooks

590.5   Biography (Collective). Genealogy (Collective)

590.6   Geography

590.7   Historic monuments (General). Illustrative material

591   General works. Histories

                                Cf. E78.W5 Indians of the West

                      By period

592   Early to 1848

                                Including United States exploring expeditions: Frémont, Lewis and Clark, Pike

                                Including biography: James Bridger, Christopher Carson, John Colter, Zebulon Montgomery Pike, Jedediah Strong Smith, William Sherley Williams, etc.

                                For Texas see F390

                                For "Indian country," 1821-1854 see F697

                                For New Mexico (1822-1848) see F800

                                For New Mexico (1848-1950) see F801

                                For California see F864

                                Cf. E123+ Spanish discoveries

                                Cf. E401+ War with Mexico, 1845-1848

                                Cf. E408 Mexican cession of 1848

                                Cf. F786 Mexican cession of 1848

                                Cf. F799 Cibola, Quivera

                                Cf. F868.N5 Donner party

                                Cf. F880 Oregon question

                      Lewis and Clark Expedition, 1804-1806

592.3   President Jefferson's message and accompanying documents

                                Subarrange by date of edition

The West. Trans-Mississippi Region. Great Plains
　By period
　　Early to 1848
　　　Lewis and Clark Expedition, 1804-1806 -- Continued
592.4　　　　　Authentic history of the expedition. Lewis and Clark
　　　　　　　journals
　　　　　　　　Subarrange by date of edition
592.5　　　　　Journals of other members of the expedition. By author
　　　　　　　　Subarrange by date of edition
592.6　　　　　Spurious publications
　　　　　　　　Subarrange by date of edition
592.7　　　　　Other works about the expedition and its members
　　　　　　　　Subarrange by author or biographee as the case may be
593　　　　1848-1860
　　　　　Including later United States expeditions; overland journeys
　　　　　　to the Pacific
　　　　　Including biography: Edward Fitzgerald Beale, William Gilpin,
　　　　　　etc.
　　　　　Cf. E83.84 wars with Pacific coast Indians, 1847-1865
　　　　　Cf. E83.857 Spirit Lake Massacre, 1857
　　　　　Cf. E83.858 Mill Creek War, 1857-1860
　　　　　Cf. F786 Gadsden Purchase, 1853
　　　　　Cf. F801 Texas cession of 1850
594　　　　1860-1880
　　　　　Including biography: Martha Canary ("Calamity Jane"),
　　　　　　William Frederick Cody ("Buffalo Bill"), James Butler
　　　　　　Hickok ("Wild Bill Hickok"), Jesse James, Moses Embree
　　　　　　Milner ("California Joe"), Cole Younger, etc.
　　　　　Cf. E83.86 Dakota Indian War, 1862-1863
　　　　　Cf. E83.863 Indian wars, 1863-1865
　　　　　Cf. E83.866 Indian wars, 1866-1898
595　　　　1880-1950
　　　　　Biography: George Le Roy Parker ("Butch Cassidy")
　　　　　Cf. E83.866 Indian Wars, 1866-1898
595.2　　　　1951-1980
595.3　　　　1981-
596　　　Frontier and pioneer life. Ranch life, cowboys, cattle trails,
　　　　　etc.
　　　　Elements in the population
596.2　　　General works
596.3.A-Z　　Individual elements
　　　　　For a list of racial, ethnic, and religious elements (with
　　　　　　Cutter numbers) see E184.A+

F1-975

597   The Northwest

Including Upper Mississippi Valley; sources of the Mississippi; northern boundary of the United States (from Lake of the Woods to Rocky Mountains), including works on region between Great Lakes and Pacific Ocean, the Oregon Trail and the Overland Trail

Biography: Jonathan Carver

For Old Northwest see F476+

For Pacific Northwest see F851.72+

For Canadian Northwest see F1060+

Cf. E78.N79 Indians of the Northwestern States

Cf. E78.N8 Indians of the Northwestern States

Cf. F612.I8 Lake Itasca and park

598   Missouri River and Valley

Cf. F472.M7 Missouri

Cf. F627.M66 Iowa

Cf. F642.M6 North Dakota

Cf. F657.M7 South Dakota

Cf. F672.M6 Nebraska

Cf. F687.M6 Kansas

Cf. F737.M7 Montana

Minnesota

Historical note from the second edition (1913) of Class F: "The entire state was visited by explorers in the 17th century and embraced in French Louisiana. That portion west of the Mississippi was ceded to Spain in 1762 and shared in the fortunes of Louisiana till the latter was purchased by the U.S. from France in 1803. The eastern part was ceded to Great Britain 1763, annexed to Quebec 1774, surrendered to the U.S. by treaty in 1783, and formed part of the Northwest Territory 1787. It belonged to Indiana Territory 1800-1809, Illinois Territory 1809-1818, Michigan Territory, 1818-1836. In the meantime, the western part of the present state of Minnesota had been included in Louisiana District (later Territory) 1804-1812, Missouri Territory 1812-1821, and after latter date in the unsettled northwestern residue of the Louisiana purchase usually known as the "Indian country." In 1834, so much of the region as lay east of the Missouri Eiver was added to Michigan Territory. In 1836 Minnesota was included in the new Wisconsin Territory. Two years later it was divided on the old Mississippi River line, the western part being set off to Iowa Territory. 1849 Minnesota Territory was organized consisting of the present state, and the Dakotas, east of the Missouri Eiver. It was admitted as a state 1858 with substantially its present limits."

601   Periodicals. Societies. Collections

603   Museums. Exhibitions, exhibits

	Minnesota -- Continued
604	Gazetteers. Dictionaries. Geographic names
604.3	Guidebooks
605	Biography (Collective). Genealogy (Collective)
605.2	Historiography
	Historians see E175.5.A+
605.5	Study and teaching
606	General works. Histories
	Including admission as a state, May 11, 1858
	Including biography: Willis Arnold Gorman, John Albert Johnson, Floyd Björnsterne Olson, Henry Hastings Sibley, etc.
	Cf. D570.85.M6+ World War I, 1914-1918
	Cf. D769.85.M6+ World War II, 1939-1945
	Cf. E83.86 Dakota Indian War, 1862-1863
	Cf. E515+ Civil War, 1861-1865 (General)
	Cf. E726.M7 War of 1898 (Spanish-American War)
606.3	Juvenile works
606.5	Pamphlets, addresses, essays
606.6	Anecdotes, legends, pageants, etc.
606.8	Geography
607	Historic monuments (General). Illustrative material
608	Antiquities (Non-Indian)
	By period
	Early through 1950 see F606
	1951-
610	General works
	Biography
610.2	Collective
610.3.A-Z	Individual, A-Z
	Subarrange each by Table F5
612.A-Z	Regions, counties, etc., A-Z
612.A15	Counties
612.A16	Mountains
612.A17	Rivers
612.A18	Lakes
612.A19	Islands
612.A3	Aitkin County
612.A6	Anoka County
612.B39	Becker County
	Including Big Cormorant Lake
612.B43	Beltrami County
	Including Star Island
612.B45	Benton County
	Big Cormorant Lake see F612.B39
	Big Fork River and Valley see F612.K7
612.B5	Big Stone County

F1-975

Minnesota

Regions, counties, etc., A-Z -- Continued

612.B6	Blue Earth County
	Including Minneopa State Park
612.B7	Boundaries
	For International boundary see F597
612.B73	Boundary Waters Canoe Area
612.B8	Brown County
612.C15	Carleton County
612.C2	Carver County
612.C25	Cass County
612.C4	Chippewa County
612.C45	Chisago County
612.C6	Clay County
612.C63	Clearwater County
	For Itasca State Park see F612.I8
612.C65	Cook County
	Including Cascade River State Park
612.C67	Cottonwood County
	Crane Island see F612.H5
612.C7	Crow Wing County
612.D2	Dakota County
612.D6	Dodge County
612.D7	Douglas County
612.F2	Faribault County
612.F25	Father Hennepin State Park
612.F4	Fillmore County
	Including Forestville State Park
	Forestville State Park see F612.F4
612.F7	Freeborn County
612.G6	Goodhue County
	Gooseberry Falls State Park see F612.L3
612.G7	Grant County
612.H5	Hennepin County
	Including Lake Minnetonka, Crane Island
612.H8	Houston County
612.H9	Hubbard County
612.I6	Isanti County
612.I7	Itasca County
612.I8	Itasca Lake. Itasca State Park
612.J2	Jackson County
612.K17	Kanabec County
612.K2	Kandiyohi County
	Including Monogalia Co.
612.K5	Kittson County
612.K7	Koochiching County
	Including Big Fork River and Valley

Minnesota
  Regions, counties, etc., A-Z -- Continued

612.L2	Lac qui Parle County
612.L3	Lake County
	Including Gooseberry Falls State Park
612.L4	Lake of the Woods County
	Including Northwest Angle
612.L5	Le Sueur County
612.L6	Lincoln County
612.L9	Lyon County
612.M25	McLeod County
612.M26	Mahnomen County
612.M266	Mankahta County
612.M27	Marshall County
612.M28	Martin County
612.M3	Meeker County
612.M36	Mesaba (Mesabi) range
612.M38	Mille Lacs County
	Minneopa State Park see F612.B6
612.M4	Minnesota River and Valley
612.M5	Mississippi River and Valley, Minn.
	Cf. F350.3+ General
	Cf. F597 Upper Mississippi Valley
	Monogalia Co. see F612.K2
612.M88	Morrison County
612.M9	Mower County
612.M95	Murray County
612.N5	Nicollet County
612.N7	Nobles County
612.N8	Norman County
	Northwest Angle see F612.L4
612.O5	Olmsted County
612.O9	Otter Tail County
	Including Pelican Lake
	Pelican Lake see F612.O9
612.P4	Pennington County
612.P42	Pepin Lake
612.P5	Pine County
612.P55	Pipestone County
612.P7	Polk County
612.P8	Pope County
612.R18	Rainy River region
612.R2	Ramsey County
612.R25	Red Lake County
612.R27	Red River of the North and Valley, Minn.
	Cf. F642.R3 North Dakota
	Cf. F1064.R3 Manitoba

F1-975

	Minnesota
	Regions, counties, etc., A-Z -- Continued
612.R28	Red River State Recreation Area
612.R3	Redwood County
612.R42	Renville County
612.R5	Rice County
612.R7	Rock County
612.R8	Roseau County
612.S2	Saint Croix River and Valley

           Class here works limited to the part of the Saint Croix River
               and Valley located in Minnesota
           For general works on the Saint Croix River and Valley,
               as well as works limited to the part located in
               Wisconsin see F587.S14

612.S25	Saint Louis County
	Including Side Lake
612.S3	Scott County
612.S4	Sherburne County
612.S5	Sibley County
	Side Lake see F612.S25
612.S64	Split Rock Creek and Valley

           Class here works limited to the part of the Split Rock Creek
               and Valley located in Minnesota
            For general works on the Split Rock Creek and Valley,
               as well as works limited to the part located in South
               Dakota see F657.S73

	Star Island see F612.B43
612.S75	Stearns County
612.S8	Steele County
612.S84	Stevens County
612.S86	Straight River and Valley (Steele and Rice Counties)
612.S9	Superior, Lake, region, Minn.
	Cf. F552 General
612.S95	Superior National Forest
612.S98	Swift County
612.T6	Todd County
612.T7	Traverse County
612.U77	Upper Iowa River and Valley

           Class here works limited to the part of the Upper Iowa River
               and Valley located in Minnesota
            For general works on the Upper Iowa River and Valley,
               as well as works limited to the part located in Iowa
               see F627.U66

612.V6	Voyageurs National Park
612.W12	Wabasha County
612.W14	Wadena County
612.W15	Wadsworth Trail

Minnesota
Regions, counties, etc., A-Z -- Continued

612.W17	Waseca County
612.W2	Washington County
612.W35	Watonwan County
612.W65	Wilkin County
612.W7	Winona County
	Including Rush Creek Valley
612.W9	Wright County
612.Y4	Yellow Medicine County
614.A-Z	Cities, towns, etc., A-Z
	e.g.
614.D8	Duluth
614.F7	Fort Snelling
614.M5-.M59	Minneapolis (Table F2)
614.M6	Minneapolis and St. Paul. "The Twin Cities"
614.R6	Rochester
614.S25	Saint Cloud
614.S4	Saint Paul
614.W7	Winona
	Elements in the population
615.A1	General works
615.A2-Z	Individual elements, A-Z

For a list of racial, ethnic, and religious elements (with
Cutter numbers) see E184.A+

Iowa

Historical note from the second edition (1913) of Class F: "Part of
the province of Louisiana down to 1803. (See note under
F366+) Included in District (later Territory) of Louisiana 1804-
1812, Missouri Territory 1812-1821 and after latter date, in
the unsettled residue of the Louisiana purchase, usually
known as the "Indian country." In 1834 it was annexed to
Michigan Territory with the rest of the region between the
Mississippi and Missouri Bivers, and 1836 formed part of the
new Wisconsin Territory. In 1838 Iowa Territory was created,
including Minnesota west of the Mississippi and the eastern
part of the Dakotas as well as modern Iowa. The state of
Iowa was admitted 1846, with substantially its present limits
(after a territorial convention had refused to accept an act of
admission passed by Congress in 1845 which left out the
western third of the present state and included a section now
part of southeast Minn.). The remainder of the territory, with
adjacent part of old Wisconsin Territory, was organized as the
territory of Minnesota in 1849."

616	Periodicals. Societies. Collections
618	Museums. Exhibitions, exhibits
619	Gazetteers. Dictionaries. Geographic names

	Iowa -- Continued
619.3	Guidebooks
620	Biography (Collective). Genealogy (Collective)
620.2	Historiography
	Historians see E175.5.A+
620.5	Study and teaching
621	General works. Histories
	Including admission as a state, December 28, 1846
	Including by period (early to 1950) as well as general
	Including biography: John Chambers, Augustus Caesar Dodge, Robert Lucas, etc.
	For 1951 and later see F625+
	Cf. D570.85.I8+ World War I, 1914-1918
	Cf. D769.85.I8+ World War II, 1939-1945
	Cf. E83.857 Spirit Lake Massacre, 1857
	Cf. E409.5.I72 War with Mexico, 1845-1848
	Cf. E507+ Civil War, 1861-1865 (General)
	Cf. E726.I4 War of 1898 (Spanish-American War)
621.3	Juvenile works
621.5	Pamphlets, addresses, essays
621.6	Anecdotes, legends, pageants
622	Historic monuments (General). Illustrative material
623	Antiquities (Non-Indian)
	By period
(624)	Early to 1950
	see F621
	1951-
625	General works
	Biography
625.4	Collective
625.42.A-Z	Individual, A-Z
	Subarrange each by Table F5
627.A-Z	Regions, counties, etc., A-Z
627.A15	Counties
627.A16	Mountains
627.A17	Rivers
627.A18	Lakes
627.A19	Islands
627.A2	Adair County
627.A3	Adams County
627.A5	Allamakee County
627.A6	Appanoose County
627.A8	Audubon County
627.B4	Benton County

	Iowa
	Regions, counties, etc., A-Z -- Continued
627.B5	Big Sioux River and Valley

Class here works limited to the part of the Big Sioux River
and Valley located in Iowa

For general works on the Big Sioux River and Valley,
as well as works limited to the part located in South
Dakota see F657.B5

627.B6	Black Hawk County
627.B67	Boone County
627.B7	Boundaries

Cf. F472.B7 Missouri boundary

627.B8	Bremer County
627.B85	Buchanan County
627.B87	Buena Vista County
627.B9	Butler County
627.C2	Calhoun County
627.C25	Carroll County
627.C3	Cass County
627.C4	Cedar County
627.C44	Cerro Gordo County
627.C47	Cherokee County
627.C5	Chickasaw County
627.C53	Clarke County
627.C54	Clay County
627.C56	Clayton County
627.C6	Clinton County
627.C8	Crawford County
627.D14	Dallas County
627.D2	Davis County
627.D26	Decatur County
627.D3	Delaware County
627.D4	Des Moines County
627.D43	Des Moines River and Valley

Class here general works on the Des Moines River and
Valley, as well as works limited to the part located in Iowa

For works limited to the part of the Des Moines River
and Valley located in Missouri see F472.D4

627.D5	Dickinson County

Including Okoboji Lake, Spirit Lake

Cf. E83.857 Spirit Lake Massacre, 1857

627.D8	Dubuque County
627.E5	Emmet County
627.F2	Fayette County
627.F5	Floyd County
627.F78	Franklin County

F1-975

Iowa

Regions, counties, etc., A-Z -- Continued

627.F8	Fremont County
	Including Waubonsie State Park
	Geode State Park see F627.H5
627.G7	Greene County
627.G75	Grundy County
627.G8	Guthrie County
627.H2	Hamilton County
627.H25	Hancock County
627.H3	Hardin County
627.H4	Harrison County
627.H5	Henry County
	Including Geode State Park
627.H7	Howard County
627.H8	Humboldt County
627.I2	Ida County
627.I6	Iowa County
627.J2	Jackson County
627.J3	Jasper County
627.J4	Jefferson County
627.J6	Johnson County
627.J7	Jones County
627.K3	Keokuk County
627.K6	Kossuth County
627.L4	Lee County
627.L7	Linn County
627.L76	Loess Hills
	Class here general works on the Loess Hills, as well as works limited to the part located in Iowa
	For works limited to the part of the Loess Hills located in Missouri see F472.L88
627.L8	Louisa County
627.L85	Lucas County
627.L9	Lyon County
627.M18	Madison County
627.M2	Mahaska County
627.M3	Marion County
627.M4	Marshall County
627.M6	Mills County
627.M64	Mississippi River and Valley, Iowa
	Cf. F350.3+ General
	Cf. F597 Upper Mississippi Valley
627.M66	Missouri River and Valley, Iowa
	Cf. F598 General
627.M7	Mitchell County
627.M75	Monona County

Iowa
    Regions, counties, etc., A-Z -- Continued

627.M8	Monroe County
627.M83	Montgomery County
627.M9	Muscatine County
627.O2	O'Brien County
	Okoboji Lakes see F627.D5
627.O8	Osceola County
627.P2	Page County
627.P3	Palo Alto County
627.P5	Plymouth County
627.P6	Pocahontas County
627.P7	Polk County
627.P8	Pottawattamie County
627.P88	Poweshiek County
627.R5	Ringgold County
627.S2	Sac County
627.S4	Scott County
627.S5	Shelby County
627.S55	Sioux County
	Spirit Lake see F627.D5
627.S8	Story County
627.T3	Tama County
627.T5	Taylor County
627.U5	Union County
627.U66	Upper Iowa River and Valley

        Class here general works on the Upper Iowa River and
           Valley, as well as works limited to the part located in Iowa
        For works limited to the part of the Upper Iowa River
           and Valley located in Minnesota see F612.U77

627.V2	Van Buren County
627.W2	Wapello County
627.W25	Warren County
627.W26	Washington County
	Waubonsie State Park see F627.F8
627.W28	Wayne County
627.W3	Webster County
627.W65	Winnebago County
627.W7	Winneshiek County
627.W8	Woodbury County
627.W86	Worth County
627.W9	Wright County
629.A-Z	Cities, towns, etc., A-Z
	e.g.
629.B9	Burlington
629.C3	Cedar Rapids
629.C8	Council Bluffs

F1-975

Iowa
 Cities, towns, etc., A-Z -- Continued

629.D2	Davenport
629.D4	Des Moines
629.D8	Dubuque
629.M9	Muscatine
629.S6	Sioux City

 Elements in the population

630.A1	General works
630.A2-Z	Individual elements

   For a list of racial, ethnic, and religious elements (with Cutter numbers) see E184.A+

North Dakota
 Historical note from the second edition (1913) of Class F: "The northern part of Dakota Territory, admitted as a state 1889. See note under South Dakota, F646+ "

631	Periodicals. Societies. Collections
633	Museums. Exhibitions, exhibits
634	Gazetteers. Dictionaries. Geographic names
634.3	Guidebooks
635	Biography (Collective). Genealogy (Collective)
635.2	Historiography

 Historians see E175.5.A+

635.5	Study and teaching
636	General works. Histories

  Including admission as a state, November 2, 1889
  Including by period (early to 1950) as well as general
  For 1951 and later see F640
  For early to 1889 see F655
  Cf. D769.85.N9+ World War II, 1939-1945

636.3	Juvenile works
636.5	Pamphlets, addresses, essays
636.6	Anecdotes, legends, pageants
637	Historic monuments (General). Illustrative material
638	Antiquities (Non-Indian)
	By period
(639)	Early to 1950

  see F636; F655

640	1951-
	Biography
641.A2	Collective
641.A3-Z	Individual, A-Z

  Subarrange each by Table F5

642.A-Z	Regions, counties, etc., A-Z
642.A15	Counties
642.A16	Mountains
642.A17	Rivers

North Dakota
Regions, counties, etc., A-Z -- Continued

642.A18	Lakes
642.A19	Islands
642.A2	Adams County
642.B3	Barnes County
642.B4	Benson County
	For Devils Lake see F642.D5
642.B5	Billings County
642.B6	Bottineau County
642.B7	Boundaries
	For International boundary see F597
642.B75	Bowman County
642.B85	Burke County
642.B9	Burleigh County
642.C34	Cass County
642.C4	Cavalier County
	Coteau du Missouri see F642.M26
642.D5	Devils Lake
642.D6	Dickey County
642.D7	Divide County
642.D9	Dunn County
	Including Killdeer Mountains, Killdeer Mountain Park
642.E2	Eddy County
642.E5	Emmons County
	Fort Abraham Lincoln State Park see F642.M7
642.F6	Foster County
642.G6	Golden Valley County
642.G7	Grand Forks County
642.G75	Grant County
642.G8	Griggs County
642.H4	Hettinger County
642.K5	Kidder County
	Killdeer Mountains see F642.D9
642.K54	Knife River and Valley
642.L3	La Moure County
642.L5	Little Missouri Badlands
	For Theodore Roosevelt National Memorial Park see F642.T5
642.L6	Logan County
642.M2	McHenry County
642.M26	McIntosh County
	Including Coteau du Missouri

F1-975

North Dakota
    Regions, counties, etc., A-Z -- Continued

642.M28	McKenzie County

        Including the part of the Yellowstone River and Valley located in North Dakota
        For general works on the Yellowstone River and Valley, as well as works limited to the part located in Montana see F737.Y4

642.M29	McLean County
642.M5	Mercer County
642.M6	Missouri River and Valley, N. Dak.

        Cf. F598 General

642.M7	Morton County

        Including Fort Abraham Lincoln State Park

642.M8	Mountrail County
642.N4	Nelson County
642.O4	Oliver County
642.P4	Pembina County
642.P5	Pierce County
642.R17	Ramsey County

        For Devils Lake see F642.D5

642.R2	Ransom County
642.R3	Red River of the North and Valley, N. Dak.

        Cf. F612.R27 Minnesota
        Cf. F1064.R3 Manitoba

642.R4	Renville County
642.R5	Richland County
642.R6	Rolette County
642.S2	Sargent County
642.S5	Sheridan County
642.S53	Sheyenne River and Valley
642.S55	Sioux County
642.S6	Slope County
642.S68	Souris River and Valley

        Class here works limited to the part of the Souris River and Valley located in North Dakota
        For works limited to the part of the Souris (Mouse) River and Valley located in Manitoba see F1064.S6
        For general works on the Souris (Mouse) River and Valley, as well as works limited to the part located in Saskatchewan see F1074.S67

642.S7	Stark County
642.S75	Steele County
642.S8	Stutsman County
642.T5	Theodore Roosevelt National Memorial Park
642.T6	Towner County
642.T7	Traill County

North Dakota
  Regions, counties, etc., A-Z -- Continued

642.W3	Walsh County
642.W35	Ward County
642.W45	Wells County
642.W6	Williams County
644.A-Z	Cities, towns, A-Z
	e.g.
644.B6	Bismarck
644.F2	Fargo
644.G8	Grand Forks

  Elements in the population

645.A1	General works
645.A2-Z	Individual elements

        For a list of racial, ethnic, and religious elements (with
           Cutter numbers) see E184.A+

South Dakota
  Including works covering both North and South Dakota

F1-975

  Historical note from the second edition (1913) of Class F: "The old
      Dakota Territory was a part of the Louisiana purchase 1803;
      included in the Louisiana District (later Territory) 1804-1812,
      Missouri Territory 1812-1834. In 1834, so much as lay east of
      the Missouri River was annexed to Michigan Territory,
      included in Wisconsin Territory 1836-1838, Iowa Territory
      1838-1849, Minnesota Territory 1849-1858. Meanwhile the
      part of modern Dakota west of the Missouri remained part of
      the unorganized "Indian country" till 1854, when it was
      included in the new territory of Nebraska. In 1861 the territory
      of Nebraska was reduced in size and the northern part, with
      the part of old Minnesota Territory not admitted as a state in
      1858, organized as Dakota Territory. This was greatly
      reduced in size by the creation of Idaho Territory in 1863.
      Divided in 1889 and admitted to the union as North and South
      Dakota."

646	Periodicals. Societies. Collections
648	Museums. Exhibitions, exhibits
649	Gazetteers. Dictionaries. Geographic names
649.3	Guidebooks
650	Biography (Collective). Genealogy (Collective)
650.2	Historiography
	Historians see E175.5.A+
650.5	Study and teaching
651	General works. Histories
651.3	Juvenile works
651.5	Pamphlets, addresses, essays
651.6	Anecdotes, legends, pageants
651.8	Geography

	South Dakota -- Continued
652	Historic monuments (General). Illustrative material
653	Antiquities (Non-Indian)
	By period
655	Early to 1889
	Including the Dakota region before 1861. Dakota Territory, 1861-1889
	Cf. E83.863 Indian wars, 1863-1865
656	1889-1950
	Including admission as a state, November 2, 1889
	Biography: Peter Norbeck
	Cf. D570.85.S7+ World War I, 1914-1918
	Cf. D769.85.S7+ World War II, 1939-1945
	Cf. E83.89 Dakota Indian War, 1890-1891
	1951-
656.2	General works
	Biography
656.3	Collective
656.4.A-Z	Individual, A-Z
	Subarrange each by Table F5
657.A-Z	Regions, counties, etc., A-Z
657.A15	Counties
657.A16	Mountains
657.A17	Rivers
657.A18	Lakes
657.A19	Islands
657.A6	Armstrong County
657.A8	Aurora County
657.B24	Badlands
657.B3	Beadle County
657.B4	Bennett County
657.B5	Big Sioux River and Valley
	Class here general works on the Big Sioux River and Valley, as well as works limited to the part located in South Dakota
	For works limited to the part of the Bix Sioux River and Valley located in Iowa see F627.B5
657.B6	Black Hills
	For Custer State Park see F657.C92
	For Mount Rushmore National Memorial see F657.R8
	For Wind Cave National Park see F657.W7
657.B65	Bon Homme County
657.B7	Boundaries
657.B75	Brookings County
657.B76	Brown County
657.B77	Brule County
657.B8	Buffalo County

South Dakota

Regions, counties, etc., A-Z -- Continued

657.B83	Buffalo Gap National Grassland
657.B9	Butte County
657.C25	Campbell County
657.C4	Charles Mix County
657.C55	Clark County
657.C6	Clay County
657.C8	Codington County
657.C83	Corson County
657.C9	Custer County
	For Jewel Cave National Monument see F657.J55
	For Wind Cave see F657.W7
657.C92	Custer State Park
657.D25	Davison County
657.D3	Day County
657.D4	Deuel County
657.D45	Dewey County
657.D7	Douglas County
657.E2	Edmunds County
657.F3	Fall River County
657.F4	Faulk County
	Fort Sisseton State Park see F657.R6
657.G7	Grant County
657.G8	Gregory County
657.H2	Haakon County
657.H3	Hamlin County
657.H35	Hand County
657.H4	Hanson County
657.H45	Harding County
657.H8	Hughes County
657.H85	Hutchinson County
657.H9	Hyde County
657.J2	Jackson County
657.J4	Jerauld County
657.J55	Jewel Cave National Monument
657.J6	Jones County
657.K5	Kingsbury County
657.L3	Lake County
657.L4	Lawrence County
657.L6	Lincoln County
657.L9	Lyman County
657.M15	McCook County
657.M2	McPherson County
657.M3	Marshall County
657.M4	Meade County
	Including Bear Butte

F1-975

South Dakota

Regions, counties, etc., A-Z -- Continued

657.M45	Mellette County
657.M55	Miner County
657.M6	Minnehaha County
657.M7	Missouri River and Valley, S. Dak.
	Cf. F598 General
657.M8	Moody County
657.P4	Pennington County
	For Mount Rushmore National Memorial see F657.R8
657.P5	Perkins County
657.P8	Potter County
657.R6	Roberts County
	Including Fort Sisseton State Park
657.R8	Mount Rushmore National Memorial
657.S3	Sanborn County
657.S5	Shannon County
657.S7	Spink County
657.S73	Split Rock Creek and Valley
	Class here general works on the Split Rock Creek and Valley, as well as works limited to the part located in South Dakota
	For works limited to the part of the Split Rock Creek and Valley located in Minnesota see F612.S64
657.S8	Stanley County
657.S9	Sully County
657.T6	Todd County
657.T7	Tripp County
657.T8	Turner County
657.U5	Union County
657.W2	Walworth County
657.W3	Washabaugh County
657.W4	Washington County
	In 1944, combined with Shannon Co.
657.W7	Wind Cave. Wind Cave National Park
657.Y2	Yankton County
657.Z5	Ziebach County
659.A-Z	Cities, towns, etc., A-Z
	e.g.
659.A14	Aberdeen
659.P6	Pierre
659.R2	Rapid City
659.S6	Sioux Falls
	Elements in the population
660.A1	General works

South Dakota
Elements in the population -- Continued
660.A2-Z Individual elements
For a list of racial, ethnic, and religious elements (with
Cutter numbers) see E184.A+
Nebraska
Historical note from the second edition (1913) of Class F: "The
entire state was embraced in the old province of Louisiana,
purchased by the U.S. 1803. It formed part of the District
(later Territory) of Louisiana 1804-1812, and part of Missouri
Territory 1812-1821, and after 1821 constituted part of the
unorganized region usually known as the "Indian country." In
1854 Nebraska Territory was organized to include the
northern part of this region, containing, besides the modern
Nebraska, the western parts of the Dakotas, Montana,
Wyoming, and part of Colorado. 1861 the northern part was
set off as Dakota Territory, and 1863 the western part of the
remainder was added to the new Idaho Territory. Nebraska
was admitted to the union in 1867, with substantially its
present limits."

F1-975

661 Periodicals. Societies. Collections
663 Museums. Exhibitions, exhibits
664 Gazetteers. Dictionaries. Geographic names
664.3 Guidebooks
665 Biography (Collective). Genealogy (Collective)
665.2 Historiography
Historians see E175.5.A+
665.5 Study and teaching
666 General works. Histories
Including admission as a state, March 1, 1867
By period (Early to 1950) as well as general
Biography: Jules Ami Sandoz, Thomas Clark White
For 1951 and later see F670+
Cf. D570.85.N19+ World War I, 1914-1918
Cf. D769.85.N19+ World War II, 1939-1945
Cf. E433 Kansas-Nebraska Bill, 1854
666.3 Juvenile works
666.5 Pamphlets, addresses, essays
666.6 Anecdotes, legends, pageants
667 Historic monuments (General). Illustrative material
668 Antiquities (Non-Indian)
By period
Early to 1950 see F666
1951-
670 General works
Biography
670.3 Collective

	Nebraska
	By period
	1951-
	Biography -- Continued
670.4.A-Z	Individual, A-Z
	Subarrange each by Table F5
672.A-Z	Regions, counties, etc., A-Z
672.A15	Counties
672.A16	Mountains
672.A17	Rivers
672.A18	Lakes
672.A19	Islands
672.A2	Adams County
	Agate Fossil Beda National Monument see F672.S6
672.A6	Antelope County
672.A7	Arthur County
672.B3	Banner County
672.B5	Blaine County
672.B6	Boone County
672.B7	Boundaries
672.B75	Box Butte County
672.B77	Boyd County
672.B8	Brown County
672.B85	Buffalo County
672.B87	Burt County
672.B9	Butler County
672.C3	Cass County
672.C35	Cedar County
672.C4	Chase County
672.C45	Cherry County
672.C5	Cheyenne County
	Chimney Rock National Historic Site see F672.M7
672.C6	Clay County
672.C7	Colfax County
672.C8	Cuming County
672.C9	Custer County
672.D2	Dakota County
672.D3	Dawes County
672.D35	Dawson County
672.D4	Deuel County
672.D58	Dixon County
672.D6	Dodge County
672.D7	Douglas County
672.D8	Dundy County
672.F48	Fillmore County
672.F7	Franklin County
672.F8	Frontier County

Nebraska

Regions, counties, etc., A-Z -- Continued

672.F9	Furnas County
672.G13	Gage County
672.G2	Garden County
672.G3	Garfield County
672.G5	Gosper County
672.G6	Grant County
672.G7	Greeley County
672.H2	Hall County
672.H25	Hamilton County
672.H3	Harlan County
672.H4	Hayes County
672.H5	Hitchcock County
672.H6	Holt County
672.H7	Hooker County
672.H8	Howard County
672.J4	Jefferson County
672.J6	Johnson County
672.K4	Kearney County
672.K45	Keith County
672.K5	Keya Paha County
672.K6	Kimball County
672.K7	Knox County
672.L2	Lancaster County
672.L4	Lincoln County
672.L6	Logan County
672.L7	Loup County
672.L8	Loup River and Valley
672.M2	McPherson County
672.M3	Madison County
672.M4	Merrick County
672.M6	Missouri River and Valley, Nebr.

Cf. F598 General

672.M7	Morrill County

Including Chimney Rock National Historic Site

672.N3	Nance County
672.N4	Nemaha County
672.N56	Niobrara River and Valley

Class here general works on the Niobrara River and Valley,
as well as works limited to the part located in Nebraska
For works limited to the part of the Niobrara River and
Valley located in Wyoming see F767.N52

	Nebraska
	Regions, counties, etc., A-Z -- Continued
672.N8	North Platte River and Valley
	Class here general works on the North Platte River and Valley, as well as works limited to the part located in Nebraska
	For works limited to the part of the North Platte River and Valley located in Wyoming see F767.N8
672.N9	Nuckolls County
672.O8	Otoe County
672.P3	Pawnee County
672.P4	Perkins County
672.P5	Phelps County
672.P54	Pierce County
672.P58	Platte County
672.P6	Platte River and Valley
672.P7	Polk County
672.R4	Red Willow County
672.R5	Richardson County
672.R6	Rock County
672.S15	Saline County
672.S17	Sandhills
672.S2	Sarpy County
672.S24	Saunders County
672.S3	Scotts Bluff County
672.S5	Seward County
672.S53	Sheridan County
672.S54	Sherman County
672.S6	Sioux County
	Including Agate Fossil Beds National Monument
672.S7	South Platte River and Valley
	Class here general works on the South Platte River and Valley, as well as works limited to the part located in Nebraska
	For works limited to the part of the South Platte River and Valley located in Colorado see F782.S7
672.S8	Stanton County
672.T3	Thayer County
672.T4	Thomas County
672.T5	Thurston County
672.V3	Valley County
672.W3	Washington County
672.W35	Wayne County
672.W4	Webster County
672.W5	Wheeler County
672.Y62	York County

	Nebraska -- Continued
674.A-Z	Cities, towns, etc., A-Z
	e.g.
674.B4	Bellevue
674.G7	Grand Island
674.H3	Hastings
674.L7	Lincoln
674.O5-.O59	Omaha (Table F2)
	Elements in the population
675.A1	General works
675.A2-Z	Individual elements
	For a list of racial, ethnic, and religious elements (with Cutter numbers) see E184.A+
	Kansas

Historical note from the second edition (1913) of Class F: "Nearly all of Kansas belonged to the Louisiana purchase of 1803. It was included in the District (later Territory) of Louisiana 1804-1812, part of Missouri Territory 1812-1821 and after 1821 formed part of the unorganized region usually known as the "Indian country." In 1854 the Kansas-Nebraska bill was passed, and Kansas Territory was organized, consisting of the present Kansas and a portion of Colorado (the southwestern portion of modern Kansas being a part of the territory purchased by the U. S. from Texas 1850). In 1861 Kansas was admitted as a state, with substantially its present limits, the western portion of the former territory forming part of the new territory of Colorado the same year."

F1-975

676	Periodicals. Societies. Collections
678	Museums. Exhibitions, exhibits
679	Gazetteers. Dictionaries. Geographic names
679.3	Guidebooks
680	Biography (Collective). Genealogy (Collective)
680.2	Historiography
	Historians see E175.5.A+
680.5	Study and teaching
681	General works. Histories
681.3	Juvenile works
681.5	Pamphlets, addresses, essays
681.6	Anecdotes, legends, pageants
682	Historic monuments (General). Illustrative material
683	Antiquities (Non-Indian)
	By period

Kansas
  By period -- Continued

685	Early to 1861

Including struggle between proslavery and antislavery parties; New England Emigrant Aid Company; armed bands from Missouri; Battle of Osawatomie, 1856; Lecompton Constitution

Including biography: James Henry Lane, Charles Robinson, etc.

Cf. E433 Kansas-Nebraska Bill, 1854

Cf. F799 Quivira

686	1861-1950

Including admission as a state, January 29, 1861

Biography: Alfred Mossman Landon, etc.

Cf. D570.85.K2+ World War I, 1914-1918

Cf. D769.85.K2+ World War II, 1939-1945

Cf. E470.9 Civil War general military operations

Cf. E471+ Civil War campaigns and battles

Cf. E474.97 Quantrill's Raid, 1863

Cf. E508+ Civil War, 1861-1865 (General)

Cf. E726.K2 War of 1898 (Spanish-American War)

1951-

686.2	General works
	Biography
686.3	Collective
686.4.A-Z	Individual, A-Z

Subarrange each by Table F5

687.A-Z	Regions, counties, etc., A-Z
687.A15	Counties
687.A16	Mountains
687.A17	Rivers
687.A18	Lakes
687.A19	Islands
687.A4	Allen County
687.A5	Anderson County
687.A7	Arkansas River and Valley

Class here works limited to the part of the Arkansas River and Valley located in Kansas

For general works on the Arkansas River and Valley, as well as works limited to the part located in Arkansas see F417.A7

687.A8	Atchison County
687.B18	Barber County
687.B2	Barton County
687.B6	Big Blue River. Blue Valley
687.B7	Boundaries
687.B73	Bourbon County

Kansas
  Regions, counties, etc., A-Z -- Continued

687.B8	Brown County
687.B9	Butler County
	Including El Dorado Lake
	Cedar Point Lake see F687.C35
687.C35	Chase County
	Including Cedar Point Lake
687.C36	Chautauqua County
687.C38	Cherokee County
687.C5	Cheyenne County
687.C52	Cimarron River and Valley

    Class here works limited to the part of the Cimarron River and
      Valley located in Kansas
    For general works on the Cimarron River and Valley, as
      well as works limited to the part located in
      Oklahoma see F702.C53
    For works limited to the part of the Cimarron River and
      Valley located in Colorado see F782.C57
    For works limited to the part of the Cimarron River and
      Valley located in New Mexico see F802.C58

687.C53	Clark County
687.C55	Clay County
	Clinton Lake see F687.W4
687.C6	Cloud County
687.C7	Coffey County
687.C75	Comanche County
687.C8	Cowley County
687.C9	Crawford County
	Davis Co. see F687.G3
687.D4	Decatur County
687.D5	Dickinson County
687.D6	Doniphan County
687.D7	Douglas County
687.E2	Edwards County
	El Dorado Lake see F687.B9
687.E28	Elk County
687.E3	Ellis County
687.E4	Ellsworth County
687.F5	Finney County
687.F55	Flint Hills

    Class here general works on Flint Hills, as well as works
      limited to the part located in Kansas
    For works limited to the part of Flint Hills located in
      Oklahoma see F702.F55

687.F6	Ford County
687.F8	Franklin County

F1-975

Kansas
  Regions, counties, etc., A-Z -- Continued

687.G3	Geary County
	Formerly Davis County
687.G72	Gove County
687.G74	Graham County
687.G75	Grant County
687.G78	Gray County
687.G8	Greeley County
687.G85	Greenwood County
687.H3	Hamilton County
687.H4	Harper County
687.H45	Harvey County
687.H5	Haskell County
687.H8	Hodgeman County
687.J2	Jackson County
687.J3	Jefferson County
687.J4	Jewell County
687.J6	Johnson County
687.K3	Kansas River and Valley
687.K4	Kearny County
687.K53	Kingman County
687.K6	Kiowa County
687.L2	Labette County
687.L3	Lane County
687.L4	Leavenworth County
687.L7	Lincoln County
687.L75	Linn County
687.L8	Logan County
687.L9	Lyon County
687.M2	McPherson County
687.M3	Marion County
	For Cedar Point Lake see F687.C35
687.M35	Marshall County
687.M48	Meade County
687.M55	Miami County
687.M6	Missouri River and Valley, Kans.
	Cf. F598 General
687.M65	Mitchell County
687.M7	Montgomery County
687.M75	Morris County
687.M8	Morton County
687.N3	Nemaha County
687.N4	Neosho County
687.N43	Ness County
687.N8	Norton County
687.O6	Osage County

Kansas

Regions, counties, etc., A-Z -- Continued

687.O7	Osborne County
687.O8	Ottawa County
687.P3	Pawnee County
687.P5	Phillips County
687.P8	Pottawatomie County
687.P9	Pratt County
687.R25	Rawlins County
687.R3	Reno County
687.R4	Republic County
687.R45	Rice County
687.R5	Riley County
687.R7	Rooks County
687.R8	Rush County
687.R9	Russell County
687.S16	Saline County
687.S3	Scott County
687.S4	Sedgwick County
687.S45	Seward County
687.S5	Shawnee County
687.S55	Sheridan County
687.S6	Sherman County
687.S8	Smith County
687.S84	Smoky Hill River and Valley

Class here general works on the Smoky Hill River and Valley,
as well as works limited to the part located in Kansas
For works limited to the part of the Smoky Hill River
and Valley located in Colorado see F782.S53

687.S85	Solomon River and Valley
687.S86	Stafford County
687.S87	Stanton County
687.S88	Stevens County
687.S9	Sumner County
687.T34	Tallgrass Prairie National Preserve
687.T7	Trego County
687.W2	Wabaunsee River and Valley
687.W4	Wakarusa River and Valley

Including Clinton Lake

687.W43	Wallace County
687.W45	Washington County
687.W6	Wichita County
687.W7	Wilson County
687.W73	Wilson Lake
687.W8	Woodson County
687.W97	Wyandotte County

F1-975

Kansas -- Continued

689.A-Z	Cities, towns, etc., A-Z
	e.g.
689.H9	Hutchinson
689.K2	Kansas City
689.L4	Lawrence
689.L5	Leavenworth
689.T6	Topeka
689.W6	Wichita
	Elements in the population
690.A1	General works
690.A2-Z	Individual elements

For a list of racial, ethnic, and religious elements (with Cutter numbers) see E184.A+

Oklahoma

Historical note from the second edition (1913) of Class F: "All of the present state of Oklahoma, except the westernmost strip, was included in the Louisiana purchase 1803. It formed part of the District (later Territory) of Louisiana 1804-1812, and territory of Missouri 1812-1819. In 1819 it was included in the new Arkansas Territory, but by acts of Congress in 1824 and 1828 was detached from Arkansas and thenceforth formed part of the Indian country, or the unsettled region west of Arkansas and Missouri. It was not till after the close of the civil war that the government succeeded in bringing to it all the Indian tribes destined to occupy the territory; no territorial government in the ordinary sense was granted. In 1890 the northwestern part, having been purchased by the government from its Indian owners, was organized as Oklahoma Territory; No-man's land, north of Texas and west of 100˚ being added to the new territory. Meanwhile the Indian Territory continued its existence till the two territories were reunited and admitted as the state of Oklahoma in 1907."

691	Periodicals. Societies. Collections
691.5	Museums. Exhibitions, exhibits
692	Gazetteers. Dictionaries. Geographic names
692.3	Guidebooks
693	Biography (Collective). Genealogy (Collective)
693.2	Historiography
	Historians see E175.5.A+
693.5	Study and teaching
694	General works. Histories
694.3	Juvenile works
694.5	Pamphlets, addresses, essays, etc.
694.6	Anecdotes, legends, pageants, etc.
694.8	Geography
695	Historic monuments (General). Illustrative material

	Oklahoma -- Continued
696	Antiquities (Non-Indian)
	By period
697	Early to 1890
	Including the "Indian country," that part of the Louisiana purchase west of Arkansas, Missouri and the Missouri River. Indian Territory before division in 1890.
	Biography: Davis Lewis Payne
	1890-1907
698	Indian Territory
699	Oklahoma Territory
700	1907-1950
	Including admission as a state, November 16, 1907
	Biography: William Henry Murray
	Cf. D570.85.O5+ World War I, 1914-1918
	Cf. D769.85.O5+ World War II, 1939-1945
701	1951-
702.A-Z	Regions, counties, etc., A-Z
702.A15	Counties
702.A16	Mountains
702.A17	Rivers
702.A18	Lakes
702.A19	Islands
702.A3	Adair County
702.A4	Alfalfa County
702.A7	Arkansas River and Valley
	Class here works limited to the part of the Arkansas River and Valley located in Oklahoma
	For general works on the Arkansas River and Valley, as well as works limited to the part located in Arkansas see F417.A7
702.A8	Atoka County
702.B4	Beaver County
702.B45	Beckham County
702.B5	Blaine County
702.B7	Boundaries
	Cf. F392.B7 Texas boundary
	Cf. F782.B7 Colorado boundary
702.B8	Bryan County
702.C15	Caddo County
702.C17	Camp Creek and Valley
702.C18	Canadian County

F1-975

Oklahoma

Regions, counties, etc. A-Z -- Continued

702.C2	Canadian River and Valley

Class here general works on the Canadian River and Valley, as well as works limited to the part located in Oklahoma

For works limited the part of the Canadian River and Valley located in Texas see F392.C27

For works limited to the part of the Canadian River and Valley located in New Mexico see F802.C2

702.C3	Carter County
702.C4	Cherokee County
702.C42	Cherokee Outlet
	Chickasaw National Recreation Area see F702.M84
702.C45	Choctaw County
702.C5	Cimarron County
702.C53	Cimarron River and Valley

Class here general works on the Cimarron River and Valley, as well as works limited to the part located in Oklahoma

For works limited to the part of the Cimarron River and Valley located in Kansas see F687.C52

For works limited to the part of the Cimarron River and Valley located in Colorado see F782.C57

For works limited to the part of the Cimarron River and Valley located in New Mexico see F802.C58

702.C6	Cleveland County
702.C65	Coal County
702.C67	Comanche County
702.C75	Cotton County
702.C8	Craig County
702.C85	Creek County
702.C9	Custer County
702.D4	Delaware County
702.D5	Dewey County
702.E4	Ellis County
702.F55	Flint Hills

Class here works limited to the part of Flint Hills located in Oklahoma

For general works on Flint Hills, as well as works limited to the part located in Kansas see F687.F55

702.G25	Garfield County
702.G3	Garvin County
702.G7	Grady County
702.G75	Grant County
702.G8	Greer County
702.H3	Harmon County
702.H35	Harper County
702.H4	Haskell County

Oklahoma

Region, counties, etc. A-Z -- Continued

702.H9	Hughes County
702.J3	Jackson County
702.J4	Jefferson County
702.J6	Johnston County
702.K23	Kay County
702.K4	Kingfisher County
702.K5	Kiowa County
702.L3	Latimer County
702.L4	Le Flore County
702.L5	Lincoln County

        Including Robinson Creek and Valley

702.L55	Little River and Valley

        Class here general works on the Little River and Valley, as
            well as works limited to the part located in Oklahoma
        For works limited to the part of the Little River and
            Valley located in Arkansas see F417.L64

702.L6	Logan County
702.L7	Love County
702.M2	McClain County
702.M3	McCurtain County
702.M35	McIntosh County
702.M4	Major County
702.M5	Marshall County
702.M55	Mayes County
702.M84	Murray County

        Including Chickasaw National Recreation Area
        For Platt National Park see F702.P7

702.M9	Muskogee County
702.N6	No Man's Land. Oklahoma Panhandle
702.N8	Noble County
702.N9	Nowata County
702.O5	Ofuskee County
702.O55	Oklahoma County

        Oklahoma Panhandle see F702.N6

702.O6	Okmulgee County
702.O7	Osage County

        Including Salt Creek and Valley

702.O8	Ottawa County
702.O9	Ouachita Mountains

        Class here general works on the Ouachita Mountains, as well
            as works limited to the part located in Oklahoma
        For works limited to the part of the Ouachita Mountains
            located in Arkansas see F417.O77

Panhandle see F702.N6

F1-975

	Oklahoma
	Regions, counties, etc. A-Z
702.P35	Pawnee County
	For Camp Creek and Valley see F702.C17
702.P4	Payne County
	For Camp Creek and Valley see F702.C17
702.P6	Pittsburg County
702.P7	Platt National Park
702.P74	Pontotoc County
702.P75	Pottawatomie County
702.P9	Pushmataha County
702.R3	Red River and Valley
	Class here works limited to the part of the Red River and Valley located in Oklahoma
	For general works on the Red River and Valley, as well as works limited to the part located in Louisiana see F377.R3
	Robinson Creek and Valley see F702.L5
702.R6	Roger Mills County
702.R7	Rogers County
	Salt Creek and Valley see F702.O7
702.S35	Seminole County
702.S4	Sequoyah County
702.S8	Stephens County
702.T4	Texas County
702.T5	Tillman County
702.T8	Tulsa County
702.W2	Wagoner County
702.W3	Washington County
702.W35	Washita County
702.W36	Washita River and Valley
	Class here works limited to the part of the Washita River and Valley located in Oklahoma
	For general works on the Washita River and Valley, as well as works limited to the part located in Texas see F392.W33
702.W55	Wichita Mountains and region
702.W7	Woods County
702.W8	Woodward County
704.A-Z	Cities, towns, etc., A-Z
	e.g.
704.E6	Enid
704.G9	Guthrie
704.M9	Muskogee
704.N6	Norman
704.O41	Oklahoma City
704.T92	Tulsa

Oklahoma -- Continued
Elements in the population
705.A1 General works
705.A2-Z Individual elements
For a list of racial, ethnic, and religious elements (with
Cutter numbers) see E184.A+
718 Pacific and Mountain States
721 Rocky Mountains. Rocky Mountains in the United States
Cf. F782.R6 Rocky Mountain region of Colorado, etc.
Cf. F1090 Rocky Mountain region of Canada
722 Yellowstone National Park
Including boundaries
Cf. F737.Y4 Yellowstone River and Valley
Montana
Historical note from the second edition (1913) of Class F: "The
greater part of Montana belonged to the Louisiana purchase
1803; the western portion being part of the Oregon country
(for many years in dispute between Gt. Brit. and U.S. and
organized as the Territory of Oregon 1846-48). The former
and larger part was included in the District (later Territory) of
Louisiana 1804-1821, in the "Indian country" 1821-1854,
Nebraska Territory 1854-1861, Dakota Territory 1861-1863.
In 1863 the Territory of Idaho was organized, including the
western parts of Dakota and Nebraska territories, and the
eastern part of Washington Territory (the present Montana,
Wyoming and Idaho). The Territory of Montana was
organized 1864 with substantially its present limits; and
admitted as a state 1889."

F1-975

726 Periodicals. Societies. Collections
728 Museums. Exhibitions, exhibits
729 Gazetteers. Dictionaries. Geographic names
729.3 Guidebooks
730 Biography (Collective). Genealogy (Collective)
730.2 Historiography
Historians see E175.5.A+
730.5 Study and teaching
731 General works. Histories
Including admission as a state, November 2, 1889
By period (Early to 1950) as well as general
Biography: Granville Stuart
For 1951 and later see F735
Cf. D570.85.M9+ World War I, 1914-1918
Cf. D769.85.M9+ World War II, 1939-1945
Cf. E83.876 Dakota Indian War, 1876
Cf. E83.877 Nez Percé War, 1877
731.3 Juvenile works
731.5 Pamphlets, addresses, essays, etc.

	Montana -- Continued
731.6	Anecdotes, legends, pageants, etc.
731.8	Geography
732	Historic monuments (General). Illustrative material
733	Antiquities (Non-Indian)
	By period
	Early to 1950 see F731
735	1951-
	Biography
735.2.A2	Collective
735.2.A3-Z	Individual, A-Z
	Subarrange each by Table F5
737.A-Z	Regions, counties, etc., A-Z
737.A15	Counties
737.A16	Mountains
737.A17	Rivers
737.A18	Lakes
737.A19	Islands
737.A3	Absaroka National Forest
737.B35	Beartooth Mountains
	Class here general works on the Beartooth Mountains, as well as works limited to the part located in Montana
	For works limited to part of the Beartooth Mountains located in Wyoming see F767.B23
737.B38	Beaverhead County
737.B48	Big Hole River and Valley
737.B49	Big Horn Canyon National Recreation Area
737.B5	Big Horn County
737.B53	Big Horn Mountains
	Class here works limited to the part of the Big Horn Mountains located in Montana
	For general works on the Big Horn Mountains, as well as works limited to the part located in Wyoming see F767.B37
	Bird-Truax Trail see F752.B64
737.B6	Bitter Root River and Valley
737.B62	Blackfoot River and Valley
737.B63	Blaine County
737.B66	Bob Marshall Wilderness
737.B7	Boundaries
	For International boundary see F597
	For Yellowstone National Park boundary see F722
	Cf. F752.B7 Idaho boundary
737.B8	Broadwater County
737.C14	Cabinet National Forest
	Camas Prairie see F737.M6
737.C25	Carbon County

	Montana
	Regions, counties, etc., A-Z -- Continued
737.C3	Carter County
737.C33	Cascade County
737.C5	Chouteau County
737.C55	Clark Fork River and Valley

               Class here general works on the Clark Fork River and Valley,
                   as well as works limited to the part located in Montana
               For works limited to the part of the Clark Fork River and
                   Valley located in Idaho see F752.C57

737.C9	Custer County
737.D3	Daniels County
737.D4	Dawson County
737.D5	Deer Lodge County
737.F2	Fallon County
737.F3	Fergus County
737.F58	Flathead County

               Including Tobacco Plains

737.F6	Flathead Lake and Valley
737.F66	Flying D Ranch
737.G18	Gallatin County
737.G2	Gallatin Valley. East and West Gallatin Rivers
737.G3	Garfield County
737.G45	Glacier County
737.G5	Glacier National Park

               Including Lake McDonald, Mount Reynolds

737.G6	Golden Valley County
737.G7	Granite County
	Grant-Kohrs Ranch National Historic Site see F737.P88
737.H55	Hi-Line Region
737.H6	Hill County
737.J4	Jefferson County

               For Lewis and Clark Cavern State Park see F737.L65
          Jocko or Flathead Indian Reservation see E99.S2

737.J8	Judith Basin County
737.J83	Judith River and Valley
737.L3	Lake County

               Including St. Ignatius Mission
               For Flathead Lake see F737.F6

| 737.L65 | Lewis and Clark Cavern State Park |

               Including Morrison Cave

737.L67	Lewis and Clark County
737.L7	Liberty County
737.L8	Lincoln County
737.M13	McCone County
737.M2	Madison County

F1-975

	Montana
	Regions, counties, etc., A-Z -- Continued
737.M24	Madison River and Valley
	Class here works limited to the part of the Madison River and Valley located in Montana
	For general works on the Madison River and Valley, as well as works limited to the part located in Wyoming see F767.M34
737.M4	Meagher County
737.M48	Milk River and Valley
	Class here works limited to the part of the Milk River and Valley located in Montana
	For general works on the Milk River and Valley, as well as works limited to the part located in Alberta see F1079.M54
737.M5	Mineral County
737.M6	Missoula County
	Including Camas Prairie
737.M7	Missouri River and Valley, Mont.
	Cf. F598 General
	Morrison Cave see F737.L65
737.M9	Musselshell County
737.P23	Park County
737.P4	Petroleum County
737.P5	Phillips County
737.P6	Pondera County
737.P8	Powder River County
737.P88	Powell County
	Including Grant-Kohrs Ranch National Historic Site
737.P9	Prairie County
737.P93	Prickly Pear Creek and Valley
737.R3	Ravalli County
	Reynolds, Mount see F737.G5
737.R5	Richland County
737.R8	Rocky Mountain region, Mont.
	Including Marias Pass
	Cf. F721 General
737.R9	Roosevelt County
737.R95	Rosebud County
737.R96	Rosebud Creek and Valley (Montana)
737.S3	Sanders County
737.S4	Sheridan County
737.S5	Silver Bow County
737.S8	Stillwater County
737.S84	Sun River and Valley
737.S88	Swan River and Valley

Montana
Regions, counties, etc., A-Z -- Continued

737.S9	Sweet Grass County
	Including West Boulder River and Valley
	Sweet Grass Hills see F737.T6
737.T4	Teton County
737.T55	Tongue River and Valley
	Class here general works on the Tongue River and Valley, as well as works limited to the part located in Montana
	For works limited to the part of the Tongue River and Valley located in Wyoming see F767.T65
737.T6	Toole County
	Including Sweet Grass Hills
737.T7	Treasure County
737.V3	Valley County
737.W4	Wheatland County
737.W5	Wibaux County
737.Y3	Yellowstone County
	Yellowstone National Park see F722
737.Y4	Yellowstone River and Valley
	Class here general works on the Yellowstone River and Valley, as well as works limited to the part located in Montana
	Including Fort Custer
	For works limited to the part of the Yellowston River and Valley located in North Dakota see F642.M28
	For works limited to the part of the Yellowston River and Valley located in Wyoming see F767.Y44
739.A-Z	Cities, towns, etc., A-Z
	e.g.
739.B5	Billings
739.B8	Butte
739.G7	Great Falls
739.H4	Helena
739.M7	Missoula
	Elements in the population
740.A1	General works
740.A2-Z	Individual elements
	For a list of racial, ethnic, and religious elements (with Cutter numbers) see E184.A+

F1-975

Idaho

Historical note from the second edition (1913) of Class F: "The present state of Idaho was a part of the Oregon country, jointly occupied by Gt. Brit. and U.S.; divided between the two countries, and the American portion organized as Oregon Territory 1846-1848. On the formation of Washington Territory in 1853, the northern part of Idaho was included in it, and on the admission of Oregon as a state in 1859, the remainder of the present Idaho was annexed to Washington Territory. In 1863 the Territory of Idaho was organized from portions of the territories of Nebraska, Dakota and Washington, so as to include what is now Idaho, Montana and Wyoming. Montana Territory was cut off in 1864 and Wyoming Territory in 1868. Idaho was admitted as a state 1890."

741	Periodicals. Societies. Collections
743	Museums. Exhibitions, exhibits
744	Gazetteers. Dictionaries. Geographic names
744.3	Guidebooks
745	Biography (Collective). Genealogy (Collective)
745.2	Historiography
	Historians see E175.5.A+
745.5	Study and teaching
746	General works. Histories

        Including admission as a state, July 3, 1890
        By period (Early to 1950) as well as general
        Biography: Frank Steunenberg
        For 1951 and later see F750+
        Cf. D769.85.I2+ World War II, 1939-1945
        Cf. E83.877 Nez Percé War, 1877

746.3	Juvenile works
746.5	Pamphlets, addresses, essays, etc.
746.6	Anecdotes, legends, pageants, etc.
747	Historic monuments (General). Illustrative material
748	Antiquities (Non-Indian)
	By period
	Early to 1950 see F746
	1951-
750	General works
	Biography
750.2	Collective
750.22.A-Z	Individual, A-Z
	Subarrange each by Table F5
752.A-Z	Regions, counties, etc., A-Z
752.A15	Counties
752.A16	Mountains
752.A17	Rivers

Idaho
Regions, counties, etc., A-Z -- Continued

752.A18	Lakes
752.A19	Islands
752.A3	Ada County
752.A4	Adams County
752.A55	Albeni Falls Dam and Region
752.A6	Alturas County (1864-1895)
752.B2	Bannock County
752.B3	Bear Lake County
752.B4	Benewah County
752.B55	Big Wood River and Valley
752.B6	Bingham County
752.B63	Birch Creek Valley
752.B64	Bird-Truax Trail
752.B65	Blaine County
	Including Sawtooth Mountains and Valley
752.B67	Boise County
752.B673	Boise River and Valley
752.B677	Bonner County
	Including Priest Lake and Region
752.B68	Bonneville County
752.B7	Boundaries
	For International boundary see F597
	For Yellowstone National Park boundary see F722
	For International boundary see F854; F880
	Cf. F897.B7 Washington boundary
752.B73	Boundary County
	Bruneau River and Valley see F752.O97
752.B9	Butte County
752.C17	Camas County
752.C2	Canyon County
752.C3	Caribou County
	Including Gem Valley
752.C35	Cassia County
	Including City of Rocks National Reserve
	City of Rocks National Reserve see F752.C35
752.C55	Clark County
752.C57	Clark Fork and Valley
	Class here works limited to the part of the Clark Fork River and Valley located in Idaho
	For general works on the Clark Fork River and Valley, as well as works limited to the part located in Montana see F737.C55
752.C6	Clearwater County
752.C62	Clearwater River and Valley
	Coeur d'Alene mining district see F752.S5

	Idaho
	Regions, counties, etc., A-Z -- Continued
752.C65	Coeur d'Alene River and Valley
	Craig Mountain see F752.N57
752.C7	Craters of the Moon National Monument
752.C9	Custer County
752.E4	Elmore County
752.F68	Frank Church-River of No Return Wilderness
752.F7	Franklin County
752.F8	Fremont County
752.G4	Gem County
	Gem Valley see F752.C3
	Gilmore Ranch see F752.I2
752.G66	Gooding County
	Including Thousand Springs State Park
	Hagerman Fossil Beds National Monument see F752.T8
752.H44	Hells Canyon National Recreation Area
	Class here works limited to the part of the Hells Canyon National Recreation Area located in Idaho.
	For general works on Hells Canyon National Recreation Area, as well as works limited to the part located in Oregon see F882.H44
752.I2	Idaho County
	Including Gilmore Ranch, Joseph Plains, Lochsa River and Valley
752.I7	Island Park region
752.J4	Jefferson County
752.J5	Jerome County
	Including Minidoka Internment National Monument
	Joseph Plains see F752.I2
752.K8	Kootenai County
	For Coeur d'Alene mining district see F752.S5
752.L3	Latah County
752.L4	Lemhi County
752.L45	Lewis County
752.L5	Lincoln County
	Lochsa River and Valley see F752.I2
752.M3	Madison County
	Mann Creek and Valley see F752.W3
752.M5	Minidoka County
	Minidoka Internment National Monument see F752.J5
752.N57	Nez Percé County
	Including Craig Mountain
752.O5	Oneida County
752.O97	Owyhee County Owyhee Mountains region
	Including Bruneau River and Valley

Idaho
    Regions, counties, etc., A-Z -- Continued

752.O98	Owyhee River and Valley

Class here works limited to the part of the Owyhee River and
Valley located in Idaho
For general works on the Owyhee River and Valley, as
well as works limited to the part located in Oregon
see F882.O98

752.P23	Pahsimeroi River and Valley
752.P25	Palouse River and Valley

Class here general works on the Palouse River and Valley,
as well as works limited to the part located in Idaho
For works limited to the part of the Palouse River and
Valley located in Washington State see F897.P24

752.P3	Payette County
752.P33	Payette River and Valley
752.P6	Power County
	Priest Lake and Region see F752.B677
752.S28	Saint Maries River and Valley
752.S35	Salmon River and Valley
752.S37	Salt Valley

Class here works limited to the part of the Salt Valley located
in Idaho
For general works on the Salt Valley, as well as works
limited to the part located in Wyoming see
F767.S37

	Sawtooth Mountains and Valley see F752.B65
752.S5	Shoshone County
	Including Coeur d'Alene mining district
752.S7	Snake River and Valley

Class here general works on the Snake River and Valley, as
well as works limited to the part located in Idaho
For works limited to the part of the Snake River and
Valley located in Oregon see F882.S6
For works limited to the part of the Snake River and
Valley located in Washington State see F897.S6

752.S74	Saint Joe River and Valley
	Sylvan Beach see F752.V3
752.T4	Teton County
752.T5	Teton River and Valley
	Thousand Springs State Park see F752.G66
752.T8	Twin Falls County
	Including Hagerman Fossil Beds National Monument
752.V3	Valley County
	Including Sylvan Beach

F1-975

Idaho
Regions, counties, etc., A-Z -- Continued
752.W27   Wasatch Range
Class here works limited to the part of the Wasatch Range located in Idaho
For general works on the Wasatch Range, as well as works limited to the part located in Utah see F832.W22
752.W3   Washington County
Including Mann Creek and Valley
Yellowstone National Park see F722
754.A-Z   Cities, towns, etc., A-Z
e.g.
754.B65   Boise
754.I2   Idaho Falls
754.L6   Lewiston
754.P7   Pocatello
754.T97   Twin Falls
Elements in the population
755.A1   General works
755.A2-Z   Individual elements
For a list of racial, ethnic, and religious elements (with Cutter numbers) see E184.A+
Wyoming
Historical note from the second edition (1913) of Class F: "The east and northeast parts (about two thirds of the area) of the present state of Wyoming formed a part of the Louisiana purchase of 1803. This was included in the District (later Territory) of Louisiana 1804-1812, in Missouri Territory 1812-1821, in the "Indian country" 1821-1854, and Territory of Nebraska 1854. The western part of Wyoming was part of the Oregon country (cf. note under F871+) and the southwest a part of the Mexican cession of 1848 (cf. note under F791+) while a small area in the south belonged to the Texas cession of 1850. In 1863 all the territory of which Wyoming is composed, previously belonging to the territories of Nebraska, Dakota, Washington and Utah, was included in the new Idaho Territory. Wyoming was organized as a separate territory in 1868 and admitted as a state in 1890."
756   Periodicals. Societies. Collections
758   Museums. Exhibitions, exhibits
759   Gazetteers. Dictionaries. Geographic names
759.3   Guidebooks
760   Biography (Collective). Genealogy (Collective)
760.2   Historiography
Historians see E175.5.A+
760.5   Study and teaching

	Wyoming -- Continued
761	General works. Histories
	Including admission as a state, July 10, 1890
	By period (Early to 1950) as well as general
	For 1951 and later see F765+
	Cf. D769.85.W8+ World War II, 1939-1945
	Cf. E83.879 Ute War, 1879
761.3	Juvenile works
761.5	Pamphlets, addresses, essays, etc.
761.6	Anecdotes, legends, pageants, etc.
762	Historic monuments (General). Illustrative material
763	Antiquities (Non-Indian)
	By period
	Early to 1950 see F761
	1951-
765	General works
	Biography
765.2	Collective
765.22.A-Z	Individual, A-Z
	Subarrange each by Table F5
767.A-Z	Regions, counties, etc., A-Z
767.A15	Counties
767.A16	Mountains
767.A17	Rivers
767.A18	Lakes
767.A19	Islands
767.A3	Albany County
767.B23	Beartooth Mountains
	Class here works limited to part of the Beartooth Mountains located in Wyoming
	For general works on the Beartooth Mountains, as well as works limited to the part located in Montana see F737.B35
	Big Horn Canyon National Recreation Area see F737.B49
767.B35	Big Horn County
767.B37	Big Horn Mountains
	Class here general works on the Big Horn Mountains, as well as works limited to the part located in Wyoming
	For works limited to the part of the Big Horn Mountains located in Montana see F737.B53
767.B4	Big Horn River and Valley, Wyo.
767.B7	Boundaries
	For Yellowstone National Park boundary see F722
	Bridger Pass Overland Trail see F767.O94
767.C16	Campbell County
767.C2	Carbon County
	Casper Mountain see F767.N2

F1-975

	Wyoming
	Regions, counties, etc., A-Z -- Continued
767.C55	Clear Creek and Valley (Big Horn County-Sheridan County)
767.C6	Converse County
767.C7	Crook County
767.D47	Devils Tower National Monument
	Eden Valley see F767.S9
767.F5	Flaming Gorge National Recreation Area

Class here general works on Flaming Gorge National Recreation Area, as well as works limited to the part located in Wyoming

For works limited to the part of the Flaming Gorge National Recreation Area located in Utah see F832.F52

767.F8	Fremont County
767.F88	Front Range

Class here works limited to the part of the Front Range located in Wyoming

For general works on the Front Range, as well as works limited to the part located in Colorado see F782.F88

	Gibbon Falls see F767.Y44
767.G6	Goshen County
	Grand Teton National Park see F767.T3
767.G7	Green River and Valley
	Including Brown's Park
767.H6	Hot Springs County
767.I38	Independence Rock
	Jackson Hole see F767.T28
767.J3	Jackson Hole National Monument (1943-1950)

Included (1950) in Grand Teton National Park, Teton National Forest, and Jackson Hole Wildlife Park

	Jackson Lake see F767.T3
	Jenny Lake see F767.T3
767.J8	Johnson County
767.L3	Laramie County
767.L5	Lincoln County
767.M34	Madison River and Valley

Class here general works on the Madison River and Valley, as well as works limited to the part located in Wyoming

For works limited to the part of the Madison River and Valley located in Montana see F737.M24

Wyoming

Regions, counties, etc., A-Z -- Continued

767.M42	Medicine Bow Mountains

Class here works limited to the part of the Medicine Bow
Mountains located in Wyoming

For general works on the Medicine Bow Mountains, as
well as works limited to the part located in Colorado
see F782.M43

767.M43	Medicine Bow National Forest
767.N2	Natrona

Including Casper Mountain

For Independence Rock see F767.I38

767.N5	Niobrara County
767.N52	Niobrara River and Valley

Class here works limited to the part of the Niobrara River and
Valley located in Wyoming

For general works on the Niobrara River and Valley, as
well as works limited to the part located in
Nebraska see F672.N56

767.N8	North Platte River and Valley

Class here works limited to the part of the North Platte River
and Valley located in Wyoming

For general works on the North Platte River and Valley,
as well as works limited to the part located in
Nebraska see F672.N8

767.O94	Overland Trail

Class here general works on the Overland Trail, as well as
works limited to the part located in Wyoming

Including Bridger Pass Overland Trail

For works limited to the part located in Colorado see
F782.O94

Cf. F597 Overland Trails (Northwest)

767.P3	Park County
767.P5	Platte County
767.P6	Powder River and Valley, Wyo.
767.S37	Salt Valley

Class here general works on the Salt Valley, as well as works
limited to the part located in Wyoming

For works limited to the part of the Salt Valley located
in Idaho see F752.S37

767.S55	Sheridan County
767.S57	Shoshone National Forest
767.S58	Shoshone River and Valley
	String Lake see F767.T3
767.S8	Sublette County
767.S9	Sweetwater County

Including Eden Valley

	Wyoming
	Regions, counties, etc., A-Z -- Continued
767.S92	Sweetwater River and Valley
767.T28	Teton County
	Including Jackson Hole
767.T29	Teton Mountains
767.T3	Grand Teton National Park
	Including Jackson Lake, String Lake, Jenny Lake
767.T65	Tongue River and Valley
	Class here works limited to the part of the Tongue River and Valley located in Wyoming
	For general works on the Tongue River and Valley, as well as works limited to the part located in Montana see F737.T55
767.T96	Two Dot Ranch
767.U3	Uinta County
767.U33	Uinta Mountains
	Class here works limited to the part of the Uinta Mountains located in Wyoming
	For general works on the Uinta Mountains, as well as works limited to the part located in Utah see F832.U39
767.W3	Washakie County
767.W4	Weston County
767.W5	Wind River and Valley. Wind River Range
	Yellowstone National Park see F722
767.Y44	Yellowstone River and Valley
	Class here works limited to the part of the Yellowstone River and Valley located in Wyoming
	Including Gibbon Falls
	For general works on the Yellowstone River and Valley, as well as works limited to the part located in Montana see F737.Y4
769.A-Z	Cities, towns, etc., A-Z
	e.g.
769.C3	Casper
769.C5	Cheyenne
769.L2	Laramie
	Elements in the population
770.A1	General works
770.A2-Z	Individual elements
	For a list of racial, ethnic, and religious elements (with Cutter numbers) see E184.A+

Colorado

Historical note from the second edition (1913) of Class F: "The present state of Colorado includes territory from three sources; the Louisiana purchase of 1803, the Mexican cession of 1848 and the Texas purchase of 1850. It was organized as a territory in 1861 from parts of the territories of Kansas, Nebraska, Utah and New Mexico, and admitted as a state 1876. "

771	Periodicals. Societies. Collections
773	Museums. Exhibitions, exhibits
774	Gazetteers. Dictionaries. Geographic names
774.3	Guidebooks
775	Biography (Collective). Genealogy (Collective)
775.2	Historiography
	Historians see E175.5.A+
775.5	Study and teaching
776	General works. Histories
776.3	Juvenile works
776.5	Pamphlets, addresses, essays, etc.
776.6	Anecdotes, legends, pageants, etc.
777	Historic monuments (General). Illustrative material
778	Antiquities (Non-Indian)
	By period
780	Early to 1876

F1-975

Including biography: John Evans, Benjamin Franklin Hall, etc.
Cf. E83.868 Battle of Beecher Island, 1868
Cf. E333 Louisiana Purchase, 1803
Cf. F786 Mexican Cession of 1848
Cf. F801 Purchase of Northwest Texas by United
States, 1850

781	1876-1950

Including admission as a state, August 1, 1876
Including biography: Robert Wilbur Steele, Davis Hanson
Waite, etc.
Cf. D570.85.C6+ World War I, 1914-1918
Cf. E83.879 Ute Indian War, 1879

781.2	1951-1980
781.3	1981-
782.A-Z	Regions, counties, etc., A-Z
782.A15	Counties
782.A16	Mountains
782.A17	Rivers
782.A18	Lakes
782.A19	Islands
782.A2	Adams County
782.A4	Alamosa County
782.A5	Arapahoe County

	Colorado
	Regions counties, etc., A-Z -- Continued
782.A6	Archuleta County
782.A7	Arkansas River and Valley

Class here works limited to the part of the Arkansas River
and Valley located in Colorado
Including Bent's Old Fort National Historic Site
For general works on the Arkansas River and Valley,
as well as works limited to the part located in
Arkansas see F417.A7
For Royal Gorge see F782.F8

782.B2	Baca County
782.B33	Battlement National Forest
	Beaver Creek and Valley see F782.E15
782.B4	Bent County
	Bent's Old Fort National Historic Site see F782.A7
782.B45	Big Thompson River and Valley

Including Big Thompson Canyon

| 782.B5 | Black Canyon of the Gunnison National Monument |
| 782.B6 | Boulder County |

Including Eldorado Canyon
For Longs Peak see F782.L83

782.B7	Boundaries
	Bridger Pass Overland Trail see F782.O94
782.C5	Chaffee County

Including Chalk Creek

782.C55	Cheyenne County
	Cheyenne Mountain see F782.E3
782.C57	Cimarron River and Valley

Class here works limited to the part of the Cimarron River and
Valley located in Colorado
For workslimited to the part of the Cimarron River and
Valley located in Kansas see F687.C52
For general works on the Cimarron River and Valley, as
well as works limited to the part located in
Oklahoma see F702.C53
For works limited to the part of the Cimarron River and
Valley located in New Mexico see F802.C58

782.C59	Clear Creek and Valley
782.C6	Clear Creek County
782.C66	Cochetopa National Forest
	Colorado National Monument see F782.M5
782.C7	Colorado River and Valley, Colo.

Formerly Grand River, Colo.
Cf. F788 General
Colorado Trail see F782.R6

| 782.C75 | Conejos County |

Colorado
Regions counties, etc., A-Z -- Continued

782.C8	Costilla County
	Including Sangre de Cristo Grant (Costilla and Trinchera estates)
782.C9	Crowley County
782.C95	Custer County
782.D4	Delta County
	Including Surface Creek and Valley
782.D45	Denver County
	Dinosaur National Monument see F832.D5
782.D57	Disappointment Creek and Valley
782.D7	Dolores County
782.D8	Douglas County
782.E15	Eagle County
	Including Beaver Creek and Valley, Eagle River and Valley
	Eagle River and Valley see F782.E15
782.E25	Elbert County
	Eldorado Canyon see F782.B6
782.E3	El Paso County
	Including Cave of the Winds, Cheyenne Mountain, Crystal Park, Garden of the Gods
	For Pikes Peak see F782.P63
782.E82	Escalante Canyon
	Estes Park region see F782.L2
782.F8	Fremont County
	Including Royal Gorge (Grand Canyon of the Arkansas)
782.F88	Front Range
	Class here general works on the Front Range, as well as works limited to the part located in Colorado
	For works limited to the part of the Front Range located in Wyoming see F767.F88
	Garden of the Gods see F782.E3
782.G3	Garfield County
	Including Glenwood Canyon
782.G4	Gilpin County
	Glenwood Canyon see F782.G3
	Grand Canyon of the Arkansas see F782.F8
782.G7	Grand County
	Including Grand Lake (Lake)
782.G73	Grand Mesa
	Grand River and Valley, Colo. see F782.C7
782.G78	Great Sand Dunes National Park and Preserve
782.G9	Gunnison County
782.H5	Hinsdale County
782.H6	Holy Cross, Mount of the
782.H8	Huerfano County

F1-975

	Colorado
	Regions, counties, etc., A-Z -- Continued
782.J3	Jackson County
	Including North Park
782.J4	Jefferson County
782.K4	Kiowa County
782.K5	Kit Carson County
782.L15	Lake County
782.L18	La Plata County
782.L2	Larimer County
	Including Estes Park region
782.L3	Las Animas County
	Including Pinon Canyon
782.L33	Las Animas Mining District
782.L4	Leadville National Forest
	Lime Creek and Valley see F782.S18
782.L6	Lincoln County
	Lodore, Canyon of see F782.M65
782.L8	Logan County
782.L83	Longs Peak
	Manti La Sal National Forest see F832.M3
	Maxwell Land Grant see F802.M38
782.M43	Medicine Bow Mountains
	Class here general works on the Medicine Bow Mountains, as well as works limited to the part located in Colorado
	For works limited to the part of the Medicine Bow Mountains located in Wyoming see F767.M42
782.M5	Mesa County
	Including Colorado National Monument
782.M52	Mesa Verde National Park
	Cf. E99.P9 Pueblo Indian antiquities
782.M6	Mineral County
782.M65	Moffat County
	Including Canyon of Lodore
	For Dinosaur National Monument see F832.D5
782.M7	Montezuma County
	Including Mancos River and Valley, Colo.
782.M8	Montrose County
	For Uncompahgre Valley see F782.U5
782.M9	Morgan County
	North Park see F782.J3
782.O8	Otero County
782.O9	Ouray County

Colorado

Regions, counties, etc., A-Z -- Continued

782.O94	Overland Trail

             Class here works on the part of the Overland Trail located in located in Colorado

             Including Bridger Pass Overland Trail

             For general works on the Overland Trail, as well as works limited to the part located in Wyoming see F767.O94

             Cf. F597 Overland Trails (Northwest)

782.P3	Park County
782.P37	Peak-to-Peak Highway
782.P5	Phillips County
782.P52	Piceance Creek and watershed
782.P63	Pikes Peak

             Including Pike National Forest

       Pinon Canyon see F782.L3

782.P7	Pitkin County
782.P8	Prowers County
782.P9	Pueblo County
782.R36	Red Mountain Mining District
782.R4	Rio Blanco County

             Including White River and Valley (General, and Colorado)

             Cf. F832.U4 White River and Valley, Utah

782.R45	Rio Grande County
782.R46	Rio Grande National Forest
782.R52	Roaring Fork Valley
782.R59	Rocky Mountain National Park

             For Estes Park region see F782.L2

             For Longs Peak see F782.L83

782.R6	Rocky Mountain region, Colo.

             Including Colorado Trail

             For Pikes Peak see F782.P63

             Cf. F721 General

782.R7	Routt County
782.R8	Routt National Forest

       Royal Gorge see F782.F8

782.S14	Saguache County
782.S15	Saint Vrain Creek and Valley
782.S17	San Juan County
782.S18	San Juan Mountains

             Including Lime Creek and Valley

782.S19	San Juan region
782.S2	San Luis Park (Valley)

             Cf. F782.C8 Sangre de Cristo Grant

782.S23	San Miguel County

       Sangre de Cristo Grant see F782.C8

F1-975

	Colorado
	Regions, counties, etc., A-Z -- Continued
782.S26	Sangre de Cristo Mountains

Class here works limited to the part of the Sangre de Cristo
Mountains located in Colorado

For general works on the Sangre de Cristo Mountains,
as well as works limited to the part located in New
Mexico see F802.S32

| 782.S4 | Sedgwick County |
| 782.S53 | Smoky Hill River and Valley |

Class here works limited to the part of the Smoky Hill River
and Valley located in Colorado

For general works on the Smoky Hill River and Valley,
as well as works limited to the part located in
Kansas see F687.S84

| 782.S6 | South Park (region) |
| 782.S7 | South Platte River and Valley |

Class here works limited to the part of the South Platte River
and Valley, as well as works limited to the part located in
Colorado

For general works on the South Platte River and Valley,
as well as works limited to the part located in
Nebraska see F672.S7

782.S76	Spanish Peaks
782.S95	Summit County
	Surface Creek and Valley see F782.D4
782.T37	Tarryall Mountains
782.T4	Teller County
782.U5	Uncompahgre Valley
	Including Uncompahgre National Forest
782.U8	Ute Pass
782.V34	Vallecito Creek and Valley
782.W3	Washington County
782.W4	Weld County
782.W46	West Elk Loop Scenic and Historic Byway
782.W49	Wet Mountain Valley
	White River and Valley, (General, and Colorado) see F782.R4
782.Y8	Yuma County
784.A-Z	Cities, towns, etc., A-Z
	e.g.
784.A7	Aspen
784.C4	Central City
784.C7	Colorado Springs
784.C8	Cripple Creek
784.D4-.D49	Denver (Table F2)
784.G7	Greeley

Colorado

Cities, towns, etc., A-Z -- Continued

784.L4	Leadville
784.M3	Manitou
784.P9	Pueblo

Elements in the population

785.A1	General works
785.A2-Z	Individual elements

For a list of racial, ethnic, and religious elements (with Cutter numbers) see E184.A+

The New Southwest. Southwestern States

785.15	Periodicals. Societies. Collections
785.3	Guidebooks
785.5	Biography (Collective). Genealogy (Collective)
785.7	Juvenile works
786	1848-1950

Including the region of the Mexican Cession of 1848, the Texas Purchase of 1850, and the Gadsden Purchase

Including Mexican boundary; Santa Fe Trail; frontier troubles with Mexico; Gadsden Purchase, 1853

Including biography: William H. Bonney (Billy the Kid), etc.

Cf. E78.S7 Indians of the New Southwest

Cf. E401+ War with Mexico, 1845-1848

Cf. E470.9 Civil War general military operations

Cf. E471+ Civil War campaigns and battles

Cf. F799+ Southwest before 1848

Cf. F1232 Mexican frontier troubles (General)

F1-975

787	1951-
788	Colorado River, Canyon, and Valley

Including Grand Canyon National Park and Lake Mead National Recreation Area

788.5	Four Corners Region
789	Great Basin

Elements in the population

790.A1	General works
790.A2-Z	Individual elements

For a list of racial, ethnic, and religious elements (with Cutter numbers) see E184.A+

New Mexico

> Historical note from the second edition (1913) of Class F: "A part of the province of New Spain and later empire and republic of Mexico down to 1836, when the eastern part was included in Texas and won its independence. The remainder was transferred to the U.S. by purchase in 1848, as a result of the Mexican war. This cession included the whole of California, Utah, Nevada, and parts of Arizona, New Mexico, Colorado and Wyoming. In 1850 the part of Texas northwest of its present limits was purchased from that state by the U.S. and from the whole of this former Mexican territory, the two territories of New Mexico and Utah and the state of California were formed the same year. In 1853 the Gadsden purchase was added to the first named. New Mexico, as thus organized, included the whole of the present New Mexico and Arizona, the southern extremity of Nevada and part of southern Colorado. The formation of the territory of Colorado in 1861, the territory of Arizona in 1863 and the state of Nevada in 1864-66 reduced New Mexico to its present limits. Admitted as a state 1912."

791	Periodicals. Societies. Collections
793	Museums. Exhibitions, exhibits
794	Gazetteers. Dictionaries. Geographic names
794.3	Guidebooks
795	Biography (Collective). Genealogy (Collective)
795.2	Historiography
	Historians see E175.5.A+
795.5	Study and teaching
796	General works. Histories
796.3	Juvenile works
796.5	Pamphlets, addresses, essays
796.6	Anecdotes, legends, pageants, etc.
797	Historic monuments (General). Illustrative material
798	Antiquities (Non-Indian)
	By period
799	Early to 1822

> > Including Spanish discoveries and settlements in the Southwest between the Mississippi River and California; seven cities of Cibola; Quivira; Spanish province; Pimería Alta
> >
> > Including biography: Eusebio Francisco Kino, Diego Dionisio de Peñalosa, etc.
> >
> > Cf. F1410 Spaniards in North America (General)

New Mexico
By period -- Continued
800   1822-1848
Including Mexican state, region between Texas and California
Cf. E405.2 Conquest by United States Troops, War
with Mexico, 1845-1848
Cf. F389 Texas
Cf. F390 Texan Santa Fe Expedition, 1841
Cf. F786 Santa Fe Trail
Cf. F826 Utah
801   1848-1950
Including admission as a state, January 6, 1912
Including purchase of northwest Texas by United States,
1850
Including biography: Octaviano Ambrosio Larrazola, Antonio
Miguel Otero, etc.
Cf. D769.85.N33+ World War II, 1939-1945
Cf. E83.88 Apache War, 1883-1886
Cf. E423 Compromise of 1850
Cf. E470.9 Civil War general military operations
Cf. E471+ Civil War campaigns and battles
Cf. E522+ Civil War, 1861-1865 (General)
Cf. E571+ Confederate history
Cf. F786 Gadsden Purchase, 1853

F1-975

1951-
801.2   General works
Biography
801.3   Collective
801.4.A-Z   Individual, A-Z
Subarrange each by Table F5
802.A-Z   Regions, counties, etc., A-Z
802.A15   Counties
802.A16   Mountains
802.A17   Rivers
802.A18   Lakes
802.A19   Islands
Aztec Ruins National Monument see E99.P9
802.B25   Bandelier National Monument
Including Frijoles Canyon
802.B5   Bernalillo County
802.B58   Bisti
802.B63   Black Range
802.B7   Boundaries
For International boundary see F786
Cf. F392.B7 Texas boundary
Cf. F782.B7 Colorado boundary

New Mexico
    Regions, counties, etc., A-Z -- Continued

802.C2	Canadian River and Valley

        Class here works limited to the part of the Canadian River
           and Valley located in New Mexico
        For general works on the Canadian River and Valley,
           as well as works limited to the part located in
           Oklahoma see F702.C2
    Capulin Volcano National Monument see F802.U5

802.C28	Carlsbad Caverns

        Including Carlsbad Caverns National Park

802.C3	Catron County
802.C4	Chaco Canyon

        Including Chaco Canyon National Monument

802.C45	Chama Valley

        Including Rio Chama

802.C5	Chaves County
802.C52	Chihuahuan Desert
802.C54	Cibola County

        Including El Malpais National Monument, El Malpais National
           Conservation Area

802.C58	Cimarron River and Valley

        Class here works limited to the part of the Cimarron River and
           Valley located in New Mexico
        For works limited to the part of the Cimarron River and
           Valley located in Kansas see F687.C52
        For general works on the Cimarron River and Valley, as
           well as works limited to the part located in
           Oklahoma see F702.C53
        For works limited to the part of the Cimarron River and
           Valley located in Colorado see F782.C57

802.C7	Colfax County

        Including Moreno Creek and Valley

802.C8	Curry County
802.D4	De Baca County
802.D6	Dona Ana County

        For Mesilla Valley see F802.M4

802.E2	Eddy County

        For Carlsbad Caverns see F802.C28
    El Malpais National Conservation Area see F802.C54
    El Malpais National Monument see F802.C54

New Mexico
Regions, counties, etc., A-Z -- Continued

802.E45	El Camino Real de Tierra Adentro National Historic Trail

Class here general works on the El Camino Real de Tierra
Adentro National Historic Trail, as well as works limited to
the part located in New Mexico
For works limited to the part of the El Camino Real de
Tierra Adentro Historic Trail located in Texas see
F392.E36

802.E5	El Morro National Monument
802.E8	Española Valley
	Frijoles Canyon see F802.B25
	Gadsden Purchase see F786
802.G54	Gila River and Valley

Class here works limited to the part of the Gila River and
Valley located in located in New Mexico
For general works on the Gila River and Valley, as well
as works limited to the part located in Arizona see
F817.G52

802.G62	Gobernador Canyon
802.G7	Grant County

Including Mimbres River and Valley

802.G9	Guadalupe County

Including Leonard Wood Co. (1903-1904), Santa Rosa Lake
and Region

802.G93	Guadalupe Mountains

Class here general works on the Guadalupe Mountains, as
well as works limited to the part located in New Mexico
For works limited to the part of the Guadalupe
Mountains located in Texas see F392.G86

802.H3	Harding County
802.H5	Hidalgo County
802.H84	Hueco Mountains

Class here works limited to the part of the Hueco Mountains
located in New Mexico
For general works on the Hueco Mountains, as well as
works limited to the part located in Texas see
F392.H82

Jemez Mountains see F802.S3
Jornada del Muerto Road see F802.J67

802.J67	Jornada del Muerto Wilderness. Jornada del Muerto Road
802.L4	Lea County
	Leonard Wood Co. (1903-1904) see F802.G9
802.L7	Lincoln County
802.L84	Los Alamos County
802.L9	Luna County
802.M2	McKinley County

New Mexico

Regions, counties, etc., A-Z -- Continued

802.M34	Manzano Mountains
802.M38	Maxwell Land Grant
802.M4	Mesilla Valley
	For Gadsden Purchase see F786
	Mimbres River and Valley see F802.G7
802.M6	Mora County
	Moreno Creek and Valley see F802.C7
	Ortiz Mountains see F802.S4
802.O7	Otero County
802.P25	Pajarito Plateau
802.P3	Pecos River and Valley, N. Mex.
	Class here works limited to the part of the Pecos River and Valley located in New Mexico
	For general works on the Pecos River and Valley, as well as works limited to the part located in Texas see F392.P3
802.P5	Pine Lawn Valley
	Pojoaque River and Valley see F802.S4
802.P83	Puerco River and Valley (General and New Mexico)
802.Q2	Quay County
	Red River see F802.T2
802.R36	Red River and Valley
	Class here works limited to the part of the Red River and Valley located in New Mexico
	For general works on the Red River and Valley, as well as works limited to the part located in Louisiana see F377.R3
802.R4	Rio Arriba County
	Rio Chama see F802.C45
802.R5	Rio Grande and Valley
	Class here works works limited to the part of the Rio Grande and Rio Grande Valley located in New Mexico
	For general works on the Rio Grande and Rio Grande Valley, as well as works limited to the part located in Texas see F392.R5
802.R68	Rocky Mountain region, N. Mex.
	Cf. F721 General
802.R7	Roosevelt County
802.S13	Salinas National Monument
802.S15	San Andres Mountains
802.S18	San Juan County
	San Mateo Mountains see F802.V3
802.S2	San Miguel County
802.S28	Sandia Mountains

New Mexico
 Regions, counties, etc., A-Z -- Continued
802.S3 Sandoval County
   Including Jemez Mountains
   For Sangre de Cristo Grant see F782.C8
   For Frijoles Canyon see F802.B25
802.S32 Sangre de Cristo Mountains
   Class here general works on the Sangre de Cristo Mountains,
    as well as works limited to the part located in New Mexico
   For works limited to the part of the Sangre de Cristo
    Mountains located in Colorado see F782.S26
802.S4 Santa Fe County
   Including Ortiz Mountains, Pojoaque River and Valley
  Santa Rosa Lake and Region see F802.G9
802.S5 Sierra County
802.S6 Socorro County
802.T2 Taos County
   Including Red River
   Cf. F782.C8 Sangre de Cristo Grant

F1-975

802.T47 Tewa Basin
802.T6 Torrance County
802.U5 Union County
   Including Capulin Volcano National Monument
802.V3 Valencia County
   Including San Mateo Mountains
   For Leonard Wood Co. (1903-1904) see F802.G9
802.W44 White Sands Missile Range
802.W45 White Sands National Monument
804.A-Z Cities, towns, etc., A-Z
   e.g.
804.A3 Albuquerque
804.L6 Los Alamos
804.S2-.S29 Santa Fe (Table F2)
804.T2 Taos
  Elements in the population
805.A1 General works
805.A2-Z Individual elements
   For a list of racial, ethnic, and religious elements (with
    Cutter numbers) see E184.A+
 Arizona
  Historical note from the second edition (1913) of Class F: "For
   early ownership and transfers of this region see note under
   New Mexico (F791+). Arizona was cut off from New Mexico
   and organized as a separate territory in 1863. The following
   year it was reduced to present limits by the transfer of its
   northern extremity to Nevada. Admitted as a state 1912"
806 Periodicals. Societies. Collections

Arizona -- Continued

808	Museums. Exhibitions, exhibits
809	Gazetteers. Dictionaries. Geographic names
809.3	Guidebooks
810	Biography (Collective). Genealogy (Collective)
810.2	Historiography
	Historians see E175.5.A+
810.5	Study and teaching
811	General works. Histories
	Including admission as a state, February 14, 1912
	By period (Early to 1950) as well as general
	For 1951 and later see F815
	Cf. D769.85.A7+ World War II, 1939-1945
	Cf. E83.88 Apache War, 1882-1886
	Cf. E470.9 Civil War, 1861-1865
	Cf. E472.3 Civil War, 1861-1865
	Cf. E473.4 Civil War, 1861-1865
	Cf. E474.1 Civil War, 1861-1865
	Cf. F786 Mexican Cession of 1848; Gadsden Purchase of 1853
811.3	Juvenile works
811.5	Pamphlets, addresses, essays
811.6	Anecdotes, legends, pageants, etc.
812	Historic monuments (General). Illustrative material
813	Antiquities (Non-Indian)
	By period
	Early to 1950 see F811
815	1951-
	Biography
815.2	Collective
815.3.A-Z	Individual, A-Z
	Subarrange each by Table F5
817.A-Z	Regions, counties, etc., A-Z
817.A15	Counties
817.A16	Mountains
817.A17	Rivers
817.A18	Lakes
817.A19	Islands
817.A6	Apache County
817.A62	Apache Trail
817.A73	Aravaipa Canyon
817.A75	Arizona Strip
817.B5	Big Sandy River and region
	Bonita Creek and Valley see F817.G7
817.B7	Boundaries
	For International boundary see F786
817.C3	Canyon de Chelly National Monument

	Arizona
	Regions, counties, etc., A-Z -- Continued
817.C35	Casa Grande National Monument
	Chiricahua Mountains see F817.C5
	Chiricahua National Monument see F817.C5
817.C5	Cochise County
	Including Chiricahua National Monument, Coronado National Memorial, Sulphur Springs Valley, Chiricahua Mountains
817.C6	Coconino County
	Including Sunset Crater Volcano National Monument, Fort Valley
817.C7	Colorado River and Valley, Ariz.
	For Grand Canyon see F788; F788
	Fort Valley see F817.C6
	Gadsden Purchase see F786
817.G5	Gila County
	Including Pleasant Valley, Tonto National Monument
817.G52	Gila River and Valley
	Class here general works on the Gila River and Valley, as well as works limited to the part located in Arizona
	For works limited to the part of the Gila River and Valley located in New Mexico see F802.G54
	Glen Canyon National Recreation Area see F832.G5
817.G7	Graham County
	Including Bonita Creek and Valley
	Grand Canyon National Park see F788
817.G8	Greenlee County
	Havasu Canyon see F788
817.L3	La Paz County
	Including McMullen Valley
	Lake Mead National Recreation Area see F788
817.L5	Little Colorado River and Valley
817.M3	Maricopa County
	Including Squaw Peak (Piestewa Peak)
	McMullen Valley see F817.L3
817.M5	Mohave County
	Including Pipe Spring National Monument
	Mohawk Valley see F817.Y9
817.M57	Montezuma Castle National Monument
817.M6	Monument Valley
817.N3	Navajo County
817.O7	Organ Pipe Cactus National Monument
817.P2	Painted Desert
817.P4	Petrified Forest National Monument
	Piestewa Peak see F817.M3

F1-975

Arizona

     Regions, counties, etc., A-Z -- Continued

817.P5	Pima County
	Including Quijotoa Mountains
	For Santa Catalina Mountains see F817.S28
817.P6	Pinal County
	Including Santan Mountains
	Pipe Spring National Monument see F817.M5
	Pleasant Valley see F817.G5
	Powell, Lake see F832.G5
817.S18	Saguaro National Park
817.S2	Salt River and Valley
817.S25	San Pedro River and Valley (General and Arizona)
	Cf. F1346 Mexico
817.S28	Santa Catalina Mountains
817.S3	Santa Cruz County
817.S33	Santa Cruz River and Valley
	Santan Mountains see F817.P6
817.S65	Sonoran Desert National Mounument
	Squaw Peak see F817.M3
	Sulphur Springs Valley see F817.C5
	Sunset Crater Volcano National Monument see F817.C6
817.S9	Superstition Mountains
	Tonto National Monument see F817.G5
817.T66	Tonto River and Valley
817.T8	Tumacacori National Monument
817.V37	Verde River and Valley
	Including Verde Wild and Scenic River
817.W47	Wet Beaver Creek and Valley
817.W8	Wupatki National Monument
817.Y3	Yavapai County
817.Y9	Yuma County
	Including Lechuguilla Desert, Mohawk Valley
819.A-Z	Cities, towns, etc., A-Z
	e.g.
819.G5	Globe
819.P57	Phoenix
819.T6	Tombstone
819.T9-.T99	Tucson (Table F2)
	Elements in the population
820.A1	General works
820.A2-Z	Individual elements
	For a list of racial, ethnic, and religious elements (with Cutter numbers) see E184.A+

Utah
> Historical note from the second edition (1913) of Class F: "The entire territory comprising the state of Utah was Spanish and Mexican property till embraced in the Mexican cession of 1848. The Mormons had settled this region in 1847 and two years later formed the state of Deseret, which, however, was not recognized. The Territory of Utah as organized in 1850 included not only the modern Utah but parts of Wyoming and Colorado on the east, and on the west all of Nevada except the southern extremity. It was reduced in size in 1861, by the formation of Colorado Territory, the extension of Nebraska Territory westward, and the formation of Nevada Territory on the west. It was reduced to present limits by the cutting out of the northeast corner on formation of territory of Idaho in 1863 and the admission of the state of Nevada on the west in 1864, with boundary line moved eastward to the 115th and later to the 114th meridian. Utah was admitted as a state in 1896."

F1-975

821	Periodicals. Societies. Collections
823	Museums. Exhibitions, exhibits
824	Gazetteers. Dictionaries. Geographic names
824.3	Guidebooks
825	Biography (Collective). Genealogy (Collective)
825.2	Historiography
	Historians see E175.5.A+
825.5	Study and teaching
826	General works. Histories

> Including admission as a state, January 4, 1896
> By period (Early to 1950) as well as general
> Including Mormon settlement; State of Deseret; Mountain Meadows Massacre, 1857; Mormon Rebellion, 1857-1859
> Including biography: Jacob Hamblin, John Doyle Lee, etc.
> For 1951 and later see F830
> Cf. BX8601+ Mormons (Church of Jesus Christ of Latter Day Saints)
> Cf. D570.85.U8+ World War I, 1914-1918
> Cf. D769.85.U8+ World War II, 1939-1945
> Cf. E423 Compromise of 1850

826.3	Juvenile works
826.5	Pamphlets, addresses, essays
826.6	Anecdotes, legends, pageants, etc.
827	Historic monuments (General). Illustrative material
828	Antiquities (Non-Indian)
	By period
	Early to 1950 see F826
830	1951-
	Biography

	Utah
	By period
	1951-
	Biography -- Continued
830.2	Collective
830.3.A-Z	Individual, A-Z
	Subarrange each by Table F5
832.A-Z	Regions, counties, etc., A-Z
832.A15	Counties
832.A16	Mountains
832.A17	Rivers
832.A18	Lakes
832.A19	Islands
832.A7	Arches National Park
832.B3	Bear River and Valley
832.B35	Beaver County
832.B6	Bonneville, Lake
832.B7	Boundaries
832.B8	Box Elder County
	For Bear River and Valley see F832.B3
	Brown's Park see F767.G7
832.B9	Bryce Canyon National Park
832.C3	Cache County
	Including Cache Valley, Logan Canyon
832.C35	Cache National Forest
832.C37	Canyonlands National Park
	Including Cataract Canyon Wilderness
	Capitol Reef National Park see F832.W27
832.C4	Carbon County
832.C45	Castle Valley
	Cataract Canyon Wilderness see F832.C37
	Cedar Breaks National Monument see F832.I6
	Cedar Mesa see F832.S4
832.C7	Colorado River and Valley, Utah
	Formerly Grand River, Utah
	Cf. F788 General
832.D2	Daggett County
832.D3	Davis County
832.D46	Desolation Canyon
832.D5	Dinosaur National Monument
	For Canyon of Lodore see F782.M65
832.D8	Duchesne County
832.E5	Emery County
832.E83	Escalante River and Valley

Utah

Regions, counties, etc., A-Z -- Continued

832.F52	Flaming Gorge National Recreation Area

Class here works limited to the part of the Flaming Gorge
National Recreation area located in Utah.

For general works on Flaming Gorge National
Recreation Area, as well as works limited to the
part located in Wyoming see F767.F5

832.G3	Garfield County
832.G5	Glen Canyon National Recreation Area

Including Lake Powell

832.G65	Grand County

Grand River and Valley see F832.C7

832.G66	Grand Staircase-Escalante National Monument
832.G7	Great Salt Lake and region

Including Great Salt Desert

Green River and Valley see F767.G7

Hole in the Rock Trail see F832.S4

832.I6	Iron County

Including Cedar Breaks National Monument

832.J8	Juab County
832.K3	Kane County

Logan Canyon see F832.C3

Manti Canyon see F832.S42

832.M3	Manti La Sal National Forest
832.M5	Millard County

Monument Valley see F817.M6

832.M6	Morgan County
832.N55	Nine Mile Canyon

Parley's Canyon see F832.S2

832.P5	Piute County

Powell, Lake see F832.G5

832.P76	Provo River and Valley
832.R3	Rainbow Bridge. Rainbow Bridge National Monument
832.R5	Rich County
832.S2	Salt Lake County

Including Parley's Canyon

832.S4	San Juan County

Including Cedar Mesa, Hole in the Rock Trail

832.S415	San Rafael River and Valley. San Rafael Swell

San Rafael Swell see F832.S415

832.S42	Sanpete County

Including Manti Canyon

832.S6	Sevier County
832.S9	Summit County

Timpanogos, Mount see F832.U8

832.T6	Tooele County

F1-975

Utah
    Regions, counties, etc., A-Z -- Continued

832.U39	Uinta Mountains
	Class here general works on the Uinta Mountains, as well as works limited to the part located in Utah
	For works limited to the part of the Uinta Mountains located in Wyoming see F767.U33
832.U4	Uintah County
	Including Uintah Basin, White River and Valley, Utah
	Cf. F782.R4 White River and Valley (General, and Colorado)
	Uncompahgre Indian Reservation see E99.U8
832.U8	Utah County
	Including Mount Timpanogos
	Utah National Park see F832.B9
832.W2	Wasatch County
832.W22	Wasatch Range
	Class here general works on the Wasatch Range, as well as works limited to the part located in Utah.
	For works limited to the part of the Wasatch Range located in Idaho see F752.W27
832.W24	Washington County
832.W27	Wayne County
	Including Capitol Reef National Park
832.W3	Weber County
	Including Ben Lomond
	White River and Valley, Utah see F832.U4
832.Z8	Zion National Park
834.A-Z	Cities, towns, etc., A-Z
	e.g.
834.L8	Logan
834.O3	Ogden
834.P3	Provo
834.S2-.S29	Salt Lake City (Table F2)
	Elements in the population
835.A1	General works
835.A2-Z	Individual elements
	For a list of racial, ethnic, and religious elements (with Cutter numbers) see E184.A+

Nevada
> Historical note from the second edition (1913) of Class F: "Under Mexico, this region was considered a part of Upper California. Ceded to the U.S. 1848, as a result of the Mexican war. On the division of the cession in 1850 all but the southern extremity of the present state of Nevada fell within the new territory of Utah. In 1861 Nevada Territory was organized. It was admitted as a state in 1864, receiving an extension to the east to the 115th meridian at the expense of Utah. Two years later the eastern line was moved still farther to the 114th meridian and the part of the modern Nevada south of 37 added at the expense of Arizona."

836	Periodicals. Societies. Collections
838	Museums. Exhibitions, exhibits
839	Gazetteers. Dictionaries. Geographic names
839.3	Guidebooks
840	Biography (Collective). Genealogy (Collective)
840.2	Historiography
	Historians see E175.5.A+

F1-975

840.5	Study and teaching
841	General works. Histories

> Including admission as a state, October 31, 1864
> By period (early to 1950) as well as general
> Including biography: John William Mackay, William Morris Stewart, etc.
> For 1951 and later see F845+
> Cf. D570.85.N22+ World War I, 1914-1918
> Cf. D769.85.N22+ World War II, 1939-1945

841.3	Juvenile works
841.5	Pamphlets, addresses, essays
841.6	Anecdotes, legends, pageants, etc.
842	Historic monuments (General). Illustrative material
843	Antiquities (Non-Indian)
	By period
	Early to 1950 see F841
	1951-
845	General works
	Biography
845.2	Collective
845.25.A-Z	Individual, A-Z
	Subarrange each by Table F5
847.A-Z	Regions, counties, etc., A-Z
847.A15	Counties
847.A16	Mountains
847.A17	Rivers
847.A18	Lakes
847.A19	Islands

Nevada
Regions, counties, etc., A-Z -- Continued

847.A42	Amargosa River and Valley (General and Nevada)
847.B53	Black Rock Desert
847.B7	Boundaries
	Cf. F868.B7 California boundary
847.C37	Carson River and Valley
847.C4	Churchill County
847.C5	Clark County
	Including Charleston Mountain, Moapa River and Valley, Valley of Fire, Red Rock Canyon National Conservation Area
847.D6	Douglas County
847.E4	Elko County
	Ellsworth Canyon see F847.N9
847.E7	Esmeralda County
847.E8	Eureka County
847.F6	Fort Churchill Historic State Monument
847.G32	Gabbs Valley
847.G64	Gold Mountain (Esmeralda County and Nye County)
847.G7	Grass Valley
847.G73	Great Basin National Park
847.H8	Humboldt County
	Including Paradise Valley
847.H85	Humboldt River and Valley
847.L3	Lander County
847.L5	Lincoln County
847.L9	Lyon County
	Lake Mead National Recreation Area see F788
847.M5	Mineral County
	Including Walker River and Valley
	Moapa River and Valley see F847.C5
	Nevada Test Site see F847.N9
847.N9	Nye County
	Including Ellsworth Canyon, Nevada Test Site
847.O6	Ormsby County
	Owyhee Mountains region see F752.O97
847.O98	Owyhee River and Valley
	Class here works limited to the part of the Owyhee River and Valley located in Nevada
	For general works on the Owyhee River and Valley, as well as works limited to the part located in Oregon see F882.O98
	Paradise Valley see F847.H8
847.P4	Pershing County
847.R33	Rainbow Canyon

	Nevada
	Regions, counties, etc., A-Z -- Continued
	Red Rock Canyon National Conservation Area see F847.C5
847.S8	Storey County
	Lake Tahoe see F868.T2
	Valley of Fire see F847.C5
	Walker River and Valley see F847.M5
847.W3	Washoe County
847.W5	White Pine County
849.A-Z	Cities, towns, etc., A-Z
	e.g.
849.A9	Austin
849.C3	Carson City
	Comstock Lode see F849.V8
849.L35	Las Vegas
849.R4	Reno
849.V8	Virginia City. Comstock Lode
	Elements in the population
850.A1	General works
850.A2-Z	Individual elements
	For a list of racial, ethnic, and religious elements (with Cutter numbers) see E184.A+
	The Pacific States
	Including the Pacific coast of North America including works on the coast of America (North and South), Pacific Northwest
	Cf. E78.P2 Indians of the Pacific States
	Cf. E83.84 Wars with the Pacific coast Indians, 1847-1865
850.5	Biography (Collective). Genealogy (Collective)
851	General works
851.5	Exploring expeditions to the Pacific coast before 1800
	For explorations since 1800, California see F864
	For Oregon see F880
	For Alaska see F907
	For British Columbia see F1088
851.7	Cascade Range
	Cf. F882.C3 Cascade Range in Oregon
	Cf. F897.C3 Cascade Range in Washington (State)
	The Pacific Northwest
	Including Washington, Oregon, Idaho, Montana, British Columbia
	By period
	Early to 1769 see F851.5
	1769-1859 see F880
852	1859-1950
	Cf. E78.N77 Indians of the Pacific Northwest
852.2	1951-1980

F1-975

	The Pacific States
	The Pacific Northwest
	By period -- Continued
852.3	1981-
853	Columbia River and Valley

> Class here general works on the Columbia River and Valley
> For works limited to the part of the Columbia River and
>   Valley located in Oregon see F882.C63
> For works limited to the part of the Columbia River and
>   Valley located in Washington State see F897.C7

854	Northwest boundary of the United States, 1846-

> Including Rocky Mountains to the Pacific
> Boundary controversy before 1846 see F880

	Elements in the population
855	General works
855.2.A-Z	Individual elements, A-Z

> For a list of racial, ethnic, and religious elements (with
>   Cutter numbers) see E184.A+

California

> Historical note from the second edition (1913) of Class F: "A part
>   of the Spanish colony of New Spain and later empire and
>   republic of Mexico. It was the "Upper California" of the
>   Mexicans, first settled about 1769. American settlers declared
>   their independence of Mexico about the same time that
>   expeditions arrived from the east in connection with the
>   Mexican war. The whole region was embraced in the Mexican
>   cession of 1848. California was admitted as a state in 1850."

856	Periodicals. Societies. Collections
858	Museums. Exhibitions, exhibits
859	Gazetteers. Dictionaries. Geographic names
859.3	Guidebooks
860	Biography (Collective). Genealogy (Collective)
860.2	Historiography
	Historians see E175.5.A+
860.5	Study and teaching
861	General works. Histories
861.3	Juvenile works
861.5	Pamphlets, addresses, essays
861.6	Anecdotes, legends, pageants, etc.
861.8	Geography
862	Historic monuments (General). Illustrative material
	Including Spanish mission buildings (General)
863	Antiquities (Non-Indian)
	By period

California

By period -- Continued

864 Early to 1869

Admission as a state, September 9, 1850

Including Spanish explorers after 1769; Spanish California, including Lower and Upper California; Indian missions; American and European intrigues before 1846; Fremont in California, 1846; and Bear Flag War, 1846

Including biography: John Bidwell, William Brown Ide, Peter Lassen, Junípero Serra, David Smith Terry, Mariano Guadalupe Vallejo, George Calvert Yount, Augustín Juan Vicente Zamorano, etc.

For Explorations before 1769 see F851.5

Cf. E83.84 Wars with Pacific coast Indians, 1847-1865

Cf. E83.858 Mill Creek War, 1857-1865

Cf. E405.2 American military conquest, 1846

Cf. E423 Compromise of 1850

Cf. E497+ Civil War, 1861-1865

Cf. F786 Mexican cession of 1848

Cf. F1089.N8 Nootka Sound Controversy, 1789-1790

Cf. F1246+ Lower California

F1-975

865 1848-1856

Including gold discoveries; Argonauts; voyages to California by Cape Horn or Central American isthmus routes; vigilance committees

Including biography: William Tell Coleman, James Wilson Marshall, John Marsh, Joaquin Murrieta, John Augustus Sutter, etc.

Cf. F593 Overland journeys from the East

866 1869-1950

Cf. D570.85.C2+ World War I, 1914-1918

Cf. E83.87 Modoc War, 1872-1873

Cf. E726.C1 War of 1898 (Spanish-American War)

1951-

866.2 General works

Biography

866.3 Collective

866.4.A-Z Individual, A-Z

Subarrange each by Table F5

867 Southern California

Cf. F864 Early Spanish missions

867.5 Northern California

868.A-Z Regions, counties, etc., A-Z

868.A15 Counties

868.A16 Mountains

868.A17 Rivers

868.A18 Lakes

	California
	Regions, counties, etc., A-Z -- Continued
868.A19	Islands
868.A3	Alameda County
	Including Livermore Valley
	Alcatraz Island see F868.S156
	Algodones Dunes see F868.I2
868.A35	Alpine County
868.A4	Amador County
	Including Shenandoah Valley
868.A44	American River and Valley
	Anacapa Island see F868.V5
	Anderson Valley see F868.M5
868.A5	Angeles National Forest
	Annadel State park see F868.S7
	Anza-Borrego Desert State Park see F868.S15
	Anza Valley see F868.R6
	Ashurst Colony see F868.S13
	Balboa Island see F868.O6
	Barona Valley see F868.S15
	Beckworth Trail see F868.S5
	Big Creek Lake see F868.S14
868.B5	Big Oak Flat Road
	Black Diamond Mines Regional Preserve see F868.C76
868.B7	Boundaries
868.B8	Butte County
868.C14	Calaveras Big Tree National Forest
868.C15	Calaveras Big Trees State Park
868.C16	Calaveras County
	For Calaveras Big Trees State Park see F868.C15
	California Redwood Park (Santa Cruz Co.) see F868.S3
	Capay Island see F868.Y5
	Cape Horn see F868.S5
	Carquinez Strait see F868.S156
	Catalina Island see F868.L8
868.C45	Central Valley
	Channel Islands see F868.S232
	Chocolate Mountains see F868.I2
	Coachella Valley see F868.R6
	Colorado Desert see F868.I2
868.C6	Colorado River and Valley, Calif.
	Cf. F788 General
868.C7	Colusa County
868.C74	Conejo Valley
868.C76	Contra Costa County
	Including Winter Island, Mount Diablo State Park, Black
	Diamond Mines Regional Preserve

California

Regions, counties, etc., A-Z -- Continued

Crane Valley Dam and Lake see F868.M2

Cuyamaca Mountains see F868.S15

868.D2	Death Valley
	Including Death Valley National Monument, Scotty's Castle
868.D4	Del Norte County
	Including Smith River National Recreation Area
868.D45	Delta Region
	Donner Lake see F868.N5
	Eagle Lake see F868.L33
868.E22	East Bay
868.E28	El Camino Real
868.E3	El Dorado County
	Including Wrights Lake
	Emerald Bay and region see F868.O6
	Emigrant Trail see F868.S5
	Empire Mine State Historic Park see F868.N5
868.F24	Farallon Islands (Farallones)
868.F3	Feather River, Canyon, and Valley
	Forest of Nisene Marks State Park see F868.S3
	French Valley see F868.R6
868.F8	Fresno County
	Including Shaver Lake
	For San Joaquin Valley see F868.S173
868.G39	Gazos Creek and Valley
	General Grant National Park see F868.K48
	Giant Sequoia National Monument see F868.S4
868.G5	Glenn County
	Goat Island see F869.S3+
	Golden Gate National Recreation Area see F868.S156
	Guenoc Valley see F868.L2
	Hearst-San Simeon State Historical Monument see F868.S18
	Huichica Creek and Valley see F868.N2
868.H8	Humboldt County
	Including Humboldt Bay, Humboldt Redwoods State Park, Shelter Cove
868.I2	Imperial County
	Including Chocolate Mountains, Colorado Desert, Imperial Valley, Algodones Dunes
	Indian Wells Valley see F868.K3
868.I6	Inyo County
	Including Manzanar National Historic Site
	For Death Valley see F868.D2
	Irvine Park see F868.O6
	Jalama Beach Park see F868.S23

F1-975

California
   Regions, counties, etc., A-Z -- Continued
      John Muir Trail see F868.S5

868.J6	Joshua Tree National Monument
868.K3	Kern County
	Including Indian Wells Valley, Tejon Ranch
868.K48	Kings Canyon National Park
	Including General Grant Grove area (General Grant National Park until 1940)
868.K5	Kings County
	Kings Mountain see F868.S19
868.K55	Klamath River and Valley
868.L2	Lake County
	Including Guenoc Valley
	Lake Elsinore and region see F868.R6
	Lanfair Valley see F868.S14
868.L33	Lassen County
	Including Eagle Lake
868.L34	Lassen Peak. Lassen Volcanic National Park
868.L38	Lava Beds National Monument
868.L8	Los Angeles County
	Including Mount Lowe, Rustic Canyon, San Fernando Valley, San Gabriel Valley, Santa Catalina Island, Santa Clarita Valley, Santa Monica Bay region, Santa Monica Canyon, Los Angeles River, Terminal Island
	For Channel Islands see F868.S232
	Los Angeles River see F868.L8
868.L83	Los Padres National Forest
	Lytle Creek Canyon see F868.S14
868.M2	Madera County
	Including Crane Valley Dam and Lake
	Malakoff Diggins State Historic Park see F868.N5
	Manzanar National Historic Site see F868.I6
868.M3	Marin County
	Including Marin Peninsula, Mount Tamalpais State Park, Muir Woods National Monument
868.M4	Mariposa County
	Including Fremont Land Grant (Mariposa estate)
868.M5	Mendocino County
	Including Anderson Valley, Mendocino Headlands State Park, and Round Valley
868.M55	Merced County
	Middle Fork Feather Wild and Scenic River see F868.P85
	Mineral King Valley see F868.T8
868.M6	Modoc County
	Including Surprise Valley
868.M65	Mohave (Mojave) Desert

California

Regions, counties, etc., A-Z -- Continued

868.M67	Mono County
	Including Mono Lake
	Mono Lake see F868.M67
	Montara, Point see F868.S19
	Montara Mountain see F868.S33
	Monterey Bay see F868.M7
868.M7	Monterey County
	Including Point Lobos, Monterey Bay, Pfeiffer Big Sur State Park
	Moreno Valley see F868.R6
	Morro Bay see F868.S18
	Morro Bay State Park see F868.S18
	Mount Diablo State Park see F868.C76
	Mount San Jacinto State Park see F868.R6
	Muir Trail see F868.S5
	Muir Woods National Monument see F868.M3
868.N16	Nacimiento River and Valley
868.N2	Napa County
	Including Huichica Creek and Valley
868.N5	Nevada County
	Including Donner Lake, Donner Party Expedition, Empire Mine State Historic Park, Malakoff Diggins State Historic Park
868.N52	New Melones Lake and region
	Nobles Trail see F868.S5
	Ojai Valley see F868.V5
	Old Emigrant Trail see F868.S5
	Ontario Colony see F869.O5
868.O6	Orange County
	Including Balboa Island, Emerald Bay and region, Irvine Park
868.O9	Owens River and Valley
868.P33	Pacific Coast
	Pajaro River and Valley see F868.S3
	Pfeiffer Big Sur State Park see F868.M7
	Pigeon Point see F868.S19
868.P6	Pinnacles National Monument
868.P7	Placer County
868.P85	Plumas County
	Including Middle Fork Feather Wild and Scenic River and Plumas Eureka State Park
	Plumas Eureka State Park see F868.P85
	Point Montara see F868.S19
	Point Piedras Blancas see F868.S18
868.P9	Point Reyes
868.P98	Putah Creek

F1-975

California
Regions, counties, etc., A-Z -- Continued

868.R32	Rand Mining District
868.R4	Redwood National Park (Humboldt and Del Norte Counties)
	Redwood Park (Santa Cruz Co.) see F868.S3
868.R6	Riverside County

Including Coachella Valley, Lake Elsinore and regions, Moreno Valley, San Jacinto River and Valley, Temecula Creek and Valley, Mount San Jacinto State Park, San Gorgonio Pass, Anza Valley, French Valley

Roosevelt-Sequoia National Park (Proposed) see F868.S4
Round Valley see F868.M5

868.R9	Russian River and Valley

Rustic Canyon see F868.L8

868.S12	Sacramento County
868.S13	Sacramento River and Valley

Including Ashurst Colony

868.S132	Saint Helena, Mount
868.S133	Salinas River and Valley
868.S136	San Benito County

Including San Juan Valley

868.S14	San Bernardino County

Including Lytle Creek Canyon, San Bernardino Valley, Bear Valley, Big Bear Valley, Big Bear Lake, Lanfair Valley, San Timoteo Canyon
For Ontario Colony see F869.O5

868.S144	San Bernardino National Forest
868.S15	San Diego County

Including Anza-Borrego Desert State Park, Barona Valley, Borrego Valley, Escondido Valley, Palomar Mountain, San Pasqual Valley, San Vicente Valley, Cuyamaca Mountains
For Imperial Valley see F868.I2

San Fernando Valley see F868.L8

868.S156	San Francisco Bay region

Including Alcatraz Island, Carquinez Strait, Golden Gate National Recreation Area, Treasure Island

868.S157	San Francisco County

For Farallon Islands see F868.F24
Cf. F869.S3+ San Francisco (City)

San Gabriel Valley see F868.L8
San Gorgonio Pass see F868.R6
San Jacinto Mountain National Monument see F868.S36
San Jacinto River and Valley see F868.R6

868.S17	San Joaquin County

California

Regions, counties, etc., A-Z -- Continued

868.S173	San Joaquin River and Valley
	Including Tulare Lake and region
	San Juan Valley see F868.S136
868.S18	San Luis Obispo County
	Including Morro Bay, Morro Bay State Park, Hearst-San Simeon State Historical Monument, Point Piedras Blancas
	For Santa Maria River and Valley see F868.S23
868.S19	San Mateo County
	Including Pigeon Point, Kings Mountain, Point Montara
	San Miguel Island see F868.S23
	San Pasqual Valley see F868.S15
868.S2	San Ramon Valley
	San Timoteo Canyon see F868.S14
	San Vicente Valley see F868.S15
868.S21	Santa Ana Mountains
868.S22	Santa Ana River and Valley
868.S23	Santa Barbara County
	Including Jalama Beach Park, San Miguel Island, Santa Barbara Valley, Santa Cruz Island, Santa Maria River and Valley, Santa Rosa Island, Santa Ynez River and Valley, Zaca Lake
	Cf. F868.S232 Santa Barbara Islands
868.S232	Santa Barbara (Channel) Islands (General)
	For individual islands, see the counties (Santa Barbara, Ventura, and Los Angeles) to which they belong
	Santa Catalina Island see F868.L8
868.S25	Santa Clara County
	Including Santa Clara Valley
	For San Juan Valley see F868.S136
	Santa Clarita Valley see F868.L8
868.S3	Santa Cruz County
	Including California Redwood Park, Forest of Nisene Marks State Park, Pajaro River and Valley
	Santa Cruz Island see F868.S23
868.S33	Santa Cruz Mountains
	Including Montara Mountain
868.S34	Santa Margarita River and Valley
	Including Rancho Santa Margarita
	Santa Maria River and Valley see F868.S23
	Santa Monica Canyon see F868.L8
868.S355	Santa Monica Mountains National Recreation Area
868.S36	Santa Rosa and San Jacinto Mountains National Monument
	Santa Rosa Island see F868.S23

F1-975

	California
	Regions, counties, etc., A-Z -- Continued
	Santa Ynez River and Valley see F868.S23
868.S37	Searles Valley
	Seiad Creek and Valley see F868.S6
868.S4	Sequoia National Park. Sequoia National Forest. Giant Sequoia National Monument
	Mount Shasta see F868.S6
868.S49	Shasta County
	Including Whiskeytown-Shasta-Trinity National Recreation Area
	For Lassen Peak see F868.L34
868.S495	Shasta Mountains
	Shaver Lake see F868.F8
	Shelter Cove see F868.H8
	Shenandoah Valley see F868.A4
868.S497	Sierra County
868.S5	Sierra Nevada Mountains (The Sierras)
	Including Beckworth Trail, Cape Horn, John Muir Trail, Old Emigrant Trail, Squaw Valley
	For Kings Canyon National Park see F868.K48
	For Lassen Peak see F868.L34
	For Donner Party Expedition see F868.N5
	For Sequoia National Park see F868.S4
	For Mount Whitney see F868.W6
	For Yosemite Valley see F868.Y6
868.S6	Siskiyou County
	Including Butte Valley, Mount Shasta, Seiad Creek and Valley, Tule Lake
	Smith River National Recreation Area see F868.D4
868.S66	Solano County
868.S7	Sonoma County
	Including Annadel State Park, Arroyo de San Antonio (Estate), Lake Sonoma
	Squaw Valley see F868.S5
868.S8	Stanislaus County
	Surprise Valley see F868.M6
868.S88	Sutter Buttes
868.S9	Sutter County
868.T2	Tahoe, Lake
	Including Tahoe National Forest
	Mount Tamalpais State Park see F868.M3
868.T3	Tehama County
	Temecula Creek and Valley see F868.R6
	Terminal Island see F868.L8
	Treasure Island see F868.S156
868.T58	Trinity Alps

	California
	Regions, counties, etc., A-Z -- Continued
868.T6	Trinity County
868.T63	Trinity River and Valley
868.T8	Tulare County
	Including Yokohl Valley
	For Sequoia National Park see F868.S4
	For Mount Whitney see F868.W6
	Tulare Lake and region see F868.S173
	Tule Lake see F868.S6
868.T9	Tuolumne County
	For Calaveras Grove see F868.C14
	For Calaveras Big Trees State Park see F868.C15
868.T92	Tuolumne River and Valley
868.V5	Ventura County
	Including Anacapa Island, Ojai Valley
	Whiskeytown-Shasta-Trinity National Recreation Area see F868.S49
868.W6	Whitney, Mount
	Winter Island see F868.C76
	Wrights Lake see F868.E3
	Yerba Buena (Goat) Island see F869.S3+
	Yokohl Valley see F868.T8
868.Y5	Yolo County
	Including Capay Valley
868.Y6	Yosemite Valley. Yosemite National Park
	Including Half Dome
868.Y8	Yuba County
	Zaca Lake see F868.S23
869.A-Z	Cities, towns, etc., A-Z
	e.g.
869.A15	General
869.B5	Berkeley
869.C27	Carmel
869.G5	Glendale
	Including Forest Lawn Memorial Park
869.H74	Hollywood
869.L7	Long Beach
869.L8-.L89	Los Angeles (Table F2)
869.O2	Oakland
869.O5	Ontario
	Including Ontario Colony
869.P3	Pasadena
869.S12	Sacramento
869.S22	San Diego
869.S3-.S39	San Francisco (Table F2)
	Including Yerba Buena (Goat) Island

F1-975

California
Cities, towns, etc., A-Z -- Continued
For Farallon Islands see F868.F24
Cf. F868.S157 San Francisco Co.
Elements in the population

870.A1	General works
870.A2-Z	Individual elements

For a list of racial, ethnic, and religious elements (with
Cutter numbers) see E184.A+
Oregon
Historical note from the second edition (1913) of Class F: "The
"Oregon country " in the later 18th and early 19th century
comprised the region between New Spain (Upper California)
and Russian America (Alaska); from 42° to 54° 40'. Both
Spanish and British claimed it by right of discovery and
exploration. In 1792 Capt. Gray explored the Columbia River,
laying the basis of the American claim. In 1818 a treaty of
joint occupation between the U.S. and Gt. Brit. was made.
The Spanish treaty of 1819 (Florida treaty) also surrendered
to the U.S. all Spanish claim to the Pacific coast above 42°.
The joint occupancy of the two countries was terminated in
1846 by agreement to divide the territory on the line of 49° and
the Straits of Fuca. The territory of Oregon was organized
1848, consisting of all the region north of 42° not included in
the old Louisiana purchase (Oregon, Washington and Idaho
and parts of Montana and Wyoming). The northern part of the
region was organized as Washington Territory in 1853, and
when Oregon was admitted as a state in 1859, the eastern
part of Oregon Territory was added temporarily to
Washington Territory."

871	Periodicals. Societies. Collections
873	Museums. Exhibitions, exhibits
874	Gazetteers. Dictionaries. Geographic names
874.3	Guidebooks
875	Biography (Collective). Genealogy (Collective)
875.2	Historiography
	Historians see E175.5.A+
875.5	Study and teaching
876	General works. Histories
876.3	Juvenile works
876.5	Pamphlets, addresses, essays
876.6	Anecdotes, legends, pageants, etc.
877	Historic monuments (General). Illustrative material
878	Antiquities (Non-Indian)
	By period

	Oregon
	By period -- Continued
879	Early to 1792
	Cf. F851.5 Exploring expeditions to the Pacific coast before 1800
	Cf. F1060.7+ Explorations in the Canadian Northwest before 1821
	Cf. F1089.N8 Nootka Sound Controversy, 1789-1790
880	1792-1859
	Including the Oregon country; "joint occupation" by Great Britain and the United States, 1818-1846; the Oregon question; Northwest boundary to 1846; Oregon Trail
	Including biography: Jesse Applegate, Jason Lee, John McLoughlin, Joseph L. Meek, Isaac Ingalls Stevens, Marcus Whitman, etc.
	Cf. E83.84 Wars with the Pacific coast Indians, 1847-1865
	Cf. F592.3+ Lewis and Clark Expedition
	Cf. F854 International boundary since 1846
	Cf. F1060+ Hudson Bay Company
	Cf. F1086+ British Columbia, the northern part of the Oregon country since 1846
881	1859-1950
	Including admission as a state, February 14, 1859
	Including biography: Harry Lane, Alfred Benjamin Meacham, etc.
	Cf. D570.85.O8+ World War I, 1914-1918
	Cf. D769.85.O8+ World War II, 1939-1945
	Cf. E83.84 Wars with Pacific coast Indians, 1847-1865
	Cf. E83.87 Modoc War, 1872-1873
	Cf. E83.877 Nez Percé War, 1877
	Cf. E526+ Civil War, 1861-1865 (General)
	1951-
881.2	General works
	Biography
881.3	Collective
881.35.A-Z	Individual, A-Z
	Subarrange each by Table F5
882.A-Z	Regions, counties, etc., A-Z
882.A15	Counties
882.A16	Mountains
882.A17	Rivers
882.A18	Lakes
882.A19	Islands
882.A65	Applegate River and Valley
882.B2	Baker County
882.B4	Benton County

F1-975

	Oregon
	Regions, counties, etc., A-Z -- Continued
882.B7	Boundaries
	Including Sand Island controversy
	For International boundary see F854; F880
	Calapooia River and Valley see F882.L7
	Camp Polk Meadow Preserve see F882.D4
882.C3	Cascade Range
	Including Spencer Butte
882.C5	Clackamas County
	For Mount Hood see F882.H85
882.C53	Clatsop County
	Including Fort Clatsop National Memorial, Fort Stevens State Park
882.C6	Columbia County
	For Sauvies Island see F882.S3
882.C63	Columbia River and Valley
	Class here works limited to the part of the Columbia River and Valley located in Oregon
	Including Columbia River Highway
	For general works on the Columbia River and Valley see F853
	For Sand Island controversy see F882.B7
	For Sauvies Island see F882.S3
882.C7	Coos County
	Including Coos Bay
	Cow Creek and Valley (Douglas County) see F882.D7
882.C8	Crater Lake. Crater Lake National Park
	Including Mount Mazama
882.C83	Crater National Forest
882.C9	Crook County
882.C95	Curry County
882.D4	Deschutes County
	Including Newberry National Volcanic Monument, Paulina Lake, Camp Polk Meadow Preserve
882.D43	Deschutes National Forest
882.D45	Deschutes River and Valley
882.D7	Douglas County
	Including Cow Creek and Valley
	Fort Clatsop National Memorial see F882.C53
	Fort Rock Valley see F882.L15
	Fort Stevens State Park see F882.C53
	French Prairie see F882.W6
882.G5	Gilliam County
882.G7	Grant County
882.H37	Harney County

	Oregon
	Regions, counties, etc., A-Z -- Continued
882.H44	Hells Canyon National Recreation Area

Class here general works on Hells Canyon National
Recreation Area, as well as works limited to the part
located in Oregon

For works limited to the part of the Hells Canyon
National Recreation Area located in Idaho see
F752.H44

| 882.H85 | Hood, Mount |

Including Timberline Lodge

| 882.H9 | Hood River County |

Including Hood River and Valley

882.J14	Jackson County
882.J4	Jefferson County
882.J73	Joaquin Miller Trail
882.J76	John Day River and Valley
882.J8	Josephine County
882.K49	Klamath Basin
882.K5	Klamath County

For Crater Lake see F882.C8

| 882.L15 | Lake County |

Including Fort Rock Valley

882.L2	Lane County
882.L49	Lewis and Clark National Historical Park
882.L6	Lincoln County
882.L7	Linn County

Including Calapooia River and Valley

882.L78	Long Tom River and Valley
882.M2	Malheur County
882.M3	Marion County
882.M8	Morrow County
882.M9	Multnomah County

For Sauvies Island see F882.S3

Neahkahnie Mountain see F882.T5

Newberry National Volcanic Monument see F882.D4

| 882.O16 | Ochoco National Forest |

Owyhee Mountains region see F752.O97

| 882.O98 | Owyhee River and Valley |

Class here general works on the Owyhee River and Valley,
as well as works limited to the part located in Oregon

For works limited to the part of the Owyhee River and
Valley located in Idaho see F752.O98

For works limited to the part of the Owyhee River and
Valley located in Nevada see F847.O98

| 882.P34 | Pacific Coast |
| 882.P7 | Polk County |

	Oregon
	Regions, counties, etc., A-Z -- Continued
882.R6	Rogue River and Valley
	Sand Island controversy see F882.B7
882.S18	Salmon River and Valley
882.S2	Santiam National Forest
882.S3	Sauvies Island
882.S5	Sherman County
882.S56	Siskiyou Mountains
882.S58	Siuslaw National Forest
882.S6	Snake River and Valley

Class here works limited to the part of the Snake River and
Valley located in Oregon

For general works on the Snake River and Valley, as
well as works limited to the part located in Idaho
see F752.S7

	Spencer Butte see F882.C3
882.T5	Tillamook County
	Including Neahkahnie Mountain
882.U4	Umatilla County
882.U43	Umpqua County
882.U5	Union County
882.W2	Wallowa County
	Including Wallowa Lake
882.W25	Wallowa National Forest
882.W3	Wasco County
	Including Mosier Hills
882.W4	Washington County
882.W5	Wheeler County
882.W6	Willamette River and Valley
	Including French Prairie
882.Y2	Yamhill County
882.Y24	Yaquina River and Valley
884.A-Z	Cities, towns, etc. A-Z
	e.g.
884.A8	Astoria
884.E9	Eugene
884.K62	Klamath Falls
884.P39	Pendleton
884.P8-.P89	Portland (Table F2)
884.S2	Salem
	Elements in the population
885.A1	General works
885.A2-Z	Individual elements

For a list of racial, ethnic, and religious elements (with
Cutter numbers) see E184.A+

Washington

Historical note from the second edition (1913) of Class F: "The state of Washington was included in the Oregon country and the U.S. territory of Oregon (cf. note under F871+) down to 1853 when Washington Territory was organized. It originally included Idaho north of 46° and a strip of western Montana, and on the admission of Oregon to statehood in 1859, received an addition of all the rest of the original Oregon Territory outside the state of Oregon (the rest of Idaho and a part of Wyoming). It was reduced to its present limits in 1863 on the formation of Idaho Territory, and admitted as a state in 1889."

886	Periodicals. Societies. Collections
888	Museums. Exhibitions, exhibits
889	Gazetteers. Dictionaries. Geographic names
889.3	Guidebooks
890	Biography (Collective). Genealogy (Collective)
890.2	Historiography
	Historians see E175.5.A+

F1-975

890.5.A-Z	Study and teaching
	For catalogs of audiovisual materials see F890.5.Z9
890.5.A1-.Z8	General works
890.5.Z9	Audiovisual materials
891	General works. Histories
	Including admission as a state, November 11, 1889
	By period (Early to 1950) as well as general
	For 1951 and later see F895+
	Cf. D570.85.W3+ World War I, 1914-1918
	Cf. D769.85.W3+ World War II, 1939-1945
	Cf. E83.84 Wars with Pacific coast Indians, 1847-1865
891.3	Juvenile works
891.5	Pamphlets, addresses, essays
891.6	Anecdotes, legends, pageants, etc.
892	Historic monuments (General). Illustrative material
893	Antiquities (Non-Indian)
	By period
	Early to 1950 see F891
	1951-
895	General works
	Biography
895.2	Collective
895.22.A-Z	Individual, A-Z
	Subarrange each by Table F5
897.A-Z	Regions, counties, etc., A-Z
897.A15	Counties
897.A16	Mountains
897.A17	Rivers

	Washington
	Regions, counties, etc., A-Z -- Continued
897.A18	Lakes
897.A19	Islands
	Adams, Mount see F897.K6
897.A2	Adams County
	Anderson Island see F897.P6
897.A7	Asotin County
	Bainbridge Island see F897.K5
	Baker, Mount see F897.W57
	Bead Lake see F897.P4
897.B4	Benton County
897.B7	Boundaries
	For International boundary see F854; F880
	Cf. F882.B7 Oregon boundary and Sand Island
	controversy
	Camano Island see F897.I7
897.C3	Cascade Range
	Including North Cascades National Park, Stevens Pass
	Chambers Creek see F897.P6
	Chehalis Co. see F897.G84
897.C4	Chelan County
897.C52	Clallam County
	Including Mount Angeles
	For Olympic National Park see F897.O5
897.C6	Clark County (Clarke County to 1925)
	For Sauvies Island see F882.S3
	Clover Creek see F897.P6
897.C68	Columbia County
897.C7	Columbia River and Valley
	Class here works limited to the part of the Columbia River
	and Valley located in Washington State
	Including Grand Coulee Dam region
	For general works on the Columbia River and Valley
	see F853
	For Sand Island controversy see F882.B7
	For Sauvies Island see F882.S3
897.C8	Columbia National Forest
	Colville River and Valley see F897.S9
897.C85	Cowlitz County
897.D7	Douglas County
	Ebey's Landing National Historical Preserve see F897.I7
897.F4	Ferry County
897.F8	Franklin County
897.G3	Garfield County
	Ginkgo Petrified Forest State Park see F897.K53
	Grand Coulee Dam region see F897.C7

Washington
  Regions, counties, etc., A-Z -- Continued
897.G75	Grant County
897.G84	Grays Harbor County (Chehalis County, 1854-1915)
	Includes Grays Harbor
897.H36	Hanford Reach National Monument
	Hartstene Island see F897.M4
897.H63	Hoh River and Valley
	Hood Canal see F897.P9
897.I7	Island County
	Including Ebey's Landing National Historical Preserve,
	Whidbey Island, Camano Island
897.J4	Jefferson County
	Including Marrowstone Island, Protection Island
897.J9	Juan de Fuca Strait region
	Cf. F897.P9 Puget Sound region
	Cf. F1089.V3 Vancouver Island
897.K3	Kettle River and Valley
	Class here works limited to the part of the Kettle River and
	Valley located in the state of Washington
	For general works on the Kettle River and Valley, as
	well as works limited to the part located in British
	Columbia see F1089.K57
	Key Peninsula see F897.P6
897.K4	King County
	Including Lake Washington, Vashon Island
897.K5	Kitsap County
	Including Bainbridge Island
897.K53	Kittitas County
	Including Ginkgo Petrified Forest State Park, Snoqualmie
	Pass
897.K6	Klickitat County
	Including Mount Adams
897.L35	Lake Roosevelt National Recreation Area
	Lake Washington see F897.K4
	Lewis and Clark National Historical Park see F882.L49
897.L6	Lewis County
897.L7	Lincoln County
	Marrowstone Island see F897.J4
897.M4	Mason County
	Including Hartstene Island
897.M44	Methow River and Valley
	Naches River and Valley see F897.Y18
	Nile Creek and Valley see F897.Y18
	North Beach Peninsula see F897.P2
	North Cascades National Park see F897.C3

	Washington
	Regions, counties, etc., A-Z -- Continued
897.O4	Okanogan County
	Including Methow River and Valley, Pine Creek
897.O5	Olympic Mountains. Olympic National Park
	For Mount Angeles see F897.C52
897.P2	Pacific County
	Including North Beach Peninsula
897.P24	Palouse River and Valley
	Class here works limited to the part of the Palouse River and Valley located in Washington State
	For general works on the Palouse River and Valley, as well as works limited to the part located in Idaho see F752.P25
897.P4	Pend Oreille County
	Including Bead Lake
897.P6	Pierce County
	Including Anderson Island, Chambers Creek, Clover Creek, Key Peninsula
	For Mount Ranier (Tacoma) see F897.R2
	Pine Creek see F897.O4
897.P65	Point Roberts
	Protection Island see F897.J4
897.P9	Puget Sound region
	Including Fort Nisqualli, Hood Canal
	Cf. F897.J9 Juan de Fuca Strait region
897.R2	Rainier, Mount (Tacoma). Mount Rainier National Park
897.S17	Saint Helens, Mount
	Samish Island see F897.S5
897.S2	San Juan County
	Including San Juan Islands, (San Juan, Orcas, Lopez, and Waldron)
	Sand Island see F882.B7
	Sauvies Island see F882.S3
897.S48	Similkameen River and Valley
	Class here works limited to the part of the Similkameen River and Valley located in the state of Washington
	For general works on the Similkameen River and Valley, as well as works limited to the part located in British Columbia see F1089.S48
897.S5	Skagit County
	Including Samish Island
897.S52	Skagit River and Valley
897.S53	Skamania County
897.S54	Skokomish River and Valley

	Washington
	Regions, counties, etc., A-Z -- Continued
897.S6	Snake River and Valley
	Class here works limited to the part of the Snake River and Valley located in Washington State
	For general works on the Snake River and Valley, as well as works limited to the part located in Idaho see F752.S7
897.S66	Snohomish County
	Including Mount Pilchuck, Three Fingers Mountain
	Snoqualmie Pass see F897.K53
897.S67	Snoqualmie River and Valley
897.S7	Spokane County
	Including Medical Lake, Spokane River and Valley
897.S9	Stevens County
	Including Colville River and Valley
897.S93	Stillaguamish River and Valley
	Stevens Pass see F897.C3
	Mount Tacoma see F897.R2
	Three Fingers Mountain see F897.S66
897.T5	Thurston County
	Vancouver Island see F1089.V3
	Vashon Island see F897.K4
897.W15	Wahkiakum County
897.W18	Walla Walla County
897.W2	Walla Walla River and Valley
897.W44	Wenatchee River and Valley
897.W57	Whatcom County
	Including Mount Baker
	Whidbey Island see F897.I7
897.W59	White River and Valley
897.W6	Whitman County
897.W65	Whitman National Monument. Whitman Mission National Historic Site
897.Y18	Yakima County
	Including Naches River and Valley, Nile Creek and Valley
897.Y2	Yakima River and Valley
899.A-Z	Cities, towns, etc., A-Z
	e.g.
899.O5	Olympia
899.P8	Port Angeles
899.S4-.S49	Seattle (Table F2)
899.S7	Spokane
899.T2	Tacoma
899.V2	Vancouver
899.Y15	Yakima
	Elements in the population

F1-975

	Washington
	Elements in the population -- Continued
900.A1	General works
900.A2-Z	Individual elements
	For a list of racial, ethnic, and religious elements (with Cutter numbers) see E184.A+
	Alaska
901	Periodicals. Societies. Collections
901.5	Museums. Exhibitions, exhibits
902	Gazetteers. Dictionaries. Geographic names
902.3	Guidebooks
903	Biography (Collective). Genealogy (Collective)
903.2	Historiography
	Historians see E175.5.A+
	Study and teaching
903.5.A1-.Z8	General works
903.5.Z9	Audiovisual materials
	Including catalogs
904	General works. Histories
904.3	Juvenile works
904.5	Pamphlets, addresses, essays
904.6	Anecdotes, legends, pageants, etc.
904.8	Geography
905	Historic monuments (General). Illustrative material
906	Antiquities (Non-Indian)
	By period
907	Early to 1867
	Including exploration; settlement by the Russians; purchase by the United States, 1867; Rossiisko-Amerikanskaia kompaniia
	Including biography: Aleksandr Andreevich Baranov, etc.
	Cf. F851.5 Early voyages to Northwest
	Cf. G600+ Polar voyages
908	1867-1896
909	1896-1959
910	1959-1981
	Admission as a state, January 3, 1959
	1981-
910.5	General works
	Biography
910.6	Collective
910.7.A-Z	Individual, A-Z
	Subarrange each by Table F5
912.A-Z	Regions, counties, etc., A-Z
912.A15	Counties
912.A16	Mountains
912.A17	Rivers

	Alaska
	Regions, counties, etc., A-Z -- Continued
912.A18	Lakes
912.A19	Islands
912.A43	Alaska, Gulf of
	Aleutian Islands see F951
912.A53	Anan Creek and Valley
912.A54	Aniakchak National Monument and Preserve
912.B14	Baranof Island
912.B2	Point Barrow
912.B24	Beaufort Sea
	Bering Sea see F951
912.B57	Bird Creek and Valley (Anchorage Borough)
912.B7	Boundaries
912.B74	Bristol Bay
912.B75	Brooks Range
912.C34	Cape Krusenstern National Monument
912.C43	Chandler River and Valley
912.C47	Clark Lake
	Including Clark Lake National Park and Preserve
912.C6	Cook Inlet region
	Including Turnagain Arm
912.C7	Copper River region
912.D58	Deadfish Lake Region
912.D6	Deborah, Mount
	Denali National Park and Reserve see F912.M23
912.D65	Denali State Park
912.D75	Douglas Island
912.F2	Fairweather, Mount
912.F67	Fortymile River and Valley
	Class here general works on Fortymile River and Valley, as well as works limited to the part located in Alaska
912.G36	Gates of the Arctic National Park and Preserve
912.G5	Glacier Bay. Glacier Bay National Monument
912.G64	Gold Creek and Valley
912.H37	Hatcher Pass
912.H8	Huntington, Mount
912.I44	Iliamna Lake and region
912.I56	Inside Passage
	Class here works limited to the part of the Inside Passage located in Alaska
	For general works on the Inside Passage, as well as works limited to the part located in British Columbia see F1089.I5
912.K26	Kachemak Bay State Park. Kachemak Bay State Wilderness Park
912.K3	Katmai National Monument

F1-975

Alaska
   Regions, counties, etc., A-Z -- Continued

912.K4	Kenai Peninsula
	Including Kenai Fjords National Park
912.K56	Klondike Gold Rush National Historical Park
	Klondike River and Valley see F1095.K5
912.K58	Knik Arm
912.K6	Kobuk River and Valley
912.K62	Kodiak Island
912.K66	Kotzebue Sound and region
912.K67	Koyukuk River and Valley
	Krusenstern, Cape, National Monument see F912.C34
912.K85	Kuskokwim River and Valley
	Lake Clark National Park and Preserve see F912.C47
912.L57	Lituya Bay
912.L65	Long Island (Prince of Wales-Outer Ketchikan Census Area)
912.M2	McKinley, Mount (Denali)
912.M23	McKinley, Mount, National Park. Denali National Park and Reserve
912.M3	Matanuska River and Valley
912.M55	Minook Creek and Valley
	Mount McKinley see F912.M2
912.M9	Muir Glacier
912.N45	Nenana River and Valley
912.N6	Noatak National Preserve
912.N7	Cape Nome region
912.N73	Nome-Taylor Highway
912.N75	Norton Sound and region
912.P9	Pribilof Islands
	Including Alaska Commercial Company, 1868-1940
912.P95	Prince of Wales Island
912.P97	Prince William Sound region
912.R48	Revillagigedo Island
912.S15	Saint Elias, Mount
912.S2	Saint Lawrence Island
912.S27	Sergief Island
912.S29	Seward Highway
912.S3	Seward Peninsula
912.S38	Shuyak Island State Park
912.S85	Stikine River and Valley
	Class here works limited to the part of the Stikine River and Valley located in Alaska
	For general works on the Similkameen River and Valley, as well as works limited to the part located in British Columbia see F1089.S85
912.S95	Susitna River and Valley

Alaska
                Regions, counties, etc., A-Z -- Continued
912.T32   Taku River and Valley
                        Class here works limited to the part of the Taku River and
                            Valley located in Alaska
                        For general works on the Taku River and Valley, as
                            well as works limited to the part located in British
                            Columbia see F1089.T14
912.T4   Thomas Bay
912.T64   Tongass National Forest
                     Turnagain Arm see F912.C6
912.T85   Twin Lakes Region (Lake and Peninsula Borough)
912.W56   Willow Creek State Recreation Area
912.W64   Wood-Tikchik State Park
912.W72   Wrangell Mountains
912.W74   Wrangell-Saint Elias National Park and Preserve
912.Y2   Yakutat Bay
912.Y9   Yukon River and Valley

F1-975

                        Class here general works on the Yukon River and Valley, as
                            well as works limited to the part located in Alaska
                        For works limited to the part of the Yukon River and
                            Valley located in the Yukon see F1095.Y9
914.A-Z   Cities, towns, etc., A-Z
                        e.g.
914.A5   Anchorage
914.F16   Fairbanks
914.J9   Juneau
914.K4   Ketchikan
914.N6   Nome
914.S6   Sitka
914.S7   Skagway
914.W8   Wrangell
                     Elements in the population
915.A1   General works
915.A2-Z   Individual elements
                     Klondike River and Valley see F1095.K5
951   Bering Sea and Aleutian Islands
                        Including discovery and exploration; antiquities
                        Cf. D769.87.A4 Aleutian Islands in World War II, 1939-
                            1945
                        Cf. F912.P9 Pribilof Islands
                     Hawaii see DU620+
965   The territories of the United States (General)
                        Including since 1912, Alaska, Hawaii, Puerto Rico

970	Insular possessions of the United States (General)
	For individual possessions, see the location
	For Hawaii see DU620+
	For Guam see DU647
	For American Samoa see DU819.A1
	For Puerto Rico see F1951+
	For Virgin Islands of the United States see F2136
975	Central American, West Indian, and other countries protected by and having close political affiliations with the United States (General)
	For Liberia see DT621+
	For Nicaragua see F1521+
	For Republic of Panama see F1561+
	For Cuba see F1751+
	For Haiti see F1912+
	For Dominican Republic see F1931+

British America
Historical note from the second edition (1913) of Class F: "Though this region, was visited by the Norse and other seamen, the first extended explorations were those of Cartier in 1534. No attempts at colonization were made till the next centuryj when Champlain, Monts and the "Company of New France" (1629-1663) established various settlements. From Quebec as centre, explorers penetrated far to the south and west, the sway of New France extending over not only eastern Canada, hut eastern Maine, western New York and Pennsylvania, the Old Northwest, the Great Lake region, the Mississippi Valley and beyond.

"Meanwhile by virtue of discovery by Frobisher and Hudson the British crown had, in 1670, established the Hudson's Bay company with almost unlimited powers over the region about the Hudson Bay and to the westward. This territory was definitely recognized as British by France in 1713, after years of conflict. Of the company's holdings, British Columbia was surrendered to the Crown in 1858, while the remainder known as Rupert's Land and the Northwest territories or Canadian Northwest, was sold to the new Dominion of Canada in 1869.

"In 1712 the province of Louisiana was formed, cutting off the southern part of New France, so as to include the Illinois country and all beyond. The record of the next half century is one of conflict between the French and English in America. The result of the final struggle (the French and Indian war of 1755-1763) was to dispossess France of her entire domain in North America; the older parts of modern Canada and Louisiana east of the Mississippi being surrendered to Great Britain, and the rest of Louisiana to Spain. Under British rule New France became Quebec, and to it there was annexed, by the Quebec act of 1774, all the territory between the settled parts of the 13 English colonies and the Mississippi River north of the Ohio. Of the maritime provinces, Nova Scotia and its dependencies continued to maintain their individual existence for a century more, and Newfoundland to the present day. In 1791 Quebec was subdivided into the provinces of Lower and Upper Canada, there being no central government in British North America till 1841, when they were reunited.

"In 1867 the Dominion of Canada was organized by the federation of the various provinces of British North America. The provinces came into the union from time to time, till now the only one remaining outside is Newfoundland, with its dependency Labrador."

Canada
1001   Periodicals. Societies. Collections (serial)
For Canadian geographical societies see G4

F1001-1145.2

	Canada -- Continued
1003	Collections (nonserial). Collected works
1003.5	Museums. Collections of Canadiana. Exhibitions, exhibits
1004	Gazetteers. Geographic names
1004.7	Directories
	Biography
1005	Collective
	Individual (Historians) see F1024.6.A+
	Individual (By period) see F1029.92+
1006	Dictionaries and encyclopedias
	Including chronological tables
1008	General works
	For New France see F1030
1008.2	Juvenile works
1008.3	Pamphlets, addresses, essays
1008.4	Anecdotes, legends, pageants, etc.
	Cf. P, Literature
	Cf. GR113+ Folklore
1009	Guidebooks. Handbooks
1010	Historic monuments (General)
1011	Parks of Canada (Collective descriptive works)
	For works on individual parks including theory, management and description, see the subject or local division
	For works on theory, management, and history, etc., of Canadian parks and public reservations in general see SB484.C2
1011.3	Geography
	Description and travel. Views
1012	General works
	Early to 1762 see F1030
1013	1763-1866
1015	1867-1950
1016	1951-1980
1017	1981-
1019	Antiquities (Non-Indian)
	For Indians of Canada see E78.C2
	For government relations see E92
	For individual tribes of Canadian Indians see E99.A+
	Social life and customs. Civilization. Intellectual life
	Including national characteristics
	For New France see F1030
	By period
1021	General works
	Early to 1945 see F1021
1021.2	1945-
	Elements in the population see F1027; F1035.A1+
	History

	Canada -- Continued
	For New France see F1030
1022	Periodicals. Yearbooks
	Chronological tables see F1006
	Historiography
1024	General works
	Biography of historians
1024.5	Collective
1024.6.A-Z	Individual, A-Z
	Subarrange each by Table F5
1025	Study and teaching
1026	General works
	Including political history
1026.4	Comic and satirical works
1026.6	Addresses, essays, lectures, etc.
1027	French Canadians. French Canadian question
	If the pertinent number provides for an A-Z arrangement for elements in the population, assign ".F83"
	For works on French Canadians in other provinces, cities, or towns, see the province, city or town
	For works on French Canadians in Quebec (Province) see F1052.92+
1027.5	Historical geography
	Including general works on boundaries, territorial expansion, geopolitics
1028	Military history
1028.5	Naval history
	Diplomatic history. Foreign and general relations
1029	General works
	Class general works on the diplomatic history of a period with the period, e.g., Foreign relations after 1945, F1034.2
	For works on relations with a specific country regardless of period see F1029.5.A+
1029.5.A-Z	Relations with individual countries, A-Z
1029.9	Other (not A-Z)
	By period
	Early to 1603 see E101+
	Jacques Cartier see E133.C3

F1001-
1145.2

Canada

History

By period -- Continued

1030   1603-1763. New France

Including history and description. English conquest of 1629;
Company of New France, 1629-1663; Royal Province,
1663; Company of the West Indies, 1665-1674; French
explorers before 1760

Including biography: François Bigot; Pierre Boucher; Louis
de Buade, comte de Frontenac; Pierre Jacques de
Taffanel, marquis de La Jonquière; François Xavier de
Laval de Montmorency; Pierre du Guast, sieur de
Monts; Jean Talon, comte d'Orsainville; Philippe de
Rigaud, marquis de Vaudreuil; Jean Baptiste Bissot,
sieur de Vincennes; etc.

Cf. E81+ Indian wars

Cf. E195+ Intercolonial wars

Cf. F350.3+ Mississippi River and Valley

Cf. F366+ Louisiana

Cf. F544 Illinois country

Cf. F1036+ Acadia, Nova Scotia

Cf. F1060+ Hudson's Bay Company and Rupert's
Land

Writings of Francis Parkman

1030.P24   Collected works

By date

1030.P245   Partial collections. Selections

By date

1030.P247   Battle for North America

California and the Oregon trail see F592

Conspiracy of Pontiac see E83.76

France and England in North America. By date

Selections see F1030.P245

Individual works

Pioneers of France

1030.P261   English editions

1030.P262   Translations

Jesuits in North America see F1030.7+

LaSalle and the discovery of the Great West see
F1030.5

Old régime in Canada

1030.P264   English editions

1030.P265   Translations

Count Frontenac and New France under Louis
XIV

1030.P267   English editions

1030.P268   Translations

	Canada
	History
	By period
	1603-1763. New France
	Writings of Francis Parkman
	France and England in North America
	Individual works
	Montcalm and Wolfe see E199
	Half century of conflict see E198
1030.1	Champlain, Samuel de
	Including Champlain Tercentenary, 1908
	For Lake Champlain Tercentenary, 1909 see
	F127.C6
1030.13	Brulé, Étienne
1030.15	Nicolet, Jean
1030.2	Marquette, Jacques
	Cf. F352 Exploration of the Mississippi
1030.3	Joliet, Louis
	Cf. F352 Exploration of the Mississippi
1030.4	Hennepin, Louis
	Cf. F352 Exploration of the Mississippi
1030.5	La Salle, Robert Cavelier, sieur de
	Cf. F352 Exploration of the Mississippi
	Jesuits in New France
	Including the adjacent regions
1030.7.A-.Z5	General works
	Jesuit relations
1030.7.Z6-.Z9	Collective
1030.8	Individual relations and other writings
	Including works about individual missionaries
1030.9	1754-1763
	Including last years of French rule; the English conquest
	Cf. E199 French and Indian War, 1755-1763;
	Quebec Campaign, 1759
	1763-
1031.5	19th century

F1001-
1145.2

Canada
History
By period
1763- -- Continued

1032   1763-1867

Province of Quebec, 1760; its expansion by Quebec Act of 1774; its division in 1791 and reunion in 1841; Canadian Rebellion, 1837-1838; burning of the "Caroline," 1837; Fenian Raids, 1866-1870; Union of British North American provinces, 1867

Including biography: George Brown, 1818-1880; Joseph Frederick Wallet Des Barres; Lord Dorchester (Guy Carleton); Sir Alexander Tilloch Galt; Sir Frederick Haldimand; Sir Francis Hincks; Sir Louis Hippolyte La Fontaine; Thomas D'Arcy McGee; William Lyon Mackenzie; Louis Joseph Papineau; Lord Sydenham (Charles Edward Poulett Thomson), etc.

Cf. E201+ American Revolution
Cf. E231 Quebec Campaign, 1775-1776
Cf. E263.C2 British North America
Cf. E263.N9 British North America
Cf. E277+ American loyalists in Canada
Cf. E355+ War of 1812, Military operations
Cf. E359.85 War of 1812
Cf. E470.95 Confederates in Canada, St. Albans Raid, 1864
Cf. F1036+ American loyalists in Acadia, Nova Scotia
Cf. F1041+ American loyalists in New Brunswick
Cf. F1056+ American loyalists in Ontario

1033   1867- . Dominion of Canada

Including annexation question; Fenian invasion of 1870-1871

Including biography: Richard Belford Bennett, Sir George Étienne Cartier, Sir George Eulas Foster, Sir Sam Hughes, William Lyon Mackenzie King, Sir Wilfrid Laurier, Sir John Alexander MacDonald, David Mills, Sir Clifford Sifton, Lord Strathcona and Mount Royal (Donald Alexander Smith), Sir John Sparrow David Thompson, Sir Charles Tupper, etc.

Cf. DT1890+ South African War, 1899-1902
Cf. F1060.9 Purchase of Northwest Territories, 1869; Riel Rebellion, 1885
Cf. F1063 Red River Rebellion, 1869-1870

	Canada
	History
	By period
	1763-
	1867-. Dominion of Canada -- Continued
1034	1914-1945
	Including New Dominion status, 1926; Statute of Westminster, 1931
	Including biography: Pierre Edouard Blondin, Henri Bourassa, etc.
	Cf. D501+ World War I, 1914-1918
	Cf. D731+ World War II, 1939-1945
	Cf. F1123 Newfoundland with Labrador established as a province, 1949
	1945-
	Cf. DT407.43 Somalia Affair, 1992-1997
1034.2	General works
	Biography
1034.3.A2	Collective
1034.3.A3-Z	Individual
	Subarrange each by Table F5
	e.g.
1034.3.D5	Diefenbaker, John George (Table F5)
1034.3.P4	Pearson, Lester B. (Table F5)
	Elements in the population
	Including racial and ethnic groups and religious bodies that have significance in the history of Canada
	The Cutter numbers are intended to be used as a guide for the best distribution of numbers and not to be used as a fixed standard or to affect numbers already assigned
	For elements in individual regions, provinces, cities, etc., see the region, province, city, etc.
	Cf. BX1+ Special churches and sects
1035.A1	General works
	Including foreign elements (General), minorities, etc.
	For Race conflicts and problems see F1027
	Acadians see F1027
1035.A5	Americans
1035.A7	Arabs
1035.A74	Armenians
1035.A75	Asians
	Asians, South see F1035.S66
1035.A87	Assyrians
1035.A94	Austrians
1035.B3	Basques
1035.B4	Belgians
	Blacks see F1035.N3

F1001-1145.2

	Canada
	Elements in the population -- Continued
1035.B7	British
	Cf. F1035.E53 Canadians, English-speaking
	Cf. F1035.I6 Irish
	Cf. F1035.S4 Scotch. Scots
1035.B84	Bulgarians
1035.C27	Cambodians
1035.C3	Catholics
1035.C4	Celts
1035.C48	Chileans
1035.C5	Chinese
1035.C64	Cornish
1035.C7	Croats
1035.C9	Czechs
1035.D3	Danes
1035.D76	Dukhobors
1035.D8	Dutch
1035.E28	East Europeans
1035.E3	East Indians
1035.E53	English-speaking Canadians
	Use only for English speakers in predominantly French-speaking areas, i.e., Quebec
1035.E85	Estonians
1035.E89	Ethiopians
1035.F48	Filipinos
1035.F5	Finns
1035.F8	French
	French Canadians (General) see F1027
	For works on French Canadians in Quebec (Province) see F1053
1035.G3	Germans
1035.G7	Greeks
1035.H34	Haitians
1035.H36	Hawaiians
1035.H54	Hindus
1035.H76	Huguenots
1035.H8	Hungarians
1035.H97	Hutterite Brethren
1035.I2	Icelanders
	Indians see E78.A+
1035.I55	Indochinese
1035.I58	Iranians
1035.I6	Irish
1035.I8	Italians
1035.J3	Japanese
1035.J5	Jews

Canada
   Elements in the population -- Continued

1035.K36	Kashubes
1035.K65	Koreans
1035.L27	Latin Americans
1035.L3	Latvians
1035.L43	Lebanese
1035.L5	Lithuanians
1035.M33	Macedonians
1035.M35	Maltese
1035.M45	Mennonites
1035.M67	Mormons
1035.M87	Muslims
1035.N3	Negroes. Blacks
1035.N52	Nigerians
1035.N58	North Africans
1035.N6	Norwegians
(1035.O6)	Orientals
	see F1035.A75
1035.P34	Pakistanis
1035.P36	Palatines
1035.P6	Poles
1035.P65	Portuguese
1035.R65	Romanians
1035.R79	Russian Germans
1035.R8	Russians
	Ruthenians see F1035.U5
1035.S3	Scandinavians
	For Danes see F1035.D3
	For Norwegians see F1035.N6
	For Swedes see F1035.S9
1035.S4	Scotch. Scots
1035.S47	Serbs
1035.S54	Sikhs
1035.S6	Slavs
1035.S63	Slovaks
1035.S64	Slovenes
1035.S65	Somalis
1035.S66	South Asians
1035.S68	Spaniards
1035.S88	Swabians
1035.S9	Swedes
1035.S94	Swiss
1035.T35	Tamils
1035.T85	Tunisians
1035.T87	Turks
1035.U5	Ukrainians

F1001-
1145.2

	Canada
	Elements in the population -- Continued
1035.U78	Uruguayans
1035.W44	Welsh
1035.W47	West Indians
1035.W5	White Russians. Belarusians
	Regions, provinces, territories
1035.8	Maritime provinces
	Including Atlantic coast of Canada
	Cf. F106 Atlantic coast of North America

Canada
  Regions, provinces, territories -- Continued
    Nova Scotia. Acadia
      Historical note from the second edition (1913) of Class F:
        "Visited by early explorers—perhaps by Norsemen; by
          Cabot, Verrazzano, etc. Cape Breton visited by French
          fishermen as early as 1504. Province of Acadia, 40° to
          46° north latitude, granted to Monts by French king; and
          explored and settled 1604-1607 by Monts, Poutrincourt,
          Champlain and others. St. Croix and Port Royal
          settlements. Jesuit station on Mt. Desert Island 1609.
      "In its broadest extent, Acadia included not only the peninsula
          of Nova Scotia, but Maine as far as the Penobscot, New
          Brunswick, Gaspe Peninsula, Cape Breton and Prince
          Edward Island. 1613 the French settlements were broken
          up by an English expedition from Virginia, and 1621 King
          James granted the region (now first called Nova Scotia)
          to Sir William Alexander. Attempts at colonization proved
          abortive and 1632 Acadia was surrendered to France. It
          was parcelled into two districts separated by the St. Croix
          River, and the next twenty years were marked by the
          feud of their two governors, La Tour and Aulnay. Acadia
          was conquered under Cromwell's orders in 1654 but
          again returned to France 1667. It was the seat of almost
          continuous fighting for a century: conquered by the
          English in 1690, returned to France 1691; conquered
          again in 1710 and all claims formally relinquished by
          France in 1713, France still reserving Cape Breton
          Island. The French fortress of Louisburg on Cape Breton
          was captured by New Englanders in 1745 but restored to
          France in 1748. Meanwhile the disputes over the limits of
          Acadia were one of the causes bringing on the French
          and Indian war. The French would restrict it to the
          peninsula of Nova Scotia, the English claiming old Acadia
          in its largest sense. Halifax was founded 1749 and
          extensive English colonization begun. The French
          Acadians still loyal to their mother country were expelled
          in 1755. Louisburg was again captured in 1758 and the
          limits of Acadia ceased to have any international
          significance with Cape Breton Island and all Canada in
          English hands by the treaty of 1763.
      "1769 Prince Edward Island was made a separate colony.
      "During the American revolution there was a large influx of
          loyalists from the U. S. to whom extensive grants of land
          were made, especially in the north; and New Brunswick
          was set off in 1784. Cape Breton Island also became
          independent of Nova Scotia the same year, but was

**F1001-
1145.2**

	Canada
	Regions, provinces, territories -- Continued
	restored, to the older province in 1820.
	"In 1867 Nova Scotia entered the Dominion."
1036	Periodicals. Societies. Collections
1036.4	Gazetteers. Dictionaries. Geographic names
1036.5	Directories
	Biography
1036.8	Collective
	Individual see F1038
1037	General works
	Including description and travel, social life and customs
1037.4	Juvenile works
1037.5	Pamphlets, addresses, essays, etc.
1037.6	Anecdotes, legends, pageants, etc.
	Cf. P, Literature
	Cf. GR113+ Folklore
1037.7	Guidebooks. Handbooks
1037.8	Historic monuments (General). Illustrative material
1037.9	Antiquities (Non-Indian)
	For Indians (General) see E78.A+
	For Indians (Specific tribes) see E99.A+
1038	History
	Including French beginnings; English conquest; Winslow's Expedition, 1755; removal of Acadians; settlement by New Englanders, 1760-1761
	Including biography: Thomas Chandler Haliburton, Sir Brenton Haliburton, Joseph Howe, Charles Amador de Saint-Étienne de la Tour, Sir William Alexander, earl of Stirling (Cf. PR2369.S5), etc.
	Cf. E78.C2 Indians in Canada
	Cf. E78.N9 Indians in Nova Scotia
	Cf. E83.72 Wars with eastern Indians, 1722-1726
	Cf. E184.A2 Acadians in the United States
	Cf. E263.N9 American Revolution, 1775-1783
	Cf. E277+ American loyalists (General)
	Cf. F16+ Maine
	Cf. F27.W3 Washington County, including St. Croix Island
	Cf. F380.A1+ Acadians in Louisiana
	Cf. F1030 New France, 1603-1763
1039.A-Z	Regions, counties, etc., A-Z
1039.A2	Annapolis County
	Fort Anne Park
1039.A25	Antigonish County
1039.A74	Atlantic Coast

	Canada
	Regions, provinces, territories
	Nova Scotia. Acadia
	Regions, counties, etc., A-Z -- Continued
1039.B7	Boundaries
	Old boundaries of Acadia
	For international boundary since 1783 see E398
	Brier Island see F1039.F9
	Cabot Trail see F1039.C2
1039.C15	Cape Breton County
1039.C2	Cape Breton Island (Île Royale)
	Including Cabot Trail
	Cf. F1039.C15 Cape Breton Co.
	Cf. F1039.I5 Inverness Co.
	Cf. F1039.R5 Richmond Co.
	Cf. F1039.V5 Victoria Co.
1039.C3	Cape Sable Island
	Chezzetcook Inlet see F1039.H3
1039.C5	Chignecto Isthmus
	Including Fort Lawrence
1039.C6	Colchester County
1039.C8	Cumberland County
1039.D5	Digby County
1039.F9	Bay of Fundy
	Including Brier Island
1039.G8	Guysborough County
1039.H3	Halifax County
	Including Chezzetcook Inlet, McNabs Island, etc.
1039.H4	Hants County
	Île Royale see F1039.C2
1039.I5	Inverness County
1039.J43	Jeddore Harbour
1039.K43	Kejimkujik Lake and region
1039.K44	Kejimkujik National Park
1039.K5	Kings County
	LaHave River and Valley see F1039.L9
1039.L9	Lunenburg County
	Including LaHave River and Valley
	McNabs Island see F1039.H3
1039.O35	Oak Island
1039.P6	Pictou County
	Including Pictou Island
	Prince Edward Island see F1046+
1039.Q3	Queens County
1039.R5	Richmond County
1039.S13	Sable Island
1039.S18	Saint Ann's Bay and region

F1001-
1145.2

Canada
Regions, provinces, territories
Nova Scotia. Acadia
Regions, counties, etc., A-Z -- Continued
Gulf of St. Lawrence see F1050
1039.S19   Saint Margaret's Bay and region
1039.S20   Saint Mary's Bay and region
1039.S27   Saint Paul Island
1039.S5   Shelburne County
1039.S55   Shubenacadie River and Valley
Surette's Island see F1039.Y3
1039.T35   Tancook Island. Big Tancook Island
1039.V5   Victoria County
1039.Y3   Yarmouth County
Including Surette's Island
1039.5.A-Z   Cities, towns, etc., A-Z
e.g.
1039.5.A16   Annapolis Royal
1039.5.D3   Dartmouth
1039.5.G5   Glace Bay
1039.5.H17   Halifax
1039.5.L8   Louisburg
Including Fortress of Louisbourg National Historic Park
For Capture of Louisburg, 1745 see E198
For Capture of Louisburg, 1758 see E199
1039.5.S9   Sydney
1039.5.Y3   Yarmouth
Elements in the population
1040.A1   General works
1040.A2-Z   Individual elements
For a list of racial, ethnic, and religious elements
(with Cutter numbers) see F1035.A1+
New Brunswick
Historical note from the second edition (1913) of Class F:
"Largely settled by American loyalists. Set off from Nova
Scotia 1784. Entered the Dominion of Canada 1867."
1041   Periodicals. Societies. Collections
1041.4   Gazetteers. Dictionaries. Geographic names
1041.5   Directories
Biography
1041.8   Collective
Individual (General) see F1043
Individual (Regions, counties, etc.) see F1044.A+
Individual (Cities, towns, etc.) see F1044.5.A+
1042   General works
Including description and travel, social life and customs
1042.4   Juvenile works

	Canada
	Regions, provinces, territories
	New Brunswick -- Continued
1042.5	Pamphlets, addresses, essays
1042.6	Anecdotes, legends, pageants, etc.
	Cf. P, Literature
	Cf. GR113+ Folklore
1042.8	Historic monuments (General). Illustrative material
1042.9	Antiquities (Non-Indian)
	For Indians see E78.A+
1043	History
	Entered the Dominion of Canada, 1867
	Cf. E263.N9 American Revolution, 1775-1783
	Cf. E277+ Loyalists
	Cf. E398 Boundary troubles with the United States
1044.A-Z	Regions, counties, etc., A-Z
1044.A4	Albert County
1044.A7	Aroostook River and Valley
	Class here works limited to the portion of the Aroostook River and Valley located in New Brunswick
	For general works on the Aroostook River and Valley, as well as works limited to the part located in Maine see F27.A7
1044.B7	Boundaries
	For international boundary since 1783 and Aroostook War see E398
1044.C2	Campobello Island
1044.C3	Carleton County
1044.C4	Chaleur Bay
1044.C5	Charlotte County
	For Campobello Island see F1044.C2
	For Deer Island see F1044.D3
	For Grand Manan Island see F1044.G7
	Chignecto Isthmus see F1044.C5
1044.D3	Deer Island
1044.F6	Fort Beauséjour National Park
1044.F86	Fundy National Park
	Fundy, Bay of see F1039.F9
	Gaspé Peninsula see F1054.G2
1044.G7	Grand Manan Island
1044.K5	Kings County
1044.K53	Kingston Peninsula
1044.L35	Lamèque Island
1044.M3	Madawaska County
	Middle Island see F1044.M5
1044.M5	Miramichi River and Valley
	Including Middle Island

F1001-1145.2

	Canada
	Regions, provinces, territories
	New Brunswick
	Regions, counties, etc., A-Z -- Continued
1044.M53	Miscou Island
1044.N7	Nepisiguit River and Valley
1044.N83	Northwest Miramichi River and Valley
1044.P3	Passamaquoddy Bay region, N.B.
	Cf. F27.P3 Maine
1044.S17	Saint Croix River and Valley
	Class here works limited to the part of the Saint Croix River and Valley located in New Brunswick
	For general works on the Saint Croix River and Valley, as well as works limited to the part located in Maine see F27.S2
1044.S2	Saint John River and Valley
	Class here general works on the Saint John River and Valley, as well as works limited to the part located in New Brunswick
	For works limited to the part of the Saint John River and Valley located in Maine see F27.S3
	Gulf of St. Lawrence see F1050
1044.S9	Sugarloaf Provincial Park
1044.T36	Tantramar River and Valley
1044.T6	Tobique River and Valley
1044.Y65	York County
1044.5.A-Z	Cities, towns, etc., A-Z
	e.g.
1044.5.F8	Fredericton
1044.5.M7	Moncton
1044.5.S14	Saint John
	Elements in the population
1045.A1	General works
1045.A2-Z	Individual elements
	For a list of racial, ethnic, and religious elements (with Cutter numbers) see F1035.A1+
	Prince Edward Island
	Historical note from the second edition (1913) of Class F: "Set off from Nova Scotia 1769."
1046	Periodicals. Societies. Collections
1046.4	Gazetteers. Dictionaries. Geographic names
1046.5	Directories
	Biography
1046.8	Collective
	Individual (General) see F1048
	Individual (Regions, counties, etc.) see F1049.A+
	Individual (Cities, towns, etc.) see F1049.5.A+

Canada

Regions, provinces, territories

Prince Edward Island -- Continued

1047	General works
	Including description and travel, social life and customs
1047.4	Juvenile works
1047.5	Pamphlets, addresses, essays
1047.6	Anecdotes, legends, pageants, etc.
	Cf. P, Literature
	Cf. GR113+ Folklore
1047.7	Guidebooks. Handbooks
1047.8	Historic monuments (General). Illustrative material
1047.9	Antiquities (Non-Indian)
	For Indians (General) see E78.A+
	For Indians (Specific tribes) see E99.A+
1048	History
	Separated from Nova Scotia, 1769
1049.A-Z	Regions, counties, etc., A-Z
1049.K5	Kings County
1049.P7	Prince County
1049.P75	Prince Edward Island National Park
1049.Q6	Queens County
1049.W47	West River
1049.5.A-Z	Cities, towns, etc. A-Z
	e.g.
1049.5.C5	Charlottetown
1049.5.S8	Summerside
	Elements in the population
1049.7.A1	General works
1049.7.A2-Z	Individual elements
	For a list of racial, ethnic, and religious elements
	(with Cutter numbers) see F1035.A1+
1050	Saint Lawrence Gulf, River, and Valley (General)
	Cf. F127.S23 Saint Lawrence Valley, N.Y.
	Cf. F127.T5 Thousand Islands
	Cf. F1054.A6 Anticosti Island
	Cf. F1054.O7 Isle of Orleans
	Cf. F1054.S26 Saint Helen's Island
	Cf. F1054.S3 Saint Lawrence Valley, Quebec
	Cf. F1059.S4 Saint Lawrence Valley, Ontario
	Cf. F1121+ Newfoundland
	Cf. F1170 Saint Pierre and Miquelon

F1001-
1145.2

Canada
   Regions, provinces, territories -- Continued
    Québec
      Historical note from the second edition (1913) of Class F:
        "The present province of Quebec is the successor of the old province of New France, comprising within its limits practically all the region actually settled by the French (except Acadia) and continuing to this day predominantly French. On the conquest of New France in 1760 the English changed the name to Quebec and in 1774 added to it, by the Quebec act, substantially all the territory earlier in dispute between France and England, lying westward of the maritime colonies (Nova Scotia, Newfoundland, and the 13 continental colonies) as far as the Mississippi and Rupert's Land. The American revolution stripped Quebec of all the southern part of this vast area by the establishment of the international boundary. In 1791 it was further reduced by division into Lower Canada (now Quebec) and Upper Canada (Ontario). The rebellion of 1837 in Lower Canada, under L. J. Papineau (F 1032), was a revolt of the French against the English government, having no real connection with the contemporary outbreak in Upper Canada. In 1867 Lower Canada came into the Dominion under her old name Quebec."

1051	Periodicals. Societies. Collections
1051.4	Gazetteers. Dictionaries. Geographic names
1051.5	Directories
	Biography
1051.8	Collective
	Individual (General) see F1052.96+
	Individual (Regions, counties, seigniories, etc.) see F1054.A+
	Individual (Cities, towns, etc.) see F1054.5.A+
1052	General works
	Including description and travel, social life and customs, etc.
1052.4	Juvenile works
1052.5	Pamphlets, addresses, essays
1052.6	Anecdotes, legends, pageants, etc.
	Cf. P, Literature
	Cf. GR113+ Folklore
1052.7	Guidebooks. Handbooks
1052.8	Historic monuments (General). Illustrative material
1052.9	Antiquities (Non-Indian)
	For Indians (General) see E78.A+
	For Indians (Specific tribes) see E99.A+

Canada
Regions, provinces, territories
Québec -- Continued
History

1052.92	Study and teaching
1052.95	General works
	By period
	Through 1791 see F1030
1053	1791-1960

Including biography: Pierre Stanislas Bedard, René Edouard Caron, Earl of Dalhousie (George Ramsay), Honoré Mercier, etc.
Cf. E184.F85 French Canadians in the United States
Cf. E231 Quebec campaign
Cf. E263.C2 American Revolution, 1775-1783
Cf. E277+ American loyalists
Cf. E355+ Military operations (War of 1812)
Cf. E359.85 Canadian participation (War of 1812)
Cf. F1027 French Canadians (General)
Cf. F1058 American loyalists

	1960-
1053.2	General works
	Biography
1053.24	Collective
1053.25.A-Z	Individual, A-Z

Subarrange each by Table F5

F1001-1145.2

1054.A-Z	Regions, counties, seigniories, etc., A-Z
1054.A3	Abitibi County Abitibi (region)
1054.A6	Anticosti Island
1054.A67	Argenteuil County
1054.A7	Arthabaska County

Including Bois-Francs

1054.B35	Baie Saint-Paul region
1054.B36	Bas-Saint-Laurent
1054.B37	Basques, Île aux
1054.B38	Beauce County
1054.B45	Bellechasse County
1054.B54	Berthier County
1054.B58	Bizard Island
	Bois-Francs see F1054.A7
1054.B6	Bonaventure County
1054.B63	Bonaventure Island
1054.B7	Boundaries

For international boundary since 1783 see E398
Cf. F42.B7 New Hampshire boundary
Cf. F127.B7 New York boundary

Canada
Regions, provinces, territories
Québec
Regions, counties, seigniories, etc., A-Z -- Continued
1054.B8   Brome County
Including general works on the Missisquoi River and
Valley, as well as the part located in Quebec
For works limited to the part of the Missisquoi
Valley located in Vermont see F57.M7
1054.C22   Caplan River and Valley
1054.C4   Cent-Iles
Chaleur Bay see F1044.C4
1054.C44   Chambly County
Including Fort Chambly
1054.C445   Charlevoix Region
1054.C45   Chateauguay County
1054.C45   Chateauguay County
Including Battle of the Châteauguay National Historic Site
1054.C49   Chicoutimi County
1054.C7   Compton County
1054.C75   Côte de Beaupré (Seigniory)
Côte-du-Sud see F1054.S3
Côte Nord see F1054.S3
1054.C8   Crane Island (Île aux Grues)
1054.D4   Deux Montagnes County
1054.D6   Dorchester County
1054.D9   Drummond County
1054.E13   Eastern Townships
For Bois-Francs see F1054.A7
1054.G2   Gaspé Peninsula. Gaspé District
Including Île Percée
For Chaleur Bay see F1044.C4
1054.G26   Gatineau River and Valley
Grosse Île see F1054.S3
Hudson Strait see F1103
1054.H9   Huntington County
1054.I3   Île aux Coudres
1054.I35   Île aux Noix
Including Fort Lennox
1054.I5   Île Verte
James Bay region see F1059.J3
1054.J47   Jesus Island
1054.K2   Kamouraska County
1054.L17   Lanaudière
1054.L2   L'Assomption County
Laurentian Mountains see F1054.S3
1054.L3   Levis County

	Canada
	Regions, provinces, territories
	Québec
	Regions, counties, seigniories, etc., A-Z -- Continued
1054.L57	L'Islet County
1054.M18	Magdalen Islands (Îles Madeleine)
1054.M19	Malbaie River and Valley
1054.M2	Mantawa River and Valley
1054.M35	Massue (Seigniory)
1054.M4	Matane County
1054.M42	Matapédia River and Valley
1054.M45	Megantic County
	For Bois-Francs see F1054.A7
1054.M5	Memphremagog, Lake, Region, Quebec
	Cf. F57.M5 Vermont
1054.M59	Mingan Islands
1054.M6	Missisquoi County
1054.M79	Montmagny County
1054.M8	Montmorency County
1054.M83	Montreal District
1054.N5	New Quebec (Ungava) District
	Ungava was created as district of Northwest Territories in 1895; in 1912 was annexed to the province of Quebec as New Quebec
	North Shore see F1054.S3
1054.N93	Nunavik
1054.O7	Isle of Orleans
1054.O9	Ottawa River and Valley
	Class here general works on the Ottawa River and Valley, as well as works limited to the part located in Quebec
	For works on the part of the Ottawa River and Valley located in Ontario see F1059.O91
1054.O94	Outaouais region
1054.P36	Parc de la Jacques-Cartier
1054.P365	Parc de Plaisance
1054.P367	Parc des Hautes-Gorges-de-la-Rivière-Malbaie
1054.P37	Parc du Mont-Orford
1054.P39	Parc du Mont-Tremblant
1054.P47	Perrot Island
1054.P54	Piémont des Appalaches
1054.P8	Pontiac County
1054.P83	Port Burwell (Island)
1054.P85	Portneuf County
1054.Q4	Quebec County
1054.Q5	Quebec District
1054.R5	Richelieu River and Valley

F1001-1145.2

	Canada
	Regions, provinces, territories
	Québec
	Regions, counties, seigniories, etc., A-Z -- Continued
1054.R615	Rivière-du-Loup County and region
1054.R87	Rupert River and Valley
1054.S13	Saguenay County
	For New Quebec District see F1054.N5
1054.S14	Saguenay River and Valley
	Cf. F1054.S267 Lake St. John
1054.S254	Saint Francis River and Valley
1054.S26	Saint Helen's Island
1054.S264	Saint Hyacinthe County
1054.S267	Saint John, Lake
1054.S3	Saint Lawrence Gulf, River, and Valley, Quebec
	Including Côte-du-Sud, Laurentian Mountains, North Shore, Grosse Île
	Cf. F1050 General
1054.S33	Saint Maurice River and Valley
1054.S34	Saint-Ours (Seigniory)
1054.S345	Saint Peter, Lake
1054.S48	Shefford County
1054.S7	Stanstead County
	Lake Tamiscamingue see F1054.T6
	Témiscamingue Co. see F1054.T6
1054.T29	Temiscouata County
1054.T4	Terrebonne County
	Thousand Islands see F127.T5
1054.T5	Three Rivers District
1054.T6	Timiskaming (region). Témiscamingue County
	Including Lake Témiskaming
	Trois Rivières Co. see F1054.T5
	Two Mountains Co. see F1054.D4
	Ungava see F1054.N5
1054.V3	Varennes (Seigniory)
1054.V47	Verchères
1054.Y3	Yamaska
1054.5.A-Z	Cities, towns, etc., A-Z
	e.g.
1054.5.H8	Hull
1054.5.M8-.M89	Montreal (Table F2)
1054.5.Q3	Québec
1054.5.S55	Sherbrooke
1054.5.T53	Three Rivers
1054.5.Y2	Yamachiche (Village and parish)
	Elements in the population
1055.A1	General works

Canada
Regions, provinces, territories
Québec
Elements in the population -- Continued
1055.A2-Z   Individual elements
For a list of racial, ethnic, and religious elements
(with Cutter numbers) see F1035.A1+
Ontario
Historical note from the second edition (1913) of Class F: "A
part of the province of New France, but not settled by the
French; save for a few forts and trading posts this region
was left to the Indians. After the English conquest in 1760
it formed part of the province of Quebec, still remaining
practically unsettled till the coming of the American
loyalists, during and immediately after the American
revolution. On the division of Quebec in 1791, this part
took the name Upper Canada. It was a battle ground
during the war of 1812. A huge immigration, especially
Scotch, poured in during the next few years. Popular
discontent over administrative abuses known as the
"Family compact" and the "Clergy reserves" led to the
outbreak of the rebellion of 1837 under W. L. Mackenzie.
(The literature of this rebellion as well as the
contemporary troubles in Lower Canada is classed in F
1032) As a result of the rebellion, certain abuses were
corrected, and Upper and Lower Canada reunited under
one government, 1841. Upper Canada was a leader in
the movement for federation of the British colonies in
North America, which brought about the formation of the
Dominion of Canada in 1867. At that time she assumed
the name Ontario."

F1001-1145.2

1056   Periodicals. Societies. Collections
1056.4   Gazetteers. Dictionaries. Collections
1056.5   Directories
Biography
1056.8   Collective
Individual (General) see F1058
Individual (Regions, counties, etc.) see F1059.A+
Individual (Cities, towns, etc.) see F1059.5.A+
1057   General works
Including description and travel, social life and customs
1057.4   Juvenile works
1057.5   Pamphlets, addresses, essays
1057.6   Anecdotes, legends, pageants, etc.
Cf. P Literature
Cf. GR113+ Folklore
1057.7   Guidebooks. Handbooks

	Canada
	Regions, provinces, territories
	Ontario -- Continued
1057.8	Historic monuments (General). Illustrative matter
1057.9	Antiquities (Non-Indian)
	For Indians see E78.O5
	For Indians (Specific tribes) see E99.A+
1058	History

Including United empire loyalists from the United States; political history.

Including biography: Richard Cartwright, Sir Oliver Mowat, Sir John Beverley Robinson, John Graves Simcoe, etc.

For Early history to 1763 see F1030

For Early history to 1791 see F1053

Cf. E78.C2 Indians

Cf. E78.O5 Indians

Cf. E277+ American loyalists (General)

Cf. E355+ War of 1812, military operations

Cf. E359.85 War of 1812

Cf. F1032 Canadian Rebellion, 1837

1059.A-Z	Regions, counties, etc., A-Z
	Addington Co. see F1059.L5
1059.A3	Algoma District
	Cf. F1059.T5 Thunder Bay District
1059.A4	Algonquin Provincial Park
	Including Opeongo Lake
1059.A44	Almaguin Highlands
1059.B36	Bathurst District
1059.B53	Blackstone Harbour Provincial Park
1059.B62	Bois Blanc Island
1059.B64	Bon Echo Provincial Park
1059.B7	Boundaries
	Cf. F550.5+ International boundary
	Cf. F1054.B7 Québec boundary
1059.B82	Brant County
1059.B95	Bruce County
1059.B98	Byng Inlet
1059.C3	Carleton County
1059.C5	Chapleau Crown Game Preserve
1059.C53	Charleston, Lake and region
1059.C7	Credit River and Valley

	Canada
	Regions, provinces, territories
	Ontario
	Regions, counties, etc., A-Z -- Continued
1059.D46	Detroit River and Valley
	Class here works limited to the part of the Detroit River and Valley located in Ontario
	For general works on the Detroit River and Valley, as well as works limited to the part located in Michigan see F572.D46
	Cf. F1059.Y6 Don River and Valley
1059.D88	Dufferin County
1059.D9	Dundas County
1059.D93	Durham County
1059.E4	Elgin County
1059.E46	Eloida, Lake, region, Ont.
1059.E6	Erie, Lake, region, Ont.
	Cf. F555 General
1059.E7	Essex County
1059.F3	Fathom Five Provincial Park
1059.F85	French River and Valley
1059.F9	Frontenac County Frontenac Provincial Park
1059.G3	Georgian Bay region
1059.G5	Glengarry County
1059.G78	Grand River and Valley
1059.G84	Grey County
1059.H27	Haliburton County
1059.H3	Hastings County
1059.H9	Humber River and Valley
1059.H92	Huron County
1059.H95	Huron, Lake, region, Ont.
	Cf. F554 General
1059.J3	James Bay region
	Joseph, Lake see F1059.M9
1059.K2	Kawartha Lakes
1059.K3	Kent County
1059.K5	Killarney Provincial Park
1059.K52	Killbear Provincial Park
1059.L2	Lake of the Woods region
	Class here general works on the Lake of the Woods region, as well as works limited to the part located in Oregon
	For works limited to the part of the Lake of the Woods region located in Manitoba see F1064.L2
1059.L23	Lambton County
1059.L3	Lanark County

F1001-
1145.2

	Canada
	Regions, provinces, territories
	Ontario
	Regions, counties, etc., A-Z -- Continued
1059.L4	Leeds County
1059.L5	Lennox and Addington County
1059.L8	Long Point
1059.M27	Manitoulin Island
1059.M6	Middlesex County
1059.M65	Mississippi River and Valley
1059.M9	Muskoka District. Muskoka Lake region
	Including Lake Joseph, Peninsula Lake, Portage Bay
	Niagara Falls see F127.N8
1059.N5	Niagara Peninsula
	Cf. F127.N6 Niagara River Region (General, and New York State)
	Cf. F1059.Q3 Queen Victoria Niagara Falls Park
	Cf. F1059.S58 Short Hills Provincial Park
1059.N55	Nipissing District
1059.N6	Norfolk County
	For Long Point see F1059.L8
1059.N65	Northumberland County
	Nym Lake and region see F1059.T5
1059.O5	Ontario County
1059.O6	Ontario, Lake, region, Ont.
	Including Toronto Islands, etc.
	Cf. F556 General
	Opeongo Lake see F1059.A4
1059.O91	Ottawa River and Valley
	Class here works limited to the part of the Ottawa River and Valley located in Ontario
	For general works on the Ottawa River and Valley, as well as works limited to the part located in Quebec see F1054.O9
1059.O98	Oxford County
1059.P25	Peel County
	Peninsula Lake (Muskoka) see F1059.M9
1059.P3	Perth County
1059.P4	Peterborough County
	Including Stony Lake
1059.P65	Polar Bear Provincial Park
	Portage Bay see F1059.M9
1059.P75	Prince Edward
1059.Q3	Queen Victoria Niagara Falls Park
	Cf. F127.N8 Niagara Falls
1059.Q4	Quetico Provincial Park
1059.Q6	Bay of Quinte

Canada
Regions, provinces, territories
Ontario
Regions, counties, etc., A-Z -- Continued

1059.R4	Renfrew County
1059.R46	Rideau River and Valley
1059.S3	Saint Clair, Lake, region, Ont.
	Cf. F572.S34 Michigan
1059.S33	Saint Joseph Island
1059.S4	Saint Lawrence River and Valley, Ont.
	Cf. F1050 General
1059.S49	Severn River and Valley
	Severn-Trent Waterway see F1059.T7
1059.S58	Short Hills Provincial Park
1059.S59	Simcoe, Lake
1059.S6	Simcoe County
1059.S63	South Nation River and Valley
1059.S65	Sparrow Lake (Muskoka District and Simcoe County)
	Stony Lake see F1059.P4
1059.S89	Stormont, Dundas and Glengarry
	Cf. F1059.D9 Dundas Co.
	Cf. F1059.G5 Glengarry Co.
1059.S9	Superior, Lake, region, Ont.
	Cf. F552 General
1059.T34	Talbot Settlement
1059.T38	Thames River and Valley
1059.T5	Thunder Bay District and region
	Including Nym Lake and region
	Cf. F1059.A3 Algoma District
1059.T53	Timagani Lake and region
1059.T56	Timiskaming
	Toronto Islands see F1059.O6
1059.T7	Trent River and Valley. Trent-Severn Waterway
	Trent-Severn Waterway see F1059.T7
1059.W32	Waterloo County
1059.W34	Wawa Lake and region
1059.W36	Welland
	Including Navy Island
1059.W37	Wellington County
1059.W4	Wentworth County
1059.W63	Woodland Caribou Provincial Park
1059.Y6	York County York Regional Municipality
	Including Don River and Valley
1059.5.A-Z	Cities, towns, etc., A-Z
	e.g.
1059.5.H2	Hamilton
1059.5.L6	London

F1001-
1145.2

	Canada
	Regions, provinces, territories
	Ontario
	Cities, towns, etc., A-Z -- Continued
1059.5.N5	Niagara
	Present name: Niagara-on-the-Lake
1059.5.N55	Niagara Falls
	Cf. F127.N8 New York
	Cf. F1059.Q3 Queen Victoria Niagara Falls Park
1059.5.O9	Ottawa
1059.5.T68-.T689	Toronto (Table F2)
1059.5.W5	Windsor
	Elements in the population
1059.7.A1	General works
1059.7.A2-Z	Individual elements
	For a list of racial, ethnic, and religious elements (with Cutter numbers) see F1035.A1+

Canada

Regions, provinces, territories -- Continued

Canadian Northwest. Northwest Territories

Region to the west and northwest of ancient New France

Including Hudson Bay, Hudson's Bay Company, Rupert's Land, Northwest Company of Canada

Historical note from the second edition (1913) of Class F: "This region, though visited in its southern parts by French explorers was never colonized or actually governed by that power. By virtue of discovery by Frobisher and Hudson it was claimed by Great Britain and in 1670 the crown chartered the Hudson's Bay company to control the region about Hudson Bay and to the west, and this claim was ultimately recognized by the French, early in the 18th century. Outside the company's own domain, Rupert's Land or the region watered by the rivers flowing into Hudson Bay, it received temporary renewable leases of the western territory to the TT. S. and the Pacific (the Northwest Territories). British Columbia was lost to the Company on its organization as a Crown colony in 1858, and in 1869 all the rest of the Company's holdings outside certain reservations were surrendered to the Dominion of Canada. In 1870 this region, excluding the district of Keewatin, was made a separate government as the "Northwest Territories." In 1882 it was subdivided by the formation of the provisional districts of Assiniboia, Saskatchewan, Alberta and Athabasca. (In 1905 these four districts were consolidated and admitted to the Dominion as the provinces of Saskatchewan and Alberta.) In 1895-97 the remaining unorganized territory in British North America was subdivided into the districts of Ungava, Franklin, Mackenzie and Yukon, of which the last was made a territory the following year. The present Northwest Territories, so-called, include Mackenzie, Keewatin, Ungava and Franklin."

For boundaries (Northwest) see F597

For boundaries (Pacific Northwest) see F854

For boundaries (Oregon) see F880

For boundaries (Alaska) see F912.B7

For boundaries (Ontario) see F1059.B7

Cf. F1060.9 Purchase of Northwest Territories, 1869

Cf. F1090 Canadian Rocky Mountains

Cf. G575+ Polar regions

Cf. G640+ Northwest Passage

1060.A1   Periodicals. Societies. Collections

F1001-1145.2

	Canada
	Regions, provinces, territories
	Canadian Northwest. Northwest Territories -- Continued
1060.A2-Z	General works
	Including history, description and travel
1060.1	Gazetteers. Dictionaries. Geographic names
1060.15	Museums. Exhibitions, exhibits
1060.2	Directories
	Biography
1060.3	Collective
	Individual see F1060.7+
1060.35	Juvenile works
1060.37	Pamphlets, addresses, essays
1060.38	Anecdotes, legends, pageants, etc.
	Cf. P, Literature
	Cf. GR113+ Folklore
1060.4	Guidebooks. Handbooks
1060.5	Historic monuments (General). Illustrative material
1060.6	Antiquities (Non-Indian)
	For Indians (General) see E78.A+
	For Indians (Specific tribes) see E99.A+
	For Eskimos see E99.E7
	By period
	Including history, explorations, description and travel
1060.7	Early to 1821
	Including biography: Médard Chouart, sieur des Grosseilliers; Matthew Cocking; Daniel Williams Harmon; Samuel Hearne; Alexander Henry, 1839-1824; Pierre Gautier de Varennes, sieur de La Vérendrye; Sir Alexander Mackenzie; Pierre Esprit Radisson; David Thompson; etc.
	Cf. F1030 New France and early French explorations (General)
	Cf. F1063 Red River Settlement, 1815-1816
	Cf. F1089.N8 Nootka Sound Controversy, 1789-1790
1060.8	1821-1867
	Including biography: John McLeod, Sir George Simpson, Thomas Simpson, etc.
	Cf. F880 Oregon question and international boundary
	Cf. F1086+ British Columbia
	Cf. F1089.V3 Vancouver Island

Canada
  Regions, provinces, territories
    Canadian Northwest. Northwest Territories
      By period -- Continued

1060.9   1867-1945
          Including purchase from the old Hudson's Bay Company,
            1869; Riel Rebellion, 1885; Alaska Highway
          Cf. F1061+ Manitoba
          Cf. F1070+ Saskatchewan
          Cf. F1075+ Alberta
          Cf. F1086+ British Columbia
          Cf. F1091+ Yukon
          Cf. F1096+ Mackenzie
          Cf. F1101+ Franklin
          Cf. F1106+ Keewatin
        1945-

1060.92   General works
         Biography
1060.93   Collective
1060.935.A-Z   Individual, A-Z
1060.94   Frontier and pioneer life. Ranch life, cowboys, cattle
         trails, etc.
1060.95.A-Z   Regions, etc., A-Z
1060.95.T85   Tuktut Nogait National Park
        Elements in the population
1060.96   General works
1060.97.A-Z   Individual elements, A-Z
          For a list of racial, ethnic, and religious elements
           (with Cutter numbers) see F1035.A1+

F1001-1145.2

      Manitoba
        Historical note from the second edition (1913) of Class F:
         "Part of the territory of the Hudson's Bay company
         (Rupert's Land). Lord Selkirk, a Scotch nobleman
         prominent in that company, colonized large numbers of
         his countrymen here, 1811-1818, but the settlement was
         broken up by the opposition of the rival Northwest
         company. Known as the Red River Settlement. Sold to
         the Dominion of Canada 1869 by the Hudson's Bay
         company with the rest of its land holdings. This sale was
         resented by the Canadian halfbreeds under Louis Riel
         who set up a government of their own but were quickly
         overthrown. Manitoba was admitted as a province of the
         Dominion 1870 and has since been greatly enlarged in
         territory."

1061   Periodicals. Societies. Collections
1061.4   Gazetteers. Dictionaries. Geographic names
1061.5   Directories

	Canada
	Regions, provinces, territories
	Manitoba -- Continued
	Biography
1061.8	Collective
	Individual (General) see F1063
	Individual (Regions, etc.) see F1064.A+
	Individual (Cities, towns, etc.) see F1064.5.A+
1062	General works
	Including description and travel, social life and customs
1062.4	Juvenile works
1062.5	Pamphlets, addresses, essays
1062.6	Anecdotes, legends, pageants, etc.
	Cf. P, Literature
	Cf. GR113+ Folklore
1062.7	Guidebooks. Handbooks
1062.8	Historic monuments (General). Illustrative material
1062.9	Antiquities (Non-Indian)
	For Indians (General) see E78.A+
	For Indians (Specific tribes) see E99.A+
	Cf. E73 Mound builders in Manitoba
1063	History
	Admission as a province, 1870
	Including Red River Settlement; Red River Rebellion, 1869-1870
	Biography: Thomas Douglas, 5th earl of Selkirk
	Cf. F1033 Fenian Raid, 1870-1871
	Cf. F1060+ Hudson Bay Company; Rupert's Land
	Cf. F1060.9 Riel and his rebellion, 1885
1064.A-Z	Regions, etc., A-Z
1064.B7	Boundaries
	For international boundary see F597
	Cf. F1059.B7 Ontario boundary
1064.C58	Churchill River and Valley
	Class here works on the part of the Churchill River and Valley located in Manitoba
	For general works on the Churchill River and Valley, as well as works limited to the part located in Saskatchewan see F1074.C58
1064.D8	Duck Mountain Provincial Park
1064.G22	Fort Garry (Lower)
1064.H42	Hecla Provincial Park

	Canada
	Regions, provinces, territories
	Manitoba
	Regions, etc., A-Z -- Continued
1064.L2	Lake of the Woods region
	Class here works limited to the part of the Lake of the Woods region located in Manitoba
	For general works on the Lake of the Woods region, as well as works limited to the part located in Oregon see F1059.L2
1064.M5	Minnedosa River and Valley
1064.M67	Morris River and Valley
1064.Q34	Qu'Appelle River and Valley
	Class here works limited to the part of the Qu'Appelle River and Valley located in Manitoba
	For general works on the Churchill River and Valley, as well as works limited to the part located in Saskatchewan see F1074.Q34
1064.R3	Red River of the North and Red River Valley, Manitoba
	Cf. F612.R27 Minnesota
	Cf. F642.R3 North Dakota
1064.R54	Riding Mountain National Park
1064.S6	Souris (Mouse) River and Valley
	Class here works limited to the part of the Souris (Mouse) River and Valley located in Manitoba
	For works limited to the part of the Souris River and Valley located in North Dakota see F642.S68
	For general works on the Souris (Mouse) River and Valley, as well as works limited to the part located in Saskatchewan see F1074.S67
1064.S79	Stuartburn
1064.S9	Swan River and Valley
	Class here works limited to the part of the Swan River and Valley located in Manitoba
	For general works on the Swan River and Valley, as well as works limited to the part located in Saskatchewan see F1074.S9
1064.W37	Wapusk National Park
1064.W47	Whiteshell Provincial Park
1064.W5	Winnipeg, Lake, region
1064.5.A-Z	Cities, towns, etc., A-Z
	e.g.
1064.5.B73	Brandon
1064.5.S13	Saint Boniface
1064.5.W7	Winnipeg
	Elements in the population
1065.A1	General works

F1001-
1145.2

	Canada
	Regions, provinces, territories
	Manitoba
	Elements in the population -- Continued
1065.A2-Z	Individual elements
	For a list of racial, ethnic, and religious elements (with Cutter numbers) see F1035.A1+
1067	Assiniboia
	Became part of province of Saskatchewan, September 1, 1905
	Saskatchewan
	Historical note from the second edition (1913) of Class F: "Province formed 1905 from eastern portions of provisional districts of Assiniboia, Saskatchewan and Athabasca."
1070	Periodicals. Societies. Collections
1070.4	Gazetteers. Dictionaries. Geographic names
1070.5	Directories
	Biography
1070.8	Collective
	Individual (General) see F1072
	Individual (Regions, counties, etc.) see F1074.A+
	Individual (Cities, towns, etc.) see F1074.5.A+
1071	General works
	Including description and travel, social life and customs
1071.4	Juvenile works
1071.5	Pamphlets, addresses, essays
1071.6	Anecdotes, legends, pageants, etc.
	Cf. P, Literature
	Cf. GR113+ Folklore
1071.8	Historic monuments (General). Illustrative matter
1071.9	Antiquities (Non-Indian)
	For Indians (General) see E78.A+
	For Indians (Specific tribes) see E99.A+
1072	History
	Province created in 1905
1074.A-Z	Regions, counties, etc., A-Z
1074.A75	Athabasca Sand Dunes Provincial Wilderness Park
	Assiniboia see F1067
	Battle Valley see F1079.B55
1074.B7	Boundaries
	For international boundary see F597
	Cf. F1064.B7 Manitoba boundary

	Canada
	Regions, provinces, territories
	Saskatchewan
	Regions, counties, etc., A-Z -- Continued
1074.C58	Churchill River and Valley
	Class here general works on the Churchill River and Valley, as well as works limited to the part located in Saskatchewan
	For works limited to the part of the Churchill River and Valley located in Manitoba see F1064.C58
	Cypress Hills see F1079.C9
1074.C92	Cypress Hills Provincial Park
1074.G72	Grasslands National Park
1074.G73	Great Sand Hills
1074.G74	Greenwater Lake Provincial Park
1074.L5	Little Pipestone Creek and Valley
1074.L65	Lovering Lake and region
1074.M4	Meadow Lake Provincial Park
1074.M66	Moose Mountain Provincial Park
	Motherwell Farmstead National Historic Park see F1074.W28
1074.P7	Prince Albert National Park
1074.Q34	Qu'Appelle River and Valley
	Class here general works on the Qu'Appelle River and Valley, as well as works limited to the part located in Saskatchewan
	For works limited to the part of the Qu'Appelle River and Valley located in Manitoba see F1064.Q34
	Red Deer River and Valley see F1079.R4
1074.R8	Russell Lake region
1074.S3	Saskatchewan River and Valley
	Class here general works on the Saskatchewan River and Valley, as well as works limited to the part located in Saskatchewan
1074.S67	Souris (Mouse) River and Valley
	Class here general works on the Souris (Mouse) River and Valley, as well as works limited to the part located in Saskatchewan
	For works limited to the part of the Souris River and Valley located North Dakota see F642.S68
	For works limited to the part of the Souris (Mouse) River and Valley located in Manitoba see F1064.S6

F1001-
1145.2

          Canada
           Regions, provinces, territories
           Saskatchewan
            Regions, counties, etc., A-Z -- Continued

1074.S9	Swan River and Valley

              Class here general works on the Swan River and Valley, as well as works limited to the part located in Saskatchewan

              For works limited to the part of the Swan River and Valley located in Manitoba see F1064.S9

1074.W28	W.R. Motherwell Farmstead National Historic Park
1074.W65	Wood Mountain (Region)
1074.5.A-Z	Cities, towns, etc., A-Z

             e.g.

1074.5.R3	Regina
1074.5.S3	Saskatoon

           Elements in the population

1074.7.A1	General works
1074.7.A2-Z	Individual elements

              For a list of racial, ethnic, and religious elements (with Cutter numbers) see F1035.A1+

          Alberta

            Historical note from the second edition (1913) of Class F: "Province formed 1905 from provisional district of Alberta and western portions of Assiniboia, Saskatchewan and Athabasca."

1075	Periodicals. Societies. Collections
1075.4	Gazetteers. Dictionaries. Geographic names
1075.5	Directories
	Biography
1075.8	Collective

            Individual (General) see F1078+

            Individual (Regions, counties, etc.) see F1079.A+

            Individual (Cities, towns, etc.) see F1079.5.A+

1076	General works

              Including description and travel, social life and customs, etc.

1076.4	Juvenile works
1076.5	Pamphlets, addresses, essays
1076.6	Anecdotes, legends, pageants, etc.

              Cf. P, Literature

              Cf. GR113+ Folklore

1076.8	Historic monuments (General). Illustrative material
1076.9	Antiquities (Non-Indian)

              For Indians (General) see E78.A+

              For Indians (Specific tribes) see E99.A+

                  Canada
                    Regions, provinces, territories
                    Alberta -- Continued
                       History
                          Class here works on the province formed in 1905

1078	General works
	By period
	Early to 1970 see F1078
	1971-
1078.2	General works
	Biography
1078.24	Collective
1078.25.A-Z	Individual, A-Z
	Subarrange each by Table F5
1079.A-Z	Regions, counties, etc., A-Z
1079.A8	Athabasca region
1079.B5	Banff National Park
	Including Mount Castleguard
1079.B55	Battle Valley
1079.B65	Blindman River and Valley
1079.B7	Boundaries
	For international boundary see F597
	Cf. F1074.B7 Saskatchewan boundary
1079.B75	Bow River and Valley
1079.B8	Buffalo Hill region
	Castleguard, Mount see F1079.B5
1079.C57	Cooking Lake-Blackfoot Grazing, Wildlife, and
	Provincial Recreation Area
1079.C6	Coyote Flats
1079.C73	Crimson Lake Provincial Park
1079.C76	Crowsnest Pass. Crowsnest River and Valley
	Class here general works on the Crowsnest Pass and
	Crowsnest River and Valley, as well as works limited
	to the part located in Alberta
	For works limited to the part of the Crowsnest Pass
	and Crowsnest River and Valley located in
	British Columbia see F1089.C77
1079.C9	Cypress Hills
1079.E24	Eagle Creek and Valley
1079.E5	Elk Island National Park
1079.F67	Forty Mile Coulee and Valley
	Including Forty Mile Coulee Reservoir
1079.I75	Island Lake
1079.J27	James River and Valley
1079.J3	Jasper National Park
	Including Maligne Lake
1079.K34	Kananaskis Country

F1001-1145.2

	Canada
	Regions, provinces, territories
	Alberta
	Regions, counties, etc., A-Z -- Continued
	Lac Ste. Anne see F1079.S25
1079.L32	Lacombe County
1079.L47	Lesser Slave Lake
	Maligne Lake and region see F1079.J3
1079.M54	Milk River and Valley
	Class here general works on the Milk River and Valley, as well as works limited to the part located in Alberta
	For works limited to the part of the Milk River and Valley located in Montana see F737.M48
1079.M57	Miquelon Lake Provincial Park
1079.P3	Peace River and Valley
	Class here general works on the Peace River and Valley, as well as works limited to the part located in Alberta
	For works limited to the part of the Peace River Valley located in British Columbia see F1089.P3
1079.R36	Pembina River and Valley
1079.R4	Red Deer River and Valley
1079.R53	Rife
1079.R62	Rocky Mountain House Region
1079.R66	Rosebud River and Valley
1079.S25	Ste. Anne, Lac
1079.S7	Strathcona
1079.T3	Tail Creek region
1079.T8	Twin Butte region
1079.W3	Waterton Lakes National Park
1079.W6	Wood Buffalo National Park
1079.W74	Writing-on-Stone Provincial Park
	Including Writing-on-Stone-Northwest Mounted Police Post
1079.Y4	Yellowhead Pass
1079.5.A-Z	Cities, towns, etc., A-Z
	e.g.
1079.5.C35	Calgary
1079.5.E3	Edmonton
1079.5.L5	Lethbridge
1079.5.M4	Medicine Hat
	Elements in the population
1080.A1	General works
1080.A2-Z	Individual elements
	For a list of racial, ethnic, and religious elements (with Cutter numbers) see F1035.A1+

Canada
  Regions, provinces, territories -- Continued
  British Columbia
    Historical note from the second edition (1913) of Class F:
      "The coast was visited by Spanish and English seamen
      in the 18th century, and the interior by traders of the
      Northwest company. The southern portion formed part of
      the " Oregon country" concerning which Great Britain and
      the U. S. made a treaty of joint occupation in 1818. On
      the union of the Northwest company with the Hudson's
      Bay company in 1821 the region was administered by the
      latter: the treaty of 1846 with the U. S. defining the
      southern limit. In 1849 Vancouver Island was made a
      British colony. And in 1858 owing to the large influx of
      population following the discovery of gold, British
      Columbia became a crown colony. In 1866 Vancouver
      Island was annexed. British Columbia joined the
      Dominion of Canada in 1871."

1086	Periodicals. Societies. Collections
1086.4	Gazetteers. Dictionaries. Geographic names
1086.5	Directories
	Biography
1086.8	Collective
	Individual (General) see F1088
	Individual (Regions, etc.) see F1089.A+
	Individual (Cities, towns, etc.) see F1089.5.A+
1087	General works

```
F1001-
1145.2
```

1087	General works
	Including description and travel, social life and customs
	Cf. F851 Pacific coast of North America
1087.4	Juvenile works
1087.5	Pamphlets, addresses, essays
1087.6	Anecdotes, legends, pageants, etc.
	Cf. P, Literature
	Cf. GR113+ Folklore
1087.7	Guidebooks. Handbooks
1087.8	Historic monuments (General). Illustrative material
1087.9	Antiquities (Non-Indian)
	For Indians (General) see E78.A+
	For Indians (Specific tribes) see E99.A+

Canada
Regions, provinces, territories
British Columbia -- Continued

1088   History

Joined the Dominion of Canada in 1871
Including biography: Sir James Douglas, etc.
Cf. E78.B9 Indians in British Columbia
Cf. E78.C2 Indians in Canada
Cf. F851.5 Exploring expeditions before 1800
Cf. F879 Northwest coast between Alaska and New
    Spain (California), 1769-1846, including the
    Oregon question
Cf. F880 Northwest coast between Alaska and New
    Spain (California), 1769-1846, including the
    Oregon question
Cf. F1060+ Hudson's Bay and Northwest companies

1089.A-Z   Regions, etc., A-Z
1089.A4   Alberni region
1089.B43   Bella Coola/Chilcotin Road
1089.B44   Bella Coola River and Valley
1089.B7   Boundaries

For international boundary see F854; F880
Cf. F912.B7 Alaska boundary
Cf. F1079.B7 Alberta boundary

1089.B74   Bowen Island
1089.B8   Bridge River and Valley
1089.B9   Bulkley River and Valley
1089.C3   Cariboo District

Including Chilako River and Valley, Deka Lake, Mitchell
    Lake

1089.C35   Cassiar District

Chilako River and Valley see F1089.C3

1089.C42   Chilcotin River and Valley
1089.C45   Chilliwack River and Valley
1089.C47   Christina Lake and region

Clayoquot Sound see F1089.V3

1089.C7   Coast Range

Including Mount Waddington (Mount George Dawson,
    Mystery Mountain)

1089.C727   Columbia Valley

Class here works limited to the Columbia Valley located
    in the New Westminster Land District of British
    Columbia

Comox Valley see F1089.V3

1089.C73   Cowichan Lake and region
1089.C75   Creston Valley

Canada
   Regions, provinces, territories
     British Columbia
       Regions, etc., A-Z -- Continued

1089.C77	Crowsnest Pass. Crowsnest River and Valley

          Class here works limited to the part of the Crowsnest Pass and Crowsnest River and Valley located in British Columbia

          For general works on the Crowsnest Pass and Crowsnest River and Valley, as well as works limited to the part located in Alberta see F1079.C76

1089.C85	Cultus Lake and region
	Deka Lake see F1089.C3
1089.D45	Denman Island
1089.D46	Departure Bay
1089.D48	Desolation Sound
1089.E38	Elk River and Valley
1089.F5	Finlay River and Valley
1089.F54	Fintry Provincial Park
1089.F7	Fraser River and Valley
1089.G3	Garibaldi Provincial Park
1089.G44	Georgia, Strait of, Region
1089.G55	Glacier National Park
1089.G8	Gulf Islands
1089.H44	Heffley Lake
1089.H6	Hope region
1089.H63	Hornby Island
1089.I5	Inside Passage

          Class here general works on the Inside Passage, as well as works limited to the part located in British Columbia

          For works limited to the part of the Inside Passage located in Alaska see F912.I56

1089.J43	Jedediah Island
	Juan de Fuca Strait region see F897.J9
1089.K4	Kamloops District
1089.K57	Kettle River and Valley

          Class here general works on the Kettle River and Valley, as well as works limited to the part located in British Columbia

          For works limited to the part of the Kettle River and Valley located in the state of Washington see F897.K3

1089.K7	Kootenay (Kootenai) River and Valley, B.C. Kootenay District

          Including Upper Arrow Lake

F1001-1145.2

Canada
Regions, provinces, territories
British Columbia
Regions, etc., A-Z -- Continued

1089.L3	Lac La Hache region
1089.L7	Lillooet District
1089.L75	Lonesome Lake and region
1089.L78	Loughborough Inlet
1089.M3	Manning Provincial Park
	Metchosin District see F1089.V3
	Mitchell Lake see F1089.C3
1089.M87	Muskwa-Kechika Management Area
1089.N48	Newcastle Island
1089.N52	Nicola River and Valley
1089.N8	Nootka Sound
	Including Nootka Sound controversy, 1789-1790
1089.O5	Okanagan River and Valley, B.C.
1089.O55	Omineca River and Valley
1089.P2	Pacific Coast
	Pacific Rim National Park see F1089.V3
1089.P3	Peace River and Valley
	Class here works limited to the part of the Peace River and Valley located in British Columbia
	For general works on the Peace River and Valley, as well as works limited to the part located in Alberta see F1079.P3
1089.P4	Pemberton Valley
1089.P5	Pitt Lake and region
1089.P77	Princess Louisa Inlet and region
1089.P8	Purcell Range
	Quadra Island see F1089.V3
1089.Q3	Queen Charlotte Islands
1089.R62	Robson River and Valley
1089.S2	Saltspring (Salt Spring) Island
	San Juan Islands see F897.S2
1089.S28	Savary Island
1089.S4	Selkirk Range
	Nakimu Caves
1089.S46	Shuswap Lake
1089.S48	Similkameen River and Valley
	Class here general works on the Similkameen River and Valley, as well as works limited to the part located in British Columbia
	For works limited to the part of the Similkameen River and Valley located in the state of Washington see F897.S48
1089.S5	Skeena River and Valley

	Canada
	Regions, provinces, territories
	British Columbia
	Regions, etc., A-Z -- Continued
1089.S77	Stein River and Valley
1089.S85	Stikine River and Valley

Class here general works on the Stikine River and Valley, as well as works limited to the part located in British Columbia

For works limited to the part of the Stikine River and Valley located in Alaska see F912.S85

1089.S88	Stuart Lake and region
1089.S94	Sunshine Coast
1089.T14	Taku River and Valley

Class here general works on the Taku River and Valley, as well as works limited to the part located in British Columbia

For works limited to the part of the Taku River and Valley located in Alaska see F912.T32

1089.T17	Tatlayoko Lake
1089.T18	Tatshenshini River and Valley
1089.T2	Telkwa River and Valley
1089.T25	Teslin River and Valley

Class here works limited to the part of the Teslin River and Valley located in British Columbia

For general works on the Teslin River and Valley, as well as works limited to the part located in the Yukon see F1095.T47

1089.T3	Texada Island
1089.T48	Thompson River and Valley
1089.T85	Tweedsmuir Provincial Park
	Upper Arrow Lake see F1089.K7
1089.V3	Vancouver Island

Including Clayoquot Sound, Metchosin District, Pacific Rim National Park, Quadra Island, Comox Valley

For Juan de Fuca Strait region see F897.J9

1089.W44	Wells Gray Provincial Park
1089.W55	Windermere Lake
1089.Y4	Yale District
	Yellowhead Pass see F1089.Y4
1089.5.A-Z	Cities, towns, etc. A-Z
	e.g.
1089.5.P7	Prince George
1089.5.V22	Vancouver
1089.5.V6	Victoria
	Elements in the population
1089.7.A1	General works

F1001-1145.2

	Canada
	Regions, provinces, territories
	British Columbia
	Elements in the population -- Continued
1089.7.A2-Z	Individual elements
	For a list of racial, ethnic, and religious elements (with Cutter numbers) see F1035.A1+
1090	Rocky Mountains of Canada
	Cf. F721 General, and in the United States
	Cf. F1011 Canadian national parks (General)
1090.5	Northern regions of Canada (General). Arctic regions
	Yukon
	District created in 1897; made a territory in 1898
	Cf. G770.A+ Arctic regions
1091.A1	Periodicals. Societies. Collections
1091.A2-Z	General works
	Including description and travel
	For Indians see E78.Y8
	For individual tribes see E99.A+
	For Inuit see E99.E7
1091.4	Juvenile works
1092	Gazetteers. Dictionaries. Geographic names
	Biography
1092.8	Collective
	Individual (General) see F1093
	Individual (Regions, etc.) see F1095.A+
	Individual (Cities, towns, etc.) see F1095.5.A+
1093	History
1095.A-Z	Regions, etc.
1095.B7	Boundaries
	Cf. F912.B7 Alaska boundary
	Cf. F1089.B7 British Columbia boundary
1095.F7	Frances Lake
1095.I98	Ivvavik National Park
1095.K5	Klondike River and Valley
1095.K54	Kluane National Park and Reserve
1095.T47	Teslin River and Valley
	Class here general works on the Teslin River and Valley, as well as works limited to the part located in the Yukon
	For works limited to the part of the Teslin River and Valley located in British Columbia see F1089.T25
1095.V86	Vuntut National Park

Canada
Regions, provinces, territories
Yukon
Regions, etc. -- Continued

1095.Y9 Yukon River and Valley
Class here works limited to the part of the Yukon River
and Valley located in the Yukon
For general works on the Yukon River and Valley,
as well as works limited to the part located in
Alaska see F912.Y9

1095.5.A-Z Cities, towns, etc., A-Z
e.g.

1095.5.D3 Dawson
1095.5.W5 Whitehorse

Mackenzie
District created in 1895; boundaries redefined in 1918
Cf. G770.A+ Arctic regions

1096.A1 Periodicals. Societies. Collections
1096.A2-Z General works
Including description and travel
For Indians (General) see E78.A+
For Indians (Specific tribes) see E99.A+
For Eskimos see E99.E7

1098 History
1100.A-Z Regions, etc., A-Z
1100.B33 Back River and Valley
Class here general works on the Back River and Valley,
as well as works limited to the part located in
Mackenzie
For works limited to the part of the Back River and
Valley located in Keewatin see F1110.B33

1100.B7 Boundaries
Cf. F1074.B7 Saskatchewan boundary
Cf. F1079.B7 Alberta boundary
Cf. F1089.B7 British Columbia boundary
Cf. F1095.B7 Yukon boundary
Cf. F1110.B7 Keewatin boundary

1100.F7 Franklin Mountains
1100.G7 Great Bear Lake
1100.K39 Kazan River and Valley
Class here general works on the Kazan River and Valley,
as well as works limited to the part located in
Mackenzie
For works limited to the part of the Kazan River and
Valley located in Keewatin see F1110.K39

1100.M3 Mackenzie River and Valley
1100.S6 South Nahanni River and Valley

**F1001-
1145.2**

	Canada
	Regions, provinces, territories
	Mackenzie
	Regions, etc., A-Z -- Continued
1100.T54	Thelon River and Valley

Class here general works on the Thelon River and Valley, as well as works limited to the part located in Mackenzie

For works limited to the part of the Thelon River and Valley located in Keewatin see F1110.T54

	Wood Buffalo National Park see F1079.W6
1100.5.A-Z	Cities, towns, etc., A-Z
	e.g.
1100.5.A4	Aklavik
1100.5.F6	Fort Smith
1100.5.N6	Norman Wells
	Franklin

District formed in 1895; boundaries redefined in 1897 and 1918; area made a game preserve in 1926

Cf. G770.A+ Arctic regions

1101.A1	Periodicals. Societies. Collections
1101.A2-Z	General works

Including description and travel

For Indians (General) see E78.A+

For Indians (Specific tribes) see E99.A+

For Eskimos see E99.E7

1103	History
1105.A-Z	Regions, etc., A-Z
	e.g.
1105.A89	Auyuittuq National Park
1105.B3	Baffin Island
	Formerly Baffin Land
1105.B7	Boundaries
	Cf. F1100.B7 Mackenzie boundary
	Cf. F1110.B7 Keewatin boundary
1105.F74	Frobisher Bay
1105.G7	Grinnell Land
1105.K5	King William Island
1105.Q44	Queen Elizabeth Islands
1105.S8	Sverdrup Islands
1105.5.A-Z	Cities, towns, etc., A-Z
	e.g.
1105.5.A7	Arctic Bay (Trading post)
1105.5.F6	Fort Ross (Trading post)
1105.7	Hudson Strait

Canada

Regions, provinces, territories -- Continued

Keewatin

District created in 1876; boundaries redefined in 1912

Cf. G770.A+ Arctic regions

1106.A1	Periodicals. Societies. Collections
1106.A2-Z	General works

Including description and travel, etc.

For Indians (General) see E78.A+

For Indians (Specific tribes) see E99.A+

For Eskimos see E99.E7

1108	History
1110.A-Z	Regions, etc., A-Z
1110.B33	Back River and Valley

Class here works limited to the part of the Back River and
Valley located in Keewatin

For general works on the Back River and Valley, as
well as works limited to the part located in
Mackenzie see F1100.B33

1110.B7	Boundaries

Cf. F1054.B7 Québec

Cf. F1064.B7 Manitoba

1110.K39	Kazan River and Valley

Class here works limited to the part of the Kazan River
and Valley located in Keewatin

For general works on the Back River and Valley, as
well as works limited to the part located in
Mackenzie see F1100.K39

F1001-
1145.2

1110.M5	Melville Peninsula
1110.S6	Southampton Island
1110.T54	Thelon River and Valley

Class here works limited to the part of the Thelon River
and Valley located in Keewatin

For general works on the Back River and Valley, as
well as works limited to the part located in
Mackenzie see F1100.T54

1110.5.A-Z	Cities, towns, etc., A-Z

e.g.

1110.5.B3	Baker Lake (Trading post)
1110.5.C5	Chesterfield Inlet (Trading post)

Ungava see F1054.N5

Canada
Regions, provinces, territories -- Continued
Newfoundland
Historical note from the second edition (1913) of Class F:
"Visited by Cabots and other early explorers. The cod
fishery attracted many seamen but few settlers. Various
grants of land were made by the British crown, but no
permanent settlements made under them. Newfoundland
became a British crown colony in 1728. In 1876 the
eastern shore of Labrador was annexed to the
government of Newfoundland. The colony has never
joined the Dominion."

1121	Periodicals. Societies. Collections
1121.4	Gazetteers. Dictionaries. Geographic names
1121.5	Directories
	Biography
1121.8	Collective
	Individual (General) see F1123
	Individual (Regions, counties, etc.) see F1124.A+
	Individual (Cities, towns, etc.) see F1124.5.A+
1122	General works
	Including description and travel, social life and customs, etc.
1122.4	Juvenile works
1122.5	Pamphlets, addresses, essays
1122.6	Anecdotes, legends, pageants, etc.
	Cf. P, Literature
	Cf. GR113+ Folklore
1122.7	Guidebooks. Handbooks
1122.8	Historic monuments (General). Illustrative material
1122.9	Antiquities (Non-Indian)
	For Indians (General) see E78.A+
	For Indians (Specific tribes) see E99.A+
1123	History
	Province created in 1949, including Labrador
	Including Baltimore colony of Avalon, political history
	Including biography: Philippe de Pastour, sieur de Costebelle, etc.
1124.A-Z	Regions, counties, etc., A-Z
	e.g.
1124.B7	Boundaries
	Cf. F1138.B7 Labrador boundary
1124.F6	Fogo Island
1124.F9	Funk Island
	Labrador see F1136
	Gulf of St. Lawrence see F1050

	Canada
	Regions, provinces, territories
	Newfoundland -- Continued
1124.5.A-Z	Cities, towns, etc., A-Z
	e.g.
1124.5.C6	Corner Brook
1124.5.G3	Gander
1124.5.G7	Grand Falls
1124.5.S14	Saint John's
	Elements in the population
1125.A1	General works
1125.A2-Z	Individual elements
	For a list of racial, ethnic, and religious elements
	(with Cutter numbers) see F1035.A1+
	Labrador
	Historical note from the second edition (1913) of Class F:
	"The eastern coast of the Labrador peninsula was
	annexed to Newfoundland as a dependency in 1876."
1135	Periodicals. Societies. Collections
1135.4	Gazetteers. Dictionaries. Geographic names
1135.5	Directories
	Biography
1135.8	Collective
	Individual (General) see F1137
	Individual (Regions, etc.) see F1138.A+
	Individual (Cities, towns, etc.) see F1139.A+
1136	General works
	Including description and travel, social life and customs
	For Indians (General) see E78.A+
	For Indians (Specific tribes) see E99.A+
1137	History
	Annexed to Newfoundland in 1876
	Including biography: Sir William Thomason Grenfell, etc.
1138.A-Z	Regions, etc., A-Z
	e.g.
1138.B7	Boundaries
	Cf. F1054.B7 Québec boundary
1138.G7	Grand Falls
1139.A-Z	Cities, towns, etc., A-Z
	e.g.
1139.B3	Battle Harbour (Fishing port)
1139.C3	Cartwright (Fishing port)
1139.H6	Hopedale (Fishing port)

F1001-
1145.2

Canada
    Regions, provinces, territories -- Continued
1140   Labrador Peninsula
           Historical note from the second edition (1913) of Class F:
             "The peninsula is at present divided into three regions for
             governmental purposes: The eastern coast as "Labrador"
             is a dependency of Newfoundland, the southern part
             belongs to Quebec, and the northwest portion, as the
             district of Ungava is one of the Northwest Territories."
           Cf. F1051+ Québec
           Cf. F1135+ Labrador (Newfoundland)
        Nunavut
1141   Periodicals. Societies. Collections
1141.4   Gazetteers. Dictionaries. Geographic names
1141.5   Directories
          Biography
1141.8   Collective
           Individual (General) see F1143
           Individual (Regions, counties, etc.) see F1144.A+
           Individual (Cities, towns, etc.) see F1144.5.A+
1142   General works
           Including description and travel, social life and customs
1142.4   Juvenile works
1142.5   Pamphlets, addresses, essays
1142.6   Anecdotes, legends, pageants, etc.
           Cf. P, Literature
           Cf. GR113+ Folklore
1142.8   Historic monuments (General). Illustrative material
1142.9   Antiquities (non-Indian)
           For Indians (General) see E78.A+
           For Indians (Specific tribes) see E99.A+
           For Eskimos see E99.E7
1143   History
1144.A-Z   Regions, counties, etc., A-Z
1144.E44   Ellesmere Island
1144.5.A-Z   Cities, towns, etc., A-Z
          Elements in the population
1145   General works
1145.2.A-Z   Individual elements, A-Z
           For a list of racial, ethnic, and religiouis elements (with
            Cutter numbers), see F1035.A+
    Other British America
      Bahamas see F1650+
      Bermudas see F1630+
      British West Florida, 1763-1783 see F301
      British East and West Florida, 1763-1783 see F314
      British Guiana see F2361+

Other British America -- Continued
  British Honduras see F1441+
  British West Indies see F2131
  Falkland Islands see F3031+
  Thirteen North American colonies before 1776 see E186+

F1001-
1145.2

Dutch America
  Colony in Brazil, 1625-1661 see F2532
  Dutch Guiana see F2401+
  Dutch West Indies see F2141
  New Netherlands to 1664 see F122.1
  New Sweden (Dutch possession, 1655-1664) see F167

French America
1170   Saint Pierre and Miquelon
                    Including overseas territory of the French union; local autonomy
                       since 1935
                 Other French America
                    Colony in Brazil, 1555-1567 see F2529
                    Colony in Florida, 1562-1565 see F314
                    French Guiana see F2441+
                    French West Indies see F2151
                    Louisiana, 1698-1803 see F372
                    New France, 1600-1753 see F1030
                    Acadia, 1600-1753 see F1038

F1170

Latin America. Spanish America
 For Saint Pierre and Miquelon see F1170
 For New Spain (Viceroyalty) see F1231
 For General see F1401+
Mexico

1201	Periodicals. Societies
	For Mexican geographical societies see G5
1202	Congresses
1203	Collections. Collected works
	Museums. Exhibitions, exhibits
1203.49	General works
1203.5.A-Z	Special institutions. By place, A-Z
	e. g.
1203.5.M43	Mexico (City). Galería de Historia - La Lucha del Pueblo Mexicano por su Libertad
1204	Gazetteers. Dictionaries. Geographic names
1204.5	Directories
	Biography
1205	Collective
	Individual see F1225.A2+
1208	General works
	Cf. F851 Pacific coast of North America
	Cf. F1410 Spaniards in North America
1208.5	Juvenile works
	Minor works see F1227
	Anecdotes, legends, pageants, etc. see F1227.2
1209	Guidebooks. Handbooks
1209.5	Historic monuments (General)
	Cf. F1218.5+ Indian antiquities
1210	Social life and customs. Civilization. Intellectual life
	Including national characteristics
	Elements in the population, other than Indian see F1392.A1+
	Indians see F1218.5+
1210.5	Mexicans in foreign countries (General)
1210.9	Geography
	Description and travel. Views
1211	1516-1809
	For early discoveries see E101+
1213	1810-1866
1215	1867-1950
	Including Inter-American Highway
1216	1951-1980
1216.5	1981-
	Antiquities. Indians
1218.5	Museums. Exhibitions
1218.6	Encyclopedias
1219	General works

F1201-3799

	Mexico
	Antiquities. Indians -- Continued
1219.1.A-Z	Local (Pre-Columbian and Modern), A-Z
	Unless otherwise provided for, class individual sites with the state in which they are located
	e.g.
	For Mayan sites see F1435.1.A+
	Cf. F799 Cibola, N. Mex.
1219.1.C25	Campeche (State)
1219.1.C3	Casas Grandes
1219.1.C35	Cerro de las Mesas
1219.1.C4	Chametla (Sinaloa)
1219.1.M5	Mexico City
1219.1.M55	Michoacán (State)
	Including Apatzingan (District)
1219.1.M6	Mitla
	Officially: San Pablo Villa de Mitla
1219.1.O11	Oaxaca (State)
	Including Monte Albán
1219.1.P9	Puebla (State)
1219.1.Q5	Quintana Roo
1219.1.S22	San Luis Potosi (State)
1219.1.T13	Tabasco (State)
	Including La Venta
1219.1.T24	Tenayuca San Bartolo (Pyramid)
1219.1.T27	Teotihucán (San Juan Teotihuacán)
1219.1.T43	Ticomán
	Including El Arbolillo
1219.1.T7	Tres Zapotes
1219.1.T8	Tula de Allende
	Including Tula Site
1219.1.U8	Usumacinta Valley
1219.1.V47	Veracruz (Vera Cruz) (State)
	Including Isla de Sacrificios
1219.1.Y8	Yucatán
1219.3.A-Z	Special topics (Pre-Columbian and Modern), A-Z
	Class here general works on specific topics only.
	For works limited to specific peoples, see the people in F1219.7 or F1221
	For works on special topics in specific localities see F1219.1.A+
1219.3.A35	Agriculture
1219.3.A42	Alcohol use
1219.3.A5	Anthropometry
1219.3.A6	Architecture
1219.3.A7	Art
1219.3.A85	Astronomy

F1201-3799

Mexico
 Antiquities. Indians
  Special topics (Pre-Columbian and Modern), A-Z --
   Continued

1219.3.B4	Beadwork
1219.3.B6	Bone carving
1219.3.C2	Calendar. Chronology
1219.3.C4	Census
1219.3.C45	Children
	Codices see F1219.5+
(1219.3.C55)	Civil rights
	see KGF1+
1219.3.C6	Commerce
1219.3.C65	Cosmogony. Cosmology
1219.3.C75	Costume. Adornment
1219.3.C8	Craniology
1219.3.C85	Cultural assimilation
	Culture see F1219
1219.3.D2	Dance
1219.3.D3	Dentistry
1219.3.D5	Diseases
1219.3.D8	Drama
1219.3.D83	Drug use
1219.3.D9	Dwellings
1219.3.E2	Economic conditions
1219.3.E3	Education
1219.3.E79	Ethnic identity
1219.3.E82	Ethnobotany
1219.3.E83	Ethnozoology
1219.3.F57	Fishing
1219.3.F6	Folklore. Legends
1219.3.F64	Food
1219.3.F85	Funeral customs and rites
1219.3.G3	Games
1219.3.G57	Goldwork
1219.3.G59	Gourds
1219.3.G6	Government relations
1219.3.H56	Historiography
1219.3.H96	Hydraulic engineering
1219.3.I4	Implements
1219.3.I5	Industries
1219.3.I56	Intellectual life
1219.3.I77	Irrigation
1219.3.J48	Jewelry
1219.3.K55	Kings and rulers
1219.3.L34	Land tenure
1219.3.L4	Law

Mexico
  Antiquities. Indians
    Special topics (Pre-Columbian and Modern), A-Z --
      Continued

1219.3.M34	Magic
1219.3.M38	Marriage customs and rites
1219.3.M4	Masks
1219.3.M42	Material culture
1219.3.M43	Mathematics
1219.3.M5	Medicine. Surgery
1219.3.M52	Metalwork
1219.3.M54	Migrations
1219.3.M55	Military science
1219.3.M58	Mines and mining. Mineralogy
1219.3.M59	Missions
1219.3.M597	Money
1219.3.M6	Monuments
1219.3.N9	Numeral systems
1219.3.P25	Painting
1219.3.P3	Paper and paper making
1219.3.P46	Petroglyphs. Rock paintings
1219.3.P5	Philosophy
1219.3.P55	Physical characteristics
1219.3.P7	Politics and government
1219.3.P73	Population
1219.3.P8	Pottery
1219.3.P84	Psychology
1219.3.P87	Public opinion
1219.3.P9	Pyramids
1219.3.R38	Religion. Mythology
1219.3.R56	Rites and ceremonies
	Rock paintings see F1219.3.P46
1219.3.S38	Sculpture
1219.3.S45	Sexual behavior
1219.3.S5	Slavery
1219.3.S57	Social conditions
1219.3.S6	Social life and customs
1219.3.S64	Societies
1219.3.S7	Statistics
1219.3.T3	Taxation
1219.3.T4	Textile fabrics
1219.3.T73	Transatlantic influences
1219.3.W37	Wars
1219.3.W6	Women
1219.3.W65	Wood carving
1219.3.W94	Writing
	Codices

F1201-
3799

	Mexico
	Antiquities. Indians
	Codices -- Continued
1219.5	General works
1219.54.A-Z	Special. By people, A-Z
	e.g.
1219.54.A98	Aztec
	Mayas see F1435.3.W75
1219.54.M59	Mixtec
1219.56.A-Z	Individual. By name, A-Z
	Under each:
	.x Texts. By date. (Including translations)
	.x2 Commentaries
1219.56.A52-.A522	Anales de Tecamachalco
1219.56.B53-.B532	Biblioteca nazionale centrale di Firenze. Manuscript. Magl. XIII, 3
1219.56.B56-.B562	Bibliothèque national de France. Manuscript 210
1219.56.B57-.B572	Bibliothèque nationale de France. Manuscript. Mexicain 22
1219.56.B58-.B582	Bibliotheque nationale (France). Manuscript. Mexicain 40
1219.56.B65-.B652	Codex Borgianus
1219.56.B67-.B672	Códice Boturini
1219.56.B74-.B742	British Library. Manuscript. Egerton 2895
1219.56.C38-.C382	Codex Azcatitlan
1219.56.C43-.C432	Codex Borbonicus
1219.56.C45-.C452	Codex Cempoallan
1219.56.C62-.C622	Codex Chimalpopocatl
1219.56.C6215-.C62152	Codex Dresdensis Maya
1219.56.C622-.C6222	Codex en croix
1219.56.C623-.C6232	Codex Fejérváry-Mayer
1219.56.C624-.C6242	Codex Laud
1219.56.C6244-.C62442	Codex López Ruiz
1219.56.C625-.C6252	Codex Mendoza
1219.56.C6253-.C62532	Codex Nuttall
1219.56.C626-.C6262	Codex Ramirez
1219.56.C627-.C6272	Codex Telleriano-Remensis
1219.56.C628-.C6282	Codex Tro-Cortesianus
1219.56.C629-.C6292	Codex Tulane
1219.56.C633-.C6332	Codex Vaticanus Lat. 3773
1219.56.C634-.C6342	Codex Veytia
1219.56.C636-.C6362	Codex Vindobonensis Mexicanus 1
1219.56.C64-.C642	Codex Xolotl

Mexico
   Antiquities. Indians
      Codices
         Individual. By name, A-Z -- Continued

1219.56.C66-.C662	Códice Azoyu 1
1219.56.C68-.C682	Códice Baranda
1219.56.C717-.C7172	Códice Chapultepec
1219.56.C7177- .C71772	Códice chugüilá
1219.56.C718-.C7182	Códice Colombino
1219.56.C72-.C722	Códice Cospi
1219.56.C725-.C7252	Códice Cozcatzin
1219.56.C73-.C732	Códice Cuauhtinchan
1219.56.C734-.C7342	Codice de Cholula
1219.56.C736-.C7362	Codice de Cutzio
1219.56.C74-.C742	Códice de Huamantla
1219.56.C743-.C7432	Códice de Jilotepec
1219.56.C746-.C7462	Códice de Metepec
1219.56.C7467- .C74672	Códice de San Antonio Techialoyan
1219.56.C747-.C7472	Códice de Santa María Asunción
1219.56.C7475- .C74752	Códice de Teloloapan
1219.56.C748-.C7482	Códice de Tlatelolco
1219.56.C7486- .C74862	Códice de Xicotepec
1219.56.C749-.C7492	Códice de Yanhuitlán
1219.56.C75-.C752	Códice Fernández Leal
1219.56.C755-.C7552	Códice florentino
1219.56.C764-.C7642	Códice Kingsborough
1219.56.C767-.C7672	Códice Muro
1219.56.C77-.C772	Códice Osuna
1219.56.C776-.C7762	Codice Porfirio Diaz
1219.56.C78-.C782	Códice Sierra
1219.56.C787-.C7872	Códice Techialoyan de Huixquilucan
1219.56.C7875- .C78752	Códice Techialoyan de San Francisco Xonacatlán
1219.56.C788-.C7882	Códice Techialoyan de San Pedro Totopec
1219.56.C79-.C792	Códice Techialoyan García Granados
1219.56.C795-.C7952	Codice Tributos de Coyoacan
1219.56.C82-.C822	Códice Xiquipilco-Temoaya
1219.56.G46-.G462	Genealogía de Zolín
1219.56.H83-.H832	Huexotzinco codex
1219.56.H84-.H842	Códice de Huichapan
1219.56.L46-.L462	Lienzo de Cuetzpala
1219.56.L48-.L482	Lienzo de Parapan
1219.56.L49-.L492	Lienzo de Quauhquechollan

F1201-
3799

Mexico
  Antiquities. Indians
    Codices
      Individual. By name, A-Z -- Continued

1219.56.L52-.L522	Lienzo de Tepetícpac
1219.56.L525-.L5252	Lienzo de Tiltepec
1219.56.L53-.L532	Lienzo de Tlaxcala
1219.56.L536-.L5362	Lienzo del pueblo del Señor San Pedro Nexicho
1219.56.L54-.L542	Lienzo of Petlacala
1219.56.L55-.L552	Lienzo Totomixtlahuaca
1219.56.L57-.L572	Lienzos de Acaxochitlán
1219.56.M32-.M322	Mapa de Cuauhtinchan núm. 2
1219.56.M33-.M332	Mapa de Cuauhtinchan núm. 3
1219.56.M36-.M362	Mapa de Santiago Guevea
1219.56.M364- .M3642	Mapa de Sigüenza
1219.56.M366- .M3662	Mapa Quinatzin
1219.56.M37-.M372	Matrícula de tributos
1219.56.O73-.O732	Ordenanza del Senor Cuauhtemoc

(1219.56.O84-.O842)	Österreichische Nationalbibliothek. Manuscript.
	  Mexicanus 1
	    see F1219.56.C636-.C6362

1219.56.P33-.P332	Padrones de Tlaxcala del siglo XVI
1219.56.P56-.P562	Plano en papel maguey
1219.56.R56-.R562	Codex Rios
1219.56.T46-.T462	Mapa de Tepechpan
1219.56.T66-.T662	Tonalámatl de Aubin
1219.56.T86-.T862	Códice Tudela

    Pre-Columbian peoples
      Class here works on the pre-Columbian period only
      For works on local archaeological sites see F1219.1.A+
      For works limited to the post-contact period, as well as
        comprehensive works on individual peoples existing
        during both periods see F1221.A+
      For works on Mayan sites see F1435.1.A+

1219.7	General works
	Aztecs
	Including works on the Nahua peoples (General)
1219.73	General works
	Biography
1219.74	Collective
1219.75.A-Z	Individual, A-Z
	Subarrange each by Table F5
	e.g.
1219.75.C83	Cuauhtemoc, Emperor of Mexico, 1495-1525 (Table F5)

	Mexico
	Antiquities. Indians
	Pre-Columbian peoples
	Aztecs
	Biography
	Individual, A-Z -- Continued
1219.75.M75	Montezuma I, Emperor of Mexico, ca. 1398-1468 (Table F5)
	Montezuma II see F1230
1219.75.N49	Nezahualcóyotl, King of Texcoco, fl. 1400-1470 (Table F5)
	For works on Nezahualcóyotl as a poet see PM4068.9.N49
1219.76.A-Z	Special topics, A-Z
1219.76.A57	Agriculture
1219.76.A59	Alcohol use
1219.76.A62	Anthropometry
1219.76.A74	Architecture
1219.76.A78	Art
1219.76.A83	Astrology
1219.76.A84	Astronomy
1219.76.B48	Beverages
1219.76.C35	Calendar. Chronology
1219.76.C37	Cartography
1219.76.C45	Census
1219.76.C53	Chalchihuitl
1219.76.C56	Children
1219.76.C59	City planning
1219.76.C65	Commerce
1219.76.C67	Cosmology
1219.76.C68	Costume. Adornment
	Customs see F1219.76.S64
1219.76.D35	Dance
1219.76.D64	Dolls
1219.76.D76	Drug use
1219.76.E36	Economic conditions
1219.76.E38	Education
1219.76.E47	Employment
1219.76.E83	Ethnobotany
1219.76.E85	Ethnozoology
1219.76.F65	Folklore. Legends
1219.76.F67	Food
1219.76.F86	Funeral customs and rites
1219.76.G35	Games
1219.76.G64	Goldwork
	Government see F1219.76.P75
1219.76.H57	Historiography

F1201-3799

Mexico
  Antiquities. Indians
    Pre-Columbian peoples
      Aztecs
        Special topics, A-Z -- Continued

1219.76.I53	Industries
1219.76.K53	Kings and rulers
1219.76.K55	Kinship
1219.76.L35	Land tenure
	Legends see F1219.76.F65
1219.76.M35	Magic
1219.76.M37	Material culture
1219.76.M38	Mathematics
1219.76.M43	Medicine
	Mythology see F1219.76.R45
1219.76.N35	Names
1219.76.P35	Painting
1219.76.P37	Paper making
1219.76.P55	Philosophy
1219.76.P75	Politics and government
1219.76.P78	Pottery
1219.76.R45	Religion. Mythology
1219.76.R57	Rites and ceremonies
1219.76.S35	Sculpture
1219.76.S53	Slavery
1219.76.S63	Social conditions
1219.76.S64	Social life and customs
1219.76.T39	Taxation
1219.76.U74	Urban residence
1219.76.W37	Wars
1219.76.W44	Weights and measures
1219.76.W75	Women
1219.76.W85	Writing
	For works limited to the Aztec codices see F1219.54.A98
1219.8.A-Z	Other individual Pre-Columbian peoples or cultures, A-Z
1219.8.A33	Acaxee
1219.8.C52	Chantuto
1219.8.C55	Chichimec
1219.8.H83	Huastec
1219.8.M38	Matlatzinca
	Mayas see F1435+
1219.8.M59	Mixtec
	Nahua see F1219.73+
1219.8.O56	Olmec
1219.8.O87	Otomi
1219.8.T37	Tarasco

Mexico
  Antiquities. Indians
    Pre-Columbian peoples
      Other individual Pre-Columbian peoples or cultures, A-Z -
        - Continued

1219.8.T43	Teco
1219.8.T47	Tepanec
1219.8.T49	Tezcucan
1219.8.T52	Tlahuica
1219.8.T53	Tlaxcalan
1219.8.T65	Toltec
1219.8.T68	Totonac
1219.8.Z37	Zapotec

      Modern Indian peoples
        For works on peoples in both Mexico and the United
          States see E99.A+

1220	General works
1221.A-Z	Individual peoples, A-Z
1221.A4	Akwa'ala
1221.A58	Amuzgo
1221.C3	Cahita
1221.C38	Cazcan
	Chañabal see F1221.T58
1221.C47	Chatino
1221.C5	Chiapanec
1221.C53	Chichimeca-Jonaz
1221.C56	Chinantec
1221.C567	Chocho
1221.C57	Chol
1221.C58	Chontal
1221.C585	Chuj
1221.C6	Cora
1221.C84	Cuicatec
1221.G79	Guachichile
1221.G82	Guarijío
1221.H8	Huastec
1221.H85	Huave
1221.H9	Huichol
	Jacalteca see F1465.2.J3
1221.K35	Kamia
1221.K5	Kiliwa
1221.L2	Lacandon
	Mam see F1465.2.M3
1221.M27	Matlatzinca
	Mayas see F1435+
1221.M3	Mayo
1221.M33	Mazahua

F1201-
3799

	Mexico
	Antiquities. Indians
	Modern Indian peoples
	Individual peoples, A-Z -- Continued
1221.M35	Mazatec
1221.M67	Mixe
1221.M7	Mixtec
1221.M74	Motozintlec
1221.N3	Nahua
1221.O6	Opata
1221.O86	Otomi
1221.P3	Pame
1221.P35	Patarabueye
1221.P5	Pima
1221.P6	Popoloca
1221.P62	Popoluca (Vera Cruz)
1221.S43	Seri
1221.T25	Tarahumara
1221.T3	Tarasco
1221.T33	Tecuexe
1221.T37	Tepecano
1221.T39	Tepehua
1221.T4	Tepehuan
1221.T5	Tlahuica
1221.T53	Tlapanec
1221.T56	Tlaxcalan
	Tohono O'Odham see E99.P25
1221.T58	Tojolabal. Chañabal
1221.T6	Totonac
1221.T7	Trique
1221.T8	Tzeltal
1221.T9	Tzotzil
1221.Y3	Yaqui
1221.Y64	Yopi
1221.Z25	Zacateca
1221.Z3	Zapotec
1221.Z6	Zoque
	History
1223	Chronological tables. Outlines, syllabi, etc.
	Including questions and answers, etc.
	Historiography
1224	General works
	Biography of historians
1225.A2	Collective
1225.A3-Z	Individual, A-Z
	Subarrange each by Table F5
1225.5	Study and teaching

	Mexico
	History -- Continued
1226	General works
	Including political history
1227	Pamphlets, addresses, essays, etc.
1227.2	Anecdotes, legends, pageants, etc.
	Cf. P, Literature
	Cf. GR115+ Folklore
	General special
1227.5	Military and naval history
	Diplomatic history (General). Foreign and general relations
1228	General works
1228.5.A-Z	Relations with individual countries, A-Z
1228.9	Other (not A-Z)
	By period
	Pre-Colombian period see F1219.1.A+
	Pre-Columbian period see F1435.1.A+
1228.98	1492-1519
1229	1519-1824
	Including end of Spanish rule, 1824
	Cf. E123+ Post-Columbian explorers and explorations (Early to 1607)
	Cf. E141+ Early descriptive works on America
1230	1519-1535
	Including the Spanish conquest; Cortés and his companions; Bernal Díaz del Castillo; Montezuma II
1231	1535-1810. New Spain (Viceroyalty)
	Including period of the viceroys; church and state; expulsion of the Jesuits
	Including biography: Luis de Carvajal; José de Iturrigaray y Aróstegui; Guillén Lombardo; Antonion de Mendoza, conde de Tendilla; Juan de Palafox y Mendoza; Melchor de Talamantes Salvador y Baeza; etc.
1231.5	1810-

F1201-
3799

Mexico
  History
    By period
      1810- -- Continued

1232   1810-1849

Including wars of Independence, 1810-1821; Empire of
Itúrbide; troubles with France, 1838-1839

Including biography: Lucas Alamán; Ignacio José Allende
y Unzaga; Nicolás Bravo; Félix María Calleja, conde
de Calderon; Míguel Hidalgo y Costilla; Augustin de
Itúrbide; José María Teclo Morelos y Pavón; Antonio
López de Santa Anna; etc.

Cf. E401+ War with United States, loss of New
Mexico and California

Cf. F390 Revolt and independence of Texas; Texan
Mier Expedition, 1842

Cf. F1438 Annexation and secession of Central
America

Cf. F1466.4 Annexation and secession of El
Salvador

1232.5   1849-1858/1861

Including revolutions; state and church; Constitution of
1857; Raousset-Boulbon and Walker Sonora
Expeditions

Including biography: Juan Álvarez; Mariano Arista;
Ignacio Comonfort; Gaston Raoux, comte Raousset-
Boulbon; etc.

1233   1849/1861-1867

Including European intervention, 1861-1867; French
army in Mexico; Empire of Maximilian, 1864-1867

Including biography: Charlotte, consort of Maximilian;
Mariana Escobedo; Benito Pablo Juárez; Maximilian,
Emperor of Mexico; etc.

For Gadsden Purchase, sale of territory south of
the Gila to the United States see F786

1233.5   1867-1910

Including biography: Porfirio Díaz, etc.

For Apache War, 1883-1886 see E83.88

	Mexico
	History
	By period
	1810- -- Continued
1234	1910-1946. Mexican Revolution (1910-1920)
	Including frontier troubles with the United States; American occupation of Veracruz, 1914; Pershing's expedition to capture Villa, 1916; Constitution of 1917
	Including biography: Plutarco Elías Calles, Manual Ávila Camacho, Lázaro Cárdenas, Venustiano Carranza, Victoriano Huerta, Francisco Indalecio Madero, Álvaro Obregón, Francisco Villa, Emiliano Zapata, etc.
	Cf. D501+ World War I, 1914-1918
	Cf. D731+ World War II, 1939-1945
	Cf. DU950.C5 Clipperton Island dispute
	1946-1970
1235	General works
1235.5.A-Z	Biography
1235.5.A2	Collective
1235.5.A3-Z	Individual
	Subarrange each by Table F5
	e.g.
1235.5.E25	Echeverría, Luis, 1922 (Table F5)
1235.5.L6	López Mateos, Adolfo (Table F5)
1235.5.L65	López Portillo, José (Table F5)
1235.5.R8	Ruiz Cortines, Adolfo (Table F5)
	1970-2000
1236	General works
	Biography
1236.5	Collective
1236.6.A-Z	Individual, A-Z
	Subarrange each by Table F5
	2000-
1236.7	General works
	Biography
1236.8	Collective
1236.9.A-Z	Individual, A-Z
	Subarrange each by Table F5
	Regions, states, territories, etc.
	Including the ecclesiastical subdivisions of New Spain, bishoprics, etc., as well as the provinces of the religious orders which are to be classed with provinces of same name even if they are not identical as to extent
	For Indian local history and antiquities see F1219.1.A+
1240	Islands of Mexico (General)

F1201-3799

Mexico
Regions, states, territories, etc. -- Continued
1241   Aguascalientes
               Baja California
                   Including Baja California (Territory)
                   Cf. F788 Colorado River
                   Cf. F864 California before 1869
1246   General works
1246.2   Baja California (State)
1246.3   Baja California Sur
1246.6   Bajío Region
1247   Balsas River
1249   Boundaries
                   Including Guatemala boundary
                   For western boundary of the Louisiana Purchase see
                       F374
                   For Gadsden Purchase, 1853 see F786
                   For Nootka Sound Controversy with Great Britain,
                       1789-1790 see F1089.N8
                   Cf. F392.B7 Republic of Texas boundary
                   Cf. F392.R5 Rio Grande and Valley (General, and
                       Texas)
                   For Gadsden Purchase, 1853 see F786
                   Cf. F1449.B7 Belize boundary
               California (Spanish and Mexican province to 1848) see
                   F864
1250   California, Gulf of
1251   Campeche
1254   Chapala, Lake
1256   Chiapas
                   Formed one of the Central American states under the
                       Audiencia of Guatemala during colonial period
                   Cf. DU950.C5 Clipperton Island
                   Cf. F1437 Central America before 1821
1261   Chihuahua
                   Province of Nueva Viscaya in colonial period
                   Including Papigochic River and Valley
                   Cf. F392.R5 Rio Grande and Valley (General, and
                       Texas)
                   Cf. F786 International boundary
1262   Chihuahuan Desert
1266   Coahuila
                   Including Laguna (Region)
                   Cf. F392.R5 Rio Grande and Valley (General, and
                       Texas)
                   Cf. F786 International boundary
                   Cf. F1234 Frontier troubles

Mexico
   Regions, states, territories, etc. -- Continued

1271	Colima
1272	Cozumel Island
1276	Durango
1279	Grijalva River
1281	Guanajuato
1286	Guerrero
1291	Hidalgo

          Including Ixmiquilpan, Metztitlán, and Pachuca Districts;
            Mezquital Valley

1294	Huasteca (Region)
1296	Jalisco

          Including Nueva Galicia (Audiencia de Guadalajara) covering
            not only the present states of Jalisco and Zacatecas but
            the provinces to the north

       Laguna Region see F1266
       Lower California see F1246+

1301	Mexico (State). Mexico (Archdiocese)

          Mexico (Federal District and City) see F1386

1302	Mexico, Valley of

          Including Federal District and parts of states of Mexico,
            Hidalgo, and Tlaxcala

1306	Michoacán

          Including Coalcomán and Jiquilpan Districts

1311	Morelos
1313	Nayarit

          In early colonial days the area was part of Nueva Galicia
            (F1296)

1314	North Mexico

       Nueva Galicia see F1296

1316	Nuevo León

          In colonial times called "Nuevo Reino de León."
          Cf. F391+ Frontier troubles
          Cf. F392.R5 Rio Grande and Valley (General, and
            Texas)
          Cf. F786 International boundary
          Cf. F1234 Frontier troubles
         Nuevo Mexico (Spanish and Mexican province to 1848)
          see F799

1321	Oaxaca

          Cf. F1359 Isthmus of Tehuantepec

1322	Occidente (State)

          Cf. F1341 Sinaloa after 1831
          Cf. F1346 Sonora after 1831

1323	Pánuco (Province)

       Papigochic River and Valley see F1261

F1201-3799

Mexico
    Regions, states, territories, etc. -- Continued
1325   Popocatepetl (Volcano)
                      Cf. QE523.P8 Geology
1326   Puebla
                      Including Sierra Norte de Puebla
                      For Popocatepetl see F1325
1331   Querétaro
1333   Quintana Roo (Territory)
                      Cf. F1272 Cozumel Island
                      Cf. F1449.B7 British Honduras boundary
1333.5   Revilla Gigedo Islands
1334   Rio Grande and Valley
                      Class here works limited to the part of the Rio Grande and
                          Rio Grande Valley located in Mexico
                      For general works on the Rio Grande and Rio Grande
                          Valley, as well as works limited to the part located
                          in Texas see F392.R5
1335   San Juan de Ulúa Island
1336   San Luis Potosí
1339   Sierra Gorda
1340   Sierra Madre
                      Including Copper Canyon
1341   Sinaloa
1346   Sonora
                      Including San Pedro River and Valley, Mexico, and Yaqui
                        River
                      Cf. F817.S25 San Pedro River and Valley, General and
                        Arizona
1348   Southeast Mexico
1351   Tabasco
1356   Tamaulipas
                      Including Nuevo Santander in colonial times
                      Cf. F391+ Frontier troubles
                      Cf. F392.R5 Rio Grande and Valley (General, and
                        Texas)
                      Cf. F786 International boundary
                      Cf. F1234 Frontier troubles
1359   Isthmus of Tehuantepec
1361   Tepic (Territory)
                  Texas (Mexican province to 1836) see F389
1366   Tlaxcala
1368   Tres Marias Islands
1371   Veracruz (Vera Cruz)
                      Including cantons: Córdoba, Jalapa (Xalapa), Orizaba,
                        Tuxpan
                      For Veracruz (Vera Cruz) (City) see F1391.V4

	Mexico
	Regions, states, territories, etc. -- Continued
1376	Yucatán Peninsula. Yucatán (State)
	For Indian history and antiquities see F1219.1.Y8
	For local Mayan antiquities see F1435.1.A+
	Cf. F1449.B7 Belize border
1381	Zacatecas
	In colonial times part of Nueva Galicia (F1286)
	Cities, towns, etc.
	For Indian local history and antiquities see F1219.1.A+
1386	Mexico (Federal District and City) (Table F1)
1391.A-Z	Other, A-Z
	e.g.
1391.G9	Guadalajara
1391.G98	Guanajuato
1391.J2	Jalapa (Xalapa)
1391.M5	Mérida
1391.M7-.M79	Monterrey (Table F2)
1391.M8	Morelia
1391.O12	Oaxaca
1391.P9	Puebla
1391.Q4	Querétaro
1391.S19	San Luis Potosí
1391.T2	Tampico
1391.T23	Taxco
1391.T3	Tepoztlán
1391.T6	Toluca
1391.V4	Veracruz (Vera Cruz)
	Xalapa see F1391.J2
1391.Z2	Zacatecas
1392.A1-Z	Elements in the population, A-Z
	Racial and ethnic groups including religious bodies that have significance in the history of Mexico
	Elements in individual regions, states, cities, etc., are classed with the region, state, city, etc.
	Cf. BX1+ Special churches and sects
1392.A1	General works
	Including foreign elements (General), minorities, race conflicts and problems
1392.A5	Americans
1392.A7	Arabs
1392.B3	Basques
1392.B55	Blacks
1392.C28	Cantabrians
1392.C3	Catalans
1392.C45	Chinese
1392.C8	Cubans

F1201-3799

Mexico
  Elements in the population, A-Z -- Continued

1392.C93	Czechs
1392.E5	English
1392.F8	French
1392.G4	Germans
1392.G74	Greeks
	Indians see F1218.5+
1392.I82	Italians
1392.J3	Japanese
1392.J4	Jews
1392.K65	Koreans
1392.L4	Lebanese
1392.M6	Mormons
	Negroes see F1392.B55
1392.P6	Poles
1392.S7	Spaniards
1392.U78	Uruguayans
1392.V45	Venezuelans

Latin America (General)
  Cf. F301 British West Florida
  Cf. F314 Florida before 1819
  Cf. F373 Louisiana, 1764-1803
  Cf. F799+ New Mexico to 1848
  Cf. F864 California to 1848
  Cf. F1201+ Mexico
  Cf. F1421+ Central America
  Cf. F1601+ West Indies
  Cf. F2201+ South America

1401	Periodicals. Societies. Collections
	For geographical societies see G5
	Organization of American States
	Publications on special subjects are to be classed with the subjects in classes B-Z
	Documents
1402.A1-.A29	Serial
	Nonserial
1402.A3	By the organization as a whole
	By date
1402.A4A-.A4Z	By subordinate bodies, departments, etc., A-Z
	For Inter-American Council for Education, Science, and Culture see F1408.4
1402.A5-Z	Nonofficial publications
	Including official publications by individual countries of the Organization

Latin America (General)
Periodicals. Societies. Collections -- Continued
Pan American Union
Formerly Bureau of the American Republics, and
International Bureau of American Republics
Official publications
1403	By the organization as a whole
1403.3	By subordinate bodies, departments, etc.
1403.5	Nonofficial publications

Including works about the organization, addresses, essays,
etc.
1403.9	Congresses

Pan American conferences
1404	American Congress, Panama, 1826
1404.4	American Congress, Lima, 1864-1865

International American Conferences, 1889-1948
Continued as Inter-American Conference, 1954-
1404.5	General works

Individual conferences. By date
Subarrange each by Table F6
e.g.
1405 1889	First conference, 1889 (Table F6)
1405.3	Inter-American Conference for the Maintenance of Peace, Buenos Aires, 1936 (Table F6)
1405.5	Meeting of Consultation of Ministers of Foreign Affairs of American States. By date

Subarrange each by Table F6
1405.9.A-Z	Other conferences, congresses, etc., A-Z

e.g.
1405.9.I5	Inter-American Conference for the Maintenance of Continental Peace and Security, Rio de Janeiro, 1947
1406	Gazetteers. Dictionaries. Geographic names
1406.5	Directories

Collected works
1406.7	Several authors
1406.8	Individual authors

Including collected papers, addresses, essays, etc.
Biography
1407	Collective

Individual (Mexico) see F1228.96+
Individual (Latin America in general) see F1411+
1408	General works
1408.2	Juvenile works
1408.25	Pamphlets, addresses, essays, etc.
1408.27	Anecdotes, legends, pageants, etc.
1408.29	Guidebooks. Handbooks

F1201-
3799

Latin America (General) -- Continued

1408.3	Social life and customs. Civilization. Intellectual life
	Including characteristics of the people
	For specific periods, see the period
1408.4	Inter-American Council for Education, Science, and Culture
	Formerly Inter-American Cultural Council
1408.5	Historic monuments (General)
	Cf. F1409.5 Antiquities
1408.8	Historical geography
1408.9	Geography
	Description and travel. Views
	Early to 1810 see E141+
1409	1811-1950
	Including Inter-American Highway
	Cf. F865 Voyages to the Pacific coast following
	discovery of gold
1409.2	1951-1980
1409.3	1981-
1409.5	Antiquities (Non-Indian)
	For Indians of Latin America see E65
	History
1409.6	Chronological tables. Outlines, syllabi, etc. Questions and
	answers, etc.
	Historiography
1409.7	General works
	Biography of historians
1409.8.A2	Collective
1409.8.A3-Z	Individual, A-Z
	Subarrange each by Table F5
	Study and teaching
1409.9.A-.Z8	General works
1409.9.Z9	Audio-visual materials catalogs
1409.95.A-Z	By region or country, A-Z
	Subarrange by author
1410	General works
	Including Spain's government of her American colonies
	Including political history
1410.5	Military history
1410.6	Naval history
	By period
1411	Early to 1601
	Including colonization, treatment of Indians, Las Casas
	tracts
	For biography of Las Casas see E125.C4
	Cf. E141+ Early accounts of America
1412	1601-1830. Wars of independence, 1806-1830
1413	1830-1898

Latin America (General)
  History
    By period -- Continued
      20th century. 1898-

1414	General works
1414.2	1948-1980
1414.3	1980-

    Diplomatic history. Foreign and general relations

1415	General works

      Including relations with several countries

1416.A-Z	Relations with individual countries, A-Z

      For United States see F1418

1418	Relations with the United States

      Including relations of United States with Latin America
      Cf. E18.85 Twentieth century America
      Cf. F975 Central American, West Indian, and other
        countries protected by and having close political
        affiliations with the United States
      Cf. F1403+ Pan American Union, Pan American
        conferences
      Cf. JZ1482 Monroe Doctrine

  Elements in the population
    For interpretation see F1392.A1+

1419.A1	General works

    Including foreign elements (General), minorities, race
    conflicts and problems, etc.

1419.A2-Z	Individual, A-Z
1419.A72	Arabs
1419.A73	Aragonese
1419.A76	Armenians
1419.A84	Asians
1419.A87	Asturians
1419.B37	Basques
	Blacks see F1419.N4
1419.C26	Canary Islanders
1419.C3	Cantabrians
1419.C94	Czechs
1419.E87	Europeans
1419.F56	Finns
1419.F75	French
1419.G2	Gallegans
1419.G3	Germans
	Indians see E65
1419.I8	Italians
1419.J3	Japanese
1419.J4	Jews
1419.K67	Koreans

F1201-3799

	Latin America (General)
	Elements in the population
	Individual, A-Z -- Continued
1419.M45	Mennonites
1419.M87	Muslims
1419.N38	Navarrese
1419.N4	Negroes. Blacks
1419.P65	Poles
1419.S26	Scots
1419.S5	Slavs
1419.S63	Spaniards
	Central America
1421	Periodicals. Societies. Collections
	For Central American geographical societies see G5
1422	Congresses
	Collected works
1423	Several authors
1423.5	Individual authors
	Including collected papers, addresses, essays, etc.
1424	Gazetteers. Dictionaries
1425	Directories
	Biography
1426	Collective
	Individual (Historians) see F1435.6.A2+
	Individual (By period) see F1436.92+
1428	General works
1428.5	Juvenile works
1428.7	Pamphlets, addresses, essays, etc.
1428.8	Anecdotes, legends, pageants, etc.
	Cf. P, Literature
	Cf. GR117+ Folklore
1429	Guidebooks. Handbooks
1430	Social life and customs. Civilization. Intellectual life
	Description and travel. Views
1431	Early to 1820
	Cf. E101+ Earliest voyages and explorations
	Cf. F1230 Earliest voyages and explorations
1432	1821-1950
	Including voyages to the Pacific coast following discovery of gold
1433	1951-1980
1433.2	1981-
	Antiquities. Indians (Ancient and modern)
1434	General works
1434.2.A-Z	Topics, A-Z
1434.2.A37	Agriculture
1434.2.A55	Anthropometry

	Central America
	Antiquities. Indians (Ancient and modern)
	Topics, A-Z -- Continued
1434.2.A7	Art
1434.2.C44	Children
(1434.2.C58)	Civil rights
	see KG3001+
1434.2.C65	Commerce
1434.2.E38	Education
1434.2.F6	Folklore. Legends
1434.2.G6	Goldwork
1434.2.G68	Government relations
1434.2.H85	Hunting
1434.2.L35	Land tenure
1434.2.M36	Masks
1434.2.M4	Metalwork
1434.2.M6	Missions
1434.2.P76	Politics and government
1434.2.P8	Pottery
1434.2.R3	Religion. Mythology
1434.2.S38	Sculpture
1434.2.S62	Social conditions
1434.2.S63	Social life and customs
1434.2.W37	Wars
1434.2.W38	Water
1434.2.W65	Women
1434.3.A-Z	Tribes (other than Mayas), A-Z
	For Aztecs see F1219.1.A+
	For guidance in classification see F2230.2.A+
	Mayas
	Cf. F1445+ British Honduras
	Cf. F1465+ Guatemala
1435.A1-.A4	Periodicals. Societies
1435.A5-Z	General works
1435.1.A-Z	Local, A-Z
1435.1.A34	Abaj Takalik
1435.1.A35	Acanceh
1435.1.A36	Agua Tibia
1435.1.A37	Aguateca
1435.1.A38	Alta Verapaz
1435.1.A4	Altar de Sacrificios
1435.1.A57	Altun Ha
1435.1.B35	Balberta
1435.1.B4	Becan
1435.1.B52	Blanca Site
1435.1.B54	Blue Creek Ruin
1435.1.B6	Bonampak

F1201-
3799

Central America
Antiquities. Indians (Ancient and modern)
Mayas
Local, A-Z -- Continued

1435.1.C32	Cacaxtla
1435.1.C33	Cahal Pech
1435.1.C34	Calakmul
1435.1.C35	Campeche
1435.1.C37	Caracol
1435.1.C38	Cayo
1435.1.C39	Ceren Site
1435.1.C43	Cerros Site
1435.1.C44	Chaguite Site
1435.1.C47	Chan Kom
1435.1.C49	Chiapa de Corso Site
1435.1.C492	Chiapas
1435.1.C494	Chicanná Site
1435.1.C5	Chichén Itzá
1435.1.C54	Chinkultic
1435.1.C546	Chunchucmil Site
1435.1.C55	Cihuatán Site
1435.1.C56	Cimientos Site
1435.1.C63	Cobá
1435.1.C65	Colha
1435.1.C67	Comalcalco Site
1435.1.C7	Copan
1435.1.C76	Cozumel Island
1435.1.C84	Cuello
1435.1.D67	Dos Pilas
1435.1.D83	Dzibanché Site
1435.1.D85	Dzibilchaltún
1435.1.D87	Dzibilnocac Site
1435.1.E32	Ecab
1435.1.E37	Edzná Site
1435.1.F45	Felipe Carrillo Puerto
1435.1.H7	Holmul
1435.1.I93	Izapa Site
1435.1.J68	Joyanca Site
1435.1.K3	Kaminaljuyu
1435.1.K35	K'axob Site
1435.1.K64	Kohunlich
1435.1.L2	Labná
1435.1.L23	Laguna de On Site
1435.1.L24	Lagunita
1435.1.L64	Loltun Cave
1435.1.L83	Lubaantun
1435.1.M22	Macanché Island

Central America
   Antiquities. Indians (Ancient and modern)
     Mayas
      Local, A-Z -- Continued

1435.1.M26	Marco Gonzalez Site
1435.1.M32	Meco Site
1435.1.M5	Minanha Site
1435.1.M54	Mirador
1435.1.M58	Mixco Viejo Site
1435.1.M64	Mojarra
1435.1.M84	Mul-Chic
1435.1.N35	Naj Tunich
1435.1.N37	Naranjo
1435.1.N55	Nim Li Punit Site
1435.1.N64	Nohmul
1435.1.O94	Oxkintok
1435.1.P2	Palenque
1435.1.P25	Pataxte
1435.1.P38	Paxil
1435.1.P47	Petén
1435.1.P52	Piedras Negras Site
1435.1.P53	Pilar Site
1435.1.P55	Planchon de las Figuras
1435.1.P66	Pomoná Site (Mexico)
1435.1.P88	Puuc Region
1435.1.Q78	Quintana Roo
1435.1.Q8	Quirigua
1435.1.R56	Rio Azul Site
1435.1.R67	Rosario Valley
1435.1.S26	San Gervasio Site
1435.1.S29	Sayil
1435.1.S44	Seibal
1435.1.S92	Sumidero
1435.1.T42	Tecoh
1435.1.T48	Tíhosuco
1435.1.T5	Tikal
1435.1.T65	Tonina
1435.1.T67	Topoxté
1435.1.T7	Tortuguero Site
1435.1.T8	Tulum
1435.1.T96	Tzutzuculi Site
1435.1.U2	Uaxactun
1435.1.U65	Utatlan Site
1435.1.U7	Uxmal
1435.1.W54	Wild Cane Cay Site
1435.1.X26	Xamanha Site
1435.1.X32	Xcan Cave

F1201-
3799

	Central America
	Antiquities. Indians (Ancient and modern)
	Mayas
	Local, A-Z -- Continued
1435.1.X35	Xcaret
1435.1.X37	Xculoc Site
1435.1.X7	Xkichmook
1435.1.X73	Xkipché Site
1435.1.X77	Xtacumbilxunaan Cave
1435.1.X82	Xunantunich
1435.1.Y3	Yaxchilán
1435.1.Y39	Yaxuná Site
1435.1.Y64	Yo'okop Site
1435.1.Y89	Yucatán (State)
1435.1.Z3	Zaculeu
1435.3.A-Z	Topics, A-Z
1435.3.A37	Agriculture
1435.3.A56	Anthropometry
1435.3.A6	Architecture
1435.3.A7	Art
1435.3.A8	Astrology
1435.3.B37	Baskets
1435.3.C14	Calender. Chronology. Astronomy
1435.3.C47	Children
1435.3.C49	Chinese influences
1435.3.C57	City planning
(1435.3.C58)	Civil rights
	see KG3001+
	Codices see F1435.3.W75
1435.3.C6	Commerce
1435.3.C69	Costume. Adornment
1435.3.C75	Crimes against
1435.3.D34	Dances
1435.3.D4	Dentistry
1435.3.D64	Domestic animals
1435.3.D84	Dwellings
1435.3.E27	Economic conditions
1435.3.E37	Education
1435.3.E52	Embroidery
1435.3.E72	Ethnic identity
1435.3.E73	Ethnobiology
1435.3.E74	Ethnobotany
1435.3.E76	Ethnozoology
1435.3.E87	Extraterrestrial influences
1435.3.F57	Fishing
1435.3.F6	Folklore. Legends
1435.3.F7	Food

Central America
  Antiquities. Indians (Ancient and modern)
    Mayas
      Topics, A-Z -- Continued

1435.3.F85	Funeral customs and rites
	Government see F1435.3.P7
1435.3.H85	Hunting
1435.3.I46	Implements
1435.3.I53	Industries
1435.3.I57	Intellectual life
1435.3.J48	Jewelry
1435.3.K57	Kinship
1435.3.L35	Land tenure
	Legends see F1435.3.F6
1435.3.M3	Masks
1435.3.M32	Material culture
1435.3.M35	Mathematics. Numeration
1435.3.M4	Medicine. Hygiene
1435.3.M49	Middle Eastern influences
1435.3.M53	Missions
1435.3.M6	Mortuary customs
	Mythology see F1435.3.R3
(1435.3.N8)	Numeration
	see F1435.3.M35
1435.3.O73	Origin
1435.3.P34	Painting
1435.3.P44	Petroglyphs. Rock paintings
1435.3.P5	Philosophy
1435.3.P7	Politics and government
1435.3.P75	Population
1435.3.P8	Pottery
1435.3.R3	Religion. Mythology
1435.3.R56	Rites and ceremonies
1435.3.R6	Roads. Trails
	Rock paintings see F1435.3.P44
1435.3.S24	Salt
1435.3.S32	Science
1435.3.S34	Sculpture
1435.3.S5	Sisal hemp
1435.3.S68	Social conditions
1435.3.S7	Social life and customs
1435.3.T48	Textile fabrics
1435.3.T63	Tobacco use
1435.3.U72	Urban residence
1435.3.W2	Wars
1435.3.W55	Women
1435.3.W6	Wood carving

F1201-
3799

	Central America
	Antiquities. Indians (Ancient and modern)
	Mayas
	Topics, A-Z -- Continued
1435.3.W75	Writing. Codices
	History
1435.4	Chronological tables. Outlines, syllabi, etc. Questions and answers, etc.
	Historiography
1435.5	General works
	Biography of historians
1435.6.A2	Collective
1435.6.A3-Z	Individual, A-Z
	Subarrange each by Table F5
1435.8	Study and teaching
1436	General works
	Including political history
	General special
1436.5	Military and naval history
	Diplomatic history. Foreign and general relations
1436.7	General works
1436.8.A-Z	Relations with individual countries, A-Z
	By period
	Pre-Columbian period see F1434+
1437	1502-1821
	Including Spanish period; Audiencia of Guatemala, 1542-1821
	Including biography: Pedro de Alvarado, Pedro Arias de Avila, Juan Vázquez de Coronado, etc.
	Cf. E101+ Early explorations and discoveries
	Cf. F1232 Mexican wars of independence, 1810-1821
	Cf. F1256 Chiapas
	Cf. F1441+ English aggressions on the coast
	Cf. F1529.M9 English aggressions on the coast
1438	1821-1950
	Including annexation to and separation from Mexico, 1822-1823; Confederación de Centro América, 1823-1838/1842; other attempts at Central American unity; Clayton-Bulwer Treaty of 1850; Filibuster wars, 1855-1860; Zeledon-Wyke Treaty of 1860; Hay-Pauncefote Treaty of 1901
	Including biography: Manuel José Arce, José Francisco Barrundia, José Simeón Cañas y Villacorta, Francisco Morazán, Rafael Heliodoro Valle, etc.
	Cf. F1526.27 Walker in Nicaragua

	Central America
	History
	By period -- Continued
1439	1951-1979
	Including organization of Central American States (Charter of Salvador, 1951)
1439.5	1979-
1440.A1-Z	Elements in the population
	Including foreign elements (General), minorities, race conflicts and problems, etc.
	For interpretation see F1392.A1+
1440.A1	General works
1440.A2-Z	Individual elements, A-Z
1440.A54	Americans
1440.B55	Blacks
1440.C84	Cubans
1440.G3	Germans
	Indians see F1434+
1440.I73	Italians
1440.J48	Jews
1440.M55	Minoans
	Negroes see F1440.B55
1440.P34	Palestinian Arabs
1440.S7	Spaniards
	British Honduras. Belize (Belice)
1441	Periodicals. Societies. Collections
1441.3	Congresses
	Collected works
1441.5	Several authors
1441.6	Individual authors
	Including collected papers, addresses, essays
1441.8	Museums. Exhibitions, exhibits
1442	Gazetteers. Dictionaries. Geographic names
1442.3	Directories
	Biography
1442.7	Collective
	Individual (Historians) see F1445.7.A2+
	Individual (By period) see F1446.92+
1443	General works
1443.2	Juvenile works
1443.3	Pamphlets, addresses, essays, etc.
1443.4	Anecdotes, legends, pageants, etc.
	Cf. P, Literature
	Cf. GR117+ Folklore
1443.5	Guidebooks. Handbooks
1443.7	Historic monuments (General)
	For Indian antiquities see F1445+

F1201-3799

	Central America
	British Honduras. Belize (Belice) -- Continued
1443.8	Social life and customs. Civilization. Intellectual life
	Including national characteristics
	Description and travel. Views
1444	Early to 1950
1444.2	1951-1980
1444.3	1981-
	Antiquities. Indians (Ancient and modern)
	Including Mayas
1445	General works
1445.1.A-Z	Local, A-Z
	For individual Mayan archaeological sites see F1435.1.A+
1445.2.A-Z	Tribes, A-Z
	Black Carib Indians see F1505.2.C3
	Kekchi see F1465.2.K5
	Mayas see F1445+
1445.3.A-Z	Topics, A-Z
	e.g.
	For topics pertaining to the Maya only see F1435.3.A+
1445.3.P6	Pottery
	History
1445.5	Chronological tables. Outlines, syllabi, etc. Questions and answers, etc.
	Historiography
1445.6	General works
	Biography of historians
1445.7.A2	Collective
1445.7.A3-Z	Individual, A-Z
	Subarrange each by Table F5
1445.8	Study and teaching
1446	General works
	Including political history
1446.3	General special
	Diplomatic history. Foreign and general relations
1446.4	General works
1446.5.A-Z	Relations with individual countries, A-Z
	By period
	Pre-Columbian period see F1445+

	Central America
	British Honduras. Belize (Belice)
	History
	By period -- Continued
1447	1506-1884
	Including self-governing British settlement, 1638-1786; colony with lieutenant governor under governor of Jamaica, 1862-1884; Crown colony, 1871; separation from Jamaica, 1884
	For disputes over claims of Spain, Guatemala, and Mexico see F1449.B7
1447.5	1884-1945
1448	1945-
	For dispute over claim of Guatemala see F1449.B7G1+
1449.A-Z	Regions, districts, etc., A-Z
1449.A53	Ambergris Cay
1449.B4	Belize
	Including Turneffe Island
1449.B7	Boundaries
1449.B7A1-.B7A9	General works
1449.B7G1-.B7G9	Guatemala
1449.B7M1-.B7M9	Mexico
1449.B7S1-.B7S9	Spain
1449.S24	Saint George's Cay
1449.T6	Toledo
	Turneffe Island see F1449.B4
1456.A-Z	Cities, towns, etc., A-Z
	e.g.
	Cf. F1445.1.A+ Indian local history and antiquities
1456.B4	Belize
	Elements in the population
	Including foreign elements (General), minorities, race conflicts and problems, etc.
	For interpretation see F1392.A1+
1457.A1	General works
1457.A2-Z	Individual elements, A-Z
1457.B4	Belgians
1457.B55	Blacks
	Indians see F1445+
1457.M45	Mennonites
	Negroes see F1457.B55
	Guatemala
	For Audiencia or captain-generalcy of Guatemala before 1821 see F1437
1461	Periodicals. Societies. Collections
	Collected works

F1201-3799

	Central America
	Guatemala
	Collected works -- Continued
1461.5	Several authors
1461.6	Individual authors
	Including collected papers, addresses, essays
1461.8	Museums. Exhibitions, exhibits
1462	Gazetteers. Dictionaries. Geographic names
1462.3	Directories
	Biography
1462.7	Collective
	Individual (Historians) see F1465.7.A+
	Individual (By period) see F1466.39+
1463	General works
1463.2	Juvenile works
1463.3	Pamphlets, addresses, essays, etc.
1463.4	Anecdotes, legends, pageants, etc.
	Cf. P, Literature
	Cf. GR117+ Folklore
1463.5	Social life and customs. Civilization. Intellectual life
	Including national characteristics
1463.6	Guidebooks. Handbooks
1463.7	Historic monuments (General)
	For Indian antiquities see F1465+
	Description and travel. Views
1464	Early to 1950
1464.2	1951-1980
1464.3	1981-
	Antiquities. Indians (Ancient and modern)
1465	General works
	Including Mayas
	Popul vuh
	Class here translations and studies of the contents
	For original text and linguistic studies see
	PM4231.Z6
(1465.P8)	Quiché text
	see PM4231.Z6
1465.P812-.P819	Translations. By language (alphabetically)
	Selections
	Quiché text see PM4231.Z6
1465.P82512- .P82519	Translations. By language (alphabetically)
1465.P83	Criticism
	For linguistic studies see PM4231.Z6

	Central America
	Guatemala
	Antiquities. Indians (Ancient and modern) -- Continued
1465.1.A-Z	Local, A-Z
	e.g.
	For individual Mayan archaeological sites see F1435.1.A+
1465.1.A8	Atitlán, Lake
1465.1.C5	Chinautla
1465.2.A-Z	Tribes, A-Z
1465.2.A23	Achi
1465.2.A34	Akatek
1465.2.A84	Awakateko
	Black Carib see F1505.2.C3
1465.2.C3	Cakchikel
1465.2.C5	Chorti
1465.2.I87	Itza
1465.2.I95	Ixil
1465.2.J3	Jacalteca
1465.2.K36	Kanjobal
1465.2.K5	Kekchi
1465.2.K68	Kowoj
	Lacandon see F1221.L2
1465.2.M3	Mam
1465.2.M65	Mopan
	Pipil see F1485.2.P5
1465.2.P6	Pokomam
1465.2.Q5	Quichés
(1465.2.R32)	Rabinal Achi
	Rabinal Achi Indians
1465.2.T9	Tzutuhil
1465.2.X5	Xinca
1465.3.A-Z	Topics, A-Z
	For topics pertaining to the Mayas only see F1435.3.A+
1465.3.A37	Agriculture
1465.3.A7	Art
(1465.3.C58)	Civil rights
	see KGD1+
1465.3.C77	Commerce
1465.3.C8	Costume. Adornment
1465.3.D3	Dance
1465.3.E2	Economic conditions
1465.3.E25	Education
1465.3.E84	Ethnic identity
1465.3.F6	Folklore. Legends
1465.3.G6	Government relations

F1201-3799

Central America
  Guatemala
    Antiquities. Indians (Ancient and modern)
      Topics, A-Z -- Continued

1465.3.I5	Industries
1465.3.M36	Masks
1465.3.M4	Medicine
1465.3.M57	Missions
1465.3.P64	Politics and government
1465.3.P68	Pottery
1465.3.R4	Religion. Mythology
1465.3.R44	Removal
1465.3.S6	Social conditions
1465.3.S62	Social life and customs
1465.3.T3	Taxation
1465.3.T4	Textile fabrics
1465.3.W37	Wars

  History
1465.5	Chronological tables. Outlines, syllabi, etc. Questions and answers, etc.

    Historiography
1465.6	General works

      Biography of historians
1465.7.A2	Collective
1465.7.A3-Z	Individual, A-Z

        Subarrange each by Table F5
1465.8	Study and teaching
1466	General works

      Including political history
    General special
1466.1	Military and naval history

      Diplomatic history. Foreign and general relations
        Cf. F1469.B7 Boundaries
1466.2	General works
1466.3.A-Z	Relations with individual countries, A-Z
1466.35	Other (not A-Z)

    By period
      Pre-Columbian period see F1465+
1466.4	1523-1838

        Including end of Spanish rule, 1821; annexation to and separation from Mexico, 1822-1823; Confederación de Centro América, 1823-1838/1842; earthquake of 1773

Central America
Guatemala
History
By period -- Continued

1466.45	1838-1945

Established as a republic, April 17, 1839; era of despots; wars with El Salvador; revolutions of 1898, 1906, 1920, 1930, 1944, etc.; epidemic of cholera, 1837; earthquakes of 1902, 1917, 1918

Including biography: Justo Rufino Barrios, Rafael Carrera, Lázaro Chacón, Manuel Estrada Cabrera, Miguel García Granados, Jorge Ubico, etc.

Cf. D731+ World War II, 1939-1945
Cf. F1507.5 Wars with Honduras

1466.5	1945-1985

Including Revolution of 1954

Including biography: Jacobo Arbenz Guzmán, Juan José Arévalo, Carlos Castillo Armas, etc.

1466.7	1985-
1469.A-Z	Regions, departments, etc., A-Z

Alta Vera Paz see F1469.V3
Baja Vera Paz see F1469.V4

1469.B7	Boundaries
1469.B7A1-.B7A5	General

British Honduras see F1449.B7

1469.B7A6-.B7Z	Honduras

Mexico see F1249
El Salvador see F1489.B7

1469.G9	Guatemala
1469.H8	Huehuetenango
1469.I9	Izabal

Cf. F1469.S2 Santo Tomas (District)

1469.J8	Jutiapa (Dept.)
1469.M68	Motagua River
1469.P4	Petén

Including Usumacinta River

1469.Q5	Quezaltenango
1469.S13	Sacatepéquez
1469.S17	San Marcos
1469.S2	Santo Tomas (District)
1469.S64	Sololá

Including Lake Atitlán

1469.T7	Totonicapán
1469.V3	Vera Paz, Alta
1469.V4	Vera Paz, Baja

Including former department of Vera Paz

1469.Z3	Zacapa

F1201-3799

	Central America
	Guatemala -- Continued
1476.A-Z	Cities, towns, etc., A-Z
	e.g.
	Cf. F1465.1.A+ Indian local history and antiquities
1476.A5	Antigua
1476.G9	Guatemala (City)
1476.P8	Puerto Barrios
1476.Q8	Quezaltenango
	Elements in the population
	For interpretation see F1392.A1+
1477.A1	General works
	Including foreign elements (General), minorities, race conflicts and problems, etc.
1477.A2-Z	Individual elements
	e.g.
1477.G3	Germans
	Indians see F1465+
1477.L33	Ladino (Latin American people)
	Salvador (El Salvador)
1481	Periodicals. Societies. Collections
	Collected works
1481.5	Several authors
1481.6	Individual authors
	Including collected papers, addresses, essays, etc.
1481.8	Museums. Exhibitions, exhibits
1482	Gazetteers. Dictionaries. Geographic names
1482.3	Directories
	Biography
1482.7	Collective
	Individual see F1485.7.A2+
1483	General works
1483.2	Juvenile works
1483.3	Pamphlets, addresses, essays, etc.
1483.4	Anecdotes, legends, pageants, etc.
	Cf. P, Literature
	Cf. GR117+ Folklore
1483.5	Guidebooks. Handbooks
1483.7	Historic monuments (General)
	For Indian antiquities see F1485+
1483.8	Social life and customs. Civilization. Intellectual life
	Including national characteristics
	Description and travel. Views
1484	Early to 1950
1484.2	1951-1980
1484.3	1981-
	Antiquities. Indians (Ancient and modern)

	Central America
	Salvador (El Salvador)
	Antiquities. Indians (Ancient and modern) -- Continued
1485	General works
1485.1.A-Z	Local, A-Z
1485.1.C8	Cuscatlán
1485.2.A-Z	Tribes, A-Z
	e.g.
	Matagalpa see F1525.2.M3
1485.2.P5	Pipil
1485.3.A-Z	Topics, A-Z
	For topics pertaining to the Mayas only see F1435.3.A+
	Government see F1485.3.P7
1485.3.N35	Names
1485.3.P7	Politics and government
1485.3.P8	Pottery
1485.3.S6	Social conditions
	History
1485.5	Chronological tables. Outlines, syllabi, etc. Questions and answers, etc.
	Historiography
1485.6	General works
	Biography of historians
1485.7.A2	Collective
1485.7.A3-Z	Individual, A-Z
	Subarrange each by Table F5
1485.8	Study and teaching
1486	General works
	Including political history
	General special
1486.1	Military and naval history
	Diplomatic history. Foreign and general relations
	Cf. F1489.B7 Boundaries
1486.2	General works
1486.3.A-Z	Relations with individual countries, A-Z
1486.9	Other (not A-Z)
	By period
	Pre-Columbian period see F1485+
1487	1524-1838
	Including end of Spanish rule, 1821; appeal to United States for annexation, 1822; Mexican rule, 1822-1823; Confederación de Centro América, 1823-1838/1842
	Including biography: José Matías Delgado, etc.

F1201-3799

	Central America
	Salvador (El Salvador)
	History
	By period -- Continued
1487.5	1838-1944. Martinez regime, 1931-1944
	Including period of internal struggles and changing constitution; wars with Guatemala; conflicts with Honduras; Revolt of 1944
	Including biography: Manuel Enrique Araujo, Maximiliano Hernandez Martinez, Alfonso Quinonez Molina, Pio Romero Bosque, etc.
1488	1944-1979
	Including earthquake of May 6, 1951
	Including biography: Salvador Castañeda Castro, Oscar Osorio, etc.
	1979-1992
1488.3	General works
	Biography
1488.4	Collective
1488.42.A-Z	Individual, A-Z
	Subarrange each by Table F5
	1992-
1488.5	General works
	Biography
1488.52	Collective
1488.53.A-Z	Individual, A-Z
	Subarrange each by Table F5
1489.A-Z	Regions, departments, etc., A-Z
	e.g.
1489.B7	Boundaries
1489.B7A1-.B7A9	General
1489.B7G1-.B7G9	Guatemala
1489.B7H1-.B7H9	Honduras
1489.C8	Cuscatlán
1489.L3	La Unión
1489.M46	Metapán (District)
1489.S2	San Salvador
	Unión see F1489.L3
1489.U8	Usulután
1496.A-Z	Cities, towns, etc., A-Z
	e.g.
	Cf. F1485.1.A+ Indian local history and antiquities
1496.S2	San Salvador
	Including fire of August 8, 1951
1496.S35	Santa Ana

	Central America
	Salvador (El Salvador) -- Continued
	Elements in the population
	Including foreign elements (General), minorities, race conflicts and problems, etc.
	For interpretation see F1392.A1+
1497.A1	General works
1497.A2-Z	Individual elements, A-Z
1497.B55	Blacks
	Indians see F1485+
	Negroes see F1497.B55
	Honduras
1501	Periodicals. Societies. Collections
	Collected works
1501.5	Several authors
1501.6	Individual authors
	Including collected papers, addresses, essays, etc.
1501.8	Museums. Exhibitions, exhibits
1502	Gazetteers. Dictionaries. Geographic names
1502.3	Directories
	Biography
1502.7	Collective
	Individual see F1505.7.A2+
1503	General works
1503.2	Juvenile works
1503.3	Pamphlets, addresses, essays, etc.
1503.4	Anecdotes, legends, pageants, etc.
	Cf. P, Literature
	Cf. GR117+ Folklore
1503.5	Guidebooks. Handbooks
1503.7	Historic monuments (General)
	For Indian antiquities see F1504.5+
1503.8	Social life and customs. Civilization. Intellectual life
	Including national characteristics
1503.9	Geography
1504	Description and travel. Views
	Antiquities. Indians (Ancient and modern)
1504.5	Museums. Exhibitions
1505	General works
1505.1.A-Z	Local, A-Z
	e.g.
1505.1.T2	Tenampua
1505.2.A-Z	Tribes, A-Z
	e.g.
1505.2.C3	Carib (Black)
1505.2.L4	Lenca
	Matagalpa see F1525.2.M3

F1201-3799

	Central America
	Honduras
	Antiquities. Indians (Ancient and modern)
	Tribes, A-Z -- Continued
	Miskito see F1529.M9
1505.2.P3	Paya
	Sumo see F1525.2.S8
1505.2.T38	Tawahka
1505.2.X5	Xicaque
1505.3.A-Z	Topics, A-Z
	For topics pertaining to the Mayas only see F1435.3.A+
1505.3.A72	Architecture
1505.3.P48	Petroglyphs. Rock paintings
1505.3.P57	Population
1505.3.P6	Pottery
	Rock paintings see F1505.3.P48
1505.3.S63	Social life and customs
	History
1505.5	Chronological tables. Outlines, syllabi, etc. Questions and answers
	Historiography
1505.6	General works
	Biography of historians
1505.7.A2	Collective
1505.7.A3-Z	Individual, A-Z
	Subarrange each by Table F5
1505.8	Study and teaching
1506	General works
	Including political history
	General special
1506.2	Military and naval history
	Diplomatic history. Foreign and general relations
	Cf. F1509.B7 Boundaries
1506.3	General works
1506.4.A-Z	Relations with individual countries, A-Z
1506.9	Other (not A-Z)
	By period
	Pre-Columbian period see F1504.5+
1507	1502-1538
	End of Spanish rule, 1821; Mexican rule, 1822-1823; Confederación de Centro América, 1823-1838/1842

Central America
  Honduras
    History
      By period -- Continued

1507.5	1838-1933
	Established as a republic, October 26, 1838; won Bay Islands and Mosquito coast, 1859; Walker's filibustering expedition, 1860; Insurrection of Amapala, 1910; wars with Guatemala and El Salvador; United States intervention, 1911, 1913, etc.
	Including biography: Manuel Bonilla, Policarpo Bonilla, Juan Nepomuceno Fernández, Marco Aurelio Soto, Vicente Tosta, etc.
	1933-1982
1508	General works
	Biography
1508.2	Collective
1508.22.A-Z	Individual, A-Z
	Subarrange each by Table F5
	1982-
1508.3	General works
	Biography
1508.32	Collective
1508.33.A-Z	Individual, A-Z
	Subarrange each by Table F5
1509.A-Z	Regions, departments, etc., A-Z
1509.B3	Bay Islands (Department)
	Including Swan Islands (Islas del Cisne)
1509.B7	Boundaries
1509.B7A1-.B7A5	General
	Guatemala see F1469.B7
1509.B7A6-.B7Z	Nicaragua
	El Salvador see F1489.B7
1509.C4	Choluteca
	Cisne, Islas del see F1509.B3
1509.C6	Colón
	Cf. F1509.M9 Mosquitia (District)
1509.M9	Mosquitia (District)
	Cf. F1529.M9 Mosquito Coast of Nicaragua
1509.O4	Olancho
	Swan Islands see F1509.B3
1509.T2	Tegucigalpa (Province)
1509.U4	Ulua (Lua) River and Valley
1509.V2	Valle
	Including Tigre Island
1509.Y6	Yoro

	Central America
	Honduras -- Continued
1516.A-Z	Cities, towns, etc., A-Z
	e.g.
	Cf. F1505.1.A+ Indian local history and antiquities
1516.C72	Comayagua
1516.G7	Gracias
1516.S3	San Pedro Sula
1516.T4	Tegucigalpa
	Elements in the population
	Including foreign elements (General), minorities, race conflicts and problems, etc.
	For interpretation see F1392.A1+
1517.A1	General works
1517.A2-Z	Individual elements, A-Z
1517.A73	Arabs
1517.B55	Blacks
	Indians see F1504.5+
	Negroes see F1517.B55
	Nicaragua
1521	Periodicals. Societies. Collections
	Collected works
1521.5	Several authors
1521.6	Individual authors
	Including collected papers, addresses, essays, etc.
1521.8	Museums. Exhibitions, exhibits
1522	Gazetteers. Dictionaries. Geographic names
1522.3	Directories
	Biography
1522.7	Collective
	Individual see F1525.7.A2+
1523	General works
1523.2	Juvenile works
1523.3	Pamphlets, addresses, essays, etc.
1523.4	Anecdotes, legends, pageants, etc.
	Cf. P, Literature
	Cf. GR117+ Folklore
1523.5	Guidebooks. Handbooks
1523.7	Historic monuments (General)
	For Indian antiquities see F1525+
1523.8	Social life and customs. Civilization. Intellectual life
	Including national characteristics
	Description and travel. Views
1524	Through 1980
1524.3	1981-
	Antiquities. Indians (Ancient and modern)
1525	General works

	Central America
	Nicaragua
	Antiquities. Indians (Ancient and modern) -- Continued
1525.1.A-Z	Local, A-Z
	e.g.
1525.1.Z3	Zapatera Island
1525.2.A-Z	Tribes, A-Z
	Carib (Black) see F1505.2.C3
	Chiapanec see F1221.C5
1525.2.C48	Chorotega
	Lenca see F1505.2.L4
1525.2.M3	Matagalpa
	Miskito see F1529.M9
1525.2.N5	Nicarao
1525.2.R3	Rama
1525.2.S7	Subtiaba
1525.2.S8	Sumo
	Terraba see F1545.2.T4
1525.2.U4	Ulva
1525.3.A-Z	Topics, A-Z
1525.3.A7	Art
1525.3.C84	Cultural assimilation
1525.3.E38	Education
1525.3.E74	Ethnic identity
1525.3.E76	Ethnobiology
1525.3.G68	Government relations
1525.3.L35	Land tenure
1525.3.M43	Medicine
1525.3.M57	Missions
	Mythology and religion see F1525.3.R44
1525.3.N35	Names
1525.3.P6	Pottery
1525.3.R44	Religion. Mythology
1525.3.S38	Sculpture
1525.3.S63	Social conditions
	History
1525.5	Chronological tables. Outlines, syllabi, etc. Questions and answers, etc.
	Historiography
1525.6	General works
	Biography of historians
1525.7.A2	Collective
1525.7.A3-Z	Individual, A-Z
	Subarrange each by Table F5
1525.8	Study and teaching
1526	General works
	Including political history

F1201-
3799

	Central America
	Nicaragua
	History -- Continued
	General special
1526.1	Military and naval history
	Diplomatic history. Foreign and general relations
	Cf. F1529.B7 Boundaries
1526.2	General works
1526.22.A-Z	Relations with individual countries, A-Z
1526.24	Other (not A-Z)
	By period
	Pre-Columbian period see F1525+
1526.25	1522-1838
	Including end of Spanish rule, 1821; Mexican rule, 1822-1823; Confederación de Centro América, 1823-1838/1842; rivalry between León and Granada; English invasion, 1780-1781
1526.27	1838-1909
	Including foreign intervention, 1848- ; Filibuster War, 1855-1860 (Battle of Rivas, 1856); transfer of Mosquito Territory by Great Britain, 1893; Nicaragua Canal (Cf. TC784)
	Including biography: Pedro Joaquín Chamorro, Roberto Sacasa, William Walker, José Santos Zelaya, etc.
	Cf. F1438 Filibusters in Central America
	Cf. F1529.M9 Mosquito coast and the English protectorate
	Cf. F1536.S2 Bombardment of Greytown, 1856
1526.3	1909-1937
	Including revolts and revolutions of 1909-1910, 1912, 1916, 1926-1929, etc.; United States intervention, 1909-1933; Bryan-Chamorro Treaty, 1916
	Including biography: Emiliano Chamorro, Adolfo Díaz, Juan Bautista Sacasa, Augusto César Sandino, etc.
1527	1937-1979
	Including invasion from El Salvador, 1944; Inter-American Highway
	Including biography: Anastasio Somoza, etc.
	Cf. D731+ World War II, 1939-1945
	1979-
1528	General works
	Biography
1528.2	Collective
1528.22.A-Z	Individual, A-Z
	Subarrange each by Table F5
1529.A-Z	Regions, departments, etc., A-Z
	Atlantic Coast see F1529.M9

	Central America
	Nicaragua
	Regions, departments, etc., A-Z -- Continued
1529.B7	Boundaries
	General
1529.B7A6-.B7Z	Costa Rica
	Honduras see F1509.B7
	Saint Andrews Island see F2281.S15
1529.C53	Chontales
1529.J4	Jinotega
1529.M9	Mosquitia (Mosquito Coast). Atlantic Coast, etc.

Including Mosquito Reservation and Miskito Indians

Cf. F1509.M9 Mosquitia (District) of Honduras

Cf. F1526.27 Transfer of Mosquito Territory by Great Britain, 1893

1529.N5	Nicaragua, Lake, region
1529.S35	San Juan River and Valley

Cf. F1549.S17 Costa Rica

1529.Z4	Zelaya

Cf. F1529.M9 Mosquitia

1536.A-Z	Cities, towns, etc., A-Z

e.g.

Cf. F1525.1.A+ Indian local history and antiquities

1536.D5	Diriamba
1536.G72	Granada

Cf. F1526.25 Early History

1536.L4	León

Cf. F1526.25 Early history

1536.M26	Managua
1536.S2	San Juan del Norte. Greytown
	Elements in the population

Including foreign elements (General), minorities, race conflicts and problems, etc.

For interpretation see F1392.A1+

1537.A1	General works
1537.A2-Z	Individual elements, A-Z
1537.A5	Americans
1537.B55	Blacks
1537.G47	Germans
	Indians see F1525+
	Negroes see F1537.B55
	Costa Rica
1541	Periodicals. Societies. Collections
	Collected works
1541.5	Several authors
1541.6	Individual authors

Including collected papers, addresses, essays, etc.

	Central America
	Costa Rica -- Continued
1541.8	Museums. Exhibitions, exhibits
1542	Gazetteers. Dictionaries. Geographic names
1542.3	Directories
	Biography
1542.7	Collective
	Individual see F1545.7.A2+
1543	General works
1543.2	Juvenile works
1543.3	Pamphlets, addresses, essays, etc.
1543.4	Anecdotes, legends, pageants, etc.
	Cf. P, Literature
	Cf. GR117+ Folklore
1543.5	Guidebooks. Handbooks
1543.7	Historic monuments (General)
	For Indian antiquities see F1545+
1543.8	Social life and customs. Civilization. Intellectual life
	Including national characteristics
1543.9	Geography
1544	Description and travel. Views
	Antiquities. Indians (Ancient and modern)
1545	General works
1545.1.A-Z	Local, A-Z
	e.g.
1545.1.V6	Volcán Irazú
1545.15	Museums. Exhibitions
1545.2.A-Z	Tribes, A-Z
1545.2.B6	Boruca
1545.2.B7	Bribri
1545.2.C33	Cabecar
1545.2.C48	Chorotega
1545.2.G77	Guatuso
	Guaymi see F1545.2.G8
1545.2.G8	Guetar
1545.2.M3	Mangue
1545.2.T4	Terraba
1545.3.A-Z	Topics, A-Z
1545.3.A7	Art
1545.3.E38	Education
1545.3.F6	Folklore. Legends
1545.3.G65	Goldwork
1545.3.J48	Jewelry
1545.3.L34	Land tenure
1545.3.P57	Politics and government
1545.3.P6	Pottery
1545.3.R4	Religion. Mythology

Central America
Costa Rica
Antiquities. Indians (Ancient and modern)
Topics, A-Z -- Continued
1545.3.R44	Reservations
1545.3.S35	Sculpture
1545.3.W2	Warfare

History
1545.5	Chronological tables. Outlines, syllabi, etc. Questions and answers, etc.

Historiography
1545.6	General works

Biography of historians
1545.7.A2	Collective
1545.7.A3-1545.Z	Individual, A-Z

Subarrange each by Table F5
1545.8	Study and teaching
1546	General works

Including political history
General special
1546.2	Military and naval history

Diplomatic history. Foreign and general relations
For boundary disputes see F1549.B7
1546.3	General works
1546.4.A-Z	Relations with individual countries, A-Z
1546.9	Other (not A-Z)

By period
Pre-Columbian period see F1545+
1547	1502-1838

Including end of Spanish rule, 1821; Mexican rule, 1822-1823; Confederación de Centro América, 1823-1838/1842
1547.5	1838-1948

Including revolutions of 1917, 1919, 1948; Inter-American Highway

Including biography: Tomás Guardia, Rafael Iglesias, Ricardo Jiménez, Juan Rafael Mora, Teodoro Picado Michalski, Bernardo Soto, etc.
1548	1948-1986

Including biography: José Figueres, Otilio Ulate Blanco, etc.

1986-
1548.2	General works

Biography
1548.22	Collective
1548.23.A-Z	Individual, A-Z

Subarrange each by Table F5

F1201-3799

	Central America
	Costa Rica -- Continued
1549.A-Z	Regions, provinces, cantons, etc., A-Z
1549.B7	Boundaries
1549.B7A1-.B7A29	General
	Nicaragua see F1549.B7
1549.B7A3-.B7Z	Panama
	Including ancient Costa Rica-Columbia boundary
1549.C6	Cocos Island
1549.D8	Golfo Dulce (Osa Gulf)
1549.G9	Guanacaste
1549.H5	Heredia
	Including Sarapiqui River
1549.I7	Irazú Volcano
1549.L55	Limón (Province)
1549.N5	Nicoya Peninsula
	Osa Gulf see F1549.D8
1549.O83	Osa Peninsula
1549.R5	Rio Grande de Térraba
1549.S15	San José
1549.S17	San Juan River and Valley
	Cf. F1529.S35 Nicaragua
1549.T13	Talamanca (District)
	Térraba River and Valley see F1549.R5
1556.A-Z	Cities, towns, etc., A-Z
	e.g.
	Cf. F1545.1.A+ Indian local history and antiquities
1556.A6	Alajuela
1556.C3	Cartago
	Including earthquake of 1910
1556.L5	Limón
1556.S2	San José
	Elements in the population
	For interpretation see F1392.A1+
1557.A1	General works
1557.A2-Z	Individual elements, A-Z
1557.B55	Blacks
1557.C66	Colombians
1557.G3	Germans
	Indians see F1545+
1557.J4	Jews
1557.L42	Lebanese
	Negroes see F1557.B55
1557.N5	Nicaraguans
1557.S7	Spaniards
	Panama
1561	Periodicals. Societies. Collections

	Central America
	Panama -- Continued
	Collected works
1561.5	Several authors
1561.6	Individual authors
	Including collected papers, addresses, essays, etc.
1561.8	Museums. Exhibitions, exhibits
1562	Gazetteers. Dictionaries. Geographic names
1562.3	Directories
	Biography
1562.7	Collective
	Individual see F1565.7.A2+
1563	General works
	Cf. F1569.C2 Canal Zone
1563.2	Juvenile works
1563.3	Pamphlets, addresses, essays, etc.
1563.4	Anecdotes, legends, pageants, etc.
	Cf. P, Literature
	Cf. GR117+ Folklore
1563.5	Guidebooks. Handbooks
1563.7	Historic monuments (General)
	For Indian antiquities see F1565+
1563.8	Social life and customs. Civilization. Intellectual life
	Including national characteristics
	Description and travel. Views
1564	Early to 1950
1564.2	1951-1980
1564.3	1981-
	Antiquities. Indians (Ancient and modern)
1565	General works
1565.1.A-Z	Local, A-Z
	e.g.
1565.1.C6	Coclé
1565.1.D26	Darien
1565.1.V47	Veraguas
1565.2.A-Z	Tribes, A-Z
	Boruca see F1545.2.B6
1565.2.C77	Cueva
1565.2.C8	Cuna
1565.2.D6	Dorask
1565.2.G8	Guaymi
	Terraba see F1545.2.T4
1565.2.W38	Waunana
1565.3.A-Z	Topics, A-Z
1565.3.A7	Art
1565.3.F64	Folklore
1565.3.G68	Government relations

F1201-3799

	Central America
	Panama
	Antiquities. Indians (Ancient and modern)
	Topics, A-Z -- Continued
1565.3.I54	Industries
1565.3.M5	Migrations
	Music (History) see ML3571+
1565.3.P45	Philosophy
1565.3.T49	Textile fabrics
	History
1565.5	Chronological tables. Outlines, syllabi, etc. Questions and answers, etc.
	Historiography
1565.6	General works
	Biography of historians
1565.7.A2	Collective
1565.7.A3-1565.Z	Individual, A-Z
	Subarrange each by Table F5
1565.8	Study and teaching
1566	General works
	Including political history
	For boundary disputes see F1569.B7
	General special
1566.2	Military history
	Diplomatic history. Foreign and general relations
	Cf. F1569.B7 Boundaries
1566.3	General works
1566.4.A-Z	Relations with individual countries, A-Z
1566.44	Other (not A-Z)
	By period
	Pre-Columbian period see F1565+
1566.45	1501-1903
	Including end of Spanish rule, 1821; part of Greater Colombia (Colombian Federation), 1821-1831; under New Granada (later Colombia), 1831-1903; independent in 1841 and 1857; secessionist revolts in 1830, 1831, 1840, 1895, 1898-1903; Massacre of 1856; Panama expeditions, 1741, 1875, 1885
1566.5	1903-1952
	Including secession from Colombia, 1903; Hay-Bunau-Varilla Treaty of 1903; Hay-Herrán Treaty of 1903; under protection of the United States, 1903-1936; revolutions of 1931, 1951
	Including biography: Manuel Amador Guerrero; Arnulfo Arias Madrid; Pablo Arosemena; Belisario Porras, etc.

	Central America
	Panama
	History
	By period -- Continued
1567	1952-1981
	Including biography: José Antonio Remón, etc.
	1981-
1567.4	General works
	Biography
1567.5	Collective
1567.6.A-Z	Individual, A-Z
	Subarrange each by Table F5
1569.A-Z	Regions, provinces, etc., A-Z
1569.B6	Bocas del Toro
	Including Laguna de Chiriquí
1569.B7	Boundaries
1569.B7A1-.B7A5	General
1569.B7A6-.B7A7	Canal Zone
1569.B7A8-.B7Z	Colombia
	Costa Rica see F1549.B7
	Caledonia (Scots' Colony) see F2281.D2
1569.C2	Canal Zone. Panama Canal
	Including Chagres River
	Cf. F1569.B7 Panama boundary
	Cf. TC774+ Panama Canal (Construction and maintenance)
	Chagres River see F1569.C2
1569.C5	Chiriquí
	For Laguna de Chiriqui see F1569.B6
1569.C6	Coclé
1569.C7	Colón
1569.D3	Darién
	Cf. F2281.D2 Scots' Colony of Darien
	Morro Island see F1569.P3
1569.P3	Panama
	Including Isla Taboga (Morro Island), Pearl Islands
	For Darién Province see F1569.D3
1569.P35	Panama Bay. Gulf of Panama
	Pearl Islands (Islas de las Perlas) see F1569.P3
1569.S3	San Blas coast
	Scots' Colony of Darien see F2281.D2
	Isla Taboga see F1569.P3
1569.V4	Veraguas (Veragua)
1576.A-Z	Cities, towns, etc., A-Z
	e.g.
	Cf. F1565.1.A+ Indian local history and antiquities
1576.C7	Colón

F1201-3799

	Central America
	Panama
	Cities, towns, etc., A-Z -- Continued
1576.P2	Panama
	Elements in the population
	Including foreign elements (General), minorities, race conflicts and problems
	For interpretation see F1392.A1+
1577.A1	General works
1577.A2-Z	Individual elements, A-Z
1577.B55	Blacks
1577.C48	Chinese
1577.E37	East Indians
	Indians see F1565.1.A+
1577.J4	Jews
	Negroes see F1577.B55
	Caribbean area see F2155+
	West Indies
1601	Periodicals. Societies. Collections
	Including conferences, congresses, etc.
	Collected works
1602	Several authors
1603	Individual authors
	Including collected papers, addresses, essays, etc.
1604	Gazetteers. Dictionaries. Geographic names
1606	Directories
	Biography
1607	Collective
	Individual (Historians) see F1620.5.A2+
	Individual (General) see F1621
	Individual (By period) see F1623
1608	General works
1608.3	Juvenile works
1608.5	Pamphlets, addresses, essays, etc.
1608.7	Anecdotes, legends, pageants, etc.
	Cf. P, Literature
	Cf. GR120+ Folklore
1609	Guidebooks. Handbooks
1609.3	Historic monuments (General)
	For Indian antiquities see F1619+
1609.5	Social life and customs. Civilization. Intellectual life
	Including characteristics of the people
1609.9	West Indians in foreign countries (General)
	For West Indians in a particular country, see the country
	Description and travel. Views
1610	Early to 1809
	Cf. E141+ Descriptive accounts of America to 1810

West Indies
    Description and travel. Views -- Continued

1611	1810-1950
1612	1951-1980
1613	1981-

    Antiquities. Indians (Ancient and modern)
        Works on the aboriginal peooples and antiquities of a group of
          islands or an individual island are classed with the group of
          islands or the individual island

1619	General works
1619.2.A-Z	Tribes, A-Z
	e.g.
	Arawak Indians see F2230.2.A7
	Carib Indians see F2001
	Lucayan Indians see F1655
1619.2.S25	Saladoid culture
1619.2.T3	Taino
1619.3.A-Z	Topics, A-Z
1619.3.A84	Astronomy
1619.3.C65	Commerce
1619.3.E83	Ethnic identity. Ethnicity
	Ethnicity see F1619.3.E83
1619.3.E85	Ethnobotany
1619.3.F6	Folklore. Legends
1619.3.G68	Government relations
1619.3.I6	Implements (Celts, axes, etc.)
1619.3.P6	Pottery
1619.3.S38	Sculpture
	History
1620	Chronological tables. Outlines, syllabi, etc. Questions and
	answers, etc.
	Historiography
1620.3	General works
	Biography of historians
1620.5.A2	Collective
1620.5.A3-Z	Individual, A-Z
	Subarrange each by Table F5
1620.7	Study and teaching

F1201-3799

West Indies
  History -- Continued
1621   General works
              Including general histories and histories of the Spanish West
                Indies to 1898; naval operations in West Indian waters;
                Audiencia of Santo Domingo; military and naval history;
                English West Indian expeditions of 1654-1655, and 1695;
                George Brydges Rodney and other commanders in the
                Seven Years' War, 1756-1763; expeditions and
                campaigns of 1793-1815
              Cf. E101+ Early discoveries
              Cf. E263.W5 American Revolution armies
              Cf. E271+ Naval operations in the American Revolution
              Cf. F1411+ Spanish America in general
              Cf. F1566.45 Panama Expedition, 1741
              Cf. F1781 Capture of Havana, 1762
              Cf. F1783 Spanish West Indies in the nineteenth
                century
              Cf. F2041 Ruyter's attack on Barbados, 1655
              Cf. F2081+ English capture of Martinique, 1809
              Cf. F2097 Rodney at St. Eustatius, 1781
              Cf. F2161 Buccaneers and pirates in the West Indies
              Cf. F2272.5 English West Indian Expedition, 1739-1742
            General special
              Military and naval history see F1621
              Diplomatic history. Foreign and general relations
1621.5   General works
1622   Relations with the United States
1622.5.A-Z   Relations with other countries, A-Z
            By period
              Early to 1898 see F1621
1623   1898-
                  Cf. F1783 Spanish West Indies, 1810-1898
            Elements in the population
              Including minorities, race conflicts, problems, etc.
              For interpretation see F1392.A1+
1628.8   General works
1629.A-Z   Individual elements, A-Z
1629.B55   Blacks
                  Cf. HT1071+ Slavery
                Indians see F1619+
                Negroes see F1629.B55
  Bermudas. Somers Islands
1630   Periodicals. Societies. Collections
            Collected works
1630.4   Several authors

	West Indies
	Bermudas. Somers Islands
	Collected works -- Continued
1630.5	Individual authors
	Including collected papers, addresses, essays, etc.
1630.6	Museums. Exhibitions, exhibits
1630.7	Gazetteers. Dictionaries. Geographic names
1630.8	Directories
	Biography
1630.9	Collective
	Individual (Historians) see F1635.6.A2+
	Individual (General) see F1636
	Individual (Islands, cities, etc.) see F1639.A+
1631	General works. Description and travel. Pictorial works
1631.2	Juvenile works
1631.3	Pamphlets, addresses, essays, etc.
1631.4	Anecdotes, legends, pageants, etc.
	Cf. P, Literature
	Cf. GR120+ Folklore
1632	Guidebooks. Handbooks
1632.5	Historic monuments (General)
1633	Social life and customs. Civilization. Intellectual life
	Including characteristics of the people
	Description and travel see F1631
1634	Antiquities
	History
1635	Chronological tables. Outlines, syllabi, etc. Questions and answers, etc.
	Historiography
1635.5	General works
	Biography of historians
1635.6.A2	Collective
1635.6.A3-1635.Z	Individual, A-Z
	Subarrange each by Table F5
1635.7	Study and teaching
1636	General works
	Including political history
1637	General special
1639.A-Z	Islands, cities, etc. A-Z
	e.g.
1639.H3	Hamilton
1639.S3	Saint George Island
	Elements in the population
	Including foreign elements (General), minorities, race conflicts and problems, etc.
	For interpretation see F1392.A1+
1640.A1	General works

F1201-3799

	West Indies
	Bermudas. Somers Islands
	Elements in the population -- Continued
1640.A2-Z	Individual elements, A-Z
1640.B55	Blacks
	Negroes see F1640.B55
1640.P67	Portuguese
	Bahamas. Bahama Islands. Lucayos
1650	Periodicals. Societies. Collections
	Collected works
1650.4	Several authors
1650.5	Individual authors
	Including collected papers, addresses, essays, etc.
1650.6	Museums. Exhibitions, exhibits
1650.7	Gazetteers. Dictionaries. Geographic names
1650.8	Directories
	Biography
1650.9	Collective
	Individual (Historians) see F1655.6.A3+
	Individual (General) see F1656
	Individual (Islands, cities, etc.) see F1659.A+
1651	General works. Description and travel. Pictorial works
1651.2	Juvenile works
1651.3	Pamphlets, addresses, essays, etc.
1651.4	Anecdotes, legends, pageants, etc.
	Cf. P, Literature
	Cf. GR120+ Folklore
1652	Guidebooks. Handbooks
1653	Historic monuments (General)
1654	Social life and customs. Civilization. Intellectual life
	Including characteristics of the people
	Description and travel see F1651
1655	Antiquities. Indians
	Including Lucayan Indians (now extinct)
	For Taino Indians see F1619.2.T3
	History
1655.3	Chronological tables. Outlines, syllabi, etc. Questions and answers, etc.
	Historiography
1655.5	General works
	Biography of historians
1655.6.A2	Collective
1655.6.A3-Z	Individual, A-Z
	Subarrange each by Table F5
1655.7	Study and teaching
1656	General works
	Including political history

	West Indies
	Bahamas. Bahama Islands. Lucayos
	History -- Continued
1657	General special
	By period
	Early to 1973 see F1656
1657.2	1973-
1659.A-Z	Islands, cities, etc., A-Z
	e.g.
1659.C37	Cat Island (Cat Cay)
1659.N3	Nassau
1659.T9	Turks and Caicos Islands
	Elements in the population
	Including foreign elements (General), minorities, race conflicts and problems, etc.
	For interpretation see F1392.A1+
1660.A1	General works
1660.A2-Z	Individual elements, A-Z
1660.B55	Blacks
	Indians see F1655
	Negroes see F1660.B55
	Greater Antilles
	Including Cuba, Haiti, Puerto Rico, Jamaica and outlying islands. The Windward Passage
1741	General works
	Including Description and travel, history, antiquities
	Cuba
1751	Periodicals. Societies. Collections
	Collected works
1752	Several authors
1753	Individual authors
	Including collected papers, addresses, essays, etc.
1753.5	Museums. Exhibitions, exhibits
1754	Gazetteers. Dictionaries. Geographic names
1754.5	Directories
1754.7	Guidebooks. Handbooks
	Biography
1755	Collective
	Individual (Historians) see F1774.A3+
	Individual (By period) see F1779
	Individual (Havana (Province)) see F1791+
1758	General works
1758.5	Juvenile works
1759	Pamphlets, addresses, essays, etc.
1759.5	Anecdotes, legends, pageants, etc.
	Cf. P, Literature
	Cf. GR120+ Folklore

F1201-3799

	West Indies
	Greater Antilles
	Cuba -- Continued
1759.7	Historic monuments
	For Indian antiquities see F1769
1760	Social life and customs. Civilization. Intellectual life
	Including national characteristics
1760.5	Cubans in foreign countries (General)
	For Cubans in a particular country, see the country
1760.9	Geography
	Description and travel. Views
1761	Early to 1810
1763	1811-1897
1765	1898-1951
1765.2	1951-1980
1765.3	1981-
1769	Antiquities. Indians
	Including inscriptions, monuments, Ciboney Indians
	For Taino Indians see F1619.2.T3
	History
1772	Chronological tables. Outlines, syllabi, etc.
	Historiography
1773	General works
	Biography of historians
1774.A2	Collective
1774.A3-Z	Individual, A-Z
	Subarrange each by Table F5
	e.g.
1774.S3	Saco, José Antonio (Table F5)
1775	Study and teaching
1776	General works
	Including political history
	General special
1776.1	Military and naval history
	Diplomatic history. Foreign and general relations
1776.2	General works
1776.3.A-1776.Z	Relations with individual countries, A-Z
1778	Other (not A-Z)
	By period
	Pre-Columbian period see F1769
1779	1492-1810
	Including Age of buccaneers (16th century); Sir Charles Knowles; Edward Vernon; capture of Spanish silver-fleet in Matanzas Bay, 1628; period of internal development (18th century)
	For discovery and exploration see E101+

West Indies
Greater Antilles
Cuba
History
By period
1492-1810 -- Continued
1781   1762-1763
Including Siege of Havana; English occupation,
1762-1763
Cf. DA510+ Anglo-Spanish War, 1762-1763
Cf. DD409+ Seven Years' War, 1756-1763
Cf. DS674.8 Philippine history, 1762-1763
Cf. E199 French and Indian War, 1755-1763
1783   1810-1898
Including general works on the Spanish West Indies;
question of annexation to the United States; Black
Eagle Conspiracy, 1830; Black Conspiracy, 1844
Including biography: Gaspar Betancourt Cisneros,
Calixto García, Máximo Gómez y Báez, José
Cipriano de la Luz y Caballero, José Martí (Cf.
PQ7389.M2), Félix Varela y Morales, etc.
Cf. E431 Ostend Manifesto, 1854
Cf. PQ7389.M2 Jose Marti
1784   Insurrection, 1849-1851. López
Including filibusters and individual biography, e.g.,
Narciso López
1785   1868-1895
Including Ten Years' War, 1868-1878; Treaty of
Zanjon, 1878; the Virginius; the "Little War,"
1879-1880
Biography: Ignacio Agramonte y Loinaz, Francisco
Vicente Aguilera, Carlos Manuel de Cespedes y
del Castillo
1786   1895-1898
Including Revolution of 1895-1898; question of
intervention to February 15, 1898
Biography: Pedro de Estanislao Betancourt y
Dávalos, Antonio Maceo, Bartolomé Masó
1787   1898-1933
Including Cuban Republic, 1902- ; Platt Amendment;
Revolution of 1906; American occupation, 1906-
1909
Including biography: Antonio Sánchez de Bustamente y
Sirvén, Tomás Estrada Palma, Juan Gualberto
Gómez, Gerardo Machado y Morales, Mario
García Menocal, Gonzalo de Quesada, Cosme de
la Torriente y Peraza, Alfredo Zayas y Alfonso, etc.

F1201-3799

	West Indies
	Greater Antilles
	Cuba
	History
	By period -- Continued
1787.5	1933-1959
	1959- . Communist regime
	Cf. E841+ Cuban missile crisis
1788	General works
1788.2	Addresses, essays, lectures
	Biography
1788.22.A2	Collective
1788.22.A3-Z	Individual
	Subarrange each by Table F5
	e.g.
1788.22.C3	Castro, Fidel (Table F5)
	Elements in the population
	For interpretation see F1392.A1+
1789.A1	General works
1789.A2-Z	Individual elements, A-Z
1789.A45	Americans
1789.A7	Asturians
1789.B37	Basques
	Blacks see F1789.N3
1789.C3	Catalans
1789.C53	Chinese
1789.D87	Dutch
1789.F7	French
1789.G3	Gallegans
	Indians see F1769
1789.J3	Japanese
1789.J4	Jews
1789.K67	Koreans
1789.N3	Negroes. Blacks
1789.S7	Spaniards
	Cf. F1789.A7 Asturians
	Cf. F1789.G3 Gallegans
1789.W47	West Indians
1789.Y6	Yoruba
	Provinces
	Cf. F1769 Indian history and antiquities
	Camagüey see F1831+
	Havana (Province)
1791	General works
1795	History
1799.A-Z	Cities, towns, etc., A-Z
	e.g.

West Indies
  Greater Antilles
    Cuba
      Provinces
        Havana (Province)
          Cities, towns, etc., A-Z -- Continued

1799.G8	Guanabacoa
1799.H3-.H39	Havana (Table F2)
1799.I8	Isle of Pines
1799.S2	San Antonio de los Baños
	Las Villas see F1821+
	Oriente see F1841+
	Pinar del Rio
1801	General works
1805	History
1809.A-Z	Cities, towns, etc., A-Z
	e.g.
1809.M4	Mantua
1809.P5	Pinar del Rio (City)
	Matanzas
1811	General works
1815	History
1819.A-Z	Cities, towns, etc., A-Z
	e.g.
1819.B4	Bellamar Cave
1819.C3	Cárdenas
1819.M4	Matanzas (City)
	Las Villas
	Formerly Santa Clara
1821	General works
1825	History
1829.A-Z	Cities, towns, etc., A-Z
	e.g.
1829.C5	Cienfuegos
1829.R4	Remedios
1829.S12	Sagua la Grande
1829.S2	Sancti Spíritus
1829.S3	Santa Clara
1829.T8	Trinidad
	Camagüey
	Formerly Puerto Principe
1831	General works
1835	History
1839.A-Z	Cities, towns, etc., A-Z
	e.g.
1839.C3	Camagüey (City)
1839.G8	Guáimaro

F1201-
3799

	West Indies
	Greater Antilles
	Cuba
	Provinces
	Camaguey
	Cities, towns, etc., A-Z -- Continued
1839.N9	Nuevitas
	Puerto Principe (City) see F1839.C3
1839.S23	Santa Cruz del Sur
	Oriente
	Formerly Santiago de Cuba
1841	General works
1845	History
1849.A-Z	Cities, towns, etc., A-Z
	e.g.
1849.B2	Baracoa
1849.B3	Bayamo
1849.G5	Gibara
1849.H6	Holguín
1849.S3	Santiago de Cuba
1849.T62	Toa River
1849.V5	Victoria de las Tunas
	Guantanamo
1850	General works
1850.5	History
1850.9.A-Z	Cities, towns, etc., A-Z
	Ciego de Avila
1851	General works
1851.5	History
1851.9.A-Z	Cities, towns, etc., A-Z
	Cienfuegos
1852	General works
1852.5	History
1852.9.A-Z	Cities, towns, etc., A-Z
	Sancti Spíritus
1853	General works
1853.5	History
1853.9.A-Z	Cities, towns, etc.. A-Z
	Holguín Province
1854	General works
1854.5	History
1854.9.A-Z	Cities, towns, etc., A-Z
	Las Tunas Province
1855	General works
1855.5	History
1855.9.A-Z	Cities, towns, etc., A-Z
	Jamaica

	West Indies
	Greater Antilles
	Jamaica -- Continued
1861	Periodicals. Societies. Collections
	Collected works
1862	Several authors
1863	Individual authors
	Including collected papers, addresses, essays, etc.
1863.5	Museums. Exhibitions, exhibits
1864	Gazetteers. Dictionaries. Geographic names
1864.5	Directories
	Biography
1865	Collective
	Individual (Historians) see F1879.5
	Individual (By period) see F1884
1868	General works
1868.2	Juvenile works
1868.3	Pamphlets, addresses, essays, etc.
1868.4	Anecdotes, legends, pageants, etc.
	Cf. P, Literature
	Cf. GR120+ Folklore
1869	Guidebooks. Handbooks
1869.5	Historic monuments (General)
	For Indian antiquities see F1875
	Description and travel. Views
1870	Early to 1810
1871	1871-1950
1872	1951-1980
1872.2	1981-
1874	Social life and customs. Civilization. Intellectual life
	Including characteristics of the people
1874.5	Geography
1875	Antiquities. Indians
	History
1878	Chronological tables. Outlines, syllabi, etc. Questions and answers, etc.
	Historiography
1879	General works
	Biography of historians
1879.5.A2	Collective
1879.5.A3-Z	Individual, A-Z
	Subarrange each by Table F5
1880	Study and teaching
1881	General works
	Including political history
	General special
1882	General works

F1201-
3799

                    West Indies
                        Greater Antilles
                            Jamaica
                                History
                                    General special -- Continued
                                        Diplomatic history. Foreign and general relations
1882.2   General works
1882.3.A-Z   Relations with individual countries, A-Z
1882.4   Other (not A-Z)
                                    By period
                                        Pre-Columbian period see F1875
1884   1494-1810
                                                Including Spanish rule, 1494-1655; British conquests of
                                                    1596, 1643, 1655; Treaty of Madrid, 1670;
                                                    attempted invasion by France and Spain, 1694, by
                                                    France alone, 1782, 1806; Maroon War, 1795-
                                                    1796; Earthquake of 1692
                                                Including biography: Sir Thomas Lynch, etc.
                                                Cf. F1526.25 British expedition from Jamaica
                                                    against Nicaragua, 1780-1781
                                                Cf. F2272.5 Admiral Vernon and the English West
                                                    Indian Expedition of 1739-1742
1886   1810-1962
                                                Including Negro insurrection, 1831; Morant Bay
                                                    Rebellion, 1865-1866; reorganization of Colony,
                                                    1844, 1866; earthquake of 1907; hurricanes, 1944,
                                                    1951; move toward British West-Indian federation
                                                Including biography: Sir John Peter Grant, Edward
                                                    John Eyre, etc.
                                                Cf. D501+ World War I, 1914-1918
                                                Cf. D731+ World War II, 1939-1945
                                                Cf. F1447 British Honduras under governor of
                                                    Jamaica, 1862-1884
1887   1962-
1891.A-Z   Regions, parishes, etc., A-Z
                                            e.g.
(1891.C5)   Cayman Islands
                                            see F2048.5
1891.H2   Hanover Parish
1891.S14   Saint James Parish
1891.S2   Saint Mary Parish
                                            For Turks and Caicos Islands see F1659.T9
1895.A-Z   Cities, towns, etc., A-Z
                                            e.g.
                                            Cf. F1875 Indian local history and antiquities
1895.K5   Kingston
                                            Including earthquake of 1907

	West Indies
	Greater Antilles
	Jamaica
	Cities, towns, etc., A-Z -- Continued
1895.M6	Montego Bay
1895.P6	Port Royal
	Including earthquake of 1692; hurricanes of 1712, 1714, 1722
1895.S7	Spanish Town
	Elements in the population
	For interpretation see F1392.A1+
1896.A1	General works
	Including race conflicts and problems, etc.
1896.A2-Z	Individual elements, A-Z
	Blacks see F1896.N4
1896.C5	Chinese
1896.E2	East Indians
1896.E87	Europeans
	Indians see F1875
1896.I6	Irish
1896.J48	Jews
1896.N4	Negroes. Blacks
	Cf. HT1096+ Slavery
	Haiti (Island). Hispaniola
1900	Periodicals. Societies. Collections
1901	General works
	Including description and travel of the whole island
1909	Antiquities. Indians
1911	History (of the island). Spanish Colony, 1492-1795
	Spanish Colony of Santo Domingo, 1808-1822 see F1938.3
	Union of the whole island, 1822-1844 see F1924
	Haiti (Republic)
1912	Periodicals. Societies. Collections, etc.
	Collected works
1912.5	Several authors
1912.6	Individual authors
	Including collected papers, addresses, essays, etc.
1912.8	Museums. Exhibitions, exhibits
1913	Gazetteers. Dictionaries, Geographic names
1913.5	Directories
	Biography
1914	Collective
	Individual see F1920
1915	General works
1915.2	Juvenile works
1915.3	Pamphlets, addresses, essays

F1201-3799

West Indies
  Greater Antilles
    Haiti (Island). Hispaniola
      Haiti (Republic) -- Continued

1915.4	Anecdotes, legends, pageants
	Cf. P, Literature
	Cf. GR120+ Folklore
1915.5	Guidebooks. Handbooks
1915.7	Historic monuments (General)
	Indian antiquities see F1909
1916	Social life and customs. Civilization. Intellectual life
	Including national characteristics
1917	Description and travel. Views
	Antiquities, Indians see F1909
	History
1918	Chronological tables. Outlines, syllabi, etc. Questions and answers
	Historiography
1919	General works
	Biography of historians
1920.A2	Collective
1920.A3-Z	Individual, A-Z
	Subarrange each by Table F5
1920.5	Study and teaching
1921	General works
	Including political history
	General special
1921.5	Military and naval history
	Diplomatic history. Foreign and general relations
1922	General works
1922.5.A-Z	Relations with individual countries, A-Z
1922.9	Other (not A-Z)
	By period
	Pre-Columbian period see F1909
1923	1492-1803
	Including French settlement, 1677-1803; Colony of Saint Domingue, 1677-1803; Treaty of Ryswick, 1697; Revolution of 1791-1803; English invasion, 1793-1798; withdrawal of Spain from island, 1795
	Including biography: François Dominique Toussaint Louverture, etc.
	For period of Spanish control see F1911

	West Indies
	Greater Antilles
	Haiti (Island). Hispaniola
	Haiti (Republic)
	History
	By period -- Continued
1924	1804-1843
	Including proclaimed independent nation, January 1, 1804; Republic, 1806; separate north and south states, 1806-1820; annexation of Santo Domingo, 1822; Revolution of 1843
	Including biography: Jean Pierre Boyer, Henri Christophe (Henri I), Jean Jacques Dessalines, Alexandre Sabés Pétion, etc.
	Cf. F1938.3 Revival of Spanish Colony in the east, 1808-1822
1926	1843-1915
	Loss of Santo Domingo, 1844; period of tumult
	Including biography: Fabre Nicolas Geffrard, Pierre Nord Alexis, Louis Étienne Félicité, Salomon; Faustino Soulouque (Faustino I, Emperor), etc.
1927	1915-1950
	United States intervention (military occupation, 1915-1934; fiscal control ended, 1947); Revolt of 1946
	Including biography: Louis Borno, Sudre Dartiguenave, Dumarsais Estimé, Élie Lescot, Sténio Vincent, etc.
1928	1950-1986
	Constitution of 1946 abrogated
	Including biography: Paul Eugène Magloire, etc.
	1986-
1928.2	General works
	Biography
1928.22	Collective
1928.23.A-Z	Individual, A-Z
	Subarrange each by Table F5
1929.A-Z	Regions, departments, cities, etc., A-Z
	e.g.
	Cf. F1909 Indian local history and antiquities
1929.B7	Boundaries
	Including boundary between Haiti and Dominican Republic
1929.C3	Cap Haïtien
1929.C8	Cul de Sac
1929.G6	Gonave Island
1929.P8	Port-au-Prince

F1201-3799

West Indies
  Greater Antilles
    Haiti (Island). Hispaniola
      Haiti (Republic) -- Continued
        Elements in the population
            Including foreign elements (General), minorities, race
               conflicts and problems, etc.
            For interpretation see F1392.A1+

1930.A1	General works
1930.A2-Z	Individual elements, A-Z
1930.B55	Blacks
1930.F7	French
	Indians see F1909
	Negroes see F1930.B55
1930.P64	Poles

      Dominican Republic. Santo Domingo

1931	Periodicals. Societies. Collections
	Collected works
1931.5	Several authors
1931.6	Individual authors
	Including collected papers, addresses, essays, etc.
1931.7	Museums. Exhibitions, exhibits
1932	Gazetteers. Dictionaries. Geographic names
1932.5	Directories
	Biography
1933	Collective
	Individual see F1937.6.A2+
1934	General works
1934.2	Juvenile works
1934.3	Pamphlets, addresses, essays
1934.4	Anecdotes, legends, pageants
	Cf. P, Literature
	Cf. GR120+ Folklore
1934.5	Guidebooks. Handbooks
1934.7	Historic monuments (General)
	Indian antiquities see F1909
1935	Social life and customs. Civilization. Intellectual life
	Including national characteristics
1935.5	Geography
	Description and travel. Views
1936	Early to 1951
1936.2	1951-1980
1936.3	1981-
	Antiquities, Indians see F1909
	History
1937	Chronological tables. Outlines, syllabi, etc. Questions and answers, etc.

    West Indies
     Greater Antilles
      Haiti (Island). Hispaniola
       Dominican Republic. Santo Domingo
        History -- Continued
         Historiography

1937.5	General works
	Biography of historians
1937.6.A2	Collective
1937.6.A3-1937.Z	Individual, A-Z
	Subarrange each by Table F5
1937.8	Study and teaching
1938	General works
	Including political history
	General special
1938.1	Military and naval history
	Diplomatic history. Foreign and general relations
1938.2	General works
1938.25.A-Z	Relations with individual countries, A-Z
1938.29	Other (not A-Z)
	By period
	Pre-Columbian period see F1909
1938.3	1492-1844
	Including under French or Haitian control, 1795-1808; Spanish colony, 1808-1822; union with Haiti, 1822-1844
	For Spanish colony, 1492-1795 see F1911
1938.4	1844-1930
	Including republic established, 1844; Spanish regime, 1861-1865; period of revolutions
	Including biography: Buenaventura Báez, Juan Pablo Duarte, Ulises Haureaux, Gregorio Luperón, Adolfo Alejandro Nouel y Bobadilla, Francisco del Rosario Sánchez, Pedro Santana, etc.
1938.45	1916-1924
	Including period of United States military occupation
1938.5	1930-1961
	Including biography: Rafael Leónidas Trujillo Molina, etc.
	1961-
1938.55	General works
	Biography
1938.57	Collective
1938.58.A-Z	Individual, A-Z
	Subarrange each by Table F5

F1201-3799

	West Indies
	Greater Antilles
	Haiti (Island). Hispaniola
	Dominican Republic. Santo Domingo -- Continued
1939.A-Z	Regions, provinces, cities, etc., A-Z
	e.g.
	Cf. F1909 Indian local history and antiquity
1939.A4	Alta Vela (Island). Isla Alto Velo
	Boundaries see F1929.B7
	Ciudad Trujillo see F1939.S4+
1939.C67	Cotuí (Town)
	Distrito Nacional see F1939.S4+
1939.I8	Isabela
	Ruined town, founded in 1493 by Columbus
	La Isabela see F1939.I8
1939.L3	La Vega (City). Concepción de la Vega
1939.M6	Monte Plata (Town)
	Monte Tina see F1939.T5
	National District see F1939.S4+
1939.P9	Puerto Plata (City). San Felipe de Puerto Plata
1939.S15	Salcedo (Province)
1939.S18	Samaná (Town). Santa Bárbara de Samaná
1939.S4-.S49	Santo Domingo (National District and City) (Table F2)
	Formerly Ciudad Trujillo from 1936 to 1961
1939.T5	Tina (mountain peak). Monte Tina or Loma Tina
	Trujillo (City) see F1939.S4+
1939.Y38	Yaque del Norte River
	Elements in the population
	Including foreign elements (General), minorities, race conflicts and problems
	For interpretation see F1392.A1+
1941.A1	General works
1941.A2-Z	Individual elements, A-Z
1941.A73	Arabs
1941.B55	Blacks
1941.C37	Catalans
1941.F5	Flemings
1941.H3	Haitians
	Indians see F1909
1941.J3	Japanese
1941.J4	Jews
	Negroes see F1941.B55
1941.S7	Spaniards
	Puerto Rico. Boriquén
1951	Periodicals. Societies. Collections
	Collected works
1952	Several authors

	West Indies
	Greater Antilles
	Puerto Rico. Boriquen
	Collected works -- Continued
1953	Individual authors
	Including collected papers, addresses, essays
1953.5	Museums. Exhibitions, exhibits
1954	Gazetteers. Dictionaries. Geographic names
1954.5	Directories
	Biography
1955	Collective
	Individual see F1970.6.A2+
1958	General works
1958.3	Juvenile works
1958.5	Pamphlets, addresses, essays
1958.7	Anecdotes, legends, pageants
	Cf. P, Literature
	Cf. GR120+ Folklore
1959	Guidebooks. Handbooks
1959.5	Historic monuments (General)
	For Indian antiquities see F1969
1960	Social life and customs. Civilization. Intellectual life
	Including national characteristics
	Description and travel. Views
1961	Early to 1897
1965	1898-1950
1965.2	1851-1980
1965.3	1981-
1969	Antiquities. Indians
	Including the Borinqueño Indians (now extinct)
	History
1970	Chronological tables. Outlines, syllabi, etc. Questions and answers, etc.
	Historiography
1970.5	General works
	Biography of historians
1970.6.A2	Collective
1970.6.A3-1970.Z	Individual, A-Z
	Subarrange each by Table F5
	e.g.
1970.6.T3	Tapia y Rivera, Alejandro (Table F5)
1970.8	Study and teaching
1971	General works
	Including political history
1972	General special
	By period
	Pre-Columbian period see F1969

F1201-
3799

	West Indies
	Greater Antilles
	Puerto Rico. Boriquen
	History
	By period -- Continued
1973	1493-1898
	Including period of Spanish rule; attacks by British in 1595, 1598, 1791; attack by Dutch, 1625; revolts against Spain in 1812, 1867; autonomous regime, 1897
	Including biography: Eugenio María de Hostos y Bonilla, etc.
	Cf. E717.3 Spanish-American War, 1898
	Cf. F1783 Spanish West Indies, 1810-1898
1975	1898-1952
	Including United States possession, 1898; United States Territory, (organized by unincorporated), 1917-1952; hurricanes of 1899, 1928, 1932, etc. Known as Porto Rico, 1898-1932
	Including biography: Jesús T. Piñero, etc.
	1952-1998
1976	General works
	Biography
1976.2	Collective
1976.3.A-Z	Individual, A-Z
	Subarrange each by Table F5
	1998-
1976.4	General works
	Biography
1976.5	Collective
1976.6.A-Z	Individual, A-Z
	Subarrange each by Table F5
1981.A-Z	Regions, departments, cities, etc., A-Z
	e.g.
	Cf. F1969 Indian local history and antiquities
1981.A26	Aguada
1981.A6	Arecibo (City)
1981.C24	Caguas
1981.C9	Culebra Island
1981.G7	Guayama
1981.M4	Mayagüez
1981.P7	Ponce
1981.R5	Río Piedras
1981.S2	San Juan
	Including La Fortaleza (Government House), San Juan National Monument
1981.U8	Utuado

West Indies
  Greater Antilles
    Puerto Rico. Boriquen
      Regions, departments, cities, etc., A-Z -- Continued

1981.V5   Vieques Island. Crab Island
      Elements in the population
         Including foreign elements (General), minorities, race
           conflicts and problems
         For interpretation see F1392.A1+

1983.A1   General works
1983.A2-Z   Individual elements, A-Z
         Blacks see F1983.N4
1983.C83   Cubans
1983.D65   Dominicans
         Indians see F1969
1983.N4   Negroes. Blacks
1983.S64   Spaniards
1983.W47   West Indians
    Other islands
1991   Navassa
  Lesser Antilles. Caribbees
2001   General works. Cariban Indians
         Cf. F2161 The Caribbean Sea with coasts and
           adjoining islands
    Groups of islands, by geographical distribution
         For Individual islands see F2033+
         For groups by political allegiance see F2130+
2006   Leeward Islands
         Including Anguilla, Antigua, Barbuda, Désirade, Dominica,
           Guadeloupe, Les Saintes, Marie Galante, Montserrat,
           Nevis, Redonda, Saba, Saint Bartholomew, Saint
           Christopher, Saint Croix, Saint Eustatius, Saint John,
           Saint Martin, Saint Thomas, Virgin Islands
2011   Windward Islands
         Including Barbados, Grenada, The Grenadines, Martinique,
           Saint Lucia, Saint Vincent
2016   Islands along the Venezuela coast
         Including Aruba, Bonaire, Curaçao, Tobago, Trinidad
         For islands belonging to Venezuela see F2331.A2
    Individual islands (alphabetically)
2033   Anguilla
2035   Antigua and Barbuda
2038   Aruba
2041   Barbados
         Including Ruyter's attack on Barbados, 1655
         Barbuda see F2035
          Basse-Terre Island see F2066

F1201-3799

	West Indies
	Lesser Antilles. Caribbees
	Individual islands (alphabetically) -- Continued
2048	Bonaire. Buen Ayre
2048.5	Cayman Islands
2049	Curaçao
2050	Désirade
2051	Dominica
2056-2056.9	Grenada (Table F3)
2061	The Grenadines
	For Saint Vincent and the Grenadines see F2106+
2066	Guadeloupe
2070	Les Saintes
2076	Marie-Galante
2081-2081.9	Martinique (Table F3)
2082	Montserrat
2084	Nevis. Saint Kitts and Nevis
	Redonda see F2035
2088	Saba
2089	Saint Bartholomew. Saint-Barthélemy
2091	Saint Christopher. Saint Kitts
	For Saint Kitts and Nevis see F2084
2096	Saint Croix
2097	Saint Eustatius. Sint Eustatius
2098	Saint John
	Saint Kitts see F2091
2100	Saint Lucia
2103	Saint Martin
	Divided between Saint-Martin (Guadeloupe) and Sint Maarten (Netherlands Antilles)
2105	Saint Thomas
	Saint Vincent. Saint Vincent and the Grenadines
2106	General works
2110.A-Z	Local, A-Z
	Sint Eustatius see F2097
2116	Tobago
	For Trinidad and Tobago see F2119+
	Trinidad. Trinidad and Tobago
2119	General works
	By period
2120	Early to 1888
2121	1888-1962
2122	1962-
2123.A-Z	Local, A-Z
2129	Virgin Islands, British
	Including the individual islands

West Indies
Lesser Antilles. Caribbees -- Continued
Groups of islands. By political allegiance or national
language
2130   English-speaking Caribbean
2131   British West Indies (Commonwealth Caribbean)
Including Bahamas, Bermudas, Cayman Islands, Jamaica,
the Leeward Islands (Anguilla, Antigua, Barbuda,
Dominica, Montserrat, Nevis, Redonda, Saint
Christopher), Tobago, Trinidad, the Windward Islands
(Barbados, Grenada, The Grenadines, Saint Lucia,
Saint Vincent)
For Bermudas see F1630+
For Bahamas see F1650+
For Jamaica see F1861+
Cf. E162 English colonies in America before 1775
(General)
Cf. E188 English colonies in America before 1775
(General)
Cf. E263.W5 West Indies in the American Revolution,
1775-1783
Cf. F1529.M9 British Protectorate of Mosquito coast
Cf. HT1091+ Slavery
2132   Description and travel, 1951-
2133   History, 1943-
2134   West Indies Federation
Came into effect January, 1958. Consists of 10 colonies
embracing 13 islands: Antigua, Barbados, Dominica,
Grenada, Jamaica, Montserrat, Saint Christopher,
Nevis, Anguilla, Saint Lucia, Saint Vincent, Trinidad,
and Tobago
2136   Virgin Islands of the United States (Table F3)
Danish West Indies before 1917
For Saint Croix see F2096
For Saint John see F2098
For Saint Thomas see F2105
Cf. E669 Proposed annexation to United States,
1867-1869
Cf. E756 Proposed annexation to United States, 1902
Cf. E768 Purchase by the United States, 1917
British Virgin Islands see F2129
2141   Netherlands Antilles. Netherlands West Indies. Dutch
West Indies
Including Aruba, Bonaire, Curaçao, Saba, Sint Eustatius,
Sint Maarten
For individual islands, see F2038+

F1201-3799

West Indies
Lesser Antilles. Caribbees
Groups of islands. By political allegiance or national
language -- Continued
2151   French West Indies
Including Leeward Islands (Guadeloupe, Marie Galante,
Saint-Barthélemy, part of Saint Martin); Martinique
(Windward Islands); Les Saintes
For individual islands, see F2066+
Saint Domingue (French colony, Haiti) see F1923
Spanish West Indies
see F1601-1623
Caribbean area. Caribbean Sea
Including the West Indies and coasts of the Caribbean Sea, the
Gulf of Mexico, and Spanish Main
2155   Periodicals. Societies. Collections
2155.3   Congresses
Collected works
2156   Several authors
2157   Individual authors
Including collected papers, addresses, essays
2158   Gazetteers. Dictionaries. Geographic names
Biography
2160   Collective
Individual (General) see F2161
Individual (By period) see F2180.2+
2161   General works
Including pirates and buccaneers
2161.5   Juvenile works
2165   Guidebooks. Handbooks
2169   Social life and customs. Civilization. Intellectual life
Including national characteristics
For specific periods after 1810 see F2181
Description and travel. Views
2171   Early through 1950
2171.2   1951-1980
2171.3   1981-
2172   Antiquities. Indians
History
Historiography
2172.5   General works
Biography of historians
2172.6   Collective
2172.7.A-Z   Individual, A-Z
Subarrange each by Table F5
2173   Study and teaching
2175   General works

	West Indies
	Caribbean area. Caribbean Sea
	History -- Continued
2176	General special
	Diplomatic history. Foreign and general relations
2177	General works
2178.A-Z	Relations with individual countries, A-Z
	By period
	Early through 1810 see F2161
2181	1811-
2183	1945-
	Elements in the population
	For interpretation see F1392.A1+
2190	General works
2191.A-Z	Individual elements, A-Z
2191.B55	Blacks
2191.C35	Canary Islanders
2191.C46	Chinese
2191.E27	East Indians
2191.J48	Jews
2191.S36	Scots
	South America
2201	Periodicals. Societies. Collections
	For South American geographic societies see G5
2204	Gazetteers. Dictionaries. Geographic names
	Biography
2205	Collective
	Individual (Historians) see F2230.5
	Individual (By period) see F2232.92+
2208	General works
2208.5	Juvenile works
2209	Pamphlets, addresses, essays, etc.
2209.5	Anecdotes, legends, pageants, etc.
	Cf. P, Literature
	Cf. GR130+ Folklore
2210	Social life and customs. Civilization. Intellectual life
	Cf. F2239.A1+ Elements in the population
2211	Guidebooks. Handbooks
2211.5	Geography
	Regions
2212	Andes Mountains (General). Altiplano (General)
	For the Andes or Altiplano in individual countries, see the region of the country, e.g., F2851 Andes in Argentina
2213	Pacific coast
	For Galápagos Islands see F3741.G2
2214	Atlantic coast
2215	Islands of South America (General)

F1201-
3799

	South America
	Regions -- Continued
2216	Northern South America
	Including Brazil, Colombia, Ecuador, Guiana, Peru, and Venezuela
	For Spanish Main see F2161
	For Amazon River see F2546
2217	Southern South America
	Including Argentina, Bolivia, Brazil (South), Chile, Paraguay, Peru and Uruguay
	Including Gauchos (General)
	For gauchos in Brazil see F2621
	For gauchos in Paraguay see F2682.9
	For gauchos in Uruguay see F2722.9
	For La Plata region see F2801+
	For Gran Chaco see F2876
	For gauchos in Argentina see F2926
	For Falkland Islands see F3031+
	Description and travel (General). Views
2221	Early to 1810
2223	1811-1950
	Cf. F865 Voyages to the Pacific coast following discovery of gold
2224	1951-1980
2225	1981-
	Antiquities. Indians
2229	General works
2230	Modern Indians (General)
2230.1.A-Z	Topics (Ancient and modern), A-Z
2230.1.A3	Agriculture
2230.1.A4	Anthropometry
2230.1.A5	Architecture
2230.1.A6	Arms and armor
2230.1.A7	Art
2230.1.A85	Astronomy
2230.1.B6	Boats. Canoes
2230.1.B7	Botany (Economics). Ethnobotany
2230.1.C5	Children
2230.1.C75	Commerce
2230.1.C76	Copperwork
2230.1.C78	Cosmology
2230.1.C8	Costume. Adornment
2230.1.C9	Culture
2230.1.D35	Dance
2230.1.D65	Domestic animals
2230.1.D75	Drinking vessels. Queros
2230.1.D78	Drug use

South America
    Antiquities. Indians
       Topics (Ancient and modern), A-Z -- Continued

2230.1.E25	Economic conditions
2230.1.E37	Education
2230.1.E84	Ethnic identity
	Ethnobotany see F2230.1.B7
2230.1.E87	Ethnozoology
2230.1.F2	Featherwork
2230.1.F56	Folk literature
2230.1.F6	Folklore. Legends
2230.1.F66	Food
2230.1.G2	Games
2230.1.G64	Goldwork
2230.1.G68	Government relations
2230.1.H84	Hunting
2230.1.I4	Implements
2230.1.I42	Industries
2230.1.I58	Intellectual life
2230.1.I77	Irrigation
2230.1.K5	Kinship
2230.1.L35	Land tenure
2230.1.M24	Magic
2230.1.M28	Marriage customs and rites
2230.1.M3	Masks
2230.1.M34	Material culture
2230.1.M4	Medicine
2230.1.M43	Metalwork
2230.1.M47	Migrations
2230.1.M5	Missions
	Including biography of missionaries
2230.1.M54	Mixed descent
2230.1.M6	Mortuary customs
	Music see ML3575.A1+
2230.1.N37	Narcotics
2230.1.P48	Petroglyphs. Rock paintings
2230.1.P53	Philosophy
2230.1.P65	Politics and government
2230.1.P8	Pottery
	Queros see F2230.1.D75
2230.1.R3	Religion. Mythology
2230.1.R6	Roads. Trails
	Rock paintings see F2230.1.P48
2230.1.S33	Science
2230.1.S37	Sculpture
2230.1.S44	Semitic influences
2230.1.S54	Shell beads. Shell engraving. Shell jewelry

F1201-
3799

	South America
	Antiquities. Indians
	Topics (Ancient and modern), A-Z -- Continued
2230.1.S68	Social conditions
2230.1.S7	Social life and customs
2230.1.T3	Textile fabrics
2230.1.T63	Tobacco use
	Trails see F2230.1.R6
2230.1.T7	Treatment of Indians
2230.1.W37	Wars
2230.1.W6	Women
2230.1.W7	Writing
2230.2.A-Z	Tribes (Ancient and modern), A-Z
	Class here tribes that do not live or are not identified with one particular country
	Tribes that live or before extinction have lived in one country or are usually identified with one country, although they may occupy or have occupied areas of one or more adjacent countries, are classed with the individual countries
2230.2.A68	Araona Indians
2230.2.A7	Arawak
2230.2.A78	Ashluslay
2230.2.A82	Avachiripá
2230.2.A9	Aymara
2230.2.C3	Caingua
	Carib see F2001
2230.2.C5	Chamacoco
	Cofán see F3722.1.C67
2230.2.G68	Guana
2230.2.G72	Guarani
2230.2.G75	Guayana
2230.2.G78	Guaycuruan. Guaycuru
2230.2.J58	Jivaran
2230.2.K4	Kechua. Quechua
2230.2.O8	Oyana. Wayana
	Quechua see F2230.2.K4
2230.2.T84	Tupi
	Wayana see F2230.2.O8
	History
2230.3	Chronological tables. Outlines, syllabi, etc. Questions and answers, etc.
	Historiography
2230.4	General works
	Biography of historians
2230.5.A2	Collective

	South America
	History
	Historiography
	Biography of historians -- Continued
2230.5.A3-Z	Individual, A-Z
	Subarrange each by Table F5
2230.6	Study and teaching
2231	General works
2231.5	General special
2231.7	Military history
2231.8	Naval history
	Diplomatic history. Foreign and general relations
2232	General works
2232.2.A-Z	Relations with individual countries, A-Z
	By period
	Pre-Columbian period see F2229+
2233	1498-1806
	Including colonial period
	Cf. E101+ Early discoveries
	1806-1830. Wars of independence
2235	General works
2235.3	Bolívar, Simón
	Including life and works
2235.36	Guayaquil meeting, 1822
2235.4	San Martín, José de
	Including life and correspondence
2235.5.A-Z	Other liberators, A-Z
2235.5.R6	Rodríguez, Simón
2235.5.S9	Sucre, Antonio Jose de
2235.5.U7	Urdaneta, Rafael
	1830-
2236	General works
2237	1939-
	Cf. D731+ World War II, 1939-1945
	Elements in the population
	Including foreign elements (General), minorities, race conflicts and problems
	For interpretation see F1392.A1+
2239.A1	General works
2239.A2-Z	Individual elements, A-Z
2239.A7	Arabs
2239.A75	Armenians
2239.B3	Basques
2239.B55	Blacks
2239.B8	British
2239.B9	Bulgarians
2239.C36	Cantabrians

F1201-3799

	South America
	Elements in the population
	Individual elements, A-Z -- Continued
2239.C48	Chinese
2239.C76	Croats
2239.D8	Dutch
2239.G3	Germans
2239.G74	Greeks
2239.H85	Hungarians
	Indians see F2229+
2239.I8	Italians
2239.J3	Japanese
2239.J5	Jews
2239.K65	Kongo
2239.K67	Koreans
2239.L7	Lithuanians
	Negroes see F2239.B55
2239.N6	Norwegians
2239.P6	Poles
2239.P67	Portuguese
2239.S8	Swedes
2239.S9	Swiss
2239.S95	Syrians
2239.Y83	Yugoslavs
	Colombia
2251	Periodicals. Societies. Collections
	Collected works
2252	Several authors
2253	Individual authors
	Including collected papers, addresses, essays
2253.5	Museums. Exhibitions, exhibits
2254	Gazetteers. Dictionaries. Geographic names
2254.5	Directories
	Biography
2255	Collective
	Individual (Historians) see F2270.6.A+
	Individual (By period) see F2271.92+
2258	General works
2258.5	Juvenile works
2259	Pamphlets, addresses, essays, etc.
2259.3	Anecdotes, legends, pageants, etc.
	Cf. P, Literature
	Cf. GR130+ Folklore
2259.5	Guidebooks. Handbooks
2259.7	Historic monuments (General)

	South America
	Colombia -- Continued
2260	Social life and customs. Civilization. Intellectual life
	Including national characteristics.
	For race conflicts and problems see F2299.A1+
2260.9	Geography
	Description and travel. Views
2261	Early to 1809
2263	1810-1950
2264	1951-1980
2264.2	1981-
	Antiquities. Indians
2269	General works
2269.1.A-Z	Local (Ancient and modern), A-Z
	e.g.
2269.1.A28	Aburrá Valley
2269.1.C95	Cundinamarca
2269.1.P66	Popayán (Province)
2269.1.S24	San Agustin
2269.1.S25	Santa Marta Lagoon region
2269.1.T54	Tierra Adentro
2269.1.V35	Valle del Cauca
2270	Modern Indians (General)
2270.1.A-Z	Topics (Ancient and modern), A-Z
2270.1.A47	Agriculture
2270.1.A58	Anthropometry
2270.1.A7	Art
2270.1.C4	Census
2270.1.C44	Children
(2270.1.C58)	Civil rights
	see KHH1+
2270.1.E3	Economic conditions
2270.1.E36	Education
2270.1.E84	Ethnic identity
2270.1.E85	Ethnobiology
2270.1.E86	Ethnobotany
2270.1.E88	Ethnozoology
2270.1.F6	Folklore. Legends
2270.1.F85	Funeral customs and rites
2270.1.G57	Goldwork
2270.1.G6	Government relations
	Including reservations (General)
2270.1.H84	Hunting
2270.1.K55	Kinship
2270.1.L3	Land tenure
	Legends see F2270.1.F6
2270.1.M43	Medicine

F1201-
3799

	South America
	Colombia
	Antiquities. Indians
	Topics (Ancient and modern), A-Z -- Continued
2270.1.M5	Missions
2270.1.N35	Narcotics. Drugs
2270.1.P4	Petroglyphs. Rock paintings
2270.1.P63	Politics and government
2270.1.P65	Pottery
2270.1.R4	Religion. Mythology
	Rock paintings see F2270.1.P4
2270.1.S63	Social conditions
2270.1.S64	Social life and customs
2270.1.T38	Taxation
2270.1.T48	Textile fabrics
2270.1.W65	Women
2270.2.A-Z	Tribes and cultures (Ancient and modern), A-Z
2270.2.A3	Achagua
2270.2.A6	Andaqui
2270.2.A62	Andoque
2270.2.A63	Anserma
	Arawak see F2230.2.A7
2270.2.A67	Arhuaco
	Aruac see F2270.2.A67
	Baniva see F2520.1.B35
2270.2.B27	Barasana
2270.2.B3	Barbacoa
2270.2.B6	Bora
2270.2.C22	Cabiyari
2270.2.C24	Calima culture
2270.2.C25	Camsa
2270.2.C26	Carapana
2270.2.C27	Carijona
2270.2.C3	Catio
2270.2.C34	Cenu
2270.2.C37	Chamí
2270.2.C4	Chibcha
2270.2.C5	Chimila
2270.2.C6	Choco
2270.2.C63	Churoya
	Cobaría see F2270.2.T8
2270.2.C65	Coconuco
2270.2.C67	Coreguaje
2270.2.C68	Coyaima
	Cuaiquer see F3722.1.C83
2270.2.C8	Cubeo
	Cuna see F1565.2.C8

South America
  Colombia
    Antiquities. Indians
      Tribes and cultures (Ancient and modern), A-Z --
        Continued

2270.2.C87	Curripaco
2270.2.D4	Desana
2270.2.E43	Embera
2270.2.E53	Epena Saija
2270.2.G6	Goajiro
	Guahibo see F2319.2.G8
2270.2.G8	Guane
2270.2.G83	Guarino
	Ijca see F2270.2.A67
2270.2.I53	Ingano
2270.2.K3	Kagaba
	Macu see F2520.1.M2
2270.2.M33	Macuna
2270.2.M5	Mocoa
2270.2.M6	Moguex
	Motilon see F2319.2.M6
2270.2.M75	Muinane
2270.2.M8	Muzo
2270.2.N8	Nukak
2270.2.P3	Paez
	Panare see F2319.2.P34
2270.2.P37	Panche
2270.2.P4	Paniquita
2270.2.P44	Pasto
	Peban see F3430.1.P4
2270.2.P64	Pijao
2270.2.P8	Puinave
2270.2.Q54	Quillacinga
2270.2.Q8	Quimbaya
	Saliva see F2319.2.S3
2270.2.S35	San Agustin culture
2270.2.T3	Tairona
2270.2.T32	Taiwano
2270.2.T34	Tanimuca-Retuama
	Timote see F2319.2.T5
	Tucano see F2520.1.T9
	Tucuna see F2520.1.T925
2270.2.T77	Tukanoan
2270.2.T8	Tunebo
2270.2.W5	Witoto
2270.2.W54	Wiwa
2270.2.Y3	Yakalamarure

F1201-
3799

	South America
	Colombia
	Antiquities. Indians
	Tribes and cultures (Ancient and modern), A-Z -- Continued
2270.2.Y42	Yebamasa
2270.2.Y87	Yucuna
2270.2.Y9	Yuko
	Yupa see F2319.2.Y8
	History
	Including political history
2270.3	Chronological tables. Outlines, syllabi, etc. Questions and answers, etc.
	Historiography
2270.4	General works
	Biography of historians
2270.5	Collective
2270.6.A-Z	Individual, A-Z
	Subarrange each by Table F5
2270.7	Study and teaching
2271	General works
	Including political history
	General special
2271.4	Military and naval history
	Diplomatic history. Foreign and general relations
2271.5	General works
2271.52.A-Z	Relations with individual countries, A-Z
2271.9	Other (not A-Z)
	By period
	Pre-Columbian period see F2269+
2272	1499-1810
	Including Viceroyalty and Audiencia of New Granada; Conquest of Chibcha Indians, 1536-1538; Siege of Cartagena, 1585, 1697; Insurrection of the Comuneros, 1781
	Including biography: Gonzalo Jiménez de Quesada, etc.
	Cf. E135.G3 The Welsers, 1529-1556
	Cf. F2272.5 Siege of Cartagena, 1741
	Cf. F2281.D2 Scot's Colony, 1698-1700
2272.5	1739-1742. English West Indian Expedition
	Including Siege of Cartagena, 1741
	Cf. F1621 English West Indian Expedition, 1654-1655, 1695
	Cf. F2272 Siege of Cartagena, 1585, 1697
2273	1810-
	Including biography: Francisco de Paula Santander, etc.

South America
 Colombia
  History
   By period
    1810- -- Continued

2274   1810-1822. War of Independence

Republic of Colombia formed by union of New
     Granada, Venezuela, and Ecuador, 1819-1822
Including Siege of Cartagena, 1815; Battle of Boyacá,
     1819
Including biography: José María Córdoba, José
     Fernández Madrid, Antonio Nariño, Antonio
     Ricaurte y Lozano, etc.

2275   1822-1832

After Venezuela and Ecuador became independent,
     the name "State of New Granada" was adopted
     (Law of 1831 and Constitution of 1832)
Including Gran Colombia-Peru War, 1828-1829; Battle
     of Tarqui, Ecuador, 1829; separatist movements,
     1829-1830

2276   1832-1886

In modification of Constitution of 1842 and 1843, the
     name changed to "Republic of New Granada";
     under Constitution of 1858, name changed to
     "Confederation of Granada"; in Pact of 1861 and
     Constitution of 1863, name changed to "United
     States of Colombia"
Including biography: Pascual Bravo, Pedro Alcántara
     Herrán, José Hilario López, Tomás Cipriano de
     Mosquera, Rafael Núñez, etc.

2276.5   1886-1903

Under the Constitution of 1886, name changed to
     "Republic of Colombia"
Including Revolution of 1899-1903; Secession of
     Panama, 1903
Including biography: José Manuel Marroquín, Próspero
     Pinzón, Manuel Antonio Sanclemente, etc.
Cf. F1566.5 Hay-Herrán Treaty, 1903

2277   1904-1946

Including Conservative rule, 1904-1930; the liberals,
     1930-1946; Thomson-Urrutia Treaty, 1914
Including biography: Miguel Antonio Caro, Alfonso
     López, Enrique Olaya Herrera, Pedro Nel Ospina,
     Rafael Reyes, Eduardo Santos, etc.
Cf. D501+ World War I, 1914-1918
Cf. D731+ World War II, 1939-1945
Cf. F2281.B7P1+ Leticia Dispute, 1932-1934

F1201-3799

	South America
	Colombia
	History
	By period
	1810- -- Continued
2278	1946-1974
	Including Conservative restoration, 1946
	Including biography: Laureano Gómez, Mariano Ospina Pérez, Gustavo Rojas Pinilla, etc.
	1974-
2279	General works
	Biography
2279.2	Collective
2279.22.A-Z	Individual, A-Z
	Subarrange each by Table F5
2281.A-Z	Regions, departments, etc., A-Z
	e.g.
2281.A4	Amazon River and Valley, Colombia
	Cf. F2546 General, and Brazil
2281.A5	Andes Mountains, Colombia
	Cf. F2212 General
2281.A6	Antioquia
2281.A7	Arauca (Dept.)
2281.A79	Atlantic Coast
2281.A8	Atlántico
	Bogotá River see F2281.C9
2281.B6	Bolívar
	Including Barú Island, Rosario Islands, Tierra Bomba Island, San Jorge River, Sinú River
2281.B7	Boundaries
2281.B7A1-.B7A9	General
	Brazil see F2554.C7
	Costa Rica (Ancient boundary) see F1549.B7
2281.B7E1-.B7E9	Ecuador
	Panama see F1569.B7
2281.B7P1-.B7P9	Peru
	Including Leticia question
	Saint Andrews Island see F2281.S15
2281.B7V1-.B7V9	Venezuela
2281.B8	Boyacá
2281.C25	Caldas
2281.C26	Caquetá
2281.C27	Cartagena (Province)
2281.C3	Cauca
	For Patí River see F2281.P37
2281.C32	Cauca River and Valley
2281.C4	César

	South America
	Colombia
	Regions, departments, etc., A-Z -- Continued
2281.C5	Chocó
2281.C6	Córdoba (Dept.)
2281.C9	Cundinamarca
	Including Bogotá River
	For San Martín (Territory) see F2281.M49
2281.D2	Darien. Scots' Colony (Caledonia)
	For modern Darién see F1569.D3
2281.G8	Goajira (Territory). La Guajira (Dept.)
	Including Goajira peninsula
2281.H8	Huila
	La Guajira (Dept.) see F2281.G8
	Leticia question see F2281.B7P1+
2281.L52	Llanos Orientales
	Cf. F2331.O7 Orinoco River and Valley
2281.M2	Magdalena (Dept.). Santa Marta Province
	Including Sierra Nevada de Santa Marta
2281.M23	Magdalena River and Valley
2281.M3	Malpelo Island
2281.M49	Meta (Territory). San Martín (Territory)
	Including Ariari River
	Morrosquillo, Gulf of see F2281.S82
2281.N3	Nariño
	For Patí River see F2281.P37
2281.N5	Neiva (Province)
2281.N6	Norte de Santander
2281.P23	Pacific Coast
2281.P3	Pamplona (Province)
2281.P37	Patí River and Valley
2281.P4	Sierra de Perijá
	Cf. F2331.P4 Perijá (District) of Venezuela
2281.P8	Popayán (Province)
	Providence Island see F2281.S15
2281.P9	Putumayo (Dept.)
	Including Sibundoy Valley and the part of the Putumayo
	River and Valley located in Colombia,
	For general works on the Putomayo River and Valley,
	as well as works limited to the part located in
	Peru see F3451.P94
2281.Q55	Quindío (Province)
2281.S15	San Andrés y Providencia (Territory)
	Including Saint Andrews Island, Providence Island
	San Martín (Territory) see F2281.M49
	Santa Marta (Province) see F2281.M2
	Santa Marta, Sierra Nevada de see F2281.M2

F1201-3799

	South America
	Colombia
	Regions, departments, etc., A-Z -- Continued
2281.S3	Santander
	Sierra de Perijá see F2281.P4
2281.S82	Sucre (Dept.)
	Including Gulf of Morrosquillo
2281.S86	Sumapaz Region
2281.T6	Tolima
2281.T8	Tunja (Province)
2281.U7	Urabá (Province)
2281.V3	Valle del Cauca
2291.A-Z	Cities, towns, etc., A-Z
	e.g.
2291.B3	Barranquilla
2291.B6-.B69	Bogotá (Table F2)
2291.B77	Bucaramanga
2291.B8	Buga
2291.C15	Cali
2291.C3	Cartagena
	For siege of 1815 see F2272
2291.M4	Medellín
2291.P28	Pasto
2291.T8	Tunja
	Elements in the population
	Including foreign elements (General), minorities, race
	conflicts and problems
	For interpretation see F1392.A1+
2299.A1	General works
2299.A2-Z	Individual elements
2299.A73	Arabs
2299.B37	Basques
2299.B55	Blacks
2299.G3	Germans
	Indians see F2269+
2299.J3	Japanese
2299.J4	Jews
2299.L42	Lebanese
	Negroes see F2299.B55
	Venezuela
2301	Periodicals. Societies. Collections
2301.5	Sources and documents
	Collected works
2302	Several authors
2303	Individual authors
	Including collected papers, addresses, essays, etc.
2303.5	Museums. Exhibitions, exhibits

	South America
	Venezuela -- Continued
2304	Gazetteers. Dictionaries. Geographic names
2304.5	Directories
	Biography
2305	Collective
	Individual (Historians) see F2320.6.A+
	Individual (By period) see F2321.92+
2308	General works
2308.5	Juvenile works
2309	Pamphlets, addresses, essays, etc.
2309.3	Anecdotes, legends, pageants, etc.
	Cf. P, Literature
	Cf. GR130+ Folklore
2309.5	Guidebooks. Handbooks
2309.7	Historic monuments (General)
2310	Social life and customs. Civilization. Intellectual life
	Including national characteristics
	For race conflicts and problems see F2349.A1+
2310.9	Geography
	Description and travel. Views
2311	Early to 1809
2313	1810-1950
2314	1951-1980
2315	1981-
	Antiquities. Indians
2318	Museums. Exhibitions
2319	General works
2319.1.A-Z	Local (Ancient and modern), A-Z
	e. g.
2319.1.M3	Maracay
2319.1.S8	Sucre (State)
2319.2.A-Z	Tribes (Ancient and modern), A-Z
	Arawak see F2230.2.A7
	Arecuna see F2380.1.A7
2319.2.A73	Arekena
	Baniva see F2520.1.B35
	Baré see F2520.1.B4
	Betoya see F2270.2.T77
2319.2.C28	Caquetio
	Carib see F2460.1.C37
	Cariban see F2001
	Churoya see F2270.2.C63
2319.2.C78	Cuiva
2319.2.C8	Cumana
	Goajiro see F2270.2.G6
2319.2.G8	Guahibo

	South America
	Venezuela
	Antiquities. Indians
	Tribes (Ancient and modern), A-Z -- Continued
2319.2.G85	Guaiqueri
2319.2.I7	Irapa
	Macu see F2520.1.M2
	Macusi see F2380.1.M3
2319.2.M3	Maipure
2319.2.M6	Motilone
2319.2.O8	Otomaco
2319.2.P3	Palenque
2319.2.P34	Panare
2319.2.P37	Paraujano
2319.2.P45	Pemon
2319.2.P5	Piaroa
2319.2.S3	Saliva
2319.2.S52	Sicuane
2319.2.T25	Tamanca
	Taurepan see F2380.1.A7
2319.2.T4	Teque
2319.2.T5	Timote
	Waica see F2520.1.W3
2319.2.W3	Warao
	Yanomamo see F2520.1.Y3
2319.2.Y3	Yaruro
2319.2.Y4	Yecuana
2319.2.Y8	Yupa
2319.3.A-Z	Topics (Ancient and modern), A-Z
2319.3.A37	Agriculture
2319.3.A5	Anthropometry
2319.3.A67	Architecture
2319.3.A7	Art
2319.3.B37	Baskets
2319.3.C4	Census
2319.3.C46	Children
2319.3.E26	Economic conditions
2319.3.E29	Education
2319.3.E46	Employment
(2319.3.F58)	Folk literature
	see F2319.3.F6
2319.3.F6	Folklore. Legends
2319.3.G6	Government relations
2319.3.L35	Land tenure
2319.3.M5	Missions
2319.3.N5	Names
2319.3.P4	Petroglyphs. Rock paintings

	South America
	Venezuela
	Antiquities. Indians
	Topics (Ancient and modern), A-Z -- Continued
2319.3.P6	Pottery
	Rock paintings see F2319.3.P4
2319.3.S6	Social conditions
2319.3.S62	Social life and customs
2319.3.T43	Teenagers
	History
2319.5	Chronological tables. Outlines, syllabi, etc. Questions and answers, etc.
	Historiography
2320	General works
	Biography of historians
2320.5	Collective
2320.6.A-Z	Individual, A-Z
	Subarrange each by Table F5
2320.7	Study and teaching
2321	General works
	Including political history
	General special
2321.1	Military and naval history
	Diplomatic history. Foreign and general relations
2321.2	General works
2321.3.A-Z	Relations with individual countries, A-Z
2321.9	Other (not A-Z)
	By period
	Pre-Columbian period see F2318+
2322	1498-1806/1810
	Including early settlement; German occupation to 1556; pillage and attacks by English and French, 1595-1798; separation from Viceroyalty of Peru, 1731. In 1777, Captain-Generalcy of Caracas established; in 1786, Audiencia of Caracas created
	Biography: Alonso Andrea de Ledesma
2322.8	1806/1810-
	Including biography: José Antonio Páez, etc.
2323	1806-1812
	Including Francisco de Miranda's attempts at independence including his biography; Treaty of San Mateo, 1812

F1201-3799

South America
  Venezuela
    History
      By period
        1806/1810- -- Continued
2324   1810-1830. War of Independence, 1810-1823
          Including Earthquake of 1812; Battle of Carabobo, 1821. Province of Republic of Colombia, 1822-1829
          Including biography: José Antonio Anzoátegui, José Tomás Boves, Pedro Luis Brión, Pablo Morillo y Morillo, José Félix Ribas, etc.
2325   1830-1935
          Including Republic of Venezuela formed in 1830; Era of civil wars, 1848-1870; Revolution, 1902-1903; Anglo-German-Italian Blockade, 1902; Dutch Blockade, 1908
          Including biography: Cipriano Castro, Joaquín Crespo, Juan Vicente Gómez, Antonio Guzmán Blanco, Santos Michelena, José Tadeo Monagas, Juan Pietri, Arístides Rojas, José María Vargas, etc.
2326   1935-1958
          Including movement toward democracy, 1935-1948; Revolution of 1945
          Including biography: Rómulo Betancourt, Carlos Delgado Chalband, Eleazar López Contreras, Isaías Medina Angarita, Marcos Pérez Jiménez, etc.
          Cf. D731+ World War II, 1939-1945
       1958-1974
2327   General works
        Biography
2327.5   Collective
2327.52.A-Z   Individual, A-Z
         Subarrange each by Table F5
       1974-1999
2328   General works
        Biography
2328.5   Collective
2328.52.A-Z   Individual, A-Z
         Subarrange each by Table F5
       1999-
2329   General works
        Biography
2329.2   Collective
2329.22.A-Z   Individual, A-Z
         Subarrange each by Table F5

	South America
	Venezuela -- Continued
2331.A-Z	Regions, states, etc., A-Z
2331.A2	Islands along the Venezuela coast (General)
	For islands off the coast, belonging to other countries see F2016
2331.A3	Amazonas
2331.A5	Andes Mountains, Venezuela
	Cf. F2212 General
2331.A55	Anzoátegui
2331.A65	Apure
2331.A7	Aragua
2331.A9	Aves Islands
2331.A93	Avila Mountain
2331.B3	Barinas (Sur de Occidente, Zamora)
2331.B6	Bolívar
	Including Great Savannah
	Boundaries
2331.B7	General
	Brazil see F2554.V4
2331.B72	British Guiana. Guyana
	Colombia see F2281.B7
	Guyana see F2331.B72
2331.B75	Bruzual
2331.C3	Carabobo
2331.C5	Chacao (Caracas) Vallley
2331.C6	Cojedes
2331.C7	Cubagua Island
2331.D44	Delta Amacuro
2331.F2	Falcón
	Including Paraguaná Peninsula
	Goajira (Guajira) peninsula see F2281.G8
	Great Savannah see F2331.B6
2331.G8	Guárico
2331.G83	Guayana Region
	Isla de Patos see F2331.P3
2331.J82	Juan José Mora
	Lake Maracaibo Region see F2331.M27
	Lake Valencia see F2331.V3
2331.L3	Lara
2331.M27	Maracaibo Lake Region
2331.M3	Margarita (Island)
2331.M5	Mérida
2331.M52	Mérida, Cordillera de (Sierra Nevada de Mérida)
2331.M6	Miranda
2331.M7	Monagas

F1201-3799

	South America
	Venezuela
	Regions, states, etc., A-Z -- Continued
2331.N8	Nueva Esparta
	For Margarita Island see F2331.M3
2331.O7	Orinoco River and Valley
	Cf. F2281.L52 Llanos Orientales
	Paraguaná Peninsula see F2331.F2
2331.P3	Islas de Patos
2331.P4	Perijá (District)
	Cf. F2281.P4 Sierra de Perija, Colombia
2331.P6	Portuguesa
	Roraima, Mount see F2609
2331.S8	Sucre
	Sur de Occidente see F2331.B3
2331.T2	Táchira
2331.T7	Trujillo
2331.V3	Valencia, Lake
2331.V35	Vargas
2331.Y3	Yaracuy
	Zamora see F2331.B3
2331.Z9	Zulia
	For Perijá (District) see F2331.P4
2341.A-Z	Cities, towns, etc., A-Z
	e.g.
2341.A2	Collective
2341.B3	Barquisimeto
2341.C2-.C29	Caracas (Table F2)
2341.C8	Cumaná
2341.M2	Maracaibó
2341.M25	Maracay
2341.M5	Mérida
2341.S13	San Cristóbal
2341.V25	Valencia
	Elements in the population
	For interpretation see F1392.A1+
2349.A1	General works
2349.A2-Z	Individual, A-Z
2349.A5	Americans
2349.A74	Argentines
2349.B3	Basques
2349.B55	Blacks
	Cf. HT1151+ Slavery
2349.C35	Canary Islanders
2349.C64	Colombians
2349.C83	Cubans
2349.D8	Dutch

	South America
	Venezuela
	Elements in the population
	Individual, A-Z -- Continued
2349.F73	French
2349.G24	Gallegans
2349.G3	Germans
	Indians see F2318+
2349.I8	Italians
2349.J48	Jews
2349.L43	Lebanese
2349.P6	Portuguese
2349.S36	Scotch. Scots
	Scots see F2349.S36
2349.S7	Spaniards
	Guiana
	The region between the Amazon and Orinoco although at present usually restricted to British, Dutch, and French Guiana
2351	General works
	Cf. E111+ Early voyages
2354	Antiquities. Indians
	Guyana. British Guiana
2361	Periodicals. Societies. Collections
	Collected works
2362	Several authors
2363	Individual authors
	Including collected papers, addresses, essays, etc.
2363.5	Museums. Exhibitions, exhibits
2364	Gazetteers. Dictionaries. Geographic names
2364.5	Directories
	Biography
2365	Collective
	Individual (Historians) see F2380.6.A+
	Individual (By period) see F2382.92+
2368	General works
2368.5	Juvenile works
2369	Pamphlets, essays
2369.3	Anecdotes, legends, pageants
	Cf. P, Literature
	Cf. GR130+ Folklore
2369.5	Guidebooks. Handbooks
2369.7	Historic monuments (General)
2369.8	Social life and customs. Civilization. Intellectual life
	Including national characteristics
	For race conflicts and problems see F2391.A1+
2369.9	Geography

F1201-
3799

	South America
	Guiana
	Guyana. British Guiana -- Continued
	Description and travel. Views
2370	Early to 1802
2371	1803-1950
2372	1951-1980
2373	1981-
	Antiquities. Indians
2379	General works
2380	Modern Indians (General)
	Including local (not A-Z)
2380.1.A-Z	Tribes (Ancient and modern), A-Z
	e.g.
2380.1.A2	Accawai
	Arawak see F2230.2.A7
2380.1.A7	Arecuna
	Carib see F2001
2380.1.M3	Macusi
2380.1.P3	Paramona
2380.1.T3	Taruma
	Trio see F2420.1.T7
2380.1.W25	Waiwai
2380.1.W3	Wapisiana
2380.2.A-Z	Topics (Ancient and modern), A-Z
2380.2.A7	Art
2380.2.F6	Folklore. Legends
2380.2.G3	Games
2380.2.G68	Government relations
2380.2.M44	Medicine
2380.2.M57	Missions
2380.2.S63	Social life and customs
2380.2.S7	String figures
2380.2.W7	Writing
	History
2380.3	Chronological tables. Outlines, syllabi, etc. Questions and answers, etc.
	Historiography
2380.4	General works
	Biography of historians
2380.5	Collective
2380.6.A-Z	Individual, A-Z
	Subarrange each by Table F5
2380.7	Study and teaching
2381	General works
	Including political history
2382	General special

	South America
	Guiana
	Guyana. British Guiana
	History
	General special -- Continued
	Diplomatic history. Foreign and general relations
2382.3	General works
2382.4.A-Z	Relations with individual countries, A-Z
	By period
	Pre-Columbian period see F2379+
2383	1580-1803

Including Dutch colonies of Essequibo, Demerara, and
Berbice; English conquests; French conquest,
1782

Cf. E129.R2 Raleigh's explorations, 1595-1617

Cf. F2423 English in Dutch Guiana

Cf. F2462 English in French Guiana

2384	1803-1966

Including Great Britain given permanent title by
Convention of London, 1814; union of three
colonies to form British Guiana, 1831

Including biography: John Smith, 1790-1824, etc.

For boundary disputes with Venezuela see
F2331.B7

For boundary disputes with Brazil see F2554.B8

Cf. D731+ World War II, 1939-1945

2385	1966-
2387.A-Z	Regions, counties, etc., A-Z
2387.B4	Berbice
2387.B7	Boundaries
2387.B7A1-.B7A5	General
	Brazil see F2554.B8
2387.B7A6-.B7Z	Suriname. Netherlands or Dutch Guiana
	Venezuela see F2331.B72
2387.D4	Demerara
2387.E8	Essequibo
	Including Kaieteur Falls
	Roraima, Mount see F2609
2389.A-Z	Cities, towns, etc., A-Z
	e.g.
2389.B3	Bartica
2389.G3	Georgetown
2389.N4	New Amsterdam
	Formerly Berbice
	Elements in the population
	For interpretation see F1392.A1+

F1201-
3799

South America
Guiana
Guyana. British Guiana
Elements in the population -- Continued

2391.A1	General works
	Including foreign elements (General), minorities, race conflicts and problems
2391.A2-Z	Individual elements, A-Z
	e.g.
2391.C5	Chinese
2391.E2	East Indians
	Indians see F2379+
2391.M37	Maroons
2391.N4	Negroes
	Cf. HT1139+ Slavery

Suriname. Netherlands or Dutch Guiana

2401	Periodicals. Societies. Collections
	Collected works
2402	Several authors
2403	Individual authors
	Including collected papers, addresses, essays
2403.5	Museums. Exhibitions, exhibits
2404	Gazetteers. Dictionaries. Geographic names
2404.5	Directories
	Biography
2405	Collective
	Individual
	see F2423+
2408	General works
2408.5	Juvenile works
2409	Pamphlets, addresses, essays
2409.4	Anecdotes, legends, pageants
	Cf. P, Literature
	Cf. GR130+ Folklore
2409.5	Guidebooks. Handbooks
2409.6	Historic monuments (General)
2409.8	Social life and customs. Civilization. Intellectual life
	Including national characteristics
	For race conflicts and problems see F2431.A1+
	Description and travel. Views
2410	Early to 1813
2411	1814-1950
2412	1951-1980
2413	1981-
	Antiquities. Indians
2419	General works

	South America
	Guiana
	Suriname. Netherlands or Dutch Guiana
	Antiquities. Indians -- Continued
2420	Modern Indians (General)
	Including local (not A-Z)
2420.1.A-Z	Tribes (Ancient and modern), A-Z
2420.1.A35	Akurio
	Arawak see F2230.2.A7
	Carib (Galibi) see F2460.1.C37
	Cariban see F2001
	Galibi see F2460.1.C37
2420.1.O8	Oyaricoulet
2420.1.T7	Trio
	Warrau see F2319.2.W3
	Wayana see F2230.2.O8
2420.2.A-Z	Topics (Ancient and modern), A-Z
2420.2.A7	Art
2420.2.P64	Politics and government
	History
2420.3	Chronological tables. Outlines, syllabi, etc. Questions, answers, etc.
	Historiography
2420.4	General works
	Biography of historians
2420.5	Collective
2420.6.A-Z	Individual, A-Z
	Subarrange each by Table F5
2420.7	Study and teaching
2421	General works
	Including political history
2422	General special
	By period
2423	1604-1814
	Early English settlements; Willoughby and Hyde's Grant, 1663; Dutch West India Company, 1621-1791. Also includes general works on the four Dutch colonies (Essequibo, Demerara, Berbice, and Suriname), 1667-1803
	Including biography: Cornelius Van Aerssen, heer van Sommelsdijk; Abraham Crijnssen; Jan Jacob Mauricius; etc.
	Cf. E129.R2 Raleigh's explorations, 1595-1617
	Cf. F2383 Essequibo, Demerara, and Berbice (Former Dutch colonies)

F1201-3799

	South America
	Guiana
	Suriname. Netherlands or Dutch Guiana
	History
	By period -- Continued
2424	1814-1950
	Including Dutch given permanent title by Treaty of Paris, 1814; member of Dutch American Union, 1828-1845
	Cf. D731+ World War II, 1939-1945
2425	1950-1975
	As of January 10, 1950, became autonomous within the Dutch Empire
	1975-
2425.2	General works
	Biography
2425.22	Collective
2425.23.A-Z	Individual, A-Z
	Subarrange each by Table F5
2427.A-Z	Regions, districts, A-Z
2427.B7	Boundaries
2427.B7A1-.B7A5	General
	Brazil see F2554.D8
	British Guiana see F2387.B7
2427.B7A6-.B7Z	French Guiana
2427.M3	Maroni River and Valley
	Class here works limited to the part of the Maroni River and Valley located in Suriname
	For general works on the Maroni River and Valley, as well as works limited to the part located in French Guiana see F2467.M3
2429.A-Z	Cities, towns, etc., A-Z
	e.g.
2429.N5	Nieuw Nickerie
2429.P3	Paramaribo
	Elements in the population
	For interpretation see F1392.A1+
2431.A1	General works
	Including foreign elements (General), minorities, race conflicts and problems
2431.A2-Z	Individual elements
2431.B64	Boni
2431.E2	East Indians
	Indians see F2419+
2431.J3	Javanese
2431.J4	Jews
2431.L4	Lebanese

South America
Guiana
Suriname. Netherlands or Dutch Guiana
Elements in the population
Individual elements -- Continued

2431.N3	Negroes. Blacks
	Cf. HT1141+ Slavery
2431.S27	Saramacca

French Guiana

2441	Periodicals. Societies. Collections
	Collected works
2442	Several authors
2443	Individual authors
	Including collected papers, addresses, essays, etc.
2443.5	Museums. Exhibitions, exhibits
2444	Gazetteers. Dictionaries. Geographic names
2444.5	Directories
	Biography
2445	Collective
	Individual (Historians) see F2460.6.A+
	Individual (By period) see F2461.92+
2448	General works
2448.5	Juvenile works
2449	Pamphlets, addresses, essays
2449.3	Anecdotes, legends, pageants
	Cf. P, Literature
	Cf. GR130+ Folklore
2449.5	Guidebooks. Handbooks
2449.7	Historic monuments (General)
2449.8	Social life and customs. Civilization. Intellectual life
	Including national characteristics
	For race conflicts and problems see F2471.A1+
	Description and travel. Views
2450	Early to 1813
2451	1814-1950
2452	1951-
	Antiquities. Indians
2459	General works
2460	Modern Indians (General)
	Including local (not A-Z)
2460.1.A-Z	Tribes (Ancient and modern), A-Z
	Arawak see F2230.2.A7
2460.1.C37	Carib (Galibi)
	Cariban see F2001
2460.1.E5	Emerillon
	Galibi see F2460.1.C37
2460.1.O9	Oyampi. Wayampi

F1201-3799

	South America
	Guiana
	French Guiana
	Antiquities. Indians
	Tribes (Ancient and modern), A-Z -- Continued
2460.1.P3	Palicur
	Wayampi see F2460.1.O9
	Wayana see F2230.2.O8
2460.2.A-Z	Topics (Ancient and modern), A-Z
2460.2.A37	Agriculture
2460.2.E38	Education
2460.2.F64	Folklore. Legends
2460.2.G68	Government relations
	Legends see F2460.2.F64
2460.2.P6	Pottery
	History
2460.3	Chronological tables. Outlines, syllabi, etc. Questions and answers, etc.
	Historiography
2460.4	General works
	Biography of historians
2460.5	Collective
2460.6.A-Z	Individual, A-Z
	Subarrange each by Table F5
2460.7	Study and teaching
2461	General works
	Including political history
	By period
	Pre-Columbian period see F2459+
2462	1626-1814
	Including early English settlements on the Oyapok; first French settlement, 1643; expedition of Kourou, 1763-1765; Portuguese (from Brazil) occupation, 1809-1817
	Cf. E129.R2 Raleigh's explorations, 1595-1617
	Cf. F2383 French in British Guiana
2463	1814-1946
	Including French given permanent title by Treaty of Paris, 1814.
	For boundary disputes with Brazil see F2554.F8
	For use as a penal colony see HV8956.G8
	Cf. D731+ World War II, 1939-1945
2464	1947-
	As of January 1, 1947, became a department of Metropolitan France
2467.A-Z	Regions, districts, etc., A-Z
2467.B7	Boundaries

	South America
	Guiana
	French Guiana
	Regions, districts, etc., A-Z
	Boundaries -- Continued
	Brazil see F2554.F8
	Suriname (Dutch Guiana) see F2427.B7
2467.I4	Îles du Salut (Devil's Island)
	For use as a penal colony see HV8956.G8
2467.I5	Inine (Territory)
2467.M25	Mana River and Valley
2467.M3	Maroni River and Valley
	Class here general works on the Maroni River and Valley, as well as works limited to the part located in French Guiana
	For works limited to the part of the Maroni River and Valley located in Suriname see F2427.M3
2467.T9	Tumuc-Humac Mountains
2469.A-Z	Cities, towns, etc., A-Z
	e.g.
2469.C3	Cayenne
2469.S3	Saint-Georges (Saint-Georges-de-l'Oyapock)
2469.S5	Saint-Laurent (Saint-Laurent-du-Maroni)
	Elements in the population
	Including foreign elements (General), minorities, race conflicts and problems
	For interpretation see F1392.A1+
2471.A1	General works
2471.A2-Z	Individual elements, A-Z
2471.B55	Blacks
2471.H56	Hmong (Asian people)
	Indians see F2459+
	Negroes see F2471.B55
	Brazil
2501	Periodicals. Societies. Serials
2501.5	Congresses
	Collected works (nonserial)
2502	Several authors
2503	Individual authors
	Including collected papers, addresses, essays, etc.
2503.5	Museums. Exhibitions, exhibits
2504	Gazetteers. Dictionaries. Geographic names
2504.5	Directories
	Biography
2505	Collective
	Individual (Historians) see F2520.6.A+
	Individual (By period) see F2523.92+

F1201-3799

	South America
	Brazil -- Continued
2508	General works
2508.5	Juvenile works
2509	Pamphlets, addresses, essays, etc.
2509.3	Anecdotes, legends, pageants, etc.
	Cf. P, Literature
	Cf. GR130+ Folklore
2509.5	Guidebooks. Handbooks
2509.7	Historic monuments (General)
2510	Social life and customs. Civilization. Intellectual life
	Including national characteristics
	For race conflicts and problems see F2659.A1+
2510.5	Brazilians in foreign countries (General)
	For Brazilians in a particular country, see the country
2510.9	Geography
	Description and travel. Views
2511	Early to 1821
2513	1822-1889
2515	1890-1950
2516	1951-1980
2517	1981-
	Antiquities. Indians
2518.5	Museums. Exhibitions
2519	General works
2519.1.A-Z	Local (Ancient and modern), A-Z
	e.g.
2519.1.A6	Amazon Valley
2519.1.B3	Bahia (State)
2519.1.G68	Goiás (State). Goyaz (State)
2519.1.L3	Lagoa Santa
2519.1.M37	Maranhão (State)
2519.1.M4	Matto Grosso (State)
2519.1.P2	Pará (State)
2519.1.P3	Paraná (State)
2519.1.P37	Parque Nacional do Xingu
2519.1.P8	Purus River
2519.1.R5	Rio de Janeiro (State)
2519.1.R6	Rio Grande do Sul (State)
2519.1.S2	São Paulo (State)
2519.1.U3	Uaupés Valley
2519.1.X56	Xingu Valley
2519.3.A-Z	Topics (Ancient and modern), A-Z
	Adornment see F2519.3.C68
2519.3.A42	Alcohol use
2519.3.A5	Anthropometry
2519.3.A7	Art

	South America
	Brazil
	Antiquities. Indians
	Topics (Ancient and modern), A-Z -- Continued
2519.3.A84	Astronomy
2519.3.B36	Baskets
2519.3.B5	Boats
2519.3.B6	Bows and arrows
2519.3.C3	Cannibalism
2519.3.C65	Communication
2519.3.C68	Costume. Adornment
2519.3.C85	Cultural assimilation
2519.3.D2	Dance
2519.3.D84	Dwellings
2519.3.E2	Education
2519.3.E83	Ethnic identity
2519.3.E85	Ethnobotany
2519.3.F4	Featherwork
2519.3.F6	Folklore. Legends
2519.3.F63	Food
2519.3.G3	Games
	Government see F2519.3.P58
2519.3.G6	Government relations
2519.3.H85	Hunting
2519.3.I4	Implements
2519.3.I5	Industries
2519.3.K53	Kings and rulers
2519.3.K55	Kinship
2519.3.L36	Land tenure
2519.3.M36	Material culture
2519.3.M37	Mathematics
2519.3.M43	Medicine
2519.3.M48	Migrations
2519.3.M5	Missions
2519.3.N35	Names
2519.3.P58	Politics and government
2519.3.P59	Population
2519.3.P6	Pottery
2519.3.R3	Religion. Mythology
2519.3.S46	Services for
2519.3.S58	Social conditions
2519.3.S6	Social life and customs
2519.3.S94	Suicidal behavior
2519.3.U73	Urban residence
2519.3.W37	Wars
2519.3.W66	Women
2519.3.W7	Writing

F1201-
3799

	South America
	Brazil
	Antiquities. Indians -- Continued
2520	Modern Indians (General)
2520.1.A-Z	Tribes (Ancient and modern), A-Z
2520.1.A4	Akwe-Shavante. Xavante
	Amahuaca see F3430.1.A5
2520.1.A6	Apalai
2520.1.A63	Apalakiri
2520.1.A632	Apapocuva
2520.1.A64	Apiacá
2520.1.A65	Apinagé
2520.1.A7	Arara
2520.1.A75	Araua
	Arawak see F2230.2.A7
2520.1.A77	Araweté
	Arecuna see F2380.1.A7
2520.1.A84	Asurini
2520.1.A93	Ava-Canoeiro
2520.1.B3	Bakairi
2520.1.B35	Baniva
2520.1.B4	Baré
	Betoya see F2270.2.T77
	Boro see F2270.2.B6
2520.1.B75	Bororo
2520.1.B76	Botocudo
2520.1.C3	Cadioeo
	Caingua see F2230.2.C3
2520.1.C316	Canamari
2520.1.C32	Canella
	Canoeiro see F2520.1.R53
2520.1.C35	Caraja
	Carib see F2001
2520.1.C37	Caripuna
2520.1.C38	Cashinawa
2520.1.C4	Catoquina
2520.1.C44	Caxixó
2520.1.C45	Cayapo
	Chamacoco see F3320.2.C5
	Chapacura see F3320.2.C38
	Charrua see F2719.2.C5
	Chavante see F2520.1.A4
(2520.1.C6)	Chipaya
	see F3320.2.C388
	Chiquito see F3320.2.C3
2520.1.C64	Cinta Larga
2520.1.C67	Craho. Kraho

South America
  Brazil
    Antiquities. Indians
      Tribes (Ancient and modern), A-Z -- Continued

2520.1.C7	Crichaná
2520.1.C84	Culina
2520.1.D47	Desana
2520.1.F8	Fulnio
2520.1.G37	Gaviões
2520.1.G4	Ge
2520.1.G6	Goyataca
2520.1.G68	Guaharibo
2520.1.G69	Guajá
	Guajajara see F2520.1.T4
2520.1.G718	Guana
2520.1.G72	Guanano
	Guarani see F2230.2.G72
2520.1.G75	Guató
	Guayana see F2230.2.G75
	Guayaqui see F2679.2.G9
	Guaycuru see F2230.2.G78
2520.1.H48	Heta
2520.1.I6	Ipurucotó
2520.1.I7	Iranxe
2520.1.J8	Juruna. Yuruna
2520.1.K3	Kaingang. Kaingangue
2520.1.K35	Kamaiurá
2520.1.K4	Kariri
	Kashinaua see F2520.1.C38
2520.1.K45	Kayabi
	Kraho see F2520.1.C67
2520.1.K7	Kreen-Akarore
2520.1.K85	Kuikuru
2520.1.M2	Macu
	Macusi see F2380.1.M3
2520.1.M24	Mamaindê
2520.1.M26	Maruba
2520.1.M27	Masacali
2520.1.M3	Maue
	Mayoruna see F3430.1.M45
	Mbaya see F2679.2.M3
2520.1.M44	Mehinacu
2520.1.M45	Mekranoti
	Mojo see F3320.2.M55
2520.1.M8	Mundurucu
2520.1.M9	Mura
	Including Pirahá Indians

F1201-
3799

	South America
	Brazil
	Antiquities. Indians
	Tribes (Ancient and modern), A-Z -- Continued
2520.1.N3	Nambicuara
	Omagua see F3430.1.O5
2520.1.O63	Opaye
	Pacaguara see F3320.2.P3
	Paingua see F2230.2.C3
2520.1.P32	Pakaa Nova
	Palicur see F2460.1.P3
2520.1.P35	Pancararu
	Pano see F3430.1.P3
	Panoan Indians see F3430.1.P33
2520.1.P38	Parakaña
2520.1.P4	Parintintin
2520.1.P43	Patasho
2520.1.P45	Pauishana
	Peban see F3430.1.P4
	Pirahá see F2520.1.M9
	Piro see F3430.1.P5
2520.1.P68	Potiguara
2520.1.P8	Puri
2520.1.R53	Rikbaktsa. Canoeiro (Mato Grosso)
2520.1.S22	Sakirabiá
2520.1.S24	Saluma
2520.1.S3	Sanavirona
	Sapuya see F2520.1.K4
2520.1.S47	Sherente
2520.1.S5	Shokleng
2520.1.S86	Surui
2520.1.S89	Suya
2520.1.T2	Tapajo
2520.1.T25	Tapirapé
2520.1.T3	Tapuya
2520.1.T32	Tariana
2520.1.T4	Tenetehara
2520.1.T43	Teremembe
2520.1.T45	Terena. Tereno
2520.1.T5	Timbira
	Trio see F2420.1.T7
2520.1.T7	Trumai
2520.1.T9	Tucano
2520.1.T925	Tucuna
	Tukanoan see F2270.2.T77
2520.1.T933	Tupari
	Tupi see F2230.2.T84

	South America
	Brazil
	Antiquities. Indians
	Tribes (Ancient and modern), A-Z -- Continued
2520.1.T94	Tupinamba
2520.1.T97	Tuxá
2520.1.T98	Tuyuca
2520.1.U3	Uaboi
2520.1.U5	Umotina
2520.1.U7	Urubu Kaapor
2520.1.U74	Uruewawau
2520.1.W3	Waica
2520.1.W34	Waimiri
	Waiwai see F2380.1.W25
	Wapisiana see F2380.1.W3
2520.1.W38	Waura
	Wayampi see F2460.1.O9
	Wayana see F2230.2.O8
2520.1.X33	Xacriaba
	Xavante see F2520.1.A4
2520.1.X5	Xikrin
2520.1.Y25	Yaminawa
2520.1.Y3	Yanomamo
	Yuruna see F2520.1.J8
2520.1.Z65	Zoró
2520.1.Z87	Zuruahá
	History
2520.3	Chronological tables. Outlines, syllabi, etc. Questions and answers, etc.
	Historiography
2520.4	General works
	Biography of historians
2520.5	Collective
2520.6.A-Z	Individual, A-Z
	Subarrange each by Table F5
	e.g.
2520.6.A2	Abreu, João Capistrano de (Table F5)
2520.6.P4	Pereira de Costa, Francisco Augusto (Table F5)
2520.7	Study and teaching
2521	General works
	Including political history
	General special
2522	Military and naval history
	Diplomatic history. Foreign and general relations
2523	General works
2523.5.A-Z	Relations with individual countries, A-Z
	United States see E183.8.A+

F1201-
3799

South America
Brazil
History
General special -- Continued
2523.9   Other (not A-Z)
By period
Pre-Columbian period see F2518.5+
2524   1500-1821
2526   1500-1548
Including discovery, exploration, and colonization by
Portuguese
Cf. E123 Demarkation line of Alexander VI
2528   1549-1762
Including Bandeiras (General); if limited to a state,
class with state); expulsion of Jesuits
Including biography: José de Anchieta, Salvador
Correia de Sá e Benavides, Mem de Sá, António
Vieira, etc.
Cf. BX4705.V55 Vieira as religious figure
Cf. F2684 Jesuit missions of Paraguay, War of
the Seven Reductions (Guarani War), 1754-
1756
Cf. F2723 Portuguese settlement at Colonia,
Uruguay
2529   French colony at Rio de Janeiro, 1555-1567
Including biography: Nicolas Durand de Villegagnon
2530   Spanish control, 1580-1640
2532   Dutch conquest, 1624-1654
Including Capture of Bahia, 1625; battles at
Guararapes, 1648 and 1649; capture of Olinda,
1630
Including biography: Henrique Dias, João Fernandes
Vieira, etc.
2534   1763-1821
Including Portuguese court in Brazil, 1801-1821; revolt
in Pernambuco, 1817
Including biography: Joaquim José da Silva Xavier
(Tiradentes), etc.
Cf. DP650+ John VI, King of Portugal
Cf. F2461 French Guiana
Cf. F2723 Expulsion of Brazilians from Colonia
2535   1822-

                    South America
                      Brazil
                        History
                          By period
                            1822- -- Continued

2536   Empire, 1822-1889
                Including Pedro I, 1822-1831; Regency, 1831-1841;
                   Pedro II, 1841-1889
                Including Brazil declared independent of Portugal on
                   September 7, 1822; Empire established on
                   October 12, 1822; Revolution of 1842; separatist
                   movement in Rio Grande do Sul, 1845
                Including biography: José Bonifacio de Andrada e Silva
                   (Cf. PQ9697 as author), Benjamin Constant
                   Botelho de Magalhães; Luiz Alves de Lima e Silva,
                   duque de Caxias; Marcillio Dias; Diogo Antonio
                   Feijo; Giuseppe Garibaldi (Cf. DG 558.2.G2 as
                   Italian patriot); Irineo Evangelista de Souza,
                   visconde de Maua; Joaquim Nabuco; Joaquim
                   Marques Lisbôa, marques de Tamandare
                Cf. F2687 Paraguayan War, 1865-1870
                Cf. F2725 War with Argentina over Uruguay,
                   1825-1828
                Cf. F2846.3 War with Argentina, 1849-1852

2537   Republic, 1889-
                Including special period, 1889-1930
                Including Brazil's declaration as a republic, November
                   15, 1889
                Including the Naval revolt of 1893-1894; Conselheiro
                   Insurrection, 1897; military revolution of 1924-
                   1925; etc.
                Including biography: Ruy Barbosa, Manuel Ferraz de
                   Campos Salles, Manuel Deodoro da Fonseca,
                   Antonio Vicente Mendes Maciel, Manuel de
                   Oliveira Lima, Floriano Peixoto, Jose Gomes
                   Pinheiro Machado, José Maria da Silva Paranhos,
                   barão do Rio Branco, etc.
                Cf. D501+ World War I, 1914-1918

2538   1930-1954. Period of Vargas
                Including Revolution of 1930; Communist Revolution of
                   1935; Integralist Revolt of 1938
                Including biography: Eurico Gasper Dutra, Getulio
                   Vargas, etc.
                Cf. D731+ World War II, 1939-1945
                    1954-1964
                Including administrations of Kubitschek, Quadros, and
                 Goulart

F1201-
3799

	South America
	Brazil
	History
	By period
	1822-
	1954-1964 -- Continued
2538.2	General works
	Biography
2538.22.A2	Collective
2538.22.A3-Z	Individual
	Subarrange each by Table F5
	e.g.
2538.22.G6	Goulart, João Belchior Marques (Table F5)
2538.22.K8	Kubitschek, Juscelino (Table F5)
	1964-1985
2538.25	General works
	Biography and memoirs
2538.26	Collective
2538.27.A-Z	Individual, A-Z
	Subarrange each by Table F5
	e.g.
2538.27.F53	Figueiredo, João Baptista de Oliveira, 1918- (Table F5)
2538.27.G44	Geisel, Ernesto (Table F5)
2538.27.P38	Paula, Francisco Juliao Arruda de, 1915- (Table F5)
	1985-
2538.3	General works
	Biography
2538.4	Collective
2538.5.A-Z	Individual, A-Z
	Subarrange each by Table F5
	Regions, states, etc.
2539	Islands of Brazil (General)
2540	Acre (Territory)
	Cf. F2546 Amazonas boundary
2541	Alagoas
2543	Amapá Territory
2546	Amazonas
	Including Amazon River and Valley; Içá River; Japurá (Yapurá) River; Javarí (Yavarí) River; Jurua River; Jutaí (Jutahy) River; Purus River; Rio Negro
	Cf. F2281.A4 Amazon River and Valley, Colombia
	Cf. F3451.A4 Amazonas (Peru)
	Cf. F3451.L8 Amazon River and Valley, Peru
2548	Atlantic Coast

	South America
	Brazil
	Regions, states, etc. -- Continued
2551	Bahia (Baía)
	Including Jacuípe River and Valley, and Diamantina Plateau
	Cf. F2601 Pernambuco boundary
	Cf. F2636 Sergipe boundary
	Boundaries
2554.A1-.A8	General
2554.A82	Argentina
	For Misiones question see F2916
2554.B6	Bolivia
	Cf. F2540 Acre (Territory)
2554.B8	British Guiana
2554.C7	Colombia
2554.D8	Dutch Guiana. Suriname
2554.F8	French Guiana
2554.P3	Paraguay
2554.P4	Peru
2554.U8	Uruguay
2554.V4	Venezuela
2556	Ceará
2557	Central West Brazil
2558	Counani
	Contested territory awarded to Brazil
	Distrito Federal see F2646
2561	Espírito Santo
	Including colonies of Germans, Poles, Swedes, Tyrolese
2564	Fernando de Noronha Island (Territory)
2566	Goyaz (Goías, Goiaz)
	Including Araguaya River, Tocantins River
2567	Guanabara
	Guaporé (Territory) see F2624
	Guartelá (Region) see F2596
2567.3	Ibiapaba
	Jalapão see F2640
2567.9	Mar Mountains
2568	Marajó (Island)
	French Colony, 1612-1618
2571	Maranhão
	Including Gurupy River, Parnahyba (Parnaíba) River
2576	Mato Grosso
	Including Araguaya River, Garças River, Xingú River
	Cf. F2566 Goyaz boundary
	Cf. F2684 Jesuit missions of Paraguay
2578	Mato Grosso do Sul

F1201-3799

South America
   Brazil
      Regions, states, etc. -- Continued

2581	Minas Geraes (Minas Gerais)
	Including Jequitinhonha River, Mucury Colony, and Paraibuna River
2582	North Brazil
2583	Northeast Brazil
2585	Pantanal
2586	Pará
	Including rivers: Araguaya, Capim,. Gurupy (Gurupi), Tapajos, Tocantins, Parú, Xingú
	For Marajó Island see F2568
	Cf. F2546 Amazonas boundary
2591	Parahyba (Paraíba)
2596	Paraná
	Including Assunguy Colony, Guartelá (Region), Guayra Falls, Iguazú River and Falls, Paraná River
	Cf. F2684 Jesuit missions of Paraguay
	Cf. F2909 Argentina
2601	Pernambuco
	Including Itamaracá Island
2606	Piauhy (Piauí)
	Including Parnahyba (Parnaíba) River
	Cf. F2571 Maranhão boundary
2609	Rio Branco (Territory). Roraima
	Including Mount Roraima
2611	Rio de Janeiro (State)
	Including Parahyba (Paraíba) do Sul River and Valley, Grande Island Bay
	For Rio de Janeiro (Federal District and City) see F2646
2616	Rio Grande do Norte
	Cf. F2556 Ceará boundary
2621	Rio Grande do Sul
	Including German colonies, Revolution of the Farrapos, 1835-1845; Taquari-Antas River and Valley
	Including Gauchos, Brazil
	Cf. F2217 Gauchos, General
	Cf. F2684 Jesuit missions; War of the Seven Reductions, 1754-1756
2624	Rondônia (Territory). Rondônia (State)
	Including Madeira River
	Roraima see F2609

	South America
	Brazil
	Regions, states, etc. -- Continued
2626	Santa Catharina (Santa Catarina)
	Part of Misiones awarded to Brazil
	Including German colonies, e.g., Blumenau; Itajahy (Itajaí River and Valley)
	Including Santa Catarina Island
	Cf. F2596 Paraná boundary
	Cf. F2916 Misiones Territory of Argentina
2629	São Francisco River and Valley
2631	São Paulo
	Including Bandeiras; Revolution of 1932; etc. Rivers: Aguapehy (Aguapeí), Juquiá, Paraná, Peixe, Piracicaba, Ribeira de Iguape, Tieté
	Cf. F2581 Minas Geraes boundary
	Cf. F2684 Jesuit missions of Paraguay; War of the Seven Reductions, 1754-1756
2636	Sergipe
2638	Sinos River and Valley
2639	South Brazil
2640	Tocantins State
	Including Jalapão
2641	Vargem Alegre (District)
	Cities, towns, etc., A-Z
2646	Rio de Janeiro (City) and Federal District until April 21, 1960 (Table F1)
2647	Brasilia (City; and Federal District, April 21, 1960-) (Table F1)
2651.A-Z	Other, A-Z
	e.g.
	Bahia see F2651.S13+
2651.B4	Belém
2651.B42	Belo Horizonte
2651.C83	Curitiba
2651.F6	Fortaleza
2651.N5	Niterói
2651.O9	Ouro Preto
2651.P15	Palmares
	Pará see F2651.B4
	Pernambuco see F2651.R4+
2651.P8	Porto Alegre
2651.R4-.R49	Recife (Table F2)
2651.S13-.S139	Salvador (Table F2)
2651.S15	Santos
2651.S2-.S29	São Paulo (Table F2)

F1201-3799

	South America
	Brazil -- Continued
	Elements in the population
	For interpretation see F1392.A1+
2659.A1	General works
	Including foreign elements (General), minorities, race conflicts and problems
2659.A2-Z	Individual elements, A-Z
2659.A5	Americans
2659.A7	Arabs
2659.A75	Armenians
2659.A84	Asians
2659.A9	Austrians
2659.B4	Belgians
	Blacks see F2659.N4
2659.B64	Bolivians
2659.B7	British
2659.C32	Caboclos
2659.D35	Danes
2659.D7	Dutch
2659.E8	Estonians
2659.E95	Europeans
2659.F8	French
2659.G3	Germans
2659.H85	Hungarians
	Indians see F2518.5+
2659.I8	Italians
2659.J3	Japanese
2659.J5	Jews
	Latin America see F2659.S65
2659.L38	Latvians
2659.L42	Lebanese
2659.L5	Lithuanians
2659.M69	Mozambicans
2659.N4	Negroes. Blacks
	Cf. HT1126+ Slavery
2659.P7	Poles
2659.P8	Portuguese
2659.S45	Slovenes
2659.S63	Spaniards
2659.S65	Spanish Americans (Latin America)
2659.S84	Swedes
2659.S85	Swiss
2659.U4	Ukrainians
	Paraguay
2661	Periodicals. Societies. Collections
2661.5	Congresses

	South America
	Paraguay -- Continued
	Collected works
2662	Several authors
2663	Individual authors
	Including collected papers, addresses, essays
2663.5	Museums. Exhibitions, exhibits
2664	Gazetteers. Dictionaries. Geographic names
2664.5	Directories
	Biography
2665	Collective
	Individual (Historians) see F2679.6.A+
	Individual (By period) see F2682.92+
2668	General works
2668.5	Juvenile works
2669	Pamphlets, addresses, essays
2669.3	Anecdotes, legends, pageants
	Cf. P, Literature
	Cf. GR130+ Folklore
2669.5	Guidebooks. Handbooks
2669.7	Historic monuments (General)
2670	Social life and customs. Civilization. Intellectual life
	Including national characteristics
	For race conflicts and problems see F2699.A1+
2670.9	Geography
	Description and travel. Views
2671	Early to 1810
2675	1810-1950
2676	1951-
	Antiquities. Indians
2678	Museums. Exhibitions
2679	General works
2679.1	Modern Indians (General)
2679.15.A-Z	Local (Ancient and modern), A-Z
	e.g.
2679.15.C48	Chaco Region
2679.15.M35	Marcelina Kue Site
2679.2.A-Z	Tribes (Ancient and modern), A-Z
2679.2.A2	Abipon Indians
	Arawak see F2230.2.A7
	Caingua see F2230.2.C3
	Chamacoco see F2230.2.C5
	Chiquito see F3320.2.C39
2679.2.C5	Chiripá Indians
	Guarani see F2230.2.G72
2679.2.G9	Guayaki Indians
	Guaycuru see F2230.2.G78

	South America
	Paraguay
	Antiquities. Indians
	Tribes (Ancient and modern), A-Z -- Continued
2679.2.L4	Lengua
2679.2.M25	Maca
2679.2.M3	Mbaya
2679.2.M34	Mbya
	Mocobi see F2823.M6
2679.2.M6	Moro Indians
2679.2.P3	Payagua
	Pilaga see F2823.P5
	Tereno see F2520.1.T45
2679.2.T65	Tomaráxo Indians
	Toba see F2823.T7
2679.3.A-Z	Topics (Ancient and modern), A-Z
2679.3.A77	Art
2679.3.C45	Census
(2679.3.C58)	Civil rights
	see KHP1+
2679.3.C64	Colonization
2679.3.E38	Education
2679.3.F42	Featherwork
2679.3.F64	Folklore. Legends
2679.3.G65	Goldwork
2679.3.G67	Government relations
	Health and hygiene see RA475+
2679.3.I53	Industries
2679.3.L35	Land tenure
	Legends see F2679.3.F64
2679.3.M5	Missions
2679.3.P64	Politics and government
2679.3.P66	Population
2679.3.R44	Religion. Mythology
2679.3.S65	Social conditions
	History
2679.35	Chronological tables. Outlines, syllabi, etc. Questions and answers, etc.
	Historiography
2679.4	General works
	Biography of historians
2679.5	Collective
2679.6.A-Z	Individual, A-Z
	Subarrange each by Table F5
2679.7	Study and teaching
2681	General works
	Including political history

	South America
	Paraguay
	History -- Continued
	General special
2681.5	Military history
	Diplomatic history. Foreign and general relations
2682	General works
2682.5.A-Z	Relations with individual countries, A-Z
2682.9	Other (not A-Z)
	Cf. F2217 Gauchos, General
	By period
	Pre-Columbian period see F2678+
2683	1527-1811
	Including before 1620, part of the La Plata region; in 1620, Province of Paraguay established under jurisdiction of viceroy at Lima; in 1776, transferred to viceroy at Buenos Aires
	Including War of Independence, 1810-1811
2684	Jesuit province. Missions or reductions, 1609-1769
	Including Treaty of Madrid, 1750; War of the Seven Reductions (Guarani War), 1754-1756
	Cf. F2621 Rio Grande do Sul
	Cf. F2723 Colonia
	Cf. F2891 Corrientes
	Cf. F2916 Misiones
2686	1811-1870. Era of three dictators
	Including independence from Buenos Aires viceroyalty, 1813; United States Paraguay Expedition, 1858-1859
	Including biography: José Gaspar Rodríguez, Francia Carlos Antonio López, Francisco Solano López, etc.
2687	Paraguayan War, 1865-1870
	Also called the "War of the Triple Alliance."
	Including battles at Campo Grande, 1869; Curupaity, 1866; Riachuelo, 1865; Tuyuty, 1866; Yatayty-Corá, 1866
2688	1870-1938
	Including biography: Eusebio Ayala, Rafael Franco, Eduardo Schaerer, etc.
	Cf. D501+ World War I, 1914-1918
2688.5	Chaco War, 1932-1935
	Including Chaco Peace Conference at Buenos Aires, 1935-1939; Treaty of Peace, 1938
	Cf. F2691.C4 Chaco Boreal

F1201-3799

	South America
	Paraguay
	History
	By period -- Continued
2689	1938-1989
	Including political revolts; Colorados; communists, Franquistas; Tiempistas
	Including biography: José Félix Estigarribia, Higinio Moríningo Martínez, etc.
	Cf. D731+ World War II, 1939-1945
	1989-
2689.2	General works
	Biography
2689.22	Collective
2689.23.A-Z	Individual, A-Z
	Subarrange each by Table F5
2691.A-Z	Regions, departments, etc., A-Z
	e.g.
2691.A4	Alto Paraná
	Including Colonia Mayntzhusen
	Boundaries
2691.B7A1-.B7A5	General
	Argentina see F2857.P2
2691.B7A6-.B7Z	Bolivia
	For Chaco Boreal dispute see F2691.C4
	Brazil see F2554.P3
2691.C4	Chaco Boreal. Paraguayan Chaco. Western Paraguay
	Including territory between the Paraguay and Pilcomayo rivers
	Cf. F2688.5 Chaco War, 1932-1935
	Cf. F2876 El Gran Chaco (General, and Argentina)
	Cf. F3341.C4 Bolivian Chaco
2691.C6	Concepción
2691.P3	Paraguay River and Valley
2695.A-Z	Cities, towns, etc., A-Z
	e.g.
2695.A8	Asunción
2695.C7	Concepción
2695.C8	Coronel Oviedo
2695.C9	Curuguaty
2695.E5	Encarnación
	Including Tornado, 1926
2695.H7	Hohenau
2695.T6	Tobatí
2695.V5	Villarrica

	South America
	Paraguay -- Continued
	Elements in the population
	Including foreign elements (General), minorities, race conflicts and problems
	For interpretation see F1392.A1+
2699.A1	General works
2699.A2-Z	Individual elements, A-Z
2699.A72	Arabs
2699.A87	Australians
2699.B67	Brazilians
2699.B7	British
2699.D34	Danes
2699.F7	French
2699.G3	Germans
	Indians see F2678+
2699.I8	Italians
2699.J35	Japanese
2699.J4	Jews
2699.M44	Mennonites
2699.R8	Russians
	Uruguay
2701	Periodicals. Societies. Collections
	Collected works
2702	Several authors
2703	Individual authors
	Including collected papers, addresses, essays
2703.5	Museums. Exhibitions, exhibits
2704	Gazetteers. Dictionaries. Geographic names
2704.5	Directories
	Biography
2705	Collective
	Individual (Historians) see F2720.6.A+
	Individual (By period) see F2722.92+
2708	General works
2708.5	Juvenile works
2709	Pamphlets, addresses, essays
2709.3	Anecdotes, legends, pageants
	Cf. P, Literature
	Cf. GR130+ Folklore
2709.5	Guidebooks. Handbooks
2709.7	Historic monuments (General)
2710	Social life and customs. Civilization. Intellectual life
	Including national characteristics
	For race conflicts and problems see F2799.A1+
	Description and travel. Views
2711	Early to 1810

	South America
	Uruguay
	Description and travel. Views -- Continued
2713	1811-1950
2714	1951-1980
2715	1981-
	Antiquities. Indians
2719	General works
2719.1.A-Z	Local (Ancient and modern), A-Z
2719.1.C65	Colonia (Dept.)
2719.1.S24	Salto Grand Dept.
2719.1.T74	Treinta y Tres (Dept.)
2719.2.A-Z	Tribes (Ancient and modern), A-Z
	Chané see F3320.2.C37
2719.2.C5	Charrua
	Guarani see F2230.2.G72
2719.2.G84	Güenoa
2719.3.A-Z	Topics (Ancient and modern), A-Z
	e.g.
2719.3.P6	Pottery
2719.3.T6	Tobacco pipes
	History
2720	Chronological tables. Outlines, syllabi, etc. Questions and answers, etc.
	Historiography
2720.3	General works
	Biography of historians
2720.5	Collective
2720.6.A-Z	Individual, A-Z
	Subarrange each by Table F5
2720.7	Study and teaching
2721	General works
	Including political history
	General special
2721.5	Military and naval history
	Diplomatic history. Foreign and general relations
2722	General works
2722.5.A-2722.5.Z	Relations with individual countries, A-Z
2722.9	Other (not A-Z)
	Including gauchos in Uruguay
	Cf. F2217 Gauchos, General
	By period
	Pre-Columbian period see F2719+

South America
Uruguay
History
By period -- Continued

2723   1516-1811

Known as the "Banda Oriental." In 1776 placed under the viceroy in Buenos Aires

Including contests over Colonia; Treaty of San Ildefonso, 1777

Cf. F2684 Jesuit missions; War of the Seven Reductions, 1754-1756

Cf. F2845 English invasion of the La Plata, 1806-1807

2724   1811-

2725   1811-1830

In 1821, incorporated in Brazil as Cisplatine Province; declared itself independent, 1825; recognized as independent, 1828

Including wars of independence; Argentine-Brazilian War, 1825-1828 (battles at Sarandi, 1825; Ituzaingó, 1827)

Including biography: José Gervasio Artigas, etc.

2726   1830-1904

Formally constituted as a republic, 1830

Including civil wars between Blancos and Colorados; foreign intervention; siege of Montevideo, 1843-1851

Including biography: Juan Lindolfo Cuestas, Juan Carlos Gómez, Julio Herrera y Obes, Juan Idiarte Borda, Lorenzo Latorre, Manuel Oribe, José Fructuoso Rivera, Máximo Santos, Aparicio Saravia, etc.

Cf. F2687 Paraguayan War, 1865-1870

Cf. F2846.3 War against Rosas, 1849-1852

2728   1904-1973. Era of Batlle, 1903-1929

Including Revolution of 1904; Battle of Tupambaé, 1904; Revolution of 1910

Including biography: Juan José Amézaga, José Batlle y Ordóñez, Baltasar Brum, Luis Alberto de Herrera, Andrés Martínez Trueba, José Serrato Gabriel Terra, etc.

Cf. D501+ World War I, 1914-1918

Cf. D731+ World War II, 1939-1945

Cf. D772.G7 Admiral Graf Spee (Battleship)

          1973-

2729   General works

          Biography

F1201-3799

South America
Uruguay
History
By period
1811-
1973-
Biography -- Continued

2729.5	Collective
2729.52.A-Z	Individual, A-Z
	Subarrange each by Table F5
2731.A-Z	Regions, departments, etc., A-Z
2731.A7	Artigas
2731.A84	Atlantic Coast
2731.B7	Boundaries (General)
	For Brazil see F2554.U8
	For Argentina see F2857.U7
2731.C22	Canelones
2731.C4	Cerro Largo
2731.C7	Colonia
	For Portuguese settlement at Colonia see F2723
2731.D8	Durazno
2731.F5	Flores
2731.F55	Florida
2731.L3	Lavalleja
	Lobos Island see F2731.M2
2731.M2	Maldonado
	Including Lobos Island, Punta Ballema
	Montevideo see F2781
2731.P3	Paysandú
2731.R4	Río Negro
2731.R5	Rivera
2731.R6	Rocha
2731.S2	Salto
2731.S3	San José
2731.S6	Soriano
2731.T3	Tacuarembó
2731.T6	Treinta y Tres
2731.U7	Uruguay River
	Cities, towns, etc.
2781	Montevideo (Table F1)
2791.A-Z	Other, A-Z
	e.g.
2791.M3	Maldonado
2791.M55	Mercedes
2791.P54	Paysandú
2791.S2	Salto

	South America
	Uruguay -- Continued
	Elements in the population
	Including foreign elements (General), minorities, race conflicts and problems
	For interpretation see F1392.A1+
2799.A1	General works
2799.A2-Z	Individual elements, A-Z
2799.A7	Armenians
2799.B2	Basques
	Blacks see F2799.N3
2799.B7	Brazilians
2799.C76	Croats
2799.F7	French
2799.G25	Galicians (Spain)
2799.G3	Germans
2799.G74	Greeks
	Indians see F2719+
2799.I8	Italians
2799.J36	Japanese
2799.J4	Jews
2799.L4	Lebanese
2799.N3	Negroes. Blacks
2799.S6	Spaniards
2799.S9	Swiss
	Argentina. La Plata region
2801	Periodicals. Societies. Collections
2801.5	Congresses
	Collected works
2802	Several authors
2803	Individual authors
	Including collected papers, addresses, essays
2803.5	Museums. Exhibitions, exhibits
2804	Gazetteers. Dictionaries. Geographic names
2804.5	Directories
	Biography
2805	Collective
	Individual (Historians) see F2829.6.A+
	Individual (By period) see F2840.2+
2808	General works
2808.2	Juvenile works
2808.3	Pamphlets, addresses, essays
2808.4	Anecdotes, legends, pageants, etc.
	Cf. P, Literature
	Cf. GR130+ Folklore
2808.5	Guidebooks. Handbooks
2809	Historic monuments (General)

F1201-3799

	South America
	Argentina. La Plata Region -- Continued
2810	Social life and customs. Civilization. Intellectual life
	Including national characteristics
	For race conflicts and problems see F3021.A1+
2810.9	Geography
	Description and travel. Views
2811	Early to 1805
2815	1806-1950
2816	1951-1980
2817	1981-
	Antiquities. Indians
2819	Study and teaching
2820	Museums. Exhibitions
2821	General works
2821.1.A-Z	Local (Ancient and modern), A-Z
	e.g.
2821.1.A3	Andalgala
2821.1.B8	Buenos Aires (Province)
2821.1.C3	Catamarca (Province)
2821.1.C5	Chubut (Territory)
2821.1.C7	Córdoba (Province)
2821.1.E5	Entre Rios (Province)
2821.1.J9	Jujuy (Province)
	La Rioja (Province) see F2821.1.R58
2821.1.N4	Neuquén (Province)
2821.1.P22	Paraná Valley
2821.1.P29	Patagonia
2821.1.R58	La Rioja (Province)
2821.1.S15	Salta (Province)
2821.1.S23	Santiago del Estero (Province)
2821.1.T89	Tucumán (Province)
2821.3.A-Z	Topics (Ancient and modern), A-Z
2821.3.A3	Agriculture
2821.3.A78	Architecture
2821.3.A8	Art
2821.3.B6	Bolas
2821.3.C35	Calendar
2821.3.C4	Census
(2821.3.C56)	Civil rights
	see KHA1+
2821.3.C73	Craniology
2821.3.D4	Dentistry
	Including dental mutilation
2821.3.D5	Diseases
2821.3.E84	Ethnic identity
2821.3.F57	First contact with Europeans

South America
  Argentina. La Plata Region
    Antiquities. Indians
      Topics (Ancient and modern), A-Z -- Continued
2821.3.F6	Folklore. Legends
2821.3.F7	Food
2821.3.G65	Government relations
2821.3.H8	Hunting
2821.3.I5	Implements
2821.3.I6	Industries
2821.3.L35	Land tenure
2821.3.M4	Medicine
2821.3.M44	Metalwork
2821.3.M5	Missions
2821.3.M6	Mortuary customs
2821.3.N3	Names
2821.3.P6	Petroglyphs. Rock paintings
2821.3.P66	Philosophy
2821.3.P74	Politics and government
2821.3.P8	Pottery
2821.3.R4	Religion. Mythology
	Rock paintings see F2821.3.P6
2821.3.S54	Silverwork
2821.3.T6	Tobacco pipes
2821.3.T65	Tombs
2821.3.U7	Urns
	Wars see F2822
2821.3.W65	Women
2822	Modern tribes (General)
	Including Indian wars
2823.A-Z	Tribes (Ancient and modern), A-Z
	Abipone see F2679.2.A2
	Alacaluf see F2986
	Araucanian see F3126
	Ashluslay see F2230.2.A78
	Aymara see F2230.2.A9
	Caingua see F2230.2.C3
2823.C2	Calchaqui
2823.C3	Candelaria culture
2823.C4	Catamarca
	Chamacoco see F2230.2.C5
	Chané see F3320.2.C37
	Charrua see F2719.2.C5
	Choroti see F3320.2.C5
2823.C5	Comechingone
2823.D5	Diaguita
	Cf. F3070.1.D5 Chile

F1201-
3799

South America
   Argentina. La Plata region
     Antiquities. Indians
       Tribes (Ancient and modern), A-Z
         Fuegian see F2986
         Guarani see F2230.2.G72

2823.G8	Guarpe
2823.H85	Humahuaca
	Kaingangue see F2520.1.K3
	Lengua see F2679.2.L4
2823.L8	Lule
2823.M3	Mataco
2823.M6	Mocobi
2823.O34	Ocloya
	Ona see F2986
2823.P3	Pampean
	Payagua see F2679.2.P3
2823.P5	Pilaga
2823.P8	Puelche
2823.Q4	Querandi
2823.R2	Ranqueles
2823.T7	Toba
2823.T8	Tonocote
	Tzoneca see F2936
2823.V5	Vilela
	Yahgan see F2986

     History

2827	Chronological tables. Outlines, syllabi, etc. Questions and answers, etc.
	Historiography
2829	General works
	Biography of historians
2829.5	Collective
2829.6.A-Z	Individual, A-Z
	Subarrange each by Table F5
2830	Study and teaching
2831	General works
	Including political history
	General special
2832	Military and naval history
	Diplomatic history. Foreign and general relations
2833	General works
	Cf. F2857 Boundaries
2833.5.A-Z	Relations with individual countries, A-Z
2834	Other (not A-Z)
	By period
	Pre-Columbian period see F2819+

         South America
          Argentina. La Plata Region
           History
            By period

2841   1516-1810

                 Including period of discovery, exploration, and settlement. Colonial period. In 1617, Buenos Aires separated from Asunción, became the province of Rio de la Plata under the viceroy of Peru; in 1776, Viceroyalty of La Plata was formed including Argentina, Uruguay, Paraguay, and Bolivia

                 Including biography: Hernando Arias de Saavedra (Hernandarias); Francisco de Céspedes; Juan de Garay; Domingo Martínez de Irala; Juan de San Martín; Rafael de Sobremonte, marqués de Sobremonte; etc.

                 Cf. F2683 Paraguay before 1811

                 Cf. F2684 Jesuit province; War of the Seven Reductions (Guarani War), 1754-1756

                 Cf. F2723 Brazil's claims to Colonia

                 Cf. F3301+ Upper Peru and the Audiencia of Charcas

2843   1810-

                 On May 25, 1810, declared independence from Spain

2845   1806-1817

                 Including English invasions, 1806-1807; War of Independence, 1810-1817

                 Including biography: Manuel Belgrano; Guillermo Brown; Martín Miguel Guüemes; Santiago Antonio María de Liniers y Bremond, conde de Buenos Aires; Bernardo Monteagudo; Mariano Moreno; Juan Martín de Pueyrredón; Cornello de Saavedra; etc.

2846   1807-1861. Civil Wars

                 Including unitarism versus federalism; secession and return of province of Buenos Aires; battles at Cepeda (1859), and Pavoń (1861)

                 Including biography: Manuel Dorrego, Esteban Echeverría, Juan Galo de Lavalle, José María Paz, Juan Facundo Quiroga, Bernardino Rivadavia, Domingo Faustino Sarmiento, Justo José de Urquiza, Dalmacio Vélez Sársfield, etc.

                 Cf. F2725 War with Brazil over Uruguay, 1825-1828

F1201-3799

South America
  Argentina. La Plata Region
    History
      By period
        1810-
          1807-1861. Civil Wars -- Continued

2846.3	1829-1852. Period of Rosas
	Including English and French blockades of Argentine coast, 1838, and of Rio de la Plata, 1845-1847; War with Brazil (War against Rosas), 1849-1852; battles at Angaco (1841), Obligado (1845)
	Including biography: Juan Manuel José Domingo Ortiz de Rosas
2847	1861-1910
	Including League of Córdoba; Civil War, 1880; oligarchy in control, 1890-1910
	Including biography: Nicolás Avellaneda, Bartolomé Mitre Carlos Pellegrini, Julio Argentino Roca, Roque Sáenz Peña, etc.
	Cf. F2687 Paraguayan War, 1865-1870
	Cf. F2822 Conquista del desierto, 1879-1880
	Cf. F2916 Misiones award, 1894
2848	1910-1943
	Including Radicals in control, 1910-1930; Revolution of 1930; oligarchy in control, 1930-1943
	Including biography: Marcelo Torcuato de Alvear, Joaquín Víctor Gonzáles, Hipólito Irigoyen, Juan Bautista Justo, Lisandro de la Torre, José Félix Uriburu
	Cf. D501+ World War I, 1914-1918
2849	1943-1955
	Including the "G.O.U." Coup, 1943; Péron regime, 1943-1955; fascism
	Including biography: Juan Domingo Péron, etc.
	Cf. D731+ World War II, 1939-1945
	1955-2002
2849.2	General works
	Biography
2849.22.A2	Collective
2849.22.A3-Z	Individual, A-Z
	Subarrange each by Table F5
	2002-
2849.3	General works
	Biography
2849.33.A2	Collective
2849.33.A3-Z	Individual, A-Z

South America
Argentina. La Plata Region -- Continued

2850-2991	Regions, provinces, etc. A-Z
	Class an individual department or partido with the province of which it is a part
2850	Territories (General)
2850.4	Aconquija Mountains
2851	Andes Mountains
	Including Chilean boundary question
2853	Los Andes (Territory)
	Before 1910 was Bolivian territory of Atacama; in 1943, departments were assigned to the province of Jujuy, Salta, and Catamarca
2857	Boundaries
2857.A2	General
2857.B6	Bolivia
	Cf. F2853 Former Bolivian territory of Atacama
	Brazil see F2554.A82; F2916
	Chaco Boreal dispute see F2688.5
	Chile see F2851; F2853
2857.P2	Paraguay
2857.U7	Uruguay
	Buenos Aires (Federal District and City) see F3001
2861	Buenos Aires (Province)
	Including Avellaneda (Partido); Lechiguanas Islands
	For Martín Garcia (Island) see F2909
	Cf. F2846 Battles of Cepeda, 1859; Pavón, 1861
	Cf. F2886 Córdoba boundary
2871	Catamarca
2876	Chaco. Chaco Austral. El Gran Chaco (General and Argentina)
	Became a province, August 8, 1951
	For Chaco War, 1932-1935 see F2688.5
	For Chaco Boreal (Paraguayan Chaco) see F2691.C4
	For Chaco Central see F2901
	For Bolivian Chaco see F3341.C4
2881	Chubut (Territory)
	For Comodoro Rivadavia see F2884
2884	Comodoro Rivadavia
	Including military zone carved out of Chubut and Santa Cruz Territories in 1946
2886	Córdoba
2891	Corrientes
	Including Battle of Caá Guazú, 1841
	Cf. F2916 Misiones boundary
	Cuyo see F2911

F1201-3799

	South America
	Argentina. La Plata Region
	Regions, provinces, etc. A-Z
2896	Entre Rios
	For Lechiguanas Islands see F2861; F2861
2901	Formosa (Territory). Chaco Central
2906	Jujuy
2909	La Plata River and Valley (Rio de la Plata). Paraná River
	Including Iguazú Falls, Martín Garcia (Island)
	Cf. F2596 Brazil
2911	Mendoza
	Including the ancient Chilean governación of Cuyo.
	Marlargüe (District); Tupungato (Department)
	Cf. F2961 San Juan boundary
2916	Misiones
	Became a province, December 9, 1953
	Including Parque national del Iguazú
	Cf. F2626 Santa Catarina, Brazil (Part of Misiones
	awarded to Brazil)
	Cf. F2684 Jesuit missions of Paraguay
	Cf. F2916 Brazil-Argentina boundary dispute
2921	Neuquén (Territory)
	Including Neuquén River, Parque nacional "Lanín"
2921.5	Northeast Argentina
	Including Chaco, Corrientes, Formosa Misiones, and
	northern Santa Fe
2922	Northwest Argentina
	Including Calchaqui River
2924	La Pampa
	Became a province, August 8, 1951
2926	Pampas (region)
	Including region south of Mendoza and San Luis, and west
	of Buenos Aires, extending to Patagonia (about 40)
	Cf. F2217 General
2936	Patagonia
	Including collective works on Patagonia, Falkland Islands,
	Tierra del Fuego, Strait of Magellan, Cape Horn
	Including Tzoneca Indians
	Argentine Patagonia is now subdivided into the territories of
	Chubut, Neuquén, Río Negro, Santa Cruz, and Tierra
	del Fuego.
	Chilean Patagonia covers the Chilean provinces of Chiloé
	and Magallanes
	Cf. F2986 Tierra del Fuego
	Cf. F3031+ Falkland Islands
	Cf. F3191 Strait of Magellan

	South America
	Argentina. La Plata Region
	Regions, provinces, etc. A-Z -- Continued
2951	Río Negro (Territory)
	Including Nahuel Huapí (Lake), Parque nacional de Nahuel Huapí
2956	La Rioja
2957	Salado River and Valley
	Including the provinces of Salta, Santiago del Esterio, and Santa Fé
2958	Salta
2961	San Juan
2966	San Luis
	Cf. F2886 Córdoba boundary
2971	Santa Cruz (Territory)
	For Comodoro Rivadavia see F2884
2976	Santa Fé
2981	Santiago del Estero
2986	Tierra del Fuego (Territory and island)
	The western part of the island forms part of the Chilean territory of Magallanes
	Including Fuegians: The Alacaluf, Ona, and Yahgan
2991	Tucumán (Province)
	In colonial times was the gobernación of Tucumán, part of upper Peru
	Cities, towns, etc.
3001	Buenos Aires (Federal District and City) (Table F1)
3011.A-Z	Other, A-Z
	e.g.
3011.A9	Avellaneda
	Formerly Barrácas al Sud
3011.B3	Bahia Blancha
3011.C7	Córdoba
3011.L4	La Plata
3011.L45	La Rioja
	Including earthquake, 1894; etc.
3011.L8	Luján
3011.M29	Mar del Plata
3011.M45	Mendoza
	Including earthquake, 1861; etc.
3011.R7	Rosario
3011.S2	Salta
3011.S218	San Juan
	Formerly San Juan de la Frontera
	Including earthquake, 1944; etc.
	San Miguel de Tucumán see F3011.T89
3011.S26	Santa Fé

F1201-3799

	South America
	Argentina. La Plata Region
	Cities, towns, etc. A-Z
	Other, A-Z -- Continued
3011.T89	Tucumán
	Elements in the population
	Including foreign elements (General), minorities, race
	conflicts and problems
	For interpretation see F1392.A1+
3021.A1	General works
3021.A2-Z	Individual elements, A-Z
3021.A5	Americans
3021.A59	Arabs
3021.A64	Armenians
3021.B2	Basques
3021.B45	Belarusians
3021.B55	Blacks
3021.B65	Bolivians
3021.B86	British
3021.B93	Bulgarians
3021.C3	Catalans
3021.C48	Chileans
3021.C7	Croats
3021.D2	Danes
3021.D87	Dutch
3021.F56	Finns
3021.F8	French
3021.G2	Gallegans
3021.G3	Germans
3021.H85	Hungarians
	Indians see F2819+
3021.I6	Irish
3021.I8	Italians
3021.J36	Japanese
3021.J5	Jews
3021.K6	Koreans
	Negroes see F3021.B55
3021.P6	Poles
3021.P8	Portuguese
3021.R87	Russian Germans
3021.S6	Slovaks
3021.S62	Slovenes
3021.S7	Spaniards
3021.S86	Swedes
3021.S88	Swiss
3021.S95	Syrians
3021.U5	Ukrainians

	South America
	Argentina. La Plata Region
	Elements in the population
	Individual elements, A-Z -- Continued
3021.U7	Uruguayans
3021.Y7	Yugoslavs
3030	South Atlantic region
3030.3	Ascension Island
	Falkland Islands. Islas Malvinas
	Including dependencies: Graham Land (Palmer Peninsula), South Orkneys, South Shetlands
	Cf. G890.P3 Palmer Peninsula (Graham Land)
3031	General works
3031.5	Falkland Islands War, 1982
	St. Helena, Tristan da Cunha, etc. see DT669+
	South Georgia and South Sandwich Islands
3032	General works
3032.5	South Georgia
	Chile
3051	Periodicals. Societies. Collections
	Collected works
3052	Several authors
3053	Individual authors
	Including collected papers, addresses, essays
3053.5	Museums. Exhibitions, exhibits
3054	Gazetteers. Dictionaries. Geographic names
3054.5	Directories
	Biography
3055	Collective
	Individual (Historians) see F3076.A+
	Individual (By period) see F3090.2+
3058	General works
3058.5	Juvenile works
3059	Pamphlets, addresses, essays, etc.
3059.3	Anecdotes, legends, pageants, etc.
	Cf. P, Literature
	Cf. GR130+ Folklore
3059.5	Guidebooks. Handbooks
3059.8	Historic monuments (General)
3060	Social life and customs. Civilization. Intellectual life
	Including national characteristics
	For race conflicts and problems see F3285.A1+
3060.5	Chileans in foreign countries (General)
	For Chileans in a specific country, see the country
3060.9	Geography
	Description and travel. Views

F1201-3799

	South America
	Chile
	Description and travel. Views -- Continued
3061	Early to 1809
3061	Early to 1809
3063	1810-1950
3064	1951-1980
3065	1981-
	Antiquities. Indians
3069	General works
3069.1.A-Z	Local (Ancient and modern), A-Z
	e.g.
	Araucania see F3126
3069.1.A8	Atacama (Province)
3069.1.H8	Huasco (Province)
3069.1.L5	Llaima (Department)
3069.1.L6	Rio Loa region
3069.1.M25	Malloa
3069.1.M6	Molle
3069.1.P5	Pichilemu
3069.1.Q6	Quilpué
3069.3.A-Z	Topics (Ancient and modern), A-Z
3069.3.A3	Agriculture
3069.3.A58	Anthropometry
3069.3.A7	Art
3069.3.C66	Commerce
3069.3.D58	Diseases
3069.3.E2	Economic conditions
3069.3.E38	Education
3069.3.E46	Employment
3069.3.E84	Ethnobotany
3069.3.F57	Fishing
3069.3.F64	Folklore. Legends
3069.3.G6	Government relations
	Legends see F3069.3.F64
3069.3.M4	Metalwork
3069.3.M5	Missions
3069.3.M55	Mixed descent
3069.3.P76	Population
3069.3.P8	Pottery
3069.3.R44	Religion. Mythology
3069.3.T4	Textile fabrics
3069.3.W37	Wars
3070	Modern Indians (General)
3070.1.A-Z	Tribes (Ancient and modern), A-Z
	Araucanians (Chilote, Huilliche, Mapuche, Pehuenche, and Picunche) see F3126

	South America
	Chile
	Antiquities. Indians
	Tribes (Ancient and modern), A-Z -- Continued
3070.1.A7	Atacameno
3070.1.C5	Chango
3070.1.C6	Chono
3070.1.D5	Diaguita
	Cf. F2823.D5 Argentina
	Fuegian (Alacaluf, Yahgan) see F2986
3072	Ciudad de los Césares
	History
3073	Chronological tables. Outlines, syllabi, etc. Questions and answers, etc.
	Historiography
3074	General works
	Biography of historians
3075	Collective
3076.A-Z	Individual, A-Z
	Subarrange each by Table F5
	e.g.
3076.B3	Barros Arana, Diego (Table F5)
3077	Study and teaching
3081	General works
	Including political history
	General special
3082	Military and naval history
	Diplomatic history. Foreign and general relations
3083	General works
3083.5.A-Z	Relations with individual countries, A-Z
3083.9	Other (not A-Z)
	By period
	Pre-Columbian period see F3069+
3091	1535-1810
	Including conquest of the Araucanian Indians; history as a Spanish colony
	Including biography: Pedro de Valdivia, etc.
	1810-
	Declared independence from Spain, July 16, 1801
3093	General works
3094	1810-1824. War of Independence
	Including battles of Rancagua (1814), Chacabuco (1817), Maipo (1818)
	Including biography: José Miguel Carrera, Juan Mackenna, Bernardo O'Higgins, etc.

F1201-
3799

	South America
	Chile
	History
	By period
	1810- -- Continued
3095	1824-1920
	Including domination of the conservatives, 1830-1861; War with Spain, 1865-1866; bombardment of Valparaiso, 1866; civil wars
	Including biography: Manuel Francisco Antonio Julián Montt, Diego José Víctor Portales, Benjamín Vicuña Mackenna, etc.
	Cf. D501+ World War I, 1914-1918
	Cf. F3447 War with Spain, 1865-1866
3097	War of the Pacific, 1879-1884
3097.3	Territorial questions growing out of the war
	Including the Tacna-Arica question (controversial topic until 1929); Treaty of Ancón, 1883; Treaty of Valparaiso, 1884
3098	Revolution of 1891
	Including biography: José Manuel Balmaceda, etc.
3099	1921-1970
	Including restoration of presidential power, 1921-1938; Popular Front, 1938-1942; earthquake of 1938
	Including biography: Pedro Aguirre Cerda, Arturo Alessandri, Carlos Ibáñez del Campo, etc.
	Cf. D731+ World War II, 1939-1945
	1970-1988
3100	General works
	Biography
3101.A2	Collective
3101.A3-Z	Individual, A-Z
	Subarrange each by Table F5
	e.g.
3101.A4	Allende, Salvador (Table F5)
	1988-
3101.3	General works
3101.4.A2-Z	Biography
3101.4.A2	Collective
3101.4.A3-Z	Individual, A-Z
	Subarrange each by Table F5
	Regions, provinces, etc.
3105	Islands of Chile (General)
3106	Aconcagua
	Aisén see F3134

	South America
	Chile
	Regions, provinces, etc., A-Z
3111	Andes Mountains in Chile
	Cf. F2212 South America
	Cf. F2851 Argentina
3116	Antofagasta
	Formerly Bolivian territory of Atacama
	For Taltal (Department) see F3238
3126	Arauco
	Including ancient and modern Mapuche Indians
	(Araucanian) and ancient and modern Araucanian
	Indians in Chile and adjacent areas of Argentina
	For Malleco, formerly part of Arauco see F3196
	Arica (Department) see F3231
3131	Atacama (Desert and Province)
	Including the islands : Gonzalez; Saint Ambrose (San
	Ambrosio); Saint Felix (San Félix), Huasco River
3134	Aysén (Aisén)
	Including Baker River
	Baker River see F3134
3136	Bío-Bío
	Including Antuco (Volcano)
	Boundaries
3139.A1-.A4	General
	Argentina see F2851; F2853
3139.A5-Z	Bolivia
	Cf. F3097.3 Tacna and Arica question
	Cf. F3116 Former Bolivian territory of Atacama
	Peru see F3451.B73
	Cape Horn see F3186
3141	Cautín
	Including Llaima (Department)
3146	Chiloé
	A province of Chilean Patagonia
	Including Wreck of the Wager (Ship)
	Cf. F2936 Patagonia
3151	Colchagua
	Including Tinguiririca (Volcano)
3156	Concepción
3159	Copiapó River and Valley
3161	Coquimbo
	Including Guayacán Bay
3166	Curicó
	Cuyo see F2911

F1201-
3799

	South America
	Chile
	Regions, provinces, etc., A-Z -- Continued
3169	Easter Island
	Isla de Pascua, L'ile de Pâques, Rapa Nui, Te Pito te Henua
3170	El Loa
3170.5	Elqui River and Valley
3171	Juan Fernández Islands
	Including earthquake of 1835
3174	Laja River and Valley
3176	Linares
	Llaima (Department) see F3141
3181	Llanquihue
	Including Llanquihue Lake, Reloncaví Bay, Rio Cisnes, Rio Puelo
	Loa see F3170
3186	Magallanes y Antártica Chilena
	Name of Region XII created in 1974 by the union of the former province of Magallanes (western part of the island of Tierra del Fuego, formed as a province of Chilean Patagonia, 1929) and the former Territorio Antártico Chileno (formally claimed by Chile in Nov. 1940)
	Including Cape Horn, etc.
	For Ultima Esperanza (Department) see F3244
	Cf. F2936 Patagonia
	Cf. F2986 Tierra del Fuego (Island)
3191	Strait of Magellan
	Cf. G286.M2 Life and travels of Fernão de Magalhães (Ferdinand Magellan)
	Cf. G420.M2 First circumnavigation of globe by Magellan and crew
3196	Malleco
	Including Tolhuaca and Lonquímay Volcanoes. Formerly a part of the Province of Arauco; formed as a separate province, 1887
3201	Maule
3205	North Chile
3206	Ñuble
	Including earthquake of 1939
3211	O'Higgins
3214	Pisagua (Department)
3218	Region de los Lagos
3221	Santiago
	Cf. F3271 Santiage de Chile (City)

	South America
	Chile
	Regions, provinces, etc., A-Z -- Continued
3231	Tacna (Department). Arica (Department)
	Between 1883 and 1929, Tacna belonged to Chile; in 1929, it became a department of Peru
	Before 1883, Arica belonged to Peru
	Cf. F3097.3 Territorial questions arising from war with Peru and Bolivia, 1879-1884
3236	Talca
3238	Taltal (Department)
3241	Tarapacá
	Before 1883, belonged to Peru
	For Pisagua (Department) see F3214
	For departments of Tacna and Arica see F3231
	Cf. F3097.3 Territorial questions arising from war with Peru and Bolivia, 1879-1884
	Tierra del Fuego (Chilean part of the island) see F3186
3244	Ultima Esperanza (Department)
3246	Valdivia
3251	Valparaiso
	For Easter Island see F3169
	For Juan Fernández Island see F3171
	Cities, towns, etc.
3271	Santiago de Chile (City) (Table F1)
3281.A-Z	Other, A-Z
3281.A45	Antofagasta
3281.A6	Arica
3281.C46	Chillán
3281.C5	Concepción
3281.I6	Iquique
3281.T17	Talca
3281.T2	Talcahuano
3281.T4	Temuco
3281.V15	Valdivia
3281.V2	Valparaiso
3281.V6	Viña del Mar
	Elements in the population
	For interpretation see F1392.A1+
3285.A1	General works
	Including foreign elements (General), minorities, race conflicts and problems
3285.A2-Z	Individual elements, A-Z
3285.A5	Americans
3285.A7	Arabs
3285.B3	Basques
3285.B53	Blacks

F1201-
3799

South America
  Chile
    Elements in the population
      Individual elements, A-Z -- Continued

3285.B7	British
3285.C76	Croats
3285.C94	Czechs
3285.F8	French
3285.G25	Galicians (Spain)
3285.G3	Germans
	Indians see F3069+
3285.I8	Italians
3285.J4	Jews
3285.N67	Norwegians
3285.P4	Peruvians
3285.S7	Spaniards
3285.S9	Swiss
3285.S95	Syrians
3285.Y8	Yugoslavs

  Bolivia

3301	Periodicals. Societies. Collections
	Collected works
3302	Several authors
3303	Individual authors
	Including collected papers, addresses, essays
3303.5	Museums. Exhibitions, exhibits
3304	Gazetteers. Dictionaries. Geographic names
3304.5	Directories
	Biography
3305	Collective
	Individual (Historians) see F3320.6.A+
	Individual (By period) see F3321.92+
3308	General works
3308.5	Juvenile works
3309	Pamphlets, addresses, essays
3309.4	Anecdotes, legends, pageants
	Cf. P, Literature
	Cf. GR130+ Folklore
3309.5	Guidebooks. Handbooks
3309.7	Historic monuments (General)
3310	Social life and customs. Civilization. Intellectual life
	Including national characteristics
3310.9	Geography
	Description and travel. Views
3311	Early to 1808
3313	1809-1950
3314	1951-1980

	South America
	Bolivia
	Description and travel. Views -- Continued
3315	1981-
	Antiquities. Indians
3319	General works
3319.1.A-Z	Local (Ancient and modern), A-Z
	e.g.
3319.1.C4	Chaco (Bolivian)
3319.1.C6	Cochabamba
3319.1.P6	Potosí
3319.1.S2	Samaypata
3319.1.T55	Tiahuanaco (Tiwanaku, Tiahuanacu)
	Including the Tiwanaku Valley and the Tiwanaku culture
3320	Modern Indians (General)
3320.1.A-Z	Topics (Ancient and modern), A-Z
3320.1.A47	Agriculture
3320.1.A68	Architecture
3320.1.A7	Art
3320.1.C45	Census
(3320.1.C57)	Civil rights
	see KHC1+
3320.1.C6	Colonization
3320.1.C64	Costume. Adornment
3320.1.D35	Dance
3320.1.D83	Dwellings
3320.1.E4	Education
3320.1.E84	Ethnic identity
3320.1.F6	Folklore. Legends
3320.1.F64	Food
3320.1.G35	Games
3320.1.G6	Government relations
3320.1.I45	Implements
3320.1.I54	Industries
3320.1.L35	Land tenure
3320.1.M37	Marriage customs and rites
3320.1.M38	Masks
3320.1.M4	Medicine
3320.1.M43	Metalwork
3320.1.M47	Missions
3320.1.M5	Mixed descent
3320.1.N37	Narcotics
3320.1.P53	Philosophy
3320.1.P56	Politics and government
3320.1.P6	Pottery
3320.1.P8	Psychology
3320.1.R3	Religion. Mythology

F1201-
3799

	South America
	Bolivia
	Antiquities. Indians
	Topics (Ancient and modern), A-Z -- Continued
3320.1.S35	Science
3320.1.S38	Sculpture
3320.1.S62	Social conditions
3320.1.T38	Taxation
3320.1.T48	Textile fabrics
3320.1.W37	Wars
3320.1.W65	Women
3320.2.A-Z	Tribes (Ancient and modern), A-Z
3320.2.A6	Apolista
3320.2.A7	Arauna
	Arawak see F2230.2.A7
	Aymara see F2230.2.A9
3320.2.C3	Callahuaya
3320.2.C33	Canichana
	Caripuna see F2520.1.C37
3320.2.C34	Cavineño
3320.2.C35	Cayubaba
3320.2.C36	Chacobo
	Chamacoco see F2230.2.C5
3320.2.C37	Chané
3320.2.C38	Chapacura
3320.2.C387	Chimane
3320.2.C388	Chipaya
3320.2.C39	Chiquito
3320.2.C4	Chiriguano
3320.2.C5	Choroti
3320.2.C62	Churumata
	Colla see F3430.1.C6
3320.2.G8	Guarayo
	Guaycuru see F2230.2.G78
3320.2.I8	Itene
3320.2.J84	Jukumani
	Kechua see F2230.2.K4
	Lengua see F2679.2.L4
3320.2.M26	Manacica
	Mataco see F2823.M3
3320.2.M55	Mojo
3320.2.M57	Mollo culture
3320.2.M6	Moseten
	Moxo see F3320.2.M55
3320.2.O3	Ocorona
3320.2.O8	Otuquis
3320.2.P3	Pacaguara

	South America
	Bolivia
	Antiquities. Indians
	Tribes and cultures (Ancient and modern), A-Z
	Pano see F3430.1.P3
	Panoan Indians see F3430.1.P33
3320.2.P37	Pauserna
	Pilaga see F2823.P5
	Puquina see F3430.1.P8
	Quechua see F2230.2.K4
3320.2.S3	Samucu
3320.2.S5	Siriono
3320.2.T3	Tacana
	Toba see F2823.T7
3320.2.T6	Toromona
	Tucuna see F2520.1.T925
3320.2.U78	Uru
3320.2.Y78	Yuqui
3320.2.Y8	Yurucari
3320.2.Z3	Zamucoan
	History
3320.3	Chronological tables. Outlines, syllabi, etc. Questions and answers
	Historiography
3320.4	General works
	Biography of historians
3320.5	Collective
3320.6.A-Z	Individual, A-Z
	Subarrange each by Table F5
3320.7	Study and teaching
3321	General works
	Including political history
	General special
3321.1	Military history
	Diplomatic history. Foreign and general relations
3321.2	General works
3321.3.A-Z	Relations with individual countries, A-Z
3321.9	Other (not A-Z)
	By period
	Pre-Columbian period see F3319+

F1201-
3799

	South America
	Bolivia
	History
	By period -- Continued
3322	1538-1809. Upper Peru

In colonial times, Bolivia was the southern part of Upper Peru, formed Audiencia of Charcas under viceroy of Peru, 1559-1776; under viceroy of Buenos Aires (La Plata), 1776-1810

Cf. F2841 Argentina, 1516-1810

Cf. F2991 Ancient gobernación of Tucumán

Cf. F3444 Insurrection of Tupac Amaru, 1780-1781

3323	1809-1825. Wars of independence
3324	1825-1884

Including independence from Peru, declared August 6, 1825. Period of civil wars and conflicts with neighboring countries

Including biography: Mariano Melgarejo, Andrés Santa-Cruz, etc.

For loss of southern Chaco to Argentina, 1878 see F2876

For war with Chile (War of the Pacific), 1879-1884 see F3097

Cf. F3447 Confederación Perú-Boliviana

3325	1884-1938

Including conflicts between the civil war and the military; rule of dictators, etc.

Including biography: Mariano Baptista, Ismael Montes, etc.

For loss of Acre District to Brazil (Treaty of Petropolis, 1903) see F2540

For Chaco War, 1932-1935 and Treaty of peace, 1938 see F2688.5

3326	1938-1982

Including biography: Victor Paz Estenssoro, Enrique Peñaranda Castillo, etc.

Cf. D731+ World War II, 1939-1945

3327	1982-
3341.A-Z	Regions, departments, etc., A-Z
3341.A1	Collective
	Acre Territory see F2540
3341.A5	Andes Mountains

Cf. F2212 General

Atacama (Argentine territory of Los Andes) see F2853

Atacama (Chilean province of Antofagasta) see F3116

3341.A9	Azero (Province)
3341.B4	Beni

	South America
	Bolivia
	Regions, departments, etc., A-Z -- Continued
3341.B7	Boundaries (General)
	For Brazil see F2554.B6
	For Paraguay see F2691.B7A+
	For Chaco Boreal dispute see F2691.C4
	For Argentina see F2857.B6
	For Peru see F3451.B71
3341.C27	Capinota (Province)
3341.C3	Caupolican (Province)
3341.C4	Chaco (Bolivian)
	For Chaco War, 1932-1935 see F2688.5
	Cf. F2691.C4 Chaco Boreal (Paraguay)
	Cf. F2876 El Gran Chaco (General, and Argentina)
3341.C5	Chiquitos (Province)
3341.C6	Chuquisaca
	For Azero (Province) see F3341.A9
3341.C7	Cochabamba
3341.C75	Cordillera (Province)
3341.I25	Ichilo (Province)
3341.L3	La Paz
	For Acre Territory see F2540
	For Caupolican (Province) see F3341.C3
	For Nor Yungas (Province) see F3341.N67
	For Lake Titicaca see F3341.T6
3341.L35	Larecaja (Province)
3341.M58	Mizque (Province)
3341.M9	Moxos (Province)
3341.N67	Nor Yungas (Province)
3341.O5	Omasuyos (Province)
3341.O6	Oriente
3341.O7	Oruro
3341.P3	Pando
	Piray River and Valley see F3341.S2
3341.P7	Potosí
3341.S2	Santa Cruz
	Including Piray River and Valley
	Cf. F2691.C4 Chaco Boreal dispute
3341.S9	Sud Chichas
3341.T2	Tarija
	Cf. F2691.C4 Chaco Boreal dispute
3341.T3	Territorio Nacional de Colonias

	South America
	Bolivia
	Regions, departments, etc., A-Z -- Continued
3341.T6	Titicaca, Lake, Region
	Class here general works on the Lake Titicaca Region, as well as works limited to the part located in Bolivia
	Including Titicaca Island
	For works limited to the part of the Lake Titicaca Region located in Peru see F3451.P9
3351.A-Z	Cities, towns, etc., A-Z
	e.g.
3351.C67	Cochabamba
3351.L2-.L29	La Paz (Table F2)
3351.O7	Oruro
3351.P85	Potosí
3351.S3	Santa Cruz
3351.S94	Sucre
	Formerly known as Charcas, Chuquisaca, and La Plata
	Elements in the population
	For interpretation see F1392.A1+
3359.A1	General works
	Including foreign elements (General), minorities, race conflicts and problems
3359.A2-Z	Individual elements, A-Z
3359.B55	Blacks
3359.B73	Brazilians
3359.C45	Chileans
3359.G3	Germans
	Indians see F3319+
3359.J3	Japanese
3359.J47	Jews
3359.R97	Ryukyuans
	Peru
3401	Periodicals. Societies. Collections
	Collected works
3402	Several authors
3403	Individual authors
	Including collected papers, addresses, essays
3403.5	Museums. Exhibitions, exhibits
3404	Gazetteers. Dictionaries. Geographic names
3404.5	Directories
	Biography
3405	Collective
	Individual (Historians) see F3430.6.A+
	Individual (By period) see F3441.2+
3408	General works
3408.5	Juvenile works

	South America
	Peru -- Continued
3409	Pamphlets, addresses, essays
3409.3	Anecdotes, legends, pageants, etc.
	Cf. P, Literature
	Cf. GR130+ Folklore
3409.5	Guidebooks. Handbooks
3409.7	Historic monuments (General)
3410	Social life and customs. Civilization. Intellectual life
	Including national characteristics
	For race conflicts and problems see F3619.A1+
3410.4	Geography
	Description and travel. Views
3410.5	History of travel
3411	Early to 1819
3423	1820-1950
3424	1951-1980
3425	1981-
	Antiquities. Indians
3429	General works
	Including Incas
3429.1.A-Z	Local (Ancient and modern), A-Z
	e.g.
3429.1.A45	Ancash (Department)
	Including Recuay culture
3429.1.A5	Ancón
3429.1.A7	Arequipa (Department)
3429.1.C3	Callejón de Huaylas
3429.1.C47	Chancay Valley
	Including Chancay culture
3429.1.C48	Chavín
	Including Chavín culture
3429.1.C497	Chiribaya Alta. Chiribaya Baja
	Including Chiribaya culture
3429.1.C5	Choqquequirau
3429.1.C8	Cuelap
3429.1.C9	Cuzco
3429.1.E7	Espiritu Pampa
3429.1.H8	Huamachuco
3429.1.H828	Huari
3429.1.K37	Kasapata
3429.1.L35	Lambayeque (Department)
	Including Sicán culture
3429.1.L7	Lima (Department)
3429.1.M3	Machu Picchu
3429.1.M35	Maranga
3429.1.N29	Ñawinpukyo

F1201-
3799

	South America
	Peru
	Antiquities. Indians
	Local (Ancient and modern), A-Z -- Continued
3429.1.N3	Nazca
	Including Nazca culture
3429.1.N5	Nievería
3429.1.P2	Pachacamac
3429.1.P25	Paracas
3429.1.P28	Paramonga
3429.1.P8	Puno (Department)
3429.1.P86	Putumayo Valley
3429.1.R55	Rimac Valley
	Sicán culture see F3429.1.L35
3429.1.T8	Trujillo (Province)
3429.1.V45	Vicús
	Including Vicús culture
3429.1.V77	Virú Valley
3429.1.V8	Vitcos
3429.3.A-Z	Topics (Ancient and modern), A-Z
3429.3.A37	Aged. Older Indians
3429.3.A4	Agriculture
3429.3.A45	Alcohol use
3429.3.A5	Anthropometry
3429.3.A65	Architecture
3429.3.A7	Art
3429.3.A76	Astronomy
3429.3.A9	Axes
3429.3.B63	Boats
	Burial customs see F3429.3.M7
3429.3.C14	Calendar. Chronology. Astrology
3429.3.C4	Census
	Ceremonies see F3429.3.R3
(3429.3.C56)	Civil rights
	see KHQ1+
3429.3.C59	Commerce
3429.3.C594	Communication
3429.3.C6	Consanguinity
3429.3.C74	Cosmology
3429.3.C8	Costume. Adornment
3429.3.C85	Craniology
3429.3.D6	Diseases
3429.3.D66	Dolls
3429.3.D69	Domestic animals
3429.3.D72	Domestic relations
3429.3.D77	Drinking vessels
3429.3.D79	Drug use

South America
  Peru
    Antiquities. Indians
      Topics (Ancient and modern), A-Z -- Continued

3429.3.E2	Economic conditions
3429.3.E3	Education
3429.3.E35	Egyptian influences
3429.3.E45	Employment
3429.3.E84	Ethnic identity
3429.3.E86	Ethnobotany
3429.3.F55	First contact with Europeans
3429.3.F57	Fishing
3429.3.F6	Folklore. Legends
3429.3.F65	Food
3429.3.F85	Funeral customs and rites
3429.3.G3	Games
3429.3.G4	Genealogy
3429.3.G5	Goldwork
	Government see F3429.3.P65
3429.3.G6	Government relations
3429.3.H5	Historiography
3429.3.I53	Industries
3429.3.I77	Irrigation
3429.3.J8	Judiciary
3429.3.K53	Kings and rulers
3429.3.K55	Kinship
3429.3.L3	Land tenure
3429.3.L45	Law and legislation
	Legends see F3429.3.F6
3429.3.L5	Litters
3429.3.M3	Magic
3429.3.M34	Marriage customs
3429.3.M35	Masks (Sculpture)
3429.3.M36	Mathematics
	For works limited to Quipu see F3429.3.Q6
3429.3.M4	Medicine
3429.3.M42	Metalwork
3429.3.M6	Missions
3429.3.M63	Mixed descent
3429.3.M7	Mortuary customs
3429.3.M8	Mummies
	Older Indians see F3429.3.A37
3429.3.P34	Painting
3429.3.P47	Petroglyphs. Rock paintings
3429.3.P55	Philosophy
3429.3.P65	Politics and government
3429.3.P68	Population

F1201-
3799

South America
Peru
Antiquities. Indians
Topics (Ancient and modern), A-Z -- Continued

3429.3.P69	Portraits, Indian
3429.3.P7	Postal service
3429.3.P8	Pottery
3429.3.P85	Psychology
3429.3.Q6	Quipu
3429.3.R27	Relations with blacks
3429.3.R3	Religion. Mythology
3429.3.R58	Rites and ceremonies
3429.3.R6	Roads. Trails
	Rock paintings see F3429.3.P47
3429.3.S39	Sculpture
3429.3.S45	Sexual behavior
3429.3.S54	Silverwork
3429.3.S59	Social conditions
3429.3.S6	Social life and customs
3429.3.T2	Tattooing
3429.3.T28	Taxation. Tribute
3429.3.T29	Teeth
3429.3.T3	Textile fabrics
3429.3.T7	Trephining
	Tribute see F3429.3.T28
3429.3.W2	Warfare
3429.3.W27	Wars
3429.3.W4	Weights and measures
3429.3.W65	Women
3429.3.W66	Wood-carving
3429.3.W7	Writing
3430	Modern Indians
3430.1.A-Z	Tribes (Ancient and modern), A-Z
	Achuale see F3430.1.A25
3430.1.A25	Achuar. Achuale
3430.1.A35	Aguaruna
3430.1.A5	Amahuaca
3430.1.A54	Amuesha
3430.1.A6	Andoa
3430.1.A7	Arabela
3430.1.A83	Ashaninca
3430.1.A85	Asto
	Aymara see F2230.2.A9
	Bora see F2270.2.B6
3430.1.C3	Campa
3430.1.C32	Candoshi
3430.1.C34	Capanahua

South America
   Peru
      Antiquities. Indians
         Tribes (Ancient and modern), A-Z -- Continued

3430.1.C35	Cashibo
	Cashinawa see F2520.1.C38
3430.1.C37	Chachapoya
3430.1.C4	Chanca
	Chavín culture see F3429.1.C48
3430.1.C43	Chayahuita
3430.1.C46	Chimu
3430.1.C48	Cholone
3430.1.C5	Chupacho
3430.1.C55	Cocama
3430.1.C6	Colla
	Conibo see F3430.1.S5
	Culina see F2520.1.C84
3430.1.C8	Cupisnique
3430.1.E78	Ese Ejja
3430.1.H78	Huambisa
3430.1.H8	Huanca
3430.1.H83	Huari
	Incas see F3429+
3430.1.I68	Iquito
3430.1.I8	Iscaycinca
3430.1.I85	Itucale
	Jivaro see F3722.1.J5
	Kechua see F2230.2.K4
3430.1.M3	Machiganga
3430.1.M38	Mashco
3430.1.M4	Mayna
3430.1.M45	Mayoruna
3430.1.M6	Mochica
3430.1.N3	Nasca
3430.1.O25	Ocaina
3430.1.O5	Omagua
3430.1.O74	Orejón
3430.1.P3	Pano
3430.1.P33	Panoan
3430.1.P4	Peban
	Pioje see F3722.1.P5
3430.1.P5	Piro
3430.1.P6	Pocra
3430.1.P8	Puquina
3430.1.Q47	Quero
3430.1.S35	Senci
3430.1.S4	Setibo

F1201-
3799

	South America
	Peru
	Antiquities. Indians
	Tribes (Ancient and modern), A-Z -- Continued
3430.1.S47	Shapra
3430.1.S48	Sharanahua
3430.1.S5	Shipibo-Conibo. Sipibo
	Tacana see F3320.2.T3
3430.1.U83	Urarina
3430.1.W35	Wamani
	Witoto see F2270.2.W5
3430.1.Y3	Yagua
3430.1.Y34	Yanaconas
3430.1.Y8	Yunca
	Zaparo see F3722.1.Z3
	History
3430.3	Chronological tables. Outlines, syllabi, etc. Questions and answers, etc.
	Historiography
3430.4	General works
	Biography of historians
3430.5	Collective
3430.6.A-Z	Individual, A-Z
	Subarrange each by Table F5
3430.7	Study and teaching
3431	General works
	Including political history
	General special
3432	Military and naval history
	Diplomatic history. Foreign and general relations
3433	General works
3434.A-Z	Relations with individual countries, A-Z
	By period
	Pre-Columbian period see F3429+
3442	1522-1548
	Including Spanish conquest, civil wars
	Including biography: Francisco Pizarro, Gonzalo Pizarro, etc.
	For Indians of Peru and the Inca Empire before 1531 see F3429
3444	1548-1820
	Including Viceroyalty of Peru, 1542-1824; Insurrection of Tupac Amaru, 1780-1781; sporadic revolts, 1805-1814
	Including biography: Vega, Garcilaso de la; Francisco de Toledo; Micaela Villegas; etc.

South America
  Peru
    History
      By period -- Continued

3446   1820-1829

          Including independence from Spain, proclaimed, 1821; battles at Zepita (1823), Colpahuaico (1824), Ayacucho (1824)

          Including biography: Juan Antonio Álvarez de Arenales, José de Lamar y Cortazar, William Miller, José Silverio Olaya, etc.

          For Battle of Tarqui, Ecuador see F2275

          For loss of upper Peru, 1825 see F3324

        1829-

3446.5   General works

3447   1829-1919

          Including civil wars; Battle of Yanacocha, 1835; Confederación Perú-Boliviana, 1835-1839; Spanish question, 1864; War with Spain, 1865-1866; Bombardment of Callao, 1866; Revolution of 1872; period of reconstruction, 1884-1919

          Including biography: Ramón Castilla, Agustín Gamarra, Augusto Bernardino Leguia, Nicolás de Piérola, Leoncio Prado, Mariano Ignacio Prado, Felípe Santiago Salaverry, etc.

          For War of the Pacific, 1879-1884 see F3097

          Cf. D501+ World War I, 1914-1918

          Cf. F3095 War with Spain, 1865-1866

          Cf. F3451.P94 Putumayo atrocities

3448   1919-1968

          Including rise of liberalism; the Apristas; anti-axis policies

          Including biography: Oscar Raimundo Benavides, Víctor Raúl Haya de la Torre, Manual Artura Odría, Manuel Prado y Ugarteche, etc.

          Cf. D731+ World War II, 1939-1945

          Cf. F2281.B7P1+ Leticia Dispute, 1932-1934

        1968-1980

3448.2   General works

         Biography

3448.3   Collective

3448.4.A-Z   Individual, A-Z

           Subarrange each by Table F5

           e. g.

3448.4.V4   Velasco Alvarado, Juan (Table F5)

        1980-

3448.5   General works

	South America
	Peru
	History
	By period
	1829-
	1980- -- Continued
	Biography
3448.6	Collective
3448.7.A-Z	Individual, A-Z
	Subarrange each by TABLE F5
	e. g.
3448.7.F85	Fujimori, Alberto (Table F5)
3451.A-Z	Regions, departments, etc., A-Z
3451.A4	Amazonas
	Amazonas, Bajos see F3451.B3
3451.A43	Anan Yauyo (Province)
3451.A45	Ancachs (Ancash)
	Including Callejón de Huaylos
3451.A48	Andahuaylas (Province)
3451.A5	Andes Mountains, Peru
	Including Cordillera Blanca
	Cf. F2212 General
3451.A54	Andrés Avelino Cáceres
3451.A6	Apurímac
3451.A7	Arequipa
	Including Coropuna, El Misti (Volcano)
	Arica (Department) see F3231
3451.A87	Ayabaca (Province)
3451.A9	Ayacucho
3451.B3	Bajo Amazonas
	Province was named Maynas in 1943
	Boundaries
3451.B7	General
3451.B71	Bolivia
	Brazil see F2554.P4
3451.B73	Chile
	Cf. F3097.3 Tacna and Arica question
	Colombia see F2281.B7
3451.B75	Ecuador
	Leticia question see F2281.B7P1+
	Cáceres Region see F3451.A54
3451.C2	Cajamarca
3451.C23	Calca (Province)
3451.C25	Callao
3451.C27	Canas (Province)
3451.C28	Canchis
3451.C3	Carabaya (Province)

	South America
	Peru
	Regions, departments, etc., A-Z -- Continued
	Cerro Salcantay see F3451.C9
3451.C46	Chancay (Province)
3451.C5	Chincha Valley
3451.C55	Chota (Province)
3451.C6	Chucuito (Province)
3451.C7	Contumazá (Province)
	Cordillera Blanca see F3451.A5
3451.C76	Corongo (Province)
3451.C85	Cutervo (Province)
3451.C9	Cuzco (Cusco)
	Including Nevado Sarcantay (Cerro Salcantay), Pampaconas River, Urubamba River
	Ene River and Valley see F3451.J9
3451.G73	Grau Region
3451.H7	Huamalies (Province)
3451.H75	Huancané (Province)
3451.H76	Huancavelica
3451.H78	Huancayo
3451.H79	Huanta
3451.H8	Huánuco
	Including Pozuzo colony
	Huaura River and Valley see F3451.L7
3451.H83	Huaral (Province)
	Huaylas, Callejon de see F3451.A45
3451.I3	Ica
3451.J33	Jaén (Province)
3451.J9	Junín
	Including Ene River and Valley
	La Libertad see F3451.L3
3451.L2	Lambayeque
3451.L23	Lampa
3451.L3	Libertad
3451.L7	Lima
	Including Huaura River and Valley, Marcahuasi Plateau
	Cf. F3601 Lima (City)
3451.L8	Loreto
	Including Amazon River and Valley, Peru, Marañón River, Pastaza River, Pichis River, and Ucayali River
3451.M2	Madre de Dios
	Including Madre de Dios River
	Marcahuasi Plateau see F3451.L7
	Maynas (Province) see F3451.B3
	Misti (Volcano) see F3451.A7
3451.M6	La Montaña (region)

F1201-3799

	South America
	Peru
	Regions, departments, etc., A-Z -- Continued
3451.M8	Moquegua
	Nevado Sarcantay see F3451.C9
3451.N67	Nor Oriental del Marañón
3451.O16	Ocsabamba (Oxapampa) colony
3451.P14	Pachitea (Province)
3451.P19	Pacific Coast
3451.P245	Parinacochas (Province)
3451.P247	Pasco
	Pastaza River see F3451.L8
3451.P25	Paucartambo (Province)
3451.P48	Pisco (Province)
3451.P5	Piura
	Pozuzo (Posuso) colony see F3451.H8
3451.P9	Puno
	Including Peruvian section of Lake Titicaca
	For general works on the Lake Titicaca Region, as well as works limited to the part located in Bolivia see F3341.T6
3451.P94	Putomayo River and Valley
	Class here general works on the Putomayo River and Valley, as well as works limited to the part located in Peru
	Including rubber atrocities
	For works limited to the part of the Putomayo River and Valley located in Colombia see F2281.P9
	Cf. F2546 Brazil, where river is called "Içá"
3451.R6	Rodríguez de Mendoza (Province)
	Salcantay, Cerro see F3451.C9
3451.S2	San Marcos (Province)
3451.S24	San Martín
3451.S244	Sandia (Province)
3451.S25	Santa Cruz (District)
	Sarcantay see F3451.C9
	Tacna (Department) see F3231
	Tarapacá see F3241
	Lake Titicaca region see F3451.P9
3451.T7	Trujillo (Province)
3451.T8	Tumbes
	Ucayali River and Valley see F3451.L8
3451.U88	Utcubamba (Province)
	White Cordillera see F3451.A5
3451.Y38	Yauyos (Province)
3451.Y47	Yerupaja (El Carnicero, The Butcher)

	South America
	Peru -- Continued
	Cities, towns, etc.
	Including individual biography
3601	Lima (Table F1)
	Including earthquakes of 1687, 1746; occupation by Chilean forces, 1881-1883
3611.A-Z	Other, A-Z
	e.g.
3611.A7	Arequipa
3611.C2	Callao
3611.C9	Cuzco
3611.H8	Huancavelica
3611.H82	Huancayo
3611.I6	Iquitos
3611.S84	Sullana
3611.T8	Trujillo
	Elements in the population
	Including foreign elements (General), minorities, race conflicts and problems
	For interpretation see F1392.A1+
3619.A1	General works
3619.A2-Z	Individual elements, A-Z
3619.A5	Americans
3619.A73	Arabs
3619.B55	Blacks
3619.B7	British
3619.C34	Canary Islanders
3619.C5	Chinese
3619.F74	French
3619.G3	Germans
	Indians see F3429+
3619.I8	Italians
3619.J3	Japanese
3619.J4	Jews
3619.M47	Mestizos
	Negroes see F3619.B55
3619.P64	Poles
3619.P67	Portuguese
3619.R87	Russians
3619.Y84	Yugoslavs
	Ecuador
3701	Periodicals. Societies. Collections
	Collected works
3702	Several authors
3703	Individual authors
	Including collected papers, addresses, essays

F1201-3799

	South America
	Ecuador -- Continued
3703.5	Museums. Exhibitions, exhibits
3704	Gazetteers. Dictionaries. Geographic names
3704.5	Directories
	Biography
3705	Collective
	Individual (Historians) see F3726.A+
	Individual (By period) see F3732.92+
3708	General works
3708.5	Juvenile works
3709	Pamphlets, addresses, essays
3709.3	Anecdotes, legends, pageants, etc.
	Cf. PN, PQ, etc., Literature
	Cf. GR130+ Folklore
3709.5	Guidebooks. Handbooks
3709.7	Historic monuments (General)
3710	Social life and customs. Civilization. Intellectual life
	Including national characteristics
	For race conflicts and problems see F3799.A1+
3710.9	Geography
	Description and travel. Views
3711	Early to 1808
3714	1809-1950
3715	1951-1980
3716	1981-
	Antiquities. Indians
3721	General works
3721.1.A-Z	Local (Ancient and modern), A-Z
	e.g.
3721.1.C2	Carchi (Province)
3721.1.G9	Guayas (Province)
3721.1.I3	Imbabura (Province)
3721.1.L36	La Plata Island
3721.1.M2	Manabí
3721.1.Q54	Quijos River Valley
3721.1.T65	Tomebamba
3721.3.A-Z	Topics (Ancient and modern), A-Z
3721.3.A35	Agriculture
3721.3.A67	Architecture
3721.3.A7	Art
3721.3.C64	Commerce
3721.3.D35	Dance
3721.3.D58	Diseases
	Drugs see F3721.3.N35
3721.3.E25	Economic conditions
3721.3.E35	Education

South America
  Ecuador
    Antiquities. Indians
      Topics (Ancient and modern), A-Z -- Continued

3721.3.E84	Ethnic identity
3721.3.E85	Ethnobotany
3721.3.F65	Folklore. Legends
3721.3.F7	Food
3721.3.G45	Genealogy
3721.3.G68	Government relations
3721.3.I4	Implements
3721.3.M37	Material culture
3721.3.M38	Mathematics
3721.3.M4	Medicine
3721.3.M45	Metalwork
3721.3.M6	Missions
	Mythology see F3721.3.R44
3721.3.N35	Narcotics. Drugs
3721.3.P35	Painting
3721.3.P74	Politics and government
3721.3.P76	Population
3721.3.P8	Pottery
3721.3.R44	Religion. Mythology
3721.3.S24	Salt
3721.3.S65	Social conditions
3721.3.S7	Social life and customs
3721.3.T18	Taxation. Tribute
3721.3.T2	Teeth mutilation and decoration
3721.3.T47	Textile fabrics
	Tribute see F3721.3.T18
3721.3.U73	Urban residence
3721.3.W35	Wars
3721.3.W65	Women
3722	Modern Indians (General)
3722.1.A-Z	Tribes (Ancient and modern), A-Z
	Achuale see F3430.1.A25
	Andoa see F3430.1.A6
	Arawak see F2230.2.A7
3722.1.C2	Cañari
3722.1.C23	Canelo
3722.1.C25	Cara
3722.1.C3	Cayapa
3722.1.C67	Cofán
3722.1.C7	Colorado
3722.1.C83	Cuaiquer
3722.1.E8	Esmeralda
3722.1.G82	Guayacundo

	South America
	Ecuador
	Antiquities. Indians
	Tribes (Ancient and modern), A-Z -- Continued
3722.1.H8	Huancavilca
3722.1.H83	Huao
	Incas see F3429
3722.1.J5	Jivaro. Shuar
	Kechua see F2230.2.K4
3722.1.M3	Manta
3722.1.O8	Otavalo
3722.1.P35	Panzaleo
	Pasto see F2270.2.P44
3722.1.P5	Pioje
3722.1.P8	Puruhá
3722.1.Q48	Quijo
3722.1.Q5	Quitu
3722.1.S43	Secoya
	Shuar see F3722.1.J5
	Tucuna see F2520.1.T925
3722.1.V34	Valdivia
3722.1.Y86	Yumbo
3722.1.Z3	Zaparo
	History
3723.3	Chronological tables. Outlines, syllabi, etc. Questions and answers, etc.
	Historiography
3724	General works
	Biography
3725	Collective
3726.A-Z	Individual, A-Z
	Subarrange each by Table F5
3731	General works
	Including political history
	General special
3731.5	Military and naval history
	Diplomatic history. Foreign and general relations
3732	General works
3732.5.A-Z	Relations with individual countries, A-Z
3732.9	Other (not A-Z)
	By period
	Pre-Columbian period see F3721+

South America
  Ecuador
    History
      By period -- Continued

3733	1526-1809. Colonial period
	Including discovery and conquest; civil war among the conquistadores; under viceroyalty of Peru, 1539-1717; under viceroyalty of Nueva Granada,1717-1723; under viceroyalty of Peru, 1723-1740; under viceroyalty of Nueva Granada, 1740 to independence
	Including biography: Sebastián de Belalcázar, Francisco Javier Eugenio, Santa Cruz y Espejo, etc.
3734	1809-1830. Wars of independence
	Including revolts against Spain, 1809-1810; Battle of Pichincha, 1822; member of Confederacy known as Republic of Colombia, 1822-1830
	Including biography: Abdón Calderón, etc.
3735	1830-
	Republic of Ecuador created in 1830 by secession from confederacy
3736	1830-1895. Age of Moreno, 1860-1895
	Including civil wars; Concordat of 1862; theocratic state, 1860-1895; etc.
	Including biography: Juan José Flores, Gabriel García Moreno, Federico González Suárez, Vicente Rocafuerte, Luis Vargas Torres, etc.
	For War with Spain, 1865-1866 see F3447
	Cf. BX1472+ Concordat of 1862
3737	1895-1944
	Including rule of liberals; restriction of church influence; loss of territory to Brazil in 1904, to Peru in 1942; etc.
	Including biography: Eloy Alfaro, Carlos Alberto Arroyo del Río, Isidro Ayora, Federico Páez, Leónidas Plaza Gutiérrez, etc.
	For Leticia dispute, 1932-1934 see F2281.B7P1+
	Cf. D501+ World War I, 1914-1918
	Cf. D731+ World War II, 1939-1945
3738	1944-1984
	Including revolts and counter revolutions; earthquake of 1949; etc.
	Including biography: Galo Plaza Lasso, José María Velasco Ibarra, etc.
	1984-
3738.2	General works
	Biography
3738.3	Collective

F1201-3799

South America
Ecuador
History
By period
1830-
1984-
Biography -- Continued

3738.4.A-Z	Individual, A-Z
	Subarrange each by Table F5
3741.A-Z	Regions, provinces, etc., A-Z
3741.A6	Andes Mountains, Ecuador
	Cf. F2212 General
	Archipiélago de Colón see F3741.G2
3741.A9	Azuay
3741.B5	Bolívar
3741.B7	Boundaries (General)
	For Colombia see F2281.B7
	For Leticia question see F2281.B7P1+
	For Peru see F3451.B75
3741.C25	Cañar
3741.C3	Carchi
	Including Rumichaca grotto
3741.C5	Chimborazo
	Colón. Archipiélago de see F3741.G2
3741.C6	Cotopaxi (León)
3741.E4	El Oro
	Enchanted Islands see F3741.G2
3741.E6	Esmeraldas
	Including Isla de la Tola (Tolita)
3741.G2	Galápagos (Encantadas, Enchanted) Islands.
	Archipiélago de Colón
3741.G9	Guayas
	Cf. F3741.G2 Galápagos Islands
3741.I6	Imbabura
	León see F3741.C6
3741.L5	Llanganati (Mountains)
3741.L6	Loja
3741.L7	Los Ríos
3741.M2	Manabí
3741.N3	Napo-Pastaza
	Including Oriente (Región oriental)
	For Peruvian boundary dispute see F3451.B7+
	Cf. F3741.S3 Santiago-Zamora
	Oriente (Región oriental) see F3741.N3
	El Oro see F3741.E4
3741.P32	Pacific Coast
3741.P4	Pichincha

	South America
	Ecuador
	Regions, provinces, etc., A-Z -- Continued
	Región oriental see F3741.N3
	Los Ríos see F3741.L7
3741.S3	Santiago-Zamora
	For Oriente (Región oriental) see F3741.N3
	Sierra see F3741.A6
3741.S93	Sucumbíos
3741.T7	Tungurahua
	Cities, towns, etc.
3781	Quito (Table F1)
3791.A-Z	Other, A-Z
	e.g.
3791.A6	Ambato
3791.C9	Cuenca
3791.G9	Guayaquil
3791.I3	Ibarra
3791.J3	Jipijapa (Canton)
3791.L3J3	Latecunga
3791.L6	Loja
3791.R6	Riobamba
3791.T8	Tulcán
3791.V7	Vinces
	Elements in the population
	For interpretation see F1392.A1+
3799.A1	General works
3799.A2-Z	Individual elements, A-Z
3799.B55	Blacks
	Indians see F3721+
3799.J4	Jews
	Negroes see F3799.B55
3799.S3	Salesians

F1201-
3799

.xA2	Collected works. By date
.xA25	Selected works. Selections. By date
	Including quotations
.xA3	Autobiography, diaries, etc. By date
.xA4	Letters. By date
.xA5	Speeches, essays, and lectures. By date
.xA6-.xZ	Biography and criticism

TABLES

.A3	Autobiography, diaries, etc. By date
.A4	Letters. By date
.A6-.Z	Biography and criticism

TABLES

.xA3	Autobiography, diaries, etc. By date
.xA4	Letters. By date
.xA6-.xZ	Biography and criticism

.x date	Collected works. By date
.x2	Selected works. Selections. By date
	Including quotations
	Autobiographies, diaries, etc.
	see the biography number for the individual, subdivided by Table
	E2, .A3
	Letters
	see the biography number for the individual, subdivided by Table
	E2, .A4
.x4	Essays. By date
.x5	Speeches. By date
.x9A-.x9Z	Special libraries. By author, A-Z

TABLES

	Official publications
.A1-.A4	Serial publications
.A5-.A69	Monographs
.A7	Nonofficial publications
.A8-.W	State branches. By state, A-W

Under each state:

	Official publications
.xA1-.xA4	*Serial publications*
.xA5-.xA7	*Monographs*
.xA8-.xZ	*Nonofficial publications*

	Official publications
.xA1-.xA4	Serial publications
.xA5-.xA7	Monographs
.xA8-.xZ	Nonofficial publications

TABLES

.A1-.A49	Official publications
.A5A-.A5Z	History of the society
.A6-.W	By state, A-W

.A2	Periodicals. Societies. Collections
.A3	Museums. Exhibitions, exhibits
.A4	Guidebooks. Gazetteers. Directories
.A5-.Z	General works. Description
.1	Monumental and picturesque
.13	Pamphlets, addresses, essays
.15	Antiquities
.2	Social life and customs. Intellectual life
	History
	Biography
.23.A2	General. Collective
.23.A3-Z	Individual
.25	Historiography. Study and teaching
.3	General works
	Sections. Districts, etc.
.4.A2	General. Collective
.4.A3-Z	Individual
	Cemeteries
.42.A2	General. Collective
.42.A3-Z	Individual
	Monuments. Statues
.5.A2	General. Collective
.5.A3-Z	Individual
	Parks. Squares. Circles
.6.A2	General. Collective
.6.A3-Z	Individual
	Streets
.7.A2	General. Collective
.7.A3-Z	Individual
	Buildings
.8.A2	General. Collective
.8.A3-Z	Individual
	Elements in the population
.9.A2	General. Collective
.9.A3-Z	Individual, A-Z
	For lists of Cutters, see E184, United States; F1035, Canada; F1392, Mexico, F1477, Guatemala; etc.

TABLES

.x	Periodicals. Societies. Collections
.x2	Museums. Exhibitions, exhibits
.x3	Guidebooks. Gazetteers. Directories
.x4	General works. Description
.x43	Monumental and picturesque
.x45	Pamphlets, addresses, essays
.x47	Antiquities
.x5	Social life and customs. Intellectual life
	History
	Biography
.x53A2-.x53A29	General. Collective
.x53A3-.x53Z	Individual
.x55	Historiography. Study and teaching
.x57	General works
	Sections. Districts, etc.
.x6A2-.x6A29	General. Collective
.x6A3-.x6Z	Individual
	Cemeteries
.x62A2-.x62A29	General. Collective
.x62A3-.x62Z	Individual
	Monuments. Statues
.x65A2-.x65A29	General. Collective
.x65A3-.x65Z	Individual
	Parks. Squares. Circles
.x7A2-.x7A29	General. Collective
.x7A3-.x7Z	Individual
	Streets
.x75A2-.x75A29	General. Collective
.x75A3-.x75Z	Individual
	Buildings
.x8A2-.x8A29	General. Collective
.x8A3-.x8Z	Individual
	Elements in the population
.x9A2-.x9A29	General. Collective
.x9A3-.x9Z	Individual

For lists of Cutters, see E184, United States; F1035, Canada; F1392, Mexico; F1477, Guatemala; etc.

.A2	Periodicals. Societies
.A3	Sources and documents. Collections
.A5-.Z	General works
.2	Description and travel. Guidebooks. Gazetteers
.3	Antiquities. Indians
.4	Social life and customs. Civilization
.42	Elements in the population
	History
.5	General works
.6	Biography and memoirs (Collective)
	Political and diplomatic history
.62	General works
.63.A-Z	Relations with individual countries, A-Z
	By period
	Early
.65	General works
	Biography and memoirs
.66	Collective
.67.A-Z	Individual, A-Z
	Colonial
.7	General works
	Biography and memoirs
.72	Collective
.73.A-Z	Individual, A-Z
	Independent
.8	General works
	Biography and memoirs
.82	Collective
.83.A-Z	Individual, A-Z
.9.A-Z	Local, A-Z

TABLES

Use this table where indicated to subarrange numbers for biography
    and memoirs of individual persons in the F schedule. In cases
    where individual biography is classed in numbers designating
    individual periods, this table does not apply. Instead, two
    Cutters are assigned, one for the name of the biographee, and
    one for the author

.A2   Collected works. By date
    Including collected or selected works by the individual on general
        historical or political topics pertaining to the period in which he
        lived
    For his collected or selected works on a special topic, see the topic

.A25   Selected works. By date
    Including collected or selected works by the individual on general
        historical or political topics pertaining to the period in which he
        lived
    For his collected or selected works on a special topic, see the topic

.A3   Autobiography, diaries, etc. By date

.A4   Letters. By date

Speeches, essays, and lectures
    Including interviews
    Including collected or selected works by the individual on general
        historical or political topics pertaining to the period in which he
        lived
    For his collected or selected works on a special topic, see the topic

.A49-.A499   Serials. By title

.A5   Monographs. By title

.A6-.Z   Biography and criticism

Use this table where indicated to subarrange Cutter numbers for biography and memoirs of individual persons in the F schedule, e.g., F1788.22.C3, Castro, Fidel. In cases where individual biography is classed in numbers designating individual periods, this table does not apply. Instead, two Cutters are assigned, one for the name of the biographee, and one for the author

.xA2	Collected works. By date

Including collected or selected works by the individual on general historical or political topics pertaining to the period in which he lived

For his collected or selected works on a special topic, see the topic

.xA25	Selected works. By date

Including collected or selected works by the individual on general historical or political topics pertaining to the period in which he lived

For his collected or selected works on a special topic, see the topic

.xA3	Autobiography, diaries, etc. By date
.xA4	Letters. By date
	Speeches, essays, lectures

Including interviews

Including collected or selected works by the individual on general historical or political topics pertaining to the period in which he lived

For his collected or selected works on a special topic, see the topic

.xA49-.xA499	Serials. By title
.xA5	Monographs. By date
.xA6-.xZ	Biography and criticism

TABLES

.A1-.A7   Official publications
.A8-.Z4   Reports of delegations from participating countries
                               Arrange alphabetically by country
.Z5   Works about the conference

NUMERALS

1976 Bicentennial celebration, U.S.: E285.3+

A

Abenaki Indians: E99.A13
Aberdeen (S. D.): F659.A14
Abipon Indians: F2679.2.A2
Abitibi County (Québec): F1054.A3
Abitibi Indians: E99.A12
Abitibi Region (Québec): F1054.A3
Abnaki Indians: E99.A13
Abolition of slavery
  United States: E453
    Agitation for: E449
Aboriginal America: E51+, E103+
Aboriginal Americans: E75+
Abreu, João Capistrano de: F2520.6.A2
Absaroka National Forest: F737.A3
Aburrá Valley (Colombia): F2269.1.A28
Acadia: F1036+
  Indians: E78.N9
Acadia National Park: F27.M9
Acadia Parish (La.): F377.A2
Acadians in Canada: F1036+
  Expulsion from Acadia: F1038
Acadians in Louisiana: F380.A1+
  "Evangeline country": F377.T4
Acadians in the United States: E184.A2
Acanceh Site (Mexico): F1435.1.A35
Acaxee Indians: F1219.8.A33
Accawai Indians: F2380.1.A2
Achagua Indians: F2270.2.A3
Achi Indians: F1465.2.A23
Achomawi Indians: E99.A15
Achuale Indians: F3430.1.A25
Achuar Indians: F3430.1.A25
Achuara Indians: F3430.1.A25
Ackia Battleground National Monument: F347.L45
Acoma Indians: E99.A16
Aconcagua, Chile (Province): F3106
Aconquija Mountains: F2850.4
Acre, Brazil (Territory): F2540
Acua-Shavante Indians: F2520.1.A4

Acuen-Xavante Indians: F2520.1.A4
Adair, John: E353.1.A19
Adams, Charles Francis, 1807-1886: E467.1.A2
Adams, Charles Francis (1835-1915): E664.A19
Adams, John: E322
  Administration, 1797-1801: E321+
  Collected works: E302.A26+
  Family: E322.1
Adams, John Quincy: E377+
  Administration, 1825-1829: E376+
  Charges of bargain with Clay: E375
  Collected works: E337.8.A2
Adams, Mount (Wash.): F897.K6
Adams, Samuel: E302.6.A2
Addicks, John Edward: F169
Addington Co. (Ont.): F1059.L5
Adena culture: E99.A18
Adet, P.A.: E313+
Adirondack Mountains (N.Y.): F127.A2
Adobe Walls, Battle of, 1864: E83.863
Adoption, Indian: E98.A15
Adornment
  Aztecs: F1219.76.C68
  Indians
    Bolivia: F3320.1.C64
    Brazil: F2519.3.C68
    Guatemala: F1465.3.C8
    Mexico: F1219.3.C75
    North America: E98.C8
    Peru: F3429.3.C8
    Pre-Columbian America: E59.C6
    South America: F2230.1.C8
  Mayas: F1435.3.C69
Aerial operations
  United States
    Civil War: E492.7
Aesthetics
  Indians: E98.A2
    Pre-Columbian America: E59.A32
Afghans in the United States: E184.A23
African American artisans: E185.8
African American business associations: E185.8
African American businessmen: E185.8
African American farmers: E185.8

African American insurrections: E447
African American race relations:
  E185.61, E185.615
African American sailors: E185.63
African American soldiers: E185.63
  Civil War
    Confederate Army: E585.A35
    Regiments: E492.9
    Union Army: E540.N3
  Revolutionary War: E269.N3
  War of 1812: E359.9.A35
  War of 1898: E725.5.N3
African American studies: E184.7.A1+
African Americans
  By region: E185.9+
  By state: E185.93.A+
  Colonization: E448
  Economic conditions: E185.8
  Emancipation: E453
  Ethnobotany: E185.89.E8
  Genealogy: E185.96+
  Intellectual life: E185.89.I56
  Moral conditions: E185.86
  Museums: E185.53.A1+
  Names: E185.89.N3
  Relations with Jews: E184.36.A34
  Slave life: E443
  Slavery: E441
  Social conditions: E185.86
  United States
    Discrimination: E185.61
    Segregation: E185.61
  Ward of the U. S.: E185.2
African Americans in the armed forces:
  E185.63
African Americans, Relations with
  United States Presidents:
    E176.472.A34
Africans
  Discovery of America: E109.A35
Africans in the United States: E184.A24
Afrikaners in the United States:
  E184.A26
Agate Fossil Beds National Monument
  (Nebraska): F672.S6
Agawam River (Mass.): F72.E7
Agramonte y Loinaz, Ignacio: F1785

Agrarian conflicts (New York): F122+
Agriculture
  Aztecs: F1219.76.A57
  Indians: E98.A3
    Argentina: F2821.3.A3
    Bolivia: F3320.1.A47
    Central America: F1434.2.A37
    Chile: F3069.3.A3
    Colombia: F2270.1.A47
    Ecuador: F3721.3.A35
    French Guiana: F2460.2.A37
    Guatemala: F1465.3.A37
    Mexico: F1219.3.A35
    Peru: F3429.3.A4
    Pre-Columbian America: E59.A35
    South America: F2230.1.A3
    Venezuela: F2319.3.A37
  Mayas: F1435.3.A37
Agua Tibia (Guatemala): F1435.1.A36
Aguada (Puerto Rico): F1981.A26
Aguapehy River (Brazil): F2631
Aguaruna Indians: F3430.1.A35
Aguascalientes, Mexico (State): F1241
Aguateca (Guatemala): F1435.1.A37
Aguilar, Jerónimo de: E125.A3
Aguilera, Francisco Vicente: F1785
Aguirre Cerda, Pedro: F3099
Aguirre, Lope de: E125.A35
Ahtena Indians: E99.A28
Aiken, S.C., Battle of, 1865: E477.7
Aisén, Chile (Province): F3134
Akan in America: E29.A43
Akatek Indians: F1465.2.A34
Aklavik (Mackenzie District):
  F1100.5.A4
Akoerio Indians: F2420.1.A35
Akron (Ohio): F499.A3
Akuri Indians: F2420.1.A35
Akuria Indians: F2420.1.A35
Akurijo Indians: F2420.1.A35
Akurio Indians: F2420.1.A35
Akwa'ala Indians: F1221.A4
Akwe-Shavante Indians: F2520.1.A4
Alabama: F321+
  African Americans: E185.93.A3
  Confederate history: E551+
  Counties: F332.A+

Alabama
  Indians: E78.A28
  Reconstruction, 1865-1877: F326
  Slavery: E445.A3
  Wars
    Civil War: E495+
      Military operations: E470.6,
        E470.7, E471+, E471.52
    War of 1898: E726.A3
Alabama (Confederate cruiser):
  E599.A3
Alabama Indians: E99.A4
Alacaluf Indians: F2986
Alachua Co. (Florida): F317.A4
Alagoas, Brazil (State): F2541
Alajuela (Costa Rica): F1556.A6
Alamán, Lucas: F1232
Alamo, Siege of the, 1836: F390
Alaska: F901+
  African Americans: E185.93.A4
  Counties, etc: F912.A+
  Indians: E78.A3
  Purchase by U.S.: F907
  Russian settlement: F907
Alaska Commercial Company, 1868-
  1940: F912.P9
Alaska, Gulf of: F912.A43
Alaska Highway: F1060.9
Albán (Mexico): F1219.1.O11
Albanians in the United States:
  E184.A3
Albany: F129.A3+
Albemarle (Ram): E599.A4
Albemarle region (N.C.): F262.A33
Albemarle settlement (N.C.): F257
Albeni Falls Dam and Region (Idaho):
  F752.A55
Alberni region (British Columbia):
  F1089.A4
Albert Co. (New Brunswick): F1044.A4
Alberta: F1075+
  Indians: E78.A34
Albuquerque (N. M.): F804.A3
Alcan Highway: F1060.9
Alcatraz Island (Calif.): F868.S156
Alcohol use
  Aztecs: F1219.76.A59

Alcohol use
  Indians: E98.L7
    Brazil: F2519.3.A42
    Mexico: F1219.3.A42
    Peru: F3429.3.A45
Aldogones Dunes (Calif.): F868.I2
Alessandri, Arturo: F3099
Aleutian Islands (Alaska): F951
Aleuts: E99.A34
Alexander, Andrew Jonathan:
  E467.1.A3
Alexander, Robert: E278.A3
Alexander VI (Pope)
  Demarcation line of: E123
Alexander, William (Lord Sterling):
  E207.A3
Alexandria (Virginia): F234.A3
Alexis, Pierre Nord: F1926
Alfaro, Eloy: F3737
Alger Hiss case: E743.5
Algeria, U.S. war with, 1815: E365
Algoma District (Ontario): F1059.A3
Algonkin Indians: E99.A349
Algonquian Indians: E99.A35
Algonquin Provincial Park (Ontario):
  F1059.A4
Alibamu Indians: E99.A4
Alien and sedition laws, 1798: E327
Alien enemies, Treatment of
  United States
    War of 1812: E358
Allagash River and Valley (Me.):
  F27.A4
Allatoona, Battle of, 1864: E476.87
Allegany State Park (New York):
  F127.A43
Alleghany Mountains: F217.A3
Allegheny Mountains: F217.A3
  Pennsylvania: F157.A45
Allegheny River and Valley (New York):
  F127.A45
Allegheny River and Valley
  (Pennsylvania): F157.A5
Allen, Charles: E340.A4
Allen, Ethan: E207.A4
Allen, Henry Watkins: E467.1.A4
Allen, Ira: F52

Allen, Jolley: E278.A4
Allen Parish (La.): F377.A4
Allen, William: F496
Allende, Salvador: F3101.A4
Allende y Unzaga, Ignacio José: F1232
Allens Creek and Valley (New York): F127.M6
Allerton, Isaac: F68
Almaguin Highlands (Ontario): F1059.A44
Alsatians in the United States: E184.A4
Alsea Indians: E99.A45
Alston, Theodosia Burr: E302.6.B954
Alta Pimería: F799
Alta Vela (Island): F1939.A4
Alta Verapaz (Guatemala): F1469.V3
  Indian antiquities: F1435.1.A38
Altamaha River and Valley (Ga.): F292.A48
Altar de Sacrificios, Guatemala (Mayas): F1435.1.A4
Altgeld, John Peter: F546
Altiplano (South America): F2212
Alto Paraná, Paraguay (Dept.): F2691.A4
Alto Velo, Isla: F1939.A4
Alton (Illinois): F549.A4
  Civil War prison: E616.A4
Altona Flat Rock (New York): F127.C77
Altun Ha site (Mayas): F1435.1.A57
Alvarado, Pedro de: F1437
Alvarado (Veracruz, Mexico), 1846, Battle of: E406.A48
Álvarez de Arenales, Juan Antonio: F3446
Álvarez, Juan: F1232.5
Alvear, Marcelo Torcuato de: F2848
Amador Guerrero, Manuel: F1566.5
Amahuaca Indians: F3430.1.A5
Amapá, Brazil (Territory): F2543
Amapala, Insurrection of, 1910: F1507.5
Amargosa River and Valley (Nevada): F847.A42
Amarillo (Texas): F394.A4
Amazon River and Valley: F2281.A4, F2546

Amazon River and Valley
  Indian antiquities: F2519.1.A6
Amazon River and Valley (Peru): F3451.L8
Amazonas
  Brazil (State): F2546
  Peru (Dept.): F3451.A4
  Venezuela (Territory): F2331.A3
Amazonas, Bajo, Peru (Province): F3451.B3
Ambato (Ecuador): F3791.A6
Ambergris Cay (Belize): F1449.A53
Ambrister, Robert
  Execution of: E83.817
Ambulance service
  United States
    Civil War: E621+
Amelia Island
  Seized by MacGregor, 1817: F314
Amelia Island (Florida): F317.N3
America: E11+
  Antiquities: E51+, E75+
  Description
    Earliest to 1810: E141+
  Discovery and exploration: E101+
  Indians: E51+
  Pan-American relations: F1415+
America Day: E120
America (The name): E125.V6
American Civil War: E461+
American colonial tracts monthly: E187.A5
American Colonization Society: E448
American conferences, International: F1404+
American Indians: E75+
  Education: E97+
American institutions, European origin of: E189
American Knights: E458.8
American loyalists: E277+
American political tracts
  Colonial history: E187.A53
American Revolution: E201+
American River and Valley (California): F868.A44

American Scenic and Historic
 Preservation Society: E151
Americanists, Societies of: E51
Americanization
 United States: E169.1+
Americanized citizens
 Argentina: F3021.A64
 Brazil: F2659.A5
Americans in Argentina: F3021.A5
Americans in Brazil: F2659.A5
Americans in Canada: F1035.A5
Americans in Central America:
 F1440.A54
Americans in Chile: F3285.A5
Americans in Cuba: F1789.A45
Americans in foreign countries: E184.2
Americans in Mexico: F1392.A5
Americans in Nicaragua: F1537.A5
Americans in Peru: F3619.A5
Americans in Venezuela: F2349.A5
Ames, Fisher: E302.6.A5
Amézaga, Juan José: F2728
Amherst College and the Civil War:
 E541.A5
Amish in the United States: E184.M45
Amishgo Indians: F1221.A58
Amistad National Recreation Area
 (Texas): F392.A195
Amistad (Slave ship): E447
Amnesty after Civil War
 United States: E668
Amucho Indians: F1221.A58
Amueixa Indians: F3430.1.A54
Amuesha Indians: F3430.1.A54
Amuexa Indians: F3430.1.A54
Amusement, Places of
 Boston: F73.627
 Chicago: F548.627
 New York: F128.627
 Philadelphia: F158.627
Amusgo Indians: F1221.A58
Amuzgo Indians: F1221.A58
Anacapa Island (Calif.): F868.V5
Anacostia River and Valley (District of
 Columbia): F202.A5
Anales de Tecamachalco:
 F1219.56.A52+

Analostan Island (District of Columbia):
 F203.4.T5
Anan Creek and Valley (Alaska):
 F912.A53
Anan Yauyo, Peru (Province):
 F3451.A43
Anasazi culture: E99.P9
Ancachs (Ancash), Peru (Dept.):
 F3451.A45
Ancash (Peru : Dept.)
 Indian antiquities: F3429.1.A45
Anchieta, José de: F2528
Anchorage (Alaska): F914.A5
Ancón, Peru
 Indian antiquities: F3429.1.A5
Ancón, Treaty of, 1883: F3097.3
Andahuaylas, Peru (Province):
 F3451.A48
Andalgala (Argentina)
 Indian antiquities: F2821.1.A3
Andaqui Indians: F2270.2.A6
Anderson Island (Wash.): F897.P6
Anderson, Richard Heron: E467.1.A54
Anderson Valley (California): F868.M5
Andersonville, Ga. Military prison
 Civil War: E612.A5
Andes, Los, Argentina (Territory):
 F2853
Andes Mountains: F2212
 Argentina: F2851
 Bolivia: F3341.A5
 Chile: F3111
 Colombia: F2281.A5
 Ecuador: F3741.A6
 Peru: F3451.A5
 Venezuela: F2331.A5
Andoa Indians: F3430.1.A6
Andoque Indians: F2270.2.A62
Andrada e Silva, José Bonifacio de:
 F2536
André, John: E280.A5
Andrés Avelino Cáceres (Peru):
 F3451.A54
Andrew, John Albion: E513+
Andrews' Railroad Raid, 1862: E473.55
Andros, Edmund: F7.5
Androscoggin Co: F27.A5

Androscoggin, Lake: F27.A5
Androscoggin River and Valley:
  F27.A53
Anecdotes, Historical
  Maine: F19.6
  U.S. revolution: E296
Angaco, Battle of, 1841: F2846.3
Angeles, Mount (Wash.): F897.C52
Angeles National Forest: F868.A5
Angell, Israel: E263.R4
Angell, James Burrill: E664.A55
Anglicans and the Revolution
  United States: E269.C5
Anglo-German Blockade, 1902
  (Venezuela): F2325
Anguilla (West Indies): F2033
Aniakchak National Monument and
  Preserve (Alaska): F912.A54
Ann Arbor (Michigan): F574.A6
Ann, Cape (Mass.): F72.E7
Annadel State Park (California):
  F868.S7
Annapolis Co. (Nova Scotia): F1039.A2
Annapolis (Maryland): F189.A6+
Annapolis Royal (Nova Scotia):
  F1039.5.A16
Anniversaries
  United States
    1976 Bicentennial: E285.3+
    Civil War: E641+
    Revolution: E285+
    War of 1812: E363
    War of 1898: E733
    War with Mexico: E413
Anserma Indians: F2270.2.A63
Ante-bellum North Carolina: F258
Ante-bellum South: F213
Ante-bellum Virginia: F230
Antes, Henry: F152
Anthony, Henry Bowen: E664.A6
Anthropology
  Indians
    North America: E51+, E75+
Anthropology, Physical
  Indians: E98.P53
Anthropometry
  Aztecs: F1219.76.A62

Anthropometry
  Indians: E98.A55
    Brazil: F2519.3.A5
    Central America: F1434.2.A55
    Chile: F3069.3.A58
    Colombia: F2270.1.A58
    Mexico: F1219.3.A5
    Peru: F3429.3.A5
    Pre-Columbian America: E59.A5
    South America: F2230.1.A4
    Venezuela: F2319.3.A5
  Mayas: F1435.3.A56
Anticosti Island (Québec): F1054.A6
Antietam, Battle of, 1862: E474.65
Antietam Creek (Md.): F187.W3
Antietam National Cemetery: E474.65
Antigonish Co. (Nova Scotia):
  F1039.A25
Antigua and Barbuda: F2035
Antigua (Guatemala): F1476.A5
Antilles, Greater: F1741+
Antilles, Lesser: F2001+
Antioquia, Colombia (Dept.): F2281.A6
Antiquities
  Aboriginal American: E51+
  Argentina: F2819+
  Bahamas: F1655
  Bolivia: F3319+
  Brazil: F2518.5+
  Caribbean Area: F2172
  Chile: F3069+
  Colombia: F2269+
  Cuba: F1769
  Ecuador: F3721+
  French Guiana: F2459+
  Guiana: F2354
  Guyana: F2379+
  Haiti: F1909
  Jamaica: F1875
  Mexico: F1218.5+
  Non-Indian
    America: E21.5
    United States: E159.5
  Panama: F1565+
  Paraguay: F2678+
  Peru: F3429+
  Puerto Rico: F1969

Antiquities
  South America: F2229+
  Suriname: F2419+
  Uruguay: F2719+
  Venezuela: F2318+
  West Indies: F1619+
Antislavery leaders
  United States: E449+
Antislavery movements
  United States: E441+, E446
    Kansas troubles: F685
Antofagasta (Chile)
  City: F3281.A45
  Province: F3116
Antuco (Volcano), Chile: F3136
Anza-Borrego Desert State Park (Calif.):
  F868.S15
Anza Valley (Calif.): F868.R6
Anzoátegui, José Antonio: F2324
Anzoátegui, Venezuela (State):
  F2331.A55
Apache Indians: E99.A6
  War, 1883-1886: E83.88
Apache Mohave (Yavapai) Indians:
  E99.Y5
Apache Trail (Arizona): F817.A62
Apalachee Indians: E99.A62
Apalachicola Indians: E99.A63
Apalachicola River and Valley: F317.A6
Apalai Indians: F2520.1.A6
Apalakiri Indians: F2520.1.A63
Apapocuva Indians: F2520.1.A632
Apapokuva Indians: F2520.1.A632
Apatzingan, Mexico (District)
  Indian antiquities: F1219.1.M55
Apiacá Indians: F2520.1.A64
Apinagé Indians: F2520.1.A65
Apolista Indians: F3320.2.A6
Apostle Islands (Wis.): F587.A8
Appalachian Mountains: F106
Appalachian Mountains, Southern:
  F217.A65
Appalachian people (General), Life and
  conditions of: F210
Appalachian Region
  Indians: E78.A66
Appalachian Trail: F106

Applegate, Jesse: F880
Applegate River and Valley (Oregon):
  F882.A65
Appomattox Campaign, 1865: E477.67
Apristas (Peru): F3448
Apure, Venezuela (State): F2331.A65
Apurímac, Peru (Dept.): F3451.A6
Apytere Indians: F2679.2.M34
Aquidneck (Island): F87.R4
Arabela Indians: F3430.1.A7
Arabs in America: E29.A73
Arabs in Argentina: F3021.A59
Arabs in Brazil: F2659.A7
Arabs in Canada: F1035.A7
Arabs in Chile: F3285.A7
Arabs in Colombia: F2299.A73
Arabs in Honduras: F1517.A73
Arabs in Latin America: F1419.A72
Arabs in Mexico: F1392.A7
Arabs in Paraguay: F2699.A72
Arabs in Peru: F3619.A73
Arabs in South America: F2239.A7
Arabs in the Dominican Republic:
  F1941.A73
Arabs in the United States: E184.A65
Aragonese in Latin America:
  F1419.A73
Aragua, Venezuela (State): F2331.A7
Araguaya River (Brazil): F2566, F2576,
  F2586
Arahuna Indians: F2230.2.A68
Araona Indians: F2230.2.A68
Arapaho Indians: E99.A7
Arara Indians: F2520.1.A7
Ararawa Indians: F2520.1.A77
Araua Indians: F2520.1.A75
Arauca Department
  Colombia: F2281.A7
Araucania (Chile): F3126
Araucanian Indians: F3126
Araucanian wars (Chile): F3091
Arauco, Chile (Province): F3126
Araujo, Manuel Enrique: F1487.5
Arauna Indians: F3320.2.A7
Aravaipa Canyon (Arizona): F817.A73
Arawak Indians: F2230.2.A7
Araweté Indians: F2520.1.A77

Arawna Indians: F2230.2.A68
Arbenz Guzmán, Jacobo: F1466.5
Arbuthnot, Alexander: E83.817
Arce, Manuel José: F1438
Archaeological Institute of America:
  E51
Archaeology
  Indians
    North America: E77.8+
  Research
    United States: E57
Archaeology, Prehistoric
  America: E61
Arches National Park (Utah): F832.A7
Archipiélago de Colón: F3741.G2
Architecture
  Aztecs: F1219.76.A74
  Indians: E98.A63
    Argentina: F2821.3.A78
    Bolivia: F3320.1.A68
    Ecuador: F3721.3.A67
    Honduras: F1505.3.A72
    Mexico: F1219.3.A6
    Peru: F3429.3.A65
    Pre-Columbian America: E59.A67
    South America: F2230.1.A5
    Venezuela: F2319.3.A67
  Mayas: F1435.3.A6
Archives, Indian: E97.9
Arctic Bay, Franklin District (Trading
  post): F1105.5.A7
Arctic regions of Canada: F1090.5
Are Indians: F2520.1.H48
Arecibo (Puerto Rico): F1981.A6
Arecuna Indians: F2380.1.A7
Arekena Indians: F2319.2.A73
Arenales, Juan Antonio Alvarez de:
  F3446
Arequipa (Peru)
  City: F3611.A7
  Department: F3451.A7
    Indian antiquities: F3429.1.A7
Arévalo, Juan José: F1466.5
Argenteuil County (Québec):
  F1054.A67
Argentina: F2801+
  La Plata region before 1806: F2841

Argentina
  Military history
    Argentine-Brazilian War, 1825-1828:
      F2725
    Argentine-Brazilian wars: F2846.3
    Civil wars: F2846, F2847
    Paraguayan War, 1865-1870:
      F2687
    Seven Reductions, War of the,
      1754-1756: F2684
    War of Independence, 1810-1817:
      F2845
  Misiones question with Brazil: F2626,
    F2916
  Péron regime, 1943-1955: F2849
  Rosas period, 1829-1852: F2846.3
Argentines in the United States:
  E184.A67
Argentines in Venezuela: F2349.A74
Argonauts (California): F865
Argyle Island (Georgia): F277.S3,
  F292.S3
Arhuaco Indians: F2270.2.A67
Ariari River (Colombia): F2281.M49
Arias de Saavedra, Hernando: F2841
Arias Madrid, Arnulfo: F1566.5
Arica, Chile (City): F3281.A6
Arica, Chile (Dept.): F3231
Aricna-Tacna question: F3097.3
Arikara Indians: E99.A8
Arikara War, 1823: E83.818
Arista, Mariano: F1232.5
Arizona: F806+
  African Americans: E185.93.A7
  Confederate history: E552+
  Counties, etc: F817.A+
  Indians: E78.A7
  Wars
    Apache War, 1883-1886: E83.88
    Civil War, 1861-1865
      Military operations: E470.9
Arizona Strip (Arizona): F817.A75
Arkansas: F406+
  African Americans: E185.93.A8
  Confederate history: E553+
  Counties, etc: F417.A+
  Indians: E78.A8

Arkansas
  Reconstruction, 1865-1877: F411
  Wars
    Civil War
      Military operations: E470.4+,
        E470.8, E470.9
      Military operations: E471.57
      War with Mexico, 1845-1848:
        E409.5.A8
Arkansas (Confederate ironclad):
  E474.11
Arkansas Delta (Ark.): F417.A67
Arkansas, Grand Canyon of the:
  F782.F8
Arkansas National Forest: F417.O8
Arkansas Post, Expedition against, Jan.
  1863: E474.48
Arkansas River and Valley: F417.A7
  Colorado: F782.A7
  Kansas: F687.A7
  Oklahoma: F702.A7
Arlington House: F234.A7
Arlington Memorial Bridge (Washington,
  D.C.): F203.7.A6
Arlington National Cemetery: F234.A7
Arlington (Virginia): F234.A7
Armand Bayou Park and Nature Center
  (Texas): F392.H38
Armenians in Argentina: F3021.A64
Armenians in Brazil: F2659.A75
Armenians in Canada: F1035.A74
Armenians in Latin America: F1419.A76
Armenians in South America:
  F2239.A75
Armenians in the United States:
  E184.A7
Armenians in Uruguay: F2799.A7
Armies
  Canada
    American Revolution: E263.C2
    Intercolonial wars: E196, E197,
      E198
    War of 1812: E359.85
  Confederate States of America
    African American troops: E585.A35
    Civil War: E470.2+, E545+, E608
      Registers: E548

Armies
  Great Britain
    American Revolution: E267+
    War of 1812: E359.8
  Mexico
    War with U.S.: E409.8
  Spain
    War of 1898: E725.9
  United States
    Civil War: E491+, E608
    Revolution: E255
    War of 1812: E359+
    War of 1898: E725+
    War with Mexico: E409+
Arms and armor
  Indians: E98.A65
    Pre-Columbian America: E59.A68
    South America: F2230.1.A6
Armstrong, John: E302.6.A7
Army life
  U.S. Civil War: E607
Army of Northern Virginia (C.S.A.):
  E470.2+
Army of Tennessee (C.S.A.): E470.5
Army of the Cumberland: E470.5
Army of the James: E470.2+
Army of the Pacific: E470.9
Army of the Potomac: E470.2+
Army of the Tennessee: E470.5
Army of Virginia: E470.2+
Army of West Virginia: E470.4+
Arnold, Benedict: E278.A7
  Treason, 1780: E236
Arnold, Margaret (Shippen): E278.A72
Aroostook River and Valley: F27.A7
  New Brunswick: F1044.A7
Aroostook War, 1839: E398
Arosaguntacook Indians: E99.A82
Arosemena, Pablo: F1566.5
Arrows
  Indians
    Brazil: F2519.3.B6
Arrowsmith, George: E467.1.A78
Arroyo de San Antonio Estate
  (California): F868.S7
Arroyo del Río, Carlos Alberto: F3737
Arsenal (Frankford, Pa.): F158.8.A7

Art
  Aztecs: F1219.76.A78
  Indians: E98.A7
    Argentina: F2821.3.A8
    Bolivia: F3320.1.A7
    Brazil: F2519.3.A7
    Central America: F1434.2.A7
    Chile: F3069.3.A7
    Colombia: F2270.1.A7
    Costa Rica: F1545.3.A7
    Ecuador: F3721.3.A7
    Guatemala: F1465.3.A7
    Guyana: F2380.2.A7
    Mexico: F1219.3.A7
    Nicaragua: F1525.3.A7
    Panama: F1565.3.A7
    Paraguay: F2679.3.A77
    Peru: F3429.3.A7
    Pre-Columbian America: E59.A7
    South America: F2230.1.A7
    Suriname: F2420.2.A7
    Venezuela: F2319.3.A7
  Mayas: F1435.3.A7
Art and the war
  War with Mexico: E415.2.A78
Arthabaska County (Québec):
  F1054.A7
Arthur, Chester A.
  Administration, 1881-1885: E691
Articles of Confederation: E303
Artigas, José Gervasio: F2725
Artigas, Uruguay (Dept.): F2731.A7
Arts
  Indians: E98.A73
    Pre-Columbian America: E59.A73
Aruac Indians: F2270.2.A67
Aruba (West Indies): F2038
Ascension Island: F3030.3
Ascension Parish (La.): F377.A7
Ash Swamp, New Jersey, Battle of,
  1777: E241.S53
Ashaninca Indians: F3430.1.A83
Ashburton Treaty, 1842: E398
Ashby, Turner: E467.1.A8
Asheville, N.C., Battle of, 1865: E477.7
Asheville (North Carolina): F264.A8

Ashley River and Valley (S.C.):
  F277.A84
Ashluslay Indians: F2230.2.A78
Ashurst Colony (Calif.): F868.S13
Asian influences, Indian: E98.A84
Asians in America: E29.A75
Asians in Brazil: F2659.A84
Asians in Canada: F1035.A75
Asians in Latin America: F1419.A84
Asians in the United States: E184.A75
Asians, South, in Canada: F1035.S66
Aspen (Colorado): F784.A7
Assassination attempt
  Franklin Delano Roosevelt: E807.3
  Ronald Reagan: E877.3
Assassination attempts
  Gerald Ford: E866.3
Assateague Indians: E99.A83
Assateague Island National Seashore
  (Maryland): F187.W7
Assiniboia: F1067
Assiniboin Indians: E99.A84
Association of the Territorial Company
  of Philadelphia: F442.1
Assumption Parish (La.): F377.A75
Assunguy Colony (Brazil): F2596
Assyrians in Canada: F1035.A87
Assyrians in the United States:
  E184.A8
Asto Indians: F3430.1.A85
Astoria (Oregon): F884.A8
Astrology
  Aztecs: F1219.76.A83
  Indians
    Peru: F3429.3.C14
  Mayas: F1435.3.A8
Astronomy
  Aztecs: F1219.76.A84
  Indians: E98.A88
    Brazil: F2519.3.A84
    Mexico: F1219.3.A85
    Peru: F3429.3.A76
    Pre-Columbian America: E59.A8
    South America: F2230.1.A85
    West Indies: F1619.3.A84
Asturians in Cuba: F1789.A7
Asturians in Latin America: F1419.A87

Asunción (Paraguay): F2695.A8
Asurini Indians: F2520.1.A84
Atacama, Chile (Province): F3131
 Indian antiquities: F3069.1.A8
Atacama Desert (Chile): F3131
Atacama (former Bolivian territory):
 F2853, F3116
Atacameno Indians: F3070.1.A7
Atchaflaya River and Swamp (La.):
 F377.A78
Athabasca region (Alberta): F1079.A8
Athabasca Sand Dunes Provincial
 Wilderness Park (Saskatchewan):
 F1074.A75
Athapascan Indians: E99.A86
Athens, Mo., Battle of, 1861: E472.2
Atikamekw Indians: E99.T33
Atitlán, Lake (Guatemala): F1469.S64
 Indian antiquities: F1465.1.A8
Atlanta Campaign, 1864: E476.7
Atlanta (Georgia): F294.A8+
 Capture of, 1864: E476.7
Atlanta (Ram): E599.A8
Atlantic City (N.J.): F144.A8
Atlantic Coast
 Brazil: F2548
 Canada: F1035.8
 Colombia: F2281.A79
 Florida: F317.A74
 Georgia: F292.A74
 Maine: F27.A75
 New England: F12.A74
 New Jersey: F142.A79
 Nicaragua: F1529.M9
 North America: F106
 Nova Scotia: F1039.A74
 South America: F2214
 South Carolina: F277.A86
 Uruguay: F2731.A84
Atlantic Coast (Conn.): F102.A85
Atlantic Provinces (Canada): F1035.8
Atlantic, South (Region): F3030
Atlantic States: F106
 Indians: E78.A88
Atlántico, Colombia (Dept.): F2281.A8
Atrocities, Putumayo: F3451.P94
Atsina Indians: E99.A87

Atsugewi Indians: E99.A875
Attacapa Indians: E99.A88
Attakapas District (La.): F377.A8
Atticmospicayes Indians: E99.T4
Au Sable Chasm (New York): F127.E8
Au Sable River and Valley (New York):
 F127.E8
Auca Indians: F3722.1.H83
Audiencia of Caracas: F2322
Audiencia of Charcas: F3322
Audiencia of Guadalajara: F1296
Audiencia of Guatemala: F1437
Audiencia of New Granada: F2272
Audiencia of Santo Domingo: F1621
Audio-visual materials catalogs (Latin
 America): F1409.9.Z9
Auditorium Building (Chicago):
 F548.8.A9
Augusta (Georgia): F294.A9
Augusta (Me.): F29.A9
Augutge Indians: F2520.1.G37
Austin (Nevada): F849.A9
Austin, Stephen Fuller: F389
Austin (Texas): F394.A9+
Austin's Colony (Texas): F389
Australians in Paraguay: F2699.A87
Austrians in Brazil: F2659.A9
Austrians in Canada: F1035.A94
Austrians in the United States: E184.A9
Auxiliaries, French
 American Revolution: E265
Auyuittuq National Park (Northwest
 Territories, Canada): F1105.A89
Ava-Canoeiro Indians: F2520.1.A93
Ava-mbiha Indians: F2679.2.M34
Avachiripá Indians: F2230.2.A82
Avakatuete Indians: F2230.2.A82
Avalon (Baltimore colony): F1123
Avellaneda (Argentina)
 City: F3011.A9
 Partido: F2861
Avellaneda, Nicolás: F2847
Avery Island (La.): F377.F57
Aves Islands (Venezuela): F2331.A9
Ávila Camacho, Manuel: F1234
Avila Mountain (Venezuela): F2331.A93
Avila, Pedro Arias de: F1437

Avoyelles Parish (La.): F377.A9
Awahun Indians: F3430.1.A35
Awakateko Indians: F1465.2.A84
Awikenox Indians: E99.O68
Awikyenoq Indians: E99.O68
Axes
  Indians
    Peru: F3429.3.A9
Ayabaca Province (Peru): F3451.A87
Ayacucho, Battle of, 1824: F3446
Ayacucho, Peru (Dept.): F3451.A9
Ayala, Eusebio: F2688
Aycock, Charles Brantley: F259
Aymara Indians: F2230.2.A9
Ayora, Isidro: F3737
Aysén, Chile (Province): F3134
Azerbaijanis in the United States:
  E184.A94
Azero, Bolivia (Province): F3341.A9
Azilia: F289
Azoreans in the United States:
  E184.A95
Aztec Club of 1847: E401.1
Aztec codices: F1219.54.A98
Aztec Ruins National Monument
  New Mexico: E99.P9
Aztecs: F1219.73+
  Wars: F1219.3.W37
Azuay, Ecuador (Province): F3741.A9

B

Babcock State Park (West Viginia):
  F247.F2
Bache, Benjamin Franklin: E302.6.B14
Back Bay (Boston): F73.68.B32
Back Creek and Valley
  Virginia: F232.B24
  West Virginia: F247.B14
Back River and Valley
  Keewatin: F1110.B33
  Mackenzie: F1100.B33
Bacon, Robert: E664.B123
Bacon's Rebellion, 1676: F229
Badlands (N.D.): F642.L5
Badlands (S.D.): F657.B24
Báez, Buenaventura: F1938.4

Baffin Island and Land: F1105.B3
Bahamas: F1650+
Bahia Blancha (Argentina): F3011.B3
Bahia (Brazil)
  City: F2651.S13+
    Capture by Dutch, 1625: F2532
  State: F2551
    Indian antiquities: F2519.1.B3
Baia (Brazil): F2651.S13+
Baie Saint-Paul region (Québec):
  F1054.B35
Bailey, Anne: F241
Bailey, Joseph Weldon: E664.B2
Bailey, Theodorus: E467.1.B14
Bainbridge Island (Wash.): F897.K5
Bainbridge, William: E353.1.B2
Baja California (Mexico): F1246+
Baja California (State)
  Mexico: F1246.2
Baja California Sur (Mexico): F1246.3
Baja Vera Paz, Guatemala (Dept.):
  F1469.V4
Bajío Region (Mexico): F1246.6
Bajo Amazonas, Peru (Province):
  F3451.B3
Bakairi Indians: F2520.1.B3
Baker, Edward Dickenson: E467.1.B16
Baker Lake (Trading post): F1110.5.B3
Baker, Mount (Wash.): F897.W57
Baker River (Chile): F3134
Balberta
  Mayas: F1435.1.B35
Balboa Island (Calif.): F868.O6
Balboa, Vasco Núñez de: E125.B2
Balcones Canyonlands National Wildlife
  Refuge (Texas): F392.B17
Bald Head Island (N.C.): F262.B9
Bald Mountains
  North Carolina: F262.B3
  Tennessee: F443.B3
Baldwin, Abraham: E302.6.B17
Baldwin, Simeon: E302.6.B19
Balize: F1441+
Ball's Bluff, Battle of, 1861: E472.63
Balmaceda, José Manuel: F3098
Balsas River (Mexico): F1247

Baltimore, Cecilius Calvert, 2d Baron of: F184

Baltimore colony of Avalon: F1123

Baltimore, George Calvert, 1st Baron of: F184

Colony of Avalon: F1123

Baltimore (Maryland): F189.B1+

Battle of, 1814: E356.B2

Conflict between U.S. troops and mob, 1861: E472.13

Riot, 1812: F189.B1+

Bancroft, George: E340.B2

Banda Oriental del Uruguay: F2723

Bandeiras: F2528

São Paulo: F2631

Bandelier National Monument: F802.B25

Banff National Park (Alberta): F1079.B5

Bangladeshis in the United States: E184.B13

Bangor (Me.): F29.B2

Baniba Indians: F2520.1.B35

Baniva Indians: F2520.1.B35

Bank of the United States

Removal of deposits: E384.7

Bankhead, John Hollis: F326

Banks, Nathaniel Prentice: E467.1.B23

Bannock Indians: E99.B33

Baptista, Mariano: F3325

Baptists and the American Revolution: E269.B2

Bar Harbor (Me.): F29.B3

Baracoa (Cuba): F1849.B2

Baranof Island (Alaska): F912.B14

Baranov, Aleksandr Andreevich: F907

Barasana Indians: F2270.2.B27

Barbacoa Indians: F2270.2.B3

Barbados (West Indies): F2041

Barbary States

Relations with U.S.: E335

War with Algeria, 1815: E365

War with Tripoli, 1801-1805: E335

Barbosa, Ruy: F2537

Barbuda: F2035

Baré Indians: F2520.1.B4

Barí Island (Colombia): F2281.B6

Barinas, Venezuela (State): F2331.B3

Barlow, Francis Channing: E467.1.B25

Barnegat Bay (N.J.): F142.O2

Barnes, James: E467.1.B26

Barney, Joshua: E353.1.B26

Barona Valley (Calif.): F868.S15

Barquisimeto (Venezuela): F2341.B3

Barrácas al Sud (Argentina): F3011.A9

Barranquilla (Colombia): F2291.B3

Barrios, Justo Rufino: F1466.45

Barron, James: E335

Barros Arana, Diego: F3076.B3

Barrow, Point (Alaska): F912.B2

Barrundia, José Francisco: F1438

Barry, John: E207.B2

Bartholdi's Statue of Liberty (New York): F128.64.L6

Bartholomew Bayou

Arkansas: F417.B27

Louisiana: F377.B37

Bartica (British Guiana): F2389.B3

Bartlett Island (Me.): F27.M9

Bartlett, Josiah: E302.6.B2

Bartlett, William Francis: E467.1.B29

Baruch, Bernard Mannes: E748.B32

Bas-Saint-Laurent (Québec): F1054.B36

Basket-Maker Indians: E99.B37

Baskets

Indians

Brazil: F2519.3.B36

North America: E98.B3

Pre-Columbian America: E59.B3

Venezuela: F2319.3.B37

Mayas: F1435.3.B37

Basques

Discovery of America: E109.B3

Basques, Île aux (Québec): F1054.B37

Basques in America: E29.B35

Basques in Argentina: F3021.B2

Basques in Canada: F1035.B3

Basques in Chile: F3285.B3

Basques in Colombia: F2299.B37

Basques in Cuba: F1789.B37

Basques in Latin America: F1419.B37

Basques in Mexico: F1392.B3

Basques in South America: F2239.B3

Basques in the United States:
E184.B15
Basques in Uruguay: F2799.B2
Basques in Venezuela: F2349.B3
Bass Islands (Ohio): F497.O8
Basse-Terre Island (Guadeloupe):
F2066
Bat Indians: F2520.1.C38
Bates, Frederick: F466
Bathurst District (Ontario): F1059.B36
Baticola Indians: F2679.2.M34
Batlle y Ordóñez, José: F2728
Baton Rouge District of West Florida:
F377.F6
Before 1812: F301
Baton Rouge (La.): F379.B33
Operations against, 1862: E474.11
Battery (New York): F128.65.B3
Battle Abbey (Richmond): F234.R5+
Battle Harbour, Labrador (Fishing port):
F1139.B3
Battle of the Châteauguay National
Historic Site (Québec): F1054.C45
Battle Valley (Alberta and
Saskatchewan): F1079.B55
Battlement National Forest (Colorado):
F782.B33
Battles
United States: E181, E182
Civil War: E470+
Indian wars: E81+
Revolution: E231+
War of 1812: E355+
War of 1898: E717+
War with Mexico: E405+
Baxter Springs, Kansas, Battle of, 1863:
E474.9
Baxter State Park (Me.): F27.P5
Bay City (Michigan): F574.B3
Bay Islands, Honduras (Dept.):
F1509.B3
Bay of Fundy (Nova Scotia): F1039.F9
Bay of Quinte (Ontario): F1059.Q6
Bayamo (Cuba): F1849.B3
Bayard, George Dashiell: E467.1.B3
Bayard, James Asheton: E302.6.B3
Bayard, John: E263.P4

Bayard, Nicholas: F122+
Bayard, Thomas Francis: E664.B3
Bayou Chene (La.): F377.A78
Bayou Teche (La.): F377.T4
Bays Mountain (Tennessee): F443.B33
Beacon Hill (Boston): F73.68.B4
Beacon Hill Monument (Boston):
F73.64.B4
Bead Lake (Wash.): F897.P4
Beadwork
Indians: E98.B46
Mexico: F1219.3.B4
Pre-Columbian America: E59.B43
Beale, Edward Fitzgerald: F593
Bean Creek and Valley
Michigan: F572.B36
Ohio: F497.B3
Bean, Roy: F391+
Bear Butte (S.D.): F657.M4
Bear Flag War, 1846: F864
Bear Mountain State Park (N.Y.):
F127.R6
Bear River and Valley (Utah): F832.B3
Bear Valley (California): F868.S14
Beard, Charles Austin: E175.5.B38
Bearlake Indians: E99.B376
Beartooth Mountains
Montana: F737.B35
Wyoming: F767.B23
Beauce County (Québec): F1054.B38
Beaufort Sea region (Alaska):
F912.B24
Beaumont (Texas): F394.B3
Beauregard Parish (La.): F377.B4
Beauregard, Pierre Gustave Toutant:
E467.1.B38
Beaver Creek and Valley (Colo.):
F782.E15
Beaver Dam Creek, Battle of, 1862:
E473.68
Beaver Dams, Ontario, Battle of, 1813:
E356.B3
Beaver Indians
Athapascan tribe: E99.T77
Beaver Island (Michigan): F572.B38
Beaver, James Addams: E467.1.B39
Beaver Kill (New York): F127.B4

Beaver Kill Valley (New York): F127.B4
Beaver Lake (Indiana): F532.N5
Beaver River and Valley (Pa.):
  F157.B23
Becan site (Mexico): F1435.1.B4
Beckworth Trail (Calif.): F868.S5
Bedard, Pierre Stanislas: F1053
Bedford Co. (Tennessee): F443.B35
Bedford, N.Y. (Westchester Co.), Battle
  of, 1779: E241.B33
Bedinger, George Michael: F455
Bedloe's Island (New York). Statue of
  Liberty: F128.64.L6
Beecher Island, Battle of, 1868:
  E83.868
B.E.F.: F199
Behaim, Martin: E110
Belalcázar, Sebastián de: F3733
Belarusians in Argentina: F3021.B45
Belarusians in Canada: F1035.W5
Belarusians in the United States:
  E184.W6
Belém (Brazil): F2651.B4
Belgians in Belize: F1457.B4
Belgians in Brazil: F2659.B4
Belgians in Canada: F1035.B4
Belgians in the United States: E184.B2
  Civil War: E540.B4
Belgrano, Manuel: F2845
Belice: F1441+
Belize (Belize)
  District: F1449.B4
Belize (British Honduras)
  City: F1456.B4
Bell, John: E415.9.B4
Bella Coola River and Valley (B.C.):
  F1089.B44
Bella Coola/Chilcotin Road (B.C.):
  F1089.B43
Bellabella Indians: E99.H45
Bellacoola Indians: E99.B39
Bellamar Cave (Cuba): F1819.B4
Belle Isle Prison, Richmond: E612.B3
Bellechasse County (Québec):
  F1054.B45
Bellevue (Nebraska): F674.B4
Bellevue Valley (Mo.): F472.B38

Belly River, Battle of, 1870: E83.8697
Belmont, August: E415.9.B45
Belmont (Missouri), Engagement at,
  1861: E472.28
Belmont, Perry: E664.B5
Belo Horizonte (Brazil): F2651.B42
Ben Lomond (Utah): F832.W3
Benavides, Oscar Raimundo: F3448
Benedict, Lewis: E467.1.B397
Bengali in the United States: E184.B26
Beni, Bolivia (Dept.): F3341.B4
Benjamin, Judah Philip: E467.1.B4
Bennett, Richard Belford: F1033
Bennington, Battle of, 1777: E241.B4
Bennington (Vermont): F59.B4
Benton, Thomas Hart: E340.B4
Bentonville, N.C., Battle of, 1865:
  E477.7
Bent's Old Fort National Historic Site
  (Colo.): F782.A7
Beothuk Indians: E99.B4
Berbice (British Guiana): F2389.N4
Berbice Co. (British Guiana): F2387.B4
Berbice (Dutch Colony): F2383, F2423
Bering Sea: F951
Berkeley (California): F869.B5
Berks Co. (Pa.): F157.B3
Berkshire Hills: F72.B5
Bermuda Hundred (Virginia), Operations
  at, 1864: E476.57
Bermudas: F1630+
  American Revolution: E263.W5
Berry, Hiram Gregory: E467.1.B5
Berthier County (Québec): F1054.B54
Betancourt Cisneros, Gaspar: F1783
Betancourt, Rómulo: F2326
Betancourt y Dávalos, Pedro de
  Estanislao: F1786
Bethel, Battle of, 1861: E472.14
Betoyan Indians: F2270.2.T77
Beverages
  Aztecs: F1219.76.B48
Biblioteca nazionale centrale di Firenze.
  Manuscript. Magl. XIII, 3:
  F1219.56.B53+

Bibliothèque national de France. Manuscript 210 (Codices): F1219.56.B56+

Bibliothèque nationale de France. Manuscript. Mexicain 22 (Codices): F1219.56.B57+

Bibliotheque nationale (France). Manuscript. Mexicain 40 (Codices): F1219.56.B58+

Bickerdyke, Mary Ann: E621

Biddle, Charles: F153

Biddle, James: E353.1.B5

Biddle, Nicholas: E207.B48

Biddle, Owen: E207.B5

Bidwell, John: F864

Bienville, Jean Baptiste Le Moyne de: F372

Bienville Parish (La.): F377.B5

Big Bald Mountain
North Carolina: F262.B3
Tennessee: F443.B3

Big Bear Lake (California): F868.S14

Big Bear Valley (California): F868.S14

Big Bend National Park (Texas): F392.B53

Big Bend Region (Florida): F317.B54

Big Bend region (Texas): F392.B54

Big Bethel, Engagement at, 1861: E472.14

Big Blue, Battle of, 1864: E477.16

Big Blue River (Kansas): F687.B6

Big Bone Lick (Kentucky): F457.B65

Big Coal River and Valley (West Virginia): F247.B54

Big Cormorant Lake (Minnesota): F612.B39

Big Fork River and Valley (Minnesota): F612.K7

Big Hole Battle: E83.877

Big Hole River and Valley (Mont.): F737.B48

Big Horn Canyon National Recreation Area (Mont. and Wyo.): F737.B49

Big Horn Post No. 2 (Mont.): F737.Y4

Big Horn River and Valley (Wyoming): F767.B4

Big Moose Lake (New York): F127.H5

Big Oak Flat Road (Calif.): F868.B5

Big Pine Creek and Valley (N.C.): F262.M25

Big Sandy River and region (Arizona): F817.B5

Big Sandy River and Valley (Kentucky): F457.B5

Big Sioux River and Valley
Iowa: F627.B5
South Dakota: F657.B5

Big Tancook Island (Nova Scotia): F1039.T35

Big Thicket (Texas): F392.H37

Big Thompson Canyon (Colo.): F782.B45

Big Thompson River and Valley (Colo.): F782.B45

Big Tree National Forest (Caliveras, Calif.): F868.C14

Big Tree, Treaty of, 1797: F127.H7

Big Wood River and Valley (Idaho): F752.B55

Bigelow, John: E664.B55

Bigelow, Timothy: E207.B58

Bigot, François: F1030

Billings (Mont.): F739.B5

Billy the Kid: F786

Billys Island (Georgia): F292.O5

Biloxi Indians: E99.B5

Biloxi (Mississippi): F349.B5

Bingham, Harry: F39

Binney, Horace, 1790-1875: E340.B57

Bío-Bío, Chile (Province): F3136

Biography (Collective)
Argentina: F2805
Bahamas: F1650.9
Belize: F1442.7
Bermudas: F1630.9
Bolivia: F3305
Brazil: F2505
British America: F1005
British Guiana: F2365
Canada: F1005
Central America: F1426
Chile: F3055
Colombia: F2255
Costa Rica: F1542.7

Biography (Collective)
  Cuba: F1755
  Dominican Republic: F1933
  Dutch Guiana: F2405
  Ecuador: F3705
  El Salvador: F1482.7
  French Guiana: F2445
  Guatemala: F1462.7
  Haiti: F1914
  Honduras: F1502.7
  Jamaica: F1865
  Latin America: F1407
  Mexico: F1205
  Nicaragua: F1522.7
  Panama: F1562.7
  Paraguay: F2665
  Peru: F3405
  Puerto Rico: F1955
  South America: F2205
  Spanish America: F1407
  United States
    1961-: E840.6
    West (U.S.): F590.5
  Uruguay: F2705
  Venezuela: F2305
  West Indies: F1607
Biology
  Indians: E98.B54
Birch Coulee, Battle of, 1862: E83.86
Birch Creek Valley (Idaho): F752.B63
Birch River and Valley (West Virignia):
  F247.B55
Bird Creek and Valley (Alaska):
  F912.B57
Bird-Truax Trail (Idaho): F752.B64
Birmingham (Alabama): F334.B6+
Birney, David Bell: E467.1.B6
Birney, James Gillespie: E340.B6
Biscayne Bay (Florida): F317.D2
Bishop Hill Colony: F549.B6
Bismarck (N.D.): F644.B6
Bissot, Jean Baptiste, sieur de
  Vincennes: F1030
Bisti (New Mexico): F802.B58
Bitter Root River and Valley (Mont.):
  F737.B6
Bizard Island (Québec): F1054.B58

Black Canyon of the Gunnison National
  Monument (Colorado): F782.B5
Black Caribs: F1505.2.C3
Black Conspiracy, 1844: F1783
Black Diamond Mines Regional
  Preserve (Calif.): F868.C76
Black Eagle Conspiracy, 1830: F1783
Black Hawk (Sauk chief): E83.83
Black Hawk War, 1832: E83.83
  Lincoln's participation: E457.35
Black Hawk War (Utah), 1865-1872:
  E83.867
Black Hills (S.D.): F657.B6
Black, Jeremiah Sutherland: E415.9.B6
Black Lake (N.Y.): F127.S2
Black Mountains (N.C.): F262.B4
Black Range (N.M.): F802.B63
Black River and Valley (Wisconsin):
  F587.B55
Black River (New York): F127.B48
Black Rock Desert (Nevada): F847.B53
Black studies: E184.7.A1+
Blackfoot River and Valley (Mont.):
  F737.B62
Blackfoot (Sihasapa) Dakota Indians:
  E99.S53
Blackfoot (Siksika) Algonquian Indians:
  E99.S54
Blacklands (Texas): F392.B546
Blacks in America: E29.N3
Blacks in Argentina: F3021.B55
Blacks in Belize: F1457.B55
Blacks in Bermuda: F1640.B55
Blacks in Bolivia: F3359.B55
Blacks in Brazil: F2659.N4
Blacks in Canada: F1035.N3
Blacks in Central America: F1440.B55
Blacks in Chile: F3285.B53
Blacks in Colombia: F2299.B55
Blacks in Costa Rica: F1557.B55
Blacks in Cuba: F1789.N3
Blacks in Ecuador: F3799.B55
Blacks in El Salvador: F1497.B55
Blacks in French Guiana: F2471.B55
Blacks in Haiti: F1930.B55
Blacks in Honduras: F1517.B55
Blacks in Jamaica: F1896.N4

Blacks in Latin America: F1419.N4
Blacks in Mexico: F1392.B55
Blacks in Nicaragua: F1537.B55
Blacks in Panama: F1577.B55
Blacks in Peru: F3619.B55
  Relations with Indians: F3429.3.R27
Blacks in Puerto Rico: F1983.N4
Blacks in South America: F2239.B55
Blacks in Suriname: F2431.N3
Blacks in the Bahamas: F1660.B55
Blacks in the Caribbean: F2191.B55
Blacks in the Dominican Republic:
  F1941.B55
Blacks in Uruguay: F2799.N3
Blacks in Venezuela: F2349.B55
Blacks in West Indies: F1629.B55
Blackstone Harbour Provincial Park
  (Ontario): F1059.B53
Blackstone River and Valley
  General and Rhode Island: F87.B55
  Massachusetts: F72.B57
Blackstone, William: F73.4
Blackwater River and Valley (Md.):
  F187.D6
Bladensburg, Battle of, 1814: E356.B5
Blaine, Harriet (Bailey): E664.B62
Blaine, James Gillespie: E660.B6+,
  E664.B6
  Foreign policy, 1881: E686
Blair House (Washington, D.C.):
  F204.B5
Blanca Site (Guatemala): F1435.1.B52
Blancos (Uruguay): F2726
Bland, Richard Parks: E664.B64
Bland, Theodorick: E263.V8
Blankets, Indian: E98.T35
Blennerhassett Island (West Virginia):
  F247.B56
Blindman River and Valley (Alberta):
  F1079.B65
Blisland Parish (Virginia): F232.B55
Bliss, Aaron Thomas: F566
Blissland Parish (Virginia): F232.B55
Block Island (R.I.): F87.B6
Blockades, Naval
  United States
    Civil War: E480, E600

Blockades, Naval
  United States
    War of 1812: E360
Blondin, Pierre Edouard: F1034
Bloom, Sol: E748.B63
Bloomingdale (New York): F128.68.B6
Bloomington (Illinois): F549.B65
Blount, William: E302.6.B6
Blue Creek Ruin (Belize): F1435.1.B54
Blue Hill Bay (Me.): F27.B49
Blue Lake (Wisconsin): F587.O5
Blue Licks, Battle of the, 1782:
  E241.B65
Blue Mountain Lake (Ark.): F417.L75
Blue Mountain Lake (New York):
  F127.H2
Blue Mountains (Pa.): F157.B65
Blue Ridge Mountains: F217.B6
  Indians: E78.A66
Blue Springs, Tenn., Battle of, 1863:
  E475.8
Blue Springs, Tenn., Battle of, 1864:
  E476.8
Blue Valley (Kansas): F687.B6
Bluegrass region (Kentucky): F457.B6
Bluff Island (Me.): F27.Y6
Blumenau (German colony in Brazil):
  F2626
Boats
  Indians: E98.B6
    Brazil: F2519.3.B5
    Peru: F3429.3.B63
    Pre-Columbian America: E59.C2
    South America: F2230.1.B6
Bob Marshall Wilderness (Mont.):
  F737.B66
Bocas del Toro, Panama (Province):
  F1569.B6
Bocootawwonauke Indians: E99.B6
Boerum, Simon: E263.N6
Bogardus, Annetje Jane: F128.4
Bogotá (Colombia): F2291.B6+
Bogotá River (Colombia): F2281.C9
Bogue Banks (N.C.): F262.C23
Bogue Island (N.C.): F262.C23
Bohemia Manor (Maryland): F187.C3

Bohemians in the United States:
E184.B67
Bois Blanc Island (Ontario): F1059.B62
Bois-Francs (Québec): F1054.A7
Boise (Idaho): F754.B65
Boise River and Valley (Idaho):
F752.B673
Bolas
Indians
Argentina: F2821.3.B6
Bolívar, Colombia (Dept.): F2281.B6
Bolívar, Ecuador (Province): F3741.B5
Bolivar Peninsula (Texas): F392.B57
Bolívar, Simón: F2235.3
Bolívar, Venezuela (State): F2331.B6
Bolivia: F3301+
Acre Territory controversy: F2540
Charcas (Audiencia): F3322
Confederacion Peru-Bolivian, 1835-
1839: F3447
Military history
Chaco War, 1932-1935: F2688.5
Civil wars: F3324, F3325
War of Independence, 1809-1825:
F3323
War of the Pacific, 1879-1884:
F3097
War with Chile, 1836-1839: F3447
Tacna-Arica question: F3097.3
Bolivians in Argentina: F3021.B65
Bolivians in Brazil: F2659.B64
Bolivians in the United States:
E184.B674
Bomoseen, Lake (Vt.): F57.R9
Bon Echo Provincial Park (Ontario):
F1059.B64
Bonaire (West Indies): F2048
Bonampak (Mexico)
Mayas: F1435.1.B6
Bonaparte, Charles Joseph: E664.B69
Bonaventure County (Québec):
F1054.B6
Bonaventure Island (Québec):
F1054.B63
Bone carving
Indians
Mexico: F1219.3.B6

Bone Cave (Mo.): F472.M45
Boni in Suriname: F2431.B64
Bonilla, Manuel: F1507.5
Bonilla, Policarpo: F1507.5
Bonita Creek and Valley
Arizona: F817.G7
Bonneville, Lake (Utah): F832.B6
Bonney, William H: F786
Bonus Expeditionary Force, 1932 and
1933: F199
Books and reading
Indians: E98.B65
Boomer, George Boardman: E467.1.B7
Boon Island (Me.): F27.Y6
Boon Lake (Mass.): F72.M7
Boone, Daniel: F454
Booth, John Wilkes: E457.5
Boquet River, Engagement at, 1814:
E356.B6
Bora Indians: F2270.2.B6
Borah, William Edgar: E748.B7
Border life: E161.5+
Border ruffians
Kansas: F685
Border Slave States, Convention of,
1861: E440.5
Border States: F217.B67
Border warfare
Indians: E81+
U.S. Civil War: E470.45
Borinqueño Indians: F1969
Boriquén: F1951+
Borno, Louis: F1927
Bororo Indians: F2520.1.B75
Borrego Desert State Park (Calif.):
F868.S15
Borrego Valley (Calif.): F868.S15
Boruca Indians: F1545.2.B6
Bosnians in the United States:
E184.B675
Bossier Parish (La.): F377.B6
Boston Common (Boston): F73.65
Boston (Massachusetts): F73
Anthony Burns case, 1854: E450
Garrison mob, 1835: E450
Massacre, 1770: E215.4
Siege, 1775-1776: E231

Boston Port Bill, 1774: E215.8
Boston Tea Party: E215.7
Boston Ten Townships: F127.T6
Botany, Economic
  Indians: E98.B7
    South America: F2230.1.B7
Botelho de Magalhães, Benjamin
  Constant: F2536
Botocudo Indians: F2520.1.B76
Boucher, Pierre: F1030
Boudinot, Elias: E302.6.B7
Bound Brook, Battle of, 1777:
  E241.B76
Boundaries
  Canada: F1027.5, F1039.B7
  United States: E179.5
    Alaska: F912.B7
    Florida: F317.B7
    Louisiana: F374
    Mexico: F786
    Northeast: E398
    Northern: F550.5+
    Northwest: F597
    Oregon: F880
    Pacific Northwest: F854
    Southwest: F786
    Texas: F392.B7
Boundary Waters Canoe Area
  (Minnesota): F612.B73
Bounties, Military
  United States
    Civil War: E491+, E545+
    Revolution: E255
    War of 1812: E359.4
    War with Mexico: E409.4
Bouquet, Henry: E83.76
Bourassa, Henri: F1034
Boves, José Tomás: F2324
Bow River and Valley (Alberta):
  F1079.B75
Bowdoin College and the Civil War:
  E541.B7
Bowdoin, James: F69
Bowen Island (B.C.): F1089.B74
Bowen, John Steven: E467.1.B73
Bowery (New York): F128.67.B6

Bows and arrows
  Indians
    Brazil: F2519.3.B6
Boyacá, Battle of, 1819: F2274
Boyacá, Colombia (Dept.): F2281.B8
Boyd's Creek and Valley (Tennessee):
  F443.B74
Boydton Plank Road, Va., Battle of,
  1864: E476.93
Boyer, Jean Pierre: F1924
Boyl, Bernardo: E125.B7
Boyle, John: F545
Braddock's defeat, 1755: E199
Braddock's Rock (Washington, D.C.):
  F203.4.B7
Bradford, William: F68
Bradley, Stephen Row: E302.6.B8
Bradley, William Albert: F198
Bradstreet, John: E199
Bragg, Braxton: E467.1.B75
Branch, John: E340.B67
Brandeis, Louis Dembitz: E664.B819
Brandon (Manitoba): F1064.5.B73
Brandy Station, Va., Battle of, 1863:
  E475.51
Brandywine, Battle of, 1777: E241.B8
Brandywine Creek and Valley
  Delaware: F172.B78
  Pennsylvania: F157.B77
Brant Co. (Ontario): F1059.B82
Brasilia, Brazil
  City: F2647
  Federal District: F2647
Brass Ankles in the United States:
  E184.B676
Brattleboro (Vermont): F59.B8
Bravo, Nicolás: F1232
Bravo, Pascual: F2276
Brazil: F2501+
  Cisplatine province, 1821-1824:
    F2725
  Contests over Colonia: F2723
  Dutch conquest, 1624-1654: F2532
  French Guiana, Occupation of (1809-
    1817): F2462

Brazil
  Military history
    Argentine-Brazilian War, 1825-1828:
      F2725
    Argentine-Brazilian wars
      1849-1852: F2846.3
    Paraguayan War, 1865-1870:
      F2687
    Revolution of 1930: F2538
    Revolution of the Farrapos, 1835-
      1845: F2621
    São Paolo Revolution, 1932: F2631
    War of Independence, 1889: F2536
    War of the Seven Reductions, 1754-
      1756: F2684
  Portuguese court in Brazil, 1808-1821:
    F2534
  Republic, 1889-: F2537
  Rio de Janeiro (French colony):
    F2529
Brazilians in Bolivia: F3359.B73
Brazilians in foreign countries: F2510.5
Brazilians in Paraguay: F2699.B67
Brazilians in the United States:
  E184.B68
Brazilians in Uruguay: F2799.B7
Brazos River and Valley (Texas):
  F392.B842
Breckinridge Creek and Valley (West
  Virginia): F247.B6
Breckinridge, John: E302.6.B84
Breckinridge, John Cabell: E415.9.B79
Breed's Hill, Battle of 1775: E241.B9
Brethren, Hutterite, in the United States:
  E184.H97
Bretons in the United States: E184.B69
Brewster, William: F68
Bribri Indians: F1545.2.B7
Brice's Crossroads, Miss., Battle of,
  1864: E476.83
Bridge River and Valley (B.C.):
  F1089.B8
Bridger, James: F592
Bridger Pass Overland Trail
  Colorado: F782.O94
  Wyoming: F767.O94

Bridges
  Boston: F73.67
  Chicago: F548.67
  Philadelphia: F158.67.A+
  Washington, D.C.: F203.7.A+
Bridgewater, Ont., Battle of, 1814:
  E356.L9
Brier Island (Nova Scotia): F1039.F9
Brighton (Massachusetts): F74.B73
Brightwood (Washington, D.C.):
  F202.B8
Brinton, John Hill: E621
Brión, Pedro Luis: F2324
Bristoe Station, Va., Battle of, 1863:
  E475.75
Bristoe (Virginia), campaign, Oct. 1863:
  E475.75
Bristol Bay (Alaska): F912.B74
Bristol Parish (Virginia): F232.B8
British America: F1001+
  Bahamas: F1650+
  Belize: F1441+
  Bermudas: F1630+
  British Guiana: F2361+
  British West Indies: F2131
  Canada: F1001+
  Falkland Islands: F3031
British Cartagena expedition, 1741:
  F2272.5
British colonies in America: E162
  British Honduras: F1447
British Columbia: F1086+
  Hudson's Bay Company: F1060+
  Indians: E78.B9
  Oregon country: F880
British Guiana: F2361+
  Dutch colonies, 1667-1803: F2383,
    F2423
British Honduras: F1441+
British in America: E29.B75
British in Argentina: F3021.B86
British in Brazil: F2659.B7
British in Canada: F1035.B7
British in Chile: F3285.B7
British in Mexico: F1392.E5
British in Paraguay: F2699.B7
British in Peru: F3619.B7

British in South America: F2239.B8
British in the United States: E184.B7
British Library. Manuscript. Egerton
  2895 (Codices): F1219.56.B74+
British North America: F1001+
British West Florida: F301
British-West Indian Federation
  (Proposed): F1886
British West Indies: F2131
  Individual islands: F1630+, F1861+,
    F2006+
Broad River and Valley
  North Carolina: F262.B89
  South Carolina: F277.B73
Broadway (New York): F128.67.B7
Brock, Sir Isaac: E353.1.B8
Brockenbrough, William Henry:
  E340.B8
Brocks Gap (Virginia): F232.R7
Broderick, David Colbreth: E415.9.B84
Brome County (Québec): F1054.B8
Bronx (Borough): F128.68.B8
Bronx Parkway (New York):
  F128.65.B8
Brookland (Washington, D.C.): F202.B9
Brooklyn (Boroughy): F129.B7
Brooks, P. S.
  Assault on Senator Sumner: E434.8
Brooks Range (Alaska): F912.B75
Broom, Jacob: F168
Brotherton Indians: E99.B7
Brown, Albert Gallatin: F341
Brown, George: F1032
Brown, Guillermo: F2845
Brown, Jacob: E353.1.B9
Brown, James: E340.B88
Brown, John (1744-1780): E207.B8
Brown, John, 1800-1859: E451
  Kansas: F685
  Raid at Harper's Ferry, W. Va., 1859:
    E451
Brown, Joseph Newton: E467.1.B77
Brown University and the Civil War:
  E541.B8
Browning, Orville Hickman: E415.9.B88
Brownlow, William Gannaway:
  E415.9.B9

Brown's Ferry, Skirmish at, 1863:
  E475.92
Brown's Hole: F767.G7
Brown's Park (Wyoming): F767.G7
Brownstown, Mich., Battle of, 1812:
  E356.B8
Bruce Co. (Ontario): F1059.B95
Brulé, Étienne: F1030.13
Brulé Indians: E99.B8
Brule River and Valley
  Michigan: F572.B86
  Wisconsin: F587.B85
Brum, Baltasar: F2728
Bruneau River and Valley (Idaho):
  F752.O97
Brunswick (Me.): F29.B9
Brunswick Proprietors: F29.B9
Bruzual (Venezuela): F2331.B75
Bryan-Chamorro Treaty, 1916: F1526.3
Bryan, William Jennings: E660.B87+,
  E664.B87
Bryce Canyon National Park: F832.B9
Bucaramanga (Colombia): F2291.B77
Buccaneers
  Caribbean Sea: F2161
  Cuba: F1779
Buchanan, James: E437
  Administration, 1857-1861: E436
  Family: E437.1
Buckeye Lake (Ohio): F497.B86
Buckingham, William Alfred: E499+
Buckshot War, 1838: F153
Buen Ayre (West Indies): F2048
Buena Vista, Mexico, Battle of, 1847:
  E406.B9
Buenos Aires
  Province: F2861
    Indian antiquities: F2821.1.B8
Buenos Aires (Argentina)
  City: F3001
  Federal District: F3001
Buenos Aires (Viceroyalty): F2841
Buffalo
  Indians: E98.B8
Buffalo Bill (W.F. Cody): F594
Buffalo Creek and Valley (Pa.):
  F157.U5

Buffalo Hill region (Alberta): F1079.B8
Buffalo (New York): F129.B8+
Buffalo River and Valley (Ark.):
  F417.B85
Buga (Colombia): F2291.B8
Bulgarians in Argentina: F3021.B93
Bulgarians in Canada: F1035.B84
Bulgarians in South America: F2239.B9
Bulgarians in United States: E184.B8
Bulkley River and Valley (B.C.):
  F1089.B9
Bull Island (S.C.): F277.C4
Bull Run, 1st Battle of, 1861: E472.18
Bull Run, 2d Battle of, 1862: E473.77
Bull Run Campaign, July 1861:
  E472.18
Bull Shoals Lake and Region
  Arkansas: F417.B86
  Missouri: F472.B94
Bullock Creek and Valley (S.C.):
  F277.Y6
Bullock, Rufus Brown: F291
Bull's Ferry, N.J., Engagement at, 1780:
  E241.B87
Bulltown, W.V., Battle of, 1863: E475.7
Buneau-Varilla-Hay Treaty, 1903:
  F1566.5
Bunker Hill, Battle of, 1775: E241.B9
Bureau of Indian Affairs School, Bethel,
  Alaska: E97.6.B87
Bureau of the American Republics:
  F1403+
Burges, Tristam: E340.B9
Burgoyne, John
  Campaign of 1777: E233
Burial customs
  Indians: E98.M8
    Peru: F3429.3.M7
Burkes Garden Basin (Va.): F232.T2
Burlington (Iowa): F629.B9
Burlington (Vermont): F59.B9
Burnet, David Gouverneur: F389
Burnet, Jacob: F495
Burnet, William: F122+
Burnett, Thomas Pendleton: F584
Burns, Anthony: E450
Burnside, Ambrose Everett: E467.1.B8

Burnside, Ambrose Everett
  Expedition to North Carolina, 1862:
    E473.3
Burr, Aaron: E302.6.B9
  Conspiracy: E334
Burr, Esther (Edwards): E302.6.B93
Burrington, George: F257
Burundians in the United States:
  E184.B89
Bush, George: E881+
Bush, George W.: E902+
Bushnell, Asa Smith: F496
Business, African Americans in: E185.8
Business enterprises
  Indians: E98.B87
Busquipani Indians: F3430.1.C34
Bustamente y Sirvén, Antonio Sánchez
  de: F1787
Butch Cassidy (F.L. Parker): F595
Butcher, The (Cerro Yerupaja):
  F3451.Y47
Butler, Benjamin Franklin (1795-1858):
  E340.B98
Butler, Benjamin Franklin, 1818-1893:
  E467.1.B87
  Government of Louisiana: E510+
Butler, Smedley Darlington: E182
Butler, Walter: E278.B9
Butler, William Orlando: E403.1.B9
Butler's Indian Campaign, 1778: E234
Butler's rangers
  Loyalist: E277.6.B9
Butte, Battle of the, 1877: E83.8765
Butte (Mont.): F739.B8
Butte Valley (California): F868.S6
Butterfield, Daniel: E467.1.B9
Butternuts: E458.8
Buzzards Bay region: F72.B9
Byng Inlet (Ontario): F1059.B98

C

Caá Guazú, Battle of, 1841: F2891
Caaygua Indians: F2679.2.M34
Cabahiba Indians: F2520.1.P4
Cabecar Indians: F1545.2.C33

Cabin Creek, Okla., 2nd Battle of, 1864: E477.1

Cabinet National Forest: F737.C14

Cabiyari Indians: F2270.2.C22

Caboclos in Brazil: F2659.C32

Cabot, George: E302.6.C11

Cabot, John: E129.C1

Cabot, Sebastian: E129.C1

Cabot Trail (Nova Scotia): F1039.C2

Cabral, Pedro Alvares: E125.C11

Cabrillo, Juan Rodríguez: E125.C12

Cacapon River and Valley (West Virginia): F247.C24

Cacaxtla
Mexico: F1435.1.C32

Cáceres Region (Peru): F3451.A54

Cache National Forest: F832.C35

Cache River and Valley (Illinois): F547.C13

Cache Valley (Utah): F832.C3

Cactus Canyon (Arizona): F788

Caddo Indians: E99.C12

Caddo Lake
Louisiana: F377.C15
Texas: F392.C17

Caddo Parish (La.): F377.C15

Caddoan Indians: E99.C13

Cadioeo Indians: F2520.1.C3

Cadron Creek and Valley (Ark.): F417.C27

Caguas (Puerto Rico): F1981.C24

Cahaba, Ala. Military Prison: E612.C2

Cahal Pech
Mexico: F1435.1.C33

Cahita Indians: F1221.C3

Cahokia Indians: E99.C15

Cahuilla Indians: E99.C155

Caicos Island: F1659.T9

Caingua Indians: F2230.2.C3

Cajamarca, Peru (Dept.): F3451.C2

Cajuns in the United States: E184.A2

Cakchikel Indians: F1465.2.C3

Caladesi Island (Florida): F317.P6

Calakmul (Mexico): F1435.1.C34

Calamity Jane (Martha Canary): F594

Calapooia River and Valley (Oregon): F882.L7

Calaveras Big Tree National Forest: F868.C14

Calaveras Big Trees State Park (Calif.): F868.C15

Calaveras Grove (Calif.): F868.C14

Calca, Peru (Province): F3451.C23

Calcasieu Parish (La.): F377.C2

Calcasieu Pass, La., Battle of, 1864: E476.3

Calchaqui Indians: F2823.C2

Calchaqui River (Argentina): F2922

Caldas, Colombia (Dept.): F2281.C25

Calderón, Abdón: F3734

Caldwell Parish (La.): F377.C23

Caledonia (Colony), Darien: F2281.D2

Calendar
Aztecs: F1219.76.C35
Indians: E98.C14
Argentina: F2821.3.C35
Mexico: F1219.3.C2
Peru: F3429.3.C14
Mayas: F1435.3.C14

Calgary (Alberta): F1079.5.C35

Calhoun, John Caldwell: E340.C15
Collected works: E337.8.C13

Cali (Colombia): F2291.C15

California: F856+
African Americans: E185.93.C2
Compromise of 1850: E423
Counties, etc: F868.A+
Gold discoveries: F865
Indians: E78.C15
Spanish missions: F864
Buildings: F862
Wars
Bear Flag War, 1846: F864
Civil War: E497+
Expedition, 1862: E473.46
Indian wars: E83.84, E83.858, E83.87
War of 1898: E726.C1
War with Mexico
Conquest by U.S. troops: E405.2

California column, 1862: E473.46

California, Gulf of: F1250

California Joe: F594

California, Lower: F864

California, Lower
  Mexico: F1246
California, Northern: F867.5
California Redwood Park: F868.S3
California, Southern: F867
California, Spanish: F864
California, Upper: F864
Calima culture, Indian: F2270.2.C24
Callahuaya Indians: F3320.2.C3
Callao (Peru)
  City: F3611.C2
  Department: F3451.C25
Calleja, Félix María, conde de Calderon:
  F1232
Callejon de Huaylas (Peru): F3451.A48
Callejón de Huaylas (Peru)
  Indian antiquities: F3429.1.C3
Calles, Plutarco Elías: F1234
Calumet region
  Illinois: F547.C7
  Indiana: F532.L2
Calusa Indians: E99.C18
Calverts, The (Proprietors of Maryland):
  F184
Camacho, Manuel Ávila: F1234
Camagüey (Cuba)
  City: F1839.C3
  Province: F1831+
Camano Island (Wash.): F897.I7
Camas Prairie (Mont.): F737.M6
Cambodians in Canada: F1035.C27
Cambodians in the United States:
  E184.K45
Cambridge (Mass.): F74.C1
Camden, Ark., expedition, 1864:
  E476.35
Camden District (S.C.): F277.C22
Camden (N.J.): F144.C2
Camden, S.C., Battle of, 1780:
  E241.C17
Cameron Parish (La.): F377.C25
Cameron, Simon: E415.9.C18
Caminha, Pedro Vaz de: E125.C2
Camino, El, Real de Tierra Adentro
  National Historic Trail: F392.E36
  New Mexico: F802.E45
  Texas: F392.E36

Camp Cady, Battle of, 1866: E83.8675
Camp Creek and Valley (Oklahoma):
  F702.C17
Camp Polk Meadow Preserve (Oregon):
  F882.D4
Campa Indians: F3430.1.C3
Campbell County (Ga.): F292.F9
Campbell, George Washington:
  E302.6.C2
Campbell, John Archibald: E415.9.C19
Campbell's Creek and Valley (W.Va.):
  F247.K2
Campbell's Island, Battle of, 1814:
  E356.C2
Campeche (Mexico): F1435.1.C35
Campeche, Mexico (State): F1251
  Indian antiquities: F1219.1.C25
Campo Grande, Battle of, 1869: F2687
Campo Indians: E99.C19
Campobello Island: F1044.C2
Campos do Jordão: F2631
Campos Salles, Manuel Ferraz de:
  F2537
Camsa Indians: F2270.2.C25
Canaan Valley (West Virginia): F247.T8
Canada: F1001+
  Annexation question: F1033
  Boundaries
    Alaska: F912.B7
    New Hampshire: F42.B7
    Northeast U.S.: E398
    Oregon: F880
    Southern: F550.5+, F597
    Southwest: F854
    Vermont: F57.B7
  Boundaries, 1763-1867: F1032
  History
    1763-1867: F1032
    Early to 1603: E101+
  Hudson's Bay Company: F1060+
  Indians: E78.C2, E92
  Military history
    American Loyalists
      New Brunswick: F1041+
      Nova Scotia: F1036+
      Ontario: F1056+
    American Revolution: E263.C2

Canada
  Military history
    American Revolution
      Canadian aid sought: E216
      Invasions from Canada, 1777:
        E233
      Invasions of Canada, 1775-1776:
        E231
    Civil War
      United States
        Confederates in Canada:
          E470.95
    Fenian invasions, 1866: F1032
    Fenian invasions, 1870-1871:
      F1033
    Indian wars: E81+
    Intercolonial wars: E196, E197,
      E198
    Rebellion, 1837: F1032
    Red River Rebellion, 1869-1870:
      F1063
    Riel Rebellion: F1060.9
    War of 1812: E355+, E359.85
  Provinces, 1763-: F1031+
  Provinces, 1763-1867: F1035.8+
Canada, Lower: F1051+
Canada, Northern regions of (General):
  F1090.5
Canada, Upper: F1056+
Canadian Arctic Archipelago: F1101+
Canadian Invasion, 1775-1776: E231
Canadian Northwest: F1060+
Canadian River and Valley: F702.C2
  New Mexico: F802.C2
  Texas: F392.C27
Canadians in the American Revolution:
  E269.C27
Canadians in the United States:
  E184.C2
  Civil War: E540.C25
Canal Zone: F1569.C2
Canamari Indians: F2520.1.C316
Canandaigua Lake (New York):
  F127.O7
Cañar, Ecuador (Province): F3741.C25
Cañari Indians: F3722.1.C2
Canary Islanders in America: E29.C35

Canary Islanders in Latin America:
  F1419.C26
Canary Islanders in Peru: F3619.C34
Canary Islanders in the Caribbean:
  F2191.C35
Canary Islanders in the United States:
  E184.C22
Canary Islanders in Venezuela:
  F2349.C35
Canary, Martha: F594
Cañas y Villacorta, Francisco Morazán:
  F1438
Canchis (Peru): F3451.C28
Candelaria culture
  Argentina: F2823.C3
Candlewood, Lake (Conn.): F102.C2
Candoshi Indians: F3430.1.C32
Candoxi Indians: F3430.1.C32
Cane Hill, Ark., Battle of, 1862: E474.9
Cane River Lake (La.): F377.N4
Canella Indians: F2520.1.C32
Canelo Indians: F3722.1.C23
Canelones, Uruguay (Dept.):
  F2731.C22
Caney, El, Battle of, 1898: E717.1
Canichana Indians: F3320.2.C33
Canisteo River (N.Y.): F127.S8
Cannibalism
  Indians
    Brazil: F2519.3.C3
    Pre-Columbian America: E59.C18
Cannon, Joseph Gurney: E664.C22
Canoeiro (Mato Grosso) Indians:
  F2520.1.R53
Canoes
  Indians: E98.B6
    Pre-Columbian America: E59.C2
    South America: F2230.1.B6
Cantabrians in Latin America:
  F1419.C3
Cantabrians in Mexico: F1392.C28
Cantabrians in South America:
  F2239.C36
Canton (Ohio): F499.C2
Canyon de Chelly National Monument:
  F817.C3
Canyon of Colorado River: F788

Canyon of Lodore (Colo.): F782.M65
Canyonlands National Park (Utah): F832.C37
Cap Français (Haiti): F1929.C3
Cap-Haïtien (Haiti): F1929.C3
Capanahua Indians: F3430.1.C34
Capanawa Indians: F3430.1.C34
Capay Valley (Calif.): F868.Y5
Cape Ann (Mass.): F72.E7
Cape Breton Co. (Nova Scotia): F1039.C15
Cape Breton Island: F1039.C2
  Siege and capture, 1745: E198
Cape Canaveral (Fla.): F317.B8
Cape Cod Bay (Mass.): F72.C3
Cape Cod (Mass.): F72.C3
Cape Fear (N.C.): F262.B9
Cape Fear River (N.C.): F262.C2
Cape Hatteras National Seashore (N.C.): F262.O96
Cape Horn
  Chile: F3186
  Voyages to California via: F865
Cape Horn (Calif.): F868.S5
Cape Krusenstern National Monument (Alaska): F912.C34
Cape Lookout National Seashore (N.C.): F262.C23
Cape Nome region (Alaska): F912.N7
Cape Romain (S.C.): F277.C4
Cape Sable Island: F1039.C3
Cape Verdeans in the United States: E184.C24
Capim River (Brazil): F2586
Capinota, Bolivia (Province): F3341.C27
Capitals (Cities)
  Alabama: F334.T9
  Massachusetts: F73
  National: F191+
  New York (State): F129.A3+
Capitol building (Washington, D.C.): F204.C2
Capitol Hill (Washington, D.C.): F202.C2
Capitol Reef National Park (Utah): F832.W27

Capitols, State
  United States: E159
Caplan River and Valley (Québec): F1054.C22
Capon River and Valley (West Virginia): F247.C24
Capote Indians: E99.C2
Captivities
  Indians
    Pre-Columbian America: E59.C22
Captivities of Indians: E85+
Caquetá (Colombia): F2281.C26
Caquetio Indians: F2319.2.C28
Cara Indians: F3722.1.C25
Carabaya, Peru (Province): F3451.C3
Carabobo, Battle of, 1821: F2324
Carabobo, Venezuela (State): F2331.C3
Caracas (Audiencia): F2322
Caracas Valley (Venezuela): F2331.C5
Caracas (Venezuela): F2341.C2+
Caracol, Belize (Mayas): F1435.1.C37
Caraja Indians: F2520.1.C35
Carapana Indians: F2270.2.C26
Carchi, Ecuador (Province): F3741.C3
  Indian antiquities: F3721.1.C2
Cárdenas (Cuba): F1819.C3
Cárdenas, Lázaro: F1234
Carib Indians: F2460.1.C37
  Black Caribs: F1505.2.C3
Cariban Indians: F2001
Caribbean, English-speaking: F2130
Caribbean Sea: F2155+
Caribbeans in the United States: E184.C27
Caribbees: F2001+
Cariboo District (B.C.): F1089.C3
Caricatures and cartoons
  United States
    Lincoln, Abraham: E457.63
    Wars
      Civil War: E647
      Revolution: E298
Carihona Indians: F2270.2.C27
Carijo Indians: F2520.1.F8
Carijona Indians: F2270.2.C27
Caripuna Indians: F2520.1.C37

Carleton Co. (New Brunswick):
F1044.C3

Carleton Co. (Ontario): F1059.C3

Carleton, Guy: F1032

Carleton Island (N.Y.): F127.T5

Carleton's Raid, 1778: E241.C2

Carlsbad Caverns National Park:
F802.C28

Carlsbad Caverns (N.M.): F802.C28

Carmel (California): F869.C27

Carnegie Institution of Washington.
Division of Historical Research:
E175.4.C3

Carnicero (Cerro Yerupaja): F3451.Y47

Carnifex Ferry, W.V., Battle of, 1861:
E472.6

Carnijo Indians: F2520.1.F8

Caro, Miguel Antonio: F2277

Carolana grant, 1629: F272

Carolina grant, 1663: F257

Carolina, Province of (1663-1712):
F272
Northern Carolina settlements: F257
Queen Anne's War, 1702-1713: E197

Carolinas
Separation: F272
Wars
Civil War
Campaign, 1865: E477.7
Revolution
Campaign, 1781: E237

Caroline (Steamer)
Burning, 1837: F1032

Caron, René Edouard: F1053

Carpenter, Matthew Hale: E664.C29

Carpenter's Hall (Philadelphia):
F158.8.C2

Carpetbag rule: E668

Carquinez Strait (Calif.): F868.S156

Carranza, Venustiano: F1234

Carrera, José Miguel: F3094

Carrera, Rafael: F1466.45

Carrier (Takulli) Indians: E99.T17

Carroll, Anna E.
Claim: E472.9

Carroll, Charles: E302.6.C3

Carroll, Daniel: E302.6.C33

Carson, Christopher: F592

Carson City (Nevada): F849.C3

Carson River and Valley (Nevada):
F847.C37

Cartagena (Colombia)
City: F2291.C3
Province: F2281.C27
Sieges
1585, 1697: F2272
1741: F2272.5

Cartagena, Siege of 1815: F2274

Cartago (Costa Rica): F1556.C3

Carter, Jimmy: E872+

Carteret, Sir George: F137

Carthage, Mo., Battle of, 1861: E472.2

Cartier, George Étienne: F1033

Cartier, Jacques: E133.C3

Cartography
Aztecs: F1219.76.C37
Indians: E98.C17
Pre-Columbian America: E59.C25

Cartwright, Labrador (Fishing port):
F1139.C3

Cartwright, Peter: F545

Cartwright, Richard: F1058

Carutana Indians: F2520.1.B35

Carvajal, Luis de: F1231

Carver, Jonathan: F597

Cary, Archibald: F230

Casa Blanca Land Grant (Texas):
F392.C287

Casa Grande National Monument
Arizona: F817.C35

Casa Yrujo, Carlos Martinez de Yrujo y
Tacon, marques de: E313+

Casas, Bartolomé de las: E125.C4

Casas Grandes culture: E99.C23

Casas Grandes (Mexico)
Indian antiquities: F1219.1.C3

Casas Revolution: F389

Cascade Range: F851.7

Cascade Range in Oregon: F882.C3

Cascade Range in Washington (State):
F897.C3

Cascade River State Park (Minnesota):
F612.C65

Casco Bay: F27.C3

Cashibo Indians: F3430.1.C35
Cashiers Valley (N.C.): F262.J2
Cashinahua Indians: F2520.1.C38
Cashinawa Indians: F2520.1.C38
Casper Mountain (Wyoming): F767.N2
Casper (Wyoming): F769.C3
Cass, Lewis: E340.C3
Cassiar District (B.C.): F1089.C35
Castañeda Castro, Salvador: F1488
Castilla, Ramón: F3447
Castillo Armas, Carlos: F1466.5
Castle Island (Mass.): F73.68.C3
Castle Valley (Utah): F832.C45
Castleguard, Mount (Alberta):
    F1079.B5
Castleton Island State Park (New York):
    F127.C28
Castro, Cipriano: F2325
Castro, Fidel: F1788.22.C3
Cat Cay and Island (Bahamas):
    F1659.C37
Catahoula Parish (La.): F377.C3
Catalans
    Discovery of America: E109.C37
Catalans in America: E29.C37
Catalans in Argentina: F3021.C3
Catalans in Cuba: F1789.C3
Catalans in Mexico: F1392.C3
Catalans in the Dominican Republic:
    F1941.C37
Catalans in the United States:
    E184.C29
Catalina Island (Calif.): F868.L8
Catamarca, Argentina (Province):
    F2871
    Indian antiquities: F2821.1.C3
Catamarca Indians: F2823.C4
Cataract, Battle of the, 1814: E356.L9
Cataract Canyon Wilderness (Utah):
    F832.C37
Catawba Indians: E99.C24
Catawba River and Valley
    North Carolina: F262.C3
    South Carolina: F277.C3
Cathedral of St. Peter and St. Paul
    (Washington, D.C.): F204.C3
Cathlamet Indians: E99.C26

Catholic orders in New France: F1030
    Jesuits: F1030.7+
Catholics, Chaldean, in the United
    States: E184.C36
Catholics in Canada: F1035.C3
Catholics in the United States: E184.C3
    Civil War: E540.C3
    Revolution: E269.C3
Catio Indians: F2270.2.C3
Catoctin Mountain (Maryland): F187.F8
Catoquina Indians: F2520.1.C4
Catskill Mountains: F127.C3
Cattle trails
    Canadian Northwest: F1060.94
    West (U.S.): F596
Cauca, Colombia (Dept.): F2281.C3
Cauca River and Valley (Colombia):
    F2281.C32
Caughnawaga Indians: E99.M8
Caulk's Field, Md., Battle of, 1814:
    E356.C3
Caupolican, Bolivia (Province):
    F3341.C3
Cautín, Chile (Province): F3141
Cave of Dry Fork of Cheat River
    (W.Va.): F247.R2
Cave of the Mounds (Wisconsin):
    F587.D3
Cave of the Winds (Colo.): F782.E3
Cavina Indians: F2230.2.A68
Cavineño Indians: F3320.2.C34
Cavite, Battle of, 1898: E717.7
Cawahib Indians: F2520.1.P4
Caxias, Luiz Alves de Lima e Silva,
    duque de: F2536
Caxixó Indians: F2520.1.C44
Cayapa Indians: F3722.1.C3
Cayapo Indians: F2520.1.C45
Cayenne (French Guiana): F2469.C3
Cayman Islands (West Indies): F2048.5
Cayo (Mexico): F1435.1.C38
Cayubaba Indians: F3320.2.C35
Cayuga Indians: E99.C3
Cayuga Lake (New York): F127.C52
Cayuse Indians: E99.C32
Cayuse War, 1847-1850: E83.84
Cazcan Indians: F1221.C38

Ceará, Brazil (State): F2556
Cedar Breaks Monument (Utah):
  F832.I6
Cedar Creek, Battle of, 1864: E477.33
Cedar Mesa (Utah): F832.S4
Cedar Mountain, Battle of, 1862:
  E473.76
Cedar Point Lake (Kansas): F687.C35
Cedar Rapids (Iowa): F629.C3
Cedar River and Valley (New York):
  F127.C56
Celeron's Expedition, 1749: F517
Celts
  Discovery of America: E109.C44
Celts in Canada: F1035.C4
Celts (Indian implements)
  West Indies: F1619.3.I6
Cemeteries
  United States
    Arlington: F234.A7
    Boston: F73.61
    Chicago: F548.61+
    National cemeteries: E160, E641
    New York: F128.61.A+
    Philadelphia: F158.61.A+
    Washington, D.C.: F203.1.A+
Censorship
  United States
    War with Mexico: E415.2.P74
Censorship of the press
  U.S. Civil War: E609
Census
  Aztecs: F1219.76.C45
  Indians: E98.C3
    Argentina: F2821.3.C4
    Bolivia: F3320.1.C45
    Colombia: F2270.1.C4
    Mexico: F1219.3.C4
    Paraguay: F2679.3.C45
    Peru: F3429.3.C4
    Venezuela: F2319.3.C4
Cent-Iles (Québec): F1054.C4
Centenary College of Louisiana,
  Shreveport, and the Civil War:
  E586.S5
Central America: F1421+

Central America
  Audiencia of Guatemala (1542-1821):
    F1437
  Confederación de Centro América,
    1823-1838/1842: F1438
  Discovery and exploration to 1600:
    E101+, F1230
  English on the coast: F1441+,
    F1529.M9
  Filibuster wars, 1855-1860: F1438
  Union question: F1438
Central American isthmus
  Voyages to California via: F865
Central American States, Organization
  of: F1439
Central-American unionism: F1438
Central Americans in the United States:
  E184.C34
Central City (Colo.): F784.C4
Central Park (N.Y.): F128.65.C3
Central Valley (Calif.): F868.C45
Cenu Indians: F2270.2.C34
Cepeda, Battle of, 1859: F2846
Ceremonies
  Indians
    Peru: F3429.3.R3
Ceremonies, Indian: E98.R3
Ceren Site
  Mayas: F1435.1.C39
Cerro de las Mesas (Mexico)
  Indian antiquities: F1219.1.C35
Cerro El Avila (Venezuela): F2331.A93
Cerro Gordo, Battle of, 1847: E406.C4
Cerro Largo, Uruguay (Dept.):
  F2731.C4
Cerro Maya Site (Belize): F1435.1.C43
Cerro Salcantay (Peru): F3451.C9
Cerroraima (Brazil): F2609
Cerros Site (Belize): F1435.1.C43
Cervera's fleet, Destruction of: E727
César, Colombia (Dept.): F2281.C4
Césares, Ciudad de los: F3072
Céspedes, Francisco de: F2841
Cespedes y del Castillo, Carlos Manuel
  de: F1785
Chacabuco, Battle of, 1817: F3094
Chacao Valley (Venezuela): F2331.C5

Chachapoya Indians: F3430.1.C37
Chaco, Argentina (Territory): F2876
Chaco Austral: F2876
Chaco (Bolivia): F3341.C4
  Indian antiquities: F3319.1.C4
Chaco Boreal, El: F2691.C4
Chaco Boreal War, 1932-1935:
  F2688.5
Chaco Canyon National Monument:
  F802.C4
Chaco Canyon (N.M.): F802.C4
Chaco Central: F2901
Chaco culture: E99.C37
Chaco dispute: F2688.5
Chaco, El Gran: F2876
Chaco, Paraguayan: F2691.C4
Chaco Peace Conference at Buenos
  Aires, 1935-1939: F2688.5
Chaco Region (Paraguay):
  F2679.15.C48
Chaco War, 1932-1935: F2688.5
Chacobo Indians: F3320.2.C36
Chacón, Lázaro: F1466.45
Chagres River (Panama): F1569.C2
Chaguite Site (Guatemala)
  Mayas: F1435.1.C44
Chain O' Lakes (Ill.): F547.C37
Chain O'Lakes (Wisconsin): F587.W3
Chakchiuma Indians: E99.C4
Chake Indians: F2319.2.M6
Chalchihuitl: F1219.76.C53
Chalchuite: F1219.76.C53
Chaldean Catholics in the United States:
  E184.C36
Chaleur Bay (New Brunswick):
  F1044.C4
Chalk Bluff, Battle of, 1863: E474.9
Chalk Creek (Colo.): F782.C5
Chalmer's raid (west Tenn. and north
  Miss., 1863): E475.88
Chalmette National Historical Park:
  E356.N5
Chama River (N.M.): F802.C45
Chama Valley (N.M.): F802.C45
Chamacoco Indians: F2230.2.C5
Chamberlain, David Henry: F274
Chambers Creek (Wash.): F897.P6

Chambers, John: F621
Chambers, Whittaker
  Alger Hiss case: E743.5
Chambersburg (Pennsylvania)
  Burning of, 1864: F159.C4
Chambly County (Québec): F1054.C44
Chametla, Mexico (Sinaloa)
  Indian antiquities: F1219.1.C4
Chamí Indians: F2270.2.C37
Chamorro, Emiliano: F1526.3
Chamorro, Pedro Joaquín: F1526.27
Champaign (Illinois): F549.C44
Champe, John: E263.V8
Champion's Hill, Battle of, 1863:
  E475.26
Champlain, Lake
  Valcour Island, Battle of, 1776:
    E241.V14
  War of 1812: E355.2+, E356.P7
Champlain, Lake (N.Y.)
  Tercentenary, 1909: F127.C6
Champlain, Lake, region
  New York: F127.C6
  Vermont: F57.C4
Champlain, Samuel de: F1030.1
  Tercentenary, 1908: F1030.1
Champlain Valley (N.Y.): F127.C6
Chan Kom, Mexico
  Mayas: F1435.1.C47
Chañabal Indians: F1221.T58
Chanca Indians: F3430.1.C4
Chancay culture (Peru)
  Indian antiquities: F3429.1.C47
Chancay, Peru (Province): F3451.C46
Chancay Valley (Peru)
  Indian antiquities: F3429.1.C47
Chancellorsville campaign, 1863:
  E475.35
Chandalar Kutchin Indians: E99.N22
Chandler, John: E278.C4
Chandler River and Valley (Alaska):
  F912.C43
Chandler, Zachariah: E664.C4
Chané Indians: F3320.2.C37
Chango Indians: F3070.1.C5
Channel Islands (Calif.): F868.S232
Chantilly, Battle of, 1862: E473.77

Chantuto Indians: F1219.8.C52
Chapa Indians: F3430.1.S47
Chapacura Indians: F3320.2.C38
Chapala, Lake (Mexico): F1254
Chaplains, Military
  United States
    Civil War: E635
Chapleau Crown Game Preserve
  (Ontario): F1059.C5
Chappaquiddick Island (Mass.): F72.M5
Chapra Indians: F3430.1.S47
Chapultepec, Battle of, 1847: E406.C47
Charcas (Audiencia): F3322
Charcas, Bolivia (City): F3351.S94
Charitable contributions
  Indians
    North America: E98.C47
Charles River (Mass.): F72.C46
Charleston Harbor (S.C.)
  Civil War
    1863: E473.96, E475.6+
    1864: E476.41
    Bombardment, 1861: E471.1
    Siege, 1863-1865: E470.65
Charleston Insurrection, 1822:
  F279.C4+
Charleston, Lake and region (Ontario):
  F1059.C53
Charleston Mountain (Nevada):
  F847.C5
Charleston (S.C.): F279.C4+
  Siege, 1780: E241.C4
  Siege, 1863: E475.62
Charleston (W.Va.): F249.C4
Charlestown (Mass.): F74.C4
Charlestown (S.C.)
  Settlement at: F272
Charlevoix Region (Québec):
  F1054.C445
Charlotte and Mecklenburg County
  (N.C.): F264.C4
Charlotte, Consort of Maximilian: F1233
Charlotte (N.C.): F264.C4
Charlottetown (Prince Edward Island):
  F1049.5.C5
Charrua Indians: F2719.2.C5

Chase, Camp (Columbus, Ohio)
  Civil War prison: E616.C4
Chase, Salmon Portland: E415.9.C4
Chase, Samuel: E302.6.C4
Chasta Indians: E99.C48
Chastacosta Indians: E99.C483
Chatata Creek and Valley (Tennessee):
  F443.B8
Chateauguay County (Québec):
  F1054.C45
Chateauguay, N.Y., Battle of, 1813:
  E356.C4
Chatino Indians: F1221.C47
Chattahoochee River and Valley:
  F292.C4
  Alabama: F332.C4
  Florida: F317.J2
Chattahoochee River Valley
  Indians: E78.C45
Chattanooga Railroad Expedition, 1862:
  E473.55
Chattanooga region
  Military operations, 1861-1865:
    E470.5
Chattanooga-Ringgold campaign, 1863:
  E475.97
Chattanooga (Tennessee): F444.C4+
  Attack on, 1862: E473.59
Chattooga River and Valley: F217.C45
Chautauqua Creek and Valley (N.Y.):
  F127.C7
Chautauqua Lake (N.Y.): F127.C7
Chavante-Akwe Indians: F2520.1.A4
Chavante Indians: F2520.1.A4
Chavín culture, (Peru)
  Indian antiquities: F3429.1.C48
Chavín (Peru)
  Indian antiquities: F3429.1.C48
Chayahuita Indians: F3430.1.C43
Cheat Mountain, W.V., Battle of, 1861:
  E472.6
Cheat Mountain (W.Va.): F247.R2
Cheat River, Cave of Dry Fork of
  (W.Va.): F247.R2
Chehalis Indians: E99.C49
Chelan Indians: E99.C4925

Chelsea, Mass., Battle of, 1775: E241.C48

Chemehuevi Indians: E99.C493

Chemung River and Valley: F127.C73
Pennsylvania: F157.C37

Chenango Canal (New York): F127.C765

Chenango River and Valley (New York): F127.C765

Cheneaux Islands (Michigan): F572.L57

Chennault, Claire Lee: E745

Chequamegon Bay (Wis.): F587.A8

Cheraw Indians: E99.C495

Cherente Indians: F2520.1.S47

Cheroenhaka Indians: E99.N93

Cherokee Indians: E99.C5

Cherokee National Female Seminary, Tahlequah, Okla: E97.6.C35

Cherokee Outlet (Oklahoma): F702.C42

Cherokee (Steamer): E595.C5

Cherokee Strip (Oklahoma): F702.C42

Cherokee War, 1759-1761: E83.759

Cherry Valley, N.Y., massacre, 1778: E241.C5

Chesapeake and Ohio Canal area: F187.C47

Chesapeake Bay and Region
Maryland: F187.C5
Virginia: F232.C43

Chesapeake Bay expedition, 1813: E355.4

Chesapeake Bay, Va., 1781, Battle of: E241.C515

Chesapeake-Leopard Affair, 1807: E357.3

Chester Parish (Maryland): F187.K3

Chesterfield Inlet, Keewatin District (Trading post): F1110.5.C5

Chestnut Hill, Battle of, 1777: E241.C52

Chesuncook Lake (Me.): F27.P5

Chetco Indians: E99.C526

Chetlain, Augustus Louis: E467.1.C52

Chew, Benjamin: F153

Cheyenne Indians: E99.C53

Cheyenne Mountain (Colo.): F782.E3

Cheyenne outbreak: E83.875

Cheyenne War, 1864: E83.863

Cheyenne (Wyoming): F769.C5

Chiapa de Corso Site (Mexico): F1435.1.C49

Chiapanec Indians: F1221.C5

Chiapas (Mexico)
Mayas: F1435.1.C492

Chiapas, Mexico (State): F1256

Chibcha Indians: F2270.2.C4
Conquest by Colombia, 1536-1538: F2272

Chicago: F548+
Massacre, 1812: E356.C53

Chicago River (Illinois): F547.C45

Chicamauga and Chattanooga National Military Park: E475.81

Chicanná Site (Mayas): F1435.1.C494

Chichén Itzá (Mexico)
Mayas: F1435.1.C5

Chichimec Indians: F1219.8.C55

Chichimeca-Jonaz Indians: F1221.C53

Chickahominy River and Valley (Virginia): F232.C54

Chickamauga campaign, 1863: E475.81

Chickamauga Lake and region (Tennessee): F443.C47

Chickasaw Indians: E99.C55

Chickasaw National Recreation Area (Oklahoma): F702.M84

Chickasaw War, 1739-1740: E83.739

Chicoutimi County (Québec): F1054.C49

Chignecto Isthmus: F1039.C5

Chihuahua campaign, 1846-1848: E405.4

Chihuahua, Mexico (State): F1261

Chihuahuan Desert (Mexico): F1262

Chihuahuan Desert (N.M.): F802.C52

Chilako River and Valley (B.C.): F1089.C3

Chilcotin Indians: E99.T78

Chilcotin River and Valley (B.C.): F1089.C42

Child soldiers
  Civil War
    Confederate Army: E585.C54
Children
  Aztecs: F1219.76.C56
  Indians: E98.C5
    Central America: F1434.2.C44
    Colombia: F2270.1.C44
    Mexico: F1219.3.C45
    Pre-Columbian America: E59.C46
    South America: F2230.1.C5
    Venezuela: F2319.3.C46
  Jews: E184.36.S65
  Mayas: F1435.3.C47
Children, African American: E185.86
Children in the United States
  Civil War: E540.C47
Children of Presidents: E176.45
Children of the American Revolution:
  E202.9
Children of the Confederacy: E483.55
Chile: F3051+
  Boundaries
    Argentina: F2851, F2853
    Peru: F3451.B73
    Tacna and Arica question: F3097.3
  Military history
    Civil wars: F3095
    Revolution of 1891: F3098
    War of Independence, 1810-1824:
      F3094
    War of the Pacific, 1879-1884:
      F3097
    War with Peru-Bolivian
      Confederation, 1836-1839: F3447
    War with Spain, 1865-1866: F3095
  Occupation of Lima, 1881-1883:
    F3601
Chileans in Argentina: F3021.C48
Chileans in Bolivia: F3359.C45
Chileans in Canada: F1035.C48
Chileans in the United States: E184.C4
Chilkat Indians: E99.C552
Chillán (Chile): F3281.C46
Chillicothe (Ohio): F499.C4
  Virginia military lands: F483
Chilliwack Indians: E99.C5523

Chilliwack River and Valley (B.C.):
  F1089.C45
Chilliwhack Indians: E99.C5523
Chiloé, Chile (Province): F3146
Chilote Indians: F3126
Chilton, William Parish: F326
Chilula Indians: E99.C553
Chimane Indians: F3320.2.C387
Chimariko Indians: E99.C56
Chimborazo, Ecuador (Province):
  F3741.C5
Chimila Indians: F2270.2.C5
Chimmesyan Indians: E99.C565
Chimney Rock National Historic Site
  (Nebraska): F672.M7
Chimney Rock Park (N.C.): F262.R9
Chimu Indians: F3430.1.C46
Chinantec Indians: F1221.C56
Chinatown
  New York: F128.68.C47
  Washington, D.C.: F202.C46
Chinautla (Guatemala)
  Indian antiquities: F1465.1.C5
Chincha Valley (Peru): F3451.C5
Chincoteague Island (Va.): F232.A2
Chinese
  Discovery of America: E109.C5
Chinese in America: E29.C5
Chinese in British Guiana: F2391.C5
Chinese in Canada: F1035.C5
Chinese in Central America
  Panama: F1577.C48
Chinese in Cuba: F1789.C53
Chinese in Jamaica: F1896.C5
Chinese in Mexico: F1392.C45
Chinese in Peru: F3619.C5
Chinese in South America: F2239.C48
Chinese in the Caribbean: F2191.C46
Chinese in the United States: E184.C5
Chinese influences
  Mayas: F1435.3.C49
Chinkultic Site (Mexico): F1435.1.C54
Chinook Indians: E99.C57
Chinookan Indians: E99.C58
Chipaya Indians: F3320.2.C388
Chippewa Indians: E99.C6

Chippewa, Ont., Battle of, 1814:
E356.C55
Chippewa River and Valley (Wisconsin):
F587.C5
Chippewa War, 1898: E83.895
Chippewyan Indians: E99.C59
Chiquito Indians: F3320.2.C39
Chiquitos, Bolivia (Province): F3341.C5
Chiribaya Alta (Peru)
Indian antiquities: F3429.1.C497
Chiribaya Baja (Peru)
Indian antiquities: F3429.1.C497
Chiribaya culture (Peru)
Indian antiquities: F3429.1.C497
Chiricahua Indians: E99.C68
Chiricahua Mountains (Arizona):
F817.C5
Chiricahua National Monument
(Arizona): F817.C5
Chiriguano Indians: F3320.2.C4
Chiripá Indians: F2679.2.C5
Chiriquí, Laguna de (Panama):
F1569.B6
Chiriquí, Panama (Province): F1569.C5
Chisholm Trail: F596
Chitimacha Indians: E99.C7
Chittenden, Thomas: F52
Choate, Joseph Hodges: E664.C45
Choate, Rufus: E340.C4
Chocho Indians: F1221.C567
Chocó, Colombia (Dept.): F2281.C5
Choco Indians: F2270.2.C6
Chocolate Mountains (Calif.): F868.I2
Choctaw Indians: E99.C8
Choke Canyon Reservoir (Texas):
F392.F92
Chol Indians: F1221.C57
Cholchagua, Chile (Province): F3151
Cholone Indians: F3430.1.C48
Cholti Indians: F1221.C57
Choluteca, Honduras (Dept.): F1509.C4
Chono Indians: F3070.1.C6
Chontal Indians: F1221.C58
Chontales (Nicaragua): F1529.C53
Choqquequirau (Peru)
Indian antiquities: F3429.1.C5
Chorotega Indians: F1545.2.C48

Chorotega Indians
Nicaragua: F1525.2.C48
Choroti Indians: F3320.2.C5
Chorti Indians: F1465.2.C5
Chota, Peru (Province): F3451.C55
Chouart, Médard, sieur des Groseilliers:
F1060.7
Christ Church Parish (Maryland):
F187.C15
Christ Church (Philadelphia):
F158.62.C5
Christian Commission, United States:
E635
Christian (Moravian) Indians: E99.M9
Christiana Riot, 1851: E450
Christians and the Civil War
United States: E540.C5
Christie, James: E278.C5
Christina Lake and region (B.C.):
F1089.C47
Christina River (Creek) (Delaware):
F172.N5
Chronological tables
America: E18.5
Argentina: F2827
Bahamas: F1655.3
Belize: F1445.5
Bermudas: F1635
Bolivia: F3320.3
Brazil: F2520.3
Central America: F1435.4
Chile: F3073
Colombia: F2270.3
Costa Rica: F1545.5
Cuba: F1772
Dominican Republic: F1937
Ecuador: F3723.3
El Salvador: F1485.5
French Guiana: F2460.3
Guatemala: F1465.5
Guyana: F2380.3
Haiti: F1918
Honduras: F1505.5
Jamaica: F1878
Latin America: F1409.6
Mexico: F1223
Nicaragua: F1525.5

Chronological tables
  Panama: F1565.5
  Paraguay: F2679.35
  Peru: F3430.3
  Puerto Rico: F1970
  South America: F2230.3
  Suriname: F2420.3
  United States: E174.5
  Uruguay: F2720
  Venezuela: F2319.5
  West Indies: F1620
Chronology
  America: E18.5
  Aztecs: F1219.76.C35
  Indians: E98.C55
    Mexico: F1219.3.C2
    Peru: F3429.3.C14
    Pre-Columbian America: E59.C5
  Mayas: F1435.3.C14
  United States: E174.5
Chubut, Argentina (Territory): F2881
  Indian antiquities: F2821.1.C5
Chucuito, Peru (Province): F3451.C6
Chuj Indians: F1221.C585
Chumash Indians: E99.C815
Chumashan Indians: E99.C815
Chunchucmil Site (Mexico):
  F1435.1.C546
Chupacho Indians: F3430.1.C5
Chuquisaca, Bolivia (City): F3351.S94
Chuquisaca, Bolivia (Dept.): F3341.C6
Church of England and the American
  Revolution: E269.C5
Churches
  Boston: F73.62
  New York City: F128.62
Churches, African American: E185.7
Churches and the Civil War, 1861-1865:
  E540.C5
Churches and the War of 1898:
  E725.5.C5
Churchill River and Valley
  Manitoba: F1064.C58
  Saskatchewan: F1074.C58
Churchill River Watershed (Sask. and
  Man.): E78.C5

Church's expedition to the eastward,
  1704: E197
Churoya Indians: F2270.2.C63
Churubusco, Battle of 1847: E406.C5
Churumata Indians
  Bolivia: F3320.2.C62
Cibola: F799
Ciboney Indians: F1769
Cicero (Illinois): F549.C56
Ciego de Avila Province (Cuba):
  F1851+
Cienfuegos (Cuba): F1829.C5
Cienfuegos Province (Cuba): F1852+
Cihuatán Site (El Salvador):
  F1435.1.C55
Cilley, Jonathan: E340.C5
Cilley, Joseph: E263.N4
Cimarron River and Valley
  Colorado: F782.C57
  Kansas: F687.C52
  New Mexico: F802.C58
Cimarron River and Valley (Oklahoma):
  F702.C53
Cimientos Site (Mexico): F1435.1.C56
Cincinnati, Daughters of the: E202.2
Cincinnati (Ohio): F499.C5+
  Symmes Tract: F483
Cincinnati, Society of the: E202.1
Cinta Larga Indians: F2520.1.C64
Cisne, Islas del: F1509.B3
Cisnes River (Chile): F3181
Cisplatine Province, 1821-1824: F2725
City Hall Park (New York): F128.65.C5
City Island (New York): F128.68.C5
City planning
  Aztecs: F1219.76.C59
  Indians
    Pre-Columbian America: E59.C55
  Mayas: F1435.3.C57
Ciudad de los Césares: F3072
Civil rights
  United States
    African Americans: E185.61
Civil War, 1861-1865: E461+
  Aerial operations: E492.7, E546.7
  Anniversaries: E641+

Civil War, 1861-1865
  Armies
    Confederate: E545+
    Union: E491+
  Biography: E467+
  Chronology: E468.3
  Commerce: E480
  Diplomatic history: E469+, E488
  Finance: E480
  Historiography: E468.5
  History: E468+
  Lee's surrender, 1865: E477.67
  Medical and hospital services: E621+
  Monuments and memorials: E641+
  Naval operations: E591+
  Opening events: E471+
  Personal narratives: E464
  Political history: E458+, E459
    Confederate: E487
  Press, censorship, etc: E609
  Prisons: E611+
  Relief: E629+
  Religious aspects: E540.A+, E635
  Secret service: E608
  Societies
    Patriotic, etc: E462+
      Confederate: E483
  Travel: E167
  Veterans' societies: E462+
    Confederate: E483
  Women: E628
  Women's work
    Nurses: E621+
Civil War Nurses, National Association
  of: E621
Claiborne Parish (La.): F377.C5
Claiborne, William: F184, F229
Claiborne, William Charles Cole: F374
Claims against the United States
  Civil War: E480
  Indians: E98.C6+
  Revolution: E249, E255
  War of 1812: E359.4
  War with Mexico: E409.4
Clallam Indians: E99.C82
Clamorgan land grant (Arkansas and
  Missouri): F417.C5

Clapps Mill, N.C., 1781, Battle of:
  E241.C56
Clarence Cannon Reservoir (Mo.):
  F472.C47
Clarendon settlement (N.C.): F257
Clarion River (Pa.): F157.C52
Clark, Abraham: E302.6.C55
Clark, Champ: E664.C49
Clark Fork and Valley
  Idaho: F752.C57
Clark Fork River and Valley
  Montana: F737.C55
Clark, George Rogers: E207.C5
  Expedition against Detroit, 1781:
    E237
  Expedition to the Illinois, 1778: E234
Clark Lake (Alaska): F912.C47
Clark Mountain (Virginia): F232.O6
Clark, William
  Lewis and Clark Expedition: F592.3+
Clarke, Elijah: F290
Clarke, John: F82
Clark's Mill, Mo., Battle of, 1862:
  E473.8
Clatsop Fort National Memorial
  (Oregon): F882.C53
Clay, Cassius Marcellus: E415.9.C55
Clay, Henry: E340.C6
  Charge of bargain with John Quincy
    Adams: E375
  Collected works: E337.8.C55
  Omnibus Bill: E423
Clayoquot Indians: E99.C83
Clayoquot Sound (B.C.): F1089.V3
Clayton, Augustin Smith: E340.C62
Clayton-Bulwer Treaty, 1860: F1438
Clayton, John Middleton: E415.9.C6
Clear Creek and Valley (Big Horn
  County-Sheridan County)
  Wyoming: F767.C55
Clear Creek and Valley (Colorado):
  F782.C59
Clear Fork River and Valley
  Kentucky: F457.C58
  Tennessee: F443.C56
Clearwater River and Valley (Idaho):
  F752.C62

Cleburne's Division
  Confederate Army: E547.C6
Clergy and the Civil War, 1861-1865:
  E540.C5
Clergy and the Revolution, 1775-1783:
  E210+
Clermont State Historic Site (New York):
  F127.L73
Clermont State Park (New York):
  F127.L73
Cleveland, Grover: E697
  Administration, 1885-1889: E696+
  Administration, 1893-1897: E706+
  Family: E697.5
Cleveland (Ohio): F499.C6+
Cliff dwellings
  America: E61
  Mesa Verde National Park (Colorado):
    F782.M52
  Pueblo Indians: E99.P9
Clifty Falls State Park (Indiana):
  F532.J5
Clinch River and Valley
  Tennessee: F443.C57
  Virginia: F232.C65
Clingman, Thomas Lanier: E415.9.C63
Clinton, Bill: E885+
Clinton, De Witt: E340.C65
Clinton, George: E302.6.C6
Clinton, James: E207.C62
Clinton Lake (Kansas): F687.W4
Clover Creek (Wash.): F897.P6
Clovis culture: E99.C832
Cloyds Mountain, Va., Battle of, 1864:
  E476.1
Coachella Valley (Calif.): F868.R6
Coahuila and Texas (State): F389
Coahuila, Mexico (State): F1266
Coahuilla Indians: E99.C155
Coahuiltecan Indians: E99.C834
Coaiker Indians: F3722.1.C83
Coaiquer Indians: F3722.1.C83
Coalcomán, Mexico (District): F1306
Coast Range (B.C.): F1089.C7
Coast Salish Indians: E99.S21
Coastal Bend (Texas): F392.C517
Cobá Indians: F1435.1.C63

Cobaría Indians: F2270.2.T8
Cobb, Howell: F290
Cobb Island (Maryland): F187.C6
Cobbeos Indians: F2270.2.C8
Cobbosseecontee, Lake (Me.): F27.K2
Coburn, Abner: E511+
Cocalico Creek and Valley (Pa.):
  F157.C67
Cocama Indians: F3430.1.C55
Cochabamba, Bolivia
  City: F3351.C67
  Department: F3341.C7
    Indian antiquities: F3319.1.C6
Cochetopa National Forest: F782.C66
Cochimi Indians: E99.C835
Cochino Bayou and Valley (Texas):
  F392.C52
Cochise Co. (Arizona): F817.C5
Cochiti Indians: E99.C84
Cocking, Matthew: F1060.7
Cockran, William Bourke: E664.C543
Coclé, Panama (Province): F1569.C6
  Indian antiquities: F1565.1.C6
Coconino Co. (Arizona): F817.C6
Coconuco Indians: F2270.2.C65
Cocopa Indians: E99.C842
Cocos Island (Costa Rica): F1549.C6
Cod, Cape (Mass.): F72.C3
Codex Azcatitlan: F1219.56.C38+
Codex Borbonicus: F1219.56.C43+
Codex Borgianus: F1219.56.B65+
Codex Cempoallan: F1219.56.C45+
Codex Chimalpopocatl: F1219.56.C62+
Codex Dresdensis Maya:
  F1219.56.C6215+
Codex en croix: F1219.56.C622+
Codex Fejérváry-Mayer:
  F1219.56.C623+
Codex Laud: F1219.56.C624+
Codex López Ruiz: F1219.56.C6244+
Codex Mendoza: F1219.56.C625+
Codex Nuttall: F1219.56.C6253+
Codex Ramírez: F1219.56.C626+
Codex Rios: F1219.56.R56+
Codex Telleriano-Remensis:
  F1219.56.C627+

Codex Tro-Cortesianus:
 F1219.56.C628+
Codex Tulane: F1219.56.C629+
Codex Vaticanus Lat. 3773:
 F1219.56.C633+
Codex Veytia: F1219.56.C634+
Codex Vindobonensis Mexicanus 1:
 F1219.56.C636+
Codex Xolotl: F1219.56.C64+
Códice Azoyu 1: F1219.56.C66+
Códice Baranda: F1219.56.C68+
Códice Boturini: F1219.56.B67+
Códice Chapultepec: F1219.56.C717+
Códice chugüilá: F1219.56.C7177+
Códice Colombino: F1219.56.C718+
Códice Cospi: F1219.56.C72+
Códice Cozcatzin: F1219.56.C725+
Códice Cuauhtinchan: F1219.56.C73+
Codice de Cholula: F1219.56.C734+
Codice de Cutzio: F1219.56.C736+
Códice de Jilotepec: F1219.56.C743+
Códice de Metepec: F1219.56.C746+
Códice de San Antonio Techialoyan:
 F1219.56.C7467+
Códice de Santa María Asunción:
 F1219.56.C747+
Códice de Teloloapan:
 F1219.56.C7475+
Códice de Tlatelolco: F1219.56.C748+
Códice de Xicotepec:
 F1219.56.C7486+
Códice de Yanhuitlán: F1219.56.C749+
Códice Fernández Leal:
 F1219.56.C75+
Códice florentino: F1219.56.C755+
Códice Huamantla: F1219.56.C74+
Códice Huichapan: F1219.56.H84+
Códice Kingsborough: F1219.56.C764+
Códice Muro: F1219.56.C767+
Códice Osuna: F1219.56.C77+
Codice Porfirio Diaz: F1219.56.C776+
Códice Sierra: F1219.56.C78+
Códice Techialoyan de Huixquilucan:
 F1219.56.C787+
Códice Techialoyan de San Francisco
 Xonacatlán: F1219.56.C7875+

Códice Techialoyan de San Pedro
 Totopec: F1219.56.C788+
Códice Techialoyan García Granados:
 F1219.56.C79+
Codice Tributos de Coyoacan:
 F1219.56.C795+
Códice Tudelo: F1219.56.T86+
Códice Xiquipilco-Temoaya:
 F1219.56.C82+
Codices
 Indians
  Mexico: F1219.5+
  Mayas: F1435.3.W75
Cody, William Frederick: F594
Coeur d'Alene Indians: E99.S63
Coeur d'Alene mining district (Idaho):
 F752.S5
Coeur d'Alene River and Valley (Idaho):
 F752.C65
Cofán Indians: F3722.1.C67
Cohuilla Indians: E99.C155
Cojedes, Venezuela (State): F2331.C6
Colchester Co. (Nova Scotia):
 F1039.C6
Cold Harbor, Battle of, 1864: E476.52
Colden, Cadwallader: F122+
Coleman, William Tell: F865
Coles, Edward: F545
Colfax Co. (N.M.): F802.C7
Colfax, Schuyler: E415.9.C68
Colha Site (Belize): F1435.1.C65
Colima, Mexico (State): F1271
Colla Indians: F3430.1.C6
Collamer, Jacob: F53
Collectibles, Political: E183.3
Colleges, Tribal: E97.55
Colleges (U.S.) and the Civil War:
 E541.A+
Colleges (U.S.) and the Revolution:
 E270.A1+
Colleges (U.S.) and the War of 1898:
 E725.6.A+
Colombia: F2251+
 English West Indian expedition,
  1700s: F2272.5
 English West Indian expeditions,
  1600s: F1621

Colombia
  Leticia Dispute, 1932-1934:
    F2281.B7P1+
  Military history
    Civil war: F2278
    Panama revolts: F1566.45, F2276.5
    War of Independence, 1810-1822:
      F2274
  New Granada (Viceroyalty): F2272
  Secession of Panama, 1903: F2276.5
  Union with Ecuador and Venezuela:
    F2274
Colombians in Costa Rica: F1557.C66
Colombians in the United States:
  E184.C58
Colombians in Venezuela: F2349.C64
Colombo, Cristoforo: E111+
Colombo family: E113
Colón, Archipiélago de: F3741.G2
Colón family: E113
Colón, Honduras (Dept.): F1509.C6
Colon (Panama)
  City: F1576.P2
Colón (Panama): F1576.C7
  Province: F1569.C7
Colonel's Island (Georgia): F292.G5
Colonia Mayntzhusen (Paraguay):
  F2691.A4
Colonia (Uruguay)
  Contests over: F2723
Colonia, Uruguay (Dept.): F2731.C7
  Indian antiquities: F2719.1.C65
Colonial Dames of America: E186.5
Colonial Dames of the XVII Century:
  E186.99.C55
Colonial Daughters of the Seventeenth
  Century: E186.7
Colonial life
  Maine: F23
  New England: F7
  New Hampshire: F37
  South Atlantic States: F212
  United States: E162
  Vermont: F52
Colonial National Historical Park:
  F232.C7
Colonial pamphlets: E187.C72

Colonias, Territorio Nacional de
  (Bolivia): F3341.T3
Colonization
  African Americans: E448
  Indians
    Bolivia: F3320.1.C6
    Paraguay: F2679.3.C64
    Pre-Columbian America: E59.C58
Colorado: F771+
  African Americans: E185.93.C6
  Counties, etc: F782.A+
  Indians: E78.C6
  Wars
    Civil War: E498+
    Indian wars: E83.868, E83.879
Colorado Desert (Calif.): F868.I2
Colorado Indians: F3722.1.C7
Colorado National Monument (Colo.):
  F782.M5
Colorado Plateau
  Indians: E78.C617
Colorado River, Canyon, and Valley:
  F788
  Arizona: F817.C7
  California: F868.C6
  Colorado: F782.C7
  Utah: F832.C7
Colorado River (Texas): F392.C6
Colorado River Valley
  Indians: E78.C62
Colorado Springs (Colorado): F784.C7
Colorado Trail
  Colorado: F782.R6
Colorados
  Paraguay: F2689
  Uruguay: F2726
Colpahuaico, Battle of, 1824: F3446
Colter, John: F592
Columbia Heights (Washington, D.C.):
  F202.C6
Columbia Indians: E99.S55
Columbia National Forest (Wash.):
  F897.C8
Columbia Plateau
  Indians: E78.C63
Columbia River and Valley: F853
  Oregon: F882.C63

Columbia River and Valley
  Washington: F897.C7
Columbia River Highway (Oregon):
  F882.C63
Columbia River Valley
  Indians: E78.C64
Columbia (S.C.): F279.C7
  Burning of, 1865: E477.75
Columbia Valley (B.C.): F1089.C727
Columbiana Co. (Ohio): F497.C6
Columbus, Christopher: E111+
  Celebrations, 1892-1893: E119
  Monument, Washington, D.C.:
    F203.4.C7
  Quincentennial, 1992-1993: E119.2
Columbus Day: E120
Columbus (Georgia): F294.C7
  Capture, 1865: E477.96
Columbus (Kentucky), Demonstration
  upon, 1861: E472.28
Columbus (Ohio): F499.C7+
Colville Indians: E99.C844
Colville River and Valley (Wash.):
  F897.S9
Comalcalco Site (Mexico): F1435.1.C67
Comanche Indians: E99.C85
Comanche War, 1840: E83.837
Comayagua (Honduras): F1516.C72
Comechingone Indians: F2823.C5
Comic histories
  United States
    Revolution, 1775-1783: E298
Commerce
  Aztecs: F1219.76.C65
  Indians: E98.C7
    Central America: F1434.2.C65
    Chile: F3069.3.C66
    Ecuador: F3721.3.C64
    Guatemala: F1465.3.C77
    Mexico: F1219.3.C6
    Peru: F3429.3.C59
    Pre-Columbian America: E59.C59
    South America: F2230.1.C75
    West Indies: F1619.3.C65
  Mayas: F1435.3.C6
Commerce Building, Department of
  (Washington, D.C.): F204.D43

Commerce, Restrictions on
  United States
    1800-1810: E336+
    Colonial period: E215.1
Committee of Seventy (Louisiana):
  F375
Committees of correspondence and
  safety: E216
Commonwealth Caribbean: F2130+
Communication
  Indians
    Brazil: F2519.3.C65
    Peru: F3429.3.C594
    Indians of North America: E98.C73
Communist Revolution of 1935 (Brazil):
  F2538
Communist spies in Canada: F1034
Communist spies in the United States:
  E743.5
Community colleges, Indian: E97.55
Comodoro Rivadavia (Argentina):
  F2884
Comonfort, Ignacio: F1232.5
Comox Indians: E99.C86
Comox Valley (B.C.): F1089.V3
Compagnie du Scioto: F483
Company of New France: F1030
Company of the West Indies: F1030
Compromise of 1850: E423
Compton County (Québec): F1054.C7
Comstock Lode (Nevada): F849.V8
Comuneros, Insurrection of the, 1781:
  F2272
Conant, Roger: F67
Concepción (Chile)
  City: F3281.C5
  Province: F3156
Concepción de la Vega (Dominican
  Republic): F1939.L3
Concepción, Paraguay
  City: F2695.C7
  Department: F2691.C6
Concho River and Valley (Texas):
  F392.C773
Concord, Battle of, 1775: E241.C7
Concord (Massachusetts): F74.C8
Concord (New Hampshire): F44.C7

Concord River (Mass.): F72.M7
Concordat of 1862: F3736
Concordia Parish (La.): F377.C7
Conejo Valley (Calif.): F868.C74
Conemaugh River and Valley:
  F157.C73
Conestoga Creek and Valley (Pa.):
  F157.L2
Conestoga Indians: E99.C87
Conewago Creek and Valley (Pa.):
  F157.C75
Coney Island (New York): F129.C75
Confederación de Centro América,
    1823-1838/1842: F1438
  Costa Rica: F1547
  Guatemala: F1466.4
  Honduras: F1507
  Nicaragua: F1526.25
Confederación de Centro América,
    1823-1848/1842
  El Salvador: F1487
Confederación Granadina: F2276
Confederación Peru-Boliviana: F3447
Confederate Memorial Day: E645
Confederate Memorial Literary Society:
  E483.75
Confederate operations in Canada:
  E470.95
Confederate States of America: E482+
  Construction of war vessels in
    England: E469+
  Description and travel: F214
  Flags: E646
  Military history: E551+
  Naval history: E591+
  Political history: E487
  Propaganda in foreign countries:
    E488.5
  Slavery: E453
  Social conditions: F214
  Travel: F214
Confederate sympathizers in the North:
  E458.8
Confederate Veteran Association of
  Kentucky: E483.2
Confederate Veterans' Association of
  Fulton County, Georgia: E483.99.C78

Confederated Southern Memorial
  Association: E483.72
Confederates in Canada: E470.95
Confederation, 1783-1789
  United States: E303
Confederation, Articles of, 1778: E303
Confederation of Granada: F2276
Confiscations
  United States
    Civil War: E480
    Revolution: E277
Congaree Swamp and Region (S.C.):
  F277.C85
Congress Hall (Philadelphia):
  F158.8.C7
Congress of Lima, 1864-1865: F1404.4
Congress of Panama, 1826: F1404
Congressional Cemetery (Washington,
  D.C.): F203.1.C7
Conkling, Roscoe: E664.C75
Conneaut Lake (Pa.): F157.C77
Connecticut: F91+
  African Americans: E185.93.C7
  Counties, etc: F102.A+
  Dutch posts: F97
  Indians: E78.C7
  Old Northwest cession: F483
  Slavery: E445.C7
  Wars
    Civil War: E499+
    French and Indian War: E199
    Indian wars: E83.63, E83.67
    Revolution: E230+, E263.C5
    War of 1812: E359.5.C7
    War of 1898: E726.C7
    War with Mexico, 1845-1848:
      E409.5.C6
  Western Reserve: F497.W5
  Wyoming Valley claims: F157.W9
Connecticut Gore: F157.W9
Connecticut Reserve (Ohio): F497.W5
Connecticut River and Valley
  Connecticut: F102.C7
  Massachusetts: F72.C7
  New England: F12.C7
  New Hampshire: F42.C65
  Vermont: F57.C7

Conner, David: E403.1.C7
Connolly, John: E278.C7
Conococheague Creek and Valley:
  F157.F8
  Maryland: F187.W3
Conoy Indians: E99.C873
Consanguinity
  Indians
    Peru: F3429.3.C6
Conselheiro Insurrection (Brazil): F2537
Consolidated province of New England:
  F7.5
Conspiracies
  U.S. Civil War: E458.8
Constitution
  United States: E303
Constitution Avenue (Washington,
  D.C.): F203.7.C7
Constitution Island (New York):
  F127.C83
Continental army
  United States: E259+
Continental Congress, 1774-1788:
  E303
Continental Hall, Memorial (Washington,
  D.C.): F204.M5
Contrabands: E453
Contracts, Government
  United States
    Civil War: E480
Contreras, Battle of, 1847: E406.C6
Contumazá, Peru (Province): F3451.C7
Convention of Border Slave States
  Frankfort, Kentucky: E440.5
Conway Cabal: E255
Cooch's Bridge, Skirmish of, 1777:
  E241.C73
Cook, Daniel Pope: E340.C7
Cook Forest Park (Pa.): F157.C76
Cook Inlet (Alaska): F912.C6
Cooking Lake-Blackfoot Grazing,
  Wildlife, and Provincial Recreation
  Area (Alberta): F1079.C57
Cook's Mills, Battle of, 1814: E356.C74
Cool Spring, Va., Battle of, 1864:
  E476.66
Coolidge, Calvin: E792

Coolidge, Calvin
  Administrations, 1923-1929: E791+
  Family: E792.1
Coolidge, Calvin, Jr: E792.1
Cooper, James: F153
Cooper Lake (Texas): F392.C79
Cooper River (S.C.): F277.B5
Cooper, Thomas: E302.6.C7
Coos Bay (Oregon): F882.C7
Coos Indians: E99.C874
Coosa Indians: E99.C87414
Coosa River and Valley (Alabama):
  F332.C75
Copiapó River and Valley (Chile):
  F3159
Copper Canyon (Mexico): F1340
Copper Falls State Park (Wis.):
  F587.A8
Copper River region (Alaska): F912.C7
Copperheads: E458.8
Copperwork
  Indians
    North America: E98.C76
    South America: F2230.1.C76
Copp's Hill Burial Ground (Boston):
  F73.61
Coquille Indians: E99.C8742
Coquimbo, Chile (Province): F3161
Cora Indians: F1221.C6
Cordillera Blanca (Peru): F3451.A5
Cordillera, Bolivia (Province):
  F3341.C75
Cordillera de Mérida: F2331.M52
Córdoba (Argentina)
  City: F3011.C7
  Province: F2886
    Indian antiquities: F2821.1.C7
Córdoba, Colombia (Dept.): F2281.C6
Córdoba, Jose Maria: F2274
Córdoba, League of: F2847
Córdoba (Mexico)
  Canton: F1371
Coree Indians: E99.C8743
Coreguaje Indians: F2270.2.C67
Corinth (Mississippi)
  Battle of, October 1862: E474.44
  Siege, 1862: E473.56

Cornell, Samuel: E278.C8
Corner Brook (Newfoundland):
  F1124.5.C6
Cornish in Canada: F1035.C64
Cornish in the United States: E184.C6
Cornwallis, C.C., 1st marquis
  Campaigns of 1780-1781: E236
  Surrender, 1781: E241.Y6
Cornwallis, C.C., 1st Marquis
  Campaigns of 1780-1781: E237
Coronado, Francisco: E125.V3
Coronado National Memorial (Arizona):
  F817.C5
Coronel Oviedo (Paraguay): F2695.C8
Corongo, Peru (Province): F3451.C76
Coropuna (Peru): F3451.A7
Corpus Christi (Texas): F394.C78
Correia de Sá e Benavides (Salvador):
  F2528
Correspondence, Colonial committees
  of: E216
Correspondents, War
  U.S. Civil War: E609
Corrientes, Argentina (Province): F2891
  Jesuit missions of Paraguay: F2684
Cortés, Hernando: F1230
Corwin, Thomas: E340.C76
Corydon, Ind., Battle of, 1863: E475.18
Cosa, Juan de la: E125.C8
Cosmogony
  Indians
    Mexico: F1219.3.C65
Cosmology
  Aztecs: F1219.76.C67
  Indians
    Mexico: F1219.3.C65
    North America: E98.C79
    Peru: F3429.3.C74
    South America: F2230.1.C78
Costa Rica: F1541+
  Battle of Rivas, 1856: F1526.27
  Confederación de Centro América:
    F1438, F1547
Costebelle, Phillipe de Pastour, sieur
  de: F1123
Costilla and Trinchera estates (Colo.):
  F782.C8

Costume
  Aztecs: F1219.76.C68
  Indians
    Bolivia: F3320.1.C64
    Brazil: F2519.3.C68
    Guatemala: F1465.3.C8
    Mexico: F1219.3.C75
    North America: E98.C8
    Peru: F3429.3.C8
    Pre-Columbian America: E59.C6
    South America: F2230.1.C8
  Mayas: F1435.3.C69
Côte de Beaupré (Seigniory) (Québec):
  F1054.C75
Côte-du-Sud (Québec): F1054.S3
Côte-Nord du Golfe Sainte-Laurent:
  F1054.S3
Coteau du Missouri: F642.M26
Cotile Lake
  Louisiana: F377.R25
Cotopaxi, Ecuador (Province):
  F3741.C6
Cotuí (Dominican Republic):
  F1939.C67
Coudres, Île aux (Québec): F1054.I3
Coulee Dam region (Wash.): F897.C7
Counani, Brazil (Territory): F2558
Council Bluffs (Iowa): F629.C8
Council for New England
  Grants in Connecticut: F97
  Grants in Massachusetts: F67
Council for New England, 1620: F7
Covenanters in the United States:
  E184.C8
Covington (Kentucky): F459.C8
Covington, Leonard: E353.1.C75
Cow Neck Creek and Valley (Oregon):
  F882.D7
Cow Neck Peninsula (New York):
  F127.N2
Cowan's Ford, Battle of, 1781: E241.C8
Cowboys
  Canadian Northwest: F1060.94
  Montana: F731
  Texas: F391
  West (U.S.): F596
Cowichan Indians: E99.C875

Cowichan Lake and region (B.C.):
F1089.C73
Cowlitz Indians: E99.C877
Cowpens, Battle of, 1781: E241.C9
Cox, George Barnsdale: F496
Cox, Jacob Dolson: E664.C78
Cox, Samuel Sullivan: E664.C8
Coxton Lake (Pa.): F157.W35
Coyaima Indians: F2270.2.C68
Coyote Flats (Alberta): F1079.C6
Cozumel Island (Mexico): F1272,
F1435.1.C76
Crab Island (Puerto Rico): F1981.V5
Crafts
Indians
North America: E98.I5
Craho Indians: F2520.1.C67
Craig Mountain (Idaho): F752.N57
Crampton's Gap, Md., Battle of, 1862:
E474.61
Crane Island (Minnesota): F612.H5
Crane Island (Québec): F1054.C8
Crane Valley Dam and Lake (Calif.):
F868.M2
Craney Island, Battle of, 1813: E356.C8
Craniology
Indians: E98.C85
Argentina: F2821.3.C73
Mexico: F1219.3.C8
Peru: F3429.3.C85
Pre-Columbian America: E59.C73
Crater, Battle of Petersburg, 1864:
E476.93
Crater Lake National Park (Oregon):
F882.C8
Crater Lake (Oregon): F882.C8
Crater National Forest: F882.C83
Crater of Diamonds State Park:
F417.P5
Craters of the Moon National Monument
(Idaho): F752.C7
Craven County (S.C.): F277.B5
Crawford, John Wallace: F154
Crawford, William
Indian Campaign, 1782: E238
Crawford, William Harris: E340.C89

Creation
Indian religion: E98.R3
Credit fund, Revolving
Indians: E98.F3
Credit River and Valley (Ontario):
F1059.C7
Cree Indians: E99.C88
Creek Indians: E99.C9
Creek War
1st, 1813-1814: E83.813
2d, 1836: E83.836
Cremation
Indians
Pre-Columbian America: E59.C9
Creole (Brig)
Mutiny: E447
Creoles in America: E29.C73
Creoles in the United States: E184.C87
Cresap, Michael: F517
Crespo, Joaquín: F2325
Creston Valley (B.C.): F1089.C75
Cretans in the United States: E184.C9
Crichaná Indians: F2520.1.C7
Crijnssen, Abraham: F2423
Crime
Indians of North America: E98.C87
Crimes against
Mayas: F1435.3.C75
Criminal justice system
Indians of North America: E98.C87
Crimson Lake Provicial Park (Alberta):
F1079.C73
Cripple Creek (Colorado): F784.C8
Crisca Indians: F2520.1.A4
Cristophe, Henri: F1924
Crittenden Compromise: E440.5
Crittenden, John Jordan: E340.C9
Crittenden Resolution: E440.5
Crixá Indians: F2520.1.A4
Croatan Indians: E99.C91
Croatians in the United States:
E184.C93
Croats in America: E29.C75
Croats in Argentina: F3021.C7
Croats in Canada: F1035.C7
Croats in Chile: F3285.C76
Croats in South America: F2239.C76

Croats in the United States: E184.C93
Croats in Uruguay: F2799.C76
Crocker's Iowa Brigade: E507.4
Crockett, David: F436
Croghan, George: E353.1.C8
Croker, Richard: F128.47
Crook, George: E83.866
Crooked Billet, Battle of the, 1778:
  E241.C94
Crooked Creek, Battle of, 1859:
  E83.8577
Crosby, Enoch: E280.C95
Cross Keys, Va., Battle of, 1862:
  E473.74
Crow Indians: E99.C92
Crown Coffee House (Boston):
  F73.8.C9
Crown Heights (New York, N.Y.):
  F128.68.C76
Crown Point (New York)
  French and Indian War: E199
Crowsnest Pass
  Alberta: F1079.C76
  British Columbia: F1089.C77
Crowsnest River and Valley
  Alberta: F1079.C76
  British Columbia: F1089.C77
Crozat's Grant, 1712-1717: F372
Cruises down the river
  Mississippi River: F354
Crystal Lake (Michigan): F572.B4
Crystal Park (Colo.): F782.E3
C.S.A.: E482+
Cuaiker Indians: F3722.1.C83
Cuaiquer Indians: F3722.1.C83
Cuauhtemoc, Emperor of Mexico:
  F1219.75.C83
Cuba: F1751+
  American occupation, 1906-1909:
    F1787
  Annexation question: F1786
  Discovery and exploration: E101+
  English occupation, 1762-1763:
    F1781
  Filibusters: F1784

Cuba
  Military history
    Insurrections
      1849-1851 (López expeditions):
        F1784
      1868-1878 (Ten Years' War):
        F1785
      Little War, 1878-1880: F1785
    Revolutions
      1895-1898: F1786
      1906: F1787
      1933: F1788
    War of 1898: E717.1
    Ostend Manifesto, 1854: E431
Cubagua Island (Venezuela): F2331.C7
Cuban missile crisis: E841+
Cuban question
  1895-1898: F1786
  1896-1898: E721
Cubans in Central America: F1440.C84
Cubans in foreign countries: F1760.5
Cubans in Mexico: F1392.C8
Cubans in Puerto Rico: F1983.C83
Cubans in United States: E184.C97
Cubans in Venezuela: F2349.C83
Cubeo Indians: F2270.2.C8
Cuelap (Peru)
  Indian antiquities: F3429.1.C8
Cuello Site (Belize): F1435.1.C84
Cuenca (Ecuador): F3791.C9
Cuesta Encantada (California):
  F868.S18
Cuestas, Juan Lindolfo: F2726
Cueva Indians: F1565.2.C77
Cuiba Indians: F2319.2.C78
Cuicatec Indians: F1221.C84
Cuiva Indians: F2319.2.C78
Cul de Sac (Haiti) (plain): F1929.C8
Culebra Island (Puerto Rico): F1981.C9
Culina Indians: F2520.1.C84
Cultural assimilation
  Indians: E98.C89
    Brazil: F2519.3.C85
    Mexico: F1219.3.C85
    Nicaragua: F1525.3.C84
Cultural relations
  Spain with Latin America: F1414

Cultural relations
  United States
    1961-: E840.2
    20th century: E744.5
Culture
  Indians
    South America: F2230.1.C9
Cultus Lake and region (B.C.):
  F1089.C85
Cumana Indians: F2319.2.C8
Cumaná (Venezuela): F2341.C8
Cumberland, Army of the: E470.5
Cumberland Caverns (Tennessee):
  F443.W2
Cumberland, Fort, N.B., Battle of, 1776:
  E241.C96
Cumberland (Frigate): E595.C9
Cumberland Gap campaign, Mar-June
  1862: E473.52
Cumberland Gap National Historical
  Park: F457.C77
Cumberland Gap (Tennessee),
  Evacuation of Sept-Oct. 1862:
  E474.38
Cumberland Island (Georgia):
  F292.C94
Cumberland Island National Seashore
  (Georgia): F292.C94
Cumberland Mountains: F457.C8
Cumberland Parish (Virginia):
  F232.C94
Cumberland River and Valley
  Kentucky: F457.C9
Cumberland Road (Pa.): F157.C85
Cumberland Valley
  Pennsylvania: F157.C9, F157.F8
Cumberland Valley (Ky. and Tenn.):
  F442.2, F457.C9
  Civil War
    Military operations: E470.5
Cuna Indians: F1565.2.C8
Cundinamarca (Colombia):
  F2269.1.C95
Cundinamarca, Colombia (Dept.):
  F2281.C9
Cunningham Chapel Parish (Va.):
  F232.C59

Cupeño Indians: E99.C94
Cupisnique Indians: F3430.1.C8
Curaçao (West Indies): F2049
Curicó, Chile (Province): F3166
Curitiba (Brazil): F2651.C83
Curler, Arent van: F122.1
Curley, James Michael: F70
Current River and Valley (General, and
  Mo.): F472.C9
Curripaco Indians: F2270.2.C87
Curtis, Benjamin Robbins: E415.9.C96
Curtis, Samuel Ryan: E467.1.C97
Curuguaty (Paraguay): F2695.C9
Curupaity, Battle of, 1866: F2687
Curwen, Samuel: E278.C9
Cuscatlán, El Salvador (Dept.):
  F1489.C8
  Indian antiquities: F1485.1.C8
Cushing, Caleb: E415.9.C98
Cushing, William Barker: E467.1.C98
Custer, Fort (Mont.): F737.Y4
Custer, George Armstrong: E467.1.C99
Custer State Park (South Dakota):
  F657.C92
Custis-Lee Mansion, Arlington, Va:
  F234.A7
Custom House (Chicago): F548.8.C9
Cutervo, Peru (Province): F3451.C85
Cutler, Manasseh: F483
Cuttyhunk Island (Mass.): F72.E5
Cuyahoga River and Valley (Ohio):
  F497.C95
Cuyamaca Mountains (Calif.):
  F868.S15
Cuyo (Province): F2911
Cuzco (Peru)
  City: F3611.C9
    Indian antiquities: F3429.1.C9
  Department: F3451.C9
Cypress Creek and Valley (Ark.):
  F417.C7
Cypress Creek and Valley (Kentucky):
  F457.U5
Cypress Hills (Alta. and Saska.):
  F1079.C9
Cypress Hills Provincial Park
  (Saskatchewan): F1074.C92

Cypriots in the United States: E184.C98
Czechs in America: E29.C94
Czechs in Canada: F1035.C9
Czechs in Chile: F3285.C94
Czechs in Latin America: F1419.C94
Czechs in Mexico: F1392.C93
Czechs in the United States: E184.B67
  Civil War: E540.C94
Czolgosz, L. F.: E711.9

D

Dahlgren, John Adolphus Bernard:
  E467.1.D13
Dahlgren, Ulric
  Raid, 1864: E476.27
Dakota Indian wars
  1855-1856: E83.854
  1862-1865: E83.86
  1876: E83.876
  1890-1891: E83.89
Dakota Indians: E99.D1
Dakota region before 1861: F655
Dakota Territory
  Indians: E78.D2
Dakota Territory (1861-1889): F655
Dale Hollow Lake and Region (Ky.):
  F457.D26
Dale Hollow Lake and Region (Tenn.):
  F443.D18
Dalhousie, George Ramsay, 9th Earl of:
  F1053
Dallas, Alexander James: E302.6.D14
Dallas, George Mifflin: E340.D14
Dallas (Texas): F394.D21+
Dalles of the Wisconsin: F587.W8
Dames of 1846: E401.7
Dames of the Loyal Legion: E462.25
Dana, Francis: E302.6.D16
Dana, Richard Henry: E415.9.D15
  Collected works: E415.6.D16+
Danbury (Connecticut)
  Burning by the British, 1777: E241.D2
Dance
  Aztecs: F1219.76.D35
  Indians: E98.D2
    Bolivia: F3320.1.D35

Dance
  Indians
    Brazil: F2519.3.D2
    Ecuador: F3721.3.D35
    Guatemala: F1465.3.D3
    Mexico: F1219.3.D2
    Pre-Columbian America: E59.D35
    South America: F2230.1.D35
  Mayas: F1435.3.D34
Danes
  Discovery of America: E109.D2
Danes in Argentina: F3021.D2
Danes in Brazil: F2659.D35
Danes in Canada: F1035.D3
Danes in Paraguay: F2699.D34
Danes in the United States: E184.S19
Daniel Island (S.C.): F277.B5
Daniels, Margaret (Truman): E814.1
Danish colonies in America
  Danish West Indies (Before 1917):
    F2136
Danish West Indies: F2136
Danube Swabians in America: E29.D25
Danville, Va. Military Prison: E612.D2
D.A.R.: E202.5
Dare, Virginia: F229
Darién: F1569.D3
Darien (Panama)
  Indian antiquities: F1565.1.D26
Darien (Scots' Colony): F2281.D2
Dartiguenave, Sudre: F1927
Dartmoor Massacre, 1815: E362
Dartmouth College and the Civil War:
  E541.D22
Dartmouth (Nova Scotia): F1039.5.D3
Daughters of Founders and Patriots of
  America: E186.8
Daughters of the American Colonists:
  E186.99.D3
Daughters of the American Revolution:
  E202.5
  Memorial Continental Hall: F204.M5
Daughters of the Cincinnati: E202.2
Daughters of the Confederacy, United:
  E483.5
Daughters of the Revolution: E202.6

Daughters of Union Veterans of the Civil War: E462.99.D2

Dauphin Island (Alabama): F332.M6

Daveiss, Joseph Hamilton: F455

Davenport (Iowa): F629.D2

Davidson, William Lee: E207.D3

Davie, William Richardson: E302.6.D2

Davis, Charles Henry: E467.1.D24

Davis, Henry Winter: E415.9.D26

Davis, Jeff: E664.D28

Davis, Jefferson: E467.1.D26
  Administration (C.S.A.): E487
  Conference with Gilmore and
    Jacquess: E469+
  Pursuit and capture: E477.98

Davis, Varina Anne Jefferson:
  E467.1.D28

Davis, Varina (Howell): E467.1.D27

Dawes, Charles Gates: E748.D22

Dawson (Yukon): F1095.5.D3

Day, John Marshall: E302.6.M4

Dayton (Ohio): F499.D2+

Dayton, William Louis: E415.9.D27

De Kalb, Jean: E207.K14

De Lancey's Brigade (Loyalist):
  E277.6.D3

De Soto, Hernando: E125.S7

De Soto Parish (La.): F377.D45

De Witt's Colony (Texas): F389

Dead River and Valley (Me.): F27.D2

Deadfish Lake Region (Alaska):
  F912.D58

Deal Lake (N.J.): F142.M7

Dean Mountain (Virginia): F232.S48

Deane, Silas: E302.6.D25

Dearborn, Fort
  Massacre, 1812: E356.C53

Dearborn, Henry: E302.6.D3
  Campaign, 1812: E355.2
  Campaigns, 1813: E355.4

Dearborn (Michigan): F574.D2

Dearborn Park (Chicago): F548.65.D2

Death Valley (Calif.): F868.D2

Death Valley National Monument
  (Calif.): F868.D2

Death's Door (Wisconsin): F587.P83

Deborah, Mount (Alaska): F912.D6

Debsconeag Lake region (Me.): F27.P5

Decatur (Illinois): F549.D3

Decatur, Stephen, 1752-1808: E182

Decatur, Stephen, 1779-1820:
  E353.1.D29

Declaration of Independence: E221

Declaration of Independence,
  Mecklenburg: E215.9

Decoration Day: E642

Deer Creek (Maryland): F187.H2

Deer Island (New Brunswick):
  F1044.D3

Deerfield (Mass.)
  Massacre, 1704: E197

Deerfield River (Mass.): F72.F8

DeForest, David Curtis: E340.D4

Deg Hit'an Indians: E99.D18

Deka Lake (B.C.): F1089.C3

Delaware: F161+
  African Americans: E185.93.D4
  Counties, etc: F172.A+
  Delmarva Peninsula: F187.E2
  Indians: E78.D3
  New Sweden: F167
  Slavery: E445.D3
  Wars
    Civil War: E500+
    Revolution: E263.D3
      Military operations: E230+

Delaware and Lehigh National Heritage
  Corridor
  Pennsylvania: F157.D28

Delaware Bay: F172.D3
  New Jersey: F142.D3

Delaware Bay Region: F172.D3
  New Jersey: F142.D3

Delaware, Fort
  Civil War prison: E616.D3

Delaware Indians: E99.D2

Delaware River: F157.D4
  Lower counties on: F167
  Swedish settlements on: F167

Delaware River and Valley: F157.D4
  Delaware: F172.D4
  New Jersey: F142.D4
  New York: F127.D4

Delaware Valley
  Indian antiquities: E78.D5
  Revolution: E263.P4
Delaware Water Gap: F157.D5
Delgado Chalband, Carlos: F2326
Delgado, José Matías: F1487
Dells of the Wisconsin: F587.W8
Delmarva Peninsula: F187.E2
  Indians: E78.D54
  Revolution: E263.D3
Delta Amacuro (Venezuela):
  F2331.D44
Delta Region
  California: F868.D45
  Louisiana: F377.D4
Demarcation line of Pope Alexander VI:
  E123
Demerara Co. (British Guiana):
  F2387.D4
Demerara (Dutch Colony): F2383,
  F2423
Dena'ina Indians: E99.T185
Denali, Mount (Alaska): F912.M2
Denali National Park and Reserve
  (Alaska): F912.M23
Denali State Park (Alaska): F912.D65
Dene Thá Indians: E99.D25
Denison, Camp (Ohio)
  Civil War prison: E616.D4
Denman Island (B.C.): F1089.D45
Denmark Vesey's Rebellion, 1822:
  F279.C4+
Denning Point (New York): F127.D8
Dental mutiliation
  Indians
    Argentina: F2821.3.D4
Dentistry
  Indians
    Argentina: F2821.3.D4
    Mexico: F1219.3.D3
    Pre-Columbian America: E59.D45
  Mayas: F1435.3.D4
Denver (Colorado): F784.D4+
Departure Bay (B.C.): F1089.D46
Depew, Chauncey Mitchell: E660.D3+,
  E664.D4
DePeyster, John Watts: F123

Des Barres, J. F. W.: F1032
Des Moines (Iowa): F629.D4
Des Moines River and Valley
  Iowa: F627.D43
  Missouri: F472.D4
Des Plaines River and Valley (Illinois):
  F547.D4
Desana Indians: F2270.2.D4,
  F2520.1.D47
Deschutes National Forest: F882.D43
Deschutes River and Valley (Oregon):
  F882.D45
Deseret: F826
Desert Island, Mount: F27.M9
Desertions, Military
  United States
    War with Mexico: E415.2.D48
Désirade (West Indies): F2050
Desolation Canyon (Utah): F832.D46
Desolation Sound (B.C.): F1089.D48
Dessalines, Jean Jacques: F1924
Desventuradas (Chile): F3131
Detroit (Michigan): F574.D4+
  Clark's Expedition against, 1781:
    E237
  Surrender to the British, 1812:
    E355.2, E356.D4
Detroit River and Valley
  Michigan: F572.D46
  Ontario: F1059.D46
Deux Montagnes County (Québec):
  F1054.D4
Devil's Island (French Guiana):
  F2467.I4
Devil's Island (Wisconsin): F587.S2
Devils Lake (Lenawee County,
  Michigan): F572.L5
Devils Lake (N.D.): F642.D5
Devils River and Valley (Texas):
  F392.D47
Devils Tower National Monument
  (Wyoming): F767.D47
Dewees Island (S.C.): F277.C4
Dewey, George: E714.6.D51
Dewey, Thomas Edmund: E748.D48
Dexter, Samuel: E302.6.D45
Dhegiha Indians: E99.D4

Dia de Colon: E120
Diaguita Indians
  Argentina: F2823.D5
  Chile: F3070.1.D5
Diamantina Plateau (Brazil): F2551
Diamond Cave (Ky.): F457.B2
Dias, Henrique: F2532
Dias, Marcillio: F2536
Díaz, Adolfo: F1526.3
Díaz del Castillo, Bernal: F1230
Díaz, Porfirio: F1233.5
Dickinson, Anna Elizabeth: E415.9.D48
Dickinson, Daniel Stevens: E415.9.D5
Dickinson, John: E302.6.D5
Dickinson, Walter Mason: E714.6.D55
Diefenbaker, John George: F1034.3.D5
Diegueño Indians: E99.D5
Digby Co. (Nova Scotia): F1039.D5
Dingley, Nelson Jr: E664.D58
Dinosaur National Monument: F832.D5
Dinosaur Valley State Park (Tex.):
  F392.S65
Dinwiddie Courthouse, Battle of, 1865:
  E477.67
Diriamba (Nicaragua): F1536.D5
Disappointment Creek and Valley
  (Colorado): F782.D57
Disasters
  United States: E179
Discoveries and exploration
  America: E101+
    Columbian: E111+
    Post-Columbian: E121+
    Pre-Columbian: E103+
Discovery Day: E120
Discrimination, Racial
  United States
    African Americans: E185.61
Diseases
  Indians: E98.D6
    Argentina: F2821.3.D5
    Chile: F3069.3.D58
    Ecuador: F3721.3.D58
    Mexico: F1219.3.D5
    Peru: F3429.3.D6
    Pre-Columbian America: E59.D58

Disloyal organizations
  U.S. Civil War: E458.8
Dismal Swamp
  North Carolina: F262.D7
  Virginia: F232.D7
District of Columbia: F191+
  African Americans: E185.93.D6
  Indians: E78.D6
  Retrocession of Alexander Co., 1846:
    F195
  Slavery: E445.D6
  Wars
    Civil War: E501+
      Military operations: E470.2+,
        E476.66
    War of 1812: E355.6
      Burning of Washington: E356.W3
    War with Mexico: E409.5.D6
District of West Augusta (Virginia):
  F157.W5
Dix, John Adams: E415.9.D6
Dix, John Alden: F124
Dixie: F206+
Djore-Xikrin Indians: F2520.1.X5
Dochet Island: F27.W3
Dodge, Augustus Caesar: F621
Dodge, Grenville Mellen: E467.1.D6
Dodge, Henry: E340.D7
Doe, Charles: F39
Dog Rib Indians: E99.T4
Dolls
  Aztecs: F1219.76.D64
  Indians: E98.D65
    Peru: F3429.3.D66
    Pre-Columbian America: E59.D66
Domestic animals
  Indians
    North America: E98.D67
    Peru: F3429.3.D69
    Pre-Columbian America: E59.D69
    South America: F2230.1.D65
  Mayas: F1435.3.D64
Domestic relations
  Indians
    Peru: F3429.3.D72
Dominica (West Indies): F2051
Dominican Republic: F1931+

Dominican Republic
  Annexation to U.S. proposed: E673
  Pre-Columbian period: F1909
  Spanish colony, 1492-1795: F1911
Dominicans (Dominican Republic) in
  United States: E184.D6
Dominicans in Puerto Rico: F1983.D65
Dominion of Canada: F1001+
Dominion of New England, 1686-1689:
  F7.5
Don River and Valley (Ontario):
  F1059.Y6
Donck, Adriaen van der: F122.1
Donelson, Emily Tennessee (Donelson):
  E382.1.D6
Donelson, Fort
  Siege and capture, 1862: E472.97
Dongan, Thomas, Earl of Limerick:
  F122+
Doniphan, Alexander William:
  E403.1.D6
  Expedition in Mexican War: E405.2
Donner, Lake (Calif.): F868.N5
Donner party expedition: F868.N5
Dorado, El: E121+
Dorask Indians: F1565.2.D6
Dorchester Co. (Md.): F187.D6
Dorchester Company: F67
Dorchester County (Québec):
  F1054.D6
Dorchester, Guy Carleton, baron:
  F1032
Dorchester (Mass.): F74.D5
Dorr, Thomas Wilson: F83.4
Dorrego, Manuel: F2846
Dos Pilas (Mexico): F1435.1.D67
Douglas, Camp (Chicago, Ill.): E616.D7
Douglas Island (Alaska): F912.D75
Douglas, Sir James: F1088
Douglas, Stephen Arnold: E415.9.D73
  Debates with Lincoln, 1858: E457.4
Douglas, Thomas, 5th earl of Selkirk:
  F1063
Douglass, Frederick: E449
Doukhobors in Canada: F1035.D76
Dover (Delaware): F174.D74
Dover (New Hampshire): F44.D7

Drachita Indians: F2823.D5
Draft riot (New York), 1863: F128.44
Drake, Sir Francis: E129.D7
Drama
  Indians: E98.D8
    Mexico: F1219.3.D8
Drayton, John: E263.S7
Dred Scott case: E450
Drew, Daniel: F124
Drewrys Bluff, Va., Battle of, 1864:
  E476.57
Drinking horns: F2230.1.D75
Drinking vessels
  Indians
    Peru: F3429.3.D77
    South America: F2230.1.D75
Droop Mountain, Battle of, 1863:
  E475.76
Drug use
  Aztecs: F1219.76.D76
  Indians: E98.N5
    Colombia: F2270.1.N35
    Ecuador: F3721.3.N35
    Mexico: F1219.3.D83
    Peru: F3429.3.D79
    South America: F2230.1.D78
Drug uses
  Indians
    South America: F2230.1.N37
Drummond Island (Mich.): F572.D88
Drummond, Lake (Virginia): F232.D7
Druzes in the United States: E184.D78
Dry Fork River and region (West
  Virginia): F247.D79
Dry Tortugas
  Civil War operations, 1861: E471.53
Du Pont, Samuel Francis: E467.1.D9
Duane, James: E302.6.D8
Duane, William: E302.6.D82
Duane, William John: F153
Duarte, Juan Pablo: F1938.4
Dubuque (Iowa): F629.D8
Duché letters: E216
Duck Creek (Ohio): F497.H2
Duck Mountain Provincial Park
  (Manitoba): F1064.D8
Dudley Indians: E99.D8

Dudley, Thomas: F67
Dudley's defeat, 1813: E356.D8
Dufferin Co. (Ontario): F1059.D88
Dukhobors in Canada: F1035.D76
Dulany, Daniel: E278.D94
Dulce, Golfo (Costa Rica): F1549.D8
Dulles, John Foster: E748.D868
Duluth (Minnesota): F614.D8
Duncan, Joseph: F545
Dunes
  Illinois: F547.M56
  Indiana: F532.M67
Dunes region (Indiana): F532.M67
Dunes State Park (Indiana): F532.I5
Dunmore, Lake (Vermont): F57.A2
Dunmore's War, 1774: E83.77
Dunn, William McKee: E415.9.D9
Dunne, Edward Fitzsimons: F546
Duportail, Louis Lebegue de Presle:
  E207.D9
Durand de Villegagnon, Nicolas: F2529
Durango, Mexico (State): F1276
Durant, Thomas Jefferson: F374
Durazno, Uruguay (Dept.): F2731.D8
Durfee, Amos: F1032
Durham Co. (Ontario): F1059.D93
Durward's Glen (Wisconsin): F587.S2
Dutch
  Discovery and exploration of America
    Post-Columbian: E135.D9
    Pre-Columbian: E109.D9
Dutch America
  Dutch Guiana: F2401+
Dutch American Union, 1828-1845
  Dutch Guiana: F2424
Dutch attack of Puerto Rico, 1625:
  F1973
Dutch Blockade of Venezuela, 1908:
  F2325
Dutch colonies in America
  Brazil (1624-1654): F2532
  Connecticut: F97
  Dutch Guiana: F2423
  Dutch West Indies: F2141
  Guiana (early colonies): F2383,
    F2423
  New Netherlands (1610-1664): F122+

Dutch colonies in America
  New Sweden (1629-1664): F167
Dutch conquest of Brazil, 1624-1652:
  F2532
Dutch conquest of Delaware, 1655:
  F167
Dutch conquest of New Sweden: F167
Dutch conquest of New York: F122+
Dutch Guiana: F2401+
  Early history of separate colonies:
    F2383
  Raleigh's explorations, 1595-1617:
    E129.R2
Dutch in Argentina: F3021.D87
Dutch in Brazil: F2659.D7
Dutch in Canada: F1035.D8
Dutch in Cuba: F1789.D87
Dutch in South America: F2239.D8
Dutch in the American Revolution:
  E269.D88
Dutch in the United States: E184.D9
Dutch in Venezuela: F2349.D8
Dutch-Indian War, 1643-1645: E83.65
Dutch West India Company
  Dutch Guiana: F2423
Dutch West Indies: F2141
Dutra, Eurico Gasper: F2538
Duwamish Indians: E99.D9
Dwellings
  Indians: E98.D9
    Bolivia: F3320.1.D83
    Brazil: F2519.3.D84
    Mexico: F1219.3.D9
    Pre-Columbian America: E59.D9
  Mayas: F1435.3.D84
Dzibanché Site (Mexico): F1435.1.D83
Dzibilchaltún (Mexico): F1435.1.D85
Dzibilnocac Site (Mexico): F1435.1.D87

E

Eagle Creek and Valley, Alberta:
  F1079.E24
Eagle Lake (California): F868.L33
Eagle River and Valley (Colo.):
  F782.E15
Eagle's Mere (Pa.): F157.S67

Earle, Thomas: F153
Early, Jubal Anderson: E467.1.E13
Earthquakes
  Costa Rica: F1556.C3
  El Salvador: F1488
  Guatemala: F1466.4, F1466.45
  Jamaica: F1884, F1886
  Venezuela: F2324
East Baton Rouge Parish (La.):
  F377.E17
East Bay (California): F868.E22
East Boston (Mass.): F73.68.E2
East Carroll Parish (La.): F377.E2
East, Dept. of the, June-Aug., 1863:
  E475.5
East Europeans in Canada: F1035.E28
East Europeans in the United States:
  E184.E17
East Feliciana Parish (La.): F377.E3
East Florida: F314
  Revolution: E263.F6
East Gallatin River (Mont.): F737.G2
East Hampton (N.Y.): F129.E13
East Indians
  Discovery of America: E109.E2
East Indians in America: E29.E37
East Indians in British Guiana:
  F2391.E2
East Indians in Canada: F1035.E3
East Indians in Central America
  Panama: F1577.E37
East Indians in Jamaica: F1896.E2
East Indians in Suriname: F2431.E2
East Indians in the Caribbean:
  F2191.E27
East Indians in United States: E184.E2
East Jersey, 1676-1702: F137
East Maine Conference Seminary,
  Bucksport, and the Civil War:
  E541.E13
East North Central States: F476+
East Orange (N.J.): F144.O6
East St. Louis (Illinois): F549.E2
East Syrians in the United States:
  E184.C36
East Tennessee: F442.1

East Tennessee campaign, 1863:
  E475.85
Easter Island (Chile): F3169
Eastern Indian wars (New England),
  1722-1726: E83.72
Eastern North American Indians:
  E78.E2
Eastern shore of Maryland: F187.E2
Eastern shore of Virginia: F232.E2
Eastern Townships (Québec):
  F1054.E13
Eaton, William: E302.6.E16
Ebey's Landing National Historical
  Preserve (Wash.): F897.I7
Ecab, Mexico (Mayas): F1435.1.E32
Ece'je Indians: F3430.1.E78
Echeverría, Esteban: F2846
Echeverría, Luis: F1235.5.E25
Ecleto Creek and Valley (Texas):
  F392.W7
Economic conditions
  African Americans: E185.8
  Aztecs: F1219.76.E36
  Indians: E98.E2
    Chile: F3069.3.E2
    Colombia: F2270.1.E3
    Ecuador: F3721.3.E25
    Guatemala: F1465.3.E2
    Mexico: F1219.3.E2
    Peru: F3429.3.E2
    Pre-Columbian America: E59.E3
    South America: F2230.1.E25
    Venezuela: F2319.3.E26
  Jews: E184.36.E25
  Mayas: F1435.3.E27
Ecuador: F3701+
  Leticia dispute, 1932-1934:
    F2281.B7P1+
  Member of Republic of Colombia,
    1822-1830: F2274, F3734
  Military history
    Civil wars: F3736
      Conquistadors: F3733
    Wars of independence, 1809-1830:
      F3734
Ecuadorians in the United States:
  E184.E28

Eden Valley (Wyoming): F767.S9
Edisto Island (S.C.): F277.B3
Edisto River and Valley (S.C.):
F277.E25
Edmonton (Alberta): F1079.5.E3
Education
Aztecs: F1219.76.E38
Indians
Bolivia: F3320.1.E4
Brazil: F2519.3.E2
Central America: F1434.2.E38
Chile: F3069.3.E38
Colombia: F2270.1.E36
Ecuador: F3721.3.E35
French Guiana: F2460.2.E38
Guatemala: F1465.3.E25
Mexico: F1219.3.E3
Nicaragua: F1525.3.E38
North America: E96+
Paraguay: F2679.3.E38
Peru: F3429.3.E3
Pre-Columbian America: E59.E4
South America: F2230.1.E37
Venezuela: F2319.3.E29
Mayas: F1435.3.E37
Educations
Indians
Costa Rica: F1545.3.E38
Edward's Ferry, Action near, 1861:
E472.63
Edwards, Ninian: F545
Edwards Plateau (Texas): F392.E33
Edzná Site (Mexico): F1435.1.E37
Egg Harbor, N.J., Skirmish of, 1778:
E241.L7
Egyptian influences
Indians
Peru: F3429.3.E35
Egyptians
Discovery of America: E109.E3
Egyptians in the United States:
E184.E38
Eiriksson, Leiv: E105
Eisenhower, Dwight David:
E742.5.E37+, E836
Administrations, 1953-1961: E835+
Family: E837

Eisenhower, Mamie (Doud): E837
Ekab, Mexico: F1435.1.E32
El Arbolillo (Mexico)
Indian antiquities: F1219.1.T43
El Beni, Bolivia (Dept.): F3341.B4
El Camino Real (Colorado): F868.E28
El Camino Real de Tierra Adentro
National Historic Trail: F392.E36
New Mexico: F802.E45
Texas: F392.E36
El Caney, Battle of, 1898: E717.1
El Dorado: E121+
El Dorado Lake (Kansas): F687.B9
El Gran Chaco: F2876
El Loa (Chile): F3170
El Malpais National Monument (N.M.):
F802.C54
El Misti (Volcano): F3451.A7
El Morrow National Monument (N.M.):
F802.E5
El Oro, Ecuador (Province): F3741.E4
El Paso Co. (Texas): F392.E38
El Paso (Texas): F394.E4
El Salvador: F1481+
Confederación de Centro América:
F1438, F1487
Military history
Wars with
Guatemala: F1466.45, F1487.5
Honduras: F1487.5, F1507.5
Wars with Nicaragua (Invasion):
F1527
Elbert, Samuel: E207.E3
Eldorado Canyon (Colo.): F782.B6
Electoral Commission, 1877: E680
Electronic information resource catalogs
United States history: E175.88
Eleven Point Wild and Scenic River
(Mo.): F472.E4
Elgin Co. (Ontario): F1059.E4
Elizabeth City (N.C.)
Capture, 1862: E473.3
Elizabeth City Parish (Virginia):
F232.E6
Elizabeth Islands (Mass.): F72.E5
Elizabeth (New Jersey): F144.E4
Battle of, 1780: E241.E39

Elizabeth River and Valley (Virginia): F232.E62

Elizabethtown, N.C., Battle of, 1781: E241.E4

Elk Island National Park (Alberta): F1079.E5

Elk River and Valley (B.C.): F1089.E38

Elk River and Valley (West Virginia: F247.E4

Ellery, William: E302.6.E3

Ellesmere Island (Nunavut): F1144.E44

Elliot, Jesse Duncan: E353.1.E4

Elliott Island (Md.): F187.D6

Elliott, Stephen: E467.1.E4

Ellsworth Canyon (Nevada): F847.N9

Ellsworth, Ephraim Elmer: E467.1.E47

Ellsworth, Oliver: E302.6.E4

Elmira (New York)
  Civil War prison: E616.E4

Elmwood (Pa.): F158.68.E4

Eloida Lake region (Ontario): F1059.E46

Elqui River and Valley (Chile): F3170.5

Elsinore, Lake and region (Calif.): F868.R6

Emancipation of slaves
  United States: E453

Emancipation Proclamation: E453

Embargo, 1794: E313+

Embera Indians: F2270.2.E43

Embroidery
  Indians: E98.E5
  Mayas: F1435.3.E52

Emerald Bay and region (Calif.): F868.O6

Emerald Coast
  Florida: F317.G8

Emerillon Indians: F2460.1.E5

Emigrant Trail (Calif.): F868.S5

Empire Mine State Historic Park (Calif.): F868.N5

Employment
  Aztecs: F1219.76.E47
  Indians: E98.E6
    Chile: F3069.3.E46
    Peru: F3429.3.E45
    Pre-Columbian America: E59.E3

Employment
  Indians
    Venezuela: F2319.3.E46

Enauenê-Nauê Indians: F2520.1.S24

Encantadas (Islands), Ecuador: F3741.G2

Encarnación (Paraguay): F2695.E5

Enchanted Hill (California): F868.S18

Enchanted Islands (Ecuador): F3741.G2

Enchanted Rock State Natural Area (Texas): F392.E64

Endecott, John: F67

Endless Caverns (Virginia): F232.S47

Endless Mountains (Pa.): F157.E45

Ene River and Valley (Peru): F3451.J9

English colonies in America: E162, E188
  Bahamas: F1650+
  Bermudas: F1630+
  British Guiana: F2383
  British West Indies: F2131
  Cuba: F1781
  Falkland Islands: F3031
  Florida (1763-1783): F314
  Florida, West and East: F301
  Jamaica (1655-): F1861+
  New Haven Colony: F98
  New Plymouth Colony: F68
  Newfoundland: F1121+
  Roanoke Colonies (Virginia), 1584-1590: F229
  To 1776: E163, E186+

English conquest of
  Delaware, 1664: F167
  New France, 1629: F1030
  New Netherlands, 1664: F122.1, F167

English explorers of America: E127+

English invasion of Nicaragua, 1780-1781: F1526.25

English settlement
  Illinois: F547.E3

English settlements
  Dutch Guiana: F2423
  French Guiana: F2462

English-speaking Canadians:
F1035.E53
English-speaking Caribbean: F2130
English West Indian expeditions
1654-1655, 1695: F1621
1739-1742: F2272.5
Enid (Oklahoma): F704.E6
Entiat Indians: E99.E42
Entre Rios, Argentina (Province):
F2896
Indian antiquities: F2821.1.E5
Epena Saija Indians: F2270.2.E53
Epidemics
Guatemala: F1466.45
Ericson (Ericsson), Leif: E105
Ericsson Monument (Washington, D.C.):
F203.4.E6
Erie, Fort
Siege, 1814: E356.E5
Erie Indians: E99.E5
Erie, Lake, Battle of, 1813: E356.E6
Erie, Lake, region: F555
New York: F127.E65
Ohio: F497.E6
Ontario: F1059.E6
Pennsylvania: F157.E6
Erie (Pa.): F159.E7
Escalante Canyon (Colorado):
F782.E82
Escalante River and Valley(Utah):
F832.E83
Escobedo, Mariana: F1233
Escondido Valley (Calif.): F868.S15
Ese Ejja Indians: F3430.1.E78
Eskimauan Indians: E99.E7
Eskimos: E99.E7
Esmeralda Indians: F3722.1.E8
Esmeraldas, Ecuador (Province):
F3741.E6
Esopus Indian wars, 1659-1664:
E83.663
Esopus Indians: E99.E8
Espanola Valley (New Mexico):
F802.E8
Espionage in the United States: E743.5
Espírito Santo (Brazil): F2561

Espiritu Pampa, Peru
Indian antiquities: F3429.1.E7
Esselen Indians: E99.E85
Essequibo Co. (British Guiana):
F2387.E8
Essequibo (Dutch Colony): F2383,
F2423
Essex Co. (Ontario): F1059.E7
Essex (U.S. ironclad): E474.11
Estates, Trust
Indians: E98.F3
Estatoe River (N.C.): F262.A9
Estes Park region (Colo.): F782.L2
Esther Mountain (N.Y.): F127.A2
Estigarribia, José Félix: F2689
Estimé, Dumarsais: F1927
Estonians in Brazil: F2659.E8
Estonians in Canada: F1035.E85
Estonians in the United States:
E184.E7
Estrada Cabrera, Manuel: F1466.45
Estrada Palma, Tomás: F1787
Ethics
Indians: E98.E83
Ethiopians in Canada: F1035.E89
Ethiopians in the United States:
E184.E74
Ethnic elements
Latin America: F1419.A1+
Mexico: F1392.A1+
Ethnic identity
Indians
Argentina: F2821.3.E84
Bolivia: F3320.1.E84
Brazil: F2519.3.E83
Colombia: F2270.1.E84
Ecuador: F3721.3.E84
Guatemala: F1465.3.E84
Mexico: F1219.3.E79
Nicaragua: F1525.3.E74
North America: E98.E85
Peru: F3429.3.E84
Pre-Columbian America: E59.E75
South America: F2230.1.E84
West Indies: F1619.3.E83
Jews: E184.36.E84
Mayas: F1435.3.E72

Ethnic relations
    Jews: E184.36.E86
Ethnicity
    Indians
        West Indies: F1619.3.E83
Ethnobiology
    Indians: E98.B54
        Colombia: F2270.1.E85
        Mayas: F1435.3.E73
        Nicaragua: F1525.3.E76
Ethnobotany
    Aztecs: F1219.76.E83
    Indians: E98.B7
        Brazil: F2519.3.E85
        Chile: F3069.3.E84
        Colombia: F2270.1.E86
        Ecuador: F3721.3.E85
        Mexico: F1219.3.E82
        Peru: F3429.3.E86
        South America: F2230.1.B7
        West Indies: F1619.3.E85
    Mayas: F1435.3.E74
Ethnobotany, African American:
    E185.89.E8
Ethnozoology
    Aztecs: F1219.76.E85
    Indians
        Colombia: F2270.1.E88
        Mexico: F1219.3.E83
        South America: F2230.1.E87
    Mayas: F1435.3.E76
Euclid Creek (Ohio): F497.C9
Eugene (Oregon): F884.E9
European intervention in Mexico, 1961-
    1867: F1233
Europeans in America: E29.E87
Europeans in Brazil: F2659.E95
Europeans in Jamaica: F1896.E87
Europeans in Latin America:
    F1419.E87
Europeans in the United States:
    E184.E95
Eutaw Springs, Battle of, S.C., 1781:
    E241.E86
Evacuation Day
    New York City: E239
Evangeline Parish (La.): F377.E8

Evans, John: F780
Evans, Robley Dunglison: E182
Evanston (Illinois): F549.E8
Evansville (Indiana): F534.E9
Evarts, William Maxwell: E664.E88
Everard, Sir Richard: F257
Everett, Edward: E340.E8
    Collected works: E337.8.E9
Everett, Mount (Mass.): F72.B5
Everglades (Florida): F317.E9
Everglades National Park: F317.E9
Ewell, Richard Stoddert: E467.1.E86
Ewing, Charles: E467.1.E9
Ewing, Thomas: E340.E9
Ex-slaves, African Americans: E185.2,
    E185.93.A+
Excavations
    Archaeology: E51+
Expansion
    United States: E179.5
Expunging resolutions, 1834-1835:
    E384.7
Extraterrestrial influences
    Mayas: F1435.3.E87
Eyak Indians: E99.E9
Eyre, Edward John: F1886

F

Fair Deal period
    United States history: E813
Fair Haven Beach State Park (N.Y.):
    F127.C5
Fair Oaks, Battle of, 1862: E473.65
Fairbanks (Alaska): F914.F16
Fairfield (Connecticut)
    Burning by the British, 1779:
        E241.F16
Fairfield, John: E340.F16
Fairmount Park (Philadelphia):
    F158.65.F2
Fairmount Parkway (Philadelphia):
    F158.67.F17
Fairweather, Mount (Alaska): F912.F2
Falcón, Venezuela (State): F2331.F2
Falkland Islands: F2936, F3031+
    War of 1982: F3031.5

Falls of Schuylkill (Pennsylvania): F158.68.F2

Falmouth (Me.): F29.P9

Family
Jews: E184.36.S65

Faneuil Hall Market (Boston): F73.8.F2

Fanning, David: E278.F2

Far Rockaway (New York): F129.R8

Far West (U.S.): F590.2+

Farallon Islands (California): F868.F24

Fargo (N.D.): F644.F2

Farley, James Aloysius: E748.F24

Farragut, David Glasgow: E467.1.F23

Farragut, George: E302.6.F24

Farrapos, Revolution of the, 1835-1841: F2621

Farrar, Edgar Howard: F375

Fascist propaganda in the United States: E743.5

Father Hennepin State Park (Minnesota): F612.F25

Fathers of U.S. Presidents: E176.25

Fathom Five Provincial Park (Ontario): F1059.F3

Faustino I, Emperor of Haiti: F1926

Fayette Co. (West Virginia)\: F247.F2

Fayetteville (Arkansas), Battle of, 1863: E474.94

Feather River, Canyon, and Valley (California): F868.F3

Featherwork
Indians
Brazil: F2519.3.F4
Paraguay: F2679.3.F42
South America: F2230.1.F2

Federalism vs. unitarism (Argentina): F2846

Federalists
Opposition to War of 1812: E357.6+

Federmann, Nikolaus: E125.F3

Feijo, Diogo Antonio: F2536

Félicité, Salomon: F1926

Felipe Carrillo Puerto (Mexico)
Mayas: F1435.1.F45

Felton, William Harrell: F291

Fenian invasion, 1870-1871: F1033

Fenian Raids, 1866-1877: F1032

Fenwick, John: F137

Fenwick's colony (N.J.): F142.S2

Fernandes Vieira, João: F2532

Fernández, Juan: E125.F35

Fernández Lindo y Zelaya, Juan Nepomuceno: F1507.5

Fernández Madrid, José: F2274

Fernando de Noronha Island, Brazil (Territory): F2564

Fessenden, William Pitt: E415.9.F4

Field, David Dudley: E415.9.F5

Field, Maunsell Bradhurst: E415.9.F55

Field, Richard Stockton: F138

Field, Stephen Johnson: E664.F46

Fifth Avenue (New York): F128.67.F4

Fifth column activity: E743.5

Figueiredo, João Baptista de Oliveira: F2538.27.F53

Figueres, José: F1548

Filibuster wars
Central America: F1438
Honduras: F1507.5
Nicaragua: F1526.27

Filibusters
Cuba: F1784

Filipinos in Canada: F1035.F48

Filipinos in the United States: E184.F4

Fillmore, Fort, Evacuation of, 1861: E472.32

Fillmore, Millard: E427
Administration, 1850-1853: E426

Film catalogs
United States history: E175.87

Finance
Indian education
United States: E97.3

Financial affairs
Indians: E98.F3

Fincastle Co. (Virginia): F232.F38

Finger Lakes region (New York): F127.F4

Finlay River and Valley (B.C.): F1089.F5

Finns in Argentina: F3021.F56

Finns in Canada: F1035.F5

Finns in Latin America: F1419.F56

Finns in the United States: E184.F5

Fintry Provincial Park (B.C.):
F1089.F54
Fire Island (N.Y.): F127.S9
Fire Island State Park (N.Y.): F127.S9
Fire use
Indians: E98.F38
Firelands (Ohio): F497.W5
Fires
Boston: F73.4
Chicago, 1871: F548.42
New York City: F128.44
Salvador: F1496.S2
First contact with Europeans
Indians
Argentina: F2821.3.F57
North America: E98.F39
Peru: F3429.3.F55
Pre-Columbian America: E59.F53
First Defenders, 1861: E493.9
First Presbyterian Church
(Philadelphia): F158.62.F5
Fish, Hamilton: E664.F52
Fisher, Fort (North Carolina)
Expeditions against, 1864: E477.28
Expeditions against, 1865: E477.63
Fisher's Hill, Battle of, 1864: E477.33
Fishers Island (New York): F127.F5,
F129.S74
Fishing
Indians: E98.F4
Chile: F3069.3.F57
Mexico: F1219.3.F57
Peru: F3429.3.F57
Mayas: F1435.3.F57
Fisk, Clinton Bowen: E664.F53
Fitzhugh's Woods, Ark., Battle of, 1864:
E476.35
FitzSimmons, Thomas: E302.6.F56
Five Civilized Tribes
After 1907: E78.O45
Before 1907: E78.I5
Five Forks (Virginia), Battle of, 1865:
E477.67
Five Islands (La.): F377.F57
Flags
United States
Civil War: E646

Flags
United States
Civil War
Alabama: E495.4
Confederate states: E551.4
Revolution: E289
War of 1898: E734
Flamborough Head (England), Battle of,
1779: E241.F55
Flaming Gorge National Recreation
Area
Utah: F832.F52
Wyoming: F767.F5
Flancs-de-Chien Indians: E99.T4
Flatbush (New York, N.Y.): F129.F5
Flatbush (Ulster County, N.Y.):
F129.F503
Flathead Indian Reservation
Montana: E99.S2
Flathead Lake and Valley (Mont.):
F737.F6
Flathead (Salish) Indians: E99.S2
Flemings in the Dominican Republic:
F1941.F5
Flemings in the United States:
E184.F57
Flint Hills
Kansas: F687.F55
Oklahoma: F702.F55
Flint River and Valley (Georgia):
F292.F57
Floods
Mississippi River: F354
Ohio River Valley: F519
United States: E179
Flores, Juan José: F3736
Flores, Uruguay (Dept.): F2731.F5
Florida: F306+
African Americans: E185.93.F5
Confederate history: E558+
Counties, etc: F317.A+
Expedition against South Carolina,
1680: F272
Huguenot colony destroyed, 1565:
F314
Indians: E78.F6
Reconstruction, 1865-1877: F316

Florida
  Slavery: E445.F6
  Spanish Florida claims: F314
  Wars
    Civil War: E502+, E558+
      Military operations: E470.7
    Indian wars: E83.813, E83.817,
      E83.835, E83.855
    Revolution: E263.F6
    War of 1812: E359.5.F6
      Military operations: E355
    War of 1898: E726.F6
    War with Mexico: E409.5.F5
Florida expedition, 1864: E476.43
Florida Keys: F317.M7
Florida National Scenic Trail: F317.F63
Florida parishes (La.): F377.F6
Florida (Privateer): E599.F6
Florida, Republic of, 1812-1816: F314
Florida, Uruguay (Dept.): F2731.F55
Florida War, 1835-1842: E83.835
Flower, Roswell Pettibone: F124
Floy, Michael: F128.44
Floyd, John: F230
Floyd, John Buchanan: E415.9.F64
Flusser, Charles Williamson:
  E467.1.F64
Flying D Ranch (Mont.): F737.F66
Flynn, Edward Joseph: F128.5
Foggy Bottom (D.C.): F202.F64
Fogo Island (Newfoundland): F1124.F6
Folk, Joseph Wingate: F466
Folk literature
  Indians: E98.F58
    South America: F2230.1.F56
Folklore
  Aztecs: F1219.76.F65
  Eskimos: E99.E7
  Indians
    Argentina: F2821.3.F6
    Bolivia: F3320.1.F6
    Brazil: F2519.3.F6
    Central America: F1434.2.F6
    Chile: F3069.3.F64
    Colombia: F2270.1.F6
    Costa Rica: F1545.3.F6
    Ecuador: F3721.3.F65

Folklore
  Indians
    French Guiana: F2460.2.F64
    Guatemala: F1465.3.F6
    Guyana: F2380.2.F6
    Mexico: F1219.3.F6
    North America: E98.F6
    Panama: F1565.3.F64
    Paraguay: F2679.3.F64
    Peru: F3429.3.F6
    Pre-Columbian America: E59.F6
    South America: F2230.1.F6
    Venezuela: F2319.3.F6
    West Indies: F1619.3.F6
  Mayas: F1435.3.F6
Folly Island (S.C.): F277.C4
Folsom culture: E99.F65
Fonseca, Manuel Deodoro da: F2537
Food
  Aztecs: F1219.76.F67
  Indians: E98.F7
    Argentina: F2821.3.F7
    Bolivia: F3320.1.F64
    Brazil: F2519.3.F63
    Ecuador: F3721.3.F7
    Mexico: F1219.3.F64
    Peru: F3429.3.F65
    Pre-Columbian America: E59.F63
    South America: F2230.1.F66
  Mayas: F1435.3.F7
Foote, Andrew Hull: E467.1.F68
Foote, Henry Stuart: E415.9.F7
Footwear
  Indians: E98.F73
Foraker, Joseph Benson: E664.F69
Forbes Road (Pa.): F157.F65
Force, Peter
  Tracts and other papers: E187.F69
Ford, Gerald R.: E865+
Ford Theatre (Washington, D.C.):
  F204.F6
Ford, Thomas: F545
Fordham Manor (N.Y.): F127.W5
Foreign intervention in Cuba: F1786
Foreign intervention in Mexico, 1861-
  1867: F1233

Foreign intervention in Nicaragua, 1848-: F1526.27

Foreign intervention in Uruguay: F2726

Foreign public opinion
  United States
    Civil War: E469.8
    Revolution: E249.3

Foreign relations
  United States: E183.7+
    By period
      1783-1789: E303
      1865-1900: E661.7
      20th century: E744+, E840+
      Civil War, 1861-1865: E469+
      Revolution, 1775-1783: E249
      War of 1812: E358
      War with Mexico, 1845-1848: E408

Foreigners in the United States
  American Revolution: E269.F67
  Civil War: E540.F6

Forest Lawn Memorial Park (Glendale, California): F869.G5

Forest of Nisene Marks State Park (Calif.): F868.S3

Forest reserve parks
  United States: E160

Forests, National
  United States: E160

Forestville State Park (Minnesota): F612.F4

Formosa, Argentina (Territory): F2901

Fornio Indians: F2520.1.F8

Forrest, Nathan Bedford: E467.1.F72
  Expedition into West Tennessee, 1861-1863: E474.46
  Expedition into west Tennessee and Kentucky: E476.17

Forrest's Cavalry Corps
  Confederate Army: E547.F6

Fort Abraham Lincoln State Park (N.D.): F642.M7

Fort Ancient culture: E99.F67

Fort Anne Park (Nova Scotia): F1039.A2

Fort Beauséjour National Park (N.B.): F1044.F6

Fort Beauséjour, Siege of, 1755: E199

Fort Chambly National Historic Park (Québec): F1054.C44

Fort Churchill Historic State Monument (Nevada): F847.F6

Fort Clatsop National Memorial (Oregon): F882.C53

Fort Custer (Mont.): F737.Y4

Fort Dearborn Massacre, 1812: E356.C53

Fort Frederica National Monument: F292.F7

Fort Jefferson National Monument: F317.M7

Fort Loudoun Lake (Tennessee): F443.L9

Fort Louisburg National Historic Park (Nova Scotia): F1039.5.L8

Fort Macon (N.C.)
  Siege, 1862: E473.3

Fort McHenry National Monument and Historic Shrine: E356.B2

Fort Pillow State Park (Tennessee): F443.L35

Fort Raleigh National Historic Site (N.C.): F262.R4

Fort Ridgeley Battle, 1862: E83.86

Fort Rock Valley (Oregon): F882.L15

Fort Ross, Franklin District (Trading post): F1105.5.F6

Fort Shaw Indian School (Great Falls, Mont.): E97.6.F66

Fort Sisseton State Park (S.D.): F657.R6

Fort Smith, Mackenzie District: F1100.5.F6

Fort Snelling (Minnesota): F614.F7

Fort Stevens State Park (Oregon): F882.C53

Fort Valley (Arizonia): F817.C6

Fort Wayne (Indiana): F534.F7

Fort Worth (Texas): F394.F7

Fortaleza (Brazil): F2651.F6

Fortress of Louisburg National Historic Park (Nova Scotia): F1039.5.L8

Forty Mile Coulee and Valley (Alberta): F1079.F67

Forty Mile Coulee Reservoir (Alberta):
F1079.F67
Forty-Second Street, New York:
F128.67.F7
Fortymile Rive and Valley
Alaska: F912.F67
Fortymile River and Valley: F912.F67
Foster, George Eulas: F1033
Founders and Patriots of America:
E186.6
Four Corners Region: F788.5
Indians: E78.S7
Fourth of July: E286.A1+
Fowler, John: E302.6.F6
Fox Indians: E99.F7
Fox Islands (Michigan): F572.L45
Fox River and Valley
Illinois: F547.F77
Wisconsin
Columbia Co.-Brown Co: F587.F72
Waukesha Co: F587.F7
France
Attacks on Venezuela, 1679: F2322
Attempted invasion of Jamaica, 1694,
1782, 1806: F1884
Blockade of
Argentine coast, 1838: F2846.3
Rio de la Plata, 1845-1848:
F2846.3
Conquest of British Guiana, 1782:
F2383
Discovery and exploration of America:
E131+
Military history in America
American Revolution: E265
Naval operations in West Indies,
1775-1783: E271
Relations with U.S., 1789-1797:
E313+
Sale of Louisiana: E333
Troubles with Mexico, 1838-1839:
F1232
Troubles with U.S., 1796-1800: E323
Frances Lake (Yukon): F1095.F7
Francia, Juan Carlos: F2686
Franciscan missions
California: F862, F864

Franco, Rafael: F2688
Franconia Notch: F41.6.F8
Frank Church-River of No Return
Wilderness (Idaho): F752.F68
Frankford Arsenal: F158.8.A7
Frankfort (Kentucky): F459.F8
Frankland: F436
Franklin, Benjamin: E302.6.F7+
Collected works: E302.6.F8
Franklin District (Canada): F1101+
Eskimos: E99.E7
Indians: E78.F73
Franklin Mountains, Mackenzie District:
F1100.F7
Franklin Parish (La.): F377.F7
Franklin Park (Boston): F73.65
Franklin (State): F436
Franklin (Tennessee), Battle of, 1864:
E477.52
Franklin, William: F137
Franklin, William Buel: E467.1.F83
Franquistas (Paraguay): F2689
Fraser River and Valley (B.C.):
F1089.F7
Frayser's Farm, Battle of, 1862:
E473.68
Frederick Parish (Va.): F232.C59
Fredericksburg and Spotsylvania
County National Military Park:
E474.85
Fredericksburg, Battle of, 1862:
E474.85
Fredericksburg (Va.): F234.F8
Fredericksville Parish (Virginia):
F232.F76
Fredericktown, Mo., Battle of, 1861:
E472.2
Fredericton (N.B.): F1044.5.F8
Fredonian Insurrection, 1826-1827:
F389
Free African Americans: E185
Biography (General): E185.97.A+
The South to 1863: E185.18
Free states (U.S.), Slaves in: E450
Freedman's Farm, Battle of, 1777:
E241.S2

Freedmen
  United States: E185.2, E185.93.A+
Freedmen's Bureau: E185.2
Freeland, Fort, Warrior Run, Pa., Battle
  of, 1779: E241.F74
Freemasons
  Abraham Lincoln: E457.2
  George Washington: E312.17
    Letters: E312.75.M4+
    Masonic Memorial (Alexandria, Va.):
      F234.A3
Frelinghuysen, Theodore: E340.F86
Fremont Co
  Iowa: F627.F8
Fremont culture: E99.F75
Frémont, John Charles: E415.9.F8
  In California: F864
  In the West: F592
  Land grant (California): F868.M4
French America: F1170+
  French Guiana: F2441+
  French West Indies: F2151
  Saint Pierre and Miquelon: F1170
French and Indian War, 1755-1763:
  E199
French army in Mexico: F1233
French auxiliaries in the American
  Revolution: E265
French Broad River and Valley
  North Carolina: F262.F85
  Tennessee: F443.F8
French Canadian families: F1051+
French Canadian question: F1027
French Canadians: F1027
  United States: E184.F85
French colonies in America
  Acadia (1600-1763): F1038
  Brazil
    Marajó Island (1612-1618): F2568
    Rio de Janeiro (1555-1567): F2529
  Florida (1562-1565): F314
    West Florida: F301
  French Guiana: F2462
  French West Indies: F2151
  Hispaniola: F1923, F1938.3
  Illinois country (before 1775): F544

French colonies in America
  La Salle's colony (Texas), 1685-1687:
    F352
  Louisiana (1698-1803): F372
  Louisiana (1764-1803): F373
  Louisiana Purchase: E333
  Mississippi Valley before 1803: F352
  Saint Domingue (1677-1803): F1923
  Saint Pierre and Miquelon: F1170
French explorers of America: E131+
French Guiana: F2441+
  Raleigh's explorations, 1595-1617:
    E129.R2
French Huguenot colonies, 1562-1565:
  F314
French in America: E29.F8
French in Argentina: F3021.F8
French in Brazil: F2659.F8
French in Canada: F1035.F8
  French Canadians: F1027
French in Chile: F3285.F8
French in Cuba: F1789.F7
French in Haiti: F1930.F7
French in Latin America: F1419.F75
French in Mexico: F1392.F8
French in Paraguay: F2699.F7
French in Peru: F3619.F74
French in the United States: E184.F8
  French Canadians: E184.F85
French in Uruguay: F2799.F7
French in Venezuela: F2349.F73
French Indians: E99.M693
French Louisiana: F372
French Prairie (Oregon): F882.W6
French River and Valley (Ontario):
  F1059.F85
French, Samuel Gibbs: E467.1.F87
French spoliation claims after 1800:
  E336+
French Valley (Calif.): F868.R6
French West Florida: F301
French West Indies: F2151
Frenchtown, Battle of, 1813: E356.R2
Friends, Society of
  Persecution in Massachusetts before
    1775: F67
  United States: E184.F89

Friends, Society of
  War work
    Civil War: E540.F8
    Revolution: E269.F8
Friendship Long Island
  Maine: F27.K7
Fries Rebellion, 1798-1799: E326
Frijoles Canyon (N.M.): F802.B25
Frio River and Valley (Texas):
  F392.F92
Fripp Island (S.C.): F277.B3
Frisians in the United States:
  E184.F894
Fritchie, Barbara (Hauer): E467.1.F9
Frobisher Bay (Franklin District)
  Canada: F1105.F74
Fromme, Lynette
  Biography: E866.3
Front Range
  Colorado: F782.F88
Front Range (Colorado and Wyoming)
  Wyoming: F767.F88
Frontenac Co. (Ontario): F1059.F9
Frontenac, Fort
  Capture, 1758: E199
Frontenac, Louis de Buade, comte de:
  F1030
Frontenac Provincial Park (Ontario):
  F1059.F9
Frontenac's Expedition, 1696: E83.69
Frontier, American: E179.5
Frontier and pioneer life
  Canadian Northwest: F1060.94
  United States: E161.5+
  West (U.S.): F596
Fuca, Juan de: E125.F9
Fuegians: F2986
Fuego, Tierra del (Island): F2986
Fugitive slaves
  United States: E450
Fujimori, Alberto: F3448.7.F85
Fulnio Indians: F2520.1.F8
Fulton Chain Lakes and Region (New
  York): F127.F88
Fundy, Bay of (Nova Scotia): F1039.F9
Fundy National Park (New Brunswick):
  F1044.F86

Funeral customs and rites
  Aztecs: F1219.76.F86
  Mayas: F1435.3.F85
Funeral rites and customs
  Indians
    Colombia: F2270.1.F85
    Mexico: F1219.3.F85
    Peru: F3429.3.F85
Funk Island (Newfoundland): F1124.F9
Furnam, Moore: E263.N5
Furniture
  Indians: E98.D9
Future life
  Indian religion: E98.R3

G

Gabbs Valley
  Nevada: F847.G32
Gabrieleño Indians: E99.G15
Gadsden, Christopher: E207.G2
Gadsden Purchase, 1853: F786
Gaines, Edmund Pendleton:
  E353.1.G14
Gaines' Mill, Battle of, 1862: E473.68
Galápagos Islands (Ecuador):
  F3741.G2
Gales, Joseph: F198
Galicia, Nueva: F1296
Galicians (Spain) in America: E29.G26
Galicians (Spain) in Chile: F3285.G25
Galicians (Spain) in Uruguay:
  F2799.G25
Gallatin, Albert: E302.6.G16
Gallatin Valley (Mont.): F737.G2
Gallegans in Argentina: F3021.G2
Gallegans in Cuba: F1789.G3
Gallegans in Latin America: F1419.G2
Gallegans in Venezuela: F2349.G24
Gallego Island (Mexico): F1335
Gallipolis (Ohio)
  Scioto Land Company: F483
Galloway, Joseph: E278.G14
Galt, Sir Alexander Tilloch: F1032
Galveston (Texas): F394.G2
Galveston (Texas), Battle of, 1863:
  E474.1

Gamarra, Agustín: F3447
Gambians in the United States:
  E184.G24
Gambling
  Indians
    North America: E98.G18
Gambling on Indian reservations
  North America: E98.G18
Games
  Aztecs: F1219.76.G35
  Indians
    Bolivia: F3320.1.G35
    Brazil: F2519.3.G3
    Guyana: F2380.2.G3
    Mexico: F1219.3.G3
    North America: E98.G2
    Peru: F3429.3.G3
    Pre-Columbian America: E59.G3
    South America: F2230.1.G2
Gander (Newfoundland): F1124.5.G3
G.A.R.: E462.1
Garay, Juan de: F2841
Garças River (Brazil): F2576
García, Calixto: F1783
García, Diego de Moguer: E125.G2
García Granados, Miguel: F1466.45
García Menocal, Mario de: F1787
García Moreno, Gabriel: F3736
Garcilaso de la Vega, el Inca: F3444
Garden of the Gods (Colo.): F782.E3
Gardiner Manor (N.Y.): F129.E13
Gardiner's Island (N.Y.): F129.E13
Gardner, Augustus Peabody: E664.G2
Garfield Co. (Colo.): F782.G3
Garfield Colony (Alabama): F332.B6
Garfield, James Abram: E660.G2+,
  E687
  Administration, 1881: E686
  Memorial, Philadelphia: F158.64.G3
  Statue, Washington, D.C.: F203.4.G2
Garibaldi, Giuseppe: F2536
Garibaldi Provincial Park (B.C.):
  F1089.G3
Garner, John Nance: E748.G23
Garrison mob, Boston, 1835: E450
Garrison, William Lloyd: E449

Garry, Fort (Lower) (Manitoba):
  F1064.G22
Gaspar Rodríguez, José: F2686
Gaspé District (Québec): F1054.G2
Gaspé Peninsula (Québec): F1054.G2
Gaspee affair, June 1772: E215.6
Gaspesie, La (Québec): F1054.G2
Gaston, William: E340.G2
Gates, Horatio: E207.G3
Gates of the Arctic National Park and
  Preserve (Alaska): F912.G36
Gateway National Recreation Area:
  F127.G15
  New Jersey: F142.G37
  New York: F127.G15
Gatineau River and Valley (Québec):
  F1054.G26
Gauchos
  Argentina: F2926
  Brazil: F2621
  Paraguay: F2682.9
  Uruguay: F2722.9
Gaviões Indians: F2520.1.G37
Gayarré, Charles Étienne Arthur: F374
Gaynor, William Jay: F128.5
Gazos Creek and Valley (California):
  F868.G39
Ge Indians: F2520.1.G4
Geary, John White: E467.1.G29
Geffrard, Fabre Nicolas: F1926
Geisel, Ernesto: F2538.27.G44
Gem Valley (Idaho): F752.C3
Genealogía de Zolín (Codices):
  F1219.56.G46+
Genealogy
  African Americans: E185.96+
  American colonists: E187.5, E302.5
  Indians: E98.G44
    Ecuador: F3721.3.G45
    Peru: F3429.3.G4
  United States
    West (U.S.): F590.5
General Grant Grove area (California):
  F868.K48
General Grant National Park
  (California): F868.K48

General Slocum (Steamboat) Disaster, 1904: F128.5
Genet, E. C.: E313+
Genoa Columbus celebration, 1892: E119
Gentile Valley (Idaho): F752.C3
Geode State Park (Iowa): F627.H5
Geography, Historical
  America: E21.7
  Latin America: F1408.8
  United States: E179.5
George Dawson, Mount (B.C.): F1089.C7
George, Fort (Ontario)
  Battle, 1812: E356.G4
George III, "Olive branch" petition to (1775): E215.95
George, James Zachariah: E664.G34
George, Lake (New York): F127.G3
  Battle, 1775: E199
George Rogers Clark Memorial Park (Ohio): F497.C5
George Washington Memorial Parkway (Virginia): F232.G38
George Washington Parkway: F232.G38
George Washington-Robert Morris-Haym Salomon Monument (Chicago, Illinois): F548.64.G4
Georgetown (British Guiana): F2389.G3
Georgetown (D.C.): F202.G3
  Saint John's Church: F203.2.S14
Georgia: F281+
  African Americans: E185.93.G4
  Cession of western lands: F290
  Confederate history: E559+
  Counties, etc: F292.A+
  Indians: E78.G3
  Reconstruction, 1865-1877: F291
  Saint Augustine expeditions, 1740, 1743: F314
  Slavery: E445.G3
  South Carolina cession, 1787: F292.B7
  Wars
    Civil War: E503+, E559+

Georgia
  Wars
    Civil War
      Military operations: E470.6, E470.65
    Indian wars: E83.813, E83.817, E83.836
    Queen Anne's War, 1702-1713: E197
    Revolution: E263.G3
      Military operations: E230+
    War of 1812: E355, E359.5.G4
Georgia (Colony): F289
Georgia, North: F291.7
Georgia, South: F291.8
Georgia, Strait of, Region (B.C.): F1089.G44
Georgian Bay region (Ontario): F1059.G3
Georgians (South Caucasians) in the United States: E184.G27
German-Anglo Blockade of Venezuela, 1902: F2325
German colonies in America
  Brazil
    Espirito Santo: F2561
    Peru (Pozuzo colony): F3451.H8
    Rio Grande do Sul: F2621
    Santa Catharina: F2626
  Venezuela
    Welser colony: F2322
German explorers of America: E135.G3
German mercenaries in the American Revolution: E268
Germans in America: E29.G3
Germans in Argentina: F3021.G3
Germans in Bolivia: F3359.G3
Germans in Brazil: F2659.G3
Germans in Canada: F1035.G3
Germans in Central America: F1440.G3
Germans in Chile: F3285.G3
Germans in Colombia: F2299.G3
Germans in Costa Rica: F1557.G3
Germans in Guatemala: F1477.G3
Germans in Latin America: F1419.G3
Germans in Mexico: F1392.G4
Germans in Nicaragua: F1537.G47

Germans in Paraguay: F2699.G3
Germans in Peru: F3619.G3
Germans in South America: F2239.G3
Germans in the United States: E184.G3
  American Revolution: E269.G3
  Civil War: E540.G3
  War of 1898: E725.5.G3
Germans in Uruguay: F2799.G3
Germans in Venezuela: F2349.G3
  Welser colony: E135.G3
  Welsers: F2322
Germantown, Battle of, 1777: E241.G3
Germantown (Pa.): F159.G3
Gerry, Elbridge: E302.6.G37
Gettysburg address: E475.55
Gettysburg, Battle of, 1853: E475.53
Gettysburg Campaign, 1863: E475.51
Gettysburg National Cemetery:
  E475.55
Gettysburg National Military Park:
  E475.56
Ghanaians in the United States:
  E184.G44
Ghent, Treaty of, 1814: E358
Giant City State Park (Illinois): F547.J2
Giant Sequoia National Monument
  (California): F868.S4
Gibara (Cuba): F1849.G5
Gibbon Falls (Wyoming): F767.Y44
Gibson, John Bannister: F153
Giddings, Joshua Reed: E415.9.G4
Gila Co. (Arizona): F817.G5
Gila River and Valley
  Arizona: F817.G52
  New Mexico: F802.G54
Gilbert, Sir Humphrey: E129.G4
Gilbert, Thomas: E278.G4
Giles, William Branch: E302.6.G47
Gillem's raid, 1865: E477.9
Gilmore, J.R.
  Conference with Davis, 1854: E469+
Gilmore Ranch (Idaho): F752.I2
Gilpin, Edward Woodward: F169
Gilpin, Henry Dilworth: E340.G48
Gilpin, William: F593
Ginkgo Petrified Forest State Park
  (Wash.): F897.K53

Girty, Simon: F517
Gitksan Indians: E99.K55
Glace Bay (Nova Scotia): F1039.5.G5
Glacier Bay (Alaska): F912.G5
Glacier Bay National Monument
  (Alaska): F912.G5
Glacier National Park: F737.G5
Glacier National Park (B.C.):
  F1089.G55
Glass, Carter: E748.G53
Glen Canyon National Recreation Area
  (Ariz. and Utah): F832.G5
Glendale, Battle of, 1862: E473.68
Glendale (California): F869.G5
Glengarry Co. (Ontario): F1059.G5
Glenwood Canyon (Colo.): F782.G3
Glenwood Cemetery (Washington,
  D.C.): F203.1.G5
Globe (Arizona): F819.G5
Glorieta Pass, N.M., Battle of, 1862:
  E473.4
Glover, John: E207.G56
Goajira, Colombia (Territory): F2281.G8
Goajira peninsula (Colombia):
  F2281.G8
Goajiro Indians: F2270.2.G6
Goat Island (Calif.): F869.S3+
Goat Island (N.Y.): F127.N8
Gobernador Canyon (New Mexico):
  F802.G62
Godfrey, Edward: F23
Goebel, William: F456
Goiás State (Brazil): F2566
  Indian antiquities: F2519.1.G68
Goiaz State (Brazil): F2566
Gold Creek and Valley (Alaska):
  F912.G64
Gold discoveries
  Alaska: F909
  California: F865
Gold Mountain (Esmeralda County and
  Nye County, Nevada): F847.G64
Golden Gate National Recreation Area
  (Calif.): F868.S156
Golden Isles (Georgia): F292.G58
Goldsborough (North Carolina),
  Expedition to, Dec. 1862: E474.52

Goldwork
  Aztecs: F1219.76.G64
  Indians
    Central America: F1434.2.G6
    Colombia: F2270.1.G57
    Costa Rica: F1545.3.G65
    Mexico: F1219.3.G57
    Paraguay: F2679.3.G65
    Peru: F3429.3.G5
    Pre-Columbian America: E59.G55
    South America: F2230.1.G64
Golfo Dulce (Costa Rica): F1549.D8
Goliad State Park (Texas): F392.G6
Gómez, Esteban: E125.G6
Gómez, Juan Carlos: F2726
Gómez, Juan Gualberto: F1787
Gómez, Juan Vicente: F2325
Gómez, Laureano: F2278
Gómez y Báez, Máximo: F1783
Gonave Island (Haiti): F1929.G6
Gonzáles, Joaquín Víctor: F2848
Gonzalez Island (Chile): F3131
González Suárez, Federico: F3736
Gooding, Oliver Paul: E467.1.G6
Goodnight, Charles: F391+
Goodpasture, Jefferson Dillard: F436
Gookin, Daniel: F67
Goose Creek Island (N.C.): F262.P2
Gorda, Sierra: F1339
Gordon, John Brown: E467.1.G66
Gore, Christopher: F69
Gorgas, Josiah: E467.1.G68
Gorham, Nathaniel: E302.6.G66
Gorman, Arthur Pue: E664.G67
Gorman, Willis Arnold: F606
Gorsuch, Edward
  Christiana Riot, 1851: E450
Gorton, Samuel: F82
Gosiute Indians: E99.G67
Gosnold, Batholomew: F7
G.O.U. coup, 1943 (Argentina): F2849
Goulart administration (Brazil):
  F2538.2+
Goulart, João Belchior Marques:
  F2538.22.G6

Gourds
  Indians
    Mexico: F1219.3.G59
Gourgues, Dominique de: F314
Government agencies dealing with
  Indians: E91+
Government relations
  Indians
    Argentina: F2821.3.G65
    Bolivia: F3320.1.G6
    Brazil: F2519.3.G6
    Central America: F1434.2.G68
    Chile: F3069.3.G6
    Ecuador: F3721.3.G68
    French Guiana: F2460.2.G68
    Guatemala: F1465.3.G6
    Guyana: F2380.2.G68
    Latin America (To 1601): F1411
    Mexico: F1219.3.G6
    Nicaragua: F1525.3.G68
    North America: E91+
    Panama: F1565.3.G68
    Paraguay: F2679.3.G67
    Peru: F3429.3.G6
    Pre-Columbian America: E59.G6
    South America: F2230.1.G68
    Venezuela: F2319.3.G6
    West Indies: F1619.3.G68
Government services for Indians: E91+
Governor Shirley's War: E198
Governor's Island (New York):
  F128.68.G7
Governor's Land Archaeological District
  (Va.): F232.C43
Goyataca Indians: F2520.1.G6
Goyaz, Brazil (State): F2566
  Indian antiquities: F2519.1.G68
Graceland Cemetery (Chicago):
  F548.612.G72
Gracias (Honduras): F1516.G7
Grady, Henry Woodfin: E664.G73
Graham Co
  Arizona: F817.G7
Graham, Joseph: E263.N8
Graham Land (Palmer Peninsula):
  F3031+
Graham, William Alexander: E415.9.G7

Gran Chaco, El: F2876

Gran Colombia-Peru War, 1828-1829: F2275

Gran Montana (Venezuela): F2331.A93

Granada, Confederation of: F2276

Granada, Nicaragua (City): F1536.G72
    Rivalry with León: F1526.25

Granary Burial Ground (Boston): F73.61

Grand Army of the Republic: E462.1

Grand Camp Confederate Veterans, Department of Virginia: E483.28

Grand Canyon National Park: F788

Grand Canyon of the Colorado River: F788

Grand Canyon of the Arkansas (Colo.): F782.F8

Grand Central Passenger Station (Chicago): F548.8.G7

Grand Coulee Dam region (Wash.): F897.C7

Grand Falls (Labrador): F1138.G7

Grand Falls (Newfoundland): F1124.5.G7

Grand Forks (N.D.): F644.G8

Grand Gulf State Military Park (Mississippi): F347.C5

Grand Island (Mic.): F572.G45

Grand Island (Neb.): F674.G7

Grand Island (N.Y.): F129.G68

Grand Isle (La.): F377.J4

Grand Lake (Colo : Lake): F782.G7

Grand Manan Island: F1044.G7

Grand Mesa (Colorado): F782.G73

Grand Rapids (Mich.): F574.G7

Grand River and Valley
    Colorado: F782.C7
    Michigan: F572.G46
    Utah: F832.C7

Grand River and Valley (Ontario): F1059.G78

Grand Staircase-Escalante National Monument (Utah): F832.G66

Grand Teton Nation Park (Wyoming): F767.T3

Grand Traverse Bay region (Michigan): F572.G5

Grandchildren of Presidents: E176.45

Grande Island Bay (Brazil): F2611

Grandfather Mountain (N.C.): F262.B6

Grant, General National Park (California): F868.K48

Grant-Kohrs Ranch National Historic Site (Mont.): F737.P88

Grant Parish (La.): F377.G7

Grant, Sir John Peter: F1886

Grant, Ulysses Simpson: E660.G756+
    Administrations, 1869-1877: E671
    Collected works: E660.G756+
    Controversy with Sumner: E671
    Memorial (Washington, D.C.): F203.4.G7
    Monument and tomb (New York): F128.64.G7

Grass Valley (Nevada): F847.G7

Grasslands National Park (Saskatchewan): F1074.G72

Grau Region
    Peru: F3451.G73

Grau San Martin, Ramon: F1788

Gravelly Run (Virginia), Battle of, 1865: E477.67

Graves-Cilley duel: E340.C5

Grays Harbor (Wash.): F897.G84

Great Basin: F789

Great Basin Indians: E78.G67

Great Basin National Park (Nevada): F847.G73

Great Bear Lake, Mackenzie District: F1100.G7

Great Bridge, Va., Battle of, 1775: E241.G6

Great Britain
    Colonies in America: E162
    Discovery and exploration of America: E127+
    Military history
        Conquests of Jamaica, 1596, 1643, 1655: F1884
        Invasion of Haiti, 1793-1798: F1923
    Military history in America
        American Revolution: E230+
        Attacks on
            Venezuela, 1595-1598: F2322

Great Britain
  Military history in America
    Blockade of
      Venezuela, 1902: F2325
    Blockade of Argentine coast, 1838:
      F2846.3
    Capture of Martinique, 1809:
      F2081+
    Conquest of British Guiana: F2383
    Invasion of La Plata: F2845
    Nicaragua, 1780-1781: F1526.25
    Siege of Havana, 1762: F1781
    West Indian expeditions: F1621
      1739-1742: F2272.5
    Naval history
      American Revolution: E271
      War of 1812: E360
    Nootka Sound Controversy, 1789-
      1790: F1089.N8
    Occupation of
      Cuba, 1762-1763: F1781
      Oregon jointly with the U.S., 1818-
        1846: F880
    Relations with U.S.: E183.8.A+
Great Falls (Mont.): F739.G7
Great Falls of the Potomac: F187.M7
Great Gott Island (Me.): F27.H3
Great Kanawha River and Valley (West
  Virginia): F247.K3
Great Lakes
  Indians: E78.G7
Great Miami River and Valley (Ohio):
  F497.M64
Great Moose Lake (Me.): F27.S7
Great Onyx Cave (Ky.): F457.B2
Great Pedee River (S.C.): F277.P3
Great Plains: F590.2+
Great Plains Indians: E78.G73
Great Sacandaga Lake (New York):
  F127.G67
Great Salt Lake, Desert, and region
  (Utah): F832.G7
Great Sand Dunes National Park and
  Preserve (Colo.): F782.G78
Great Sand Hills (Saskatchewan):
  F1074.G73

Great Savannah (Venezuela):
  F2331.B6
Great Smoky Mountains National Park:
  F443.G7
Great Smoky Mountains (Tennessee):
  F443.G7
Greater Antilles: F1741+
Greater New York: F128.5
Greeks
  Discovery of America: E109.G7
Greeks in Canada: F1035.G7
Greeks in Mexico: F1392.G74
Greeks in South America: F2239.G74
Greeks in the United States: E184.G7
Greeks in Uruguay: F2799.G74
Greeley (Colorado): F784.G7
Greeley, Horace: E415.9.G8
Green, Andrew Haswell: F128.47
Green Bay Region: F587.G6
  Michigan: F572.G87
Green Bay (Wisconsin): F589.G7
Green Island (Québec): F1054.I5
Green Mountain boys: F52
Green Mountains (Vt.): F57.G8
Green River and Valley
  Kentucky: F457.G85
Green River and Valley (Wyoming):
  F767.G7
Green Valley (Texas): F392.D4
Greenbrier River Trail (West Virginia):
  F247.G73
Greenbrier River, W.V., Battle of, 1861:
  E472.6
Greene, George Sears: E467.1.G79
Greene, Nathaneal: E207.G9
Greenhalge Frederic Thomas: F70
Greenville (S.C.): F279.G79
Greenwater Lake Provincial Park
  (Saskatchewan): F1074.G74
Greenwich Village (New York):
  F128.68.G8
Grenada (West Indies): F2056+
Grenadians in the United States:
  E184.G75
Grenadines (West Indies): F2061
Grenell Island (N.Y.): F127.T5
Grenfell, Sir William Thomason: F1137

Grey Co. (Ontario): F1059.G84
Greylock Mountain (Mass.): F72.B5
Greytown (Nicaragua): F1536.S2
Grierson's Cavalry Raid, 1863: E475.23
Grijalva, Juan de: E125.G8
Grijalva River (Mexico): F1279
Grimes, James Wilson: E415.9.G85
Grindstone Island
  New York: F127.T5
Grinnell, Josiah Bushnell: E415.9.G86
Grinnell Land: F1105.G7
Griswoldville, Ga., Battle of, 1864:
  E477.41
Gros Ventre Indians (Montana):
  E99.A87
Groseilliers, Médard Chouart, sieur de:
  F1060.7
Grosse Île (Québec): F1054.S3
Groton Heights, Battle of, 1781:
  E241.G8
Groton (Massachusetts): F74.G9
Grout, William Wallace: E467.1.G88
Groveton, Battle of, 1862: E473.77
Grow, Galusha Aaron: E415.9.G89
Grues, Île aux (Québec): F1054.C8
Grundy, Felix: E340.G8
Grupo oficiales unidos (Argentina)
  Coup, 1943: F2849
Guacanahua Indians: F3430.1.E78
Guachichile Indians: F1219
  Modern: F1221.G79
Guachos: F2217
Guadalajara (Audiencia): F1296
Guadalajara (Mexico): F1391.G9
Guadalupe Club of 1838, Washington,
  D.C.: E401.2
Guadalupe Hidalgo, Treaty of, 1848:
  E408
Guadalupe Mountains
  New Mexico: F802.G93
  Texas: F392.G86
Guadalupe Mountains National Park:
  F392.G86
Guadeloupe (West Indies): F2066
Guaharibo Indians: F2520.1.G68
Guahibo Indians: F2319.2.G8
Guaica Indians: F2520.1.W3

Guáimaro (Cuba): F1839.G8
Guaiqueri Indians: F2319.2.G85
Guaíra Falls (Brazil): F2596
Guajá Indians: F2520.1.G69
Guajajara Indians: F2520.1.T4
Guajira, Colombia (Territory): F2281.G8
Guale Indians: E99.G82
Guana Indians: F2230.2.G68,
  F2520.1.G718
Guanabacoa (Cuba): F1799.G8
Guanabara: F2567
Guanacaste, Costa Rica (Province):
  F1549.G9
Guanajuato (Mexico)
  City: F1391.G98
  State: F1281
Guanano Indians: F2520.1.G72
Guane Indians: F2270.2.G8
Guantanamo, Cuba (Province): F1850+
Guaporé, Brazil (Territory): F2624
Guaraira Repans (Venezuela):
  F2331.A93
Guarani Indians: F2230.2.G72
Guarani War, 1754-1756: F2684
Guararapes, Battles at, 1648, 1649:
  F2532
Guarasu Indians: F3320.2.P37
Guarayo Indians: F3320.2.G8
Guarayo Indians (Tacanan):
  F3430.1.E78
Guarayú-tá Indians: F3320.2.P37
Guardia, Tomás: F1547.5
Guarequena Indians: F2319.2.A73
Guárico, Venezuela (State): F2331.G8
Guarijío Indians: F1221.G82
Guarino Indians: F2270.2.G83
Guarpe Indians: F2823.G8
Guartelà (Brazil)
  Region: F2596
Guasco River (Chile): F3131
Guatemala: F1461+
  Claims in British Honduras:
    F1449.B7G1+
  Confederación de Centro América:
    F1466.4
  Wars with
    El Salvador: F1466.45

Guatemala
  Wars with
    Honduras: F1466.45, F1507.5
  Wars with El Salvador: F1487.5
Guatemala Antigua: F1476.A5
Guatemala (Audiencia): F1437
Guatemala City (Guatemala):
  F1476.G9
Guatemala (Dept.): F1469.G9
Guatemalans in the United States:
  E184.G82
Guató Indians: F2520.1.G75
Guatuso Indians: F1545.2.G77
Guayacán Bay (Chile): F3161
Guayacundo Indians: F3722.1.G82
Guayaki Indians: F2679.2.G9
Guayama (Puerto Rico): F1981.G7
Guayana Indians: F2230.2.G75
Guayana Region (Venezuela):
  F2331.G83
Guayaqui Indians: F2679.2.G9
Guayaquil (Ecuador): F3791.G9
Guayaquil meeting, 1822: F2235.36
Guayas, Ecuador (Province): F3741.G9
  Indian antiquities: F3721.1.G9
Guaycuru Indians: F2230.2.G78
Guaycuruan Indians: F2230.2.G78
Guaymi Indians: F1565.2.G8
Guayra Falls (Brazil): F2596
Güemes, Martín Miguel: F2845
Güenoa Indians: F2719.2.G84
Guenoc Valley (California): F868.L2
Guerrero, Mexico (State): F1286
Guerrillas
  U.S. Civil War: E470.45
Guetar Indians: F1545.2.G8
Guiana: F2351+
  Discovery and exploration: E111+,
    E121+, E129.R2
  Dutch settlements: F2383, F2423
  English settlements: F2383, F2423,
    F2461
  French settlements: F2462
  Raleigh's expedition: E129.R2
  Willoughby and Hyde grant, 1663:
    F2423
  Guiana, British: F2361+

Guiana, Dutch: F2401+
Guiana, French: F2441+
Guilford Court House, Battle of, 1781:
  E241.G9
Guiteau, C. J.: E687.9
Gujaratis in the United States:
  E184.G84
Gulf coast (U.S.): F296, F372
  Alabama: F332.G9
  Florida: F317.G8
  Louisiana: F377.G9
  Mississippi: F347.G9
  Texas: F392.P14
Gulf, Department of the, 1862: E510+
Gulf Islands (B.C.): F1089.G8
Gulf Islands National Seashore
  Florida: F317.G8
  Mississippi: F347.G9
Gulf of Morrosquillo (Colombia):
  F2281.S82
Gulf of Panama: F1569.P35
Gulf States: F296
Gunby, John: E263.M3
Gunnison National Monument
  (Colorado): F782.B5
Gurupy River (Brazil): F2571, F2586
Guthrie (Oklahoma): F704.G9
Guyana: F2361+
Guyanese in the United States:
  E184.G86
Guysborough Co. (Nova Scotia):
  F1039.G8
Guzmán Blanco, Antonio: F2325
Gwinnett, Button: E302.6.G95
Gwynn Island (Virginia): F232.M3
Gwynns Falls Watershed (Md.):
  F187.G89
Gwynn's Island (Virginia): F232.M3
Gyitkshan Indians: E99.K55

H

Habeas corpus, Suspension of writ of
  U.S. Civil War: E458.8
Hackensack Indians: E99.H15
Hackensack Meadowlands (N.J.):
  F142.H35

Hackensack River and Valley (New Jersey): F142.B4

Hacker's Creek and Valley (West Virginia): F247.H17

Hackett, William Henry Young: F38

Hagerman Fossil Beds National Monument (Idaho): F752.T8

Haida Indians: E99.H2

Haisla Indians: E99.H23

Haiti (Island): F1900+
French colony: F1923, F1938.3
Pre-Columbian history: F1909
Spanish colony, 1492-1795: F1911
Withdrawal of Spain 1795: F1923
Spanish colony, 1808-1822: F1938.3
Union of whole island, 1822-1844: F1924, F1938.3

Haiti (Republic): F1912+
Military history
War of Independence, 1791-1804: F1923

Haitians in Canada: F1035.H34

Haitians in the American Revolution: E269.H3

Haitians in the Dominican Republic: F1941.H3

Haitians in the United States: E184.H27

Haldimand, Sir Frederick: F1032

Hale, John Parker: E415.9.H15

Hale, Nathan: E280.H2

Hales Bar Dam Region
Tennessee: F443.M32

Half Dome (California): F868.Y6

Haliburton Co. (Ontario): F1059.H27

Haliburton, Sir Brenton: F1038

Haliburton, Thomas Chandler: F1038

Halifax Co. (Nova Scotia): F1039.H3

Halifax (Nova Scotia): F1039.5.H17

Hall, Benjamin Franklin: F780

Hall, Lyman: E263.G3

Hall of Fame, New York University: E176.6

Halleck, Henry Wager: E467.1.H18

Hamblin, Jacob: F826

Hamer, Thomas Lyon: E403.1.H2

Hamilton, Alexander
Collected works: E302.6.H2

Hamilton, Andrew: F152

Hamilton (Bermuda Islands): F1639.H3

Hamilton, Elizabeth (Schuyler): E302.6.H22

Hamilton (Ontario): F1059.5.H2

Hamilton Parish (Virginia): F232.H2

Hamlin, Hannibal: E415.9.H2

Hammond, Charles: E340.H2

Hammond, James Henry: F273

Hampton Institute, Hampton, Virginia: E97.6.H3

Hampton National Historic Site (Maryland): F187.B2

Hampton Plantation (S.C.): F277.C4

Hampton Plantation State Park (S.C.): F277.C4

Hampton Roads Conference, 1865: E469+

Hampton Roads (Virginia): F232.H23
Naval engagement in, 1862: E473.2

Hampton, Wade, 1754-1835: E353.1.H2
Lake Champlain Campaign, 1813: E355.4

Hampton, Wade, 1818-1902: E467.1.H19

Hampton's Cavalry Division
Confederate Army: E547.H2

Han Indians: E99.H26

Hancock, Dorothy (Quincy): E302.6.H24

Hancock, John: E302.6.H23+

Hancock, Winfield Scott: E467.1.H2

Handicraft
Indians
North America: E98.I5

Hanford Reach National Monument (Wash.): F897.H36

Hanging Rock iron region, Ohio: F497.H35

Hanna, Marcus Alonzo: E664.H24

Hanover Court House, Va., Battle of, 1862: E473.6

Hanover, Pa., Battle of, 1863: E475.51

Hanover Parish (Jamaica): F1891.H2

Hanson, John: E302.6.H27

Hants Co. (Nova Scotia): F1039.H4

Hanway trial: E450
Harakmbet Indians: F3430.1.M38
Harbor
  Boston: F73.63
Harbors
  New York: F128.63
  Philadelphia: F158.63
Hardin, Benjamin: E340.H26
Harding, Florence Kling: E786.2
Harding, Warren Gamaliel: E786
  Administration, 1921-1923: E785
Hare Indians: E99.K28
Hare's Hill (Virginia), Battle of, 1865:
  E477.61
Harkers Island (N.C.): F262.C23
Harlan, James: E664.H27
Harlem Heights, Battle of, 1776:
  E241.H2
Harlem (New York): F128.68.H3
Harlem River: F128.68.H4
Harmar's Expedition, 1790: E83.79
Harmon, Daniel Williams: F1060.7
Harney, William Selby: E181
Harney's Expedition: E83.854
Harper, Robert Goodloe: E302.6.H29
Harpers Ferry (West Virginia): F249.H2
  John Brown Raid, 1859: E451
  Military operations, 1864: E476.66
  Siege, 1862: E474.61
Harris, Benjamin Gwinn: E415.9.H28
  Court-martial, 1865: E458.8
Harris, Isham Green: E664.H31
Harrisburg Convention, 1788: F153
Harrisburg Insurrection, 1838: F153
Harrisburg (Pennsylvania): F159.H3
Harrison, Benjamin
  Administration, 1889-1893: E701
  Biography: E702+
  Collected works: E660.H29+
Harrison, Fort
  Battle of, 1812: E356.H3
  Capture of, Sept. 1864: E477.21
Harrison, William Henry
  Administration, 1841: E391
  Biography: E392
  Expedition, 1812: E355.2

Harrison, William Henry
  Northwestern campaign, 1813:
    E355.4
Harrod, James: F454
Harry S. Truman Dam and Reservoir
  (Mo.): F472.B4
Hartford (Conn.): F104.H3
Hartford Convention, 1814: E357.7
Hartford (Sloop): E595.H2
Hartranft, John Frederick: E467.1.H4
Hartstene Island (Wash.): F897.M4
Harvard University and the Civil War:
  E541.H2
Harvard University and the War of 1898:
  E725.6.H3
Hasinai Indians: E99.H28
Haskin, John Bussing: E415.9.H35
Hastings (Nebraska): F674.H3
Hatcher Pass (Alaska): F912.H37
Hatteras Indians: E99.C91
Hatton, Robert: E467.1.H44
Haureaux, Ulises: F1938.4
Havana (City): F1799.H3+
  Siege, 1762-1763: F1781
Havana (Province): F1791+
Havasu Canyon (Arizona): F788
Havasupai Indians: E99.H3
Haverhill (Massachusetts)
  Massacre, 1697: E196
  Massacre, 1708: E197
Hawaii
  African Americans: E185.93.H3
Hawaiians in Canada: F1035.H36
Hawaiians in the United States:
  E184.H3
Hawes Shops, Va., Battle of, 1864:
  E476.52
Hawkins, Sir Richard: E129.H4
Hawley, Joseph: E263.M4
Hay-Buneau-Varilla Treaty, 1903:
  F1566.5
Hay-Herrán Treaty of 1903: F1566.5
Hay, John: E664.H41
Hay-Pauncefote Treaty, 1901: F1438
Haya de la Torre, Víctor Raúl: F3448
Hayes, Rutherford Birchard: E682
  Administration, 1877-1881: E681

Hayes, Rutherford Birchard
  Family: E682.1
Hayne, Robert Young: E340.H4
Hazard, Ebenezer
  Historical collections: E187.H42
Hazel Creek and Valley (N.C.):
  F262.S95
Health
  Indians
    North America: E98.D6
Health statistics
  Civil War, 1861-1865: E621+
Hearne, Samuel: F1060.7
Hearst Castle (California): F868.S18
Hearst-San Simeon State Historical
  Monument (California): F868.S18
Heathcote, Caleb: F122+
Hecla Provincial Park (Manitoba):
  F1064.H42
Heffley Lake (B.C.): F1089.H44
Heiltsuk Indians: E99.H45
Hein, Pieter Pieterszoon
  Capture of the Spanish silver-fleet:
    F1779
Helderberg Mountains (N.Y.): F127.A3
Helena, Arkansas, Battle of, 1863:
  E474.9
Helena (Mont.): F739.H4
Hells Canyon National Recreation Area
  Idaho: F752.H44
  Oregon: F882.H44
Hemlock Lake (New York): F127.L7
Henderson, Richard: F454
Hendricks, Thomas Andrews:
  E664.H49
Hennepin, Louis: F1030.4
  In Mississippi Valley: F352
Henrico Parish (Virginia): F232.H5
Henry, Alexander (1739-1824): F1060.7
Henry Co. (Iowa): F627.H5
Henry, Fort
  Capture of, 1862: E472.96
Henry, John: E302.6.H4
Henry, John (British): E360.6.H5
Henry, Patrick: E302.6.H5
Henshaw, David: F69

Heredia, Costa Rica (Province):
  F1549.H5
Hereditary Order of Descendants of
  Colonial Governors: E186.99.H55
Hereditary patriotic societies
  United States: E172.7+
Hereditary societies
  United States
    War of 1812: E351.3+
Herrán-Hay Treaty of 1903: F1566.5
Herrán, Pedro Alcántara: F2276
Herrera, Luis Alberto de: F2728
Herrera y Obes, Julio: F2726
Herring Lake (Michigan): F572.B4
Hessians in the American Revolution:
  E268
Heta Indians: F2520.1.H48
Hewitt, Abram Stevens: F128.47
Heyn, Piet: F1779
Hiawatha Island (N.Y.): F127.S96
Hickey Plot, 1776: E277
Hickok, James Butler: F594
Hicks, Thomas Holliday: E415.9.H6
Hicksford Raid, 1864: E477.21
Hidalgo, Mexico (State): F1291
Hidalgo y Costilla, Míguel: F1232
Hidatsa Indians: E99.H6
Hiester, Joseph: F153
Higginson, Stephen: F69
Highland Lake (Conn.): F102.L6
Highlands (New York): F127.H8
Hill, Benjamin Harvey: E664.H53
Hill Country (Texas): F392.T47
Hill, Isaac: F38
Hillegas, Michael: E302.6.H6
Hillhouse, James: E302.6.H63
Hilliard, Henry Washington: E415.9.H65
Hilton Head Island (S.C.): F277.B3
Hinckley, John
  Biography: E877.3
Hincks, Sir Francis: F1032
Hindham, William: E302.6.H65
Hindman, Fort, Arkansas
  Operations against, Jan. 1863:
    E474.48
Hindu influences, Indian
    Pre-Columbian America: E59.H54

Hindus in Canada: F1035.H54
Hispanic Americans in the United
  States: E184.S75
Hispaniola: F1900+
Hispano-American War, 1898: E714+
Hiss case, Alger: E743.5
Historians, American: E175.45+
Historic monuments
  Maine: F20
  United States: E159
Historiography
  Aztecs: F1219.76.H57
  Central America: F1445.5+
  Indians
    Mexico: F1219.3.H56
    Peru: F3429.3.H5
History, Local, of the United States: F1+
Hitchiti Indians: E99.H65
Hmong (Asian people) in French
  Guiana: F2471.H56
Hmong (Asian people) in the United
  States: E184.H55
Hoar, George Frisbie: E664.H65
Hoar, Samuel: F70
Hobart, Garret Augustus: E664.H73
Hobcaw Barony (S.C.): F277.G35
Hocking River and Valley, Ohio:
  F497.H7
Hodgenville (Kentucky). Lincoln
  Memorial Building: E457.32
Hoffman, Harold Giles: F139
Hoh River and Valley (Wash.):
  F897.H63
Hohenau (Paraguay): F2695.H7
Hohokam culture: E99.H68
Holden, William Woods: F259
Hole in the Rock Trail (Utah): F832.S4
Holguín (Cuba): F1849.H6
Holguín Province (Cuba): F1854+
Holland Purchase (New York): F127.H7
Hollywood (California): F869.H74
Holmans Creek (Virginia): F232.S47
Holmes Creek and Valley
  Alabama: F332.H56
  Florida: F317.H73
Holston River and Valley (Tennessee):
  F443.H7

Holy Cross, Mount of the (Colorado):
  F782.H6
Holyoke, Mount (Mass.): F72.H3
Home Island (Conn.): F102.F2
Hominy Creek and Valley (N.C.):
  F262.H74
Homosexuality
  Indians
    North America: E98.S48
Hondurans in the United States:
  E184.H66
Honduras: F1501+
  Confederación de Centro América:
    F1507
  Wars with
    El Salvador: F1487.5, F1507.5
    Guatemala: F1466.45, F1507.5
Hone, Philip: F128.44
Honey Hill (South Carolina),
  Engagement at, 1864: E477.44
Honey Springs, Okla., Battle of, 1863:
  E474.9
Hood Canal region (Wash.): F897.P9
Hood, John Bell: E467.1.H58
Hood, Mount (Oregon): F882.H85
Hood River and Valley (Oregon):
  F882.H9
Hooker, Joseph: E467.1.H6
Hooper Islands (Md.): F187.D6
Hooper, William: E302.6.H7
Hoosic River and Valley: F127.H73
  Massachusetts: F72.B5
  Vermont: F57.B4
Hoosier National Forest (Ind.):
  F532.H75
Hoover, Herbert Clark: E802+
  Administration, 1929-1933: E801
  Collected works: E742.5.H66+
  Family: E802.1
Hoover, Lou (Henry): E802.1
Hopatcong, Lake (N.J.): F142.H7
Hope Region (B.C.): F1089.H6
Hopedale, Labrador (Fishing port):
  F1139.H6
Hopewell culture: E99.H69
Hopi Indians: E99.H7
Hopkins, Benjamin Franklin: F586

Hopkins, Ezek: E207.H7
Hopkins, Samuel
  Expedition, 1812: E355.2
Hopkins, Stephen: E302.6.H78
Hornby Island (B.C.): F1089.H63
Horses
  Indians: E98.H55
Horseshoe Lake (Illinois): F547.A3
Hosmer, Titus: E302.6.H8
Hospital services, Military
  United States
    Civil War: E621+
    Revolution: E283
    War of 1812: E362.5
    War of 1898: E731
    War with Mexico: E412.5
Hostos y Bonilla, Eugenio María de:
  F1973
Hot Springs (Arkansas): F419.H8
Hotels, taverns, etc
  Boston: F73.625
  New York: F128.625
  Philadelphia: F158.625
  Washington, D.C.: F203.35
Houghton Lake (Michigan): F572.R6
Houma Indians: E99.H72
Housatonic River and Valley: F102.H7
  Massachusetts: F72.H7
House of Representatives
  United States
    Election of speaker, 1856: E434.5
Housing
  Indians: E98.H58
Houston, Samuel: F390
Houston (Texas): F394.H8+
Houston, William Churchill: F138
Hovey, Alvin Peterson: E467.1.H7
Howard, John Eager: E263.M3
Howard, Oliver Otis: E467.1.H8
Howe, John: E280.H8
Howe, Joseph: F1038
Howe, Robert: E207.H85
Howe, Samuel: F69
Howe, William Howe, 5th Viscount,
  Occupation of Philadelphia, 1777:
  E233
Hualapai Indians: E99.H75

Huamachuco, Peru (Province)
  Indian antiquities: F3429.1.H8
Huamalies, Peru (Province): F3451.H7
Huambisa Indians: F3430.1.H78
Huanca Indians: F3430.1.H8
Huancané, Peru (Province): F3451.H75
Huancavelica (Peru)
  City: F3611.H8
  Department: F3451.H76
Huancavilca Indians: F3722.1.H8
Huancayo (Peru)
  City: F3611.H82
  Province: F3451.H78
Huanta, Peru (Province): F3451.H79
Huánuco (Peru): F3451.H8
Huao Indians: F3722.1.H83
Huaorani Indians: F3722.1.H83
Huaral Province (Peru): F3451.H83
Huarayo Indians (Tacanan):
  F3430.1.E78
Huari Indians: F3430.1.H83
Huari (Peru)
  Indian antiquities: F3429.1.H828
Huasco, Chile (Province)
  Indian antiquities: F3069.1.H8
Huasco River (Chile): F3131
Huastec Indians
  Modern: F1221.H8
  Pre-Columbian: F1219.8.H83
Huasteca, Mexico (Region): F1294
Huatuso Indians: F1545.2.G77
Huaura River and Valley (Peru):
  F3451.L7
Huave Indians: F1221.H85
Hubbardton, Battle of, 1777: E241.H8
Hudson Bay: F1060+
Hudson-Fulton Celebration, 1909:
  F127.H8
Hudson, Henry: E129.H8
Hudson River and Valley: F127.H8
  New Jersey: F142.H83
Hudson River Palisades: F127.H8
Hudson Strait: F1105.7
Hudson Valley: F127.H8
  Dutch colony, 1610-1664: F122+
  Indians: E78.H83

Hudson Valley
  Revolution, 1775-1783
    Military operations: E230.5.N4
    Washington's retreat, 1776: E232
Hudson's Bay Company: F1060+
Hueco Mountains
  New Mexico: F802.H84
  Texas: F392.H82
Huehuetenango, Guatemala (Dept.):
  F1469.H8
Huerta, Victoriano: F1234
Huetar Indians: F1545.2.G8
Huexotzinco codex: F1219.56.H83+
Hughes, Charles Evans: E664.H86
Hughes, Sir Sam: F1033
Huguenots in America: E29.H9
Huguenots in Canada: F1035.H76
Huguenots in the United States:
  E184.H9
  Florida, 1562-1565: F314
Huichica Creek and Valley
  California: F868.N2
Huichol Indians: F1221.H9
Huila, Colombia (Dept.): F2281.H8
Huilliche Indians: F3126
Hull, Cordell: E748.H93
Hull, Isaac: E353.1.H8
Hull (Québec): F1054.5.H8
Hull, William: E353.1.H9
Hullicos Indians: F3126
Hul'q'umi'num Indians: E99.H77
Humahuaca Indians: F2823.H85
Humber River and Valley (Ontario):
  F1059.H9
Humboldt Bay (California): F868.H8
Humboldt River and Valley (Nevada):
  F847.H85
Humor
  Indians: E98.H77
Humor of American history: E178.4
Humphreys, Andrew Atkinson:
  E467.1.H885
Humphreys, David: E302.6.H89
Hungarians in Argentina: F3021.H85
Hungarians in Brazil: F2659.H85
Hungarians in Canada: F1035.H8

Hungarians in South America:
  F2239.H85
Hungarians in the United States:
  E184.H95
  Civil War: E540.H6
Hungerford, Daniel Elihu: E403.1.H87
Hungry Mother Creek and Valley
  (Virginia): F232.S6
Hunkpapa Indians: E99.H795
Hunt, Henry Jackson: E467.1.H89
Hunter, David: E467.1.H9
Hunter, Robert Mercer Taliaferro:
  E415.9.H9
Hunting
  Indians: E98.H8
    Argentina: F2821.3.H8
    Brazil: F2519.3.H85
    Central America: F1434.2.H85
    Colombia: F2270.1.H84
    Mayas: F1435.3.H85
    South America: F2230.1.H84
Hunting Island (S.C.): F277.B3
Huntingdon, Benjamin: E302.6.H9
Huntingdon, Jabez Williams: E340.H9
Huntington County (Québec): F1054.H9
Huntington, Mount (Alaska): F912.H8
Huntington (W.Va.): F249.H95
Hupa Indians: E99.H8
Huron Co. (Ontario): F1059.H92
Huron Indians: E99.H9
Huron, Lake, region: F554
  Michigan: F572.H92
  Ontario: F1059.H95
Huron-Manistee National Forests
  Michigan: F572.H93
Huron Mountains (Michigan): F572.M33
Hurricanes
  Florida, 1926-1927: F316
  Jamaica: F1895.P6
  New England, 1938: F9
  United States: E179
Husbands, Herman: E302.6.H93
Hutchinson, Anne (Marbury): F67
Hutchinson (Kansas): F689.H9
Hutchinson, Thomas: F67
Hutterite Brethren in Canada:
  F1035.H97

Hutterite Brethren in the United States: E184.H97

Hyde and Willoughby's grant, 1663 (Guiana): F2423

Hyde Park (New York): F129.H99

Hydraulic engineering
Indians
Mexico: F1219.3.H96

Hygiene
Mayas: F1435.3.M4

I

Ibáñez del Campo, Carlos: F3099

Ibarra (Ecuador): F3791.I3

Iberia Parish (La.): F377.I15

Iberville Parish (La.): F377.I2

Iberville, Pierre Le Moyne d': F372

Ibiapaba (Brazil): F2567.3

Ica, Peru (Dept.): F3451.I3

Içá River (Brazil): F2546

Icelanders in Canada: F1035.I2

Icelanders in the United States: E184.I3

Ichetucknee River (Fla.): F317.I24

Ichilo, Bolivia (Province): F3341.I25

Ickes, Harold Le Claire: E748.I28

Idaho: F741+
African Americans: E185.93.I15
Counties, etc: F752.A+
Indians: E78.I118
Wars
Indian wars: E83.83, E83.877

Idaho Co: F752.I2

Idaho Falls (Idaho): F754.I2

Ide, William Brown: F864

Idiarte Borda, Juan: F2726

Iglesias, Rafael: F1547.5

Iguape, Ribeira de (Brazil): F2631

Iguazú Falls (Argentina): F2909

Iguazú Falls (Brazil): F2596

Iguazú, Parque Nacional del (Argentina): F2916

Iguazú River and Falls (Brazil): F2596

Ijca Indians: F2270.2.A67

Île aux Basques (Québec): F1054.B37

Île aux Coudres (Québec): F1054.I3

Île aux Grues (Québec): F1054.C8

Île aux Noix (Québec): F1054.I35

Île Bizard (Québec): F1054.B58

Île Jésus (Québec): F1054.J47

Île Percée (Québec): F1054.G2

Île Royale (Nova Scotia): F1039.C2

Île Verte (Québec): F1054.I5

Îles de Mingan (Québec): F1054.M59

Îles du Salut (French Guiana): F2467.I4

Îles Madeleine (Québec): F1054.M18

Iliamna Lake and region (Alaska): F912.I44

Illinois: F536+
African Americans: E185.93.I2
Clark's campaign, 1778-1779: E234
Counties, etc: F547.A+
Indians: E78.I3
Quebec Act, 1774: F1032
Slavery: E445.I2
Wars
Civil War: E470.4+, E470.8, E505+
Indian wars: E83.83
War of 1812: E355+, E359.5.A+
War of 1898: E717, E726.I2
War with Mexico: E405+, E409.5.I4

Illinois and Michigan Canal National Heritage Corridor (Illinois): F547.I13

Illinois country: F544

Illinois Indians: E99.I2

Illinois military tract: F547.M6

Illinois River and Valley: F547.I2

Imbabura, Ecuador (Province): F3741.I6
Indian antiquities: F3721.1.I3

Immigrant lists, English
U. S. colonial period: E187.5

Immigrants in the United States
Civil War: E540.F6

Impeachment of President Johnson: E666

Impeachment, Proposed, of Richard Nixon: E861

Imperial Valley (Calif.): F868.I2

Imperialism
United States: E713

Implements
Indians: E98.I4
Argentina: F2821.3.I5

Implements
  Indians
    Bolivia: F3320.1.I45
    Brazil: F2519.3.I4
    Ecuador: F3721.3.I4
    Mexico: F1219.3.I4
    Pre-Columbian America: E59.I4
    South America: F2230.1.I4
    West Indies: F1619.3.I6
  Mayas: F1435.3.I46
Impresarios (Texas): F389
Impressment
  War of 1812: E357.2
Incas: F3429+
  Insurrection of Tupac-Amaru, 1780-1781: F3444
Independence Day: E286.A1+
Independence, Declaration of: E221
Independence Hall (Philadelphia): F158.8.I3
Independence, Mount
  Revolution, 1775-1783: E230.5.V3
Independence National Historical Park (Philadelphia): F158.65.I3
Independence Rock (Wyoming): F767.I38
Independence Square (Philadelphia): F158.67.I33
Indian campaigns
  Revolution, 1775-1783: E230+
  War of 1812: E355
Indian community colleges
  North America: E97.55
Indian country: F697
Indian Creek and Valley (W. Va.): F247.R6
Indian masonry: E98.S75
Indian massacres: E81+
  Virginia: F229
Indian reservation police
  North America: E98.C87
Indian reservations: E91+
Indian rights associations: E91+
Indian River (Fla.): F317.B8
Indian sandpaintings: E98.S3
Indian schools
  Canada: E96.6.A+

Indian schools
  United States: E97.5+
Indian soldiers
  Mexico: F1219.3.M55
  North America: E98.M5
  Civil War
    Confederate Army: E585.I53
    Union Army: E540.I3
Indian Stream (N.H.): F42.C7
Indian Territory
  History
    1890-1907: F698
    To 1890: F697
  Indians: E78.I5
  Wars
    Civil War, 1861-1865: E470.9, E471.57, E505.95, E561
Indian tribal government: E98.T77
Indian tribes
  Argentina: F2823.A+
  Belize: F1445.2.A+
  Bolivia: F3320.2.A+
  Brazil: F2520.1.A+
  Central America: F1434.3.A+
  Chile: F3070.1.A+
  Colombia: F2270.2.A+
  Costa Rica: F1545.2.A+
  Ecuador: F3722.1.A+
  El Salvador: F1485.2.A+
  French Guiana: F2460.1.A+
  Guatemala: F1465.2.A+
  Guyana: F2380.1.A+
  Honduras: F1505.2.A+
  Mexico: F1221.A+
    Mayas: F1435.1.A+
    Pre-Columbian: F1219.1.A+
  Nicaragua: F1525.2.A+
  North America: E99.A+
  Panama: F1565.2.A+
  Paraguay: F2679.2.A+
  Peru: F3430.1.A+
  South America: F2230.2.A+
  Suriname: F2420.1.A+
  Uruguay: F2719.2.A+
  Venezuela: F2319.2.A+
  West Indies: F1619.2.A+
Indian warfare: E98.W2

Indian warfare
  Scalping: E98.W2
Indian wars
  Aztecs: F1219.76.W37
  Brazil: F2519.3.W37
  Guatemala: F1465.3.W37
  Mayas: F1435.3.W2
  Mexico: F1219.3.W37
  North America: E81+
    Chronological list: E83.63+
  Peru: F3429.3.W27
  South America: F2230.1.W37
Indian Wells Valley (California):
  F868.K3
Indiana: F521+
  African Americans: E185.93.I4
  Counties, etc: F532.A+
  Indians: E78.I53
  Slavery: E445.I3
  Wars
    Civil War: E506+
      Military operations: E470.4+
    Indian wars: E83.81
    Morgan's raid, 1863: E475.18
    Revolution: E263.I5
    War of 1812: E359.5.I53
    War of 1898: E726.I3
    War with Mexico: E405.1+,
      E409.5.I7
Indiana Dunes State Park: F532.I5
Indianapolis (Indiana): F534.I3+
Indians: E51+, E75+
  Antiquities
    Local: E78.A+
  Argentina: F2819+
  Bahamas: F1655
  Belize: F1445+
  Bolivia: F3319+
  Brazil: F2518.5+
  Caribbean Area: F2172
  Central America: F1434+
  Chile: F3069+
  Colombia: F2269+
  Costa Rica: F1545+
  Cuba: F1769
  Ecuador: F3721+

Indians
  Education
    Canada: E96.2+
    United States: E97+
  El Salvador: F1485+
  French Guiana: F2459+
  Guatemala: F1465+
  Guiana: F2354
  Guyana: F2379+
  Haiti: F1909
  Honduras: F1504.5+
  Jamaica: F1875
  Latin America: E65
  Mexico: F1218.5+
  Military administration: E98.M5
  Nicaragua: F1525+
  North America
    Biography: E89+
  Origin: E61
  Panama: F1565+
  Paraguay: F2678+
  Peru: F3429+
  Pre-Columbian America: E61
  Puerto Rico: F1969
  Relations with African Americans:
    E98.R28
  South America: F2229+
  Suriname: F2419+
  Treatment of: E91+
  Uruguay: F2719+
  Venezuela: F2318+
  West Indies: F1619+
Indians and libraries: E97.8
Indians and the American Revolution:
  E269.I5
Indochinese in Canada: F1035.I55
Indochinese in the United States:
  E184.I43
Indonesians
  Discovery of America: E109.I57
Indonesians in the United States:
  E184.I45
Industries
  Aztecs: F1219.76.I53
  Indians
    Argentina: F2821.3.I6
    Bolivia: F3320.1.I54

Industries
  Indians
    Brazil: F2519.3.I5
    Guatemala: F1465.3.I5
    Mexico: F1219.3.I5
    North America: E98.I5
    Panama: F1565.3.I54
    Paraguay: F2679.3.I53
    Peru: F3429.3.I53
    Pre-Columbian America: E59.I5
    South America: F2230.1.I42
    Mayas: F1435.3.I53
Influence on other civilizations, Indian
  Pre-Columbian America: E59.I53
Ingalik Indians: E99.D18
Ingalls, John James: E664.I4
Ingano Indians: F2270.2.I53
Ingersoll, Charles Jared: E340.I5
Ingersoll, Jared: E302.6.I6
Ingersoll, Joseph Reed: E340.I53
Ingles Ferry (N.C.): F262.N6
Ingram's Rebellion (Va.): F229
Inine, French Guiana (Territory):
  F2467.I5
Innes, Harry: F455
Inside Passage
  Alaska: F912.I56
  British Columbia: F1089.I5
Insular possessions (U.S.): F970
Insurrection of Amapala, 1910: F1507.5
Insurrection of the Comuneros, 1781:
  F2272
Insurrection of Tupac-Amaru, 1780-
  1781: F3444
Integralism in Brazil: F2538
Integralist Revolt of 1938: F2538
Intellectual life
  African Americans: E185.89.I56
  Indians
    Mayas: F1435.3.I57
    Mexico: F1219.3.I56
    Pre-Columbian America: E59.I58
    South America: F2230.1.I58
  Jews: E184.36.I58
Inter-American Conference: F1404.5+

Inter-American Conference for the
  Maintenance of Continental Peace
  and Security, Rio de Janeiro, 1947:
  F1405.9.I5
Inter-American Conference for the
  Maintenance of Peace, Buenos Aires,
  1936: F1405.3
Inter-American Council for Education,
  Science, and Culture: F1408.4
Inter-American Cultural Council:
  F1408.4
Inter-American Highway
  Costa Rica: F1547.5
  Latin America: F1409
  Mexico: F1215
  Nicaragua: F1527
Inter-American relations: F1415+
Intercolonial wars
  North America: E195+
Internal security
  United States: E743.5
Internal slave trade
  United States: E442
International American Conference:
  F1404.5+
International Bureau of American
  Republics: F1403+
International Conference of American
  States: F1404.5+
Interracial cooperation
  United States
    African Americans: E185.61
Interracial marriage: E185.62
Intervention by the United States in
  Cuba: E721, F1786, F1787
Intervention by the United States in
  European affairs, 1848-1853: E429
Interviews
  Indians: E98.I54
Inuit: E99.E7
Inverness Co. (Nova Scotia): F1039.I5
Iowa: F616+
  African Americans: E185.93.I64
  Counties, etc: F627.A+
  Indians: E78.I6
  Wars
    Civil War: E507+

Iowa
  Wars
    Indian wars: E83.857
    War of 1898: E726.I4
    War with Mexico: E409.5.I72
Iowa Indians: E99.I6
Iowa University and the Civil War:
  E541.I6
Ipswich River (Mass.): F72.E7
Ipurucotó Indians: F2520.1.I6
Iquique (Chile): F3281.I6
Iquito Indians: F3430.1.I68
Iquitos (Peru): F3611.I6
Irala, Domingo Martínez de: F2841
Iranche Indians: F2520.1.I7
Iranians in Canada: F1035.I58
Iranians in the United States: E184.I5
Irantxe Indians: F2520.1.I7
Iranxe Indians: F2520.1.I7
Irapa Indians: F2319.2.I7
Iraqis in the United States: E184.I55
Irazú Volcano (Costa Rica): F1549.I7
  Indian antiquities: F1545.1.V6
Iredell, James: E302.6.I7
Ireland
  Aid sought in the American
    Revolution: E216
Irigoyen, Hipólito: F2848
Irish
  Discovery of America: E109.I6
Irish in America: E29.I74
Irish in Argentina: F3021.I6
Irish in Canada: F1035.I6
Irish in Jamaica: F1896.I6
Irish in the United States: E184.I6
  Civil War: E540.I6
  Revolution: E269.I6
Irish soldiers
  North America
    Civil War
      Confederate Army: E585.I75
Irondequoit Creek and Valley (New
  York): F127.M6
Iroquoian Indians: E99.I69
Iroquois Indians: E99.I7
Iroquois (N.Y.). Thomas Indian School:
  E97.6.T4

Irrigation
  Indians: E98.I75
    Mexico: F1219.3.I77
    Peru: F3429.3.I77
    South America: F2230.1.I77
Irvine Park (Calif.): F868.O6
Irvine Regional Park (Calif.): F868.O6
Irving Park (Ill.): F548.68.I7
Isabela (Dominican Republic): F1939.I8
Iscaycinca Indians: F3430.1.I8
Island Lake (Alberta): F1079.I75
Island No. 10
  Military operations, 1862: E473.15
Island Park region (Idaho): F752.I7
Islas de Cisne (Honduras): F1509.B3
Islas de las Perlas (Panama): F1569.P3
Isle of Orleans (Québec): F1054.O7
Isle of Pines (Cuba): F1799.I8
Isle Royale (Michigan): F572.I8
Isle Verte (Québec): F1054.I5
Isles de Pierres Indians: E99.S55
Isles Derniers (La.): F377.T5
Isles of Shoals: F42.I8
Islesboro Island (Me.): F27.W16
Isleta Indians: E99.I8
Israelis in the United States: E184.I7
Isthmus of Panama: F1561+
Isthmus of Tehuantepec: F1359
Itajahy (Itajai) River and Valley (Brazil):
  F2626
Italian Jews in the United States:
  E184.3+
Italians
  Discovery and exploration of America:
    E109.I8
    Post-Columbian: E135.I8
Italians in America: E29.I8
Italians in Argentina: F3021.I8
Italians in Brazil: F2659.I8
Italians in Canada: F1035.I8
Italians in Central America: F1440.I73
Italians in Chile: F3285.I8
Italians in Latin America: F1419.I8
Italians in Mexico: F1392.I82
Italians in Paraguay: F2699.I8
Italians in Peru: F3619.I8
Italians in South America: F2239.I8

Italians in the United States: E184.I8
  Civil War: E540.I8
Italians in Uruguay: F2799.I8
Italians in Venezuela: F2349.I8
Italy
  Anglo-German-Italian Blockade of
    Venezuela, 1902: F2325
Itamaracá Island (Brazil): F2601
Itasca Lake (Minnesota): F612.I8
Itasca State Park (Minnesota): F612.I8
Itene Indians: F3320.2.I8
Itucale Indians: F3430.1.I85
Itúrbide, Augustin de: F1232
Iturrigaray y Aróstegui, José de: F1231
Ituzaingó, Battle of, 1827: F2725
Itza Indians: F1465.2.I87
Iuka (Mississippi), Engagement at, Sept.
  1862: E474.42
Ivapare Indians: F2520.1.H48
Ivoirians in the United States: E184.I96
Ivvavik National Park (Yukon):
  F1095.I98
Ixil Indians: F1465.2.I95
Ixmiquilpan, Mexico (District): F1291
Izabal, Guatemala (Dept.): F1469.I9
Izapa Site (Mexico)
  Mayas: F1435.1.I93

J

Jacalteca Indians: F1465.2.J3
Jackson, Andrew: E337.8.J3, E382
  Administrations, 1829-1837: E381+
  Execution of the Tennessee
    militiamen: E83.813
  Family: E382.1.A1+
  Governor of Florida: F315
  Vote of censure, 1834: E384.7
Jackson Co. (Colo.): F782.J3
Jackson, Fort
  Bombardment and capture, 1862:
    E472.88
Jackson Hole National Monument
  (Wyoming): F767.J3
Jackson Hole (Wyoming): F767.T28
Jackson, John Peter: F139
Jackson Lake (Wyoming): F767.T3

Jackson, Miss., Battle of, 1863 (May
  13): E475.29
Jackson (Mississippi): F349.J13
  Campaign, 1863: E475.29
Jackson, Mississippi
  Siege, 1863: E475.29
Jackson Parish (La.): F377.J2
Jackson Purchase region (Kentucky):
  F457.J23
Jackson, Rachel (Donelson): E382.1.J2
Jackson River and Valley
  Virginia: F232.J13
  West Virginia: F247.J22
Jackson, Thomas Jonathan:
  E467.1.J15
Jackson Whites: E184.R3
Jacksonville (Florida): F319.J1
Jacob's Cavern (Mo.): F472.M13
Jacques Cartier Park (Québec):
  F1054.P36
Jacuhype River (Brazil): F2551
Jacuípe River (Brazil): F2551
Jaén (Peru)
  Province: F3451.J33
Jalama Beach Park (California):
  F868.S23
Jalapa (Mexico)
  Canton: F1371
  City: F1391.J2
Jalapão (Brazil): F2640
Jalisco, Mexico (State): F1296
Jamaica: F1861+
  Separation of British Honduras from,
    1884: F1447
Jamaicans in the United States:
  E184.J27
James, Army of the: E470.2+
James Bay region (Ontario and
  Québec): F1059.J3
James Island (S.C.): F277.C4
James Island (South Carolina)
  Engagement at, 1862: E473.92
James, Jesse: F594
James River and Valley (Alberta):
  F1079.J27
James River and Valley (Virginia):
  F232.J2

James River (Virginia)
  Campaign from the Rapidan, 1864: E476.52
  Operations on south side, 1864: E476.57
Jamestown settlement: F229
Jamestown (Virginia): F234.J3
Japanese in America: E29.J3
Japanese in Argentina: F3021.J36
Japanese in Bolivia: F3359.J3
Japanese in Brazil: F2659.J3
Japanese in Canada: F1035.J3
Japanese in Colombia: F2299.J3
Japanese in Cuba: F1789.J3
Japanese in Latin America: F1419.J3
Japanese in Mexico: F1392.J3
Japanese in Paraguay: F2699.J35
Japanese in Peru: F3619.J3
Japanese in South America: F2239.J3
Japanese in the Dominican Republic: F1941.J3
Japanese in the United States: E184.J3
Japanese in Uruguay: F2799.J36
Japurá River (Brazil): F2546
Jaquess, J. F.
  Conference with Davis, 1864: E469+
Jarvis, Leonard: E340.J3
Jasper National Park (Alberta): F1079.J3
Javanese in Dutch Guiana: F2431.J3
Javarí River (Brazil): F2546
Jay, John: E302.6.J4
  Treaty with Great Britain: E314
Jay, William: E449
Jeddore (Nova Scotia): F1039.J43
Jedediah Island (B.C.): F1089.J43
Jefferson City (Mo.): F474.J4
Jefferson Davis Parish (La.): F377.J43
Jefferson, Fort (Dry Tortugas)
  Civil War operations, 1861: E471.53
  Fort Jefferson National Monument: F317.M7
Jefferson Parish (La.): F377.J4
Jefferson, Thomas: E332
  Administrations, 1801-1809: E331+
  Family: E332

Jefferson, Thomas
  Memorial, Washington, D.C.: F203.4.J4
Jehossee Island (S.C.): F277.C4
Jekyl Island (Georgia): F292.G58
Jemez Indians: E99.J4
Jemez Mountains (N.M.): F802.S3
Jenckes, Thomas Allen: E415.9.J5
Jenkins, Charles Jones: F291
Jenkins' Ferry, Ark., Battle of, 1864: E476.35
Jenny Lake (Wyoming): F767.T3
Jequitinhonha River (Brazil): F2581
Jersey City: F144.J5+
Jersey Shore: F142.J4
Jesuit province of Paraguay: F2684
Jesuit reductions: F2684
Jesuit relations (North America): F1030.7+
Jesuits
  Expulsion from
    Brazil: F2528
    Mexico: F1231
  Missions
    Mount Desert Island station, 1609: F1038
    New France: F1030.7+
    Paraguay reductions (1609-1769): F2684
    Primería Alta: F799
    War of the Seven Reductions, 1854-1856: F2684
Jesup, Thomas Sidney: E83.836
Jesus Island (Québec): F1054.J47
Jewel Cave National Monument (South Dakota): F657.J55
Jewelry
  Indians
    Costa Rica: F1545.3.J48
    Mexico: F1219.3.J48
    North America: E98.J48
    Mayas: F1435.3.J48
Jewish colony in British Guiana, 1658-1666: F2381
Jews in America: E29.J5
Jews in Argentina: F3021.J5
Jews in Bolivia: F3359.J47

Jews in Brazil: F2659.J5
Jews in Canada: F1035.J5
Jews in Central America: F1440.J48
Jews in Chile: F3285.J4
Jews in Colombia: F2299.J4
Jews in Costa Rica: F1557.J4
Jews in Cuba: F1789.J4
Jews in Dutch Guiana: F2431.J4
Jews in Ecuador: F3799.J4
Jews in Jamaica: F1896.J48
Jews in Latin America: F1419.J4
Jews in Mexico: F1392.J4
Jews in Panama: F1577.J4
Jews in Paraguay: F2699.J4
Jews in Peru: F3619.J4
Jews in South America: F2239.J5
Jews in the Caribbean: F2191.J48
Jews in the Dominican Republic:
  F1941.J4
Jews in the United States: E184.3+
  Civil War: E540.J5
  Revolution: E269.J5
  War of 1812: E359.9.J5
  War of 1898: E725.5.J4
Jews in Uruguay: F2799.J4
Jews in Venezuela: F2349.J48
Jews, Relations with
  United States Presidents:
    E176.472.J47
Jicarilla Indians: E99.J5
Jim Thorpe (Pa.): F159.M4
Jiménez de Quesada, Gonzalo: F2272
Jiménez, Ricardo: F1547.5
Jinotega, Nicaragua (Dept.): F1529.J4
Jipijapa, Ecuador (Canton): F3791.J3
Jiquilpan, Mexico (District): F1306
Jivaran Indians: F2230.2.J58
Jivaro Indians: F3722.1.J5
João, King of Portugal
  VI
    Court in Brazil, 1808-1821: F2534
Joaquin Miller Trail (Oregon): F882.J73
Jocko Indian Reservation
  Montana: E99.S2
John Brown's Raid, 1859: E451
John Day River and Valley (Oregon):
  F882.J76

John Fenwick's colony: F142.S2
John Marshall Day: E302.6.M4
John Muir Trail (Calif.): F868.S5
Johns Island (S.C.): F277.C4
Johnson, Andrew: E667+
  Administration, 1865-1869: E666+
  Collected works: E415.6.J65+
  Impeachment: E666
  Military governor of Tennessee:
    E531+
Johnson, Herschel Vespasian: F290
Johnson, John Albert: F606
Johnson, Lyndon Baines: E847
  Administration, 1963-1969: E846+
  Family: E848
Johnson, Richard Mentor: E340.J69
Johnson, Sir William: E195+
Johnson, Thomas: E302.6.J65
Johnson, Tom Loftin: F496
Johnson, William Samuel: E302.6.J7
Johnson's Indian School, White Sulphur
  (Kentucky): E97.6.J69
Johnson's Island (Lake Erie)
  Civil War prison: E616.J7
Johnsonville, Battle of, 1864: E476.8
Johnston, Albert Sidney: E467.1.J73
Johnston, Joseph Eggleston:
  E467.1.J74
Johnstown (Pennsylvania): F159.J7
Joliet (Illinois): F549.J7
Joliet, Louis: F1030.3
  In Mississippi Valley: F352
Jonathan Lemmon slave case, 1860:
  E450
Jonaz-Chichimeca Indians: F1221.C53
Jones, Anson: F389
Jones Beach State Park (New York):
  F127.N2
Jones, George Wallace: E415.9.J6
Jones, J. Glancy: E415.9.J7
Jones, Jacob: E353.1.J7
Jones, John Paul: E207.J7
Jones Mountain (Virginia): F232.S48
Jones, William: E57
Jonesboro (Jonesborough), Battle of,
  1864: E476.7
Jordão, Campos do (Brazil): F2631

Jornada del Muerto Road (N.M.):
F802.J67
Jornada del Muerto Wilderness (N.M.):
F802.J67
Joseph, Lake (Ontario): F1059.M9
Joseph Plains (Idaho): F752.I2
Joshua Tree National Monument
(California): F868.J6
Joyanca Site (Guatemala)
Mayas: F1435.1.J68
Juan de Fuca Strait region (Wash.):
F897.J9
Juan Fernández Islands (Chile): F3171
Juan José Mora District (Venezuela):
F2331.J82
Juaneño Indians: E99.J8
Juárez, Benito Pablo: F1233
Jubilee College State Park (Illinois):
F547.P4
Judiciary
Indians
Peru: F3429.3.J8
Judith River and Valley (Mont.):
F737.J83
Jujuy, Argentina (Province): F2906
Indian antiquities: F2821.1.J9
Jukumani Indians: F3320.2.J84
Julian, George Washington: E415.9.J95
Collected works: E415.6.J94+
July Fourth: E286.A1+
Jumano Indians: E99.J9
Jumel, Eliza (Bowen): E302.6.B91
Jumel Mansion (New York): F128.8.M8
Juneau (Alaska): F914.J9
Juniata River and Valley (Pa.): F157.J7
Junín, Peru (Dept.): F3451.J9
Junipero, Father: F864
Jupiter Inlet (Florida): F317.P2
Juquiá River (Brazil): F2631
Jurua River (Brazil): F2546
Juruna Indians: F2520.1.J8
Justo, Juan Bautista: F2848
Jutahy River (Brazil): F2546
Jutaí River (Brazil): F2546
Jutiapa (Guatemala) (Dept.): F1469.J8
Juvenile delinquency among Indians:
E98.C87

K

Kaaterskill Park (New York): F127.C3
Kachemak Bay State Park (Alaska):
F912.K26
Kachemak Bay State Wilderness Park
(Alaska: F912.K26
Kadiak Island (Alaska): F912.K62
Kagaba Indians: F2270.2.K3
Kagwahiv Indians: F2520.1.P4
Kaieteur Falls (British Guiana):
F2387.E8
Kainah Indians: E99.K15
Kaingang Indians: F2520.1.K3
Kaingangue Indians: F2520.1.K3
Kalamazoo (Michigan): F574.K1
Kalamazoo River and Valley (Michigan):
F572.K22
Kalapuyan Indians: E99.K16
Kalb, Jean, baron de: E207.K14
Kalispel Indians: E99.K17
Kalmyks in the United States: E184.K3
Kamaiurá Indians: F2520.1.K35
Kamia Indians: E99.K18, F1221.K35
Kamloops District (B.C.): F1089.K4
Kamouraska County (Québec):
F1054.K2
Kananaskis Country (Alberta):
F1079.K34
Kanarese in the United States:
E184.K35
Kanawha River and Valley (West
Virginia): F247.K3
Kandoshi Indians: F3430.1.C32
Kanjobal Indians: F1465.2.K36
Kankakee River and Valley: F532.K2
Illinois: F547.K27
Indians: E78.K15
Kankakee-St. Joseph portage (Indiana):
F532.S2
Kansa Indians: E99.K2
Kansas: F676+
African Americans: E185.93.K16
Counties, etc: F687.A+
Indians: E78.K16
Slavery: E445.K16

Kansas
  Slavery
    Pro- and anti-slavery party
      struggles: F685
  Wars
    Civil War: E508+
      Military operations: E470.9
    War of 1898: E726.K2
Kansas City (Kansas): F689.K2
Kansas City (Mo.): F474.K2+
Kansas (Kansa) Indians: E99.K2
Kansas-Nebraska Bill, May, 1854: E433
Kansas River and Valley: F687.K3
Karankawa Indians: E99.K23
Karijona Indians: F2270.2.C27
Kariri Indians: F2520.1.K4
Karok Indians: E99.K25
Karutana Indians: F2520.1.B35
Kasapata (Peru)
  Indian antiquities: F3429.1.K37
Kashaya Indians: E99.K258
Kashinaua Indians: F2520.1.C38
Kashubes in Canada: F1035.K36
Kashubes in the United States:
  E184.K37
Kaska Indians: E99.K26
Kaskaskia Indians: E99.K264
Katcinas: E98.R3
Kathadin, Mount (Me.): F27.P5
Katmai National Monument (Alaska):
  F912.K3
Kato Indians: E99.K267
Kavanagh, Edward: E302.6.K3
Kawaiisu Indians: E99.K269
Kawartha Lakes (Ontario): F1059.K2
Kawchodinne Indians: E99.K28
Kawchottine Indians: E99.K28
Kawia Indians
  Shoshoneans: E99.C155
K'axob Site (Belize)
  Mayas: F1435.1.K35
Kayabi Indians: F2520.1.K45
Kazan River and Valley (General and
  Mackenzie): F1100.K39
Kazan River and Valley (Keewatin):
  F1110.K39
Kearny, Fort: E83.866

Kearny, Philip: E467.1.K24
Kearny, Stephen Watts: E403.1.K2
  New Mexico campaign: E405.2
Kearsarge (Corvette): E595.K2
Kearsarge, Mount (New Hampshire):
  F42.C3, F42.M5
Kechua Indians: F2230.2.K4
Keeche Indians: E99.K3
Keewatin District (Canada): F1106+
  Eskimos: E99.E7
  Indians: E78.K25
  Ontario boundary: F1059.B7
Keith, Sir William: F152
Kejimkujik Lake and region (Nova
  Scotia): F1039.K43
Kejimkujik National Park (Nova Scotia):
  F1039.K44
Kekchi Indians: F1465.2.K5
Kelley, Alfred: F495
Kelleys Island (Ohio): F497.E5
Kelly, John: F128.47
Kelly's Ford (Virginia), Battle of, 1863:
  E475.3
Kenai Fjords National Park (Alaska):
  F912.K4
Kenai Peninsula (Alaska): F912.K4
Kendall, Amos: E340.K33
Kennebago Lake (Me.): F27.R2
Kennebec Patent (Me.): F27.K3
Kennebec Purchase (Me.): F27.K3
Kennebec River and Valley: F27.K32
Kennebunk (Me.): F29.K3
Kennedy, John Fitzgerald: E842+
  Administration, 1961-1963: E841+
  Family: E843
Kennedy, John Pendleton: E415.9.K35
Kennedy, Robert F.: E840.8.K4
Kennesaw Mountain, Battle of, 1864:
  E476.7
Kennesaw Mountain National Battlefield
  Park: E476.7
Kenosha (Wisconsin): F589.K3
Kensington rune stone: E105
Kent Co. (Ontario): F1059.K3
Kent Island (Maryland)
  Kent Island and Claiborne: F184
Kent Island (Md.): F187.C5

Kent, James: F123
Kenton, Simon: F517
Kentucky: F446+
  African Americans: E185.93.K3
  Confederate history: E564+
  Counties, etc: F457.A+
  Indians: E78.K3
  Slavery: E445.K5
  Virginia claims withdrawn: F454
  Wars
    Civil War: E509+, E564+
      Military operations: E472.4
    Indian wars: E83.79
    Revolution: E263.K4
    War of 1812: E359.5.K5
    War of 1898: E726.K37
    War with Mexico: E409.5.K4
Kentucky and Virginia Resolutions:
  E328
Kentucky County and District (Virginia):
  F454
Kentucky (District): F454
Kentucky Lake: F457.K29
Kentucky River and Valley: F457.K3
Kenyans in the United States:
  E184.K43
Keresan Indians: E99.K39
Kernstown, Battle of, 1862: E473.72
Kernstown, Va., 2nd Battle of, 1864:
  E476.66
Kerr, Michael Crawford: E664.K4
Kessler's Cross Lanes, W.V., Battle of,
  1861: E472.6
Ketchikan (Alaska): F914.K4
Kettle Creek, Georgia, Battle of, 1779:
  E241.K48
Kettle River and Valley
  British Columbia: F1089.K57
  Washington: F897.K3
Keuka Lake: F127.K4
Keweenaw Peninsula (Michigan):
  F572.K43
Key Peninsula (Wash.): F897.P6
Key West (Florida): F319.K4
Khmers in Canada: F1035.C27
Khmers in the United States: E184.K45
Khotana Indians: E99.K79

Kiawah Island (S.C.): F277.B3
Kichai Indians: E99.K396
Kicho Indians: F3722.1.Q48
Kickapoo Indians: E99.K4
Kickapoo River and Valley (Wisconsin):
  F587.K4
Kidnapping of slaves: E450
Kieft's War: E83.65
Kilby, Thomas Erby: F326
Kiliwa Indians: F1221.K5
Killarney Provincial Park (Ontario):
  F1059.K5
Killbear Provincial Park (Ontario):
  F1059.K52
Killdeer Mountain, Battle of, 1864:
  E83.86
Killdeer Mountain Park (N.D.): F642.D9
Killdeer Mountains (N.D.): F642.D9
Kilpatrick's expedition against
  Richmond, 1864: E476.27
King, Ernest Joseph: E182
King George's Parish (Maryland):
  F187.P9
King George's War, 1744-1748: E198
King, Horatio: E415.9.K52
King, John Alsop: F123
King Philip's War, 1675-1676: E83.67
King Ranch (Texas): F392.K47
King, Rufus: E302.6.K5
King, William: F24
King William Island (Franklin District):
  F1105.K5
King, William Lyon Mackenzie: F1033
King, William Rufus: E340.K54
King William's War, 1689-1697: E196
Kings and rulers
  Aztecs: F1219.76.K53
  Indians
    Brazil: F2519.3.K53
    Mexico: F1219.3.K55
    Peru: F3429.3.K53
Kings Bay (Georgia): F292.C17
Kings Canyon National Park: F868.K48
King's Chapel Burial Ground (Boston):
  F73.61
Kings Co
  New Brunswick: F1044.K5

Kings Co
  Nova Scotia: F1039.K5
  Prince Edward Island: F1049.K5
Kings Mountain, Battle of, 1780:
  E241.K5
Kings Mountain (Calif.): F868.S19
Kings Mountain National Military Park
  (S.C.): F277.K5
Kingston (Jamaica): F1895.K5
Kingston (New York)
  Burning by the British, 1777: E241.K6
Kingston Parish (Virginia): F232.K54
Kingston Peninsula (New Brunswick):
  F1044.K53
Kino, Eusebio Francisco: F799
Kinship
  Aztecs: F1219.76.K55
  Indians
    Brazil: F2519.3.K55
    Colombia: F2270.1.K55
    North America: E98.K48
    Peru: F3429.3.K55
    South America: F2230.1.K5
  Mayas: F1435.3.K57
Kiowa Apache Indians: E99.K52
Kiowa Indians: E99.K5
Kirkpatrick, Andrew: F138
Kirkwood, Samuel Jordan: E507+
Kissimmee River and Valley (Florida):
  F317.K57
Kissinger, Henry: E840.8.K58
Kitksan Indians: E99.K55
Kittochtinny Valley (Pa.): F157.C9
Kiyuksa Indians: E99.K59
Klamath Basin (Oregon): F882.K49
Klamath Falls (Oregon): F884.K62
Klamath Indians: E99.K7
Klamath River and Valley (California):
  F868.K55
Klikitat Indians: E99.K76
Klondike Gold Rush National Historical
  Park (Alaska): F912.K56
Klondike River (Yukon): F1095.K5
Klondike Valley (Yukon): F1095.K5
Kluane National Park and Reserve
  (Yukon): F1095.K54

Knife River and Valley (North Dakota):
  F642.K54
Knights of the Golden Circle: E458.8
Knights of the Order of the Sons of
  Liberty: E458.8
Knik Arm (Alaska): F912.K58
Knives
  Indians: E98.K54
Knott, Aloysius Leo: F186
Knowles, Sir Charles, in Cuba: F1779
Knox, Henry: E207.K74
Knoxville campaign, 1863: E475.94
Knoxville (Tenn.)
  Siege, 1863: E475.94
Knoxville (Tennessee): F444.K7
Koaiker Indians: F3722.1.C83
Koasati Indians: E99.K77
Kobena Indians: F2270.2.C8
Kobuk River and Valley (Alaska):
  F912.K6
Kodiak Island (Alaska): F912.K62
Kofán Indians: F3722.1.C67
Kohunlich Site (Mexico)
  Mayas: F1435.1.K64
Kokomish Indians: E99.S64
Kongo (African people) in South
  America: F2239.K65
Kościuszko, Tadeusz Andrzej: E207.K8
Kootenay District, River and Valley
  (B.C.): F1089.K7
Korean Air Lines Incident, 1983:
  E183.8.A+
Koreans in Argentina: F3021.K6
Koreans in Canada: F1035.K65
Koreans in Cuba: F1789.K67
Koreans in Latin America: F1419.K67
Koreans in Mexico: F1392.K65
Koreans in South America: F2239.K67
Koreans in the United States: E184.K6
Korekaru Indians: F2520.1.B35
Körner, Gustave Philip: E415.9.K7
Kotzebue Sound and region (Alaska):
  F912.K66
Kourou expedition in French Guiana,
  1763-1765: F2462
Kowoj Indians: F1465.2.K68
Koyukon Indians: E99.K79

Koyukuk River and Valley (Alaska):
  F912.K67
Koyukukkhotana Indians: E99.K79
Kraho Indians: F2520.1.C67
Kreen-Akarore Indians: F2520.1.K7
Krusenstern, Cape, National Monument
  (Alaska): F912.C34
Ku-Klux Klan: E668
  Alabama: F326
  Louisiana: F375
Kubitschek administration (Brazil):
  F2538.2+
Kubitschek, Juscelino: F2538.22.K8
Kuikuru Indians: F2520.1.K85
Kuitsh Indians: E99.K82
Kurds in the United States: E184.K87
Kuskokwim River and Valley (Alaska):
  F912.K85
Kusso Indians: E99.K83
Kutchin Indians: E99.K84
Kutenai Indians: E99.K85
Kwaiker Indians: F3722.1.C83
Kwakiutl Indians: E99.K9

L

La Antigua (Guatemala): F1476.A5
La Crosse (Wisconsin): F589.L1
La Fontaine, Sir Louis Hippolyte: F1032
La Guajira Dept. (Colombia): F2281.G8
La Guardia, Fiorello Henry: E748.L23
La Jonquière, P. J. de Taffanel, marquis
  de: F1030
La Junta de los Rios (Texas): F392.L33
La Lagunita Site (Guatemala):
  F1435.1.L24
La Libertad, Peru (Dept.): F3451.L3
La Pampa, Argentina (Province): F2924
La Paz (Bolivia)
  City: F3351.L2+
  Department: F3341.L3
La Plata (Argentina): F3011.L4
La Plata, Bolivia (City): F3351.S94
La Plata Island (Ecuador)
  Indian antiquities: F3721.1.L36
La Plata region: F2801+
La Plata River (South America): F2909

La Plata (Viceroyalty): F2841
La Rioja (Argentina)
  City: F3011.L45
  Province: F2956
    Indian antiquities: F2821.1.R58
La Sal National Forest: F832.M3
La Salle National Forest: F832.M3
La Salle Parish (La.): F377.L3
La Salle, Robert Cavelier, sieur de:
  F1030.5
  In Mississippi Valley: F352
La Salle's Colony, 1685-1687: F352
La Tour, C.A. de Saint-Étienne, sieur
  de: F1038
La Unión, El Salvador (Dept.):
  F1489.L3
La Vega (Dominican Republic) (City):
  F1939.L3
La Venta, Mexico (Tabasco)
  Indian antiquities: F1219.1.T13
La Vérendrye, Pierre Gautier de
  Varennes, sieur de: F1060.7
Labrador: F1135+
  Eskimos: E99.E7
  Indians: E78.L3
  Ungava: F1054.N5
Labrador Peninsula: F1140
  Newfoundland: F1135+
Lac La Hache region (B.C.): F1089.L3
Lacandon Indians: F1221.L2
Lackawanna River and Valley (Pa.):
  F157.L17
Lacombe County (Alberta): F1079.L32
Ladies of the Grand Army of the
  Republic: E462.17
Ladino (Latin American people) in
  Guatemala: F1477.L33
Lafayette, Fort (New York)
  Civil War prison: E616.L2
Lafayette, Marquis de: E207.L2
Lafayette National Park: F27.M9
Lafayette, Order of: E202.99.O63
Lafayette Parish (La.): F377.L2
Lafayette Park (Washington, D.C.):
  F203.5.L2
Lafitte, Jean: F374
LaFollette, Robert Marion: E664.L16

Lafourche Bayou (La.): F377.L24
Lafourche Parish (La.): F377.L25
Lagoa Santa (Brazil)
  Indian antiquities: F2519.1.L3
Laguna de Chiriquí (Panama): F1569.B6
Laguna de On Site (Belize): F1435.1.L23
Laguna Indians: E99.L2
Laguna region (Mexico): F1266
Lagunita Site (Guatemala): F1435.1.L24
LaHave River and Valley (Nova Scotia): F1039.L9
Laja River and Valley (Chile): F3174
Lake Boon (Mass.): F72.M7
Lake Clark National Park and Preserve (Alaska): F912.C47
Lake Co. (California): F868.L2
Lake Meredith National Recreation Area (Texas): F392.H95
Lake Quinsigamond (Mass.): F72.W9
Lake region (U.S.): F550.5+
Lake Roosevelt National Recreation Area (Wash.): F897.L35
Lakes Indians: E99.S546
Lamar culture: E99.L25
Lamar, Lucius Quintus Cincinnatus: E664.L2
Lamar, Mirabeau Bonaparte: F390
Lamar y Cortazar, José de: F3446
Lamb, John: E207.L22
Lambayeque (Peru)
  Department
    Indian antiquities: F3429.1.L35
Lambayeque, Peru (Dept.): F3451.L2
Lambton Co. (Ontario): F1059.L23
Lamèque Island (New Brunswick): F1044.L35
Lamoille River and Valley (Vermont): F57.L22
Lampa (Peru): F3451.L23
Lanark Co. (Ontario): F1059.L3
Lanaudière (Québec): F1054.L17
Land tenure
  Aztecs: F1219.76.L35
  Indians: E98.L3

Land tenure
  Indians
    Argentina: F2821.3.L35
    Bolivia: F3320.1.L35
    Brazil: F2519.3.L36
    Central America: F1434.2.L35
    Colombia: F2270.1.L3
    Costa Rica: F1545.3.L34
    Mexico: F1219.3.L34
    Nicaragua: F1525.3.L35
    Paraguay: F2679.3.L35
    Peru: F3429.3.L3
    Pre-Columbian America: E59.L3
    South America: F2230.1.L35
    Venezuela: F2319.3.L35
  Mayas: F1435.3.L35
Land transfers
  Indians: E91+
Landon, Alfred Mossman: F686
Lane, Harriet: E437.1
Lane, Harry: F881
Lane, James Henry: F685
Lane, Joseph: E415.9.L2
Lanfair Valley (California): F868.S14
Langdon, John: E302.6.L26
Lanier, James Franklin Doughty: F526
Lanier, Lake (Georgia): F292.S53
Lanín, Parque Nacional (Argentina): F2921
Lansing (Michigan): F574.L2
Laos in the United States: E184.L27
Lara, Venezuela (State): F2331.L3
Laramie (Wyoming): F769.L2
Larecaja Province (Bolivia): F3341.L35
Laredo Brú, Federico: F1788
Larrazolo, Octaviano Ambrosio: F801
Las Animas Mining District (Colo.): F782.L33
Las Casas Revolution: F389
Las Tunas Province (Cuba): F1855+
Las Vegas (Nevada): F849.L35
Las Villas, Cuba (Province): F1821+
Lassen Peak (Calif.): F868.L34
Lassen, Peter: F864
Lassen Volcanic National Park: F868.L34
Lassik Indians: E99.L3

L'Assomption County (Québec):
  F1054.L2
Latecunga (Ecuador): F3791.L3J3
Latin America: F1401+
  Aboriginal peoples: E65
  Description
    1607-1810: E141+
    Since 1810: F1409
  Discovery and exploration to 1600:
    E101+
  Foreign and general relations:
    F1415+
  History: F1409.6+
  Indians: E65, F1434+
  Relations with United States: F1418
Latin Americans in Brazil: F2659.S65
Latin Americans in Canada: F1035.L27
Latorre, Lorenzo: F2726
Latrobe, Benjamin Henry
  U.S. Capitol: F204.C2
Latvians in Brazil: F2659.L38
Latvians in Canada: F1035.L3
Latvians in the United States: E184.L4
Laudonnière, R.G. de: F314
Laurens, Henry: E302.6.L3
Laurentian Mountains: F1054.S3
Laurier, Wilfrid: F1033
Lava Beds National Monument
  (California): F868.L38
Laval de Montmorency, F. X. de: F1030
LaValle, Juan Galo de: F2846
Lavalleja, Uruguay (Dept.): F2731.L3
Law and legislation
  Indians
    Peru: F3429.3.L45
Lawrence, Abbott: E340.L4
Lawrence, Amos: F69
Lawrence, Amos Adams: E415.9.L38
Lawrence, Fort (Nova Scotia):
  F1039.C5
Lawrence, James: E353.1.L4
Lawrence (Kansas): F689.L4
  Haskell Institute
    Massacre, 1863: E474.97
Lawrence, William Beach: E415.9.L4
Le Conte, Mount (Tennessee):
  F443.S45

Le Droit Park (Washington, D.C.):
  F202.L4
Le Moyne de Bienville, Jean Baptiste:
  F372
Le Moyne d'Iberville, Pierre: F372
Leadville (Colorado): F784.L4
Leadville National Forest: F782.L4
League Island (Pa.): F158.68.L4
League of Córdoba: F2847
Leather District (Boston): F73.68.L43
Leatherwood Creek and Valley
  Ohio: F497.L4
Leatherwork
  Indians: E98.L4
    Pre-Columbian America: E59.L4
Leavenworth, Elias Warner: F123
Leavenworth (Kansas): F689.L5
Lebanese in Brazil: F2659.L42
Lebanese in Canada: F1035.L43
Lebanese in Colombia: F2299.L42
Lebanese in Costa Rica: F1557.L42
Lebanese in Mexico: F1392.L4
Lebanese in Suriname: F2431.L4
Lebanese in the United States:
  E184.L34
Lebanese in Uruguay: F2799.L4
Lebanese in Venezuela: F2349.L43
Lebanon (Connecticut). Moor's Indian
  Charity School: E97.6.M5
Lechiguanas Islands (Argentina):
  F2861
Lechuguilla Desert (Ariz.): F817.Y9
Lecompton Constitution
  Kansas: F685
LeConte, Mount (Tenn.): F443.S45
Ledesma, A.A. de: F2322
Lee, Charles: E207.L47
Lee, Henry: E207.L5
Lee, Jason: F880
Lee, John Doyle: F826
Lee, Richard Henry: E302.6.L4
Lee, Robert Edward: E467.1.L4
  Gettysburg Campaign: E475.53
  Mansion (Arlington, Va.): F234.A7
  Memorial (Arlington, Va.): F234.A7
  Surrender, 1865: E477.67
Lee, Thomas: F273

Lee, Thomas
  Ohio Company (1747-1779): F517
Leeds Co. (Ontario): F1059.L4
Leelanau Co. (Michigan): F572.L45
Lee's legion
  Continental Army: E260
Leesburg (Virginia)
  Military operations near, 1861:
    E472.63
Leetes island (Conn.): F102.N5
Leeward Islands: F2006
Legal status, laws, etc
  Indians
    Mexico: F1219.3.L4
Legaré, Hugh Swinton: E340.L5
Legends
  Aztecs: F1219.76.F65
  Indians
    Argentina: F2821.3.F6
    Bolivia: F3320.1.F6
    Brazil: F2519.3.F6
    Central America: F1434.2.F6
    Chile: F3069.3.F64
    Colombia: F2270.1.F6
    Costa Rica: F1545.3.F6
    Ecuador: F3721.3.F65
    French Guiana: F2460.2.F64
    Guatemala: F1465.3.F6
    Guyana: F2380.2.F6
    Mexico: F1219.3.F6
    North America: E98.F6
    Paraguay: F2679.3.F64
    Peru: F3429.3.F6
    Pre-Columbian America: E59.F6
    South America: F2230.1.F6
    Venezuela: F2319.3.F6
    West Indies: F1619.3.F6
  Mayas: F1435.3.F6
Legion of Loyal Women, Washington,
  D.C.: E462.18
Leguia, Augusto Bernardino: F3447
Lehigh (Monitor): E595.L5
Lehigh River and Valley (Pa.): F157.L6
Lehman, Herbert Henry: F124
Leif the Lucky: E105
Leisler, Jacob: F122+
Leisler's Rebellion, 1689: F122+

Leiv Eiriksson: E105
Lekwungen Indians: E99.L35
Lemmon, Jonathan: E450
Lemon, John A.: F154
Lenca Indians: F1505.2.L4
L'Enfant, Pierre C.
  Plan for Washington, D.C.: F195
Lengua Indians: F2679.2.L4
Lennox and Addington Co. (Ont.):
  F1059.L5
Lennox Co. (Ont.): F1059.L5
Lennox, Fort (Québec): F1054.I35
Lenox, Walter: F198
León, Ecuador (Province): F3741.C6
León (Nicaragua): F1536.L4
León, Nicaragua (City)
  Rivalry with Granada: F1526.25
León, Nuevo: F1316
Leonard, Daniel: E278.L5
Les Cheneaux Islands (Michigan):
  F572.L57
Les Saintes (West Indies): F2070
Lescot, Élie: F1927
Lesser Antilles: F2001+
Lesser Slave Lake (Alberta): F1079.L47
Letchworth State Park (N.Y.): F127.L57
Lethbridge (Alberta): F1079.5.L5
Leticia question: F2281.B7P1+
Levis County (Québec): F1054.L3
Lévis, François Gaston: E199
Lewis and Clark Cavern State Park
  (Mont.): F737.L65
Lewis and Clark Expedition: F592.3+
Lewis and Clark National Historical Park
  (Oregon): F882.L49
Lewis, Ellis: F153
Lewis, Francis: E302.6.L6
Lewis Mountain (Virginia): F232.S48
Lewisburg (W.Va.), Expeditions against,
  1863: E475.76
Lewiston (Idaho): F754.L6
Lexington (Kentucky): F459.L6
Lexington (Massachusetts), Battle of,
  1775: E241.L6
Lexington (Missouri), Seige of, 1861:
  E472.25
Libby Prison (Richmond): E612.L6

Liberal Republicans
  United States history: E671
Liberia
  American Colonization Society: E448
Liberians in the United States:
  E184.L53
Libertad, Peru (Dept.): F3451.L3
Liberty and Union Convention
  Nashville, Tennessee: E531+
Liberty Bell: F158.8.I3
Liberty Gap (Tennessee): F443.B35
Liberty, Statue of (New York):
  F128.64.L6
Libraries and Indians: E97.8
Lieber, Francis: E415.9.L7
Liechtensteiners in the United States:
  E184.L55
Lienzo de Cuetzpala (Codices):
  F1219.56.L46+
Lienzo de Parapan (Codices):
  F1219.56.L48+
Lienzo de Quauhquechollan (Codices):
  F1219.56.L49+
Lienzo de Tepetícpac (Codices):
  F1219.56.L52+
Lienzo de Tiltepec: F1219.56.L525+
Lienzo de Tlaxcala (Codices):
  F1219.56.L53+
Lienzo del pueblo del Señor San Pedro
  Nexicho (Codices): F1219.56.L536+
Lienzo of Petlacala (Codices):
  F1219.56.L54+
Lienzo Totomixtlahuaca (Codices):
  F1219.56.L55+
Lienzos de Acaxochitlán:
  F1219.56.L57+
Liggon's Tobacco Warehouse Prison,
  Richmond: E612.L7
L'ile de Pâques (Chile): F3169
Lilienthal, David Eli: E748.L7
Lillooet District (B.C.): F1089.L7
Lillooet Indians: E99.L4
Lima (City)
  American Congress, 1864-1865:
    F1404.4
Lima Congress, 1864-1865: F1404.4

Lima (Peru)
  City: F3601
  Department: F3451.L7
    Indian antiquities: F3429.1.L7
Lime Creek and Valley (Colorado):
  F782.S18
Limerick, Thomas Dongan, Earl of:
  F122+
Limón (Costa Rica): F1556.L5
Limón Province (Costa Rica):
  F1549.L55
Linares, Chile (Province): F3176
Lincoln, Abraham: E456+
  Administrations, 1861-1865: E456
  Cooper Institute address: E438
  Douglas debates: E457.4
  Election 1860: E440
  Election 1864: E458.4
  Emancipation Proclamation: E453
  Family: E457.25, E457.32
  Gettysburg address: E475.55
  Home in Springfield: F549.S7
  Memorial (Washington, D.C.):
    F203.4.L73
  Museum, Washington, D.C.: E457.65
  Tomb (Springfield, Illinois): E457.52
  Writings: E457.91+
Lincoln Boyhood National Memorial
  (Indiana): F532.S6
Lincoln Day: E457.7
Lincoln-Douglas debates: E457.4
Lincoln, Mary (Todd): E457.25
Lincoln, Nancy (Hanks): E457.32
Lincoln (Nebraska): F674.L7
Lincoln Parish (La.): F377.L6
Lincoln Park (Chicago): F548.65.L7
Lincoln, Sarah (Bush) Johnston:
  E457.32
Lincoln, Thomas: E457.32
Lincoln, Thomas (Tad): E457.25
Lincoln's Birthday: E457.7
Lindley's Mill, Battle of, 1781: E241.L65
Lindo, Juan: F1507.5
Liniers y Bremond, Santiago Antonio
  María de: F2845
Linn, Lewis Fields: E340.L7

Linville Gorge Wilderness (N.C.):
F262.P57

Lipan Indians: E99.L5

Liquor use
Indians: E98.L7

Lisbôa, Joaquim Nabuco, marques de
Tamandare: F2536

L'Islet County (Québec): F1054.L57

Litchfield (Conn.): F104.L7

Litchfield Hills (Conn.): F102.L6

Lithuanians in Brazil: F2659.L5

Lithuanians in Canada: F1035.L5

Lithuanians in South America:
F2239.L7

Lithuanians in the United States:
E184.L7

Litters
Indians
Peru: F3429.3.L5

Little Big Horn Battle, 1876: E83.876

Little Colorado River and Valley
Indians: E78.L58

Little Colorado River and Valley
(Arizona): F817.L5

Little Cranberry Island (Me.): F27.H3

Little Egg Harbor, N.J., Skirmish of,
1778: E241.L7

Little Gott Island (Me.): F27.H3

Little Italy (New York): F128.68.L5

Little Laurel Creek and Valley (North
Carolina): F262.L64

Little Long Island (Conn.): F102.F2

Little Miami River and Valley (Ohio):
F497.L7

Little Missouri Badlands (N.D.):
F642.L5

Little Nine Partners Patent (New York):
F127.D8

Little Pedee River (S.C.): F277.P3

Little Pipestone Creek and Valley
(Sask.): F1074.L5

Little River and Valley
Arkansas: F417.L64
Oklahoma: F702.L55
Tennessee: F443.L63

Little Rock (Arkansas): F419.L7

Little Rock (Arkansas)
Advance of Union forces upon, 1863:
E474.96

Little Tennessee River and Valley
(Georgia and Tennessee): F443.L64

Little Traverse Bay region: F572.L7

Little War, 1879-1880 (Cuba): F1785

Littlefield, George Washington: F391+

Lituya Bay (Alaska): F912.L57

Livermore, Edward St. Loe: E302.6.L66

Livermore Valley (Calif.): F868.A3

Livingston, Anne Home (Shippen):
E302.6.L67

Livingston, Edward: E302.6.L68

Livingston, Louise (Davezac) Moreau:
E302.6.L684

Livingston Manor (New York): F127.L73

Livingston Parish (La.): F377.L6

Livingston, Philip: E302.6.L7

Livingston, Robert R.: E302.6.L72

Livingston, William: E302.6.L75

Llaima, Chile (Dept.): F3141
Indian antiquities: F3069.1.L5

Llanganati Mountains (Ecuador):
F3741.L5

Llano Estacado (Texas): F392.L62

Llanos Orientales (Colombia):
F2281.L52

Llanquihue, Chile (Province): F3181

Llanquihue Lake (Chile): F3181

Loa (Chile): F3170

Loa River and Valley
Indian antiquities: F3069.1.L6

Lobos Island (Maldonado, Uruguay):
F2731.M2

Lobos, Point (Monterey Co., Calif.):
F868.M7

Local history of the United States: F1+

Lochsa River and Valley (Idaho):
F752.I2

Locke, John
Fundamental constitutions (South
Carolina): F272

Locust Grove, Okla, Battle of, 1862:
E473.8

Lodge, Henry Cabot: E660.L75+,
E664.L7

Lodore, Canyon of (Colo.): F782.M65
Loess Hills
  General and Iowa: F627.L76
  Missouri: F472.L88
Logan Canyon (Utah): F832.C3
Logan, George: E302.6.L8
Logan, James: F152
Logan, John Alexander: E664.L83
Logan, Thomas Muldrup: E467.1.L5
Logan (Utah): F834.L8
Loja (Ecuador)
  City: F3791.L6
  Province: F3741.L6
Loltun Cave (Mexico): F1435.1.L64
Loma Tina: F1939.T5
Lombardo, Guillén: F1231
London (Ontario): F1059.5.L6
London, Virginia Company of: F229
Lonesome Lake and region (B.C.):
  F1089.L75
Long Beach (Calif.): F869.L7
Long Beach Island (N.J.): F142.L65
Long Beach (N.J.): F142.O2
Long Branch Lake and region (Mo.):
  F472.M2
Long Bridge (Washington, D.C.):
  F203.7.L8
Long Cove (Texas): F392.L66
Long, Huey Pierce: E748.L86
Long Island, Battle of, 1776: E241.L8
Long Island census area Alaska:
  F912.L65
Long Island City (New York): F129.L78
Long Island (Conn.): F102.F2
Long Island (Me.): F27.H3
Long Island (New York): F127.L8
Long Lake (Michigan): F572.I6
Long Lake (New York): F127.H2
Long Point (Ontario): F1059.L8
Long Tom River and Valley
  Oregon: F882.L78
Longs Peak (Colorado): F782.L83
Longstreet, James: E467.1.L55
Lonquímay (Volcano): F3196
Lookout Mountain
  Battle of: E475.97
Lookout Mountain (Tenn.): F443.L8

Lookout, Point (Arenac Co., Michigan):
  F572.A7
Lookout, Point (Maryland)
  Civil War prison: E616.L8
López, Alfonso: F2277
López Contreras, Eleazar: F2326
López expeditions to Cuba, 1849-1851:
  F1784
López, Francia Carlos Antonio: F2686
López, Francisco Solano: F2686
Lopez Island (Wash.): F897.S2
López, José Hilario: F2276
López Mateos, Adolfo: F1235.5.L6
López, Narciso: F1784
López Portillo, José: F1235.5.L65
Lorenzan Indians: F3430.1.A54
Loreto, Peru (Dept.): F3451.L8
Lorretto Indians: F3722.1.C23
Los Alamos Co. (New Mexico):
  F802.L84
Los Alamos (N.M.): F804.L6
Los Andes, Argentina (Territory): F2853
Los Angeles (Calif.): F869.L8+
Los Angeles River (Calif.): F868.L8
Los Padres National Forest (California):
  F868.L83
Los Rios (Ecuador)
  Province: F3741.L7
Losantiville (Ohio): F499.C5+
Lost Cove (Tennessee): F443.C32
Lost River and Valley (Indiana):
  F532.O63
Loudoun, Fort (Tenn.): F443.M7
Loughborough Inlet: F1089.L78
Louisburg National Historic Park (Nova
  Scotia): F1039.5.L8
Louisburg (Nova Scotia): F1039.5.L8
  Siege and capture, 1745, 1748: E198
Louisiana: F366+
  African Americans: E185.93.L6
  Confederate history: E565+
  French control: F372, F373
  Indians: E78.L8
  Parishes (counties), etc: F377.A+
  Purchase by U.S., 1803: E333
  Reconstruction, 1865-1877: F375
  Slavery: E445.L8

Louisiana
Spanish control: F372, F373
Wars
Civil War: E510+, E565+
Military operations: E470.7
Indian wars: E83.739
Revolution: E263.L68
War of 1812: E359.5.L8
War of 1898: E726.L8
Louisiana (Colony): F372, F373
Louisiana, French: F372
Louisiana (Province), 1803-1804: F374
Louisiana Purchase, 1803: E333
Boundary question with Spanish
territory: F374
Louisiana, Spanish: F373
Louisville (Kentucky): F459.L8+
Loup River and Valley (Nebraska):
F672.L8
Lovejoy, Owen: E415.9.L89
Lovering Lake and region
(Saskatchewan): F1074.L65
Low, Seth: F128.5
Lowden, Frank Orren: F546
Lowe, Enoch Louis: F185
Lowe, Mount (Calif.): F868.L8
Lowell, Charles Russell: E467.1.L6
Lower Canada: F1051+
Lower counties on the Delaware: F167
Lower Mississippi River and Valley:
F396
Lower Peninsula, Michigan (Northern
part): F572.N7
Lowes area (Va.): F232.L8
Lowes Island (Va.): F232.L8
Loyada Lake region (Ontario):
F1059.E46
Loyal League of Union Citizens: E463
Loyal Legion of the United States,
Military Order of the: E462.2
Loyal National League of the State of
New York: E463
Loyal Publication Society: E463
Collected pamphlets: E458
Loyalists, American: E277+
Lua River and Valley (Honduras):
F1509.U4

Lubaantun, Belize (Mayas):
F1435.1.L83
Lucas, Robert: F621
Lucas, Scott Wike: E748.L893
Lucayan Indians: F1655
Lucayos: F1650+
Ludington, Henry: E263.N6
Luiseño Indians: E99.L9
Luján (Argentina): F3011.L8
Lule Indians: F2823.L8
Lumbee Indians: E99.C91
Lummi Indians: E99.L95
Lundy's Lane, Battle of, 1814: E356.L9
Lunenburg Co. (Nova Scotia):
F1039.L9
Luperón, Gregorio: F1938.4
Luray Caverns (Virginia): F232.P2
Lusatian Sorbs in the United States:
E184.S68
Lutuamian Indians: E99.L98
Luxemburgers in the United States:
E184.L88
Luz y Caballero, J.C. de la: F1783
Luzerne, Lake (N.Y.): F127.W2
Lygonia (Colony): F23
Lynch, Sir Thomas: F1884
Lynchburg campaign, 1864: E476.65
Lynches Scenic River (S.C.): F277.L94
Lyndon B. Johnson Historical Park
(Texas): F392.L87
Lynn (Massachusetts): F74.L98
Lynnhaven Parish (Virginia): F232.P87
Lyon, Nathaniel: E467.1.L9
Lytle Creek Canyon (California):
F868.S14

M

Maca Indians: F2679.2.M25
Macanché Island (Guatemala):
F1435.1.M22
MacArthur, Douglas: E745
Macauley, Edward Yorke: E182
MacDonald, John Alexander: F1033
Macdonough, Thomas: E353.1.M2
Macedonians in Canada: F1035.M33

Macedonians in the United States:
E184.M3
Maceo, Antonio: F1786
MacGregor, Gregor
Invasion of Florida, 1817: F314
Machaculi Indians: F2520.1.M27
Machado, Jose Gomes Pinheiro
Machado: F2537
Machado y Norales, Gerardo: F1787
Machias Bay (Me.): F27.W3
Machiganga Indians: F3430.1.M3
Machu Picchu (Peru)
Indian antiquities: F3429.1.M3
Maciel, Antonio Vicente Mendes: F2537
Mackay, John William: F841
Mackenna, Juan: F3094
Mackenzie District (Canada): F1096+
Eskimos: E99.E7
Indians: E78.M16
Mackenzie River and Valley: F1100.M3
Mackenzie, Sir Alexander: F1060.7
Mackenzie, William Lyon: F1032
Mackinac, Fort: F572.M14
Mackinac Island: F572.M16
Capture, 1812: E356.M15
Mackinac Island, Mich. (City):
F572.M16
Mackinac region: F572.M14
Mackinac, Straits of: F572.M14
Mackinaw Island: F572.M16
Mackinaw (Michigan): F574.M17
Maclay, William: E302.6.M14
Maclay, William Brown: E415.9.M16
Macomb, Alexander: E353.1.M3
Macon Co. (N.C.): F262.M2
Macon (Georgia): F294.M2
Military Prison
Civil War: E612.M1
Wilson's raid, 1865: E477.96
Macon, Nathaniel: E302.6.M17
Macu Indians: F2520.1.M2
Macuna Indians: F2270.2.M33
Macusi Indians: F2380.1.M3
Mad River and Valley (Vermont):
F57.M25
Madawaska Co. (New Brunswick):
F1044.M3

Madehsi Indians: E99.M115
Madeira River (Brazil): F2624
Madeleine, Îles (Québec): F1054.M18
Madeline Island (Wis.): F587.A8
Madero, Francisco Indalecio: F1234
Madison, Dolly: E342.1
Madison, Dorothy (Payne) Todd:
E342.1
Madison (Georgia) Military Prison:
E612.M2
Madison, James: E342
Administrations, 1801-1817: E341+
Collected works: E302.M19+
Family: E342.1
Madison Parish (La.): F377.M2
Madison River and Valley
Montana: F737.M24
Wyoming: F767.M34
Madison (Wisconsin): F589.M1+
Madre de Dios, Peru (Dept.): F3451.M2
Madre de Dios River (Peru): F3451.M2
Madrid
Columbus celebration, 1892: E119
Madrid, José Fernandez: F2274
Madrid, Treaty of
1670: F1884
1750: F2684
Maffitt, John Newland: E467.1.M35
Magallanes y Antártica Chilena: F3186
Magalloway Valley (Me.): F27.M18
Magdalen Islands (Québec):
F1054.M18
Magdalena, Colombia (Dept.):
F2281.M2
Magdalena River and Valley (Colombia):
F2281.M23
Magellan, Strait of: F3191
Maggie Valley (North Carolina):
F262.H35
Magic
Aztecs: F1219.76.M35
Indians: E98.M2
Mexico: F1219.3.M34
Peru: F3429.3.M3
South America: F2230.1.M24
Magloire, Paul Eugène: F1928

Magothy River and Valley (Md.):
F187.C5
Mahan, Alfred Thayer: E182
Mahican Indians: E99.M12
Mahone, William: F231
Mahoning River and Valley: F497.M2
Pennsylvania: F157.M3
Maidu Indians: E99.M18
Maine: F16+
African Americans: E185.93.M15
Ancient boundary of Acadia:
F1039.B7
Annexed to Massachusetts: F23, F24
Aroostook War, 1839: E398
Counties, etc: F27.A+
Indian wars, 1722-1726: E83.72
Indians: E78.M2
Land patents
Kennebec: F27.K3
Muscongus: F27.M95
Pejepscot: F29.B9
Wars
Civil War: E511+
Revolution: E263.M4
Military operations: E230+
Maine (Battleship)
Destruction, 1898: E721.6
Maine (Colony): F23
Maiongking Indians: F2319.2.Y4
Maipo, Battle of, 1818: F3094
Maipure Indians: F2319.2.M3
Makah Indians: E99.M19
Makka Indians: E99.M19
Malakoff Diggins State Historic Park
(Calif.): F868.N5
Malargüe, Argentina (Province): F2911
Malbaie River and Valley: F1054.M19
Maldonado (Uruguay)
City: F2791.M3
Department: F2731.M2
Malecite Indians: E99.M195
Malians
Pre-Columbian discovery of America:
E109.M34
Malians in the United States: E184.M33
Maligne Lake and region (Alberta):
F1079.J3

Mall, The (Washington, D.C.):
F203.5.M2
Malleco, Chile (Province): F3196
Malloa (Chile)
Indian antiquities: F3069.1.M25
Malpelo Island (Colombia): F2281.M3
Maltese in Canada: F1035.M35
Maltese in the United States: E184.M34
Malungeons in the United States:
E184.M44
Malvern Hill, Battle of, 1862: E473.68
Malvinas, Islas: F3031+
Mam Indians: F1465.2.M3
Mamaindê Indians: F2520.1.M24
Mammoth Cave (Ky.): F457.M2
Mammoth Cave National Park (Ky.):
F457.M2
Mana River and Valley (French Guiana):
F2467.M25
Manabí, Ecuador (Province): F3741.M2
Indian antiquities: F3721.1.M2
Manacica Indians: F3320.2.M26
Managua (Nicaragua): F1536.M26
Manahoac Indians: E99.M198
Manasota Key (Florida): F317.M18
Manassas
1st Battle of, 1861: E472.18
2d Battle of, 1862: E473.77
Manassas Battlefield Confederate Park:
E472.182
Manassas National Battlefield Park:
E472.183
Manatee River (Fla.): F317.M2
Manchac, Bayou (La.): F377.M23
Manche Indians: F1465.2.M65
Manchester (N.H.): F44.M2
Mancos River and Valley (Colo.):
F782.M7
Mandan Indians: E99.M2
Mangue Indians: F1545.2.M3
Mangum, Willie Person: E340.M3
Manhasset Neck (New York): F127.N2
Manhattan Indians: E99.M22
Manhattan (New York, N.Y.): F128+
Maniba Indians: F2520.1.B35
Manila Bay, Battle of, 1898: E717.7
Manisees Island (R.I.): F87.B6

Manitoba: F1061+
  Indians: E78.M25
  Riel Rebellion, 1885: F1060.9
Manitou (Colorado): F784.M3
Manitoulin Island: F1059.M27
Maniva Indians: F2520.1.B35
Manley, Charles: F258
Mann Creek and Valley (Idaho):
  F752.W3
Manning Provincial Park (B.C.):
  F1089.M3
Mansfield, La., Battle of, 1864: E476.33
Mansfield, Mount (Vermont): F57.M3
Mansions, Historic
  United States: E159
Manso Indians: E99.M23
Manta Indians: F3722.1.M3
Mantawa River and Valley: F1054.M2
Manti Canyon (Utah): F832.S42
Manti La Sal National Forest (Utah and
  Colorado): F832.M3
Manti National Forest: F832.M3
Mantua (Cuba): F1809.M4
Manzanar National Historic Site
  (California): F868.I6
Manzano Mountains (New Mexico):
  F802.M34
Mapa de Cuauhtinchan núm. 2:
  F1219.56.M32+
Mapa de Cuauhtinchan núm. 3:
  F1219.56.M33+
Mapa de Santiago Guevea (Codices):
  F1219.56.M36+
Mapa de Sigüenza (Codices):
  F1219.56.M364+
Mapa de Tepechpan (Codices):
  F1219.56.T46+
Mapa Quinatzin (Codices):
  F1219.56.M366+
Mapuche Indians: F3126
Maquiritare Indians: F2319.2.Y4
Mar del Plata (Argentina): F3011.M29
Mar Mountains (Brazil): F2567.9
Maracaibo Lake Region (Venezuela):
  F2331.M27
Maracaibó (Venezuela): F2341.M2
Maracay (Venezuela): F2341.M25

Maracay (Venezuela)
  Indian antiquities: F2319.1.M3
Marajó, Brazil (Island): F2568
Maraka Indians: F2319.2.Y8
Maranga (Peru)
  Indian antiquities: F3429.1.M35
Maranhão, Brazil (State): F2571
  Indian antiquities: F2519.1.M37
Marañón River (Peru): F3451.L8
Marathas in the United States:
  E184.M37
Marcahuasi Plateau (Peru): F3451.L7
Marcelina Kue Site (Paraguay):
  F2679.15.M35
Marco da Nizza, Father: E125.M3
Marco Gonzalez Site (Belize):
  F1435.1.M26
Marco Island (Florida): F317.C7
Marcy, Mount (N.Y.): F127.A2
Marcy, William Learned: E415.9.M18
Margarita (Island) Venezuela:
  F2331.M3
Marias Pass (Mont.): F737.R8
Maricopa Indians: E99.M25
Maricopa Wells, Battle of, 1857:
  E83.8565
Marie Galante (West Indies): F2076
Marietta College and the Civil War:
  E541.M3
Marietta (Georgia)
  Chattanooga Railroad Expedition,
    1862: E473.55
Marietta (Ohio): F499.M3
  Ohio Company (1786-1795): F483
Marin Peninsula (California): F868.M3
Marion, Francis: E207.M3
Mariposa estate (California): F868.M4
Maritime Provinces (Canada): F1035.8
  Indians: E78.M28
Market Street (Philadelphia):
  F158.67.M34
Marks' Mill, Ark., Battle of, 1864:
  E476.35
Maroba Indians: F2520.1.M26
Maroni River and Valley
  Dutch Guiana: F2427.M3
  French Guiana: F2467.M3

Maroon War, 1795-1796: F1884
Maroons in British Guiana: F2391.M37
Marova Indians: F2520.1.M26
Marquette, Jacques: F1030.2
  In Mississippi Valley: F352
Marriage customs and rites
  Indians
    Bolivia: F3320.1.M37
    Mexico: F1219.3.M38
    North America: E98.M27
    Peru: F3429.3.M34
    South America: F2230.1.M28
Marroquín, José Manuel: F2276.5
Marrowstone Island (Wash.): F897.J4
Marsh, John: F865
Marshall, George Catlett: E745
Marshall, Humphrey: E302.6.M35
Marshall, James Wilson: F865
Marshall, John: E302.6.M4
Martha's Vineyard (Mass.): F72.M5
Martí, José: F1783
Martiau, Nicolas: F229
Martín Garcia (Island): F2909
Martin, Morgan Lewis: F586
Martínez de Irala, Domingo: F2841
Martinez, Macimiliano Hernandez:
  F1487.5
Martínez Trueba, Andrés: F2728
Martinique (West Indies): F2081+
Martis culture: E99.M27
Maruba Indians: F2520.1.M26
Marubo Indians: F2520.1.M26
Maryland: F176+
  African Americans: E185.93.M2
  Cession to the District of Columbia:
    F197, F202.G3
  Confederate history: E566+
  Counties, etc: F187.A+
  Indians: E78.M3
  Reconstruction, 1865-1877: F186
  Slavery: E445.M3
  Wars
    Civil War: E512+, E566+
      Military operations: E470.2+
    French and Indian War: E199
    Revolution: E230+, E263.M3
    War of 1812: E359.5.M2

Maryland
  Wars
    War of 1812
      Baltimore Riot, 1812: F189.B1+
    War with Mexico: E409.5.M2
Maryland campaigns
  1862: E474.61
  1863: E475.51
  1864: E476.66
Maryland Heights (Md.): F187.W3
Maryland Loyalists Regiment:
  E277.6.M2
Maryland, Western: F186.9
Masacali Indians: F2520.1.M27
Masco Indians: F3430.1.M38
Mascouten Indians: E99.M3
Mashacali Indians: F2520.1.M27
Mashco Indians: F3430.1.M38
Mashpee Indians: E99.M4
Masko Indians: F3430.1.M38
Masks
  Indians: E98.M3
    Bolivia: F3320.1.M38
    Central America: F1434.2.M36
    Mexico: F1219.3.M4
    Peru: F3429.3.M35
    Pre-Columbian America: E59.M3
    South America: F2230.1.M3
  Mayas: F1435.3.M3
Masks, Indian
  Guatemala: F1465.3.M36
Masó, Bartolomé: F1786
Mason and Dixon's line: F157.B7
Mason, Armistead Thomson:
  E302.6.M432
Mason, Charles: E415.9.M19
Mason, George: E302.6.M45
Mason, James Murray: E415.9.M2
Mason, Jeremiah: E340.M34
Mason, John: F37
Mason, Stevens Thomson: F566
Mason's Grant (N.H.): F37
Massabesic, Lake (New Hampshire):
  F42.R7
Massachuset Indians: E99.M42
Massachusetts: F61+

Massachusetts
  African American citizens of
    Massachusetts in South Carolina,
    1845: F273
  African Americans: E185.93.M3
  Counties, etc: F72.A+
  Indians: E78.M4
  Lands in western New York: F127.H7,
    F127.T6
  Maine separated from, 1820: F24
  Revolution: E263.M4
  Shays' Rebellion: F69
  Slavery: E445.M4
  Wars
    Civil War: E513+
    Indian wars: E83.67, E83.72
    Intercolonial wars, 1689-1763:
      E196, E197, E199
    Revolution
      Military operations: E230+
      Preliminaries: E210+
    War of 1812: E359.5.M3
    War of 1898: E726.M4
  Western lands ceded, 1787: E309,
    F483
Massachusetts Bay Company: F67
Massachusetts (Province): F67
Massachusetts Ten Townships:
  F127.T6
Massacre of 1856 (Panama): F1566.45
Massawomeck Indians: E99.M424
Massey, John Edward: F231
Massie, Nathaniel: F483
Massue Seigniory (Québec):
  F1054.M35
Mataco Indians: F2823.M3
Matagorda Bay (Texas): F392.M4
Matamoros, Battle of, 1846: E406.M3
Matane County (Québec): F1054.M4
Matanuska River and Valley (Alaska):
  F912.M3
Matanzas Bay (Cuba)
  Capture of the Spanish silver-fleet,
    1628: F1779
Matanzas (Cuba)
  City: F1819.M4
  Province: F1811+

Matapédia River and Valley:
  F1054.M42
Material culture
  Aztecs: F1219.76.M37
  Indians: E98.M34
    Brazil: F2519.3.M36
    Ecuador: F3721.3.M37
    Mexico: F1219.3.M42
    Pre-Columbian America: E59.M33
    South America: F2230.1.M34
  Mayas: F1435.3.M32
Mathematics
  Indians
    Aztecs: F1219.76.M38
    Brazil: F2519.3.M37
    Ecuador: F3721.3.M38
    Mayas: F1435.3.M35
    Mexico: F1219.3.M43
    Peru: F3429.3.M36
    Pre-Columbian America: E59.M34
Mather, Cotton: F67
Mather, Increase: F67
Matheson Cove (N.C.): F262.C47
Matinicus Island (Me.): F27.M3
Matlatzinca Indians
  Modern: F1221.M27
  Pre-Columbian: F1219.8.M38
Mato Grosso (Brazil): F2576
  Jesuit missions of Paraguay: F2684
Mato Grosso do Sul (Brazil): F2578
Matrícula de tributos (Codices):
  F1219.56.M37+
Matthew, Lyon: E302.6.L9
Matto Grosso (Brazil)
  Indian antiquities: F2519.1.M4
Mattole Indians: E99.M43
Maua, Irineo Evangelista de Souza,
  visconde ne: F2536
Mauch Chunk (Pa.): F159.M4
Maue Indians: F2520.1.M3
Maule, Chile (Province): F3201
Maumee River and Valley
  Indiana: F532.M62
  Ohio: F497.M4
Mauricius, Jan Jacob: F2423
Maury, Dabney Herndon: E415.9.M3
Maury, Lake (Va.): F232.W27

Maxakali Indians: F2520.1.M27
Maximilian, Emperor of Mexico: F1233
Maxwell Land Grant: F802.M38
Maya astrology: F1435.3.A8
Mayagüez (Puerto Rico): F1981.M4
Mayan folklore and legends:
  F1435.3.F6
Mayas: F1435+
  Belize: F1445+
  Guatemala: F1465
  North America: E99.M433
  Yucatán: F1376
Mayflower Descendants, Society of:
  F68
Mayflower (Ship): F68
Mayna Indians: F3430.1.M4
Maynas, Peru (Province): F3451.B3
Mayntzhusen, Colonia: F2691.A4
Mayo Indians: F1221.M3
Mayoruna Indians: F3430.1.M45
Mazahua Indians: F1221.M33
Mazama, Mount (Oregon): F882.C8
Mazatec Indians: F1221.M35
Mazzei, Filippo: E263.V8
Mbaya Indians: F2679.2.M3
Mbwiha Indians: F2679.2.M34
Mbya Indians: F2679.2.M34
McAlpine, John: E278.M13
McArthur, Duncan: E353.1.M15
McCarren, Patrick Henry: F124
McCarthyism: E743.5
McClellan, George Brinton: E467.1.M2
McCrea, Jane: E233
McCulloch, Ben: E467.1.M24
McDonald, Charles James: F290
McDonald, Lake (Mont.): F737.G5
McDonald, William Jesse: F391+
McDowell, Va., Battle of, 1862: E473.7
McDuffie, George: E340.M17
McEnery, Samuel Douglas: F375
McGee, Thomas D'Arcy: F1032
McGregor, Mount (N.Y.): F127.S26
McHenry, Fort
  Bombardment of, 1814: E356.B2
McHenry, James: E302.6.M12
McKean, Thomas: E302.6.M13
McKinley, Ida (Saxton): E711.95

McKinley, Mount (Alaska): F912.M2
McKinley, Mount, National Park
  (Alaska): F912.M2
McKinley, William: E660.M14+,
  E711.6+
  Administrations, 1897-1901: E711+,
    E751+
  Statue (Philadelphia): F158.64.M2
McLean, John: E340.M2
McLemore Cove (Georgia): F292.W16
McLeod, Alexander
  Murder of Amos Durfee: F1032
McLeod, John: F1060.8
McLoughlin, John: F880
McMahon, John Van Lear: F185
McMullen Valley (Ariz.): F817.L3
McNabs Island (Nova Scotia):
  F1039.H3
McRae, Thomas Chipman: F411
Mdewakanton Indians: E99.M435
Meacham, Alfred Benjamin: F881
Mead, Lake, National Recreation Area
  (Arizona, Colorado, and Nevada):
  F788
Meade, George Gordon: E467.1.M38
  Monument (Washington, D.C.):
    F203.4.M5
Meade, Richard Worsam: E182
Meadow Lake Provincial Park
  (Saskatchewan): F1074.M4
Meagher, Thomas Francis: E467.1.M4
Mechanicsville, Va., Battle of, 1862:
  E473.68
Mecklenburg Resolves, 1775: E215.9
Meco Indians: F1221.C53
Meco Site (Mexico): F1435.1.M32
Medal of Honor Legion of the United
  States: E181
Medals
  Indians: E98.M35
Medellín (Colombia): F2291.M4
Medical Lake (Wash.): F897.S7
Medical services, Military
  United States
    Civil War: E621+
    Revolution: E283
    War of 1812: E362.5

Medical services, Military
  United States
    War of 1898: E731
    War with Mexico: E412.5
Medicine
  Aztecs: F1219.76.M43
  Indians: E98.M4
    Argentina: F2821.3.M4
    Bolivia: F3320.1.M4
    Brazil: F2519.3.M43
    Colombia: F2270.1.M43
    Ecuador: F3721.3.M4
    Guatemala: F1465.3.M4
    Guyana: F2380.2.M44
    Mexico: F1219.3.M5
    Nicaragua: F1525.3.M43
    Peru: F3429.3.M4
    Pre-Columbian America: E59.M4
    South America: F2230.1.M4
  Mayas: F1435.3.M4
Medicine Bow Mountains
  Colorado: F782.M43
  Wyoming: F767.M42
Medicine Bow National Forest
  (Wyoming): F767.M43
Medicine Hat (Alberta): F1079.5.M4
Medicine-man
  Indians: E98.M4
Medina Angarita, Isaías: F2326
Meek, Joseph L.: F880
Meenahga, Mount (N.Y.): F127.U4
Meeting of Consultation of Ministers of
  Foreign Affairs of American States:
  F1405.5
Megantic County (Québec): F1054.M45
Mehinacu Indians: F2520.1.M44
Meigs, Fort, Battle of, 1813: E356.M5
Mekranoti Indians: F2520.1.M45
Melgarejo, Mariano: F3324
Mellon, Andrew William: E748.M52
Melungeons in the United States:
  E184.M44
Melville Peninsula: F1110.M5
Memminger, Christopher Gustavus:
  E415.9.M4
Memorial Bridge (Washington, D.C.):
  F203.7.A6

Memorial Continental Hall (Washington,
  D.C.): F204.M5
Memorial Day: E642
Memphis, Tenn., Battle of, 1862:
  E473.5
Memphis (Tennessee): F444.M5+
Memphremagog, Lake, region
  Quebec: F1054.M5
Memphremagog, Lake, region
  (Vermont): F57.M5
Mendocino Headlands State Park
  (California): F868.M5
Mendota, Lake (Wisconsin): F587.D3
Mendoza, Antonio de, conde de
  Tendilla: F1231
Mendoza (Argentina)
  City: F3011.M45
  Province: F2911
Menefee, Richard Hickman: E340.M4
Menendez de Avila, Pedro: F314
Mennonites in Belize: F1457.M45
Mennonites in Canada: F1035.M45
Mennonites in Latin America:
  F1419.M45
Mennonites in Paraguay: F2699.M44
Mennonites in the United States:
  E184.M45
Menocal, Mario García: F1787
Menominee Indians: E99.M44
Menominee Range
  Michigan: F572.M516
  Wisconsin: F587.M49
Menominee River and Valley:
  F572.M52
  Wisconsin: F587.M5
Meo (Asian people) in the United States:
  E184.H55
Mercedes (Uruguay): F2791.M55
Mercenaries, German, in the American
  Revolution: E268
Mercer, Charles Fenton: E340.M5
Mercer, Fort, N.J. Battle of, 1777:
  E241.M5
Mercer, Hugh: E207.M5
Mercier, Honoré: F1053
Meredith, Lake, National Recreation
  Area (Texas): F392.H95

Meredith, William Morris: E415.9.M5

Mérida, Cordillera de: F2331.M52

Mérida (Mexico): F1391.M5

Mérida (Venezuela)
  City: F2341.M5
  State: F2331.M5

Meridian (Mississippi): F349.M5
  Expedition, 1864: E476.14

Merrimac and Monitor, Battle between,
  1862: E473.2

Merrimac (Frigate): E599.M5

Merrimac River and Valley
  Massachusetts: F72.M6
  New Hampshire: F42.M4

Merritt Island (Fla.): F317.B8

Mesa Verde National Park (Colorado):
  F782.M52

Mesaba range (Minnesota): F612.M36

Mescalero Indians: E99.M45

Mesilla (New Mexico), Skirmish at,
  1861: E472.32

Mesilla Valley (N.M.): F802.M4

Messiah War: E83.89

Mestizos in Peru: F3619.M47

Mestizos in the United States:
  E184.M47

Meta Department (Colombia):
  F2281.M49

Metalwork
  Indians
    Argentina: F2821.3.M44
    Bolivia: F3320.1.M43
    Central America: F1434.2.M4
    Chile: F3069.3.M4
    Ecuador: F3721.3.M45
    Mexico: F1219.3.M52
    North America: E98.M45
    Peru: F3429.3.M42
    Pre-Columbian America: E59.M47
    South America: F2230.1.M43

Metapán, El Salvador (District):
  F1489.M46

Metchosin District (B.C.): F1089.V3

Methodists and the Civil War
  United States: E540.M5

Methow Indians: E99.M46

Methow River and Valley (Wash.):
  F897.O4

Methow River and Valley (Washington):
  F897.M44

Métis: E99.M47

Métis Rebellion, 1869-1870: F1063

Métis Rebellion, 1885: F1060.9

Metztitlán, Mexico (District): F1291

Mexican War, 1846-1848: E401+

Mexicans and the Civil War
  United States: E540.M54

Mexicans in foreign countries: F1210.5
  United States: E184.M5

Mexico: F1201+
  Annexation and separation of
    Guatemala (1822-1823): F1466.4
  Annexation and separation of Central
    America (1822-1823): F1438
  Boundaries: F1249
  Cession of 1848: E408, F786
  Claims in British Honduras:
    F1449.B7M1+
  European intervention, 1861-1867:
    F1233
  Frontier troubles: F1232, F1234
    United States: F786
      Texas: F391
  Mayas: F1435.1.A+
  Military history
    Spanish conquest of, 1519-1550:
      F1230
    Texan Mier Expedition, 1842: F390
    Texan War of Independence, 1835-
      1836: F390
    War with the United States, 1845-
      1848: E405+
    Wars of Independence, 1810-1821:
      F1232
  Naval history
    War with the United States: E410
  Revolution of 1910-: F1234
  Rule over Honduras, 1822-1823:
    F1507
  Troubles with France, 1838-1839:
    F1232

Mexico (Archdiocese): F1301

Mexico (City): F1386

Mexico (City)
  Capture of, 1847: E406.M6
  Indian antiquities: F1219.1.M5
Mexico (Empire)
  Iturbide, 1821-1823: F1232
  Maximilian, 1864-1867: F1233
Mexico (Federal District): F1386
Mexico, Gulf of: F296
Mexico, Gulf of (Caribbean area):
  F2155+
Mexico (State): F1301
Mexico, Valley of: F1302
Mexico (Viceroyalty): F1231
Mezquital Valley (Mexico): F1291
Miami (Florida): F319.M6
Miami Indians: E99.M48
Miami Purchase: F483
Miami River and Valley (Ohio):
  F497.M64
Miao (Asian people) in the United
  States: E184.H55
Miccosukee Indians: E99.M615
Michaelius, Jonas: F122.1
Michelena, Santos: F2325
Michigan: F561+
  African Americans: E185.93.M5
  Counties, etc: F572.A+
  Indians: E78.M6
  Wars
    Civil War: E514+
    Indian wars: E83.76, E83.81
    Revolution
      Clark's Expedition against Detroit,
        1781: E237
    Toledo War, 1836: F497.B7
    War of 1812: E355+
    War of 1898: E726.M6
Michigan Association of Veterans of the
  War with Mexico: E401.34
Michigan, Lake, Region: F553
  Illinois: F547.M56
  Indiana: F532.M67
  Michigan: F572.M57
  Wisconsin: F587.M57
Michilimackinac: F572.M16
Michilimackinac Island (Michigan):
  F572.M16

Michoacán, Mexico (State): F1306
Micmac Indians: E99.M6
Middle America: F1421+
Middle Atlantic States: F106
  Colonial history: E188
  Indians: E78.M65
  Revolution: E230.5.M6
Middle Columbia Salish Indians:
  E99.S55
Middle Creek, Ky., Battle of, 1862:
  E472.9
Middle Eastern influences
  Mayas: F1435.3.M49
Middle Easterners in the United States:
  E184.M52
Middle Fork Feather Wild and Scenic
  River (California): F868.P85
Middle Island (New Brunswick):
  F1044.M5
Middle Tennessee: F442.2
Middle West: F350.3+
  Indians: E78.M67
Middleburg, Battle of, 1863: E475.5
Middlesex Co. (Ontario): F1059.M6
Middlesex Fells Reservation (Mass.):
  F72.M7
Middletown (Virginia), Battle of, 1864:
  E477.33
Midwest (Midwestern States): F350.3+
Mier Expedition, 1842: F390
Mifflin, Thomas: E207.M6
Migrations
  Indians
    Brazil: F2519.3.M48
    Mexico: F1219.3.M54
    Panama: F1565.3.M5
    Pre-Columbian America: E59.M58
    South America: F2230.1.M47
Mikasuki Indians: E99.M615
Mikinakwadshiwininiwak Indians:
  E99.M62
Miles, Nelson Appleton: E83.866
Military biography
  United States: E181
    20th century: E745
    Civil War: E457, E467+
    Revolution: E206+

Military biography
  United States
    War of 1812: E353+
    War of 1898: E714.5+
    War with Mexico: E403+
Military history in America
  Attacks on
    Puerto Rico, 1585, 1598, 1791:
    F1973
Military lands
  Illinois: F547.M6
  New York: F127.M4
Military museums
  United States
    Civil War: E646
    Revolution: E289
    War of 1898: E734
Military Order of Foreign Wars of the
  United States: E181
Military Order of Pulaski: E202.99.M64
Military Order of the Loyal Legion of the
  United States: E462.2
  Papers read before: E464
Military Order of the Medal of Honor:
  E462.3
Military Order of the Purple Heart: E181
Military service, Compulsory
  United States
    Civil War
      Alabama: E551.4
      Confederate Army: E545
      Union Army: E491
Military societies
  United States: E181
Military Society of the War of 1812:
  E351.5
Military tracts
  Illinois: F547.M6
  New York: F127.M4
  Virginia
    Old Northwest: F483
Militia
  United States
    War of 1812: E359.3
Milk River and Valley: F737.M48,
  F1079.M54
Mill Creek and Valley (Pa.): F157.L2

Mill Creek Indians: E99.M625
Mill Creek (Ohio): F497.H2
Mill Creek War, 1857-1865: E83.858
Mill River (Mass.): F72.H3
Mill Springs, Ky., Battle of, 1862:
  E472.9
Miller, William: F3446
Millers River and Valley (Mass.):
  F72.M73
Milliken's Bend, Battle of 1863: E475.4
Mills, David: F1033
Millstone River and Valley (New Jersey):
  F142.M64
Milner, Moses Embree: F594
Miluk Indians: E99.C8742
Milwaukee (Wisconsin): F589.M6+
Mimbreño Indians: E99.M63
Mimbres culture: E99.M76
Mimbres River and Valley (N.M.):
  F802.G7
Minaco Indians: F2520.1.M44
Minanha Site (Belize): F1435.1.M5
Minas Geraes, Brazil (State): F2581
Mine Creek., Kan., Battle of, 1864:
  E477.16
Mine Run (Virginia), campaign, 1863:
  E475.78
Mineral Co. (Nevada): F847.M5
Mineral King Valley (California):
  F868.T8
Mineralogy
  Indians
    Mexico: F1219.3.M58
Mines and mining
  Indians
    Mexico: F1219.3.M58
Mingan Islands (Québec): F1054.M59
Mingo Indians: E99.M64
Mingo Swamp (Mo.): F472.M48
Miniconjou Indians: E99.M642
Minidoka Internment National
  Monument (Idaho): F752.J5
Minisink Indians: E99.M65
Minisink, N.Y., Battle of, 1779: E241.M6
Minisink Patent (1704): F142.B7
Minisink region (New York): F127.M5

Minneapolis and St. Paul (Minnesota):
F614.M6
Minneapolis (Minnesota): F614.M5+
Minnedosa River and Valley (Manitoba):
F1064.M5
Minneopa State Park (Minn.): F612.B6
Minnesota: F601+
African Americans: E185.93.M55
Counties, etc: F612.A+
Indians: E78.M7
Wars
Civil War: E515+
Indian wars: E83.86, E83.863
War of 1898: E726.M7
Minnesota River and Valley: F612.M4
Minnetonka, Lake (Minnesota):
F612.H5
Minnewaska, Lake (N.Y.): F127.U4
Minoans in Central America:
F1440.M55
Minook Creek and Valley: F912.M55
Minorcans in the United States:
E184.M53
Minorities
America: F1035.A1+
Argentina: F3021.A1+
Central America: F1440.A1+
Latin America: F1419.A1+
South America: F2239.A1+
West Indies: F1629.A+
Minuit, Peter: F122.1
Minute Man National Historical Park
(Mass.): F72.M7
Minute Men of 1861: E493.9
Minutemen
United States Revolution: E263.A+
Miquelon: F1170
Miquelon Lake Provicial Park (Alberta):
F1079.M57
Mirador (Guatemala): F1435.1.M54
Miramichi River and Valley (New
Brunswick): F1044.M5
Miranda, Francisco de: F2323
Miranda, Venezuela (State): F2331.M6
Miranda's Expedition to Venezuela,
1806: F2323
Miró, Esteban: F373

Miscegenation
African Americans
United States: E185.62
Miscou Island (New Brunswick):
F1044.M53
Mishikhwutmetunne Indians:
E99.C8742
Misiones, Argentina (Province): F2916
Jesuit missions of Paraguay: F2684
Part awarded to Brazil: F2626
Miskigula Indians: E99.P26
Miskito Indians: F1529.M9
Mission buildings, Spanish: F862
Missionary Ridge, Battle of, 1863:
E475.97
Missions
Indians
Argentina: F2821.3.M5
Bolivia: F3320.1.M47
Brazil: F2519.3.M5
Central America: F1434.2.M6
Chile: F3069.3.M5
Colombia: F2270.1.M5
Ecuador: F3721.3.M6
Guatemala: F1465.3.M57
Guyana: F2380.2.M57
Mexico: F1219.3.M59
Nicaragua: F1525.3.M57
North America: E98.M6
Paraguay: F2679.3.M5
Peru: F3429.3.M6
Pre-Columbian America: E59.M65
South America: F2230.1.M5
United States: F864
Venezuela: F2319.3.M5
Mayas: F1435.3.M53
Missisauga Indians: E99.M68
Missisquoi County (Québec): F1054.M6
Missisquoi River and Valley
Vermont: F57.M7
Missisquoi River and Valley (Québec):
F1054.B8
Mississippi: F336+
African Americans: E185.93.M6
Confederate history: E568+
Counties, etc: F347.A+
Indians: E78.M73

Mississippi
  Natchez District of West Florida: F341
  Reconstruction, 1865-1877: F341
  Slavery: E445.M6
  Wars
    Civil War: E516+, E568+
      Military operations: E470.7
    Indian war, 1813-1814: E83.813
    War with Mexico: E409.5.M56
Mississippi River: F350.3+
  Right of navigation: F373
  Sources: F597
Mississippi River and Valley: F350.3+
  Arkansas: F417.M6
  Illinois: F547.M65
  Iowa: F627.M64
  Kentucky: F457.M6
  Louisiana: F377.M6
  Minnesota: F612.M5
  Mississippi: F347.M6
  Missouri: F472.M6
  Tennessee: F443.M6
  Wisconsin: F587.M63
Mississippi River and Valley (Ontario): F1059.M65
Mississippi Valley: F350.3+
  French explorations: F350.3+
  Indians: E78.M75
  Wars
    Black Hawk War, 1832: E83.83
    Civil War: E569+
      Military operations: E470.8, E476.3, E477.1
    Revolution
      Clark's expedition, 1778: E234
Mississippi Valley, Lower: F396
Mississippi Valley, Upper: F597
Mississippian culture: E99.M6815
Missoula Co. (Mont.): F737.M6
Missoula (Mont.): F739.M7
Missouri: F461+
  African Americans: E185.93.M7
  Counties, etc: F472.A+
  Indians: E78.M8
  Kansas troubles, 1854-1859: F685
  Missouri Compromise, 1820: E373
  Slavery: E445.M67

Missouri
  Wars
    Civil War: E517+, E569+
      Military operations: E470.4+, E470.8, E470.9
    War of 1898: E726.M8
Missouri Compromise, 1820: E373
  Repeal, 1854: E433
Missouri Indians: E99.M682
Missouri River and Valley: F598
  Iowa: F627.M66
  Kansas: F687.M6
  Missouri: F472.M7
  Montana: F737.M7
  Nebraska: F672.M6
  North Dakota: F642.M6
  South Dakota: F657.M7
Missouri Valley
  Indian antiquities: E78.M82
Mistassin Indians: E99.M683
Misti (Volcano): F3451.A7
Mitchel, Ormsby Macknight: E467.1.M6
Mitchell Lake (B.C.): F1089.C3
Mitchell, Mount (N.C.): F262.B4
Mitla, Mexico (Oaxaca)
  Indian antiquities: F1219.1.M6
Mitre, Bartolomé: F2847
Miwok Indians: E99.M69
Mixco Viejo Site (Guatemala): F1435.1.M58
Mixe Indians: F1221.M67
Mixed descent
  Indians: E99.M693
    Bolivia: F3320.1.M5
    Chile: F3069.3.M55
    North America: E98.M63
    Peru: F3429.3.M63
    Pre-Columbian America: E59.M66
    South America: F2230.1.M54
Mixtec codices: F1219.54.M59
Mixtec Indians
  Modern: F1221.M7
  Pre-Columbian: F1219.8.M59
Mizque Province (Bolivia): F3341.M58
Moache Indians: E99.M697
Moapa River and Valley (Nevada): F847.C5

Mobile (Alabama): F334.M6
  Military operations, 1864: E476.85
Mobile Bay (Alabama): F332.M58
Mobile campaign, 1865: E477.94
Mobile District (West Florida): F301,
  F341
Mobile Indians: E99.M698
Mochica Indians: F3430.1.M6
Mocho Indians: F1221.M74
Mocoa Indians: F2270.2.M5
Mocobi Indians: F2823.M6
Modoc Indians: E99.M7
Modoc War, 1872-1873: E83.87
Moena Indians: F3430.1.M38
Mogollon Apache: E99.M75
Mogollon culture: E99.M76
Moguex Indians: F2270.2.M6
Mohammedans in Latin America:
  F1419.M87
Mohammedans in the United States:
  E184.M88
Mohave Desert (California): F868.M65
Mohave Indians: E99.M77
Mohawk Indians: E99.M8
Mohawk River and Valley (New York):
  F127.M55
Mohawk Trail
  Massachusetts: F72.B5
  New York: F127.M55
Mohawk Valley (Ariz.): F817.Y9
Mohegan Indians: E99.M83
Mohonk Lake (N.Y.): F127.U4
Mojarra
  Mayas: F1435.1.M64
Mojo Indians: F3320.2.M55
Molala Indians: E99.M84
Molino del Rey, Battle of, 1847:
  E406.M65
Molle (Chile)
  Indian antiquities: F3069.1.M6
Mollo culture: F3320.2.M57
Monacan Indians: E99.M85
Monadnock, Mount (New Hampshire):
  F42.C5
Monagas, José Tadeo: F2325
Monagas, Venezuela (State):
  F2331.M7

Moncton (New Brunswick): F1044.5.M7
Money
  Indians: E98.M7
    Mexico: F1219.3.M597
    Pre-Columbian America: E59.M7
Monhegan Island (Me.): F27.M7
Monica Bay region (Calif.): F868.L8
Monitor and Merrimac, Battle between,
  1862: E473.2
Monitor (Ironclad): E595.M7
Moniz family: E113
Monmouth, Battle of, 1778: E241.M7
Monmouth Patent (N.J.): F142.M7
Mono Indians: E99.M86
Mono Lake (Calif.): F868.M67
Monocacy, Battle of the, 1864: E476.66
Monogalia Co. (Minnesota): F612.K2
Monongahela National Forest (West
  Virginia): F247.M59
Monongahela River and Valley
  Pennsylvania: F157.M58
  West Virginia: F247.M6
Monroe, James: E302.M74+
Monroe, James, 1758-1831
  Administrations, 1817-1825: E371+
Monroe, James, 1799-1870: E340.M7
Monroe Street (Chicago): F548.67.M75
Monroe's Crossroads, N.C., Battle of,
  1865: E477.7
Mont Castleguard (Alberta): F1079.B5
Mont-Orford Park (Québec): F1054.P37
Montagnais Indians: E99.M87
Montana: F726+
  African Americans: E185.93.M8
  Counties, etc: F737.A+
  Indian wars: E83.877
  Indians: E78.M9
Montaña, La (region): F3451.M6
Montara Mountain (California):
  F868.S33
Montauk Indians: E99.M88
Montcalm-Gozon, Louis Joseph de:
  E199
Monte Albán (Mexico)
  Indian antiquities: F1219.1.O11
Monte Irazú (Costa Rica): F1549.I7

Monte Plata (Dominican Republic): F1939.M6

Monte Roraima (Brazil): F2609

Monte Tina: F1939.T5

Monteagudo, Bernardo: F2845

Montego Bay (Jamaica): F1895.M6

Montenegrins in the United States: E184.M66

Monterey Bay (Calif.): F868.M7

Monterrey (Mexico): F1391.M7+
Battle of, 1846: E406.M7

Montes, Ismael: F3325

Montevideo (Uruguay): F2781
Siege, 1843-1851: F2726

Montezuma Castle National Monument (Arizona): F817.M57

Montezuma I, Emperor of Mexico: F1219.75.M75

Montezuma II, Emperor of Mexico: F1219, F1230

Montgomery (Alabama): F334.M7+

Montgomery, Richard: E207.M7

Montgomery, Sir Robert: F289
Margravate of Azilia: F289

Monticello (Virginia): E332.74

Montmagny County (Québec): F1054.M79

Montmorency County (Québec): F1054.M8

Montpelier (Vermont): F59.M7

Montreal District (Québec): F1054.M83

Montreal (Québec): F1054.5.M8+

Monts, Pierre de Guast, sieur de: F1030

Montserrat (West Indies): F2082

Montt, Manuel F. A. J.: F3095

Monument Cemetery (Philadelphia): F158.61.M8

Monument Valley (Arizona): F817.M6

Monuments
Indians
Mexico: F1219.3.M6
United States
Persons: E312.45+, E332.73
Wars and battles: E641+, E733

Moody, James: E278.M8

Moore's Creek Bridge, N.C., Battle of, 1776: E241.M8

Moor's Indian Charity School (Lebanon, Connecticut): E97.6.M5

Moose Mountain Provincial Park (Saskatchewan): F1074.M66

Moosehead Lake region (Me.): F27.M8

Mopan Indians: F1465.2.M65

Moquegua, Peru (Dept.): F3451.M8

Moquelumnan Indians: E99.M89

Mora, Juan Rafael: F1547.5

Morant Bay Rebellion, 1865-1866: F1886

Moravian Indians: E99.M9

Moravians in the United States: E184.M7
Revolution: E269.M6

Morazán, Francisco: F1438

Morehead, John Motley: F258

Morehouse Parish (La.): F377.M7

Morelia (Mexico): F1391.M8

Morelos, Mexico (State): F1311

Morelos y Pavón, José María Teclo: F1232

Moreno Creek and Valley (N.M.): F802.C7

Moreno, Mariano: F2845

Moreno Valley (Calif.): F868.R6

Morgan, Daniel: E207.M8

Morgan, George: E302.6.M6

Morgan, John Hunt: E467.1.M86
Kentucky raid, 1862-1863: E474.75
Kentucky raid, July 1862: E474.32
Kentucky raid, May-June 1864: E476.82
Raid in Kentucky, Indiana, and Ohio, 1863: E475.18

Morgan's Cavalry Division
Confederate Army: E547.M8

Morillo y Morillo, Pablo: F2324

Moriníngo Martínez, Higinio: F2689

Mormon settlement
Utah: F826

Mormons
Utah
Rebellion, 1857-1859: F826

Mormons in Canada: F1035.M67

Mormons in Mexico: F1392.M6
Mormons in the United States:
E184.M8
Moro Indians: F2679.2.M6
Morrill Co. (Nebraska): F672.M7
Morrill, Justin Smith: E664.M8
Morris, Charles: E353.1.M8
Morris Creek and Valley (West Virginia):
F247.B6
Morris, Gouverneur: E302.6.M7
Morris Island (S.C.), Military operations
on, 1863: E475.63
Morris Mansion (New York): F128.8.M8
Morris, Margaret (Hill): E263.N5
Morris, Mary (White): E302.6.M81
Morris, Richard Valentine: E335
Morris River and Valley (Manitoba):
F1064.M67
Morris, Robert: E302.6.M8
Morris, Thomas: E340.M8
Morrisania Manor (New York):
F128.68.B8
Morrison Cave (Mont.): F737.L65
Morristown National Historical Park
(N.J.): F142.M85
Morro Bay (California): F868.S18
Morro Bay State Park (California):
F868.S18
Morro, El, National Monument (N.M.):
F802.E5
Morro Island (Panama): F1569.P3
Morrow, Dwight Whitney: E748.M75
Morrow, Jeremiah: E340.M83
Mortality and health statistics
United States
Civil War: E621+
Morton, Camp, Indianapolis
Civil War prison: E616.M8
Morton, Julius Sterling: E664.M82
Morton, Levi Parsons: E664.M85
Morton, Oliver Perry: E506+
Mortuary customs
Indians: E98.M8
Argentina: F2821.3.M6
Peru: F3429.3.M7
Pre-Columbian America: E59.M8
South America: F2230.1.M6

Mortuary customs
Mayas: F1435.3.M6
Mosby, John Singleton: E467.1.M87
Moseten Indians: F3320.2.M6
Mosier Hills (Oregon): F882.W3
Moslems in Latin America: F1419.M87
Moslems in the United States:
E184.M88
Mosquera, Tomás Cipriano de: F2276
Mosquitia, Honduras (District):
F1509.M9
Mosquitia, Nicaragua (region):
F1529.M9
Mosquito Coast (Nicaragua): F1529.M9
Transfer to Nicaragua by Great
Britain, 1893: F1526.27
Mosquito Indians: F1529.M9
Mosquito Reservation (Nicaragua):
F1529.M9
Mossy Creek, Tenn., Battle of, 1863:
E475.9
Motagua River (Guatemala):
F1469.M68
Mother Neff State Park (Texas):
F392.C8
Mothers of U.S. Presidents: E176.3
Motherwell Farmstead National Historic
Park (Saskatchewan): F1074.W28
Motilon Indians: F2319.2.M6
Motilone Indians: F2319.2.M6
Motilones Indians: F2319.2.M6
Motion pictures about the war
Civil War, 1861-1865: E656
Motochintlec Indians: F1221.M74
Motozintlec Indians: F1221.M74
Motoztintlec Indians: F1221.M74
Mott, Lucretia (Coffin): E449
Moultrie, Fort, Battle of, 1776: E241.M9
Moultrie, William: E207.M85
Mound builders: E73, E78.A+
Mounds: E73, E78.A+
Mounds, Cave of the (Wisconsin):
F587.D3
Mount Adams (Wash.): F897.K6
Mount Castleguard (Alberta): F1079.B5
Mount Desert Island
Jesuit station, 1609: F1038

Mount Desert Island (Me.): F27.M9
Mount Diable State Park (Calif.):
F868.C76
Mount Hope Cemetery (Boston):
F73.61
Mount LeConte (Tennessee): F443.S45
Mount Marcy (N.Y.): F127.A2
Mount McKinley National Park (Alaska):
F912.M23
Mount Moosilaukee (N.H.): F42.G7
Mount Orford Park (Québec):
F1054.P37
Mount Pleasant (District of Columbia):
F202.M9
Mount Rainier National Park (Wash.):
F897.R2
Mount Reynolds (Mont.): F737.G5
Mount Rushmore National Memorial:
F657.R8
Mount San Jacinto State Park (Calif.):
F868.R6
Mount Tamalpais State Park
(California): F868.M3
Mount Timpanogos (Utah): F832.U8
Mount Vernon: E312.5
Mount Vernon Memorial Highway
(Virginia): F232.G38
Mountain Lake (Va.): F232.G4
Mountain Meadows Massacre, 1857:
F826
Mountain people: E184.M83
Ramapo Mountains: E184.R3
Mountaineer (Montagnais) Indians:
E99.M87
Mouse River and Valley
Manitoba: F1064.S6
Saskatchewan: F1074.S67
Mowat, Sir Oliver: F1058
Moxie Pond (Me.): F27.S7
Moxos, Bolivia (Province): F3341.M9
Moylan, Stephen: E207.M9
Mozambicans in Brazil: F2659.M69
Mt. Castleguard (Alberta): F1079.B5
Mt. LeConte (Tenn.): F443.S45
Muckleshoot Indians: E99.M917
Mucury Colony (Brazil): F2581
Muename Indians: F2270.2.M75

Muenane Indians: F2270.2.M75
Muhlenberg, John Peter Gabriel:
E207.M95
Muinana Indians: F2270.2.M75
Muinane-Bora Indians: F2270.2.M75
Muinane Indians: F2270.2.M75
Muinani Indians: F2270.2.M75
Muir Glacier (Alaska): F912.M9
Muir Trail (Calif.): F868.S5
Muir Woods National Monument
(California): F868.M3
Mul-Chic (Mexico): F1435.1.M84
Mulattoes
United States: E185.62
Mulberry Island (Virginia): F232.J2
Mullica River (N.J.): F142.M9
Mulligan, Hercules: E302.6.M88
Mulluk Indians: E99.C8742
Multnomah Indians: E99.M92
Mummies
Indians
Peru: F3429.3.M8
Mundurucu Indians: F2520.1.M8
Munku Indians: F2520.1.I7
Munsee Indians: E99.M93
Mura Indians: F2520.1.M9
Murfreesboro campaign, 1862-1863:
E474.77
Murfreesboro (Tennessee), Action at
and surrender of, July 1862: E474.34
Murphy, Henry Cruse: F123
Murphys Lake (La.): F377.N4
Murray, James: E278.M98
Murray, Lake, and Region (S.C.):
F277.M87
Murray, William Henry: F700
Murrell, John A.: F396
Murrieta, Joaquin: F865
Muscatatuck National Wildlife Refuge
(Ind.): F532.M87
Muscatine (Iowa): F629.M9
Muscle Shoals (Tenn.): F332.T2
Muscongus lands (Me.): F27.M95
Muscongus Patent (Me.): F27.M95
Muskeget Island ((Mass.): F72.N2
Muskegon (Michigan): F574.M9

Muskegon River and Valley (Michigan): F572.M93

Muskhogean Indians: E99.M95

Muskingum River and Valley (Ohio): F497.M92

Muskogee (Oklahoma): F704.M9

Muskoka District (Ontario): F1059.M9

Muskoka Lake region (Ontario): F1059.M9

Muskwa-Kechika Management Area (British Columbia): F1089.M87

Muslims in Canada: F1035.M87

Muslims in Latin America: F1419.M87

Muslims in the United States: E184.M88

Mustang Island State Park (Texas): F392.N8

Mutilones (Indians): F2319.2.M6

Mutiny Act, 1765: E215.4

Mutiny of the Pennsylvania line, 1781: E255

Muzo Indians: F2270.2.M8

Myakka River State Park (Florida): F317.M92

Mystery Mountain (B.C.): F1089.C7

Mythology
  Aztecs: F1219.76.R45
  Indians: E98.R3
    Argentina: F2821.3.R4
    Bolivia: F3320.1.R3
    Brazil: F2519.3.R3
    Central America: F1434.2.R3
    Chile: F3069.3.R44
    Colombia: F2270.1.R4
    Costa Rica: F1545.3.R4
    Ecuador: F3721.3.R44
    Guatemala: F1465.3.R4
    Mexico: F1219.3.R38
    Nicaragua: F1525.3.R44
    Paraguay: F2679.3.R44
    Peru: F3429.3.R3
    Pre-Columbian America: E59.R38
    South America: F2230.1.R3
  Mayas: F1435.3.R3

N

Nabesnatana Indians: E99.T187

Nabuco, Joaquim: F2536

Naches River and Valley (Wash.): F897.Y18

Nacimiento River and Valley (California): F868.N16

Nacogdoches District (Texas): F392.N24

Nahane Indians: E99.N125

Nahoas: F1221.N3

Nahua Indians
  Modern: F1221.N3
  Pre-Columbian: F1219.73+

Nahuatl Indians: F1221.N3

Nahuatlecas: F1221.N3

Nahuel Huapí, Lake (Argentina): F2951

Nahuel Huapí, Parque Nacional de (Argentina): F2951

Naj Tunich
  Mayas: F1435.1.N35

Nakimu Caves (B.C.): F1089.S4

Nambicuara Indians: F2520.1.N3

Names
  Aztecs: F1219.76.N35
  Indians: E98.N2
    Argentina: F2821.3.N3
    Brazil: F2519.3.N35
    El Salvador: F1485.3.N35
    Nicaragua: F1525.3.N35
    Venezuela: F2319.3.N5

Names, African American: E185.89.N3

Nancy Hanks Lincoln Memorial (Indiana): F532.S6

Nanticoke Indians: E99.N14

Nanticoke River and Valley
  Delaware: F172.N35
  Maryland: F187.N35

Nantucket Island (Mass.): F72.N2

Napo Indians: F3722.1.Q48

Napo-Pastaza, Ecuador (Province): F3741.N3

Naranjo Site (Guatemala): F1435.1.N37

Narcotics
  Indians: E98.N5
    Bolivia: F3320.1.N37

Narcotics
  Indians
    Colombia: F2270.1.N35
    Ecuador: F3721.3.N35
    Pre-Columbian America: E59.N5
    South America: F2230.1.N37
Nariño, Antonio: F2274
Nariño, Colombia (Dept.): F2281.N3
Narragansett Bay region: F87.N2
Narragansett country: F82
Narranganset Indians: E99.N16
Narváez, Pánfilo de: E125.N3
Nasca Indians: F3430.1.N3
Nash, Francis: E207.N2
Nashawena Island (Mass.): F72.E5
Nashua (New Hampshire): F44.N2
Nashville (Tennessee): F444.N2+
  Battle of, 1864: E477.52
  Southern Convention, 1850: E423
Naskapi Indians: E99.N18
Nassau (Bahamas): F1659.N3
Nat Turner's Insurrection, 1831:
  F232.S7
Natchesan Indians: E99.N19
Natchez District of West Florida: F341
Natchez Indians: E99.N2
Natchez Massacre, 1729: E83.73
Natchez (Mississippi): F349.N2
Natchez Trace: F217.N37
Natchitoches Parish (La.): F377.N4
National Alliance, Daughters of
  Veterans: E462.99.D2
National Association of Army Nurses of
  the Civil War: E621
National Association of Naval Veterans:
  E462.5
National Association of Veterans of the
  Mexican War: E401.3
National capital, Location of
  United States: F195
National Cathedral (Washington, D.C.):
  F204.C3
National characteristics
  America: E169.1
National Convention of the Soldiers of
  the War of 1812: E351.2

National parks
  United States: E160
National Road (Pa.): F157.C85
National Society of the Colonial Dames
  of America: E186.4
National Society of the Colonial
  Daughters of America: E186.99.N33
National Society of United States
  Daughters of 1812: E351.6
National Soldiers Historical Association:
  E462.98
National Theatre (Washington, D.C.):
  F204.N23
National Veteran Club of the United
  States: E462.99.N27
Natsitkutchin Indians: E99.N22
Natural Bridge (Va.): F232.R68
Natural Tunnel State Park (Virginia):
  F232.S3
Natural Tunnel (Virginia): F232.S3
Naugatuck Indians: E99.N23
Naugatuck River and Valley (Conn.):
  F102.N2
Nauset Beach (Mass.): F72.C3
Nauset Indians: E99.N25
Naushon Island (Mass.): F72.E5
Navaho War, 1858-1868: E83.859
Navajo Indians: E99.N3
Naval and Military Order of the Spanish-
  American War: E714.3.N2+
Naval biography
  United States: E182
    20th century: E746
    Civil War: E467+
    Revolution: E206+
    War of 1812: E353+
    War of 1898: E714.5+
    War with Mexico: E403+
Naval blockades
  Civil War: E480
Naval Order of the United States: E182
Naval revolt (Brazil): F2537
Naval societies
  United States: E182
Naval veterans' organizations
  United States: E182

Naval war with France (U.S.), 1798-1800: E323
Navarrese in Latin America: F1419.N38
Navassa: F1991
Navesink River and Valley (N.J.): F142.M7
Navies
  Spain
    War of 1898: E727.8
  United States
    Revolution: E271
    War of 1812: E360
    War of 1898: E727
Navigation laws, British Enforcement (1775-1783): E215.1
Navy Island (Ontario): F1059.W36
Ñawinpukyo (Peru)
  Indian antiquities: F3429.1.N29
Nayarit, Mexico (State): F1313
Nazareth Hall, Nazareth, Pa. and the Civil War: E541.N2
Nazca culture (Peru)
  Indian antiquities: F3429.1.N3
Nazca (Peru)
  Indian antiquities: F3429.1.N3
Neahkahnie Mountain (Oregon): F882.T5
Nebraska: F661+
  African Americans: E185.93.N5
  Civil War: E518+
  Counties, etc: F672.A+
  Indians: E78.N3
  Slavery: E445.N2
Nebraska-Kansas Bill, May 1854: E433
Necessity, Fort: E199
Neches River and Valley (Texas): F392.N35
Negro emancipation
  Haiti: F1923
  Jamaica: F1886
Negro insurrections
  Jamaica, 1831: F1886
Negro River (Brazil): F2546
Negroes in British Guiana: F2391.N4
Nehalem Indians: E99.N45
Neiva, Colombia (Province): F2281.N5
Nelson, Knute: E664.N4

Nenana River and Valley (Alaska): F912.N45
Nendiume Site (Mexico): F1435.1.C49
Nepisiguit River and Valley (New Brunswick): F1044.N7
Nespelim Indians: E99.N46
Netherlands
  Attack on Puerto Rico, 1625: F1973
  Blockade of Venezuela, 1908: F1923
Netherlands Antilles: F2141
Netherlands Guiana: F2401+
Netherlands West Indies: F2141
Netsikutchin Indians: E99.N22
Neuquén, Argentina (Territory): F2921
  Indian antiquities: F2821.1.N4
Neuquén River (Argentina): F2921
Neuse River and Valley (N.C.): F262.N48
Neutral Nation Indians: E99.N48
Neutral trade, American, 1800-1810: E336+
Neutrality proclamation, 1793: E313+
Nevada: F836+
  African Americans: E185.93.N52
  Civil War: E519+
  Counties, etc: F847.A+
  Indians: E78.N4
Nevada Test Site (Nev.): F847.N9
Nevado Sarcantay (Peru): F3451.C9
Nevis (West Indies): F2084
New Albion Grant: F137
New Amsterdam (British Guiana): F2389.N4
New Amsterdam (New York before 1775): F128.4
New Bern, N.C., Battle of, March 1862: E473.34
New Bern (North Carolina)
  Expedition against, 1864: E476.23
  Expedition from, Dec. 1862: E474.52
New Brunswick (Canada): F1041+
  American Revolution: E263.N9
    Loyalists: E277
  Boundary troubles with U.S.: E398
  Indians: E78.N46
New Deal period
  United States history: E806

New England: F1+
  Colony and province: F7, F7.5
  Council for: F7
  Dominion of, 1686-1689: F7.5
  Hurricane, 1938: F9
  Indians: E78.N5
  Nova Scotia settlement, 1760-1761:
    F1038
  United colonies, 1643-1684: F7
  Wars
    Indian wars: E83.63, E83.67,
      E83.72
    Intercolonial wars, 1689-1763:
      E196, E197, E198, E199
    Revolution of 1689: F7.5
    War of 1812, Federalist opposition
      to: E357.6+
New England Association of Soldiers of
  the War of 1812: E351.27
New England Emigrant Aid Company:
  F685
New France
  Acadia: F1036+
  Conflicts with British colonies, 1689-
    1763: E196, E197, E199
  English conquests: F1030, F1030.9
  Explorations: E131+
    Mississippi River and Valley: F351
  Hudson's Bay Company: F1060+
  Indian wars: E81+
  Intercolonial wars: E199
    Quebec campaign, 1759: E199
New France, Company of, 1629-1663:
  F1030
New Granada
  Audiencia: F2272
  Republic, 1842-1858: F2276
  State, 1831-1842: F2275
  United Provinces, 1811-1816: F2274
  Viceroyalty: F2272
New Hampshire: F31+
  African Americans: E185.93.N53
  Counties, etc: F42.A+
  Indians: E78.N54
  Wars
    Civil War: E520+
    French and Indian War: E199

New Hampshire
  Wars
    Indian wars: E83.72
    Revolution: E263.N4
      Military operations: E230+
    War of 1812: E359.5.N3
    War of 1898: E726.N3
New Hampshire Grants: F52
New Harmony (Indiana): F534.N5
New Haven Colony: F98
New Haven (Conn.): F104.N6+
  Invasion, 1779: E241.N5
New Hope Church, Battle of, 1864:
  E476.7
New Jersey: F131+
  African Americans: E185.93.N54
  Counties, etc: F142.A+
  East Jersey, 1676-1702: F137
  Fenwick's colony: F142.S2
  Indians: E78.N6
  Slavery: E445.N54
  Wars
    Civil War: E521+
    Colonial wars: E199
    Revolution: E263.N5
      Military operations: E230+
      Washington's retreat, 1776: E232
    War of 1812: E359.5.N4
    War of 1898: E726.N4
New Jersey Coastal Heritage Trail (New
  Jersey): F142.N48
New Jersey Palisades: F142.B4
New Jersey Volunteers
  Loyalist regiment: E277.6.N5
New London (Conn.): F104.N7
New Madrid (Missouri)
  Military operations, 1862: E473.15
New Market Endless Caverns (Virginia):
  F232.S47
New Market (Virginia): F234.N48
  Engagement at, 1864: E476.64
New Melones Lake and region
  (California): F868.N52
New Mexico: F791+
  African Americans: E185.93.N55
  Confederate history: E571+
  Counties, etc: F802.A+

New Mexico
  Indians: E78.N65
  Mexican state, 1822-1848: F800
  New Southwest: F786, F799+
  Occupation by U.S.
    War with Mexico: E405.2
  Slavery: E445.N55
  Spanish province before 1822: F799
  Texan Santa Fe Expedition, 1841:
    F390
  Texas purchase of 1850: F801
  Wars
    Civil War: E522+, E571+
      Military operations: E470.9
    Indian wars: E83.88
    War with Mexico: E405.2
New Netherlands: F122+
  Conquests of New Sweden: F167
  Hudson Valley: F127.H8
  Indian wars: E83.655
  Posts on Connecticut River: F97
New Northwest: F597
New Orleans: F379.N5+
  Battle of 1815: E356.N5
  General Butler's administration, 1862:
    E510+
  Occupation of, 1862: E472.88
  War of 1812: E355.6
New Plymouth Colony: F68
New Providence (Bahamas): F1659.N3
New Québec District (Québec):
  F1054.N5
New River and Valley
  North Carolina: F262.N6
  Virginia: F232.N5
  West Virginia: F247.N5
New River and Valley (Onslow Co.,
  N.C.): F262.O5
New River, N.C., Battle of, 1862:
  E474.5
New Southwest: F785.15+
New Spain (Viceroyalty): F1231
New Sweden: F167
New Ulm Battle, 1862: E83.86
New World, Allusions to the: E139
New York Avenue Presbyterian Church
  (Washington, D.C.): F203.2.N4

New York (City)
  British occupation, 1776: E232
  Draft riots, 1863: F128.44
  Evacuation, 1783: E239
New York City: F128+
New York City College and the Civil
  War: E541.N5
New York County: F128+
New York Indian Uprising, 1655:
  E83.655
New York military tracts: F127.M4
New York (State): F116+
  African Americans: E185.93.N56
  Counties, etc: F127.A+
  Dutch conquest, 1673: F122+
  Hudson's explorations: E129.H8
  Indians: E78.N7
  New Hampshire Grants: F52
  Slavery: E445.N56
  Wars
    Civil War: E523+
    Indian wars: E83.655, E83.663
    Intercolonial wars: E199
    Revolution: E263.N6
      Military operations: E230+
    War of 1812: E359.5.N6
    War of 1898: E726.N5
    War with Mexico: E409.5.N6
  Western lands ceded, 1787: E309,
    F483
New York State Convention of the
  Soldiers of the War of 1812: E351.28
New York State Seaway Trail (New
  York): F127.N38
New York University. Hall of Fame:
  E176.6
Newark (N.J.): F144.N6+
Newbern (North Carolina): E474.52
Newberry District (S.C.): F277.N5
Newberry National Volcanic Monument
  (Oregon): F882.D4
Newburgh addresses: E255
Newburgh Bay (N.Y.): F127.O8
Newcastle Island (British Columbia):
  F1089.N48
Newfound Lake (N.H.): F42.G7
Newfoundland: F1121+

Newfoundland
  Annexation of Labrador: F1137
  Indians: E78.N72
  Provincial status, 1949: F1123
Newport (Rhode Island): F89.N5
  Union of plantations: F82
Newsmen
  U.S. Civil War: E609
Newtown, New York, Battle of, 1779:
  E241.N59
Nez Percé Indians: E99.N5
Nez Percé War, 1877: E83.877
Nezahualcóyotl, King of Texcoco:
  F1219.75.N49
Niagara campaign, 1759: E199
Niagara Falls, Battle of, 1814: E356.L9
Niagara Falls (N.Y.): F127.N8
Niagara Falls (Ontario): F1059.5.N55
Niagara Falls Park, Queen Victoria:
  F1059.Q3
Niagara, Fort
  French and Indian War, 1755-1763:
    E199
Niagara Frontier: F127.N6
Niagara-on-the-Lake (Ontario):
  F1059.5.N5
Niagara (Ontario): F1059.5.N5
Niagara peninsula (Ontario): F1059.N5
Niagara region
  War of 1812: E355.6
Niagara River region
  New York: F127.N6
  Ontario: F1059.N5
Niantic Indians: E99.N6
Nicaragua: F1521+
  Confederación de Centro América:
    F1438, F1526.25
  Conflicts with El Salvador: F1527
  English invasion, 1780-1781:
    F1526.25
  Filibuster War, 1855-1860: F1526.27
  Revolutions of 1909-1910, 1912,
    1926-1929: F1526.3
  United States intervention, 1909-1933:
    F1526.3
Nicaragua Canal: F1526.27
Nicaragua, Lake, region: F1529.N5

Nicaraguans in Costa Rica: F1557.N5
Nicaraguans in the United States:
  E184.N53
Nicarao Indians: F1525.2.N5
Nicola River and Valley (British
  Columbia): F1089.N52
Nicolet, Jean: F1030.15
Nicoya Peninsula (Costa Rica):
  F1549.N5
Nictheroy (Brazil): F2651.N5
Nieuw Nickerie (Dutch Guiana):
  F2429.N5
Nievería (Peru)
  Indian antiquities: F3429.1.N5
Nigerians in Canada: F1035.N52
Nigerians in the United States:
  E184.N55
Nile Creek and Valley (Wash.):
  F897.Y18
Nim Li Punit Site (Belize): F1435.1.N55
Nimrod Lake and Region (Ark.):
  F417.N56
Nine Mile Canyon (Utah): F832.N55
Nine Partners Patent (New York):
  F127.D8
Nineteen Seventy Six (1976)
  Bicentennial
  United States: E285.3+
Ninety-Six District (S.C.): F277.N6
Niobrara River and Valley
  Nebraska: F672.N56
  Wyoming: F767.N52
Nipissing District (Ontario): F1059.N55
Nipissing Indians: E99.N65
Nipmuc Indians: E99.N7
Nippenose Valley (Pa.): F157.N57
Niquiranos: F1525.2.N5
Nisenan Indians: E99.N73
Nishenam Indians: E99.N73
Niska Indians: E99.N734
Nisqualli, Fort (Wash.): F897.P9
Nisqually Indians: E99.N74
Niterói (Brazil): F2651.N5
Nixon, Richard Milhous: E855+
No Mans Land Island (Mass.): F72.N6
No Man's Land (Oklahoma): F702.N6
Noah, Mordecai Manuel: E335

Noatak National Preserve (Alaska): F912.N6

Nobles Trail (Calif.): F868.S5

Nohmul Site (Belize): F1435.1.N64

Noix, Île aux (Québec): F1054.I35

Nome (Alaska): F914.N6

Nome, Cape: F912.N7

Nome-Taylor Highway (Alaska): F912.N73

Nomlaki Indians: E99.N815

Nonamesset Island (Mass.): F72.E5

Nonimportation agreements of 1768-1769: E215.3

Nooksack Indians: E99.N84

Nootka Indians: E99.N85

Nootka Sound (B.C.): F1089.N8

Nootka Sound Controversy, 1789-1790: F1089.N8

Nor Oriental del Marañón (Peru): F3451.N67

Nor Yungas, Bolivia (Province): F3341.N67

Norbeck, Peter: F656

Nord Alexis, Pierre: F1926

Nordeste brasileiro: F2583

Nordeste do Brasil (Region): F2583

Norfolk Co. (Ontario): F1059.N6

Norfolk (Virginia): F234.N8
 Expedition against, 1813: E355.4
 Occupation of, 1862: E473.64

Norman, Lake (N.C.): F262.N67

Norman (Oklahoma): F704.N6

Norman Wells (Mackenzie District): F1100.5.N6

Norridgewock Indians: E99.N9

Norris, George William: E748.N65

Norris Lake (Tenn.): F443.N67

Norsemen
 Pre-Columbian discovery of America: E105

Norte de Santander, Colombia (Dept.): F2281.N6

North Africans in Canada: F1035.N58

North America: E31+
 Aboriginal peoples: E75+
 Anthropology: E51+
 Atlantic Coast: F106

North America
 Discovery: E101+
 Pacific coast: F851.72+

North Anna River, Va., Battle of, 1864: E476.52

North Beach Peninsula (Washington): F897.P2

North Carolina: F251+
 African Americans: E185.93.N6
 Confederate history: E573+
 Counties, etc: F262.A+
 Indians: E78.N74
 Raleigh's colonies, 1584-1590: F229
 Reconstruction, 1865-1877: F259
 Slavery: E445.N8
 Wars
  Civil War: E524+, E573+
   Military operations: E470.6, E470.65, E477.7
  Indian wars: E83.71, E83.759
  Regulator Insurrection, 1766-1771: F257
  Revolution: E236, E237, E241.A+, E263.N8
  War of 1812: E359.5.N7
  War of 1898: E726.N8
  War with Spaniards of Florida, 1740: F314
 Western lands ceded to the U.S.: E309, F483

North Carolina University and the Civil War: E586.N8

North Carolina, Western: F261

North Cascades National Park: F897.C3

North Central States: F476+, F597

North Chile: F3205

North Dakota: F631+
 African Americans: E185.93.N7
 Counties, etc: F642.A+
 Dakota Indian War, 1890-1891: E83.89
 Indians: E78.N75

North End (Boston): F73.68.N65

North Fork, Coeur d'Alene River (Idaho): F752.C65

North Fork Skokomish River (Wash.): F897.S54

North Georgia: F291.7

North Mexico: F1314

North Park (Colo.): F782.J3

North Penn Village (Philadelphia): F158.68.N8

North Platte River and Valley: F672.N8
  Wyoming: F767.N8

North Point, Battle of 1814: E356.B2

North River (Mass.): F72.P7

North Shore (Chicago): F548.68.N7

North Shore (Mass.): F72.E7

North Shore of the Saint Lawrence Gulf: F1054.S3

North Shore (Québec): F1054.S3

North Shrewsbury River (N.J.): F142.M7

North Toe River and Valley (N.C.): F262.A9

Northeast Argentina: F2921.5

Northeast Brazil: F2583

Northeast coast region (N.C.): F262.A33

Northeast Washington (D.C.): F202.N5

Northeastern boundary
  Maine: F27.B7
  New Hampshire: F42.B7
  United States
    Disputes, 1783-1845: E398

Northeastern States
  Indians: E78.E2

Northern boundary (U.S.): F550.5+, F597

Northern California: F867.5

Northern Liberties (Philadelphia): F158.68.N9

Northern Michigan: F572.N7
  Upper Peninsula: F572.N8

Northern Neck (Virginia): F232.N86

Northern Peninsula (Michigan): F572.N8

Northern regions of Canada (General): F1090.5

Northern Virginia: F232.N867

Northern Virginia, Army of (C.S.A.): E470.2+

Northmen
  Pre-Columbian discovery of America: E105

Northumberland Co. (Ontario): F1059.N65

Northwest Angle (Minnesota): F612.L4

Northwest Argentina: F2922

Northwest boundary (U.S.): F854, F880

Northwest, Canadian: F1060+

Northwest coast Indians: E78.N78

Northwest Company of Canada: F1060+

Northwest, Department of the
  United States Army
    Military operations, 1862: E473.8
    Military operations, 1863: E474.9

Northwest Miramichi River and Valley (N.B.): F1044.N83

Northwest, New: F597

Northwest, Old: F476+
  Indians: E78.N76

Northwest Ordinance, 1787: E309

Northwest Rebellion, 1885: F1060.9

Northwest Territories (Canada): F1060+

Northwest Territories, Indians of: E78.N79

Northwest Territory (U.S.): F476+

Northwest (U.S.): F597

Northwest Washington (District of Columbia): F202.N7

Northwestern Conspiracy, 1864: E458.8

Northwestern Indian wars (Ohio Valley), 1790-1795: E83.79

Norton Sound and region (Alaska): F912.N75

Norwalk Islands (Conn.): F102.F2

Norwegians in Canada: F1035.N6

Norwegians in Chile: F3285.N67

Norwegians in South America: F2239.N6

Norwegians in the United States: E184.S2

Norwich (Conn.): F104.N93

Norwich (Vermont): F59.N9

Nottoway Indians: E99.N93

Nouel y Bobadilla, Adolfo Alejandro: F1938.4
Nova Scotia: F1036+
  American Revolution: E263.N9
    Loyalists: E277, F1038
  Indians: E78.N9
    Wars: E83.72
  Settlement by New Englanders, 1760-1761: F1038
Ntlakyapamuk Indians: E99.N96
Ñuble, Chile (Province): F3206
Nueces River and Valley (Texas): F392.N82
Nueces River, Battle of, 1862: E473.4
Nueva Esparta, Venezuela (State): F2331.N8
Nueva Galicia: F1296
Nueva Viscaya: F1261
Nuevitas (Cuba): F1839.N9
Nuevo Reino de León: F1316
Nuevo Santander: F1356
Nukak Indians: F2270.2.N8
Nullification
  United States
    Jackson's administration: E384.3
Numa Indians: E99.N97
Numeral systems
  Indians
    Mexico: F1219.3.N9
    Pre-Columbian America: E59.N8
Numeration
  Indians
    Mayas: F1435.3.M35
Numic Indians: E99.N97
Nunavik
  Quebec: F1054.N93
Nunavut: F1141+
Núñez Cabeza de Vaca, Alvar: E125.N9
Núñez, Rafael: F2276
Nurses
  United States Civil War: E621+
    Confederate: E625
Nutley area (N.J.): F142.E8
Nym Lake and region (Ontario): F1059.T5

O

O-wee-kay-no Indians: E99.O68
Oaica Indians: F2520.1.W3
OAK: E458.8
Oak Hill Cemetery (Washington, D.C.): F203.1.O12
Oak Island (Nova Scotia): F1039.O35
Oak Park (Illinois): F549.O13
Oak Ridge (Tennessee): F444.O3
Oakland (California): F869.O2
OAS: F1402.A1+
Oaxaca (Mexico)
  City: F1391.O12
  State: F1321
    Indian antiquities: F1219.1.O11
Oberlin College and the Civil War: E541.O2
Oberlin-Wellington rescue, 1858: E450
Obligado, Battle of, 1845: F2846.3
Obregón, Álvaro: F1234
O'Brien, Jeremiah: E207.O13
Ocaina Indians: F3430.1.O25
Ocala National Forest (Florida): F317.O25
Occaneechi Indians: E99.O22
Occidente, Mexico (State): F1322
Occultism, Indian: E98.R3
Ocean Pond, Florida, Battle of, 1864: E476.43
Ochoco National Forest: F882.O16
Ocloya Indians: F2823.O34
Ocmulgee River (Georgia): F292.O27
Ocoee District (Tennessee): F442.1
Oconee River and Valley (Georgia): F292.O33
Ocorona Indians: F3320.2.O3
Ocracoke Island (N.C.): F262.H9
Ocsabamba colony (Peru): F3451.O16
Octagon House (Washington, D.C.): F204.O2
Octoraro Creek and Valley
  Maryland: F187.O27
  Pennsylvania: F157.O26
O'Daniel, Wilbert Lee: F391+
Odiorne Point State Park (New Hampshire): F42.R7

Odría, Manual Artura: F3448
Ogden (Utah): F834.O3
Ogeechee River and Valley (Georgia):
   F292.O38
Oglala Indians: E99.O3
Oglethorpe, James Edward: F289
O'Gorman, James Aloysius: F124
O'Higgins, Bernardo: F3094
O'Higgins, Chile (Province): F3211
Ohio: F486+
   African Americans: E185.93.O2
   Counties, etc: F497.A+
   Indians: E78.O3
   Old Northwest: F476+
   Wars
      Civil War: E470.4+, E525+
         Morgan's raid, 1863: E475.18
      Indian wars: E83.81
      Revolution: E263.O3
      Toledo War, 1836: F497.B7
      War of 1812: E359.5.O2
      War of 1898: E726.O3
      War with Mexico: E409.5.O3
Ohio Company (1747-1779): F517
Ohio Company (1786-1795): F483
Ohio Company of Virginia: F517
Ohio Land Company: F483
Ohio River and Valley: F516+
   Illinois: F547.O4
   Indiana: F532.O4
   Kentucky: F457.O3
   Ohio: F497.O3
   Pennsylvania: F157.B2
   West Virginia: F247.O4
Ohio State Association of Mexican War
   Veterans: E401.36
Ohio Valley: F516+
   Indians: E78.O4
   Wars
      Civil War: E470.4+
      French and Indian War: E199
      Indian wars: E83.79
      Revolution: E230.5.O3
Ohlone Indians: E99.O32
Ojai Valley (Calif.): F868.V5
Ojarikoelle Indians: F2420.1.O8
Ojibwa Indians: E99.C6

Okaloacoochee Slough (Florida):
   F317.O27
Okanagan River and Valley (B.C.):
   F1089.O5
Okeechobee, Lake (Florida): F317.O4
Okefenokee Swamp (Georgia):
   F292.O5
Okinagan Indians: E99.O35
Oklahoma: F691+
   African Americans: E185.93.O4
   Counties, etc: F702.A+
   Indian country: F697
   Indian Territory: F697, F698
   Indians: E78.I5, E78.O45
   Oklahoma Territory: F699
Oklahoma City (Oklahoma): F704.O41
Oklahoma Panhandle (Oklahoma):
   F702.N6
Oklawaha River and Valley (Florida):
   F317.O46
Okoboji Lake (Iowa): F627.D5
Okolona, Battle of, 1864: E476.14
Olancho, Honduras (Dept.): F1509.O4
Olaya Herrera, Enrique: F2277
Olaya, José Silverio: F3446
Old Capitol Prison, Washington, D.C.
   Civil War prison: E616.O4
Old Colony Historical Society
   (Massachusetts): F74.T2
Old Emigrant Trail (Calif.): F868.S5
Old Man of the Mountain (New
   Hampshire): F41.6.P9
Old Northwest: F476+
Old Order Amish in the United States:
   E184.M45
Old Southwest: F396
Old State House (Boston): F73.8.O4
Old Westmoreland Co. (Pa.): F157.W5
Older Indians: E98.A27
   Peru: F3429.3.A37
Oldroyd Collection of Lincoln Relics:
   E457.65
Oley Valley (Pa.): F157.B3
Olinda (Brazil)
   Capture by Dutch, 1630: F2532
Olive branch petition to George III,
   1775: E215.95

Oliveira Lima, Manuel de: F2537
Oliver Dam (Alabama): F332.T9
Oliver, Peter: F67
Olmec Indians: F1219.8.O56
Olmsted, Arthur George: F154
Olson, Floyd Björnsterne: F606
Olustee, Florida, Battle of, 1864:
  E476.43
Olympia (Washington): F899.O5
Olympic Mountains: F897.O5
Olympic National Park: F897.O5
Omagua Indians: F3430.1.O5
Omaha Indians: E99.O4
Omaha (Nebraska): F674.O5+
Omasuyos, Bolivia (Province):
  F3341.O5
Omineca River and Valley
  British Columbia: F1089.O55
Omnibus Bill, Clay's: E423
Ompompanoosuc Parish (Vermont):
  F57.O56
Ona Indians: F2986
Oneida Indians: E99.O45
Oneida Lake (New York): F127.O52
O'Neill Ranch (California): F868.S34
Oneota Indians
  Great Plains: E99.O5
Onondaga Indians: E99.O58
Onondaga Lake (N.Y.): F127.O6
Ontario: F1056+
  American loyalists: F1058
  Canadian Rebellion, 1837-1838:
    F1032
  History to 1791: F1030, F1031+,
    F1032
  Indians: E78.O5
  War of 1812: E355+
Ontario (Calif.): F869.O5
Ontario Co. (Ontario): F1059.O5
Ontario Colony (Calif.): F869.O5
Ontario, Lake, region: F556
  New York: F127.O72
  Ontario: F1059.O6
Ontonagon River and Valley
  Michigan: F572.O62
Oohenonpa Indians: E99.O63
Oowekeeno Indians: E99.O68

Opata Indians: F1221.O6
Opaye Indians: F2520.1.O63
Opeongo Lake (Ontario): F1059.A4
Opequan Creek, Battle of, 1864:
  E477.33
Orange County Park (Calif.): F868.O6
Orange Lake (N.Y.): F127.O8
Orange (N.J.): F144.O6
Orangeburgh District (S.C.): F277.O6
Oratory
  Indians: E98.O7
Orcas Island (Wash.): F897.S2
Ord, Edward Otho Cresap: E467.1.O7
Ordás, Diego de: E125.O58
Ordenanza del Senor Cuauhtemoc:
  F1219.56.O73+
Order of American Freemen: E462.94
Order of American Knights: E458.8
Order of Colonial Lords of Manors in
  America: E186.99.O6
Order of Lafayette: E202.99.O63
Order of Stars and Stripes:
  E462.99.O65
Order of the Descendants of the Signers
  of the Secret Pact or prior Declaration
  of Independence: E202.99.O65
Order of the Founders and Patriots of
  America: E186.6
Order of the Lone Star: E458.8
Order of the Purple Heart, Military:
  E181
Order of the Sons of Liberty: E458.8
Order of Washington: E202.7
Orderly books
  American Revolution: E231+
Ordinance of 1787: E309
Oregon: F871+
  African Americans: E185.93.O7
  Counties, etc: F882.A+
  Indians: E78.O6
  International boundary: F854
  Wars
    Civil War: E526+
    Indian wars: E83.84, E83.87,
      E83.877
Oregon country: F880
Oregon question: F880

Oregon Trail: F597
  Oregon: F880
Orejón Indians: F3430.1.O74
Orellano, Francisco de: E125.O6
Organ Pipe Cactus National Monument
  (Arizona): F817.O7
Organization of American States:
  F1402.A1+
Organization of Central American
  States: F1439
Oribe, Manuel: F2726
Oriente (Bolivia): F3341.O6
Oriente, Cuba (Province): F1841+
Oriente region (Ecuador): F3741.N3
Origin
  Mayas: F1435.3.O73
Original narratives of early American
  history: E187.O7
Orinoco River and Valley (Venezuela):
  F2331.O7
Oriskany, Battle of, 1777: E241.O6
Oriskany Campaign, 1777: E233
Orizaba (Mexico)
  Canton: F1371
Orleans, Isle of (Québec): F1054.O7
Orleans Parish (La.): F377.O7
Orleans, Territory of, 1804-1812: F374
Ornaments
  Indians
    North America: E98.C8
Oro, El, Ecuador (Province): F3741.E4
Orphanages
  Indians: E98.O76
Orr's Island (Me.): F27.C9
Orsainville, Jean Talon, comte d':
  F1030
Ortiz de Rosas, J.M.J.D.: F2846.3
Ortiz Mountains (N.M.): F802.S4
Oruro (Bolivia)
  City: F3351.O7
  Department: F3341.O7
Osa Gulf (Costa Rica): F1549.D8
Osa Peninsula (Costa Rica):
  F1549.O83
Osage Indians: E99.O8
Osage River and Valley (Mo.):
  F472.O74

Osawatomie, Battle of, 1856: F685
Osborn, Chase Salmon: F566
Oshkosh (Wisconsin): F589.O8
Osorio, Oscar: F1488
Ospina, Pedro Nel: F2277
Ospino Pérez, Mariano: F2278
Ossabaw Island (Georgia): F292.C36
Ossipee Mountain (New Hampshire):
  F42.C3
Ossipee Mountain Park (New
  Hampshire): F42.C3
Ostend Manifesto, October 1854: E431
Oswegatchie River (New York):
  F127.O908
Otavalo Indians: F3722.1.O8
Otero, Antonio Miguel: F801
Otis, Harrison Gray: E340.O8
Otis, James: E302.6.O8
Oto Indians: E99.O87
Otomaco Indians: F2319.2.O8
Otomi Indians
  Modern: F1221.O86
  Pre-Columbian: F1219.8.O87
Ottawa Indians: E99.O9
Ottawa (Ontario): F1059.5.O9
Ottawa region (Québec): F1054.O94
Ottawa River and Valley
  Ontario: F1059.O91
  Quebec: F1054.O9
Otuquis Indians: F3320.2.O8
Ouachita Mountains
  Arkansas: F417.O77
  Oklahoma: F702.O9
Ouachita National Forest: F417.O8
Ouachita Parish (La.): F377.O78
Ouachita River and Valley
  Arkansas: F417.O83
  Louisiana: F377.O8
Ouayeoue Indians: F2380.1.W25
Ouro Preto (Brazil): F2651.O9
Outaouais region (Québec): F1054.O94
Outer Banks (N.C.): F262.O96
Overland journeys to the Pacific (1848-
  1860): F593
Overland Trail: F597
  Colorado: F782.O94
  Wyoming: F767.O94

Overwharton Parish (Louisiana):
  F232.O9
Oweekano Indians: E99.O68
Oweekayo Indians: E99.O68
Owens River and Valley (California):
  F868.O9
Owikeno Indians: E99.O68
Owyhee Mountains region (Idaho,
  Nevada, Oregon): F752.O97
Owyhee River and Valley
  Idaho: F752.O98
  Nevada: F847.O98
  Oregon: F882.O98
Owyhees in the United States: E184.H3
Oxapampa colony (Peru): F3451.O16
Oxford Co. (Ontario): F1059.O98
Oxford Hills (Me.): F27.O9
Oxford Township (Pennsylvania):
  F158.68.O8
Oxkintok (Mexico): F1435.1.O94
Oyambi Indians: F2460.1.O9
Oyampi Indians: F2460.1.O9
Oyana Indians: F2230.2.O8
Oyapok River (French Guiana)
  English settlements: F2462
Oyaricoulet Indians: F2420.1.O8
Oyster Bay (New York): F129.O98
Ozark Mountains
  Arkansas: F417.O9
  Indians: E78.O9
  Missouri: F472.O9
Ozarks, Lake of the (Missouri):
  F472.O93
Ozonia Lake (N.Y.): F127.S2

P

Pacaguara Indians: F3320.2.P3
Pachacamac, Peru
  Indian antiquities: F3429.1.P2
Pachitea, Peru (Province): F3451.P14
Pachuca, Mexico (District): F1291
Pacific and Mountain States
  History: F718
Pacific, Army of the: E470.9

Pacific Coast
  Alaska
    Exploring expeditions: F907
  British Columbia: F1089.P2
    Exploring expeditions: F1088
  California: F868.P33
    Exploring expeditions: F864
  Colombia: F2281.P23
  Ecuador: F3741.P32
  North America: F850.5+
    Exploring expeditions: F851.5
    Indians: E78.P2
    Overland journeys to: F593
    Voyages by Cape Horn or the
      isthmus: F865
  Oregon: F882.P34
    Exploring expeditions: F880
  Peru: F3451.P19
  South America: F2213
  United States: F851
Pacific Crest Trail
  Indians: E78.P24
Pacific Islanders in the United States:
  E184.P25
Pacific Northwest: F851.72+
Pacific Ocean
  U.S. insular possessions: F970
Pacific Rim National Park (B.C.):
  F1089.V3
Pacific States: F850.5+
Padre Island (Texas): F392.P14
Padrones de Tlaxcala del siglo XVI
  (Codices): F1219.56.P33+
Paducah (Kentucky)
  Demonstration from, 1861: E472.28
Páez, Federico: F3737
Paez Indians: F2270.2.P3
Páez, José Antonio: F2322.8
Page, Walter Hines: E664.P15
Pageants
  United States history: E179, F4.6
    Colonial: E189
    Wars
      War with Mexico: E415
Pahsimeroi River and Valley
  Idaho: F752.P23
Paia Indians: E99.P32

Paiaia Indians: E99.P32
Paialla Indians: E99.P32
Paiaya Indians: E99.P32
Paine, Robert Frost: E302.6.P14
Paingua Indians: F2230.2.C3
Paint Rock River
  Alabama: F332.P34
  Tennessee: F443.P34
Painted Desert (Arizona): F817.P2
Painting
  Aztecs: F1219.76.P35
  Indians: E98.P23, F3721.3.P35
    Mexico: F1219.3.P25
    Peru: F3429.3.P34
  Mayas: F1435.3.P34
Paiute Indians: E99.P2
Pajarito Plateau (N.M.): F802.P25
Pajaro River and Valley (Calif.):
  F868.S3
Pakaa Nova Indians: F2520.1.P32
Pakistanis in Canada: F1035.P34
Pakistanis in the United States:
  E184.P28
Palafox y Mendoza, Juan de: F1231
Palaihnihan Indians: E99.P215
Palatines in Canada: F1035.P36
Palatines in the United States: E184.P3
Palenque Indians: F1435.1.P2,
  F2319.2.P3
Palermo
  Columbus celebration, 1892: E119
Palestinian Arabs in Central America:
  F1440.P34
Palestinians in the United States:
  E184.P33
Palicur Indians: F2460.1.P3
Palisades of New Jersey: F142.B4
Palisades of the Hudson (Interstate
  park): F127.H8
Palmares, Brazil: F2651.P15
Palmer House, Chicago: F548.8.P17
Palmer, John McAuley: E664.P2
Palmer Peninsula: F3031+
Palmito Ranch, Tex., Battle of, 1865:
  E477.8
Palo Alto, Battle of, 1846: E406.P3
Palo Duro Canyon (Texas): F392.P16

Palo Duro State Park (Texas):
  F392.P16
Palomar Mountain (Calif.): F868.S15
Paloos Indians: E99.P22
Palouse River and Valley
  Idaho: F752.P25
  Washington: F897.P24
Pame Indians: F1221.P3
Pamlico Indians: E99.P225
Pampa, Argentina (Province): F2924
Pampaconas River (Peru): F3451.C9
Pampas, Argentina (region): F2926
Pampean Indians: F2823.P3
Pamplona, Colombia (Province):
  F2281.P3
Pamunkey Indians: E99.P23
Pamunkey River and Valley (Virginia):
  F232.P25
Pan-American conferences: F1404+
Pan-American Highway: F1409,
  F1547.5
Pan American Union: F1403+
Panama: F1561+
  Scots' Colony of Darien: F2281.D2
  Secession from Colombia: F2276.5
  Under U.S. protection, 1903-1936:
    F1566.5
  War of Independence, 1903:
    F1566.45
Panama Bay: F1569.P35
Panama Canal: F1569.C2
Panama Canal Zone: F1569.C2
Panama (City): F1576.P2
  American Congress, 1826: F1404
Panama Congress, 1826: F1404
Panama Expeditions: F1566.45
Panama, Gulf of: F1569.P35
Panama, Isthmus of: F1561+
Panama (Province): F1569.P3
Panamanians in the United States:
  E184.P35
Panamint Indians: E99.P24
Panare Indians: F2319.2.P34
Pancaldo, León: E125.P2
Pancararu Indians: F2520.1.P35
Panche Indians: F2270.2.P37
Pando, Bolivia (Department): F3341.P3

Panhandle culture
  Indians: E99.P244
Panhandle, Texas: F392.P168
Paniquita Indians: F2270.2.P4
Panjabis in the United States:
  E184.P36
Pano Indians: F3430.1.P3
Panoan Indians: F3430.1.P33
Pánuco, Mexico (Province): F1323
Panzaleo Indians: F3722.1.P35
Paoli Massacre, 1777: E241.P2
Papago Indians: E99.P25
Paper and paper making
  Aztecs: F1219.76.P37
  Indians
    Mexico: F1219.3.P3
Papigochic River and Valley: F1261
Papineau, Louis Joseph: F1032
Papineau Rebellion, 1837-1838: F1032
Pâques, L'ile de (Chile): F3169
Pará (Brazil)
  City: F2651.B4
  State: F2586
    Indian antiquities: F2519.1.P2
Paracas, Peru
  Indian antiquities: F3429.1.P25
Paradise Valley (Nevada): F847.H8
Paraguaná Peninsula (Venezuela):
  F2331.F2
Paraguay: F2661+
  Chaco region: F2691.C4
  Jesuit province: F2684
  Military history
    Chaco War, 1932-1935: F2688.5
    Paraguayan War, 1865-1870:
      F2687
    War of Independence, 1810-1811:
      F2683
    War of the Seven Reductions, 1754-
      1756: F2684
  Reductions (1609-1769): F2684
  United States Expedition, 1858-1859:
    F2686
Paraguay (Province): F2683, F2684
Paraguay River and Valley: F2691.P3
Paraguayan War, 1865-1870: F2687
Parahyba, Brazil (State): F2591

Parahyba do Sul River (Brazil): F2611
Paraíba, Brazil (State): F2591
Paraibuna River (Brazil): F2581
Parakaña Indians: F2520.1.P38
Paramaribo, Dutch Guiana: F2429.P3
Paramona Indians: F2380.1.P3
Paramonga (Peru)
  Indian antiquities: F3429.1.P28
Paraná, Brazil (State): F2596
  Indian antiquities: F2519.1.P3
Paraná River
  Argentina: F2909
  Brazil: F2596, F2631
Paraná Valley, Argentina
  Indian antiquities: F2821.1.P22
Paraphernalia, Political: E183.3
Paraujano Indians: F2319.2.P37
Parc de la Jacques-Cartier (Québec):
  F1054.P36
Parc de Plaisance (Québec):
  F1054.P365
Parc des Hautes-Gorges-de-la-Rivière-
  Malbaie (Québec): F1054.P367
Parc du Mont-Orford (Québec):
  F1054.P37
Parc du Mont-Tremblant (Québec):
  F1054.P39
Parinacochas, Peru (Province):
  F3451.P245
Parintintin Indians: F2520.1.P4
Park Avenue (New York): F128.67.P3
Park Street (Boston): F73.67.P3
Parkateyê Indians: F2520.1.G37
Parker, George Le Roy: F595
Parker House (Boston): F73.8.P3
Parker, Joel: E521+
Parks
  Boston: F73.65
  Canada: F1011
  Chicago: F548.65
  New York City: F128.65.A+
  Philadelphia: F158.65.A+
  United States: E160
  Washington (D.C.): F203.5.A+
Parmachenee Lake (Me.): F27.O9
Parnahyba River (Brazil): F2606

Parque Nacional del Iguazú (Argentina): F2916

Parque Nacional do Xingu (Brazil): F2519.1.P37

Parque Nacional "Lanín" (Argentina): F2921

Parris Island (S.C.): F277.B3

Parsons' Cause, 1763: F229

Parsons, Lewis Baldwin: E467.1.P26

Parsons, Samuel Holden: E207.P2

Parsons, Theophilus: F69

Parú River (Brazil): F2586

Pasadena (California): F869.P3

Pascagoula Indians: E99.P26

Pascagoula River and Valley (Mississippi): F347.P26

Pasco, Peru (Dept.): F3451.P247

Pascua, Isla de (Chile): F3169

Pasquaney Lake (N.H.): F42.G7

Pasque Island (Mass.): F72.E5

Pass Manchac (La.): F377.P27

Passaic River and Valley: F142.P3

Passamaquoddy Bay and region: F27.P3

New Brunswick: F1044.P3

Passamaquoddy Indians: E99.P27

Pastaza River (Peru): F3451.L8

Pasto (Colombia): F2291.P28

Pasto Indians: F2270.2.P44

Pastorius, Francis Daniel: F152

Pastour, Philippe de, sieur de Costebelle: F1123

Patachó Indians: F2520.1.P43

Patagonia

Argentina: F2936

Indian antiquities: F2821.1.P29

Chilean: F3146

Patapsco Neck and River (Maryland): F187.B2

Patarabueye Indians: F1221.P35

Patashó Indians: F2520.1.P43

Pataxó Indians: F2520.1.P43

Pataxte (Guatemala)

Mayas: F1435.1.P25

Paterson, John: E207.P3

Paterson (N.J.): F144.P4

Paterson, William: E302.6.P3

Patí River and Valley, Colombia: F2281.P37

Patos, Isla de (Venezuela): F2331.P3

Patriotic hereditary societies

United States: E172.7+

Patriotic societies

United States

Civil War: E462+, E483

Colonial period: E186.3+

War of 1812: E351.3+

War of 1898: E714.3.A+

War with Mexico: E401.1+

Patriots' Day, April 19: E231

Patton, George Smith: E745

Patuxent River and Valley (Maryland): F187.P38

Patwin Indians: E99.P29

Paucartambo, Peru (Province): F3451.P25

Paugusset Indians: E99.P292

Pauishana Indians: F2520.1.P45

Pauisiana Indians: F2520.1.P45

Pauixana Indians: F2520.1.P45

Paul Revere's ride: E216

Paula, Francisco Julião Arruda de: F2538.27.P38

Paula Santander, Francisco de: F2273

Paulding, Hiram: E182

Paulding, John: E280.A5

Paulina Lake (Oregon): F882.D4

Paulint, Antoine: E263.C2

Paulmier de Gonneville, Binot: E133.P3

Paulus Hook, Battle of, 1779: E241.P24

Paunceforte-Hay Treaty, 1901: F1438

Pauserna Indians: F3320.2.P37

Pavón, Battle of, 1861: F2846

Paw Paw Lake (Michigan): F572.B5

Paw Paw River and Valley (Michigan): F572.P38

Pawleys Island (S.C.): F277.G35

Pawnee Indians: E99.P3

Pawtucket (Wamesit) Indians: E99.W19

Pawtuxet River and Valley (Rhode Island): F87.P3

Paxil (Mexico)

Mayas: F1435.1.P38

Paxton boys: F152

Paya Indians: F1505.2.P3
Payagua Indians: F2679.2.P3
Payai Indians: E99.P32
Payalla Indians: E99.P32
Payay Indians: E99.P32
Payaya Indians: E99.P32
Payaye Indians: E99.P32
Payette River and Valley (Idaho):
 F752.P33
Payne, Davis Lewis: F697
Payne Hollow (Ky.): F457.T65
Paynes Prairie (Florida): F317.A4
Paysandú (Uruguay)
 City: F2791.P54
 Department: F2731.P3
Paz Estenssoro, Victor: F3326
Paz, José María: F2846
Pea Ridge, Battle of, 1862: E473.17
Pea River and Valley (Alabama):
 F332.P37
Peace Conference at Washington:
 E440.5
Peace River and Valley (Canada)
 Alberta: F1079.P3
 British Columbia: F1089.P3
Peachtree Creek, Ga., Battle of, 1864:
 E476.7
Peak Island (Me.): F27.C9
Peak-to-Peak Highway (Colorado):
 F782.P37
Pearce, James Alfred: E340.P3
Pearl Islands (Panama): F1569.P3
Pearl River
 Louisiana: F377.P3
 Mississippi: F347.P3
Pearson, Lester B.: F1034.3.P4
Pease River, Battle of, 1860: E83.8596
Peaux-de-Lievres Indians: E99.K28
Peay, Austin: F436
Peban Indians: F3430.1.P4
Pecos Indians: E99.P34
Pecos River and Valley
 New Mexico: F802.P3
 Texas: F392.P3
Peddocks Island (Mass.): F72.P7
Pedee River
 North Carolina: F262.Y2

Pedee River
 South Carolina: F277.P3
Pedro I, Emperor of Brazil: F2536
Pedro II, Emperor of Brazil: F2536
Pedro IV, Emperor of Brazil: F2536
Pee Dee Indians: E99.P35
Pee Dee River and Valley
 North Carolina: F262.Y2
 South Carolina: F277.P3
Peel Co. (Ontario): F1059.P25
Peguenche Indians: F3126
Pehuenche Indians: F3126
Peirpont, Francis Harrison: E534+
Peixe River (Brazil): F2631
Peixoto, Floriano: F2537
Pejepscot Company: F29.B9
Pejepscot Patent and Purchase
 (Brunswick), Maine: F29.B9
Pelham Manor (New York): F128.68.B8
Pelican Lake (Minnesota): F612.O9
Pellegrini, Bartolomé Mitre Carlos:
 F2847
Pell's Point, Battle of, 1776: E241.P3
Peltier Creek and Valley (N.C.):
 F262.P35
Pemaquid (Maine): F22
Pemberton, John Clifford: E467.1.P365
Pemberton Valley (British Columbia):
 F1089.P4
Pembina River and Valley (Alberta):
 F1079.R36
Pemon Indians: F2319.2.P45
Peñalosa, Diego Dionisio de: F799
Peñaranda Castillo, Enrique: F3326
Pendleton District (S.C.): F277.P35
Pendleton, Edmund: F230
Pendleton, George Hunt: E415.9.P4
Pendleton (Oregon): F884.P39
Pendleton, William Nelson: E467.1.P37
Penikese Island (Mass.): F72.E5
Peninsula Lake (Muskoka, Ontario):
 F1059.M9
Peninsula State Park (Wisconsin):
 F587.D7
Peninsular campaign, 1862: E473.6
Penn family (Proprietors of
 Pennsylvania): F152.2

Penn, William: F152.2
  Grant to, 1681: F152, F167
Pennacook Indians: E99.P4
Penn's Cave (Pa.): F157.C3
Pennsylvania: F146+
  African Americans: E185.93.P41
  Connecticut claims in northeast:
    F157.W9
  Counties, etc: F157.A+
  Fries' Rebellion, 1798-1799: E326
  Indians: E78.P4
  Lower counties on the Delaware:
    F167
  New Sweden: F167
  Slavery: E445.P3
  Virginia claims in southwest:
    F157.W5
  Wars
    Buckshot War, 1838: F153
    Civil War: E527+
      Military operations: E470.2+
    French and Indian War: E199
    Indian wars: E83.76
    King George's War: E199
    Revolution: E263.P4
    War of 1812: E359.5.P3
    War of 1898: E726.P4
    War with Mexico: E409.5.P3
    Whiskey Rebellion: E315
Pennsylvania Association of the
  Defenders of the Country in the War of
  1812: E351.23
Pennsylvania Avenue (Washington,
  D.C.): F203.7.P4
Pennsylvania Dutch Country (Pa.):
  F157.P44
Pennsylvania German region (Pa.):
  F157.P44
Pennsylvania Hall (Philadelphia):
  F158.8.P4
Pennsylvania, Insurrection of, 1795:
  E315
Pennsylvania Invasion, 1863: E475.51
Pennsylvania line mutiny: E255
Pennsylvania Station (New York):
  F128.8.P4

Pennsylvania University and the Civil
  War: E541.P4
Pennypacker Memorial (Philadelphia):
  F158.64.P4
Pennypacker, Samuel Whitaker: F154
Penobscot Bay region (Me.): F27.P37
Penobscot Expedition, 1779: E235
Penobscot Indians: E99.P5
Penobscot River and Valley (Me.):
  F27.P4
Penrose, Boies: E664.P41
Pensacola District of West Florida
  First Seminole War, 1817-1818:
    E83.817
  History
    Before 1819: F301
    Since 1819: F317.W5
  Treaty of 1819: F314
Pensacola, Fla., Battle of, 1781:
  E241.P46
Pensacola (Florida): F319.P4
Pensions
  Indians: E98.P3
Pensions, Military
  United States
    Lists of pensioners
      Revolution: E255
      War of 1812: E359.4
      War with Mexico: E409.4
    Veterans' march, Washington, D.C.:
      F199
Pensions, Slave: E185.2
People with disabilities
  Indians: E98.H35
Peoria (Illinois): F549.P4
Peoria Indians: E99.P515
Pepin, Lake (Minn.): F612.P42
Pepperell, Sir William: E198
Pequawket Indians: E99.P52
Pequawket, Mount (New Hampshire):
  F42.C3
Pequea Creek (Pa.): F157.L2
Pequot Indians: E99.P53
Pequot War, 1636-1638: E83.63
Percée, Île (Québec): F1054.G2
Perdido River and Valley
  Alabama: F332.P4

Perdido River and Valley
  Florida: F317.P4
Pere Marquette River and Valley
  Michigan: F572.P46
Pereira de Costa, Francisco Augusto:
  F2520.6.P4
Perestrello family: E113
Pérez Jiménez, Marcos: F2326
Perijá District (Venezuela): F2331.P4
Perijá, Sierra de: F2331.P4
Periodicals, Historical
  America: E11
  Canada: F1001
  Latin America: F1201
  United States: E151
Perkins, George Hamilton: E467.1.P4
Perkiomen River and Valley (Pa.):
  F157.M7
Perlas, Islas de las (Panama):
  F1569.P3
Pernambuco (Brazil)
  City: F2651.R4+
  Province: F2601
  State: F2601
Péron, Juan Domingo: F2849
Péron regime, Argentina, 1943-1955:
  F2849
Perrot Island (Québec): F1054.P47
Perry, Benjamin Franklin: F274
Perry, Matthew: E182
Perry, Oliver Hazard: E353.1.P4
  Battle of Lake Erie, 1813: E356.E6
  Memorial, Put-in-Bay (Ohio): E356.E6
Perryville (Kentucky), Battle of, October
  1862: E474.39
Pershing, John Joseph: E181
Pershing's expedition, 1916: F1234
Personal liberty laws: E450
Personal narratives
  Early American history: E187.O7
  Early explorers, traders, etc: E88
  Fugitive slaves: E450
  Slaves: E444
Personal narratives, Military
  United States
    Civil War
      Noncombatants: E487

Personal narratives, Military
  United States
    Civil War
      Nurses: E621+
      Sailors: E591+
      Soldiers: E464
    Prisoners: E281, E611+
    Revolution: E231+, E275.A2+
      British soldiers: E267+
      French auxiliaries: E265
      German mercenaries: E268
      Loyalists: E277+
      Privateers: E271
      Sailors: E271
      State troops: E263.A+
    War of 1898: E727+
    War with Mexico, 1845-1848: E411
Perth Co. (Ontario): F1059.P3
Peru: F3401+
  Leticia question, 1932-1934:
    F2281.B7P1+
  Loss of Upper Peru: F3324
  Military history
    1522-1548: F3442
    1548-1820: F3444
    1820-1829: F3446
    Civil wars: F3442, F3447
    War of the Pacific, 1879-1884:
      F3097
    War with Spain, 1865-1866: F3447
  Tacna-Arica question: F3097.3
Peru-Bolivian Confederation War with
  Chile, 1836-1839: F3447
Peru, Upper: F3322
Peru (Viceroyalty): F3444
Peruvians in Chile: F3285.P4
Peruvians in the United States:
  E184.P47
Petén: F1435.1.P47
Petén, Guatemala (Dept.): F1469.P4
Peterborough Co. (Ontario): F1059.P4
Peters, Richard: F152
Petersburg National Military Park:
  E476.93
Petersburg (Virginia)
  Battle at Petersburg Crater, 1864:
    E476.93

Petersburg (Virginia)
  Engagement at, June 1864: E476.59
  Evacuation of, 1865: E477.61
  Expedition to, 1865: E477.65
  Siege, June-July 1864: E476.93
Petersen House (Washington, D.C.):
  F204.P47
Petigru, James Louis: F273
Petión, Alexandre Sabés: F1924
Petit Jean Mountain (Arkansas):
  F417.P43
Petrified Forest National Monument:
  F817.P4
Petroglyphs
  Indians: E98.P34
    Argentina: F2821.3.P6
    Colombia: F2270.1.P4
    Honduras: F1505.3.P48
    Mexico: F1219.3.P46
    Peru: F3429.3.P47
    Pre-Columbian America: E59.P42
    South America: F2230.1.P48
    Venezuela: F2319.3.P4
  Mayas: F1435.3.P44
Petropolis, Treaty of, 1903: F2540
Petsworth Parish (Virginia): F232.P45
Pettaquamscutt Purchase: F87.P5
Pettigrew, James Johnston:
  E467.1.P51
Peyaya Indians: E99.P32
Peyton, John Howe: F230
Pfeiffer Big Sur State Park (California):
  F868.M7
Phelps, Charles Edward: F186
Phelps-Gorham Purchase (1788):
  F127.G2
Phelps, Samuel Shethar: E340.P54
Phelps, William Walter: E664.P53
Phil Kearny, Fort
  Massacre at, 1866: E83.866
Philadelphia, Association of the
  Territorial Company of: F442.1
Philadelphia (Frigate)
  Capture and destruction: E335
Philadelphia (Pennsylvania): F158
  Howe's occupation, 1777: E233
  Philadelphia County merger: F158.44

Philadelphia. War Veterans' Club:
  E462.97
Philanthropy
  Indians
    North America: E98.C47
Philip, John Woodward: E182
Philippine Campaign, 1898: E717.7
Philippine Islands
  Wars
    War of 1898: E717.7
Philip's War, King, 1675-1676: E83.67
Philipsburg Manor (N.Y.): F127.W5
Phillips, Samuel: F69
Phillips, Wendell: E449
  Collected works: E415.6.P55+
Phillips, William: F69
Philosophy
  Aztecs: F1219.76.P55
  Indians: E98.P5
    Argentina: F2821.3.P66
    Bolivia: F3320.1.P53
    Costa Rica: F1565.3.P45
    Mexico: F1219.3.P5
    Peru: F3429.3.P55
    Pre-Columbian America: E59.P45
    South America: F2230.1.P53
  Mayas: F1435.3.P5
Philosophy of American history: E175.9
Phoenicians
  Pre-Columbian discovery of America:
    E109.P5
Phoenix (Arizona): F819.P57
Physical characteristics
  Indians: E98.P53
    Mexico: F1219.3.P55
Piankashaw Indians: E99.P57
Piaroa Indians: F2319.2.P5
Piatt, Donn: F496
Piauhy, Brazil (State): F2606
Picado Michalski, Teodoro: F1547.5
Piceance Creek and watershed
  (Colorado): F782.P52
Pichilemu (Chile)
  Indian antiquities: F3069.1.P5
Pichincha, Battle of, 1822: F3734
Pichincha, Ecuador (Province):
  F3741.P4

Pichis River (Peru): F3451.L8
Pickens, Andrew: E207.P63
Pickering, Timothy: E302.6.P5
Pickett, George Edward: E467.1.P57
Pickett's Division
    Confederate Army: E547.P5
Pickwick Landing Reservoir: F217.T3
Pico do Monte Roraima (Brazil): F2609
Pictou Co. (Nova Scotia): F1039.P6
Pictou Island (Nova Scotia): F1039.P6
Picture writing
    Indians
        Pre-Columbian America: E59.W9
Pictured Rocks National Lakeshore
    (Mich.): F572.P5
Picunche Indians: F3126
Picuris Indians: E99.P575
Piedmont Region: F217.P53
Piedmont Region (Va.): F232.P5
Piedmont, Va., Battle of, 1864: E476.6
Piedras Negras Site (Guatemala)
    Mayas: F1435.1.P52
Piegan Indians: E99.P58
Piémont des Appalaches (Québec):
    F1054.P54
Pierce, Franklin: E432
    Administration, 1853-1857: E431+
    Family: E432.2
Piérola, Nicolás de: F3447
Pierpont, Francis Harrison: E534+
Pierre (S. D.): F659.P6
Piestewa Peak (Arizona): F817.M3
Pietri, Juan: F2325
Pigeon Point (Calif.): F868.S19
Pigeon River and Valley (Michigan):
    F572.P53
Pigeon River Country State Forest
    (Michigan): F572.P53
Pigeon Roost Massacre, 1812:
    E356.P6
Pigwacket Fight, 1725: E83.72
Pijao Indians: F2270.2.P64
Pike Lake Chain (Wisconsin): F587.P9
Pike National Forest (Colorado):
    F782.P63
Pike, Zebulon Montgomery: F592
Pikes Peak (Colorado): F782.P63

Pilaga Indians: F2823.P5
Pilar Site (Belize): F1435.1.P53
Pilchuck, Mount (Wash.): F897.S66
Pilcomayo River
    Paraguay-Argentina boundary
        question: F2857.P2
Pilgrim Society (Plymouth): F68
Pilgrims: F7, F68
Pilgrims (Patriotic society): E186.99.P6
Pillow, Fort, Massacre at, 1864:
    E476.17
Pillow, Gideon Johnson: E403.1.P6
    Court-martial: E405.6
Pilot Knob, Battle of, 1864: E477.16
Pima Indians: E99.P6, F1221.P5
Piman Indians: E99.P62
Pinao Indians: F2270.2.P64
Pinar del Rio (Cuba)
    City: F1809.P5
    Province: F1801+
Pinchot, Gifford: E664.P62
Pinckney, Charles: E302.6.P54
Pinckney, Charles Cotesworth:
    E302.6.P55
Pinckney, Eliza (Lucas): F272
Pinckney, Thomas: E302.6.P57
Pine Barrens (N.J.): F142.P5
Pine Creek and Valley (Potter County-
    Lycoming County)
    Pennsylvania: F157.P63
Pine Creek Gorge Natural Area (Pa.):
    F157.P64
Pine Creek (Washington): F897.O4
Pine Ford Dam and Reservoir (Mo.):
    F472.P64
Pine Ford Lake (Mo.): F472.P64
Pine Island (Florida): F317.L3
Pine Lawn Valley (N.M.): F802.P5
Pinelands National Reserve (N.J.):
    F142.P5
Piñero, Jesús T.: F1975
Piney Woods (Mississippi): F347.P63
Pinkney, William: E302.6.P6
Pinnacles National Monument
    (California): F868.P6
Pinon Canyon (Colo.): F782.L3
Pinzón, Martín Alonso: E125.P5

Pinzón, Próspero: F2276.5
Pinzón, Vincente Yáñez: E125.P52
Piocobgês Indians: F2520.1.G37
Pioje Indians: F3722.1.P5
Pioneer life: E161.5+
Pioneer Valley (Mass.): F72.C7
Pipe Spring National Monument
  (Arizona): F817.M5
Pipes, Tobacco
  Indians: E98.T6
    Pre-Columbian America: E59.T6
Pipil Indians: F1485.2.P5
Piqua, Ohio, Battle of, 1780: E241.P55
Piracicaba River (Brazil): F2631
Pirahá Indians: F2520.1.M9
Pirates
  Caribbean Sea: F2161
  Tripolitan War, 1801-1815: E335
  U.S. War with Algeria, 1815: E365
Piray River and Valley (Bolivia):
  F3341.S2
Piro Indians: F3430.1.P5
Piro Pueblo Indians: E99.P63
Pisagua, Chile (Dept.): F3214
Piscataqua River and Valley
  Maine: F27.P48
  New Hampshire: F42.P4
Piscataway Indians: E99.C873
Piscataway Park (Md.): F187.P56
Pisco, Peru (Province): F3451.P48
Pishgah National Forest (N.C.):
  F262.P57
Pisinahua Indians: F3430.1.S48
Pitcairn, John: E207.P68
Pitney, Henry Cooper: F139
Pitt Lake and region (British Columbia):
  F1089.P5
Pittsburgh Landing, Battle of, 1862:
  E473.54
Pittsburgh (Pa.): F159.P6+
Piura, Peru (Dept.): F3451.P5
Pizarro, Francisco: F3442
Pizarro, Gonzalo: F3442
Placentia Island (Me.): F27.H3
Places of amusement
  Boston: F73.627
  Chicago: F548.627

Places of amusement
  New York: F128.627
  Philadelphia: F158.627
Placilla, Battle of, 1891: F3098
Plains Indians: E78.G73
Plaisted, Harris Merrill: F25
Planchon de las Figuras (Mexico)
  Mayas: F1435.1.P55
Plano en papel maguey (Codices):
  F1219.56.P56+
Plantation life
  South Atlantic States: F214
  United States: F213
    Slave life: E443
Plantations, Union of, 1636-1643: F82
Plaquemine culture: E99.P635
Plaquemines Parish (La.): F377.P45
Plate River: F2909
Plateau Indians: E78.G67
Plateau Shoshonean Indians: E99.N97
Plats-Côtes-de Chien Indians: E99.T4
Platt Amendment (Cuba): F1787
  Abrogation, 1934: F1788
Platt National Park (Oklahoma):
  F702.P7
Platt, Orville Hitchcock: E664.P7
Platt, Thomas Collier: E664.P72
Platte Bridge Fight, July 1865: E83.86
Platte Purchase: F466
Platte River and Valley (Nebraska):
  F672.P6
Plattsburg, N.Y., Battle of, 1814:
  E356.P7
Plaza Gutiérrez, Leónidas: F3737
Plaza Lasso, Galo: F3738
Pleasant Hill, Battle of, 1864: E476.33
Pleasant Valley (Ariz.): F817.G5
Plough (Patent): F23
Plowden's New Albion Grant (New
  Jersey): F137
Plum Island (Mass.): F72.P6
Plumas Eureka State Park (California):
  F868.P85
Plumb, Preston B.: E664.P73
Plumer, William: E302.6.P73
Plymouth Colony: F68
Plymouth Company (1606): F7

Plymouth Company (1749-1816): F27.K3

Plymouth (Massachusetts): F74.P8

Plymouth, Va., Battle of, 1864: E476.2

Pocahontas: E99.P85

Pocasset Indians: E99.P64

Pocatello (Idaho): F754.P7

Poco Sabo Plantation (S.C.): F277.C8

Pocomoke River (Md.): F187.E2

Pocono Mountains: F157.M6

Pocotaligo, S.C., Battle of, 1862: E473.9

Pocra Indians: F3430.1.P6

Pocumtuck Valley (Mass.): F72.F8

Poesten Kill (N.Y.): F127.R3

Poetical works
United States history: E178.9

Poetry
Indians: E98.P74

Poindexter, George: E340.P75

Poinsett, Joel Roberts: E340.P77

Point Barrow (Alaska): F912.B2

Point Lobos (Calif.): F868.M7

Point Lookout (Arenac Co., Michigan): F572.A7

Point Lookout (Maryland)
Civil War prison: E616.L8

Point Montara (Calif.): F868.S19

Point Piedras Blancas (Calif.): F868.S18

Point Pleasant Battle, 1774: E83.77

Point Reyes (California): F868.P9

Point Roberts (Wash.): F897.P65

Pointe Coupee Parish (La.): F377.P55

Poison Spring, Ark., Battle of, 1864: E476.35

Pojoaque River and Valley (N.M.): F802.S4

Pokagon State Park (Indiana): F532.S8

Pokomam Indians: F1465.2.P6

Polar Bear Provincial (Ontario): F1059.P65

Poles in America: E29.P6

Poles in Argentina: F3021.P6

Poles in Brazil: F2659.P7
Espírito: F2561

Poles in Canada: F1035.P6

Poles in Haiti: F1930.P64

Poles in Latin America: F1419.P65

Poles in Mexico: F1392.P6

Poles in Peru: F3619.P64

Poles in South America: F2239.P6

Poles in the United States: E184.P7
Civil War: E540.P64

Police
Indians
North America: E98.C87

Political Americana: E183.3

Political collectibles: E183.3

Political paraphernalia: E183.3

Political refugees
United States
1850-1853: E429

Politics and government
Aztecs: F1219.76.P75
Indians
Argentina: F2821.3.P74
Bolivia: F3320.1.P56
Brazil: F2519.3.P58
Central America: F1434.2.P76
Colombia: F2270.1.P63
Costa Rica: F1545.3.P57
Ecuador: F3721.3.P74
El Salvador: F1485.3.P7
Guatemala: F1465.3.P64
Mexico: F1219.3.P7
Paraguay: F2679.3.P64
Peru: F3429.3.P65
Pre-Columbian America: E59.P73
South America: F2230.1.P65
Suriname: F2420.2.P64
Jews: E184.36.P64
Mayas: F1435.3.P7

Polk, James K.: E417
Administration, 1845-1849: E416

Polk, Leonidas: E467.1.P7

Polk, Sarah (Childress): E417.1

Pollock, Oliver: E302.6.P84

Polynesian
Discovery and exploration of America: E109.P65

Pomeroy, Samuel Clarke: E415.9.P78

Pomeroy, Seth: E207.P7

Pomo Indians: E99.P65

Pomoná Site (Mexico)
  Mayas: F1435.1.P66
Ponca Indians: E99.P7
Ponce de León, Juan: E125.P7
Ponce (Puerto Rico): F1981.P7
Pond Mountain (N.C.): F262.A7
Pontchartrain, Lake (La.): F377.P6
Pontiac County (Québec): F1054.P8
Pontiac's Conspiracy, 1763-1765:
  E83.76
Popayán (Colombia): F2281.P8
  Indian antiquities: F2269.1.P66
Pope, John, 1770-1845: E302.6.P86
Pope, John, 1822-1892
  Virginia campaign, 1862: E473.7
Popham Colony (Maine): F22
Popocatepetl: F1325
Popoloca Indians: F1221.P6
Popoluca Indians (Vera Cruz):
  F1221.P62
Popul vuh
  Translations: F1465.P8+
Popular attitudes toward Indians
  General: E59.P89
  North America: E98.P99
Popular Front (Chile): F3099
Population
  Indians: E98.P76
    Brazil: F2519.3.P59
    Chile: F3069.3.P76
    Ecuador: F3721.3.P76
    Honduras: F1505.3.P57
    Mexico: F1219.3.P73
    Paraguay: F2679.3.P66
    Peru: F3429.3.P68
    Pre-Columbian America: E59.P75
  Mayas: F1435.3.P75
Porras, Belisario: F1566.5
Port Angeles (Wash.): F899.P8
Port-au-Prince (Haiti): F1929.P8
Port Burwell (Island), Québec:
  F1054.P83
Port Gibson (Miss.), Battle of: E475.24
Port Hudson (Louisiana)
  Operations against, March 1863:
    E474.17
  Siege, May-July 1863: E475.42

Port Republic, Va., Battle of, 1862:
  E473.7
Port Royal Farm (Pa.): F158.68.P8
Port Royal Island (S.C.): F277.B3
Port Royal (Jamaica): F1895.P6
Port Royal (Nova Scotia)
  Capture, 1690: E196
  Expedition against, 1701: E197
Port Royal (S.C.)
  Expedition, 1861: E472.7
Portage Bay (Ontario): F1059.M9
Portage Path (Ohio): F497.S9
Portage Trail (N.Y.): F127.C7
Portales, Diego José Víctor: F3095
Porte des Morts Strait (Wisconsin):
  F587.P83
Porter, Alexander: F374
Porter, David: E353.1.P7
Porter, David Dixon: E467.1.P78
Porter, Fitz-John: E467.1.P8
  Court-martial: E473.772
Porter, Horace: E467.1.P82
Portland (Maine)
  Burning of: E241.P8
Portland (Me.): F29.P9
Portland (Oregon): F884.P8+
Portneuf County (Québec): F1054.P85
Porto Alegre (Brazil): F2651.P8
Porto Rico: F1951+
Portraits
  Indians: E89+
    Peru: F3429.3.P69
Portraits, African American: E444
Portraits, African Americans: E185.96+
Portraits, American: E176.5
Portsmouth Island (N.C.): F262.C23
Portsmouth (N.H.): F44.P8
Portsmouth (Rhode Island)
  Union of plantations: F82
Portsmouth (Virginia)
  Occupation of, 1862: E473.64
Portugal
  Colonies: F2501+
  Court in Brazil, 1808-1821: F2534
Portuguesa, Venezuela (State):
  F2331.P6

Portuguese
  Discovery and exploration
    America: E109.P8
      Post-Columbian: E123+
    Brazil: F2526
Portuguese colonies
  Brazil: F2501+
  Uruguay (Colonia): F2723
Portuguese in Argentina: F3021.P8
Portuguese in Bermuda: F1640.P67
Portuguese in Brazil: F2659.P8
Portuguese in Canada: F1035.P65
Portuguese in Peru: F3619.P67
Portuguese in South America:
  F2239.P67
Portuguese in the United States:
  E184.P8
Portuguese in Venezuela: F2349.P6
Possum Trot Hollow (Tennessee):
  F443.P75
Post-Columbian discovery and
  exploration of America: E121+
Postal service
  Indians
    Peru: F3429.3.P7
Posuso colony (Peru): F3451.H8
Potawatomi Indians: E99.P8
Potiguara Indians: F2520.1.P68
Potivara Indians: F2520.1.P68
Potomac, Army of the: E470.2+
Potomac, Great Falls of the: F187.M7
Potomac Indians: E99.P83
Potomac Park (Washington, D.C.):
  F203.5.P86
Potomac River and Valley
  District of Columbia: F202.P8
  Maryland: F187.P8
  Virginia: F232.P8
  West Virginia: F247.P8
Potosí (Bolivia)
  City: F3351.P85
  Department: F3341.P7
    Indian antiquities: F3319.1.P6
Potter's Raid, N.C., 1865: E477.7
Pottery
  Aztecs: F1219.76.P78
  Indians: E98.P8

Pottery
  Indians
    Argentina: F2821.3.P8
    Belize: F1445.3.P6
    Bolivia: F3320.1.P6
    Brazil: F2519.3.P6
    Central America: F1434.2.P8
    Chile: F3069.3.P8
    Colombia: F2270.1.P65
    Costa Rica: F1545.3.P6
    Ecuador: F3721.3.P8
    El Salvador: F1485.3.P8
    French Guiana: F2460.2.P6
    Guatemala: F1465.3.P68
    Honduras: F1505.3.P6
    Mexico: F1219.3.P8
    Nicaragua: F1525.3.P6
    Peru: F3429.3.P8
    Pre-Columbian America: E59.P8
    South America: F2230.1.P8
    Uruguay: F2719.3.P6
    Venezuela: F2319.3.P6
    West Indies: F1619.3.P6
  Mayas: F1435.3.P8
Potts, Jonathan: E283
Poverty Point culture: E99.P84
Powder River and Valley (Wyoming):
  F767.P6
Powder River Campaign, 1865: E83.86
Powell, Lake (Arizona and Utah):
  F832.G5
Powell, Leven: E263.V8
Powell River and Valley
  Tennessee: F443.P78
  Virginia: F232.P816
Power Island
  Michigan: F572.G5
Powhatan Indians: E99.P85
Pownall, Thomas: F67
Powwows
  Indians: E98.P86
Pozuzo colony (Peru): F3451.H8
Prado, Leoncio: F3447
Prado, Mariano Ignacio: F3447
Prado y Ugarteche, Manuel: F3448
Prairie du Chien (Wisconsin): F589.P8

Prairie Grove (Arkansas), Battle of, 1862: E474.92
Prairie Provinces
  Indians: E78.P7
Prayers, Wartime
  United States
    Civil War: E649+
    Revolution: E297
    War of 1812: E364.5
Pre-Columbian America: E51+, E103+
Pre-Columbian discovery and exploration: E103+
Pre-Columbian peoples (Mexico): F1219.7+
Preble, Edward: E335
Preble, George Henry: E182
Prehistoric archaeology
  America: E61
Prentiss, Samuel: E340.P88
Prentiss, Seargent Smith: E340.P9
Prentiss-Tucker Duel: E340.P9
Presbyterians (U.S.) and the Civil War: E540.P9
Presbyterians (U.S.) and the Revolution: E269.P9
Prescott, William: E207.P75
Presidential campaigns (U.S.)
  1796: E320
  1800: E330
  1804: E333.7
  1808: E337
  1812: E349
  1816: E370
  1824: E375
  1828: E380
  1832: E383
  1836: E385
  1840: E390
  1844: E400
  1848: E420
  1852: E430
  1856: E435
  1860: E440
  1864: E458.4
  1868: E670
  1872: E675
  1876: E680

Presidential campaigns (U.S.)
  1880: E685
  1884: E695
  1888: E700
  1892: E705
  1896: E710
  1900: E738
  1904: E758
  1908: E760
  1912: E765
  1916: E769
  1920: E783
  1924: E795
  1928: E796
  1932: E805
  1936: E810
  1940: E811
  1944: E812
  1948: E815
  1952: E816
  1956: E837.5
  1960: E837.7
  1964: E850
  1968: E851
  1972: E859
  1976: E868
  1980: E875
  1984: E879
  1988: E880
  1992: E884
  1996: E888
  2000: E889
  2004: E905
  2008: E906
Presidents
  United States
    Biography: E176.1
      Pets: E176.48
    Fathers: E176.25
    Inaugural ceremonies
      New York City, 1789: F128.44
      Philadelphia, 1793, 1797: F158.44
      Washington, D.C., 1801-1957: F197+
    Mothers: E176.3
    Wives: E176.2

Press
  United States
    War with Mexico: E415.2.P74
Press censorship
  U.S. Civil War: E609
Preston, Francis: E302.6.P93
Pribilof Islands (Alaska): F912.P9
Price's Missouri Expedition, 1864:
  E477.16
Prickly Pear Creek and Valley (Mont.):
  F737.P93
Priest Lake and Region
  Idaho: F752.B677
Primería Alta: F799
Prince Albert National Park
  (Saskatchewan): F1074.P7
Prince Co. (Prince Edward Island):
  F1049.P7
Prince Edward Island: F1046+
Prince Edward Island National Park
  (Canada): F1049.P75
Prince Edward (Ontario): F1059.P75
Prince Frederick Parish (S.C.):
  F277.P95
Prince George (British Columbia):
  F1089.5.P7
Prince George's Parish
  Frederick Co. (Maryland): F187.F8
  Montgomery Co. (Maryland):
    F187.M7
Prince of Wales Island (Alaska):
  F912.P95
Prince of Wales-Outer Ketchikan
  Census Area
  Alaska: F912.L65
Prince William Forest Park (Virginia):
  F232.P86
Prince William Sound region (Alaska):
  F912.P97
Prince William's Parish (S.C.):
  F277.P97
Princess Louisa Inlet and region (British
  Columbia): F1089.P77
Princeton, Battle of, 1777: E241.P9
Princeton (Frigate)
  Explosion: E396

Princeton University and the Civil War:
  E541.P9
Princeton University and the Revolution:
  E270.P9
Princeton University and the War of
  1898: E725.6.P7
Prison ships
  United States Revolution: E281
Prisoners of state
  United States
    Civil War: E458.8
Prisoners of war
  United States
    Civil War: E611+
    Revolution: E281
    War of 1812: E362
    War of 1898: E730
    War with Mexico: E412
Prisons, Military
  United States
    Civil War: E611+
    Revolution: E281
    War of 1812: E362
    War of 1898: E730
    War with Mexico: E412
Privateers
  United States
    Civil War: E596+
    Revolution: E271
    War of 1812: E360
Profile (New Hampshire): F41.6.P9
Promised Land State Park
  (Pennsylvania): F157.P6
Propaganda
  United States: E743.5
    Civil War: E468.9
Propaganda, Confederate, in foreign
  countries: E488.5
Property
  Indians: E98.P9
Proprietors of Kennebec Purchase:
  F27.K3
Prosperity Lake and region (Mo.):
  F472.J3
Prosperity Reservoir (Mo.): F472.J3
Protection Island (Wash.): F897.J4

Providence Island (Colombia):
  F2281.S15
Providence plantations: F82
Providence (R.I.): F89.P9+
Providence (U.S. sloop): E273.P75
Provincetown (Massachusetts):
  F74.P96
Provo River and Valley (Utah):
  F832.P76
Provo (Utah): F834.P3
Psychology
  Indians: E98.P95
    Bolivia: F3320.1.P8
    Mexico: F1219.3.P84
    Peru: F3429.3.P85
    Pre-Columbian America: E59.P87
Psychosocial factors, African American:
  E185.625
Public buildings, Historic
  United States: E159, F5
Public domain
  United States: E179.5
Public opinion
  War with Mexico: E415.2.P82
Public opinion about Indians
  General: E59.P89
  Mexico: F1219.3.P87
  North America: E98.P99
Public opinion, Foreign
  United States
    Civil War: E469.8
    Revolution: E249.3
Public welfare
  Indians
    Pre-Columbian America: E59.P92
Puebla (Mexico)
  City: F1391.P9
  State: F1326
Puebla (Mexico: State)
  Indian antiquities: F1219.1.P9
Pueblo (Colorado): F784.P9
Pueblo Indians: E99.P9
Puelche Indians: F2823.P8
Puelo River (Chile): F3181
Puerco River and Valley (General and
  New Mexico): F802.P83
Puerto Barrios (Guatemala): F1476.P8

Puerto Plata, Dominican Republic (City):
  F1939.P9
Puerto Principe (Cuba)
  City: F1839.C3
  Province: F1831+
Puerto Rican campaign, 1898: E717.3
Puerto Ricans in the United States:
  E184.P85
Puerto Rico: F1951+
  Annexation by U.S.: F1975
  Commonwealth: F1976+
  Military history
    Revolts against Spain in 1812, 1867:
      F1973
    Spanish-American War, 1898
      Puerto Rican campaign: E717.3
  Spanish rule: F1973
  Territory of the U.S.: F1975
Pueyrredón, Juan Martín de: F2845
Puget Sound region (Wash.): F897.P9
  Indians: E78.P8
Puget Sound Salish Indians: E99.S21
Puinave Indians: F2270.2.P8
Pukobye Indians: F2520.1.G37
Pulaski, Fort
  Bombardment and capture, 1862:
    E472.79
Pulaski, Military Order of: E202.99.M64
Pulpos Island (Mexico): F1335
Puławski, Kazimierz: E207.P8
Puno, Peru (Dept.): F3451.P9
  Indian antiquities: F3429.1.P8
Punta Ballema (Uruguay): F2731.M2
Puquina Indians: F3430.1.P8
Purcell Range (British Columbia):
  F1089.P8
Puri Indians: F2520.1.P8
Puritans
  Massachusetts: F67
  New England: F7
Purple Heart, Military Order of the:
  E181
Puruhá Indians: F3722.1.P8
Purus River (Brazil): F2546
  Indian antiquities: F2519.1.P8
Put-in-Bay (Ohio): F497.O8
  Perry Memorial: E356.E6

Putah Creek (Calif.): F868.P98
Putnam, Israel: E207.P9
Putnam, Rufus: F483
  French and Indian War, 1755-1763:
    E199
Putumayo atrocities: F3451.P94
Putumayo Department (Colombia):
  F2281.P9
Putumayo River and Valley
  Colombia: F2281.P9
  Peru: F3451.P94
Putumayo River Valley (Peru)
  Indian antiquities: F3429.1.P86
Puuc Region (Mexico)
  Antiquities: F1435.1.P88
Puxiti Indians: F2520.1.A4
Puyallup Indians: E99.P98
Pyramids
  Indians
    Mexico: F1219.3.P9

Q

Quabbin Reservoir (Mass.): F72.S94
Quadra Island (B.C.)): F1089.V3
Quadros administration (Brazil):
  F2538.2+
Quaichs: F2230.1.D75
Quakers
  United States: E184.F89
Quantrill's raid into Kansas, August
  1863: E474.97
Quapaw Indians: E99.Q2
Qu'Appelle River and Valley
  Manitoba: F1064.Q34
  Saskatchewan: F1074.Q34
Quay, Matthew Stanley: E664.Q2
Québec
  Wars
    American Revolution: E231
Quebec Act, 1774: F1032
Quebec campaign, 1759: E199
Quebec (City)
  Capture, 1759: E199
Québec (City): F1054.5.Q3
  Siege, 1775-1776: E231, E241.Q3
Québec County (Québec): F1054.Q4

Québec District: F1054.Q5
Québec District, New: F1054.N5
Quebec expeditions
  1711: E197
Québec expeditions
  1775: E231
Quebec (Province)
  American loyalists: E278.A+
  Treaty of Paris: E249
  Wars
    French and Indian War: E199
    Intercolonial wars: E197
    Rebellion, 1837-1838: F1032
Québec (Province): F1051+
  American loyalists: F1058
  History to 1791: F1030
  Indians: E78.Q3
  Wars
    American Revolution: E263.C2
    War of 1812: E355+, E359.85
Quechua Indians: F2230.2.K4
Queen Anne's Parish (Maryland):
  F187.P9
Queen Anne's War, 1702-1713: E197
Queen Charlotte Islands (British
  Columbia): F1089.Q3
Queen Elizabeth Islands: F1105.Q44
Queen Victoria Niagara Falls Park
  (Ontario): F1059.Q3
Queens (Borough): F128.68.Q4
Queens Co. (Nova Scotia): F1039.Q3
Queens Co. (Prince Edward Island):
  F1049.Q6
Queen's Rangers
  Loyalist: E277.6.Q6
Queenston Heights, Battle of, 1812:
  E356.Q3
Querandi Indians: F2823.Q4
Querétaro (Mexico)
  City: F1391.Q4
  State: F1331
Quero Indians: F3430.1.Q47
Queros
  Indians
    South America: F2230.1.D75
Quesada, Gonzalo de: F1787

Quetico Provincial Park (Ontario): F1059.Q4

Quezaltenango (Guatemala)
City: F1476.Q8
Department: F1469.Q5

Quichés: F1465.2.Q5

Quichua Indians: F2230.2.K4

Quijeros Mountains (Arizona): F817.P5

Quijo Indians: F3722.1.Q48

Quijos River Valley (Indian antiquities): F3721.1.Q54

Quijotoa Mountains (Arizona): F817.P5

Quileute Indians: E99.Q5

Quillacinga Indians: F2270.2.Q54

Quilpué (Chile)
Indian antiquities: F3069.1.Q6

Quimbaya Indians: F2270.2.Q8

Quinaielt Indians: E99.Q6

Quincy (Illinois): F549.Q6

Quincy, Josiah (1744-1775): E263.M4

Quincy, Josiah (1772-1864): E302.6.Q7

Quindío, Colombia (Province): F2281.Q55

Quinnipiac Indians: E99.Q7

Quinonez Molina, Alfonso: F1487.5

Quintana Roo (Mexico)
Indians: F1219.1.Q5
Mayas: F1435.1.Q78
Territory: F1333

Quinte, Bay of (Ontario): F1059.Q6

Quipu
Indians
Peru: F3429.3.Q6

Quirigua
Antiquities: F1435.1.Q8

Quiroga, Juan Facundo: F2846

Quitman, John Anthony: E403.1.Q8

Quito (Ecuador): F3781

Quitu Indians: F3722.1.Q5

Quivera: F799

Quixo Indians: F3722.1.Q48

R

Race identity, African American: E185.625

Race relations
Canada: F1027
Latin America: F1419.A1+
United States: E184.A1
African Americans: E185.61, E185.615

Racial discrimination
United States
African Americans: E185.61

Racial elements in the population
America: F1035.A1+

Racine (Wisconsin): F589.R2

Radisson, Pierre Esprit: F1060.7

Railroads
Boston: F73.67
Philadelphia: F158.67.A+
Washington, D.C.: F203.7.A+

Rainbow Bridge National Monument (Utah): F832.R3

Rainbow Bridge (Utah): F832.R3

Rainbow Canyon (Nevada): F847.R33

Rainier, Mount (Wash.): F897.R2

Rainsford Island (Mass.): F73.68.R2

Rainy River region (Minnesota): F612.R18

Raisin River, Battle of, 1813: E356.R2

Râle, Sébastien: E83.72

Raleigh (N.C.): F264.R1

Raleigh, Sir Walter
Explorations, 1595-1617: E129.R2
Virginia colonies, 1584-1590: F229

Rama Indians: F1525.2.R3

Ramapo Mountain people: E184.R3

Ramapo River and Valley (N.J.): F142.R16

Ramsay, George, earl of Dalhousie: F1053

Ramseur, Stephen Dodson: E467.1.R2

Rancagua, Battle of, 1814: F3094

Ranch life
Canadian Northwest: F1060.94
North Dakota: F636
Texas: F391+
West (U.S.): F596
Wyoming: F761

Rancho El Tejon (California): F868.K3

Rancho Santa Margarita (Calif.):
F868.S34
Rancocas Valley (New Jersey):
F142.B9
Rand Mining District (California):
F868.R32
Randolph, Edmund: E302.6.R18
Randolph, John: E302.6.R2
Rangeley Lakes (Me.): F27.R2
Ranqueles Indians: F2823.R2
Ransom, Truman Bishop: E403.1.R2
Raousset-Boulbon, Gaston Raoux,
comte de: F1232.5
Rapa Nui (Chile): F3169
Rapid City Indian School: E97.6.R35
Rapid City (S. D.): F659.R2
Rapidan River and Valley (Virginia):
F232.R18
Rapides Parish (La.): F377.R25
Rappahannock Indians: E99.R18
Rappahannock Station, Va., 2nd Battle
of, 1863: E475.7
Raquette Lake (New York): F127.H2
Raritan River and Valley (New Jersey):
F142.R2
Rasles (Rasle), Sébastien: E83.72
Raven Rocks (Ohio): F497.B4
Rawlins, John Aaron: E467.1.R25
Ray Roberts Lake (Texas): F392.R22
Read, George: E302.6.R27
Read, John: F67
Reading (Pennsylvania): F159.R2
Reagan, Ronald: E876+
Ream's Station, Va., Battle of, 1864:
E476.93
Recife (Brazil): F2651.R4+
Reconstruction (U.S.), 1865-1877:
E668
The South: F216
Recreation
Indians
North America: E98.G2
Pre-Columbian America: E59.G3
Recuay culture (Peru)
Indian antiquities: F3429.1.A45
Red Bank, Battle of, 1777: E241.R3
Red Cloud War, 1866-1867: E83.866

Red Cross
War of 1898: E731
Red Deer River and Valley (Alberta):
F1079.R4
Red Hills (Florida): F317.R43
Red Mountain Mining District
(Colorado): F782.R36
Red River and Valley
Arkansas: F417.R3
Kentucky: F457.R4
Louisiana: F377.R3
New Mexico: F802.R36
Oklahoma: F702.R3
Texas: F392.R3
Red River expedition, 1864: E476.33
Red River Gorge (Kentucky): F457.R4
Red River (Louisiana), campaign, 1864:
E476.33
Red River (N.M.): F802.T2
Red River of the North
Manitoba: F1064.R3
Minnesota: F612.R27
North Dakota: F642.R3
Red River Parish (La.): F377.R32
Red River Rebellion, 1869-1870: F1063
Red River Settlement: F1063
Red River State Recreation Area
(Minnesota): F612.R28
Red River War, 1874-1875: E83.875
Red Rock Canyon National
Conservation Area (Nevada):
F847.C5
Reductions, Jesuit (1609-1769): F2684
Redwood National Park (Humboldt and
Del Norte Counties) (California):
F868.R4
Redwood Park (Calif.): F868.S3
Reed Gold Mine State Historic Site
(N.C.): F262.R25
Reed, James: E207.R32
Reed, Joseph: E302.6.R3
Reed, Thomas Brackett: E664.R3
Reelfoot Lake and region (Tennessee):
F443.R34
Reemelin, Charles: F496

Refugees, Political
  United States
    1850-1853: E429
Refugees, Southern: E458.7
Regimental histories
  United States
    Civil War
      Confederate Army: E545+
      Union Army: E491+
    Revolution
      Loyalists: E277.6.A+
    War of 1812: E359
    War of 1898: E725+
    War with Mexico: E409
Regiments, African American
  Civil War: E492.9
Regina (Saskatchewan): F1074.5.R3
Region de los Lagos (Chile): F3218
Region oriental (Ecuador): F3741.N3
Registers, lists, etc., Military
  Confederate States Army: E548
    Prisoners: E611
  Great Britain. Army
    American Revolution: E267+
  Spain. Army
    War of 1898: E725.9
  United States
    Civil War: E494
    Revolution: E255
      Auxiliaries: E265
      By state: E263.A+
    War of 1898: E725.8
    War with Mexico: E409.7
Regulars
  United States Army
    War of 1812: E359.2
    War with Mexico: E409.2
Regulator Insurrection, 1766-1771:
  F257
Regulators
  Vigilante groups: E179
Reid, Whitelaw: E664.R35
Relations of seceded states to the
  Union, 1865-1877: E668
Relations with blacks
  Peruvian Indians: F3429.3.R27

Relations with women
  United States presidents: E176.4
Relief agencies
  United States
    Civil War: E629+
Relief, Financial
  Indians: E98.F3
Religion
  Abraham Lincoln: E457.2
  Aztecs: F1219.76.R45
  George Washington
    Letters: E312.75.R3+
  Indians: E98.R3
    Argentina: F2821.3.R4
    Bolivia: F3320.1.R3
    Brazil: F2519.3.R3
    Central America: F1434.2.R3
    Chile: F3069.3.R44
    Colombia: F2270.1.R4
    Costa Rica: F1545.3.R4
    Ecuador: F3721.3.R44
    Guatemala: F1465.3.R4
    Mexico: F1219.3.R38
    Nicaragua: F1525.3.R44
    Paraguay: F2679.3.R44
    Peru: F3429.3.R3
    Pre-Columbian America: E59.R38
    South America: F2230.1.R3
  Mayas: F1435.3.R3
Religion in the armed forces
  United States
    Civil War: E635
Religious elements in the population
  United States
    Civil War
      Confederate Army: E585.A+
      Union Army: E540.A+
      Revolution: E269.A+
Religious toleration in colonial Maryland:
  F184
Remedios (Cuba): F1829.R4
Remón, José Antonio: F1567
Removal
  Indians: E98.R4
    Guatemala: F1465.3.R44
Removal of deposits
  Bank of the United States: E384.7

INDEX

Renfrew Co. (Ontario): F1059.R4
Reno (Nevada): F849.R4
Rensselaerswyck (N.Y.): F127.R32
Reparations
  African-Americans: E185.89.R45
Reporters, News
  U.S. Civil War: E609
Republic of Florida, 1812-1816: F314
Republic of Texas, 1836-1846: F390
Republican River Valley (Nebraska and
  Kansas)
  Indians: E78.R37
Republicans, Liberal
  United States history: E671
Resaca, Battle of, 1864: E476.7
Resaca de la Palma, Battle of, 1846:
  E406.R4
Reservations
  Indians: E91+
    Colombia: F2270.1.G6
    Costa Rica: F1545.3.R44
    North America: E78.A+, E99.A+
Reservations, National
  United States: E160
Resignation of Richard Nixon: E861
Revere, Paul: F69
  Paul Revere's ride: E216
Revilla Gigedo Islands (Mexico):
  F1333.5
Revillagigedo Island (Alaska):
  F912.R48
Revolution, 1775-1783: E201+
  Anniversaries: E285+
  Armies
    American
      French participation: E265
    British: E267+, E268
      Loyalist regiments: E277.6.A+
    Biography: E206+
      Regiments: E263.A+, E275.A2+
      Spies: E279+
      Statesmen: E302.5+
  Causes: E210+
  Chronology: E209
  Commerce: E215
  Diplomatic history: E249
  Historiography: E209

Revolution, 1775-1783
  Indian wars: E83.775
  Loyalists: E277+
  Medical and hospital services: E283
  Naval operations: E271+, E271
  Political history: E210+
  Prisons and prisoners: E281
  Registers, lists, etc: E255, E263.A+,
    E265
  Religious aspects: E209
  Secret service: E279+
  Travel during period: E163
  Women's work: E276
Revolution of 1689 (New England):
  F7.5
Revolution of the Farrapos, 1835-1841:
  F2621
Revolving credit fund
  Indians: E98.F3
Reyes, Rafael: F2277
Reynolds, John Fulton: E467.1.R4
Rhett, Robert Barnwell: F273
Rhode Island: F76+
  African Americans: E185.93.R4
  Counties, etc: F87.A+
  Gaspee affair, 1772: E215.6
  Indians: E78.R4
  Slavery: E445.R4
  Wars
    Civil War: E528.1+
    King Philip's War, 1675-1676:
      E83.67
    Revolution: E263.R4
      Military operations: E230+
    War of 1898: E726.R4
Rhode Island, Battle of, 1778: E241.R4
Rhode Island (Colony): F82
Rhode Island (Island): F87.R4
Riachuelo, Battle of, 1865: F2687
Ribas, José Félix: F2324
Ribaut (Ribault), Jean: F314
Ribeira de Iguape River (Brazil): F2631
Ricaurte y Lozano, Antonio: F2274
Rich Mountain, Battle of, 1861: E472.17
Richard B. Russell Lake and Region
  Georgia: F292.R49
  South Carolina: F277.R49

Richelieu River and Valley: F1054.R5

Richland-Chambers Dam and Reservoir (Texas): F392.R48

Richland Creek and Valley (Texas): F392.R48

Richland Parish (La.): F377.R5

Richmond campaigns
  1864, Aug.-Dec: E477.21
  1864, June-July: E476.91
  1865: E477.61

Richmond Co. (Nova Scotia): F1039.R5

Richmond (Kentucky), Battle of, August 1862: E474.37

Richmond (New York) (Borough): F234.R5+

Richmond (Virginia): F234.R5+
  Dahlgren's raid, 1864: E476.27
  Insurrection, 1800: F234.R5+

Richmond (Virginia). Battle Abbey: F234.R5+

Richmond (Virginia). Confederate Memorial Institute: F234.R5+

Rickwood Caverns State Park (Alabama): F332.B6

Rideau River and Valley (Ontario): F1059.R46

Ridgefield, Conn., 1777: E241.R53

Riding gear
  Indians: E98.R5

Riding Mountain National Park (Man.): F1064.R54

Riel Rebellion, 1885: F1060.9

Rife (Alberta): F1079.R53

Rigaud, Philippe de, marquis de Vaudreuil: F1030

Right of search
  War of 1812: E357.2

Rikbaktsa Indians: F2520.1.R53

Rimac Valley (Peru)
  Indian antiquities: F3429.1.R55

Ringwood Manor (N.J.): F142.P2

Rio Azul Site (Guatemala)
  Mayas: F1435.1.R56

Rio Branco, Brazil (Territory): F2609

Rio Chama (N.M.): F802.C45

Rio Cisnes (Chile): F3181

Rio de Janeiro, Brazil (State): F2611

Rio de Janeiro, Brazil (State)
  Indian antiquities: F2519.1.R5

Rio de Janeiro (City): F2646
  Columbus celebration, 1892: E119
  French colony, 1555-1567: F2529

Rio de Janeiro (Federal District to April 21, 1960): F2646

Rio de la Plata: F2909
  Blockade, 1845-1847: F2846.3

Rio de la Plata (Province): F2841

Rio de la Plata (Viceroyalty): F2841

Rio de las Balsas (Mexico): F1247

Rio Grande
  Mexico: F1334
  New Mexico: F802.R5
  Texas: F392.R5

Rio Grande de Térraba (Costa Rica): F1549.R5

Rio Grande do Norte, Brazil (State): F2616

Rio Grande do Sul, Brazil (State): F2621
  Indian antiquities: F2519.1.R6
  Jesuit missions of Paraguay: F2684

Río Grande (Guatemala): F1469.M68

Rio Grande National Forest (Colorado): F782.R46

Rio Grande Valley
  Indians: E78.R56

Río Huasco (Chile): F3131

Rio Jacuhype (Brazil): F2551

Rio Jacuípe (Brazil): F2551

Rio Loa (Chile): F3069.1.L6

Río Negro, Argentina (Territory): F2951

Rio Negro (Brazil): F2546

Río Negro (Uruguay): F2731.R4

Río Piedras (Puerto Rico): F1981.R5

Rio Puelo (Chile): F3181

Rio San Juan (Nicaragua): F1529.S35

Río Yaqui (Mexico): F1346

Riobamba (Ecuador): F3791.R6

Rioja (Argentina): F3011.L45

Ríos, Los, Ecuador (Province): F3741.L7

Rip Van Winkle Trail: F127.C3

Ripley, Eleanor Wheelock: E353.1.R5

Rising, Johan Classon: F167

Ritchie, Thomas: E340.R6
Rites and ceremonies
  Indians
    Aztecs: F1219.76.R57
    Mexico: F1219.3.R56
    North America: E98.R53
    Peru: F3429.3.R58
    Pre-Columbian America: E59.R56
  Mayas: F1435.3.R56
Ritner, Joseph: F153
Rivadavia, Bernardino: F2846
Rivas, Battle of, 1856: F1526.27
River Indians
  New England
    Mahican Indians: E99.M12
    Mohegan Indians: E99.M83
    Stockbridge Indians: E99.S8
River Road
  Louisiana: F377.R58
Rivera, José Fructuoso: F2726
Rivera, Uruguay (Dept.): F2731.R5
Riverside Drive (New York):
  F128.67.R6
Riverside Park (New York): F128.65.R5
Rivière-du-Loup County and region
  (Québec): F1054.R615
Roads
  Indians
    Peru: F3429.3.R6
    Pre-Columbian America: E59.R6
    South America: F2230.1.R6
  Mayas: F1435.3.R6
Roan Mountain
  North Carolina: F262.R39
  Tennessee: F443.R49
Roane, Archibald: F436
Roanoke colonies, 1584-1590: F229
Roanoke Island: F262.R4
Roanoke Island, Battle of, 1862:
  E473.31
Roanoke River and Valley
  North Carolina: F262.R5
  Virginia: F232.R63
Roanoke (Steamer): E595.R6
Roaring Fork Valley (Colorado):
  F782.R52

Robert E. Lee Memorial, Arlington, Va:
  F234.A7
Robertson, George: E340.R7
Robertson, James: F436
Robeson, Paul: E185.97.R63
Robins Island (N.Y.): F127.S9
Robinson, Charles: F685
Robinson Creek and Valley (Oklahoma):
  F702.L5
Robinson, Sir John Beverley: F1058
Robson River and Valley (British
  Columbia): F1089.R62
Roca, Julio Argentino: F2847
Rocafuerte, Vicente: F3736
Rocha, Uruguay (Dept.): F2731.R6
Rochambeau, J.B.D. de Vineur, comte
  de: E265
Roche de la Croix (Mo.): F472.P4
Rochester (Minnesota): F614.R6
Rochester (New York): F129.R7+
Rock Creek Park (Washington, D.C.):
  F203.5.R6
Rock Island (Illinois): F549.R6
Rock Island (Illinois). Military Prison
  Civil War prison: E616.R6
Rock Island Trail State Park (Illinois):
  F547.R64
Rock Island (Wisconsin): F587.D7
Rock paintings
  Indians: E98.P34
    Argentina: F2821.3.P6
    Colombia: F2270.1.P4
    Honduras: F1505.3.P48
    Mexico: F1219.3.P46
    Peru: F3429.3.P47
    Pre-Columbian America: E59.P42
    South America: F2230.1.P48
    Venezuela: F2319.3.P4
  Mayas: F1435.3.P44
Rock River and Valley: F547.R7
  Wisconsin: F587.R63
Rockaway Beach (New York): F129.R8
Rockaway Peninsula (New York):
  F129.R8
Rockefeller Center (New York):
  F128.8.R7
Rockford (Illinois): F549.R7

Rocking Chair Ranche (Texas):
F392.R64
Rocky Mountain House Region
(Alberta): F1079.R62
Rocky Mountain National Park (Colo.):
F782.L2
Rocky Mountain National Park
(Colorado): F782.R59
Rocky Mountains and region: F721
Canada: F1090
Colorado: F782.R6
Indians: E78.R63
Montana: F737.R8
New Mexico: F802.R68
Rocky River and Valley (Ohio):
F497.R7
Roddey's Raid, 1863: E475.87
Rodgers, John: E353.1.R7
Rodman, William: F153
Rodney, Caesar: E302.6.R6
Rodney, Caesar Augustus: E302.6.R61
Rodney, George Brydges
Saint Eustatius, 1781: F2097
West Indies: F1621
Rodney, Thomas: E263.D3
Rodríguez de Mendoza, Peru
(Province): F3451.R6
Rodríguez, José Gaspar: F2686
Rodríguez, Simón: F2235.5.R6
Roe, Francis Asbury: E182
Rogers, Robert: E199
Rogue River and Valley: F882.R6
Rogue River War, 1850: E83.84
Rojas, Arístides: F2325
Rojas Pinilla, Gustavo: F2278
Rollins, Edward Henry: E415.9.R75
Rollins, James Sidney: E415.9.R76
Romanians in Canada: F1035.R65
Romanians in the United States:
E184.R8
Romero Bosque, Pio: F1487.5
Romney Campaign, 1861-1862: E470.3
Rondônia State (Brazil): F2624
Roosevelt, Eleanor: E807.1
Roosevelt, Franklin Delano: E807
Administrations, 1933-1945: E806
Collected works: E742.5.R6+

Roosevelt, Franklin Delano
Family: E807.1
Hyde Park Home (National Historic
Site): F129.H99
Roosevelt Island (District of Columbia):
F203.4.T5
Roosevelt-Sequoia National Park
(Proposed): F868.S4
Roosevelt, Theodore: E757
Administrations: E756+
Collected works: E660.R7+
Family: E757.3
Rough Riders
War of 1898: E725.45
Sagamore Hill (Oyster Bay, New
York): F129.O98
Root, Elihu: E664.R7
Roque Island: F27.W3
Roraima (Brazil): F2609
Roraima Mountain (Brazil): F2609
Rosario (Argentina): F3011.R7
Rosario Islands (Colombia): F2281.B6
Rosario Valley (Mexico): F1435.1.R67
Rosas, J.M.J.D. Ortiz de: F2846.3
War against: F2846.3
Rosbrugh, John: E263.P4
Rosebud Creek and Valley (Mont.):
F737.R96
Rosebud River and Valley (Alberta):
F1079.R66
Rosecrans, William Starke: E467.1.R7
Roseland (Illinois): F548.68.R8
Rosemont Plantation (S.C.): F277.L3
Roslindale (Boston): F73.68.R67
Ross, Betsy (Griscom): E302.6.R77
Ross, George: F154
Ross, George (1730-1779):
E302.6.R79
Ross, James: E302.6.R8
Rossiisko-Amerikanskaia kompaniia:
F907
Rouges Creek and Valley (Alabama):
F332.J4
Rough Riders: E725.45
Round Valley (California): F868.M5
Routt National Forest (Colorado):
F782.R8

Rowan, Andrews Summers: E714.6.R8
Rowan, Stephen Clegg: E182
Rowlett's Station, Ky., Battle of, 1861: E472.9
Roxbury (Massachusetts): F74.R9
Royal Gorge (Colo.): F782.F8
Royale, Île (Nova Scotia): F1039.C2
Royale, Isle (Michigan): F572.I8
Royall, Anne (Newport): E340.R88
Rubber industry
  Peru: F3451.P94
Ruffin, Edmund: F230
Ruffin, Thomas: F258
Ruggles, Timothy: F67
Rugs, Indian: E98.T35
Ruins
  Aboriginal America: E51+
Ruiz Cortines, Adolfo: F1235.5.R8
Rulers
  Aztecs: F1219.76.K53
  Indians
    Peru: F3429.3.K53
Rumichaca grotto (Ecuador): F3741.C3
Rupert River and Valley (Québec): F1054.R87
Rupert's Land: F1060+
Rush, Benjamin: E302.6.R85
Rush Creek Valley (Minnesota): F612.W7
Rush, Richard: E340.R9
Rushmore, Mount, National Memorial: F657.R8
Rusk, Jeremiah McLain: E664.R93
Rusk, Thomas Jefferson: F389
Russell Lake region (Sask.): F1074.R8
Russia
  Sale of Alaska to the United States: E669, F907
Russian-American Company: F907
Russian exploration and settlement in Alaska: F907
Russian Germans in America: E29.R83
Russian Germans in Argentina: F3021.R87
Russian Germans in Canada: F1035.R79

Russian Jews in the United States: E184.3+
Russian River and Valley (California): F868.R9
Russians in Canada: F1035.R8
Russians in Paraguay: F2699.R8
Russians in Peru: F3619.R87
Russians in the United States: E29.R84, E184.R9
Russo-Japanese War, 1904-1905
  U.S. policy: E756
Rustic Canyon (Calif.): F868.L8
Ruthenians in Canada: F1035.U5
Ruthenians in the United States: E184.U5
Rutherford's Farm, Va., Battle of, 1864: E476.66
Rutledge, Ann: E457.35
Rutledge, John, 1739-1800: E302.6.R89
Rutledge, John, 1766-1819: E302.6.R9
Ruyter's attack on Barbados, 1655: F2041
Rwandans in the United States: E184.R93
Ryswick, Treaty of, 1697: F1923
Ryukyuans in Bolivia: F3359.R97
Ryukyuans in the United States: E184.R97

S

Sá, Mem de: F2528
Saavedra, Cornelio de: F2845
Saba (West Indies): F2088
Sabine Parish (La.): F377.S115
Sabine Pass, Battle of, 1863: E475.4
Sabine Pass Battlefield State Historical Park (Texas): F392.J33
Sabine River and Valley
  Louisiana: F377.S116
  Texas: F392.S12
Sable Island (Nova Scotia): F1039.S13
Sacasa, Juan Bautista: F1526.3
Sacasa, Roberto: F1526.27
Sacatepéquez, Guatemala (Dept.): F1469.S13

Sackets Harbor, N.Y., Battle of, 1813: E356.S34

Saclan Indians: E99.S14

Saco Bay (Me.): F27.Y6

Saco, José Antonio: F1774.S3

Saco River and Valley: F27.S15

Saconet Indians: E99.S16

Saconnet Indians: E99.S16

Sacramento (California): F869.S12

Sacramento River and Valley (Calif.): F868.S13

Sacrificios, Isla de (Mexico)
Indian antiquities: F1219.1.V47

Sáenz Peña, Roque: F2847

Sagamore Hill (Oyster Bay, N.Y.): F129.O98

Saginaw Bay region: F572.S15

Saginaw, Fort (Michigan): F572.S15

Saginaw (Michigan): F574.S15

Saginaw River and Valley (Michigan): F572.S2

Sagua la Grande (Cuba): F1829.S12

Saguaro National Park (Arizona): F817.S18

Saguenay County (Québec): F1054.S13

Saguenay River and Valley (Québec): F1054.S14

Sailly, Peter: E302.6.S13

Sailors
United States
Impressment
War of 1812: E357.2

Sailor's Creek, Va., Battle of, 1865: E477.67

Saint Albans Confederate Raid, 1864: E470.95

Saint Ambrose Island (Chile): F3131

Saint Andrews Bay (Florida): F317.W3

Saint Andrews Island (Colombia): F2281.S15

Saint Anne's Parish (Maryland): F187.A6

Saint Ann's Bay and region (Nova Scotia): F1039.S18

Saint Augustine colony: F314

Saint Augustine expeditions, 1740, 1743: F314

Saint Augustine (Florida): F319.S2

Saint-Barthélemy (West Indies): F2089

Saint Bartholomew (West Indies): F2089

Saint Bernard Parish (La.): F377.S12

Saint Boniface (Manitoba): F1064.5.S13

Saint Catherine Island (Md.): F187.S2

Saint Charles Parish (La.): F377.S124

Saint Christopher (West Indies): F2091

Saint Clair, Arthur: F483
Campaign, November 1791: E83.79

Saint Clair, Lake, region
Michigan: F572.S34
Ontario: F1059.S3

Saint Cloud (Minnesota): F614.S25

Saint Croix Island (Me.): F27.W3

Saint Croix River and Valley (General and Wisconsin): F587.S14

Saint Croix River and Valley (Me.): F27.S2

Saint Croix River and Valley (Minnesota): F612.S2

Saint Croix River and Valley (New Brunswick): F1044.S17

Saint Croix (West Indies) (Island): F2096

Saint Domingue, 1677-1803: F1923

Saint Elias, Mount (Alaska): F912.S15

Saint Elias-Wrangell National Park and Preserve (Alaska): F912.W74

Saint Eustatius (West Indies): F2097

Saint Felix Island (Chile): F3131

Saint Francis River and Valley (Ark.): F417.S2

Saint Francis River and Valley (Missouri): F472.S25

Saint Francis River and Valley (Québec): F1054.S254

Saint George Island (Bermudas): F1639.S3

Saint George River (Me.): F27.S25

Saint George's Cay (Belize): F1449.S24

Saint-Georges-de-l'Oyapock (French Guiana): F2469.S3
Saint-Georges (French Guiana): F2469.S3
Saint George's Parish
  Maryland: F187.H2
  Virginia: F232.S15
Saint Helena Island (S.C.): F277.B3
Saint Helena, Mount (California): F868.S132
Saint Helena Parish (La.): F377.S13
Saint Helen's Island (Québec): F1054.S26
Saint Helens, Mount (Wash.): F897.S17
Saint Hyacinthe County (Québec): F1054.S264
Saint Ignatius Mission (Mont.): F737.L3
Saint James Parish
  Jamaica: F1891.S14
  Louisiana: F377.S134
Saint James' Parish (Maryland): F187.A6
Saint Joe River and Valley (Idaho): F752.S74
Saint John Lake (Québec): F1054.S267
Saint John (New Brunswick): F1044.5.S14
Saint John River and Valley
  Maine: F27.S3
  New Brunswick: F1044.S2
Saint John the Baptist Parish (La.): F377.S135
Saint John (West Indies): F2098
Saint John's Church (Georgetown, D.C.): F203.2.S14
Saint John's (Newfoundland): F1124.5.S14
Saint Johns River and Valley (Florida): F317.S2
Saint Joseph Island (Ontario): F1059.S33
Saint Joseph-Kankakee portage (Indiana): F532.S2
Saint Joseph (Mo.): F474.S18
Saint Joseph River and Valley
  Indiana: F532.S3
  Michigan: F572.S43

Saint Kitts and Nevis (West Indies): F2084
Saint Kitts (West Indies): F2091
Saint Landry Parish (La.): F377.S14
Saint-Laurent-du-Maroni (French Guiana): F2469.S5
Saint-Laurent (French Guiana): F2469.S5
Saint Lawrence Co. (N.Y.): F127.S2
Saint Lawrence, Gulf of: F1050
Saint Lawrence Island (Alaska): F912.S2
Saint Lawrence River and Valley: F1050
  New York: F127.S23
  Ontario: F1059.S4
  Quebec: F1054.S3
Saint Lawrence River campaign, 1813
  War of 1812: E355.4
Saint Leger's invasion, 1777: E233
Saint Louis (Mo.): F474.S2+
Saint Lucia (West Indies): F2100
Saint Margaret's Bay and region (Nova Scotia): F1039.S19
Saint Maries River and Valley (Idaho): F752.S28
Saint Mark's Parish
  South Carolina: F277.S2
  Virginia: F232.S2
Saint Martin Parish (La.): F377.S16
Saint Martin (West Indies): F2103
Saint Mary Anne's Parish (Maryland): F187.C3
Saint Mary Parish
  Jamaica: F1891.S2
  Louisiana: F377.S2
Saint Marys Bay and region (Nova Scotia): F1039.S20
Saint Mary's River and Valley
  Florida: F317.S3
  Georgia: F292.S2
Saint Maurice River and Valley (Québec): F1054.S33
Saint-Ours (Seigniory) (Québec): F1054.S34
Saint Paul Island (Nova Scotia): F1039.S27

Saint Paul (Minnesota): F614.S4

Saint Peter and Saint Paul, Cathedral of (Washington, D.C.): F204.C3

Saint Peter, Lake (Québec): F1054.S345

Saint Peter's Parish (Virginia): F232.N3

Saint Petersburg (Florida): F319.S24

Saint Philip, Fort
Bombardment and capture, 1862: E472.88

Saint Pierre and Miquelon: F1170

Saint Regis Indians: E99.M8

Saint Simon's Island (Georgia): F292.G58

Saint Tammany Parish (La.): F377.S3

Saint Thomas and Saint Denis Parish (S.C.): F277.S24

Saint Thomas (West Indies): F2105

Saint Vincent and the Grenadines (West Indies): F2106

Saint Vincent (West Indies): F2106+, F2106

Saint Vrain Creek and Valley (Colorado): F782.S15

Sainte-Foy, Battle of, 1760: E199

Saintes, Les (West Indies): F2070

Sakirabiá Indians: F2520.1.S22

Saklan Indians: E99.S14

Sakonnet Indians: E99.S16

Sakonnet River and Region (Rhode Island): F87.S25

Salado culture: E99.S547

Salado River and Valley (Argentina): F2957

Saladoid culture: F1619.2.S25

Salaverry, Felípe Santiago: F3447

Salcantay, Cerro (Peru): F3451.C9

Salcedo, Dominican Republic (Province): F1939.S15

Salem Church, Va., Battle of, 1863: E475.35

Salem (Massachusetts): F74.S1
Columbus celebration 1892: E119

Salem (Oregon): F884.S2

Salem Raid, Salem, Va., 1863: E475.7

Salesians in Ecuador: F3799.S3

Salinan Indians: E99.S17

Salinas National Monument (N.M.): F802.S13

Salinas River and Valley (California): F868.S133

Salisbury (North Carolina). Military Prison: E612.S15

Salish Indians: E99.S2

Salishan Indians: E99.S21

Saliva Indians: F2319.2.S3

Salmon River and Valley (Idaho): F752.S35

Salmon River and Valley (Oregon): F882.S18

Salomon, Haym: E302.6.S17

Salomon, Louis Étienne Félicité: F1926

Salonde Indians: F2520.1.S24

Salt
Indians: E98.S26
Ecuador: F3721.3.S24
Mayas: F1435.3.S24

Salt Creek and Valley (Oklahoma): F702.O7

Salt Lake City (Utah): F834.S2+

Salt Lick Creek and Valley (Kentucky): F457.S24

Salt River and Valley (Arizona): F817.S2

Salt Spring Island (British Columbia): F1089.S2

Salt Valley
Idaho: F752.S37
Wyoming: F767.S37

Salta (Argentina)
City: F3011.S2
Province: F2958
Indian antiquities: F2821.1.S15

Salto Grande Department (Uruguay)
Indian antiquities: F2719.1.S24

Salto (Uruguay)
City: F2791.S2
Department: F2731.S2

Saltonstall, Leverett: E340.S18

Saltspring Island (British Columbia): F1089.S2

Saluma Indians: F2520.1.S24

Salut, Îles du (French Guiana): F2467.I4

Salvador: F1481+
Salvador (Brazil): F2651.S13+
Salvador, Charter of, 1951: F1439
Salvadorans in the United States:
    E184.S15
Salzburgers in Georgia: F295.S1
Samaná (Dominican Republic):
    F1939.S18
Samaypata (Bolivia)
    Indian antiquities: F3319.1.S2
Sambrano Revolution: F389
Sami Americans in the United States:
    E184.S16
Samish Indians: E99.S2115
Samish Island (Wash.): F897.S5
Samoan Americans: E184.S17
Sampson State Park (New York):
    F127.S235
Samucan Indians: F3320.2.S3
Samucu Indians: F3320.2.S3
San Agustin (Colombia): F2269.1.S24
San Agustin culture: F2270.2.S35
San Ambrosio Island (Chile): F3131
San Andres Mountains (N.M.):
    F802.S15
San Andrés y Providencia, Colombia
    (Territory): F2281.S15
San Antonio, Arroyo de (Estate)
    (California): F868.S7
San Antonio de los Baños (Cuba):
    F1799.S2
San Antonio River and Valley (Texas):
    F392.S19
San Antonio (Texas): F394.S211+
San Augustine, Surrender of Union
    forces at, 1861: E472.32
San Bernardino National Forest
    (California): F868.S144
San Bernardino Valley (California):
    F868.S14
San Blas coast (Panama): F1569.S3
San Cristóbal (Venezuela): F2341.S13
San Diego (California): F869.S22
San Felipe de Puerto Plata (Dominican
    Republic): F1939.P9
San Felipe Indians: E99.S212
San Félix Island (Chile): F3131

San Fernando Valley (Calif.): F868.L8
San Francisco Bay Region (Calif.):
    F868.S156
San Francisco (Calif.): F869.S3+
San Gabriel River and Valley (Texas):
    F392.S234
San Gabriel Valley (Calif.): F868.L8
San Gervasio Site (Mexico)
    Indians: F1435.1.S26
San Gorgonio Pass (Calif.): F868.R6
San Ildefonso Indians: E99.S213
San Ildefonso, Treaty of, 1777: F2723
San Jacinto Mountain National
    Monument (California): F868.S36
San Jacinto River and Valley (Calif.):
    F868.R6
San Joaquin River and Valley
    (California): F868.S173
San Jorge River (Colombia): F2281.B6
San José (Costa Rica)
    City: F1556.S2
    Province: F1549.S15, F1549.S17
San José, Uruguay (Dept.): F2731.S3
San Juan (Argentina)
    City: F3011.S218
    Province: F2961
San Juan Co. (Utah): F832.S4
San Juan de la Frontera (Argentina):
    F3011.S218
San Juan de Ulúa Island (Mexico):
    F1335
San Juan del Norte (Nicaragua):
    F1536.S2
San Juan Hill, Battle of, 1898: E717.1
San Juan Island (Mexico): F1335
San Juan Islands (Wash.): F897.S2
San Juan Mountains (Colorado):
    F782.S18
San Juan National Monument (Puerto
    Rico): F1981.S2
San Juan (Puerto Rico): F1981.S2
San Juan region (Colorado): F782.S19
San Juan River and Valley (Nicaragua):
    F1529.S35
San Juan Teotihuacán (Mexico)
    Indian antiquities: F1219.1.T27

San Juan Valley (California): F868.S136

San Luis, Argentina (Province): F2966

San Luis Park (Colorado) (Valley): F782.S2

San Luis Potosi (Mexico)
Indian antiquities: F1219.1.S22

San Luis Potosí (Mexico)
City: F1391.S19
State: F1336

San Marcos, Guatemala (Dept.): F1469.S17

San Marcos (Province)
Peru: F3451.S2

San Marcos River and Valley (Texas): F392.S236

San Martín, Colombia (Territory): F2281.M49

San Martín, José de: F2235.4

San Martín, Juan de: F2841

San Martín, Peru (Dept.): F3451.S24

San Martin, Ramon Grau: F1788

San Mateo Mountains (N.M.): F802.V3

San Mateo, Treaty of, 1812: F2323

San Miguel de Tucumán (Argentina): F3011.T89

San Miguel Island (California): F868.S23

San Pablo Villa de Mitla, Mexico (Oaxaca)
Indian antiquities: F1219.1.M6

San Pasqual, Battle of, 1846: E406.S2

San Pasqual Valley (Calif.): F868.S15

San Pedro River and Valley (Arizona): F817.S25

San Pedro River and Valley (Mexico): F1346

San Pedro Sula (Honduras): F1516.S3

San Rafael River and Valley (Utah): F832.S415

San Rafael Swell (Utah): F832.S415

San Ramon Valley (California): F868.S2

San Salvador (Salvador)
City: F1496.S2
Department: F1489.S2

San Simeon Estate (California): F868.S18

San Timoteo Canyon (Calif.): F868.S14

San Vicente Valley (Calif.): F868.S15

Sanavirona Indians: F2520.1.S3

Sánchez, Francisco del Rosario: F1938.4

Sanchez, Gabriel
Columbus letter to: E116

Sanclemente, Manuel Antonio: F2276.5

Sancti Spíritus (Cuba)
City: F1829.S2
Province: F1853+

Sand Creek Massacre, 1864: E83.863

Sand Hills (Nebraska): F672.S17

Sand Island boundary controversy: F882.B7

Sanders, Fort, Attack upon, 1863: E475.94

Sandhills
Georgia: F292.S25
North Carolina: F262.S34
South Carolina: F277.S27

Sandhills (Nebraska): F672.S17

Sandia Indians: E99.S214

Sandia Mountains (N.M.): F802.S28

Sandia, Peru (Province): F3451.S244

Sandino, Augusto César: F1526.3

Sandoz, Jules Ami: F666

Sandpaintings
Indians: E98.S3

Sands, Benjamin Franklin: E182

Sandusky Bay (Ohio): F497.S23

Sandusky River and Valley (Ohio): F497.S23

Sandy Beaver Canal (Ohio): F497.C6

Sangamon River and Valley (Illinois): F547.S33

Sangre de Cristo grant (Colo.): F782.C8

Sangre de Cristo Mountains
Colorado: F782.S26
New Mexico: F802.S32

Sanibel Island (Florida): F317.S37

Sanitary commissions
United States
Civil War: E631+

Sanitary fairs
  United States
    Civil War: E632
Sanitary services, Military
  United States
    Civil War: E621+
    War of 1898: E731
Sanpoil Indians: E99.S215
Sans Arc Indians: E99.S217
Santa Ana Mountains (California): F868.S21
Santa Ana River and Valley (California): F868.S22
Santa Ana (Salvador): F1496.S35
Santa Anna, Antonio López de: F1232
Santa Bárbara de Samaná (Dominican Republic): F1939.S18
Santa Barbara Islands (Calif.): F868.S232
Santa Barbara Valley (California): F868.S23
Santa Catalina Island (Calif.): F868.L8
Santa Catalina Mountains (Arizona): F817.S28
Santa Catarina (Catharina), Brazil (State): F2626
Santa Catarina Island (Brazil): F2626
Santa Clara, California, Battle of, 1847: E406.S25
Santa Clara (Cuba)
  City: F1829.S3
  Province: F1821+
Santa Clara Valley (Calif.): F868.S25
Santa Clarita Valley (Calif.): F868.L8
Santa-Cruz, Andrés: F3324
Santa Cruz, Argentina (Territory): F2971
Santa Cruz (Bolivia)
  City: F3351.S3
  Department: F3341.S2
Santa Cruz del Sur (Cuba): F1839.S23
Santa Cruz Island (California): F868.S23
Santa Cruz Mountains (California): F868.S33
Santa Cruz, Peru (District): F3451.S25

Santa Cruz River and Valley (Arizona): F817.S33
Santa Cruz y Espejo, F.J.E.: F3733
Santa Fé (Argentina)
  City: F3011.S26
  Province: F2976
Santa Fe Expedition, 1841: F390
Santa Fe (N.M.): F804.S2+
Santa Fe Trail: F786
Santa Margarita River and Valley (Calif.): F868.S34
Santa Maria River and Valley (California): F868.S23
Santa Marta Lagoon region (Colombia)
  Indian antiquities: F2269.1.S25
Santa Marta, Sierra Nevada de (Colombia): F2281.M2
Santa Monica Bay region (Calif.): F868.L8
Santa Monica Canyon (Calif.): F868.L8
Santa Monica Mountains National Recreation Area (California): F868.S355
Santa Rosa and San Jacinto Mountains National Monument (California): F868.S36
Santa Rosa Island (California): F868.S23
Santa Rosa Lake and Region (N.M.): F802.G9
Santa Rosa Mountain National Monument (California): F868.S36
Santa Rosino Indians: F3722.1.Q48
Santa Ynez River and Valley (California): F868.S23
Santan Mountains (Az.): F817.P6
Santana, Pedro: F1938.4
Santander, Colombia (Dept.): F2281.S3
Santander, Francisco de Paula: F2273
Santander, Norte de, Colombia (Dept.): F2281.N6
Santangel, Luis de
  Columbus letter to: E115+
Santee Indians: E99.S22
Santee Normal Training School, Santee (Nebraska): E97.6.S2

Santee River and system (S.C.):
F277.S28

Santiago, Battle of, 1898: E717.1, E727

Santiago campaign, 1898: E717.1

Santiago, Chile (Province): F3221

Santiago de Chile (City): F3271
Columbus celebration, 1892: E119

Santiago de Cuba
City: F1849.S3
Province: F1841+

Santiago de Cuba, Society of the Army
of: E714.3.S67+

Santiago del Estero, Argentina
(Province): F2981
Indian antiquities: F2821.1.S23

Santiago-Zamora, Ecuador (Province):
F3741.S3

Santiam National Forest (Oregon):
F882.S2

Santo Domingo (Audiencia): F1621

Santo Domingo (French colony), 1677-
1803: F1923

Santo Domingo Indians: E99.S223

Santo Domingo (National District and
City): F1939.S4+

Santo Domingo (Spanish colony):
F1911
1808-1822: F1938.3
Withdrawal of Spain, 1795: F1923

Santo Tomas, Guatemala (District):
F1469.S2

Santos (Brazil): F2651.S15

Santos, Eduardo: F2277

Santos, Máximo: F2726

São Francisco River and Valley (Brazil):
F2629

São Paulo (Brazil)
City: F2651.S2+
State
Indian antiquities: F2519.1.S2
Revolution, 1932: F2631

Sao Salvador (Brazil): F2651.S13+

Saone Indians: E99.S225

Sapelo Island (Georgia): F292.M15

Saponi Indians: E99.S226

Sapuya Indians: F2520.1.K4

Saramacca (Suriname people):
F2431.S27

Saramaccaner (Suriname people):
F2431.S27

Saramaka (Suriname people):
F2431.S27

Saranac Lakes (New York): F127.F8

Sarandi, Battle of, 1825: F2725

Sarapiqui River (Costa Rica): F1549.H5

Saratoga, Battle of, 1777: E241.S2

Saratoga Campaign, 1777: E241.S2

Saratoga Springs (New York): F129.S3

Saravia, Aparicio: F2726

Sarcantay (Peru): F3451.C9

Sargent, Winthrop: F341

Sarmiento de Gamboa, Pedro:
E125.S23

Sarmiento, Domingo Faustino: F2846

Sarsi Indians: E99.S227

Saruma Indians: F2520.1.S24

Saskatchewan: F1070+
Assiniboia: F1067
Indians: E78.S2

Saskatchewan Rebellion, 1885:
F1060.9

Saskatchewan River and Valley:
F1074.S3

Saskatoon (Sask.): F1074.5.S3

Saugus River (Mass.): F72.E7

Sauk Indians: E99.S23

Sault Ste. Marie (Michigan): F574.S3

Sauquoit Valley (N.Y.): F127.O5

Sauvies Island (Oregon): F882.S3

Savage Station, Battle of, 1862:
E473.68

Savannah (Georgia): F294.S2
Campaign, 1864: E477.41
Siege, 1779: E241.S26

Savannah (Privateer): E599.S2

Savannah River and Valley
Georgia: F292.S3
South Carolina: F277.S3

Savary Island (British Columbia):
F1089.S28

Sawtooth Mountains and Valley (Idaho):
F752.B65

Sawyer, Frederick Adolphus: F274

Sawyer, Lemuel: E302.6.S3
Sayil Site (Mexico)
  Mayas: F1435.1.S29
Scalping by Indians: E98.W2
Scandinavians in Canada: F1035.N6,
  F1035.S3
Scandinavians in South America:
  F2239.N6
Scandinavians in the United States:
  E184.S18, E184.S2
Scary Creek, Battle of, 1861: E472.17
Scaticook Indians: E99.S252
Schaerer, Eduardo: F2688
Schenck, Robert Cumming:
  E467.1.S32
Schenectady (New York)
  Destruction, 1690: E196
Schlatter, Michael: F152
Schley, Winfield Scott: E714.6.S3
  Courtmartial: E727
Schmidel, Ulrich: E125.S3
Schofield, John McAllister: E467.1.S35
Schoharie Creek and Valley (New York):
  F127.S3
Schokleng Indians: F2520.1.S5
Schroon River and Valley (New York):
  F127.S33
Schurz, Carl: E660.S3+, E664.S39
Schuyler, Philip John: E207.S3
Schuylkill, Falls of (Pennsylvania):
  F158.68.F2
Schuylkill River and Valley (Pa.):
  F157.S33
Science
  Indians
    Bolivia: F3320.1.S35
    North America: E98.S43
    Pre-Columbian America: E59.S35
    South America: F2230.1.S33
  Mayas: F1435.3.S32
Scioto Land Company: F483
Scioto River and Valley (Ohio):
  F497.S32
Scocomish Indians: E99.S64
Scots' Colony at Darien: F2281.D2
Scots in Canada: F1035.S4
Scots in Latin America: F1419.S26

Scots in the Caribbean: F2191.S36
Scots in the United States: E184.S3
Scots in Venezuela: F2349.S36
Scots-Irish in the American Revolution:
  E269.S36
Scots-Irish in the United States:
  E184.S4
Scott, Charles
  Expedition, May 1791: E83.79
Scott, Dred: E450
Scott, Hugh Lenox: E181
Scott, Winfield: E403.1.S4
  Campaign in Mexico, 1847: E405.6
Scott's Expedition, 1791: E83.79
Scotty's Castle (Calif.): F868.D2
Scouts, Military
  United States
    Civil War: E608
    Revolution: E279+
· Scranton (Pennsylvania): F159.S4
Sculpture
  Aztecs: F1219.76.S35
  Indians
    Bolivia: F3320.1.S38
    Central America: F1434.2.S38
    Costa Rica: F1545.3.S35
    Mexico: F1219.3.S38
    Nicaragua: F1525.3.S38
    Peru: F3429.3.S39
    Pre-Columbian America: E59.S37
    South America: F2230.1.S37
    West Indies: F1619.3.S38
  Mayas: F1435.3.S34
Sea Islands (S.C.): F277.B3
Sea Islands (South Carolina)
  African Americans: E185.93.S7
Seabrook Island (S.C.): F277.C4
Seaconnet Indians: E99.S16
Search, Right of
  War of 1812: E357.2
Searcy Landing, Ark., Battle of, 1862:
  E473.8
Searles Valley (California): F868.S37
Seattle (Wash.): F899.S4+
Seaway Trail (New York): F127.N38
Sebastian, Benjamin: F455
Sebasticook River and Valley: F27.S42

Sebec Lake (Me.): F27.P5

Secession
  North Carolina: F258
  Southern States: F213
  United States
    Civil War period: E440.5, E458.1
  Virginia: F230

Secessionville (South Carolina)
  Engagement at, 1862: E473.92

Sechelt Indians: E99.S258

Seconet Indians: E99.S16

Secoya Indians: F3722.1.S43

Secret service
  War with Mexico: E415.2.S43

Secret service, Military
  United States
    Civil War: E608
    Revolution: E279+
    War of 1812: E360.5+

Sectionalism
  North Carolina: F258
  Southern States: F213
  United States
    Civil War period: E440.5, E458.1,
      E468+
  Virginia: F230

Sedgwick, John: E467.1.S4

Sedition laws, 1798: E327

Seiad Creek and Valley: F868.S6

Seibal, Guatemala (Mayas):
  F1435.1.S44

Seigneuries
  New France: F1030
  Quebec: F1054.M35

Sekani Indians: E99.S26

Sekoya Indians: F3722.1.S43

Self-destruction
  North American Indians: E98.S9

Selkirk Range (B.C.): F1089.S4

Selkirk, Thomas Douglas, 5th earl of:
  F1063

Selma (Alabama)
  Wilson's raid, 1865: E477.96

Seminole Indians: E99.S28

Seminole War, 1st, 1817-1818:
  E83.817

Seminole War, 2d, 1835-1842: E83.835

Seminole War, 3d, 1855-1858: E83.855

Semitic influences
  Indians
    South America: F2230.1.S44

Semmes, Raphael: E467.1.S47

Senci Indians: F3430.1.S35

Seneca Indians: E99.S3

Seneca Lake (New York): F127.S43

Senegalese in the United States:
  E184.S48

Senijextee Indians: E99.S546

Sequatchie River and Valley
  (Tennessee): F443.S36

Sequoia National Forest: F868.S4

Sequoia National Park: F868.S4

Serbs in Canada: F1035.S47

Serbs in the United States: E184.S5

Serente Indians: F2520.1.S47

Sergief Island (Alaska): F912.S27

Sergipe, Brazil (State): F2636

Seri Indians: F1221.S43

Sermons, Wartime
  United States
    Civil War: E649+
    Revolution: E297
    War of 1812: E364.5
    War with Mexico: E415

Serra, Junípero (Miguel José): F864

Serrano Indians: E99.S31

Serrato, José: F2728

Service Men of the Spanish War (1899-
  1904): E714.3.S48+

Services for Indians
  Brazil: F2519.3.S46
  North America: E98.S46

Setá Indians: F2520.1.H48

Sete Quedas (Guayra Falls): F2596

Setibo Indians: F3430.1.S4

Seven cities of Cibola: F799

Seven Days' Battles, 1862: E473.68

Seven Pines, Battle of, 1862: E473.65

Seven Ranges
  Old Northwest: F483

Seven Reductions, War of the, 1754-
  1756: F2684

Seven Years' War, 1756-1763
  West Indies: F1621

Severn River and Valley (Maryland): F187.A6

Severn River and Valley (Ontario): F1059.S49

Severn-Trent Waterway (Ontario): F1059.T7

Sevier, John: E302.6.S45

Sewall, Samuel: F67

Seward Highway (Alaska): F912.S29

Seward, Mount (New York): F127.F8

Seward Peninsula (Alaska): F912.S3

Seward, William Henry: E415.9.S4
  Collected works: E415.6.S51+

Sewee Indians: E99.S32

Sexual behavior
  Indians
    Mexico: F1219.3.S45
    North America: E98.S48
    Peru: F3429.3.S45
    Pre-Columbian America: E59.S45

Seymour, Horatio: E415.9.S5

Shahaptian Indians: E99.S325

Shakamak State Park (Indiana): F532.S47

Shakers in the United States: E184.S53

Shamanism: E98.R3

Shapra Indians: F3430.1.S47

Sharanahua Indians: F3430.1.S48

Shark River (N.J.): F142.M7

Sharpshooters
  United States
    Civil War: E492.7

Shasta Indians: E99.S33

Shasta, Mount (California): F868.S6

Shasta Mountains (California): F868.S495

Shastan Indians: E99.S332

Shaver Lake (California): F868.F8

Shawangunk Mountains (N.Y.): F127.U4

Shawnee Indians: E99.S35

Shay's Rebellion, 1786-1787: F69

Sheepscot River and Valley (Me.): F27.W16

Sheffield Island (Conn.): F102.F2

Sheffort County (Québec): F1054.S48

Shelburne Co. (Nova Scotia): F1039.S5

Shelby, Isaac: F455

Shelby's raid in Arkansas and Missouri, 1863: E474.98

Shell beads
  Indians
    South America: F2230.1.S54

Shell engraving
  Indians
    Pre-Columbian America: E59.S54
    South America: F2230.1.S54

Shell jewelry
  Indians
    South America: F2230.1.S54

Shelter Cove (California): F868.H8

Shelter Island (New York): F127.S54

Shelton Laurel Creek and Valley (N.C.): F262.M25

Shenandoah (Cruiser): E599.S5

Shenandoah National Park: F232.S48

Shenandoah River and Valley
  Virginia: F232.S5
  West Virginia: F247.S5

Shenandoah Valley
  Civil War
    Military operations: E470.3
      1861: E472.16
      1862: E473.74
      1864: E476.66, E477.33
      1865: E477.65

Shenandoah Valley (Calif.): F868.A4

Shenango River and Valley (Pa.): F157.S47

Shepherd, Alexander Robey: F198

Sherbrooke (Québec): F1054.5.S55

Sherente Indians: F2520.1.S47

Sheridan, Philip Henry: E467.1.S54

Sherman, Ellen (Ewing): E467.1.S552

Sherman, John: E664.S57

Sherman, Roger: E302.6.S5

Sherman, William Tecumseh: E467.1.S55
  March to the sea (May 1864-April 1865): E476.69

Sherman's March through the Carolinas, 1865: E477.7

Sheta Indians: F2520.1.H48

Sheyenne River and Valley (North Dakota): F642.S53
Shields, James: E403.1.S5
Shiloh, Battle of, 1862: E473.54
Shiloh National Military Park: E473.54
Shinnecock Indians: E99.S38
Ship Island (Mississippi): F347.H3
Shipibo-Conibo Indians: F3430.1.S5
Shirianan Indians: F2520.1.Y3
Shirley, William: E195+
Shoals, Isles of: F42.I8
Shokleng Indians: F2520.1.S5
Short Hills, New Jersey, Battle of, 1777: E241.S53
Short Hills Provincial Park (Ontario): F1059.S58
Shoshone National Forest: F767.S57
Shoshone River and Valley (Wyoming): F767.S58
Shoshonean Indians: E99.S39
Shoshoni Indians: E99.S4
Shoshoni War, 1863-1865: E83.863
Shreveport, La. Centenary College of Louisiana and the Civil War: E586.S5
Shreveport (Louisiana): F379.S4
Shuar Indians: F3722.1.J5
Shubenacadie River and Valley (Nova Scotia): F1039.S55
Shuswap Indians: E99.S45
Shuswap Lake (British Columbia): F1089.S46
Shuyak Island State Park (Alaska): F912.S38
Sia Indians: E99.Z52
Sibley, Henry Hastings: F606
Sibundoy Valley (Colombia): F2281.P9
Sicán culture (Peru): F3429.1.L35
Sickles, Daniel Edgar: E415.9.S53
Sicuane Indians: F2319.2.S52
Side Lake (Minnesota): F612.S25
Sidney Lanier, Lake (Georgia): F292.S53
Sierra de la Espuma: F817.S9
Sierra de Perijá (Colombia): F2281.P4
Sierra Gorda: F1339
Sierra Leoneans in the United States: E184.S54

Sierra Madre (Mexico): F1340
Sierra Nevada de Mérida: F2331.M52
Sierra Nevada de Santa Marta (Colombia): F2281.M2
Sierra Nevada Mountains (Calif.): F868.S5
Sierra Norte de Puebla: F1326
Sierra Populuca Indians: F1221.P62
Sierras, The (Calif.): F868.S5
Sieur de Monte National Monument (Me.): F27.M9
Sifton, Sir Clifford: F1033
Sigel, Franz: E467.1.S58
Sign language, Indian: E98.S5
Signal Corps United States Civil War: E608
Signers of the Declaration of Independence: E221
Sihasapa Indians: E99.S53
Sikhs in Canada: F1035.S54
Sikhs in the United States: E184.S55
Siksika Indians: E99.S54
Siletz Indians: E99.S544
Silva, José Bonifacio de Andrada e: F2536
Silva Paranhos, José Maria da: F2537
Silva Xavier, Joaquim José da: F2534
Silversmithing Indians: E98.S55
Silverwork Indians Argentina: F2821.3.S54 Peru: F3429.3.S54
Simcoe Co. (Ontario): F1059.S6
Simcoe, John Graves: F1058
Simcoe, Lake (Ontario): F1059.S59
Similkameen River and Valley British Columbia: F1089.S48 Washington: F897.S48
Simpson, Sir George: F1060.8
Simpson, Thomas: F1060.8
Sin Aikst Indians: E99.S546
Sinagua culture: E99.S547
Sinaloa, Mexico (State): F1341
Sincayuse Indians: E99.S55
Sinissippi Valley (Wisconsin): F587.R63
Sinkiuse-Columbia Indians: E99.S55

Sinkyone Indians: E99.S56
Sinnamahoning Creek (Pa.): F157.S49
Sinos River and Valley (Brazil): F2638
Sint Eustatius (West Indies): F2097
Sinú River (Colombia): F2281.B6
Siouan Indians: E99.S6
Sioux City (Iowa): F629.S6
Sioux (Dakota) Indians: E99.D1
Sioux Falls (S. D.): F659.S6
Sioux wars: E83.854
   1862-1865: E83.86
   1876: E83.876
Sipibo Indians: F3430.1.S5
Siriono Indians: F3320.2.S5
Sisal hemp
   Mayas: F1435.3.S5
Siskiyou Mountains (Oregon):
   F882.S56
Sisseton, Fort (S.D.): F657.R6
Sisseton Indians: E99.S62
Sisseton State Park (S.D.): F657.R6
Sitka (Alaska): F914.S6
Sitting Bull (Dakota chief): E99.D1
   Death: E83.89
Siuslaw Indians: E99.S622
Siuslaw National Forest: F882.S58
Siwanoy Indians: E99.S623
Sixteenth Street (Washington, D.C.):
   F203.7.S6
Skagit Indians: E99.S627
Skagit River and Valley (Wash.):
   F897.S52
Skagway (Alaska): F914.S7
Skakamish Indians: E99.S64
Skakobish Indians: E99.S64
Skaquamish Indians: E99.S64
Skasquamish Indians: E99.S64
Skeena River and Valley (British
   Columbia): F1089.S5
Skiquamish Indians: E99.S64
Skitswish Indians: E99.S63
Skokamish Indians: E99.S64
Skokobc Indians: E99.S64
Skokomish Indians: E99.S64
Skokomish River and Valley (Wash.):
   F897.S54
S'Komish Indians: E99.S64

Skoskomish Indians: E99.S64
Slave auctions
   United States: E442
Slave insurrections
   British Guiana, 1823: F2384
   Haiti, 1791-1804: F1923
   Jamaica
      Maroon War, 1795-1796: F1884
   Jamaica, 1831, 1865: F1886
   United States: E447, E450
      Charleston (S.C.), 1822: F279.C4+
      New York Negro plot, 1741: F128.4
      Richmond Insurrection, 1800:
         F234.R5+
      Southampton Insurrection, 1831:
         F232.S7
Slave masters
   United States: E443
Slave overseers
   United States: E443
Slave trade
   Jamaica (Trade abolished, 1807):
      F1884
   United States: E442
      Attempts to revive: E438, E446
      Mutiny on slave ships: E447
Slavery
   Aztecs: F1219.76.S53
   Confederate States of America: E453
   Indians: E98.S6
      Mexico: F1219.3.S5
      Pre-Columbian America: E59.S63
   United States: E441+
      Abolition: E453
      Abolition agitation, 1830-1863:
         E449
      Antislavery movements: E441+
         Kansas: F685
      Civil War: E453
      Compromise attempts: E440.5
      Economic aspects: E441+
      Extension to Kansas: F685
      Extension to the territories
         1845-1861: E415.7
         1845-1949: E416+
         1849-1853: E423
         1856-1861: E438

Slavery
  United States
    Free state slaves: E450
    Fugitive slaves: E450
    History: E441
      1830-1863: E449+
      To 1830: E446+
    Justification: E449
    Lincoln's attitude: E457.2
    Moral aspects: E441+
    Personal liberty laws: E450
    Political aspects
      1801-1845: E338
      1830-1863: E449
      1845-1849: E416+
      1845-1861: E415.7
      1849-1853: E423
      1853-1857: E433
      1857-1861: E438, E440.5
      Civil War: E453, E458+
Slaves
  Pensions: E185.2
  United States
    Biography: E444
    Colonization: E448
    Emancipation: E453
    Free state slaves: E450
    Fugitive slaves: E450
    Kidnapping: E450
    Legal status in free states: E450
    Life, duties, etc: E443
    Markets and auctions: E442
    Personal liberty laws: E450
    Personal narratives: E444
Slavey Indians: E99.S65
Slavs in Canada: F1035.S6
Slavs in Latin America: F1419.S5
Slavs in the United States: E184.S6
Sleeping Bear Dunes National
  Lakeshore (Michigan): F572.S8
Slidell, John: E415.9.S58
Sloat, John Drake: E403.1.S6
Slocum, Henry Warner: E467.1.S63
Slovaks in Argentina: F3021.S6
Slovaks in Canada: F1035.S63
Slovaks in the United States: E184.S64
Slovenes in Argentina: F3021.S62

Slovenes in Brazil: F2659.S45
Slovenes in Canada: F1035.S64
Slovenes in the United States:
  E184.S65
Smith, Alfred Emanuel: E748.S63
Smith, Benjamin: F258
Smith, Gerrit: E415.9.S64
Smith, Henry: F390
Smith Island (Md.): F187.C5
Smith Island (N.C.): F262.B9
Smith, Jedediah Strong: F592
Smith, Jeremiah: E302.6.S57
Smith, John: F7, F229
Smith River National Recareation
  (Calif.): F868.D4
Smith, William Farrar: E467.1.S75
Smith, William Stephens: E302.6.S59
Smith's Island (Conn.): F102.F2
Smokies, The (Tennessee): F443.G7
Smoking
  Indians: E98.T6
Smoky Hill River and Valley
  Colorado: F782.S53
  Kansas: F687.S84
Smoky Mountains (Tennessee):
  F443.G7
Smoot, Reed: E664.S68
Smyth, Alexander
  Niagara campaign, 1812: E355.2
Smyth, John Ferdinand Dalziel:
  E278.S6
Snake River and Valley
  Idaho: F752.S7
  Oregon: F882.S6
  Washington: F897.S6
Snake (Shoshoni) Indians: E99.S4
Snake War, 1864-1868: E83.864
Snoqualmie Indians: E99.S66
Snoqualmie Pass (Wash.): F897.K53
Snoqualmie River and Valley (Wash.):
  F897.S67
Snow Falls
  Maine: F27.A5
Snow's Pond, Ky., Battle of, 1862:
  E474.3
Snows, The, Islands (Michigan):
  F572.L57

Snowy Cross Mountain (Colorado):
  F782.H6
Snyder, Adam Wilson: F545
Sobremonte, Rafael de, marqués de
  Sobremonte: F2841
Social conditions
  Aztecs: F1219.76.S63
  Indians: E98.S67
    Bolivia: F3320.1.S62
    Brazil: F2519.3.S58
    Central America: F1434.2.S62
    Colombia: F2270.1.S63
    Ecuador: F3721.3.S65
    El Salvador: F1485.3.S6
    Guatemala: F1465.3.S6
    Mexico: F1219.3.S57
    Nicaragua: F1525.3.S63
    Paraguay: F2679.3.S65
    Peru: F3429.3.S59
    Pre-Columbian America: E59.S64
    South America: F2230.1.S68
    Venezuela: F2319.3.S6
  Jews: E184.36.S65
  Mayas: F1435.3.S68
Social life and customs
  America: E20
  Aztecs: F1219.76.S64
  Bahamas: F1654
  Belize: F1443.8
  Bermudas: F1633
  Canada: F1021+
  Central America: F1430
  Costa Rica: F1543.8
  Cuba: F1760
  El Salvador: F1483.8
  Guatemala: F1463.5
  Honduras: F1503.8
  Indians
    Brazil: F2519.3.S6
    Central America: F1434.2.S63
    Colombia: F2270.1.S64
    Ecuador: F3721.3.S7
    Guatemala: F1465.3.S62
    Guyana: F2380.2.S63
    Honduras: F1505.3.S63
    Mexico: F1219.3.S6
    North America: E98.S7

Social life and customs
  Indians
    Peru: F3429.3.S6
    Pre-Columbian America: E59.S65
    South America: F2230.1.S7
    Venezuela: F2319.3.S62
  Jews: E184.36.S65
  Mayas: F1435.3.S7
  Mexico: F1210
  Nicaragua: F1523.8
  Panama: F1563.8
  United States: E161.5+
  West Indies: F1609.5
Societies
  Indians: E98.S75
    Mexico: F1219.3.S64
Society for Correct Civil War
  Information: E462.99.S6
Society of American Wars of the United
  States: E181
Society of Colonial Wars: E186.3
Society of Mayflower Descendants: F68
Society of the Army and Navy of the
  Confederate States, Maryland:
  E483.25
Society of the Army and Navy of the
  Gulf: E462.99.S62
Society of the Army of Santiago de
  Cuba: E714.3.S67+
Society of the Cincinnati: E202.1
  Washington's letters: E312.75.S6+
Society of the Second War with Great
  Britain in the State of New York:
  E351.32
Society of the War of 1812: E351.3
Sokoki Indians: E99.S665
Sol, Isla del (Bolivia): F3341.T6
Solano López, Francisco: F2686
Soldiers
  Almanacs
    U.S. Civil War: E468.8
  Indians: E98.M5
  Lincoln's relations with: E457.2
Soldiers' and Sailors' National Union
  League of Washington, D.C.: E462.92
Sololá (Guatemala): F1469.S64

Solomon River and Valley (Kansas): F687.S85

Solomon's Fork, Battle of, 1857: E83.8575

Solomons Island (Maryland): F187.C15

Somalis in Canada: F1035.S65

Somalis in the United States: E184.S67

Somers Islands: F1630+

Somers, Richard: E335

Somoza, Anatasio: F1527

Songhees Indians: E99.L35

Sonoma, Lake (California): F868.S7

Sonora, Mexico (State): F1346
  Pimería Alta: F799
  Walker expedition: F1232.5

Sonoran Desert National Monument (Arizona): F817.S65

Sons and Daughters of the Pilgrims: E186.99.S5

Sons of Confederate Veterans: E483.4

Sons of Liberty
  United States
    Revolution: E216
  U.S. Civil War: E458.8

Sons of the American Revolution: E202.3

Sons of Union Veterans of the Civil War: E462.9

Sons of Veterans of the United States of America: E462.9

Sorbians in the United States: E184.S68

Sorbs in the United States: E184.S68

Soriano, Uruguay (Dept.): F2731.S6

Soto, Bernardo: F1547.5

Soto, Hernando de: E125.S7
  In Mississippi Valley: F352

Soto, Marco Aurelio: F1507.5

Soulé, Pierre: E415.9.S72

Soulouque, Faustino: F1926

Souris River and Valley
  Manitoba: F1064.S6
  North Dakota: F642.S68
  Saskatchewan: F1074.S67

South America: F2201+
  Indians: F2229+

South Asians in Canada: F1035.S66

South Asians in the United States: E184.S69

South Atlantic coast
  United States
    Civil War military operations: E470.65

South Atlantic region: F3030

South Atlantic States: F206+

South Bend (Indiana): F534.S7

South Bend Reservoir (Texas): F392.B842

South Boston (Massachusetts): F73.68.S7

South Carolina: F266+
  African Americans: E185.93.S7
  Carolana grant of 1629: F272
  Counties, etc: F277.A+
  Georgia settlement: F289
  Huguenot colony at Port Royal, 1562: F314
  Indians: E78.S6
  Northern Carolina settlements: F257
  Nullification: E384.3
  Reconstruction: F274
  Slavery: E445.S7
  St. Augustine expedition, 1740: F314
  Wars
    Civil War
      Military operations: E470.6, E470.65
      Port Royal mission: E185.93.S7
    Indian wars: E83.759
    Queen Anne's War, 1702-1713: E197
    Revolution: E236, E237, E241.A+, E263.S7
    War with Mexico: E409.5.S7
  Western lands ceded, 1787: F292.B7

South Carolina University and the Civil War: E586.S7

South Central States: F296

South Dakota: F646+
  African Americans: E185.93.S8
  Counties, etc: F657.A+
  Dakota Indian War, 1890-1891: E83.89
  Indians: E78.S63

South George and South Sandwich
   Islands: F3032+
South Georgia: F291.8
South Georgia (Island): F3031, F3032.5
South Manitou Island (Michigan):
   F572.S86
South Mills, N.C., Battle of, 1862:
   E473.3
South Mountain, Md., Battle of, 1862:
   E474.61
South Nahanni River and Valley
   (Mackenzie District): F1100.S6
South Nation River and Valley (Ontario):
   F1059.S63
South Orange (N.J.): F144.O6
South Orkney Island: F3031+
South Park (Chicago): F548.65.S7
South Park region (Colorado): F782.S6
South Platte River and Valley: F672.S7
   Colorado: F782.S7
South Sandwich Islands: F3032+
South Shetland Islands: F3031+
South Shore (Chicago): F548.68.S7
South Shore (Mass.): F72.P7
Southampton Insurrection, 1831:
   F232.S7
Southampton Island: F1110.S6
Southeast Asians in the United States:
   E184.S695
Southeast Mexico: F1348
Southeast Washington (District of
   Columbia): F202.S6
Southern Appalachian Mountains:
   F217.A65
Southern California: F867
Southern Convention, Nashville, 1850:
   E423
Southern federals
   Union Army: E491+
Southern Historical Society: E483.7
Southern relief agencies
   U.S. Civil War: E634
Southern States: F206+
   Indians: E78.S65
   Mason and Dixon's line: F157.B7
   Reconstruction, 1861-1877: E216

Southern States
   Wars
      Civil War: E461+
      Revolution: E231+
      War of 1812: E355.1.A+
Southold (New York): F129.S74
Southwark (Philadelphia): F158.68.S6
Southwest, New: F785.15+
   Government of newly acquired
      Spanish possessions, 1845-1849:
      E416
Southwest, Old: F396
Southwest Washington (District of
   Columbia): F202.S7
Southwestern States: F785.15+
Souza, Irineo Evangelista de Souza:
   F2536
Soviet espionage in the United States:
   E743.5
Spaight, Richard Dobbs: E302.6.S7
Spain
   Attempted invasion of Jamaica, 1694:
      F1884
   Cession of
      Florida: F314
   Military history
      War with Ecuador, 1865-1866:
         F3447
      War with Peru, 1865-1866: F3447
   Relations with United States, 1789-
      1797: E313+
   Treaty with the United States
      1819: F314
Spalding, Thomas: F290
Spaniards
   Discovery of America: E109.S7
      Columbus: E111+
      Post-Columbian: E123+
Spaniards in America: E29.S65
Spaniards in Argentina: F3021.S7
Spaniards in Brazil: F2659.S63
Spaniards in Canada: F1035.S68
Spaniards in Central America:
   F1440.S7
Spaniards in Chile: F3285.S7
Spaniards in Costa Rica: F1557.S7
Spaniards in Cuba: F1789.S7

Spaniards in Latin America: F1419.S63
Spaniards in Mexico: F1392.S7
Spaniards in Puerto Rico: F1983.S64
Spaniards in the American Revolution: E269.S63
Spaniards in the Dominican Republic: F1941.S7
Spaniards in the United States: E184.S7
Spaniards in Uruguay: F2799.S6
Spaniards in Venezuela: F2349.S7
Spanish-American War, 1898: E714+
Spanish Americans in Brazil: F2659.S65
Spanish Americans in the United States: E184.S75
Spanish California: F864
Spanish colonies
  California: F864
  Florida: F314
  Louisiana: F372
  New Mexico: F799
  Southwest: F799
Spanish explorers
  America: E109.S7, E123+
  California: F851.5, F864
  Southwest: F799
Spanish Florida claims: F314
Spanish Main: F2155+
Spanish mission buildings (U.S.): F862
Spanish Peaks (Colorado): F782.S76
Spanish silver-fleet (Capture, 1628): F1779
Spanish Town (Jamaica): F1895.S7
Spanish War Veterans (1899-1904): E714.3.A12
Spanish West Florida: F301
Spanish West Indies
  History
    1810-1898: F1783
    1898-: F1623
    To 1898: F1621
Sparrow-hawk (Ship)
  Wreck, 1826: F72.C3
Sparrow Lake (Ontario)
  Muskoka District and Simcoe County: F1059.S65

Sparta Mine (Ark.): F417.C3
Spartanburg (S.C.): F279.S7
Speaker of the House, Election of, 1856: E434.5
Speed, James: E415.9.S74
Spencer Butte (Oregon): F882.C3
Spencer's Butte (Oregon): F882.C3
Spies in the United States: E743.5
  Wars
    Civil War: E608
    Revolution: E279+
    War of 1812: E360.5+
Spirit Lake (Iowa): F627.D5
Spirit Lake Massacre, 1857: E83.857
Split Rock Creek and Valley
  Minnesota: F612.S64
  South Dakota: F657.S73
Spokan Indians: E99.S68
Spokane Expedition, 1858: E83.84
Spokane River and Valley (Wash.): F897.S7
Spokane (Washington): F899.S7
Spoon River and Valley (Illinois): F547.S65
Sports
  Indians
    North America: E98.G2
    Pre-Columbian America: E59.G3
Spotswood, Alexander: F229
Spotsylvania, Va., Battle of, 1864: E476.52
Spring Hill (Tennessee), Battle of, 1864: E477.52
Spring Mill State Park (Indiana): F532.L4
Springfield
  Illinois: F549.S7
  Massachusetts: F74.S8
  Missouri: F474.S7
  New Jersey
    Battle of, 1780: E241.S6
  Ohio: F499.S7
Squatter sovereignty: E415.7
Squaw Peak (Arizona): F817.M3
Squaw Valley (Calif.): F868.S5
Squawmish Indians: E99.S7

Staff
  United States Presidents: E176.47
Staked Plain (Texas): F392.L62
Stalo Indians: E99.S72
Stamford (Conn.): F104.S8
Stamp Act, 1765: E215.2
Stamp Act Congress, Oct. 1765:
  E215.2
Standish, Miles: F68
Stanford, Leland: E664.S78
Stanstead County (Québec): F1054.S7
Stanton, Edwin McMasters: E467.1.S8
Stanwix, Fort, N.Y. Siege, 1777:
  E241.S7
Star Island (Minnesota): F612.B43
Stark, John: E207.S79
Starved Rock State Park (Illinois):
  F547.L3
State House (Boston): F73.8.S8
State militia
  United States
    Revolution: E263.A+
    War of 1812: E359.5.A+
    War of 1898: E726.A+
    War with Mexico: E409.5.A+
State, Prisoners of
  United States
    Civil War: E458.8
State Street (Boston): F73.67.S7
Staten Island (N.Y.): F127.S7
Statesmen
  United States
    Biography
      19th century: E339+, E415.8+
      Revolutionary period: E302.5+
Statistics
  Indians
    Mexico: F1219.3.S7
    Pre-Columbian America: E59.S7
Statue of Liberty (New York):
  F128.64.L6
Ste. Anne, Lac (Alberta): F1079.S25
Stedman, Fort, Battle of, 1865: E477.61
Steedman, Charles: E182
Steedman, James Barrett: E467.1.S84
Steele, Robert Wilbur: F781

Stein River and Valley (British
  Columbia): F1089.S77
Stephens, Alexander Hamilton:
  E467.1.S85
Stephens, Linton: F290
Stephenson, Fort, Ohio, Defense of,
  1813: E356.S7
Sterling (Mass.): F74.S84
Steuben, Friedrich Wilhelm, Baron von:
  E207.S8
Steunenberg, Frank: F746
Stevens, Fort, Battle of, 1864: E476.66
Stevens, Isaac Ingalls: F880
Stevens Pass (Wash.): F897.C3
Stevens, Thaddeus: E415.9.S84
Stevenson, Adlai Ewing: F546
Stevenson, Andrew: E340.S75
Stewart, Charles: E353.1.S8
Stewart, William Morris: F841
Stikine River and Valley
  Alaska: F912.S85
  British Columbia: F1089.S85
Stillaguamish River and Valley
  (Washington): F897.S93
Stillaquamish Indians: E99.S75
Stillwater, Battle of, 1777: E241.S2
Stimson, Frederic Jesup: E748.S88
Stirling, William Alexander, called Lord:
  E207.A3
Stirling, William Alexander, Earl of:
  F1038
Stockbridge Indians: E99.S8
Stockton, Richard: E302.6.S85
Stockton, Robert Field: E403.1.S8
  California campaign
    Mexican War: E405.2
Stone, Charles Pomeroy: E467.1.S87
Stone Mountain Memorial (Georgia):
  F292.S85
Stoneham (Mass.): F74.S88
Stoneman, George
  Raid, 1863: E475.38
  Raid, 1865: E477.9
Stone's River campaign, 1862-1863:
  E474.77
Stones River National Military Park:
  E474.77

Stonington (Connecticut)
  Bombardment, 1814: E356.S8
Stony Point, Battle of, 1779: E241.S8
Stormont, Dundas and Glengarry
  (Ontario): F1059.S89
Stow (Mass.): F74.S89
Straight River and Valley (Steele and
  Rice Counties): F612.S86
Strait of Magellan: F3191
Stratford Hall (Virginia): F234.S865
Strathcona (Alberta): F1079.S7
Strathcona and Mount Royal, Donald
  Alexander Smith, 1st baron: F1033
Stratton Island (Me.): F27.Y6
Straus, Oscar Solomon: E664.S896
Strawberry Mansion (Philadelphia):
  F158.8.S8
Street cries
  New York City: F128.37
Streets
  Boston: F73.67
  Chicago: F548.67
  New York: F128.67.A+
  Philadelphia: F158.67.A+
  Washington, D.C.: F203.7.A+
Streight, A. D.
  Raid toward Rome, Ga., 1863:
    E475.1
String figures
  Indians
    Guyana: F2380.2.S7
String Lake (Wyoming): F767.T3
Strong, Caleb: F69
Stuart, Alexander Hugh Holmes:
  E415.9.S88
Stuart, Granville: F731
Stuart, James Ewell Brown: E467.1.S9
  Expedition into Maryland and
    Pennsylvania, Oct. 1862: E474.67
  Raid, June 1862: E473.66
Stuart Lake and region (British
  Columbia): F1089.S88
Stuartburn (Manitoba): F1064.S79
Study and teaching
  Canadian history: F1025
  Indians
    Argentina: F2819

Study and teaching
  Maine history: F18.5
  United States history: E175.8
Sturbridge (Mass.): F74.S93
Stuyvesant, Peter: F122.1
Stuyvesant Village (New York):
  F128.68.S9
Subtiaba Indians: F1525.2.S7
Suburbs
  Boston: F73.68.A+
  Chicago: F548.68
  New York: F128.68.A+
  Philadelphia: F158.68.A+
Subversive activities
  United States: E743.5
Sucre, Antonio Jose de: F2235.5.S9
Sucre, Bolivia (City): F3351.S94
Sucre Department (Colombia):
  F2281.S82
Sucre, Venezuela (State): F2331.S8
  Indian antiquities: F2319.1.S8
Sucumbíos, Ecuador: F3741.S93
Sud Chichas (Bolivia): F3341.S9
Sudanese in the United States:
  E184.S77
Sudbury River and Valley
  (Massachusetts): F72.S86
Suffolk (Va.)
  Siege, 1862: E474.5
Suffrage
  Indians: E91+
Sugar Creek and Valley, Macoupin
  County and Sangamon County
  (Illinois): F547.S94
Sugar Loaf Mountain (Maryland):
  F187.F8
Sugarlands (Tenn.): F443.S45
Sugarloaf Provincial Park (New
  Brunswick): F1044.S9
Sugliak: F1110.S6
Suicidal behavior
  Indians
    Brazil: F2519.3.S94
Suicide
  North American Indians: E98.S9
Sulgrave Manor House: E312.195
Sullana, Peru: F3611.S84

Sullivan, John: E207.S9
  Indian campaign: E235
Sullivan's Island, Battle of, 1776:
  E241.M9
Sullivans Island (S.C.): F277.S77
Sulphur Springs Valley (Arizona):
  F817.C5
Sumapaz Region (Colombia):
  F2281.S86
Sumidero (Mexico)
  Mayas: F1435.1.S92
Summerside (Prince Edward Island):
  F1049.5.S8
Summit Springs, Battle of, 1869:
  E83.8695
Sumner, Charles: E415.9.S9
  Brooks' assault on: E434.8
  Collected works: E415.6.S93+
  Controversy with President Grant:
    E671
Sumo Indians: F1525.2.S8
Sumter (Cruiser): E599.S8
Sumter, Fort
  Bombardment, 1861: E471.1
  Bombardment, 1863: E475.65
Sumter, Thomas: E207.S95
Sun, Island of the (Bolivia): F3341.T6
Sun River and Valley (Mont.): F737.S84
Sunapee Lake (New Hampshire):
  F42.S9
Sunset Crater Volcano National
  Monument (Arizona): F817.C6
Sunshine Coast (British Columbia):
  F1089.S94
Superior, Lake, region: F552
  Indian antiquities: E78.S87
  Michigan: F572.S9
  Minnesota: F612.S9
  Ontario: F1059.S9
  Wisconsin: F587.S9
Superior National Forest: F612.S95
Superior Roadless Primitive Area
  (Minnesota): F612.B73
Superior (Wisconsin): F589.S95
Superstition Mountains (Arizona):
  F817.S9

Supreme Court Building (Washington,
  D.C.): F204.S9
Suquamish Indians: E99.S85
Sur de Occidente, Venezuela (State):
  F2331.B3
Surette's Island (Nova Scotia):
  F1039.Y3
Surface Creek and Valley (Colo.):
  F782.D4
Surgery
  Indians
    Mexico: F1219.3.M5
Suriname: F2401+
Suriname (Dutch colony): F2423
Surini Indians: F2520.1.A84
Surprise Valley (California): F868.M6
Surratt, J.H.: E457.5
Surratt, Mary E. (Jenkins): E457.5
Surui Indians: F2520.1.S86
Susitna River and Valley (Alaska):
  F912.S95
Susquehanna claims: F157.W9
Susquehanna Company: F157.W9
Susquehanna Indians: E99.S95
Susquehanna River and Valley
  Maryland: F187.S8
  New York: F127.S96
  Pennsylvania: F157.S8
Susquehanna Valley
  Indian antiquities: E78.S9
Sutter Buttes (Calif.): F868.S88
Sutter, John Augustus: F865
Suwannee River and Valley (Florida):
  F317.S8
Suya Indians: F2520.1.S89
Sverdrup Islands: F1105.S8
Swabians in Canada: F1035.S88
Swabians in the United States:
  E184.S78
Swan Islands (Honduras): F1509.B3
Swan River and Valley
  Manitoba: F1064.S9
  Saskatchewan: F1074.S9
Swan River and Valley (Mont.):
  F737.S88
Swans Island (Me.): F27.H3

Sweatbaths
  Indians: E98.S94
Sweden, New: F167
Swedes in America: E29.S83
Swedes in Argentina: F3021.S86
Swedes in Brazil: F2659.S84
Swedes in Brazil (Espírito Santo):
  F2561
Swedes in Canada: F1035.S9
Swedes in South America: F2239.S8
Swedes in the United States: E184.S23
  Civil War: E540.S8
  Revolution: E269.S8
Swedish settlements on the Delaware:
  F167
Sweet Grass Hills (Mont.): F737.T6
Sweetwater River and Valley
  (Wyoming): F767.S92
Sweetwater Valley (Tennessee):
  F443.S97
Swift River Valley (Mass.): F72.S94
Swiss in Argentina: F3021.S88
Swiss in Brazil: F2659.S85
Swiss in Canada: F1035.S94
Swiss in Chile: F3285.S9
Swiss in South America: F2239.S9
Swiss in the United States: E184.S9
Sydenham, C. E. P. Thomson, Baron:
  F1032
Sydney (Nova Scotia): F1039.5.S9
Sylvan Beach (Idaho): F752.V3
Sylvia Lake (N.Y.): F127.S2
Symmes, John Cleves: E302.6.S98
  Symmes Purchase: F483
Syrians in Argentina: F3021.S95
Syrians in Chile: F3285.S95
Syrians in South America: F2239.S95
Syrians in the United States: E184.S98

T

Tabasco, Mexico (State): F1351
  Indian antiquities: F1219.1.T13
Tabeguache Indians: E99.T114
Taboga, Isla (Panama): F1569.P3
Tacana Indians: F3320.2.T3
Táchira, Venezuela (State): F2331.T2

Tacna Arica question: F3097.3
Tacna, Chile (Dept., 1883-1929): F3231
Tacna, Peru (Dept.): F3231
Tacoma, Mount (Wash.): F897.R2
Tacoma (Washington): F899.T2
Taconic Mountains (N.Y.): F127.R3
Tacuarembó, Uruguay (Dept.):
  F2731.T3
Taensa Indians: E99.T115
Taft, Alphonso: E415.9.T12
Taft, Helen (Herron): E762.1
Taft, Robert Alphonso: E748.T2
Taft, William Howard: E660.T11+,
  E762+
  Administration, 1909-1913: E761+
  Family: E762.1
Tahlequah, Okla. Cherokee National
  Female Seminary: E97.6.C35
Tahltan Indians: E99.T12
Tahoe, Lake (California): F868.T2
Tahoe National Forest (California):
  F868.T2
Tail Creek Region (Alberta): F1079.T3
Taino Indians: F1619.2.T3
Tairona Indians: F2270.2.T3
Tait, Charles: E302.6.T18
Taiwanese in the United States:
  E184.T35
Taiwano Indians: F2270.2.T32
Takelma Indians: E99.T15
Taku River and Valley (Alaska):
  F912.T32
Taku River and Valley (British
  Columbia): F1089.T14
Takulli Indians: E99.T17
Talamanca, Costa Rica (District):
  F1549.T13
Talamantes Salvador y Baeza, Melchor
  de: F1231
Talbot Settlement (Ontario): F1059.T34
Talbot, Silas: E207.T13
Talca (Chile)
  City: F3281.T17
  Province: F3236
Talcahuano (Chile): F3281.T2
Tallahassee (Florida): F319.T14

Tallgrass Prairie National Preserve
(Kansas): F687.T34
Tallmadge, Benjamin: E302.6.T2
Talmadge, Eugene: F291
Talon, Jean, comte d'Orsainville: F1030
Taltal, Chile (Dept.): F3238
Tamanca Indians: F2319.2.T25
Tamandare, J. M. Lisbôa, marques de:
F2536
Tamaroa Indians: E99.T18
Tamaulipas, Mexico (State): F1356
Tamils in Canada: F1035.T35
Tamiscamingue, Lake (Québec):
F1054.T6
Tampa (Florida): F319.T2
Tampico (Mexico): F1391.T2
Tanai Indians: E99.T185
Tanana Indians: E99.T187
Tancook Island (Nova Scotia):
F1039.T35
Tangier Island (Virginia): F232.T15
Tangipahoa Parish (La.): F377.T3
Tanglewood Park (N.C.): F262.F7
Tanimuca-Retuama Indians:
F2270.2.T34
Tannehill Historical State Park
(Alabama): F332.T17
Tanner, John Riley: F546
Tanning
Indians: E98.L4
Pre-Columbian America: E59.L4
Tanoan Indians: E99.T189
Tantramar River and Valley (N.B.):
F1044.T36
Taos Indians: E99.T2
Taos (N.M.): F804.T2
Tapajo Indians: F2520.1.T2
Tapajos River (Brazil): F2586
Tapia y Rivera, Alejandro: F1970.6.T3
Tapirapé Indians: F2520.1.T25
Tapuya Indians: F2520.1.T3
Taquari-Antas River and Valley, Brazil:
F2621
Tarahumara Indians: F1221.T25
Tarapacá, Chile (Province): F3241
Tarasco Indians
Modern: F1221.T3

Tarasco Indians
Pre-Columbian: F1219.8.T37
Taria Indians: F2520.1.T32
Tariana Indians: F2520.1.T32
Tarija, Bolivia (Dept.): F3341.T2
Tarqui, Battle of, Ecuador, 1829: F2275
Tarryall Mountains (Colorado):
F782.T37
Taruma Indians: F2380.1.T3
Tatham, William: F436
Tatlayoko Lakc (B.C.): F1089.T17
Tatshenshini River and Valley (British
Columbia): F1089.T18
Tattooing
Indians: E98.T2
Peru: F3429.3.T2
Taunton (Massachusetts): F74.T2
Taurepan Indians: F2380.1.A7
Tawahka Indians: F1505.2.T38
Tawakoni Indians: E99.T315
Taxation
Aztecs: F1219.76.T39
Indians: E98.T24
Bolivia: F3320.1.T38
Colombia: F2270.1.T38
Ecuador: F3721.3.T18
Guatemala: F1465.3.T3
Mexico: F1219.3.T3
Peru: F3429.3.T28
Taxation and representation
American colonies: E215.5
Taxco (Mexico): F1391.T23
Taylor, Alfred Alexander: F436
Taylor, John: E302.6.T23
Taylor, Robert Love: F436
Taylor, Zachary: E422
Administration, 1849-1950: E421+
Campaign in Mexico, 1846-1847:
E405.1
Te Pito te Henua (Chile): F3169
Tea Farm Park (S.C.): F277.C4
Tea tax
American colonies: E215.7
Teapot Dome oil scandal: E785
Teche, Bayou (La.): F377.T4
Teco Indians: F1219.8.T43
Tecoh Site (Mexico): F1435.1.T42

Tecuexe Indians: F1221.T33
Teenagers
  Indians
    Venezuela: F2319.3.T43
Teeth
  Indians
    Peru: F3429.3.T29
Teeth mutilation and decoration
  Indians
    Ecuador: F3721.3.T2
Tegakouita, Catharine: E90.T2
Tegucigalpa (Honduras)
  City: F1516.T4
  Province: F1509.T2
Tehuantepec, Isthmus of: F1359
Tehuexe Indians: F1221.T33
Tejon Ranch (California): F868.K3
Telegraph service, Military
  United States
    Civil War: E608
Telkwa River and Valley (British
  Columbia): F1089.T2
Teller, Henry Moore: E664.T2
Tellico Creek and Valley (N.C.):
  F262.M2
Temecula Creek and Valley (Calif.):
  F868.R6
Temecula Massacre, 1847: E83.838
Témiscaming Lake (Québec): F1054.T6
Témiscamingue County (Québec):
  F1054.T6
Temiscouata County (Québec):
  F1054.T29
Temiskaming County (Québec):
  F1054.T6
Temple Heights (Washington, D.C.):
  F202.T4
Temple Mound culture: E99.M6815
Temple Stream (Me.): F27.F8
Temuco (Chile): F3281.T4
Ten Years' War, 1868-1878: F1785
Tenampua (Honduras)
  Indian antiquities: F1505.1.T2
Tenankutchin Indians: E99.T187
Tenayuca San Bartolo, Mexico
  (Pyramid): F1219.1.T24

Tendilla, Antonio de Mendoza, conde
  de: F1231
Tenetehara Indians: F2520.1.T4
Tenino Indians: E99.T32
Tenleytown (Washington, D.C.):
  F202.T43
Tenmile Creek and Valley (West
  Virginia): F247.T4
Tennessee: F431+
  African Americans: E185.93.T3
  Confederate history: E579+
  Counties, etc: F443.A+
  Franklin (State): F436
  Indians: E78.T3
  Reconstruction: F436
  Slavery: E445.T3
  Wars
    Civil War: E531+, E579+
      Military operations: E470.4+,
        E470.5, E470.8
    Indian wars: E83.813
    Revolution: E263.T4
    War of 1898: E726.T4
    War with Mexico: E409.5.T4
Tennessee, Army of (C.S.A.): E470.5
Tennessee, Army of the: E470.5
Tennessee, East: F442.1
Tennessee, Middle: F442.2
Tennessee militiamen, Jackson's
  execution of: E83.813
Tennessee River and Valley: F217.T3
  Alabama: F332.T2
  Kentucky: F457.T3
  Tennessee: F443.T3
Tennessee River Region
  Indians: E78.T33
Tennessee River Reopening, 1863:
  E475.92
Tennessee Valley
  Military operations
    Civil War: E470.5
  Texas: F392.B34
Tennessee, West: F442.3
Tensas Parish (La.): F377.T45
Teotihuacán (Mexico): F1301
Teotihucán (Mexico)
  Indian antiquities: F1219.1.T27

Tepanec Indians: F1219.8.T47
Tepecano Indians: F1221.T37
Tepehua Indians: F1221.T39
Tepehuan Indians: F1221.T4
Tepic, Mexico (Territory): F1361
Tepoztlán (Mexico): F1391.T3
Teque Indians: F2319.2.T4
Tequesta Indians: E99.T325
Teremembe Indians: F2520.1.T43
Terena Indians: F2520.1.T45
Tereno Indians: F2520.1.T45
Terminal Island (Calif.): F868.L8
Terra, Gabriel: F2728
Terraba Indians: F1545.2.T4
Térraba River and Valley (Costa Rica):
    F1549.R5
Terre Haute (Indiana): F534.T3
Terrebonne County (Québec):
    F1054.T4
Terrebonne Parish (La.): F377.T5
Territorial Company of Philadelphia,
    Association of: F442.1
Territorial expansion
  Canada: F1027.5
  United States: E179.5
    Alaska purchase, 1867: E669, F907
    Canal Zone: F1569.C2
    Danish West Indies: E768
    Danish West Indies purchase:
      F2136
    Florida cessions (1798-1819):
      F301, F314
    Gadsden Purchase, 1853: F786
    New Southwest: F786
    Northwest Ordinance, 1787: E309
    Old Northwest: E309, F483
    Oregon: F314
    Political question: E713
    Proposed annexations
      Canada: F1033
    Western lands, 1787: E309, F483
Territorio Nacional de Colonias (Bolivia):
    F3341.T3
Territory of Orleans, 1804-1812: F374
Territory south of the Ohio: F431+
Terry, David Smith: F864

Teslin River and Valley
    British Columbia: F1089.T25
Teslin River (Yukon): F1095.T47
Teslin Valley (Yukon): F1095.T47
Têtes de Boule Indians: E99.T33
Teton Indians: E99.T34
Teton Mountains (Wyoming): F767.T29
Teton River and Valley (Idaho):
    F752.T5
Tewa Basin (N.M.): F802.T47
Tewa Indians: E99.T35
Texada Island (British Columbia):
    F1089.T3
Texan Mier Expedition, 1842: F390
Texas: F381+
  African Americans: E185.93.T4
  Burr Conspiracy, 1805-1807: E334
  Confederate history: E580+
  Counties, etc: F392.A+
  Fredonian Insurrection: F389
  Indians: E78.T4
  International boundary: F786
  La Salle's Colony, 1685-1687: F352
  New Mexico (1836-1848): F800
  Northwest lands sold to U.S.: F801
  Reconstruction, 1867-1877: F391
  Santa Fe Expedition, 1841: F390
  Slavery: E445.T47
  Wars
    Civil War: E532+, E580+
      Military operations: E470.7,
        E470.9
    Revolution: E263.T45
    War of 1812: E359.5.T47
    War of Independence, 1835-1836:
      F390
    War with Mexico: E409.5.T45
Texas Hill Country: F392.T47
Texas Panhandle: F392.P168
Texas (Province): F389
Texas, Purchase of Northwest, 1850:
    F801
Texas Rangers: F391
Texas, Republic of, 1836-1846: F390
Textile fabrics
  Indians
    Bolivia: F3320.1.T48

Textile fabrics
  Indians
    Chile: F3069.3.T4
    Colombia: F2270.1.T48
    Costa Rica: F1565.3.T49
    Ecuador: F3721.3.T47
    Guatemala: F1465.3.T4
    Mexico: F1219.3.T4
    North America: E98.T35
    Peru: F3429.3.T3
    Pre-Columbian America: E59.T35
    South America: F2230.1.T3
  Mayas: F1435.3.T48
Tezcucan Indians: F1219.8.T49
Thais in the United States: E184.T4
Thames, Battle of, 1813: E356.T3
Thames River and Valley (Ontario): F1059.T38
Thanksgiving Day: F7
Thanksgiving Day and customs
  Colonial America: E162
Thatcher, John Boyd: F124
Thelon River and Valley
  Keewatin: F1110.T54
  Mackenzie: F1100.T54
Theocratic state, 1860-1895 (Ecuador): F3736
Theodore Roosevelt Island (District of Columbia): F203.4.T5
Theodore Roosevelt National Memorial Park (North Dakota): F642.T5
Thetford (Vermont): F59.T4
Thevet, André: E133.T47
Thimbles (Conn.): F102.T4
Third Army Corps Union: E493.1
Third Brigade Association: E493.5
Thirteen American Colonies: E186+
  Revolution: E263.A+
Thirteen North American colonies (before 1776): E162
Thlingchadinne Indians: E99.T4
Thomas Bay (Alaska): F912.T4
Thomas, Ebenezer Smith: E302.6.T4
Thomas, George Henry: E467.1.T4
Thomas Indian School, Iroquois, N.Y.: E97.6.T4
Thomas, John: E207.T45

Thompson, David: F1060.7
Thompson Island (Massachusetts): F73.68.T5
Thompson, Jacob: E415.9.T45
Thompson Lake and Region (Me.): F27.T48
Thompson, Richard Wiggington: E340.T47
Thompson River and Valley (British Columbia): F1089.T48
Thompson, Sir John Sparrow David: F1033
Thompson's Station, Tenn., Battle of, 1863: E475.1
Thomson, C.E.P.T. (Lord Sydenham): F1032
Thomson, Charles: E302.6.T48
Thomson-Urrutia Treaty, 1914: F2277
Thousand Islands: F127.T5
Thousand Springs State Park (Idaho): F752.G66
Three Fingers Mountain (Wash.): F897.S66
Three Rivers District (Québec): F1054.T5
Three Rivers (Québec): F1054.5.T53
Thumb Area (Michigan): F572.T58
Thumb District (Michigan): F572.T58
Thunder Bay District (Ontario): F1059.T5
Thunder Bay (Michigan): F572.A4
Thunder Bay region (Ontario): F1059.T5
Tiahuanaco (Bolivia)
  Indian antiquities: F3319.1.T55
Tiatinagua Indians: F3430.1.E78
Tibetans in the United States: E184.T53
Ticomán, Mexico (Guadalupe Hidalgo)
  Indian antiquities: F1219.1.T43
Ticonderoga (New York)
  Capture: E241.T5
  Military operations: E199
Tidewater Region (Virginia): F232.T54
Tiempistas (Paraguay): F2689
Tierra Adentro
  Indian antiquities: F2269.1.T54

Tierra Bomba Island (Colombia): F2281.B6

Tierra del Fuego, Argentina: F2986

Tierra Firme: F2155+

Tieté River (Brazil): F2631

Tiffin, Edward: F495

Tiffin River and Valley (Ohio): F497.B3

Tigre Island (Honduras): F1509.V2

Tigua Indians: E99.T52

Tíhosuco (Mexico): F1435.1.T48

Tikal (Guatemala)
 Mayas: F1435.1.T5

Tilden, Samuel J.
 Presidential campaign, 1876: E680

Tilden, Samuel Jones: E415.9.T5
 Collected works: E415.6.T57+

Tilghman, Tench: E207.T57

Tillamook Indians: E99.T53

Tillman, Benjamin Ryan: E664.T57

Timagani Lake and region (Ontario): F1059.T53

Timberline Lodge (Oregon): F882.H85

Timbira Indians: F2520.1.T5

Timiskaming Co
 Ontario: F1059.T56

Timiskaming County (Québec): F1054.T6

Timiskaming Indians: E99.T54

Timiskaming, Lake (Québec): F1054.T6

Timiskaming Region (Québec): F1054.T6

Timote Indians: F2319.2.T5

Timucua Indians: E99.T55

Timucuan Ecological and Historic Preserve (Florida): F317.S2

Tina (Peak): F1939.T5

Tinguiririca (Volcano): F3151

Tinkers Creek and Valley (Ohio): F497.C95

Tinne Indians: E99.T56

Tionontati Indians: E99.T57

Tippecanoe, Battle of, 1811: E83.81

Titicaca Island: F3341.T6

Titicaca, Lake, region
 Peru: F3451.P9

Titicaca, Lake, Region: F3341.T6

Tiwa Indians: E99.T52

Tiwanaku (Bolivia)
 Indian antiquities: F3319.1.T55

Tlahuica Indians: F1221.T5
 Pre-Columbian: F1219.8.T52

Tlakluit Indians: E99.T58

Tlapanec Indians: F1221.T53

Tlaxcala (Mexico): F1366

Tlaxcalan Indians
 Modern: F1221.T56
 Pre-Columbian: F1219.8.T53

Tlaxcaltecan Indians: F1219.8.T53

Tlingit Indians: E99.T6

Toa River (Cuba): F1849.T62

Toba Indians: F2823.T7

Tobacco pipes
 Indians: E98.T6
  Argentina: F2821.3.T6
  Pre-Columbian America: E59.T6
  Uruguay: F2719.3.T6

Tobacco Plains (Mont.): F737.F58

Tobacco use
 Indians
  South America: F2230.1.T63
  Mayas: F1435.3.T63

Tobago (West Indies): F2116

Tobatí (Paraguay): F2695.T6

Tobico Marsh (Michigan): F572.B3

Tobique River and Valley (New Brunswick): F1044.T6

Tocantins River (Brazil)
 Goyaz (State): F2566
 Pará (State): F2586

Tocantins State (Brazil): F2640

Toe River (N.C.): F262.A9

Tohono O'Odham Indians: E99.P25

Tojolabal Indians: F1221.T58

Tola, Isla de la (Ecuador): F3741.E6

Toledo Bend region (La.): F377.T6

Toledo Bend region (Texas): F377.T6

Toledo Bend Reservoir (La.): F377.T6

Toledo, British Honduras (District): F1449.T6

Toledo, Francisco de: F3444

Toledo (Ohio): F499.T6

Toledo War, 1836: F497.B7

Tolhuaca (Volcano): F3196

Tolima, Colombia (Dept.): F2281.T6

Tolita, Isla de la (Ecuador): F3741.E6
Tolowa Indians: E99.T7
Toltec Indians: F1219.8.T65
Toluca (Mexico): F1391.T6
Tom, Mount (Mass.): F72.H3
Tomaráxo Indians: F2679.2.T65
Tombigbee River and Valley
  Alabama: F332.T6
  Mississippi: F347.T6
Tombs
  Indians
    Argentina: F2821.3.T65
Tombstone (Arizona): F819.T6
Tomebamba (Indian antiquities):
  F3721.1.T65
Tomlinson Run State Park (Virginia):
  F247.H24
Tomlinson Run (West Virginia):
  F247.H24
Tomoka River (Florida): F317.V7
Tompkins, Daniel D.: E302.6.T8, F123
Tonalámatl de Aubin (Codices):
  F1219.56.T66+
Tongass National Forest (Alaska):
  F912.T64
Tongue River and Valley
  Montana: F737.T55
  Wyoming: F767.T65
Tongue River, Battle of, 1877:
  E83.8765
Tonikan Indians: E99.T73
Tonina (Guatemala)
  Mayas: F1435.1.T65
Tonkawa Indians: E99.T75
Tonocote Indians: F2823.T8
Tonto National Monument (Arizona):
  F817.G5
Tonto River and Valley (Arizona):
  F817.T66
Toombs, Robert Augustus: E415.9.T6
Topeka (Kansas): F689.T6
Topoxté: F1435.1.T67
Topsail Island (N.C.): F262.O5
Torch Lake (Michigan): F572.A5
Tories, American: E277+
Toromona Indians: F3320.2.T6
Toronto Islands (Ontario): F1059.O6

Toronto (Ontario): F1059.5.T68+
  Capture, 1813: E356.T68
Torre, Lisandro de la: F2848
Torriente y Peraza, Cosme de la:
  F1787
Tortuguero Site (Mexico): F1435.1.T7
Tory estates, Sale of: E277
Tory regiments: E277.6.A+
Toscanelli, Paolo del Pozzo: E110
Tosta, Vicente: F1507.5
Totem poles
  Indians: E98.T65
Totems
  Indians: E98.T65
Totonac Indians
  Modern: F1221.T6
  Pre-Columbian: F1219.8.T68
Totonicapán, Guatemala (Dept.):
  F1469.T7
Totopotomoy Creek, Va., Battle of,
  1864: E476.52
Toussaint Louverture, François
  Dominique: F1923
Tower Rock (Mo.): F472.P4
Townsend, Robert: E280.T7
Townshend Acts, 1763: E215.3
Trade laws, British
  Enforcement in American colonies:
    E215.1
Trails
  Indians
    North America: E98.T7
    Peru: F3429.3.R6
    Pre-Columbian America: E59.R6
    South America: F2230.1.R6
  Mayas: F1435.3.R6
Traitors
  United States
    Civil War: E458.8
    Revolution: E277
Trans-Mississippi Department
  Confederate Army: E470.9
Trans-Mississippi Region: F590.2+
Transatlantic influences
  Indian: E98.T73
  Indians
    Mexico: F1219.3.T73

Transcontinental journeys (U.S.), 1848-1860: F593

Transpacific influences, Indian
Pre-Columbian America: E59.T73

Transylvania: F454

Trapping
Indians: E98.T75

Traverse region (Michigan): F572.G5

Treasure Island (San Francisco County, Calif.): F868.S156

Treatment of Indians: F1411
South America: F2230.1.T7

Treaty of Paris, 1778: E249

Treaty of Paris, 1783: E249

Treaty of Paris, 1803: E333

Treaty of Tordesillas, 1494: E123

Treaty of Washington, 1819: F314

Treinta y Tres, Uruguay (Dept.): F2731.T6
Indian antiquities: F2719.1.T74

Trelawney Plantation (Maine): F23

Tremont Street (Boston): F73.67.T7

Trent Affair, Nov. 8, 1861: E469+

Trent Canal (Ontario): F1059.T7

Trent River and Valley (North Carolina): F262.T73

Trent River and Valley (Ontario): F1059.T7

Trent-Severn Waterway (Ontario): F1059.T7

Trent Valley (Ontario): F1059.T7

Trenton, Battle of, 1776: E241.T7

Trenton (N.J.): F144.T7+

Trephining
Indians
Peru: F3429.3.T7

Tres Marias Islands (Mexico): F1368

Tres Zapotes (Mexico)
Indian antiquities: F1219.1.T7

Trevilian Station, Va., Battle of, 1864: E476.6

Tribal colleges
North America: E97.55

Tribal government
Indians: E98.T77
Pre-Columbian America: E59.T75

Tribute
Indians
Ecuador: F3721.3.T18

Tribute (Taxation)
Indians
Peru: F3429.3.T28

Trike Indians: F1221.T7

Trimble, Allen: F495

Trinidad and Tobago (West Indies): F2119+

Trinidad (Cuba): F1829.T8

Trinidad (West Indies): F2119+

Trinity Alps (California): F868.T58

Trinity River and Valley (California): F868.T63

Trinity River and Valley (Texas): F392.T83

Trio Indians: F2420.1.T7

Triometesem Indians: F2420.1.A35

Triple Alliance, War of the, 1865-1870: F2687

Tripoli, War with, 1801-1805: E335

Tripoline War: E335

Tripolitan War: E335

Trique Indians: F1221.T7

Trois Rivières County (Québec): F1054.T5

Trojans
Pre-Columbian discovery of America: E109.T74

Trophies, Military
United States
Civil War: E646
War of 1898: E734

Trujillo Molina, Rafael Leónidas: F1938.5

Trujillo (Peru)
City: F3611.T8
Province: F3451.T7
Indian antiquities: F3429.1.T8

Trujillo, Venezuela (State): F2331.T7

Trumai Indians: F2520.1.T7

Truman, Harry S.: E814
Administrations, 1945-1953: E813+
Collected works: E742.5.T6+
Family: E814.1

Trumbell, Jonathan: E263.C5

Trumbell, Lyman: E415.9.T86
Truro Parish (Virginia): F232.T8
Trust estates
  Indians: E98.F3
Trustee for establishing the colony of
  Georgia: F289
Truth, Sojourner: E185.97.T8
Truxtun, Thomas: E182
Tryon, William: F257
Tsattine Indians: E99.T77
Tsetsaut Indians: E99.T772
Tsilkotin Indians: E99.T78
Tsimshian Indians: E99.T8
Tsuva Indians: F2520.1.S89
Tubatulabal Indians: E99.T83
Tucano Indians: F2520.1.T9
Tucanoan Indians: F2270.2.T77
Tuck, Amos: E415.9.T88
Tucker, John Randolph: E467.1.T8
Tucker-Prentiss Duel: E340.P9
Tucker, Samuel: E207.T8
Tuckernuck Island (Mass.): F72.N2
Tucson (Arizona): F819.T9+
Tucumán (Argentina)
  City: F3011.T89
  Province: F2991
    Indian antiquities: F2821.1.T89
Tucuna Indians: F2520.1.T925
Tug Hill region (New York): F127.T83
Tukanoan Indians: F2270.2.T77
Tukkuthkutchin Indians: E99.T845
Tuktut Nogait National Park (N.W.T.):
  F1060.95.T85
Tukuarika Indians: E99.T85
Tula de Allende (Mexico): F1219.1.T8
Tula Site (Mexico): F1219.1.T8
Tulalip Indians: E99.T87
Tulare Lake and region (California):
  F868.S173
Tulcán (Ecuador): F3791.T8
Tule Lake (California): F868.S6
Tullahoma campaign, 1863: E475.16
Tulsa (Oklahoma): F704.T92
Tulum (Mexico)
  Mayas: F1435.1.T8
Tumacacori National Monument:
  F817.T8

Tumbes, Peru (Dept.): F3451.T8
Tumuc-Humac Mountains (French
  Guiana): F2467.T9
Tunebo Indians: F2270.2.T8
Tungurahua, Ecuador (Province):
  F3741.T7
Tunica Indians: E99.T875
Tunisians in Canada: F1035.T85
Tunja (Colombia)
  City: F2291.T8
  Province: F2281.T8
Tunxis Indians: E99.T88
Tuolumne River and Valley (California):
  F868.T92
Tupac Amaru, Insurrection of, 1780-
  1781: F3444
Tupambaé, Battle of, 1904: F2728
Tupari Indians: F2520.1.T933
Tupelo, Miss., Battle of, 1864: E476.84
Tupelo (Mississippi), Expedition to,
  1864: E476.84
Tupi Indians: F2230.2.T84
Tupinamba Indians: F2520.1.T94
Tupper, Sir Charles: F1033
Tupungato, Argentina (Dept.): F2911
Turkey Run State Park (Indiana):
  F532.P2
Turks and Caicos Islands (Bahamas):
  F1659.T9
Turks in Canada: F1035.T87
Turks in the United States: E184.T88
Turnagain Arm (Alaska): F912.C6
Turneffe Island (Belize): F1449.B4
Turner, Nat
  Negro Insurrection, 1831: F232.S7
Turtle Creek and Valley (West Virginia):
  F247.B6
Tuscaloosa (Alabama): F334.T9
Tuscarawas River and Valley (Ohio):
  F497.T93
Tuscarora Indians: E99.T9
Tuscarora War, 1711-1713: E83.71
Tutchone Indians: E99.T92
Tutelo Indians: E99.T96
Tuttle, Stephen: E278.T9
Tututni Indians: E99.T97
Tuxá Indians: F2520.1.T97

Tuxpan (Mexico)
  Canton: F1371
Tuyuca Indians: F2520.1.T98
Tuyuty, Battle of, 1866: F2687
Tuzantec Indians: F1221.M74
Twana Indians: E99.T98
Tweed, William Marcy: F128.47
Tweedsmuir Provincial Park (British
  Columbia): F1089.T85
Twenties, The
  United States history: F784
Twin Butte region (Alberta): F1079.T8
Twin Cities (Minneapolis and St. Paul):
  F614.M6
Twin Falls (Idaho): F754.T97
Twin Lakes Region (Lake and Peninsula
  Borough, Alaska): F912.T85
Twin Valley (Ohio): F497.M7
Two Dot Ranch (Wyoming): F767.T96
Two Mountains County (Québec):
  F1054.D4
Tybee Island (Georgia): F292.C36
Tye River and Valley (Virginia):
  F232.N25
Tygart River and Valley (West Virginia):
  F247.T86
Tyler, Daniel: E467.1.T9
Tyler, John: E397
  Administration: E396+
Tyler, Mary Hunt (Palmer): E302.6.T93
Tyler, Robert: E415.9.T93
Tyler, Tex. Camp Ford
  Civil War prison: E612.T9
Tyndale, Hector: E467.1.T98
Tyrolese in Brazil (Espírito Santo):
  F2561
Tzeltal Indians: F1221.T8
Tzoneca Indians: F2936
Tzotzil Indians: F1221.T9
  North America: E99.T986
Tzutuhil Indians: F1465.2.T9
Tzutzuculi Site (Mexico): F1435.1.T96

U

Uaboi Indians: F2520.1.U3
Uaica Indians: F2520.1.W3

Uajaribo Indians: F2520.1.G68
Uarequena Indians: F2319.2.A73
Uaupés Valley (Brazil)
  Indian antiquities: F2519.1.U3
Uaxactun (Guatemala)
  Mayas: F1435.1.U2
Ubico, Jorge: F1466.45
Ucayali River (Peru): F3451.L8
Uinta Basin (Utah): F832.U4
Uinta Indians: E99.U35
Uinta Mountains
  Utah: F832.U39
  Wyoming: F767.U33
Ukrainians in Argentina: F3021.U5
Ukrainians in Brazil: F2659.U4
Ukrainians in Canada: F1035.U5
Ukrainians in the United States:
  E184.U5
Ulate Blanco, Otilio: F1548
Ulloa, San Juan de, Island (Mexico):
  F1335
Ulmecs: F1219
Ultima Esperanza, Chile (Dept.): F3244
Ulúa Island (Mexico): F1335
Ulua River and Valley (Honduras):
  F1509.U4
Ulustee, Florida, Battle of, 1864:
  E476.43
Ulva Indians: F1525.2.U4
Umatilla Indians: E99.U4
Umawa Indians: F2270.2.C27
Umotina Indians: F2520.1.U5
Umpqua Indians: E99.U45
Un-American activities in the United
  States: E743.5, E839.8
Unadilla River and Valley (New York):
  F127.U54
Uncanoonuc Mountains (New
  Hampshire): F42.H6
Uncompahgre Indian Reservation:
  E99.U8
Uncompahgre National Forest:
  F782.U5
Uncompahgre Valley (Colorado):
  F782.U5
Underground railroad: E450
Ungava: F1054.N5

Ungava
  Indians: E78.Q3
Union City (Tennessee)
  Descent upon, 1862: E473.15
Union clubs: E462.84, E463
Unión, La, El Salvador (Dept.):
  F1489.L3
Union League of America: E462.7
Union men in the South
  Civil War: E458.7
Union Navy
  United States Civil War: E591+
Union Parish (La.): F377.U5
Union River and Valley (Me.): F27.H3
Union River Bay (Me.): F27.H3
Union River (Me.): F27.H3
Union Society of the Civil War:
  E462.99.U53
Union Soldiers' Alliance, Washington,
  D.C.: E462.99.U57
Union Station (Washington, D.C.):
  F204.U5
Union University, Schenectady, N.Y.
  and the Civil War: E541.U5
Union Veteran Legion of the United
  States: E462.4
Union Veterans' Union: E462.99.U63
Union White Boys in Blue: E462.96
Unitarism vs. federalism (Argentina):
  F2846
United Colonies of New England, 1643-
  1684: F7
United Confederate Veterans: E483.1
United Daughters of the Confederacy:
  E483.5
United Empire loyalists
  American loyalists: E277
  New Brunswick: F1043
  Nova Scotia: F1038
  Upper Canada: F1058
United Sons of Confederate Veterans:
  E483.4
United Spanish War Veterans:
  E714.3.U57+
United States: E151+
  Air force history: E840.4
  Annexations: E179.5

United States
  Anniversaries: E285+
    1976 Bicentennial: E285.2+
  Articles of Confederation, 1778: E303
  Chronology, Historical: E468.3,
    E470.1
  Civilization: E162+, E169.1+
  Constitution: E303
  Cuba, Occupation of, 1906-1909:
    F1787
  Declaration of Independence: E221
  Description and travel: E151+
  Directories: E154.5+
  Frontier troubles with Mexico: F1234
  Gazetteers: F17
  History: E178+
    Research: E175.7
    Study and teaching: E175.8
  Intellectual life: E162+, E169.1
  Intervention in Cuba, 1898-1902:
    E721, F1786
  Intervention in Cuba, 1898-1902,
    1906-1909: F1787
  Intervention in Dominican Republic,
    1916-1924: F1938.45
  Intervention in European affairs, 1849-
    1853: E429
  Intervention in Haiti, 1915-1947:
    F1927
  Intervention in Honduras, 1911, 1913:
    F1507.5
  Intervention in Nicaragua, 1909-1933:
    F1526.3
  Intervention in Panama, 1903-1936:
    F1566.5
  Military history: E181, E745, E840.4,
    E897+
    Civil War, 1861-1865: E470+
    French and Indian War, 1755-1763:
      E199
    King George's War, 1744-1748:
      E198
    King Philip's War, 1675-1676:
      E83.67
    King William's War, 1675-1676:
      E196

United States
  Military history
    Queen Anne's War, 1702-1713:
     E197
    Revolution, 1775-1786: E230+
    War of 1812: E355+
    War of 1898: E726.A+
    War with Algeria: E365
    War with France, 1798-1800: E323
    War with Mexico, 1845-1848:
     E405+
    War with Tripoli, 1801-1805: E335
  National parks: E160
  Naval history: E182, E746, E840.4
    Civil War: E591+
    Conflicts with France: E323
    Revolution: E271
    War of 1812: E360
    War of 1898: E727
    War with Algeria: E365
    War with Mexico: E410
    War with Tripoli: E335
  Oregon occupied jointly with Great
   Britain, 1818-1846: F880
  Paraguay expedition, 1858-1859:
   F2686
  Regionalism: E179.5
  Relations with areas, regions, etc:
   E183.75
  Relations with individual countries:
   E183.8.A+
  Secret service
    Civil War: E608
    Revolution: E279+
  Travel: E141, E161.5+, F214
United States. Adjutant General's Office
 Reports
 Civil War
  By state: E495+
United States. Army
 Battles: E181
 Biography: E181
 Veterans' organizations: E181
United States. Army. Signal Corps
 Civil War: E608
 War of 1898: E725.47

United States. Bureau of American
  Ethnology: E51
United States. Bureau of Refugees,
  Freedmen, and Abandoned Lands:
  E185.2
United States Christian Commission:
  E635
United States. Congress. House.
  Committee on Un-American Activities:
  E743.5
United States. Continental Army:
  E259+, E260
United States. Continental Congress:
  E303
United States Daughters of 1812:
  E351.6
United States. Dept. of State. Office of
  Information and Educational
  Exchange: E744.5
United States. Dept. of State. Voice of
  America
  Radio program: E744.5
United States. Freedmen's Bureau:
  E185.2
United States Information Agency:
  E744.5
United States local history: F1+
United States Military Telegraph Corps:
  E608
United States. Navy
  Battles: E182
  Biography: E182
  Veterans' organizations: E182
United States Navy Veteran
  Association: E182
United States Navy veterans' societies:
  E182
United States Paraguay Expedition,
  1858-1859: F2686
United States Presidents, Relations with
  African Americans: E176.472.A34
  Jews: E176.472.J47
United States Sanitary Commission:
  E631+
United States Veteran Signal Corps
  Association: E608

Universities (U.S.) and the Civil War:
E541.A+
Confederate: E586.A+
Universities (U.S.) and the Revolution:
E270.A1+
University of California. Tecumseh
Center: E97.6.U54
Unzaga, Ignacio José Allende y: F1232
Upper Arrow Lake (British Columbia):
F1089.K7
Upper California: F864
Upper Canada: F1056+
Upper Iowa River and Valley (Iowa):
F627.U66
Upper Iowa River and Valley (Minn.):
F612.U77
Upper Mississippi River and Valley:
F597
Upper Nine Partners Patent (New York):
F127.D8
Upper Peninsula (Michigan): F572.N8
Upper Peru: F3322
Upper Tanana Indians: E99.T187
Urarina Indians: F3430.1.U83
Urban residence
Aztecs: F1219.76.U74
Indians: E98.U72
Brazil: F2519.3.U73
Ecuador: F3721.3.U73
Mayas: F1435.3.U72
Urdaneta, Rafael: F2235.5.U7
Uriburu, José Félix: F2848
Urns
Indians
Argentina: F2821.3.U7
Urquiza, Justo José de: F2846
Ursúa, Pedro de: E125.U8
Uru Indians: F3320.2.U78
Urubá, Colombia (Province): F2281.U7
Urubamba River (Peru): F3451.C9
Urubu Kaapor Indians: F2520.1.U7
Uruewawau Indians: F2520.1.U74
Uruguay: F2701+
English invasions of the La Plata,
1806-1807: F2845
Jesuit missions of Paraguay: F2684,
F2723

Uruguay
La Plata region before 1806: F2841
Contests over Colonia: F2723
Military history
Argentine-Brazilian War, 1825-1828:
F2725
Civil war (Blancos and Colorados):
F2726
Paraguayan War, 1865-1870:
F2687
Seven Reductions, War of the,
1754-1756: F2684
War against Rosas, 1849-1852:
F2846.3
War of Independence, 1811-1828:
F2725
Uruguay (Cisplatine province, 1821-
1824): F2725
Uruguay River: F2731.U7
Uruguayans in Argentina: F3021.U7
Uruguayans in Canada: F1035.U78
Uruguayans in Mexico: F1392.U78
U.S. Military Academy and the Civil
War: E586.U5
USIA: E744.5
Usulután, Salvador (Dept.): F1489.U8
Usumacinta River (Guatemala):
F1469.P4
Usumacinta Valley (Mexico)
Indian antiquities: F1219.1.U8
Utah: F821+
African Americans: E185.93.U8
Civil War: E532.95
Counties, etc: F832.A+
Indians: E78.U55
Mormon Rebellion, 1857-1859: F826
Utatlan Site (Guatemala)
Mayas: F1435.1.U65
Utcubamba, Peru (Province):
F3451.U88
Ute Indians: E99.U8
Ute Pass (Colorado): F782.U8
Ute War, 1879: E83.879
Utensils
Indians: E98.I4
Uto-Aztecan Indians: E99.U85
Utuado (Puerto Rico): F1981.U8

Uxmal, Mexico (Mayas): F1435.1.U7

V

Valcour Island, Battle of, 1776:
  E241.V14
Valdivia (Chile)
  City: F3281.V15
  Province: F3246
Valdivia culture: F3722.1.V34
Valdivia, Pedro de: F3091
Valencia, Lake, Venezuela: F2331.V3
Valencia (Venezuela): F2341.V25
Vallandigham, Clement Laird:
  E415.9.V2
Valle del Cauca, Colombia (Dept.):
  F2281.V3
  Indian antiquities: F2269.1.V35
Valle, Honduras (Dept.): F1509.V2
Valle, Rafael Heliodoro: F1438
Vallecito Creek and Valley (Colorado):
  F782.V34
Vallejo, Mariano Guadalupe: F864
Valley Forge (Pennsylvania)
  Revolution: E234
Valley of Fire (Nevada): F847.C5
Valley of Virginia: F232.S5
Valparaiso, Battle of, 1891: F3098
Valparaiso (Chile)
  City: F3281.V2
    Bombardment, 1866: F3095
  Province: F3251
Valparaiso, Treaty of, 1884: F3097.3
Valverde, N.M., Battle of, 1862: E473.4
Van Buren, Martin: E387
  Administration, 1837-1841: E386+
Van Cortlandt Manor (N.Y.): F127.W5
Van Cortlandt Mansion (New York):
  F128.8.V2
Van Rensselaer Manor (N.Y.):
  F127.R32
Van Rensselaer, Stephen: F123
Van Schaack, Henry Cruger: E278.V27
Van Wart, Isaac: E280.A5
Vance, Zebulon Baird: E664.V2
Vancouver (B.C.): F1089.5.V22
Vancouver Island (B.C.): F1089.V3

Vancouver (Wash.): F899.V2
Vaqueros: F596
Varela y Morales, Félix: F1783
Varennes (Seigniory), Québec:
  F1054.V3
Vargas, Getulio: F2538
Vargas, José María: F2325
Vargas Torres, Luis: F3736
Vargas (Venezuela): F2331.V35
Vargem Alegre District (Brazil): F2641
Varnum, James Mitchell: E302.6.V33
Varnum, Joseph Bradley: E302.6.V4
Vashon Island (Wash.): F897.K4
Vaudreuil, Philippe de Rigaud, marquis
  de: F1030
Vaupés Valley (Brazil): F2519.1.U3
Vaz de Caminha, Pedro de: E125.C2
Vazquez de Coronado, Francisco
  Cibola: F799
Vázquez de Coronado, Francisco:
  E125.V3
Vázquez de Coronado, Juan: F1437
Vega, Garcilaso de la: F3444
Vega, La, Dominican Republic (City):
  F1939.L3
Velasco Alvarado, Juan: F3448.4.V4
Velasco Ibarra, José María: F3738
Vélez Sársfield, Dalmacio: F2846
Venezuela: F2301+
  Anglo-German-Italian Blockade, 1902:
    F2325
  Caracas (Audiencia): F2322
  Dutch Blockade, 1908: F2325
  English and French attacks, 1596-
    1798: F2322
  German occupation to 1556: F2322
  Islands along the coast: F2016
  Military history
    Civil wars, 1848-1879: F2325
    Revolution 1902-1903: F2325
    Revolution of 1945: F2326
    War of Independence, 1810-1823:
      F2324
  Miranda's Expedition, 1806: F2323
Venezuelans in Mexico: F1392.V45
Vera Cruz (Mexico)
  City: F1391.V4

Vera Paz, Alta, Guatemala (Dept.):
F1469.V3
Vera Paz, Baja, Guatemala (Dept.):
F1469.V4
Veracruz (Mexico)
City: F1391.V4
Occupation, 1914: F1234
Surrender, 1847: E406.V4
State: F1371
Indian antiquities: F1219.1.V47
Veraguas (Veragua), Panama
(Province): F1569.V4
Indian antiquities: F1565.1.V47
Verchères County (Québec):
F1054.V47
Verde River and Valley (Arizona):
F817.V37
Verde Wild and Scenic River (Arizona):
F817.V37
Vermillion Parish (La.): F377.V5
Vermont: F46+
African Americans: E185.93.V4
Counties, etc: F57.A+
Indians: E78.V5
New Hampshire Grants: F52
Wars
Civil War: E533+
St. Alban's Raid: E470.95
Revolution: E263.V5
Military operations: E230+
War of 1812: E359.5.V3
War of 1898: E726.V5
Vernon, Edward
In Cuba: F1779
Siege of Cartagena: F2272.5
Vernon Parish (La.): F377.V6
Vernon, Thomas: E278.V54
Verrazzano, Giovanni: E133.V5
Verte, Île (Québec): F1054.I5
Vesey, Denmark
Rebellion, 1822: F279.C4+
Vespucci, Amerigo: E125.V5
Veteran Brotherhood of the State of
Kansas: E462.6
Veteran Nurses of the Civil War: E621

Veterans
United States
Registers, lists, etc
Civil War: E548
Societies: E182
Civil War: E462+
Confederate: E483
Revolution: E202.1
War of 1812: E351.2+
War of 1898: E714.3.A+
War with Mexico: E401.1+
Veterans' bonus march, Washington,
D.C.: F199
Veterans of Foreign Wars of the United
States: E181
Vice-Presidents
Biography: E176.49
Viceroyalty of
Mexico: F1231
New Granada: F2272
Rio de la Plata: F2841
Viceroyalty of Peru: F3444
Vicksburg (Miss.)
Operations against, 1862: E474.11
Vicksburg (Mississippi): F349.V6
Operations against: E474.47
Siege, 1863: E475.27
Vicksburg National Military Park:
E475.27
Victoria (B.C.): F1089.5.V6
Victoria Co. (Nova Scotia): F1039.V5
Victoria de las Tunas (Cuba): F1849.V5
Vicuña Mackenna, Benjamín: F3095
Vicús culture (Peru)
Indian antiquities: F3429.1.V45
Vicús (Peru)
Indian antiquities: F3429.1.V45
Vieira, António: F2528
Vieira, João Fernandes: F2532
Vieques Island (Puerto Rico): F1981.V5
Vietnamese in the United States:
E184.V53
Vigilance committees: E179
California: F865
Vilela Indians: F2823.V5
Villa, Francisco: F1234

Village Creek and Valley (Arkansas):
F417.V55
Villarrica (Paraguay): F2695.V5
Villas, Las, Cuba (Province): F1821+
Villegas, Micaela: F3444
Viña del Mar (Chile): F3281.V6
Vincennes (Indiana): F534.V7
Vincennes, Jean Baptiste Bissot, sieur
de: F1030
Vincent, Sténio: F1927
Vinces (Ecuador): F3791.V7
Vinland
Pre-Columbian discovery of America:
E105
Vinton, Samuel Finley: E340.V7
Virgin Islands, British: F2129
Virgin Islands of the United States:
F2136
Individual islands: F2096, F2098,
F2105
Proposed annexation (1867-1869,
1902): E669, E756
Purchase, 1917: E768
Virginia: F221+
African Americans: E185.93.V8
Claims in southwestern Pennsylvania:
F157.W5
Claims to Kentucky withdrawn: F454
Confederate history: E581.1+
Counties, etc: F232.A+
Delmarva Peninsula: F187.E2
Indians: E78.V7
John Brown at Harper's Ferry: E451
Kentucky County and District: F454
Nat Turner's Insurrection, 1831:
F232.S7
Ohio Valley explorations: F517
Raleigh's explorations and colonies,
1584-1590: F229
Reconstruction, 1865-1877: F231
Rectrocession of Alexandria County
from the District of Columbia: F195
Slavery: E445.V8
Union government of Virginia: E534+
Wars
Cherokee War, 1759-1761:
E83.759

Virginia
Wars
Civil War: E534+
Military operations: E470.2+,
E470.65
French and Indian War, 1755-1763:
E199
Revolution: E263.V8
Campaign, 1781: E237
War of 1812: E359.5.V8
West Virginia, Separation of: F241
Western lands ceded to the U.S.:
F483
Western lands ceded to the U.S.,
1781-1786: E309
Virginia and Tennessee Railroad,
Expedition against, 1864: E476.62
Virginia, Army of: E470.2+
Virginia, Army of Northern (C.S.A.):
E470.2+
Virginia City (Nevada): F849.V8
Virginia Company of London: F229
Virginia, Grand Camp Confederate
Veterans of: E483.28
Virginia Military Institute, Lexington, and
the Civil War: E586.V5
Virginia military lands: F483
Virginia Resolutions: E328
Virginia University and the Civil War:
E586.V6
Virginia, Valley of: F232.S5
Virginius (Steamer) affair: F1785
Virú Valley (Peru)
Indian antiquities: F3429.1.V77
Vitcos (Peru)
Indian antiquities: F3429.1.V8
Voice of America
Radio program: E744.5
Volcan Irazú (Costa Rica): F1545.1.V6
Volcán Irazú (Costa Rica): F1549.I7
Volcanic eruptions (Guatemala):
F1466.45
Vote of censure, 1834: E384.7
Voyages to the Pacific coast: F865
Voyageurs National Park (Minnesota):
F612.V6
Vuntakutchin Indians: E99.V8

Vuntut National Park (Yukon): F1095.V86

W

Wabash and Erie Canal
General and Indiana: F532.W16
Ohio: F497.W13
Wabash River and Valley: F532.W2
Illinois: F547.W14
Waccamaw Indians: E99.W114
Waccamaw River and Valley
North Carolina: F262.W18
South Carolina: F277.W33
Wachovia (N.C.): F262.F7
Wachuset Indians: E99.W12
Wachusett Mountain (Mass.): F72.W9
Waco Indians: E99.W125
Waco (Texas): F394.W12
Waddington, Mount (B.C.): F1089.C7
Wade, Benjamin Franklin: E415.9.W16
Wadsworth, Fort (S.D.): F657.R6
Wadsworth, James Samuel:
E467.1.W13
Wadsworth Trail (Minnesota):
F612.W15
Wager (Ship), Wreck of: F3146
Wagner, Battery, 1863: E475.63
Wahpekute Indians: E99.W13
Wahpeton Indians: E99.W135
Waica Indians: F2520.1.W3
Waika Indians: F2520.1.W3
Wailaki Indians: E99.W15
Waimiri Indians: F2520.1.W34
Wainright, Jonathan Mayhew: E745
Waite, Davis Hanson: F781
Waiwai Indians: F2380.1.W25
Waiwe Indians: F2380.1.W25
Wakarusa River and Valley (Kansas):
F687.W4
Wakashan Indians: E99.W16
Walden Pond (Mass.): F72.M7
Walden Ridge (Tennessee): F443.W17
Waldo Patent (Me.): F27.M95
Waldron Island (Wash.): F897.S2
Walker, Frank C.: E748.W225
Walker, James John: F128.5

Walker River and Valley (Nevada):
F847.M5
Walker, Robert James: E415.9.W2
Walker, William: F1526.27
Filibuster expeditions: F1232.5,
F1507.5
Wall Street (New York): F128.67.W2
Walla Walla Indians: E99.W18
Walla Walla River and Valley (Wash.):
F897.W2
Wallace, Henry Agard: E748.W23
Wallace, Lewis: E467.1.W2
Wallace, William Alexander Anderson:
F390
Wallace, William Henry Lamme:
E467.1.W3
Wallenpaupack Creek and Valley
(Pennsylvania): F157.P6
Walloomsac, New York, Battle of, 1777:
E241.B4
Walloon Lake (Michigan): F572.W24
Walloons in the United States:
E184.W35
Wallowa Lake (Oregon): F882.W2
Wallowa National Forest: F882.W25
Walpapi Indians: E99.W185
Wama Indians: F2420.1.A35
Wamani Indians: F3430.1.W35
Wamesit Indians: E99.W19
Wampanoag Indians: E99.W2
Wampum: E98.M7, F1219.3.M597
Pre-Columbian America: E59.M7
Wanamaker, John: E664.W24
Wanapum Indians: E99.W3
Wao Indians: F3722.1.H83
Waodadi Indians: F3722.1.H83
Wapisiana Indians: F2380.1.W3
Wappinger Indians: E99.W34
Wappo Indians: E99.W35
Wapusk National Park (Manitoba):
F1064.W37
War against Rosas, 1849-1852:
F2846.3
War between the States: E461+
War correspondents
U.S. Civil War: E609
War of 1812: E351+

War of 1898: E714+
War of Independence, 1861-1865 (Texas): F390
War of the American Revolution: E201+
War of the Pacific, 1879-1884: F3097
War of the Regulators (N.C.): F257
War of the Seven Reductions, 1754-1756: F2684
War of the Triple Alliance, 1865-1870: F2687
War, Prisoners of
  Civil War: E611+
  Revolution: E281
  War of 1812: E362
  War of 1898: E730
  War with Mexico: E412
War relief work
  United States
    Civil War: E629+
    War of 1898: E731
War songs
  United States
    Songs and ballads
      Civil War: E647
      War of 1898: E735
      War with Mexico: E415
Warao Indians: F2319.2.W3
Ward, Artemas: E207.W2
Ward, Samuel: E207.W26
Ware River Valley (Mass.): F72.S94
Warekena Indians: F2319.2.A73
Warfare
  Indians
    Costa Rica: F1545.3.W2
    Peru: F3429.3.W2
    Pre-Columbian America: E59.W3
Warm Springs Apache Indians: E99.W36
Warner, Seth: E207.W27
Warrau Indians: F2319.2.W3
Warren, Gouverneur Kemble: E467.1.W4
  Court-martial: E477.675
Warren, Joseph: E263.M4
Warren Wagon Train Massacre, 1871: E83.866

Wars
  Indians
    Bolivia: F3320.1.W37
    Central America: F1434.2.W37
    Chile: F3069.3.W37
    Ecuador: F3721.3.W35
Wars of independence, Latin America, 1806-1830: F1412
Warwick (Rhode Island)
  Union of plantations: F82
Wasatch Range (Idaho): F752.W27
Wasatch Range (Utah): F832.W22
Wasco Indians: E99.W37
Washburn, Cadwallader Colden: F586
Washburn, Israel: E511+
Washington, Booker Taliaferro: E185.97.W4
Washington, Bushrod: E302.6.W15
Washington (D.C.): F191+
  Bonus Expeditionary Force, 1932, 1933: F199
  Burning by British, 1814: E356.W3
  L'Enfant's plan: F195
  Monuments, memorials, statues: F203.4.A+
  Peace Conference, 1861: E440.5
  Princeton (Frigate) explosion, 1844: E396
Washington (D.C.). Old Capitol Prison
  Civil War prison: E616.O4
Washington (D.C.). Old Guard: E462.93
Washington, Fort, Capture of, 1776: E241.W3
Washington, George: E312+
  Administrations 1789-1797: E311
  Expeditions to the Ohio: E312.23
  Family: E312.19
  Mansion (Philadelphia, Pa.): F158.8.W3
  Masonic Memorial (Alexandria, Va.): F234.A3
  Military career: E312.25
    French and Indian War: E312.23
    Northwestern Indian wars: E83.79
    Revolution: E201+
  Monuments (Philadelphia): F158.64.W3

Washington, George
  Presidential speeches and messages:
    E312.9
  Writings: E312.7+
Washington Heights (New York):
  F128.68.W2
Washington Island (Wisconsin):
  F587.D7
Washington, Lake (Wash.): F897.K4
Washington, Martha (Dandridge) Custis:
  E312.19
Washington Memorial Parkway
  (Virginia): F232.G38
Washington Monument (Washington,
  D.C.): F203.4.W3
Washington-Morris-Salomon Monument
  (Chicago, Illinois): F548.64.G4
Washington, Mount (New Hampshire):
  F41.6.W3
Washington (North Carolina)
  Siege, 1863: E474.55
Washington, Order of: E202.7
Washington Parish (La.): F377.W3
Washington Society of Maryland:
  E202.8
Washington (State): F886+
  African Americans: E185.93.W3
  Columbia River Highway: F882.C63
  Counties, etc: F897.A+
  Indians: E78.W3
  Sand Island controversy: F882.B7
  Sauvies Island: F882.S3
  Vancouver Island: F1089.V3
  Wars
    Civil War: E535+
    Indian wars: E83.84
Washington Street (Boston):
  F73.67.W3
Washington, Treaty of
  1819: F314
  1842: E398
Washington's birthday: E312.6
Washita Campaign, 1868-1869:
  E83.869
Washita River and Valley
  General and Texas: F392.W33
  Oklahoma: F702.W36

Washo Indians: E99.W38
Washoan Indians: E99.W38
Washoe Indians: E99.W38
Watauga Association: F436
Watauga colony: F436
Water
  Indians
    Central America: F1434.2.W38
Watergate Affair: E860
Waterloo Co. (Ontario): F1059.W32
Waterton Lakes National Park (Alberta):
  F1079.W3
Waterville (New Hampshire): F44.W32
Waterville Valley (New Hampshire):
  F44.W32
Watkins Glen (N.Y.): F127.S34
Watson, Thomas Edward: E664.W337
Watts Bar Reservoir and region
  (Tennessee): F443.W33
Watts, Thomas Hill: F326
Waubonsie State Park
  Iowa: F627.F8
Wauhatchie (Tennessee)
  Engagement at, 1863: E475.92
Waunana Indians: F1565.2.W38
Waupaca Co. (Wisconsin): F587.W3
Waura Indians: F2520.1.W38
Wawa Lake and region (Ontario):
  F1059.W34
Wawayanda Patent (1703): F142.B7
Wawenock Indians: E99.W4
Waxhaws (N.C.): F262.W37
Waxhaws (S.C): F277.W39
Wayampi Indians: F2460.1.O9
Wayana Indians: F2230.2.O8
Waymouth, George: F7
Wayne, Anthony: E207.W35
  Campaign, 1793-1795: E83.794
Wayne Co. (Utah): F832.W27
Wayne, James Moore: E340.W3
Wea Indians: E99.W45
Weapons
  Indians: E98.A65
    Pre-Columbian America: E59.A68
Weaving
  Indians
    North America: E98.T35

Webster, Daniel: E340.W4
  Collected works: E337.8.W24
  Webster-Ashburton Treaty, 1842:
    E398
Webster Parish (La.): F377.W4
Webster, Pelatiah: E302.6.W2
Wee-kee-mock Indians: E99.O68
Weed, Thurlow: E415.9.W39
Weeden Island culture
  Indians: E99.W48
Weekenock Indians: E99.O68
Weems, Mason Locke: E302.6.W4
Weights and measures
  Aztecs: F1219.76.W44
  Indians
    Peru: F3429.3.W4
Weir, Lake (Florida): F317.M3
Weiser, Conrad: F152
Weiss Lake (Ala.): F332.C44
Welch Island (N.H.): F42.W7
Weldon Railroad in military operations,
  1864: E477.21
Welfare, Public
  Indians
    Pre-Columbian America: E59.P92
Welland Co. (Ontario): F1059.W36
Welles, Gideon: E467.1.W46
Wellington Co. (Ontario): F1059.W37
Wellington-Oberlin rescue, 1858: E450
Wells Gray Provincial Park (British
  Columbia): F1089.W44
Welsers, The
  Grant in Venezuela: F2322
Welsh
  Pre-Columbian discovery of America:
    E109.W4
Welsh in Canada: F1035.W44
Welsh in the American Revolution:
  E269.W4
Welsh in the United States: E184.W4
Welsh Indians
  Tradition: E99.W5
Wenatchee River and Valley
  (Washington): F897.W44
Wenatchi Indians: E99.W53
Wendell Phillip Statue (Boston):
  F73.64.W4

Wends in the United States: E184.S68
Wenrohronon Indians: E99.W54
Wentworth Co. (Ontario): F1059.W4
Wesorts: E184.W5
West Augusta, District of (Virginia):
  F157.W5
West Baton Rouge Parish (La.):
  F377.W45
West Boulder River and Valley (Mont.):
  F737.S9
West Brookland (Washington, D.C.):
  F202.W5
West Canada Creek (New York):
  F127.H5
West Carroll Parish (La.): F377.W47
West Elk Loop Scenic and Historic
  Byway (Colorado): F782.W46
West End (Boston): F73.68.W47
West Feliciana Parish (La.): F377.W5
West Florida: F301
  Baton Rouge district (after 1812):
    F377.F6
  Mobile District: F301, F341
  Natchez District: F341
  Pensacola District (after 1819):
    F317.W5
  Wars
    Civil War: E472.8, E474.1, E475.4,
      E477.9
    Revolt, 1810: F301
    Revolution, 1775-1783: E263.F6
West Florida parishes (La.): F377.F6
West Florida region (Florida): F317.W5
West Gallatin River (Mont.): F737.G2
West India Company, Dutch: F2423
West Indian expeditions (English), 1654-
  1655: F1621
West Indians in Canada: F1035.W47
West Indians in Cuba: F1789.W47
West Indians in foreign countries:
  F1609.9
West Indians in Puerto Rico:
  F1983.W47
West Indians in the United States:
  E184.W54
West Indies: F1601+
  Blacks: F1629.B55

West Indies
  Buccaneers and pirates: F2161
  Caribbean Sea: F2155+
  Discovery and exploration: F1621
  English expeditions: F1621
  English expeditions of 1739-1742:
    F2272.5
  Indians: F1619+
  Naval operations (General): F1621
  Santo Domingo (Audiencia): F1621
  Wars
    American Revolution: E263.W5
      Naval operations: E271+
    Queen Anne's War, 1702-1713:
      E197
    Seven Years' War, 1756-1763:
      F1621
West Indies Federation: F2134
West Jersey, 1676-1702: F137
West North Central States (U.S.): F597
West Orange (N.J.): F144.O6
West Philadelphia (Pennsylvania):
  F158.68.W5
West Point and the Confederate Army:
  E586.U5
West Point, Ga., Battle of, 1865:
  E477.96
West River (Prince Edward Island):
  F1049.W47
West Roxbury (Massachusetts):
  F74.W59
West South Central States: F396
West Tennessee: F442.3
West (U.S.): F590.2+
West Virginia: F236+
  African Americans: E185.93.W5
  Counties, etc: F247.A+
  History
    1951-: F245
    To 1951: F229+, F241
  Indians: E78.W6
  Wars
    Civil War: E534+, E536+, E582+
      Military operations: E470.2+
West Virginia, Army of: E470.4+
West Virginia campaign, July 1861:
  E472.17

Western Gaviões Indians: F2520.1.G37
Western Hemisphere: E11+
Western Insurrection, 1794: E315
Western lands ceded to U.S.
  government: E309
  Georgia cession, 1802: F290, F296,
    F321+
  Old Northwest: F483
  South Carolina cession, 1787:
    F292.B7
Western Maryland: F186.9
Western New York: F126.9
Western North Carolina: F261
Western Reserve (Ohio): F497.W5
Western Sanitary Commission:
  E631.5.A1+
Western states: F590.2+
Westfield, New Jersey, Battle of, 1777:
  E241.S53
Westminister, Statute of, 1931: F1034
Westport, Battle of, 1864: E477.16
Westward expansion
  United States: E179.5
Wet Beaver Creek and Valley (Arizona):
  F817.W47
Wet Mountain Valley (Colorado):
  F782.W49
Wet'suwet'en Indians: E99.W56
Wetzel, Lewis: F517
Weyer's Cave (Virginia): F232.A9
Wharton Estate (N.J.): F142.W47
Wharton, Francis: E664.W55
Wharton State Forest (N.J.): F142.W47
Wharton Tract (N.J.): F142.W47
Wheeler and Roddey's raid, 1863:
  E475.87
Wheeler, Joseph: E467.1.W5
Wheeler Lake and region (Alabama):
  F332.W48
Wheeler's Cavalry Corps
  Confederate Army: E547.W5
Wheeling (West Virginia): F249.W5
Whidbey Island (Wash.): F897.I7
Whipple, William: E302.6.W5
Whiskey Insurrection, 1794: E315

Whiskeytown-Shasta-Trinity National Recreation Area (California): F868.S49

White Cordillera (Peru): F3451.A5

White House (Washington, D.C.): F204.W5

White, Hugh Lawson: E340.W53

White Mountains: F41

White Oak Swamp, Va., Battle of, 1862: E473.68

White Plains, Battle of, 1776: E241.W5

White River and Valley (Arkansas and Missouri): F417.W5
   Arkansas: F417.W5
   Missouri: F472.W5

White River and Valley (Colorado and Utah): F782.R4
   Colorado: F782.R4
   Utah: F832.U4

White River and Valley (Wash.): F897.W59

White River Massacre
   Indian wars: E83.879

White Russians in Canada: F1035.W5

White Russians in the United States: E184.W6

White Sands Missile Range
   New Mexico: F802.W44

White Sands National Monument
   New Mexico: F802.W45

White Sulphur (Kentucky). Johnson's Indian School: E97.6.J69

White Sulphur Springs (West Virginia): F249.W6

White, Thomas Clark: F666

White Walnut Creek and Valley (Illinois): F547.P45

Whitehall, N.C., Battle of, 1862: E474.5

Whitehorse (Yukon): F1095.5.W5

White's Island (Conn.): F102.F2

Whiteshell Provincial Park (Manitoba): F1064.W47

Whiteside Cove (N.C.): F262.J2

Whitestone Hill, Battle of, 1863: E83.86

Whitewater River and Valley (Indiana): F532.W59

Whiting, William Henry Chase: E467.1.W61

Whitman, Marcus: F880

Whitman Mission National Historic Site (Wash.): F897.W65

Whitman National Monument: F897.W65

Whitney, Mount (Calif.): F868.W6

Wichita Indians: E99.W6

Wichita (Kansas): F689.W6

Wichita Mountains and region (Oklahoma): F702.W55

Wickes, Lambert: E207.W63

Wiechquaeskeck Indians: E99.W63

Wier's Cave (Virginia): F232.A9

Wife abuse
   Indians: E98.W49

Wikanee Indians: E99.O68

Wikeinoh Indians: E99.O68

Wikeno Indians: E99.O68

Wild Bill Hickok (J.B. Hickok): F594

Wild Cane Cay Site (Belize): F1435.1.W54

Wilder, John Thomas: E467.1.W69

Wilderness, Battle of, 1864: E476.52

Wilke, Wendell Lewis: E748.W7

Wilkes-Barre (Pennsylvania): F159.W6

Wilkins, Isaac: E278.W6

Wilkinson, Eliza (Yonge): E263.S7

Wilkinson, James: E353.1.W6
   Burr's conspiracy: E334
   Campaigns, 1813: E355.4
   Expedition, Aug. 1791: E83.79

Willamette River and Valley (Oregon): F882.W6

Willett, Marinus: E207.W65

William B. Bankhead National Forest (Alabama): F332.W54

William Bacon Oliver Dam (Alabama): F332.T9

William Henry, Fort
   French and Indian War: E199

Williams, Alpheus Starkey: E467.1.W72

Williams College and the Civil War: E541.W7

Williams, David: E280.A5

Williams, John Sharp: E664.W675

Williams, Otho Holland: E207.W7
Williams, Roger: F82
Williams, William: E302.6.W55
Williams, William Sherley: F592
Williamsburg, Battle of, 1862: E473.63
Williamsburg (Virginia): F234.W7
Williamson, Hugh: E302.6.W6
Willing, Thomas: E302.6.W62
Willoughby and Hyde's Grant, 1663
    (Guiana): F2423
Willoughby Lake (Vermont): F57.O7
Willow Creek and Valley (Illinois):
    F547.K27
Willow Creek State Recreation Area
    (Alaska): F912.W56
Wills
    Indians: E98.P9
Wilmot, David: E340.W65
Wilmot Proviso, 1846: E416+
Wilson, Edith (Bolling): E767.3
Wilson, Henry: E415.9.W6
Wilson, James: E302.6.W64
Wilson, James Harrison: E467.1.W74
Wilson-Kautz Raid, 1864: E476.91
Wilson Lake (Kansas): F687.W73
Wilson Reservoir (Kansas): F687.W73
Wilson, Woodrow
    Administrations, 1913-1921: E766+
    Collected works: E660.W71+
    Family: E767.3
Wilson's Creek, Battle of, 1861:
    E472.23
Wilson's raid to Selma. Ala., and Macon,
    Ga., 1865: E477.96
Wilson's Wharf, Va., Battle of, 1864:
    E476.52
Wiminuche Indians: E99.W65
Wina Indians: F2270.2.D4
Winchester, Battle of
    Mar. 1862: E473.72
    Sept. 1864: E477.33
Winchester, Expedition from, 1865:
    E477.65
Winchester, Va., 1st Battle of, 1862
    (May 25): E473.74
Winchester, Va., 2nd Battle of, 1863:
    E475.5

Wind Cave National Park (S.D.):
    F657.W7
Wind Cave (S.D.): F657.W7
Wind River and Valley (Wyoming):
    F767.W5
Wind River Valley (Wyoming): F767.W5
Windermere Lake (British Columbia):
    F1089.W55
Windmill Island (Pennsylvania):
    F158.68.W7
Windom, William: E664.W76
Windsor (Ontario): F1059.5.W5
Windward Islands: F2011
Windward Passage (West Indies):
    F1741
Wingate, Paine: E302.6.W67
Winn Parish (La.): F377.W6
Winnebago Indians: E99.W7
Winnipauk Island (Conn.): F102.F2
Winnipeg, Lake, region (Manitoba):
    F1064.W5
Winnipeg (Manitoba): F1064.5.W7
Winnipesaukee, Lake: F42.W7
Winona (Minnesota): F614.W7
Winooski River (Vermont): F57.W73
Winslow, John Ancrum: E467.1.W77
Winslow's expedition for the expulsion of
    the Acadians, 1755: F1038
Winston-Salem (North Carolina):
    F264.W8
Winter Island (Calif.): F868.C76
Winthrop, John (1588-1649): F67
Winthrop, John (1606-1676): F97
Winthrop, Robert Charles: E340.W73
Wintu Indians: E99.W78
Wintun Indians: E99.W79
Wiregrass Country: F217.W57
Wirt, William: E340.W79
Wisconsin: F576+
    African Americans: E185.93.W58
    Counties, etc: F587.A+
    French rule and exploration: F584
    Indians: E78.W8
    Slavery: E445.W8
    Wars
        Civil War: E537+
        War of 1898: E726.W6

Wisconsin River and Valley: F587.W8
Wisconsin Territory: F585
Wise, Henry Alexander: E415.9.W8
Wisner, Henry: E302.6.W68
Wissahickon Creek: F158.68.W8
Wissahickon Creek and Valley
  (Pennsylvania): F157.W62
Wistar, Isaac Jones: E467.1.W81
Witherspoon, John: E302.6.W7
Withlacoochee River and Valley
  (Florida): F317.W57
Witoto Indians: F2270.2.W5
Wives of U.S. presidents: E176.2
  Madison: E342.1
  Washington: E312.19
Wiwa Indians: F2270.2.W54
Wiyat Indians: E99.W8
Wolcott, Edward Oliver: E664.W8
Wolcott, Oliver: E302.6.W85
Wolcott, Roger: F70
Wolf Mountain, Battle of, 1877:
  E83.8765
Wolf National Scenic Riverway
  (Wisconsin): F587.W86
Wolf River (Wisconsin): F587.W86
Wolfe, James
  Capture of Quebec: E199
Wolf's Point (Chicago): F548.68.W8
Women
  Aztecs: F1219.76.W75
  Indians: E98.W8
    Argentina: F2821.3.W65
    Bolivia: F3320.1.W65
    Brazil: F2519.3.W66
    Central America: F1434.2.W65
    Colombia: F2270.1.W65
    Ecuador: F3721.3.W65
    Mexico: F1219.3.W6
    Peru: F3429.3.W65
    Pre-Columbian America: E59.W8
    South America: F2230.1.W6
  Jews: E184.36.W64
  Mayas: F1435.3.W55
Women, African American: E185.86
Women in the American Civil War:
  E628
Women's Relief Corps: E462.15

Women's work
  United States
    War of 1812: E362.7
Women's work in the American
  Revolution: E276
Wood Buffalo National Park (Alberta):
  F1079.W6
Wood carving
  Indians
    Mexico: F1219.3.W65
    Mayas: F1435.3.W6
Wood-carving
  Indians
    Peru: F3429.3.W66
Wood, Fernando: F128.44
Wood, James: E207.W78
Wood Lake Battle, 1862: E83.86
Wood, Leonard: E181
Wood Mountain (Region)
  Saskatchewan: F1074.W65
Wood-Tikchik State Park (Alaska):
  F912.W64
Woodbridge, William: F566
Woodbury, Levi: E340.W8
Woodhull, Nathaniel: E207.W8
Woodland Caribou Provincial Park
  (Ontario): F1059.W63
Woodland culture: E99.W84
Woodlands Indians: E78.E2
Woodlawn Cemetery (New York):
  F128.61.W8
Woodlawn (Chicago): F548.68.W82
Woodrow Wilson Foundation: E772
Woods, Lake of the, region
  Manitoba: F1064.L2
  Ontario: F1059.L2
Woodward, George Washington: F153
Wool, John Ellis: E403.1.W8
  March to Saltillo: E405.4
Woolworth Building (New York):
  F128.8.W82
Wooster, David: E207.W9
Worcester (Massachusetts): F74.W9
Worsell Manor (Maryland): F187.C3
Worth, Jonathan: F259
Worth, Lake (Florida): F317.D2
Worth, William Jenkins: E403.1.W9

Worthington, Thomas: F495
Wounded Knee Massacre, 1890: E83.89
Woyamana Indians: F2380.1.W25
W.R. Motherwell Farmstead National Historic Park (Saskatchewan): F1074.W28
Wrangell (Alaska): F914.W8
Wrangell Mountains (Alaska): F912.W72
Wrangell-Saint Elias National Park and Preserve (Alaska): F912.W74
Wright, Marcus Joseph: E467.1.W94
Wright, Silas: E340.W95
Writing
  Aztecs: F1219.76.W85
  Indians: E98.W86
    Brazil: F2519.3.W7
    Guyana: F2380.2.W7
    Mexico: F1219.3.W94
    Peru: F3429.3.W7
    Pre-Columbian America: E59.W9
    South America: F2230.1.W7
Writing-on-Stone Northwest Mounted Police Post (Alberta): F1079.W74
Writing-on-Stone Provincial Park (Alberta): F1079.W74
Writs of assistance: E215.1
Wupatki National Monument (Arizona): F817.W8
Wyam Indians: E99.W9
Wyandot Indians: E99.H9
Wyandotte Cave (Indiana): F532.C8
Wykenas Indians: E99.O68
Wyoming: F756+
  African Americans: E185.93.W9
  Counties, etc: F767.A+
  Indian wars: E83.879
  Indians: E78.W95
Wyoming Massacre, 1763: E83.7595
Wyoming Massacre, 1778: E241.W9
Wyoming Valley (Pa.): F157.W9

X

Xacriaba Indians: F2520.1.X33

Xalapa (Mexico)
  Canton: F1371
  City: F1391.J2
Xamanha Site
  Mayas: F1435.1.X26
Xavante-Acuen Indians: F2520.1.A4
Xavante Indians: F2520.1.A4
Xcan Cave (Mexico): F1435.1.X32
Xcaret, Mexico (Mayas): F1435.1.X35
Xculoc Site (Mexico)
  Mayas: F1435.1.X37
Xeta Indians: F2520.1.H48
Xicaque Indians: F1505.2.X5
Xikrin Indians: F2520.1.X5
Xinca Indians: F1465.2.X5
Xingú River (Brazil)
  Matto Grosso (State): F2576
  Pará (State): F2586
Xingu Valley (Brazil)
  Indian antiquities: F2519.1.X56
XIT Ranch (Texas): F392.X2
Xkichmook (Yucatan)
  Mayas: F1435.1.X7
Xkipché Site (Mexico)
  Mayas: F1435.1.X73
Xtacumbilxunaan Cave (Mexico): F1435.1.X77
Xunantunich Site (Belize): F1435.1.X82
XYZ letters: E323

Y

Yadkin River and Valley (N.C.): F262.Y2
Yagua Indians: F3430.1.Y3
Yahgan Indians: F2986
Yahuskin Indians: E99.Y18
Yakalamarure Indians: F2270.2.Y3
Yakama Indians: E99.Y2
Yakima Indians: E99.Y2
Yakima River and Valley (Wash.): F897.Y2
Yakima War, 1855-1858: E83.84
Yakima (Washington): F899.Y15
Yakonan Indians: E99.Y212
Yakutat Bay (Alaska): F912.Y2

Yale District (British Columbia):
F1089.Y4

Yale University and the Civil War:
E541.Y2

Yale University and the Revolution:
E270.Y2

Yamachiche, Québec (Village and
parish): F1054.5.Y2

Yamaska County (Québec): F1054.Y3

Yamassee Indians: E99.Y22

Yamassee War, 1715-1716: E83.713

Yaminawa Indians: F2520.1.Y25

Yampa Indians: E99.Y225

Yana Indians: E99.Y23

Yanacocha, Battle of, 1835: F3447

Yanaconas Indians
Peru: F3430.1.Y34

Yancey, William Lowndes: E415.9.Y2

Yankton Indians: E99.Y25

Yanktonai Indians: E99.Y26

Yanomamo Indians: F2520.1.Y3

Yao (Southeast Asian people) in the
United States: E184.Y36

Yapurá River (Brazil): F2546

Yaque del Norte River (Dominican
Republic): F1939.Y38

Yaqui Indians: F1221.Y3

Yaqui River (Mexico): F1346

Yaquina River and Valley (Oregon):
F882.Y24

Yaracuy, Venezuela (State): F2331.Y3

Yarmouth Co. (Nova Scotia): F1039.Y3

Yarmouth (Nova Scotia): F1039.5.Y3

Yaruro Indians: F2319.2.Y3

Yatayty-Corá, 1866: F2687

Yates, Richard: F545

Yauyos (Peru)
Province: F3451.Y38

Yavapai Indians: E99.Y5

Yavarí River (Brazil): F2546

Yaxchilán (Mexico)
Mayas: F1435.1.Y3

Yaxuná Site (Mexico): F1435.1.Y39

Yazoo fraud: F341

Yazoo Indians: E99.Y54

Yazoo land companies: F341

Yazoo Pass expedition, 1863: E475.22

Yazoo River and Valley (Mississippi):
F347.Y3

Yazoo River expedition, 1864: E476.14

Yebamasa Indians: F2270.2.Y42

Yecuana Indians: F2319.2.Y4

Yellow Creek (Ohio): F497.J4

Yellowhead Pass (Alta. and B.C.):
F1079.Y4

Yellowstone National Park: F722
Indians: E78.Y44

Yellowstone River and Valley
Montana: F737.Y4
North Dakota: F642.M28
Wyoming: F767.Y44

Yellowstone River Valley
Indians: E78.Y44

Yemenis in the United States:
E184.Y44

Yemenites in the United States:
E184.Y44

Yerba Buena Island (Calif.): F869.S3+

Yerupaja, Cerro: F3451.Y47

YMCA: E635

Yokayo Indians: E99.Y7

Yokohl Valley (Calif.): F868.T8

Yokuts
Indians: E99.Y75

Yoncalla Indians: E99.Y77

Yo'okop Site (Mexico): F1435.1.Y64

Yopi Indians: F1221.Y64

York Co. (New Brunswick): F1044.Y65

York Co. (Ontario): F1059.Y6

York District (S.C.): F277.Y62

York (Me.): F29.Y6

York, Ontario, Battle of, 1813:
E356.T68

York Regional Municipality (Ontario):
F1059.Y6

York Road (Pa.): F157.Y7

Yorktown (Virginia): F234.Y6
Siege, 1862: E473.61
Surrender of Cornwallis, 1781:
E241.Y6

Yoro, Honduras (Dept.): F1509.Y6

Yoruba in America: E29.Y67

Yoruba in Cuba: F1789.Y6

Yoruba in the United States: E184.Y66

Yosemite National Park (California): F868.Y6

Yosemite Valley (California): F868.Y6

Youghiogheny River and Valley
Maryland: F187.Y68
Pennsylvania: F157.Y72
West Virginia: F247.Y68

Young Men's Christian Associations and the Civil War: E635

Young, Owen D.: E748.Y74

Younger, Cole: F594

Youngstown (Ohio): F499.Y8

Yount, George Calvert: F864

Youth
Indians: E98.Y68
Jews: E184.36.S65

Youth, African American: E185.86

Yucatán, Mexico (State): F1376
Indian antiquities: F1219.1.Y8
Mayas: F1435.1.Y89

Yucatán Peninsula (Mexico): F1376

Yuchi Indians: E99.Y9

Yuco Indians: F2319.2.Y8

Yucpa Indians: F2319.2.Y8

Yucuna Indians: F2270.2.Y87

Yugoslavs in Argentina: F3021.Y7

Yugoslavs in Chile: F3285.Y8

Yugoslavs in Peru: F3619.Y84

Yugoslavs in South America: F2239.Y83

Yugoslavs in the United States: E184.Y7

Yukian Indians: E99.Y92

Yuko Indians: F2270.2.Y9

Yukon River and Valley
Alaska: F912.Y9

Yukon River (Yukon): F1095.Y9

Yukon Territory: F1091+
Alaska boundary: F912.B7
Eskimos: E99.E7
Indians: E78.Y8

Yukon Valley (Yukon): F1095.Y9

Yukpa Indians: F2319.2.Y8

Yulee, David Levy: E415.9.Y9

Yuma Indians: E99.Y94

Yuman Indians: E99.Y95

Yumbo Indians: F3722.1.Y86

Yunca Indians: F3430.1.Y8

Yupa Indians: F2319.2.Y8

Yuqui Indians: F3320.2.Y78

Yurok Indians: E99.Y97

Yurucari Indians: F3320.2.Y8

Yuruna Indians: F2520.1.J8

Yvapare Indians: F2520.1.H48

Z

Zaca Lake (California): F868.S23

Zacapa, Guatemala (Dept.): F1469.Z3

Zacateca Indians: F1221.Z25

Zacatecas (Mexico)
City: F1391.Z2
State: F1381

Zaculeu (Guatemala)
Mayas: F1435.1.Z3

Zamora, Venezuela (State): F2331.B3

Zamorano, Augustín Juan Vicente: F864

Zamucoan Indians: F3320.2.Z3

Zangara, Giuseppe
Biography: E807.3

Zanjon, Treaty of, 1878: F1785

Zaparo Indians: F3722.1.Z3

Zapata, Emiliano: F1234

Zapetera Island
Indian antiquities: F1525.1.Z3

Zapotec Indians
Modern: F1221.Z3
Pre-Columbian: F1219.8.Z37

Zayas y Alfonso, Alfredo: F1787

Zelaya, José Santos: F1526.27

Zelaya, Nicaragua (Dept.): F1529.Z4

Zeledon-Wyke Treaty, 1860: F1438

Zeno, Antonio: E109.I8

Zeno, Niccolò: E109.I8

Zepita, Battle of, 1823: F3446

Zia Indians: E99.Z52

Zion National Park: F832.Z8

Zoological Park (New York): F128.65.Z6

Zoque Indians: F1221.Z6

Zoró Indians: F2520.1.Z65

Zulia, Venezuela (State): F2331.Z9

Zuñi Indians: E99.Z9

INDEX

INDEX

Zuruahá Indians: F2520.1.Z87